ECONOMICS

CANADA IN THE GLOBAL ENVIRONMENT

FOURTH EDITION

MICHAEL PARKIN
ROBIN BADE

Addison
Wesley
Longman

Toronto

Canadian Cataloguing in Publication Data

Parkin, Michael, 1939-
    Economics: Canada in the global environment

4th ed.
Includes index.
ISBN 0-201-61384-0

1. Economics. 2. Canada—Economic conditions—1991- . I. Bade, Robin.
II. Title.

HB171.5.P26 2000   330   C99-931979-5

ISBN: 0-201-61384-0

Vice President and Editorial Director: Patrick Ferrier
Senior Acquisitions Editor: Dave Ward
Developmental Editor: Suzanne Schaan
Marketing Manager: Steve Iacovelli
Production Editor: Nicole Mellow
Copy Editor: Gail Marsden
Production Coordinator: Deborah Starks
Permissions: Susan Wallace-Cox
Photo Research: Cheryl Freedman
Art Director: Mary Opper
Cover and Interior Design: Anthony Leung
Cover Image (globe): Tony May TSI Imaging/Tony Stone Images
Cover Image (inset): Frederick Charles/Tony Stone Images
Page Layout: Bill Renaud
Illustrator: Richard Parkin

1 2 3 4 5   04 03 02 01 00

Printed and bound in the United States of America.

Statistics Canada information is used with the permission of the Minister of Industry, as Minister responsible for Statistics Canada. Information on the availability of the wide range of data from Statistics Canada's regional offices, its World Wide Web site at **http://www.statcan.ca**, and its toll-free access number **1-800-263-1136**.

About the Authors

Michael Parkin received his training as an economist at the Universities of Leicester and Essex in England. Currently in the Department of Economics at the University of Western Ontario, Canada, Professor Parkin has held faculty appointments at Brown University, the University of Manchester, the University of Essex, and Bond University. He is a past president of the Canadian Economics Association and has served on the editorial boards of the *American Economic Review* and the *Journal of Monetary Economics* and as managing editor of the *Canadian Journal of Economics*. Professor Parkin's research on macroeconomics, monetary economics, and international economics has resulted in over 160 publications in journals and edited volumes, including the *American Economic Review*, the *Journal of Political Economy*, the *Review of Economic Studies*, the *Journal of Monetary Economics*, and the *Journal of Money, Credit and Banking*. He became most visible to the public with his work on inflation that discredited the use of wage and price controls. Michael Parkin also spearheaded the movement toward European monetary union.

Robin Bade earned degrees in mathematics and economics at the University of Queensland and her Ph.D. at the Australian National University. She has held faculty appointments in the business school at the University of Edinburgh and Bond University and in the economics departments at the University of Manitoba, the University of Toronto, and the University of Western Ontario. Her research on international capital flows appears in the *International Economic Review* and the *Economic Record*.

Professor Parkin and Dr. Bade are joint authors of *Modern Macroeconomics* (Prentice-Hall), an intermediate text, and have collaborated on many research and textbook writing projects. They are both experienced and dedicated teachers of introductory economics.

Preface

This book presents economics as a serious, lively, and evolving science. Its goal is to help the student to develop the "economic way of thinking" and to gain insights into how the economy works and how it might be made to work better. ◆ Our goal is to make economics as accessible as possible, yet to provide a thorough and complete coverage of the subject, not a slimmed-down or oversimplified selection. ◆ We are conscious that many students find economics hard, so we place the student at centre stage and write for the student. We use a style and language that doesn't intimidate and that allows the student to concentrate on the substance. ◆ We open each chapter with a clear statement of learning objectives, a real-world student-friendly vignette to grab attention, and a brief preview. We illustrate principles with examples that are selected to hold the student's interest and to make the subject lively. And we put principles to work by using them to illuminate current real-world problems and issues. ◆ We present some new ideas, such as dynamic comparative advantage, game theory, the modern theory of the firm, public choice theory, rational expectations, new growth theory, and real business cycle theory. But we explain these topics with familiar core ideas and tools. ◆ Today's course springs from today's issues—the information revolution, the Asian recession, and the expansion of global trade and investment. But the principles that we use to understand these issues remain the core principles of our science. ◆ Governments and international agencies place renewed emphasis on long-term fundamentals as they seek to sustain economic growth. This book reflects this emphasis. ◆ To enable students to access the latest information on the national and global economy, we have developed a companion Web site. And to provide active learning opportunities, we have developed the tutorials and quizzes on the accompanying *Economics in Action* CD.

The Fourth Edition Revision

Economics: Canada in the Global Environment, Fourth Edition, retains all the improvements achieved in its predecessor with its emphasis on core principles, coverage of recent economic developments, brief yet accessible explanations, and strong pedagogy. New to this edition are:

- Revised and updated micro content
- Revised and updated macro content
- In-text review quiz
- Parallel end-of-chapter problems
- Part wrap-up

Revised and Updated Micro Content

The major revisions in the micro chapters are:

1. What Is Economics? (Chapter 1): A new photo-intensive introduction to the issues and methods of economics.
2. The Economic Problem (Chapter 3): Improved explanation of increasing opportunity cost and simplified explanation of the gains from trade.
3. Elasticity (Chapter 5): A new predictions-oriented treatment of the elasticity of demand and supply.
4. Efficiency and Equity (Chapter 6): New chapter studies the efficiency and the fairness of market outcomes using the tools of demand and supply.
5. Markets in Action (Chapter 7): Now includes explicit discussion of efficiency and equity issues.
6. Organizing Production (Chapter 10): A briefer and more complete statement of the nature of the firm, the essence of its problem, its objectives and constraints, its costs and economic profit.
7. Monopoly (Chapter 13): New explanations of single-price and price discriminating cases including efficiency and distributional aspects of each type and monopoly policy issues.
8. Monopolistic Competition (Chapter 14): A more extensive discussion of the role and effects of selling costs and advertising.
9. Demand and Supply in Resource Markets (Chapter 15): New compact yet complete coverage of all factor markets and now includes simple explanation of net present value and investment decision.
10. Market Failure and Public Choice (Chapter 18): Includes a simpler treatment of public goods and more extensive coverage on taxes.

Revised and Updated Macro Content

The major revisions in the macro chapters are:

1. Measuring Employment and Unemployment (Chapter 23): A new chapter (based on Chapter 31 of the Third Edition) that covers the measurement issues in the labour market.
2. Aggregate Supply and Aggregate Demand (Chapter 24): Reorganized and simplified to better explain the supply-side fundamentals.
3. Money, Banking, and Interest Rates (Chapter 27): New section on interest rates and expenditure plans.
4. Monetary Policy (Chapter 28): A new explanation of the distinction between interest rate targeting and money supply targeting.
5. Fiscal and Monetary Interactions (Chapter 29): First part extensively revised and now organized around the *AS–AD* and money market models to provide greater continuity.
6. The Economy at Full Employment (Chapter 31): A new chapter that begins to build the story of the aggregate supply side of the economy and that explains how changes in population, capital, and technology change potential GDP, employment, and the real wage rate. This chapter provides the foundation for the theory of aggregate supply and is the jumping-off point for Chapter 32 on economic growth.
7. The Business Cycle (Chapter 33): Simplified explanation of aggregate demand theories and a new section, the Japanese recession of the 1990s.
8. Thorough and extensive updating to reflect the Canadian economy and the global economy at the end of the 1990s including events such as the evolution of the federal budget from deficit to surplus, the ongoing expansion of the North American economy, recession in Asia, and turmoil in global financial markets.

In-Text Review Quiz

We have replaced the in-text Review of the previous editions with a Review Quiz. These brief quizzes invite students to revisit the material they have just studied with a set of questions in mind. We hope that these quizzes will encourage a more critical and thoughtful rereading of any material that proves difficult for the student.

Parallel End-of-Chapter Problems

We have reworked the end-of-chapter problems and created pairs of parallel problems. We have provided the solutions to the odd-numbered problems on the Student Resource CD and on the Parkin-Bade Web site. Also, these solutions together with those to the even-numbered problems are available to instructors on the Instructor Resource CD. This arrangement provides help to students and flexibility to instructors who want to assign problems for credit.

Part Wrap-Up

A new feature at the *end* of each part:

- Explains how the chapters relate to each other and fit into the larger picture.
- Provides a biographical sketch of the economist who developed the central idea and places the original contribution in its historical context.
- Presents an interview with a leading contemporary economist.

Features to Enhance Teaching and Learning

HERE, WE DESCRIBE THE CHAPTER FEATURES that are designed to enhance teaching and learning. Each chapter contains:

Chapter Objectives

A list of learning objectives enables students to see exactly where the chapter is going and to set their goals before they begin the chapter. We link these goals directly to the chapter's major headings.

After studying this chapter, you will be able to:

- **Explain the fundamental economic problem**
- **Define the production possibility frontier**
- **Define and calculate opportunity cost**
- **Explain the conditions in which resources are used efficiently**
- **Explain how economic growth expands production possibilities**
- **Explain how specialization and trade expand production possibilities**

Chapter Opener

A one-page student-friendly, attention-grabbing vignette raises questions that both motivate and focus the chapter.

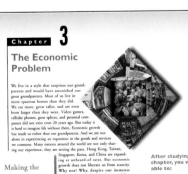

In-Text Review Quiz

A review quiz at end of most major sections enables students to determine whether a topic needs further study before moving on.

R E V I E W   Q U I Z

- What is marginal cost and how is it measured?
- What is marginal benefit and how is it measured?
- How does the marginal benefit from a good change as the quantity of that good increases? Why?
- What is the relationship between marginal cost and the production possibility frontier?
- What conditions must be satisfied if resources are used efficiently? Why?

Key Terms

Highlighted terms within the text simplify the student's task of learning the vocabulary of economics. Each highlighted term appears in an end-of-chapter list with page numbers, an end-of-book glossary, bold-faced in the index, in the *Economics in Action* software on the Student Resource CD, and on the Parkin-Bade Web site.

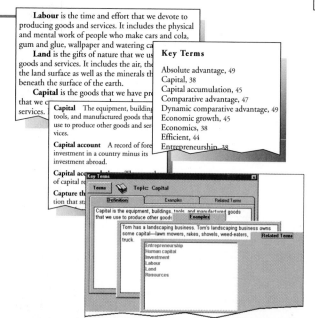

Key Figures and Tables

An icon ◆ identifies the most important figures and tables, and the end-of-chapter summary lists them. Instructor's overhead transparencies also contain enlarged images of most of these key figures.

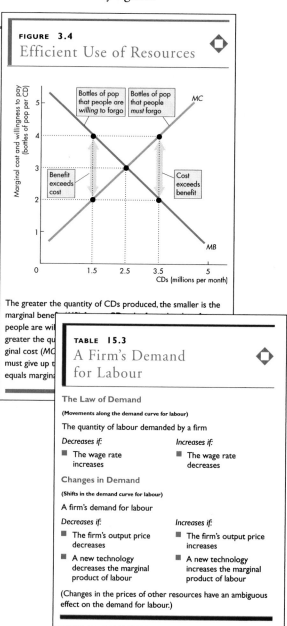

FIGURE 3.4
Efficient Use of Resources

The greater the quantity of CDs produced, the smaller is the marginal benef... people are wil... greater the qu... ginal cost (MC... must give up t... equals margina...

TABLE 15.3
A Firm's Demand for Labour

The Law of Demand

(Movements along the demand curve for labour)

The quantity of labour demanded by a firm

Decreases if:	Increases if:
■ The wage rate increases	■ The wage rate decreases

Changes in Demand

(Shifts in the demand curve for labour)

A firm's demand for labour

Decreases if:	Increases if:
■ The firm's output price decreases	■ The firm's output price increases
■ A new technology decreases the marginal product of labour	■ A new technology increases the marginal product of labour

(Changes in the prices of other resources have an ambiguous effect on the demand for labour.)

Diagrams That Show the Action

This book has set new standards of clarity in its diagrams. Our goal has always been to show "where the economic action is." The diagrams in this book continue to generate an enormously positive response, which confirms our view that graphical analysis is the most important tool available for teaching and learning economics. But many students find graphs hard to work with. For this reason, we have developed the entire art program with the study and review needs of the student in mind. The diagrams feature:

■ Shifted curves, equilibrium points, and other important features highlighted in red
■ Colour-blended arrows to suggest movement
■ Graphs paired with data tables
■ Diagrams labelled with boxed notes
■ Extended captions that make each diagram and its caption a self-contained object for study and review

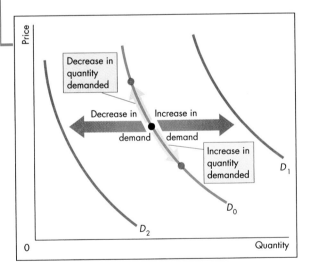

Reading Between the Lines

Each chapter contains an economic analysis of a significant news article together with a set of critical thinking questions that relate to the issues raised in the article.

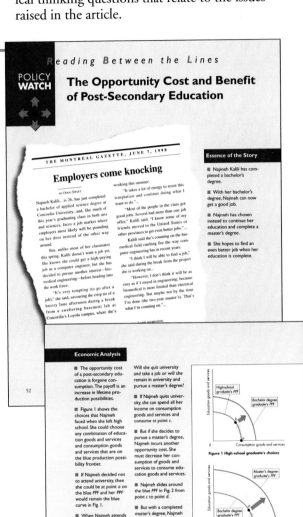

End-of-Chapter Study Material

Each chapter has a concise summary organized by major topics, lists of key terms, figures, and tables (all with page references), problems, and critical thinking questions. Items identified by an icon 💻 link to the *Economics in Action* software CD included with the text. Items identified by an icon 🕸 link to the Parkin-Bade Web site at **http://www.econ100.com**. Our hope is to encourage students to keep up-to-date and to become comfortable and efficient in their use of the Internet to access information.

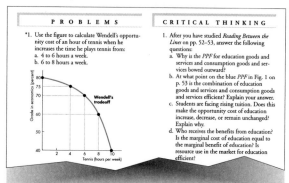

For the Instructor

THIS BOOK ENABLES YOU TO ACHIEVE THREE objectives in your principles course:

- Focus on the core ideas.
- Explain the issues and problems of our time.
- Choose your own course structure.

Focus on the Core Ideas

You know how hard it is to encourage a student to think like an economist. But that is your goal. Consistent with this goal, the text focuses on and repeatedly uses the central ideas: choice, tradeoff, opportunity cost, the margin, incentives, the gains from voluntary exchange, the forces of demand, supply, and equilibrium, the pursuit of economic rent, and the effects of government actions on the economy.

Explain the Issues and Problems of Our Time

Students must use the core ideas and tools if they are to begin to understand them. And there is no better way to motivate students than by using the tools of economics to explain the issues that confront students in today's world. These issues include the environment, immigration, widening income gaps, the productivity growth slowdown, budget surpluses and deficits, restraining inflation, watching for the next recession, avoiding protectionism, and the long-term growth of output and incomes.

Choose Your Own Course Structure

You want to teach your own course. We have organized this book to enable you to do so. We demonstrate the book's flexibility in the "Flexibility Chart" and "Alternative Sequences" tables that appear on pp. xx–xxv. You can use this book to teach a traditional course that blends theory and policy or a current policy issues course. Your micro course can emphasize theory or policy. You can structure your macro course to emphasize long-term growth and supply-side fundamentals. Or you can follow a traditional macro sequence and emphasize short-term fluctuations. The choices are yours.

Instructor's Resource CD

Our *Instructor's Resource CD* contains an Instructor's Manual, Computerized Test Bank, and PowerPoint Lecture Presentations.

Instructor's Manual

An Instructor's Manual includes teaching notes and solutions to end-of-chapter problems.

Computerized Test Bank

The Test Bank by Harvey King has been revised and updated by Kam Hon Chu of Memorial University and Glen Stirling of the University of Western Ontario. The Test Bank is accessed using Diploma, a highly acclaimed test generating and grade management software. The questions in the computerized Test Bank are also available in a printed Test Bank.

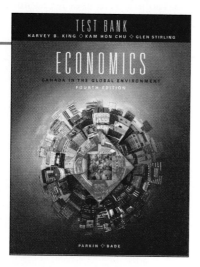

PowerPoint Lecture Presentations

A full-colour Microsoft PowerPoint Lecture Presentation breaks the chapters into lecture-size bites and includes key figures from the text, animated graphs, and speaking notes. The presentation can be used electronically in the classroom or can be printed to create hard-copy Transparency Masters. The lecture presentation is available for Windows to qualified adopters of the text (contact your Pearson Education sales representative).

Other Instructor Resources

Economics in Action Software

Instructors can use *Economics in Action* interactive software in the classroom. Its full-screen display option turns its many analytical graphs into "electronic transparencies" for live graph manipulation in lectures. Its real-world data sets and graphing utility bring animated time-series graphs and scatter diagrams to the classroom.

Overhead Transparencies

Full-colour overhead transparencies of enlarged key figures from the text will improve the clarity of your lectures. They are available to qualified adopters of the text (contact your Pearson Education sales representative).

For the Student

Study Guide

The fourth edition *Study Guide* by Avi Cohen (York University) and Harvey King (University of Regina) is carefully coordinated with the main text and the Test Bank. Each chapter of the Study Guide contains:

- Key concepts
- Helpful hints
- Self-Test with True/false/uncertain and Multiple-choice questions, and Short-answer problems, many of which are Critical Thinking problems.
- Detailed solutions.

Each part allows students to test their cumulative understanding with questions that go across chapters and work a sample mid-term examination.

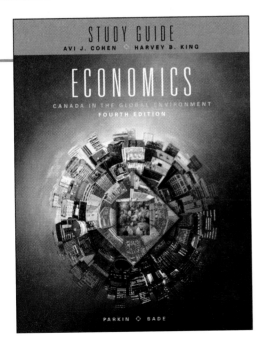

Economics in Action Interactive Software

With *Economics in Action* Release 4.0 that accompanies the Fourth Edition, students will have fun working the tutorials, answering questions that give instant explanations, and testing themselves ahead of their midterm tests. One of our students told us that using *EIA* is like having a private professor in your dorm room!

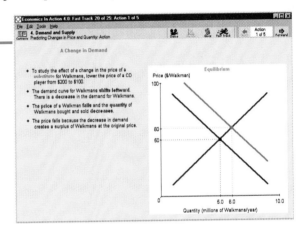

The Parkin-Bade Web Site

The Parkin-Bade Web site provides online quizzes, study tips, office hours, links, electronic *Reading Between the Lines*, a *Point-Counterpoint* feature that encourages students to participate in contemporary policy debates, and much more. You can reach the site at **http://www.econ100.com**.

Acknowledgments

WE THANK OUR CURRENT AND FORMER COLLEAGUES and friends at the University of Western Ontario who have taught us a great deal. They are: Audra Bowlus, Jim Davies, Jeremy Greenwood, Ig Horstmann, Peter Howitt, Greg Huffman, David Laidler, Phil Reny, Chris Robinson, John Whalley, and Ron Wonnacott. We also thank Doug McTaggart and Christopher Findlay, co-authors of the Australian edition, and Melanie Powell and Kent Matthews, co-authors of the European edition. Suggestions arising from their adaptations of earlier editions have been helpful in preparing this edition.

We thank the several thousand students whom we have been privileged to teach. The instant response that comes from the look of puzzlement or enlightenment has taught us, more than anything else, how to teach economics.

This new edition has been developed during the merger of two outstanding Canadian publishers, Addison-Wesley Canada and Prentice-Hall Canada into the new Pearson Education Canada. We have been privileged to work with both publishers for many years and have come to know well their contrasting styles and strengths. Chief Executive Officer Tony Vander Woude and Chief Operating Officer Alan Reynolds have managed this merger with vision and sensitivity both to the individuals involved and the economic realities that the publishing industry faces today. Tony and Alan have been champions of our project from its inception in the mid-1980s and we want to place on record once more our deep gratitude to them for their support and for ensuring that despite upheavals, we are provided with the best editors in the industry.

We first want to say thank you to those of our former Addison-Wesley team who did not join the new company. They are John More, Ron Doleman, and Linda Scott. John and Ron worked with us from day one and became (and remain) dear friends. We can see their stamp on this edition and believe that it will survive and be visible in many subsequent editions. Linda died during the development of this edition, but she, too left many indelible marks. She was a truly outstanding editor and friend who we greatly miss.

Second, we thank our new editors and helpers at Pearson Education. Patrick Ferrier, Vice President and Editorial Director, has provided overall direction.

Dave Ward, Senior Acquisitions Editor and our sponsoring editor, has ably coordinated the arrangements for this edition and worked tirelessly to champion our cause. Suzanne Schaan, Developmental Editor, and Joan MacMillan have brought creative and professional direction to the development effort on this edition. Nicole Mellow, our Production Editor, has managed a tight production schedule and been extremely responsive to our need to keep revising up to the last possible minute.

We thank our outstanding colleagues and friends who have written the supplements and in other ways helped to make this text and package as accurate and useful as possible. Avi Cohen and Harvey King have written a superb Study Guide. And once again, they have played a crucial role in the creation of other supplements and in the overall revision process. Kit Pasula and Glen Stirling have provided valuable suggestions and caught slips and errors in their accuracy review of near-final pages. Lutz-Alexander Busch pointed out an error in the entry deterrence game that is described on pp. 308-309 and suggested how it might be fixed.

Finally, we thank the people who work directly with us. Our assistant, Jeannie Gillmore, has performed too many tasks to list. A few include finding news articles and writing the first drafts of most of the *Reading Between the Lines* features, checking the end-of-chapter problems and solutions, preparing and checking the glossary, and ensuring the accuracy of *Economics in Action* and the quizzes on our Web site.

Jane McAndrew provided excellent library help. Richard Parkin created the electronic art files for the text, CD, and Web site and offered many ideas that improved the illustrations. Laurel Davies created, edited, and checked the accuracy of the *Economics in Action* database. Jessica Dooley read and suggested improvements to the interview with Martin Dooley that appears on pp. 198–200.

Classroom experience will test the value of this book. We would appreciate hearing from teachers and students about how we can continue to improve it in future editions.

Robin Bade
Michael Parkin
London, Ontario, Canada
michael.parkin@uwo.ca
robin@econ100.com

Reviewers

Syed Ahmed, Red Deer Community College
Benjamin Amoah, University of Guelph
Terri Anderson, Fanshawe College
Torben Andersen, Red Deer College
Syed Ashan, Concordia University
Keith Baxter, Bishop's University
Andy Baziliauskas, University of Winnipeg
Karl Bennett, University of Waterloo
Ronald Bodkin, University of Ottawa
Caroline Boivin, Concordia University
Paul Booth, University of Alberta
John Boyd, University of British Columbia
John Brander, University of New Brunswick
Larry Brown, Selkirk College
Lutz-Alexander Busch, University of Waterloo
Beverly Cameron, University of Manitoba
Norman Cameron, University of Manitoba
Emanuel Carvalho, University of Waterloo
Francois Casas, University of Toronto
Robert Cherneff, University of Victoria
Saud Choudhry, Trent University
Louis Christofides, University of Guelph
Kam Hon Chu, Memorial University of
    Newfoundland
George Churchman, University of Manitoba
Avi Cohen, York University
Rosilyn Coulson, Douglas College
Brian Coulter, University College of the Fraser
    Valley
Stanya Cunningham, Concordia University College
    of Alberta
Douglas Curtis, Trent University
Garth Davies, Olds College
Vaughan Dickson, University of New Brunswick
    (Fredericton)
Mohammed Dore, Brock University
Byron Eastman, Laurentian University
Fahira Eston, Humber College
Brian Ferguson, University of Guelph
Len Fitzpatrick, Carleton University
Peter Fortura, Algonquin College
Donald Garrie, Georgian College
David Gray, University of Ottawa
Michael Hare, University of Toronto

Rod Hill, University of New Brunswick
Susan Kamp, University of Alberta
Peter Kennedy, Simon Fraser University
Harvey King, University of Regina
Patricia Koss, Concordia University
Robert Kunimoto, Mt. Royal College
David Johnson, Wilfrid Laurier University
Eva Lau, University of Waterloo
Gordon Lee, University of Alberta
Scott Lynch, Memorial University
Dan MacKay, SIAST
Keith MacKinnon, York University
S. Manchouri, University of Alberta
Raimo Martalla, Malaspina University College
Dennis McGuire, Okanagan University College
Rob Moir, University of New Brunswick (St. John)
Joseph Muldoon, Trent University
David Murrell, University of New Brunswick
    (Fredericton)
Robin Neill, Carleton University
A. Gyasi Nimarko, Vanier College
Sonia Novkovic, Saint Mary's University
John O'Brien, Concordia University
Kit Pasula, Okanagan University College
Arne Paus-Jenssen, University of Saskatchewan
Stephen Rakoczy, Humber College
Don Reddick, Kwantlen University College
E. Riser, Memorial University
Roberta Robb, Brock University
Nick Rowe, Carleton University
Michael Rushton, University of Regina
Balbir Sahni, Concordia University
Brian Scarfe, University of Regina
Marlyce Searcy, SIAST Palliser
Judith Skuce, Georgian College
Peter Sinclair, Wilfred Laurier University
Stan Shedd, University of Calgary
Ian Skaith, Fanshawe College
George Slasor, University of Toronto
Bert Somers, John Abbott College
Lewis Soroka, Brock University
Glen Stirling, University of Western Ontario
Tony Ward, Brock University
Bruce Wilkinson, University of Alberta
Russell Uhler, University of British Columbia
A. Wong, Grant McEwan Community College
Ayoub Yousefi, University of Waterloo
Weiqiu Yu, University of New Brunswick
    (Fredericton)

Flexibility Guide

Core	Policy	Optional
1 What Is Economics?		2 Making and Using Graphs [A good chapter to assign to the student with a fear of graphs.]
3 The Economic Problem		
4 Demand and Supply		
5 Elasticity		
6 Efficiency and Equity [A chapter that provides a non-technical explanation of efficiency and equity that unifies the micro coverage and permits early coverage of policy issues.]	7 Markets in Action [A unique chapter that gives extensive applications of demand and supply.]	8 Utility and Demand [Although this chapter is optional, it may be covered if desired *before* demand in Chapter 4.]
		9 Possibilities, Preferences, and Choices [A full chapter on this strictly optional topic to ensure that it is covered clearly with intuitive explanations and illustrations. The standard short appendix treatment of this topic makes it indigestible.]
		10 Organizing Production [This chapter may be skipped or assigned as a reading.]
11 Output and Costs		
12 Perfect Competition		
13 Monopoly		
14 Monopolistic Competition and Oligopoly		
15 Demand and Supply in Resource Markets [Enables you to cover all the resource market issues in a single chapter. Includes an explanation of present value.]		16 Labour Markets
	17 Inequality and Redistribution	

Core	Policy	Optional

18 Market Failure and Public Choice
[Introduces the role of government in the economy and explains the positive theory of government.]

19 Competition Policy

20 Externalities, the Environment, and Knowledge

21 A First Look at Macroeconomics

22 Measuring GDP, Inflation, and Economic Growth

23 Measuring Employment and Unemployment

24 Aggregate Supply and Aggregate Demand

25 Expenditure Multipliers

26 Fiscal Policy

[Chapters 25–30 may be delayed and studied after either or both of Chapters 31 and 32.]

27 Money, Banking, and Interest Rates

28 Monetary Policy

29 Fiscal and Monetary Interactions

30 Inflation

31 The Economy at Full Employment
[This chapter may be studied any time after Chapter 23.]

32 Economic Growth
[The section on growth theory is optional.]

33 The Business Cycle

34 Macroeconomic Policy Challenges

35 Trading with the World

36 International Finance

Four Alternative Micro Sequences

Four Alternative Macro Sequences

Brief Contents

Contents

Summary (Key Points, Key Figures and Tables, and Key Terms), Problems, and Critical Thinking appear at the end of each chapter.

Chapter **1**

What Is Economics?

From the moment you wake up each morning to the moment you fall asleep again each night, your life is filled with *choices*. Your first choice is when to get up. Will you start running the moment the alarm goes off, or will you linger for a few minutes and listen to the radio? What will you wear today? You check the weather forecast and make that decision. Then, what will you have for breakfast? Will you drive to school or take the bus? Which classes will you attend? Which assignments will you complete? What will you do for lunch? Will you play tennis, swim, run, or skate today? How will you spend your evening? Will you study, relax at home with a video, or go to the movies? ◆ You face decisions like these every day. But on some days, you face choices that can change the entire direction of your life. What will you study? Will you major in economics, business, law, or film? ◆ While you are making your own decisions, other people are making theirs. And some of the decisions that other people make will have an impact on your own subsequent decisions. Your school decides its course offerings for next year. Steven Spielberg decides what his next movie will be. General Motors decides what new models to introduce and how many of this year's models to produce. A team of eye doctors decides on a new experiment that will lead them to a cure for nearsightedness. Parliament decides to cut defence spending and to lower taxes. The Bank of Canada decides to lower interest rates. ◆ All these choices and decisions by you and everyone else are examples of economics in your life.

A Day in Your Life

◆ This chapter takes a first look at the subject you are about to study. It defines economics. Then it expands on that definition with five big questions that economists try to answer and eight big ideas that define the economic way of thinking. These questions and ideas are the foundation on which your course is built. The chapter concludes with a description of how economists go about their work, the scientific method they use, and the pitfalls they try to avoid. When you have completed your study of this chapter, you will have a good sense of what economics is about and you'll be ready to start learning economics and using it to gain a new view of the world.

After studying this chapter, you will be able to:

■ Define economics

■ Explain the five big questions that economists seek to answer

■ Explain eight ideas that define the economic way of thinking

■ Describe how economists go about their work

A Definition of Economics

ALL ECONOMIC QUESTIONS AND PROBLEMS ARISE from **scarcity**—they arise because our wants exceed the resources available to satisfy them.

We want good health and long life, material comfort, security, physical and mental recreation, and knowledge. None of these wants is completely satisfied for everyone, and everyone has some unsatisfied wants. While many people have all the material comfort they want, many others do not. And no one feels entirely satisfied with her or his state of health and expected length of life. No one feels entirely secure, even in the post–Cold War era, and no one has enough time for sport, travel, vacations, movies, theatre, reading, and other leisure pursuits.

The poor and the rich alike face scarcity. A child wants a 75¢ can of soft drink and a 50¢ pack of gum but has only $1.00 in her pocket. She experiences scarcity. A student wants to go to a party on Saturday night but also wants to spend that same night catching up on late assignments. He experiences scarcity. A millionaire wants to spend the weekend playing golf *and* attending a business strategy meeting and cannot do both. She experiences scarcity. Even parrots face scarcity—there just aren't enough crackers to go around!

Faced with scarcity, we must *choose* among the available alternatives. Economics is sometimes called the *science of choice*. More formally, **economics** is the science that studies the choices that people make when wants exceed the available resources—when resources are scarce.

Not only do I want a cracker—we all want a cracker!

Big Economic Questions

ALL ECONOMIC CHOICES CAN BE SUMMARIZED IN five big questions about the goods and services we produce. These questions are: What? How? Who? Where? When?

1. What?

What goods and services are produced and in what quantities? **Goods and services** are all the things that we value and are willing to pay for. We produce a dazzling array of goods and services that range from necessities such as houses to leisure items such as camping vehicles and equipment. We build more than a million new homes every year. And these homes are more spacious and better equipped than they were 20 years ago. We make several million new leisure vehicles, tents, portable microwaves, refrigerators, telephones, television sets, and VCRs, all of which make outdoor living and vacations more attractive and more comfortable.

What determines whether we build more homes or make more camping gear and develop more campsites? How do these choices change over time? And how are they affected by the ongoing changes in technology that make an ever-wider array of goods and services available to us?

others, they use a laser scanner. One farmer keeps track of his livestock feeding schedules and inventories by using paper and pencil records, while another uses a personal computer. GM hires workers to weld auto bodies in some of its plants and uses robots to do the job in others.

Why do we use machines in some cases and people in others? Do mechanization and technological change destroy more jobs than they create? Do they make us better off or worse off?

2. How?

How are goods and services produced? In a vineyard in France, basket-carrying workers pick the annual grape crop by hand. In a vineyard in Ontario, a machine and a few workers do the same job that a hundred French grape harvesters do. Look around you and you will see many examples of this phenomenon—the same job being done in different ways. In some supermarkets, checkout clerks key in prices. In

3. Who?

Who consumes the goods and services that are produced? Who consumes the goods and services produced depends on the incomes that people earn. Doctors earn much higher incomes than nurses and medical assistants. So, doctors get more of the goods and services produced than nurses and medical assistants.

You probably know about many other persistent differences in incomes. Men, on the average, earn more than women. College graduates, on the average, earn more than high school graduates do. Canadians, on the average, earn more than Europeans, who in turn earn more on the average than Asians and Africans. But there are some significant exceptions. The people of Japan and Hong Kong now earn an amount similar to that of Canadians. And there is a lot of income inequality throughout the world.

What determines the incomes we earn? Why do doctors earn larger incomes than nurses? Why do women and minorities earn less than white males?

4. Where?

Where are goods and services produced? The Kellogg Company, of Battle Creek, Michigan, makes breakfast cereals in 20 countries and sells them in 160 countries. Kellogg's business in Japan is so huge that it has a Japanese language Web site to promote its products! Honda, the Japanese auto producer, makes cars and motorcycles on most continents. "Globalization through localization" is its slogan. But it produces some cars in one country and ships them for sale in another. Canadians even import some cars from Japan.

In today's global economy, people who are separated by thousands of miles cooperate to produce many goods and services. Software engineers in the Ottawa Valley work via the Internet with programmers in India. American Express card charge slips are processed in Barbados. But there is a lot of local concentration of production as well. Most North American carpets are made in Dalton, Georgia. And most Canadian movies are made in Toronto.

What determines where goods and services are produced? And how are changing patterns of production location changing the jobs we do and the wages we earn?

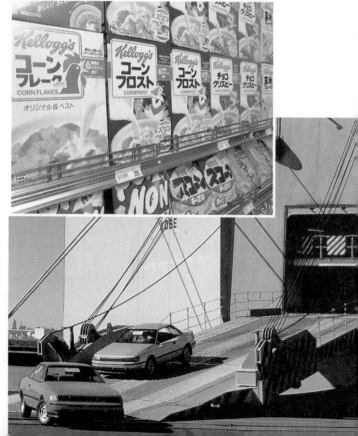

5. When?

When are goods and services produced? On a building site, there is a surge of production activity and people must work overtime to keep production flowing fast enough. An auto factory closes for the summer, temporarily lays off its workers, and its production dries up.

Sometimes, economy-wide production slackens off and even shrinks in what is called a *recession*. At other times, economy-wide production expands rapidly. We call these ebbs and flows of production the *business cycle*. When production falls, jobs are lost and unemployment climbs. Once, during the Great Depression of the 1930s, production fell so much that 20 percent of the work force was jobless.

During the past few years, production has decreased in Russia and its Central and Eastern European neighbours as these countries try to change the way they organize their economies.

In contrast, in Canada and the United States, production has expanded rapidly during the 1990s and unemployment has fallen. Is this burst of rapid expansion a sign of a "new economy" as some people claim, or is it just another example of a period of temporary expansion that will eventually end?

What makes production rise and fall? When will production fall again in Canada? Can the government prevent production from falling?

REVIEW QUIZ

- How would you define economics?
- What is scarcity? Give some examples of rich people and poor people facing scarcity.
- Give some examples, different from those in the chapter, of each of the five big economic questions.
- Why do you care about *what* goods and services are produced? Give some examples of goods that you value highly and goods on which you place a low value.
- Why do you care about *how* goods and services are produced? [Hint: Think about cost.]
- Why do you care about *who* gets the goods and services that are produced?
- Why do you care about *where* or *when* goods and services are produced?

These five big economic questions give you a sense of what economics is *about*. They tell you about the *scope of economics*. But they don't tell you what economics *is*. They don't tell you how economists *think* about these questions and seek answers to them. Let's find out how economists approach economic questions by looking at some big ideas that define the *economic way of thinking*.

Big Ideas of Economics

WE CAN SUMMARIZE THE ECONOMIC WAY OF thinking in eight big ideas. Let's study them.

1. Choice, Tradeoff, and Opportunity Cost

A choice is a tradeoff—we give up something to get something else—and the highest-valued alternative we give up is the opportunity cost of the activity we choose.

Whatever we choose to do, we could have done something else instead. We trade off one thing for another. **Tradeoff** means giving up something to get something else. The highest-valued alternative we give up to get something is the **opportunity cost** of the activity chosen. "There's no such thing as a free lunch" is not just a clever throwaway line. It expresses the central idea of economics—that every choice involves a cost.

We use the term *opportunity cost* to emphasize that when we make a choice in the face of scarcity, we give up an opportunity to do something else. The opportunity cost of any action is the highest-valued alternative forgone. The action that you choose not to do—the highest-valued alternative forgone—is the cost of the action that you choose to do.

You can quit school right now or you can remain in school. If you quit and take a job at McDonald's, you might earn enough to buy some CDs, go to the movies, and spend lots of free time with your friends. If you remain in school, you can't afford these things. You will be able to buy these things later, and that is one of the payoffs from being in school. But for now, when you've bought your books, you have nothing left for CDs and movies. And doing assignments means that you've got less time for hanging around with your friends. The opportunity cost of being in school is the alternative things that you would have done if you had quit school.

Opportunity cost is the highest-valued alternative forgone. It is not *all* the possible alternatives forgone. For example, your economics lecture is at 8:30 on a Monday morning. You contemplate two alternatives to the lecture: staying in bed for an hour or jogging for an hour. You can't stay in bed and jog for that same hour. The opportunity cost of attending the lecture is the forgone hour in bed *or* the forgone hour of jogging. If these are the only alternatives you consider, then you have to decide which one you would do if you did not go to the lecture. The opportunity cost of attending a lecture for a jogger is a forgone hour of exercise; the opportunity cost of attending a lecture for a late sleeper is a forgone hour in bed.

2. Margins and Incentives

We make choices in small steps, or at the margin, and choices are influenced by incentives. Everything that we do involves a decision to do a little bit more or a little bit less of an activity. You can allocate the next hour between studying and e-mailing your friends. But the choice is not "all-or-nothing." You must decide how many minutes to allocate to each activity. To make this decision, you compare the benefit of a little bit more study time with its cost—you make your choice at the **margin**.

The mother of a young child must decide how to allocate her time between being with her child and working for an income. Like your decision about study time, this decision too involves comparing the benefit of a little bit more income with the cost of a little bit less time with her child.

The benefit that arises from an increase in an activity is called **marginal benefit**. For example, suppose that a mother is working 2 days a week and is thinking about increasing her work to 3 days. Her marginal benefit is the benefit she will get from the additional day of work. It is *not* the benefit she gets from all 3 days. The reason is that she already has the benefit from 2 days work, so she doesn't count this benefit as resulting from the decision she is now making.

The cost of an increase in an activity is called **marginal cost**. For the mother of the young child, the marginal cost of increasing her work to 3 days a week is the cost of the additional day not spent with her child. It does not include the cost of the 2 days she is already working.

To make her decision, the mother compares the marginal benefit from an extra day of work with its marginal cost. If the marginal benefit exceeds the marginal cost, she works the extra day. If the marginal cost exceeds the marginal benefit, she does not work the extra day.

By evaluating marginal benefits and marginal costs and choosing only those actions that bring greater benefit than cost, we use our scarce resources in the way that makes us as well off as possible.

Our choices respond to incentives. An **incentive** is an inducement to take a particular action. The inducement can be a benefit—a carrot—or a cost—a stick. A change in opportunity cost—in marginal cost—and a change in marginal benefit changes the incentives that we face and leads to changes in our actions.

For example, suppose the daily wage rate rises and nothing else changes. With a higher daily wage rate, the marginal benefit of working increases. For the young mother, the opportunity cost of spending a day with her child has increased. She now has a bigger incentive to work an extra day a week. Whether or not she does so depends on how she evaluates the marginal benefit of the additional income and the marginal cost of spending less time with her child.

Similarly, suppose the cost of day care rises and nothing else changes. The higher cost of day care increases the marginal cost of working. For the young mother, the opportunity cost of spending a day with her child has decreased. She now has a smaller incentive to work an extra day a week. Again, whether or not she changes her actions in response to a change in incentives depends on how she evaluates the marginal benefit and marginal cost.

The central idea of economics is that by looking for changes in marginal cost and marginal benefit, we can predict the way choices will change in response to changes in incentives.

3. Voluntary Exchange and Efficient Markets

Voluntary exchange makes both buyers and sellers better off, and markets are generally an efficient way to organize exchange.

When you shop for food, you give up some money in exchange for a basket of vegetables. But the food is worth the price you have to pay. You are better off having exchanged some of your money for the vegetables. The food store receives a payment that makes its operator happy too. Both you and the food store operator gain from your purchase.

Similarly, when you work at a summer job, you receive a wage that you've decided is sufficient to compensate you for the leisure time you must give up. But the value of your work to the firm that hires you is at least as great as the wage it pays you. So again, both you and your employer gain from a **voluntary exchange**.

You are better off when you buy your food. And you are better off when you sell your labour during the summer vacation. Whether you are a buyer or a seller, you gain from voluntary exchange with others. What is true for you is true for everyone. Everyone gains from voluntary exchange.

In our economy, exchanges take place in **markets** and for money. We sell our labour in exchange for an income in the labour market. And we buy the goods and services we've chosen to consume in a wide variety of markets—markets for vegetables, coffee, movies, videos, muffins, haircuts, and so on. At the other side of these transactions, firms buy our labour and sell us the hundreds of different consumer goods and services we buy.

Markets are **efficient** in the sense that they send resources to the place where they are valued most highly. For example, a frost kills Florida's orange crop and sends the price of orange juice through the roof. This increase in price, with all other prices remaining unchanged, increases the opportunity cost of drinking orange juice. The people who place the highest value on orange juice are the ones who keep drinking it. People who place a lower value on orange juice now have an incentive to substitute other fruit juices.

Markets are not the only way to organize the economy. An alternative is called a command system. In a **command system**, some people give orders (commands) and other people obey those orders. A command system is used in the military and in many firms. And it was used in the former Soviet Union to organize the entire economy. But the market is a superior method of organizing an entire economy.

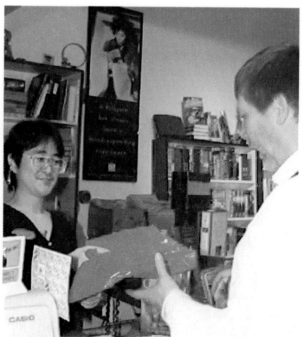

4. Market Failure

The market does not always work efficiently and government action is sometimes necessary to make the use of resources efficient.

Market failure is a state in which the market does not use resources efficiently. If you pay attention to the news media, you might get the impression that the market almost never does a good job. It makes credit card interest rates too high. It makes the wages of fast-food workers too low. It causes the price of coffee to go through the ceiling every time Brazil has a serious frost. It increases the world price of oil when political instability threatens the Middle East. These examples are not cases of market failure. They are examples of the market doing its job of helping us to allocate our scarce resources and ensure that they are used in the activities in which they are most highly valued.

Buyers never like it when prices rise. But sellers love it. And sellers never like it when prices fall. But buyers are happy. Rising and falling prices make news because they bring changes in fortunes. Some people win and some lose. Everyone gains from voluntary exchange, as you've just seen, but other things remaining the same, the higher the price, the more the seller gains and the less the buyer gains.

Because a high price brings a bigger gain to the seller, there is an incentive for sellers to try to control a market. When a single producer controls an entire market, the producer can restrict the quantity available and raise the price. This action brings market failure. The quantity of the good available is too small. Some people believe that Intel restricts the quantity of computer chips when it introduces a new design in order to get a high price for it. Eventually, the price falls, but at first, Intel sells its new design for a high price and makes a bigger profit.

Market failure can also arise when producers don't take into account the costs they impose on other people. For example, when foreign boats take huge quantities of cod from the North Atlantic, they deplete the stock of fish and destroy jobs and fishing communities in Newfoundland. If these costs were taken into account, the cod catch would be smaller.

Market failure can also arise because some goods, such as national defence, must be consumed equally by everyone. None of us has an incentive voluntarily to pay our share of the cost of such a good. Instead, we try to free ride on everyone else. But if everyone tries to free ride, no one gets a ride!

To overcome market failure, governments intervene in markets. They discourage the production and consumption of some goods and services (such as tobacco and alcohol) by taxing them. They encourage the production and consumption of some goods and services (such as health care and education) by subsidizing them. And they directly provide some goods and services (such as national defence).

5. Expenditure, Income, and the Value of Production

For the economy as a whole, expenditure *equals* income and *equals* the value of production.

When you buy a coffee milk shake, you spend $2. But what happens to that money? The server gets some of it in wages, the owner of the building gets some of it as rent, and the owner of the milk bar gets some of it as profit. The suppliers of the milk, ice cream, and coffee also get some of your $2. But these suppliers spend part of what they receive on wages and rent. And they keep part of it as profit. Your $2 of **expenditure** creates exactly $2 of **income** for all the people who have contributed to making the milk shake, going all the way back to the farmer in Brazil who grew the coffee beans.

Your expenditure generates income of an equal amount. The same is true for everyone else's expenditure. So, for the economy as a whole, total expenditure on goods and services equals total income. One way to value the things you buy is to use the prices you pay for them. So the value of all of the goods and services bought equals total expenditure. Another way to value the items you buy is to use the cost of production. This cost is the total amount paid to the people who produced the items—the total income generated by your expenditure. But we've just seen that total expenditure and total income are equal, so they also equal the **value of production**.

6. Living Standards and Productivity Growth

Living standards improve when production per person increases.

By automating a car production line, one worker can produce a greater output. But if one worker can produce more cars, then more people can enjoy owning a car. The same is true for all goods and services. With increased output per person, we enjoy a higher standard of living and buy more goods and services.

The dollar value of production can increase for any of three reasons: because prices rise, because production per person—**productivity**—increases, or because the population increases.

But only an increase in productivity brings an improvement in living standards. A rise in prices brings higher incomes, but only in dollars. The extra income is just enough to pay the higher prices, not enough to buy more goods and services. An increase in population brings an increase in *total* production, but not an increase in production per person.

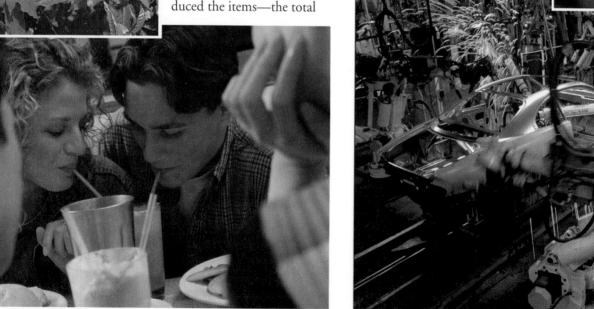

7. Inflation: A Monetary Problem

Prices rise in a process called **inflation** when the quantity of money increases faster than production. This process leads to a situation in which "too much money is chasing too few goods." As people bring more money to market, sellers see that they can raise their prices. But when these sellers go to buy their supplies, they find that the prices they face increase. With too much money around, money starts to lose value.

In some countries, inflation has been rapid. One such country is Poland. Since 1990, prices in Poland have risen more than seven-fold. In Canada, we have moderate inflation of about 1 percent a year.

Some people say that by increasing the quantity of money, we can create jobs. The idea is that if more money is put into the economy, when it is spent, businesses sell more and so hire more labour to produce more goods and services.

Initially, an increase in money might increase production and create jobs. But eventually, it only increases prices and leaves production and jobs unchanged.

8. Unemployment: Productive and Wasteful

Unemployment can result from market failure and be wasteful. But some unemployment is productive.

Unemployment is ever present. Sometimes its rate is low and sometimes it is high. Also, unemployment fluctuates over the business cycle.

Some unemployment is normal and efficient. We choose to take our time finding a suitable job rather than rushing to accept the first one that comes along. Similarly, businesses take their time in filling vacancies. The unemployment that results from these careful searches for jobs and workers improves productivity because it helps to assign people to their most productive jobs.

Some unemployment results from fluctuations in expenditure and can be wasteful.

REVIEW QUIZ

- Give some examples of *tradeoffs* that you have made and the *opportunity costs* you've incurred today.
- Give some examples of *marginal cost* and *marginal benefit*.
- How do markets enable both buyers and sellers to gain from exchange and why do markets sometimes fail?
- For the economy as a whole, why does expenditure equal income and the value of production?
- What makes living standards rise?
- What makes prices rise?
- Is unemployment always a problem?

What Economists Do

ECONOMISTS USE THE EIGHT BIG IDEAS THAT YOU have just studied to search for answers to the five big questions that you reviewed at the start of this chapter. But how do they go about their work? What special problems and pitfalls do they encounter? And do they always agree on the answers?

Microeconomics and Macroeconomics

Economists approach their work from either a micro or a macro perspective. These two perspectives define the two major branches of the subject:

■ Microeconomics
■ Macroeconomics

Microeconomics is the study of the decisions of individual people and businesses and the interaction of those decisions in markets.

Macroeconomics is the study of the national economy and the global economy. It seeks to explain *average* prices and *total* employment, income, and production.

You can take either a micro or a macro view of the spectacular display of national flags in a Korean sports stadium. The micro view is of a single participant and the actions he or she is taking. The macro view is the patterns formed by the joint actions of all the individuals participating in the entire display.

Microeconomics seeks to explain the prices and quantities of individual goods and services. It also studies the effects of government regulation and taxes on the prices and quantities of individual goods and services. For example, microeconomics studies the forces that determine the prices of cars and the quantities of cars produced and sold. It also studies the effects of regulations and taxes on the prices and quantities of cars.

Macroeconomics studies the effects of taxes, government spending, and the government budget surplus or deficit on total jobs and incomes. It also studies the effects of money and interest rates.

Economic Science

Economics is a social science (along with political science, psychology, and sociology). A major task of economists is to discover how the economic world works. In pursuit of this goal, economists (like all scientists) distinguish between two types of statements:

■ What *is*
■ What *ought* to be

Statements about what *is* are called *positive* statements. They say what is currently believed about the way the world operates. A positive statement might be right or wrong. And we can test a positive statement by checking it against the facts. When a chemist does an experiment in her laboratory, she is attempting to check a positive statement against the facts.

Statements about what *ought* to be are called *normative* statements. These statements depend on values and cannot be tested. When Parliament debates a motion, it is ultimately trying to decide what ought to be. It is making a normative statement.

To see the distinction between positive and normative statements, consider the controversy over global warming. Some scientists believe that centuries of the burning of coal and oil are increasing the carbon dioxide content of the earth's atmosphere and leading to higher temperatures that eventually will have devastating consequences for life on this planet. "Our planet is warming because of an increased carbon dioxide buildup in the atmosphere" is a positive statement. It can (in principle and with sufficient data) be tested. "We ought to cut back on our use of carbon-based fuels such as coal and oil" is a normative statement. You may agree with or disagree with this statement, but you can't test it. It is based on values. Health-care reform provides an economic example of the distinction. "Universal health care will cut the amount of work time lost to illness" is a positive statement. "Every Canadian should have equal access to health care" is a normative statement.

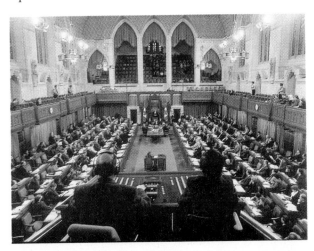

The task of economic science is to discover and catalogue positive statements that are consistent with what we observe in the world and that enable us to understand how the economic world works. This task is a large one that can be broken into three steps:

- Observation and measurement
- Model building
- Testing models

Observation and Measurement   First, economists keep track of the amounts and locations of natural and human resources, of wages and work hours, of the prices and quantities of the different goods and services produced, of taxes and government spending, and of the quantities of goods and services bought from and sold to other countries. This list gives a flavour of the array of things that economists can observe and measure.

Model Building   The second step toward understanding how the economic world works is to build a model. An **economic model** is a description of some aspect of the economic world that includes only those features of the world that are needed for the purpose at hand. A model is simpler than the reality it describes. What a model includes and what it leaves out result from *assumptions* about what is essential and what are inessential details.

You can see how ignoring details is useful—even essential—to our understanding by thinking about a model that you see every day, the TV weather map. The weather map is a model that helps to predict the temperature, wind speed and direction, and precipitation over a future period. The weather map shows lines called isobars—lines of equal barometric pressure. It doesn't show the highways. The reason is that our theory of the weather tells us that the pattern of air pressure, not the location of the highways, determines the weather.

An economic model is similar to a weather map. It tells us how a number of variables are determined by a number of other variables. For example, an economic model of the 1994 Los Angeles earthquake might tell us the effects of the earthquake and the government's relief efforts on the number of houses and apartments, rents and prices, jobs, and commuting times.

Testing   The third step is testing the model. A model's predictions may correspond to or be in conflict with the facts. By comparing the model's predictions with the facts, we are able to test a model and develop an economic theory. An **economic theory** is a generalization that summarizes what we think we understand about the economic choices that people make and the performance of industries and entire economies. It is a bridge between an economic model and the real economy.

A theory is created by a process of building and testing models. For example, meteorologists have a theory that if the isobars form a particular pattern at a particular time of the year (a model), then it will snow (reality). They have developed this theory by repeated observation and by carefully recording the weather that follows specific pressure patterns.

Economics is a young science. It was born in 1776 with the publication of Adam Smith's *The Wealth of Nations* (see pp. 58–59). Over the past 225 years, economics has discovered many useful theories. But in many areas, economists are still looking for answers. The gradual accumulation of economic knowledge gives most economists some faith that their methods will, eventually, provide usable answers to the big economic questions.

But progress in economics comes slowly. Let's look at some of the obstacles to progress in economics.

Obstacles and Pitfalls in Economics

We cannot easily do economic experiments. And most economic behaviour has many simultaneous causes. For these two reasons, it is difficult in economics to unscramble cause and effect.

Unscrambling Cause and Effect By changing one factor at a time and holding all the other relevant factors constant, we isolate the factor of interest and are able to investigate its effects in the clearest possible way. This logical device, which all scientists use to identify cause and effect, is called *ceteris paribus*. *Ceteris paribus* is a Latin term that means "other things being equal" or "if all other relevant things remain the same." Ensuring that other things are equal is crucial in many activities, including athletic events, and all successful attempts to make scientific progress use this device.

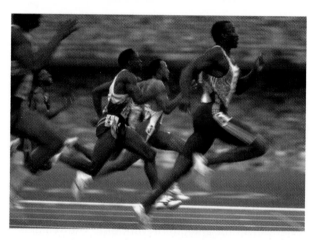

Economic models (like the models in all other sciences) enable the influence of one factor at a time to be isolated in the imaginary world of the model. When we use a model, we are able to imagine what would happen if only one factor changed. But *ceteris paribus* can be a problem in economics when we try to test a model.

Laboratory scientists, such as chemists and physicists, perform experiments by actually holding all the relevant factors constant except for the one under investigation. In the non-experimental sciences such as economics (and astronomy), we usually observe the outcomes of the *simultaneous* operation of many factors. Consequently, it is hard to sort out the effects of each individual factor and to compare the effects with what a model predicts. To cope with this problem, economists take three complementary approaches.

First, they look for pairs of events in which other things were equal (or similar). An example might be to study the effects of employment insurance on the unemployment rate by comparing Canada with the United States on the presumption that the people in the two economies are sufficiently similar. Second, economists use statistical tools—called *econometrics.* And third, when they can, they perform experiments. This relatively new approach puts real subjects (usually students) in a decision-making situation and varies their incentives in some way to discover how they respond to one factor at a time.

Economists try to avoid *fallacies*—errors of reasoning that lead to a wrong conclusion. But two fallacies are common, and you need to be on your guard to avoid them. They are the

■ Fallacy of composition
■ *Post hoc* fallacy

Fallacy of Composition   The fallacy of composition is the (false) statement that what is true of the parts is true of the whole or that what is true of the whole is true of the parts. Think of the true statement, "Speed kills," and its implication, going more slowly saves lives. If an entire freeway moves at a lower speed, everyone on the highway has a safer ride.

But suppose that one driver only slows down and all the other drivers try to maintain their original

speed. In this situation, there will probably be more accidents because more cars will change lanes to overtake the slower vehicle. So, in this example, what is true for the whole is not true for a part.

The fallacy of composition arises mainly in macroeconomics, and it stems from the fact that the parts interact with each other to produce an outcome for the whole that might differ from the intent of the parts. For example, a firm lays off some workers to cut costs and improve its profits. If all firms take similar actions, incomes fall

and so does spending. The firm sells less, and its profits don't improve.

Post Hoc Fallacy   Another Latin phrase—*post hoc ergo propter hoc*—means "after this, therefore because of this." The *post hoc* fallacy is the error of reasoning

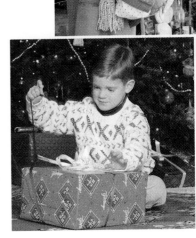

that a first event *causes* a second event because the first occurred before the second. Suppose you are a visitor from a far-off world. You observe lots of people shopping in early December and then you see them opening gifts and partying on Christmas day. Does the shopping cause Christmas, you wonder. After a deeper study, you discover that Christmas causes the shopping. A later event causes an earlier event.

Unravelling cause and effect is difficult in economics. And just looking at the timing of events often doesn't help. For example, the stock market booms, and some months later the economy expands—jobs and incomes grow. Did the stock market boom cause the economy to expand? Possibly, but perhaps businesses started to plan the expansion of production because a new technology that lowered costs had become available. As knowledge of the plans spread, the stock market reacted to *anticipate* the economic expansion. To disentangle cause and effect, economists use economic models and data and, to the extent that they can, perform experiments.

Economics is a challenging science. Does the difficulty of getting answers in economics mean that anything goes and that economists disagree on most questions? Perhaps you've heard the joke: "If you laid all the economists in the world end to end, they still wouldn't reach agreement." Does the joke make a valid point?

Agreement and Disagreement

Economists agree on a remarkably wide range of questions. And surprisingly, the agreed view of economists often disagrees with the popular and sometimes politically correct view. When Bank of Canada Governor Gordon Thiessen testifies before Parliament, his words are rarely controversial among economists, even when they generate endless debate in the media.

Here are 12 propositions[1] with which at least 7 out of every 10 economists broadly agree:

■ Tariffs and import restrictions make most people worse off.

■ A large federal budget deficit has an adverse effect on the economy.

■ Cash payments to welfare recipients make them better off than do transfers-in-kind of equal cash value.

■ A minimum wage increases unemployment among young workers and low skilled workers.

■ A tax cut can help to lower unemployment when the unemployment rate is high.

■ The distribution of income should be more equal.

■ Inflation is primarily caused by a rapid rate of money creation.

■ The government should restructure welfare along the lines of a "negative income tax."

■ Rent ceilings cut the availability of housing.

■ Pollution taxes are more effective than pollution limits.

■ The redistribution of income is a legitimate role for the federal government.

■ The federal budget should be balanced on the average over the business cycle, but not every year.

Which are positive and which are normative? Notice that economists are willing to offer their opinions on normative issues as well as their professional views on positive questions. Be on the lookout for normative propositions dressed up as positive propositions.

---

[1]These are propositions generally supported or supported with provisions by more than 7 out of 10 economists according to a survey by Richard M. Alston, J.R. Kearl, and Michael B. Vaughan, "Is There a Consensus Among Economists," *American Economic Review*, 82, (May 1992), pp. 203–209. We have simplified the language in some cases and you should check the original for the exact propositions and percentages agreeing.

REVIEW QUIZ

▨ What is the distinction between microeconomics and macroeconomics? Provide an example (not in the chapter) of a micro issue and a macro issue.

▨ What is the distinction between a positive statement and a normative statement? Provide an example (different from those in the chapter) of each type of statement.

▨ What is a model? Can you think of a model that you might use (probably without thinking of it as a model) in your everyday life?

▨ What is a theory? Why is the statement, "It might work in theory but it doesn't work in practice" a silly statement? [Hint: Think about what a theory is and how it is used.]

▨ What is the *ceteris paribus* assumption and how is it used?

▨ Try to think of some everyday examples of fallacies.

◇ You are now ready to start *doing* economics. As you get into the subject, you will see that we rely heavily on graphs. You must be comfortable with this method of reasoning. If you need some help with it, take your time in working carefully through Chapter 2. If you are already comfortable with graphs, then you are ready to jump right into Chapter 3 and begin to study the fundamental economic problem, scarcity.

S U M M A R Y

Key Points

A Definition of Economics (p. 2)

- Economics is the *science of choice*—the science that explains the choices that we make to cope with scarcity.

Big Economic Questions (pp. 2–5)

- Economists try to answer five big questions about goods and services:
  1. What?
  2. How?
  3. Who?
  4. Where?
  5. When?

  What are the goods and services produced, *how*, are they produced, *who* consumes them, and *where* and *when* are they produced?
- These questions interact to determine the standards of living and the distribution of well-being in Canada and around the world.

Big Ideas of Economics (pp. 6–11)

- A choice is a tradeoff and the highest-valued alternative forgone is the opportunity cost of what is chosen.
- Choices are made at the margin and are influenced by incentives.
- Markets enable both buyers and sellers to gain from voluntary exchange.
- Sometimes government actions are needed to overcome market failure.
- For the economy as a whole, expenditure equals income and equals the value of production.
- Living standards rise when production per person increases.
- Prices rise when the quantity of money increases faster than production.
- Unemployment can result from market failure but can also be productive.

What Economists Do (pp. 12–16)

- Microeconomics is the study of individual decisions, and macroeconomics is the study of the economy as a whole.
- Positive statements are about what *is* and normative statements are about what *ought* to be.
- To explain the economic world, economists build and test economic models.
- Economists use the *ceteris paribus* assumption to try to disentangle cause and effect, and they are careful to avoid the fallacy of composition and the *post hoc* fallacy.
- Economists agree on a wide range of questions about how the economy works.

Key Terms

Ceteris paribus, 14
Command system, 8
Economic model, 13
Economic theory, 13
Economics, 2
Efficient, 8
Expenditure, 10
Goods and services, 2
Incentive, 7
Income, 10
Inflation, 11
Macroeconomics, 12
Margin, 7
Marginal benefit, 7
Marginal cost, 7
Markets, 8
Market failure, 9
Microeconomics, 12
Opportunity cost, 6
Productivity, 10
Scarcity, 2
Tradeoff, 6
Unemployment, 11
Value of production, 10
Voluntary exchange, 8

PROBLEMS

*1. You plan to go to school this summer. If you do, you won't be able to take your usual job that pays $6,000 for the summer and you won't be able to live at home for free. The cost of your tuition will be $2,000, textbooks $200, and living expenses $1,400. What is the opportunity cost of going to summer school?

2. You plan a major adventure trip for the summer. You won't be able to take your usual summer job that pays $6,000 and you won't be able to live at home for free. The cost of your travel on the trip will be $3,000, film and video tape will cost you $200, and your food will cost $1,400. What is the opportunity cost of taking this trip?

*3. The local mall has free parking, but the mall is always very busy and it usually takes 30 minutes to find a parking space. Today when you found a vacant spot, Harry also wanted it. Is parking really free at this mall? If not, what did it cost you to park today? When you parked your car today, did you impose any costs on Harry? Explain your answers.

4. A city has built a new parking garage. There is always a free parking spot but it costs $1 a day. Before the new garage was built, it usually took 15 minutes of cruising to find a parking space. Compare the opportunity cost of parking in the new garage with that in the old parking lot. Which is less costly and by how much?

CRITICAL THINKING

1. Use the link on the Parkin-Bade Web site to visit *Resources for Economists on the Internet*. This site is a good place from which to search for economic information on the Internet. Visit the "general interest" sites and become familiar with the types of information that they contain.

2. Use the link on the Parkin-Bade Web site to visit *Statistics Canada*. Use this site to keep informed about the Canadian economy and about the economy of your own province and city.

a. What is the number of people employed in your area?
b. Has employment increased or decreased?
c. What is income per person in your area?

3. This man is homeless and you can see all his possessions in the photograph.

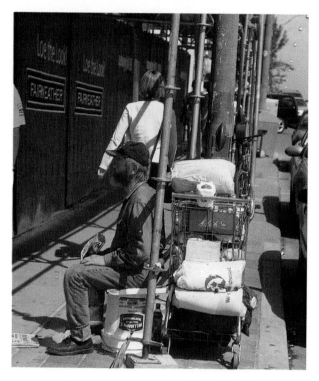

Use the five big questions and the eight big ideas of economics to organize a short essay about the economic life of the man in the photograph. Does he face scarcity? Does he make choices? Can you interpret his choices as being in his own best interest? Can either his own choices or the choices of others make this man better off? If so, how?

4. Use the link on the Parkin-Bade Web site to visit the *National Post*.
a. What is the top economic news story today?
b. With which of the five big questions does it deal? [Hint: It must deal with at least one of them and might deal with more than one.]
c. Which of the eight big ideas seem to be relevant to understanding this news item?
d. Write a summary of the news item using as much as possible of the economic vocabulary that you have learned in this chapter and that is in the key terms list on p. 17.

2

Making and Using Graphs

British Prime Minister Benjamin Disraeli is reputed to have said that "There are three kinds of lies: lies, damned lies, and statistics." One of the most powerful ways of conveying statistical information is in the form of a graph. And like statistics, graphs can lie. But the right graph does not lie. It reveals a relationship that would otherwise be obscure. ◆ Graphs are a modern invention. They first appeared in the late eighteenth century, long after the discovery of logarithms and calculus. But today, in the age of the personal computer and video display, graphs have become as important as

Three Kinds of Lies

words and numbers. How do economists use graphs? What types of graphs do they use? What do graphs reveal and what can they hide? ◆ The big questions that economics tries to answer—questions that you studied in Chapter 1—are difficult ones. They involve relationships among a large number of variables. Almost nothing in economics has a single cause. Instead, a large number of variables interact with each other. It is often said that in economics, everything depends on everything else. Changes in the quantity of ice cream consumed are caused by changes in the price of ice cream, the temperature, and many other factors. How can we make and interpret graphs of relationships among several variables?

◇ In this chapter, you are going to look at the kinds of graphs that economists use. You are going to learn how to make them and read them. You are also going to learn how to determine the magnitude of the influence of one variable on another by calculating the slope of a line and of a curve. ◆ There are no graphs or techniques used in this book that are more complicated than those explained and described in this chapter. If you are already familiar with graphs, you may want to skip (or skim) this chapter. Whether you study this chapter thoroughly or give it a quick pass, you can use it as a handy reference and return to it whenever you feel that you need extra help understanding the graphs that you encounter in your study of economics.

After studying this chapter, you will be able to:

■ Make and interpret a time-series graph, a scatter diagram, and a cross-section graph

■ Distinguish between linear and nonlinear relationships and between relationships that have a maximum and a minimum

■ Define and calculate the slope of a line

■ Graph relationships among more than two variables

Graphing Data

GRAPHS REPRESENT A QUANTITY AS A DISTANCE on a line. Figure 2.1 gives two examples. A distance on the horizontal line represents temperature, measured in degrees Celsius. A movement from left to right shows an increase in temperature. A movement from right to left shows a decrease in temperature. The point marked 0 represents zero degrees Celsius. To the right of 0, the temperatures are positive. To the left of 0, the temperatures are negative (as indicated by the minus sign in front of the numbers).

A distance on the vertical line represents altitude or height, measured in thousands of metres above sea level. The point marked 0 represents sea level. Points above 0 represent metres above sea level. Points below 0 (indicated by a minus sign) represent metres below sea level.

There are no rigid rules about the scale for a graph. The range of the variables being graphed determines the scale.

The main point of a graph is to enable us to visualize the relationship between two variables. And to accomplish this, we set two scales perpendicular to each other, like those in Fig. 2.1.

The two scale lines are called *axes*. The horizontal line is called the *x*-axis or horizontal axis, and the vertical line is called the *y*-axis or vertical axis. The letters *x* and *y* appear on the axes of Fig. 2.1. Each axis has a zero point, which is shared by the two axes. This zero point, common to both axes, is called the *origin*.

To show something in a two-variable graph, we need two pieces of information. We need the value of the variable *x* and the value of the variable *y*. For example, off the coast of British Columbia on a winter's day, the temperature is 10 degrees. Call this value *x*. A fishing boat is located at 0 metres above sea level. We'll call this value *y*. These two bits of information appear as point *a* in Fig. 2.1. A climber at the top of Mount McKinley on a very cold day is 6,194 metres above sea level in a zero degree gale. These two pieces of information appear as point *b*. The position of the climber on a warmer day might be at the point marked *c*. This point represents the peak of Mt. McKinley when the temperature is 10 degrees.

Two lines, called coordinates, can be drawn from point *c* in the graph. One of these lines runs from *c* to the horizontal axis. This line is called the *y*-coordinate. Its length is the same as the value marked off on the *y*-axis. The other of these lines

FIGURE 2.1

Making a Graph

All graphs have axes that measure quantities as distances. Here, the horizontal axis (*x*-axis) measures temperature. A rightward movement shows an increase in temperature. The vertical axis (*y*-axis) measures height. An upward movement shows an increase in height. Point *a* represents a fishing boat at sea level (0 on the *y*-axis) on a day when the temperature is 10° (10° on the *x*-axis). Point *b* represents a climber at the top of Mt. McKinley (6,194 metres above sea level on the *y*-axis) on a day when the temperature on Mt. McKinley is 0° (0° on the *x*-axis). Point *c* represents a climber at the top of Mt. McKinley, 6,194 metres above sea level (on the *y*-axis) on a day when the temperature on Mt. McKinley is 10° (on the *x*-axis).

runs from *c* to the vertical axis. This line is called the *x*-coordinate. Its length is the same as the value marked off on the *x*-axis. To describe a point in a graph, we simply use the values of its *x*- and *y*-coordinates.

Graphs like that in Fig. 2.1 can be used to show any type of quantitative data about two variables. Economists use graphs similar to the one in Fig. 2.1 to reveal and describe the relationships among economic variables. To do so, they use three main types of graph, which we'll now study. They are:

■ Scatter diagrams
■ Time-series graphs
■ Cross-section graphs

Scatter Diagrams

A **scatter diagram** plots the value of one economic variable against the value of another variable. Such a graph is used to reveal whether a relationship exists between two economic variables. It is also used to describe a relationship.

Consumption and Income   Figure 2.2(a) shows a scatter diagram of the relationship between consumption and income. The *x*-axis measures average income, and the *y*-axis measures average consumption. Each point shows consumption per person and income per person (on the average) in Canada in a given year from 1985 to 1998. The points for the fourteen years are "scattered" within the graph. Each point is labelled with a two-digit number that shows us its year. For example, the point marked 88 shows us that in 1988, income per person was $25,750 and consumption per person was $14,700.

The dots in this graph form a pattern, which reveals a positive relationship between these two variables. That is, when income increases, consumption also increases.

Phone Calls and Price   Figure 2.2(b) shows a scatter diagram of the relationship between the number of international phone calls made from Canada and the average price per minute.

The dots in this graph reveal that as the price per minute falls, the number of calls increases.

Unemployment and Inflation   Figure 2.2(c) shows a scatter diagram of inflation and unemployment in Canada. The dots in this graph form a pattern that shows us there is no clear relationship between these two variables. By its lack of a distinct pattern, the graph shows us there is no simple relationship between inflation and unemployment in Canada.

Correlation and Causation   A scatter diagram that shows a clear relationship between two variables, such as Fig. 2.2(a) or Fig. 2.2(b), tells us that the two variables have a high correlation. When a high correlation is present, we can predict the value of one variable from the value of the other variable. But correlation does not imply causation. Sometimes a high correlation is just a coincidence, but sometimes

---

FIGURE 2.2

Scatter Diagrams

(a) Consumption and income

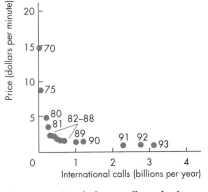

(b) International phone calls and prices

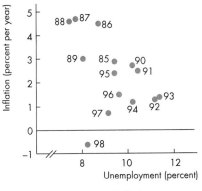

(c) Unemployment and inflation

A scatter diagram reveals the relationship between two variables. Part (a) shows the relationship between consumption and income between 1985 to 1998. Each point shows the values of the two variables in a specific year. For example, in 1988, average income was $25,750 and average consumption was $14,700. The pattern formed by the points shows that as income increases, so does consumption. Part (b) shows the relationship between the price of an international phone call and the number of phone calls made per year between 1970 and 1993. This graph shows that as the price of a phone call has fallen, the number of calls made has increased. Part (c) shows the inflation rate and unemployment rate in Canada between 1985 and 1998. This graph shows that inflation and unemployment are not closely related.

it does arise from a causal relationship. It is likely, for example, that increasing income causes increasing consumption (Fig. 2.2a) and that falling phone call prices cause more calls to be made (Fig. 2.2b).

Breaks in the Axes Two of the graphs you've just looked at, Fig. 2.2(a) and Fig. 2.2(c), have breaks in their axes, as shown by the small gaps. The breaks indicate that there are jumps from the origin, 0, to the first values recorded.

In Fig. 2.2(a), the breaks are used because the lowest value of consumption exceeds $10,000 and the lowest value of income exceeds $15,000. With no breaks in the axes, there would be a lot of empty space, all the points would be crowded into the top right corner, and we would not be able to see whether a relationship exists between these two variables. By breaking the axes, we are able to see the relationship.

Putting a break in the axes is like using a zoom lens to bring the relationship into the centre of the graph and magnify it so that it fills the graph.

Misleading Graphs Breaks can be used to highlight a relationship. But they can also be used to mislead and create a wrong impression—to make a graph that lies. The most common way of making a graph lie is to use axis breaks and to either stretch or compress a scale. The most effective way to see the power of this kind of lie is to make some graphs that use this technique. For example, redraw Fig. 2.2(a) but make the *y*-axis that measures consumption run from zero to $45,000 and keep the *x*-axis the same as the one shown. The graph will now create the impression that despite huge income growth, consumption has barely changed.

To avoid being misled, it is a good idea to get into the habit of always looking closely at the values and the labels on the axes of a graph before you start to interpret it.

Time-Series Graphs

A **time-series graph** measures time (for example, months or years) on the *x*-axis and the variable or variables in which we are interested on the *y*-axis. Figure 2.3 shows an example of a time-series graph. In this graph, time (on the *x*-axis) is measured in years, which run from 1968 to 1998. The variable that we are interested in is the price of coffee and it is measured on the *y*-axis.

A time-series graph conveys an enormous amount of information quickly and easily, as this example illustrates. It shows:

- The *level* of the price of coffee—when it is *high* and *low*. When the line is a long way from the *x*-axis, the price is high. When the line is close to the *x*-axis, the price is low.

- How the price *changes*—whether it *rises* or *falls*. When the line slopes upward, as in 1976, the price is rising. When the line slopes downward, as in 1978, the price is falling.

- The *speed* with which the price is changing—whether it is rising or falling *quickly* or *slowly*. If the line is very steep, then the price is rising or falling quickly. If the line is not steep, the price rises or falls slowly. For example, the price rose very quickly in 1976 and 1977. The price went up again in 1993 but slowly. Similarly, when the price was falling in 1978, it fell quickly, but during the early 1980s, it fell more slowly.

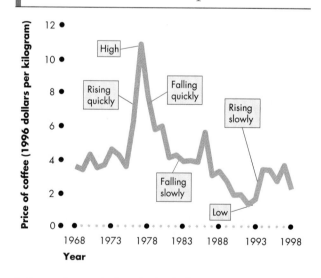

FIGURE 2.3
A Time-Series Graph

A time-series graph plots the level of a variable on the *y*-axis against time (day, week, month, or year) on the *x*-axis. This graph shows the price of coffee (in 1996 dollars per kilogram) each year from 1968 to 1998. It shows us when the price of coffee was *high* and when it was *low*, when the price *rose* and when it *fell*, and when it changed *quickly* and when it changed *slowly*.

A time-series graph also reveals whether there is a trend. A **trend** is a general tendency for a variable to rise or fall. You can see that the price of coffee had a general tendency to fall from the mid-1970s to the early 1990s. That is, although there were ups and downs in the price, there was a general tendency for it to fall.

A time-series graph also lets us compare different periods quickly. Figure 2.3 shows that the 1980s were different from the 1970s. The price of coffee fluctuated more violently in the 1970s than it did in the 1980s. This graph conveys a wealth of information, and it does so in much less space than we have used to describe only some of its features.

Comparing Two Time Series   Sometimes we want to use a time-series graph to compare two different variables. For example, suppose you want to know whether the balance of the government's budget fluctuates with the unemployment rate. You can examine the government's budget balance and the unemployment rate by drawing a graph of each of them on the same time scale. But we can measure the government's budget balance either as a surplus or as a deficit. Figure 2.4(a) plots the budget surplus. The scale of the unemployment rate is on the left side of the figure, and the scale of the government's budget surplus is on the right. The orange line shows unemployment, and the blue line shows the government's budget surplus. This figure shows that the unemployment rate and the government's budget surplus move in opposite directions. For example, when the unemployment rate decreases, the budget surplus increases.

Figure 2.4(b) uses a scale for the government's budget balance measured as a deficit. That is, we flip the right-side scale over. This figure shows that the unemployment rate and the budget deficit move in the same direction. The budget deficit and the unemployment rate increase together and decrease together.

Scatter Diagram for Comparing Two Time Series We can compare two time series in a graph like Fig. 2.4 or in a scatter diagram like Fig. 2.2. Which is better? There is no right answer to this question. If the purpose of the graph is to show *both* the way two variables have changed over time and how they are related to each other, then the time-series graph does the better job. But if the purpose of the graph is to check the strength of the relationship between two variables, then a scatter diagram does a better job. A relationship that looks strong in a time-series graph often looks weak in a scatter diagram.

FIGURE 2.4

Time-Series Relationships

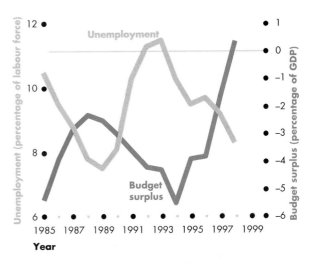

(a) Unemployment and budget surplus

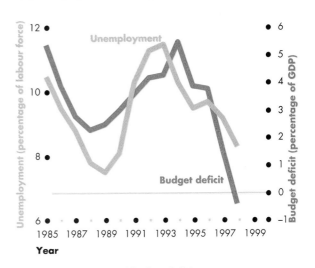

(b) Unemployment and budget deficit

These two graphs show the unemployment rate and the balance of the government's budget. The unemployment line is identical in the two parts. Part (a) shows the budget surplus—taxes *minus* spending—on the right scale. It is hard to see a relationship between the budget surplus and unemployment. Part (b) shows the budget as a deficit—spending *minus* taxes. It inverts the scale of part (a). With the scale for the budget balance inverted, the graph reveals a tendency for unemployment and the budget deficit to move together.

Cross-Section Graphs

A **cross-section graph** shows the values of an economic variable for different groups in a population at a point in time. Figure 2.5 is an example of a cross-section graph. It shows the unemployment rate across ten cities in Canada in 1998. This graph uses bars rather than dots and lines, and the length of each bar indicates the percentage of the labour force in the city unemployed. Figure 2.5 enables you to compare the unemployment rates in these ten cities. And you can do so much more quickly and clearly than by looking at a list of numbers.

The cross-section graph in Fig. 2.5 is also an example of a *bar chart*. We often use bars rather than lines in cross-section graphs, but there are no fixed rules about whether to use lines, dots, or bars. It is a matter of taste.

You've now seen how we can use graphs in economics to show economic data and to reveal relationships between variables. Next, we're going to learn how to use graphs in a more abstract way. We'll learn how economists use graphs to construct and display economic models.

FIGURE 2.5
A Cross-Section Graph

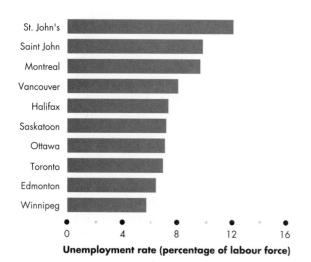

A cross-section graph shows the level of a variable across the members of a population. This graph shows the unemployment rate in ten Canadian cities in May 1998.

Graphs Used in Economic Models

THE GRAPHS USED IN ECONOMICS ARE NOT always designed to show real-world data. Often they are used to show general relationships among the variables in an economic model.

An **economic model** is a stripped down, simplified description of an economy or of a component of an economy such as a business or a household. It consists of statements about economic behaviour that can be expressed as equations or as curves in a graph. Economists use models to explore the effects of different policies or other influences on the economy in ways that are similar to the use of model airplanes in wind tunnels and models of the climate.

You will encounter many different kinds of graphs in economic models, but there are some repeating patterns and once you've learned to recognize these patterns, you will instantly understand the meaning of a graph. Here, we'll look at the different types of curves that are used in economic models, and we'll see some everyday examples of each type of curve. The patterns to look for in graphs are:

- Variables move in the same direction
- Variables move in opposite directions
- Variables have a maximum or a minimum
- Variables are unrelated

Let's look at these four cases.

Variables That Move in the Same Direction

Figure 2.6 shows graphs of the relationships between two variables that move up and down together. A relationship between two variables that move in the same direction is called a **positive relationship** or a **direct relationship**. Such a relationship is shown by a line that slopes upward.

Figure 2.6 shows three types of relationships, one that has a straight line and two that have curved lines. But all the lines in these three graphs are called curves. Any line on a graph—no matter whether it is straight or curved—is called a *curve*.

A relationship shown by a straight line is called a **linear relationship**. Figure 2.6(a) shows a linear relationship between the distance travelled in 5 hours

FIGURE 2.6

Positive (Direct) Relationships

(a) Positive linear relationship

(b) Positive becoming steeper

(c) Positive becoming less steep

Each part of this figure shows a positive (direct) relationship between two variables. That is, as the value of the variable measured on the x-axis increases, so does the value of the variable measured on the y-axis. Part (a) shows a linear relationship—as the two variables increase together, we move along a straight line. Part (b) shows a positive relationship such that as the two variables increase together, we move along a curve that becomes steeper. Part (c) shows a positive relationship such that as the two variables increase together, we move along a curve that becomes flatter.

and speed. For example, point *a* shows us that we will travel 200 kilometres in 5 hours if our speed is 40 kilometres an hour. If we double our speed to 80 kilometres an hour, we will travel 400 kilometres in 5 hours.

Part (b) shows the relationship between distance sprinted and recovery time (the time it takes the heart rate to return to its normal resting rate). This relationship is shown by a curved upward-sloping line that starts out quite flat but becomes steeper as we move along the curve away from the origin. The reason this curve slopes upward and becomes steeper is because the additional recovery time needed from sprinting an additional 100 metres increases. It takes less than five minutes to recover from 100 metres but more than 10 minutes to recover from the third 100 metres.

Part (c) shows the relationship between the number of problems worked by a student and the amount of study time. This relationship is shown by an upward-sloping curved line that starts out quite steep and becomes flatter as we move away from the origin. Study time becomes less productive as you increase the hours worked and become more tired.

Variables That Move in Opposite Directions

Figure 2.7 shows relationships between things that move in opposite directions. A relationship between variables that move in opposite directions is called a **negative relationship** or an **inverse relationship**.

Part (a) shows the relationship between the number of hours available for playing squash and the number of hours for playing tennis. One extra hour spent playing tennis means one hour less playing squash and vice versa. This relationship is negative and linear.

Part (b) shows the relationship between the cost per kilometre travelled and the length of a journey. The longer the journey, the lower is the cost per kilometre. But as the journey length increases, the cost per kilometre decreases, and the fall in the cost is smaller, the longer the journey. This feature of the relationship is shown by the fact that the curve slopes downward, starting out steep at a short journey length and then becoming flatter as the journey

FIGURE 2.7

Negative (Inverse) Relationships

(a) Negative linear relationship

(b) Negative becoming less steep

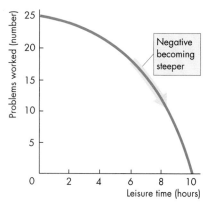

(c) Negative becoming steeper

Each part of this figure shows a negative (inverse) relationship between two variables. Part (a) shows a linear relationship—as one variable increases and the other variable decreases, we move along a straight line. Part (b) shows a negative relationship such that as the journey length increases the curve becomes less steep. Part (c) shows a negative relationship such that as leisure time increases, the curve becomes steeper.

length increases. This relationship arises because some of the costs are fixed, such as auto insurance, and the fixed costs are spread over a longer journey.

Part (c) shows the relationship between the amount of leisure time and the number of problems worked by a student. Increasing leisure time produces an increasingly large reduction in the number of problems worked. This relationship is a negative one that starts out with a gentle slope at a small number of leisure hours and becomes steeper as the number of leisure hours increases. This relationship is a different view of the idea shown in Fig. 2.6(c).

Variables That Have a Maximum or a Minimum

Many relationships in economic models have a maximum or a minimum. For example, firms try to make the maximum possible profit and to produce at the lowest possible cost. Figure 2.8 shows relationships that have a maximum or a minimum.

Part (a) shows the relationship between rainfall and wheat yield. When there is no rainfall, wheat will

not grow, so the yield is zero. As the rainfall increases up to 10 days a month, the wheat yield also increases. With 10 rainy days a month, the wheat yield reaches its maximum at 2 tonnes per hectare (point *a*). Rain in excess of 10 days a month starts to lower the yield of wheat. If every day is rainy, the wheat suffers from a lack of sunshine and the yield falls back to zero. This relationship is one that starts out sloping upward, reaches a maximum, and then slopes downward.

Part (b) shows the reverse case—a relationship that begins sloping downward, falls to a minimum, and then slopes upward. An example of such a relationship is the gasoline cost per kilometre as the speed of travel varies. At low speeds, the car is creeping along in a traffic snarl-up. The number of kilometres per litre is low, so the gasoline cost per kilometre is high. At very high speeds, the car is travelling faster than its most efficient speed, and again the number of kilometres per litre is low and the gasoline cost per kilometre is high. At a speed of 100 kilometres an hour, the gasoline cost per kilometre travelled is at its minimum (point *b*). This relationship starts out sloping downward, reaches a minimum, and then slopes upward.

FIGURE 2.8

Maximum and Minimum Points

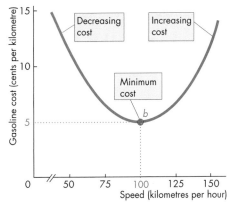

Part (a) shows a relationship that has a maximum point, *a*. The curve slopes upward as it rises to its maximum point, is flat at its maximum, and then slopes downward. Part (b) shows a relationship with a minimum point, *b*. The curve slopes downward as it falls to its minimum, is flat at its minimum, and then slopes upward.

(a) Relationship with a maximum

(b) Relationship with a minimum

Variables That Are Unrelated

There are many situations in which no matter what happens to the value of one variable, the other variable remains constant. Sometimes we want to show the independence between two variables in a graph and Fig. 2.9 shows two ways of achieving this.

In describing the graphs in Fig. 2.6 through 2.9, we have talked about the slopes of curves. Let's look more closely at the concept of slope.

FIGURE 2.9

Variables That Are Unrelated

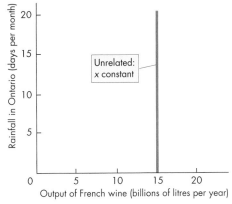

This figure shows how we can graph two variables that are unrelated to each other. In part (a), a student's grade in economics is plotted at 75 percent regardless of the price of bananas on the *x*-axis. The curve is horizontal. In part (b), the output of the vineyards of France in a year does not vary with the rainfall in Ontario. The curve is vertical.

(a) Unrelated: *y* constant

(b) Unrelated: *x* constant

The Slope of a Relationship

WE CAN MEASURE THE INFLUENCE OF ONE variable on another by the slope of the relationship. The **slope** of a relationship is the change in the value of the variable measured on the y-axis divided by the change in the value of the variable measured on the x-axis—or, slope equals rise over run. We use the Greek letter Δ (*delta*) to represent "change in." Thus Δy means the change in the value of the variable measured on the y-axis, and Δx means the change in the value of the variable measured on the x-axis. Therefore the slope of the relationship is

$$\Delta y / \Delta x.$$

If a large change in the variable measured on the y-axis (Δy) is associated with a small change in the variable measured on the x-axis (Δx), the slope is large and the curve is steep. If a small change in the variable measured on the y-axis (Δy) is associated with a large change in the variable measured on the x-axis (Δx), the slope is small and the curve is flat.

We can make the idea of slope sharper by doing some calculations.

The Slope of a Straight Line

The slope of a straight line is the same regardless of where on the line you calculate it. Thus the slope of a straight line is constant. Let's calculate the slopes of the lines in Fig. 2.10. In part (a), when x increases from 2 to 6, y increases from 3 to 6. The change in x is +4—that is, Δx is 4. The change in y is +3—that is,

---

FIGURE 2.10

The Slope of a Straight Line

(a) Positive slope

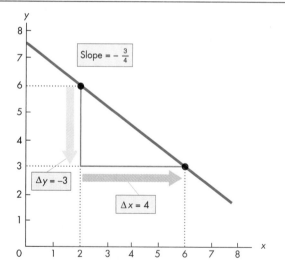

(b) Negative slope

To calculate the slope of a straight line, we divide the change in the value of the variable measured on the y-axis (Δy) by the change in the value of the variable measured on the x-axis (Δx), as we move along the curve. Part (a) shows the calculation of a positive slope. When x increases from 2 to 6, Δx equals 4. That change in x brings about an increase in y from 3

to 6, so Δy equals 3. The slope (Δy/Δx) equals 3/4. Part (b) shows the calculation of a negative slope. When x increases from 2 to 6, Δx equals 4. That increase in x brings about a decrease in y from 6 to 3, so Δy equals −3. The slope (Δy/Δx) equals −3/4.

Δy is 3. The slope of that line is

$$\frac{\Delta y}{\Delta x} = \frac{3}{4}.$$

In part (b), when x increases from 2 to 6, y decreases from 6 to 3. The change in y is *minus* 3—that is, Δy is –3. The change in x is *plus* 4—that is, Δx is 4. The slope of the curve is

$$\frac{\Delta y}{\Delta x} = \frac{-3}{4}.$$

Notice that the two slopes have the same magnitude (3/4), but the slope of the line in part (a) is positive (+3/+4 = 3/4), while the slope in part (b) is negative (–3/+4 = – 3/4). The slope of a positive relationship is positive; the slope of a negative relationship is negative.

The Slope of a Curved Line

The slope of a curved line is trickier. The slope of a curved line is not constant. Its slope depends on where on the line we calculate it. There are two ways to calculate the slope of a curved line: You can calculate the slope at a point or you can calculate the slope across an arc of the line. Let's look at the two alternatives.

Slope at a Point   To calculate the slope at a point on a curve, you need to construct a straight line that has the same slope as the curve at the point in question. Figure 2.11 shows how this is done. Suppose you want to calculate the slope of the curve at point a. Place a ruler on the graph so that it touches point a and no other point on the curve, then draw a straight line along the edge of the ruler. The straight red line is this line, and it is the tangent to the curve at point a. If the ruler touches the curve only at point a, then the slope of the curve at point a must be the same as the slope of the edge of the ruler. If the curve and the ruler do not have the same slope, the line along the edge of the ruler will cut the curve instead of just touching it.

Now that you have found a straight line with the same slope as the curve at point a, you can calculate the slope of the curve at point a by calculating the slope of the straight line. Along the straight line, as x increases from 0 to 4 ($\Delta x = 4$), y increases from 2 to 5

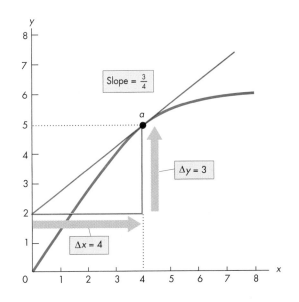

FIGURE 2.11

Slope at a Point

To calculate the slope of the curve at point a, draw the red line that just touches the curve at a—the tangent. The slope of this straight line is calculated by dividing the change in y by the change in x along the line. When x increases from 0 to 4, Δx equals 4. That change in x is associated with an increase in y from 2 to 5, so Δy equals 3. The slope of the red line is 3/4. So the slope of the curve at point a is 3/4.

(Δy = 3). Therefore the slope of the line is

$$\frac{\Delta y}{\Delta x} = \frac{3}{4}.$$

Thus the slope of the curve at point a is 3/4.

Slope Across an Arc   An arc of a curve is a piece of a curve. In Fig. 2.12, you are looking at the same curve as in Fig. 2.11. But instead of calculating the slope at point a, we are going to calculate the slope across the arc from b to c. You can see that the slope at b is greater than the slope at c. When we calculate the slope across an arc, we are calculating the average slope between two points. As we move along the arc from b to c, x increases from 3 to 5 and y increases from 4 to 5.5. The change in x is 2 ($\Delta x = 2$), and the

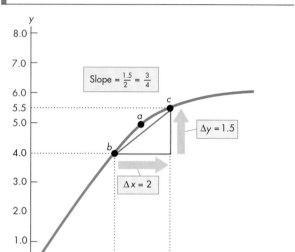

To calculate the average slope of the curve along the arc *bc*, draw a straight line from *b* to *c*. The slope of the line *bc* is calculated by dividing the change in *y* by the change in *x*. In moving from *b* to *c*, Δx equals 2 and Δy equals 1.5. The slope of the line *bc* is 1.5 divided by 2, or 3/4. So the slope of the curve across the arc *bc* is 3/4.

change in *y* is 1.5 ($\Delta y = 1.5$). Therefore the slope of the line is

$$\frac{\Delta y}{\Delta x} = \frac{1.5}{2} = \frac{3}{4}.$$

Thus the slope of the curve across the arc *bc* is 3/4.

This calculation gives us the slope of the curve between points *b* and *c*. The actual slope calculated is the slope of the straight line from *b* to *c*. This slope approximates the average slope of the curve along the arc *bc*. In this particular example, the slope across the arc *bc* is identical to the slope of the curve at point *a*. But the calculation of the slope of a curve does not always work out so neatly. You might have some fun constructing counterexamples.

You now know how to make and interpret a graph. But so far, we've limited our attention to graphs of two variables. We're now going to learn how to graph more than two variables.

Graphing Relationships Among More Than Two Variables

WE HAVE SEEN THAT WE CAN GRAPH THE relationship between two variables as a point formed by the *x*- and *y*-coordinates in a two-dimensional graph. You may be thinking that although a two-dimensional graph is informative, most of the things in which you are likely to be interested involve relationships among many variables, not just two. For example, the amount of ice cream consumed depends on the price of ice cream and the temperature. If ice cream is expensive and the temperature is low, people eat much less ice cream than when ice cream is inexpensive and the temperature is high. For any given price of ice cream, the quantity consumed varies with the temperature, and for any given temperature, the quantity of ice cream consumed varies with its price.

Figure 2.13 shows a relationship among three variables. The table shows the number of litres of ice cream consumed each day at various temperatures and ice cream prices. How can we graph these numbers?

To graph a relationship that involves more than two variables, we use the *ceteris paribus* assumption.

Ceteris Paribus The Latin phrase **ceteris paribus** means "other things remaining the same." Every laboratory experiment is an attempt to create *ceteris paribus* and isolate the relationship of interest. We use the same method to make a graph.

Figure 2.13(a) shows what happens to the quantity of ice cream consumed when the price of ice cream varies while the temperature is held constant. The line labelled 21°C shows the relationship between ice cream consumption and the price of ice cream if the temperature is 21°C. The numbers used to plot that line are those in the third column of the table in Fig. 2.13. For example, if the temperature is 21°C, 10 litres are consumed when the price is 60¢ a scoop, and 18 litres are consumed when the price is 30¢ a scoop. The curve labelled 32°C shows consumption as the price varies if the temperature is 32°C.

We can also show the relationship between ice cream consumption and temperature while the price of ice cream remains constant, as shown in Fig. 2.13(b). The curve labelled 60¢ shows how the con-

FIGURE 2.13

Graphing a Relationship Among Three Variables

(a) Price and consumption at a given temperature

(b) Temperature and consumption at a given price

(c) Temperature and price at a given consumption

Price (cents per scoop)	Ice cream consumption (litres per day)			
	−10°C	**10°C**	**21°C**	**32°C**
15	12	18	25	50
30	10	12	18	37
45	7	10	13	27
60	5	7	10	20
75	3	5	7	14
90	2	3	5	10
105	1	2	3	6

The quantity of ice cream consumed depends on its price and the temperature. The table gives some hypothetical numbers that tell us how many litres of ice cream are consumed each day at different prices and different temperatures. For example, if the price is 60¢ a scoop and the temperature is 21°C, 10 litres of ice cream are consumed. This set of values is highlighted in the table and each part of the figure. To graph a relationship among three variables, the value of one variable is held constant.

Part (a) shows the relationship between price and consumption when temperature is held constant. One curve holds temperature at 32°C and the other at 21°C. Part (b) shows the relationship between temperature and consumption when price is held constant. One curve holds the price at 60¢ a scoop and the other at 15¢ a scoop. Part (c) shows the relationship between temperature and price when consumption is held constant. One curve holds consumption at 10 litres and the other at 7 litres.

sumption of ice cream varies with the temperature when the price of ice cream is 60¢ a scoop, and a second curve shows the relationship when ice cream costs 15¢ a scoop. For example, at 60¢ a scoop, 10 litres are consumed when the temperature is 21°C and 20 litres when the temperature is 32°C.

Figure 2.13(c) shows the combinations of temperature and price that result in a constant consumption of ice cream. One curve shows the combination that results in 10 litres a day being consumed, and the other shows the combination that results in 7

litres a day being consumed. A high price and a high temperature lead to the same consumption as a lower price and a lower temperature. For example, 10 litres of ice cream are consumed at 32°C and 90¢ a scoop, at 21°C and 60¢ a scoop and at 10°C and 45¢ a scoop.

◆ With what you have learned about graphs, you can move forward with your study of economics. There are no graphs in this book that are more complicated than those that have been explained here.

MATHEMATICAL NOTE: EQUATIONS TO STRAIGHT LINES

IF A STRAIGHT LINE IN A GRAPH DESCRIBES THE relationship between two variables, we call it a **linear relationship**. Figure 1 shows the linear relationship between a person's expenditure and income. This person spends $100 a week (by borrowing or spending previous savings) when income is zero. And out of each dollar earned, this person spends 50 cents (and saves 50 cents).

All linear relationships are described by the same general equation. We call the quantity that is measured on the horizontal (or x-axis) x and we call the quantity that is measured on the vertical (or y-axis) y. In the case of Fig. 1, x is income and y is expenditure.

A Linear Equation

The equation that describes a straight-line relationship between x and y is:

$$y = a + bx.$$

In this equation, a and b are fixed numbers and they are called *constants*. The values of x and y vary so these numbers are called *variables*. Because the equation describes a straight line, it is called a **linear equation**.

The equation tells us that when the value of x is zero, the value of y is a. We call the constant a the y-axis intercept. The reason is that on the graph the straight line hits the y axis at a value equal to a. Figure 1 illustrates the y-axis intercept.

For positive values of x, the value of y exceeds a. The constant b tells us by how much y increases above a as x increases. The constant b is the slope of the line.

Slope of Line

As we explain in the chapter, the **slope** of a relationship is the change in the value of y divided by the change in the value of x. We use the Greek letter Δ (*delta*) to represent "change in." Thus Δy means the change in the value of the variable measured on the y-axis, and Δx means the change in the value of the variable measured on the x-axis. Therefore the slope of the relationship is

$$\Delta y \, / \, \Delta x.$$

To see why the slope is b, suppose that initially the value of x is x_1, or $200 in Fig. 2. The corresponding value of y is y_1, also $200 in Fig. 2. The equation to the line tells us that

$$y_1 = a + bx_1. \qquad (1)$$

Now the value of x increases by Δx to $x_1 + \Delta x$ (or $400 in Fig. 2). And the value of y increases by Δy to $y + \Delta y$ (or $300 in Fig. 2).

Figure 1 Linear relationship

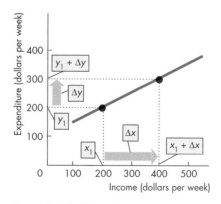

Figure 2 Calculating slope

The equation to the line now tells us that

$$y_1 + \Delta y = a + b(x_1 + \Delta x) \qquad (2)$$

To calculate the slope of the line, subtract equation (1) from equation (2) to obtain:

$$\Delta y = b\Delta x \qquad (3)$$

and now divide equation (3) by Δx to obtain:

$$\frac{\Delta y}{\Delta x} = b.$$

So, the slope of the line is b.

Position of Line

The y-axis intercept determines the position of the line on the graph. Figure 3 illustrates the relationship between the y-axis intercept and the position of the line on the graph. The y-axis measures saving and the x-axis measures income. When the y-axis intercept, a, is positive, the line hits the y-axis at a positive value of y—as the blue line does. When the y-axis intercept, a, is zero, the line hits the y-axis at the origin—as the purple line does. When the y-axis intercept, a, is negative, the line hits the y-axis at a negative value of y—as the red line does. As the equations to the three lines show, the value of the y-axis intercept does not influence the slope of the line.

Positive Relationships

Figure 1 shows a positive relationship—the two variables x and y move in the same direction. All positive relationships have a slope that is positive. In the equation to the line, the constant b is positive. In this example, the y-axis intercept, a, is 100. The slope b equals $\Delta y/\Delta x$, which is 100/200 or 0.5. The equation to the line is:

$$y = 100 + 0.5x.$$

Negative Relationships

Figure 4 shows a negative relationship—the two variables x and y move in the opposite direction. All negative relationships have a slope that is negative. In the equation to the line, the constant b is negative. In the example in Fig. 4, the y-axis intercept, a, is 30. The slope, b, equals $\Delta y/\Delta x$, which is $-20/2$ or -10. The equation to the line is:

$$y = 30 + (-10)x$$

or,

$$y = 30 - 10x.$$

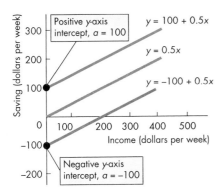

Figure 3 The y-axis intercept

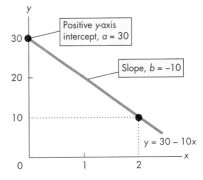

Figure 4 Negative relationship

S U M M A R Y

Key Points

Graphing Data (pp. 20–24)

- Time-series graphs show trends, cycles, and other fluctuations in economic data.
- Scatter diagrams show the relationship between two variables. They show whether two variables are positively related, negatively related, or unrelated.
- Cross-section graphs show how variables change across the members of a population.

Graphs Used in Economic Models (pp. 24–27)

- Graphs are used to show relationships among variables in economic models.
- Relationships can be positive (an upward-sloping curve), negative (a downward-sloping curve), positive and then negative (have a maximum point), negative and then positive (have a minimum point), or unrelated (a horizontal or vertical curve).

The Slope of a Relationship (pp. 28–30)

- The slope of a relationship is calculated as the change in the value of the variable measured on the y-axis divided by the change in the value of the variable measured on the x-axis—that is, $\Delta y/\Delta x$.
- A straight line has a constant slope.
- A curved line has a varying slope. To calculate the slope of a curved line, we calculate the slope at a point or across an arc.

Graphing Relationships Among More Than Two Variables (pp. 30–31)

- To graph a relationship among more than two variables, we hold constant the values of all the variables except two.
- We then plot the value of one of the variables against the value of another.

Key Figures ◆

Key Terms

R E V I E W   Q U I Z

- What are the three types of graphs used to show economic data?
- Give an example of a time-series graph.
- List three things that a time-series graph shows quickly and easily.
- Give three examples, different from those in the chapter, of scatter diagrams that show a positive relationship, a negative relationship, and no relationship.
- Draw some graphs to show the relationships between two variables:
  a. That move in the same direction.
  b. That move in opposite directions.
  c. That have a maximum.
  d. That have a minimum.
- Which of the relationships in the previous question is a positive relationship and which is a negative relationship?
- What are the two ways of calculating the slope of a curved line?
- How do we graph a relationship among more than two variables?

P R O B L E M S

Use the following data on the Canadian economy in problems 1, 2, 3, and 4. Column A is the year, column B is the inflation rate, column C is the interest rate, column D is the growth rate of output, column E is the unemployment rate.

	A	B	C	D	E
1	1980	9.6	12.7	1.4	7.5
2	1981	10.8	17.8	3.8	7.6
3	1982	8.7	13.8	-3.4	11.0
4	1983	5.0	9.3	3.3	11.9
5	1984	3.1	11.1	6.4	11.3
6	1985	2.6	9.5	5.4	10.5
7	1986	2.4	9.0	2.6	9.5
8	1987	4.7	8.2	4.1	8.8
9	1988	4.6	9.4	4.9	7.8
10	1989	4.8	12.0	2.5	7.5
11	1990	3.1	12.8	0.0	8.1
12	1991	2.7	8.9	−1.9	10.3
13	1992	1.4	6.5	1.0	11.3
14	1993	1.8	4.9	2.3	11.5
15	1994	0.2	5.4	4.7	10.3
16	1995	2.2	7.0	2.6	9.5
17	1996	1.6	4.2	1.2	9.7
18	1997	1.6	3.3	3.8	9.2
19	1998	1.0	4.7	4.2	8.3

*1. a. Draw a time-series graph of the inflation rate.
   b. In which year(s) (i) was inflation highest? (ii) was inflation lowest? (iii) did it increase? (iv) did it decrease? (v) did it increase most? and (vi) did it decrease most?
   c. What was the main trend in inflation?

2. a. Draw a time-series graph of the interest rate.
   b. In which year(s) (i) was the interest rate highest? (ii) was it lowest? (iii) did it increase? (iv) did it decrease? (v) did it increase most? and (vi) did it decrease most?
   c. What was the main trend in the interest rate?

3. Draw a scatter diagram to show the relationship between the inflation rate and the interest rate. Describe the relationship.

4. Draw a scatter diagram to show the relationship between the growth rate of output and the unemployment rate. Describe the relationship.

*5. Draw a graph to show the relationship between the two variables x and y:

x	0	1	2	3	4	5	6	7	8
y	0	1	4	9	16	25	36	49	64

   a. Is the relationship positive or negative?
   b. Does the slope of the relationship increase or decrease as the value of x increases?
   c. Think of some economic relationships that might be similar to this one.

6. Draw a graph that shows the relationship between two variables x and y:

x	0	1	2	3	4	5
y	50	48	44	32	16	0

   a. Is the relationship positive or negative?
   b. Does the slope of the relationship increase or decrease as the value of x increases?
   c. Think of some economic relationships that might be similar to this one.

*7. In problem 5, calculate the slope of the relationship between x and y when x equals 4.

8. In problem 6, calculate the slope of the relationship between x and y when x equals 3.

*9. In problem 5, calculate the slope of the relationship across the arc when x increases from 3 to 4.

10. In problem 6, calculate the slope of the relationship across the arc when x increases from 4 to 5.

*11. Calculate the slope of the relationship shown at point a in the following figure.

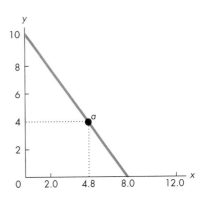

12. Calculate the slope of the relationship shown at point *a* in the following figure.

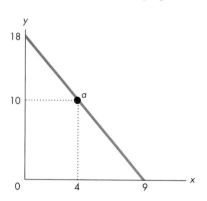

☐*13. Use the following figure to calculate the slope of the relationship:

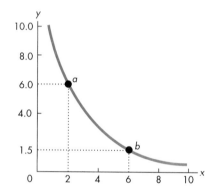

a. At points *a* and *b*.
b. Across the arc *ab*.

14. Use the following figure to calculate the slope of the relationship:

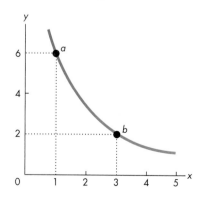

a. At points *a* and *b*.
b. Across the arc *ab*.

☐*15. The table gives the price of a balloon ride, the temperature, and the number of rides a day.

Price	Balloon rides (number per day)		
(dollars per ride)	10°C	20°C	30°C
5.00	32	40	50
10.00	27	32	40
15.00	18	27	32
20.00	10	18	27

Draw graphs to show the relationship between
a. The price and the number of rides, holding the temperature constant.
b. The number of rides and temperature, holding the price constant.
c. The temperature and price, holding the number of rides constant.

16. The table gives the price of umbrellas, rainfall, and the umbrellas purchased.

Price	Umbrellas (number per day)		
(dollars per umbrella)	0 mm	2 mm	10 mm
10	7	8	12
20	4	7	8
30	2	4	7
40	1	2	4

Draw graphs to show the relationship between
a. The price and the number of umbrellas purchased, holding rainfall constant.
b. The number of umbrellas purchased and rainfall, holding the price constant.
c. Rainfall and the price, holding the number of umbrellas purchased constant.

17. Visit the Parkin-Bade Web site and find the Consumer Price Index (CPI) for the latest 12 months. Make a graph to show whether the CPI is rising or falling and whether the rate of rise or fall is increasing or decreasing.

18. Visit the Parkin-Bade Web site and find the unemployment rate for the latest 12 months. Make a graph to show whether the unemployment rate is rising or falling and whether the rate of rise or fall is increasing or decreasing.

3

The Economic Problem

Making the Most of It

We live in a style that surprises our grandparents and would have astonished our great grandparents. Most of us live in more spacious homes than they did. We eat more, grow taller, and are even born larger than they were. Video games, cellular phones, gene splices, and personal computers did not exist even 20 years ago. But today it is hard to imagine life without them. Economic growth has made us richer than our grandparents. And we are not alone in experiencing an expansion in the goods and services we consume. Many nations around the world are not only sharing our experience, they are setting the pace. Hong Kong, Taiwan, Singapore, Korea, and China are expanding at unheard-of rates. But economic growth does not liberate us from scarcity. Why not? Why, despite our immense wealth, must we still make choices and face costs? Why are there no "free lunches"?
◆ We see an incredible amount of specialization and trade in the world. Each one of us specializes in a particular job—as a lawyer, a car maker, a homemaker. We have become so specialized that one farm worker can feed 100 people. Less than one-sixth of the Canadian work force is employed in manufacturing. More than half of the work force is employed in wholesale and retail trade, banking and finance, government, and other services. Why do we specialize? How do we benefit from specialization and trade?
◆ Over many centuries, institutions and social arrangements have evolved that we take for granted. One of them is property rights and a political and legal system that protects them. Another is markets. Why have these social arrangements evolved? How do they extend our ability to specialize and increase production?

◇ These are the questions that we study in this chapter. We begin with the core economic problem: scarcity and choice and the concept of the production possibility frontier. We then learn about the central idea of economics—efficiency. We also discover how we can expand production by accumulating capital and by specializing and trading with each other.
◆ What you will learn in this chapter is the foundation on which all economics is built. You will receive big dividends from a careful study of this material.

After studying this chapter, you will be able to:

- Explain the fundamental economic problem

- Define the production possibility frontier

- Define and calculate opportunity cost

- Explain the conditions in which resources are used efficiently

- Explain how economic growth expands production possibilities

- Explain how specialization and trade expand production possibilities

Resources and Wants

TWO FACTS DOMINATE OUR LIVES:

- We have limited resources.
- We have unlimited wants.

These two facts define **scarcity**, a condition in which the resources available are insufficient to satisfy people's wants.

Scarcity is a universal fact. It confronts each one of us individually, and it confronts our families, local communities, and nations.

The fundamental economic problem is to use our limited resources to produce the items that we value most highly. **Economics** is the study of the *choices* people make to cope with *scarcity*. It is the study of how we each individually try to get the most out of our own limited resources and of how in that endeavour we interact with each other. Let's look a bit more closely at our limited resources and unlimited wants.

Limited Resources

The resources that can be used to produce goods and services are grouped into four categories:

1. Labour
2. Land
3. Capital
4. Entrepreneurship

Labour is the time and effort that we devote to producing goods and services. It includes the physical and mental work of people who make cars and cola, gum and glue, wallpaper and watering cans.

Land is the gifts of nature that we use to produce goods and services. It includes the air, the water, and the land surface as well as the minerals that lie beneath the surface of the earth.

Capital is the goods that we have produced and that we can now use to produce other goods and services. It includes highways, buildings, dams and power projects, airports and jumbo jets, car production lines, shirt factories, and cookie shops.

Capital also includes **human capital**, which is the knowledge and skill that people obtain from education and on-the-job training. You are building human capital right now as you work on your economics course and other subjects. And your human capital will continue to grow when you get a full-time job and become better at it. Human capital improves the *quality* of labour.

Entrepreneurship is the resource that organizes labour, land, and capital. Entrepreneurs make business decisions, bear the risks that arise from these decisions, and come up with new ideas about what, how, where, and when to produce.

Our limited resources are converted into goods and services by using the technologies available. These technologies are limited by our knowledge—our human capital—and by our other resources.

Unlimited Wants

Our wants are limited only by our imaginations and are effectively unlimited. We want food and drink, clothing, housing, education, and health care. We want some of these things so badly that we call them *necessities*. But we also want many other things. We want cars and airplanes, movie theatres and videos, popcorn and pop, Walkmans and CDs, books and magazines, restaurant meals, vacations at the beach and in the mountains, music and poetry, and instant telecommunication across the globe.

Some of these wants are less pressing than others, but they are all wants. We even want things that are technologically impossible today but about which we fantasize. We want to live longer and healthier lives. Some of us want to hitch-hike the galaxy and be beamed around the universe.

Because our wants exceed our resources, we must make choices. We must rank our wants and decide which wants to satisfy and which to leave unsatisfied. We try to get the most out of our resources.

R E V I E W   Q U I Z

- What is scarcity?
- What is the fundamental economic problem?
- Can you provide a definition of economics?
- What are the resources that can be used to produce goods and services?
- How do we cope with the fact that our wants cannot be satisfied with the resources available?

We'll begin our study of the choices people make by looking at the limits to production and at a fundamental implication of choice—opportunity cost.

Resources, Production Possibilities, and Opportunity Cost

EVERY WORKING DAY, IN MINES, FACTORIES, shops, and offices and on farms and construction sites across Canada, 15 million people produce a vast variety of goods and services valued at around $27 billion. The quantities of goods and services that can be produced are limited by our available resources and by technology. That limit is described by the production possibility frontier.

The **production possibility frontier** (*PPF*) is the boundary between those combinations of goods and services that can be produced and those that cannot.

To illustrate the production possibility frontier in a graph, we focus our attention on two goods at a time. In focusing on two goods, we hold the quantities produced of all the other goods and services constant—a device called the *ceteris paribus* assumption. That is, we look at a *model* of the economy in which everything remains the same except for the production of the two goods we are currently considering.

Let's look at the production possibility frontier for two goods that most students buy—bottles of pop and CDs.

Production Possibility Frontier

The *production possibility frontier* for pop and CDs shows the limits to the production of these two goods, given the total resources available to produce them. Figure 3.1 shows this production possibility frontier. The table lists some combinations of the quantities of CDs and pop that can be produced given the resources available, and the figure graphs these combinations. The quantity of CDs produced is shown on the *x*-axis and the quantity of pop produced is shown on the *y*-axis. (The numbers are hypothetical.)

Because the *PPF* shows the *limits* to production, we cannot attain the points outside the frontier. They are points that describe wants that cannot be satisfied. We can produce at all the points *inside* the *PPF* and *on* the *PPF*. They are attainable points.

Suppose that in a typical month, 4 million CDs and 5 million bottles of pop are produced. Figure 3.1 shows this combination as point *e* and as possibility *e* in the table. Figure 3.1 also shows other production possibilities. For example, we might stop producing

FIGURE 3.1

Production Possibility Frontier

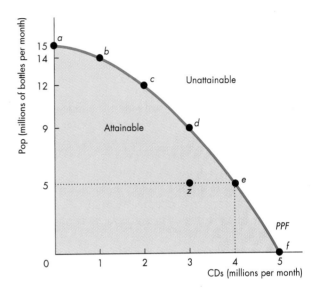

Possibility	CDs (millions per month)		Pop (millions of bottles per month)
a	0	and	15
b	1	and	14
c	2	and	12
d	3	and	9
e	4	and	5
f	5	and	0

The table lists six points on the production possibility frontier for CDs and pop. Row *a* tells us that if we produce no CDs, the maximum quantity of pop we can produce is 15 million bottles a month. The rows of the table are graphed as points *a, b, c, d, e,* and *f* in the figure. The line passing through these points is the production possibility frontier (*PPF*). It separates the attainable from the unattainable. We can produce at any point inside the orange area or on the frontier. Points outside the frontier are unattainable. Points inside the frontier such as point *z* are inefficient because it is possible to use the available resources to produce more of either or both goods.

CDs and move all the people who produce them into bottling pop. This case is shown as point *a* in the figure and possibility *a* in the table. The quantity of pop produced increases to 15 million bottles a month, and CD production dries up. Alternatively, we might close down the bottling plants and switch all the resources into producing CDs. In this situation, we produce 5 million CDs a month. This case is shown as point *f* in the figure and possibility *f* in the table.

Production Efficiency

We achieve **production efficiency** if we cannot produce more of one good without producing less of some other good. When production is efficient, we are at a point *on* the *PPF*. If we are at a point *inside* the *PPF*, such as point *z*, production is *inefficient* because we have some *unused* resources or we have some *misallocated* resources or both.

Resources are unused when they are idle but could be working. For example, we might leave some of the bottling plants idle or some workers might be unemployed.

Resources are *misallocated* when they are assigned to tasks for which they are not the best match. For example, we might assign skilled bottling machine operators to work in a CD factory and skilled CD makers to work in a bottling plant. We could get more CDs *and* more bottles of pop from these same workers if we reassigned them to the tasks that more closely match their skills.

If we produce at a point inside the *PPF* such as *z*, we can use our resources more efficiently to produce more CDs, more pop, or more of *both* CDs and pop. But if we produce at a point *on* the *PPF*, we are using our resources efficiently and we can produce more of one good only if we produce less of the other. We face a *tradeoff*.

Tradeoff

On the production possibility frontier, every choice involves a **tradeoff**—we must give up something to get something else. On the *PPF* in Fig. 3.1, we must give up some pop to get more CDs (or give up some CDs to get more pop).

Tradeoffs arise from scarcity and occur in every imaginable real-world situation. At any given point in time, we have a fixed amount of labour, land, capital, and entrepreneurship. By using our available technologies, we can employ these resources to produce goods and services. But we are limited in what we can produce. This limit defines a boundary between what we can attain and what we cannot attain. This

boundary is the real-world's production possibility frontier, and it defines the tradeoffs that we must make. On our real-world *PPF*, we can produce more of any one good or service only if we produce less of some other goods or services.

When doctors say we must spend more on AIDS and cancer research, they are suggesting a tradeoff—more medical research for less of some other things. When Jean Chrétien says he wants to spend more on education and health care, he is suggesting a tradeoff: more education and health care for less national defence or less private spending (because of higher taxes). When your parents say that you should study more, they are suggesting a tradeoff: more study time for less leisure or less sleep. When an environmental group argues for less logging, it is suggesting a tradeoff: greater conservation of endangered wildlife for less paper.

All tradeoffs involve a cost—an opportunity cost.

Opportunity Cost

The **opportunity cost** of an action is the highest-valued alternative forgone. We can make the concept of opportunity cost more precise by using the production possibility frontier. Along the frontier, there are only two goods, so there is only one alternative forgone—some quantity of the other good. Given our current resources and technology, we can produce more CDs only if we produce fewer bottles of pop. The opportunity cost of producing an additional CD is the number of bottles of pop we must forgo. Similarly, the opportunity cost of producing an additional bottle of pop is the quantity of CDs we must forgo.

For example, at point *c* in Fig. 3.1, we produce fewer CDs and more bottles of pop than at point *d*. If we choose point *d* over point *c*, the additional 1 million CDs *cost* 3 million bottles of pop. One CD costs 3 bottles of pop.

We can also work out the opportunity cost of choosing point *c* over point *d* in Fig. 3.1. If we move from point *d* to point *c*, the quantity of pop produced increases by 3 million bottles and the quantity of CDs produced decreases by 1 million. So if we choose point *c* over point *d*, the additional 3 million bottles of pop *cost* 1 million CDs. One bottle of pop costs 1/3 of a CD.

Opportunity Cost Is a Ratio Opportunity cost is a ratio. It is the decrease in the quantity produced of one good divided by the increase in the quantity produced of another good as we move along the production possibility frontier.

Because opportunity cost is a ratio, the opportunity cost of producing pop is equal to the *inverse* of the opportunity cost of producing CDs. Check this proposition by returning to the calculations we've just worked through. When we move along the *PPF* from *c* to *d*, the opportunity cost of a CD is 3 bottles of pop. The inverse of 3 is 1/3, so if we decrease the production of CDs and increase the production of pop by moving from *d* to *c*, the opportunity cost of a bottle of pop must be 1/3 of a CD. You can check that this number is correct. If we move from *d* to *c*, we produce 3 million more bottles of pop and 1 million fewer CDs. Because 3 million bottles cost 1 million CDs, the opportunity cost of 1 bottle of pop is 1/3 of a CD.

Increasing Opportunity Cost   The opportunity cost of a CD increases as the quantity of CDs produced increases. Also, the opportunity cost of pop increases as the quantity of pop produced increases. This phenomenon of increasing opportunity cost is reflected in the *shape* of the *PPF*—it is bowed outward.

When a large quantity of pop and a small quantity of CDs are produced—between points *a* and *b* in Fig. 3.1—the frontier has a gentle slope. A given increase in the quantity of CDs *costs* a small decrease in the quantity of pop, so the opportunity cost of a CD is a small amount of pop.

When a large quantity of CDs and a small quantity of pop are produced—between points *e* and *f* in Fig. 3.1—the frontier is steep. A given increase in the quantity of CDs *costs* a large decrease in the quantity of pop, so the opportunity cost of a CD is a large amount of pop.

The production possibility frontier is bowed outward because resources are not all equally productive in all activities. Production workers with many years of experience working for PepsiCo are very good at producing pop but not very good at making CDs. So if we move these people from PepsiCo to Maxell, we get a small increase in the quantity of CDs but a large decrease in the quantity of pop.

Similarly, plastics engineers and production workers who have spent many years working for Maxell are good at producing CDs but not so good at bottling pop. So if we move these people from Maxell to PepsiCo, we get a small increase in the quantity of pop but a large decrease in the quantity of CDs. The more we try to produce of either good, the less productive are the additional resources we use to produce that good and the larger is the opportunity cost of a unit of that good.

Increasing Opportunity Costs Are Everywhere
Just about every activity that you can think of is one with an *increasing* opportunity cost. Two examples are the production of food and the production of health-care services. We allocate the most skilful farmers and the most fertile land to the production of food. And we allocate the best doctors and least fertile land to the production of health-care services. If we shift fertile land and tractors away from farming to hospitals and ambulances and ask farmers to become hospital porters, the production of food drops drastically and the increase in the production of health-care services is small. The opportunity cost of a unit of health-care services rises. Similarly, if we shift our resources away from health-care towards farming, we must use more doctors and nurses as farmers and more hospitals as hydroponic tomato factories. The decrease in the production of health-care services is large, but the increase in food production is small. The opportunity cost of a unit of food rises.

This example is extreme and unlikely, but these same considerations apply to any pair of goods that you can imagine: housing and diamonds, wheelchairs and golf carts, pet food and breakfast cereals.

R E V I E W   Q U I Z

- How does the production possibility frontier illustrate scarcity?
- How does the production possibility frontier illustrate production efficiency?
- How does the production possibility frontier show that every choice involves a tradeoff?
- How does the production possibility frontier illustrate opportunity cost?
- Why is opportunity cost a ratio?
- Why does the *PPF* for most goods bow outward so that opportunity cost increases as the quantity produced of a good increases?

We've seen that production possibilities are limited by the production possibility frontier. And we've seen that production on the *PPF* is efficient. But there are many possible quantities we can produce on the *PPF*. How do we choose among them? How do we know which point on the frontier is the best one?

Using Resources Efficiently

H OW DO WE DECIDE WHETHER TO SPEND MORE on AIDS and cancer research? Whether to vote for an education and health-care package or a tax cut? Whether to join an environmental group and press for a greater conservation of endangered wildlife?

These are big questions that have enormous consequences. But you can see the essence of the answer by thinking about the simpler question: How do we decide how many CDs and how many bottles of pop to produce?

We decide by calculating and comparing two numbers:

■ Marginal cost
■ Marginal benefit

Marginal Cost

Marginal cost is the opportunity cost of producing *one more unit* of a good or service. You've seen how we can calculate opportunity cost as we move along the production possibility frontier. The marginal cost of a CD is the opportunity cost of *one* CD—the quantity of pop that must be given up to get one more CD—as we move along the *PPF*.

Figure 3.2 illustrates the marginal cost of a CD. If all the available resources are used to produce pop, 15 million bottles of pop and no CDs are produced. If we now decide to produce 1 million CDs, how much pop do we have to give up? You can see the answer in Fig. 3.2(a). To produce 1 million more CDs, we move from *a* to *b* and the quantity of pop decreases by 1 million bottles to 14 million a month. So the opportunity cost of the first 1 million CDs is 1 million bottles of pop.

If we decide to increase the production of CDs to 2 million, how much pop must we give up? This time, we move from *b* to *c* and the quantity of pop decreases by 2 million bottles. So the second million CDs costs 2 million bottles of pop.

You can repeat this calculation for an increase in the quantity of CDs produced from 2 million to 3 million, then to 4 million, and finally to 5 million. Figure 3.2(a) shows these opportunity costs as a series of steps. Each additional million CDs costs more bottles of pop then the preceding million did.

We've just calculated the opportunity cost of CDs in blocks of 1 million at a time and generated the steps

FIGURE 3.2

Opportunity Cost and Marginal Cost

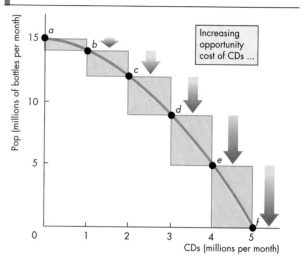

(a) PPF and opportunity cost

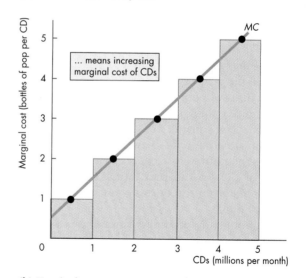

(b) Marginal cost

Opportunity cost is measured along the *PPF* in part (a). If the production of CDs increases from zero to 1 million, the opportunity cost of the first 1 million CDs is 1 million bottles of pop. If the production of CDs increases from 1 million to 2 million, the opportunity cost of the second 1 million CDs is 2 million bottles of pop. The opportunity cost of CDs increases as the production of CDs increases. Marginal cost is the opportunity cost of producing one more unit. Part (b) shows the marginal cost of a CD as the *MC* curve.

in Fig. 3.2(a). If we now calculate the opportunity cost of CDs one at a time, we obtain the *marginal cost* of a CD. In Fig. 3.2(b), the line labelled *MC* shows the marginal cost of a CD. The marginal cost of each additional CD in terms of forgone bottles of pop increases, so the marginal cost curve slopes upward.

Marginal Benefit

To use our resources efficiently, we must compare the marginal cost of a CD with its marginal benefit. **Marginal benefit** is the benefit that a person receives from consuming one more unit of a good or service. The marginal benefit from a good or service is measured as the maximum amount that a person is willing to pay for one more unit of it. It is a general principle that the more we have of any good or service, the smaller is our marginal benefit from it —the principle of *decreasing marginal benefit*.

To understand the principle of decreasing marginal benefit, think about your own marginal benefit from CDs. If CDs were very hard to come by and you can buy only one or two a year, you might be willing to pay a high price to get one more CD. But if CDs are readily available and you have as many as you can use, you are willing to pay almost nothing for yet one more CD.

In everyday life, we think of prices as money—as dollars per CD. But you have just been thinking about cost as opportunity cost, which is not a dollar cost but a cost in terms of a forgone alternative. You can also think about prices in the same terms. The price you pay for something is not the number of dollars you give up, but the goods and services that you would have bought with those dollars.

To see this idea more clearly, let's continue with the example we used to study the *PPF* and opportunity cost—CDs and pop. The marginal benefit from a CD can be expressed as the number of bottles of pop that a person is willing to forgo to get a CD. Figure 3.3 illustrates the marginal benefit from CDs. Marginal benefit is the way people feel about different quantities of goods and we can't derive it from the *PPF*. The numbers in Fig. 3.3 are *assumed*.

In row *a*, 0.5 million CDs a month are available and at that quantity, people are willing to pay 5 bottles of pop for a CD. As the quantity of CDs available increases, the amount that people are willing to pay for a CD falls. When 4.5 million CDs a month are available, people are willing to pay only 1 bottle of pop for a CD.

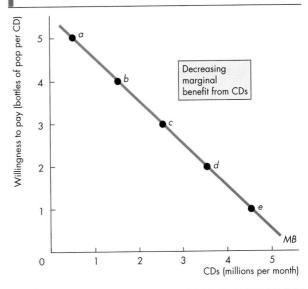

FIGURE 3.3
Marginal Benefit

Possibility	CDs (millions per month)	Willingness to pay (bottles per CD)
a	0.5	5
b	1.5	4
c	2.5	3
d	3.5	2
e	4.5	1

The fewer the number of CDs available, the more pop people are willing to give up to get an additional CD. If only 0.5 million CDs a month are available, people are willing to pay 5 bottles of pop for a CD. But if 4.5 million CDs a month are available, people will pay only 1 bottle of pop for a CD. Decreasing marginal benefit is a universal feature of people's preferences.

The marginal benefit from a CD and the opportunity cost of a CD are both measured in bottles of pop. But they are not the same concept. The *opportunity cost* of a CD is the amount of pop that people *must forgo* to get another CD. The *marginal benefit* from a CD is the amount of pop that people are *willing to forgo* to get another CD.

You now know how to calculate marginal cost and marginal benefit. Let's use these concepts to discover the efficient quantity of CDs to produce.

Efficient Use of Resources

Resource use is **efficient** when we produce the goods and services that we value most highly. That is, when we are using our resources efficiently, we cannot produce more of any good without giving up something that we value even more highly.

We always choose *at the margin*. We compare marginal cost and marginal benefit. If the marginal benefit from a good exceeds the marginal cost of the good, we increase production of that good. If marginal cost exceeds marginal benefit, we decrease production of the good. And if marginal benefit equals marginal cost, we stick with the current production.

This principle is just like the decisions you make when you go shopping. You have $10 to spend and are thinking about buying a CD or a box of floppy disks. You figure that you will get more value from the CD than from the floppy disks, so you spend your $10 on the CD. You have allocated scarce resources to their highest-value use. The marginal benefit from a CD is greater than (or equal to) its marginal cost, the box of floppy disks. The marginal benefit from a box of floppy disks is less than its marginal cost. No matter what the goods or services, if you can afford it and you think it is worth the price, you buy it. If you think it not worth its price, you pass it up.

We can illustrate an efficient use of resources by continuing to use the example of pop and CDs. Figure 3.4 shows the marginal cost and marginal benefit of CDs. Suppose we produce 1.5 million CDs a month. The marginal cost of a CD is 2 bottles of pop. But the marginal benefit from a CD is 4 bottles of pop. Because someone values an additional CD more highly than it costs to produce, we can get more value from our resources by moving some of them out of pop production and into CD production.

Now suppose we produce 3.5 million CDs a month. The marginal cost of a CD is now 4 bottles of pop. But the marginal benefit from a CD is only 2 bottles of pop. Because an additional CD costs more to produce than anyone thinks it is worth, we can get more value from our resources by moving some of them away from CD production and into pop production.

But suppose we produce 2.5 million CDs a month. Marginal cost and marginal benefit are now equal at 3 bottles of pop. This allocation of resources between CDs and pop is efficient. If more CDs are produced, the forgone pop is worth more than the additional CDs. If fewer CDs are produced, the forgone CDs are worth more than the additional pop.

FIGURE 3.4
Efficient Use of Resources

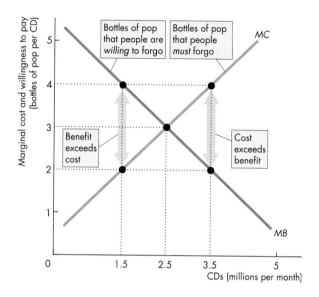

The greater the quantity of CDs produced, the smaller is the marginal benefit (*MB*) from a CD—the fewer bottles of pop people are willing to give up to get an additional CD. But the greater the quantity of CDs produced, the greater is the marginal cost (*MC*) of a CD—the more bottles of pop people must give up to get an additional CD. When marginal benefit equals marginal cost, resources are being used efficiently.

R E V I E W   Q U I Z

- What is marginal cost and how is it measured?
- What is marginal benefit and how is it measured?
- How does the marginal benefit from a good change as the quantity of that good increases? Why?
- What is the relationship between marginal cost and the production possibility frontier?
- What conditions must be satisfied if resources are used efficiently? Why?

You now understand the limits to production and the conditions under which resources are used efficiently. Your next task is to study the expansion of production possibilities.

Economic Growth

DURING THE PAST 30 YEARS, PRODUCTION PER person in Canada has doubled. Such an expansion of production is called **economic growth**. Can economic growth enable us to overcome scarcity and avoid opportunity cost? You are going to see that economic growth does not overcome scarcity and avoid opportunity cost. You are also going to see that the faster we make production grow, the greater is the opportunity cost of economic growth.

The Cost of Economic Growth

Two key factors influence economic growth: technological change and capital accumulation. **Technological change** is the development of new goods and of better ways of producing goods and services. **Capital accumulation** is the growth of capital resources.

As a consequence of technological change and capital accumulation, we have an enormous quantity of cars that enable us to produce more transportation than when we had only horses and carriages. We have satellites that make global communications possible on a scale that is much larger than that produced by the earlier cable technology. But new technologies and new capital have an opportunity cost. To use resources in research and development and to produce new capital, we must decrease our production of consumption goods and services. Let's look at this opportunity cost.

Instead of studying the *PPF* of CDs and pop, we'll hold the quantity of pop produced constant and examine the *PPF* for CDs and CD-making machines. Figure 3.5 shows this *PPF* as the blue curve *abc*. If we devote no resources to producing CD-making machines, we produce at point *a*. If we produce 3 million CDs a month, we can produce 6 CD-making machines at point *b*. If we produce no CDs, we can produce 10 CD-making machines a month at point *c*.

The amount by which our production possibilities expand depends on the resources we devote to technological change and capital accumulation. If we devote no resources to this activity (point *a*), the frontier remains at *abc*—the blue curve in Fig. 3.5. If we cut the current production of CDs and produce 6 machines a month (point *b*), then in the future, we'll have more capital and our *PPF* rotates outward to the

FIGURE 3.5

Economic Growth

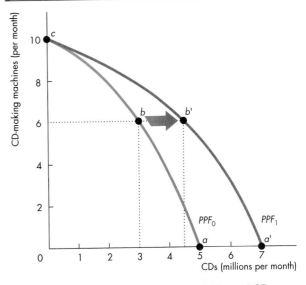

PPF_0 shows the limits to the production of CDs and CD-making equipment, with the production of all other goods and services remaining the same. If we devote no resources to producing CD-making machines and produce 5 million CDs a month, we remain stuck at point *a*. But if we decrease CD production to 3 million a month and produce 6 CD-making machines a month, at point *b*, our production possibilities will expand. After a year, the production possibility frontier shifts outward to PPF_1 and we can produce at point *b'*, a point outside the original *PPF*. We can shift the *PPF* outward but we cannot avoid opportunity cost. The opportunity cost of producing more CDs in the future is fewer CDs today.

position shown by the red curve. The fewer resources we devote to producing CDs and the more resources we devote to producing machines, the greater is the expansion of our production possibilities.

Economic growth is not free. To make it happen, we devote resources to producing new machines and fewer resources to producing CDs. In Fig. 3.5, we move from *a* to *b*. There is no free lunch. The opportunity cost of more CDs in the future is fewer CDs today. Also, economic growth is no magic formula for abolishing scarcity. On the new *PPF*, we continue to face opportunity costs.

The ideas about economic growth that we have explored in the setting of the CD industry also apply to nations. Let's look at two examples.

Economic Growth in Canada and Hong Kong

If as a nation we devote all our resources to producing consumer goods and none to research and capital accumulation, our production possibilities in the future will be the same as they are today. To expand our production possibilities in the future, we must devote fewer resources to producing consumption goods and some resources to accumulating capital and developing technologies so we can produce more consumption goods in the future. The decrease in today's consumption is the opportunity cost of an increase in future consumption.

The experiences of Canada and Hong Kong make a striking example of the effects of our choices on the rate of economic growth. In 1968, the production possibilities per person in Canada were two and a half times those in Hong Kong (see Fig. 3.6). Canada devoted one-fifth of its resources to accumulating capital and the other four-fifths to consumption. In 1968, Canada was at point *a* on its *PPF*. Hong Kong devoted two-fifths of its resources to accumulating capital and three-fifths to consumption. In 1968, Hong Kong was at point *a* on its *PPF*.

Since 1968, both countries have experienced economic growth, but growth in Hong Kong has been more rapid than in Canada. Because Hong Kong devoted a bigger fraction of its resources to accumulating capital, its production possibilities have expanded more quickly than Canada's production possibilities expanded.

In 1998, the *PPF* per person in Canada and Hong Kong are similar. If Hong Kong continues to devote a similar proportion of its resources to accumulating capital (at point *b* on the 1998 *PPF*), it will continue to grow more rapidly than Canada and its frontier will move out beyond our own. But if Hong Kong increases its consumption and decreases its capital accumulation (moving to point *c* on its 1998 production possibility frontier), then its rate of economic growth will slow.

Canada is typical of the rich industrial countries, which include the United States, Western Europe, and Japan. Hong Kong is typical of the fast-growing Asian economies, which include Taiwan, Thailand, South Korea, and China. Growth in these countries has slowed during the past two years, but before the slowdown, these countries expanded production by between 5 percent and almost 10 percent a year. If these high growth rates are restored, these other

countries will eventually close the gap on Canada as Hong Kong has done.

FIGURE 3.6

Economic Growth in Canada and Hong Kong

In 1968, the production possibilities per person in Canada were much larger than those in Hong Kong. But Hong Kong devoted more of its resources to accumulating capital than did Canada, so its production possibility frontier has shifted out more quickly than has that of Canada. In 1998, the two production possibilities per person were similar.

R E V I E W   Q U I Z

- What are the two key factors that generate economic growth?
- How does economic growth influence the production possibility frontier?
- What is the opportunity cost of economic growth?
- Why has Hong Kong experienced faster economic growth than Canada has?

Next, we're going to study another way we expand our production possibilities—the amazing fact that buyers and sellers gain from specialization and trade.

Gains from Trade

PEOPLE CAN PRODUCE FOR THEMSELVES ALL THE goods that they consume, or they can concentrate on producing one good (or perhaps a few goods) and then trade with others—exchange some of their own goods for those of others. Concentrating on the production of only one good or a few goods is called *specialization*. We are going to discover how people gain by specializing in the production of the good in which they have a *comparative advantage* and trading with each other.

Comparative Advantage

A person has a **comparative advantage** in an activity if that person can perform the activity at a lower opportunity cost than anyone else. Differences in opportunity costs arise from differences in individual abilities and from differences in the characteristics of other resources.

The range of individual ability is enormous. But no one excels at *everything*. One person is an outstanding pitcher but a poor catcher; another person is a brilliant lawyer but a poor teacher. In almost all human endeavours, what one person does easily, someone else finds difficult. The same applies to land and capital. One plot of land is fertile but has no mineral deposits; another plot of land has outstanding views but is infertile. One machine has great precision but is difficult to operate; another machine is fast but often breaks down.

Although no one excels at everything, some people excel and can outperform others in many activities. But such a person does not have a *comparative* advantage in every activity. For example, Robertson Davies was a better actor than most people. But he was an even better writer. So his *comparative* advantage was writing.

Because people's abilities and the quality of their resources differ, they have different opportunity costs of producing various goods. Such differences give rise to comparative advantage. Let's explore the idea of comparative advantage by looking at two CD factories, one operated by Tom and the other operated by Trish.

Tom's Factory   To simplify the story, suppose that CDs have just two components: a disc and a plastic case. Suppose that Tom has two production lines: one

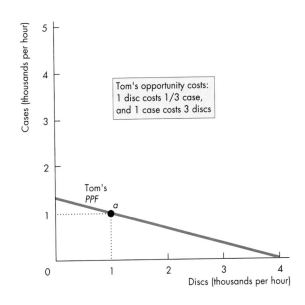

Production Possibilities in Tom's Factory

Tom's opportunity costs:
1 disc costs 1/3 case,
and 1 case costs 3 discs

Tom can produce discs and cases along the production possibility frontier *PPF*. For Tom, the opportunity cost of 1 disc is 1/3 of a case and the opportunity cost of 1 case is 3 discs. If Tom produces at point *a*, he can produce 1,000 cases and 1,000 discs an hour.

for discs and one for cases. Figure 3.7 shows Tom's production possibility frontier for discs and cases.

Tom's *PPF* in Fig. 3.7 is a straight line rather than a bowed out curve. This situation arises when resources are equally useful in each activity. We use this situation here because it lets us focus on comparative advantage without worrying about varying opportunity cost along the *PPF*.

Tom's *PPF* in Fig. 3.7 tells us that if Tom uses all his resources to make discs, he can produce 4,000 discs an hour. It also tells us that if Tom uses all his resources to make cases, he can produce 1,333 cases an hour. But to produce cases, Tom must decrease his production of discs. For each 1 case produced, he must decrease his production of discs by 3.

Tom's opportunity cost of producing 1 case is 3 discs.

Similarly, if Tom wants to increase his production of discs, he must decrease his production of cases. And for each 1,000 discs produced, he must decrease his production of cases by 333. So

Tom's opportunity cost of producing 1 disc is 0.333 cases.

Trish's Factory   The other factory, operated by Trish, can also produce cases and discs. But Trish's factory has machines that are custom-made for case production, so they are more suitable for producing cases than discs. Also, Trish's work force is more skilled in making cases.

This difference between the two factories means that Trish's production possibility frontier—shown along with Tom's *PPF* in Fig. 3.8—is different from Tom's. If Trish uses all her resources to make discs, she can produce 1,333 discs an hour. If she uses all her resources to make cases, she can produce 4,000 cases an hour. To produce discs, Trish must decrease her production of cases. For each 1,000 additional discs produced, she must decrease her production of cases by 3,000.

Trish's opportunity cost of producing 1 disc is 3 cases.

Similarly, if Trish wants to increase her production of cases, she must decrease her production of discs. For each 1,000 additional cases produced, she must decrease her production of discs by 333. So

Trish's opportunity cost of producing 1 case is 0.333 discs.

Suppose that Tom and Trish produce both discs and cases and that each produces 1,000 discs and 1,000 cases—1,000 CDs—an hour. That is, each produces at point *a* on their production possibility frontiers. Total production is 2,000 CDs an hour.

In which of the two goods does Trish have a comparative advantage? Recall that comparative advantage is a situation in which one person's opportunity cost of producing a good is lower than another person's opportunity cost of producing that same good. Trish has a comparative advantage in producing cases. Trish's opportunity cost of a case is 0.333 discs, whereas Tom's is 3 discs.

You can see her comparative advantage by looking at the production possibility frontiers for Trish

FIGURE 3.8

The Gains from Trade

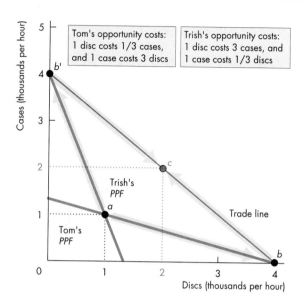

Tom and Trish each produce at point *a* on their respective *PPF*s. Trish has a comparative advantage in cases, and Tom has a comparative advantage in discs. If Trish specializes in cases, she produces at point *b'* on her *PPF*. If Tom specializes in discs, he produces at point *b* on his *PPF*. They exchange cases for discs along the red "Trade line." Trish buys discs from Tom for less than her opportunity cost of producing them, and Tom buys cases from Trish for less than his opportunity cost of producing them. Each goes to point *c*—a point outside his or her *PPF*—where each has 2,000 CDs an hour. Tom and Trish increase production with no change in resources.

and Tom in Fig. 3.8. Trish's production possibility frontier is steeper than Tom's. To produce one more case, Trish gives up fewer discs than Tom. Hence Trish's opportunity cost of a case is less than Tom's. This means that Trish has a comparative advantage in producing cases.

Tom's comparative advantage is in producing discs. His production possibility frontier is less steep than Trish's. This means that Tom gives up fewer cases to produce one more disc than Trish does. Tom's opportunity cost of producing a disc is 0.33 cases, which is less than Trish's 3 cases. So Tom has a comparative advantage in producing discs.

Achieving the Gains from Trade

Because Trish has a comparative advantage in cases and Tom in discs, they can both gain from specialization and exchange. If Tom, who has a comparative advantage in disc production, puts all his resources into that activity, he can produce 4,000 discs an hour—point *b* on his *PPF*. If Trish, who has a comparative advantage in producing cases, puts all her resources into that activity, she can produce 4,000 cases an hour—point *b'* on her *PPF*. By specializing, Tom and Trish together can produce 4,000 cases and 4,000 discs an hour, double their total production without specialization. By specialization and exchange, Tom and Trish can get *outside* their production possibility frontiers.

To achieve the gains from specialization, Tom and Trish must trade with each other. Suppose they agree to the following deal: Each hour, Trish produces 4,000 cases, Tom produces 4,000 discs, and Trish supplies Tom with 2,000 cases in exchange for 2,000 discs. With this deal in place, Tom and Trish move along the red "Trade line" to point *c*. At this point, each produces 2,000 CDs an hour—double their previous production rate. These are the gains from specialization and trade.

Both parties share the gains. Trish, who can produce discs at an opportunity cost of 3 cases per disc can buy discs from Tom for a price of 1 case per disc. Tom, who can produce cases at an opportunity cost of 3 discs per case, can buy cases from Trish at a price of 1 disc per case. Trish gets her discs more cheaply, and Tom gets his cases more cheaply.

Absolute Advantage

Suppose that Trish invents and patents a production process that makes her *four* times as productive as she was before in the production of both cases and discs. With her new technology, Trish can produce 16,000 cases an hour (4 times the original 4,000) if she puts all her resources into that activity. Alternatively, she can produce 5,332 discs (4 times the original 1,333) if she puts all her resources into that activity. Trish now has an **absolute advantage** in producing *both* goods—she can produce more of both goods than Tom can produce.

But Trish does not have a *comparative* advantage in both goods. She can produce four times as much of *both* goods as before, but her *opportunity cost* of 1

disc is still 3 cases. And this opportunity cost is higher than Tom's. So Trish can still get discs at a lower cost by exchanging cases for discs with Tom.

A key point to recognize is that it is *not* possible for *anyone* to have a comparative advantage in *everything*. So gains for specialization and trade are always available when opportunity costs diverge.

Dynamic Comparative Advantage

At any given point in time, the resources and technologies available determine the comparative advantages that individuals and nations have. But just by repeatedly producing a particular good or service, people become more productive in that activity, a phenomenon called **learning-by-doing**. Learning-by-doing is the basis of *dynamic* comparative advantage. **Dynamic comparative advantage** is a comparative advantage that a person (or country) possesses as a result of having specialized in a particular activity and, as a result of learning-by-doing, having become the producer with the lowest opportunity cost.

Hong Kong and Singapore are two countries that have pursued dynamic comparative advantage vigorously. They have developed industries in which initially they did not have a comparative advantage but, through learning-by-doing, became low opportunity cost producers in those industries. A specific example is Singapore's decision to develop a genetic engineering industry. Singapore probably did not have a comparative advantage in genetic engineering initially. But it might develop one as its scientists and production workers become more skilled in this activity.

R E V I E W   Q U I Z

- What gives a person a comparative advantage in producing a good?
- Why is it not possible for anyone to have a comparative advantage at everything?
- What are the gains from specialization and trade?
- Explain the source of the gains from specialization and trade.
- Distinguish between comparative advantage and absolute advantage.
- What is dynamic comparative advantage and how does it arise?

The Market Economy

INDIVIDUALS AND COUNTRIES GAIN BY SPECIALIZing in the production of those goods and services in which they have a comparative advantage and then trading with each other. This source of economic wealth was identified by Adam Smith in his *Wealth of Nations*, published in 1776—see pp. 58–59.

To enable billions of people who specialized in producing millions of different goods and services to reap these gains, trade must be organized. But trade need not be *planned* or *managed* by a central authority. In fact, when such an arrangement has been tried, as it was for 60 years in Russia, the result has been less than dazzling.

Trade is organized by using social institutions. Two key ones are:

■ Property rights
■ Markets

Property Rights

Property rights are social arrangements that govern the ownership, use, and disposal of resources, goods, and services. *Real property* includes land and buildings—the things we call property in ordinary speech—and durable goods such as plant and equipment. *Financial property* includes stocks and bonds and money in the bank. *Intellectual property* is the intangible product of creative effort. This type of property includes books, music, computer programs, and inventions of all kinds and is protected by copyrights and patents.

If property rights are not enforced, the incentive to specialize and produce the goods in which each person has a comparative advantage is weakened, and some of the potential gains from specialization and trade are lost. If people can easily steal the production of others, then time, energy, and resources are devoted not to production, but to protecting possessions.

Establishing property rights is one of the greatest challenges facing Russia and other Eastern European nations as they seek to develop market economies. Even in countries where property rights are well established, such as Canada, protecting intellectual property is proving to be a challenge in the face of modern technologies that make it relatively easy to copy audio and video material, computer programs, and books.

Markets

In ordinary speech, the word *market* means a place where people buy and sell goods such as fish, meat, fruits, and vegetables. In economics, a *market* has a more general meaning. A **market** is any arrangement that enables buyers and sellers to get information and to do business with each other. An example is the market in which oil is bought and sold—the world oil market. The world oil market is not a place. It is the network of oil producers, oil users, wholesalers, and brokers who buy and sell oil. In the world oil market, decision makers do not meet physically. They make deals throughout the world by telephone, fax, and direct computer link.

In the example we've just studied, Trish and Tom get together and do a deal. They agree to exchange cases for discs. But in a market economy, Trish sells cases to a dealer in plastic products and she buys discs from a dealer in electronic recording media. Similarly, Tom buys cases and sells discs in these same two markets. Tom can use Trish's cases and Trish can use Tom's discs and yet be unaware of the other's existence.

Circular Flows in the Market Economy

Figure 3.9 identifies two types of markets: goods markets and resource markets. *Goods markets* are those in which goods and services are bought and sold. *Resource markets* are those in which productive resources are bought and sold.

Households decide how much of their labour, land, capital, and entrepreneurship to sell or rent in resource markets. They receive incomes in the form of wages, rent, interest, and profit. Households also decide how to spend their incomes on goods and services produced by firms. Firms decide the quantities of resource to hire, how to use them to produce goods and services, what goods and services to produce, and in what quantities.

Figure 3.9 shows the flows that result from these decisions by households and firms. The red flows are the resources that go from households through resource markets to firms and the goods and services that go from firms through goods markets to households. The green flows in the opposite direction are the payments made in exchange for these items.

How do markets coordinate all these decisions?

FIGURE 3.9
Circular Flows in the Market Economy

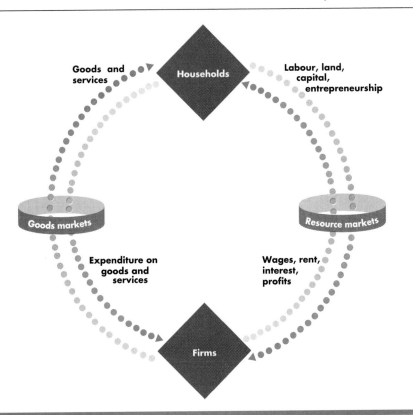

Households and firms make economic choices. Households choose the quantities of labour, land, capital, and entrepreneurship to sell or rent to firms in exchange for wages, rent, interest, and profits. Households also choose how to spend their incomes on the various types of goods and services available. Firms choose the quantities of resources to hire and the quantities of the various goods and services to produce. Goods markets and resource markets coordinate these choices of households and firms. Resources and goods flow clockwise (red) and money payments flow counterclockwise (green).

Coordinating Decisions

Markets coordinate individual decisions through price adjustments. To see how, think about your local market for hamburgers. Suppose that some people who want to buy hamburgers are not able to do so. To make the choices of buyers and sellers compatible, buyers must scale down their appetites or more hamburgers must be offered for sale (or both must happen). A rise in the price of hamburgers produces this outcome. A higher price encourages producers to offer more hamburgers for sale. It also encourages some people to change their lunch plans. Fewer people buy hamburgers, and more buy hot dogs. More hamburgers (and more hot dogs) are offered for sale.

Alternatively, suppose that more hamburgers are available than people want to buy. In this case, to make the choices of buyers and sellers compatible, more hamburgers must be bought or fewer hamburgers must be offered for sale (or both). A fall in the price of a hamburger achieves this outcome. A lower price encourages

firms to produce a smaller quantity of hamburgers. It also encourages people to buy more hamburgers.

R E V I E W Q U I Z

■ Why are social arrangements such as markets and property rights necessary?
■ What are the main functions of markets?

◆ You have now begun to see how economists approach economic questions. Scarcity, choice, and divergent opportunity cost explain why we specialize and trade and why property rights and markets have developed. You can see the lessons you've learned in this chapter all around you. *Reading Between the Lines* on pp. 52–53 gives an example. It explores the *PPF* of a student like you and the choices that students must make that influence their own economic growth—the growth of their incomes.

The Opportunity Cost and Benefit of Post-Secondary Education

THE MONTREAL GAZETTE, JUNE 7, 1998

Employers come knocking

BY DOUG SWEET

Najmeh Kalili…is 26, has just completed a bachelor of applied science degree at Concordia University…and, like much of this year's graduating class in both arts and sciences, faces a job market where employers most likely will be pounding on her door instead of the other way around.

But, unlike most of her classmates this spring, Kalili doesn't want a job yet. She knows she could get a high-paying job as a computer engineer, but she has decided to pursue another interest—biomedical engineering—before heading into the work force.

"It's very tempting (to go after a job)," she said, savouring the crisp air of a breezy June afternoon during a break from a sweltering basement lab at Concordia's Loyola campus, where she's working this summer.

"It takes a lot of energy to resist this temptation and continue doing what I want to do."…

"Most of the people in the class got good jobs. Several had more than one job offer," Kalili said. "I know some of my friends moved to the United States or other provinces to get even better jobs."…

Kalili said she's counting on the biomedical field catching fire the way computer engineering has in recent years.

"I think I will be able to find a job," she said during the break from the project she is working on…

"However, I don't think it will be as easy as if I stayed in engineering, because biomedical is more limited than electrical engineering. But maybe not by the time I'm done (the two-year master's). That's what I'm counting on."…

Essence of the Story

■ Najmeh Kalili has completed a bachelor's degree.

■ With her bachelor's degree, Najmeh can now get a good job.

■ Najmeh has chosen instead to continue her education and complete a master's degree.

■ She hopes to find an even better job when her education is complete.

The opportunity cost of a post-secondary education is forgone consumption. The payoff is an increase in lifetime production possibilities.

Figure 1 shows the choices that Najmeh faced when she left high school. She could choose any combination of education goods and services and consumption goods and services that are on the blue production possibility frontier.

If Najmeh decided not to attend university, then she could be at point *a* on the blue *PPF* and her *PPF* would remain the blue curve in Fig. 1.

When Najmeh attends university she consumes at point *b* on the blue *PPF*.

By attending university, Najmeh incurs an opportunity cost. She decreases her consumption of goods and services to increase her consumption of education goods and services.

With a completed bachelor's degree, Najmeh's consumption possibilities expand to the red *PPF* in Fig. 1.

The blue curve in Fig. 2 is the same *PPF* as the red *PPF* in Fig. 1. It is Najmeh's *PPF* following the completion of her bachelor's degree.

Now Najmeh must make another decision.

Will she quit university and take a job or will she remain in university and pursue a master's degree?

If Najmeh quits university, she can spend all her income on consumption goods and services and consume at point *c*.

But if she decides to pursue a master's degree, Najmeh incurs another opportunity cost. She must decrease her consumption of goods and services to consume education goods and services.

Najmeh slides around the blue *PPF* in Fig. 2 from point *c* to point *d*.

But with a completed master's degree, Najmeh will expand her production possibilities further.

The red *PPF* in Fig. 2 shows the expanded possibilities that Najmeh faces with a graduate degree. Following graduation, she can consume at any point on the red *PPF*.

The greater the resources that Najmeh devotes to education, the greater are her future consumption possibilities.

Najmeh is expanding her personal *PPF* by incurring a cost. Her economic growth has a cost, but it results in her reaping large returns.

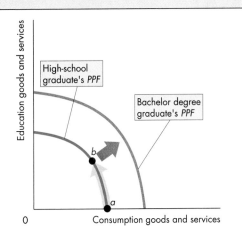

Figure 1 High-school graduate's choices

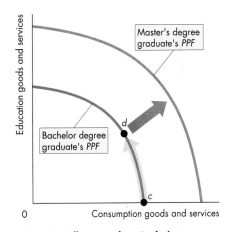

Figure 2 College graduate's choices

In September 1997, Prime Minister Chrétien announced the establishment of a Canada Millennium Scholarship Endowment Fund, which will provide thousands of scholarships each year for low- and moderate-income Canadians to attend post-secondary institutions.

Why do you think the Prime Minister is concerned about post-secondary education?

With such huge returns from education, why don't more people remain in university for longer?

What is the opportunity cost of the Prime Minister's plan?

Would you vote for or against a tax increase to fund the Millennium Scholarship Endowment Fund?

SUMMARY

Key Points

Resources and Wants (p. 38)

■ Economic activity arises from scarcity—resources are insufficient to satisfy people's wants.

■ Resources are labour, land, capital (including human capital), and entrepreneurship.

■ We choose how to use our resources and try to get the most out of them.

Resources, Production Possibilities, and Opportunity Cost (pp. 39–41)

■ The production possibility frontier, *PPF*, is the boundary between production levels that are attainable and those that are not attainable when all the available resources are used to their limit.

■ Production efficiency occurs at points on the *PPF*.

■ Along the *PPF*, the opportunity cost of producing more of one good is the amount of the other good that must be given up.

■ The opportunity cost of all goods increases as the production of the good increases.

Using Resources Efficiently (pp. 42–44)

■ The marginal cost of a good is the opportunity cost of producing one more unit.

■ The marginal benefit from a good is the maximum amount of another good that a person is willing to forgo to obtain more of the first good.

■ The marginal benefit of a good decreases as the amount available increases.

■ Resources are used efficiently when the marginal cost of each good is equal to its marginal benefit.

Economic Growth (pp. 45–46)

■ Economic growth, which is the expansion of production possibilities, results from capital accumulation and technological change.

■ The opportunity cost of economic growth is forgone current consumption.

Gains from Trade (pp. 47–49)

■ A person has a comparative advantage in producing a good if that person can produce the good at a lower opportunity cost than everyone else can.

■ It is *not* possible for *anyone* to have a comparative advantage at *everything*.

■ People gain by specializing in the activity in which they have a comparative advantage and trading with others.

The Market Economy (pp. 50–51)

■ Property rights and markets enable people to gain from specialization and trade.

■ Markets coordinate decisions and help to allocate resources to *higher* valued uses.

Key Figures

Key Terms

PROBLEMS

*1. Use the figure to calculate Wendell's opportunity cost of an hour of tennis when he increases the time he plays tennis from:
  a. 4 to 6 hours a week.
  b. 6 to 8 hours a week.

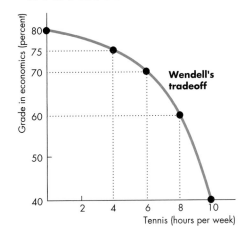

2. Use the figure to calculate Mary's opportunity cost of an hour of skating when she increases her time spent skating from:
  a. 2 to 4 hours a week.
  b. 4 to 6 hours a week.

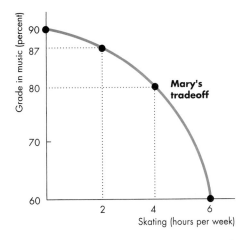

*3. In problem 1, describe the relationship between the time Wendell spends playing tennis and the opportunity cost of an hour of tennis.

4. In problem 2, describe the relationship between the time Mary spends skating and the opportunity cost of an hour of skating.

*5. Wendell, in problem 1, has the following marginal benefit curve:

  a. If Wendell uses his time efficiently, what grade will he get?
  b. Why would Wendell be worse off getting a higher grade?

6. Mary, in problem 2, has the following marginal benefit curve:

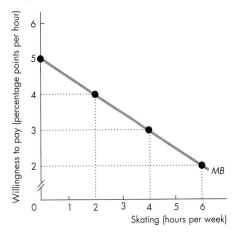

  a. If Mary uses her time efficiently, how much skating will she do?
  b. Why would Mary be worse off spending fewer hours skating?

*7. Leisureland's production possibilities are

Food (kilograms per month)		Sunscreen (litres per month)
300	and	0
200	and	50
100	and	100
0	and	150

  a. Draw a graph of Leisureland's production possibility frontier.

b. What are Leisureland's opportunity costs of producing food and sunscreen at each output in the table?

8. Jane's Island's production possibilities are:

Corn (kilograms per month)		Cloth (metres per month)
3	and	0
2	and	2
1	and	4
0	and	6

a. Draw a graph of the *PPF* on Jane's Island.
b. What are Jane's opportunity costs of producing corn and cloth at each output in the table?

*9. In problem 7, to get a litre of sunscreen people are willing to give up 5 kilograms of food if they have 25 litres of sunscreen; 2 kilograms of food if they have 75 litres of sunscreen; and 1 kilogram of food if they have 125 litres of sunscreen.
   a. Draw a graph of Leisureland's marginal benefit from sunscreen.
   b. What is the efficient use of sunscreen?

10. In problem 8, to get a metre of cloth Jane is willing to give up 0.75 kilograms of corn if she has 2 metres of cloth; 0.50 kilograms of corn if she has 4 metres of cloth; and 0.25 kilograms of corn if she has 6 metres of cloth.
   a. Draw a graph of Jane's marginal benefit from cloth.
   b. What is Jane's efficient quantity of cloth?

*11. Busyland's production possibilities are:

Food (kilograms per month)		Sunscreen (litres per month)
150	and	0
100	and	100
50	and	200
0	and	300

Calculate Busyland's opportunity costs of food and sunscreen at each output in the table?

12. Joe's Island's production possibilities are:

Corn (kilograms per month)		Cloth (metres per month)
6	and	0
4	and	1
2	and	2
0	and	3

What are Joe's opportunity costs of producing corn and cloth at each output in the table?

*13. In problems 7 and 11, Leisureland and Busyland each produce and consume 100 kilograms of food and 100 litres of sunscreen per month; and they do not trade. Now the countries begin to trade with each other.
   a. What good does Leisureland sell to Busyland and what good does it buy from Busyland?
   b. If Leisureland and Busyland divide the total output of food and sunscreen equally, what are the gains from trade?

14. In problems 8 and 12, Jane's Island produces and consumes 1 kilogram of corn and 4 metres of cloth. Joe's Island produces and consumes 4 kilograms of corn and 1 metre of cloth. Now the islands begin to trade.
   a. What good does Jane sell to Joe and what good does Jane buy from Joe?
   b. If Jane and Joe divide the total output of corn and cloth equally, what are the gains from trade?

CRITICAL THINKING

1. After you have studied *Reading Between the Lines* on pp. 52–53, answer the following questions:
   a. Why is the *PPF* for education goods and services and consumption goods and services bowed outward?
   b. At what point on the blue *PPF* in Fig. 1 on p. 53 is the combination of education goods and services and consumption goods and services efficient? Explain your answer.
   c. Students are facing rising tuition. Does this make the opportunity cost of education increase, decrease, or remain unchanged? Explain why.
   d. Who receives the benefits from education? Is the marginal cost of education equal to the marginal benefit of education? Is resource use in the market for education efficient?

2. Use the links on the Parkin-Bade Web site and obtain data on the tuition and other costs of enrolling in a graduate program and on job opportunities for graduates. Why doesn't everyone go to graduate school?

Understanding the Scope of Economics

You are living at a time that future historians will call the *Information Revolution*. We reserve the word "Revolution" for big events that influence all future generations. ◆ During the *Agricultural Revolution*, which occurred 10,000 years ago, people learned to domesticate animals and plant crops. They stopped roaming in search of food and settled in villages and eventually towns and cities, where they developed markets in which to exchange their products. ◆ During the *Industrial Revolution*,

Your Economic Revolution

which began 240 years ago, people used science to create new technologies. This revolution brought extraordinary wealth for some but created conditions in which others were left behind. It brought social and political tensions that we still face today. ◆ During today's *Information Revolution*, people who have the ability and opportunity to embrace the new technologies are prospering on an unimagined scale. But the incomes and living standards of the less educated are falling behind and social and political tensions are increasing. Today's revolution has a global dimension. Some of the winners live in previously poor countries in Asia, and some of the losers live here in Canada. ◆ So you are studying economics at an interesting

time. Whatever *your* motivation is for studying economics, *our* objective is to help you to do well in your course, to enjoy it, and to develop a deeper understanding of the economic world around you. ◆ There are three reasons why we hope that we both succeed. ◆ First, a decent understanding of economics will help you become a full participant in the Information Revolution. Second, an understanding of economics will help you play a more effective role as a citizen and voter and enable you to add your voice to those who are looking for solutions to our social and political problems. And third, you will enjoy the sheer fun of *understanding* the forces at play and how they are shaping our world. ◆ If you do find economics interesting, think seriously about majoring in the subject. A degree in economics gives the best training available in problem solving, offers lots of opportunities to develop conceptual skills, and opens doors to a wide range of graduate courses, including the MBA, and to a wide range of jobs. You can read more about the benefits of an economics degree in Robert Whaples' essay in your *Study Guide*.

◆ Economics as a discipline was born during the Industrial Revolution. We'll look at its birth and meet its founder, Adam Smith. Then we'll talk with one of today's leading economists, Professor John Whalley of the University of Western Ontario.

Probing the Ideas

The Sources of Economic Wealth

Adam Smith *was a giant of a scholar who contributed to ethics and jurisprudence as well as economics. Born in 1723 in Kirkcaldy, a small fishing town near Edinburgh, Scotland, Smith was the only child of the town's customs officer (who died before Adam was born).*

His first academic appointment, at age 28, was as Professor of Logic at the University of Glasgow. He subsequently became tutor to a wealthy Scottish duke, whom he accompanied on a two-year grand European tour, following which he received a pension of £300 a year—ten times the average income at that time.

With the financial security of his pension, Smith devoted ten years to writing An Inquiry into the Nature and Causes of **The Wealth of Nations**, *which was published in 1776. Many people had written on economic issues before Adam Smith, but he made economics a science. Smith's account was so broad and authoritative that no subsequent writer on economics could advance ideas without tracing their connections to those of Adam Smith.*

"It is not from the benevolence of the butcher, the brewer, or the baker that we expect our dinner, but from their regard to their own interest."

ADAM SMITH,
The Wealth of Nations

The Issues

Why are some nations wealthy while others are poor? This question lies at the heart of economics. And it leads directly to a second question: What can poor nations do to become wealthy?

Adam Smith, who is regarded by many scholars as the founder of economics, attempted to answer these questions in his book *The Wealth of Nations*. Smith was pondering these questions at the height of the Industrial Revolution. During those years, new technologies were invented and applied to the manufacture of cotton and wool cloth, iron, transportation, and agriculture.

Smith wanted to understand the sources of economic wealth, and he brought his acute powers of observation and abstraction to bear on the question. His answer:

- The division of labour
- Free markets

The division of labour—breaking tasks down to simple tasks and becoming skilled in those tasks—is the source of "the greatest improvement in the productive powers of labour," said Smith. The division of labour became even more productive when it was applied to creating new technologies. Scientists and engineers, trained in extremely narrow fields, became specialists at inventing. Their powerful skills accelerated the advance of technology, so by the 1820s, machines could make consumer goods faster and more accurately than any craftsman could. And by the 1850s, machines could make other machines that labour alone could never have made.

But, said Smith, the fruits of the division of labour are limited by the extent of the market. To make the market as large as possible, there must be no impediments to free trade both within a country and among countries. Smith argued that when each person makes the best possible economic choice, that choice leads as if by "an invisible hand" to the best outcome for society as a whole. The butcher, the brewer, and the baker each pursue their own interests but, in doing so, also serve the interests of everyone else.

Then ...

Adam Smith speculated that one person, working hard, using the hand tools available in the 1770s, might possibly make 20 pins a day. Yet, he observed, by using those same hand tools but breaking the process into a number of individually small operations in which people specialize—by the **division of labour**—ten people could make a staggering 48,000 pins a day. One draws out the wire, another straightens it, a third cuts it, a fourth points it, a fifth grinds it. Three specialists make the head, and a fourth attaches it. Finally, the pin is polished and packaged. But a large market is needed to support the division of labour: one factory employing ten workers would need to sell more than 15 million pins a year to stay in business.

... and Now

If Adam Smith were here today, the computer chip would fascinate him. He would see it as an extraordinary example of the productivity of the division of labour and of the use of machines to make machines that make other machines. From a design of a chip's intricate circuits, cameras transfer an image to glass plates that work like stencils. Workers prepare silicon wafers on which the circuits are printed. Some slice the wafers, others polish them, others bake them, and yet others coat them with a light-sensitive chemical. Machines transfer a copy of the circuit onto the wafer. Chemicals then etch the design onto the wafer. Further processes deposit atom-sized transistors and aluminum connectors. Finally, a laser separates the hundreds of chips on the wafer. Every stage in the process of creating a computer chip uses other computer chips. And like the pin of the 1770s, the computer chip of the 1990s benefits from a large market—a global market—to buy chips in the huge quantities in which they are produced efficiently.

Many economists have worked to refine the big themes that Smith began. One of these economists is John Whalley, whom you can meet on the following pages.

Talking with
John Whalley

new tools for computing the quantitative effects of policy actions.

Professor Whalley is an all-round economist. He works on theoretical problems, he measures the quantitative effects of policies, and he advises governments and international agencies on the consequences of alternative policy choices.

Robin Bade and Michael Parkin talked with Professor Whalley about his work, how it connects with the insights of Adam Smith, and the contribution that he and other economists are making to try to improve living standards and economic relations among nations in today's world.

John Whalley *is Professor of Economics and Director of the Centre for the Study of International Economic Relations at the University of Western Ontario and Professor of International and Development Economics and Director of the Development and International Economics Research Centre at the University of Warwick, England. He is also a Research Associate at the National Bureau of Economic Research. Born in England in 1947, Professor Whalley was an undergraduate at the University of Essex and a graduate student at Yale University. He received his Ph.D. in 1973 and began his academic career at the London School of Economics. He came to Canada in 1976. Professor Whalley is a prolific scholar. He has published 30 books and more than 200 articles on globalization, economic development, taxes, global environmental issues, and income and wealth distribution and has developed*

Professor Whalley, what first attracted you to economics?
I was attracted to economics by the opportunity to make some small contribution to improving the economic well-being of individuals and communities around the world. It seems at first sight simply unbelievable that so many people live in such appalling conditions, and that the world is such an unequal place. And yet understanding the how and why of where we are, and what to do about it, involves many subtleties of argument that only economics as a discipline offers.

What have economists learned during the past 200 years about the "nature and causes of the wealth of nations" that would surprise Adam Smith?
There are many surprises: One is that since Smith's day the period which has seen the most rapid elevation of living standards has been that with the highest (not lowest) degree of government intervention in

the economy; and that the richest countries (in the OECD) have substantially more regulation, control, and taxation than the very poorest. Another is the level and sophistication of formal argument in economic logic relative to Smith's time.

What are the challenges and benefits of globalization in today's world?

The great challenge of globalization is to exploit and harness the gains of economic integration for the greater good. This includes increased trade, investment flows, and global production for a single market. For now, removal of transborder restrictions on labour flows is the missing element in globalization. This has to be done in such a way that regulatory functions within existing nation states are taken up by new global institutions (globally redistributive taxation, global regulation of banks, global antitrust arrangements). The greatest challenge posed by globalization is marginalization; the lack of progress in and even regress in the very poorest countries (many in Africa). Other challenges involve the global environment, which is deteriorating both within countries, and globally; and the volatility we have seen on global financial markets of late (Asia 1997).

You have made many visits to Russia and studied at close hand that country's economic problems. How bad is Russia's economic performance? Why can't the Russian economy deliver for its people a standard of living that is similar to that in Canada?

By most statistical measures, Russia has suffered a fall in per capita income since the end of communism of nearly 50 percent (the World Bank puts it closer to 35 percent). This has been mirrored in other former Soviet Union countries, such as Ukraine, Belorusse, and Moldova; but in more remote former republics (Georgia, Armenia, Azerbaijan, Tadjikstan) the fall has been even larger (up to 70 percent). How and why this has occurred is a major challenge for the next generation of economists to understand. At one level, Russia followed almost exactly what Western neo-classical economists prescribed (privatization, establish legal structures, open up to trade, remove price controls). The result has been little short of catastrophic.

Why is Russian doing so much worse than China?

In China, few of the prescriptions of Western neo-classical economists have been followed and the economy has grown rapidly (up to 10 percent in some years). The contrast between Russia and China could hardly be more dramatic. It is true that Russia has had trouble collecting taxes, and it experienced hyperinflation in 1993–1995. Also, the equipment and machinery that Russia inherited from communism was not able to produce products that could compete on world markets, and it has had to be scrapped to a large degree. China has had large foreign investment, Russia almost none. In my view, modern neo-classical economics has no clear explanations for why these phenomena have occurred, just as it does not for the onset of Asian growth first in Korea and Taiwan in the late 1950s, and then in Singapore and Hong Kong later. Any discipline needs unsolved mysteries to give it focus and dynamism, and explaining the economic performance in Russia in the late 1990s is certainly one.

The greatest challenge posed by globalization is marginalization; the lack of progress in and even regress in the very poorest countries

What is your assessment of NAFTA? Has it raised living standards in Canada, the United States, and Mexico?

Like Russia, NAFTA is also a great paradox. When Canada signed the Free Trade Agreement with the United States in 1987, the average tariff that Canadian products faced in U.S. markets was less than 1 percent. We had good access to U.S. markets, and we were trying to make that access more secure.

But many of the same trade irritants and conflicts that troubled us before NAFTA (such as those in softwood lumber and steel) have remained. But equally since the days of NAFTA, Canada's trade with the United States has grown from 75 percent to 85 percent of our total trade. And our international trade has increased from 30 percent to almost 45 percent of our total production.

Something has clearly happened, but at the same time other OECD countries have experienced

61

increases in the percentage of their production traded. Studies seem to indicate that rationalization has happened in Canada since 1987 (a smaller number of larger plants producing for an integrated North American market, rather than for a smaller Canadian market). But it is hard to see how this has been driven principally by reductions in trade barriers. Some people talk about the psychological effect of NAFTA raising awareness of larger markets, but this is an unsatisfactory explanation for economists. More challenges!

Like Russia, NAFTA is also a great paradox.

China would like to join the World Trade Organization. What exactly is the WTO, and why is China so anxious to join it?
The World Trade Organization is a body in Geneva that oversees the main agreements between governments not to restrict international trade and organizes periodic negotiating rounds to lower trade barriers. It also arbitrates trade disputes between countries.

China wants to join the WTO principally to receive the WTO benefit of most favoured nation status (a guarantee that a nation will not be discriminated against in trade by other WTO countries). There are many other factors, but an equally interesting question is why so many countries are reluctant to let China into the WTO.

With your graduate school friend and colleague John Shoven (Charles R. Schwab Professor of Economics at Stanford University), you developed quantitative general equilibrium analysis, a branch of economics that now keeps hundreds of economists around the world busy. Can you describe the purpose of this work and perhaps provide a glimpse at how it is done?
You are right that I have worked a lot on numerical general equilibrium analysis, much of it with my

friend John Shoven at Stanford. This work seeks to apply theoretical structures to real-world policy and other issues using computer-based models of economics, and computational techniques. These techniques include calibration procedures that we developed during the 1970s, and counterfactual equilibrium solution methods pioneered by Herbert Scarf of Yale. John and I were both students of Scarf, and he influenced us greatly.

What are some of the main lessons that we have learned from quantitative general equilibrium analysis? Have these lessons been used in any concrete ways to make the world economy more efficient?
The applications of these methods are all over the discipline: tax policy, trade policy, environmental policy, economic history, and developmental policy. Macroeconomics began to use similar techniques during the 1980s, though macroeconomists calibrate and use their models in different ways.

There are many policy implications that have been drawn from this work. They were influential in the Canada–U.S. Free Trade debate during the 1980s, for example, and in higher-level economics courses you may encounter them.

What is your advice to a student who is just setting out to study economics? How should he or she approach the subject? What are the other subjects that should be studied alongside economics?
My advice is to strike a balance between analysis (application of deductive logic) and accumulation of information/facts. Don't let analytics become the sole driver of your work. Keep focussed and relevant. On the other hand, don't adopt an approach that is descriptive; look for analytical content and lines of logical development. Most policy debates, in my view, are settled by some convincing analytical argument but it must be supported by factual material and be placed in the right context.

Other subjects to study should also, in my view, reflect balance. These days math and computer science are very important, but so too are history and sociology. Build a portfolio of mutually reinforcing subjects once you know what sub-discipline in economics you want to study: geography for economic development, law for industrial organization, statistics for macroeconomics.

Chapter 4

Demand and Supply

Slide, rocket, and roller coaster—rides at Canada's Wonderland? No. Commonly used descriptions of price changes. ◆ CD players have taken a price slide from around $1,100 (in today's money) in 1983 to less than $200 today. And during these years, the quantity of CD players bought has increased steadily. What caused this price slide? Why didn't brisk buying keep the price high? ◆ Occasionally, a price will rocket upward. But a price rocket, like a satellite-launching rocket, has a limited life. It eventually runs out of fuel. One spectacular price rocket occurred in 1993 and 1994 when the price of coffee shot skyward from $1.30 a kilogram in 1993 to $4.60 a kilogram in 1994. Why did the price of coffee rise so spectacularly? ◆ Over longer periods, the price of coffee along with the prices of bananas and other agricultural commodities rise and fall like a roller coaster ride. ◆ The prices of some things are steady. For example, the price of an audiocassette tape has not changed much. But despite its steady price, people buy more and more tapes each year. Why do we buy more tapes even though their price is no lower than it was a decade ago? And why do firms sell more tapes even though they can't get higher prices for them? ◆ Economics is about the choices people make to cope with scarcity. These choices are guided by costs and benefits and are coordinated through markets. ◆ The tool that explains how markets work is demand and supply. It is the main tool of economics and it is used to study issues as diverse as wages and jobs, rents and housing, pollution, crime, consumer protection, education, welfare, the value of money, and interest rates.

Slide, Rocket, and Roller Coaster

◇ Your careful study of this topic will bring big rewards in both your further study of economics and your everyday life. Once you understand demand and supply, you will view the world through new eyes. When you have completed your study of demand and supply, you will be able to explain how prices are determined and make predictions about price slides, rockets, and roller coasters. But first, we're going to take a closer look at the idea of price. Just what is a price?

After studying this chapter, you will be able to:

- **Distinguish between a money price and a relative price**
- **Explain the main influences on demand**
- **Explain the main influences on supply**
- **Explain how prices and quantities bought and sold are determined by demand and supply**
- **Explain why some prices fall, some rise, and some fluctuate**
- **Use demand and supply to make predictions about price changes**

Price and Opportunity Cost

ECONOMIC ACTIONS ARISE FROM SCARCITY— wants exceed the resources available to satisfy them. Faced with *scarcity*, we must make choices. And to make choices, we compare *costs* and *benefits*. Choices are influenced by opportunity costs. Producers only offer items for sale if the price is high enough to cover their opportunity cost. And consumers respond to changing opportunity cost by seeking cheaper alternatives to expensive items.

We are going to study the way people respond to *prices* and the forces that determine prices. But to pursue these tasks, we need to understand the relationship between a price and an opportunity cost.

In everyday life, the *price* of an object is the number of dollars that must be given up in exchange for it. Economists refer to this price as the *money price*.

The *opportunity cost* of an action is the highest-valued alternative forgone. If, when you buy a cup of coffee, the highest-valued thing you forgo is some gum, then the opportunity cost of buying a coffee is the *quantity* of gum forgone. We can calculate this quantity from the money prices of coffee and gum.

If the money price of coffee is $1 a cup and the money price of gum is 50¢ a pack, then the opportunity cost of one cup of coffee is two packs of gum. To calculate this opportunity cost, we divide the price of a cup of coffee by the price of a pack of gum and find the *ratio* of one price to the other. The ratio of one price to another is called a **relative price**, and a *relative price is an opportunity cost*.

We can express the relative price of coffee in terms of gum or any other good. The normal way of expressing a relative price is in terms of a "basket" of all goods and services. To calculate this relative price, we divide the money price of a good by the money price of a "basket" of all goods (called a *price index*). The resulting relative price is expressed in the buying power of money in a particular year. It tells us the opportunity cost of an item in terms of how much of the "basket" we must give up to buy it.

Figure 4.1 shows the money price and the relative price of wheat. The money price (green) has fluctuated but has tended to rise. The relative price (red) peaked in 1974 and has tended to fall since that year.

The theory of demand and supply that we are about to study determines *relative prices*, and the word "price" means *relative* price. When we predict

FIGURE 4.1

The Price of Wheat

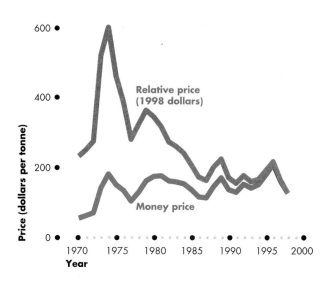

The money price of wheat—the number of dollars that must be given up for a tonne of wheat—has fluctuated between $55 and $207. But the *relative* price or *opportunity cost* of wheat, expressed in 1998 dollars, has fluctuated between $126 and $596 and has tended to fall. The behaviour of the money price obscures the fall in the relative price of wheat.

Sources: International Monetary Fund, *International Financial Statistics*, Washington, DC, 1999

that a price will fall, we do not mean that its *money* price will fall—although it might. We mean that its *relative* price will fall. That is, its price will fall *relative* to the average price of other goods and services.

REVIEW QUIZ

- Explain the distinction between a money price and a relative price.
- Why is a relative price an opportunity cost?
- Can you think of an example of a good whose money price and relative price have risen?
- Can you think of an example of a good whose money price and relative price have fallen?

Let's now begin our study of demand and supply, starting with demand.

Demand

IF YOU DEMAND SOMETHING, THEN YOU

■ Want it,
■ Can afford it, and
■ Have made a definite plan to buy it.

Wants are the unlimited desires or wishes that people have for goods and services. How many times have you thought that you would like something "if only you could afford it" or "if it weren't so expensive"? Scarcity guarantees that many—perhaps most—of our wants will never be satisfied. Demand reflects a decision about which wants to satisfy.

The **quantity demanded** of a good or service is the amount that consumers plan to buy during a given time period at a particular price. The quantity demanded is not necessarily the same amount as the quantity actually bought. Sometimes the quantity demanded is greater than the amount of goods available, so the quantity bought is less than the quantity demanded.

The quantity demanded is measured as an amount per unit of time. For example, suppose that you consume one cup of coffee a day. The quantity of coffee that you demand can be expressed as 1 cup per day or 7 cups per week or 365 cups per year. Without a time dimension, we cannot tell whether a particular quantity demanded is large or small.

What Determines Buying Plans?

The amount of any particular good or service that consumers plan to buy depends on many factors. The main ones are:

■ The price of the good
■ The prices of related goods
■ Expected future prices
■ Income
■ Population
■ Preferences

We first look at the relationship between the quantity demanded and the price of a good. To study this relationship, we keep all other influences on consumers' planned purchases the same and ask: How does the quantity demanded of the good vary as its price varies, other things remaining the same?

The Law of Demand

The law of demand states:

Other things remaining the same, the higher the price of a good, the smaller is the quantity demanded.

Why does a higher price reduce the quantity demanded? For two reasons:

■ Substitution effect
■ Income effect

Substitution Effect When the price of a good rises, other things remaining the same, its *relative* price—its opportunity cost—rises. Although each good is unique, it has *substitutes*—other goods that can be used in its place. As the opportunity cost of a good rises, people buy less of that good and more of its substitutes.

Income Effect When a price changes and all other influences on buying plans remain unchanged, the price rises *relative* to people's incomes. So faced with a higher price and an unchanged income, people cannot afford to buy all the things they previously bought. They must decrease the quantities demanded of at least some goods and services. Normally, the good whose price has increased is one of those that people buy in a smaller quantity.

To see the substitution effect and the income effect at work, think about the effects of a change in the price of tapes. Many different goods provide a service similar to that provided by a tape. For example, a compact disc, a pre-recorded tape, a radio or television broadcast, and a live concert all provide similar services to a tape. Suppose that a tape initially sells for $3 each and then the price doubles to $6. People now substitute compact discs and pre-recorded tapes for blank tapes—the substitution effect. And faced with a tighter budget, they buy fewer tapes as well as less of other goods and services—the income effect. The quantity of tapes demanded decreases for these two reasons.

Now suppose the price of a tape falls to $1. People now substitute blank tapes for compact discs and pre-recorded tapes—the substitution effect. And with a budget that now has some slack from the lower price of a tape, they buy more tapes as well as more of other goods and services—the income effect. The quantity of tapes demanded increases for these two reasons.

Demand Curve and Demand Schedule

You are now about to study one of the two most used curves in economics, the demand curve. And you are going to encounter one of the most critical distinctions: the distinction between *demand* and *quantity demanded*.

The term **demand** refers to the entire relationship between the quantity demanded and the price of a good, and it is illustrated by the demand curve and the demand schedule. The term *quantity demanded* refers to a point on a demand curve—the quantity demanded at a particular price.

Figure 4.2 shows the demand curve for tapes. A **demand curve** shows the relationship between the quantity demanded of a good and its price, when all other influences on consumers' planned purchases remain the same.

The table in Fig. 4.2 is the demand schedule for tapes. A *demand schedule* lists the quantities demanded at each different price when all the other influences on consumers' planned purchases—such as other prices, income, population, and preferences—remain the same. For example, if the price of a tape is $1, the quantity demanded is 9 million tapes a week. If the price of a tape is $5, the quantity demanded is 2 million tapes a week. The other rows of the table show the quantities demanded at prices of $2, $3, and $4.

We graph the demand schedule as a demand curve with the quantity demanded on the horizontal axis and the price on the vertical axis. The points on the demand curve labelled *a* through *e* represent the rows of the demand schedule. For example, point *a* on the graph represents a quantity demanded of 9 million tapes a week at a price of $1 a tape.

Willingness and Ability to Pay Another way of looking at the demand curve is as a willingness-and-ability-to-pay curve. And the willingness-and-ability-to-pay is a measure of *marginal benefit*.

If a small quantity is available, the highest price that someone is willing and able to pay for one more unit is high. But as the quantity available increases, the marginal benefit of each additional unit falls and the highest price that someone is willing and able to pay also falls along the demand curve.

In Fig. 4.2, if 2 million tapes are available each week, the highest price that someone is willing to pay for the 2 millionth tape is $5. But if 9 million tapes are available each week, someone is willing to pay $1 for the last tape bought.

FIGURE 4.2

The Demand Curve

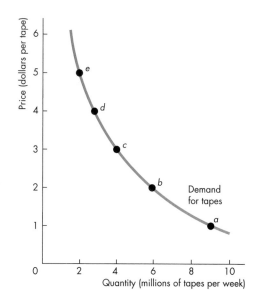

	Price (dollars per tape)	Quantity (millions of tapes per week)
a	1	9
b	2	6
c	3	4
d	4	3
e	5	2

The table shows a demand schedule listing the quantity of tapes demanded at each price if all other influences on buyers' plans remain the same. At a price of $1 a tape, 9 million tapes a week are demanded; at a price of $3 a tape, 4 million tapes a week are demanded. The demand curve shows the relationship between quantity demanded and price, everything else remaining the same.

The demand curve slopes downward: As price decreases, the quantity demanded increases. The demand curve can be read in two ways. For a given price, it tells us the quantity that people plan to buy. For example, at a price of $3 a tape, people plan to buy 4 million tapes a week. For a given quantity, the demand curve tells us the maximum price that consumers are willing and able to pay for the last tape available. For example, the maximum price that consumers will pay for the 6 millionth tape is $2.

A Change in Demand

When any factor that influences buying plans changes, other than the price of the good, there is a **change in demand**. Figure 4.3 illustrates an increase in demand. When demand increases, the demand curve shifts rightward and the quantity demanded is greater at each price. For example, at a price of $5, on the original (blue) demand curve, the quantity demanded is 2 million tapes a week. On the new (red) demand curve, the quantity demanded is 6 million tapes a week. Look closely at the numbers in the table in Fig. 4.3 and check that the quantity demanded is greater at each price.

Let's look at the factors that bring a change in demand. There are five key factors to consider.

1. Prices of Related Goods The quantity of tapes that consumers plan to buy depends in part on the prices of substitutes for tapes. A **substitute** is a good that can be used in place of another good. For example, a bus ride is a substitute for a train ride; a hamburger is a substitute for a hot dog; and a CD is a substitute for a tape. If the price of a substitute for a tape increases, people buy less of the substitute and more tapes. For example, if the price of a CD rises, people buy fewer CDs and more tapes. The demand for tapes increases.

The quantity of tapes that people plan to buy also depends on the prices of complements with tapes. A **complement** is a good that is used in conjunction with another good. Hamburgers and fries are complements. So are spaghetti and meat sauce, and so are tapes and Walkmans. If the price of a Walkman falls, people buy more Walkmans *and more tapes*. It is a fall in the price of a Walkman that increases the demand for tapes in Figure 4.3.

2. Expected Future Prices If the price of a good is expected to rise in the future and if the good can be stored, the opportunity cost of obtaining the good for future use is lower now than it will be when the price has increased. So people retime their purchase—they substitute over time. They buy more of the good before its price is expected to rise (and less after), so the current demand for the good increases.

For example, suppose that Florida is hit by a severe frost that damages the season's orange crop. You expect the price of orange juice to rise. So, anticipating a higher price, you fill your freezer with enough frozen juice to get you through the next six months. Your current demand for frozen orange juice has increased (and your future demand has decreased).

FIGURE 4.3

An Increase in Demand

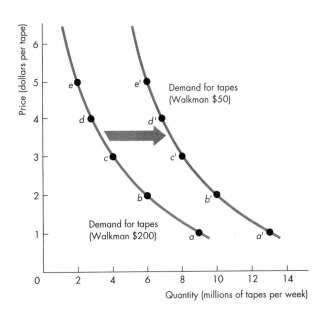

Original demand schedule Walkman $200			New demand schedule Walkman $50		
	Price (dollars per tape)	**Quantity** (millions of tapes per week)		**Price** (dollars per tape)	**Quantity** (millions of tapes per week)
a	1	9	a'	1	13
b	2	6	b'	2	10
c	3	4	c'	3	8
d	4	3	d'	4	7
e	5	2	e'	5	6

A change in any influence on buyers' plans other than the price of the good itself results in a new demand schedule and a shift of the demand curve. A change in the price of a Walkman changes the demand for tapes. At a price of $3 a tape (row c of the table), 4 million tapes a week are demanded when the Walkman costs $200 and 8 million tapes a week are demanded when the Walkman costs only $50. A *fall* in the price of a Walkman *increases* the demand for tapes because the Walkman is a complement of tapes. When demand *increases*, the demand curve shifts *rightward*, as shown by the shift arrow and the resulting red curve.

Similarly, if the price of a good is expected to fall in the future, the opportunity cost of buying the good now is high relative to what it is expected to be in the future. So again, people retime their purchases. They buy less of the good now before its price falls (and more after), so the current demand for the good decreases.

Computer prices are constantly falling, and this fact poses a dilemma. Will you buy a new computer now, in time for the start of the school year, or will you wait until the price has fallen some more? Because people expect computer prices to keep falling, the current demand for computers is less (and the future demand is greater) than it otherwise would be.

3. Income Another influence on demand is consumer income. When income increases, consumers buy more of most goods, and when income decreases, they buy less of most goods. Although an increase in income leads to an increase in the demand for *most* goods, it does not lead to an increase in the demand for *all* goods. A **normal good** is one for which demand increases as income increases. An **inferior good** is one for which demand decreases as income increases. Long-distance transportation has examples of both normal goods and inferior goods. As incomes increase, the demand for air travel (a normal good) increases and the demand for long-distance bus trips (an inferior good) decreases.

4. Population Demand also depends on the size and the age structure of the population. The larger the population, the greater is the demand for all goods and services. And the smaller the population, the smaller is the demand for all goods and services.

For example, the demand for car parking spaces or movies or tapes or just about anything that you can imagine is much greater in Toronto than it is in Thunder Bay.

Also the larger the proportion of the population in a given age group, the greater is the demand for the types of goods and services used by that age group.

For example, in 1995, there were 1.9 million 20–24 year olds in Canada compared with 2.3 million in 1985. As a result, the demand for college places decreased between 1985 and 1995. During these same years, the number of Canadians aged 85 years and over increased. As a result, the demand for nursing home services increased.

5. Preferences Demand depends on preferences. *Preferences* are an individual's attitudes towards goods

---

TABLE 4.1

The Demand for Tapes

The Law of Demand

The quantity of tapes demanded

Decreases if:	*Increases if:*
■ The price of a tape rises	■ The price of a tape falls

Changes in Demand

The demand for tapes

Decreases if:	*Increases if:*
■ The price of a substitute falls	■ The price of a substitute rises
■ The price of a complement rises	■ The price of a complement falls
■ The price of a tape is expected to fall in the future	■ The price of a tape is expected to rise in the future
■ Income falls*	■ Income rises*
■ The population decreases	■ The population increases

*A tape is a normal good.

---

and services. For example, a rock music fanatic has a much greater preference for tapes than does a tone-deaf workaholic. As a consequence, even if they have the same incomes, their demands for tapes will be very different.

Table 4.1 summarizes the influences on demand and the direction of those influences.

A Change in the Quantity Demanded Versus a Change in Demand

Changes in the factors that influence buyers' plans cause either a change in the quantity demanded or a change in demand. Equivalently, they cause either a movement along the demand curve or a shift of the demand curve.

The distinction between a change in the quantity demanded and a change in demand is the same as that between a movement along the demand curve and a shift of the demand curve.

A point on the demand curve shows the quantity demanded at a given price. So a movement along the demand curve shows a **change in the quantity demanded**. The entire demand curve shows demand. So a shift of the demand curve shows a **change in demand**. Figure 4.4 illustrates and summarizes these distinctions.

Movement Along the Demand Curve   If the price of a good changes but everything else remains the same, there is a movement along the demand curve. Because the demand curve slopes downward, a fall in the price of a good or service increases the quantity demanded and a rise in the price of the good or service decreases the quantity demanded— the law of demand.

In Fig. 4.4, if the price of a good falls when everything else remains the same, the quantity demanded of that good increases and there is a movement down the demand curve D_0. If the price rises when everything else remains the same, the quantity demanded decreases and there is a movement up the demand curve D_0.

A Shift of the Demand Curve   If the price of a good remains constant but some other influence on buyers' plans changes, there is a change in demand for that good. We illustrate a change in demand as a shift of the demand curve. For example, a fall in the price of the Walkman—a complement of tapes— increases the demand for tapes. We illustrate this increase in demand for tapes with a new demand schedule and a new demand curve. If the price of the Walkman falls, consumers buy more tapes regardless of whether the price of a tape is high or low. That is what a rightward shift of the demand curve shows— that more tapes are bought at each and every price.

In Fig. 4.4, when any influence on buyers' planned purchases changes, other than the price of the good, there is a *change in demand* and the demand curve shifts.

Demand *increases* and the demand curve *shifts rightward* (to the red demand curve D_1) if the price of a substitute rises, the expected future price of the good rises, the price of a complement falls, income increases (for a normal good), or the population increases.

Demand *decreases* and the demand curve *shifts leftward* (to the red demand curve D_2) if the price of a substitute falls, the expected future price of the good falls, the price of a complement rises, income decreases (for a normal good), or the population decreases.

For an inferior good, the effects of changes in income are in the direction opposite to those described above.

FIGURE   4.4

A Change in the Quantity Demanded Versus a Change in Demand

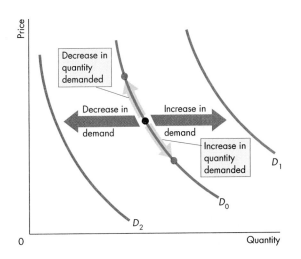

When the price of the good changes, there is a movement along the demand curve and *a change in the quantity demanded*, shown by the blue arrows on demand curve D_0. When some other influence on buying plans changes, there is a *change in demand* and the demand curve shifts. An increase in demand shifts the demand curve rightward (from D_0 to D_1) and a decrease in demand shifts the demand curve leftward (from D_0 to D_2).

R E V I E W   Q U I Z

- Can you define the *quantity demanded* of a good or service?
- What is the *law of demand* and how do we illustrate it?
- If a fixed amount of a good is available, what does the demand curve tell us about the price that consumers are willing to pay for that fixed quantity?
- Can you list all the influences on buying plans that *change demand* and for each influence say whether it increases demand or decreases demand?
- What happens to the quantity of CDs demanded and the demand for CDs if the price of a CD falls and all other influences on buying plans remain the same?

Supply

IF A FIRM SUPPLIES A GOOD OR SERVICE, THE FIRM

- Has the resources and technology to produce it,
- Can profit from producing it, and
- Has made a definite plan to produce it and sell it.

A supply is more than just having the *resources* and the *technology* to produce something. *Resources and technology* are the constraints that limit what is possible.

Many useful things can be produced, but they are not produced unless it is profitable to do so. Supply reflects a decision about which technologically feasible items to produce.

The **quantity supplied** of a good or service is the amount that producers plan to sell during a given time period at a particular price. The quantity supplied is not necessarily the same amount as the quantity actually sold. Sometimes the quantity supplied is greater than the quantity demanded, so the quantity bought is less than the quantity supplied.

Like the quantity demanded, the quantity supplied is measured as an amount per unit of time. For example, suppose that GM produces 1,000 cars a day. The quantity of cars supplied by GM can be expressed as 1,000 a day, or 7,000 a week, or 365,000 a year. Without the time dimension, we cannot tell whether a particular number is large or small.

What Determines Selling Plans?

The amount of any particular good or service that producers plan to sell depends on many factors. The main ones are:

- The price of the good
- The prices of resources used to produce the good
- The prices of related goods produced
- Expected future prices
- The number of suppliers
- Technology

Let's first look at the relationship between the price of a good and the quantity supplied. To study this relationship, we keep all the other influences on the quantity supplied the same. We ask: How does the quantity supplied of a good vary as its price varies?

The Law of Supply

The law of supply states:

> Other things remaining the same, the higher the price of a good, the greater is the quantity supplied.

Why does a higher price increase the quantity supplied? It is because of *increasing marginal cost*. As the quantity produced of any good increases, the marginal cost of producing the good increases. (You can refresh your memory of increasing marginal cost in Chapter 3, p. 42.)

It is never worth producing a good if the price received for it does not at least cover marginal cost. So when the price of a good rises, other things remaining the same, producers are willing to incur the higher marginal cost and increase production. The higher price brings forth an increase in the quantity supplied.

Let's now illustrate the law of supply with a supply curve and a supply schedule.

Supply Curve and Supply Schedule

You are now going to study the second of the two most used curves in economics, the supply curve. And you're going to learn about the critical distinction between *supply* and *quantity supplied*.

The term **supply** refers to the entire relationship between the quantity supplied and the price of a good, and it is illustrated by the supply curve and the supply schedule. The term *quantity supplied* refers to a point on a supply curve—the quantity supplied at a particular price.

Figure 4.5 shows the supply curve of tapes. A **supply curve** shows the relationship between the quantity supplied of a good and its price, when all other influences on producers' planned sales remain the same. It is a graph of a supply schedule.

The table in Fig. 4.5 sets out the supply schedule for tapes. A *supply schedule* lists the quantities supplied at each different price when all the other influences on producers' planned sales remain the same. For example, if the price of a tape is $1, the quantity supplied is zero—on row *a* of the table. If the price of a tape is $2, the quantity supplied is 3 million tapes a week—on row *b*. The other rows of the table show the quantities supplied at prices of $3, $4, and $5.

FIGURE 4.5

The Supply Curve

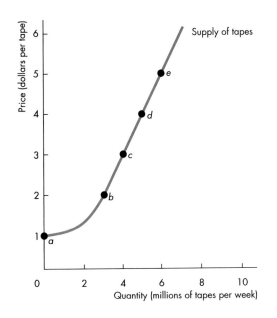

	Price (dollars per tape)	Quantity (millions of tapes per week)
a	1	0
b	2	3
c	3	4
d	4	5
e	5	6

The table shows the supply schedule of tapes. For example, at $2 a tape, 3 million tapes a week are supplied; at $5 a tape, 6 million tapes a week are supplied. The supply curve shows the relationship between the quantity supplied and price, everything else remaining the same. The supply curve usually slopes upward: As the price of a good increases, so does the quantity supplied.

A supply curve can be read in two ways. For a given price, it tells us the quantity that producers plan to sell. For example, at a price of $3 a tape, producers plan to sell 4 million tapes a week. And for a given quantity, it tells us the minimum price that producers are willing to accept for that quantity. For example, the minimum price that producers are willing to accept for the 6 millionth tape is $5.

To make a supply curve, we graph the quantity supplied on the horizontal axis and the price on the vertical axis, just as in the case of the demand curve. The points on the supply curve labelled *a* through *e* represent the rows of the supply schedule. For example, point *a* on the graph represents a quantity supplied of zero at a price of $1 a tape.

Minimum Supply Price Just as the demand curve has two interpretations, so too does the supply curve. The demand curve can be interpreted as a willingness-and-ability-to-pay curve. The supply curve can be interpreted as a minimum-supply-price curve. It tells us the lowest price at which someone can profitably sell another unit.

If a small quantity is produced, the lowest price at which someone can profitably produce one more unit is low. But if a large quantity is produced, the lowest price at which someone can profitably sell one more unit is high.

In Fig. 4.5, if 6 million tapes a week are produced, the lowest price that a producer is willing to accept for the 6 millionth tape is $5. But if only 4 million tapes are produced each week, the lowest price that a producer is willing to accept for the 4 millionth tape is $3.

A Change in Supply

When any factor that influences selling plans changes, other than the price of the good, there is a **change in supply**. Let's look at the five key factors that change supply.

1. Prices of Productive Resources The prices of productive resources influence supply. The easiest way to see this influence is to think about the supply curve as a minimum-supply-price curve. If the price of a productive resource rises, the lowest price a producer is willing to accept rises so supply decreases. For example, during 1996, the price of jet fuel increased and the supply of air transportation decreased. Similarly, a rise in the minimum wage decreases the supply of hamburgers. If the wages of tape producers rise, the supply of tapes decreases.

2. Prices of Related Goods Produced The prices of related goods and services that firms produce influence supply. For example, if the price of pre-recorded tapes rises, the supply of blank tapes decreases. Blank tapes and pre-recorded tapes are *substitutes in produc-*

tion—goods that can be produced by using the same resources. If the price of beef rises, the supply of cowhide increases. Beef and cowhide are *complements in production*—goods that must be produced together.

3. Expected Future Prices   If the price of a good is expected to rise, the return from selling the good in the future is higher than it is in the present. So the current supply decreases.

4. The Number of Suppliers   Supply also depends on the number of suppliers. The larger the number of firms that produce a good, the greater is the supply of the good. As firms enter an industry, the supply in that industry increases. As firms leave an industry, the supply in that industry decreases. For example, over the past two years there has been a huge increase in the number of firms that produce and manage Web sites. As a result, the supply of Internet and World Wide Web services has increased enormously.

5. Technology   New technologies create new products and lower the costs of producing existing products. As a result, new technologies change supply. For example, the development of a new technology for tape production by Sony and Minnesota Mining and Manufacturing (3M) has lowered the cost of producing tapes and increased the supply of tapes.

Figure 4.6 illustrates an increase in supply. When supply increases, the supply curve shifts rightward and the quantity supplied is larger at each and every price. For example, at a price of $2, on the original (blue) supply curve, the quantity supplied is 3 million tapes a week. On the new (red) supply curve, the quantity supplied is 6 million tapes a week. Look closely at the numbers in the table in Fig. 4.6 and check that the quantity supplied is larger at each price.

Table 4.2 summarizes the influences on supply and the directions of those influences.

A Change in Quantity Supplied Versus a Change in Supply

Changes in the factors that influence producers' planned sales cause either a change in the quantity supplied or a change in supply. Equivalently, they cause either a movement along the supply curve or a shift of the supply curve.

FIGURE 4.6

An Increase in Supply

| Original supply schedule | | | New supply schedule | | |
Old technology			New technology		
	Price (dollars per tape)	Quantity (millions of tapes per week)		Price (dollars per tape)	Quantity (millions of tapes per week)
a	1	0	a'	1	3
b	2	3	b'	2	6
c	3	4	c'	3	8
d	4	5	d'	4	10
e	5	6	e'	5	12

A change in any influence on sellers' plans other than the price of the good itself results in a new supply schedule and a shift of the supply curve. For example, if Sony and 3M invent a new, cost-saving technology for producing tapes, the supply of tapes changes.

At a price of $3 a tape, 4 million tapes a week are supplied when producers use the old technology (row c of the table) and 8 million tapes a week are supplied when producers use the new technology. An advance in technology *increases* the supply of tapes and the supply curve shifts *rightward*, as shown by the shift arrow and the resulting red curve.

A point on the supply curve shows the quantity supplied at a given price. A movement along the supply curve shows a **change in the quantity supplied**. The entire supply curve shows supply. A shift of the supply curve shows a **change in supply**.

Figure 4.7 illustrates and summarizes these distinctions. If the price of a good falls and everything else remains the same, the quantity supplied of that good decreases and there is a movement down the supply curve S_0. If the price of a good rises and everything else remains the same, the quantity supplied increases and there is a movement up the supply curve S_0. When any other influence on selling plans changes, the supply curve shifts and there is a change in supply. If the supply curve is S_0 and if production costs fall, supply increases and the supply curve shifts to the red supply curve S_1. If the supply curve is S_0 and if production costs rise, supply decreases and the supply curve shifts to the red supply curve S_2.

TABLE 4.2
The Supply for Tapes

The Law of Supply

The quantity of tapes supplied

Decreases if:
- The price of a tape falls

Increases if:
- The price of a tape rises

Changes in Supply

The supply of tapes

Decreases if:
- The price of a resource used to produce tapes rises
- The price of a substitute in production rises
- The price of a complement in production falls
- The price of a tape is expected to rise in the future
- The number of tape producers decreases

Increases if:
- The price of a resource used to produce tapes falls
- The price of a substitute in production falls
- The price of a complement in production rises
- The price of a tape is expected to fall in the future
- The number of tape producers increases
- More efficient technologies for producing tapes are discovered

FIGURE 4.7
A Change in the Quantity Supplied Versus a Change in Supply

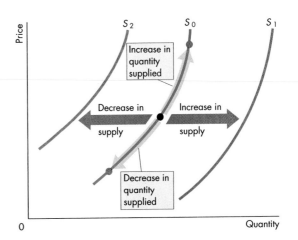

When the price of the good changes, there is a movement along the supply curve and *a change in the quantity supplied*, shown by the blue arrows on supply curve S_0. When any other influence on selling plans changes, there is a shift of the supply curve and a *change in supply*. An increase in supply shifts the supply curve rightward (from S_0 to S_1) and a decrease in supply shifts the supply curve leftward (from S_0 to S_2).

R E V I E W   Q U I Z

- Can you define the *quantity supplied* of a good or service?
- What is the *law of supply* and how do we illustrate it?
- If consumers are willing to buy only a given quantity, what does the supply curve tell us about the price at which firms will supply that quantity?
- Can you list all the influences on selling plans that *change supply* and for each influence say whether it increases supply or decreases supply?

Your next task is to use what you've learned about demand and supply and learn how prices and quantities are determined.

Market Equilibrium

WE HAVE SEEN THAT WHEN THE PRICE OF A good *rises*, the quantity demanded *decreases* and the quantity supplied *increases*. We are now going to see how prices coordinate the plans of buyers and sellers and achieve an equilibrium.

An *equilibrium* is a situation in which opposing forces balance each other. Equilibrium in a market occurs when the price balances the plans of buyers and sellers. The **equilibrium price** is the price at which the quantity demanded equals the quantity supplied. The **equilibrium quantity** is the quantity bought and sold at the equilibrium price. A market moves towards its equilibrium because:

■ Price regulates buying and selling plans
■ Price adjusts when plans don't match

Price As a Regulator

The price of a good regulates the quantities demanded and supplied. If the price is too high, the quantity supplied exceeds the quantity demanded. If the price is too low, the quantity demanded exceeds the quantity supplied. There is one price at which the quantity demanded equals the quantity supplied. Let's work out what that price is.

Figure 4.8 shows the market for tapes. The table shows the demand schedule (from Fig. 4.2) and the supply schedule (from Fig. 4.5). If the price of a tape is $1, the quantity demanded is 9 million tapes a week, but no tapes are supplied. The quantity demanded exceeds the quantity supplied by 9 million tapes a week. In other words, at a price of $1 a tape, there is a shortage of 9 million tapes a week. This shortage is shown in the final column of the table. At a price of $2 a tape, there is still a shortage, but only of 3 million tapes a week. If the price of a tape is $5, the quantity supplied exceeds the quantity demanded. The quantity supplied is 6 million tapes a week, but the quantity demanded is only 2 million. There is a surplus of 4 million tapes a week. The one price at which there is neither a shortage nor a surplus is $3 a tape. At that price, the quantity demanded is equal to the quantity supplied: 4 million tapes a week. The equilibrium price is $3 a tape, and the equilibrium quantity is 4 million tapes a week.

Figure 4.8 shows that the demand curve and supply curve intersect at the equilibrium price of

FIGURE 4.8

Equilibrium

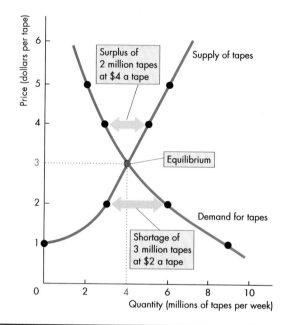

Price (dollars per tape)	Quantity demanded	Quantity supplied	Shortage (−) or surplus (+)
		(millions of tapes per week)	
1	9	0	−9
2	6	3	−3
3	4	4	0
4	3	5	+2
5	2	6	+4

The table lists the quantities demanded and quantities supplied as well as the shortage or surplus of tapes at each price. If the price is $2 a tape, 6 million tapes a week are demanded and 3 million are supplied. There is a shortage of 3 million tapes a week, and the price rises. If the price is $4 a tape, 3 million tapes a week are demanded and 5 million are supplied. There is a surplus of 2 million tapes a week, and the price falls. If the price is $3 a tape, 4 million tapes a week are demanded and 4 million are supplied. There is neither a shortage nor a surplus. Neither buyers nor sellers have any incentive to change the price. The price at which the quantity demanded equals the quantity supplied is the equilibrium price.

$3 a tape. At each price *above* $3 a tape, there is a surplus of tapes. For example, at $4 a tape the surplus is 2 million tapes a week, as shown by the blue arrow. At each price *below* $3 a tape, there is a shortage of tapes. For example, at $2 a tape, the shortage is 3 million tapes a week, as shown by the red arrow.

Price Adjustments

You've seen that if the price is below equilibrium there is shortage and if the price is above equilibrium there is a surplus. But can we count on the price to change and eliminate shortages or surpluses? We can, because such price changes are mutually beneficial to both buyers and sellers. Let's see why the price changes when there is a shortage or a surplus.

A Shortage Forces the Price Up Suppose the price of a tape is $2. Consumers plan to buy 6 million tapes a week, and producers plan to sell 3 million tapes a week. Consumers can't force producers to sell more than they plan, so the quantity actually offered for sale is 3 million tapes a week. In this situation, powerful forces operate to increase the price and move it towards the equilibrium price. Some producers, noticing lines of unsatisfied consumers, move their prices up. Some producers increase their output. As producers push their prices up, the price rises towards its equilibrium. The rising price reduces the shortage because it decreases the quantity demanded and increases the quantity supplied. When the price has increased to the point at which there is no longer a shortage, the forces moving the price stop operating and the price comes to rest at its equilibrium.

A Surplus Forces the Price Down Suppose the price of a tape is $4. Producers plan to sell 5 million tapes a week, and consumers plan to buy 3 million tapes a week. Producers cannot force consumers to buy more than they plan, so the quantity that is actually bought is 3 million tapes a week. In this situation, powerful forces operate to lower the price and move it towards the equilibrium price. Some producers, unable to sell the quantities of tapes that they planned to sell, cut their prices. In addition, some producers scale back production. As producers cut prices, the price falls towards its equilibrium. The falling price decreases the surplus because it increases the quantity demanded and decreases the quantity supplied. When the price has fallen to the point at

which there is no longer a surplus, the forces moving the price stop operating, and the price comes to rest at its equilibrium.

The Best Deal Available for Buyers and Sellers
When the price is below equilibrium, it is forced upward towards the equilibrium. Why don't buyers resist the increase and refuse to buy at the higher price? Because they value the good more highly than the current price and they cannot satisfy all their demands at the current price. In some markets—an example is the market for rental accommodation in Sydney, Australia, as we approach the 2000 Olympic Games—the buyers might even be the ones who force the price upward by offering higher prices to divert the limited quantities away from other buyers.

When the price is above equilibrium, it is bid downward towards the equilibrium. Why don't sellers resist this decrease and refuse to sell at the lower price? Because their minimum supply price is below the current price and they cannot sell all they would like to at the current price. Normally, it is the sellers who force the price downward by offering lower prices to gain market share from their competitors.

At the price at which the quantity demanded and the quantity supplied are equal, neither buyers nor sellers can do business at a better price. Buyers pay the highest price they are willing to pay for the last unit bought, and sellers receive the lowest price at which they are willing to supply the last unit sold.

When people freely make offers to buy and sell, and when demanders try to buy at the lowest possible price and suppliers try to sell at the highest possible price, the price at which trade takes place is the equilibrium price—the price at which the quantity demanded equals the quantity supplied. The price coordinates the plans of buyers and sellers.

R E V I E W   Q U I Z

- What is the *equilibrium price* of a good or service?
- Over what range of prices does a shortage arise?
- Over what range of prices does a surplus arise?
- What happens to the price when there is a shortage?
- What happens to the price when there is a surplus?
- Why is the price at which the quantity demanded equals the quantity supplied the equilibrium price?
- Why is the equilibrium price the best deal available for both buyers and sellers?

Predicting Changes in Price and Quantity

THE DEMAND AND SUPPLY THEORY WE HAVE JUST studied provides us with a powerful way of analysing influences on prices and the quantities bought and sold. According to the theory, a change in price stems from either a change in demand or a change in supply or a change in both. Let's look first at the effects of a change in demand.

A Change in Demand

What happens to the price and quantity of tapes if the demand for tapes increases? We can answer this question with a specific example. Suppose the price of a Walkman falls from $200 to $50. Because the Walkman and tapes are complements, the demand for tapes increases, as is shown in the table in Fig. 4.9. The original demand schedule and the new one are set out in the first three columns of the table. The table also shows the supply schedule for tapes.

The original equilibrium price is $3 a tape. At that price, 4 million tapes a week are demanded and supplied. When demand increases, the price that makes the quantity demanded equal the quantity supplied is $5 a tape. At this price, 6 million tapes are bought and sold each week. When demand increases, both the price and the quantity increase.

Figure 4.9 shows these changes. The figure shows the original demand for and supply of tapes. The original equilibrium price is $3 a tape, and the quantity is 4 million tapes a week. When demand increases, the demand curve shifts rightward. The equilibrium price rises to $5 a tape, and the quantity supplied increases to 6 million tapes a week, as highlighted in the figure. There is an *increase in the quantity supplied* but *no change in supply*—a movement along, but no shift of, the supply curve.

We can reverse the exercise that we've just conducted. If we start at a price of $5 a tape with 6 million tapes a week being bought and sold, we can work out what happens if demand decreases to its original level. Such a decrease in demand might arise from a fall in the price of a CD or a CD player (both substitutes for tapes). The decrease in demand shifts the demand curve leftward. The equilibrium price falls to $3 a tape, and the equilibrium quantity decreases to 4 million tapes a week.

FIGURE 4.9

The Effects of a Change in Demand

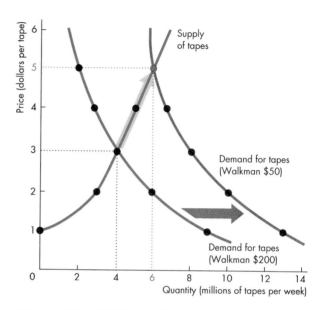

Price	Quantity demanded (millions of tapes per week)		Quantity supplied (millions of tapes per week)
(dollars per tape)	Walkman $200	Walkman $50	
1	9	13	0
2	6	10	3
3	4	8	4
4	3	7	5
5	2	6	6

With the price of a Walkman at $200, the demand for tapes is the blue curve. The equilibrium price is $3 a tape and the equilibrium quantity is 4 million tapes a week. When the price of a Walkman falls from $200 to $50, the demand for tapes increases and the demand curve shifts rightward to become the red curve.

At $3 a tape, there is now a shortage of 4 million tapes a week. The price of a tape rises to a new equilibrium of $5 a tape. As the price rises to $5, the quantity supplied increases, as shown by the blue arrow along the supply curve, to the new equilibrium quantity of 6 million tapes a week. Following an increase in demand, the quantity supplied increases but supply does not change—the supply curve does not shift.

We can now make our first two predictions:

1. When demand increases, both the price and the quantity increase.
2. When demand decreases, both the price and the quantity decrease.

A Change in Supply

Suppose that Sony and 3M introduce a new cost-saving technology in their tape production plants. The new technology increases the supply of tapes. The new supply schedule (the same one that was shown in Fig. 4.6) is presented in the table in Fig. 4.10. What are the new equilibrium price and quantity? The answer is highlighted in the table: The price falls to $2 a tape, and the quantity increases to 6 million a week. You can see why by looking at the quantities demanded and supplied at the original price of $3 a tape. The quantity supplied at that price is 8 million tapes a week, and there is a surplus of tapes. The price falls. Only when the price is $2 a tape does the quantity supplied equal the quantity demanded.

Figure 4.10 illustrates the effect of an increase in supply. It shows the demand curve for tapes and the original and new supply curves. The initial equilibrium price is $3 a tape, and the quantity is 4 million tapes a week. When the supply increases, the supply curve shifts rightward. The equilibrium price falls to $2 a tape, and the quantity demanded increases to 6 million tapes a week, highlighted in the figure. There is an *increase in the quantity demanded* but *no change in demand*—a movement along, but no shift of, the demand curve.

The exercise that we've just conducted can be reversed. If we start out at a price of $2 a tape with 6 million tapes a week being bought and sold, we can work out what happens if supply decreases to its original level. Such a decrease in supply might arise from an increase in the cost of labour or raw materials. The decrease in supply shifts the supply curve leftward. The equilibrium price rises to $3 a tape, and the equilibrium quantity decreases to 4 million tapes a week.

We can now make two more predictions:

1. When supply increases, the quantity increases and the price falls.
2. When supply decreases, the quantity decreases and the price rises.

FIGURE 4.10

The Effects of a Change in Supply

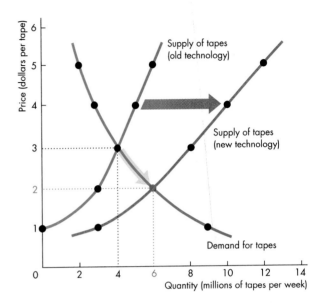

Price (dollars per tape)	Quantity demanded (millions of tapes per week)	Quantity supplied (millions of tapes per week)	
		old technology	new technology
1	9	0	3
2	6	3	6
3	4	4	8
4	3	5	10
5	2	6	12

With the old technology, the supply of tapes is shown by the blue supply curve. The equilibrium price is $3 a tape, and the equilibrium quantity is 4 million tapes a week. When the new technology is adopted, the supply of tapes increases and the supply curve shifts rightward to become the red curve.

At $3 a tape, there is now a surplus of 4 million tapes a week. The price of a tape falls to a new equilibrium of $2 a tape. As the price falls to $2, the quantity demanded increases, as shown by the blue arrow on the demand curve, to the new equilibrium quantity of 6 million tapes a week. Following an increase in supply, the quantity demanded increases but demand does not change—the demand curve does not shift.

A Change in Both Demand and Supply

You can now predict the effects of a change in either demand or supply on the price and the quantity. But what happens if *both* demand and supply change together? To answer this question, we look first at the case in which demand and supply move in the same direction—either both increase or both decrease. Then we look at the case in which they move in opposite directions—demand decreases and supply increases or demand increases and supply decreases.

Demand and Supply Change in the Same Direction   We've seen that an increase in the demand for tapes increases the price of tapes and increases the quantity bought and sold. And we've seen that an increase in the supply of tapes lowers the price of tapes and increases the quantity bought and sold. Let's now examine what happens when both of these changes happen to occur together.

The table in Fig. 4.11 brings together the numbers that describe the original quantities demanded and supplied and the new quantities demanded and supplied after the fall in the price of the Walkman and the improved tape production technology. These same numbers are illustrated in the graph. The original (blue) demand and supply curves intersect at a price of $3 a tape and a quantity of 4 million tapes a week. The new (red) supply and demand curves also intersect at a price of $3 a tape but at a quantity of 8 million tapes a week.

An increase in either demand or supply increases the quantity. So when both demand and supply increase, so does quantity.

An increase in demand raises the price, and an increase in supply lowers the price, so we can't say whether the price will rise or fall when demand and supply increase together. In this example, the price does not change. But notice that if demand increases by slightly more than the amount shown in the figure, the price will rise. And if supply increases by slightly more than the amount shown in the figure, the price will fall.

We can now make two more predictions:

1. When *both* demand and supply increase, the quantity increases and the price might increase, decrease, or remain the same.
2. When *both* demand and supply decrease, the quantity decreases and the price might increase, decrease, or remain the same.

FIGURE 4.11

The Effects of an Increase in Both Demand and Supply

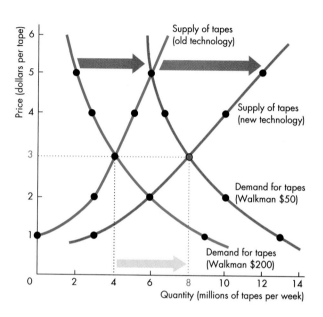

	Original quantities (millions of tapes per week)		**New quantities** (millions of tapes per week)	
Price (dollars per tape)	**Quantity demanded** Walkman $200	**Quantity supplied** old technology	**Quantity demanded** Walkman $50	**Quantity supplied** new technology
1	9	0	13	3
2	6	3	10	6
3	4	4	8	8
4	3	5	7	10
5	2	6	6	12

When a Walkman costs $200 and firms use the old technology to produce tapes, the price of a tape is $3 and the quantity is 4 million tapes a week. A fall in the price of a Walkman increases the demand for tapes, and improved technology increases the supply of tapes. The new supply curve intersects the new demand curve at $3 a tape, the same price as before, but the quantity increases to 8 million tapes a week. These increases in demand and supply increase the quantity but leave the price unchanged.

Demand and Supply Change in Opposite Directions Let's now see what happens when demand and supply change together but move in *opposite* directions. An improved production technology increases the supply of tapes as before. But now the price of a CD player falls. A CD player is a substitute for tapes. With cheaper CD players, more people buy them and switch from buying tapes to buying CDs, and the demand for tapes decreases.

The table in Fig. 4.12 describes the original and new demand and supply schedules. These schedules are shown as the original (blue) and new (red) demand and supply curves in the graph. The original demand and supply curves intersect at a price of $5 a tape and a quantity of 6 million tapes a week. The new supply and demand curves intersect at a price of $2 a tape and at the original quantity of 6 million tapes a week.

A decrease in demand or an increase in supply lowers the price. So when a decrease in demand and an increase in supply occur together, the price falls.

A decrease in demand decreases the quantity and an increase in supply increases the quantity, so we can't say for sure which way the quantity will change when demand decreases and supply increases at the same time. In this example, the decrease in demand and the increase in supply are such that the increase in quantity brought about by an increase in supply is offset by the decrease in quantity brought about by a decrease in demand—so the quantity does not change. But notice that if demand had decreased by slightly more, the quantity would have decreased. And if supply had increased by slightly more, the quantity would have increased.

We can now make two more predictions:

1. When demand decreases and supply increases, the price falls and the quantity might increase, decrease, or remain the same.
2. When demand increases and supply decreases, the price rises and the quantity might increase, decrease, or remain the same.

R E V I E W   Q U I Z

■ What is the effect on the price of a tape and the quantity of tapes if: (a) the price of a CD rises or (b) the price of a Walkman rises or (c) more firms start to produce tapes or (d) tape producers' wages rise or (e) if any pair of these events occur at the same time? (Draw the diagrams!)

FIGURE 4.12

The Effects of a Decrease in Demand and an Increase in Supply

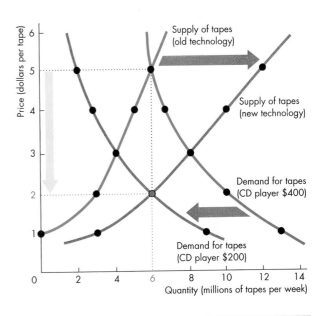

	Original quantities (millions of tapes per week)		New quantities (millions of tapes per week)	
Price (dollars per tape)	**Quantity demanded** CD player $400	**Quantity supplied** old technology	**Quantity demanded** CD player $200	**Quantity supplied** new technology
1	13	0	9	3
2	10	3	6	6
3	8	4	4	8
4	7	5	3	10
5	6	6	2	12

When the price of a CD player is $400 and firms use the old technology to produce tapes, the price of a tape is $5 and the quantity is 6 million tapes a week. A fall in the price of a CD player decreases the demand for tapes, and improved technology increases the supply of tapes. The new supply curve intersects the new demand curve at $2 a tape, a lower price, but in this case the quantity remains constant at 6 million tapes a week. This decrease in demand and increase in supply lower the price but leave the quantity unchanged.

CD Players, Coffee, and Bananas

Earlier in this chapter, we looked at some facts about prices and quantities of CD players, coffee, and bananas. Let's use the theory of demand and supply that we have just studied to explain the movements in the prices and quantities of those goods.

A Price Slide: CD Players Figure 4.13(a) shows the market for CD players. In 1983, when CD players were first manufactured, very few producers made them and the supply was small. The supply curve was S_0. In 1983, there weren't many titles on CDs and the demand for CD players was small. The demand curve was D_0. The quantities supplied and demanded in 1983 were equal at Q_0, and the price was $1,100 (1994 dollars).

As the technology for making CD players improved and as more and more factories began to produce CD players, the supply increased by a large amount and the supply curve shifted rightward from S_0 to S_1. At the same time, increases in incomes, a decrease in the price of a CD, and an increase in the number of titles on CDs increased the demand for CD players. But the increase in demand was much smaller than the increase in supply. The demand curve shifted rightward from D_0 to D_1. With the new demand curve D_1 and the new supply curve S_1, the equilibrium price fell to $170 in 1994, and the quantity increased to Q_1.

The large increase in supply combined with a smaller increase in demand resulted in an increase in the quantity of CD players and a dramatic fall in the price. Figure 4.13(a) shows the CD player price slide.

A Price Rocket: Coffee Figure 4.13(b) shows the market for coffee. In the second quarter of 1993, the supply curve for coffee was S_0 and the demand for coffee was D_0. The price of coffee was $1.30 a kilogram and the quantity was Q_0.

Serious back-to-back frosts in Brazil damaged coffee plants and severely cut the harvest. As a result, the supply of coffee decreased. This decrease in supply shifted the supply curve leftward from S_0 to S_1. At the same time that the supply of coffee decreased, the demand for coffee increased. The increase in demand was not large, but higher incomes and a larger population brought some increase in demand. The demand curve shifted rightward from D_0 to D_1. The combined effect of a large decrease in supply and a small increase in demand was a rapid rise in price from $1.30 a kilogram in the second quarter of 1993

to $4.60 a kilogram in the third quarter of 1994. The quantity decreased from Q_0 to Q_1. Figure 4.13(b) shows the coffee price rocket.

A Price Roller Coaster: Bananas Figure 4.13(c) shows the market for bananas. The demand for bananas—curve D—does not change much over the years. But the supply of bananas, which depends mainly on the weather, fluctuates between S_0 and S_1. With good growing conditions, the supply curve is S_1. With bad growing conditions, supply decreases and the supply curve is S_0. As a consequence of fluctuations in supply, the quantity fluctuates between Q_0 and Q_1. The price of bananas fluctuates between 44 cents per kilogram (1995 cents), the minimum price, and 73 cents per kilogram, the maximum price. Figure 4.13(c) shows the banana price roller coaster.

◆ You now know the basic theory of demand and supply. By using this theory, you can explain past fluctuations in prices and quantities and also make predictions about future fluctuations. *Reading Between the Lines* on pp. 82–83 shows you the theory in action in the world market for luxury cruises during the New Year vacation season at the turn of the millennium.

You will see lots of news articles that you can better understand by using your knowledge of demand and supply. Watch for stories on frosts in Brazil and the price of coffee, on frosts in Florida and the price of orange juice, or on hurricanes and earthquakes and their effects on the prices of many necessities.

Adam Smith said that each buyer and seller in a market "is led by an invisible hand to promote an end which was no part of his intention." What did he mean? He meant that when each one of us makes decisions to buy or sell in order to achieve the best outcome for ourselves and when our decisions are co-ordinated in free markets, we end up achieving the best outcome for everyone.

Although markets are amazing instruments, it turns out that they do not always work quite so perfectly as Adam Smith imagined. If you go on to study *micro*economics, you will discover the conditions under which markets are efficient and why they sometimes fail to achieve the best possible outcome for everyone. If you go on to study *macro*economics, you will discover the reasons why the market economy produces fluctuations in output and employment and sometimes creates persistent unemployment.

FIGURE 4.13

Price Slide, Rocket, and Roller Coaster

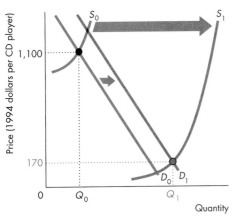

(a) Price slide: CD players

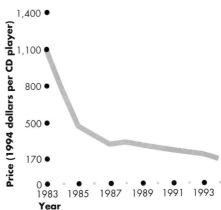

A large increase in the supply of CD players, from S_0 to S_1 combined with a small increase in demand, from D_0 to D_1, resulted in an increase in the quantity of CD players bought and sold from Q_0 to Q_1. The average price of a CD player fell from $1,100 in 1983 to $170 in 1994—a price slide.

(b) Price rocket: coffee

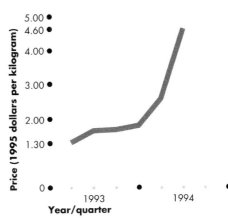

A large decrease in the supply of coffee, from S_0 to S_1, combined with a small increase in the demand, from D_0 to D_1, resulted in a decrease in the quantity, from Q_0 to Q_1, and a rise in the price of coffee from $1.30 a kilogram in the second quarter of 1993 to $4.60 a kilogram in the third quarter of 1994—a price rocket.

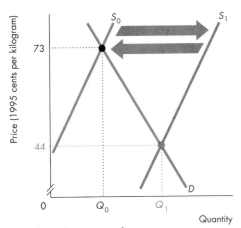

(c) Price roller coaster: bananas

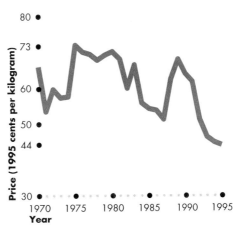

The demand for bananas remains at D. But supply fluctuates between S_0 and S_1. As a result, the price of bananas has fluctuated between 44 cents per kilogram and 73 cents per kilogram—a price roller coaster.

Supply and Demand: The Millennium Party

VANCOUVER SUN, JULY 18, 1998

Prepare to pay big for millennium party cruise tickets

When Richard Ramlall, of Herndon, Va., started shopping around for a millennium New Year's Eve cruise for himself and 31 friends a couple of months ago, he figured a guy who was willing to shell out $96,000 (based on $3,000 US per person) would be a pretty important client to some dutiful, commission-hungry travel agent. Wrong. After approaching eight different local agencies, Ramlall didn't even merit a return call. He's decided to spend the cash in landlocked Times Square instead.

The problem: While travel industry price-gouging during the "first" millennium celebration (Jan. 1, 2000; the real one, purists insist, follows a year later) isn't limited to cruise lines, Ramlall and numerous other cruisers are finding themselves caught in the kind of once-in-a-thousand-years seller's market in which cruise lines, anticipating a tidal wave of demand, are playing "punish the passengers."...

Expect high prices. Millennium cruisers will pay 25 per-cent more on top of the ... premium already charged for holiday periods. The cheapest cabin on a seven-day Caribbean cruise on Holland America on a slow week costs $1,128; this year's holiday rate is $1,600. For New Year's Eve 1999? The cheapest inside berth on a ship like the Volendam costs $2,740 —but the ship's booked. ...

Early booking discounts are minuscule or absent. Windstar and Princess offer a whopping 10 per cent discount if you book "soon."...

Grand Princess is reportedly sold out for its millennium cruise. Carnival's five-day Caribbean cruise on Jubilee, one of the shortest millennium itineraries available, is almost fully booked. ...

Essence of the Story

■ Demand for millennium cruise tickets is high.

■ During holiday periods, cruise ticket prices are 25 to 35 percent higher than during other periods.

■ Millennium cruisers will pay an additional 25 percent.

■ A 7-day Caribbean cruise in the cheapest cabin costs $1,128 during a slow week, $1,600 during the 1998 holiday period, and $2,740 on the millennium cruise.

■ Figure 1 shows the market for cabins on weekly Caribbean cruises. The supply curve is S and initially the demand curve is D_0. The equilibrium is at point a. The price of a cabin is $1,128 and the quantity of cabins occupied is 30,000 a week.

■ During the winter holiday season, the demand for cruises increases. The demand curve shifts rightward from D_0 to D_1.

■ The supply of cabins does not increase, but the quantity of cabins supplied increases. There is a movement up along the supply curve. The equilibrium is at point b. The price of a cabin rises to $1,600 and the quantity of cabins occupied increases to 40,000 a week.

■ The price increase between a normal week and the 1998 holiday season is more than 40 percent.

■ During the millennium holiday period, many people want to experience the "once-in-a-thousand-years" party cruise. The demand for cabins for New Year's celebrations in 1999 is greater than the demand for cabins for New Year's celebrations in 1998.

■ The demand curve shifts rightward from D_1 to D_2.

■ The supply of cabins does not increase, but the quantity of cabins supplied increases. There is a movement up along the supply curve. The equilibrium is at point c. The price of a cabin rises to $2,740 and the quantity of cabins occupied increases to 50,000 a week.

■ Suppose that the price of a cabin on a millennium cruise is $1,600, the same price as the cabin in the 1998 holiday season.

■ Figure 2 shows that when the price is $1,600 60,000 cabins are demanded, but only 40,000 cabins are supplied. There is a shortage of 20,000 cabins.

■ Figure 2 also shows that when only 40,000 cabins are supplied, the highest price that someone is willing to pay for the 40,000th cabin is $3,880.

■ Some people, unable to find a cabin at $1,600, offer to pay more and some cruise ships, noticing lists of prospective passengers, raise their prices.

■ The price rise reduces the shortage because the quantity demanded decreases and the quantity supplied increases.

■ The price will rise until there is no shortage. The equilibrium price is $2,740.

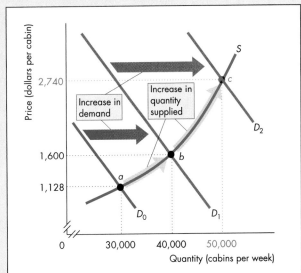

Figure 1 The market for cruises

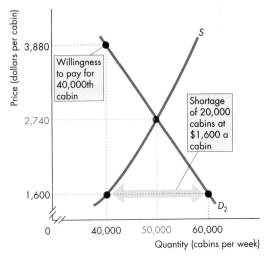

Figure 2 The market for millennium cruises

MATHEMATICAL NOTE: DEMAND, SUPPLY, AND EQUILIBRIUM

Demand Curve

The law of demand states that as the price of a good or service falls, the quantity demanded of it increases. A demand schedule, a demand curve, or a demand equation illustrates the law of demand. When the demand curve is a straight line, a linear equation describes it. A demand equation is

$$P = a - bQ_D,$$

where P is the price and Q_D is the quantity demanded. The a and b are positive constants.

Figure 1   Demand curve

The demand equation tells us three things:

1. The price at which no one is willing to buy the good (Q_D is zero). If the price is a, then the quantity demanded is zero. You can see the price a on the graph. It is the price at which the demand curve hits the y-axis—what we call the demand curve's "intercept on the y-axis."

2. As the price falls, the quantity demanded increases. If Q_D is a positive number, then the price P must be less than a. And as Q_D gets larger, the price P becomes smaller. That is, as the quantity increases, the maximum price that buyers are willing to pay of the good falls.

3. The constant b tells us how fast the maximum price that someone is willing to pay for the good falls as the quantity increases. That is, the constant b tells us about the steepness of the demand curve. The equation tells us that the slope of the demand curve is $-b$.

Supply Curve

The law of supply states that as the price of a good or service rises, the quantity supplied of it increases. A supply schedule, a supply curve, or a supply equation illustrates the law of supply. When the supply curve is a straight line, a linear equation describes it. A supply equation is

$$P = c + dQ_S,$$

where P is the price and Q_S the quantity supplied. The c and d are positive constants.

Figure 2   Supply curve

The supply equation tells us three things:

1. The price at which no one is willing to sell the good (Q_S is zero). If the price is c, then the quantity supplied is zero. You can see the price c on the graph. It is the price at which the supply curve hits the y-axis—what we call the supply curve's "intercept on the y-axis."

2. As the price rises, the quantity supplied increases. If Q_S is a positive number, then the price P must be greater than c. And as Q_S increases, the price P gets larger. That is, as the quantity increases, the minimum price that sellers are willing to accept rises.

3. The constant d tells us how fast the minimum price at which someone is willing to sell the good rises as the quantity increases. That is, the constant d tells us about the steepness of the supply curve. The equation tells us that the slope of the supply curve is d.

Market Equilibrium

Demand and supply determined the equilibrium price (P^*) and equilibrium quantity (Q^*) at the intersection of the demand curve and the supply curve.

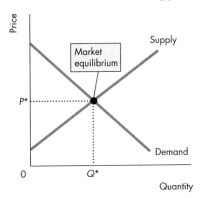

Figure 3 Market equilibrium

We can use the equations to find the equilibrium price and equilibrium quantity. The price of a good will adjust until the quantity demanded equals the quantity supplied. That is,

$$Q_D = Q_S.$$

So at the equilibrium price (P^*) and equilibrium quantity (Q^*),

$$Q_D = Q_S = Q^*.$$

To find the equilibrium price and equilibrium quantity: First substitute Q^* for Q_D in the demand equation and Q^* for Q_S in the supply equation. Then the price is the equilibrium price (P^*), which gives

$$P^* = a - bQ^*$$

$$P^* = c + dQ^*.$$

Notice that

$$a - bQ^* = c + dQ^*.$$

Now solve for Q^*

$$a - c = bQ^* + dQ^*$$

$$a - c = (b + d)Q^*$$

$$Q^* = \frac{a - c}{b + d}.$$

To find the equilibrium price (P^*), substitute for Q^* in either the demand equation or the supply equation.

Using the demand equation,

$$P^* = a - b\left(\frac{a - c}{b + d}\right)$$

$$P^* = \frac{a(b + d) - b(a - c)}{b + d}$$

$$P^* = \frac{ad + bc}{b + d}.$$

Alternatively, using the supply equation,

$$P^* = c + d\left(\frac{a - c}{b + d}\right)$$

$$P^* = \frac{c(b + d) + d(a - c)}{b + d}$$

$$P^* = \frac{ad + bc}{b + d}.$$

An Example

The demand for ice cream cones is

$$P = 800 - 2Q_D.$$

The supply of ice cream cones is

$$P = 200 + 1Q_S.$$

The price of a cone is expressed in cents and the quantities are expressed in cones per day.

To find the equilibrium price (P^*) and equilibrium quantity (Q^*), substitute Q^* for Q_D and Q_S and P^* for P.

That is,

$$P^* = 800 - 2Q^*$$

$$P^* = 200 + 1Q^*.$$

Now solve for Q^*:

$$800 - 2Q^* = 200 + 1Q^*$$

$$600 = 3Q^*$$

$$Q^* = 200.$$

And

$$P^* = 800 - 2Q^*$$

$$P^* = 400.$$

The equilibrium price is $4 a cone, and the equilibrium quantity is 200 cones a day.

S U M M A R Y

Key Points

Price and Opportunity Cost (p. 64)

▪ Opportunity cost is a relative price. We measure a relative price by dividing the price of one good by the price (index) of a basket of all goods.

▪ Demand and supply determines relative prices.

Demand (pp. 65–69)

▪ Demand is the relationship between the quantity demanded of a good and its price when all other influences on buying plans remain the same.

▪ The higher the price of a good, other things remaining the same, the smaller is the quantity demanded—the law of demand.

▪ Demand depends on the prices of substitutes and complements, expected future prices, income, population, and preferences.

Supply (pp. 70–73)

▪ Supply is the relationship between the quantity supplied of a good and its price when all other influences on selling plans remain the same.

▪ The higher the price of a good, other things remaining the same, the greater is the quantity supplied—the law of supply.

▪ Supply depends on the prices of resources used to produce a good, the prices of related goods produced, expected future prices, the number of producers, and technology.

Market Equilibrium (pp. 74–75)

▪ At the equilibrium price, the quantity demanded equals the quantity supplied.

▪ At prices above equilibrium, there is a surplus and the price falls.

▪ At prices below equilibrium, there is a shortage and the price rises.

Predicting Changes in Price and Quantity (pp. 76–81)

▪ An increase in demand brings a rise in price and an increase in the quantity supplied. (A decrease in demand brings a fall in price and a decrease in the quantity supplied.)

▪ An increase in supply brings a fall in price and an increase in the quantity demanded. (A decrease in supply brings a rise in price and a decrease in the quantity demanded.)

▪ An increase in demand and an increase in supply bring an increase in the quantity but the price might rise, fall, or remain the same. An increase in demand and a decrease in supply bring a higher price but the quantity might increase, decrease, or remain the same.

Key Figures ◆

Key Terms

P R O B L E M S

*1. What is the effect on the price of a tape and the quantity of tapes sold if:
  a. The price of a CD rises?
  b. The price of a Walkman rises?
  c. The supply of CD players increases?
  d. Consumers' incomes increase?
  e. Workers who make tapes get a pay raise?
  f. The price of a Walkman rises at the same time as workers who make tapes get a raise?

2. What is the effect on the price of hot dogs and the quantity of hot dogs sold if:
  a. The price of a hamburger rises?
  b. The price of a hot dog bun rises?
  c. The supply of hot dog sausages increases?
  d. Consumers' incomes decrease?
  e. The wage of the hot dog seller increases?
  f. The wage of the hot dog seller rises and at the same time prices of ketchup, mustard, and relish fall?

*3. Suppose that one of the following events occurs:
  i. The price of crude oil rises.
  ii. The price of a car rises.
  iii. All speed limits on highways are abolished.
  iv. Robot production cuts car production costs.
  Which of the above events increases or decreases (state which):
  a. The demand for gasoline?
  b. The supply of gasoline?
  c. The quantity of gasoline demanded?
  d. The quantity of gasoline supplied?

4. Suppose that one of the following events occurs:
  i. The price of wool rises.
  ii. The price of a sweater falls.
  iii. A close substitute for wool is invented.
  iv. A new high-speed loom is invented.
  Which of the above events increases or decreases (state which):
  a. The demand for wool?
  b. The supply of wool?
  c. The quantity of wool demanded?
  d. The quantity of wool supplied?

*5. The figure illustrates the market for pizza.
  a. Label the curves in the figure.
  b. What are the equilibrium price of a pizza and the equilibrium quantity of pizza?

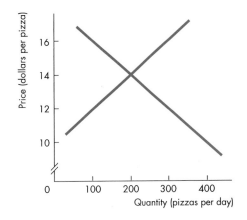

6. The figure illustrates the market for bread.

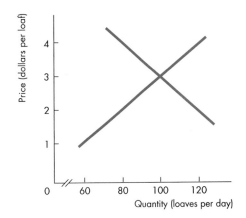

  a. Label the curves in the figure.
  b. What are the equilibrium price of bread and the equilibrium quantity of bread?

*7. The demand and supply schedules for gum are:

Price (cents per pack)	Quantity demanded	Quantity supplied
	(millions of packs a week)	
20	180	60
30	160	80
40	140	100
50	120	120
60	100	140
70	80	160
80	60	180

  a. What are the equilibrium price and quantity of gum?
  b. If gum was 70 cents a pack, describe the situation in the gum market and explain what would happen to the price of gum.

8. The demand and supply schedules for potato chips are:

Price (cents per bag)	Quantity demanded	Quantity supplied
	(millions of bags per week)	
40	170	90
50	160	100
60	150	110
70	140	120
80	130	130
90	120	140
100	110	150
110	100	160

a. What are the equilibrium price and equilibrium quantity of potato chips?
b. If the price of chips was 60 cents a bag, describe the situation in the market for potato chips and explain what would happen to the price of a bag of chips.

*9. In problem 7, suppose that a fire destroys some gum-producing factories and the supply of gum decreases by 40 million packs a week.
a. Has there been a shift in or a movement along the supply curve of gum?
b. Has there been a shift in or a movement along the demand curve for gum?
c. What are the new equilibrium price and quantity of gum?

10. In problem 8, suppose that a new snack food comes onto the market and as a result the demand for potato chips decreases by 40 million bags a week.
a. Has there been a shift in or a movement along the supply curve of chips?
b. Has there been a shift in or a movement along the demand curve for chips?
c. What are the new equilibrium price and quantity of chips?

*11. In problem 9, suppose an increase in the teenage population increases the demand for gum by 40 million packs per week at the same time as the fire occurs. What are the new equilibrium price and quantity of gum?

12. In problem 10, suppose that a flood destroys several potato farms and as a result supply decreases by 20 million bags a week at the same time as the new snack food comes onto the market. What are the new equilibrium price and quantity of chips?

CRITICAL THINKING

1. Study *Reading Between the Lines*, pp. 82–83, and then:
a. Describe how the millennium changes the price of a Caribbean cruise.
b. Draw a figure of demand and supply to explain what happens when there is an increase in demand and no change in supply.
c. Explain why the millennium results in an increase in the quantity of cabins supplied but no change in the supply of cabins.
d. What do you think is happening to bring about an increase in the quantity of cabins supplied? Describe what the cruise line companies are doing to increase the quantity supplied.
e. What do you predict would happen to the price of a cruise if air fares to Australia and the South Pacific were to decrease?
f. What do you predict would happen to the price of a cruise if there were an increase in the price of oil?

2. Use the links on the Parkin-Bade Web site and obtain data on the prices and quantities of wheat.
a. Draw a demand and supply diagram to illustrate the market for wheat in 1998.
b. Show the changes since 1998 in demand and supply and the changes in the quantity demanded and the quantity supplied that are consistent with the price and quantity data.

3. Use the link on the Parkin-Bade Web site to obtain information about the market for California navel oranges in 1999.
a. Explain why the supply of oranges decreased but the demand for oranges did not change. How can the demand not change when the quantity available decreases?
b. Explain the forces that determine the wholesale price and the retail price of oranges.
c. What, if anything, can be done to keep the price of oranges down when a frost occurs?
d. Use the links on the Parkin-Bade Web site and obtain the latest data on the quantity and price of oranges produced and use the demand and supply model to explain the changes in price during the past year.

5

Elasticity

Your pizza business is earning you a good profit but you are worried. You've just learned that a major pizza franchise is planning a big expansion in your neighbourhood. You know that the resulting increase in supply will lower the price of pizza and bring tough competition for you. But how big a price fall will you have to cope with? Will there be little change in pizza consumption and a large fall in price? Or will there be a huge increase in pizza consumption and little change in the price? To answer these questions, you need a measure of the responsiveness of the quantity of pizza demanded to the price of pizza. ◆ Faced with tough competition from your

Predicting Prices

pizzeria, the burger shop next door has cut its prices. How will the lower price of burgers affect the demand for your pizza? Will it wipe you out of business or make only a small dent in your sales? To answer this question, you need a measure of the responsiveness of the demand for your pizza to the price of burgers, a substitute for pizza. ◆ The economy is booming and people's incomes are rising. You know that with more income to spend, people will buy more pizza. But how much more pizza will people buy? Will the higher incomes bring a large increase in your sales or will they make only a small difference? To answer this question, you need a measure of the responsiveness of the demand for pizza to consumers' incomes. ◆ As incomes increase, you expect the demand for pizza to increase. But will the increase in demand bring a rise in price with little change in the quantity bought? Or will it bring a huge increase in pizza consumption with little change in the price? To answer this question, you need a measure of the responsiveness of the quantity of pizza supplied to a change in the price of pizza.

◆ In this chapter, you will learn how to answer questions like the ones just posed. You will learn about elasticity, a measure of the responsiveness of quantities bought and sold to changes in prices and other influences on buyers' and sellers' plans.

After studying this chapter, you will be able to:

■ **Define and calculate the price elasticity of demand**

■ **Use a total revenue test and an expenditure test to estimate the price elasticity of demand**

■ **Explain the factors that influence the price elasticity of demand**

■ **Define and calculate the cross elasticity of demand**

■ **Define and calculate the income elasticity of demand**

■ **Define and calculate the elasticity of supply**

The Price Elasticity of Demand

YOU KNOW THAT WHEN SUPPLY INCREASES, THE equilibrium price falls and the equilibrium quantity increases. But does the price fall by a large amount and the quantity increase by a little? Or does the price barely fall and the quantity increase by a large amount?

The answer depends on the responsiveness of the quantity demanded to a change in the price. You can see why by studying Fig. 5.1, which shows two possible scenarios in a local pizza market. Figure 5.1(a) shows one scenario and Fig. 5.1(b) shows the other.

In both cases, supply is initially S_0. In part (a), the demand for pizza is shown by the demand curve D_a. In part (b), the demand for pizza is shown by the demand curve D_b. Initially, in both cases, the price is $20 a pizza and the quantity of pizza produced and consumed is 10 pizzas an hour.

Now a large pizza franchise opens up and the supply of pizza increases. The supply curve shifts rightward to S_1. In case (a), the price of a pizza falls by an enormous $15 to $5 and the quantity increases by only 3 to 13 pizzas an hour. In contrast, in case (b), the price falls by only $5 to $15 a pizza and the quantity increases by 7 to 17 pizzas an hour.

The different outcomes arise from differing degrees of responsiveness of the quantity demanded to a change in the price. But what do we mean by responsiveness? One possible answer is slope. The slope of demand curve D_a is steeper than the slope of demand curve D_b.

In this example, we can compare the slopes of the two demand curves. But we can't always do so. The reason is that the slope of a demand curve depends on the units in which we measure the price and quantity. And we often must compare the demand curves for different goods and services that are measured in unrelated units. For example, a pizza producer might want to compare the demand for pizza with the demand for pop. Which quantity demanded is more responsive to a price change? This question can't be answered by comparing the slopes of two demand curves. The units of measurement of pizza and pop are unrelated. The question can be answered with a measure of responsiveness that is independent of units of measurement. Elasticity is such a measure.

The **price elasticity of demand** is a units-free measure of the responsiveness of the quantity demanded of a good to a change in its price when all other influences on buyers' plans remain the same.

FIGURE 5.1

How a Change in Supply Changes Price and Quantity

(a) Large price change and small quantity change

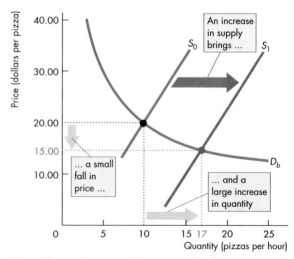

(b) Small price change and large quantity change

Initially, the price is $20 a pizza and the quantity sold is 10 pizzas an hour. Then supply increases from S_0 to S_1. In part (a), the price falls by $15 to $5 a pizza and the quantity increases by only 3 to 13 pizzas an hour. In part (b), the price falls by only $5 to $15 a pizza and the quantity increases by 7 to 17 pizzas an hour. This price change is smaller and quantity change is larger than in case (a). The quantity demanded is more responsive to price in case (b) than in case (a).

Calculating Elasticity

We calculate the *price elasticity of demand* by using the formula:

$$\text{Price elasticity of demand} = \frac{\text{Percentage change in quantity demanded}}{\text{Percentage change in price}}.$$

To use this formula, we need to know the quantities demanded at different prices when all other influences on buyers' plans remain the same. Suppose we have the data on prices and quantities demanded of pizza and calculate the price elasticity of demand for pizza.

Figure 5.2 zooms in on the demand curve for pizza and shows how the quantity demanded responds to a small change in the price. Initially, the price is $20.50 a pizza and 9 pizzas an hour are sold—the original point in the figure. The price then falls to $19.50 a pizza and the quantity demanded increases to 11 pizzas an hour—the new point in the figure. When the price falls by $1 a pizza, the quantity demanded increases by 2 pizzas an hour.

To calculate the price elasticity of demand, we express the changes in price and quantity demanded as percentages of the *average price* and the *average quantity*. By using the average price and average quantity, we calculate the elasticity at a point on the demand curve midway between the original point and the new point. The original price is $20.50 and the new price is $19.50, so the average price is $20. The $1 price decrease is 5 percent of the average price. That is,

$$\Delta P/P_{ave} = (\$1/\$20) \times 100 = 5\%.$$

The original quantity demanded is 9 pizzas and the new quantity demanded is 11 pizzas, so the average quantity demanded is 10 pizzas. The 2 pizza increase in the quantity demanded is 20 percent of the average quantity. That is,

$$\Delta Q/Q_{ave} = (2/10) \times 100 = 20\%.$$

So the price elasticity of demand, which is the percentage change in the quantity demanded (20 percent) divided by the percentage change in the price (5 percent), is 4. That is,

$$\text{Price elasticity of demand} = \frac{\%\Delta Q}{\%\Delta P}$$

$$= \frac{20\%}{5\%} = 4.$$

FIGURE 5.2
Calculating the Elasticity of Demand

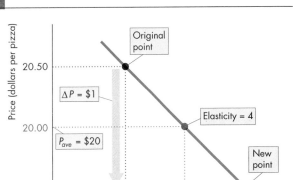

The elasticity of demand is calculated by using the formula*

$$\text{Price elasticity of demand} = \frac{\text{Percentage change in quantity demanded}}{\text{Percentage change in price}}$$

$$= \frac{\%\Delta Q}{\%\Delta P}$$

$$= \frac{\Delta Q/Q_{ave}}{\Delta P/P_{ave}}$$

$$= \frac{2/10}{1/20}$$

$$= 4.$$

This calculation measures the elasticity at an average price of $20 a pizza and an average quantity of 10 pizzas an hour.

*In the formula, the Greek letter delta (Δ) stands for "change in" and %Δ stands for "percentage change in."

Average Price and Quantity We use the *average* price and *average* quantity to avoid having two values for the elasticity of demand at a single point on the demand curve, depending on whether the price falls or rises. If the price falls from $20.50 to $19.50, the $1 price change is 4.9 percent of $20.50. The 2 pizza change in quantity is 22.2 percent of 9, the original quantity. If we use these numbers, the elasticity is 22.2 divided by 4.9, which equals 4.5. If the price rises from $19.50 to $20.50, the $1 price change is

5.1 percent of $19.50. The 2 pizza change in quantity is 18.2 percent of 11, the original quantity. If we use these numbers, the elasticity is 18.2 divided by 5.1, which equals 3.6. By using the *average* price and *average* quantity, we get the same value for the elasticity regardless of whether the price falls or rises.

Percentages and Proportions   Elasticity is the ratio of the *percentage* change in the quantity demanded to the percentage change in the price. It is also, equivalently, the proportionate change in the quantity demanded, $\Delta Q/Q_{ave}$, divided by the proportionate change in the price, $\Delta P/P_{ave}$. The percentage changes are the proportionate changes multiplied by 100. So when we divide one percentage change by another, the 100s cancel and the result is the same as we get by using the proportionate changes.

A Units-Free Measure   Now that you've calculated a price elasticity of demand, you can see why it is a *units-free measure*. Elasticity is a units-free measure because the percentage change in each variable is independent of the units in which the variable is measured. And the ratio of the two percentages is a number without units.

Minus Sign and Elasticity   When the price of a good *rises*, the quantity demanded *decreases* along the demand curve. Because a *positive* change in the price brings a *negative* change in the quantity demanded, the price elasticity of demand is a negative number. But it is the magnitude, or *absolute value*, of the price elasticity of demand that tells us how responsive—how elastic—demand is. To compare elasticities, we use the magnitude of the price elasticity of demand and ignore the minus sign.

Inelastic and Elastic Demand

Figure 5.3 shows three demand curves that cover the entire range of possible elasticities of demand. In Fig. 5.3(a), the quantity demanded is constant regardless of the price. In this case, the price elasticity of demand is zero and the good is said to have **perfectly inelastic demand**. One good that has a very low price elasticity of demand (perhaps zero over some price range) is insulin. Insulin is of such importance to some diabetics that if the price rises or falls, they do not change the quantity they buy.

If the percentage change in the quantity demanded equals the percentage change in the price, then the price elasticity equals 1 and the good is said to have **unit elastic demand**. The demand in Fig. 5.3(b) is an example of unit elastic demand.

Between the cases shown in parts (a) and (b) of Fig. 5.3 is the general case in which the percentage

---

FIGURE   5.3

Inelastic and Elastic Demand

(a) Perfectly inelastic demand

(b) Unit elastic demand

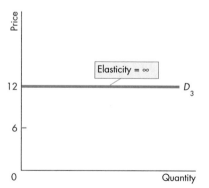

(c) Perfectly elastic demand

Each demand illustrated here has a constant elasticity. The demand curve in part (a) illustrates the demand for a good that has a zero elasticity of demand. The demand curve in part (b) illustrates the demand for a good with a unit elasticity of demand. And the demand curve in part (c) illustrates the demand for a good with an infinite elasticity of demand.

change in the quantity demanded is less than the percentage change in the price. In this case, the price elasticity of demand is between zero and 1, and the good is said to have **inelastic demand**. Food and housing are examples of goods with inelastic demand.

If the quantity demanded changes by an infinitely large percentage in response to a tiny price change, then the price elasticity of demand is infinity, and the good is said to have **perfectly elastic demand**. Fig. 5.3(c) shows perfectly elastic demand. An example of a good that has a very high elasticity of demand (almost infinite) is marker pens from the campus bookstore and from the convenience store next door to the bookstore. If the two stores offer pens for the same price, some people buy from one and some from the other. But if the bookstore's price is higher than the convenience store's price, even by a small amount, the bookstore will not sell many pens. Pens from the two stores are perfect substitutes.

Between the cases in parts (b) and (c) of Fig. 5.3 is the general case in which the percentage change in the quantity demanded exceeds the percentage change in the price. In this case, the price elasticity is greater than 1 and the good is said to have **elastic demand**. Automobiles and furniture are examples of goods that have elastic demand.

Elasticity Along a Straight-Line Demand Curve

Elasticity and slope are not the same but are related. To understand how they are related, let's look at elasticity along a straight-line demand curve—a demand curve that has a constant slope.

Figure 5.4 illustrates the calculation of elasticity along a straight-line demand curve. First, let's calculate the elasticity when the price falls by $10 from $20 to $10. The average price in this case is $15 and

$$\Delta P/P_{ave} = \$10/\$15.$$

When the price falls from $20 to $10, the quantity demanded increases by 20 pizzas an hour from zero to 20, so the average quantity demanded is 10 and

$$\Delta Q/Q_{ave} = 20/10.$$

Now divide the proportionate change in the quantity demanded by the proportionate change in the price to obtain the elasticity as

$$\frac{\Delta Q/Q_{ave}}{\Delta P/P_{ave}} = \frac{20/10}{10/15} = 3.$$

We can repeat the calculation that we've just done at any price and quantity along the demand curve. Because the demand curve is a straight line, a $10 price fall always increases the quantity demanded by 20 pizzas an hour. So in the elasticity formula, ΔP is $10 and ΔQ is 20 for every average price and average quantity. But the lower the average price, the greater is the average quantity. So the lower the average price, the less elastic is demand.

Check this proposition by calculating the elasticity when the price falls by $10 from $10 to zero. Now the average price is $5 and

$$\Delta P/P_{ave} = \$10/\$5.$$

When the price falls from $10 to zero, the quantity demanded increases by 20 pizzas an hour from 20 to 40, so the average quantity demanded is 30 and

$$\Delta Q/Q_{ave} = 20/30.$$

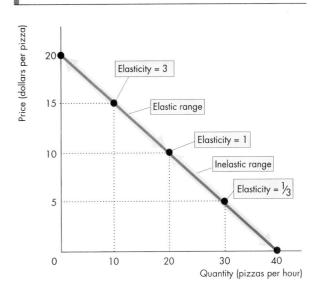

FIGURE 5.4

Elasticity Along a Straight-Line Demand Curve

On a straight-line demand curve, elasticity decreases as the price falls and the quantity demanded increases. Demand is unit elastic at the midpoint of the demand curve (elasticity is 1). Above the midpoint, demand is elastic; and below the midpoint, demand is inelastic.

To obtain the elasticity of demand, divide the proportionate change in the quantity demanded by the proportionate change in the price

$$\frac{\Delta Q/Q_{ave}}{\Delta P/P_{ave}} = \frac{20/30}{10/5} = 1/3.$$

Finally, let's calculate the elasticity when the price falls by $10 from $15 to $5. Now the average price is $10 and

$$\Delta P/P_{ave} = \$10/\$10.$$

When the price falls from $15 to $5, the quantity demanded increases by 20 pizzas an hour from 10 to 30, so the average quantity demanded is 20 and

$$\Delta Q/Q_{ave} = 20/20.$$

To obtain the elasticity of demand, divide the proportionate change in the quantity demanded by the proportionate change in the price

$$\frac{\Delta Q/Q_{ave}}{\Delta P/P_{ave}} = \frac{20/20}{10/10} = 1.$$

You've now seen how elasticity changes along a straight-line demand curve. At the midpoint of the curve, the elasticity is 1. Above the midpoint, demand is elastic; and below the midpoint, demand is inelastic.

Total Revenue and Elasticity

Total revenue from the sale of a good equals the price of the good multiplied by the quantity sold. When a price changes, total revenue changes. But a rise in price does not always increase total revenue. The change in total revenue depends on the elasticity of demand.

- If demand is elastic, a 1 percent price cut increases the quantity sold by more than 1 percent and total revenue increases.
- If demand is unit elastic, a 1 percent price cut increases the quantity sold by 1 percent and so total revenue does not change.
- If demand is inelastic, a 1 percent price cut increases the quantity sold by less than 1 percent and total revenue decreases.

Figure 5.5 shows how we can use this relationship between elasticity and total revenue to estimate elasticity using the total revenue test. The **total revenue test** is a method of estimating the price elasti-

FIGURE 5.5

Elasticity and Total Revenue

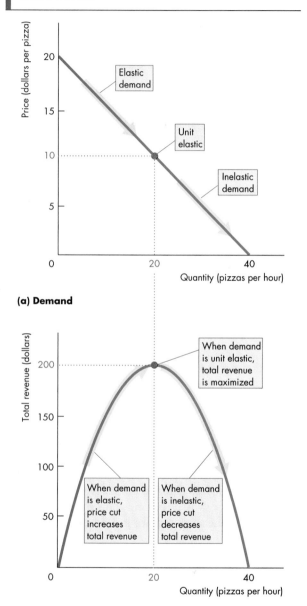

(a) Demand

(b) Total revenue

When demand is elastic, in the price range from $20 to $10, a decrease in the price (part a) brings an increase in total revenue (part b). When demand is inelastic, in the price range from $10 to zero, a decrease in the price (part a) brings a decrease in total revenue (part b). When demand is unit elastic, at a price of $10 (part a), total revenue is at a maximum (part b).

city of demand by observing the change in total revenue that results from a price change (with all other influences on the quantity sold remaining unchanged).

■ If a price cut increases total revenue, demand is elastic.

■ If a price cut decreases total revenue, demand is inelastic.

■ If a price cut leaves total revenue unchanged, demand is unit elastic.

In Fig. 5.5(a), over the price range from $20 to $10, demand is elastic. Over the price range from $10 to zero, demand is inelastic. At a price of $10, demand is unit elastic. In Fig. 5.5(b), you can see how total revenue changes. At a price of $20, the quantity sold is zero, so total revenue is also zero. At a price of zero, the quantity demanded is 40 pizzas an hour but total revenue is again zero. A price cut in the elastic range brings an increase in total revenue—the percentage increase in the quantity demanded is greater than the percentage decrease in the price. A price cut in the inelastic range brings a decrease in total revenue—the percentage increase in the quantity demanded is less than the percentage decrease in the price. At a unit elasticity, total revenue is at a maximum.

So if when the price of an item falls, you spend more on it, your demand for that item is elastic; if you spend the same amount, your demand is unit elastic; and if you spend less, your demand is inelastic.

The Factors That Influence the Elasticity of Demand

Table 5.1 lists some estimates of actual elasticities in the real world. You can see that these real-world elasticities of demand range from 1.52 for metals, the good with the most elastic demand in the table, to 0.12 for food, the good with the most inelastic demand in the table. What makes the demand for some goods elastic and the demand for others inelastic?

Elasticity depends on three main factors:

■ The closeness of substitutes

■ The proportion of income spent on the good

■ The time elapsed since a price change

Closeness of Substitutes The closer the substitutes for a good or service, the more elastic is the demand for it. For example, oil has substitutes but none that are very close (imagine a steam-driven,

TABLE 5.1

Some Real-World Price Elasticities of Demand

Good or Service	Elasticity
Elastic Demand	
Metals	1.52
Electrical engineering products	1.39
Mechanical engineering products	1.30
Furniture	1.26
Motor vehicles	1.14
Instrument engineering products	1.10
Professional services	1.09
Transportation services	1.03
Inelastic Demand	
Gas, electricity, and water	0.92
Oil	0.91
Chemicals	0.89
Beverages (all types)	0.78
Clothing	0.64
Tobacco	0.61
Banking and insurance services	0.56
Housing services	0.55
Agricultural and fish products	0.42
Books, magazines, and newspapers	0.34
Food	0.12

Sources: Ahsan Mansur and John Whalley, "Numerical Specification of Applied General Equilibrium Models: Estimation, Calibration, and Data," in *Applied General Equilibrium Analysis*, eds. Herbert E. Scarf and John B. Shoven (New York: Cambridge University Press, 1984), 109, and Henri Theil, Ching-Fan Chung, and James L. Seale, Jr., *Advances in Econometrics, Supplement 1, 1989, International Evidence on Consumption Patterns* (Greenwich, Conn.: JAI Press Inc., 1989). Reprinted with permission.

coal-fuelled car or a nuclear-powered jetliner). So the demand for oil is inelastic. Metals have substitutes such as plastics, so the demand for metals is elastic.

The degree of substitutability between two goods also depends on how narrowly (or broadly) we define them. For example, the elasticity of demand for meat is low, but the elasticity of demand for beef, lamb, or chicken is high. The elasticity of demand for personal computers is low, but the elasticity of demand for a Compaq, Dell, or IBM is high.

In everyday language we talk about *necessities* and *luxuries*. A necessity is a good that has poor substitutes and that is crucial for our well-being. So generally, a necessity has an inelastic demand. A luxury is a good that usually has many substitutes, one of which is not buying it. So a luxury generally has an elastic demand.

Proportion of Income Spent on the Good
Other things remaining the same, the greater the proportion of income spent on a good, the more elastic is the demand for it.

Think about your own elasticity of demand for chewing gum and housing. If the price of chewing gum doubles, you consume almost as much gum as before. Your demand for gum is inelastic. If apartment rents double, you shriek and look for more students to share accommodation with you. Your demand for housing is more elastic than your demand for gum. Why the difference? Housing takes a large proportion of your budget and gum takes only a tiny proportion. You don't like either price increase, but you hardly notice the higher price of gum, while the higher rent puts your budget under severe strain.

Figure 5.6 shows the proportion of income spent on food and the price elasticity of demand for food in 10 countries. This figure confirms the general tendency we have just described. The larger the proportion of income spent on food, the larger is the price elasticity of demand for food. For example, in Tanzania, where 62 percent of income is spent on food, the price elasticity of demand for food is 0.77. In contrast, in Canada, where 14 percent of income is spent on food, the elasticity of demand for food is 0.13.

Time Elapsed Since Price Change   The longer the time that has elapsed since a price change, the more elastic is demand. When a price rises, consumers often continue to buy similar quantities of a good for a while. But given enough time, they find acceptable and less costly substitutes. As this process of substitution occurs, the quantity purchased of a good or service that has become more expensive gradually decreases. When a price falls, consumers buy more of the good. But as time passes, they find ever more creative ways of using inexpensive items and demand becomes more elastic. For example, some Japanese farmers have discovered that they can use an inexpensive pager to tell their cows when it is milking time!

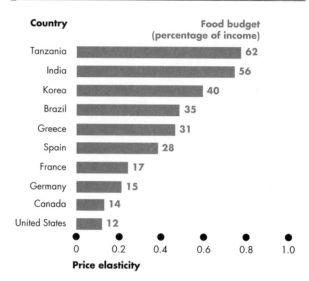

FIGURE 5.6

Price Elasticities in 10 Countries

As income increases and the proportion of income spent on food decreases, the demand for food becomes less elastic.

Source: Henri Theil, Ching-Fan Chung, and James L. Seale, Jr., *Advances in Econometrics, Supplement 1, 1989, International Evidence on Consumption Patterns* (Greenwich, Conn.: JAI Press Inc., 1989).

REVIEW QUIZ

- Why do we need a units-free measure of the responsiveness of the quantity demanded of a good or service to a change in its price?
- Define and calculate the price elasticity of demand.
- Why, when we calculate the price elasticity of demand, do we express the change in the price as a percentage of the *average* price and the change in quantity as a percentage of the *average* quantity?
- What is the total revenue test and why does it work?
- What are the main influences on the elasticity of demand that make the demand for some goods elastic and the demand for other goods inelastic?

You've now completed your study of the *price* elasticity of demand. Two other elasticity concepts tell us about the effects of other influences on demand. Let's look at these other elasticities of demand.

More Elasticities of Demand

BACK AT THE PIZZERIA, YOU ARE TRYING TO WORK out how a price cut by the burger shop next door will affect the demand for your pizza. You know that pizzas and burgers are substitutes. And you know that when the price of a substitute for pizza falls, the demand for pizza decreases. But by how much?

You also know that pizza and pop are complements. And you know that if the price of a complement of pizza falls, the demand for pizza increases. So you wonder whether you might keep your customers by cutting the price you charge for pop. But you want to know by how much you must cut the price of pop to hold on to your customers in the face of the cheaper burgers next door.

To answer these questions, you need to calculate the cross elasticity of demand. Let's examine this elasticity measure.

Cross Elasticity of Demand

We measure the influence of a change in the price of substitutes or complements by using the concept of the cross elasticity of demand. The **cross elasticity of demand** is a measure of the responsiveness of the demand for a good to a change in the price of a substitute or complement, other things remaining the same. It is calculated by using the formula

$$\text{Cross elasticity of demand} = \frac{\text{Percentage change in quantity demanded}}{\text{Percentage change in price of a substitute or complement}}.$$

The cross elasticity of demand can be positive or negative. It is positive for a substitute and negative for a complement.

Figure 5.7 illustrates the cross elasticity of demand. Pizza and burgers are substitutes. Because they are substitutes, when the price of a burger falls, the demand for pizza decreases. The demand curve for pizza shifts leftward from D_0 to D_1. Because a *fall* in the price of a burger brings a *decrease* in the demand for pizza, the cross elasticity of demand for pizza with respect to the price of a burger is *positive*. Both the price and the quantity change in the same direction.

FIGURE 5.7

Cross Elasticity of Demand

A burger is a *substitute* for pizza. When the price of a burger falls, the demand for pizza decreases and the demand curve for pizza shifts leftward from D_0 to D_1. The cross elasticity of the demand for pizza with respect to the price of a burger is *positive*. Pop is a *complement* of pizza. When the price of pop falls, the demand for pizza increases and the demand curve for pizza shifts rightward from D_0 to D_2. The cross elasticity of the demand for pizza with respect to the price of pop is *negative*.

Pizza and pop are complements. Because they are complements, when the price of pop falls, the demand for pizza increases. The demand curve for pizza shifts rightward from D_0 to D_2. Because a *fall* in the price of pop brings an *increase* in the demand for pizza, the cross elasticity of demand for pizza with respect to the price of pop is *negative*. The price and quantity change in *opposite* directions.

The magnitude of the cross elasticity of demand determines how far the demand curve shifts. The larger the cross elasticity (absolute value), the greater is the change in demand and the larger is the shift in the demand curve.

If two items are very close substitutes, such as two brands of spring water, the cross elasticity is large. If two items are close complements, such as movies and popcorn, the cross elasticity is large. If two items are somewhat unrelated, such as newspapers and orange juice, the cross elasticity is small, and perhaps zero.

Income Elasticity of Demand

The economy is expanding and people are enjoying rising incomes. This prosperity is bringing an increase in the demand for all types of goods and services. But by how much will the demand for pizza increase?

The answer depends on the income elasticity of demand for the good. The **income elasticity of demand** is a measure of the responsiveness of the demand for a good or service to a change in income, other things remaining the same. It is calculated by using the formula

$$\text{Income elasticity of demand} = \frac{\text{Percentage change in quantity demanded}}{\text{Percentage change in income}}.$$

Income elasticities of demand can be positive or negative and fall into three interesting ranges:

1. Greater than 1 (*normal* good, income elastic)
2. Between zero and 1 (*normal* good, income inelastic)
3. Less than zero (*inferior* good)

Figure 5.8(a) shows an income elasticity of demand that is greater than 1. As income increases, the quantity demanded increases, but the quantity demanded increases faster than income. Examples of goods in this category are ocean cruises, international travel, jewellery, and works of art.

Figure 5.8(b) shows an income elasticity of demand that is between zero and 1. In this case, the quantity demanded increases as income increases, but income increases faster than the quantity demanded. Examples of goods in this category are food, clothing, newspapers, and magazines.

Figure 5.8(c) shows an income elasticity of demand that eventually becomes negative. In this case, the quantity demanded increases as income increases until it reaches a maximum at income m. As income continues to increase above m, the quantity demanded decreases. The elasticity of demand is positive but less than 1 up to income m. Beyond income m, the income elasticity of demand is negative. Examples of goods in this category are small motorcycles, potatoes, and rice. Low-income consumers buy most of these goods. At low income levels, the demand for such goods increases as income increases. But as income increases above m, consumers replace these goods with superior alternatives. For example, a small car replaces the motorcycle; fruit, vegetables, and meat begin to appear in a diet that was heavy in rice or potatoes.

FIGURE 5.8

Income Elasticity of Demand

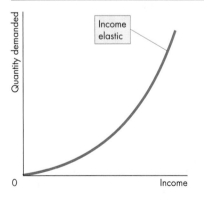

(a) Elasticity greater than 1

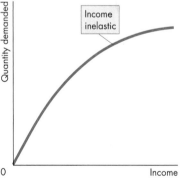

(b) Elasticity between zero and 1

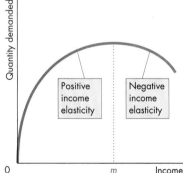

(c) Elasticity less than 1 and becomes negative

Income elasticity of demand has three ranges of values. In part (a), income elasticity of demand is greater than 1. As income increases along the x-axis, the quantity demanded increases but by a bigger percentage than the increase in income. In part (b), income elasticity of demand is between zero and 1. As income increases, the quantity demanded increases but by a smaller percentage than the increase in income. In part (c), the income elasticity of demand is positive at low incomes but becomes negative as income increases above level m. Maximum consumption of this good occurs at the income m.

Real-World Income Elasticities of Demand

Table 5.2 shows estimates of some real-world income elasticities of demand. Necessities such as food and clothing are income inelastic, while luxuries such as airline and foreign travel are income elastic.

But what is a necessity and what is a luxury depends on the level of income. For people with a low income, food and clothing can be luxuries. So the *level* of income has a big effect on income elasticities of demand. Figure 5.9 shows this effect on the income elasticity of demand for food in 10 countries. In countries with low incomes, such as Tanzania and India, the income elasticity of demand for food is high. In countries with high incomes, such as Canada and the United States, it is low.

TABLE 5.2
Some Real-World Income Elasticities of Demand

Elastic Demand

Airline travel	5.82
Movies	3.41
Foreign travel	3.08
Electricity	1.94
Restaurant meals	1.61
Local buses and trains	1.38
Haircuts	1.36
Cars	1.07

Inelastic Demand

Tobacco	0.86
Alcoholic beverages	0.62
Furniture	0.53
Clothing	0.51
Newspapers and magazines	0.38
Telephone	0.32
Food	0.14

Sources: H.S. Houthakker and Lester D. Taylor, *Consumer Demand in the United States* (Cambridge, Mass.: Harvard University Press, 1970), and Henri Theil, Ching-Fan Chung, and James L. Seale, Jr., *Advances in Econometrics, Supplement 1, 1989, International Evidence on Consumption Patterns* (Greenwich, Conn.: JAI Press Inc., 1989). Reprinted with permission.

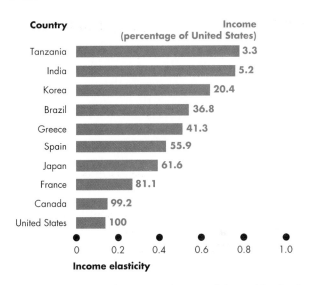

FIGURE 5.9
Income Elasticities in 10 Countries

As income increases, the income elasticity of demand for food decreases. For low-income consumers, a larger percentage of any increase in income is spent on food than for high-income consumers.

Source: Henri Theil, Ching-Fan Chung, and James L. Seale, Jr., *Advances in Econometrics, Supplement 1, 1989, International Evidence on Consumption Patterns* (Greenwich, Conn.: JAI Press Inc., 1989).

REVIEW QUIZ

- What does the cross elasticity of demand measure?
- What does the sign (positive versus negative) of the cross elasticity of demand tell us about the relationship between two goods?
- What does the income elasticity of demand measure?
- What does the sign (positive versus negative) of the income elasticity of demand tell us about a good?
- Why does the level of income influence the magnitude of the income elasticity of demand?

You've now completed your study of the *cross elasticity* of demand and the *income elasticity* of demand. Let's look at the other side of a market and examine the elasticity of supply.

Elasticity of Supply

YOU KNOW THAT WHEN DEMAND INCREASES, THE equilibrium price rises and the equilibrium quantity increases. But does the price rise by a large amount and the quantity increase by a little? Or does the price barely rise and the quantity increase by a large amount?

The answer depends on the responsiveness of the quantity supplied to a change in the price. You can see why by studying Fig. 5.10, which shows two possible scenarios in a local pizza market. Figure 5.10(a) shows one scenario and Fig. 5.10(b) shows the other.

In both cases, demand is initially D_0. In part (a), the supply of pizza is shown by the supply curve S_a. In part (b), the supply of pizza is shown by the supply curve S_b. Initially, in both cases, the price is $20 a pizza and the quantity produced and consumed is 10 pizzas an hour.

Now an increase in income and population increase the demand for pizza. The demand curve shifts rightward to D_1. In case (a), the price rises by $20 to $30 a pizza and the quantity increases by only 3 to 13 an hour. In contrast, in case (b), the price rises by only $1 to $21 a pizza and the quantity increases by 10 to 20 pizzas an hour.

The different outcomes arise from differing degrees of responsiveness of the quantity supplied to a change in the price. We measure the degree of responsiveness by using the concept of the elasticity of supply.

Calculating the Elasticity of Supply

The **elasticity of supply** measures the responsiveness of the quantity supplied to a change in the price of a good when all other influences on selling plans remain the same. It is calculated by using the formula

$$\frac{\text{Elasticity}}{\text{of supply}} = \frac{\text{Percentage change in quantity supplied}}{\text{Percentage change in price}}.$$

We use the same method that you learned when you studied the elasticity of demand. Let's calculate the elasticity of supply for the supply curves in Fig. 5.10.

In Fig. 5.10(a), when the price rises from $20 to $30, the price rise is $10 and the average price is $25, so the price rises by 40 percent of the average price. The quantity increases from 10 to 13, so the increase

FIGURE 5.10

How a Change in Demand Changes Price and Quantity

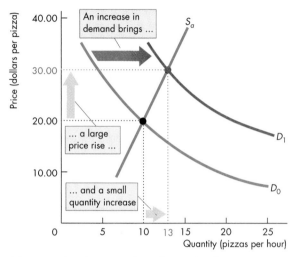

(a) Large price change and small quantity change

(b) Small price change and large quantity change

Initially, the price is $20 a pizza and the quantity sold is 10 pizzas an hour. Then incomes and population increase and demand increases from D_0 to D_1. In part (a), the price rises by $10 to $30 a pizza and the quantity increases by only 3 to 13 pizzas an hour. In part (b), the price rises by only $1 to $21 a pizza and the quantity increases by 10 to 20 pizzas an hour. This price change is smaller and quantity change is larger than in case (a). The quantity supplied is more responsive to price in case (b) than in case (a).

is 3, the average quantity is 11.5, and the quantity increases by 26 percent. The elasticity of supply is equal to 26 percent divided by 40 percent, which equals 0.65.

In Fig. 5.10(b), when the price rises from $20 to $21, the price rise is $1 and the average price is $20.50, so the price rises by 4.9 percent of the average price. The quantity increases from 10 to 20, so the increase is 10, the average quantity is 15, and the quantity increases by 67 percent. The elasticity of supply is equal to 67 percent divided by 4.9 percent, which equals 13.67.

Figure 5.11 shows the range of supply elasticities. If the quantity supplied is fixed regardless of the price, the supply curve is vertical and the elasticity of supply is zero. Supply is perfectly inelastic. This case is shown in Fig. 5.11(a). A special intermediate case is when the percentage change in the price equals the percentage change in quantity. Supply is then unit elastic. This case is shown in Fig. 5.11(b). No matter how steep the supply curve is, if it is linear and passes through the origin, supply is unit elastic. If there is a price at which sellers are willing to offer any quantity for sale, the supply curve is horizontal and the elasticity of supply is infinite. Supply is perfectly elastic. This case is shown in Fig. 5.11(c).

The Factors That Influence the Elasticity of Supply

The magnitude of the elasticity of supply depends on:

- Resource substitution possibilities
- Time frame for supply decisions

Resource Substitution Possibilities   Some goods and services can be produced only by using unique or rare productive resources. These items have a low, and perhaps a zero, elasticity of supply. Other goods and services can be produced by using commonly available resources that could be allocated to a wide variety of alternative tasks. Such items have a high elasticity of supply.

A Van Gogh painting is an example of a good with a vertical supply curve and an elasticity of supply of zero. At the other extreme, wheat can be grown on land that is almost equally good for growing corn. So it is just as easy to grow wheat as corn, and the opportunity cost of wheat in terms of forgone corn is almost constant. As a result, the supply curve of wheat is almost horizontal and its elasticity of supply is very large. Similarly, when a good is produced in many different countries (for example, sugar and beef), the supply of the good is highly elastic.

FIGURE 5.11

Inelastic and Elastic Supply

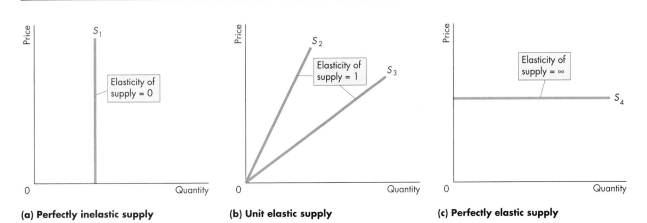

(a) Perfectly inelastic supply

(b) Unit elastic supply

(c) Perfectly elastic supply

Each supply illustrated here has a constant elasticity. The supply curve in part (a) illustrates the supply of a good that has a zero elasticity of supply. The supply curves in part (b) illustrate the supply of goods that have a unit elasticity of supply.

All linear supply curves that pass through the origin have a unit elasticity. The supply curve in part (c) illustrates the supply of a good that has an infinite elasticity of supply.

The supply of most goods and services lies between the two extremes. The quantity produced can be increased but only by incurring higher cost. If a higher price is offered, the quantity supplied increases. Such goods and services have an elasticity of supply between zero and infinity.

Time Frame for Supply Decisions To study the influence of the length of time elapsed since a price change, we distinguish three time frames of supply:

■ Momentary supply
■ Long-run supply
■ Short-run supply

When the price of a good rises or falls, the *momentary supply curve* shows the response of the quantity supplied immediately following a price change.

Some goods, such as fruits and vegetables, have a perfectly inelastic momentary supply—a vertical supply curve. The quantities supplied depend on crop-planting decisions made earlier. In the case of oranges, for example, planting decisions have to be made many years in advance of the crop being available. The momentary supply curve is vertical because, on a given day, no matter what the price of oranges, producers cannot change their output. They have picked, packed, and shipped their crop to market, and the quantity available for that day is fixed.

In contrast, some goods have a perfectly elastic momentary supply. Long-distance phone calls are an example. When many people simultaneously make a call, there is a big surge in the demand for telephone cables, computer switching, and satellite time, and the quantity bought increases (up to the physical limits of the telephone system). But the price remains constant. Long-distance carriers monitor fluctuations in demand and re-route calls to ensure that the quantity supplied equals the quantity demanded without changing the price.

The *long-run supply curve* shows the response of the quantity supplied to a change in the price after all the technologically possible ways of adjusting supply have been exploited. In the case of oranges, the long run is the time it takes new plantings to grow to full maturity—about 15 years. In some cases, the long-run adjustment occurs only after a completely new production plant has been built and workers have been trained to operate it—typically a process that might take several years.

The *short-run supply curve* shows how the quantity supplied responds to a price change when only *some* of the technologically possible adjustments to production have been made. The first adjustment that is usually made is in the amount of labour employed. To increase output in the short run, firms work their labour force overtime and perhaps hire additional workers. To decrease their output in the short run, firms lay off workers or reduce their hours of work. With the passage of time, firms can make additional adjustments, perhaps training additional workers or buying additional tools and other equipment. The short-run response to a price change, unlike the momentary and long-run responses, is not a unique response but a sequence of adjustments.

The short-run supply curve slopes upward because producers can take actions quite quickly to change the quantity supplied in response to a price change. For example, if the price of oranges falls, growers can stop picking and leave oranges to rot on the tree. Or if the price rises they can use more fertilizer and improved irrigation to increase the yields of their existing trees. In the long run, they can plant more trees and increase the quantity supplied even more in response to a given price rise.

R E V I E W   Q U I Z

■ Why do we need to measure the responsiveness of the quantity supplied of a good or service to a change in its price?
■ Can you define and calculate the elasticity of supply?
■ What are the main influences on the elasticity of supply that make the supply of some goods elastic and the supply of other goods inelastic?
■ Can you provide examples of goods or services whose elasticity of supply are: (a) zero, (b) greater than zero but less than infinity, and (c) infinity?
■ How does the time frame over which a supply decision is made influence the elasticity of supply?

◆ You have now studied the theory of demand and supply, and you have learned how to measure the elasticities of demand and supply. All the elasticities that you've met in this chapter are summarized in Table 5.3. In the next chapter, we are going to study the efficiency of competitive markets. But before doing that, take a look at *Reading Between the Lines*, on pp. 104–105, to see elasticity in action.

TABLE 5.3

A Compact Glossary of Elasticities

Price Elasticities of Demand

A relationship is described as	When its magnitude is	Which means that
Perfectly elastic or infinitely elastic	Infinity	The smallest possible increase in the price causes an infinitely large decrease in the quantity demanded*
Elastic	Less than infinity but greater than 1	The percentage decrease in the quantity demanded exceeds the percentage increase in the price
Unit elastic	1	The percentage decrease in the quantity demanded equals the percentage increase in the price
Inelastic	Greater than zero but less than 1	The percentage decrease in the quantity demanded is less than the percentage increase in the price
Perfectly inelastic or completely inelastic	Zero	The quantity demanded is the same at all prices

Cross Elasticities of Demand

A relationship is described as	When its value is	Which means that
Perfect substitutes	Infinity	The smallest possible increase in the price of one good causes an infinitely large increase in the quantity demanded of the other good
Substitutes	Positive, less than infinity	If the price of one good increases, the quantity demanded of the other good also increases
Independent	Zero	The quantity demanded of one good remains constant, regardless of the price of the other good
Complements	Less than zero	The quantity demanded of one good decreases when the price of the other good increases

Income Elasticities of Demand

A relationship is described as	When its value is	Which means that
Income elastic (normal good)	Greater than 1	The percentage increase in the quantity demanded is greater than the percentage increase in income
Income inelastic (normal good)	Less than 1 but greater than zero	The percentage increase in the quantity demanded is less than the percentage increase in income
Negative income elastic (inferior good)	Less than zero	When income increases, quantity demanded decreases

Elasticities of Supply

A relationship is described as	When its value is	Which means that
Perfectly elastic	Infinity	The smallest possible increase in the price causes an infinitely large increase in the quantity supplied
Elastic	Less than infinity but greater than 1	The percentage increase in the quantity supplied exceeds the percentage increase in the price
Inelastic	Greater than zero but less than 1	The percentage increase in the quantity supplied is less than the percentage increase in the price
Perfectly inelastic	Zero	The quantity supplied is the same at all prices

*In each description, the directions of change may be reversed. For example, in this case: The smallest possible *decrease* in the price causes an infinitely large *increase* in the quantity demanded.

The Price Elasticity of Demand for Computers

THE GLOBE AND MAIL, JUNE 22, 1998

Students show their shopping smarts

University students have been doing their homework when it comes to computer shopping, according to retailers who say more and more students are coming into stores with a clear idea of what they need.

Luckily for students, who tend to shop on a fairly tight budget, computer manufacturers also have been hitting the books to come up with an interesting array of powerful entry-level models at prices that have dropped considerably over the past year.

"Students always want the biggest bang for their buck," says computer salesman Tom Lam at the University of British Columbia Computer Shop.

"They want the most processing power they can get for the least number of dollars."

Manufacturers are battling for market share in the home computer market and that is good news right now for students looking to make their first computer purchase before classes begin in the fall. Prices have dropped and if that's not enough for bargain hunters, incentives aimed at students include package deals to provide hardware and software upgrades, plus easy terms and low-cost financing.

The average price of a consumer desktop fell about 21 per cent to about $1,800 in the first quarter of this year compared with a year earlier, according to market research firm AC Nielsen Canada. That helped to boost home computer sales in that period by about 17 per cent overall, says AC Nielsen spokesman Kelvin Wayne. Within the postsecondary-school education market, sales were up 22 per cent. ...

UBC's Mr. Lam says students coming into his store on the UBC campus want well-equipped computers with enough power and speed to easily handle the applications they need...

"Pricing is usually the prime concern but students won't pay a low price and take lower quality," Mr. Lam says. "They want the most current specs." That includes fast microprocessing, CD-ROM drives and modems, plus plenty of memory. ...

Essence of the Story

■ The price of a desktop computer fell 21 percent between the first quarter of 1997 and the first quarter of 1998.

■ Home computer sales in the same period increased by 17 percent overall.

■ Computer sales in the same period in the post-secondary student market increased by 22 percent.

■ Students tend to shop on a tight budget but still buy the most processing power they can get for the smallest price.

Economic Analysis

■ The price elasticity of demand equals the percentage change in the quantity demanded divided by the percentage change in price, using the *average* quantity and *average* price.

■ The percentage changes in price and quantity demanded reported in the news article are most likely percentages of the 1997 price and quantities.

■ The table uses the information in the news article to work out the numbers we need. (The news article does not give quantity data, but our assumptions are consistent with the information in the article.)

■ The first row of the table shows the price and assumed quantities for 1998. The second row shows the percentage changes from 1997. The third row calculates the implied quantities in 1977.

■ The fourth row shows the changes in price and quantities. The fifth row shows the average price and average quantities. The final row shows the implied elasticities of demand.

■ Figure 1 illustrates this calculation for the overall market for computers.

■ When the price falls from $2,280 to $1,800, the quantity demanded

increases from 641,000 to 750,000.

■ The price falls by 23.5 percent of the average price. And the quantity demanded increases by 15.7 percent of the average quantity. So the elasticity of demand is 15.7 percent divided by 23.5 percent, which is 0.67.

■ Figure 2 illustrates the calculation for the post-secondary student market.

■ When the price falls from $2,280 to $1,800, the quantity demanded increases from 82,000 to 100,000.

■ The price falls by 23.5 percent of the average price. And the quantity demanded increases by 19.8 percent of the average quantity. So the elasticity of demand is 19.8 percent divided by 23.5 percent, which is 0.84.

■ The student demand for computers is inelastic. But it is less inelastic than the overall demand. Why?

■ Students tend to have smaller budgets than do other buyers and so spend a greater proportion of their budgets on computers. The greater the proportion of income spent on a good, the more elastic is the demand for it. This is the reason why the students' demand for computers is more elastic than the overall demand.

Figure 1 Canadian demand

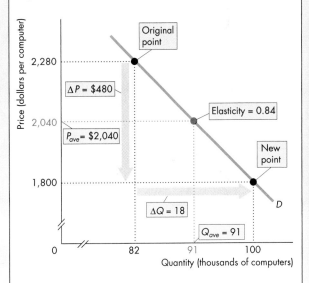

Figure 2 Post-secondary students' demand

	Price	Overall quantity	Students' quantity
1998	$1,800	750,000	100,000
% Δ from 1997	21	17	22
1997	$2,280	641,000	82,000
Change	$480	109,000	18,000
Average	$2,040	696,000	91,000
% of average	23.5	15.7	19.8
Elasticity		0.67	0.84

Table 1 Canadian Computer Markets

SUMMARY

Key Points

The Price Elasticity of Demand (pp. 90–96)

- Elasticity is a measure of the responsiveness of the quantity demanded of a good to a change in its price.
- Price elasticity of demand equals the percentage change in the quantity demanded divided by the percentage change in the price.
- The larger the magnitude of the elasticity of demand, the greater is the responsiveness of the quantity demanded to a given change in the price.
- Price elasticity of demand depends on how easily one good serves as a substitute for another, the proportion of income spent on the good, and the length of time elapsed since the price change.
- If demand is elastic, a decrease in price leads to an increase in total revenue. If demand is unit elastic, a decrease in price leaves total revenue unchanged. And if demand is inelastic, a decrease in price leads to a decrease in total revenue.

More Elasticities of Demand (pp. 97–99)

- Cross elasticity of demand measures the responsiveness of demand for one good to a change in the price of a substitute or a complement.
- The cross elasticity of demand with respect to the price of a substitute is positive. The cross elasticity of demand with respect to the price of a complement is negative.
- Income elasticity of demand measures the responsiveness of demand to a change in income. For a normal good, the income elasticity of demand is positive. For an inferior good, the income elasticity of demand is negative.
- When the income elasticity is greater than 1, as income increases, the percentage of income spent on the good increases.
- When the income elasticity is less than 1 but greater than zero, as income increases, the percentage of income spent on the good decreases.

Elasticity of Supply (pp. 100–102)

- Elasticity of supply measures the responsiveness of the quantity supplied of a good to a change in its price.
- Elasticities of supply are usually positive and range between zero (vertical supply curve) and infinity (horizontal supply curve).
- Supply decisions have three time frames: momentary, long run, and short run.
- Momentary supply refers to the response of sellers to a price change at the instant that the price changes.
- Long-run supply refers to the response of sellers to a price change when all the technologically feasible adjustments in production have been made.
- Short-run supply refers to the response of sellers to a price change after some adjustments in production have been made.

Key Figures and Table

Key Terms

PROBLEMS

*1. Rain spoils the strawberry crop. As a result, the price rises from $4 to $6 a box and the quantity demanded decreases from 1,000 to 600 boxes a week. Over this price range,
   a. What is the price elasticity of demand?
   b. Describe the demand for strawberries.

2. Good weather brings a bumper tomato crop. The price falls from $6 to $4 a basket and the quantity demanded increases from 200 to 400 baskets a day. Over this price range,
   a. What is the price elasticity of demand?
   b. Describe the demand for tomatoes.

*3. The figure shows the demand for videotape rentals.

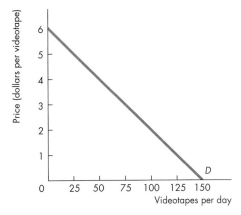

   a. Calculate the elasticity of demand for a rise in rental price from $3 to $5.
   b. At what price is the elasticity of demand equal to 1?

4. The figure shows the demand for pens.

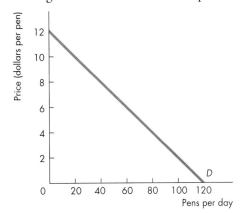

   a. Calculate the elasticity of demand for a rise in price from $2 to $4.

   b. At what prices is the elasticity of demand equal to 1, greater than 1, and less than 1?

*5. If the quantity of dental services demanded increases by 10 percent when the price of dental services falls by 10 percent, is the demand for dental services inelastic, elastic, or unit elastic?

6. If the quantity of fish demanded decreases by 5 percent when the price of fish rises by 10 percent, is the demand for fish elastic, inelastic, or unit elastic?

*7. The demand schedule for computer chips is:

Price (dollars per chip)	Quantity demanded (millions of chips per year)
200	50
250	45
300	40
350	35
400	30

   a. What will happen to total revenue if the price of a chip falls from $400 to $350?
   b. What will happen to total revenue if the price of a chip falls from $350 to $300?
   c. At what price is total revenue maximized?
   d. What quantity of chips will be sold at the price that answers problem 7(c)?
   e. At an average price of $350, is the demand for chips elastic or inelastic? Use the total revenue test to answer this question.

8. The demand schedule for coffee is:

Price (dollars per kilogram)	Quantity demanded (millions of kilograms per year)
10	30
15	25
20	20
25	15

   a. What will happen to total revenue if the price rises from $10 to $20 per kilogram?
   b. What will happen to total revenue if the price rises from $15 to $25 per kilogram?
   c. At what price is total revenue maximized?
   d. What quantity of coffee will be sold at the price that answers problem 8(c)?
   e. At an average price of $15 a kilogram, is the demand for coffee elastic or inelastic? Use the total revenue test to answer this question.

*9. In problem 7, at $250 a chip, is the demand for chips elastic or inelastic? Use the total revenue test to answer this question.

10. In problem 8, at $15 a kilogram, is the demand for coffee elastic or inelastic? Use the total revenue test to answer this question.

*11. If a 12 percent rise in the price of orange juice decreases the quantity of orange juice demanded by 22 percent and increases the quantity of apple juice demanded by 14 percent, calculate the cross elasticity of demand between orange juice and apple juice.

12. If a 10 percent fall in the price of beef increases the quantity of beef demanded by 15 percent and decreases the quantity of chicken demanded by 20 percent, calculate the cross elasticity of demand between beef and chicken.

*13. Last year Alex's income increased from $3,000 to $5,000. Alex increased his consumption of bagels from 4 to 8 a month and decreased his consumption of donuts from 12 to 6 a month. Calculate Alex's income elasticity of demand for (i) bagels and (ii) donuts.

14. Last year Judy's income increased from $10,000 to $12,000. Judy increased her demand for concert tickets by 10 percent and decreased her demand for bus rides by 5 percent. Calculate Judy's income elasticity of demand for (i) concert tickets and (ii) bus rides.

*15. The table gives the supply schedule for long-distance phone calls:

Price (cents per minute)	Quantity supplied (millions of minutes per day)
10	200
20	400
30	600
40	800

Calculate the elasticity of supply when
a. The price falls from 40 cents to 30 cents a minute.
b. The price is 20 cents a minute.

16. The table gives the supply schedule for shoes.

Price (dollars per pair)	Quantity supplied (millions of pairs per year)
120	1,200
125	1,400
130	1,600
135	1,800

Calculate the elasticity of supply when
a. The price rises from $125 to $135 a pair.
b. The price is $125 a pair.

CRITICAL THINKING

1. Study *Reading Between the Lines* on pp. 104–105 on the markets for computers in Canada and then answer the following questions:
a. What happened to the total revenue from computer sales to post-secondary students during 1997 and 1998?
b. What happened to the total revenue from computer sales to home computer buyers during 1997 and 1998?
c. Do you think that the overall computer market has an inelastic demand? Explain why.
d. If you were a retailer, how would you try to take advantage of the difference in the elasticities of demand between students and other computer buyers?

2. Thinking about the computer market in Canada, what do you predict will happen to the price and quantity during the coming year? Set out your assumptions about changes in supply, changes in demand, the price elasticity of demand, the relevant cross elasticities of demand, the income elasticity of demand, and the elasticity of supply.

3. Use the link on the Parkin-Bade Web site and:
a. Find the price of gasoline during 1999. Did the price rise or fall?
b. Use the tools of demand and supply and the concept of elasticity to explain the recent changes in the price of gasoline.
c. Find the latest price of crude oil.
d. Use the tools of demand and supply and the concept of elasticity to explain the recent changes in the price of crude oil.

4. Use the link on the Parkin-Bade Web site and:
a. Find the number of litres in a barrel.
b. What is the cost of the crude oil in one litre of gasoline?
c. What are the other costs that make up the total cost of a litre of gasoline?
d. If the price of crude oil falls by 10 percent, by what percentage would you expect the price of gasoline to change, other things remaining the same?
e. In light of your answer to part (d), do you think the elasticity of demand for crude oil is greater than, less than, or equal to the elasticity of demand for gasoline?

Efficiency and Equity

People constantly strive to get more for less. As consumers, we love to get a bargain. We enjoy telling our friends about the great deal we got on CDs or some other item we bought at a surprisingly low price. Every time we buy something, or decide *not* to buy something, we express our view about how scarce resources should be used. We try to spend our incomes in ways that get the most out of our scarce resources. For example, we balance the pleasure we get from our expenditure on movies against that we get from our textbooks.

More for Less

◆ Is the allocation of our resources between leisure and education, pizza and submarine sandwiches, inline skates and squash balls, and all the other things we buy the right one? Could we get more out of our resources if we spent more on some goods and services and less on others? ◆ Scientists and engineers devote enormous efforts to finding new and more productive ways of using our scarce land, labour, and capital resources to produce goods and services. Workers in factories and on assembly lines make suggestions that increase productivity. Is our economy efficient at producing goods and services? Do we get the most out of our scarce resources in our factories, offices, and shops? ◆ Some firms make huge profits year after year. Microsoft, for example, has generated enough profit over the past ten years to rocket Bill Gates, one of its founders, into the position of being one of the richest people in the world. Is that kind of business success a sign of efficiency? ◆ And is it fair that Bill Gates is so incredibly rich, while others live in miserable poverty?

◆ These are the kinds of questions you'll explore in this chapter. You will first learn some concepts that enable you to think about efficiency more broadly than the everyday use of that word. You will discover that competitive markets can be efficient. But you will also discover some sources of inefficiency that can be addressed with government action. You will also discover that firms that make huge profits, while efficient in one sense, might be inefficient in a broader sense.

After studying this chapter, you will be able to:

- ■ Define efficiency
- ■ Distinguish between value and price and define consumer surplus
- ■ Distinguish between cost and price and define producer surplus
- ■ Explain the conditions in which competitive markets move resources to their highest-valued uses
- ■ Explain the obstacles to inefficiency in our economy
- ■ Explain the main ideas about fairness and evaluate claims that competitive markets result in unfair outcomes

Efficiency: A Refresher

IT IS HARD TO TALK ABOUT EFFICIENCY IN ordinary conversation without generating both disagreement and misunderstanding. Many people see efficiency as a clearly desirable goal. To an engineer, an entrepreneur, a politician, a working mother, or an economist, getting more for less seems like a sensible thing to aim for. But some people think that the pursuit of efficiency conflicts with other goals. They believe the other goals are more worthy of pursuit. Environmentalists worry about contamination from "efficient" nuclear power plants. Car producers worry about competition from "efficient" foreign producers.

Economists use the idea of efficiency in a special way that avoids these disagreements. An **efficient allocation** of resources occurs when we produce the goods and services that people value most highly (see Chapter 3, pp. 42–44). Equivalently, resource use is efficient when we cannot produce more of a good or service without giving up some other good or service that we value more highly.

If people value a nuclear-free environment more highly than they value cheap electric power, it is efficient to use higher-cost, non-nuclear technologies to produce electricity. Efficiency is not a cold, mechanical concept. It is a concept based on value, and value is based on people's feelings.

Think about the efficient quantity of pizza. To produce more pizza, we must give up some other goods and services. For example, we might give up some submarine sandwiches. To get more pizzas, we forgo submarines. If we have fewer pizzas, we can have more submarines. What is the efficient quantity of pizza to produce? The answer depends on marginal benefit and marginal cost.

Marginal Benefit

If we consume one more pizza, we receive a marginal benefit. **Marginal benefit** is the benefit that a person receives from consuming one more unit of a good or service. The marginal benefit from a good or service is measured as the maximum amount that a person is willing to pay for one more unit of it. So the marginal benefit from a pizza is the maximum amount of other goods and services that people are willing to give up in order to get one more pizza. The marginal benefit from pizza decreases as the quantity of pizza consumed increases—the principle of *decreasing marginal benefit*.

We can express the marginal benefit from a pizza as the number of submarine sandwiches that people are willing to forgo to get one more pizza. But we can also express marginal benefit as the dollar value of other goods and services that people are willing to forgo. Figure 6.1 shows the marginal benefit from pizza expressed in this way. As the quantity of pizza increases, the value of other items that people are willing to forgo to get yet one more pizza decreases.

Marginal Cost

If we produce one more pizza, we incur a marginal cost. **Marginal cost** is the opportunity cost of producing *one more unit* of a good or service. The marginal cost of a good or service is measured as

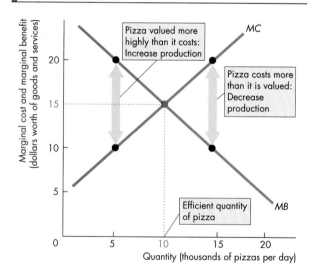

FIGURE 6.1

The Efficient Quantity of Pizza

The marginal benefit curve (MB) shows what people *are willing* to forgo to get one more pizza. The marginal cost curve (MC) shows what people *must* forgo to get one more pizza. If fewer than 10,000 pizzas a day are produced, marginal benefit exceeds marginal cost. Greater value can be obtained by producing more pizzas. If more than 10,000 pizzas a day are produced, marginal cost exceeds marginal benefit. Greater value can be obtained by producing fewer pizzas. If 10,000 pizzas a day are produced, marginal benefit equals marginal cost and the efficient quantity of pizza is available.

the value of the best alternative forgone. So the marginal cost of a pizza is the value of the best alternative forgone to get one more pizza. The marginal cost of a pizza increases as the quantity of pizza produced increases—the principle of *increasing marginal cost*.

We can express marginal cost as the number of submarine sandwiches we must forgo to get one more pizza. But we can also express marginal cost as the dollar value of other goods and services we must forgo. Figure 6.1 shows the marginal cost of pizza expressed in this way. As the quantity of pizza produced increases, the value of other items we must forgo to get yet one more pizza increases.

Efficiency and Inefficiency

To determine the efficient quantity of pizza, we compare the marginal cost of a pizza with the marginal benefit from a pizza. There are three possible cases:

- Marginal benefit exceeds marginal cost.
- Marginal cost exceeds marginal benefit.
- Marginal benefit equals marginal cost.

Marginal Benefit Exceeds Marginal Cost

Suppose the quantity of pizza produced is 5,000 a day. Figure 6.1 shows that at this quantity, the marginal benefit of a pizza is $20. That is, when the quantity of pizza available is 5,000 a day, people are willing to pay $20 for the 5,000th pizza.

Figure 6.1 also shows that the marginal cost of the 5,000th pizza is $10. That is, to produce one more pizza, the value of other goods and services that we must forgo is $10. If pizza production increases from 4,999 to 5,000, the value of the additional pizza is $20 and its marginal cost is $10. By producing this pizza, the value of the pizza produced exceeds the value of the goods and services forgone by $10. Resources are used more efficiently—they create more value—if we produce an extra pizza and fewer other goods and services. This same reasoning applies all the way up to the 9,999th pizza. Only when we get to the 10,000th pizza does marginal benefit not exceed marginal cost.

Marginal Cost Exceeds Marginal Benefit

Suppose the quantity of pizza produced is 15,000 a day. Figure 6.1 shows that at this quantity, the marginal benefit of a pizza is $10. That is, when the quantity of pizza available is 15,000 a day, people are willing to pay $10 for the 15,000th pizza.

Figure 6.1 also shows that the marginal cost of the 15,000th pizza is $20. That is, to produce one

more pizza, the value of the other goods and services that we must forgo is $20.

If pizza production decreases from 15,000 to 14,999, the value of the one pizza forgone is $10 and its marginal cost is $20. So by not producing this pizza, the value of the other goods and services produced exceeds the value of the pizza forgone by $10. Resources are used more efficiently—they create more value—if we produce one fewer pizza and more other goods and services. This same reasoning applies all the way down to the 10,001st pizza. Only when we get to the 10,000th pizza does marginal cost not exceed marginal benefit.

Marginal Benefit Equals Marginal Cost   Suppose the quantity of pizza produced is 10,000 a day. Figure 6.1 shows that at this quantity, the marginal benefit of a pizza is $15. That is, when the quantity of pizza available is 10,000 a day, people are willing to pay $15 for the 10,000th pizza.

Figure 6.1 also shows that the marginal cost of the 10,000th pizza is $15. That is, to produce one more pizza, the value of other goods and services that we must forgo is $15.

In this situation, we cannot increase the value of the goods and services produced by either increasing or decreasing the quantity of pizza. If we increase the quantity of pizza, the 10,001st pizza costs more to produce than it is worth. If we decrease the quantity of pizza produced, the 9,999th pizza is worth more than it costs to produce. So when marginal benefit equals marginal cost, resource use is efficient.

R E V I E W   Q U I Z

- If the marginal benefit of pizza exceeds the marginal cost of pizza, are we producing too much pizza and too little of other goods, or too little pizza and too much of other goods? Explain.
- If the marginal cost of pizza exceeds the marginal benefit of pizza, are we producing too much pizza and too little of other goods, or too little pizza and too much of other goods? Explain.
- Explain the relationship between the marginal benefit of pizza and the marginal cost of pizza when we are producing the efficient quantity of pizza.

Does a competitive market in pizza produce the efficient quantity of pizza? Let's answer this question.

Value, Price, and Consumer Surplus

TO INVESTIGATE WHETHER A COMPETITIVE market is efficient, we need to learn about the connection between demand and marginal benefit and between supply and marginal cost.

Value, Willingness to Pay, and Demand

In everyday life we talk about "getting value for money." When we use this expression we are distinguishing between *value* and *price*. Value is what we get, and the price is what we pay.

The **value** of one more unit of a good or service is its *marginal benefit*. Marginal benefit can be expressed as the maximum price that people are willing to pay for another unit of the good or service. The willingness to pay for a good or service determines the demand for it.

In Fig. 6.2(a), the demand curve shows the quantity demanded at each price. For example, when the price of a pizza is $15, the quantity demanded is 10,000 pizzas a day. In Fig. 6.2(b), the demand curve shows the maximum price that people are willing to pay when there is a given quantity. For example, when 10,000 pizzas a day are available, the most that people are willing to pay for a pizza is $15. This second interpretation of the demand curve means that the marginal benefit from the 10,000th pizza is $15.

When we draw a demand curve, we use a *relative* price, not a *money* price. A relative price is expressed in dollar units, but it measures the number of dollars-worth of other goods and services forgone to obtain one more unit of the good in question (see Chapter 4, p. 64). So a demand curve tells us the quantity of other goods and services that people are willing to forgo to get an additional unit of a good. But this is what a marginal benefit curve tells us too. So:

A demand curve is a marginal benefit curve.

We don't always have to pay the maximum price that we are willing to pay. When we buy something, we often get a bargain. Let's see how.

FIGURE 6.2

Demand, Willingness to Pay, and Marginal Benefit

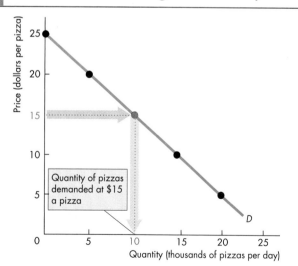

(a) Price determines quantity demanded

(b) Quantity determines willingness to pay

The demand curve for pizza, *D*, shows the quantity of pizza demanded at each price, other things remaining the same. It also shows the maximum price that consumers are willing to pay if a given quantity of pizza is available. At a price of $15 a

pizza, the quantity demanded is 10,000 pizzas a day (part a). If 10,000 pizzas a day are available, the maximum price that consumers are willing to pay for the 10,000th pizza is $15 (part b).

Consumer Surplus

When people buy something for less than it is worth to them, they receive a consumer surplus. A **consumer surplus** is the value of a good minus the price paid for it.

To understand consumer surplus, look at Lisa's demand for pizza, which is shown in Fig. 6.3. Lisa likes pizza, but the marginal benefit she gets from it decreases quickly as her consumption increases.

Suppose Lisa can buy pizza by the slice and that there are 10 slices in a pizza. If a pizza costs $2.50 a slice (or $25 a pizza), Lisa buys no pizza. She spends her fast-food budget on items that she values more highly than pizza. At $2 a slice, she buys 10 slices (one pizza) a week. At $1.50 a slice, she buys 20 slices a week; at $1 a slice, she buys 30 slices a week; and at 50 cents a slice she buys 40 slices a week.

Lisa's demand curve for pizza in Fig. 6.3 is also her *willingness-to-pay* or marginal benefit curve. It tells us that if Lisa can have only 10 slices a week, she is willing to pay $2 a slice. Her marginal benefit from the 10th slice is $2. If she can have 20 slices (2 pizzas) a week, she is willing to pay $1.50 for the 20th slice. Her marginal benefit from the 20th slice is $1.50.

Figure 6.3 also shows Lisa's consumer surplus from pizza when its price is $1.50 a slice. At this price, she buys 20 slices a week. A price of $1.50 a slice is the most she is willing to pay for the 20th slice, so its marginal benefit is exactly the price she pays for it. But Lisa is willing to pay almost $2.50 for the first slice. Her marginal benefit from this slice is close to $1 more than she pays for it, so her *consumer surplus* from the first slice is almost $1. Lisa's marginal benefit from the 10th slice is $2, so on the 10th slice her consumer surplus is 50 cents.

To calculate Lisa's consumer surplus, we find the consumer surplus on each slice and add these surpluses together. This sum is the area of the green triangle in Fig. 6.3. The base of the triangle is 20 slices a week and the height is $1 a slice, so consumer surplus is

$$\frac{20 \text{ slices per week} \times \$1 \text{ per slice}}{2} = \$10 \text{ per week.}$$

The blue rectangle in Fig. 6.3 is the amount that Lisa pays for pizza, which is $30 a week—20 slices at $1.50 a slice.

All goods and services are like the pizza example you've just studied. Because of decreasing marginal

FIGURE 6.3
A Consumer's Demand and Consumer Surplus

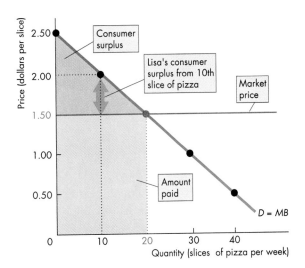

Lisa's demand curve for pizza tells us that at $2.50 a slice, she does not buy pizza. At $2 a slice, she buys 10 slices a week; at $1.50 a slice, she buys 20 slices a week. Lisa's demand curve also tells us that she is willing to pay $2 for the 10th slice and $1.50 for the 20th. She actually pays $1.50 a slice—the market price—and buys 20 slices a week. Her consumer surplus from pizza is $10—the area of the green triangle.

benefit, people receive more benefit from their consumption than the amount they pay.

REVIEW QUIZ

- Explain how we measure the value or marginal benefit of a good or service.
- Explain the relationship between marginal benefit and the demand curve.
- What is consumer surplus and how do we measure it?

You've seen how we distinguish between value—marginal benefit—and price. And you've seen that buyers receive a consumer surplus when marginal benefit exceeds price. Next, we're going to study the connection between supply and marginal cost and learn about producer surplus.

Cost, Price, and Producer Surplus

WHAT YOU ARE NOW GOING TO LEARN ABOUT cost, price, and producer surplus parallels the related ideas about value, price, and consumer surplus that you've just studied.

Firms are in business to make a profit. To do so, they must sell their output for a price that exceeds the cost of production. Let's investigate the relationship between cost and price.

Cost, Minimum Supply Price, and Supply

Firms undertake elaborate schemes to earn profits. Earning a profit means receiving more (or at least receiving no less) for the sale of a good or service than the cost of producing it. Just as consumers distinguish between *value* and *price*, so producers distinguish between *cost* and *price*. Cost is what a producer gives up, and price is what a producer receives.

The cost of producing one more unit of a good or service is its *marginal cost*. Marginal cost is the minimum price that producers must receive to induce them to produce another unit of the good or service. This minimum acceptable price determines supply.

In Fig. 6.4(a), the supply curve shows the quantity supplied at each price. For example, when the price of a pizza is $15, the quantity supplied is 10,000 pizzas a day. In Fig. 6.4(b), the supply curve shows the minimum price that producers must be offered to produce a given quantity of pizza. For example, the minimum price that producers must be offered to get them to produce 10,000 pizzas a day is $15 a pizza. This second view of the supply curve means that the marginal cost of the 10,000th pizza is $15.

Because the price is a relative price, a supply curve tells us the quantity of other goods and services that *sellers must forgo* to produce one more unit of the good. But a marginal cost curve also tells us the quantity of other goods and services that we must

---

FIGURE 6.4

Supply, Minimum Supply Price, and Marginal Cost

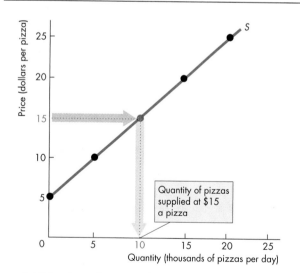

(a) Price determines quantity supplied

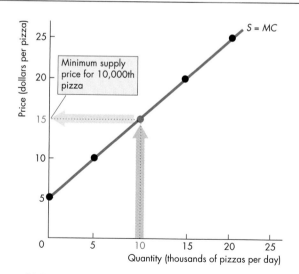

(b) Quantity determines minimum supply price

The supply curve of pizza, S, shows the quantity of pizza supplied at each price, other things remaining the same. The supply curve also shows the minimum price that producers must be offered to get them to produce a given quantity of pizza. At a price of $15 a pizza, the quantity supplied is 10,000 pizzas a day (part a). To get firms to produce 10,000 pizzas a day, the minimum price they must be offered for the 10,000th pizza is $15 (part b).

forgo to get one more unit of the good. So:

> A supply curve is a marginal cost curve.

Producers don't always receive their minimum supply price. If the price they receive exceeds the cost they incur, producers earn a surplus. This producer surplus is analogous to consumer surplus. Let's look at producer surplus.

Producer Surplus

When a firm sells something for more than it costs to produce, the firm obtains a producer surplus. A **producer surplus** is the price of a good minus the opportunity cost of producing it. To understand producer surplus, look at Max's supply of pizza in Fig. 6.5.

Max can produce pizza or bake bread. The more pizza he bakes, the less bread he can bake. His opportunity cost of pizza is the value of the bread he must forgo. This opportunity cost increases as Max increases his production of pizza. If a pizza sells for only $5, Max produces no pizza. He uses his kitchen to bake bread. Pizza just isn't worth producing. But at $10 a pizza, Max produces 50 pizzas a day, and at $15 a pizza, he produces 100 a day.

Max's supply curve of pizza is also his *minimum supply price* curve. It tells us that if Max can sell only 1 pizza a day, the minimum that he must be paid for it is $5. If he can sell 50 pizzas a day, the minimum that he must be paid for the 50th pizza is $10, and so on.

Figure 6.5 also shows Max's producer surplus. If the price of a pizza is $15, Max plans to sell 100 pizzas a day. The minimum that he must be paid for the 100th pizza is $15. So its opportunity cost is exactly the price he receives for it. But his opportunity cost of the first pizza is only $5. So this first pizza costs $10 less to produce than he receives for it. Max receives a *producer surplus* from his first pizza of $10. He receives a slightly smaller producer surplus on the second pizza, less on the third, and so on until he receives no producer surplus on the 100th pizza.

Figure 6.5 shows Max's producer surplus as the blue triangle formed by the area above the supply curve and beneath the price line. The base of the triangle is 100 pizzas a week and the height is $10 a pizza, so producer surplus is

$$\frac{100 \text{ pizzas per week} \times \$10 \text{ per pizza}}{2} = \$500 \text{ per week.}$$

FIGURE 6.5

A Producer's Supply and Producer Surplus

Max's supply curve of pizza tells us that at a price of $5, Max plans to sell no pizza. At a price of $10, he plans to sell 50 pizzas a day; and at a price of $15, he plans to sell 100 pizzas a day. Max's supply curve also tells us the minimum that he must be offered is $10 for the 50th pizza a day and $15 for the 100th pizza a day. If the market price is $15 a pizza, he sells 100 pizzas a day and receives $1,500. The red area shows Max's cost of producing pizza, which is $1,000 a day, and the blue area shows his producer surplus, which is $500 a day.

Figure 6.5 also shows Max's opportunity costs of production as the red area beneath the supply curve.

REVIEW QUIZ

- Explain the relationship between the marginal cost or opportunity cost of producing a good or service and the minimum supply price.
- Explain the relationship between marginal cost and the supply curve.
- What is producer surplus and how do we measure it?

Consumer surplus and producer surplus can be used to measure the efficiency of a market. Let's see how we can use these concepts to study the efficiency of a competitive market.

Is the Competitive Market Efficient?

FIGURE 6.6 SHOWS THE MARKET FOR PIZZA. THE demand curve, *D*, shows the demand for pizza. The supply curve, *S*, shows the supply of pizza. The equilibrium price is $15 a pizza, and the equilibrium quantity is 10,000 pizzas a day.

The market forces that you studied in Chapter 4 (pp. 74–75) will pull the pizza market to this equilibrium. If the price is greater than $15 a pizza, a surplus will force the price down. If the price is less than $15 a pizza, a shortage will force the price up. Only if the price is $15 a pizza is there neither a surplus nor a shortage and no forces operating to change the price.

So the market price and quantity are pulled towards their equilibrium values. But is this competitive equilibrium efficient? Does it produce the efficient quantity of pizza?

Efficiency of Competitive Equilibrium

The equilibrium in Fig. 6.6 is efficient. Resources are being used to produce the quantity of pizza that people value most highly. It is not possible to produce more pizza without giving up some other good or service that is valued more highly. And if a smaller quantity of pizza is produced, resources are used to produce some other good that is not valued as highly as the pizza forgone.

To see why the equilibrium in Fig. 6.6 is efficient, think about the interpretation of the demand curve as a marginal benefit curve and the supply curve as a marginal cost curve. The demand curve tells us the marginal benefit from pizza. The supply curve tells us the marginal cost of pizza. So where the demand curve and the supply curve intersect, marginal benefit equals marginal cost.

But this condition—marginal benefit equals marginal cost—is the condition that delivers an efficient use of resources. It puts resources to work in the activities that create the greatest possible value. So a competitive equilibrium is efficient.

If production is less than 10,000 pizzas a day, the marginal pizza is valued more highly than its opportunity cost. If production exceeds 10,000 pizzas a day, the marginal pizza costs more to produce than the value that consumers place on it. Only when 10,000

FIGURE 6.6

An Efficient Market for Pizza

Resources are used efficiently when the sum of consumer surplus and producer surplus is maximized. Consumer surplus is the area below the demand curve and above the market price line—the green triangle. Producer surplus is the area below the price line and above the supply curve—the blue triangle. Here consumer surplus is $50,000 and producer surplus is also $50,000. Total surplus is $100,000. Total surplus is maximized when the willingness to pay equals the opportunity cost. The efficient quantity of pizza is 10,000 per day.

pizzas a day are produced is the marginal pizza worth exactly what it costs. The competitive market pushes the quantity of pizza produced to its efficient level of 10,000 a day. If production is less than 10,000 a day, a shortage raises the price, which stimulates an increase in production. If production exceeds 10,000 a day, a surplus lowers the price, which decreases production.

When the market is using resources efficiently at the competitive equilibrium, the sum of consumer surplus and producer surplus is maximized. At this equilibrium, resources are used in the activities in which they are valued most highly.

Buyers and sellers each attempt to do the best they can for themselves and no one plans for an efficient outcome for society as a whole. Buyers seek the lowest possible price and sellers seek the highest possible price. And the market comes to an equilibrium in which the gains from trade are as large as possible.

The Invisible Hand

Writing in his *Wealth of Nations* in 1776, Adam Smith was the first to suggest that competitive markets send resources to the uses in which they have the highest value—see pp. 58–59. Smith believed that each participant in a competitive market is "led by an invisible hand to promote an end [the efficient use of resources] which was no part of his intention."

You can see the invisible hand at work in the cartoon. The cold drinks vendor has both cold drinks and shade. He has an opportunity cost of each and a minimum supply price of each. The park-bench reader has a marginal benefit from a cold drink and from shade. You can see that the marginal benefit from shade exceeds the marginal cost, but the marginal cost of a cold drink exceeds its marginal benefit. The transaction that occurs creates producer surplus and consumer surplus. The vendor obtains a producer surplus from selling the shade for more than its opportunity cost and the reader obtains a consumer surplus from buying the shade for less than its marginal benefit. In the third frame of the cartoon, both the consumer and the producer are better off than they were in the first frame. The umbrella has moved to its highest-value use.

The Invisible Hand at Work Today

The market economy relentlessly performs the activity illustrated in the cartoon and in Fig. 6.6 to achieve an efficient allocation of resources. And rarely has the market been working as hard as it is today. Think about a few of the changes taking place in our economy that the market is guiding towards an efficient use of resources.

New technologies have cut the cost of producing computers. As these advances have occurred, supply has increased and the price has fallen. Lower prices have encouraged an increase in the quantity demanded of this now less costly tool. The marginal benefit from computers is brought to equality with their marginal cost.

A Florida frost cuts the supply of oranges. With fewer oranges available, the marginal benefit from an orange increases. A shortage of oranges raises their price and so the market allocates the smaller quantity available to the people who value them most highly.

Market forces persistently bring marginal cost and marginal benefit to equality and maximize the sum of consumer surplus and producer surplus.

Obstacles to Efficiency

ALTHOUGH MARKETS GENERALLY DO A GOOD JOB at sending resources to where they are most highly valued, they do not always get the correct answer. Sometimes markets overproduce a good or service, and sometimes they underproduce. The most significant obstacles to achieving an efficient allocation of resources in the market economy are

- Price ceilings and price floors
- Taxes, subsidies, and quotas
- Monopoly
- Public goods
- External costs and external benefits

Price Ceilings and Price Floors   A **price ceiling** is a regulation that makes it illegal to charge a price higher than a specified level. An example is a price ceiling on apartment rents, which some cities impose. A **price floor** is a regulation that makes it illegal to pay a lower price than a specified level. An example is the minimum wage. (We study both of these restrictions on buyers and sellers in Chapter 7.)

The presence of a price ceiling or a price floor blocks the forces of demand and supply and results in a quantity produced that might exceed or fall short of the quantity determined in an unregulated market.

Taxes, Subsidies, and Quotas   Taxes increase the prices paid by buyers and lower the prices received by sellers. Taxes decrease the quantity produced (for reasons that are explained in Chapter 7, on p. 137). All kinds of goods and services are taxed, but the highest taxes are on gasoline, alcohol, and tobacco.

Subsidies, which are payments by the government to producers, decrease the prices paid by buyers and increase the prices received by sellers. Subsidies increase the quantity produced.

Quotas, which are limits to the quantity that a firm is permitted to produce, restrict output below the quantity that a competitive market produces. Farms are sometimes subject to quotas.

Monopoly   A **monopoly** is a firm that has sole control of a market. For example, Microsoft has a near monopoly on operating systems for personal computers. Although monopolies earn large profits, they prevent markets from achieving an efficient use of resources. The goal of a monopoly is to maximize profit. To achieve this goal, it restricts production and raises price. (We study monopoly in Chapter 13.)

Public Goods   A **public good** is a good or service that is consumed simultaneously by everyone, even if they don't pay for it. Examples are national defence and the enforcement of law and order. Competitive markets would produce too small a quantity of public goods because of a *free-rider problem*. It is not in each person's interest to buy her or his share of a public good. So a competitive market produces less than the efficient quantity. (We study public goods in Chapter 18.)

External Costs and External Benefits   An **external cost** is a cost not borne by the producer but borne by other people. The cost of pollution is an example of an external cost. When an electric power utility burns coal to generate electricity, it puts sulfur dioxide into the atmosphere. This pollutant falls as acid rain and damages vegetation and crops. The utility does not consider the cost of pollution when it decides the quantity of electric power to supply. Its supply curve is based on its own costs, not on the costs that they inflict on others. As a result, the utility produces more power than the efficient quantity.

An **external benefit** is a benefit that accrues to people other than the buyer of a good. An example is when someone in a neighbourhood paints her home or landscapes her yard. The homeowner does not consider her neighbour's marginal benefit when she decides whether to do this type of work. So the demand curve for house painting and yard improvement does not include all the benefits that accrue. In this case, the quantity falls short of the efficient quantity. (We study externalities in Chapter 20.)

The impediments to efficiency that we've just reviewed and that you will study in greater detail in later chapters result in two possible outcomes:

■ Underproduction
■ Overproduction

Underproduction

Suppose that one firm owned all the pizza outlets in a city and that it restricted the quantity of pizza produced to 5,000 a day. Figure 6.7(a) shows that at this quantity, consumers are willing to pay $20 for the marginal pizza—marginal benefit is $20. The marginal cost of a pizza is only $10. So there is a gap between what people are willing to pay and what producers must be offered—between marginal benefit and marginal cost.

The sum of consumer surplus and producer surplus is decreased by the amount of the grey triangle in Fig. 6.7(a). This triangle is called deadweight loss. **Deadweight loss** is the decrease in consumer surplus and producer surplus that results from an inefficient level of production.

The 5,000th pizza brings a benefit of $20 and costs only $10 to produce. If we don't produce this pizza, we are wasting almost $10. Similar reasoning applies all the way up to the 9,999th pizza. By producing more pizza and less of other goods and services, we get more value from our resources.

The deadweight loss is borne by the entire society. It is not a loss for the consumers and a gain for the producer. It is a *social* loss.

FIGURE 6.7

Underproduction and Overproduction

(a) Underproduction

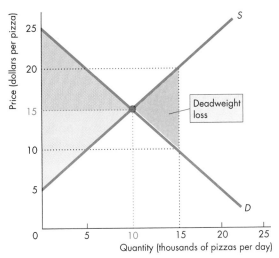

(b) Overproduction

If pizza production is restricted to 5,000 a day, a deadweight loss (the grey triangle) arises. Consumer surplus and producer surplus are reduced to the green and blue areas. At 5,000 pizzas, the benefit of one more pizza exceeds its cost. The same is true for all levels of production up to 10,000 pizzas a day. If production increases to 15,000, a deadweight loss arises. At 15,000 pizzas a day, the cost of the 15,000th pizza exceeds its benefit. The cost of each pizza above 10,000 exceeds its benefit. Consumer surplus plus producer surplus equals the green and blue areas minus the deadweight loss.

Overproduction

Suppose the pizza lobby gets the government to pay the pizza producers a fat subsidy and that production increases to 15,000 a day. Figure 6.7(b) shows that at this quantity, consumers are willing to pay only $10 for that marginal pizza but the opportunity cost of that pizza is $20. It now costs more to produce the marginal pizza than consumers are willing to pay for it. The gap gets smaller as production approaches 10,000 pizzas a day, but it is present at all quantities greater than 10,000 a day.

Again, the grey triangle shows the deadweight loss. The sum of consumer surplus and producer surplus is smaller than its maximum by the amount of deadweight loss. The 15,000th pizza brings a benefit of $10 but costs $20 to produce. If we produce this pizza, we are wasting almost $10. Similar reasoning applies all the way down to the 10,001st pizza. By producing less pizza and more of other goods and services, we get more value from our resources.

REVIEW QUIZ

- Do competitive markets use resources efficiently? Explain why or why not.
- Do markets with a price ceiling or price floor, taxes, subsidies, or quotas, monopoly power, public goods, or externalities result in the quantity produced being the efficient quantity? Explain.
- What is deadweight loss and in what conditions does it occur?
- Does a deadweight loss occur in a competitive market when the quantity produced equals the competitive equilibrium quantity and the resource allocation is efficient? Explain why or why not.

You now know the conditions under which the resource allocation is efficient. You've seen how a competitive market can be efficient, and you've seen some impediments to efficiency. But is an efficient allocation of resources fair? Does the competitive market provide people with fair incomes for their work? And do people always pay a fair price for the things they buy? Don't we need the government to step into some competitive markets to prevent the price from rising too high or falling too low? Let's now study these questions.

Is the Competitive Market Fair?

WHEN A NATURAL DISASTER STRIKES, SUCH AS A severe winter storm or a hurricane, the prices of many essential items jump. The reason the prices jump is that some people have a greater demand and greater willingness to pay while the items are in limited supply. So the higher prices achieve an efficient allocation of scarce resources. News reports of these price hikes almost never talk about efficiency. Instead, they talk about fairness, or more particularly, unfairness. The claim is that it is unfair for profit-seeking dealers to cheat the victims of natural disaster.

Similarly, when low-skilled people work for a wage that is below what most would regard as a "living wage," the media and politicians talk of employers taking unfair advantage of their workers.

How do we decide if something is fair or unfair? You know when *you* think something is unfair. But how do you know? What are the *principles* of fairness?

Philosophers have tried for centuries to answer this question. Economists have offered their answers too. But before we look at the proposed answers, you should know that there is no universally agreed answer.

Economists agree about efficiency. That is, they agree that it makes sense to make the economic pie as large as possible and to bake it at the lowest possible cost. But they do not agree about fairness. That is, they do not agree about what are fair shares of the economic pie for all the people who make it. The reason is that ideas about fairness are not exclusively economic ideas. They touch on politics, ethics, and religion. Nevertheless, economists have thought about these issues and have a contribution to make. So let's examine the views of economists on this topic.

To think about fairness, think of economic life as a game—a serious game. All ideas about fairness can be divided into two broad groups. They are:

- It's not fair if the *result* isn't fair
- It's not fair if the *rules* aren't fair

It's Not Fair If the *Result* Isn't Fair

The earliest efforts to establish a principle of fairness were based on the view that the result is what matters. And the idea was that it is unfair if people's incomes are too unequal. It is unfair that bank chairpersons earn millions of dollars a year while bank tellers earn only thousands of dollars a year. It is unfair that a storeowner enjoys a larger profit and her customers pay higher prices in the aftermath of a winter storm.

There was a lot of excitement during the nineteenth century when economists thought they had made the incredible discovery that equality of incomes was not only fair, but also efficient. If the economic pie is shared equally, it will be the largest it can possibly be. This idea turns out to be wrong, but there is a lesson in the reason that it is wrong. So this nineteenth century idea is worth a closer look.

Utilitarianism The nineteenth century idea that equality is both fair and efficient is called utilitarianism. **Utilitarianism** is a principle that states that we should strive to achieve "the greatest happiness for the greatest number." The people who developed this idea were known as utilitarians. They included the most eminent minds such as David Hume, Adam Smith, Jeremy Bentham, and John Stuart Mill.

Utilitarians argued that to achieve "the greatest happiness for the greatest number," income must be transferred from the rich to the poor up to the point of complete equality—to the point that there are no rich and no poor.

They reasoned in the following way: First, everyone has the same basic wants and a similar capacity to enjoy life. Second, the greater a person's income, the smaller is the marginal benefit of a dollar. The millionth dollar spent by a rich person brings a smaller marginal benefit to that person than the marginal benefit of the thousandth dollar spent by a poorer person. So by transferring a dollar from the millionaire to the poorer person, more is gained than is lost and the two people added together are better off.

Figure 6.8 illustrates this utilitarian idea. Tom and Jerry each have the same marginal benefit curve, *MB*. (Marginal benefit is measured on the same scale of 1 to 3 for both Tom and Jerry.) Tom is at point *a*. He earns $5,000 a year and his marginal benefit of a dollar of income is 3. Jerry is at point *b*. He earns $45,000 a year and his marginal benefit of a dollar of income is 1. If a dollar is transferred from Jerry to Tom, Jerry loses 1 unit of marginal benefit and Tom gains 3 units. So if we take Tom and Jerry together, they are better off. They are sharing the economic pie more efficiently. If a second dollar is transferred, the same thing happens: Tom gains more than Jerry loses. And the same is true for every dollar transferred until they each reach point *c*. At point *c*, Tom and Jerry

FIGURE 6.8

Utilitarian Fairness

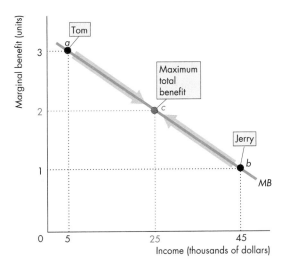

Tom earns $5,000 and has 3 units of marginal benefit at point a. Jerry earns $45,000 and has 1 unit of marginal benefit at point b. If income is transferred from Jerry to Tom, Jerry's loss is less than Tom's gain. Only when each of them has $25,000 and 2 units of marginal benefit (at point c) can the sum of their total benefit increase no further.

each have $25,000 and each have a marginal benefit of 2 units. Now they are sharing the economic pie in the most efficient way. It is bringing the greatest attainable happiness to Tom and Jerry together.

The Big Tradeoff A big problem with the utilitarian ideal of complete equality is that it ignores the costs of making income transfers. Recognizing the cost of making income transfers leads to what is called "the **big tradeoff**," which is a tradeoff between efficiency and fairness.

The big tradeoff is based on the following facts. Income can be transferred from people with high incomes to people with low incomes only by taxing incomes. Taxing people's income from employment makes them work less. It results in the quantity of labour being less than the efficient quantity. Taxing people's income from capital makes them save less. It results in the quantity of capital being less than the efficient quantity. With smaller quantities of both labour and capital, the quantity of goods and services produced is less than the efficient quantity. The economic pie shrinks.

The tradeoff is between the size of the economic pie and the degree of equality with which it is shared. The greater the amount of income redistribution through income taxes, the greater is the inefficiency—the smaller is the economic pie.

There is a second source of inefficiency. A dollar taken from a rich person does not end up as a dollar in the hands of a poorer person. Some of it is spent on administration of the tax and transfer system. The cost of tax-collecting agencies, such as Revenue Canada, and welfare-administering agencies, such as Health Canada and the provincial government welfare departments, must be paid with some of the taxes collected. Also, taxpayers hire accountants, auditors, and lawyers to help them ensure that they pay the correct amount of tax. These activities use skilled labour and capital resources that could otherwise be used to produce goods and services that people value.

You can see that when all these costs are taken into account, transferring a dollar from a rich person does not give a dollar to a poor person. It is even possible that with high taxes, those with low incomes end up being worse off. Suppose, for example, that highly taxed entrepreneurs decide to work less hard and shut down some of their businesses. Low-income workers get fired and must seek other, perhaps even lower-paid, work.

Because of the big tradeoff, those who say that fairness is equality propose a modified version of utilitarianism.

Make the Poorest As Well Off As Possible A Harvard philosopher, John Rawls, proposed a modified version of utilitarianism in a classic book entitled *A Theory of Justice*, published in 1971. Rawls says that, taking all the costs of income transfers into account, the fair distribution of the economic pie is the one that makes the poorest person as well off as possible. The incomes of rich people should be taxed and, after paying the costs of administering the tax and transfer system, what is left should be transferred to the poor. But the taxes must not be so high that they make the economic pie shrink to the point that the poorest person ends up with a smaller piece of pie. A bigger share of a smaller pie can be less than a smaller share of a bigger pie. The goal is to make the piece of pie enjoyed by the poorest person as big as possible. Most likely this piece will not be an equal share.

The "fair results" ideas require a change in the results after the game is over. Some economists say these changes are themselves unfair and propose a different way of thinking about fairness.

It's Not Fair If the *Rules* Aren't Fair

The idea that it's not fair if the rules aren't fair is based on a fundamental principle that seems to be hard wired into the human brain. It is the symmetry principle. The **symmetry principle** is the requirement that people in similar situations be treated similarly. It is the moral principle that lies at the centre of all the big religions and that says, in some form or other, "behave towards other people in the way you expect them to behave towards you."

In economic life, this principle translates into *equality of opportunity*. But equality of opportunity to do what? This question is answered by another Harvard philosopher, Robert Nozick, in a book entitled *Anarchy, State, and Utopia*, published in 1974.

Nozick argues that the idea of fairness as an outcome or result cannot work and that fairness must be based on the fairness of the rules. He suggests that fairness obeys two rules:

1. The state must enforce laws that establish and protect private property.
2. Private property may be transferred from one person to another only by voluntary exchange.

The first rule says that everything that is valuable must be owned by individuals and that the state must ensure that theft is prevented. The second rule says that the only legitimate way a person can acquire property is to buy it in exchange for something else that the person owns. If these rules, which are the only fair rules, are followed, the result is fair. It doesn't matter how unequally the economic pie is shared provided it is baked by people each one of whom voluntarily provides services in exchange for the share of the pie offered in compensation.

These rules satisfy the symmetry principle. And if these rules are not followed, the symmetry principle is broken. You can see these facts by imagining a world in which the laws are not followed.

First, suppose that some resources or goods are not owned. They are common property. Then everyone is free to participate in a grab to use these resources or goods. The strongest will prevail. But when the strongest prevails, the strongest effectively *owns* the resources or goods in question and prevents others from enjoying them.

Second, suppose that we do not insist on voluntary exchange for transferring ownership of resources from one person to another. The alternative is *involuntary* transfer. In simple language, the alternative is theft.

Both of these situations violate the symmetry principle. Only the strong get to acquire what they want. The weak end up with only the resources and goods that the strong don't want.

In contrast, if the two rules of fairness are followed, everyone, strong and weak, is treated in a similar way. Individuals are free to use their resources and human skills to create things that are valued by themselves and others and to exchange the fruits of their efforts with each other. This is the only set of arrangements that obeys the symmetry principle.

Fairness and Efficiency If private property rights are enforced and if voluntary exchange takes place in a competitive market, resources will be allocated efficiently if there are no:

- Price ceilings and price floors
- Taxes, subsidies, and quotas
- Monopolies
- Public goods
- External costs and external benefits

According to the Nozick rules, the resulting distribution of income and wealth will be fair. Let's study a concrete example to examine the claim that if resources are allocated efficiently, they are also allocated fairly.

A Price Hike in a Natural Disaster An earthquake has broken the pipes that deliver drinking water to a city. The price of bottled water jumps from $1 to $8 a bottle in the 30 or so shops that have water for sale.

First, let's agree that the water is being used *efficiently*. There is a fixed amount of bottled water in the city and given the quantity available, some people are willing to pay $8 to get a bottle. The water goes to the people who value it most highly. Consumer surplus and producer surplus are maximized.

So the water resources are being used efficiently. But are they being used fairly? Shouldn't people who can't afford to pay $8 a bottle get some of the available water for a lower price that they can afford? Isn't the fair solution for the shops to sell the water for a lower price that people can afford? Or perhaps it might be fairer if the government bought the water and then made it available to people through a government store at a "reasonable" price. Let's think about these alternative solutions to the water problem of this city.

The first answer that jumps into your mind is that the water should somehow be made available at a more reasonable price. But is this the correct answer?

Shop Offers Water for $5 Suppose that Chip, a shop owner, offers water at $5 a bottle. Who will buy it? There are two types of buyers. Chuck is an example of one type. He values water at $8—is willing to pay $8 a bottle. Recall that given the quantity of water available, the equilibrium price is $8 a bottle. If Chuck buys the water for $5, he consumes it. Chuck ends up with a consumer surplus of $3 on the bottle and Chip receives $3 *less* of producer surplus.

Mitch is an example of the second type of buyer. Mitch would not pay $8 for a bottle. In fact, he wouldn't even pay $5 to consume a bottle of water. But he buys a bottle for $5. Why? He plans to sell the water to someone who is willing to pay $8 to consume it. When Mitch buys the water, Chip again receives a producer surplus of $3 *less* than he would receive if he charged the going market price. Mitch now becomes a water dealer. He sells the water for the going price of $8 and earns a producer surplus of $3.

So by being public spirited and offering water for less than the market price, Chip ends up $3 a bottle worse off and the buyers end up $3 a bottle better off. In both situations, the same people consume the water—those who value it at $8 a bottle. But the distribution of consumer surplus and producer surplus is different in the two cases. When Chip sells water for $5 a bottle, he gets a smaller producer surplus, Chuck gets a larger consumer surplus, and Mitch gets a larger producer surplus.

So which arrangement is fair? The one that favours Chip or the one that favours Chuck and Mitch? The fair-rules view is that both arrangements are fair. Chip voluntarily sells the water for $5, so in effect, he is helping the community to cope with its water problem. It is fair that he should help. But the choice is his. He owns the water. It is not fair that he should be compelled to help.

Government Buys Water Now suppose instead that the government buys all the water. The going price is $8 a bottle, so that's what the government pays. Now they offer the water for sale for $1 a bottle, its "normal" price. The quantity of water supplied is exactly the same as before. But now, at $1 a bottle, the quantity demanded is much larger than the quantity supplied. There is a shortage of water.

Because there is a large water shortage, the government decides to ration the amount that anyone may buy to one bottle. So everyone lines up to collect his or her bottle. Two of these people are Chuck and Mitch. Chuck, you'll recall, is willing to pay $8 a

bottle. Mitch is willing to pay less than $5. But they both get a bargain. Chuck drinks his $1 bottle and enjoys a $7 consumer surplus. What does Mitch do? Does he drink his bottle? He does not. He sells it to someone who values the water at $8. And he enjoys a $7 producer surplus from his temporary water trading business.

So the people who value the water most highly consume it. But the consumer and producer surpluses are distributed in a different way from what the free market would have delivered. Again, the question arises, which arrangement is fair?

The main difference between the government scheme and Chip's private charitable contributions lies in the fact that to buy the water for $8 and sell it for $1, the government must tax someone $7 for each bottle sold. So whether this arrangement is fair depends on whether the taxes are fair.

Taxes are an involuntary transfer of private property, so according to the fair-rules view, they are unfair. But most economists, and most other people, think that there is such a thing as a fair tax. So it seems that the fair-rules view needs to be weakened a bit. Agreeing that there is such a thing as a fair tax is the easy part. Agreeing on what is a fair tax brings endless disagreement and debate.

REVIEW QUIZ

- What are the two big approaches to fairness?
- Explain the utilitarian idea of fairness and what is wrong with it.
- Explain the big tradeoff and the idea of fairness developed to deal with it.
- What is the main idea of fairness based on fair rules? Explain your answer.

◆ You've now studied the two biggest issues that run right through the whole of economics: efficiency and equity, or fairness. In the next chapter, we study some sources of inefficiency and unfairness. And at many points throughout this book—and in your life—you will return to and use the ideas about efficiency and equity that you've learned in this chapter. *Reading Between the Lines* on pp. 124–125 looks at an example of an inefficiency, and some would argue an inequity, in our economy today.

Inefficiency in Software

THE FINANCIAL POST, JANUARY 18, 1997

Microsoft earnings beat predictions

SEATTLE—Microsoft Corp. said Friday it earned US$741 million in its latest quarter, up sharply from year-before results, but the software giant warned of slower earnings growth in the next fiscal year.

The second-quarter earnings, equal to US57¢ a share, compared with US$575 million (US45¢ a share) in the year-ago quarter.

The results for the quarter ended Dec. 31 beat analysts' forcasts. Wall Street on average had expected Microsoft to report earnings equal to US51¢ a share for the quarter, with estimates ranging from US47¢ to US55¢.

Analysts had said results in that range would be impressive considering that Microsoft had no major new products in the quarter and was up against difficult comparisons with the year-earlier period, which was the first full quarter that its Windows 95 operating system was available. ...

"The company performed solidly in all of our businesses, including operating systems, desktop applications, enterprise software, tools, hardware and content," Microsoft chief financial officer Mike Brown said. ...

Essence of the Story

■ In January 1997, Microsoft reported earnings for the quarter ended December 31, 1996, that exceeded Wall Street analysts' expectations.

■ Profits were also up on the same quarter of the previous year.

■ Microsoft earned solid profits on all its lines of business.

Economic Analysis

■ Figure I shows the demand curve for Windows 95, labelled D. The demand curve is also the marginal benefit curve, so it is also labelled MB. It tells us the value to users of one more copy of Windows 95.

■ Figure I also shows Microsoft's marginal cost curve, MC, for producing Windows 95. The curve has a gentle slope, which reflects the assumption that the marginal cost of software does not increase by much as the quantity produced increases.

■ If Windows 95 was produced in a competitive market, the marginal cost curve would also be a supply curve. In this case, equilibrium would occur at point a, where the demand curve and the supply curve intersect.

■ At point a, production is efficient—marginal benefit equals marginal cost.

■ The consumer surplus arising from Windows 95 is shown by the green area. The producer surplus arising from Windows 95 is shown by the blue area.

■ But Microsoft does not produce at point a. Instead, it produces at point b in Fig. 2.

■ Microsoft knows that it can make a bigger profit by reducing its output and charging a higher price.

■ By reducing output to Q_b, Microsoft can raise the price of Windows 95 to $90 per unit.

■ Point b is good for Microsoft but it is ineffi-cient. Marginal benefit exceeds marginal cost and a deadweight loss arises, as shown by the grey area.

■ With the higher price and smaller quantity at point b, Microsoft's pro-ducer surplus is greater than at point a. But con-sumer surplus is smaller. And the decrease in con-sumer surplus is larger than the increase in pro-ducer surplus by the size of the deadweight loss.

■ The reason why Microsoft's earnings were greater than expected is that the demand for Windows 95 was greater than Wall Street analysts expected. The demand was greater than expected because the marginal benefit from Windows 95 exceeded expectations.

■ The increase in the marginal benefit arose most likely from the lower cost of computers and the availability of more highly valued applications.

Figure 1 Efficient quantity

Figure 2 Inefficient quantity

125

SUMMARY

Key Points

Efficiency: A Refresher (pp. 110–111)

- The marginal benefit received from a good or service—the benefit of consuming one additional unit—is the *value* of the good or service to its consumers.
- The marginal cost of a good or service—the cost of producing one additional unit—is the *opportunity cost* of one more unit to its producers.
- Resources allocation is efficient when marginal benefit equals marginal cost.
- If marginal benefit exceeds marginal cost, an increase in production uses resources more efficiently.
- If marginal cost exceeds marginal benefit, a decrease in production uses resources more efficiently.

Value, Price, and Consumer Surplus (pp. 112–113)

- Marginal benefit is measured by the maximum price that consumers are willing to pay for a good or service.
- Marginal benefit determines demand, and a demand curve is a marginal benefit curve.
- Value is what people are *willing to* pay; price is what people *must* pay.
- Consumer surplus equals value minus price, summed over the quantity consumed.

Cost, Price, and Producer Surplus (pp. 114–115)

- Marginal cost is measured by the minimum price producers must be offered to increase production by one unit.
- Marginal cost determines supply, and a supply curve is a marginal cost curve.
- Opportunity cost is what producers pay; price is what producers receive.
- Producer surplus equals price minus opportunity cost, summed over the quantity produced.

Is the Competitive Market Efficient? (pp. 116–117)

- In a competitive equilibrium, marginal benefit equals marginal cost and resource allocation is efficient.

Obstacles to Efficiency (pp. 117–119)

- Monopoly restricts production and creates deadweight loss.
- A competitive market provides too small a quantity of public goods because of the free-rider problem.
- A competitive market provides too large a quantity of goods and services that have external costs and too small a quantity of goods and services that have external benefits.

Is the Competitive Market Fair? (pp. 120–123)

- Ideas about fairness divide into two groups: fair *results* or fair *rules*.
- Fair-results ideas require income transfers from the rich to the poor.
- Fair-rules ideas require property rights and voluntary exchange.

Key Figures

Key Terms

P R O B L E M S

*1. The figure shows the demand for and supply of floppy disks.

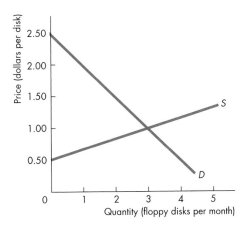

a. What are the equilibrium price and equilibrium quantity of floppy disks?
b. What is the consumer surplus?
c. What is the producer surplus?
d. What is the efficient quantity of floppy disks?

2. The figure shows the demand for and supply of cans of beans.

a. What are the equilibrium price and equilibrium quantity of cans of beans?
b. What is the consumer surplus?
c. What is the producer surplus?
d. What is the efficient quantity of beans?

*3. The table gives the demand and supply schedules for sandwiches.

Price (dollars per sandwich)	Quantity demanded	Quantity supplied
	(sandwiches per hour)	
0	400	0
1	350	50
2	300	100
3	250	150
4	200	200
5	150	250
6	100	300
7	50	350
8	0	400

a. What is the maximum price that consumers are willing to pay for the 250th sandwich?
b. What is the minimum price that producers are willing to accept for the 250th sandwich?
c. Are 250 sandwiches an hour less than or greater than the efficient quantity?
d. What is the consumer surplus if the efficient quantity of sandwiches is produced?
e. What is the producer surplus if the efficient quantity of sandwiches is produced?
f. What is the deadweight loss if 250 sandwiches are produced?

4. The table gives the demand and supply schedules for spring water.

Price (dollars per bottle)	Quantity demanded	Quantity supplied
	(bottles per day)	
0	80	0
0.50	70	10
1.00	60	20
1.50	50	30
2.00	40	40
2.50	30	50
3.00	20	60
3.50	10	70
4.00	0	80

a. What is the maximum price that consumers are willing to pay for the 30th bottle?
b. What is the minimum price that producers are willing to accept for the 30th bottle?
c. Are 30 bottles a day less than or greater than the efficient quantity?
d. What is the consumer surplus if the efficient quantity of spring water is produced?

e. What is the producer surplus if the efficient quantity of spring water is produced?

f. What is the deadweight loss if 30 bottles are produced?

*5. The table gives the demand and supply schedules for train travel for Ben, Beth, and Bo.

Price (cents per passenger kilometre)	Quantity demanded (passenger kilometres)		
	Ben	**Beth**	**Bo**
10	500	300	60
20	450	250	50
30	400	200	40
40	350	150	30
50	300	100	20
60	250	50	10
70	200	0	0

a. If the price of train travel is 40 cents a passenger kilometre, what is the consumer surplus of each traveller?

b. Which traveller has the largest consumer surplus? Explain why.

c. If the price of train travel rises to 50 cents a passenger kilometre, what is the change in consumer surplus of each traveller?

6. The table gives the demand and supply schedules for bus travel for Joe, Jean, and Joy.

Price (cents per passenger kilometre)	Quantity demanded (passenger kilometres)		
	Joe	**Jean**	**Joy**
10	50	600	300
20	45	500	250
30	40	400	200
40	35	300	150
50	30	200	100
60	25	100	50
70	20	0	0

a. If the price of train travel is 50 cents a passenger kilometre, what is the consumer surplus of each passenger?

b. Which passenger has the largest consumer surplus? Explain why.

c. If the price of train travel falls to 30 cents a passenger kilometre, what is the change in consumer surplus of each passenger?

CRITICAL THINKING

1. Study *Reading Between the Lines* on pp. 124–125 on Microsoft and then answer the following questions:

a. Is the quantity of Microsoft software greater than, less than, or equal to the efficient quantity? Explain your answer by using the concepts of marginal benefit, marginal cost, price, consumer surplus, and producer surplus.

b. What, if anything, do you think could be done to increase the quantity of software and decrease its price?

c. Microsoft sells copies of its programs in campus software stores at a huge educational discount. Does this practice increase or decrease consumer surplus? Does it increase or decrease Microsoft's producer surplus? Does it bring the quantity of software closer to the efficient quantity? Explain your answer by using the concepts of marginal benefit, marginal cost, price, consumer surplus, and producer surplus.

d. Chinese software producers have been accused of making illegal copies of Microsoft products and selling them at much lower prices than Microsoft's own price. Does this practice increase or decrease consumer surplus? Does it increase or decrease Microsoft's producer surplus? Does it bring the quantity of software closer to the efficient quantity? Explain your answer by using the concepts of marginal benefit, marginal cost, price, consumer surplus, and producer surplus.

2. Use the link on the Parkin-Bade Web site to visit Agriculture and Agri-Food Canada and obtain information on the Agricultural Income Disaster Assistance (AIDA) program. Describe the main provisions of the program and explain why you think the program is efficient or inefficient, and fair or unfair.

3. How would you set about determining whether the allocation of your time between studying different subjects is efficient? In what units would you measure marginal benefit and marginal cost? Explain your answer by using the concepts of marginal benefit, marginal cost, price, consumer surplus, and producer surplus.

Markets in Action

In 1906, San Francisco suffered a devastating earthquake that destroyed more than half the city's homes but killed few people. How did the people of San Francisco cope with this enormous shock? Did rents have to be controlled to keep housing affordable? Were scarce housing resources allocated to their highest-valued uses? ◆ Almost every day, a new machine is invented that saves labour and increases productivity. How do labour markets cope with labour-saving technological change? Does decreasing demand for low-skilled labour drive wages lower and lower? Do we need minimum wage laws to prevent wages from falling?

Turbulent Times

Do minimum wages enable us to use labour efficiently? ◆ Almost everything we buy is taxed. How do taxes affect the prices? Do they increase by the full amount of the tax so that we, the buyers, pay all the tax? Or does the seller pay part of the tax? Do taxes help or hinder the market in its attempt to move resources to where they are valued most highly? ◆ Trade in items such as drugs, automatic firearms, and enriched uranium is illegal. What are the effects of laws that make trading in a good or service illegal on the amounts of such items consumed? And how do such laws affect the prices paid by those who trade illegally? ◆ In 1991, ideal conditions brought high grain yields. But in 1996, crops were devastated by drought and grain yields were low. How do farm prices and revenues react to such output fluctuations? And how do the actions of speculators and farm marketing boards influence farm revenues?

◆ In this chapter, we study a variety of markets. We use the theory of demand and supply (Chapter 4) and the concepts of elasticity (Chapter 5) and efficiency (Chapter 6) to answer the questions just posed. We're going to begin by studying two markets that have the biggest impacts on our lives: the housing market and the labour market. Because these markets are so vital to the economic welfare of everyone, governments often intervene in them to try to control prices. They impose rent ceilings and minimum wages. To set the scene for each, we're going to see how a market responds to turbulent events.

After studying this chapter, you will be able to:

- Explain how housing markets work and how price ceilings create housing shortages and inefficiency
- Explain how labour markets work and how minimum wage laws create unemployment and inefficiency
- Explain the effects of the sales tax
- Explain how markets for illegal goods work
- Explain why farm prices and revenues fluctuate
- Explain how speculation limits price fluctuations
- Explain how farm marketing boards influence prices, quantities produced, and farm revenues

Housing Markets and Rent Ceilings

To see how a market copes with a supply shock, let's transport ourselves to San Francisco in April 1906, as the city is suffering from a massive earthquake and fire. You can sense the enormity of San Francisco's problems by reading a headline from the *New York Times* on the first days of the crisis. On April 19, 1906:

Over 500 Dead, $200,000,000 Lost in San Francisco Earthquake
Nearly Half the City Is in Ruins and 50,000 Are Homeless

The commander of federal troops in charge of the emergency described the magnitude of the problem:

> Not a hotel of note or importance was left standing. The great apartment houses had vanished . . . two hundred-and-twenty-five thousand people were . . . homeless.[1]

Almost overnight, more than half the people in a city of 400,000 had lost their homes. Temporary shelters and camps alleviated some of the problem, but it was also necessary to utilize the apartment buildings and houses left standing. As a consequence, they had to accommodate 40 percent more people than they had before the earthquake.

The *San Francisco Chronicle* was not published for more than a month after the earthquake. When the newspaper reappeared on May 24, 1906, the city's housing shortage—what would seem to be a major news item that would still be of grave importance—was not mentioned. Milton Friedman and George Stigler describe the situation:

> *There is not a single mention of a housing shortage!* The classified advertisements listed sixty-four offers of flats and houses for rent, and nineteen of houses for sale, against five advertisements of flats or houses wanted. Then and thereafter a considerable number of all types of accommodation except hotel rooms were offered for rent.[2]

How did San Francisco cope with such a devastating reduction in the supply of housing?

[1]Reported in Milton Friedman and George J. Stigler, "Roofs or Ceilings? The Current Housing Problem," in *Popular Essays on Current Problems*, vol. 1, no. 2 (New York: Foundation for Economic Education, 1946), 3–159.
[2]*Ibid*, 3.

The Market Response to a Decrease in Supply

Figure 7.1 shows the market for housing in San Francisco. The demand curve for housing is *D*. There is a short-run supply curve, labelled *SS*, and a long-run supply curve, labelled *LS*.

The short-run supply curve shows the change in the quantity of housing supplied as the rent changes while the number of houses and apartment buildings remains constant. The short-run supply response arises from changes in the intensity with which existing buildings are used. The quantity of housing supplied increases if families rent out rooms that they previously used themselves, and it decreases if families use rooms that they previously rented out to others.

The long-run supply curve shows how the quantity of housing supplied responds to a change in price after enough time has elapsed for new apartment buildings and houses to be erected or for existing ones to be destroyed. In Fig. 7.1, the long-run supply curve is *perfectly elastic*. We do not actually know that the long-run supply curve is perfectly elastic, but it is a reasonable assumption. It implies that the cost of building an apartment is pretty much the same regardless of whether there are 50,000 or 150,000 apartments in existence.

The equilibrium price (rent) and quantity are determined at the point of intersection of the *short-run* supply curve and the demand curve. Before the earthquake, the equilibrium rent is $16 a month and the quantity is 100,000 units of housing.

Figure 7.1(a) shows the situation immediately after the earthquake. The destruction of buildings decreases the supply of housing and shifts the short-run supply curve *SS* leftward to SS_A. If the rent remains at $16 a month, only 44,000 units of housing are available. But with only 44,000 units of housing available, the maximum rent that someone is willing to pay for the last available apartment is $24 a month. So rents rise. In Fig. 7.1(a), the rent rises to $20 a month.

As the rent rises, the quantity of housing demanded decreases and the quantity supplied increases to 72,000 units. These changes occur because people economize on their use of space and make spare rooms, attics, and basements available to others. The higher rent allocates the scarce housing to those people who value it most highly and are willing to pay most for it.

But the higher rent has other, long-run effects. Let's look at these long-run effects.

FIGURE 7.1

The San Francisco Housing Market in 1906

(a) After earthquake

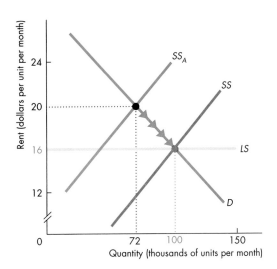

(b) Long-run adjustment

Part (a) shows that before the earthquake 100,000 housing units were rented at $16 a month. After the earthquake, the short-run supply curve shifts from SS to SS_A. The rent rises to $20 a month, and the quantity of housing decreases to 72,000 units. With rent at $20 a month, there is profit in building new apartments and houses. As the building program proceeds, the short-run supply curve shifts rightward (part b). The rent gradually falls to $16 a month, and the quantity of housing increases to 100,000 units—as the arrowed line shows.

Long-Run Adjustments With sufficient time for new apartments and houses to be constructed, supply increases. The long-run supply curve tells us that in the long run, housing is supplied at a rent of $16 a month. Because the rent of $20 a month exceeds the long-run supply price, there is a building boom. Apartments and houses are built, and the short-run supply curve shifts gradually rightward.

Figure 7.1(b) shows the long-run adjustment. As more housing is built, the short-run supply curve shifts rightward and intersects the demand curve at lower rents and larger quantities. The market equilibrium follows the arrows down the demand curve. When the process ends, there is no further profit in building. The rent is back at $16 a month, and 100,000 units of housing are available.

We've just seen how a housing market responds to a decrease in supply. And we've seen that a key part of the adjustment process is a rise in the rent. Suppose the government passes a law to stop the rent from rising. What happens then?

A Regulated Housing Market

We're now going to study the effects of a price ceiling in the housing market. A **price ceiling** is a regulation that makes it illegal to charge a price higher than a specified level. When a price ceiling is applied to housing markets, it is called a **rent ceiling**. How does a rent ceiling affect the housing market?

The effect of a price (rent) ceiling depends on whether it is imposed at a level that is above or below the equilibrium price (rent). A price ceiling set above the equilibrium price has no effect. The reason is that the price ceiling does not constrain the market forces. The force of the law and the market forces are not in conflict. But a price ceiling below the equilibrium price has powerful effects on a market. The reason is that it attempts to prevent the price from regulating the quantities demanded and supplied. The force of the law and the market forces are in conflict, and one (or both) of these forces must yield to some degree. Let's study the effects of a price ceiling set below the equilibrium price by returning to San Francisco. What would have happened in San Francisco if a rent ceiling of $16 a month—the rent before the earthquake—had been imposed?

Figure 7.2 enables us to answer this question. At a rent of $16 a month, the quantity of housing supplied is 44,000 units and the quantity demanded is

FIGURE 7.2
A Rent Ceiling

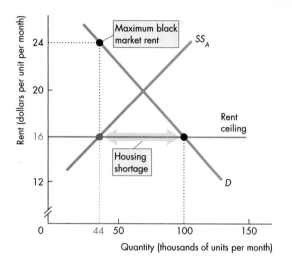

If there had been a rent ceiling of $16 a month, then the quantity of housing supplied after the earthquake would have been stuck at 44,000 units. People would willingly have paid $24 a month for the 44,000th unit. Because the last unit of housing available is worth more than the rent ceiling, frustrated renters will spend time searching for housing and frustrated renters and landlords will make deals in a black market.

100,000 units. So there is a shortage of 56,000 units of housing.

But the story does not end here. Somehow, the 44,000 units of available housing must be allocated among people who demand 100,000 units. How is this allocation achieved? When a rent ceiling creates a housing shortage, two developments occur. They are:

■ Search activity
■ Black markets

Search Activity

The time spent looking for someone with whom to do business is called **search activity**. We spend some time in search activity almost every time we buy something. You want the latest hot CD, and you know four stores that stock it. But which store has the best deal? You need to spend a few minutes on the telephone finding out. In some markets, we

spend a lot of time searching. An example is the used car market. People spend a lot of time checking out alternative dealers and cars.

But when a price is regulated and there is a shortage, search activity increases. In the case of rent-controlled housing markets, frustrated would-be renters scan the newspapers, not only for housing ads but also for death notices! Any information about newly available housing is useful. And they race to be first on the scene when news of a possible supplier breaks.

The *opportunity cost* of a good is equal not only to its price but also to the value of the search time spent finding the good. So the opportunity cost of housing is equal to the rent (a regulated price) plus the time and other resources spent searching for the restricted quantity available. Search activity is costly. It uses time and other resources, such as telephones, cars, and gasoline that could have been used in other productive ways. A rent ceiling controls the rent portion of the cost of housing, but it does not control the opportunity cost, which might even be *higher* than the rent would be if the market were unregulated.

Black Markets

A **black market** is an illegal market in which the price exceeds the legally imposed price ceiling. Black markets occur in rent-controlled housing and scalpers run black markets in tickets for big sporting events and rock concerts.

When rent ceilings are in force, frustrated renters and landlords constantly seek ways of increasing rents. One common way is for a new tenant to pay a high price for worthless fittings, such as $2,000 for threadbare drapes. Another is for the tenant to pay an exorbitant price for new locks and keys—called "key money."

The level of a black market rent depends on how tightly the rent ceiling is enforced. With loose enforcement, the black market rent is close to the unregulated rent. But with strict enforcement, the black market rent is equal to the maximum price that renters are willing to pay.

With strict enforcement of the rent ceiling in the San Francisco example shown in Fig. 7.2, the quantity of housing available remains at 44,000 units. A small number of people offer housing for rent at $24 a month—the highest rent that someone is willing to pay—and the government detects and punishes some of these black market traders.

Inefficiency of Rent Ceilings

In an unregulated market, resources are allocated efficiently. The sum of *consumer surplus* and *producer surplus* is maximized (see Chapter 6, p. 116).

Figure 7.3 shows the inefficiency of a rent ceiling. If the rent is fixed at $16 per unit per month, 44,000 units are supplied. The producer surplus is shown by the blue triangle above the supply curve and below the rent line. Because the quantity of housing is less than the competitive quantity, there is a deadweight loss shown by the grey triangle. This loss is borne by the consumers who can't find housing and by producers who can't supply housing at the new lower price. Consumers who do find housing at the controlled rent gain. If no one incurs search cost, consumer surplus could be as large as the sum of the green triangle and the red rectangle. But consumer surplus can be smaller than this amount because in a regulated housing market, there is no guarantee that the people who find housing are those who value it most highly. The worst case outcome is that in the struggle to find homes people incur search costs that eat up the entire consumer surplus.

Equity? So rent ceilings prevent scarce resources from flowing to their highest-valued use. But don't rent ceilings ensure that scarce housing goes to the people whose need is greatest and make the allocation of scarce housing fair?

The complex ideas about fairness are explored in Chapter 6 (pp. 120–123). Blocking rent adjustments that bring the quantity of housing demanded into equality with the quantity supplied don't end scarcity. So when the law prevents rents from adjusting and blocks the price mechanism from allocating scarce housing, some other allocation mechanism must be used. One of these factors is discrimination on the basis of race, ethnicity, or sex.

Paris, New York, and Toronto are three examples of cities that have rent ceilings but the best example is New York. One consequence of New York's rent ceilings is that families that have lived in the city for a long time—including some rich and famous ones—enjoy low rents, while newcomers pay high rents for hard-to-find apartments. At the same time, landlords in rent-controlled Harlem abandon entire city blocks to rats and drug dealers.

The effects of rent ceilings have led Swedish economist Assar Lindbeck to suggest that rent ceilings are the most effective means yet for destroying cities, even more effective than the hydrogen bomb.

FIGURE 7.3

The Inefficiency of a Rent Ceiling

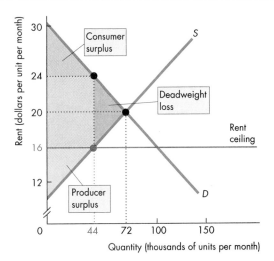

A rent ceiling of $16 a month decreases the quantity of housing supplied to 44,000 units. Producer surplus shrinks to the blue triangle and a deadweight loss (the grey triangle) arises. If people use no resources in search activity, the green triangle plus the red rectangle show consumer surplus. But people might use resources in search activity equal to the amount that they are willing to pay for available housing, the red rectangle.

REVIEW QUIZ

- How does a decrease in the supply of housing change the equilibrium rent in the short run? Who gets to consume the scarce housing resources?
- What are the long-run effects of higher rents following a decrease in the supply of housing?
- What is a rent ceiling and what are the effects of a rent ceiling set above the equilibrium rent?
- What are the effects of a rent ceiling set below the equilibrium rent?
- How do scarce housing resources get allocated when a rent ceiling is in place? Is the allocation fair?

You now know how a price ceiling (rent ceiling) works. Next, we'll learn about the effects of a price floor by studying minimum wages in the labour market.

The Labour Market and the Minimum Wage

FOR EACH ONE OF US, THE LABOUR MARKET IS the market that influences the jobs we get and the wages we earn. Firms decide how much labour to demand, and the lower the wage rate, the greater is the quantity of labour demanded. Households decide how much labour to supply, and the higher the wage rate, the greater is the quantity of labour supplied. The wage rate adjusts to make the quantity of labour demanded equal to the quantity supplied.

But the labour market is constantly hit by shocks, and wages and employment prospects constantly change. The most pervasive source of these shocks is the advance of technology.

New labour-saving technologies become available every year. As a result, the demand for some types of labour, usually the least skilled types, decreases. During the 1980s and 1990s, for example, the demand for telephone operators and television repair persons decreased. Throughout the past 200 years, the demand for low-skilled farm labourers has steadily decreased.

How does the labour market cope with this continuous decrease in the demand for low-skilled labour? Doesn't it mean that the wages of the low-skilled workers are constantly falling?

To answer these questions, we must study the market for low-skilled labour. And just like we did when we studied the housing market, we must look at both the short run and the long run.

In the short run, there are a given number of people who have a given skill, training, and experience. Short-run supply of labour describes how the number of hours of labour supplied by this given number of workers changes as the wage rate changes. To get workers to work more hours, they must be offered a higher wage rate.

In the long run, people can acquire new skills and find new types of jobs. The number of people in the low-skilled labour market depends on the wage rate in this market compared with other opportunities. If the wage rate of low-skilled labour is high enough, people will enter this market. If the wage rate is too low, people will leave it. Some will seek training to enter higher-skilled labour markets, and others will stop working and stay at home or retire.

Long-run supply of labour is the relationship between the quantity of labour supplied and the wage rate after enough time has passed for people to enter or leave the low-skilled labour market. If people can freely enter and leave the low-skilled labour market, the long-run supply of labour is *perfectly elastic*.

Figure 7.4 shows the market for low-skilled labour. Other things remaining the same, the lower the wage rate, the greater is the quantity of labour demanded by firms. The demand curve for labour, D in part (a), shows this relationship between the wage rate and the quantity of labour demanded. Other things remaining the same, the higher the wage rate, the greater is the quantity of labour supplied by households. But the longer the period of adjustment, the greater is the *elasticity of supply* of labour. The short-run supply curve is SS, and a long-run supply curve is LS. In the figure, long-run supply is assumed to be perfectly elastic (the LS curve is horizontal). This market is in equilibrium at a wage rate of $5 an hour and with 22 million hours of labour employed.

What happens if a labour-saving invention decreases the demand for low-skilled labour? Figure 7.4(a) shows the short-run effects of such a change. The demand curve before the new technology is introduced is the curve labelled D. After the introduction of the new technology, the demand curve shifts leftward to D_A. The wage rate falls to $4 an hour, and the quantity of labour employed decreases to 21 million hours. This short-run effect on the wage rate and employment is not the end of the story.

People who are now earning only $4 an hour look around for other opportunities. They see many other jobs (in markets for other types of skills) that pay more than $4 an hour. One by one, workers decide to go back to school or take jobs that pay less but offer on-the-job training. As a result, the short-run supply curve begins to shift leftward.

Figure 7.4(b) shows the long-run adjustment. As the short-run supply curve shifts leftward, it intersects the demand curve D_A at higher wage rates and lower levels of employment. The process ends when workers have no incentive to leave the market for low-skilled labour and the short-run supply curve has shifted all the way to SS_A. At this point, the wage rate has returned to $5 an hour and employment has decreased to 20 million hours a year.

Sometimes, the adjustment process that we've just described is rapid. At other times, it is slow and wages remain low for a long period. To boost the incomes of the lowest paid workers, the government intervenes in the labour market and sets the minimum wage that employers are required to pay. Let's look at the effects of the minimum wage.

FIGURE 7.4
A Market for Low-skilled Labour

(a) After invention

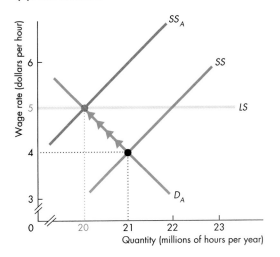

(b) Long-run adjustment

Part (a) shows the immediate effect of a labour-saving invention on the market for low-skilled labour. Initially, the wage rate is $5 an hour and 22 million hours of labour a year are employed. A labour-saving invention shifts the demand curve from D to D_A. The wage rate falls to $4 an hour, and employment decreases to 21 million hours a year. With the lower wage rate, some workers leave this market, and the short-run supply curve starts to shift gradually to SS_A (part b). The wage rate gradually increases, and the employment level decreases. In the long run, the wage rate returns to $5 an hour, and employment decreases to 20 million hours a year.

The Minimum Wage

A **price floor** is a regulation that makes it illegal to trade at a price lower than a specified level. When a price floor is applied to labour markets, it is called a **minimum wage**. If the minimum wage is set *below* the equilibrium wage, the minimum wage has no effect. The minimum wage law and market forces are not in conflict. But if a minimum wage is set *above* the equilibrium wage, the minimum wage is in conflict with the market forces and does have some effects on the labour market. Let's study these effects by returning to the market for low-skilled labour.

Suppose that with an equilibrium wage of $4 an hour (Fig. 7.4a), the government imposes a minimum wage of $5 an hour. What are the effects of this law? Figure 7.5 answers this question. It shows the minimum wage as the horizontal red line labelled "Minimum wage." At this minimum wage, 20 million hours of labour are demanded (point *a*) and 22 million hours of labour are supplied (point *b*), so 2 million hours of available labour go unemployed.

FIGURE 7.5
Minimum Wage and Unemployment

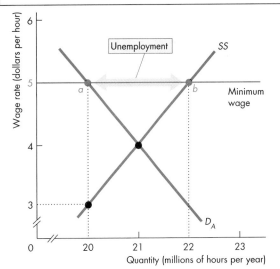

The demand curve for labour is D_A, and the supply curve is SS. In an unregulated market, the wage rate is $4 an hour and 21 million hours of labour a year are employed. If a minimum wage of $5 an hour is imposed, only 20 million hours are hired but 22 million hours are available. Unemployment—*ab*— of 2 million hours a year is created.

The Minimum Wage in Practice

The provincial governments set minimum wages in Canada. In 1999, the minimum wage rates ranged from a low of $5.25 an hour in Newfoundland to a high of $7.20 an hour in Yukon.

Figure 7.5 shows that the minimum wage brings unemployment. But how much unemployment does it bring? Economists do not agree on the answer to this question. Until recently, most economists believed that the minimum wage was a big contributor to high unemployment among low-skilled young workers. But recently this view has been challenged and the challenge rebutted.

David Card, a Canadian economist who works at the University of California at Berkeley, and Alan Krueger of Princeton University say that increases in the minimum wage have not decreased employment and created unemployment. Studying minimum wages in the United States, they say that in California, New Jersey, and Texas, the employment rate of low-income workers increased following an increase in the minimum wage. Card and Krueger suggest three reasons why higher wages might increase employment. First, workers become more conscientious and productive. Second, workers are less likely to quit, so labour turnover, which is costly, is reduced. Third, managers make a firm's operations more efficient.

Most economists are skeptical about the suggestions by Card and Krueger. They ask two questions. First, if higher wages make workers more productive and reduce labour turnover, why don't firms freely pay wage rates above the equilibrium wage to encourage more productive work habits? Second, are there other explanations for the employment responses that Card and Krueger have found?

According to Daniel Hamermesh of the University of Texas at Austin, Card and Krueger got the timing wrong and fell into the trap of the *post hoc* fallacy (described on p. 15). Hamermesh says that firms cut employment *before* the minimum wage is increased in anticipation of the increase. If he is correct, looking for the effects of an increase in the minimum wage *after* the minimum wage rate has increased misses its main effects.

Finis Welch of Texas A&M University and Kevin Murphy of the University of Chicago say the employment effects that Card and Krueger found are caused by regional differences in economic growth, not changes in the minimum wage.

One effect of the minimum wage, according to Fig. 7.5, is an increase in the quantity of labour supplied. If this effect occurs, it might show up as an increase in the number of people who quit school before completing high school. Some economists say that this response does occur.

Inefficiency of the Minimum Wage

An unregulated labour market allocates scarce labour resources to the jobs in which they are valued most highly. The minimum wage frustrates the market mechanism and results in unemployment—wasted labour resources—and an inefficient amount of job search.

In Fig. 7.5, with firms employing only 20 million hours of labour at the minimum wage, many people who are willing to supply labour are unable to get hired. You can see that the 20 millionth hour of labour is available for $3. That is, the lowest wage at which someone is willing to supply the 20 millionth hour—read off from the supply curve—is $3. Someone who manages to find a job earns $5 an hour—$2 an hour more than the lowest wage rate at which someone is willing to work. So it pays unemployed people to spend time and effort searching for one of the hard-to-find jobs.

REVIEW QUIZ

- How does a decrease in the demand for low-skilled labour change the wage rate in the short run?
- What are the long-run effects of a lower wage rate for low-skilled labour?
- What is a minimum wage and what is the effect of a minimum wage that is set above the equilibrium wage?
- What is the effect of a minimum wage that is set below the equilibrium wage?

Next we're going to study a more widespread government intervention in markets: taxes, such as the provincial sales tax. We'll see how taxes change prices and quantities. We'll discover that the sales tax is not paid entirely by the consumer. And we'll see that usually a tax creates a deadweight loss.

Taxes

ALMOST EVERYTHING YOU BUY IS TAXED. BUT who really pays the tax? Because the sales tax is added to the price of a good or service when it is sold, isn't it obvious that *you*, the buyer, pay the tax? Isn't the price higher than it otherwise would be by an amount equal to the tax? It can be, but usually it isn't. And it is even possible that you actually pay none of the tax! Let's see how we can make sense of these apparently absurd statements.

Who Pays the Sales Tax?

Suppose the government puts a $10 sales tax on CD players. What are the effects of the sales tax on the price and quantity of CD players? To answer this question, we need to work out what happens to demand and supply in the market for CD players.

Figure 7.6 shows this market. The demand curve is *D*, and the supply curve is S. With no sales tax, the equilibrium price is $100 per CD player and 5,000 players are bought and sold each week.

When a good is taxed, it has two prices: a price that excludes the tax and a price that *includes* the tax. Buyers respond only to the price that includes the tax, because that is the price they pay. Sellers respond only to the price that excludes the tax, because that is the price they receive. The tax is like a wedge between these two prices.

Think of the price on the vertical axis of Fig. 7.6 as the price paid by buyers—the price that *includes* the tax. When a tax is imposed and the price changes, there is a change in the quantity demanded but no change in demand. That is, there is a movement along the demand curve and no shift of the demand curve.

But the supply changes and the supply curve shifts. The sales tax is like an increase in cost, so supply decreases and the supply curve shifts leftward to *S + tax*. To determine the position of this new supply curve, we add the tax to the minimum price that sellers are willing to accept for each quantity sold. For example, with no tax, sellers are willing to offer 5,000 players a week for $100 a player. So with a $10 tax, they will supply 5,000 players a week for $110—a price that includes the tax. The curve *S + tax* describes the terms on which sellers are willing to offer players for sale now that there is a $10 tax.

Equilibrium occurs where the new supply curve intersects the demand curve—at a price of $105 and

FIGURE 7.6

The Sales Tax

With no sales tax, 5,000 CD players a week are bought and sold at $100 each. A sales tax of $10 a CD player is imposed, and the supply curve shifts leftward to *S + tax*. In the new equilibrium, the price rises to $105 a player and the quantity decreases to 4,000 CD players a week. The sales tax raises the price by less than the tax, lowers the price received by the seller, and decreases the quantity. The sales tax brings in revenue to the government equal to the blue rectangle.

a quantity of 4,000 CD players a week. The $10 sales tax increases the price paid by the buyer by $5 a player. And it decreases the price received by the seller by $5 a player. So the buyer and the seller pay the $10 tax equally.

The tax brings in tax revenue to the government equal to the tax per item multiplied by the number of items sold. The blue area in Fig. 7.6 illustrates the tax revenue. The $10 tax on CD players brings in a tax revenue of $40,000 a week.

In this example, the buyer and the seller split the tax equally: The buyer pays $5 a player and so does the seller. This equal sharing of the tax is a special case and does not usually occur. But some sharing of the tax between the buyer and seller is usual. Also, there are other special cases in which either the buyer or the seller pays the entire tax. The division of the tax between the buyer and the seller depends on the elasticities of demand and supply.

Tax Division and Elasticity of Demand

The division of the tax between the buyer and the seller depends, in part, on the elasticity of demand. There are two extreme cases:

- Perfectly inelastic demand—buyer pays.
- Perfectly elastic demand—seller pays.

Perfectly Inelastic Demand Figure 7.7(a) shows the market for insulin, a vital daily medication of diabetics. Demand is perfectly inelastic at 100,000 doses a day, regardless of the price, as shown by the vertical curve *D*. That is, a diabetic would sacrifice all other goods and services rather than not consume the insulin dose that provides good health. The supply curve of insulin is *S*. With no tax, the price is $2 a dose and the quantity is 100,000 doses a day.

If insulin is taxed at 20¢ a dose, we must add the tax to the minimum price at which drug companies are willing to sell insulin. The result is a new supply curve *S* + *tax*. The price rises to $2.20 a dose, but the quantity does not change. The buyer pays the entire sales tax of 20¢ a dose.

Perfectly Elastic Demand Figure 7.7(b) shows the market for pink marker pens. Demand is perfectly elastic at $1 a pen as shown by the horizontal curve *D*. If pink pens are less expensive than the others, everyone uses pink. If pink pens are more expensive than the others, no one uses them. The supply curve of pink pens is *S*. With no tax, the price of a pink marker is $1, and the quantity is 4,000 pens a week.

If a sales tax of 10¢ a pen is imposed on pink marker pens, we add the tax to the minimum price at which sellers are willing to offer them for sale and the new supply curve is *S* + *tax*. The price remains at $1 a pen, and the quantity decreases to 1,000 a week. The 10¢ sales tax leaves the price paid by the buyer unchanged but lowers the amount received by the seller by the full amount of the sales tax. As a result, sellers decrease the quantity offered for sale.

We've seen that when demand is perfectly inelastic, the buyer pays the entire tax, and when demand is perfectly elastic, the seller pays it. In the usual case, demand is neither perfectly inelastic nor perfectly elastic, and the tax is split between the buyer and the seller. But the division depends on the elasticity of demand. The more inelastic the demand, the larger is the amount of the tax paid by the buyer.

FIGURE 7.7

Sales Tax and the Elasticity of Demand

(a) Inelastic demand

(b) Elastic demand

Part (a) shows the market for insulin, where demand is perfectly inelastic. With no tax, the price is $2 a dose and the quantity is 100,000 doses a day. A sales tax of 20¢ a dose shifts the supply curve to *S* + *tax*. The price rises to $2.20 a dose, but the quantity bought does not change. Buyers pay the entire tax. Part (b) shows the market for pink marker pens. The demand for pink pens is perfectly elastic. With no tax, the price is $1 a pen and the quantity is 4,000 pens a week. A sales tax of 10¢ a pink pen shifts the supply curve to *S* + *tax*. The price remains at $1 a pen, and the quantity of pink pens sold decreases to 1,000 a week. Sellers pay the entire tax.

Tax Division and Elasticity of Supply

The division of the tax between the buyer and the seller also depends, in part, on the elasticity of supply. Again, there are two extreme cases:

■ Perfectly inelastic supply—seller pays.
■ Perfectly elastic supply—buyer pays.

Perfectly Inelastic Supply   Figure 7.8(a) shows the market for water from a spring that flows at a constant rate that can't be controlled. Supply is perfectly inelastic at 100,000 bottles a week as shown by the supply curve S. The demand curve for this spring water is D. With no tax, the price is 50¢ a bottle and the 100,000 bottles that flow from the spring are sold.

Suppose this spring water is taxed at 5¢ a bottle. The supply curve does not change because the spring owners still produce 100,000 bottles a week even though the price they receive falls. But buyers are willing to buy the 100,000 bottles only if the price is 50¢ a bottle. So the price remains at 50¢ a bottle, and the seller pays the entire tax. The sales tax reduces the price received by sellers to 45¢ a bottle.

Perfectly Elastic Supply   Figure 7.8(b) shows the market for sand from which computer-chip makers extract silicon. Supply of this sand is perfectly elastic at a price of 10¢ a kilogram as shown by the supply curve S. The demand curve for sand is D. With no tax, the price is 10¢ a kilogram and 5,000 kilograms a week are bought.

If this sand is taxed at 1¢ a kilogram, we must add the tax to the minimum supply price. Sellers are now willing to offer any quantity at 11¢ a kilogram along the curve S + tax. A new equilibrium is determined where the new supply curve intersects the demand curve—at a price of 11¢ a kilogram and a quantity of 3,000 kilograms a week. The sales tax has increased the price paid by the buyer by the full amount of the tax—1¢ a kilogram—and decreased the quantity sold.

We've seen that when supply is perfectly inelastic, the seller pays the entire tax, and when supply is perfectly elastic, the buyer pays it. In the usual case, supply is neither perfectly inelastic nor perfectly elastic and the tax is split between the buyer and the seller. But the division between the buyer and the seller depends on the elasticity of supply. The more elastic the supply, the larger is the amount of the tax paid by the buyer.

FIGURE 7.8
Sales Tax and the Elasticity of Supply

(a) Inelastic supply

(b) Elastic supply

Part (a) shows the market for water from a mineral spring. Supply is perfectly inelastic. With no tax, the price is 50¢ a bottle. With a sales tax of 5¢ a bottle, the price remains at 50¢ a bottle. The number of bottles bought remains the same, but the price received by the seller decreases to 45¢ a bottle. The seller pays the entire tax. Part (b) shows the market for sand. Supply is perfectly elastic. With no tax, the price is 10¢ a kilogram and 5,000 kilograms a week are bought. The sales tax of 1¢ a kilogram increases the minimum supply price to 11¢ a kilogram. The supply curve shifts to S + tax. The price increases to 11¢ a kilogram. The buyer pays the entire tax.

Sales Taxes in Practice

We've looked at the range of possible effects of a sales tax by studying the extreme cases. In practice, supply and demand are rarely perfectly elastic or perfectly inelastic. They lie somewhere in between. But some items tend towards one of the extremes. For example, a heavily taxed item such as alcohol, tobacco, or gasoline has a low elasticity of demand. Consequently, the buyer pays most of the tax. Also, because demand is inelastic, the quantity bought does not decrease much and the government collects a large tax revenue. It is unusual to heavily tax an item if its demand is elastic. Such a good or service has close substitutes. If a tax is levied on such a good or service, people will reduce their purchases of the taxed good and increase their purchases of an untaxed substitute. That is, the quantity of the taxed good bought decreases by a large amount and the government will not collect much tax revenue. This explains why the items that are taxed are those that have inelastic demands and why, in practice, buyers pay most of the taxes.

Taxes and Efficiency

You've seen that a sales tax places a wedge between the price paid by buyers and the price received by sellers. The price paid by buyers is also the buyers' willingness to pay, which measures marginal benefit. And the price received by sellers is the sellers' minimum supply price, which equals marginal cost.

So, because a tax places a wedge between the buyers' price and the sellers' price, it also puts a wedge between marginal benefit and marginal cost and creates inefficiency. With a higher buying price and a lower selling price, the tax decreases the quantity produced and consumed and a deadweight loss arises. Figure 7.9 shows the inefficiency of taxes. Both the consumer surplus and producer surplus shrink. Part of each surplus goes to the government in tax revenue—the light blue area in the figure. And part of each surplus becomes a deadweight loss—the grey area.

In the extreme cases of perfectly inelastic demand and perfectly inelastic supply, the quantity does not change and there is no deadweight loss. The more inelastic is either demand or supply, the smaller is the decrease in quantity and the smaller is the deadweight loss. When demand or supply is perfectly inelastic, the quantity remains constant and there is no deadweight loss.

FIGURE 7.9
Taxes and Efficiency

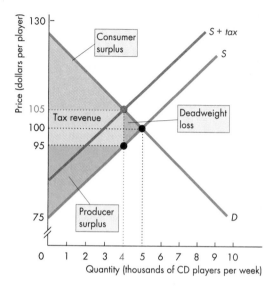

With no sales tax, 5,000 players a week are bought and sold at $100 each. With a sales tax of $10 a player, the buyers' price rises to $105 a player, the sellers' price falls to $95, and the quantity decreases to 4,000 CD players a week. Consumer surplus shrinks to the green area and producer surplus shrinks to the dark blue area. Part of the loss of consumer surplus and producer surplus goes to the government as tax revenue, which is shown as the light blue area. A deadweight loss also arises, which is shown by the grey area.

R E V I E W   Q U I Z

- How does the elasticity of demand influence the effect of a sales tax on the price paid by the buyer, the price received by the seller, the quantity, the tax revenue, and the deadweight loss?
- How does the elasticity of supply influence the effect of a sales tax on the price paid by the buyer, the price received by the seller, the quantity, the tax revenue, and the deadweight loss?
- Why do taxes create a deadweight loss?

Governments make some types of goods such as drugs illegal. Let's see how the market works when trade in an illegal good takes place.

Markets for Illegal Goods

THE MARKETS FOR MANY GOODS AND SERVICES are regulated, but buying and selling some goods is illegal. The best known examples of illegal goods are drugs, such as marijuana, cocaine, and heroin.

Despite the fact that these drugs are illegal, trade in them is a multibillion-dollar business. This trade can be understood by using the same economic model and principles that explain trade in legal goods. To study the market for illegal goods, we're first going to examine the prices and quantities that would prevail if these goods were not illegal. Next, we'll see how prohibition works. Then we'll see how a tax might be used to limit the consumption of these goods.

A Free Market for Drugs

Figure 7.10 shows the market for drugs. The demand curve, D, shows that, other things remaining the same, the lower the price of drugs, the larger is the quantity of drugs demanded. The supply curve, S, shows that, other things remaining the same, the lower the price of drugs, the smaller is the quantity supplied. If drugs were not illegal, the quantity bought and sold would be Q_c and the price would be P_c.

A Market for Illegal Drugs

When a good is illegal, the cost of trading in the good increases. By how much the cost increases and on whom the cost falls depend on the penalties for violating the law and the effectiveness with which the law is enforced. The larger the penalties and the more effective the policing, the higher are the costs. Penalties might be imposed on sellers, buyers, or both.

Penalties on Sellers Drug dealers in Canada face large penalties if their activities are detected. For example, a marijuana dealer could pay a $200,000 fine and serve a 15-year prison term. A heroin dealer could pay a $500,000 fine and serve a 20-year prison term. These penalties are part of the cost of supplying illegal drugs, and they bring a decrease in supply—a leftward shift in the supply curve. To determine the new supply curve, we add the cost of breaking the law to the minimum price that drug dealers are willing to accept. In Fig. 7.10, the cost of breaking the law by selling drugs (CBL) is added to the minimum

FIGURE 7.10

A Market for an Illegal Good

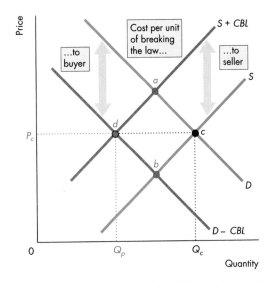

The demand curve for drugs is D, and the supply curve is S. If drugs are not illegal, the quantity bought and sold is Q_c at a price of P_c—point c. If selling drugs is illegal, the cost of breaking the law by selling drugs (CBL) is added to the minimum supply price and supply decreases to $S + CBL$. The price rises and the quantity bought decreases—point a. If buying drugs is illegal, the cost of breaking the law is subtracted from the maximum price that buyers are willing to pay, and demand decreases to $D - CBL$. The price falls, and the quantity bought decreases—point b. If both buying and selling are illegal, both the supply and demand curves shift and the quantity bought decreases even more, but (in this example) the price remains at its unregulated level—point d.

price that dealers will accept, and the supply curve shifts leftward to $S + CBL$. If penalties are imposed only on sellers, the market moves from point c to point a. The price increases, and the quantity bought decreases.

Penalties on Buyers In Canada, it is illegal to *possess* drugs such as marijuana, cocaine, and heroin. For example, possession of marijuana can bring a prison term of 1 year and possession of heroin can bring a prison term of 2 years. Penalties fall on buyers and the cost of breaking the law must be subtracted from the value of the good to determine the maximum price buyers are willing to pay for the drugs. Demand decreases, and the demand curve shifts leftward. In Fig. 7.10, the demand curve shifts to $D - CBL$. With penalties imposed on only buyers, the market moves from point c to point b. The price and the quantity bought decrease.

Penalties on Both Sellers and Buyers

If penalties are imposed on sellers *and* buyers, both supply and demand decrease and both the supply curve and the demand curve shift. In Fig. 7.10, the costs of breaking the law are the same for both buyers and sellers, so both curves shift leftward by the same amounts. The market moves to point d. The price remains at the competitive market price P_c but the quantity bought decreases to Q_p.

The larger the penalties and the greater the degree of law enforcement, the larger is the decrease in demand and/or supply and the greater is the shift of the demand and/or supply curve. If the penalties are heavier on sellers, the supply curve shifts farther than the demand curve and the price rises above P_c. If the penalties are heavier on buyers, the demand curve shifts farther than the supply curve and the price falls below P_c. In Canada, the penalties on sellers are larger than on buyers so the quantity of drugs traded decreases and the price increases compared with an unregulated market.

With high enough penalties and effective law enforcement, it is possible to decrease demand and/or supply to the point at which the quantity bought is zero. But in reality, such an outcome is unusual. It does not happen in the case of illegal drugs. The key reason is the high cost of law enforcement and insufficient resources for the police to achieve effective enforcement. Because of this situation, some people suggest that drugs (and other illegal goods) should be legalized and sold openly but also be taxed at a high rate in the same way that legal drugs such as alcohol are taxed. How would such an arrangement work?

Legalizing and Taxing Drugs

From your study of the effects of taxes, it is easy to see that the quantity of drugs bought could be decreased if drugs were legalized and taxed. A sufficiently high tax could be imposed to decrease supply, raise the price, and achieve the same decrease in the quantity bought as with a prohibition on drugs. The government would collect a large tax revenue.

Illegal Trading to Evade the Tax

It is likely that an extremely high tax rate would be needed to cut the quantity of drugs bought to the level prevailing with a prohibition. It is also likely that many drug dealers and consumers would try to cover up their activities to evade the tax. If they did act in this way, they would face the cost of breaking the law—the tax law. If the penalty for tax law violation is as severe and as effectively policed as drug-dealing laws, the analysis we've already conducted applies also to this case. The quantity of drugs bought would depend on the penalties for law breaking and on the way in which the penalties were assigned to buyers and sellers.

Taxes Versus Prohibition: Some Pros and Cons

So which works more effectively: making drugs illegal and imposing penalties on people who trade in drugs, or legalizing drugs and taxing them?

In favour of taxes and against making drug trading an offence is the fact that the tax revenue can be used to make law enforcement more effective. It can also be used to run a more effective education campaign against addictive drugs.

In favour of prohibition and against taxes is the fact that a prohibition sends a signal that might influence preferences, decreasing the demand for drugs. Also, some people dislike the idea of the government profiting from trade in harmful substances.

REVIEW QUIZ

- How does the imposition of a penalty for selling a drug influence demand, supply, price, and the quantity of the drug consumed?
- How does the imposition of a penalty for buying a drug influence demand, supply, price, and the quantity of the drug consumed?
- How does the imposition of a penalty for selling *or* buying a drug influence demand, supply, price, and the quantity of the drug consumed?
- Is there any case for legalizing drugs?

You've seen how price ceilings, price floors, and taxes limit the quantity and create inefficient resource use. You've also seen how in a market for an illegal good, the quantity can be decreased by imposing penalties on either buyers or sellers or by legalizing and taxing the good. In the next and final section of this chapter, we look at agricultural markets and see how governments try to stabilize farm revenues.

Stabilizing Farm Revenues

EARLY FROST, DROUGHT, HEAVY RAIN AND FLOOD, all contribute to fill the lives of farmers with uncertainty. Fluctuations in the weather bring big fluctuations in farm output. How do changes in farm output affect farm prices and farm revenues? And how might farm revenues be stabilized? Let's begin to answer these questions by looking at an agricultural market.

An Unregulated Agricultural Market

Figure 7.11 shows the market for wheat. In both parts, the demand curve for wheat is *D*. Once farmers have harvested their crop, they have no control over the quantity supplied, and supply is inelastic along a *momentary supply curve*. In normal climate conditions, the momentary supply curve is MS_0 (in both parts of the figure).

The price is determined at the point of intersection of the momentary supply curve and the demand curve. In normal conditions, the price is $200 a tonne. The quantity of wheat produced is 20 million tonnes, and farm revenue is $4 billion. Suppose the opportunity cost to farmers of producing wheat is also $4 billion. Then in normal conditions, farmers just cover their opportunity cost.

Poor Harvest Suppose there is a bad growing season, resulting in a poor harvest. What happens to the price of wheat and the revenue of farmers? These questions are answered in Fig. 7.11(a). Supply decreases, and the momentary supply curve shifts leftward to MS_1, where 15 million tonnes of wheat are produced. With a decrease in supply, the price increases to $300 a tonne.

What happens to total farm revenue? It *increases* to $4.5 billion. A decrease in supply has brought an increase in price and an increase in farm revenue. It does so because the demand for wheat is *inelastic*. The percentage decrease in the quantity demanded is less than the percentage increase in price. You can verify this fact by noticing in Fig. 7.11(a) that the increase in revenue from the higher price ($1.5 billion light blue area) exceeds the decrease in revenue from the smaller quantity ($1.0 billion red area). Farmers are now making a revenue in excess of their opportunity cost.

FIGURE 7.11

Harvests, Farm Prices, and Farm Revenue

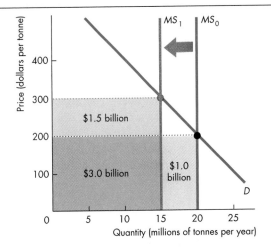

(a) Poor harvest: revenue increases

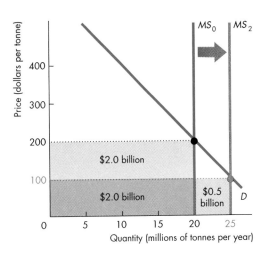

(b) Bumper harvest: revenue decreases

The demand curve for wheat is *D*. In normal times, the supply curve is MS_0 and 20 million tonnes are sold for $200 a tonne. In part (a), a poor harvest decreases supply to MS_1. The price rises to $300 a tonne, and farm revenue increases to $4.5 billion—the $1.5 billion increase from the higher price (light blue area) exceeds the $1.0 billion decrease from the smaller quantity (red area). In part (b), a bumper harvest increases supply to MS_2. The price falls to $100 a tonne, and farm revenue decreases to $2.5 billion—the $2.0 billion decrease from the lower price (red area) exceeds the $0.5 billion increase from the increase in the quantity sold (light blue area).

Although total farm revenue increases when there is a poor harvest, some farmers, whose entire crop is wiped out, suffer a decrease in revenue. Others, whose crop is unaffected, make an enormous gain.

Bumper Harvest Figure 7.11(b) shows what happens in the opposite situation, when there is a bumper harvest. Now supply increases to 25 million tonnes, and the momentary supply curve shifts rightward to MS_2. With the increased quantity supplied, the price falls to $100 a tonne. Farm revenue decreases to $2.5 billion. It does so because the demand for wheat is inelastic. To see this fact, notice in Fig. 7.11(b) that the decrease in revenue from the lower price ($2.0 billion red area) exceeds the increase in revenue from the increase in the quantity sold ($0.5 billion light blue area).

Elasticity of Demand In the example we've just worked through, demand is inelastic. If demand is elastic, the price fluctuations go in the same directions as those we've worked out, but revenue fluctuates in the opposite direction. Bumper harvests increase revenue, and poor harvests decrease it. But the demand for most agricultural products is inelastic, and the case we've studied is the relevant one.

Because farm prices fluctuate, two types of institutions have evolved to stabilize them:

■ Speculative markets in inventories
■ Farm marketing boards

Speculative Markets in Inventories

Many goods, including a wide variety of agricultural products, can be stored. These inventories provide a cushion between production and consumption. If production decreases, goods can be sold from inventory; if production increases, goods can be put into inventory.

In a market that has inventories, we must distinguish production from supply. The quantity produced is not the same as the quantity supplied. The quantity supplied exceeds the quantity produced when goods are sold from inventory. And the quantity supplied is less than the quantity produced when goods are put into inventory. Supply therefore depends on the behaviour of inventory holders.

The Behaviour of Inventory Holders Inventory holders speculate. They hope to buy at a low price

and sell at a high price. That is, they hope to buy goods and put them into inventory when the price is low and sell them from inventory when the price is high. They make a profit or incur a loss equal to their selling price minus their buying price and minus the cost of storage.

But how do inventory holders know when to buy and when to sell? How do they know whether the price is high or low? To decide whether a price is high or low, inventory holders forecast the future price. If the current price is above the forecasted future price, inventory holders sell goods from inventory. If the current price is below the forecasted future price, inventory holders buy goods to put into inventory. This behaviour by inventory holders makes the supply perfectly elastic at the price forecasted by inventory holders.

Let's work out what happens to price and quantity in a market in which inventories are held when production fluctuates. Let's look again at the wheat market.

Fluctuations in Production In Fig. 7.12, the demand curve for wheat is D. Inventory holders expect the future price to be $200 a tonne. The supply curve is S—supply is perfectly elastic at the price expected by inventory holders. Production fluctuates between Q_1 and Q_2.

When production fluctuates and there are no inventories, the price and the quantity fluctuate. We saw this result in Fig. 7.11. But if there are inventories, the price does not fluctuate. When production decreases to Q_1 or 15 million tonnes, inventory holders sell 5 million tonnes from inventory and the quantity bought by consumers is 20 million tonnes. The price remains at $200 a tonne. When production increases to Q_2 or 25 million tonnes, inventory holders buy 5 million tonnes and consumers continue to buy 20 million tonnes. The price remains at $200 a tonne. Inventories reduce price fluctuations. In Fig. 7.12, price fluctuations are entirely eliminated. When there are costs of carrying inventories and when inventories become almost depleted, some price fluctuations do occur, but they are smaller than those occurring in a market without inventories.

Farm Revenue Even if inventory speculation succeeds in stabilizing prices, it does not stabilize farm revenue. With the price stabilized, farm revenue fluctuates as production fluctuates. But now bumper harvests bring larger revenues than poor harvests. The reason is that now farmers, in effect, face a perfectly elastic demand for their output.

FIGURE 7.12
How Inventories Limit Price Changes

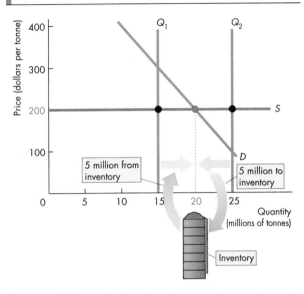

Inventory holders sell wheat from inventory if a poor harvest causes the price to rise above $200 a tonne and buy wheat to hold in inventory if a bumper harvest causes the price to fall below $200 a tonne. So supply (S) is perfectly elastic. When production decreases to Q_1, 5 million tonnes are sold from inventory; when production increases to Q_2, 5 million tonnes are added to inventory. The price remains at $200 a tonne.

Farm Marketing Boards

Most governments intervene in agricultural markets. The most extensive such intervention occurs in the European Union. But intervention also occurs in Canada and the United States, where it is designed to stabilize the prices of agricultural products that include grains, milk, eggs, tobacco, rice, peanuts, cotton, and poultry meats. In Canada, more than 100 farm marketing boards operate and influence more than one-half of total farm sales. A **farm marketing board** is a regulatory agency that intervenes in an agricultural market to stabilize the price of an agricultural product. Farm marketing boards are often supported by governments. How do agricultural markets work when a stabilization program is in place? The answer depends on which type of intervention takes place. There are three types of intervention:

- Price floor
- Quota
- Subsidy

Price Floor   A price floor operates in an agricultural market in much the same way that it operates in other markets. Earlier in this chapter we examined a price floor in the labour market when we studied the effect of minimum wages. The principles are the same in the case of agricultural markets.

Figure 7.13 shows how a price floor works in the market for skim milk powder. The competitive equilibrium price of skim milk powder is $3 a tonne, and 16 million tonnes are produced and bought. If the Canadian Dairy Commission imposes a price floor of $4 a tonne, then the price increases to $4 a tonne and

FIGURE 7.13
A Price Floor

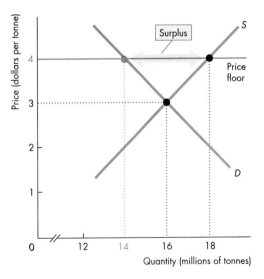

The competitive equilibrium price is $3 a tonne and the equilibrium quantity produced and bought is 16 million tonnes. A price floor of $4 a tonne increases the price to $4 a tonne, decreases the quantity sold to 14 million tonnes, and increases the quantity produced to 18 million tonnes. The price floor creates a surplus of 4 million tonnes. If the Canadian Dairy Commission does not buy the surplus and allows farmers to find their own market, the price will return to its competitive level of $3 a tonne.

the quantity demanded decreases to 14 million tonnes. The quantity supplied increases to 18 million tonnes. Farmers produce a surplus of 4 million tonnes.

This method of supporting the price of an agricultural product will fail unless there is some method of taking up the surplus produced. If farmers are left to find a market for their surplus, then the price will fall below the price floor to the competitive price—$3 a tonne. If, on the other hand, the Canadian Dairy Commission purchases the surplus at the support price, then the price will remain at the price floor. If the marketing board systematically buys more than it sells, then it will end up with a large inventory. Such has been the outcome in the European Union where stabilization agencies have mountains of butter and lakes of wine! The cost of buying and storing the inventory falls on taxpayers, and the main gainers from the support price are the large, efficient farms.

Quota A **quota** is a restriction on the quantity of a good that a farm is permitted to produce. If a quota restricts farm production, then the supply curve becomes perfectly inelastic at the quota quantity.

Figure 7.14 illustrates how a quota works in the market for skim milk. The competitive price is $3 a tonne and the competitive quantity is 16 million tonnes. If the Canadian Dairy Commission imposes a quota that restricts total production to 14 million tonnes, the supply curve becomes the vertical line labelled "Quota." With output restricted by the quota, the quantity produced is now 14 million tonnes and the price increases to $4 a tonne.

But this might not be the end of the story. Farmers are willing to produce skim milk at $2 a tonne, so at a market price of $4 a tonne, they will want to increase their output. If the Canadian Dairy Commission does not prevent quotas from being exceeded, a gradual increase in the quantity of skim milk supplied will eventually restore the competitive equilibrium.

Subsidy A **subsidy** is a payment made by the government to the producer. A subsidy is like a tax—a payment made by a producer to the government—but it goes in the reverse direction. Therefore a subsidy works in a similar way to a tax, but instead of adding something to the price paid by the consumer, a subsidy lowers the price to below what it would be in the absence of a subsidy.

FIGURE 7.14

A Quota

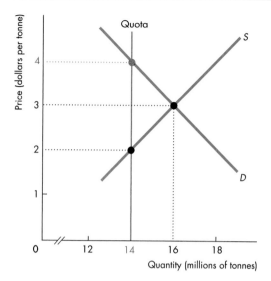

The competitive equilibrium price is $3 a tonne and the equilibrium quantity produced and bought is 16 million tonnes. A quota is set at 14 million tonnes. As a result, the price rises to $4 a tonne and the quantity sold decreases to 14 million tonnes. Producers are willing to supply 14 million tonnes at $2 a tonne, so they will want to increase the quantity that they supply. If the regulatory agency cannot control the quantity produced, then the quantity produced will increase and the price will fall to its competitive level of $3 a tonne.

Figure 7.15 illustrates how a subsidy works in the market for (liquid) milk. The competitive equilibrium is at 30¢ a litre with 16 billion litres produced and bought. The Canadian Dairy Commission then offers a subsidy of 10¢ a litre. The subsidy increases the supply of milk and shifts the supply curve rightward. The magnitude of the shift depends on the size of the subsidy. In this case, farmers are willing to sell each litre for 10¢ less than they would be willing to accept in the absence of a subsidy. The equilibrium price falls to 25¢ a litre, and the quantity produced and bought increases to 17 billion litres. Farmers receive 35¢ a litre, which is the market price of 25¢ a litre plus the subsidy of 10¢ a litre. Thus farmers gain, but taxpayers pay the subsidy. The total subsidy paid is $1.7 billion, which is the 10¢ a litre subsidy multiplied by the 17 billion litres of milk produced.

FIGURE 7.15

A Subsidy

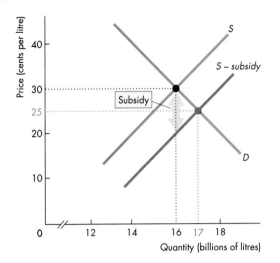

The competitive equilibrium price is 30¢ a litre and the equilibrium quantity produced and bought is 16 billion litres. The Canadian Dairy Commission introduces a subsidy of 10¢ a litre. As a result, producers are now willing to supply each quantity at 10¢ a litre less. The supply curve shifts rightward such that the vertical distance between the supply curve S and the supply curve S – subsidy is 10¢ a litre. The price falls to 25¢ a litre, and the quantity produced and sold increases to 17 billion litres. Producers receive 35¢ a litre, which is the market price of 25¢ a litre plus the subsidy of 10¢ a litre. The total subsidy paid is $1.7 billion, which taxpayers will have to pay.

This method of agricultural support can impose major costs on taxpayers.

Efficiency and Equity in Farm Markets

Are farm marketing boards efficient and are they fair? It is easy to answer the first question. They are generally inefficient. It is harder to answer the second question.

Inefficiency of Farm Marketing Boards You can see that farm marketing boards are inefficient by looking at what they do to the relationship between marginal cost and marginal benefit. A price floor that exceeds the competitive equilibrium price decreases

the quantity demanded and results in a price that equals marginal benefit but that exceeds marginal cost. So both consumer surplus and producer surplus shrink and there is a deadweight loss.

A quota restricts output below the quantity that maximizes the sum of consumer surplus and producer surplus. So it, too, creates deadweight loss.

A subsidy increases production above the competitive level. So it results in marginal cost exceeding marginal benefit and creates deadweight loss.

All the methods of intervention, then, are inefficient. But are they fair?

Equity of Farm Marketing Boards Farm marketing boards increase the incomes of farmers and decrease the incomes of taxpayers and consumers of farm products compared with what the unregulated market would provide. Because the actions of farm marketing boards create deadweight loss, the gains by farmers are smaller than the losses borne by everyone else.

Whether this redistribution of economic wellbeing towards farmers is fair is a controversial matter. Most farmers probably think it perfectly fair and most other people probably have their doubts. Whatever the merits of either view, it is a curious and perhaps surprising fact that farmers throughout the world manage to persuade the non-farming majority that redistribution towards the farmers is necessary.

R E V I E W   Q U I Z

- Can you explain how poor harvests and bumper harvests influence farm prices and farm revenues?
- Can you explain how the existence of inventories and speculation influence farm prices and farm revenues?
- What are the main actions that farm marketing boards take and how do these actions influence farm prices and farm revenues?

◇ You now know how to use the demand and supply model to predict prices, to study government intervention in markets, and to study the sources and costs of inefficiency. Before you leave this topic, take a look at *Reading Between the Lines* on pp. 148–149 and see what is happening in the illegal market for pirated software today.

POLICY WATCH

The Illegal Market for Pirated Software

GLOBE AND MAIL, JUNE 22, 1998

Stealing programs on Canada's campuses

Steve, a student at Ryerson Polytechnic University in Toronto, keeps his computer humming with the latest games, sophisticated business applications and expensive graphics programs.

The array of software at his disposal would cost several thousand dollars to buy in stores. But for Steve, 20, it's simply a matter of copying borrowed programs onto a blank, recordable CD. Total cost? About $2.50.

Sure, it's illegal, Steve said, but the economics outweigh the legal constraints. ... "We're students. We don't have any money. Can each of us afford to spend $400 for a program like Office 97?"

Software piracy in Canada—counterfeiting and illegal copying of software—costs manufacturers and the Canadian economy an estimated $500-million a year, according to the Canadian Alliance Against Software Theft. CAAST is a coalition of Canadian software makers...

CAAST, formed in 1990 to battle software piracy, said that about four out of every 10 software programs now in use in Canada were not purchased. ...

But tougher legislation to combat piracy is on the way and software firms are hoping that the threat of penalties of up to $20,000—plus antipiracy hot lines and an ongoing campaign to educate the public—will help to cut the hefty losses this year. ...

"We know that there is definitely a higher rate of piracy on university campuses than there is in Canada in general," said CAAST spokesperson Kimberley Lauder, ...

Popular with students, she said, are so-called compilation CDs that contain an array of programs. ...

For about $50, students can buy a compilation CD that might contain up to $40,000 worth of programs—everything from costly new operating systems and graphics programs, worth hundreds of dollars each, to the newest games that sell for $60 each in stores. ...

Under changes to copyright legislation that are expected to take effect in the fall, software makers will be able to pursue statutory damages... Firms will need to simply show that a loss occurred, and a judge could then set a penalty of $500 to $20,000 for each violation.

Tougher laws and penalties in the United States have helped keep the software piracy rate there down to about half of what it is in Canada, so firms are optimistic that they can significantly reduce piracy here, ...

Essence of the Story

■ Software piracy in Canada costs an estimated $500 million per year.

■ Tougher legislation to fight software piracy by increasing penalties up to $20,000 is anticipated.

■ Currently, students can buy a compilation CD for $50 that contains up to $40,000 worth of pirated programs.

■ Tougher laws and penalties in the United States have kept the piracy rate at half the Canadian level.

Economic Analysis

On university campuses, students can buy illegal CDs that contain numerous software programs.

Because an illegal CD is cheap to make, the minimum price that software pirates are willing to accept for an illegal CD is low.

Figure 1 illustrates the campus market for illegal CDs. In this example, the price is $50 a CD and 12,500 CDs are bought each year—at point *a*.

If each CD contains software worth $40,000, the software industry loses $500 million a year.

If the sellers of illegal CDs are penalized $100 for each CD sold, then the minimum price that sellers will accept increases and the supply of illegal CDs decreases.

Figure 2 shows the new supply curve, *S* + *CBL*. The vertical distance between the supply curve, *S*, and the supply curve,

S + *CBL*, equals the $100 penalty on sellers.

With the penalty on sellers, the price of a CD rises to $100 and the quantity decreases to 7,500 CDs—at point *b*.

But if a penalty of $50 per CD is also imposed on buyers, then the maximum price that buyers are willing to pay falls and demand decreases.

Figure 3 shows the new demand curve, *D* – *CBL*. The vertical distance between the demand curve, *D*, and the demand curve, *D* – *CBL*, equals the $50 penalty imposed on buyers.

With penalties on both sellers and buyers, the price rises to $75 a CD and the quantity decreases to 5,000 CDs—at point *c*.

By imposing penalties on sellers and buyers of illegal CDs, software piracy on Canadian campuses will decrease.

Figure 1 Illegal market for pirated software

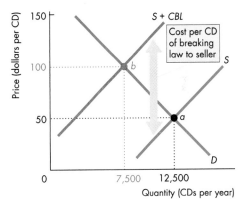

Figure 2 Software market with copyright law enforced on sellers

Figure 3 Software market with copyright law enforced on buyers and sellers

You're The Voter

Would you support legislation that imposes penalties on sellers of pirated software but not on buyers?

Would you support legislation that imposes penalties on buyers of pirated software but not on sellers?

List all policy actions you can think of that would decrease the amount of software piracy.

S U M M A R Y

Key Points

Housing Markets and Rent Ceilings (pp. 130–133)

- A decrease in the supply of housing decreases short-run supply and raises the equilibrium rent.
- Higher rents stimulate building and, in the long run, the quantity of housing increases and rents fall.
- A rent ceiling set below the equilibrium rent creates a housing shortage, wasteful search, and a black market.

The Labour Market and the Minimum Wage (pp. 134–136)

- A decrease in the demand for low-skilled labour lowers the wage rate and reduces employment.
- The lower wage rate encourages people with low skill to acquire more skill, which decreases the supply of low-skilled labour and, in the long run, raises their wage rate.
- A minimum wage set above the equilibrium wage creates unemployment and increases the amount of time people spend searching for jobs.
- Minimum wages hit low-skilled young people hardest.

Taxes (pp. 137–140)

- When a good or service is taxed, usually the price increases and the quantity bought decreases but the price increases by less than the tax. The buyer pays part of the tax, and the seller pays part of the tax.
- The share of a tax paid by the buyer and by the seller depends on the elasticity of demand and the elasticity of supply.
- The less elastic the demand and the more elastic the supply, the greater is the price increase, the smaller is the quantity decrease, and the larger is the share of the tax paid by the buyer.
- If demand is perfectly elastic or supply is perfectly inelastic, the seller pays the entire tax. And if demand is perfectly inelastic or supply is perfectly elastic, the buyer pays the entire tax.

Markets for Illegal Goods (pp. 141–142)

- Penalties on sellers of an illegal good increase the cost of selling the good and decrease its supply. Penalties on buyers decrease their willingness to pay and decrease the demand for the good.
- The higher the penalties and the more effective the law enforcement, the smaller is the quantity bought. The price is higher or lower than the unregulated price, depending on whether the penalties on sellers or buyers are higher.
- A tax set at a sufficiently high rate will decrease the quantity of a drug consumed, but there will be a tendency for the tax to be evaded.

Stabilizing Farm Revenues (pp. 143–147)

- Farm revenues fluctuate because supply fluctuates.
- The demand for most farm products is inelastic, so a decrease in supply increases the price and increases farm revenues, while an increase in supply decreases price and decreases farm revenues.
- Inventory holders and government agencies act to stabilize farm prices and revenues.
- Farm marketing boards use price floors, quotas, and subsidies to increase farm prices and revenues.

Key Figures

Key Terms

PROBLEMS

*1. The figure below shows the demand for and supply of rental housing in the Village:

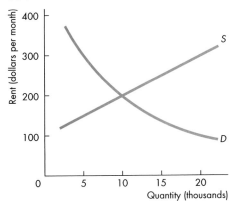

a. What are the equilibrium rent and the equilibrium quantity of rented housing?

If a rent ceiling is set at $150 a month, what is:

b. The quantity of housing rented?
c. The shortage of housing?
d. The maximum price that someone is willing to pay for the last unit of housing available?

2. The figure below shows the demand for and supply of rental housing in Township:

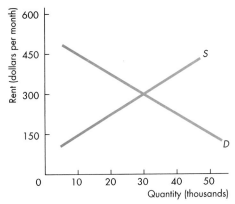

a. What is the equilibrium rent and equilibrium quantity of rented housing?

If a rent ceiling is set at $150 a month, what is:

b. The quantity of housing rented?
c. The shortage of housing?
d. The maximum price that someone is willing to pay for the last unit available?

*3. The table gives the demand for and supply of teenage labour.

Wage rate (dollars per hour)	Quantity demanded	Quantity supplied
	(hours per month)	
2	3,000	1,000
3	2,500	1,500
4	2,000	2,000
5	1,500	2,500
6	1,000	3,000

a. What are the equilibrium wage rate and level of employment?
b. What is the quantity of unemployment?
c. If a minimum wage of $3 an hour is set for teenagers, how many hours do they work?
d. If a minimum wage of $3 an hour is set for teenagers, how many hours of their labour are unemployed?
e. If a minimum wage is set at $5 an hour for teenagers, how many hours of their labour are employed and unemployed?
f. If a minimum wage is set at $5 an hour and demand increases by 500 hours a month, what is the wage rate paid to teenagers and how many hours of their labour are unemployed?

4. The table gives the demand for and supply of high-school graduates.

Wage rate (dollars per hour)	Quantity demanded	Quantity supplied
	(hours per month)	
6	9,000	4,000
7	8,000	5,000
8	7,000	6,000
9	6,000	7,000
10	5,000	8,000

a. What are the equilibrium wage rate and level of employment?
b. What is the level of unemployment?
c. If a minimum wage is set at $7 an hour, how many hours do high-school graduates work?
d. If a minimum wage is set at $7 an hour, how many hours of labour are unemployed?
e. If a minimum wage is set at $9 an hour, how many hours of their labour are employed and unemployed?
f. If the minimum wage is $9 an hour and demand increases by 500 hours a month, what is the wage rate paid to high-school graduates and how many hours of their labour are unemployed?

*5. The table gives the demand and supply schedules for chocolate brownies:

Price (cents per brownie)	Quantity demanded	Quantity supplied
	(millions per day)	
50	5	3
60	4	4
70	3	5
80	2	6
90	1	7

a. If brownies are not taxed, what is the price of a brownie and how many are consumed?
b. If brownies are taxed at 20¢ each, what is the price and how many brownies are consumed? Who pays the tax?

6. The table gives the demand and supply schedules for coffee.

Price (dollars per cup)	Quantity demanded	Quantity supplied
	(cups per hour)	
1.50	90	30
1.75	70	40
2.00	50	50
2.25	30	60
2.75	10	70

a. If there is no tax on coffee, what is the price and how much coffee is consumed?
b. If a tax of 75¢ a cup is introduced, what is the price, how much coffee is consumed, and who pays the tax?

*7. The demand for and supply of eggs on Turtle Island is:

Price (dollars per dozen)	Quantity demanded	Quantity supplied
	(dozens per week)	
1.20	3,000	500
1.30	2,750	1,500
1.40	2,500	2,500
1.50	2,250	3,500
1.60	2,000	4,500

If the government sets a floor price of $1.50 a dozen, what is the market price, the quantity sold, farm revenue, and surplus of eggs?

8. If in the Turtle Island egg market of problem 7, the government sets a quota of 1,500 dozen eggs a week but sets no floor price, what is the market price, the quantity sold, farm revenues, and shortage of eggs?

CRITICAL THINKING

1. Study *Reading Between the Lines* on the market for illegal pirated software on pp. 148-149 and answer the following questions:
a. Draw the diagrams using a $50 penalty on the sellers and a $100 penalty on the buyers. What changes occur in the quantity of CDs bought and sold each year and in the price?
b. What size of penalty would be required to eliminate software piracy?
c. If the price elasticity of demand is greater than estimated in the diagrams, would the quantity of CDs bought and sold decrease or increase when a $100 penalty on sellers is imposed?
d. Would possible incarceration change the positions of the shifted supply and demand curves?

2. Rent ceilings exist in many Canadian cities. What impact do you think rent ceilings have on the rent that students have to pay for rented accommodation and the amount and quality of that accommodation?

3. Use the links on the Parkin-Bade Web site to obtain information on the minimum wage rates across the provinces. In which province do you think the minimum wage might be causing the most unemployment and why?

4. Use the links on the Parkin-Bade Web site to obtain information and views on taxes on cigarettes. For many years, the provinces have increased the tax on cigarettes. But recently, Quebec and Ontario cut this tax. What do you think will be the change in the price of cigarettes, the quantity of cigarettes sold, and provincial tax revenue? Who will gain from the tax cut—buyers or sellers of cigarettes?

5. Use the links on the Parkin-Bade Web site to obtain information about markets in grain. Some grain growers in Western Canada would like to sell their grain on the world market. Under Canadian law, such action is prohibited. The Wheat Board is the sole seller of these grains. What would be the change in the farm revenues if the law were changed and farmers were allowed to market their own grain?

Understanding How Markets Work

The four chapters that you've just studied explain how markets work. The market is an amazing instrument. It enables people who have never met and who know nothing about each other to interact and do business. It also enables us to allocate our scarce resources to the uses that we value most highly. Markets can be very simple or highly organized. ◆ A simple market is one that the American historian Daniel J. Boorstin describes in *The Discoverers* (p. 161). In the late 14th century,

The Amazing Market

The Muslim caravans that went southward from Morocco across the Atlas Mountains arrived after twenty days at the shores of the Senegal River. There the Moroccan traders laid out separate piles of salt, of beads from Ceutan coral, and cheap manufactured goods. Then they retreated out of sight. The local tribesmen, who lived in the strip mines where they dug their gold, came to the shore and put a heap of gold beside each pile of Moroccan goods. Then they, in turn, went out of view, leaving the Moroccan traders either to take the gold offered for a particular pile or to reduce the pile of their merchandise to suit the offered price in gold. Once again the Moroccan traders withdrew, and the process went on. By this system of commercial etiquette, the Moroccans collected their gold.

Organized markets are the Toronto Exchange that trades many millions of stocks each day and monthly auctions at which governments sell bonds to finance their debts. ◆ Whether simple, or highly organized, all of these markets determine the prices at which exchanges take place and enable both buyers and sellers to benefit. ◆ Everything and anything that can be exchanged is traded in markets. There are markets for goods and services; for resources such as labour, capital, and raw materials; for dollars, pounds, and yen; for goods to be delivered now and for goods to be delivered in the future. Only the imagination places limits on what can be traded in markets. ◆ You began your study of markets in Chapter 4, by learning about the laws of demand and supply. There, you discovered the forces that make prices adjust to coordinate buying plans and selling plans. In Chapter 5, you learned how to calculate and use the concept of elasticity to predict the responsiveness of prices and quantities to changes in supply and demand. In Chapter 6, you studied efficiency and discovered the conditions under which a market sends resources to uses in which they are valued most highly. And finally, in Chapter 7, you studied markets in action. There, you learned how markets cope with change and discovered how they operate when governments intervene to fix prices, impose taxes, or make some goods illegal.

◇ The laws of demand and supply were discovered during the nineteenth century by some remarkable economists. We conclude our study of demand and supply and markets by looking at the lives and times of some of these economists. We also talk with Richard Harris, one of Canada's most influential economists today.

Probing the Ideas

Discovering the Laws of Demand and Supply

Alfred Marshall

(1842–1924) grew up in an England that was being transformed by the railroad and by the expansion of manufacturing. Mary Paley was one of Marshall's students at Cambridge and when Alfred and Mary married, in 1877, celibacy rules barred Marshall from continuing to teach at Cambridge. By 1884, with more liberal rules, the Marshalls returned to Cambridge where Alfred became Professor of Political Economy.

Many others had a hand in refining the theory of demand and supply, but the first thorough and complete statement of the theory as we know it today was set out by Alfred Marshall, with the acknowledged help of Mary. Published in 1890, the monumental treatise, Principles of Economics, *became the textbook on economics on both sides of the Atlantic for almost half a century. Marshall was an outstanding mathematician, but he kept mathematics and even diagrams in the background. His supply and demand diagram appears only in a footnote.*

> "The forces to be dealt with are … so numerous, that it is best to take a few at a time. … Thus we begin by isolating the primary relations of supply, demand, and price…"
>
> ALFRED MARSHALL,
> THE PRINCIPLES OF
> ECONOMICS

The Issues

The laws of demand and supply that you studied in Chapter 4 were discovered during the 1830s by Antoine-Augustin Cournot (1801–1877), a professor of mathematics at the University of Lyon, France. Although Cournot was the first to use demand and supply, it was the development and expansion of the railroads during the 1850s that gave the newly emerging theory its first practical applications. Railroads then were at the cutting edge of technology just as airlines are today. And as in the airline industry today, competition among the railroads was fierce.

Dionysius Lardner (1793–1859), an Irish professor of philosophy at the University of London, used demand and supply to show railroad companies how they could increase their profits by cutting rates on long-distance business on which competition was fiercest and by raising rates on short-haul business on which they had less to fear from other transportation suppliers. Today, economists use the principles that Lardner worked out during the 1850s to calculate the freight rates and passenger fares that will give airlines the largest possible profit. And the rates calculated have a lot in common with the railroad rates of the nineteenth century. On local routes on which there is little competition, fares per kilometre are highest, and on long-distance routes on which the airlines compete fiercely, fares per kilometre are lowest.

Known satirically among scientists of the day as "Dionysius Diddler," Lardner worked on an amazing range of problems from astronomy to railway engineering to economics. A colourful character, he would have been a regular guest on late-night TV talk shows had they been around in the 1850s. Lardner visited the École des Ponts et Chaussées (the School of Bridges and Roads) in Paris and must have learned a great deal from Jules Dupuit.

In France, Jules Dupuit (1804–1866), a French engineer/economist, used demand to calculate the benefits from building a bridge and, once the bridge was built, for calculating the toll to charge for its use. His work was the forerunner of what is today called *cost-benefit analysis*. Working with the principles invented by Dupuit, economists today calculate the costs and benefits of highways and airports, dams, and power stations.

... and Now

Today, using the same principles that Dupuit devised, economists calculate whether the benefits of expanding airports and air-traffic control facilities are sufficient to cover their costs. Airline companies use the principles developed by Lardner to set their prices and to decide when to offer "seat sales." Like the railroads before them, the airlines charge a high price per kilometre on short flights, for which they face little competition, and a low price per kilometre on long flights, for which competition is fierce.

Then ...

Dupuit used the law of demand to determine whether a bridge or canal would be valued enough by its users to justify the cost of building it. Lardner first worked out the relationship between the cost of production and supply and used demand and supply theory to explain the costs, prices, and profits of railroad operations. He also used the theory to discover ways of increasing revenue by raising rates on short-haul business and lowering them on long-distance freight.

Markets do an amazing job. And the laws of demand and supply help us to understand how markets work. But in some situations, a market must be designed and institutions must be created to enable the market to operate. In recent years, economists have begun to use their tools to design and create markets. One of Canada's leading economists who has studied how markets work in many different contexts is Richard Harris, whom you can meet on the following pages.

Talking with
Richard Harris

Richard G. Harris *is the B.C. Telephone Professor of Economics at Simon Fraser University, and Fellow of the Canadian Institute for Advanced Research. He began his academic career at Queen's University, where he became Director of the John Deutsch Institute for the Study of Economic Policy, and held visiting appointments at the University of California at Berkeley, MIT, and the University of New South Wales. Professor Harris specializes in international economics and was a special advisor to the Canadian government during the negotiations that lead to the Canada–U.S. Free Trade Agreement. He has served as consultant to the World Bank and the OECD.*

Professor Harris has published many books and articles on Canadian international trade, economic growth, and Canadian economic policy as well as on more technical topics. A recently published volume entitled The Asia-Pacific Region in the Global Economy: A Canadian Perspective

summarizes the results of a two-year research program that he headed.

Robin Bade and Michael Parkin talked with Professor Harris about his work and the contribution that he and other economists are making to try to improve economic policy in Canada.

Professor Harris, what first attracted you to economics?
I was an undergraduate at Queen's University studying mathematics and philosophy and became a bit disenchanted with the level of abstraction in both those disciplines. In my introductory economics course, I was fascinated by the idea that the organization of society could be studied in a scientific way using a few basic principles that had universal applicability—a concept that was completely novel to me at the time. I also was very much of the view, which was typical of most in my generation, that governments effectively controlled all aspects of the economy. The idea that markets were social institutions that promoted the productive use of resources was a fairly radical idea for an undergraduate to be exposed to in the 1960s. While quite critical of the pure free market view at the time, it was a major intellectual challenge to think systematically about the issues rather than to simply express an opinion.

When Alfred Marshall first described the laws of demand and supply, he said that "the forces to be dealt with are ... so numerous, that it is best to take a few at a time ... [and] ... begin by isolating the primary relations of *demand, supply,* and *price*." Was Marshall correct? Do the laws of demand and supply have the same force and relevance today that they did when Marshall first explained them?
Absolutely. I don't think one could prove that the laws of supply and demand are of more or less force or rele-

vance today than in the past—these are universal laws. Occasionally, they are pushed into the background during periods of great social or political upheaval, but they are as inevitable in their relevance to human affairs just as the laws of electromagnetics are to the functioning of your computer. Marshall's emphasis on isolating a few critical channels of influence on supply or demand is good advice and absolutely necessary if a theory is to be of any practical use. In looking at the Canada–U.S. Free Trade Agreement, for example, I found that economies of scale were one of the few factors that figured importantly on the anticipated supply response of industry to the agreement; although people were convinced that large numbers of other influences would matter—such as who owned the firms, what city they were located in, and so forth. Keep your theories simple!

Do the laws of demand and supply apply to the international economy?

Yes, but with some interesting twists. At the international level, an increase in the supply of a good in one country (say Canada) can have important ramifications on the prices of goods consumed or produced in countries that are far removed from Canada. The connection, of course, is that international trade links countries directly and indirectly. If there is discovery of a diamond mine in the Yukon Territory in Canada (which happened recently), this will ultimately impact on wages and incomes in South Africa. Why? Because South Africa is a major world supplier of diamonds and the Yukon mine is a source of competitive supply to the global market of diamonds. This new supply will put downward pressure on the price of diamonds throughout the world and, in particular, will affect the major diamond-producing country—South Africa. International trade allows the laws of supply and demand to have global applicability. If South Africa did not export or import any diamonds, then the Yukon diamond discovery would have had no effect on South Africa.

You've recently studied Canada's place in the Asia–Pacific economy. Can Canadians compete with low-cost Asian producers? Would we be better off if we taxed cheap foreign-produced goods so that Canadian producers could compete more effectively?

Absolutely not. The notion that providing "protection" for domestic producers will lead to an improvement in national well-being is one of the oldest and most discredited ideas in economics. Almost all economists agree that policies, which improve international trade or move the economy towards "freer trade" on average, tend to lead to increases in national income. The Asian example comes up often because the very low wages in Asia suggest that Canadian producers would be wiped out if Asian exporters had free access to the Canadian market. Let's suppose for the moment that Asian clothing producers pay wages much lower than is the case in Canada. Most people recognize that the Canadian consumer would be better off if we allowed cheaper clothing imports from Asia. But many fail to recognize the very important benefits that would come about from having valuable resources —capital and labour—that are being utilized in the clothing industry move to other industries where they are more productive—for example, the automobile industry. This is the law of comparative advantage and it is arguably the most important principle that economics has to teach after opportunity cost.

> *The notion that providing "protection" for domestic producers will lead to an improvement in national well-being is one of the oldest and most discredited ideas in economics.*

You attracted a lot of attention in 1999 by suggesting that the market for the Canadian dollar does not work well and that we would be better off if we closed it down and started using the U.S. dollar. What is wrong with letting the Canadian dollar find its equilibrium price on the foreign exchange market?

There are two basic problems with the current Canadian dollar regime. First, from the point of view of promoting trade and investment between Canada and other countries and, in particular, the United States, there would be enormous benefits from having a single currency—for many of the same reasons that we all benefit from working in a single language. The costs of writing contracts, organizing exchange, managing accounting systems, and so forth are enormously complicated by the use of multiple currencies. Think of anybody organizing an e-commerce business in Canada. The hassle of having to deal with currency exchange for U.S. customers is a tremendous barrier to Canadian entry in that business. Practically speaking, we are not yet ready for a "world money" and Canada trades predominantly with the United States, so that harmonizing on a currency obviously means in this case the U.S. dollar.

> *...from the point of view of promoting trade and investment between Canada and other countries and, in particular, the United States, there would be enormous benefits from having a single currency*

The second reason is that the foreign exchange market is an asset market, analogous to the stock market for example, which is extremely forward looking but whose outcome has immediate and important effects on goods and labour markets in Canada. For example, the depreciation of the Canadian dollar has had an enormous impact in terms of increasing the cost of imported information technology in the last few years. A "floating" or market-determined exchange rate is necessary if a country wishes to set its own monetary policy and inflation rates. But offset against this potential "benefit" are the costs imposed on the economy by the rapid up-and-down movements of the exchange rate. In my opinion, these costs now substantially outweigh the benefits of an independent monetary policy. Small trading countries, such as the Netherlands, gave up using the exchange rate as an instrument of national economic policy a long time ago. It's now time for Canada to do the same.

The world is a long way from achieving free trade in agricultural products. Why can't we let supply and demand work in agricultural markets? What reforms in Canadian and global markets for farm products do you think are needed?

That unfortunately is not an easy question to answer simply because all countries have tended to intervene heavily in their agricultural markets. While the WTO has made some progress in getting commitments to lower agricultural trade barriers, particularly subsidies, remarkably little has been achieved. I think the politics of trade policy is such that it is reasonable to ask a sector such as agriculture to accept lower domestic trade barriers if our trading partners do likewise. But in the absence of a willingness of Europe and the United States to reduce their subsidies, politically why should Canada move first? The problem is compounded because the current agricultural "trade wars" between the European Union and United States have severely depressed the price of a number of products that Canada exports, such as wheat, which in turn has increased the demands for the government to do "something." Agricultural trade policy is more like "disaster relief" these days. Perhaps in the future we can make some progress analogous to that made in the case of industrial products.

Do you think that economics is a good subject in which to major? Why? What else should be studied alongside economics?

Economics is a great major for those who are interested in the forces behind the newspaper headlines, but with an inclination to think systematically about an issue both in terms of looking at the facts and in the application of basic theories to what may appear as a novel problem. It is also extremely useful to anyone interested in a career in business or government. Business, because understanding your market and where it might be going is crucial. Government, for the obvious reason that virtually every government policy must be examined in light of it's economic consequences. If you are interested ultimately in being a professional economist it is very important to get a firm foundation in mathematics and statistics. However, a general knowledge of history and politics is very important—I strongly recommend courses in those areas as well.

Chapter **8**

Utility and Demand

We need water to live. We don't need diamonds for much besides decoration. If the benefits of water far outweigh the benefits of diamonds, why does water cost practically nothing while diamonds are expensive? ◆ When a winter storm cuts off the power supply, the prices of alternative sources of heat, such as firewood, and alternative sources of light, such as candles, rise dramatically. But people buy as much firewood and as many candles as they can get their hands on. Our demand for goods that provide heat and light is price inelastic. But why? ◆ When the CD player was introduced in

Water, Water, Everywhere

1983, it cost more than $1,000, and consumers didn't buy very many. Since then, the price has decreased dramatically, and people are buying CD players in enormous quantities. Our demand for CD players is price elastic. What makes the demand for some things price elastic while the demand for others is price inelastic? ◆ Over the past 20 years, after the effects of inflation are removed, incomes in Canada have increased by 40 percent. Over that same period, expenditure on electricity has increased by more than 60 percent, while expenditure on transportation has increased by less than 20 percent. Thus the proportion of income spent on electricity has increased, and the proportion spent on transportation has decreased. Why, as incomes rise, does the proportion of income spent on some goods rise and that spent on others fall?

◇ In the preceding four chapters, we saw that demand has an important effect on the price of a good. But we did not analyse what exactly shapes a person's demand. This chapter examines household behaviour and its influence on demand. It explains why demand for some goods is elastic and demand for other goods is inelastic. It also explains why the prices of some things, such as diamonds and water, are so out of proportion to their total benefits.

After studying this chapter, you will be able to:

■ Explain the household's budget constraint

■ Define total utility and marginal utility

■ Explain the marginal utility theory of consumer choice

■ Use marginal utility theory to predict the effects of changing prices and incomes

■ Explain the connection between individual demand and market demand

■ Explain the paradox of value

Household Consumption Choices

A HOUSEHOLD'S CONSUMPTION CHOICES ARE determined by many factors, but we can summarize all of these factors under two concepts:

- Budget constraint
- Preferences

Budget Constraint

A household's consumption choices are constrained by the household's income and by the prices of the goods and services it buys. The household has a given amount of income to spend and cannot influence the prices of the goods and services it buys.

A household's *budget line* describes the limits to its consumption choices. Let's consider Lisa's household. Lisa has an income of $30 a month and she plans to buy only two goods—movies and pop. Movies cost $6 each; pop costs $3 a six-pack. If Lisa spends all her income, she will reach the limits to her consumption of movies and pop.

Figure 8.1 illustrates Lisa's possible consumption of movies and pop. Rows *a* through *f* in the table show six possible ways of allocating $30 to these two goods. For example, Lisa can see 2 movies for $12 and buy 6 six-packs for $18 (row *c*). Points *a* through *f* in the figure illustrate the possibilities presented in the table. The line passing through these points is Lisa's budget line.

Lisa's budget line is a constraint on her choices. It marks the boundary between what she can afford and what she cannot afford. She can afford all the points on the line and inside it. She cannot afford the points outside the line. The constraint on her consumption depends on prices of movies and pop and on her income. The constraint changes when the price of movies or pop changes or her income changes.

Preferences

How does Lisa divide her $30 between these two goods? The answer depends on her likes and dislikes—her *preferences*. Economists use the concept of utility to describe preferences. The benefit or satisfaction that a person gets from the consumption of a good or service is called **utility**. Let's now see how we can use the concept of utility to describe preferences.

FIGURE 8.1
Consumption Possibilities

	Movies		Pop	
		Expenditure		**Expenditure**
Possibility	**Quantity**	**(dollars)**	**Six-packs**	**(dollars)**
a	0	0	10	30
b	1	6	8	24
c	2	12	6	18
d	3	18	4	12
e	4	24	2	6
f	5	30	0	0

Rows *a* through *f* in the table show six possible ways that Lisa can allocate $30 to movies and pop. For example, Lisa can buy 2 movies and 6 six-packs (row *c*). The combination in each row costs $30. These possibilities are points *a* through *f* in the figure. The line through those points is a boundary between what Lisa can afford and what she cannot afford. Her choices must lie along the line *af* or inside the orange area.

Total Utility

Total utility is the total benefit that a person gets from the consumption of goods and services. The units in which we measure utility are arbitrary, like the units in which we measure temperature. Total utility depends on the level of consumption—more consumption generally gives more total utility. Table 8.1 shows Lisa's total utility from movies and pop. If she sees no movies, she gets no utility from movies. If

TABLE 8.1
Lisa's Total Utility from Movies and Pop

Movies		Pop	
Quantity per month	Total utility	Six-packs per month	Total utility
0	0	0	0
1	50	1	75
2	88	2	117
3	121	3	153
4	150	4	181
5	175	5	206
6	196	6	225
7	214	7	243
8	229	8	260
9	241	9	276
10	250	10	291
11	256	11	305
12	259	12	318
13	261	13	330
14	262	14	341

she sees 1 movie in a month, she gets 50 units of utility. As the number of movies she sees in a month increases, her total utility increases; if she sees 10 movies a month, she gets 250 units of total utility. The other part of the table shows Lisa's total utility from pop. If she drinks no pop, she gets no utility from pop. As the amount of pop she drinks increases, her total utility increases.

Marginal Utility

Marginal utility is the change in total utility that results from a one-unit increase in the quantity of a good consumed. When the number of six-packs Lisa buys increases from 4 to 5 a month, her total utility from pop increases from 181 units to 206 units. Thus for Lisa, the marginal utility of consuming a fifth six-pack each month is 25 units. The table in Fig. 8.2 shows Lisa's marginal utility for pop. Notice that in the table, marginal utility appears midway between the quantities of pop. It does so because it is the *change* in consumption from 4 to 5 packs that produces the *marginal* utility of 25 units. The table dis-

plays calculations of marginal utility for each number of six-packs that Lisa buys from 1 to 5.

Figure 8.2(a) illustrates the total utility that Lisa gets from pop. The more pop Lisa drinks in a month, the more total utility she gets. Part (b) illustrates her marginal utility. This graph tells us that as Lisa drinks more pop, the marginal utility that she gets from pop decreases. For example, her marginal utility decreases from 75 units for the first six-pack to 42 units from the second and 36 units from the third. We call this decrease in marginal utility as the quantity of the good consumed increases the principle of **diminishing marginal utility**.

Marginal utility is positive but diminishes as the consumption of a good increases. Why does marginal utility have these two features? In Lisa's case, she likes pop, and the more she drinks the better. That's why marginal utility is positive. The benefit that Lisa gets from the last six-pack consumed is her marginal utility. To see why marginal utility diminishes, think about the following two situations: In one, you've been studying all through the day and evening and you've been too busy finishing an assignment to go shopping. A friend drops by with a six-pack of pop. The utility you get from that pop is the marginal utility from one six-pack. In the second situation, you've been on a pop binge. You've been working on an assignment all day but you've guzzled three six-packs while doing so. You are up to your eyeballs in pop. You are happy enough to have one more can. But the thrill that you get from it is not very large. It is the marginal utility of the nineteenth can in a day.

Temperature—An Analogy

Utility is similar to temperature. Both are abstract concepts, and both have units of measurement that are arbitrary. You know when you feel hot, and you know when you feel cold. But you can't *observe* temperature. You can observe water turning to steam if it is hot enough or turning to ice if it is cold enough. And you can construct an instrument, called a thermometer, which can help you to predict when such changes will occur. The scale on the thermometer is what we call temperature. But the units in which we measure temperature are arbitrary. For example, we can accurately predict that when a Celsius thermometer shows a temperature of 0, water will turn to ice. But the units of measurement do not matter because this same event also occurs when a Fahrenheit thermometer shows a temperature of 32.

162

FIGURE 8.2
Total Utility and Marginal Utility

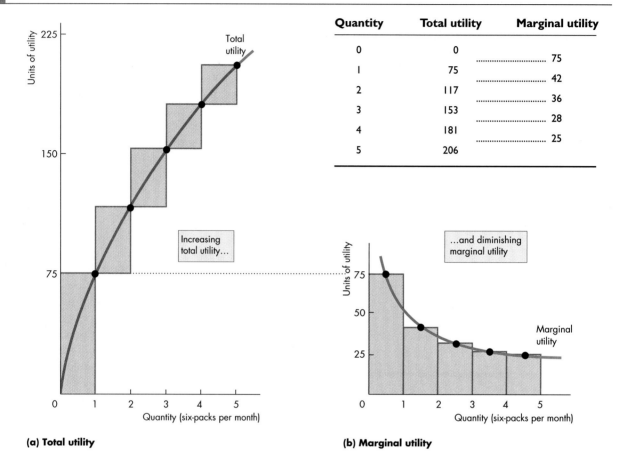

Quantity	Total utility	Marginal utility
0	0	
		75
1	75	
		42
2	117	
		36
3	153	
		28
4	181	
		25
5	206	

(a) Total utility

(b) Marginal utility

The table shows that as Lisa drinks more pop her total utility from pop increases. The table also shows her marginal utility—the change in total utility resulting from the last six-pack that she consumes. Marginal utility declines as consumption increases. The figure graphs Lisa's total utility and marginal

utility from pop. Part (a) shows her total utility. It also shows as a bar the extra total utility she gains from each additional six-pack—her marginal utility. Part (b) shows how Lisa's marginal utility from pop diminishes by placing the bars shown in part (a) side by side as a series of declining steps.

The concept of utility helps us make predictions about consumption choices in much the same way that the concept of temperature helps us make predictions about physical phenomena.

Admittedly marginal utility theory does not enable us to predict how buying plans change with the same precision that a thermometer enables us to predict when water will turn to ice or steam. But the theory provides important insights into buying plans and has some powerful implications, as you are about to discover.

REVIEW QUIZ

- Explain how a consumer's income and the prices of goods limit consumption possibilities.
- What is utility and how do we use the concept of utility to describe a consumer's preferences?
- What is the distinction between total utility and marginal utility?
- What is the key assumption about marginal utility?

Maximizing Utility

A HOUSEHOLD'S INCOME AND THE PRICES THAT it faces limit the household's consumption choices and the household's preferences determine the utility that it can obtain from each consumption possibility. Marginal utility theory assumes that the household chooses the consumption possibility that maximizes its total utility. This assumption of utility maximization is a way of expressing the fundamental economic problem—scarcity. People's wants exceed the resources available to satisfy those wants, so they must make hard choices. In making choices, they try to get the maximum attainable benefit—they try to maximize total utility.

Let's see how Lisa allocates $30 a month between movies and pop to maximize her total utility. We'll continue to assume that movies cost $6 each and pop costs $3 a six-pack.

The Utility-Maximizing Choice

The most direct way to calculate how Lisa spends her income to maximize her total utility is by making a table like Table 8.2. The rows of this table show the affordable combinations of movies and pop that lie along her budget line in Fig. 8.1. The table records three things: first, the number of movies seen and the total utility derived from them (the left-side of the table); second, the number of six-packs consumed and the total utility derived from them (the right-side of the table); and third, the total utility derived from both movies and pop (the centre column).

The first row of Table 8.2 records the situation when Lisa watches no movies and buys 10 six-packs. In this case, Lisa gets no utility from movies and 291 units of total utility from pop. Her total utility from movies and pop (the centre column) is 291 units. The rest of the table is constructed in the same way.

The consumption of movies and pop that maximizes Lisa's total utility is highlighted in the table. When Lisa sees 2 movies and buys 6 six-packs of pop, she gets 313 units of total utility. This is the best Lisa can do, given that she has only $30 to spend and given the prices of movies and six-packs. If she buys 8 six-packs of pop, she can see only 1 movie. She gets 310 units of total utility, 3 less than the maximum attainable. If she sees 3 movies, she can drink only 4 six-packs. She gets 302 units of total utility, 11 less than the maximum attainable.

TABLE 8.2

Lisa's Utility-Maximizing Combination

	Movies		Total utility	Pop	
	Quantity per month	Total utility	from movies and pop	Total utility	Six-packs per month
a	0	0	291	291	10
b	1	50	310	260	8
c	2	88	313	225	6
d	3	121	302	181	4
e	4	150	267	117	2
f	5	175	175	0	0

We've just described Lisa's consumer equilibrium. A **consumer equilibrium** is a situation in which a consumer has allocated all his or her available income in the way that, given the prices of goods and services, maximizes his or her total utility. Lisa's consumer equilibrium is 2 movies and 6 six-packs.

In finding Lisa's consumer equilibrium, we measured her *total* utility from movies and pop. But there is a better way of determining a consumer equilibrium—one that does not involve measuring total utility at all. Let's look at this alternative.

Equalizing Marginal Utility per Dollar Spent

Another way to find out the allocation that maximizes a consumer's total utility is to make the marginal utility per dollar spent on each good equal for all goods. The **marginal utility per dollar spent** is the marginal utility obtained from the last unit of a good consumed divided by the price of the good. For example, Lisa's marginal utility from seeing the first movie is 50 units of utility. The price of a movie is $6, which means that the marginal utility per dollar spent on movies is 50 units divided by $6, or 8.33 units of utility per dollar.

Total utility is maximized when all the consumer's available income is spent and when the marginal utility per dollar spent is equal for all goods.

Lisa maximizes total utility when she spends all her income and consumes movies and pop such that

$$\frac{\text{Marginal utility}}{\text{Price of a movie}} = \frac{\text{Marginal utility}}{\text{Price of pop}}.$$

Call the marginal utility from movies MU_m, the marginal utility from pop MU_p, the price of a movie P_m, and the price of pop P_p. Then Lisa maximizes her utility when she spends all her income and when

$$\frac{MU_m}{P_m} = \frac{MU_p}{P_p}.$$

Let's use this formula to find Lisa's utility-maximizing consumption choice. Table 8.3 sets out Lisa's marginal utilities (which are calculated from Table 8.1) and her marginal utility per dollar spent on each good. For example, in row b, Lisa's marginal utility from movies is 50 units, and because movies cost $6 each, her marginal utility per dollar spent on movies is 8.33 units per dollar (50 units divided by $6). Each row exhausts Lisa's income of $30. You can see that Lisa's marginal utility per dollar spent on each good, like marginal utility itself, decreases as more of the good is consumed.

Lisa maximizes her total utility when the marginal utility per dollar spent on movies is equal to the marginal utility per dollar spent on pop—possibility c. Lisa consumes 2 movies and 6 six-packs.

Figure 8.3 shows why the rule "equalize marginal utility per dollar spent on all goods" works. Suppose that instead of consuming 2 movies and 6 six-packs (possibility c), Lisa consumes 1 movie and 8 six-packs (possibility b). She then gets 8.33 units of utility per dollar spent on movies and 5.67 units per dollar spent on pop. Lisa can increase her total utility by buying less pop and seeing more movies. If she spends less on pop and more on movies, her total utility from pop decreases by 5.67 units per dollar and her total utility from movies increases by 8.33 units per dollar. Her total utility increases by 2.66 units per dollar.

TABLE 8.3

Equalizing Marginal Utilities per Dollar Spent

	Movies ($6 each)			Pop ($3 per six-pack)		
	Quantity	Marginal utility	Marginal utility per dollar spent	Six-packs	Marginal utility	Marginal utility per dollar spent
a	0	0		10	15	5.00
b	1	50	8.33	8	17	5.67
c	2	38	6.33	6	19	6.33
d	3	33	5.50	4	28	9.33
e	4	29	4.83	2	42	14.00
f	5	25	4.17	0	0	

FIGURE 8.3

Equalizing Marginal Utilities per Dollar Spent

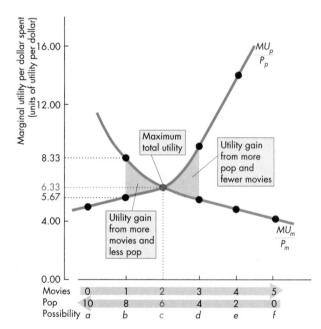

If Lisa consumes 1 movie and 8 six-packs (possibility b), she gets 8.33 units of utility from the last dollar spent on movies and 5.67 units of utility from the last dollar spent on pop. She can get more total utility by seeing one more movie. If she consumes 4 six-packs and 3 movies (possibility d), she gets 5.50 units of utility from the last dollar spent on movies and 9.33 units of utility from the last dollar spent on pop. She can increase her total utility by seeing one fewer movie. When Lisa's marginal utility per dollar spent on both goods is equal, her total utility is maximized.

Or suppose that Lisa consumes 3 movies and 4 six-packs (possibility *d*). In this situation, her marginal utility per dollar spent on movies (5.50) is less than her marginal utility per dollar spent on pop (9.33). Lisa can now increase her total utility by spending less on movies and more on pop.

The Power of Marginal Analysis The method we've just used to find Lisa's utility-maximizing choice of movies and pop is an example of the power of marginal analysis. By comparing the marginal gain from having more of one good with the marginal loss from having less of another good, Lisa is able to ensure that she gets the maximum attainable utility.

In the example, Lisa consumes at the point at which the marginal utility per dollar spent on movies and pop are equal. Because we buy goods and services in indivisible lumps, the numbers don't always work out so precisely. But the basic approach always works.

The rule to follow is very simple: If the marginal utility per dollar spent on movies exceeds the marginal utility per dollar spent on pop, see more movies and buy less pop; if the marginal utility per dollar spent on pop exceeds the marginal utility per dollar spent on movies, buy more pop and see fewer movies.

More generally, if the marginal gain from an action exceeds the marginal loss, take the action. You have met this principle before and you will meet it time and again in your study of economics. And you will find yourself using it when you make your own economic choices, especially when you must make a big decision.

Units of Utility In calculating Lisa's utility-maximizing choice in Table 8.3 and Fig. 8.3, we have not used the concept of total utility at all. All our calculations use marginal utility and price. By making the marginal utility per dollar spent equal for both goods, we know that Lisa maximizes her total utility.

This way of viewing maximum utility is important; it means that the units in which utility is measured do not matter. We could double or halve all the numbers measuring utility, or multiply them by any other positive number, or square them, or take their square roots. None of these transformations of the units used to measure utility makes any difference to the outcome. It is in this respect that utility is analogous to temperature. Our prediction about the freezing of water does not depend on the temperature scale; our prediction about the household's consumption choice does not depend on the units of utility.

R E V I E W   Q U I Z

- What is Lisa's goal when she chooses the quantities of movies and pop to consume?
- What are the two conditions that are met if a consumer is maximizing utility?
- Explain why equalizing the marginal utility of each good does *not* maximize utility.
- Explain why equalizing the marginal utility per dollar spent on each good *does* maximize utility.

Predictions of Marginal Utility Theory

LET'S NOW USE MARGINAL UTILITY THEORY TO make some predictions. What happens to Lisa's consumption of movies and pop when their prices change and when her income changes?

To work out the effect of a change in price or income on the consumption choice: First, determine the combinations of movies and pop that just exhaust the new income at the new prices. Second, calculate the new marginal utilities per dollar spent. Third, determine the combinations that make the marginal utilities per dollar spent on movies and pop equal.

A Fall in the Price of Movies

Suppose that the price of a movie falls from $6 to $3. The rows of Table 8.4 show the combinations of movies and pop that exactly exhaust Lisa's $30 of income when movies cost $3 each and pop costs $3 a six-pack. Lisa's preferences do not change when prices change, so her marginal utility schedule remains the same as before. Now divide her marginal utility from movies by $3 to get the marginal utility per dollar spent on movies.

To find how Lisa responds to the fall in the price of a movie compare her new utility-maximizing choice (Table 8.4) with her original choice (Table 8.3). Lisa sees more movies (up from 2 to 5 a month) and drinks less pop (down from 6 to 5 six-packs a month). That is, Lisa *substitutes* movies for pop. Figure 8.4 shows these effects. The fall in the price of a movie produces a movement along Lisa's demand curve for movies (part a) and shifts her demand curve for pop (part b).

TABLE 8.4

How a Change in Price of Movies Affects Lisa's Choices

Movies ($3 each)		Pop ($3 per six-pack)	
Quantity	Marginal utility per dollar spent	Six-packs	Marginal utility per dollar spent
0		10	5.00
1	16.67	9	5.33
2	**12.67**	8	5.67
3	11.00	7	6.00
4	9.67	**6**	**6.33**
5	8.33	5	8.33
6	7.00	4	9.33
7	6.00	3	12.00
8	5.00	2	14.00
9	4.00	1	25.00
10	3.00	0	

FIGURE 8.4

A Fall in the Price of Movies

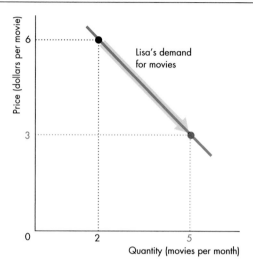

Lisa's demand for movies

(a) Movies

A Rise in the Price of Pop

Now suppose that the price of pop rises from $3 to $6 a six-pack. The rows of Table 8.5 show the combinations of movies and pop that exactly exhaust Lisa's $30 of income when movies cost $3 each and pop costs $6 a six-pack. Lisa's preferences don't change when the price of pop changes. Now divide Lisa's marginal utility from pop by $6 to get her marginal utility per dollar spent on pop.

To find the effect of the rise in the price of pop on Lisa's utility-maximizing choice compare her new choice (Table 8.5) with her previous choice (Table 8.4). When the price of pop increases, Lisa drinks less pop (down from 5 to 2 six-packs a month) and sees more movies (up from 5 to 6 a month). That is, Lisa *substitutes* movies for pop. Figure 8.5 shows these effects. The rise in the price of pop produces a movement along Lisa's demand curve for pop (part a) and shifts her demand curve for movies (part b).

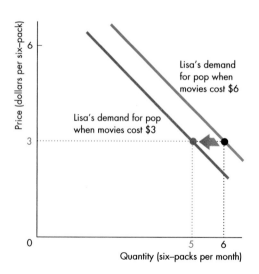

Lisa's demand for pop when movies cost $6

Lisa's demand for pop when movies cost $3

(b) Pop

When the price of a movie falls and the price of pop remains the same, the quantity of movies demanded by Lisa increases and, in part (a), Lisa moves along her demand curve for movies. Also, Lisa decreases her demand for pop and, in part (b), her demand curve for pop shifts leftward.

TABLE 8.5

How a Change in Price of Pop Affects Lisa's Choices

Movies ($3 each)		Pop ($6 per six-pack)	
Quantity	Marginal utility per dollar spent	Six-packs	Marginal utility per dollar spent
0		5	4.17
2	12.67	4	4.67
4	9.67	3	6.00
6	7.00	2	7.00
8	5.00	1	12.50
10	3.00	0	

Marginal utility theory predicts these two results:

1. When the price of a good rises, the quantity demanded of that good decreases.
2. If the price of one good rises, the demand for another good that can serve as a substitute increases.

Does this sound familiar? It should. These predictions of marginal utility theory correspond to the assumptions that we made about demand in Chapter 4. There we *assumed* that the demand curve for a good sloped downward, and we *assumed* that a rise in the price of a substitute increases demand.

You've now seen that marginal utility theory predicts how the quantities demanded respond to price changes. The theory helps us to understand the shape and the position of a demand curve and how the demand curve for one good shifts when the price of another good changes.

Marginal utility theory also helps us to understand how demand changes when income changes. Let's study the effects of a change in income on demand.

FIGURE 8.5

A Rise in the Price of Pop

(a) Pop

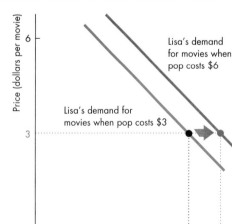

(b) Movies

When the price of pop rises and the price of a movie remains the same, the quantity of pop demanded by Lisa decreases and, in part (a), Lisa moves along her demand curve for pop.

Also, Lisa's demand for movies increases and, in part (b), her demand curve for movies shifts rightward.

A Rise in Income

Let's suppose that Lisa's income increases to $42 a month and that a movie costs $3 and a six-pack costs $3. We saw in Table 8.4 that with these prices and with an income of $30 a month, Lisa sees 5 movies and drinks 5 six-packs a month. We want to compare this choice of movies and pop with Lisa's choice when her income is $42. Table 8.6 shows the calculations needed to make the comparison. With $42, Lisa can see 14 movies a month and buy no pop or buy 14 six-packs a month and see no movies or choose any combination of the two goods in the rows of the table. We calculate the marginal utility per dollar spent in exactly the same way as we did before

and find the quantities at which the marginal utilities per dollar spent on movies and on pop are equal. With an income of $42, the marginal utility per dollar spent on each good is equal when Lisa sees 7 movies and drinks 7 six-packs of pop a month.

By comparing this situation with that in Table 8.4, we see that with an additional $12 a month, Lisa buys 2 more six-packs and sees 2 more movies a month. Lisa's response arises from her preferences, as described by her marginal utilities. Different preferences would produce different quantitative responses. With a larger income, the consumer always buys more of a *normal* good and less of an *inferior* good. For Lisa, pop and movies are normal goods. When her income increases, Lisa buys more of both goods.

You have now completed your study of the marginal utility theory of a household's consumption choices. Table 8.7 summarizes the key assumptions, implications, and predictions of the theory.

TABLE 8.6

Lisa's Choices with an Income of $42 a Month

Movies ($3 each)		Pop ($3 per six-pack)	
Quantity	Marginal utility per dollar spent	Six-packs	Marginal utility per dollar spent
0		14	3.67
1	16.67	13	4.00
2	12.67	12	4.33
3	11.00	11	4.67
4	9.67	10	5.00
5	**8.33**	9	5.33
6	7.00	8	5.67
7	6.00	7	6.00
8	5.00	6	6.33
9	4.00	5	**8.33**
10	3.00	4	9.33
11	2.00	3	12.00
12	1.00	2	14.00
13	0.67	1	25.00
14	0.33	0	

TABLE 8.7

Marginal Utility Theory

Assumptions

■ A consumer derives utility from the goods consumed.

■ Each additional unit of consumption yields additional total utility; marginal utility is positive.

■ As the quantity of a good consumed increases, marginal utility decreases.

■ A consumer's aim is to maximize total utility.

Implication

■ Total utility is maximized when all the available income is spent and when the marginal utility per dollar spent is equal for all goods.

Predictions

■ Other things remaining the same, the higher the price of a good, the smaller is the quantity bought (the law of demand).

■ The higher the price of a good, the greater is the quantity bought of substitutes for that good.

■ The larger the consumer's income, the greater is the quantity demanded of normal goods.

Individual Demand and Market Demand

Marginal utility theory explains how an individual household spends its income and enables us to derive an individual household's demand curve. In earlier chapters, we have been using *market* demand curves. We can derive a *market* demand curve from individual demand curves. Let's see how.

The relationship between the total quantity demanded of a good and its price is called **market demand**. The market demand curve is what you studied in Chapter 4. The relationship between the quantity demanded of a good by a single individual and its price is called *individual demand*.

Figure 8.6 illustrates the relationship between individual demand and market demand. In this example, Lisa and Chuck are the only people. The market demand is the total demand of Lisa and Chuck. At $3 a movie, Lisa demands 5 movies a month and Chuck demands 2, so the total quantity demanded by the market is 7 movies a month. Lisa's demand curve for movies in part (a) and Chuck's in part (b) sum *horizontally* to give the market demand curve in part (c).

The market demand curve is the horizontal sum of the individual demand curves and is formed by adding the quantities demanded by each individual at each price.

Because marginal utility theory predicts that individual demand curves slope downward, it also predicts that market demand curves slope downward.

FIGURE 8.6

Individual and Market Demand Curves

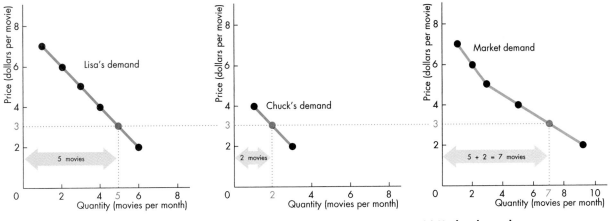

(a) Lisa's demand   **(b) Chuck's demand**   **(c) Market demand**

Price	Quantity of movies demanded		
(dollars per movie)	Lisa	Chuck	Market
7	1	0	1
6	2	0	2
5	3	0	3
4	4	1	5
3	5	2	7
2	6	3	9

The table and figure illustrate how the quantity of movies demanded varies as the price of a movie varies. In the table, the market demand is the sum of the individual demands. For example, at a price of $3, Lisa demands 5 movies and Chuck demands 2 movies, so the total quantity demanded in the market is 7 movies. In the figure, the market demand curve is the horizontal sum of the individual demand curves. Thus when the price is $3, the market demand curve shows that the quantity demanded is 7 movies, the sum of the quantities demanded by Lisa and Chuck.

Marginal Utility and the Real World

Marginal utility theory can be used to answer a wide range of questions about the real world. The theory sheds light on why the demand for CD players is price elastic while the demand for oil is price inelastic and why the demand for electricity is income elastic while the demand for transportation is income inelastic. Elasticities are determined by preferences. The feature of our preferences that determines elasticity is the step size with which marginal utility declines—the steepness of the marginal utility steps in Fig. 8.2(b).

If marginal utility declines in big steps, a small change in the quantity bought brings a big change in the marginal utility per dollar spent. So it takes a big change in price or income to bring a small change in the quantity demanded—demand is inelastic. Conversely, if marginal utility diminishes slowly, even a large change in the quantity bought brings a small change in the marginal utility per dollar spent. So it takes only a small price change to bring a large quantity change—demand is elastic.

But marginal utility theory can do much more than explain households' *consumption* choices. It can be used to explain *all* the choices made by households. One of these choices, the allocation of time between work in the home, office, or factory and leisure, is the theme of Probing the Ideas on pp. 196–197.

REVIEW QUIZ

■ When the price of a good falls and the prices of other goods and a consumer's income remain the same, explain what happens to the consumption of the good whose price has fallen and to the consumption of other goods.

■ Elaborate your answer to the previous question by using demand curves. For which good is there a change in demand and for which is there a change in the quantity demanded?

■ If a consumer's income increases and if all goods are normal goods, how does the quantity bought of each good change?

We're going to end this chapter by returning to a recurring theme throughout your study of economics: the concept of efficiency and the distinction between price and value.

Efficiency, Price, and Value

MARGINAL UTILITY THEORY HELPS US TO DEEPEN our understanding of the concept of efficiency and also helps us to see more clearly the distinction between *value* and *price*. Let's see how.

Consumer Efficiency and Consumer Surplus

When Lisa allocates her limited budget to maximize utility, she is using her resources efficiently. Any other allocation of her budget wastes some resources.

But when Lisa has allocated her limited budget to maximize utility, she is *on* her demand curve for each good. A demand curve is a description of the quantity demanded at each price when utility is maximized. When we studied efficiency in Chapter 6, we learned that value equals marginal benefit and that a demand curve is also a willingness-to-pay curve. It tells us a consumer's *marginal benefit*—the benefit from consuming an additional unit of a good. You can now give the idea of marginal benefit a deeper meaning:

Marginal benefit is the maximum price a consumer is willing to pay for an extra unit of a good or service when utility is maximized.

The Paradox of Value

For centuries, philosophers have been puzzled by a paradox that we raised at the start of this chapter. Water, which is essential to life itself, costs little, but diamonds, which are useless compared to water, are expensive. Why? Adam Smith tried to solve this paradox. But not until the theory of marginal utility had been developed could anyone give a satisfactory answer.

You can solve this puzzle by distinguishing between *total* utility and *marginal* utility. The total utility that we get from water is enormous. But remember, the more we consume of something, the smaller is its marginal utility. We use so much water that its marginal utility—the benefit we get from one more glass of water—diminishes to a small value. Diamonds, on the other hand, have a small total utility relative to water, but because we buy few diamonds, they have a high marginal utility. When a household has maximized its total utility, it has allocated its budget in the way that makes the marginal utility per dollar spent equal for all goods.

FIGURE 8.7

The Paradox of Value

(a) Water

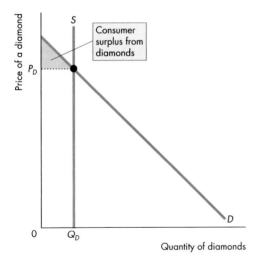

(b) Diamonds

Part (a) shows the demand for water, D, and the supply of water, S. The supply is (assumed to be) perfectly elastic at the price P_W. At this price, the quantity of water consumed is Q_W and the consumer surplus from water is the large green triangle. Part (b) shows the demand for diamonds, D, and the supply of diamonds, S. The supply is (assumed to be) perfectly inelastic at the quantity Q_D. At this quantity, the price of diamonds is P_D and the consumer surplus from diamonds is the small green triangle. Water is valuable—has a large consumer surplus—but cheap. Diamonds are less valuable than water—have a smaller consumer surplus—but are expensive.

That is, the marginal utility from a good divided by the price of the good is equal for all goods. This equality of marginal utilities per dollar spent holds true for diamonds and water: Diamonds have a high price and a high marginal utility. Water has a low price and a low marginal utility. When the high marginal utility of diamonds is divided by the high price of diamonds, the result is a number that equals the low marginal utility of water divided by the low price of water. The marginal utility per dollar spent is the same for diamonds as for water.

Another way to think about the paradox of value uses *consumer surplus*. Figure 8.7 explains the paradox of value by using this idea. The supply of water (part a) is perfectly elastic at price P_W, so the quantity of water consumed is Q_W and the consumer surplus from water is the large green area. The supply of diamonds (part b) is perfectly inelastic at quantity Q_D, so the price of diamonds is P_D and the consumer surplus from diamonds is the small green area. Water is cheap but brings a large consumer surplus, while diamonds are expensive but bring a small consumer surplus.

REVIEW QUIZ

- Explain why, along a demand curve, a consumer's choices are efficient.
- Explain the paradox of value and provide an example (different from diamonds and water).
- Does water or diamonds have the greater marginal utility? Does water or diamonds have the greater total utility? Does water or diamonds have the greater consumer surplus?

◇ You have now completed your study of the marginal utility theory. And you've seen how the theory can be used to explain our real-world consumption choices. You can see the theory in action once again in *Reading Between the Lines* on pp. 172–173, where it is used to interpret some recent trends in choices about coffee consumption.

The next chapter presents an alternative theory of household behaviour. To help you see the connection between the two theories of consumer behaviour, we'll continue with the same example. We'll meet Lisa again and discover another way of understanding how she gets the most out of her $30 a month.

The Utility of Coffee

VANCOUVER SUN, JULY 25, 1998

Cashing in on coffee craze

As a rule, Jerry Wennes starts his day at Bean Around the World Coffees on West 10th in Point Grey with a steaming double cafe mocha—two shots of espresso, chocolate syrup and steamed milk, topped with a dollop of foam and garnished with chocolate sprinkles—a bowlful of pleasure for $3.10.

"I call it my energy stop," says the owner of Tap-Roots Ltd., a plumbing company in the Dunbar area. "I don't take coffee at home. The coffee shop is my neighborhood pub where I meet people."

Wennes, who drinks decaffeinated coffee on doctor's orders, can easily spend $10 a day on his favourite brew for an annual total of $3,650, including weekends and holidays.

Based on that figure, going out for coffee is the fifth largest household expense after taxes, shelter, food and transportation, according to Statistics Canada data.

Wennes is not alone in his passion for premium-priced coffee. A growing number of coffee lovers seems willing to shell out $3 and more for specialty coffees and companion confections, creating a market estimated to be worth at least $100 million in the Greater Vancouver area.

And this lucrative and expanding pool of coffee consumers has drawn giant Starbucks Coffee Co. of Seattle, with 80 outlets in the region, into pitched battle with more than 150 independent coffee houses scattered hither and yon. ...

The success of speciality coffee houses is due partly to people treating themselves to small indulgences despite money being tight, said Peter Hume of Hume Consulting.

"After the extravagant spending of the late 1980s followed by the recession in 1991, consumers became more price conscious, as evidenced by the success of big-box retailers," Hume says.

"But people are now prepared to go into Starbucks with a friend and drop $10 on a couple of cappuccinos and a biscotti. It's become very social." ...

Essence of the Story

■ For some people, going out for coffee is the fifth highest household expense after taxes, shelter, food, and transportation.

■ The price of a cup of specialty coffee is approximately $3.

■ Drinking coffee in a coffee house has become a popular outing.

■ Jerry Wennes spends $10 a day on coffee. Assume that a coffee costs $2.50 and that Jerry drinks 4 cups a day. (Some coffee costs more than $2.50 and some less, but $2.50 is an average price.)

■ Figure 1 shows Jerry's total utility and Fig. 2 shows his marginal utility of coffee and of meals. His marginal utility of meals is greater than his marginal utility of coffee for small quantities but diminishes more quickly. Beyond three meals a day, Jerry is more interested in coffee than in food.

■ Suppose that Jerry has $20 a day to spend on coffee and meals and that meals cost $5 each.

■ Jerry maximized utility by equalizing the marginal utility per dollar spent on coffee and meals. The table (top half) shows that he consumes 4 coffees and 2 meals a day. Figure 3 shows Jerry's marginal utility per dollar spent and his utility-maximizing decision.

■ But Jerry's liking for coffee doesn't mean that he's not sensitive to prices. Suppose the price of an average cup of coffee increases to $5.

■ The table (bottom half) shows that Jerry now decreases his consumption of coffee to 1 cup a day and consumes 3 meals a day.

Figure 1 Total utility

Figure 2 Marginal utility

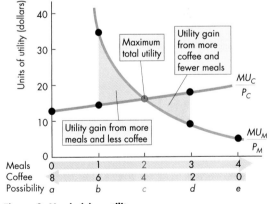

Figure 3 Maximizing utility

Jerry Wennes' Consumption Choices

	Meals ($5 each)			**Coffee** ($2.50 per cup)		
	Quantity	Marginal utility	Marginal utility per dollar	Cups	Marginal utility	Marginal utility per dollar
a	0			8	32	12.8
b	1	175	35	6	36	14.4
c	2	80	16	4	40	16.0
d	3	45	9	2	45	18.0
e	4	25	5	0		

	Meals ($5 each)			**Coffee** ($5.00 per cup)		
	Quantity	Marginal utility	Marginal utility per dollar	Cups	Marginal utility	Marginal utility per dollar
a'	0			4	38	7.6
b'	1	175	35	3	40	8.0
c'	2	80	16	2	42	8.4
d'	3	45	9	1	45	9.0
e'	4	25	5	0	50	10.0

S U M M A R Y

Key Points

Household Consumption Choices (pp. 160–162)

- A household's choices are determined by its consumption possibilities and preferences.
- A household's consumption possibilities are constrained by its income and by prices. Some combinations of goods are affordable, and some are not affordable.
- A household's preferences can be described by marginal utility.
- The key assumption of marginal utility theory is that the marginal utility of a good or service decreases as consumption of the good or service increases.

Maximizing Utility (pp. 163–165)

- Marginal utility theory assumes that people buy the affordable combination of goods and services that maximizes total utility.
- Total utility is maximized when all the available income is spent and when the marginal utility per dollar spent on each good is equal.
- If the marginal utility per dollar spent on good *A* exceeds that on good *B*, the consumer can increase total utility by buying more of good *A* and less of good *B*.

Predictions of Marginal Utility Theory (pp. 165–170)

- Marginal utility theory predicts the law of demand. That is, other things remaining the same, the higher the price of a good, the smaller is the quantity demanded of that good.
- Marginal utility theory also predicts that other things remaining the same, the higher the income of a consumer, the larger is the quantity demanded of a normal good.
- Market demand is the sum of all individual demands, and the market demand curve is found by summing horizontally all the individual demand curves.

Efficiency, Price, and Value (pp. 170–171)

- When a consumer maximizes utility, he or she is using resources efficiently.
- Marginal utility theory resolves the paradox of the relative value of water and diamonds.
- When we talk loosely about value, we are thinking of *total* utility or consumer surplus. But price is related to *marginal* utility.
- Water, which we consume in large amounts, has a high total utility and a large consumer surplus but a low marginal utility and a low price.
- Diamonds, which we consume in small amounts, have a low total utility and a small consumer surplus but a high marginal utility and a high price.

Key Figures and Table

Key Terms

P R O B L E M S

⌨ *1. Jason enjoys rock CDs and spy novels and spends $60 a month on them. The following table shows the utility he gets from each good:

Quantity per month	Utility from rock CDs	Utility from spy novels
1	60	20
2	110	38
3	150	53
4	180	64
5	200	70
6	206	75

a. Draw graphs showing Jason's utility from rock CDs and from spy novels.
b. Compare the two utility graphs. Can you say anything about Jason's preferences?
c. Draw graphs that show Jason's marginal utility from rock CDs and from spy novels.
d. What do the two marginal utility graphs tell you about Jason's preferences?
e. If rock CDs and spy novels both cost $10 each, how does Jason spend the $60?

2. Mary enjoys classical CDs and travel books and spends $50 a month on them. The following table shows the utility she gets from each good:

Quantity per month	Utility from classical CDs	Utility from travel books
1	30	30
2	40	38
3	48	44
4	54	46
5	58	47

a. Draw graphs showing Mary's utility from classical CDs and from travel books.
b. Compare the two utility graphs. Can you say anything about Mary's preferences?
c. Draw graphs that show Mary's marginal utility from classical CDs and from travel books.
d. What do the two marginal utility graphs tell you about Mary's preferences?
e. If a classical CD and a travel book cost $10 each, how does Mary spend the $50 a month?

⌨ *3. Max enjoys windsurfing and snorkelling. He obtains the following utility from each of these sports:

Hours per day	Utility from windsurfing	Utility from snorkelling
1	120	40
2	220	76
3	300	106
4	360	128
5	400	140
6	412	150
7	422	158

Max has $35 to spend and he can spend as much time as he likes on his leisure pursuits. Windsurfing equipment rents for $10 an hour, and snorkelling equipment rents for $5 an hour.
a. Draw a graph that shows Max's budget line.
b. How long does he spend windsurfing and how long does he spend snorkelling?

4. Rob enjoys rock concerts and the opera. The table shows the utility he gets from each activity:

Concerts per month	Utility from rock concerts	Utility from operas
1	100	60
2	180	110
3	240	150
4	280	180
5	300	200
6	310	210

Rob has $100 a month to spend on concerts. A rock concert ticket is $20, and an opera ticket is $10.
a. Draw a graph that shows Rob's budget line.
b. How many rock concerts and how many operas does he attend?

⌨ *5. In problem 3, Max's sister gives him $20 to spend on his leisure pursuits, so he now has $55.
a. Draw a graph that shows Max's budget line.
b. How many hours does Max choose to windsurf and how many hours does he choose to snorkel now that he has $55 to spend?

6. In problem 4, if Rob's uncle gives him $30 to spend on concert tickets, he now has $130.
   a. Draw a graph that shows Rob's budget line.
   b. How many rock concerts and how many operas does he now attend?

*7. In problem 5, if windsurfing equipment now rents for $5 an hour, how long does Max windsurf and how long does he snorkel?

8. In problem 4, if the price of a rock concert decreases to $10, how many rock concerts and operas will Rob attend?

*9. Max takes a Club Med vacation, the cost of which includes unlimited sports activities. There is no extra charge for equipment. If Max windsurfs and snorkels for 6 hours a day, how many hours does he windsurf and how many hours does he snorkel?

10. Rob wins a lottery and has more than enough money to satisfy his desires for rock concerts and opera. He decides that he would like to see 5 concerts each month. How many rock concerts and how many operas does he now attend?

⌨ *11. Shirley's and Dan's demand schedules for popcorn are:

Price (cents per carton)	Quantity demanded by	
	Shirley	Dan
	(cartons per week)	
10	12	6
30	9	5
50	6	4
70	3	3
90	1	2

If Shirley and Dan are the only two individuals, what is the market demand for popcorn?

12. Ben's and Jerry's demand schedules for ice cream cones are:

Price (dollars per cone)	Quantity demanded by	
	Ben	Jerry
	(cones per week)	
1.00	8	10
1.30	7	8
1.50	6	6
1.70	5	4
1.90	4	2

If Ben and Jerry are the only two individuals, what is the market demand for ice cream cones?

CRITICAL THINKING

1. Study *Reading Between the Lines* on pp. 172–173 on coffee consumption in Canada and then answer the following questions:
   a. What are the facts about coffee consumption reported in the news article?
   b. How can we account for the consumption of a large quantity of coffee using marginal utility theory?
   c. What does marginal utility theory predict will happen to coffee consumption if the price of coffee rises sharply?
   d. What does marginal utility theory predict will happen to coffee consumption as people's incomes rise?
   e. Why do you think special coffee varieties have become more popular in recent years? Can marginal utility theory account for this trend?

2. In recent years, bottled water, fruit drinks, and sports drinks—new age drinks—have become popular. Use the marginal utility theory you have learned in this chapter to explain the rise in popularity of new age drinks.

3. Use the links on the Parkin-Bade Web site and read what Henry Schimberg, CEO of Coca-Cola Enterprises, says about the market for bottled water in North America. Use the marginal utility theory you have learned in this chapter to interpret and explain Mr. Schimberg's remarks about the bottled water market.

4. Smoking is banned on all airline flights in Canada and on most international flights. Use marginal utility theory to explain:
   a. What effect this ban has on the utility of smokers.
   b. How you expect the ban to influence the decisions of smokers.
   c. What effect this ban has on the utility of non-smokers.
   d. How you expect the ban to influence the decisions of non-smokers.

   In your answer to this question, consider decisions about smoking, flying, and the willingness to pay for a flight.

Possibilities, Preferences, and Choices

Like the continents floating on the earth's mantle, our spending patterns change steadily over time. On such subterranean movements, business empires rise and fall. Goods such as home videos and microwave popcorn now appear on our shopping lists, while 78 rpm phonograph records and horse-drawn carriages have disappeared. Miniskirts appear, disappear, and reappear in cycles of fashion.

Subterranean Movements

◆ But the glittering surface of our consumption obscures deeper and slower changes in how we spend. In the last few years, we've seen a proliferation of gourmet food shops and designer clothing boutiques. Yet we spend a smaller percentage of our income today on food and clothing than we did in 1950. At the same time, the percentage of our income spent on housing, transportation, and recreation has grown steadily. Why does consumer spending change over the years? How do people react to changes in income and changes in the prices of the things they buy? ◆ Similar subterranean movements govern the way we spend our time. For example, the average workweek has fallen steadily from 70 hours a week in the nineteenth century to 35 hours a week today. Although the average workweek is now much shorter than it once was, far more people now have jobs. This change has been especially dramatic for women, who are much more likely to work outside the home than they were in previous generations. Why has the average workweek declined? And why do more women work?

⬦ We're going to study a model of choice that predicts the effects of changes in prices and incomes on what people buy and how much work they do.

After studying this chapter, you will be able to:

■ Calculate and graph a household's budget line

■ Work out how the budget line changes when prices or income changes

■ Make a map of preferences by using indifference curves

■ Explain the choices that households make

■ Predict the effects of price and income changes on consumption choices

■ Predict the effects of wage changes on work-leisure choices

Consumption Possibilities

CONSUMPTION CHOICES ARE LIMITED BY INCOME and by prices. A household has a given amount of income to spend and cannot influence the prices of the goods and services it buys. A household's **budget line** describes the limits to its consumption choices.

Let's look at Lisa's budget line.[1] Lisa has an income of $30 a month to spend. She buys two goods—movies and pop. Movies cost $6 each; pop costs $3 for a six-pack. Figure 9.1 shows alternative affordable ways for Lisa to consume movies and pop. Row *a* says that she can buy 10 six-packs of pop and see no movies, a combination of movies and pop that exhausts her monthly income of $30. Row *f* says that Lisa can watch 5 movies and drink no pop—another combination that exhausts the $30 available. Each of the other rows in the table also exhausts Lisa's income. (Check that each of the other rows costs exactly $30.) The numbers in the table define Lisa's consumption possibilities. We can graph Lisa's consumption possibilities as points *a* through *f* in Fig. 9.1.

Divisible and Indivisible Goods Some goods—called divisible goods—can be bought in any quantity desired. Examples are gasoline and electricity. We can best understand household choice if we suppose that all goods and services are divisible. For example, Lisa can consume a half a movie a month *on the average* by seeing one movie every two months. When we think of goods as being divisible, the consumption possibilities are not just the points *a* through *f* shown in Fig. 9.1, but those points plus all the intermediate points that form the line running from *a* to *f*. Such a line is a budget line.

Lisa's budget line is a constraint on her choices. It marks the boundary between what is affordable and what is unaffordable. She can afford any point on the line and inside it. She cannot afford any point outside the line. The constraint on her consumption depends on prices and her income, and the constraint changes when prices or her income changes. Let's see how by studying the budget equation.

---

[1] If you have studied Chapter 8 on marginal utility theory, you have already met Lisa. This tale of her thirst for pop and zeal for movies will sound familiar to you—up to a point. But in this chapter, we're going to use a different method for representing preferences—one that does not require us to resort to the idea of utility.

FIGURE 9.1

The Budget Line

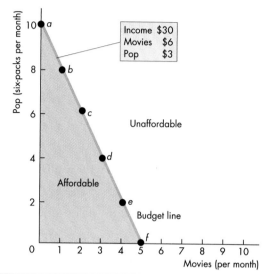

Income	$30
Movies	$6
Pop	$3

Consumption possibility	Movies (per month)	Pop (six-packs per month)
a	0	10
b	1	8
c	2	6
d	3	4
e	4	2
f	5	0

Lisa's budget line shows the boundary between what she can and cannot afford. The rows of the table list Lisa's affordable combinations of movies and pop when her income is $30, the price of pop is $3 a six-pack, and the price of a movie is $6. For example, row *a* tells us that Lisa exhausts her $30 income when she buys 10 six-packs and sees no movies. The figure graphs Lisa's budget line. Points *a* through *f* on the graph represent the rows of the table. For divisible goods, the budget line is the continuous line *af*. To calculate the equation for Lisa's budget line, start with expenditure equal to income:

$$\$3Q_p + \$6Q_m = \$30.$$

Divide by $3 to obtain

$$Q_p + \$2Q_m = 10.$$

Subtract $2Q_m$ from both sides to obtain

$$Q_p = 10 - 2Q_m.$$

The Budget Equation

We can describe the budget line by using a *budget equation*. The budget equation starts with the fact that

$$\text{Expenditure} = \text{Income}.$$

Expenditure is equal to the sum of the price of each good multiplied by the quantity bought. For Lisa,

Expenditure = (Price of pop × Quantity of pop)
            + (Price of movie × Quantity of movies).

Call the price of pop P_p, the quantity of pop Q_p, the price of a movie P_m, the quantity of movies Q_m, and income y. Using these symbols, Lisa's budget equation is

$$P_p Q_p + P_m Q_m = y.$$

Or, using the prices Lisa faces, $3 for a six-pack and $6 for a movie, and Lisa's income, $30, we get

$$\$3 Q_p + \$6 Q_m = \$30.$$

Lisa can choose any quantities of pop (Q_p) and movies (Q_m) that satisfy this equation. To find the relationship between these quantities, first divide both sides of the equation by the price of pop (P_p) to get

$$Q_p + \frac{P_m}{P_p} \times Q_m = \frac{y}{P_p}.$$

Now subtract the term (P_m/P_p) × Q_m from both sides of this equation to give

$$Q_p = \frac{y}{P_p} - \frac{P_m}{P_p} \times Q_m.$$

For Lisa, income (y) is $30, the price of a movie (P_m) is $6, and the price of a six-pack (P_p) is $3. So Lisa must choose the quantities of movies and pop to satisfy the equation

$$Q_p = \frac{\$30}{\$3} - \frac{\$6}{\$3} \times Q_m.$$

or

$$Q_p = 10 - 2 Q_m.$$

To interpret the equation, go back to the budget line of Fig. 9.1 and check that the equation delivers that budget line. First set Q_m equal to zero. In this case, the budget equation tells us that Q_p, the quantity of pop, is y/P_p, which is 10 six-packs. This combination of Q_m and Q_p is the same as that shown in row *a* of the table in Fig. 9.1. Next set Q_m equal to 5. Q_s is now equal to zero (row *f* of the table). Check that you can derive the other rows.

The budget equation contains two variables chosen by the household (Q_m and Q_p) and two variables (y/P_p and P_m/P_p) that the household takes as given. Let's look more closely at these variables.

Real Income A household's **real income** is the household's income expressed not as money but as a quantity of goods the household can afford to buy. Expressed in terms of pop, Lisa's real income is y/P_p. This quantity is the maximum number of six-packs that she can buy. It is equal to her money income divided by the price of pop. Lisa's income is $30 and the price of pop is $3 a six-pack, so her real income in terms of pop is 10 six-packs, which is shown in Fig. 9.1 as the point at which the budget line intersects the y-axis.

Relative Price A **relative price** is the price of one good divided by the price of another good. In Lisa's budget equation, the variable P_m/P_p is the relative price of a movie in terms of pop. For Lisa, P_m is $6 a movie and P_p is $3 a six-pack, so P_m/P_p is equal to 2 six-packs per movie. That is, to see one more movie, Lisa must give up 2 six-packs.

You've just calculated Lisa's opportunity cost of a movie. Recall that the opportunity cost of an action is the best alternative forgone. For Lisa to see 1 more movie a month, she must forgo 2 six-packs. You've also calculated Lisa's opportunity cost of pop. For Lisa to consume 2 more six-packs a month, she must give up seeing 1 movie. So her opportunity cost of 2 six-packs is 1 movie.

The relative price of a movie in terms of pop is the magnitude of the slope of Lisa's budget line. To calculate the slope of the budget line, recall the formula for slope (Chapter 2): Slope equals the change in the variable measured on the y-axis divided by the change in the variable measured on the x-axis as we move along the line. In Lisa's case (Fig. 9.1), the variable measured on the y-axis is the quantity of pop, and the variable measured on the x-axis is the quantity of movies. Along Lisa's budget line, as pop decreases from 10 to 0 six-packs, movies increase from 0 to 5. Therefore the magnitude of the slope of the budget line is 10 six-packs divided by 5 movies, or 2 six-packs per movie. The magnitude of this slope is exactly the same as the relative price we've just calculated. It is also the opportunity cost of a movie.

A Change in Prices When prices change, so does the budget line. The lower the price of the good measured on the horizontal axis, other things

FIGURE 9.2

Changes in Prices and Income

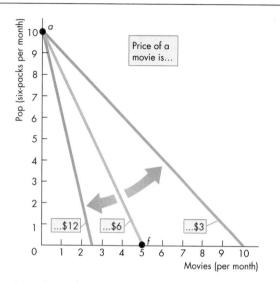

(a) A change in price

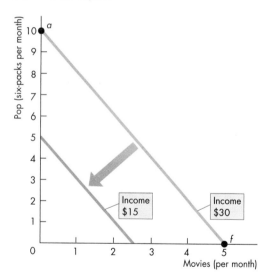

(b) A change in income

In part (a), the price of a movie changes. A fall in the price from $6 to $3 rotates the budget line outward and makes it flatter. A rise in the price from $6 to $12 rotates the budget line inward and makes it steeper.

In part (b), income falls from $30 to $15 while the prices of movies and pop remain constant. The budget line shifts leftward, but its slope does not change.

remaining the same, the flatter is the budget line. For example, if the price of a movie falls from $6 to $3, real income in terms of pop does not change but the relative price of a movie falls. The budget line rotates outward and becomes flatter, as shown in Fig. 9.2(a). The higher the price of the good measured on the horizontal axis, other things remaining the same, the steeper is the budget line. For example, if the price of a movie rises from $6 to $12, the relative price of a movie increases. The budget line rotates inward and becomes steeper as shown in Fig. 9.2(a).

A Change in Income A change in *money income* changes real income but does not change relative prices. The budget line shifts, but its slope does not change. The bigger a household's money income, the bigger is real income and the farther to the right is the budget line. The smaller a household's money income, the smaller is real income and the farther to the left is the budget line. Figure 9.2(b) shows the effect of a change in money income on Lisa's budget line. The initial budget line is the same one that we began with in Fig. 9.1 when Lisa's income is $30. The new budget line shows how much Lisa can consume if her income falls to $15 a month. The two budget lines have the same slope because they have the same relative price. The new budget line is closer to the origin than the initial one because Lisa's real income has decreased.

REVIEW QUIZ

- What does Lisa's budget line show?
- What is Lisa's real income in terms of movies?
- What is Lisa's opportunity cost of pop?
- If a household has an income of $40 and consumes only bus rides at $4 each and magazines of $2 each, what is the equation that describes its budget line?
- If the price of one good changes, what happens to the relative price and to the slope of the budget line?
- If a household's money income changes and no prices change, what happens to the household's real income and its budget line?

We've studied the limits to what a household can consume. Let's now learn how we can describe preferences and make a map that contains a lot of information about a household's preferences.

Preferences and Indifference Curves

YOU ARE GOING TO DISCOVER A VERY NEAT IDEA—
that of drawing a map of a person's preferences. A
preference map is based on the intuitively appealing
assumption that people can sort all the possible combinations of goods into three groups: preferred, not
preferred, and indifferent. To make this idea more
concrete, let's ask Lisa to tell us how she ranks various
combinations of movies and pop.

Figure 9.3(a) shows part of Lisa's answer. She tells
us that she currently consumes 2 movies and 6 six-
packs a month at point c. She then lists all the combinations of movies and pop that she says are equally
acceptable to her as her current consumption. When
we plot these combinations of movies and pop we get
the green curve in Fig. 9.3(a). This curve is the key
element in a map of preferences and is called an
indifference curve.

An **indifference curve** is a line that shows combinations of goods among which a consumer is *indifferent*. The indifference curve in Fig. 9.3(a) tells us
that Lisa is just as happy to consume 2 movies and 6
six-packs a month at point c as to consume the combination of movies and pop at point g or at any other
point along the curve.

Lisa also says that she prefers all the combinations of movies and pop in the yellow area above the
indifference curve in Fig. 9.3(a) to any combination
on the indifference curve. And she prefers any combination on the indifference curve to any combination
in the grey area below the indifference curve.

The indifference curve in Fig. 9.3(a) is just one
of a whole family of such curves. This indifference
curve appears again in Fig. 9.3(b) labelled I_1. The
curves labelled I_0 and I_2 are two other indifference
curves. Lisa prefers any point on indifference curve I_2
to any point on indifference curve I_1, and she prefers
any point on I_1 to any point on I_0. We refer to I_2 as
being a higher indifference curve than I_1, and I_1 as
being higher than I_0.

A preference map is a series of indifference curves
that resemble the contour lines on a map. By looking
at the shape of the contour lines on a map, we can
draw conclusions about the terrain. Similarly, by
looking at the shape of indifference curves, we can
draw conclusions about a person's preferences.

Let's learn how to "read" a preference map.

FIGURE 9.3

A Preference Map

(a) An indifference curve

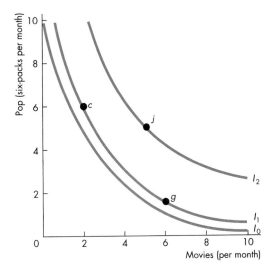

(b) Lisa's preference map

In part (a), Lisa consumes 6 six-packs of pop and 2 movies a
month at point c. She is indifferent between all the points on
the green indifference curve such as c and g. She prefers any
point above the indifference curve (yellow area) to any point
on it, and she prefers any point on the indifference curve to
any point below it (grey area). A preference map is a number
of indifference curves. Part (b) shows three—I_0, I_1, and I_2—that
are part of Lisa's preference map. She prefers point j to point c
or g, so she prefers any point on I_2 to any point on I_1.

Marginal Rate of Substitution

The **marginal rate of substitution** (*MRS*) is the rate at which a person will give up good *y* (the good measured on the *y*-axis) to get one additional unit of good *x* (the good measured on the *x*-axis) and at the same time remain indifferent (remain on the same indifference curve). The marginal rate of substitution is measured by the magnitude of the slope of an indifference curve.

- If the indifference curve is *steep*, the marginal rate of substitution is *high*. The person is willing to give up a large quantity of good *y* to get a small quantity of good *x* while remaining indifferent.

- If the indifference curve is *flat*, the marginal rate of substitution is *low*. The person is willing to give up only a small amount of good *y* to get a large amount of good *x* to remain indifferent.

Figure 9.4 shows you how to calculate the marginal rate of substitution. Suppose that Lisa consumes 6 six-packs and 2 movies at point *c* on indifference curve I_1. Her marginal rate of substitution is calculated by measuring the magnitude of the slope of the indifference curve at point *c*. To measure this magnitude, place a straight line against, or tangent to, the indifference curve at point *c*. Along that line, as pop consumption decreases by 10 six-packs, movie consumption increases by 5. So at point *c*, Lisa is willing to give up pop for movies at the rate of 2 six-packs per movie. Her marginal rate of substitution is 2.

Now, suppose that Lisa consumes 6 movies and 1.5 six-packs at point *g* in Fig. 9.4. Her marginal rate of substitution is now measured by the slope of the indifference curve at point *g*. That slope is the same as the slope of the tangent to the indifference curve at point *g*. Here, as pop consumption decreases by 4.5 six-packs, movie consumption increases by 9. So at point *g*, Lisa is willing to give up pop for movies at the rate of 1/2 six-pack per movie. Her marginal rate of substitution is 1/2.

As Lisa's consumption of movies increases and her consumption of pop decreases, her marginal rate of substitution diminishes. Diminishing marginal rate of substitution is the key assumption of consumer theory. The assumption of **diminishing marginal rate of substitution** is a general tendency for the marginal rate of substitution to diminish as the consumer moves along an indifference curve, increasing consumption of the good measured on the *x*-axis and decreasing consumption of the good measured on the *y*-axis.

FIGURE 9.4
The Marginal Rate of Substitution

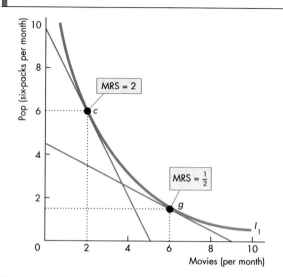

The magnitude of the slope of an indifference curve is called the marginal rate of substitution (MRS). The red line at point *c* tells us that Lisa is willing to give up 10 six-packs to see 5 movies. Her marginal rate of substitution at *c* is 10 divided by 5, which equals 2. The red line at point *g* tells us that Lisa is willing to give up 4.5 six-packs to see 9 movies. Her marginal rate of substitution at *g* is 4.5 divided by 9, which equals 1/2.

Your Own Diminishing Marginal Rate of Substitution   You may be able to appreciate why we assume the principle of a diminishing marginal rate of substitution by thinking about your own preferences. Imagine that in a week, you consume 10 six-packs of pop and no movies. Most likely you are willing to give up a lot of pop so that you can go to the movies just once. But now imagine that in a week, you consume 1 six-pack and 6 movies. Most likely you will now not be willing to give up much pop to see a seventh movie. As a general rule, the greater the number of movies you see, the smaller is the quantity of pop you are willing to give up to see one additional movie.

The shape of a person's indifference curves incorporates the principle of the diminishing marginal rate of substitution because the curves are bowed towards the origin. The tightness of the bend of an indifference curve tells us how willing a person is to substitute one good for another while remaining indifferent. Let's look at some examples that make this point clear.

Degree of Substitutability

Most of us would not regard movies and pop as being close substitutes for each other. We probably have some fairly clear ideas about how many movies we want to see each month and how many cans of pop we want to drink. Nevertheless, to some degree, we are willing to substitute between these two goods. No matter how big a pop freak you are, there is surely some increase in the number of movies you can see that will compensate you for being deprived of a can of pop. Similarly, no matter how addicted you are to the movies, surely some number of cans of pop will compensate you for being deprived of seeing one movie. A person's indifference curves for movies and pop might look something like those shown in Fig. 9.5(a).

Close Substitutes Some goods substitute so easily for each other that most of us do not even notice which we are consuming. The different brands of personal computers are an example. So long as it has an "Intel inside" and runs Windows, most of us don't care whether our PC is a Dell, a Compaq, a Toshiba, or any of a dozen other brands. The same holds true for marker pens. Most of us don't care whether we use a marker pen from the campus bookstore or the local supermarket. When two goods are perfect substitutes for each other, their indifference curves are straight lines that slope downward, as Fig. 9.5(b) illustrates. The marginal rate of substitution is constant.

Complements Some goods cannot substitute for each other at all. Instead they are complements. The complements in Fig. 9.5(c) are left and right running shoes. Indifference curves of perfect complements are L-shaped. One left running shoe and one right running shoe are as good as one left shoe and two right ones. Having two of each is preferred to having one of each, but having two of one and one of the other is no better than having one of each.

The extreme cases of perfect substitutes and perfect complements shown here don't often happen in reality. They do, however, illustrate that the shape of the indifference curve shows the degree of substitutability between two goods. The more perfectly

---

FIGURE 9.5

The Degree of Substitutability

(a) Ordinary goods

(b) Perfect substitutes

(c) Perfect complements

The shape of the indifference curves reveals the degree of substitutability between two goods. Part (a) shows the indifference curves for two ordinary goods: movies and pop. To consume less pop and remain indifferent, one must see more movies. The number of movies that compensates for a reduction in pop increases as less pop is consumed. Part (b) shows the indifference curves for two perfect substitutes. For the consumer to remain indifferent, one fewer marker pen from the local supermarket must be replaced by one extra marker pen from the campus bookstore. Part (c) shows two perfect complements—goods that cannot be substituted for each other at all. Having two left running shoes with one right running shoe is no better than having one of each. But having two of each is preferred to having one of each.

"With the pork I'd recommend an Alsatian white or a Coke."

substitutable the two goods, the more nearly are their indifference curves straight lines and the less quickly does the marginal rate of substitution fall. Poor substitutes for each other have tightly curved indifference curves, approaching the shape of those shown in Fig. 9.5(c).

As you can see in the cartoon, according to the waiter's preferences, Coke and Alsatian white wine are perfect substitutes and each is a complement with pork. We hope the customers agree with him.

R E V I E W   Q U I Z

■ What is an indifference curve and how does an indifference map show preferences?
■ Why does an indifference curve slope downward and why is it bowed towards the origin?
■ What do we call the magnitude of the slope of an indifference curve?
■ What is the key assumption about a consumer's marginal rate of substitution?

The two components of the model of household choice are now in place: the budget line and the preference map. We will now use these components to work out the household's choice and to predict how choices change when prices and income change.

Predicting Consumer Behaviour

WE ARE NOW GOING TO PREDICT THE QUANTITIES of movies and pop that Lisa *chooses* to buy. Figure 9.6 shows Lisa's budget line from Fig. 9.1 and her indifference curves from Fig. 9.3(b). We assume that Lisa consumes at her best affordable point, which is 2 movies and 6 six-packs—at point *c*. Here, Lisa

■ Is on her budget line
■ Is on her highest attainable indifference curve
■ Has a marginal rate of substitution between movies and pop equal to the relative price of movies and pop.

For every point inside the budget line, such as point *i*, there are points *on* the budget line that Lisa

FIGURE 9.6
The Best Affordable Point

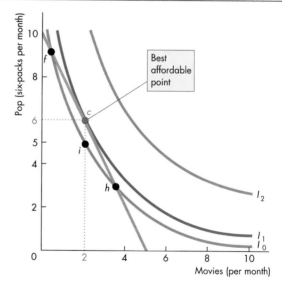

Lisa's best affordable point is *c*. At that point, she is on her budget line and also on the highest attainable indifference curve. At a point such as *h*, Lisa is willing to give up more movies in exchange for pop than she has to. She can move to point *i*, which is just as good as point *h* and have some unspent income. She can spend that income and move to *c*, a point that she prefers to point *i*.

prefers. For example, she prefers all the points on the budget line between *f* and *h* to point *i*. So she chooses a point on the budget line.

Every point on the budget line lies on an indifference curve. For example, point *h* lies on the indifference curve I_0. At point *h*, Lisa's marginal rate of substitution is less than the relative price. Lisa is willing to give up more movies in exchange for pop than the budget line says she must give up. So she moves along her budget line from *h* towards *c*. As she does so, she passes through a number of indifference curves (not shown in the figure) located between indifference curves I_0 and I_1. All of these indifference curves are higher than I_0, and therefore Lisa prefers any point on them to point *h*. But when Lisa gets to point *c*, she is on the highest attainable indifference curve. If she keeps moving along the budget line, she starts to encounter indifference curves that are lower than I_1. So Lisa chooses point *c*.

At the chosen point, the marginal rate of substitution (the magnitude of the slope of the indifference curve) equals the relative price (the magnitude of the slope of the budget line).

Let's use this model of household choice to predict the effects on consumption of changes in prices and income. We'll begin by studying the effect of a change in price.

A Change in Price

The effect of a change in price on the quantity of a good consumed is called the **price effect**. We will use Fig. 9.7(a) to work out the price effect of a fall in the price of a movie. We start with movies costing $6 each, pop costing $3 a six-pack, and Lisa's income at $30 a month. In this situation, she consumes 6 six-packs and 2 movies a month at point *c*.

Now suppose that the price of a movie falls to $3. With a lower price of a movie, the budget line rotates outward and becomes flatter. (Check back with Fig. 9.2 (a) for a refresher on how a price change affects the budget line.) The new budget line is the dark orange one in Fig. 9.7(a).

Lisa's best affordable point is now point *j*, where she consumes 5 movies and 5 six-packs of pop. Lisa drinks less pop and watches more movies now that movies cost less. She cuts her pop consumption from 6 to 5 six-packs and increases the number of movies she sees from 2 to 5 a month. Lisa substitutes movies for pop when the price of a movie falls and the price of pop and her income remain constant.

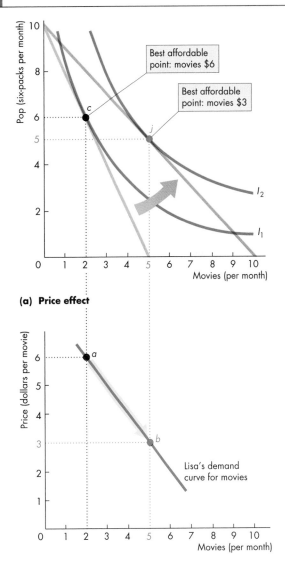

FIGURE 9.7

Price Effect and Demand Curve

(a) Price effect

(b) Demand curve

Initially, Lisa consumes at point *c* (part a). If the price of a movie falls from $6 to $3, she consumes at point *j*. The move from *c* to *j* is the price effect.

Part (b) shows Lisa's demand curve for movies. At a price of $6 a movie, Lisa sees 2 movies a month, at point *a*. At a price of $3 a movie, she sees 5 movies a month, at point *b*. Lisa's demand curve traces out her best affordable quantity of movies as the price of a movie varies.

The Demand Curve   In Chapter 4, we asserted that the demand curve slopes downward. We can now derive a demand curve from a consumer's budget line and indifference curves. By doing so, we can see that the law of demand and the downward-sloping demand curve are consequences of the consumer's choosing his or her best affordable combination of goods.

To derive Lisa's demand curve for movies, lower the price of a movie and find her best affordable point at different prices. We've just done this for two movie prices in Fig. 9.7(a). Figure 9.7(b) highlights these two prices and two points that lie on Lisa's demand curve for movies. When the price of a movie is $6, Lisa sees 2 movies a month at point *a*. When the price falls to $3, she increases the number of movies she sees to 5 a month at point *b*. The demand curve is made up of these two points plus all the other points that tell us Lisa's best affordable consumption of movies at each movie price, given the price of pop and Lisa's income. As you can see, Lisa's demand curve for movies slopes downward. The lower the price of a movie, the more movies she watches each month. This is the law of demand.

Next, let's examine how Lisa changes her consumption of movies and pop when her income changes.

A Change in Income

The effect of a change in income on consumption is called the **income effect**. Let's work out the income effect by examining how consumption changes when income changes and prices remain constant. Figure 9.8(a) shows the income effect when Lisa's income falls. With an income of $30 and with a movie costing $3 and pop $3 a six-pack, she consumes at point *j*—5 movies and 5 six-packs. If her income falls to $21, she consumes at point *k*—consuming 4 movies and 3 six-packs. When Lisa's income falls, she consumes less of both goods. Movies and pop are normal goods.

The Demand Curve and the Income Effect
A change in income leads to a shift in the demand curve, as shown in Fig. 9.8(b). With an income of $30 and a movie costing $3, Lisa's demand curve is D_0, the same curve as in Fig. 9.7. But when her income falls to $21, Lisa sees only 4 movies at point *c*. With less income, she plans to see fewer movies at each price, so her demand curve shifts leftward to D_1.

FIGURE 9.8

Income Effect and Change in Demand

(a) Income effect

(b) Demand curve

A change in income shifts the budget line and changes the best affordable point and changes consumption. In part (a), when Lisa's income decreases from $30 to $21, she consumes less of both movies and pop. In part (b), Lisa's demand curve for movies when her income is $30 is D_0. When Lisa's income decreases to $21, her demand curve for movies shifts leftward to D_1. Lisa's demand for movies decreases because she now sees fewer movies at each price.

Substitution Effect and Income Effect

For a normal good, a fall in price *always* increases the quantity bought. We can prove this assertion by dividing the price effect into two parts:

- Substitution effect
- Income effect.

Figure 9.9(a) shows the price effect, and Fig. 9.9(b) divides the price effect into its two parts.

Substitution Effect The **substitution effect** is the effect of a change in price on the quantity bought when the consumer (hypothetically) remains indifferent between the original and the new situation. To work out Lisa's substitution effect, we imagine that when the price of a movie falls, Lisa's income also falls by an amount that leaves her on the same indifference curve as before.

Figure 9.9 shows the substitution effect. When the price of a movie falls from $6 to $3, suppose (hypothetically) that Lisa's income falls to $21. What's special about $21? It is the income that is just enough, at the new price of a movie, to keep Lisa's best affordable point on the *same* indifference curve as her original consumption point *c*. Lisa's budget line in this situation is the light orange line shown in Fig. 9.9(b). With the new price of a movie and the new smaller income, Lisa's best affordable point is *k* on indifference curve I_1. The move from *c* to *k* isolates the substitution effect of the price change. The substitution effect of the fall in the price of a movie is an increase in the consumption of movies from 2 to 4. The direction of the substitution effect never varies: When the relative price of a good falls, the consumer substitutes more of that good for the other good.

Income Effect To calculate the substitution effect, we gave Lisa a $9 pay cut. Now let's give Lisa her $9 back. The $9 increase in income shifts Lisa's budget line outward, as shown in Fig. 9.9(b). The slope of the budget line does not change because both prices remain constant. This change in Lisa's budget line is similar to the one illustrated in Fig. 9.8. As Lisa's budget line shifts outward, her best affordable point becomes *j* on indifference curve I_2. The move from *k* to *j* isolates the income effect of the price change. The income effect of the fall in the price of a movie is the increase in the quantity of movies seen from 4 to 5. As Lisa's income increases, she increases her consumption of movies. For

FIGURE 9.9

Substitution Effect and Income Effect

(a) Price effect

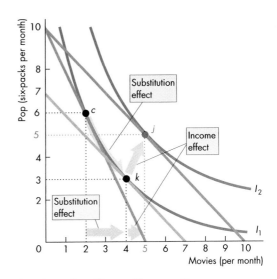

(b) Substitution effect and income effect

The price effect in part (a) can be separated into a substitution effect and an income effect in part (b). To isolate the substitution effect, we confront Lisa with the new price but keep her on her original indifference curve, I_1. The substitution effect is the move from *c* to *k*. To isolate the income effect, we confront Lisa with the new price of movies but increase her income so that she can move from the original indifference curve, I_1, to the new one, I_2. The income effect is the move from *k* to *j*.

Lisa, a movie is a normal good. For a normal good, the income effect reinforces the substitution effect.

Inferior Goods The example that we have just studied is that of a change in the price of a normal good. The effect of a change in the price of an inferior good is different. Recall that an inferior good is one whose consumption decreases as income increases. For an inferior good, the income effect is negative. Thus for an inferior good, a lower price does not always lead to an increase in the quantity demanded. The lower price has a substitution effect that increases the quantity demanded. But the lower price also has a negative income effect that reduces the demand for the inferior good. Thus the income effect offsets the substitution effect to some degree. If the negative income effect exceeded the positive substitution effect, the demand curve would slope upward. This case does not appear to occur in the real world.

Back to the Facts

We started this chapter by observing how consumer spending has changed over the years. The indifference curve model explains those changes. Spending patterns are determined by best affordable choices. Changes in prices and incomes change the best affordable choice and change consumption patterns.

R E V I E W   Q U I Z

- When a consumer chooses the combination of goods and services to buy, what is she or he trying to achieve?
- Can you explain the conditions that are met when a consumer has found the best affordable combination of goods to buy? (Use the terms "budget line," "marginal rate of substitution," and "relative price" in your explanation.)
- If the price of a normal good falls, what happens to the quantity demanded of that good?
- Into what two effects can we divide the effect of a price change?
- For a normal good, does the income effect reinforce the substitution effect or does it partly offset the substitution effect?

The model of household choice can explain many other household choices. Let's look at one of them.

Work-Leisure Choices

HOUSEHOLDS MAKE MANY CHOICES OTHER THAN those about how to spend their income on the various goods and services available. We can use the model of consumer choice to understand many other household choices. Some of these choices are discussed on pp. 158–159. Here we'll study a key choice: How much labour to supply.

Labour Supply

Every week, we allocate our 168 hours between paid work—called *labour*—and all other activities—called *leisure*. How do we decide how to allocate our time between labour and leisure? We can answer this question by using the theory of household choice.

The more hours we spend on *leisure*, the smaller is our income. The relationship between leisure and income is described by an *income-time budget line*. Figure 9.10(a) shows Lisa's income-time budget line. If Lisa devotes the entire week to leisure—168 hours—she has no income and is at point z. By supplying labour in exchange for a wage, she can convert hours into income along the income-time budget line. The slope of that line is determined by the hourly wage rate. If the wage rate is $5 an hour, Lisa faces the flattest budget line. If the wage rate is $10 an hour, she faces the middle budget line. And if the wage rate is $15 an hour, she faces the steepest budget line.

Lisa buys leisure by not supplying labour and by forgoing income. The opportunity cost of an hour of leisure is the hourly wage rate forgone.

Figure 9.10(a) also shows Lisa's indifference curves for income and leisure. Lisa chooses her best attainable point. This choice of income and time allocation is just like her choice of movies and pop. She gets onto the highest possible indifference curve by making her marginal rate of substitution between income and leisure equal to her wage rate. Lisa's choice depends on the wage rate she can earn. At a wage rate of $5 an hour, Lisa chooses point a and works 20 hours a week (168 minus 148) for an income of $100 a week. At a wage rate of $10 an hour, she chooses point b and works 35 hours a week (168 minus 133) for an income of $350 a week. And at a wage rate of $15 an hour, she chooses point c and works 30 hours a week (168 minus 138) for an income of $450 a week.

The Labour Supply Curve

Figure 9.10(b) shows Lisa's labour supply curve. This curve shows that as the wage rate increases from $5 an hour to $10 an hour, Lisa increases the quantity of labour supplied from 20 hours a week to 35 hours a week. But when the wage rate increases to $15 an hour, she decreases her quantity of labour supplied to 30 hours a week.

Lisa's supply of labour is similar to that described for the economy as a whole at the beginning of this chapter. As wage rates have increased, work hours have decreased. At first, this pattern seems puzzling. We've seen that the hourly wage rate is the opportunity cost of leisure. So a higher wage rate means a higher opportunity cost of leisure. This fact on its own leads to a decrease in leisure and an increase in work hours. But instead, we've cut our work hours. Why? Because our incomes have increased. As the wage rate increases, incomes increase, so people demand more of all normal goods. Leisure is a normal good, so as incomes increase, people demand more leisure.

The higher wage rate has both a *substitution effect* and an *income effect*. The higher wage rate increases the opportunity cost of leisure and so leads to a substitution effect away from leisure. And the higher wage rate increases income and so leads to an income effect towards more leisure.

This theory of household choice can explain the facts about work patterns described at the beginning of this chapter. First, it can explain why the average workweek has fallen steadily from 70 hours in the nineteenth century to 35 hours today. The reason is that as wage rates have increased, although people have substituted work for leisure, they have also decided to use their higher incomes in part to consume more leisure. Second, the theory can explain why more women now have jobs in the labour market. The reason is that increases in their wage rates and improvements in their job opportunities have led to a substitution effect away from working at home and towards working in the labour market.

◆ This theory of household choice can also explain trends in the furniture industry, as you can see in *Reading Between the Lines* on pp. 190–191. In the chapters that follow, we're going to study the choices made by firms. We'll see how, in the pursuit of profit, firms make choices that determine the supply of goods and services and the demand for productive resources.

FIGURE 9.10

The Supply of Labour

(a) Time allocation decision

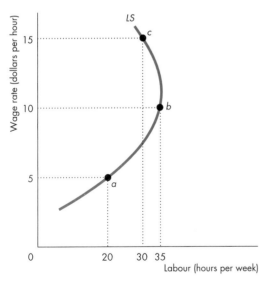

(b) Labour supply curve

In part (a), at a wage rate of $5 an hour, Lisa takes 148 hours of leisure and works 20 hours a week at point *a*. If the wage rate increases from $5 to $10, she decreases her leisure to 133 hours and increases her work to 35 hours a week at point *b*. But if the wage rate increases from $10 to $15, Lisa *increases* her leisure to 138 hours and *decreases* her work to 30 hours a week at point *c*. Part (b) shows Lisa's labour supply curve. Points *a*, *b*, and *c* on the supply curve correspond to Lisa's choices on her income-time budget line in part (a).

Indifference Curves for Furniture

THE CALGARY HERALD, JULY 25, 1998

Inflatable furniture returns with a BANG!

It's back. It's bold. And it's blown up.

"It" is inflatable furniture and home fashions made from this heavy-duty PVC vinyl are one of the hottest retro decorating crazes around these days. "It's an exciting product to have," says Maureen Reid, of Reid Stationers, which is selling plenty of these perky plastics. ...

People apparently have an instant reaction to the inflatable furniture when they see the Day-Glo decorating pieces.

"They notice and comment on it right away," says Seabird Urtasun, owner of the Land and Sea store in Eau Claire Market. "Everybody want(s) to interact with it—squeezing it, sitting and bouncing on it. And you can't miss it, because of the colors."...

"We have the sofas and chairs, which are the bigger pieces, but also lots of other things to go with them," says Urtasun. "There are love seats, side tables, pillows, a chaise, and even a mirror." ...

This fun and funky furniture trend is taking furniture sales by storm with local retailers saying they can't stock it fast enough because it interests such a wide segment of the population. ...

Of course, it...has a lot of appeal to the younger set. ...

"The new generation is really taking to it," says Reid. "People are buying it for teens' rooms as gifts and young adults like the look of it and the fact it's affordable as a first furniture purchase. It's also practical if you move a lot."

Prices for inflatable furniture range from about $100 to $150 for a sofa, while chairs, which can pack down to the size of a large book and weigh less than a pound, can be found for around $65 to $100. ...

They're tough, but comfy, say air furniture aficionados, while also being easy to move around. ...

So if you're looking for lots of quirkiness and comfort, and want a piece that's super-in right now, inflatable furniture is in your future. Just add air.

Essence of the Story

■ Teens and young adults like the look and the price of inflatable furniture.

■ Retailers say that inflatable furniture also appeals to other segments of the population.

■ Many types of traditional furniture such as sofas, chairs, and tables are available as inflatable furniture.

Lisa, a student, is furnishing her first apartment. She can choose traditional furniture or inflatable furniture.

Figure 1 shows Lisa's indifference curves for inflatable furniture and conventional furniture.

The magnitude of the slope of an indifference curve is the marginal rate of substitution (*MRS*).

The marginal rate of substitution tells how many units of conventional furniture Lisa is willing to give up to gain more inflatable furniture while remaining on the same indifference curve.

If Lisa consumes on indifference curve I_0, at point *a*, she is willing to give up one unit of conventional furniture to get one additional unit of inflatable furniture—the move from *a* to *b*.

If Lisa consumes on indifference curve I_1, at point *c*, she is willing to give up less than one unit of conventional furniture to get one additional unit of inflatable furniture—the move from *c* to *d*.

And if Lisa consumes on indifference curve I_2, at point *e*, she is willing to give up almost no conventional furniture to get one additional unit of inflatable furniture—the move from *e* to *f*.

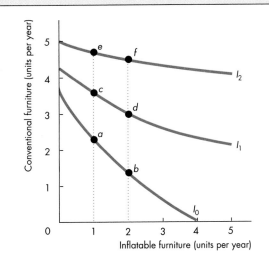

Figure 1 Preferences for furniture

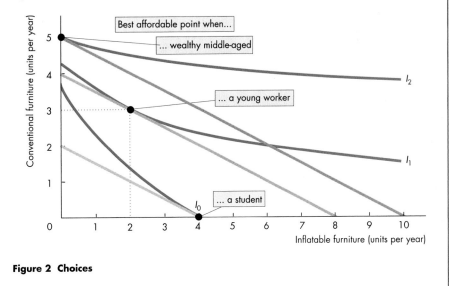

Figure 2 Choices

Figure 2 shows Lisa's choices.

While she is a student, she has a low income and the highest indifference curve she can reach is I_0. Her best affordable point is at 4 units of inflatable furniture and no conventional furniture.

But Lisa knows that when she is a twenty-something–year-old worker, she will have an income that enables her to reach indifference curve I_1. Her preferences don't change but her best affordable point will then be at 2 units of inflatable furniture and 3 units of conventional furniture.

And Lisa knows that when she is a wealthy middle-aged woman, she will have an income that enables her to reach indifference curve I_2. Her best affordable point will then be at no units of inflatable furniture and 5 units of conventional furniture.

For Lisa, inflatable furniture is an *inferior good*. As her income increases, her consumption of inflatable furniture decreases.

SUMMARY

Key Points

Consumption Possibilities (pp. 178–180)

- The budget line is the boundary between what the household can and cannot afford given its income and the prices of goods.
- The point at which the budget line intersects the *y*-axis is the household's real income in terms of the good measured on that axis.
- The magnitude of the slope of the budget line is the relative price of the good measured on the *x*-axis in terms of the good measured on the *y*-axis.
- A change in price changes the slope of the budget line. A change in income shifts the budget line but does not change its slope.

Preferences and Indifference Curves (pp. 181–184)

- A consumer's preferences can be represented by indifference curves. An indifference curve joins all the combinations of goods among which the consumer is indifferent.
- A consumer prefers any point above an indifference curve to any point on it and any point on an indifference curve to any point below it.
- The magnitude of the slope of an indifference curve is called the marginal rate of substitution.
- The marginal rate of substitution diminishes as consumption of the good measured on the *y*-axis decreases and consumption of the good measured on the *x*-axis increases.

Predicting Consumer Behaviour (pp. 184–188)

- A household consumes at its best affordable point. This point is on the budget line and on the highest attainable indifference curve and has a marginal rate of substitution equal to relative price.
- The effect of a price change (the price effect) can be divided into a substitution effect and an income effect.
- The substitution effect is the effect of a change in price on the quantity bought when the consumer (hypothetically) remains indifferent between the original and the new situation.

- The substitution effect always results in an increase in consumption of the good whose relative price has fallen.
- The income effect is the effect of a change in income on consumption.
- For a normal good, the income effect reinforces the substitution effect. For an inferior good, the income effect works in the opposite direction to the substitution effect.

Work-Leisure Choices (pp. 188–189)

- The indifference curve model of household choice enables us to understand how a household allocates its time between work and leisure.
- Work hours have decreased and leisure hours have increased because the income effect on the demand for leisure has been greater than the substitution effect.

Key Figures

Key Terms

PROBLEMS

*1. Sara has an income of $12 a week. Popcorn costs $3 a bag, and cola costs $3 a can.
 a. What is Sara's real income in terms of cola?
 b. What is her real income in terms of popcorn?
 c. What is the relative price of cola in terms of popcorn?
 d. What is the opportunity cost of a can of cola?
 e. Calculate the equation for Sara's budget line (placing bags of popcorn on the left side).
 f. Draw a graph of Sara's budget line with cola on the x-axis.
 g. In part (f), what is the slope of Sara's budget line? What does it represent?

2. Marc has an income of $20 per week. CDs cost $10 each and root beer costs $5 a can.
 a. What is Marc's real income in terms of root beer?
 b. What is his real income in terms of CDs?
 c. What is the relative price of root beer in terms of CDs?
 d. What is the opportunity cost of a can of root beer?
 e. Calculate the equation for Marc's budget line (placing cans of root beer on the left side).
 f. Draw a graph of Marc's budget line with CDs on the x-axis.
 g. In part (f), what is the slope of Marc's budget line? What does it represent?

*3. Sara's income and the prices she faces are the same as in problem 1. The figure illustrates Sara's preferences.

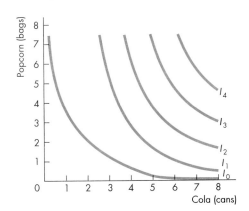

 a. What are the quantities of popcorn and cola that Sara buys?
 b. What is Sara's marginal rate of substitution of popcorn for cola at the point at which she consumes?

4. Marc's income and the prices he faces are the same as in problem 2. The figure illustrates his preferences.

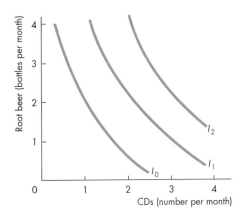

 a. What are the quantities of root beer and CDs that Marc buys?
 b. What is Marc's marginal rate of substitution of CDs for root beer at the point at which he consumes?

*5. Now suppose that in the situation described in problem 3, the price of cola falls to $1.50 per can and the price of popcorn and Sara's income remain constant.
 a. Find the new quantities of cola and popcorn that Sara buys.
 b. Find two points on Sara's demand curve for cola.
 c. Find the substitution effect of the price change.
 d. Find the income effect of the price change.
 e. Is cola a normal good or an inferior good for Sara?
 f. Is popcorn a normal good or an inferior good for Sara?

6. Now suppose that in problem 4, the price of a CD falls to $5 and the price of root beer and income remain constant.
 a. Find the new quantities of root beer and CDs that Marc buys.
 b. Find two points on Marc's demand curve for CDs.

c. Find the substitution effect of the price change.

d. Find the income effect of the price change.

e. Are CDs a normal good or an inferior good for Marc?

f. Is root beer a normal good or an inferior good for Marc?

*7. Pam buys cookies and comic books. The price of a cookie is $1 and the price of a comic book is $2. Each month, Pam spends all of her income and buys 30 cookies and 5 comic books. Next month, the price of a cookie will fall to 50¢ and the price of a comic book will rise to $5. Assume that Pam's preference map is similar to that in Fig. 9.3(b).

a. Will Pam be able to buy 30 cookies and 5 comic books next month?

b. Will Pam want to buy 30 cookies and 5 comic books?

c. Which situation does Pam prefer: cookies at $1 and comic books at $2 or cookies at 50¢ and comic books at $3?

d. If Pam changes the quantities that she buys, which good will she buy more of and which less of?

e. When the prices change next month, will there be an income effect and a substitution effect at work or just one of them?

8. Pete buys tuna and golf balls. The price of tuna is $2 a can, and the price of golf balls is $1 each. Each month, Pete spends all of his income and buys 20 cans of tuna and 40 golf balls. Next month, the price of tuna will rise to $3 a can and the price of golf balls will fall to 50¢ each. Assume that Pete's preference map is similar to that in Fig. 9.3(b).

a. Will Pete be able to buy 20 cans of tuna and 40 golf balls next month?

b. Will Pete want to buy 20 cans of tuna and 40 golf balls?

c. Which situation does Pete prefer: tuna at $2 a can and golf balls at $1 each or tuna at $3 a can and golf balls at 50¢ each?

d. If Pete changes the quantities that he buys, which good will he buy more of and which less of?

e. When the prices change next month, will there be an income effect and a substitution effect at work or just one of them?

CRITICAL THINKING

1. Study *Reading Between the Lines* about inflatable furniture on pp. 190–191, and then answer the following questions.

a. What types of people buy inflatable furniture?

b. Do the people who buy inflatable furniture have different preferences from the people who buy conventional furniture?

c. Use the indifference curve model to explain the buying patterns that we observe in the markets for inflatable and conventional furniture.

d. What do you predict would happen to the quantity of inflatable furniture bought if its price fell with the price of conventional furniture remaining the same?

2. The GST is a tax on goods and services. It replaced a federal sales tax on goods only. When we replaced the federal sales tax with the GST:

a. What happened to the relative price of CDs and haircuts?

b. What happened to the budget line showing the quantities of CDs and haircuts you can afford to buy?

c. How would you change your purchases of CDs and haircuts?

d. Which type of tax is best for the consumer and why?

e. Show in a figure the changes and show the substitution effect and the income effect.

3. Jim spends his income on apartment rent, food, clothing, and vacations. He gets a pay raise from $3,000 a month to $4,000 a month. At the same time, airfares and other vacation-related costs increase by 50 percent while other prices remain the same.

a. How do you think Jim will change his spending pattern as a result of the changes in his income and prices?

b. Can you say whether Jim is better off or worse off in his new situation?

c. If *all* prices rise by 50 percent, how does Jim change his purchases? Is he better off or worse off? Why?

d. Show in a figure the changes in Jim's choices that the change in income and changes in prices induce.

Understanding Households' Choices

The powerful forces of demand and supply shape the fortunes of families, businesses, nations, and empires in the same unrelenting way that the tides and winds shape rocks and coastlines. You saw in Chapters 4 through 7 how these forces raise and lower prices, increase and decrease quantities bought and sold, cause revenues to fluctuate, and send resources to their most valuable uses. ◆ These powerful forces begin quietly and privately with the choices that each one of us makes. Chapters 8 and 9 probe these individual

Making the Most of Life

choices. In Chapter 8, you learned about the marginal utility theory of human decisions. This theory explains people's consumption plans. It also explains people's consumption of leisure time and its flip side, the supply of work time. Marginal utility theory can even be used to explain "non-economic" choices, such as whether to marry and how many children to have. In a sense, there are no non-economic choices.

If there is scarcity, there must be choice. And economics studies all such choices. Chapter 9 describes a tool that enables us to make a map of people's likes and dislikes, a tool called an *indifference curve*. Indifference curves are considered an advanced topic, so this chapter is *strictly optional*. But the presentation of indifference curves in Chapter 9 is the clearest and most straightforward available, so if you want to learn about this tool, this chapter is the place to do so.

◇ The earliest economists (Adam Smith and his contemporaries) did not have a very deep understanding of households' choices. It was not until the nineteenth century that progress was made in this area. On the following pages, you can spend some time with Jeremy Bentham, the person who pioneered the use of the concept of utility to study human choices, and with Martin Dooley of McMaster University, who is one of Canada's most influential students of human behaviour.

Probing the Ideas

People as Rational Decision Makers

Jeremy Bentham

(1748–1832), who lived in London, was the son and grandson of a lawyer and was himself trained as a barrister. But he rejected the opportunity to maintain the family tradition and instead, spent his life as a writer, activist, and Member of Parliament, in the pursuit of rational laws that would bring the greatest happiness to the greatest number.

Bentham, whose embalmed body is preserved to this day in a glass cabinet in the University of London, was the first person to use the concept of utility to explain human choices. But in Bentham's day, the distinction between explaining and prescribing was not a sharp one, and Bentham was ready to use his ideas to tell people how they ought to behave. He was one of the first to propose pensions for the retired, guaranteed employment, minimum wages, and social benefits such as free education and free medical care.

" ... it is the greatest happiness of the greatest number that is the measure of right and wrong."

JEREMY BENTHAM,
FRAGMENT ON GOVERNMENT

The Issues

The economic analysis of human behaviour in the family, the workplace, the markets for goods and services, the markets for labour services, and financial markets is based on the idea that our behaviour can be understood as a response to scarcity. Everything we do can be understood as a choice that maximizes total benefit subject to the constraints imposed by our limited resources and technology. If people's preferences are stable in the face of changing constraints, then we have a chance of predicting how they will respond to an evolving environment.

The economic approach explains the incredible change that has occurred during the past 100 years in the way women allocate their time as the consequence of changing constraints, not of changing attitudes. Technological advances have equipped the nation's farms and factories with machines that have increased the productivity of both women and men, thereby raising the wages they can earn. The increasingly technological world has increased the return to education for both women and men and has led to a large increase in high school and college graduates of both sexes. And equipped with an ever-widening array of gadgets and appliances that cut the time taken to do household jobs, an increasing proportion of women have joined the labour force.

The economic explanation might not be correct, but it is a powerful one. And if it is correct, the changing attitudes are a consequence, not a cause, of the economic advancement of women.

By 1997, more than 60 percent of women were in the labour force, and although many had low-paying jobs, increasingly women were found in the professions and in executive positions. What brought about this dramatic change compared with 100 years earlier? Was it a change in preferences or a change in the constraints that women face?

Then ...

Economists explain people's actions as the consequences of choices that maximize total utility subject to constraints. In the 1890s, fewer than 20 percent of women chose market employment, and most of those who did had low-paying and unattractive jobs. The other 80 percent of women chose non-market work in the home. What were the constraints that led to these choices?

Many economists stand on the shoulders of Jeremy Bentham and study the choices of individuals and families. One of these is Martin Dooley of McMaster University. Professor Dooley's work shows the power of viewing human choices as being rational ones that respond to incentives. You can meet him on the following pages.

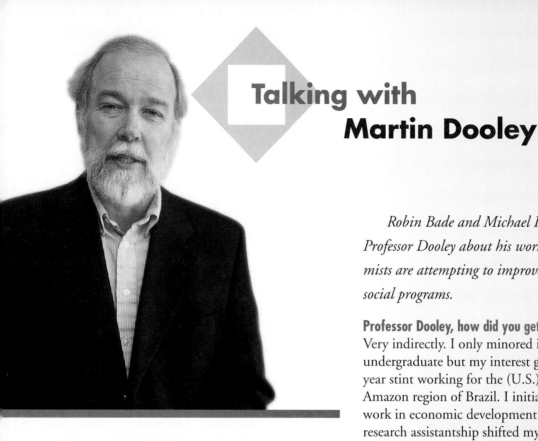

Talking with
Martin Dooley

Martin D. Dooley *is Professor of Economics at McMaster University. Born in South Bend, Indiana in 1947, Professor Dooley was an undergraduate at Indiana University, a graduate student at the University of Wisconsin, and a Postdoctoral Fellow at the University of Chicago. He received his Ph.D. in 1977 and has been on the faculty of McMaster University since 1981. Professor Dooley studies labour economics, health economics, and the economics of the family. He is currently working on the social and economic determinants of child health and development, welfare use, and the stability of marriages.*

Professor Dooley's work is a good example of how the theory of consumer choice has been extended and applied to choices that are broader than those about how to spend a fixed budget, and of how economic incentives influence a wide range of decisions.

198

Robin Bade and Michael Parkin talked with Professor Dooley about his work and how economists are attempting to improve the effectiveness of social programs.

Professor Dooley, how did you get into economics?
Very indirectly. I only minored in economics as an undergraduate but my interest grew during a two-year stint working for the (U.S.) Peace Corps in the Amazon region of Brazil. I initially pursued graduate work in economic development but a summer research assistantship shifted my focus to my current interests.

What is the connection between the three major areas in which you currently work: labour economics, health economics, and the economics of the family?
There are many connections. The character of our lives and work influence our health status and our health influences our lives and work. An important factor linking all three areas is the fact that we spend most of our lives either residing in a family unit or at least in close contact with relatives. We care for our relations and are cared for by them. We share with them both our personal income and personal services such as health care, childcare, and others. That family members share time and money is, I am sure, more than obvious to the reader, but discussions of both labour market policy and health policy often ignore this fact, at least when it is convenient to do so. For example, the beneficiaries of efforts to raise female earnings include the male family members with whom women share their pay cheques. The "cost savings" achieved by shortening hospital stays may be partially or even fully offset by increased money and time burdens on the family. These examples and many others show that a necessary ingredient for good policy analysis is a full accounting of

the benefits and costs, including the less obvious effects that work through the family.

What exactly is health economics? Isn't health care so vital that it stands above economics?

One is strongly tempted to think that economic factors have little impact on health-care decisions because "your good health is everything." A bit of reflection indicates that we do indeed care about our health, but much else besides. I routinely drive on four-lane highways at (legal) speeds that pose a minor risk to my health in order to economize on time. I enjoy my trips to the food court even though my doctor tells me it would be better for my health to go to the squash court.

Health economists deal with many issues. One is how to deliver health-care services in an efficient and fair manner. This requires the study of how health-care consumers and providers react to incentives. What would be, for example, the impact on preventative health care of a fee for routine physical examinations? What is the superior way to reimburse physicians—fee-for-service or a salary? The health economics question with which I am involved is how socioeconomic factors influence child health and development. The data clearly show that children from poor families have more psychiatric disorders and schooling problems than do children from non-poor families. But what should we infer from this finding?

One interpretation is that the problems are directly attributable to low income, that is, due either to inadequate levels of consumption or the stress brought on by economic insecurity. This suggests that providing better cash transfers to poor parents will directly improve outcomes for their children. An alternative interpretation, however, is that some other variable, such as poor parental health or education, is responsible for both low income and poor child health. This interpretation suggests that greater cash transfers might not be an effective way to improve the well-being of the children concerned and that alternatives should be considered. Both interpretations will likely have some merit but we are just beginning to understand the key policy issue of the relative importance of each interpretation.

What issues in the economics of the family are you working on?

One issue is the way in which economic factors influence marital stability. Research shows that wives suffer much greater income loss after separation and divorce than do husbands even after accounting for alimony and child support payments. One implication is that wives who have higher personal earnings relative to the earnings of their husbands have less to lose economically from a split and less need to stick with a bad marriage for fear of the economic consequences of single life. My work with Pierre Lefebvre and Phil Merrigan of UQAM confirms that marriages in which the wife's earnings more closely approximate (or exceed) those of her husband are less stable—other things being equal.

People on welfare face some hard choices. Does welfare keep them from getting jobs and developing human capital?

The disincentives are strong. "Welfare taxes" result from the fact that benefit cheques are reduced when income from virtually any source is increased. And the rate of taxation is commonly equal to or

Health economists deal with many issues. One is how to deliver health care services in an efficient and fair manner.

close to 100 percent. As a result, most welfare clients perform little paid work. Of course, some earnings are not reported but the evidence indicates that this is not a major issue. The welfare tax clearly makes paid-work not pay!

So why don't we lower this tax rate?

Some provinces have done so but only to 75–80 percent. This means that an $8 an hour job, not uncommon among welfare clients, still only pays $2 an hour once the welfare reduction is taken into account— an offer that is easy to refuse.

So why not lower the welfare tax to 25 percent or less?

The main reason is that this step will be very costly for governments at least in the foreseeable future. Some existing welfare clients may get jobs and see their benefit cheques shrink. But the lower tax rate means that clients can earn a lot more without exhausting their welfare cheque and leaving the welfare rolls.

Can you give us an example to show the effects of lowering the tax rate?

If the monthly welfare benefit for non-workers is $1,000 and the tax rate is 100 percent, then monthly earnings of $1,000 will reduce the actual welfare payment to zero and cause an exit from the welfare rolls. At a tax rate of 25 percent, however, it will take $4,000 of monthly earnings to fully "tax away" this same benefit (because $1,000 is 25 percent of $4,000). Hence, many more families will potentially qualify for a welfare benefit—possibly all those earning between $1,000 and $4,000 per month. The effect might be to increase total welfare expenditures greatly. Furthermore, the work incentives of any new clients will worsen because the welfare tax they face has risen from zero percent (not on welfare) to 25 percent (on welfare). Lowering the welfare tax rate improves the work incentive for existing clients but lowers it for any newly attracted or retained clients—and there is no easy way around this dilemma.

I believe that few corners of human behaviour are untouched by economic factors …

Why do you think so many lone mothers are on welfare?

The work incentives for lone mothers on welfare are especially weak. Paid work means high child-care costs and leaving the welfare rolls also means the loss of valuable subsidies for drugs, dental care, and housing. My research shows that the response of lone mothers to the incentives is strong. Over the last 25 years, for example, Canadian lone mothers under age 35 increased their welfare participation and decreased their labour force participation, but that just the opposite was true of lone mothers age 35 and over. An important reason for this was that, relative to welfare benefits, the typical labour market earnings of young, unskilled workers fell substantially during this period but the earnings of older workers did not.

Can we hope to design an economic policy program towards the family that brings genuinely equal opportunities for all and that does not confront the poorest people with disincentives to work?

For lone-mother families at least, it is very hard to do so in a way that is both inexpensive and does not penalize poor children. As I indicated above, simply lowering the welfare tax is likely to be expensive. Mandatory work requirements for mothers on welfare bring the day-care problem to the fore. Government could pay for child care, which would increase public expenditures, or force the lone mothers to pay for it, which would lower further the well-being of Canada's least fortunate children.

One suggestion, which is currently being implemented, is to "take kids off welfare." The federal child tax benefit for low-income families is being enriched to the point where welfare benefits for children can and will be eliminated in all provinces without lowering the disposable income of families with children on welfare. This policy is not without drawbacks but it will lower the incentive, especially for larger families, to leave the labour market, where pay cheques do not depend on the number of dependents, and go on welfare, where benefit cheques do depend on this factor.

Is there any way in which economists can measure the disincentives experimentally?

Yes. An interesting idea is being tested in a social experiment now underway in New Brunswick and British Columbia. A randomly selected group of lone mothers on welfare have been permitted to keep an unusually large portion of their welfare benefits after entering the labour market but only if they take a full-time job. The goal is to attract more lone mothers into employment that offers advancement opportunities sufficient to escape what for some is a recurring cycle of welfare and dead-end jobs.

Do you think that economics is a good subject in which to major? Why? What else should be studied alongside it?

I believe that few corners of human behaviour are untouched by economic factors and that equally few are untouched by non-economic factors. The insights one gets from the study of economics are widely applicable. And the study of every other social science complements and enriches the insights provided by economics.

Chapter 10

Organizing Production

In the fall of 1990, a British scientist named Tim Berners-Lee invented the World Wide Web. This remarkable idea paved the way for the creation and growth of thousands of profitable businesses. One of these businesses is CANOE—Canadian Online Explorer—founded by Sun Media, one of Canada's largest news organizations, and BCE Media. ◆ How do CANOE and the other 2 million firms that operate in Canada make their business decisions? How do they operate efficiently? ◆ Businesses range from multinational giants, such as Microsoft, to small family restaurants and local Internet service providers. Three-quarters of all firms are operated by their owners. But corporations like CANOE and Microsoft account for 90 percent of all business sales. What are the different types a firm can take? Why do some remain small while others become giants? Why are most firms owner-operated? ◆ Many businesses operate in a highly competitive environment and struggle to earn their profits. Others, like Microsoft, seem to have cornered the market on their products and earn large profits. What are the different types of market in which firms operate and why is it harder to make a profit in some markets than in others? ◆ Most of the components of an IBM personal computer are made by other firms. Microsoft created its Windows operating system and Intel makes its processor chip. Other firms make hard drives and modems, and yet others make CD drives, sound cards, and so on. Why doesn't IBM make all its own computer components? Why does it leave these activities to other firms and buy from them in markets? How do firms decide what to make themselves and what to buy in the marketplace from other firms?

◆ In this chapter, we are going to learn about firms and the choices they make to cope with scarcity. We begin by studying the economic problems and choices that *all* firms face.

Spinning a Web

After studying this chapter, you will be able to:

■ Explain what a firm is and describe the economic problems that *all* firms face

■ Distinguish between technological efficiency and economic efficiency

■ Define and explain the principal–agent problem

■ Describe and distinguish between different types of business organization

■ Describe and distinguish between different types of markets in which firms operate

■ Explain why firms coordinate some economic activities and markets coordinate others

The Firm and Its Economic Problem

THE 2 MILLION FIRMS IN CANADA DIFFER IN SIZE and in the scope of what they do. But they all perform the same basic economic functions. Each **firm** is an institution that hires productive resources and that organizes those resources to produce and sell goods and services.

Our goal is to predict firm behaviour. To do so, we need to know a firm's goals and the constraints it faces. We begin with the goals.

The Firm's Goal

If you asked a group of entrepreneurs what they are trying to achieve, you would get many different answers. Some would talk about making a quality product, others about business growth, others about market share, and others about the job satisfaction of their work force. All of these goals might be pursued, but they are not the fundamental goal. They are means to a deeper goal.

A firm's goal is to *maximize profit*. A firm that does not seek to maximize profit is either eliminated or bought out by firms that do seek to maximize profit.

What exactly is the profit that a firm seeks to maximize? To answer this question, let's look at Sidney's Sweaters.

Measuring a Firm's Profit

Sidney runs a successful business that makes sweaters. Sidney's Sweaters receives $400,000 a year for the sweaters it sells. Its expenses are $80,000 a year for wool, $20,000 for utilities, $120,000 for labour, and $10,000 in interest on a bank loan. With receipts of $400,000 and expenses of $230,000, Sidney's Sweaters' annual surplus is $170,000.

Sidney's accountant lowers this number by $20,000, which he says is the depreciation (fall in value) of the firm's buildings and knitting machines during the year. (Accountants use Revenue Canada rules based on standards established by the accounting profession to calculate the depreciation.) So the accountant reports that the profit of Sidney's Sweaters is $150,000 a year.

Sidney's accountant measures cost and profit to ensure that the firm pays the correct amount of income tax and to show the bank how its loan has been used. But we want to predict the decisions that a firm makes. These decisions respond to *opportunity cost* and *economic profit*.

Opportunity Cost

The **opportunity cost** of any action is the highest-valued alternative forgone. The action that you choose not to do—the highest-valued alternative forgone—is the cost of the action that you choose to do. For a firm, the opportunity cost of production is the value of the firm's best alternative use of its resources.

Opportunity cost is a real alternative forgone. But so that we can compare the cost of one action with that of another action, we express opportunity cost in money units. A firm's opportunity costs are:

- Explicit costs
- Implicit costs

Explicit Costs   Explicit costs are paid in money. The amount paid for a resource could have been spent on something else, so it is the opportunity cost of using the resource. For Sidney, his expenditures on wool, utilities, wages, and bank interest are explicit costs.

Implicit Costs   A firm incurs implicit costs when it forgoes an alternative action but does not make a payment. A firm incurs implicit costs when it:

1. Uses its own capital.
2. Uses its owner's time or financial resources.

The cost of using its own capital is an implicit cost—and an opportunity cost—because the firm could rent the capital to another firm. The rental income forgone is the firm's opportunity cost of using its own capital. This opportunity cost is called the **implicit rental rate** of capital.

People rent houses, apartments, cars, telephones, and videotapes. And firms rent photocopiers, earth-moving equipment, satellite launching services, and so on. If a firm rents capital, it incurs an *explicit* cost. If a firm buys the capital it uses, it incurs an *implicit* cost. The implicit rental rate of capital is made up of:

1. Economic depreciation
2. Interest forgone

Economic depreciation is change in the *market* value of capital over a given period. It is calculated as the market price of the capital at the beginning of the period minus its market price at the end of the period. For example, suppose that Sidney could have sold his buildings and knitting machines on December 31, 1998, for $400,000. If he can sell the same capital on December 31, 1999, for $375,000, his economic depreciation during 1999 is $25,000—the fall in the market value of the machines. This $25,000 is an implicit cost of using the capital during 1999.

The funds used to buy capital could have been used for some other purpose. And in their next best use, they would have yielded a return—an interest income. This forgone interest is part of the opportunity cost of using the capital. For example, Sidney's Sweaters could have bought government bonds instead of a knitting factory. The interest forgone on the government bonds is an implicit cost of operating the knitting factory.

Cost of Owner's Resources   A firm's owner often supplies *entrepreneurial ability*—the productive resource that organizes the business, makes business decisions, innovates, and bears the risk of running the business. The return to entrepreneurship is profit and the *average* return for supplying entrepreneurial ability is called **normal profit**. Normal profit is part of a firm's opportunity cost, because it is the cost of a forgone alternative—running another firm. If normal profit in the textile business is $50,000 a year, this amount must be added to Sidney's costs to determine his opportunity cost.

The owner of a firm also can supply labour (in addition to entrepreneurship). The return to labour is a wage. And the opportunity cost of the owner's time spent working for the firm is the wage income forgone by not working in the best alternative job. Suppose that Sidney could take another job that pays $40,000 a year. By working for his knitting business and forgoing this income, Sidney incurs an opportunity cost of $40,000 a year.

Economic Profit

What is the bottom line—the profit or loss of the firm? A firm's **economic profit** is equal to its total revenue minus its opportunity cost. The firm's opportunity cost is the sum of its explicit costs and implicit costs. And the implicit costs, remember, include *normal profit*. The return to entrepreneurial ability is greater than normal in a firm that makes a positive economic profit. And the return to entrepreneurial

ability is less than normal in a firm that makes a negative economic profit—a firm that incurs an economic loss.

Economic Accounting: A Summary

Table 10.1 summarizes the economic accounting concepts that you've just studied. Sidney's Sweaters' total revenue is $400,000. Its opportunity cost (explicit costs plus its implicit costs) is $365,000. And its economic profit is $35,000.

To achieve the objective of maximum profit—maximum economic profit—a firm must make five basic decisions:

1. What goods and services to produce and in what quantities
2. How to produce—the techniques of production to use
3. How to organize and compensate its managers and workers
4. How to market and price its products
5. What to produce itself and what to buy from other firms

In all these decisions, a firm's actions are limited by the constraints that it faces. Our next task is to learn about these constraints.

TABLE 10.1
Economic Accounting

Item		Amount
Total Revenue		**$400,000**
Opportunity Costs		
Wool	$ 80,000	
Utilities	20,000	
Wages paid	120,000	
Bank interest paid	10,000	
Total Explicit Costs		$ 230,000
Sidney's wages forgone	40,000	
Sidney's interest forgone	20,000	
Economic depreciation	25,000	
Normal profit	50,000	
Total Implicit Costs		$ 135,000
Total Cost		**$365,000**
Economic Profit		**$ 35,000**

The Firm's Constraints

Three features of its environment limit the maximum profit a firm can make. They are:

■ Technology constraints
■ Information constraints
■ Market constraints

Technology Constraints   Economists define technology broadly. A **technology** is any method of producing a good or service. Technology includes the detailed designs of machines. It also includes the layout of the workplace. And it includes the organization of the firm. For example, the shopping mall is a technology for producing retail services. It is a different technology from the catalogue store, which in turn is different from the downtown store.

It might seem surprising that a firm's profits are limited by technology. For it seems that technological advances are constantly increasing profit opportunities. Almost every day, we learn about some new technological advance that amazes us. With computers that speak and recognize our own speech and cars that can find the address we need in a city we've never visited before, we are able to accomplish ever more.

Technology is advancing. But at each point in time, to produce more output and gain more revenue, a firm must hire more resources and incur greater costs. The increase in profit that the firm can achieve is limited by the technology available for transforming resources into output. For example, using its current plant and work force, Ford can produce some maximum number of cars per day. To produce more cars per day, Ford must hire more resources and incur greater costs, which limits the increase in profit that Ford can make by selling the additional cars.

Information Constraints   We never possess all the information we would like to make decisions. We lack information about both the future and the present. For example, suppose you plan to buy a new computer. When should you buy it? The answer depends on how the price is going to change in the future. Where should you buy it? The answer depends on the prices at hundreds of different computer shops. To get the best deal, you must compare the quality and prices in every shop. But the opportunity cost of this comparison exceeds the cost of the computer!

Similarly, a firm is constrained by limited information about the quality and effort of its work force, the current and future buying plans of its customers, and the plans of its competitors. Workers slacken off when managers believe they are working hard. Customers switch to competing suppliers. Firms must compete against competition from a new firm.

Firms try to create incentive systems for workers to ensure they work hard even when no one is monitoring their efforts. And firms spend millions of dollars on market research. But none of these efforts and expenditures eliminates the problems of incomplete information and uncertainty. And the cost of coping with limited information itself limits profit.

Market Constraints   What each firm can sell and the price it can obtain is constrained by the willingness to pay of its customers and by the prices and marketing efforts of other firms. Similarly, the resources that each firm can buy and the prices it must pay are limited by the willingness of people to work for and invest in the firm. Firms spend billions of dollars a year marketing and selling their products. Some of the most creative minds strive to find the right message that will produce a knockout television advertisement. Market constraints and the expenditures firms make to overcome them limit the profit a firm can make.

R E V I E W   Q U I Z

■ Why do firms seek to maximize profit? What happens to firms that don't pursue this goal?
■ Why do accountants and economists calculate a firm's cost and profit in different ways?
■ What are the items that make opportunity cost depart from the accountants' measure of cost?
■ Why is normal profit an opportunity cost?
■ What are the three types of constraint that firms face? How does each constraint limit the profit that a firm can make?

In the rest of this chapter and in Chapters 11 through 14, we study the decisions that firms make. We're going to learn how we can predict a firm's behaviour as the response to the constraints that it faces and to changes in those constraints. We begin by taking a closer look at the technology constraints, information constraints, and market constraints that firms face.

Technology and Economic Efficiency

MICROSOFT EMPLOYS A LARGE WORK FORCE. And most Microsoft workers possess a large amount of human capital. But the firm uses a small amount of physical capital. In contrast, a coal mining company employs a huge amount of mining equipment (physical capital) and almost no labour. Why? The answer lies in the concept of efficiency. There are two concepts of production efficiency: technological efficiency and economic efficiency. **Technological efficiency** occurs when the firm produces a given output by using the least inputs. **Economic efficiency** occurs when the firm produces a given output at least cost. Let's explore the two concepts of efficiency by studying an example.

Suppose that there are four alternative techniques for making TV sets:

a. *Robot production.* One person monitors the entire computer-driven process.
b. *Production line.* Workers specialize in a small part of the job as the emerging TV set passes them on a production line.
c. *Bench production.* Workers specialize in a small part of the job but walk from bench to bench to perform their tasks.
d. *Hand-tool production.* A single worker uses a few hand tools to make a TV set.

Table 10.2 sets out the amounts of labour and capital required by each of these four methods to make 10 TV sets a day.

Which of these alternative methods are technologically efficient?

Technological Efficiency

Recall that technological efficiency occurs when the firm produces *a* given output by using the least inputs. Inspect the numbers in the table and notice that method *a* uses the most capital but the least labour. Method *d* uses the most labour but the least capital. Methods *b* and *c* lie between the two extremes. They use less capital but more labour than method *a* and less labour but more capital than method *d*. Compare methods *b* and *c*. Method *c* requires 100 workers and 10 units of capital to pro-

duce 10 TV sets. Those same 10 TV sets can be produced by method *b* with 10 workers and the same 10 units of capital. Because method *c* uses the same amount of capital and more labour than method *b*, method *c* is not technologically efficient.

Are any of the other methods not technologically efficient? The answer is no. Each of the others is technologically efficient. Method *a* uses more capital but less labour than method *b*, and method *d* uses more labour but less capital than method *b*.

Which of the methods are economically efficient?

Economic Efficiency

Recall that economic efficiency occurs when the firm produces a given output at least cost. Suppose that labour costs $75 per person-day and that capital costs $250 per machine-day. Table 10.3(a) calculates the costs of using the different methods. By inspecting the table, you can see that method *b* has the lowest cost. Although method *a* uses less labour, it uses too much expensive capital. And although method *d* uses less capital, it uses too much expensive labour.

Method *c*, which is technologically inefficient, is also economically inefficient. It uses the same amount of capital as method *b* but 10 times as much labour, so it costs more. A technologically inefficient method is never economically efficient.

Although *b* is the economically efficient method in this example, method *a* or *d* could be economically efficient with different input prices.

First, suppose that labour costs $150 a person-day and capital costs only $1 a machine-day. Table 10.3(b) now shows the costs of making a TV set. In this case,

TABLE 10.2

Four Ways of Making 10 TV Sets a Day

| Method | Quantities of inputs | |
	Labour	Capital
a Robot production	1	1,000
b Production line	10	10
c Bench production	100	10
d Hand-tool production	1,000	1

TABLE 10.3

The Costs of Different Ways of Making 10 TV Sets a Day

(a) Four ways of making TVs

Method	Labour cost ($75 per day)		Capital cost ($250 per day)		Total cost	Cost per TV set
a	$75	+	$250,000	=	$250,075	$25,007.50
b	750	+	2,500	=	3,250	325.00
c	7,500	+	2,500	=	10,000	1,000.00
d	75,000	+	250	=	75,250	7,525.00

(b) Three ways of making TVs: High Labour Costs

Method	Labour cost ($150 per day)		Capital cost ($1 per day)		Total cost	Cost per TV set
a	$150	+	$1,000	=	$1,150	$115.00
b	1,500	+	10	=	1,510	151.00
d	150,000	+	1	=	150,001	15,000.10

(c) Three ways of making TVs: High Capital Costs

Method	Labour cost ($1 per day)		Capital cost ($1000 per day)		Total cost	Cost per TV set
a	$1	+	$1,000,000	=	$1,000,001	$100,000.10
b	10	+	10,000	=	10,010	1,001.00
d	1,000	+	1,000	=	2,000	200.00

method *a* is economically efficient. Capital is now so cheap relative to labour that the method that uses the most capital is the economically efficient method.

Second, suppose that labour costs only $1 a person-day while capital costs $1,000 a machine-day. Table 10.3(c) shows the costs in this case. Method *d*, which uses a lot of labour and little capital, is now the least-cost method and economically efficient method.

From these examples, you can see that while technological efficiency depends only on what is feasible, economic efficiency depends on the relative costs of resources. The economically efficient method is the one that uses the smaller amount of a more expensive resource and a larger amount of a less expensive resource.

A firm that is not economically efficient does not maximize profit. Natural selection favours efficient firms and opposes inefficient firms. Inefficient firms go out of business or are taken over by firms that lower costs. Profit-maximizing firms are better able to survive temporary adversity than inefficient ones.

REVIEW QUIZ

- How do we define technological efficiency? Is a firm technologically efficient if it uses the latest technology? Why?

- How do we define economic efficiency? Is a firm economically inefficient if it can cut costs by producing less? Why?

- Explain the key distinction between technological efficiency and economic efficiency.

- Why do some firms use large amounts of capital and small amounts of labour while others use small amounts of capital and large amounts of labour?

You have now seen how the technology constraints that a firm faces influence the amounts of capital and labour that it employs. Next we study information constraints and the diversity of *organization structures* they generate.

Information and Organization

EACH FIRM ORGANIZES THE PRODUCTION OF goods and services by combining and coordinating the productive resources it hires. But there is variety across firms in how they organize production. Firms use a mixture of two systems:

- Command systems
- Incentive systems

Command Systems

A **command system** is a method of organizing production that uses a managerial hierarchy. Commands pass downward through the managerial hierarchy and information passes upward. Managers spend most of their time collecting and processing information about the performance of the people under their control and making decisions about commands to issue and how best to get those commands implemented.

The military uses the purest form of command system. A commander-in-chief makes the big decisions about strategic objectives. Beneath this highest level, generals organize their military resources. Beneath the generals, successively lower ranks organize smaller and smaller units but pay attention to ever increasing degrees of detail. At the bottom of the managerial hierarchy are the people who operate weapons systems.

Command systems in firms are not as rigid as they are in the military. But they share some similar features. A chief executive officer (CEO) sits at the top of a firm's command system. Senior executives who report to and receive commands from the CEO specialize in managing production, marketing, finance, personnel, and perhaps other aspects of the firm's operations. Beneath these senior managers might be several tiers of middle management ranks that stretch downward to the managers that supervise the day-to-day operations of the business. Beneath these managers are the people who operate the firm's machines and who make and sell goods and services.

Small firms have one or two layers of managers while large firms have several layers. As production processes have become ever more complex, management ranks have swollen. Today, more people have management jobs than ever before. But the information revolution of the 1990s slowed the growth of management and, in some industries, it decreased the number of layers of managers and brought a shakeout of middle managers.

Managers make enormous efforts to be well informed. And they try hard to make good decisions and issue commands that end up using resources efficiently. But managers always have incomplete information about what is happening in the divisions of the firm for which they are responsible. It is for this reason that firms use incentive systems as well as command systems to organize production.

Incentive Systems

An **incentive system** is a method of organizing production that uses a market-like mechanism inside the firm. Instead of issuing commands, senior managers create compensation schemes that will induce workers to perform in ways that maximize the firm's profit.

Selling organizations use incentive systems most extensively. Sales representatives who spend most of their working time alone and unsupervised are induced to work hard by being paid a small salary and a large performance-related bonus.

But incentive systems operate at all levels in a firm. A CEO's compensation plan includes a share in the firm's profit, and factory floor workers sometimes receive compensation based on the quantity they produce.

Mixing the Systems

Firms use a mixture of commands and incentives. And they choose the mixture to maximize profit. They use commands when it is easy to monitor performance or when a small deviation from an ideal performance is very costly. They use incentives when monitoring performance is either not possible or too costly to be worth doing.

For example, it is easy and not very costly to monitor the performance of workers on a production line. And if one person works too slowly, the entire line slows. So a production line is organized with a command system.

In contrast, it is costly to monitor a CEO. What, for example, did Matthew Barrett (a former president of the Bank of Montreal) contribute to the success in the global market of that bank? This question cannot be answered with certainty, yet a big bank must put someone in charge of operations and provide this person the *incentive* to be efficient. Incentives and the contracts that create them are an attempt to cope with a general problem called the principal–agent problem.

The Principal–Agent Problem

The **principal–agent problem** is the problem of devising compensation rules that induce an *agent* to act in the best interest of a *principal*. For example, the stockholders of the Royal Bank are *principals* and the bank's managers are *agents*. The stockholders (the principals) must induce the managers (agents) to act in the stockholders' best interest. Similarly, Bill Gates, (a principal) must induce the programmers working on Windows 2000 (agents) to work efficiently.

Agents, whether they are managers or workers, pursue their own goals and often impose costs on a principal. For example, the goal of a stockholder of the Royal Bank (a principal) is to maximize the bank's profit. But the bank's profit depends on the actions of its managers (agents), who have their own goals. Perhaps a manager takes a customer to a ball game on the pretence that she is building customer loyalty, when in fact she is simply taking on-the-job leisure. This same manager is also a principal and her tellers are agents. The manager wants the tellers to work hard and attract new customers so she can meet her operating targets. But the tellers enjoy conversations with each other and keep customers waiting in line. Nonetheless, the bank constantly strives to find ways of improving performance and increasing profits.

Coping with the Principal–Agent Problem

Issuing commands does not address the principal–agent problem. In most firms, the shareholders can't monitor the managers and often the managers can't monitor the workers. Each principal must create incentives that induce each agent to work in the interests of the principal. Three ways of attempting to cope with the principal–agent problem are:

■ Ownership
■ Incentive pay
■ Long-term contracts

Ownership By assigning to a manager or worker ownership (or part-ownership) of a business, the principal can sometimes induce a job performance that increases a firm's profits. Part-ownership schemes for senior managers are quite common, and they are less common but not unknown for workers. For example, in 1995 Canadian Pacific Ltd. sold off CP Express and Transport, a coast-to-coast trucking operation, to its 3,500 employees.

Incentive Pay Incentive pay schemes—pay related to performance—are very common. They are based on a variety of performance criteria such as profits or production or sales targets. Promoting an employee for good performance is another example of an incentive pay scheme.

Long-Term Contracts Long-term contracts tie the long-term fortunes of managers and workers (agents) to the success of the principal(s)—the owner(s) of the firm. For example, a multi-year employment contract for a CEO encourages that person to take a long-term view and devise strategies that achieve maximum profit over a sustained period.

These three ways of coping with the principal–agent problem give rise to different types of business organization. Each type of business organization is a different response to the principal–agent problem. It uses ownership, incentives, and long-term contracts in different ways. Let's look at the main types of business organization.

Types of Business Organization

The three main types of business organization are:

■ Sole proprietorship
■ Partnership
■ Corporation

Sole Proprietorship A *sole proprietorship* is a firm with a single owner—a proprietor—who has unlimited liability. *Unlimited liability* is the legal responsibility for all the debts of a firm up to an amount equal to the entire wealth of the owner. If a sole proprietorship cannot pay its debts, those to whom the firm owes money can claim the personal property of the owner. Corner stores, computer programmers, and artists are all examples of sole proprietorships.

The proprietor makes management decisions, receives the firm's profits, and is responsible for its losses. Profits from a sole proprietorship are taxed at the same rate as other sources of the proprietor's personal income.

Partnership   A *partnership* is a firm with two or more owners who have unlimited liability. Partners must agree on an appropriate management structure and on how to divide the firm's profits among themselves. The profits of a partnership are taxed as the personal income of the owners. But each partner is legally liable for all the debts of the partnership (limited only by the wealth of an individual partner). Liability for the full debts of the partnership is called *joint unlimited liability*. Most law firms are partnerships.

Corporation   A *corporation* is a firm owned by one or more limited liability stockholders. *Limited liability* means that the owners have legal liability only for the value of their initial investment. This limitation of liability means that if the corporation becomes bankrupt, its owners are not required to use their personal wealth to pay the corporation's debts.

Corporation profits are taxed independently of stockholders' incomes. Because stockholders pay taxes on the income they receive as dividends on stocks, corporate profits are taxed twice. The stockholders also pay capital gains tax on the profit they earn by selling a stock for a higher price than they paid for it. Corporate stocks generate capital gains when a corporation retains some of its profit and reinvests it in profitable activities. So even retained earnings are taxed twice because the capital gains they generate are taxed.

Pros and Cons of Different Types of Firms

The different types of business organization arise as different ways of trying to cope with the principal–agent problem. Each has advantages in particular situations. And because of its special advantages, each type continues to exist. Each type also has its disadvantages, which explains why it has not driven out the other two.

Table 10.4 summarizes these pros and cons of the different types of firm.

TABLE 10.4

The Pros and Cons of Different Types of Firms

Type of Firm	Pros	Cons
Sole Proprietorship	▪ Easy to set up ▪ Simple decision making ▪ Profits taxed only once as owner's income	▪ Bad decisions not checked by need for consensus ▪ Owner's entire wealth at risk ▪ Firm dies with owner ▪ Capital is expensive ▪ Labour is expensive
Partnership	▪ Easy to set up ▪ Diversified decision making ▪ Can survive withdrawal of partner ▪ Profits taxed only once as owners' incomes	▪ Achieving consensus may be slow and expensive ▪ Owners' entire wealth at risk ▪ Withdrawal of partner may create capital shortage ▪ Capital is expensive
Corporation	▪ Owners have limited liability ▪ Large-scale, low-cost capital available ▪ Professional management not restricted by ability of owners ▪ Perpetual life ▪ Long-term labour contracts cut labour costs	▪ Complex management structure can make decisions slow and expensive ▪ Profits taxed twice as company profit and as stockholders' income

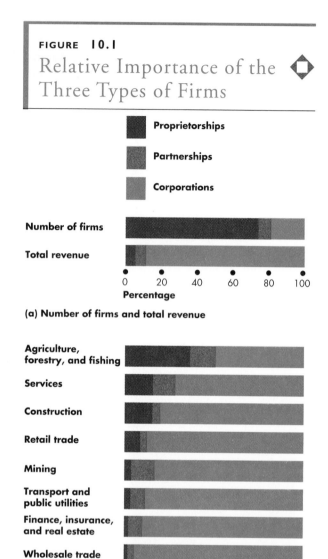

FIGURE 10.1

Relative Importance of the Three Types of Firms

(a) Number of firms and total revenue

(b) Total revenue in various industries

The data shown are for the United States because we do not have comparable data for Canada. In the United States, three-quarters of all firms are sole proprietorships, almost one-fifth are corporations, and only a twentieth are partnerships. Corporations account for 86 percent of business revenue (part a). But sole proprietorships and partnerships account for a significant percentage of business revenue in some industries (part b).

Source: U.S. Bureau of the Census, *Statistical Abstract of the United States: 1998*, 118th ed. CD-ROM. (Washington, DC: 1998): 855, 856, and 1103.

The Relative Importance of Different Types of Firms

Figure 10.1(a) shows the relative importance of the three main types of firms in the U.S. economy. The figure also shows that the revenue of corporations is much larger than that of the other types of firms. Although only 18 percent of all firms are corporations, they generate 86 percent of revenue.

Figure 10.1(b) shows the percentage of revenue generated by the different types of firms in various industries. Sole proprietorships in agriculture, forestry, and fishing generate about 36 percent of the total revenue in those sectors. Sole proprietorships in the service sector, construction, and retail trades also generate a large percentage of total revenue. Partnerships in agriculture, forestry, and fishing generate about 14 percent of total revenue. Partnerships are more prominent in services; mining; and finance, insurance, and real estate than in other sectors. Corporations are important in all sectors and in manufacturing have the field almost to themselves.

Why do corporations dominate the business scene? Why do the other types of business survive? And why are sole proprietorships and partnerships more prominent in some sectors? The answer to these questions lies in the pros and cons of the different types of business organization that are summarized in Table 10.4 above. Corporations dominate where a large amount of capital is used. But sole proprietorships dominate where flexibility in decision making is critical.

REVIEW QUIZ

- Explain the distinction between a command system and an incentive system.
- What is the principal–agent problem and what are the three ways in which firms try to cope with it?
- What are the three types of firm? Explain the major advantages and disadvantages of each type.
- Why do all three types of firm survive and in which sectors are the three types most prominent?

You've now seen how technology constraints influence a firm's use of capital and labour and how information constraints influence a firm's organization. We'll now look at market constraints and see how they influence the environment in which firms compete for business.

Markets and the Competitive Environment

THE MARKETS IN WHICH FIRMS OPERATE VARY A great deal. Some are highly competitive and profits are hard to come by. Some appear to be almost free from competition and firms earn large profits. Some markets are dominated by fierce advertising campaigns in which each firm seeks to persuade buyers that it has the best products. And some markets display a war-like character.

Economists identify four market types:

1. Perfect competition
2. Monopolistic competition
3. Oligopoly
4. Monopoly

Perfect competition arises when there are many firms each selling an identical product; many buyers; and no restrictions on the entry of new firms into the industry. The many firms and buyers are all well informed about the prices of the products of each firm in the industry. The worldwide markets for corn, rice, and other grain crops are examples of perfect competition.

Monopolistic competition is a market structure in which a large number of firms compete by making similar but slightly different products. Making a product slightly different from the product of a competing firm is called **product differentiation**. Product differentiation gives a monopolistically competitive firm an element of monopoly power. The firm is the sole producer of the particular version of the good in question. For example, in the market for running shoes, Nike, Reebok, Fila, and Asics all make their own version of the perfect shoe. Each of these firms has a monopoly on a particular brand of shoe. Differentiated products are not necessarily different products. What matters is that consumers *perceive* them to be different. For example, different brands of aspirin are chemically identical (salicylic acid) and differ only in their packaging.

Oligopoly is a market structure in which a small number of firms compete. Computer software, airplane manufacture, and international air transportation are examples of oligopolistic industries. Oligopolies might produce almost identical products, such as the colas produced by Coke and Pepsi. Or they might produce differentiated products such as Chevrolet's Lumina and Ford's Taurus.

A **monopoly** is an industry that produces a good or service for which no close substitute exists and in which there is one supplier that is protected from competition by a barrier preventing the entry of new firms. In some places, the phone, gas, electricity, and water suppliers are local monopolies—monopolies restricted to a given location. Microsoft Corp., the software developer that created Windows, the operating system used by PCs, is an example of a global monopoly.

Perfect competition is the most extreme form of competition. Monopoly is the most extreme absence of competition. The other two market types fall between these extremes.

Many factors must be taken into account to determine which market structure describes a particular real-world market. One of these factors is the extent to which the market is dominated by a small number of firms. To measure this feature of markets, economists use indexes called measures of concentration. Let's look at these measures.

Measures of Concentration

Economists use two measures of concentration:

■ The four-firm concentration ratio
■ The Herfindahl-Hirschman Index

The Four-Firm Concentration Ratio The **four-firm concentration ratio** is the percentage of the value of sales accounted for by the four largest firms in an industry. The range of the concentration ratio is from almost zero for perfect competition to 100 percent for monopoly. This ratio is the main measure used to assess market structure.

Table 10.5 shows two calculations of the four-firm concentration ratio, one for tires and one for

printing. In this example, 14 firms produce tires. The largest four have 80 percent of the sales, so the four-firm concentration ratio is 80 percent. In the printing industry, with 1,004 firms, the largest four firms have only 0.5 percent of the sales, so the four-firm concentration ratio is 0.5 percent.

A low concentration ratio indicates a high degree of competition, and a high concentration ratio indicates an absence of competition. A monopoly has a concentration ratio of 100 percent—the largest (and only) firm has 100 percent of the sales. A four-firm concentration ratio that exceeds 60 percent is regarded as an indication of a market that is highly concentrated and dominated by a few firms in an oligopoly. A ratio of less than 40 percent is regarded as an indication of a competitive market.

The Herfindahl-Hirschman Index The Herfindahl-Hirschman Index—also called the HHI—is the square of the percentage market share of each firm summed over the largest 50 firms (or summed over all the firms if there are fewer than 50) in a market. For example, if there are four firms in a market and the market shares of the firms are 50 percent, 25 percent, 15 percent, and 10 percent, the Herfindahl-Hirschman Index is

$$\text{HHI} = 50^2 + 25^2 + 15^2 + 10^2 = 3,450.$$

In perfect competition, the HHI is small. For

TABLE 10.5

Concentration Ratio Calculations

Tiremakers		Printers	
Firm	**Sales** (millions of dollars)	**Firm**	**Sales** (millions of dollars)
Top, Inc.	200	Fran's	2.5
ABC, Inc.	250	Ned's	2.0
Big, Inc.	150	Tom's	1.8
XYZ, Inc.	100	Jill's	1.7
Largest 4 firms	700	Largest 4 firms	8.0
Other 10 firms	175	Other 1,000 firms	1,592.0
Industry	**875**	Industry	**1,600.0**

Four-firm concentration ratios:

Tiremakers: $\dfrac{700}{875} \times 100 = 80\%$

Printers: $\dfrac{8}{1,600} \times 100 = 0.5\%$

example, if each of the largest 50 firms in an industry has a market share of 0.1 percent, the HHI is $0.1^2 \times 50 = 0.5$. In a monopoly, the HHI is 10,000—the firm has 100 percent of the market: $100^2 = 10,000$.

The HHI can be used to classify markets across the spectrum of types. A market in which the HHI is less than 1,000 is regarded as being competitive and the smaller the number, the greater is the degree of competition. A market in which the HHI lies between 1,000 and 1,800 is regarded as being moderately competitive—a form of monopolistic competition. Although the HHI of 10,000 is needed for a pure monopoly, a market in which the HHI exceeds 1,800 is regarded as being uncompetitive and a potential matter for concern by competition regulators.

Concentration Measures for the Canadian Economy

Figure 10.2 shows a selection of concentration ratios calculated by Statistics Canada.

Industries that produce tobacco products, petroleum and coal products, transport equipment, communications, and beverages have a high degree of concentration and are oligopolies. Services, clothing, furniture, retail trade, and knitting mills have low concentration measures and are highly competitive. Industries that produce food and electrical products are moderately concentrated. These industries are examples of monopolistic competition.

Concentration measures are a useful indicator of the degree of competition in a market. But they must be supplemented by other information to determine a market's structure. Table 10.6 summarizes the range of other information along with the measures of concentration that determine which market structure describes a particular real-world market.

Limitations of Concentration Measures

The three main limitations of concentration measures alone as determinants of market structure are their failure to take proper account of:

- The geographical scope of the market
- Barriers to entry and firm turnover
- The correspondence between a market and an industry

FIGURE 10.2

Concentration Measures in Canada

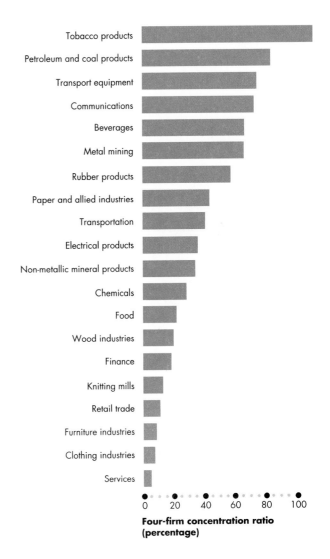

Four-firm concentration ratio (percentage)

The industries that produce tobacco products, petroleum and coal products, transport equipment, communications, and beverages are highly concentrated, while those that produce services, clothing, furniture, retail trade services, and knitware are highly competitive. The industries that produce food and electrical products have an intermediate degree of concentration.

Source: Statistics Canada, *StatCan: CANSIM Disc,* March 1999.

TABLE 10.6

Market Structure

Characteristics	Perfect competition	Monopolistic competition	Oligopoly	Monopoly
Number of firms in industry	Many	Many	Few	One
Product	Identical	Differentiated	Either identical or differentiated	No close substitutes
Barriers to entry	None	None	Moderate	High
Firm's control over price	None	Some	Considerable	Considerable or regulated
Concentration ratio	0	Low	High	100
HHI (approx. ranges)	Less than 100	101 to 999	More than 1,000	10,000
Examples	Wheat, corn	Food, clothing	Automobiles, cereals	Local water supply

---

Geographical Scope of Market Concentration measures take a *national* view of the market. Many goods are sold in a national market, but some are sold in a *regional* market and some in a *global* one. The newspaper industry consists of local markets. The concentration measures for newspapers are low, but there is a high degree of concentration in the newspaper industry in most cities. The auto industry is a global market. The big three North American car makers don't have much domestic competition, either in Canada or in the United States. But they face tough competition from foreign producers both here and more especially in foreign markets.

Barriers to Entry and Turnover Concentration measures don't measure barriers to entry. Some industries are highly concentrated but have easy entry and an enormous amount of turnover of firms. For example, many small towns have few restaurants but there are no restrictions on opening a restaurant and many firms attempt to do so.

Also, an industry might be competitive because of *potential entry*—because a few firms in a market face competition from many firms that can easily enter the market and will do so if economic profits are available.

Market and Industry To calculate concentration ratios, Statistics Canada classifies each firm as being in a particular industry. But markets do not always correspond closely to industries for three reasons.

First, markets are often narrower than industries. For example, the pharmaceutical industry, which has a low concentration ratio, operates in many separate markets for individual products—for example, measles vaccine and AIDS fighting drugs. These drugs do not compete with each other, so this industry, which looks competitive, includes firms that are monopolies (or near monopolies) in markets for individual drugs.

Second, most firms make several or even many products. For example, Labatt produces beer and milk, among many other items. So this one firm operates in several separate markets. But Statistics Canada classifies Labatt as being in the brewing industry. The fact that Labatt competes with other producers of milk does not show up in the concentration ratios for the milk market.

Third, firms switch from one market to another depending on profit opportunities. For example, Canadian Pacific Ltd., which today provides hotel services, forest products, coal and petroleum products, as well as rail services, has diversified from being just a railroad company. Publishers of newspapers and magazines are today diversifying into Internet and multimedia products. These switches among industries show that there is much scope for entering and exiting an industry and so measures of concentration have limited usefulness.

Despite their limitations, concentration measures do provide a basis for determining the degree of competition in an industry when they are combined with information about the geographical scope of the market, barriers to entry, and the extent to which large, multiproduct firms straddle a variety of markets.

FIGURE 10.3

The Market Structure of the North American Economy

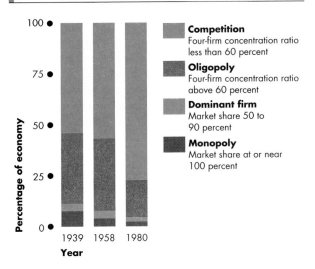

Competition
Four-firm concentration ratio less than 60 percent

Oligopoly
Four-firm concentration ratio above 60 percent

Dominant firm
Market share 50 to 90 percent

Monopoly
Market share at or near 100 percent

Three-quarters of the North American economy is effectively competitive (perfect competition or monopolistic competition), one fifth is oligopoly, and the rest is monopoly. The economy became more competitive between 1939 and 1980. (Professor Shepherd, whose 1982 study remains the latest word on this topic, suspects that although some industries have become more concentrated, others have become less concentrated, so the net picture has probably not changed much since 1980.)

Source: William G. Shepherd, "Causes of Increased Competition in the U.S. Economy, 1939–1980," *Review of Economics and Statistics*, November 1982, pp. 613–626.

Market Structures in the North American Economy

How competitive are the markets of North America? Do most firms operate in competitive markets or in markets with monopoly elements?

Figure 10.3 provides part of the answer to these questions. It shows the market structure of the U.S. economy and the trends in market structure between 1939 and 1980. (Unfortunately, comparable data for Canada alone and data for the 1980s and 1990s are not available.)

In 1980, three-quarters of the value of goods and services bought and sold in the United States was traded in markets that are essentially competitive—markets that have almost perfect competition or monopolistic competition. Monopoly and the dominance of a single firm accounted for about 5 percent of sales. Oligopoly, which is found mainly in manufacturing, accounted for about 18 percent of sales.

Over the period covered by the data in Fig. 10.3, the U.S. economy became increasingly competitive. You can see that the competitive markets have expanded most (the blue areas) and the oligopoly markets have shrunk most (the red areas).

But also, during the past decade, the U.S. economy has become much more exposed to competition from the rest of the world. Figure 10.3 does not capture this international competition.

R E V I E W   Q U I Z

■ What are the four market types? Explain the distinguishing characteristics of each.
■ What are the two measures of concentration? Explain how each measure is calculated.
■ Under what conditions do the measures of concentration give a good indication of the degree of competition in a market?
■ Is our economy competitive? Is it becoming more competitive or less competitive?

You now know the variety of market types and the way we classify firms and industries into the different market types. Our final question in this chapter is what determines the items that firms decide to buy from other firms rather than produce for themselves?

Firms and Markets

AT THE BEGINNING OF THIS CHAPTER, WE defined a firm as an institution that hires productive resources and organizes them to produce and sell goods and services. To organize production, firms coordinate the economic decisions and activities of many individuals. But firms are not the only co-ordinators of economic decisions. You learned in Chapter 4 that markets also coordinate decisions. By adjusting prices, markets make the decisions of buyers and sellers consistent—make the quantities demanded equal to the quantities supplied for different goods and services.

Markets can coordinate production. An example of market coordination versus firm coordination is the production of a rock concert. A promoter hires a stadium, some stage equipment, audio and video recording engineers and technicians, some rock groups, a superstar, a publicity agent, and a ticket agent—all market transactions—and sells tickets to thousands of rock fans, audio rights to a recording company, and video and broadcasting rights to a television network—another set of market transactions. If rock concerts were produced like corn flakes, the firm producing them would own all the capital used (stadiums, stage, sound and video equipment) and would employ all the labour needed (singers, engineers, sales people, and so on).

Another example of market coordination versus firm coordination is *outsourcing*. A firm uses outsourcing when it buys parts or products from another firm rather than making them itself. The major automakers use outsourcing for windshields and windows, gearboxes, tires, and many other car parts.

What determines whether a firm or markets coordinate a particular set of activities? How do firms decide whether to buy from another firm or manufacture an item themselves? The answer is cost. Taking account of the opportunity cost of time as well as the costs of the other inputs, people use the method that costs least. In other words, they use the economically efficient method.

Firms coordinate economic activity when they can perform a task more efficiently than markets. In such a situation, it is profitable to set up a firm. If markets can perform a task more efficiently than a firm can, people will use markets, and any attempt to set up a firm to replace such market coordination will be doomed to failure.

Why Firms?

There are four key reasons why, in many instances, firms are more efficient than markets as coordinators of economic activity. Firms can achieve:

■ Lower transactions costs
■ Economies of scale
■ Economies of scope
■ Economies of team production

Transactions Costs The idea that firms exist because there are activities in which they are more efficient than markets was first suggested by University of Chicago economist and Nobel Laureate Ronald Coase. Coase focused on the firm's ability to reduce or eliminate transactions costs. **Transactions costs** are the costs arising from finding someone with whom to do business, of reaching an agreement about the price and other aspects of the exchange, and of ensuring that the terms of the agreement are fulfilled. *Market* transactions require buyers and sellers to get together and to negotiate the terms and conditions of their trading. Sometimes, lawyers have to be hired to draw up contracts. A broken contract leads to still more expenses. A *firm* can lower such transactions costs by reducing the number of individual transactions undertaken.

Consider, for example, two ways of getting your creaking car fixed.

Firm coordination: You take the car to the garage. The garage owner coordinates parts and tools as well as the mechanic's time, and your car gets fixed. You pay one bill for the entire job.

Market coordination: You hire a mechanic who diagnoses the problems and makes a list of the parts and tools needed to fix them. You buy the parts from the local wrecker's yard and rent the tools from ABC Rentals. You hire the mechanic again to fix the problems. You return the tools and pay your bills—wages to the mechanic, rental to ABC, and the cost of the parts used to the wrecker.

What determines the method that you use? The answer is cost. Taking account of the opportunity cost of your own time as well as the costs of the other inputs that you would have to buy, you will use the method that costs least. In other words, you will use the economically efficient method.

The first method requires that you undertake only one transaction with one firm. It's true that the firm has to undertake several transactions—hiring the labour and buying the parts and tools required to do the job. But the firm doesn't have to undertake those transactions simply to fix your car. One set of such transactions enables the firm to fix hundreds of cars. Thus there is an enormous reduction in the number of individual transactions that take place if people get their cars fixed at the garage rather than going through an elaborate sequence of market transactions.

Economies of Scale   When the cost of producing a unit of a good falls as its output rate increases, economies of scale exist. Automakers, for example, experience economies of scale because as the scale of production increases, the firm can use cost saving equipment and highly specialized labour. An automaker that produces only a few cars a year must use hand-tool methods that are costly. Economies of scale arise from specialization and the division of labour that can be reaped more effectively by firm coordination rather than market coordination.

Economies of Scope   A firm experiences **economies of scope** when it uses specialized (and often expensive) resources to produce *a range of goods and services*. For example, Microsoft hires specialist programmers, designers, and marketing experts, and uses their skills across a range of software products. As a result, Microsoft coordinates the resources that produce software at a lower cost than an individual can who buys all these services in markets.

Economies of Team Production   A production process in which the individuals in a group specialize in mutually supportive tasks is *team production*. Sport provides the best example of team activity. Some team members specialize in pitching and some in batting, some in defence and some in offence. The production of goods and services offers many examples of team activity. For example, production lines in automobile and TV manufacturing plants work most efficiently when individual activity is organized in teams, each specializing in a small task. You can also think of an entire firm as being a team. The team has buyers of raw material and other inputs, production workers, and salespeople. There are even specialists within these various groups. Each individual member of the team specializes, but the value of the output of the team and the profit that it earns depend on the coordinated activities of all the team's members. The idea that firms arise as a consequence of the economies of team production was first suggested by

Armen Alchian and Harold Demsetz of the University of California at Los Angeles.

Because firms can economize on transactions costs, reap economies of scale, and organize efficient team production, it is firms rather than markets that coordinate most of our economic activity. But there are limits to the economic efficiency of firms. If a firm becomes too big or too diversified in the things that it seeks to do, the cost of management and monitoring per unit of output begins to rise, and at some point, the market becomes more efficient at coordinating the use of resources. IBM is an example of a firm that became too big to be efficient. In an attempt to restore efficient operations, IBM split up its large organization into a number of "Baby Blues," each of which specializes in a segment of the computer market.

Sometimes firms enter into long-term relationships with each other that effectively cut out ordinary market transactions and make it difficult to see where one firm ends and another begins. For example, GM has long-term relationships with suppliers of windows, tires, and other parts. Wal-Mart has long-term relationships with suppliers of the goods it sells in its stores. Such relationships make transactions costs lower than they would be if GM or Wal-Mart went shopping on the open market each time it wanted new supplies.

REVIEW QUIZ

- What are the two ways in which economic activity can be coordinated?
- What determines whether a firm or markets coordinate production?
- What are the main reasons why firms can often coordinate production at a lower cost than markets?

◆ *Reading Between the Lines* on pp. 218–219 explores the economic problem faced by Levi Strauss, the firm that produces denim jeans. We continue to study firms and their decisions in the next four chapters. In Chapter 11, we learn about the relationships between cost and output at different output levels. These cost-output relationships are common to all types of firms in all types of markets. We then turn to problems that are special to firms in different types of markets—perfect competition in Chapter 12, monopoly in Chapter 13, and monopolistic competition and oligopoly in Chapter 14.

Levi Strauss's Economic Problem

WALL STREET JOURNAL, FEBRUARY 23, 1999

Levi Strauss to close one-half of plants in North America, cut staff in area

BY REBECCA QUICK

Taking the ax to its operations for the second time in just over a year, Levi Strauss and Co. said it will close half of its 22 manufacturing plants in North America, laying off about 5,900 employees, or 30% of its total in the U.S. and Canada. ...

The ... denim empire has seen sales of its pioneering jeans shrink, caught in a market squeeze between trendy, expensive jeans from designers like Ralph Lauren, and cheaper brands from department stores like J.C. Penney. Since 1990, Levi's market share of men's jeans dropped to 25% from 48%, according to Tactical Retail Solutions, a market-research firm in New York. And last week, Levi Strauss said its sales slumped 13% in 1998, to $6 billion from $6.9 billion a year earlier. ...

But the company said the latest round of closings wouldn't lower its production because it intends to shift much of the work to independent contractors in other countries. Many of Levi Strauss's competitors, including Guess and Tommy Hilfiger, have most if not all of their jeans produced overseas. There, labor costs are frequently much lower than the $10.12 an hour in wages and benefits paid to the average U.S. garment worker.

Aside from chopping its labor bills, Levi Strauss said it will also be able to reduce the time it takes to get apparel into stores. "The drawback to owning your own plant is that changing the line a plant produces is very time- and cost-consuming," said Clarence Grebey, a spokesman for Levi Strauss. "If we go to contractors to do that, we can get our consumers into the product more quickly." ...

Essence of the Story

■ Since 1990, Levi Strauss and Company's share of the market for men's jeans has shrunk from 48 percent to 25 percent as the market shares of designer and department store brands have expanded.

■ Most of Levi's competitors produce their jeans overseas where labour costs are lower than those in North America.

■ Levi plans to cut production in North America and transfer the work to independent contractors in other countries.

■ Besides cutting labour costs, Levi says it can get its products into stores more quickly from contractors than from its own plants.

Economic Analysis

■ Figure 1 shows how Levi Strauss's market share has shrunk from 48 percent to 25 percent, squeezed by designer brands (like Calvin Klein, Tommy Hilfiger, Mossimo, Ralph Lauren, and Donna Karan) and other brands (like Lee and Wrangler, and The Gap) and store brands (like J.C. Penney and Sears).

■ The predicament faced by Levi Strauss illustrates all the aspects of the firm and its economic problem described in this chapter.

■ Levi Strauss and Company is in business to maximize profit. The firm might engage in philanthropic acts but to do so, it must first maximize profit.

■ During the 1990s, the market for jeans has become more competitive and the company's profit has been squeezed.

■ Most large suppliers of jeans are publicly-owned companies with many stockholders. Levi Strauss is a privately-owned company that remains under the control of the descendants of Levi Strauss, who created the firm more than 100 years ago.

■ Jeans can be supplied to the consumer at the lowest possible cost if some firms specialize in *designing* jeans, some in *manufacturing* jeans, some in *marketing*, and some in *information* services.

■ The technology for *designing* and *marketing* jeans is sophisticated and uses the latest information systems. Firms link computers to retailers to manage inventories and use the Internet to obtain customers' measurements.

■ The technology for *manufacturing* jeans involves a small number of operations and basic parts. It uses simple machines and relatively low-skilled labour.

■ Because of the technology for manufacturing jeans, they can be made at least cost in countries that have low labour costs and by achieving economies from long production runs of one particular type of jean.

■ By closing some of its factories in North America and buying jeans from specialist manufacturers, Levi Strauss is capturing these cost savings and economies.

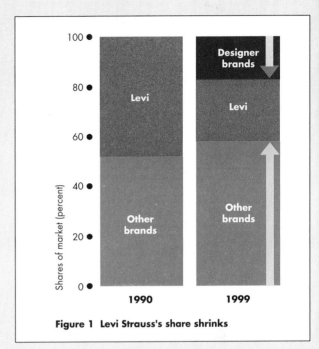

Figure 1 Levi Strauss's share shrinks

SUMMARY

Key Points

The Firm and Its Economic Problem (pp. 202–204)

- Firms hire and organize resources to produce and sell goods and services.
- Firms seek to maximize economic profit, which is total revenue minus opportunity cost.
- Technology, information, and markets limit a firm's profit.

Technology and Economic Efficiency (pp. 205–206)

- A method of production is technologically efficient when it is not possible to increase output without using more inputs.
- A method of production is economically efficient when the cost of producing a given output is as low as possible.

Information and Organization (pp. 207–210)

- Firms use a combination of command systems and incentive systems to organize production.
- Faced with incomplete information and uncertainty, firms induce managers and workers to perform in ways consistent with the firm's goals.
- Sole proprietorships, partnerships, and corporations use ownership, incentives, and long-term contracts to cope with the principal–agent problem.

Markets and the Competitive Environment (pp. 211–215)

- Perfect competition occurs when there are many buyers and sellers of an identical product and when new firms can easily enter a market.
- Monopolistic competition occurs when a large number of firms compete with each other by making slightly different products.
- Oligopoly is a situation in which a small number of producers compete with each other.

- Monopoly is a firm that produces a good or service for which there are no close substitutes and that is protected by a barrier that prevents the entry of competitors.

Firms and Markets (pp. 216–217)

- Firms coordinate economic activities when they can perform a task more efficiently—at lower cost—than markets.
- Firms economize on transactions costs and achieve the benefits of economies of scale, economies of scope, and economies of team production.

Key Figure and Tables

Key Terms

PROBLEMS

*1. One year ago, Jack and Jill set up a vinegar bottling firm (called JJVB). Use the following information to calculate JJVB's explicit costs and implicit costs during its first year of operation:
   a. Jack and Jill put $50,000 of their own money into the firm.
   b. They bought equipment for $30,000.
   c. They hired one employee to help them for an annual wage of $20,000.
   d. Jack gave up his previous job, at which he earned $30,000, and spent all his time working for JJVB.
   e. Jill kept her old job, which paid $30 an hour, but gave up 10 hours of leisure each week (for 50 weeks) to work for JJVB.
   f. JJVB bought $10,000 of goods and services from other firms.
   g. The market value of the equipment at the end of the year was $28,000.

2. One year ago, Ms. Moffat and Mr. Spieder opened a cheese firm (called MSCF). Use the following information to calculate MSCF's explicit costs and implicit costs during its first year of operation:
   a. Moffat and Spieder put $70,000 of their own money into the firm.
   b. They bought equipment for $40,000.
   c. They hired one employee to help them for an annual wage of $18,000.
   d. Moffat gave up her previous job, at which she earned $22,000, and spent all her time working for MSCF.
   e. Spieder kept his old job, which paid $20 an hour, but gave up 20 hours of leisure each week (for 50 weeks) to work for MSCF.
   f. MSCF bought $5,000 of goods from other firms.
   g. The market value of the equipment at the end of the year was $37,000.

*3. Four methods for doing a tax return are: personal computer, pocket calculator, pocket calculator with pencil and paper, pencil and paper. With a PC, the job takes an hour; with a pocket calculator, it takes 12 hours; with a pocket calculator and pencil and paper, it takes 12 hours; and with a pencil and paper,

it takes 16 hours. The PC and its software cost $1,000, the pocket calculator costs $10, and the pencil and paper cost $1.
   a. Which, if any, of the methods is technologically efficient?
   b. Which method is economically efficient if the wage rate is
      i) $5 an hour?
      ii) $50 an hour?
      iii) $500 an hour?

4. Sue can do her accounting assignment by using: a personal computer; a pocket calculator; a pocket calculator and a pencil and paper; or a pencil and paper. With a PC, Sue completes the job in half an hour; with a pocket calculator, it takes 4 hours; with a pocket calculator and with a pencil and paper, it takes 5 hours; and with a pencil and paper, it takes 14 hours. The PC and its software cost $2,000, the pocket calculator costs $15, and the pencil and paper cost $3.
   a. Which, if any, of the methods is technologically efficient?
   b. Which method is economically efficient if Sue's wage rate is
      i) $10 an hour?
      ii) $20 an hour?
      iii) $50 an hour?

*5. Alternative ways of laundering 100 shirts are:

Method	Labour (hours)	Capital (machines)
a	1	10
b	5	8
c	20	4
d	50	1

   a. Which methods are technologically efficient?
   b. Which method is economically efficient if the hourly wage rate and rental rate are:
      i) Wage rate $1, rental rate $100?
      ii) Wage rate $5, rental rate $50?
      iii) Wage rate $50, rental rate $5?

6. Alternative ways of making 100 shirts a day are:

Method	Labour (hours)	Capital (machines)
a	10	50
b	20	40
c	50	20
d	100	10

a. Which methods are technologically efficient?
b. Which method is economically efficient if the hourly wage rate and rental rate are:
   i) Wage rate $1, rental rate $100?
   ii) Wage rate $5, rental rate $50?
   iii) Wage rate $50, rental rate $5?

*7. Sales of the firms in the tattoo industry are:

Firm	Sales (dollars)
Bright Spots	450
Freckles	325
Love Galore	250
Native Birds	200
Other 15 firms	800

a. Calculate the four-firm concentration ratio.
b. What is the structure of the tattoo industry?

8. Sales of the firms in the pet food industry are:

Firm	Sales (thousands of dollars)
Big Collar, Inc.	50
Shiny Coat, Inc.	75
Friendly Pet, Inc.	60
Nature's Way, Inc.	65
Other 8 firms	400

a. Calculate the four-firm concentration ratio.
b. What is the structure of the industry?

*9. Market shares of chocolate makers are:

Firm	Market share (percent)
Mayfair, Inc.	15
Bond, Inc.	10
Magic, Inc.	20
All Natural, Inc.	15
Truffles, Inc.	25
Gold, Inc.	15

a. Calculate the Herfindahl-Hirschman Index.
b. What is the structure of the industry?

10. Market shares of mat makers are:

Firm	Market share (percent)
Made-to-Last, Inc.	20
Big Wheel, Inc.	17
Magic Carpet, Inc.	22
Supreme, Inc.	17
Copra, Inc.	24

a. Calculate the Herfindahl-Hirschman Index.
b. What is the structure of the industry?

CRITICAL THINKING

 1. Study the news article about Levi Strauss and Company in *Reading Between the Lines* on pp. 218–219 and then:
   a. Describe the economic problem that the firm faced in 1998.
   b. Use the links on the Parkin-Bade Web site to find information about some of Levi Strauss's main competitors. What do you think the economic problems of these competitors are?
   c. Consider the market share of Levi Strauss in 1990 and 1998. Do you think the market for blue jeans is an example of monopoly, oligopoly, monopolistic competition, or perfect competition? Explain your answer.
   d. Use the links on the Parkin-Bade Web site to find information about *where* Levi Strauss and Co. is closing factories. Which Canadian plant closed, and what special problems do you think arose?
   e. Compare and contrast how Levi Strauss achieves technological efficiency and economic efficiency.
   f. If more and more manufacturing leaves Canada and goes to other countries, what do you think the effect will be on the Canadian economy? [Hint: Think about the *PPF* and efficiency.]

 2. Use the links on the Parkin-Bade Web site to obtain information about the auto industry.
   a. What are the main economic problems faced by auto producers?
   b. Why are auto producers merging?

 3. Use the links on the Parkin-Bade Web site to obtain information about the steel industry.
   a. What are the main economic problems faced by steel producers?
   b. Why are steel producers seeking protection from international competition?
   c. Is the number of steel producers likely to increase or decrease during the next few years? Why?

Output and Costs

Size does not guarantee survival in business. True, the Hudson's Bay Company has been around a long time and has grown pretty large. But most of the giants of fifty years ago don't even exist today. Remaining small does not guarantee survival either. Every year, millions of small businesses close down. Call a random selection of restaurants and fashion boutiques from *last* year's yellow pages and see how many have vanished. What does a firm have to do to be one of the survivors? ◆ Firms differ in lots of ways—from Mom-and-Pop's convenience store to multinational giants producing hi-tech goods. But regardless of their size or what they produce, all firms must decide how much to produce and how to produce it. How do firms make these decisions? ◆ Most automakers in North America could produce more cars than they can sell. Why do automakers have expensive equipment lying around that isn't fully used? Many electric utilities don't have enough production equipment on hand to meet demand on the coldest and hottest days and must buy power from other producers. Why don't these firms install more equipment so that they can supply the market themselves?

◇ We are going to answer these questions in this chapter. To do so, we are going to study the economic decisions of a small, imaginary firm—Sidney's Sweaters Inc., a producer of knitted sweaters. The firm is owned and operated by Sidney. By studying the economic problems of Sidney's Sweaters and the way Sidney copes with them, we will be able to get a clear view of the problems that face *all* firms—small ones like Sidney's Sweaters as well as the giants. We're going to begin by setting the scene and describing the time frames in which Sidney makes his business decisions.

Survival of the Fittest

After studying this chapter, you will be able to:

- Distinguish between the short run and the long run

- Explain the relationship between a firm's output and labour employed in the short run

- Explain the relationship between a firm's output and costs in the short run

- Derive and explain a firm's short-run cost curves

- Explain the relationship between a firm's output and costs in the long run

- Derive and explain a firm's long-run average cost curve

Decision Time Frames

PEOPLE WHO OPERATE FIRMS MAKE MANY decisions. And all of the decisions are aimed at one overriding objective: maximum attainable profit. But the decisions are not all equally critical. Some of the decisions are big ones. Once made, they are costly (or impossible) to reverse. If such a decision turns out to be incorrect, it might lead to the failure of the firm. Some of the decisions are small ones. They are easily changed. If one of these decisions turns out to be incorrect, the firm can change its actions and survive.

The biggest decision that any firm makes is what industry to enter. For most entrepreneurs, their background knowledge and interests drive this decision. But the decision also depends on profit prospects. No one sets up a firm without believing it will be profitable. And profit depends on total revenue and opportunity cost (see Chapter 10, pp. 202–203).

The firm that we study has already chosen the industry in which to operate. It has also chosen its most effective method of organization. But it has not decided the quantity to produce, the quantities of resources to hire, or the price at which to sell its output.

Decisions about the quantity to produce and the price to charge depend on the type of market in which the firm operates. Perfect competition, monopolistic competition, oligopoly, and monopoly all confront the firm with their own special problems.

But decisions about how to produce a given output do not depend on the type of market in which the firm operates. These decisions are similar for *all* types of firms in *all* types of markets.

The actions that a firm can take to influence the relationship between output and cost depend on how soon the firm wants to act. A firm that plans to change its output rate tomorrow has fewer options than one that plans to change its output rate six months from now.

To study the relationship between a firm's output decision and its costs, we distinguish two decision time frames:

- The short run
- The long run

The Short Run

The **short run** is a time frame in which the quantities of some resources are fixed. For most firms, the fixed resources are the firm's technology, buildings, and capital. The management organization is also fixed in the short run. We call the collection of fixed resources the firm's *plant*. So in the short run, a firm's plant is fixed.

For Sidney's Sweaters, the fixed plant is its factory building and its knitting machines. For an electric power utility, the fixed plant is its buildings, generators, computers, and control systems. For an airport, the fixed plant is the runways, terminal buildings, and traffic control facilities.

To increase output in the short run, a firm must increase the quantity of variable inputs it uses. Labour is usually the variable input. So to produce more output, Sidney's Sweaters must hire more labour and operate its knitting machines for more hours per day. Similarly, an electric power utility must hire more labour and operate its generators for more hours per day. And an airport must hire more labour and operate its runways, terminals, and traffic control facilities for more hours per day.

Short-run decisions are easily reversed. The firm can increase or decrease output in the short run by increasing or decreasing the labour hours it hires.

The Long Run

The **long run** is a time frame in which the quantities of *all* resources can be varied. That is, the long run is a period in which the firm can change its *plant*.

To increase output in the long run, a firm is able to choose whether to change its plant as well as whether to increase the quantity of labour it hires. Sidney's Sweaters can decide whether to install some additional knitting machines, use a new type of machine, reorganize its management, or hire more labour. An electric power utility can decide whether to install more generators. And an airport can decide whether to build more runways, terminals, and traffic-control facilities.

Long-run decisions are *not* easily reversed. Once a plant decision is made, the firm must live with it for some time. To emphasize this fact, we call the *past* cost of buying a new plant a **sunk cost**. A sunk cost is irrelevant to the firm's decisions. The only costs that influence its decisions are the short-run cost of changing its labour inputs and the long-run cost of changing its plant in the future.

We're going to study costs in the short run and the long run. We begin with the short run and describe the technology constraint the firm faces.

Short-Run Technology Constraint

To increase output in the short run, a firm must increase the quantity of labour employed. We describe the relationship between output and the quantity of labour employed by using three related concepts:

■ Total product
■ Marginal product
■ Average product

These product concepts can be illustrated either by product schedules or by product curves. Let's look first at the product schedules.

TABLE 11.1

Total Product, Marginal Product, and Average Product

	Labour (workers per day)	Total product (sweaters per day)	Marginal product (sweaters per additional worker)	Average product (sweaters per worker)
a	0	0		
			4	
b	1	4		4.00
			6	
c	2	10		5.00
			3	
d	3	13		4.33
			2	
e	4	15		3.75
			1	
f	5	16		3.20

Total product is the total amount produced. Marginal product is the change in total product that results from a one-unit increase in labour. For example, when labour increases from 2 to 3 workers a day (row c to row d), total product increases from 10 to 13 sweaters. (Marginal product is shown between the rows to emphasize that it is the result of *changing* the quantity of labour.) The marginal product of going from 2 to 3 workers is 3 sweaters. Average product is total product divided by the quantity of labour employed. For example, the average product of 3 workers is 4.33 sweaters per worker (13 sweaters a day divided by 3 workers).

Product Schedules

Table 11.1 shows some data that describe Sidney's Sweaters' total product, marginal product, and average product. The numbers tell us how Sidney's Sweaters' production changes as more workers are employed. They also tell us about the productivity of Sidney's Sweaters' labour force.

Focus first on the columns headed "Labour" and "Total product." **Total product** is the total output produced. You can see from the numbers in these columns that as Sidney employs more labour, total product increases. For example, when Sidney employs 1 worker, total product is 4 sweaters a day and when he employs 2 workers, total product is 10 sweaters a day. Each increase in employment brings an increase in total product.

Marginal product tells us by how much total product increases when employment increases. The **marginal product** of labour is the change in total product that results from a one-unit increase in the quantity of labour employed. For example, in Table 11.1, when Sidney increases employment from 2 to 3 workers, the marginal product of the third worker is 3 sweaters—total product goes from 10 to 13 sweaters.

Average product tells how productive workers are on the average. The **average product** of labour is equal to total product divided by the quantity of labour employed. For example, in Table 11.1, the average product of 3 workers is 4.33 sweaters per worker—13 sweaters a day divided by 3 workers.

If you look closely at the numbers in Table 11.1, you can see some patterns. For example, as employment increases, marginal product at first increases and then begins to decrease. For example, marginal product increases from 4 sweaters a day when the first worker is hired to 6 sweaters a day when the second worker is hired. It then decreases to 3 sweaters a day when the third worker is hired. Average product also at first increases and then decreases. The relationships between employment and the three product concepts can be seen more clearly by looking at the product curves.

Product Curves

The product curves are graphs of the relationships between employment and the product concepts you've just studied. They show how total product, marginal product, and average product change as employment changes. They also show the relationships among the three concepts. Let's look at the product curves.

Total Product Curve

Figure 11.1 shows Sidney's Sweaters' total product curve, *TP*. As employment increases, so does the number of sweaters knitted. Points *a* through *f* on the curve correspond to the same rows in Table 11.1.

The total product curve is similar to the *production possibility frontier* (explained in Chapter 3). It separates the attainable output levels from those that are unattainable. All the points that lie above the curve are unattainable. Points that lie below the curve, in the orange area, are attainable. But they are inefficient—they use more labour than is necessary to produce a given output. Only the points *on* the total product curve are technologically efficient.

Notice especially the shape of the total product curve. As employment increases from zero to 1 worker per day, the curve becomes steeper. Then, as employment continues to increase to 3, 4, and 5 workers a day, the curve becomes less steep. The steeper the slope of the total product curve, the greater is marginal product, as you are about to see.

FIGURE 11.1
Total Product Curve

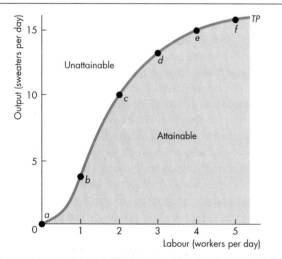

The total product curve (*TP*), based on the data in Table 11.1, shows how the quantity of sweaters produced changes as the quantity of labour employed changes. For example, 2 workers can produce 10 sweaters a day (point *c*). Points *a* through *f* on the curve correspond to the rows of Table 11.1. The total product curve separates attainable outputs from unattainable outputs. Points below the *TP* curve are inefficient.

Marginal Product Curve

Figure 11.2 shows the marginal product of labour. Part (a) reproduces the total product curve, which is the same as the total product curve in Fig. 11.1. Part (b) shows the marginal product curve, *MP*.

In part (a), the orange bars illustrate the marginal product of labour. The height of each bar measures marginal product. Marginal product is also measured by the slope of the total product curve. Recall that the slope of a curve is the change in the value of the variable measured on the *y*-axis—output—divided by the change in the variable measured on the *x*-axis—labour input—as we move along the curve. A one-unit increase in labour input, from 2 to 3 workers, increases output from 10 to 13 sweaters, so the slope from point *c* to point *d* is 3, the same as the marginal product that we've just calculated.

We've calculated the marginal product of labour for a series of unit increases in the quantity of labour. But labour is divisible into smaller units than one person. It is divisible into hours and even minutes. By varying the amount of labour in the smallest imaginable units, we can draw the marginal product curve shown in Fig. 11.2(b). The *height* of this curve measures the *slope* of the total product curve at a point. Part (a) shows that an increase in employment from 2 to 3 workers increases output from 10 to 13 sweaters (an increase of 3). The increase in output of 3 sweaters appears on the vertical axis of part (b) as the marginal product of going from 2 to 3 workers. We plot that marginal product at the midpoint between 2 and 3 workers. Notice that marginal product shown in Fig. 11.2(b) reaches a peak at 1.5 workers, and at that point, marginal product is more than 6. The peak occurs at 1.5 workers because the total product curve is steepest when employment increases from 1 worker to 2 workers.

The total product and marginal product curves are different for different firms and different types of goods. Ford Motor Company's product curves are different from those of Jim's Burger Stand, which in turn are different from those of Sidney's sweater factory. But the shapes of the product curves are similar, because almost every production process has two features:

■ Increasing marginal returns initially
■ Diminishing marginal returns eventually

Increasing Marginal Returns Increasing marginal returns occur when the marginal product of an additional worker exceeds the marginal product of the

FIGURE 11.2
Marginal Product

(a) Total product

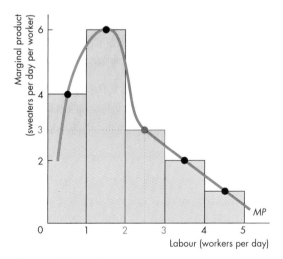

(b) Marginal product

Marginal product is illustrated by the orange bars. For example, when labour increases from 2 to 3, marginal product is the orange bar whose height is 3 sweaters. (Marginal product is shown midway between the labour inputs to emphasize that it is the result of *changing* inputs.) The steeper the slope of the total product curve (*TP*) in part (a), the larger is marginal product (*MP*) in part (b). Marginal product increases to a maximum in this example when the second worker is employed and then declines—diminishing marginal product.

previous worker. Increasing marginal returns arise from increased specialization and division of labour in the production process.

For example, if Sidney employs just one worker, that person must learn all the aspects of sweater production: running the knitting machines, fixing breakdowns, packaging and mailing sweaters, buying and checking the type and colour of the wool. That one person must perform all these tasks.

If Sidney hires a second person, the two workers can specialize in different parts of the production process. As a result, two workers produce more than twice as much as one. The marginal product of the second worker is greater than the marginal product of the first worker. Marginal returns are increasing.

Diminishing Marginal Returns Most production processes experience increasing marginal returns initially. But all production processes eventually reach a point of *diminishing* marginal returns. **Diminishing marginal returns** occur when the marginal product of an additional worker is less than the marginal product of the previous worker.

Diminishing marginal returns arise from the fact that more and more workers are using the same capital and working in the same space. As more workers are added, there is less and less for the additional workers to do that is productive. For example, if Sidney hires a third worker, output increases but not by as much as it did when he added the second worker. In this case, after two workers are hired, all gains from specialization and the division of labour have been exhausted. By hiring a third worker, the factory produces more sweaters, but the equipment is being operated closer to its limits. There are even times when the third worker has nothing to do because the machines are running without the need for further attention. Adding yet more and more workers continues to increase output but by successively smaller amounts. Marginal returns are diminishing. This phenomenon is such a pervasive one that it is called a "law"—"the law of diminishing returns." The **law of diminishing returns** states that

As a firm uses more of a variable input, with a given quantity of fixed inputs, the marginal product of the variable input eventually diminishes.

You are going to return to the law of diminishing returns when we study a firm's costs. But before we do that, let's look at the average product of labour and the average product curve.

Average Product Curve

Figure 11.3 illustrates Sidney's Sweaters' average product of labour, *AP*. It also shows the relationship between average product and marginal product. Points *b* through *f* on the average product curve correspond to those same rows in Table 11.1. Average product increases from 1 to 2 workers (its maximum value at point *c*) but then decreases as yet more workers are employed. Notice also that average product is largest when average product and marginal product are equal. That is, the marginal product curve cuts the average product curve at the point of maximum average product. For employment levels at which marginal product exceeds average product, average product is increasing. For employment levels at which marginal product is less than average product, average product is decreasing.

The relationship between the average and marginal product curves is a general feature of the relationship between the average and marginal values of any variable. Let's look at a familiar example.

FIGURE 11.3
Average Product

The figure shows the average product of labour and the connection between the average product and marginal product. With 1 worker, marginal product exceeds average product, so average product is increasing. With 2 workers, marginal product equals average product, so average product is at its maximum. With more than 2 workers, marginal product is less than average product, so average product is decreasing.

Marginal Grade and Grade Point Average

To see the relationship between average product and marginal product, think about the similar relationship between Sidney's average grade and marginal grade over five semesters. (Suppose Sidney is a part-time student who takes just one course each semester.) In the first semester, Sidney takes calculus and his grade is a 2. This grade is his marginal grade. It is also his average grade—his GPA. In the next semester, Sidney takes French and gets a 3. French is Sidney's marginal course and his marginal grade is 3. His GPA rises to 2.5. Because his marginal grade exceeds his average grade, it pulls his average up. In the third semester, Sidney takes economics and gets a 4—his new marginal grade. Because his marginal grade exceeds his GPA, it again pulls his average up. Sidney's GPA is now 3, the average of 2, 3, and 4. The fourth semester, he takes history and gets a 3. Because his marginal grade is equal to his average, his GPA does not change. In the fifth semester, Sidney takes English and gets a 2. Because his marginal grade, a 2, is below his GPA of 3, his GPA falls.

This everyday relationship between marginal and average values agrees with that between marginal and average product. Sidney's GPA increases when his marginal grade exceeds his GPA. His GPA falls when his marginal grade is below his GPA. And his GPA is constant when his marginal grade equals his GPA. The relationship between marginal product and average product is exactly the same as that between Sidney's marginal and average grades.

REVIEW QUIZ

- Explain how the marginal product of labour and the average product of labour change as the quantity of labour employed increases (a) initially and (b) eventually.
- What is the law of diminishing returns? Why does marginal product eventually diminish?
- Explain the relationship between marginal product and average product. How does average product change when marginal product exceeds average product? How does average product change when average product exceeds marginal product? Why?

Sidney cares about his product curves because they influence his costs. Let's look at Sidney's costs.

Short-Run Cost

To produce more output in the short run, a firm must employ more labour, which means it must increase its costs. We describe the relationship between output and cost by using three cost concepts:

- Total cost
- Marginal cost
- Average cost

Total Cost

A firm's **total cost** (TC) is the cost of the productive resources it uses. Total cost includes the cost of land, capital, and labour. It also includes the cost of entrepreneurship, which is *normal profit* (see Chapter 10, p. 203). We divide total cost into total fixed cost and total variable cost.

Total fixed cost (TFC) is the cost of the firm's fixed inputs. Because the quantity of a fixed input does not change as output changes, fixed cost does not change as output changes.

Total variable cost (TVC) is the cost of the firm's variable inputs. Because to change its output, a firm must change the quantity of variable inputs, total variable cost changes as output changes.

Total cost is the sum of total fixed cost and total variable cost. That is,

$$TC = TFC + TVC.$$

The table in Fig. 11.4 shows Sidney's total costs. With one knitting machine that costs $25 a day, TFC is $25. To produce more sweaters, Sidney hires more labour, which costs $25 a day. TVC, which increases as output increases, is the number of workers multiplied by $25. For example, to produce 13 sweaters a day, Sidney hires 3 workers and TVC is $75. TC is the sum of TFC and TVC, so to produce 13 sweaters a day, Sidney's total cost, TC, is $100. Check the calculation in each row of the table.

Figure 11.4 graphs Sidney's total cost curves. These curves graph total cost against total product. The green total fixed cost curve (TFC) is horizontal because total fixed cost does not change when output changes. It is a constant at $25. The purple total variable cost curve (TVC) and the blue total cost curve (TC) both increase as output increases. The vertical distance between the TVC and TC curve is total fixed cost as shown by the arrows.

Let's now look at Sidney's Sweaters' marginal cost.

FIGURE 11.4

Total Cost Curves

			Total fixed cost	Total variable cost	Total cost
	Labour (workers per day)	**Output** (sweaters per day)	**(TFC)**	**(TVC)**	**(TC)**
				(dollars per day)	
a	0	0	25	0	25
b	1	4	25	25	50
c	2	10	25	50	75
d	3	13	25	75	100
e	4	15	25	100	125
f	5	16	25	125	150

Sidney rents a knitting machine for $25 a day. This amount is Sidney's Sweaters' total fixed cost. Sidney hires workers at a wage rate of $25 a day, and this cost is Sidney's Sweaters' total variable cost. For example, if Sidney employs 3 workers, total variable cost is (3 × $25), which equals $75. Total cost is the sum of total fixed cost and total variable cost. For example, when Sidney employs 3 workers, total cost is $100—total fixed cost of $25 plus total variable cost of $75. The graph shows Sidney's Sweaters' total cost curves. Total fixed cost (TFC) is constant—it graphs as a horizontal line—and total variable cost (TVC) increases as output increases. Total cost (TC) also increases as output increases. The vertical distance between the total cost curve and the total variable cost curve is total fixed cost, as illustrated by the two arrows.

Marginal Cost

In Fig. 11.4, total variable cost and total cost increase at a decreasing rate at small levels of output and begin to increase at an increasing rate as output increases. To understand these patterns in the changes in total cost, we need to use the concept of *marginal cost.*

A firm's **marginal cost** is the change in total cost that results from a one-unit increase in output. We calculate marginal cost (*MC*) as the change in total cost (ΔTC) divided by the change in output (ΔQ). That is:

$$MC = \frac{\Delta TC}{\Delta Q}.$$

The table in Fig. 11.5 shows this calculation. When, for example, output increases from 10 sweaters to 13 sweaters, total cost increases from $75 to $100. The change in output is 3 sweaters, and the change in total cost is $25. The marginal cost of one of those 3 sweaters is ($25 ÷ 3), which equals $8.33.

Figure 11.5 graphs the marginal cost data in the table as the red marginal cost curve, *MC.* This curve is U-shaped because, when Sidney hires a second worker, marginal cost decreases, but when he hires a third, a fourth, and a fifth worker, marginal cost successively increases.

Marginal cost decreases at low outputs because of economies from greater specialization. It eventually increases because of *the law of diminishing returns.* The law of diminishing returns means that each additional worker produces a successively smaller addition to output. So to get an additional unit of output, ever more workers are required. Because more workers are required to produce one additional unit of output, the cost of the additional output—marginal cost—must eventually increase.

Marginal cost tells us how total cost changes as output changes. The final cost concept tells us what it costs, on the average, to produce a unit of output. Let's now look at Sidney's Sweaters' average costs.

Average Cost

There are three average costs:

1. Average fixed cost
2. Average variable cost
3. Average total cost

Average fixed cost (*AFC*) is total fixed cost per unit of output. **Average variable cost** (*AVC*) is total variable cost per unit of output. **Average total cost** (*ATC*) is total cost per unit of output. To calculate the average cost concepts, begin with total cost:

$$TC = TFC + TVC.$$

Divide each total cost term by the quantity produced, *Q*, to give

$$\frac{TC}{Q} + \frac{TFC}{Q} = \frac{TVC}{Q}$$

or,

$$ATC = AFC + AVC.$$

The table in Fig. 11.5 shows the calculation of average total cost. For example, when output is 10 sweaters, average fixed cost is ($25 ÷ 10), which equals $2.50, average variable cost is ($50 ÷ 10), which equals $5.00, and average total cost is ($75 ÷ 10), which equals $7.50. Note that average total cost is equal to average fixed cost ($2.50) plus average variable cost ($5.00).

Figure 11.5 shows the average cost curves. The green average fixed cost curve (*AFC*) slopes downward. As output increases, the same constant fixed cost is spread over a larger output. The blue average total cost curve (*ATC*) and the purple average variable cost curve (*AVC*) are U-shaped. The vertical distance between the average total cost and average variable cost curves is equal to average fixed cost—as indicated by the two arrows. That distance shrinks as output increases because average fixed cost declines with increasing output.

The marginal cost curve intersects the average variable cost curve and the average total cost curve at their minimum points. That is, when marginal cost is less than average cost, average cost is decreasing, and when marginal cost exceeds average cost, average cost is increasing. This relationship holds for both the *ATC* curve and the *AVC* curve and is another example of the relationship you saw in Fig. 11.3 for average product and marginal product and for course grades.

Why the Average Total Cost Curve Is U-Shaped

Average total cost, *ATC*, is the sum of average fixed cost, *AFC*, and average variable cost, *AVC*. So the shape of the *ATC* curve combines the shapes of the

FIGURE 11.5

Marginal Cost and Average Costs

Marginal cost is calculated as the change in total cost divided by the change in output. When output increases from 4 to 10, an increase of 6, total cost increases by $25 and marginal cost is $25 ÷ 6, which equals $4.17. Each average cost concept is calculated by dividing the related total cost by output. When 10 sweaters are produced, AFC is $2.50 ($25 ÷ 10), AVC is $5 ($50 ÷ 10), and ATC is $7.50 ($75 ÷ 10).

The figure shows the marginal cost curve and the average cost curves. The marginal cost curve (MC) is U-shaped and intersects the average variable cost curve and the average total cost curve at their minimum points. Average fixed cost (AFC) decreases as output increases. The average total cost curve (ATC) and average variable cost curve (AVC) are U-shaped. The vertical distance between these two curves is equal to average fixed cost, as illustrated by the two arrows.

	Labour (workers per day)	Output (sweaters per day)	Total fixed cost (TFC)	Total variable cost (TVC)	Total cost (TC)	Marginal cost (MC) (dollars per additional sweater)	Average fixed cost (AFC)	Average variable cost (AVC)	Average total cost (ATC)
			(dollars per day)				(dollars per sweater)		
a	0	0	25	0	25		—	—	—
						.... 6.25			
b	1	4	25	25	50		6.25	6.25	12.50
						.... 4.17			
c	2	10	25	50	75		2.50	5.00	7.50
						.... 8.33			
d	3	13	25	75	100		1.92	5.77	7.69
						...........12.50			
e	4	15	25	100	125		1.67	6.67	8.33
						...........25.00			
f	5	16	25	125	150		1.56	7.81	9.38

AFC and AVC curves. The U-shape of the ATC curve arises from two opposing forces:

- Spreading fixed cost over a larger output
- Eventually diminishing returns

When output increases, the firm spreads its fixed costs over a larger output and its average fixed cost decreases—its average fixed cost curve slopes downward.

Diminishing returns means that as output increases, ever-larger amounts of labour are needed to produce an additional unit of output. So average

variable cost eventually increases, and the AVC curve eventually slopes upward.

The shape of the average total cost curve combines these two effects. Initially, as output increases, both average fixed cost and average variable cost decrease, so average total cost decreases and the ATC curve slopes downward. But as output increases further and diminishing returns set in, average variable cost begins to increase. Eventually, average variable cost increases more quickly than average fixed cost decreases, so average total cost increases and the ATC curve slopes upward.

Cost Curves and Product Curves

The technology that a firm uses determines its costs. Figure 11.6 shows the links between the firm's technology constraint (its product curves) and its cost curves. The upper part of the figure shows the average product curve and the marginal product curve—like those in Fig. 11.3. The lower part of the figure shows the average variable cost curve and the marginal cost curve—like those in Fig. 11.5.

The figure highlights the links between technology and costs. As labour increases initially, marginal product and average product rise and marginal cost and average variable cost fall. Then, at the point of maximum marginal product, marginal cost is a minimum. As labour increases further, marginal product diminishes and marginal cost increases. But average product continues to rise and average variable cost continues to fall. Then, at the point of maximum average product, average variable cost is a minimum. As labour increases further, average product diminishes and average variable cost increases.

Shifts in the Cost Curves

The position of a firm's short-run cost curves depends on two factors:

■ Technology
■ Prices of productive resources

Technology A technological change that increases productivity shifts the total product curve upward. It also shifts the marginal product curve and the average product curve upward. Because with a better technology, the same inputs can produce more output, technological change lowers costs and shifts the cost curves downward.

For example, advances in robot production techniques have increased productivity in the automobile industry. As a result, the product curves of Chrysler, Ford, and GM have shifted upward, and their cost curves have shifted downward. But the relationships between their product curves and cost curves have not changed. The curves are still linked in the way shown in Fig. 11.6.

Often a technological advance results in a firm using more capital (a fixed input) and less labour (a variable input). For example, today the telephone

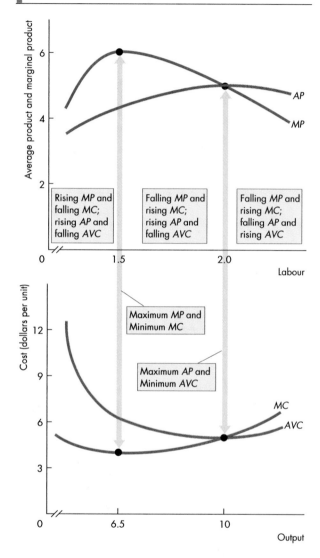

A firm's marginal product curve is linked to its marginal cost curve. If marginal product rises, marginal cost falls. If marginal product is a maximum, marginal cost is a minimum. If marginal product diminishes, marginal cost rises. A firm's average product curve is linked to its average variable cost curve. If average product rises, average variable cost falls. If average product is a maximum, average variable cost is a minimum. If average product diminishes, average variable cost rises.

TABLE 11.2

A Compact Glossary of Costs

Term	Symbol	Definition	Equation
Fixed cost		Cost that is independent of the output level; cost of a fixed input	
Variable cost		Cost that varies with the output level; cost of a variable input	
Total fixed cost	TFC	Cost of the fixed inputs	
Total variable cost	TVC	Cost of the variable inputs	
Total cost	TC	Cost of all inputs	$TC = TFC + TVC$
Total product (output)	TP	Total quantity produced (output Q)	
Marginal cost	MC	Change in total cost resulting from a one-unit increase in total product	$MC = \Delta TC \div \Delta Q$
Average fixed cost	AFC	Total fixed cost per unit of output	$AFC = TFC \div Q$
Average variable cost	AVC	Total variable cost per unit of output	$AVC = TVC \div Q$
Average total cost	ATC	Total cost per unit of output	$ATC = AFC + AVC$

companies use computers to connect long-distance calls in place of the human operators they used in the 1980s. When such a technological change occurs, costs decrease, but fixed costs increase and variable costs decrease. This change in the mix of fixed cost and variable cost means that at low output levels average total cost might increase, while at high output levels, average total cost decreases.

Prices of Resources An increase in the price of a productive resource increases costs and shifts the cost curves. But how the curves shift depends on which resource price changes. An increase in rent or some other component of *fixed* cost shifts the fixed cost curves (*TFC* and *AFC*) upward and shifts the total cost curve (*TC*) upward but leaves the variable cost curves (*AVC* and *TVC*) and the marginal cost curve (*MC*) unchanged. An increase in the wage rate or some other component of *variable* cost shifts the variable curves (*TVC* and *AVC*) upward and shifts the (*MC*) upward but leaves the fixed cost curves (*AFC* and *TFC*) unchanged. So, for example, if truck drivers' wage rates increase, the variable cost and mar-

ginal cost of transportation services increase. If the interest expense paid by a trucking company increases, the fixed cost of transportation services increases.

You've now completed your study of short-run costs. All the concepts that you've met are summarized in a compact glossary in Table 11.2.

> **R E V I E W   Q U I Z**

■ What relationships do a firm's short-run cost curves show?
■ How does marginal cost change as output increases (a) initially, and (b) eventually?
■ What does the law of *diminishing returns* imply for the shape of the marginal cost curve?
■ What is the shape of the average fixed cost curve and why?
■ What are the shapes of the average variable cost curve and the average total cost curve and why?

Long-Run Cost

IN THE SHORT RUN, A FIRM CAN VARY THE quantity of labour but the quantity of capital is fixed. In the long run, a firm can vary both the quantity of labour and the quantity of capital. We are now going to see how costs vary when the quantities of labour and capital vary. That is, we are going to study a firm's long-run costs. *Long-run cost* is the cost of production when a firm uses the economically efficient quantities of labour and capital.

The behaviour of long-run cost depends on the firm's *production function*, which is the relationship between the maximum output attainable and the quantities of both labour and capital.

The Production Function

Table 11.3 shows Sidney's Sweaters' production function. The table lists total product schedules for four different quantities of capital. We identify the quantity of capital by the plant size. The numbers for Plant 1 are for a factory with one knitting machine—the case we've just studied. The other three plants have 2, 3, and 4 machines. If Sidney's Sweaters doubles its capital to 2 knitting machines, the various amounts of labour can produce the outputs shown in the second column of the table. The other two columns show the outputs of yet larger quantities of capital. Each column of the table could be graphed as a total product curve for each plant.

Diminishing Returns Diminishing returns occur at all four quantities of capital as the quantity of labour increases. You can check that fact by calculating the marginal product of labour in plants with 2, 3, and 4 machines. At each plant size, as the quantity of labour increases, its marginal product (eventually) diminishes.

Diminishing Marginal Product of Capital Diminishing returns also occurs as the quantity of capital increases. You can check that fact by calculating the marginal product of capital at a given quantity of labour. The *marginal product of capital* is the change in total product divided by the change in capital when the quantity of labour is constant—equivalently, the change in output resulting from a one-unit increase in the quantity of capital. For example, if

TABLE 11.3
The Production Function

Labour (workers per day)	Output (sweaters per day)			
	Plant 1	Plant 2	Plant 3	Plant 4
1	4	10	13	15
2	10	15	18	21
3	13	18	22	24
4	15	20	24	26
5	16	21	25	27
Knitting machines (number)	1	2	3	4

The table shows the total product data for four quantities of capital. The greater the plant size, the larger is the total product for any given quantity of labour. But for a given plant size, the marginal product of labour diminishes. And for a given quantity of labour, the marginal product of capital diminishes.

Sidney has 3 workers and increases capital from 1 machine to 2 machines, output increases from 13 to 18 sweaters a day. The marginal product of capital is 5 sweaters per day. If Sidney increases the number of machines from 2 to 3, output increases from 18 to 22 sweaters per day. The marginal product of the third machine is 4 sweaters per day, down from 5 sweaters per day for the second machine.

Let's now see what the production function implies for long-run costs.

Short-Run Cost and Long-Run Cost

Continue to assume that labour costs $25 per worker per day and capital costs $25 per machine per day. Using these input prices and the data in Table 11.3, we can calculate and graph the average total cost curves for factories with 1, 2, 3, and 4 knitting machines. We've already studied the costs of a factory with 1 machine in Figs. 11.4 and 11.5. In Fig. 11.7, the average total cost curve for that case is ATC_1. Figure 11.7 also shows the average total cost curve for a factory with 2 machines, ATC_2, with 3 machines, ATC_3, and with 4 machines, ATC_4.

You can see, in Fig. 11.7, that plant size has a big effect on the firm's average total cost. Two things stand out:

FIGURE 11.7

Short-Run Costs of Four Different Plants

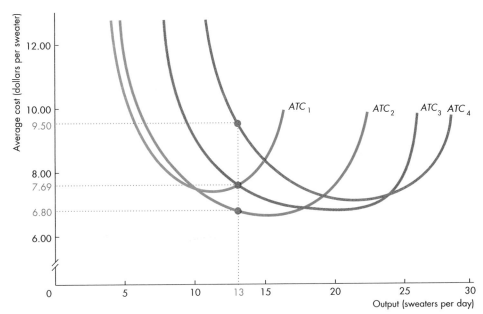

The figure shows short-run average total cost curves for four different quantities of capital. Sidney's Sweaters can produce 13 sweaters a day with 1 knitting machine on ATC_1 or with 3 knitting machines on ATC_3 for an average cost of $7.69 per sweater. Sidney's Sweaters can also produce 13 sweaters by using 2 knitting machines on ATC_2 for $6.80 per sweater or with 4 machines on ATC_4 for $9.50 per sweater. If Sidney's Sweaters produces 13 sweaters a day, the least-cost method of production—the long-run method—is with 2 machines on ATC_2.

- Each short-run average total cost curve is U-shaped.
- For each short-run average total cost curve, the larger the plant, the greater is the output at which average total cost is a minimum.

Each short-run average total cost curve is U-shaped because, as the quantity of labour increases, its marginal product at first increases and then diminishes. And these patterns in the marginal product of labour, which we examined in some detail for the plant with 1 knitting machine on pp. 226–227, occur at all plant sizes.

The minimum average total cost for a larger plant occurs at a greater output than it does for a smaller plant because the larger plant has a higher fixed cost and therefore, for any given output level, a higher average fixed cost.

Which short-run average cost curve Sidney's Sweaters operates on depends on its plant size. But in the long run, Sidney chooses the plant size. And which plant size he chooses depends on the output he plans to produce. The reason is that the average total cost of producing a given output depends on the plant size.

To see why, suppose that Sidney plans to produce 13 sweaters a day. With 1 machine, the average total cost curve is ATC_1 (in Fig. 11.7) and the average total cost of 13 sweaters a day is $7.69 per sweater. With 2 machines, on ATC_2, average total cost is $6.80 per sweater. With 3 machines on ATC_3, average total cost is $7.69 per sweater, the same as with 1 machine. Finally, with 4 machines, on ATC_4, average total cost is $9.50 per sweater.

The economically efficient plant size for producing a given output is the one that has the lowest average total cost. For Sidney, the economically efficient plant to use to produce 13 sweaters a day is the one with 2 machines.

In the long run, Sidney chooses the plant size that minimizes average total cost. When a firm is producing a given output at the least possible cost, it is operating on its *long-run average cost curve*.

The **long-run average cost curve** is the relationship between the lowest attainable average total cost and output when both the plant size and labour are varied. The long-run average cost curve is a planning curve. It tells the firm the plant size and the quantity of labour to use at each output to minimize cost. Once the plant size is chosen, the firm operates on the short-run cost curves that apply to that plant size.

The Long-Run Average Cost Curve

Figure 11.8 shows Sidney's Sweaters' long-run average cost curve $LRAC$. This long-run average cost curve is derived from the short-run average total cost curves in Fig. 11.7. For output rates up to 10 sweaters a day, average total cost is the lowest on ATC_1. For output rates between 10 and 18 sweaters a day, average total cost is the lowest on ATC_2. For output rates between 18 and 24 sweaters a day, average total cost is the lowest on ATC_3. And for output rates in excess of 24 sweaters a day, average total cost is the lowest on ATC_4. The segment of each of the four average total cost curves along which average total cost is lowest is highlighted in dark blue in Fig. 11.8. The scallop-shaped curve made up of these four segments is the long-run average cost curve.

Economies and Diseconomies of Scale

Economies of scale are features of a firm's technology that lead to falling long-run average cost as output increases. When economies of scale are present, the

$LRAC$ curve slopes downward. The $LRAC$ curve in Fig. 11.8 shows that Sidney's Sweaters experiences economies of scale for outputs up to 15 sweaters a day.

With given input prices, economies of scale occur if the percentage increase in output exceeds the percentage increase in all inputs. For example, if when a firm increases both its labour and capital by 10 percent, output increases by more than 10 percent, its average total cost falls. Economies of scale are present.

The main source of economies of scale is greater specialization of both labour and capital. For example, if GM produces 100 cars a week, each worker must perform many different tasks and the capital must be general-purpose machines and tools. But if GM produces 10,000 cars a week, each worker specializes and becomes highly proficient in a small number of tasks. Also, the capital is specialized and productive.

Diseconomies of scale are features of a firm's technology that lead to rising long-run average cost as output increases. When diseconomies of scale are present, the $LRAC$ curve slopes upward. In Fig. 11.8, Sidney's Sweaters experiences diseconomies of scale at outputs greater than 15 sweaters a day.

With given input prices, diseconomies of scale occur if the percentage increase in output is less than

FIGURE 11.8

Long-Run Average Cost Curve

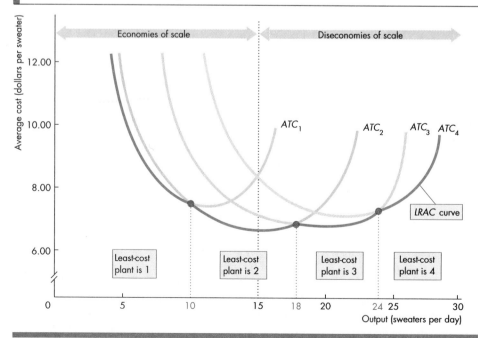

In the long run, Sidney's Sweaters can vary both capital and labour inputs. The long-run average cost curve traces the lowest attainable average total cost of production. Sidney's Sweaters produces on its long-run average cost curve, if it uses 1 machine to produce up to 10 sweaters a day, 2 machines to produce between 10 and 18 sweaters a day, 3 machines to produce between 18 and 24 sweaters a day, and 4 machines to produce more than 24 sweaters a day. Within these ranges, Sidney's Sweaters varies its output by varying its labour input.

the percentage increase in all inputs. For example, if when a firm increases both its labour and capital by 10 percent, output increases by less than 10 percent, its average total costs rises. Diseconomies of scale are present.

The main source of diseconomies of scale is the difficulty of managing a very large enterprise. The larger the firm, the greater is the challenge of organizing it and the greater is the cost of communicating up and down the management ladder and among managers. Eventually, management complexity brings rising average cost. Diseconomies of scale occur in all production processes but perhaps at only a very large output rate.

Constant returns to scale are features of a firm's technology that lead to constant long-run average cost as output increases. When constant returns to scale are present, the *LRAC* curve is horizontal.

With given input prices, constant returns to scale occur if the percentage increase in output equals the percentage increase in inputs. For example, if when a firm increases its labour and capital by 10 percent, output increases by 10 percent, its average total cost is constant. Constant returns to scale are present.

For example, General Motors can double its production of Chevy Cavaliers by doubling its production facility for those cars. It can build an identical production line and hire an identical number of workers. With the two identical production lines, GM produces exactly twice as many cars.

Minimum Efficient Scale   A firm experiences economies of scale up to some output level. Beyond that level, it moves into constant returns to scale or diseconomies of scale. A firm's **minimum efficient scale** is the smallest quantity of output at which long-run average cost reaches its lowest level.

The minimum efficient scale plays a role in determining market structure, as you will learn in the next three chapters. The minimum efficient scale also helps to answer some questions about real businesses.

Economies of Scale at Sidney's Sweaters
Sidney's production technology, shown in Table 11.3, illustrates economies of scale and diseconomies of scale. If Sidney's inputs increase from 1 machine and 1 worker to 2 of each, a 100 percent increase in all inputs, output increases by more than 100 percent from 4 sweaters to 15 sweaters a day. Sidney experiences economies of scale and his long-run average cost decreases. But if Sidney's inputs increase to 3 machines and 3 workers, a 50 percent increase, out-

put increases by less than 50 percent from 15 sweaters to 22 sweaters a day. Now Sidney's experiences diseconomies of scale and its long-run average cost increases. Sidney's minimum efficient scale is at 15 sweaters a day.

Producing Cars and Generating Electric Power
At the beginning of this chapter, we posed the question: Why do automakers have expensive equipment lying around that isn't fully used? You can now answer this question. An automaker uses the plant that minimizes the average total cost of producing the output that it can sell. But it operates below the efficient minimum scale. Its short-run average total cost curve looks like ATC_1. If it could sell more cars, it would produce more cars and its average total cost would fall.

We also noted that many electric utilities don't have enough production equipment to meet demand on the coldest and hottest days and have to buy power from other producers. You can now see why this happens and why an electric utility doesn't build more generating capacity. A power producer uses the plant size that minimizes the average total cost of producing the output that it can sell on a normal day. But it produces above the minimum efficient scale and experiences diseconomies of scale. Its short-run average total cost curve looks like ATC_3. With a larger plant size, its average total costs of producing its normal output would be higher.

REVIEW QUIZ

- What does a firm's production show and how is it related to a total product curve?
- Does the law of diminishing returns apply to capital as well as labour? Explain why.
- What does a firm's long-run average cost curve show? How is it related to the firm's short-run average cost curves?
- What are economies of scale and diseconomies of scale? How do they arise? And what do they imply for the shape of the long-run average cost curve?
- How is a firm's minimum efficient scale determined?

◆ *Reading Between the Lines* on pp. 238–239 applies what you've learned about a firm's product curves and cost curves. It looks at the total product curves and cost curves of some big aluminum producers.

Lowering the Cost of Aluminum

GLOBE AND MAIL, AUGUST 12, 1999

Merger to save Alcan and partners $600-million a year

BY ALAN FREEMAN

The mega-merger of aluminum producers Alcan Aluminium Ltd., Pechiney SA and Alusuisse Lonza Group AG (Algroup) will lead to annual cost savings of $600-million (U.S.) and the loss of as many as 4,500 jobs worldwide. …

After 3½ months of secret talks, the chiefs of Montreal-based Alcan, France's Pechiney and Switzerland's Algroup yesterday announced details of the complex transaction that will create the world's largest aluminum company, with combined 1998 revenue of $21.6-billion and 91,000 employees in 59 countries. …

The $600-million in savings are expected to come within two years… As much as 5 per cent of the combined company's 91,000 employees are to be eliminated.

"We will be eliminating overheads, we will be saving on the sales side because of overlapping of our sales organizations and there will be streamlining of our production facilities," Mr. Rodier said. "Whether this results in plant closures or not has yet to be seen. We may have some closures but we don't know exactly and we don't know when."

Not only will head office functions be merged but there will be a combination of research facilities, technical services and information technology functions. …

DEAL HIGHLIGHTS

- The new company will be temporarily referred to as Alcan-Pechiney-Algroup or APA.
- APA will be a Canadian corporation with legal headquarters in Montreal and regional headquarters in Europe. The office of the CEO will be in New York City.
- Deals should lead to annual cost savings of $600-million (U.S.) within two years.
- Five per cent of APA's employees or about 4,500 people will be let go.

Reprinted with permission from *The Globe and Mail*.

Further reproduction prohibited.

Essence of the Story

■ Alcan Aluminium Ltd., Pechiney SA, and Alusuisse Lonza Group AG plan to merge.

■ The goal of the merger is to achieve cost savings, and the companies say that with the merger, costs can be cut by $600 million within two years.

■ The labour force of the merged company would be 4,500 workers fewer than the existing combined labour forces of the three companies.

■ Alcan Aluminium Ltd., Pechiney SA, and Alusuisse Lonza Group AG are huge firms that operate bauxite mines, aluminum refiners, and 27 smelters on six continents.

■ These firms are large because there are economies of scale in many of their production activities.

■ Figure 1 shows the technology these firms face in the form of a total product curve for aluminum production. Alcan, Pechiney, and Alusuisse operate on total product curve TP_0.

■ Alcan employs 36,000 people and produces 4.5 million tonnes of aluminum a year.* Pechiney employs 11,550 people and produces 2.5 million tonnes of aluminum a year. Alusuisse employs 10,300 employees and produces 1.5 million tonnes of aluminum a year.

■ If Alcan, Alusuisse, and Pechiney merge into a single very large firm, they will be able to operate on a new total product curve. The new curve is TP_1 in Fig. 1.

*The numbers of persons employed in aluminum production and the number of tonnes of aluminum produced are based on data from Alcan, Pechiney, and Alusuisse and the authors' calculations and assumptions.

■ You can interpret the statement, "We will be eliminating overheads, we will be saving on the sales side because of overlapping of our sales organizations and there will be streamlining of our production facilities," as meaning that the combined firm does not move along the existing total product curve but jumps to a new higher total product curve TP_1 and increases productivity.

■ Figure 2 shows the effect of the merger on average total cost.

■ The average total cost curve on which the three firms operate before the merger is ATC_0. This curve uses an average of fixed costs for the three firms. Given the assumed total product curve in Fig. 1, Alusuisse and Pechiney operate in the region of falling average total cost and Alcan operates in the region of rising average total cost.

■ After the merger, the average total cost curve shifts to ATC_1. The bigger merged firm has greater fixed costs than the three separate firms, so at small output rates, average total cost is higher in the new firm than in the existing firms.

Figure 1 Total product

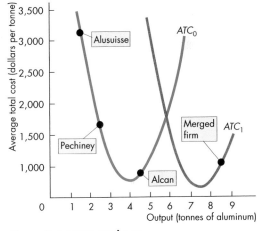

Figure 2 Average total cost

■ But at the large output rate at which the combined firm will operate, average total cost is lower for the merged firm than it was for Alusuisse and Pechiney, but slightly higher than it was for Alcan.

■ Notice that the new combined firm might operate on the upward-sloping portion of its new ATC curve, as in this example, even though it has benefited from economies of scale.

SUMMARY

Key Points

Decision Time Frames (p. 224)

- In the short run, the quantity of one resource is fixed and the quantities of the other resources can be varied.
- In the long run, the quantities of all resources can be varied.

Short-Run Technology Constraint (pp. 225–228)

- A total product curve shows the output a firm can produce with a given quantity of capital and different quantities of labour.
- Initially, the marginal product of labour increases as the quantity of labour increases, but eventually marginal product diminishes—the law of diminishing returns.
- Average product also increases initially and eventually diminishes.

Short-Run Cost (pp. 229–233)

- As output increases, total fixed cost is constant and total variable cost and total cost increase.
- As output increases, average fixed cost decreases; average variable cost, average total cost, and marginal cost decrease at small outputs and increase at large outputs. These cost curves are U-shaped.

Long-Run Cost (pp. 234–237)

- Long-run cost is the cost of production when all inputs—labour and capital—have been adjusted to their economically efficient levels.
- There is a set of short-run cost curves for each different plant size. There is one least-cost plant size for each output. The larger the output, the larger is the plant size that will minimize average total cost.
- The long-run average cost curve traces out the lowest attainable average total cost at each output when both capital and labour inputs can be varied.

- With economies of scale, the long-run average cost curve slopes downward. With diseconomies of scale, the long-run average cost curve slopes upward.

Key Figures and Table

Key Terms

PROBLEMS

*1. Rubber Duckies' total product schedule is:

Labour (workers per week)	Output (rubber boats per week)
1	1
2	3
3	6
4	10
5	15
6	21
7	26
8	30
9	33
10	35

a. Draw the total product curve.
b. Calculate the average product of labour and draw the average product curve.
c. Calculate the marginal product of labour and draw the marginal product curve.
d. What is the relationship between average product and marginal product when Rubber Duckies produces (i) fewer than 30 boats a week and (ii) more than 30 boats a week?

2. Charlie's Chocolates' total product schedule is:

Labour (workers per day)	Output (boxes per day)
1	12
2	24
3	48
4	84
5	132
6	192
7	240
8	276
9	300
10	312

a. Draw the total product curve.
b. Calculate the average product of labour and draw the average product curve.
c. Calculate the marginal product of labour and draw the marginal product curve.
d. What is the relationship between the average product and marginal product when Charlie's Chocolates produces (i) fewer than 276 boxes a day and (ii) more than 276 boxes a day?

*3. In problem 1, the price of labour is $400 a week and total fixed cost is $1,000 a week.
a. Calculate total cost, total variable cost, and total fixed cost for each output in the table and draw the short-run total cost curves.
b. Calculate average total cost, average fixed cost, average variable cost, and marginal cost at each output in the table and draw the short-run average and marginal cost curves.

4. In problem 2, the price of labour is $50 per day and total fixed costs are $50 per day.
a. Calculate total cost, total variable cost, and total fixed costs for each output in the table and draw the short-run total cost curves.
b. Calculate average total cost, average fixed cost, average variable cost, and marginal cost at each output in the table and draw the short-run average and marginal cost curves.

*5. In problem 3, suppose that Rubber Duckies' total fixed cost increases to $1,100 a week. Explain what changes occur to the short-run average and marginal cost curves.

6. In problem 4, suppose that the price of labour increases to $70 per day. Explain what changes occur to the short-run average and marginal cost curves.

*7. In problem 3, Rubber Duckies buys a second plant and now the total product of each quantity of labour doubles. The total fixed cost of operating each plant is $1,000 a week. The wage rate is $400 a week.
a. Set out the average total cost schedule when Rubber Duckies operates two plants.
b. Draw the long-run average cost curve.
c. Over what output range is it efficient to operate one plant and two plants?

8. In problem 4, Charlie's Chocolates buys a second plant and now the total product of each quantity of labour doubles. The total fixed cost of operating each plant is $50 a day. The wage rate is $50 a day.
a. Set out the average total cost curve when Charlie's operates two plants.
b. Draw the long-run average cost curve.
c. Over what output range is it efficient to operate one plant and two plants?

*9. The table shows the production function of Bonnie's Balloon Rides.

Labour (workers per day)	Output (rides per day)			
	Plant 1	Plant 2	Plant 3	Plant 4
1	4	10	13	15
2	10	15	18	21
3	13	18	22	24
4	15	20	24	26
5	16	21	25	27
Balloons (number)	1	2	3	4

Bonnie must pay $500 a day for each balloon she rents and $250 a day for each balloon operator she hires.
a. Find and graph the average total cost curve for each plant size.
b. Draw Bonnie's long-run average cost curve.
c. What is Bonnie's minimum efficient scale?
d. Explain how Bonnie uses her long-run average cost curve to decide how many balloons to rent.

10. The table shows the production function of Mario's Pizza-to-Go.

Labour (workers per day)	Output (pizzas per day)			
	Plant 1	Plant 2	Plant 3	Plant 4
1	4	8	11	13
2	8	12	15	17
3	11	15	18	20
4	13	17	20	22
Ovens (number)	1	2	3	4

Mario must pay $100 a day for each oven he rents and $75 a day for each kitchen hand he hires.
a. Find and graph the average total cost curve for each plant size.
b. Draw Mario's long-run average cost curve.
c. Over what output range does Mario experience economies of scale?
d. Explain how Mario uses his long-run average cost curve to decide how many ovens to rent.

CRITICAL THINKING

1. Study *Reading Between the Lines* on pp. 238–239 and then answer the following questions:
   a. Sketch the average product curve and the marginal product curve that correspond to the total product curve TP_0.
   b. Sketch the average product curve and the marginal product curve that correspond to the total product curve TP_1.
   c. Why does Fig. 2 show Alusuisse and Pechiney operating on the downward-sloping portion of the *ATC* curve and Alcan operating on the upward-sloping portion?
   d. Use the links on the Parkin-Bade Web site to obtain information about the labour force, revenue, and cost of other big aluminum companies.
   e. Using the size of the labour force and total cost data, how does the merged Alcan-Alusuisse-Pechiney compare with the other big aluminum companies?
   f. Which of the big aluminum companies do you think is the most efficient and why?

2. A telecommunication company is considering replacing human telephone operators with computers. This change will increase total fixed cost and decrease total variable cost. Either use the spreadsheet on the Parkin-Bade Web site or create your own example and sketch:
   a. The total cost curves for the original technology that uses human operators.
   b. The average cost curves for the original technology that uses human operators.
   c. The marginal cost curves for the original technology that uses human operators.
   d. The total cost curves for the new technology that uses computers.
   e. The average cost curves for the new technology that uses computers.
   f. The marginal cost curves for the new technology that uses computers.

3. A spreadsheet on the Parkin-Bade Web site provides information about the cost of operating an ATM. Use this data to work out the average cost curves for an ATM. Under what conditions might a bank *not* install an ATM but use a human teller instead?

Perfect Competition

It is morning rush hour and a six-vehicle pile-up snarls the traffic on Toronto's busiest section of Highway 401. Human injuries are light, but the toll in dented car bodies, buckled wheels and damaged tires, and crushed mufflers is huge. Competition to clean up the mess begins. Fifty towing companies compete for the initial clean-up. Several hundred body shops and repair shops battle for a place in a crowded market. How does competition affect prices and profits? ◆ Whether you want your car fixed or a pizza delivered, you have lots of choice. Just look in the Yellow Pages if you're not

Collision Course in Car Repairs

convinced! In this competitive environment, new firms enter and try their luck while other firms are squeezed out of business. ◆ In August 1995, almost 1.5 million people were unemployed. Of these, 900,000 were unemployed because they had lost their

jobs or were laid off by firms seeking to trim their costs and avoid bankruptcy. Retailers, computer manufacturers, and firms in almost every sector of the economy laid workers off even though the economy was expanding and the total number of jobs was growing. Why do firms lay off workers? When will a firm temporarily shut down and lay off its workers? ◆ The price of a personal computer keeps falling. A slow computer cost $5,000 a few years ago, and a fast one costs only $2,000 today. What goes on in an industry when the price of its output falls sharply? What happens to the profits of the firms producing such goods?

◇ Car repairs, computers, and most other goods are produced by more than one firm, and these firms compete with each other for sales. To study competitive markets, we are going to build a model of a market in which competition is as fierce and extreme as possible—more extreme than in the examples we've just considered. We call this situation "perfect competition."

After studying this chapter, you will be able to:

- ■ **Define perfect competition**
- ■ **Explain how price and output are determined in a competitive industry**
- ■ **Explain why firms sometimes shut down temporarily and lay off workers**
- ■ **Explain why firms enter and leave an industry**
- ■ **Predict the effects of a change in demand and of a technological advance**
- ■ **Explain why perfect competition is efficient**

Competition

THE FIRMS THAT YOU STUDY IN THIS CHAPTER face the force of raw competition. We call this extreme form of competition perfect competition. **Perfect competition** is an industry in which

- Many firms sell identical products to many buyers.
- There are no restrictions on entry into the industry.
- Established firms have no advantage over new ones.
- Sellers and buyers are well informed about prices.

Farming, fishing, wood pulping and paper milling, the manufacture of paper cups and plastic shopping bags, grocery retailing, photo finishing, lawn service, plumbing, painting, dry cleaning, and the provision of laundry services are all examples of highly competitive industries.

How Perfect Competition Arises

First, perfect competition arises if the minimum efficient scale of a single producer is small relative to the demand for a good or service (see Chapter 11, p. 237). The **minimum efficient scale** is the smallest quantity of output at which long-run average cost reaches its lowest level. Where the minimum efficient scale of a firm is small relative to the demand, there is room for many firms in an industry.

Second, perfect competition arises if each firm is perceived to produce a good or service that has no unique characteristics so that consumers don't care which firm they buy from.

Price Takers

Firms in perfect competition must make many decisions. But one thing they do *not* decide is the price at which to sell their output. Firms in perfect competition are price takers. A **price taker** is a firm that cannot influence the price of the good or service that it sells.

The reason why a perfectly competitive firm is a price taker is that it produces a tiny proportion of the total output of a particular good and buyers are well informed about the prices of other firms.

Imagine that you are a farmer in Saskatchewan. You have 500 hectares of wheat under cultivation—which sounds like a lot. But then you go on a drive.

Westward towards the Rocky Mountains, eastward through Manitoba, and southward through the Dakotas you find unbroken stretches of wheat. You would find similar scenes in Argentina, Australia, and Ukraine. Your 500 hectares is a drop in the ocean.

Nothing makes your wheat any better than any other farmer's, and all the buyers of wheat know the price at which they can do business. If everybody else sells their wheat for $300 a tonne and you want $310, why would people buy from you? They can simply go to the next farmer, and the one after that, and the next and buy all they need for $300. This price is determined in the market for wheat, and you are a *price taker*.

The *market* demand for wheat is not perfectly elastic. The market demand curve is downward sloping, and its elasticity depends on the substitutability of wheat for other grains such as barley, rye, corn, and rice. But the demand for wheat from farm A is perfectly elastic because wheat from farm B is a *perfect substitute* for wheat from farm A. A price taker faces a perfectly elastic demand curve.

Economic Profit and Revenue

A firm's goal is to maximize **economic profit**, which is equal to total revenue minus total cost. Total cost is the *opportunity cost* of production, which includes the firm's **normal profit**, the return that the firm's entrepreneur can obtain in the best alternative business.

A firm's **total revenue** equals the price of its output multiplied by the number of units of output sold (price × quantity). **Marginal revenue** is the change in total revenue that results from a one-unit increase in the quantity sold. Marginal revenue is calculated by dividing the change in total revenue by the change in the quantity sold.

Figure 12.1 illustrates these revenue concepts. Sidney's Sweaters is one of a thousand similar small firms. In Fig. 12.1(a), demand and supply in the sweater market determine the price, which is $25 a sweater. Sidney must take this price. He cannot influence it by changing the quantity of sweaters he produces.

The table shows three different quantities of sweaters produced. As the quantity varies, the price remains constant—in this example at $25 a sweater. Total revenue is equal to the price multiplied by the quantity sold. For example, if Sidney sells 8 sweaters, his total revenue is 8 × $25, which equals $200.

FIGURE 12.1

Demand, Price, and Revenue in Perfect Competition

(a) Sweater market

(b) Sidney's demand and marginal revenue

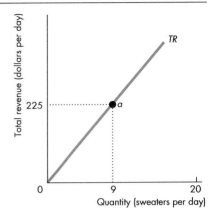

(c) Sidney's total revenue

Quantity sold (Q) (sweaters per day)	Price (P) (dollars per sweater)	Total revenue (TR = P × Q) (dollars)	Marginal revenue (MR = ΔTR/ΔQ) (dollars per additional sweater)
8	25	200	
			25
9	25	225	
			25
10	25	250	

Market demand and supply determine the market price. In part (a), the market price is $25 a sweater and 9,000 sweaters are bought and sold. Sidney faces a perfectly elastic demand at the market price of $25 a sweater. The table calculates total revenue and marginal revenue. Part (b) of the figure shows Sidney's demand curve, which is also its marginal revenue curve (MR). Part (c) shows Sidney's total revenue curve (TR). Point a corresponds to the second row of the table.

Marginal revenue is the change in total revenue that results from a one-unit increase in quantity. For example, when the quantity sold increases from 8 to 9, total revenue increases from $200 to $225, so marginal revenue is $25 a sweater. (Notice that in the table, marginal revenue appears *between* the lines for the quantities sold to remind you that marginal revenue results from the *change* in the quantity sold.)

Because the price remains constant when the quantity sold changes, the change in total revenue resulting from a one-unit increase in the quantity sold equals price. Therefore in perfect competition, marginal revenue equals price.

Figure 12.1(b) shows Sidney's marginal revenue curve (MR). This curve tells us the change in total revenue that results from selling one more sweater. This same curve is also the firm's demand curve. The firm, being a price taker, can sell any quantity it chooses at this price. The firm faces a perfectly elastic demand for its output.

The total revenue curve (TR), in part (c), shows the total revenue at each quantity sold. For example, if Sidney sells 9 sweaters, total revenue is $225 (point a). Because each additional sweater sold brings in a constant amount—$25—the total revenue curve is an upward-sloping straight line.

R E V I E W   Q U I Z

- Explain why a firm in perfect competition is a price taker.
- In perfect competition, what is the relationship between a firm's demand curve and the market demand curve?
- In perfect competition, why is a firm's demand curve also its marginal revenue curve?
- Why is the total revenue curve in perfect competition an upward-sloping straight line?

The Firm's Decisions in Perfect Competition

FIRMS IN A PERFECTLY COMPETITIVE INDUSTRY face a given market price and have the revenue curves that you've studied. These revenue curves summarize the market constraint faced by a perfectly competitive firm.

Firms also face a technology constraint, which is described by the product curves (total product, average product, and marginal product) that you studied in Chapter 11. The technology available to the firm determines its costs, which are described by the cost curves (total cost, average cost, and marginal cost) that you also studied in Chapter 11.

The task of the competitive firm is to make the maximum economic profit possible, given the constraints it faces. To achieve this objective, a firm must make four key decisions: two in the short run and two in the long run.

Short-Run Decisions   The short run is a time frame in which each firm has a given plant and the number of firms in the industry is fixed. But many things can change in the short run and the firm must react to these changes. For example, the price for which the firm can sell its output might have seasonal fluctuations, or it might fluctuate with general business fluctuations. The firm must react to short-run price fluctuations and decide:

1. Whether to produce or to shut down
2. If the decision is to produce, what quantity to produce

Long-Run Decisions   The long run is a time frame in which each firm can change the size of its plant and decide whether to leave the industry. Other firms can decide to enter the industry. So in the long run, both the plant size of each firm and the number of firms in the industry can change. Also in the long run, the constraints facing firms can change. For example, the demand for the good can permanently decrease, or technological advance can change the industry's costs. The firm must react to such long-run changes and decide:

1. Whether to increase or decrease its plant size
2. Whether to remain in an industry or leave it

The Firm and the Industry in the Short Run and the Long Run   To study a competitive industry, we begin by looking at an individual firm's short-run decisions. We then see how the short-run decisions of all firms in a competitive industry combine to determine the industry price, output, and economic profit. Then we turn to the long run and study the effects of long-run decisions on the industry price, output, and economic profit. All the decisions that we study are driven by a single objective: to maximize economic profit.

Profit-Maximizing Output

A perfectly competitive firm maximizes economic profit by choosing its output level. One way of finding the profit-maximizing output is to study a firm's total revenue and total cost curves and to find the output level at which total revenue exceeds total cost by the largest amount. Figure 12.2 shows how to do this for Sidney's Sweaters. The table lists Sidney's total revenue and total cost at different outputs, and part (a) of the figure shows Sidney's total revenue and total cost curves. These curves are graphs of the numbers shown in the first three columns of the table. The total revenue curve (TR) is the same as that in Fig. 12.1(c). The total cost curve (TC) is similar to the one that you met in Chapter 11. As output increases, so does total cost.

Economic profit equals total revenue minus total cost. The fourth column of the table in Fig. 12.2 shows Sidney's economic profit, and part (b) of the figure illustrates these numbers as Sidney's profit curve. This curve shows that Sidney makes an economic profit at outputs between 4 and 12 sweaters a day. At outputs less than 4 sweaters a day, Sidney incurs an economic loss. Sidney also incurs an economic loss if output exceeds 12 sweaters a day. At outputs of 4 sweaters and 12 sweaters a day, total cost equals total revenue and Sidney's economic profit is zero. An output at which total cost equals total revenue is called a *break-even point*. The firm's economic profit is zero but because normal profit is part of total cost, a firm makes normal profit at a break-even point. That is, at the break-even point, the entrepreneur makes an income equal to the best alternative return forgone.

Notice the relationship between the total revenue, total cost, and profit curves. The vertical distance between the total revenue and total cost curves measures economic profit. When the total revenue

FIGURE 12.2
Total Revenue, Total Cost, and Economic Profit

(a) Revenue and cost

(b) Economic profit and loss

Quantity (Q) (sweaters per day)	Total revenue (TR) (dollars)	Total cost (TC) (dollars)	Economic profit (TR – TC) (dollars)
0	0	22	–22
1	25	45	–20
2	50	66	–16
3	75	85	–10
4	100	100	0
5	125	114	11
6	150	126	24
7	175	141	34
8	200	160	40
9	225	183	42
10	250	210	40
11	275	245	30
12	300	300	0
13	325	360	–35

The table lists Sidney's total revenue, total cost, and economic profit. Part (a) graphs the total revenue and total cost curves. Economic profit, in part (a), is the height of the blue area between the total cost and total revenue curves. Sidney's makes maximum economic profit, $42 a day ($225 – $183), when it produces 9 sweaters—the output at which the vertical distance between the total revenue and total cost curves is at its largest. At outputs of 4 sweaters a day and 12 sweaters a day, Sidney makes zero economic profit—these are break-even points. At outputs less than 4 and greater than 12 sweaters a day, Sidney incurs an economic loss. Part (b) of the figure shows Sidney's profit curve. The profit curve is at its highest when economic profit is at a maximum and cuts the horizontal axis at the break-even points.

curve in part (a) is above the total cost curve, between 4 and 12 sweaters, the firm is making an economic profit, and the profit curve in part (b) is above the horizontal axis. At the break-even point, where the total cost and total revenue curves inter-

sect, the profit curve intersects the horizontal axis. The profit curve is at its highest when TR exceeds TC by the largest amount. In this example, profit maximization occurs at an output of 9 sweaters a day. At this output, Sidney's economic profit is $42 a day.

Marginal Analysis

Another way of finding the profit-maximizing output is to use *marginal analysis* and compare marginal revenue, *MR*, with marginal cost, *MC*. As output increases, marginal revenue remains constant but marginal cost changes. At low output levels, marginal cost decreases, but it eventually increases. So where the marginal cost curve intersects the marginal revenue curve, marginal cost is rising.

If marginal revenue exceeds marginal cost (if *MR* > *MC*), then the extra revenue from selling one more unit exceeds the extra cost incurred to produce it. The firm makes an economic profit on the marginal unit, so its economic profit increases if output *increases*.

If marginal revenue is less than marginal cost (if *MR* < *MC*), then the extra revenue from selling one more unit is less than the extra cost incurred to produce it. The firm incurs an economic loss on the marginal unit, so its economic profit decreases if output increases and its economic profit increases if output *decreases*.

Economic profit is maximized when the firm produces the quantity at which marginal revenue equals marginal cost (*MR* = *MC*).

The rule *MR* = *MC* is a prime example of marginal analysis. To check that the rule works, look at Fig. 12.3. The table lists Sidney's marginal revenue and marginal cost and the figure shows the marginal revenue and marginal cost curves. Marginal revenue is a constant $25 a sweater. Over the range of outputs shown in the table, marginal cost increases from $19 a sweater to $35 a sweater.

Focus on the highlighted rows of the table. If Sidney increases output from 8 sweaters to 9 sweaters, marginal revenue is $25 and marginal cost is $23. Because marginal revenue exceeds marginal cost, economic profit increases. The last column of the table shows that economic profit increases from $40 to $42, an increase of $2. This economic profit from the ninth sweater is shown as the blue area in the figure.

If Sidney increases output from 9 sweaters to 10 sweaters, marginal revenue is still $25, but marginal cost is $27. Because marginal revenue is less than marginal cost, economic profit decreases. The last column of the table shows that economic profit decreases from $42 to $40. This loss from the tenth sweater is shown as the red area in the figure.

Sidney maximizes economic profit by producing 9 sweaters a day, the quantity at which marginal revenue equals marginal cost.

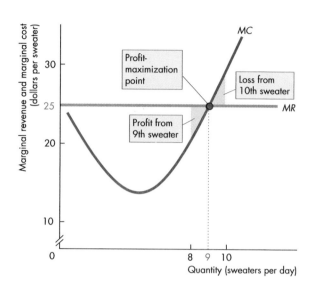

FIGURE 12.3
Profit-Maximizing Output

Quantity (Q) (sweaters per day)	Total revenue (TR) (dollars)	Marginal revenue (MR) (dollars per additional sweater)	Total cost (TC) (dollars)	Marginal cost (MC) (dollars per additional sweater)	Economic profit (TR − TC) (dollars)
7	175		141		34
		25		19	
8	200		160		40
		25		23	
9	225		183		42
		25		27	
10	250		210		40
		25		35	
11	275		245		30

Another way of finding the profit-maximizing output is to determine the output at which marginal revenue equals marginal cost. The table shows that if output increases from 8 to 9 sweaters, marginal cost is $23, which is less than the marginal revenue of $25. If output increases from 9 to 10 sweaters, marginal cost is $27, which exceeds the marginal revenue of $25. The figure shows that marginal cost and marginal revenue are equal when Sidney produces 9 sweaters a day. If marginal revenue exceeds marginal cost, an increase in output increases economic profit. If marginal revenue is less than marginal cost, an increase in output decreases economic profit. If marginal revenue equals marginal cost, economic profit is maximized.

Profits and Losses in the Short Run

In the short run, although the firm produces the profit-maximizing output, it does not necessarily end up making an economic profit. It might do so, but it might alternatively break even (with a normal profit), or incur an economic loss. To determine which of these outcomes occurs, we compare the firm's total revenue and total cost or, equivalently, we compare price with average total cost. If price equals average total cost, the firm breaks even—makes normal profit. If price exceeds average total cost, the firm makes an economic profit. If price is less than average total cost, the firm incurs an economic loss. Figure 12.4 shows these three possible short-run profit outcomes.

Three Possible Profit Outcomes In part (a), the price of a sweater is $20. Sidney produces 8 sweaters a day. Average total cost is also $20 a sweater, so Sidney makes normal profit and zero economic profit. Sidney breaks even.

In part (b), the price of a sweater is $25. Profit is maximized when output is 9 sweaters a day. Here, price exceeds average total cost (*ATC*), so Sidney

makes an economic profit. This economic profit is $42 a day. It is made up of $4.67 per sweater ($25.00 – $20.33), multiplied by the number of sweaters ($4.67 × 9 = $42). The blue rectangle shows this economic profit. The height of that rectangle is profit per sweater, $4.67, and the length is the quantity of sweaters produced, 9 a day, so the area of the rectangle measures Sidney's economic profit of $42 a day.

In part (c), the price of a sweater is $17. Here, price is less than average total cost and Sidney incurs an economic loss. Price and marginal revenue are $17 a sweater, and the profit-maximizing (in this case, loss-minimizing) output is 7 sweaters a day. Sidney's total revenue is $119 a day (7 × $17). Average total cost is $20.14 a sweater so the economic loss is $3.14 per sweater ($20.14 – $17.00). This loss per sweater multiplied by the number of sweaters is $22 ($3.14 × 7 = $22). The red rectangle shows this economic loss. The height of that rectangle is economic loss per sweater, $3.14, and the length is the quantity of sweaters produced, 7 a day, so the area of the rectangle measures Sidney's economic loss of $22 a day.

FIGURE 12.4

Three Possible Profit Outcomes in the Short Run

(a) Normal profit

(b) Economic profit

(c) Economic loss

In the short run, the firm might break even (making a normal profit), make an economic profit, or incur an economic loss. If the price equals minimum average total cost, the firm breaks even and makes a normal profit (part a). If the price exceeds the average total cost of producing the profit-maximizing output, the firm makes an economic profit (the blue rectangle in part b). If the price is below minimum average total cost, the firm incurs an economic loss (the red rectangle in part c).

The Firm's Short-Run Supply Curve

A perfectly competitive firm's short-run supply curve shows how its profit-maximizing output varies as the market price varies, other things remaining the same. Figure 12.5 (a) shows Sidney's marginal cost and average variable cost curves, and part (b) shows the firm's supply curve. There is a direct link between the marginal cost and average variable cost curves and the supply curve. Let's see what that link is.

Temporary Plant Shutdown In the short run, a firm cannot avoid incurring its fixed cost. But the firm can avoid variable costs by temporarily laying off its workers and shutting down. If a firm shuts down, it produces no output and it incurs a loss equal to total fixed cost. This loss is the largest that a firm need incur. A firm shuts down if price falls below the minimum of average variable cost. The **shutdown point** is the output and price at which the firm just covers its total variable cost—point s in Fig. 12.5(a). If the price is \$17, the marginal revenue curve is MR_0 and the profit-maximizing output is 7 sweaters a day at point s. But both price and average variable cost equal \$17, so Sidney's total revenue equals its total variable cost. Sidney incurs an economic loss equal to total fixed cost. At a price below \$17, no matter what quantity Sidney produces, average *variable* cost exceeds price and the firm's loss exceeds total fixed cost. At a price below \$17, Sidney shuts down.

The Short-Run Supply Curve If the price is above minimum average variable cost, Sidney maximizes profit by producing the output at which marginal cost equals price. We can determine the quantity produced at each price from the marginal cost curve. At a price of \$25, the marginal revenue curve is MR_1 and Sidney maximizes profit by producing 9 sweaters. At a price of \$31, the marginal revenue curve is MR_2 and Sidney produces 10 sweaters.

Sidney's short-run supply curve, shown in Fig. 12.5(b), has two separate parts: First, at prices that exceed minimum average variable cost, the supply curve is the same as the marginal cost curve above the shutdown point (s). Second, at prices below minimum average variable cost, Sidney shuts down and produces nothing. Its supply curve runs along the vertical axis. At a price of \$17, Sidney is indifferent between shutting down and producing 7 sweaters a day. Either way, Sidney incurs a loss of \$22 a day.

FIGURE 12.5
A Firm's Supply Curve

(a) Marginal cost and average variable cost

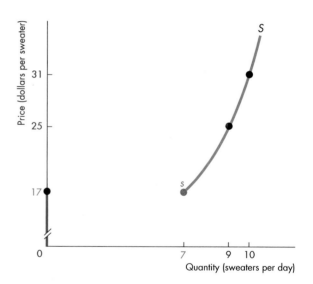

(b) Sidney's supply curve

Part (a) shows Sidney's profit-maximizing output at various market prices. At \$25 a sweater, Sidney produces 9 sweaters. At \$17 a sweater, Sidney produces 7 sweaters. At any price below \$17 a sweater, Sidney produces nothing. Sidney's shutdown point is s. Part (b) shows Sidney's supply curve—the number of sweaters Sidney will produce at each price. It is made up of its marginal cost curve (part a) at all points above its average variable cost curve and the vertical axis at all prices below minimum average variable cost.

Short-Run Industry Supply Curve

The **short-run industry supply curve** shows the quantity supplied by the industry at each price when the plant size of each firm and the number of firms remain constant. The quantity supplied by the industry at a given price is the sum of the quantities supplied by all firms in the industry at that price.

Figure 12.6 shows the supply curve for the competitive sweater industry. In this example, the industry consists of 1,000 firms exactly like Sidney's Sweaters. At each price, the quantity supplied by the industry is 1,000 times the quantity supplied by a single firm.

The table in Fig. 12.6 shows the firm's and the industry's supply schedule and how the industry supply curve is constructed. At prices below $17, every firm in the industry shuts down; the quantity supplied by the industry is zero. At a price of $17, each firm is indifferent between shutting down and producing nothing or operating and producing 7 sweaters a day. Some firms will shut down and others will supply 7 sweaters a day. The quantity supplied by each firm is *either* 0 *or* 7 sweaters, but the quantity supplied by the industry is *between* 0 (all firms shut down) and 7,000 (all firms produce 7 sweaters a day each).

To construct the industry supply curve, we sum the quantities supplied by the individual firms at each price. Each of the 1,000 firms in the industry has a supply schedule like Sidney's. At prices below $17, the industry supply curve runs along the price axis. At a price of $17, the industry supply curve is horizontal—supply is perfectly elastic. As the price rises above $17, each firm increases its quantity supplied and the quantity supplied by the industry increases by 1,000 times that of each firm.

FIGURE 12.6

Industry Supply Curve

	Price (dollars) per sweater)	Quantity supplied by Sidney's Sweaters (sweaters per day)	Quantity supplied by industry (sweaters per day)
a	17	0 or 7	0 to 7,000
b	20	8	8,000
c	25	9	9,000
d	31	10	10,000

The industry supply schedule is the sum of the supply schedules of all individual firms. An industry that consists of 1,000 identical firms has a supply schedule similar to that of the individual firm but the quantity supplied by the industry is 1,000 times as large as that of the individual firm (see table). The industry supply curve is S_I. Points a, b, c, and d correspond to the rows of the table. At the shutdown price of $17, each firm produces either 0 or 7 sweaters per day. The industry supply curve is perfectly elastic at the shutdown price.

R E V I E W   Q U I Z

- Why does a firm in perfect competition produce the quantity at which marginal cost equals price?
- What is the lowest price at which a firm will produce an output? Explain why.
- What is the largest economic loss that a firm incurs in the short run and why?
- What is the relation among a firm's supply curve, its marginal cost curve, and its average variable cost curve?
- How do we derive an industry supply curve?

So far, we have studied a single firm in isolation. We have seen that the firm's profit-maximizing actions depend on the market price, which the firm takes as given. But how is the market price determined? Let's find out.

Output, Price, and Profit in Perfect Competition

TO DETERMINE THE MARKET PRICE AND THE quantity bought and sold in a perfectly competitive market, we need to study how market demand and market supply interact. We begin by studying a perfectly competitive market in the short run when the number of firms is fixed and each firm has a given plant size.

Short-Run Equilibrium

Industry demand and industry supply determine the market price and industry output. Figure 12.7(a) shows a short-run equilibrium. The supply curve S is the same as S_I in Fig. 12.6. If the demand curve D_1 illustrates the industry demand, then the equilibrium price is $20. Although industry demand and supply determines this price, each firm takes the price as given and produces its profit-maximizing output, which is 8 sweaters a day. Because the industry has 1,000 firms, industry output is 8,000 sweaters a day.

A Change in Demand

Changes in demand bring changes to short-run industry equilibrium. Figure 12.7(b) shows these changes.

If demand increases and the demand curve shifts rightward to D_2, the price rises to $25. At this price, each firm maximizes profit by increasing output. The new output level is 9 sweaters a day for each firm and 9,000 sweaters a day for the industry.

If demand decreases and the demand curve shifts leftward to D_3, the price now falls to $17. At this price, each firm maximizes profit by decreasing its output. The new output level is 7 sweaters a day for each firm and 7,000 sweaters a day for the industry.

If the demand curve shifts farther leftward than D_3, the price remains constant at $17. Some firms continue to produce 7 sweaters a day, and others temporarily shut down. Firms are indifferent between these two activities, and, whichever they choose, they incur an economic loss equal to total fixed cost. The number of firms continuing to produce is just enough to satisfy the market demand at a price of $17.

Let's now look at the profits that firms make and losses they can incur in a short-run equilibrium.

FIGURE 12.7

Short-Run Equilibrium

(a) Equilibrium

(b) Change in equilibrium

In part (a), the industry supply curve is S. Demand is D_1 and the price is $20. At this price, each firm produces 8 sweaters a day and the industry produces 8,000 sweaters a day. In part (b), when demand increases to D_2, the price rises to $25 and

each firm increases its output to 9 sweaters a day. Industry output is 9,000 sweaters a day. When demand decreases to D_3, the price falls to $17 and each firm decreases its output to 7 sweaters a day. Industry output is 7,000 sweaters a day.

Long-Run Adjustments

In short-run equilibrium, a firm might make an economic profit, incur an economic loss, or break even (make normal profit). Although each of these three situations is a short-run equilibrium, only one of them is a long-run equilibrium. To see why, we need to examine the forces at work in a competitive industry in the long run.

In the long run, an industry adjusts in two ways:

- Entry and exit
- Changes in plant size

Let's look first at entry and exit.

Entry and Exit

In the long run, firms respond to economic profit and economic loss by either entering or exiting an industry. Firms enter an industry in which firms are making an economic profit and they exit an industry in which firms are incurring an economic loss. Temporary economic profit and temporary economic loss like the win or loss at a casino do not trigger entry and exit. But the prospect of persistent economic profit or loss does.

Entry and exit influence price, the quantity produced, and economic profit. The immediate effect of these decisions is to shift the industry supply curve. If more firms enter an industry, supply increases and the industry supply curve shifts rightward. If firms exit an industry, supply decreases and the industry supply curve shifts leftward.

Let's see what happens when new firms enter an industry.

The Effects of Entry Figure 12.8 shows the effects of entry. Suppose that all the firms in this industry have cost curves like those in Fig. 12.4. At any price greater than $20, firms make an economic profit. At any price less than $20, firms incur an economic loss. And at a price of $20, firms make zero economic profit. Also suppose that the demand curve for sweaters is D. If the industry supply curve is S_1, sweaters sell for $23, and 7,000 sweaters a day are produced. Firms in the industry make an economic profit. This economic profit is a signal for new firms to enter the industry. As these events unfold, supply increases and the industry supply curve shifts rightward to S_0. With the greater supply and unchanged demand, the market price falls from $23 to $20 a

sweater and the quantity produced by the industry increases from 7,000 to 8,000 sweaters a day.

Industry output increases but Sidney's Sweaters and the other firms in the industry *decrease* output! Because the price falls, each firm produces less. But because the number of firms in the industry increases, the industry as a whole produces more.

Because price falls, each firm's economic profit decreases. When the price falls to $20, economic profit disappears and each firm makes a normal profit.

You have just discovered a key proposition:

As new firms enter an industry, the price falls and the economic profit of each existing firm decreases.

An example of this process occurred in recent years in the personal computer industry. When IBM introduced its first PC in the early 1980s, there was little competition and the price of PCs gave IBM a big profit. But new firms such as Compaq, NEC, Dell, and a host of others entered the industry with

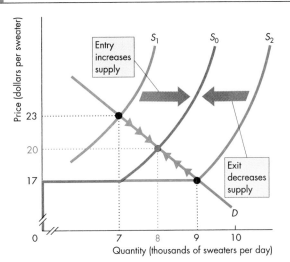

FIGURE 12.8

Entry and Exit

When new firms enter the sweater industry, the industry supply curve shifts rightward, from S_1 to S_0. The equilibrium price falls from $23 to $20, and the quantity produced increases from 7,000 to 8,000 sweaters. When firms exit the sweater industry, the industry supply curve shifts leftward, from S_2 to S_0. The equilibrium price rises from $17 to $20, and the quantity produced decreases from 9,000 to 8,000 sweaters.

machines that were technologically identical to IBM's. In fact, they were so similar that they came to be called "clones." The massive wave of entry into the personal computer industry shifted the supply curve rightward and lowered the price and the economic profit for all firms.

Let's now look at the effects of exit.

The Effects of Exit Figure 12.8 shows the effects of exit. Suppose that firm's costs and market demand are the same as before. But now suppose the supply curve is S_2. The market price is $17 and 9,000 sweaters a day are produced. Firms now incur an economic loss. This economic loss is a signal for some firms to exit the industry. As firms exit, the supply curve shifts leftward to S_0. With the decrease in supply, industry output decreases from 9,000 to 8,000 sweaters and the price rises from $17 to $20.

As the price rises, Sidney's Sweaters, like each other firm in the industry, moves up along its supply curve and increases output. That is, for each firm that remains in the industry, the profit-maximizing output increases. Because the price rises and each firm sells more, economic loss decreases. When the price rises to $20, each firm makes a normal profit.

You have just discovered a second key proposition:

As firms leave an industry, the price rises and the economic loss of each remaining firm decreases.

An example of a firm leaving an industry is International Harvester, a manufacturer of farm equipment. For decades, people associated the name "International Harvester" with tractors, combines, and other farm machines. But International Harvester wasn't the only maker of farm equipment. The industry became intensely competitive, and the firm began losing money. Now the company has a new name, Navistar International, and it doesn't make tractors any more. After years of losses and shrinking revenues, it got out of the farm business in 1985 and started to make trucks.

International Harvester exited because it was incurring an economic loss. Its exit decreased supply and made it possible for the remaining firms in the industry to break even.

You've now seen how economic profits induce entry, which in turn lowers profits and how economic losses induce exit, which in turn eliminates losses. Let's now look at changes in plant size.

Changes in Plant Size

A firm changes its plant size if, by doing so, it can lower its costs and increase its economic profit. You can probably think of lots of examples of firms changing their plant size.

One example that has almost certainly happened near your campus in recent years is a change in the plant size of Kinko or similar copy shops. Another is the number of FedEx vans that you see on the streets and highways. And another is the number of square metres of retail space devoted to selling computers and video games. These are examples of firms increasing their plant size to seek larger profits.

There are also many examples of firms decreasing their plant size to avoid economic losses. One of these is Eaton's, the department store company, before it finally closed down. As competition from other retailers become tougher, Eaton's closed some lines of business. Many firms have scaled back in a process called *downsizing* in recent years.

Figure 12.9 shows a situation in which Sidney's Sweaters can increase its profit by increasing its plant size. With its current plant, Sidney's marginal cost curve is MC_0, and its short-run average total cost curve is $SRAC_0$. The market price is $25 a sweater, so Sidney's marginal revenue curve is MR_0, and Sidney maximizes profit by producing 6 sweaters a day.

Sidney's Sweaters' long-run average cost curve is *LRAC*. By increasing its plant size—installing more machines—Sidney can move along its long-run average cost curve. As Sidney's Sweaters increases its plant size, its short-run marginal cost curve shifts rightward.

Recall that a firm's short-run supply curve is linked to its marginal cost curve. As Sidney's marginal cost curve shifts rightward, so does its supply curve. If Sidney's Sweaters and the other firms in the industry increase their plants, the short-run industry supply curve shifts rightward and the market price falls. The fall in the market price limits the extent to which Sidney can profit from an increase in plant size.

Figure 12.9 also shows Sidney's Sweaters in a long-run competitive equilibrium. This situation arises when the market price has fallen to $20 a sweater. Marginal revenue is MR_1, and Sidney maximizes profit by producing 8 sweaters a day. In this situation, Sidney's Sweaters cannot increase its profit by changing its plant size. Sidney's Sweaters is producing at minimum long-run average cost (point *m* on *LRAC*).

Because Sidney's Sweaters is producing a mini-

FIGURE 12.9

Plant Size and Long-Run Equilibrium

Initially, Sidney's plant has marginal cost curve MC_0 and short-run average total cost curve $SRAC_0$. The market price is $25 a sweater, and Sidney's marginal revenue is MR_0. The short-run profit-maximizing quantity is 6 sweaters a day. Sidney can increase his profit by increasing the plant size. If all firms in the sweater industry increase their plant sizes, the short-run industry supply increases and the market price falls. In long-run equilibrium, a firm operates with the plant size that minimizes its average cost. Here, Sidney operates the plant with short-run marginal cost MC_1 and short-run average cost $SRAC_1$. Sidney is also on the long-run average cost curve $LRAC$ and produces at point m. Output is 8 sweaters a day, and its average total cost equals the price of a sweater—$20.

mum long-run average cost, it has no incentive to change its plant size. Either a bigger plant or a smaller plant has a higher long-run average cost. If Fig. 12.9 describes the situation of all firms in the sweater industry, the industry is in long-run equilibrium. No firm has an incentive to change its plant size. Also, because each firm is making zero economic profit (normal profit), no firm has an incentive to enter the industry or to leave it.

Long-Run Equilibrium

Long-run equilibrium occurs in a competitive industry when economic profit is zero (when firms earn normal profit). If the firms in a competitive industry are making an economic profit, new firms enter the

industry. If firms can lower their costs by increasing their plant size, they expand. Each of these actions increases industry supply, shifts the industry supply curve rightward, lowers the price, and decreases economic profit.

Firms continue to enter and economic profit continues to decrease as long as firms in the industry are earning positive economic profits. When economic profit has been eliminated, firms stop entering the industry. And when firms are operating with the least-cost plant size, they stop expanding.

If the firms in a competitive industry are incurring an economic loss, some firms exit the industry. If firms can lower their costs by decreasing their plant size, they downsize. Each of these actions decreases industry supply, shifts the industry supply curve leftward, raises the price, and decreases economic loss.

Firms continue to exit and economic loss continues to decrease as long as firms in the industry are incurring economic losses. When economic loss has been eliminated, firms stop exiting the industry. And when firms are operating with the least-cost plant size, they stop downsizing.

So in long-run equilibrium in a competitive industry, firms neither enter nor exit the industry and neither expand nor downsize. Each firm earns normal profit.

R E V I E W   Q U I Z

- When a firm in perfect competition produces the quantity that maximizes profit, what is the relationship between the firm's marginal cost, marginal revenue, and price?
- If the firms in a competitive industry earn an economic profit, what happens to supply, price, output, and economic profit?
- If the firms in a competitive industry incur an economic loss, what happens to supply, price, output, and economic profit?

You've seen how a competitive industry adjusts towards its long-run equilibrium. But a competitive industry is rarely *in* a state of long-run equilibrium. It is constantly and restlessly evolving towards such an equilibrium. But the constraints that firms in the industry face are constantly changing. Two persistent sources of change are in tastes and technology. Let's see how a competitive industry reacts to such changes.

Changing Tastes and Advancing Technology

INCREASED AWARENESS OF THE HEALTH HAZARD of smoking has caused a decrease in the demand for tobacco and cigarettes. The development of inexpensive car and air transportation has caused a huge decrease in the demand for long-distance trains and buses. Solid-state electronics have caused a large decrease in the demand for TV and radio repair. The development of good-quality inexpensive clothing has decreased the demand for sewing machines. What happens in a competitive industry when there is a permanent decrease in the demand for its products?

The development of the microwave oven has produced an enormous increase in demand for paper, glass, and plastic cooking utensils and for plastic wrap. The widespread use of the personal computer has brought a huge increase in the demand for floppy disks. What happens in a competitive industry when the demand for its output increases?

Advances in technology are constantly lowering the costs of production. New biotechnologies have dramatically lowered the costs of producing many food and pharmaceutical products. New electronic technologies have lowered the cost of producing just about every good and service. What happens in a competitive industry when technological change lowers its production costs?

Let's use the theory of perfect competition to answer these questions.

A Permanent Change in Demand

Figure 12.10(a) shows a competitive industry that initially is in long-run equilibrium. The demand curve is D_0, the supply curve is S_0, the market price is P_0, and industry output is Q_0. Figure 12.10(b) shows a single firm in this initial long-run equilibrium. The firm produces q_0 and makes a normal profit and zero economic profit.

Now suppose that demand decreases and the demand curve shifts leftward to D_1, as shown in part (a). The price falls to P_1, and the quantity supplied by the industry decreases from Q_0 to Q_1 as the industry slides down its short-run supply curve S_0. Part (b) shows the situation facing a firm. Price is now below the firm's minimum average total cost, so the firm incurs an economic loss. But to keep its loss to a

minimum, the firm adjusts its output to keep marginal cost equal to price. At a price of P_1, each firm produces an output of q_1.

The industry is now in short-run equilibrium but not long-run equilibrium. It is in short-run equilibrium because each firm is maximizing profit. But it is not in long-run equilibrium because each firm is incurring an economic loss—its average total cost exceeds the price.

The economic loss is a signal for some firms to leave the industry. As they do so, short-run industry supply decreases and the supply curve gradually shifts leftward. As industry supply decreases, the price rises. At each higher price, a firm's profit-maximizing output is greater, so the firms remaining in the industry increase their output as the price rises. Each firm slides up its marginal cost or supply curve (part b). That is, as firms exit the industry, industry output decreases but the output of the firms that remain in the industry increases. Eventually, enough firms leave the industry for the industry supply curve to have shifted to S_1 (part a). At this time, the price has returned to its original level, P_0. At this price, the firms remaining in the industry produce q_0, the same quantity that they produced before the decrease in demand. Because firms are now making normal profits and zero economic profit, no firm wants to enter or exit the industry. The industry supply curve remains at S_1, and industry output is Q_2. The industry is again in long-run equilibrium.

The difference between the initial long-run equilibrium and the final long-run equilibrium is the number of firms in the industry. A permanent decrease in demand has decreased the number of firms. Each remaining firm produces the same output in the new long-run equilibrium as it did initially and earns a normal profit. In the process of moving from the initial equilibrium to the new one, firms incur economic losses.

We've just worked out how a competitive industry responds to a permanent *decrease* in demand. A permanent increase in demand triggers a similar response, except in the opposite direction. The increase in demand brings a higher price, economic profit, and entry. Entry increases industry supply and eventually lowers the price to its original level.

The demand for airline travel in the world economy has increased permanently in recent years and the deregulation of the airlines has freed up firms to seek profit opportunities in this industry. The result has been a massive rate of entry of new airlines. The

FIGURE 12.10

A Decrease in Demand

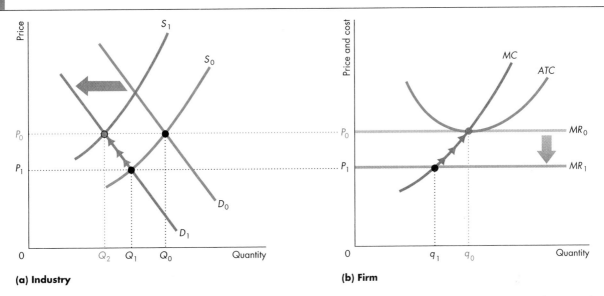

(a) Industry	(b) Firm

An industry starts out in long-run competitive equilibrium. Part (a) shows the industry demand curve D_0, the industry supply curve S_0, the equilibrium quantity Q_0, and the market price P_0. Each firm sells its output at price P_0, so its marginal revenue curve is MR_0 in part (b). Each firm produces q_0 and makes a normal profit. Demand decreases permanently from D_0 to D_1 (part a). The equilibrium price falls to P_1, each firm decreases its output to q_1 (part b), and industry output decreases to Q_1 (part a).

In this new situation, firms incur economic losses and some firms leave the industry. As they do so, the industry supply curve gradually shifts leftward, from S_0 to S_1. This shift gradually raises the market price from P_1 back to P_0. While the price is below P_0, firms incur economic losses and some firms leave the industry. Once the price has returned to P_0, each firm makes a normal profit. Firms have no further incentive to leave the industry. Each firm produces q_0, and industry output is Q_2.

process of competition and change in the airline industry is similar to what we have just studied (but with an increase in demand rather than a decrease in demand).

We've now studied the effects of a permanent change in demand for a good. To study these effects, we began and ended in a long-run equilibrium and examined the process that takes a market from one equilibrium to another. It is this process, not the equilibrium points, that describes the real world.

One feature of the predictions that we have just generated seems odd: In the long run, regardless of whether demand increases or decreases, the price returns to its original level. Is this outcome inevitable? In fact, it is not. It is possible for the long-run equilibrium price to remain the same, rise, or fall.

External Economies and Diseconomies

The change in the long-run equilibrium price depends on external economies and external diseconomies. **External economies** are factors beyond the control of an individual firm that lower its costs as the *industry* output increases. **External diseconomies** are factors outside the control of a firm that raise the firm's costs as *industry* output increases. With no external economies or external diseconomies, a firm's costs remain constant as the industry output changes.

Figure 12.11 illustrates these three cases and introduces a new supply concept: the long-run industry supply curve.

A **long-run industry supply curve** shows how the quantity supplied by an industry varies as the market price varies after all the possible adjustments have been made, including changes in plant size and the number of firms in the industry.

Part (a) shows the case we have just studied—no external economies or diseconomies. The long-run industry supply curve (LS_A) is perfectly elastic. In this case, a permanent increase in demand from D_0 to D_1 has no effect on the price in the long run. The increase in demand brings a temporary increase in price to P_S and a short-run quantity increase from Q_0 to Q_S. Entry increases short-run supply from S_0 to S_1, which lowers the price to its original level, P_0, and increases the quantity to Q_1.

Part (b) shows the case of external diseconomies. The long-run supply industry curve (LS_B) slopes upward. A permanent increase in demand from D_0 to D_1 increases the price in both the short run and the long run. As in the previous case, the increase in demand brings a temporary increase in price to P_S and a short-run quantity increase from Q_0 to Q_S. Entry increases short-run supply from S_0 to S_2, which lowers the price to P_2 and increases the quantity to Q_2.

One source of external diseconomies is congestion. The airline industry provides a good example. With bigger airline industry output, there is more congestion of airports and airspace, which results in longer delays and extra waiting time for passengers and airplanes. These external diseconomies mean that as the output of air transportation services increases (in the absence of technological advances), average cost increases. As a result, the long-run supply curve is upward sloping. So a permanent increase in demand brings an increase in quantity and a rise in the price. (Industries with external diseconomies might nonetheless have a falling price because technological advances shift the long-run supply curve downward.)

Part (c) shows the case of external economies. In this case, the long-run industry supply curve (LS_C) slopes downward. A permanent increase in demand from D_0 to D_1 increases the price in the short run and lowers it in the long run. Again, the increase in demand brings a temporary increase in price to P_S, and a short-run quantity increase from Q_0 to Q_S. Entry increases short-run supply from S_0 to S_3, which lowers the price to P_3 and increases the quantity to Q_3.

FIGURE 12.11
Long-Run Changes in Price and Quantity

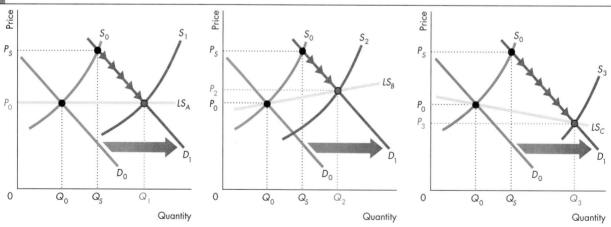

(a) Constant-cost industry

(b) Increasing-cost industry

(c) Decreasing-cost industry

Three possible changes in price and quantity occur in the long run. When demand increases from D_0 to D_1, entry occurs and the industry supply curve shifts from S_0 to S_1. In part (a), the long-run supply curve, LS_A, is horizontal. The quantity increases from Q_0 to Q_1 and the price remains constant at P_0. In part (b), the long-run supply curve is LS_B; the price rises to P_2, and the quantity increases to Q_2. This case occurs in an industry with external diseconomies. In part (c), the long-run supply curve is LS_C; the price falls to P_3, and the quantity increases to Q_3. This case occurs in an industry with external economies.

One of the best examples of external economies is the growth of specialist support services for an industry as it expands. As farm output increased in the nineteenth and early twentieth centuries, the services available to farmers expanded and average farm costs fell. For example, new firms specialized in the development and marketing of farm machinery and fertilizers. As a result, average farm costs decreased. Farms enjoyed the benefits of external economies. As a consequence, as the demand for farm products increased, the output increased but the price fell.

Over the long term, the prices of many goods and services have fallen, not because of external economies but because of technological change. Let's now study this influence on a competitive market.

Technological Change

Industries are constantly discovering lower-cost techniques of production. Most cost-saving production techniques cannot be implemented, however, without investing in new plant and equipment. As a consequence, it takes time for a technological advance to spread through an industry. Some firms whose plants are on the verge of being replaced will be quick to adopt the new technology, while other firms whose plants have recently been replaced will continue to operate with an old technology until they can no longer cover their average variable cost. Once average variable cost cannot be covered, a firm will scrap even a relatively new plant (embodying an old technology) in favour of a plant with a new technology.

New technology allows firms to produce at a lower cost. As a result, as firms adopt a new technology, their cost curves shift downward. With lower costs, firms are willing to supply a given quantity at a lower price, or, equivalently, they are willing to supply a larger quantity at a given price. In other words, industry supply increases, and the industry supply curve shifts rightward. With a given demand, the quantity produced increases and the price falls.

Two forces are at work in an industry undergoing technological change. Firms that adopt the new technology make an economic profit. So there is entry by new-technology firms. Firms that stick with the old technology incur economic losses. They either exit the industry or switch to the new technology.

As old-technology firms disappear and new-technology firms enter, the price falls and the quantity produced increases. Eventually, the industry arrives at a long-run equilibrium in which all the firms use the new technology and make a zero economic profit (a normal profit). Because in the long run competition eliminates economic profit, technological change brings only temporary gains to producers. But the lower prices and better products that technological advances bring are permanent gains for consumers.

The process that we've just described is one in which some firms experience economic profits and others experience economic losses. It is a period of dynamic change for an industry. Some firms do well, and others do badly. Often, the process has a geographical dimension—the expanding new technology firms bring prosperity to what was once the boondocks and traditional industrial regions decline. Sometimes, the new-technology firms are in a foreign country, while the old-technology firms are in the domestic economy. The information revolution of the 1990s has produced many examples of changes like these. The computer programming industry, traditionally concentrated in the United States, now flourishes in Canada, Britain, and India. Television shows and movies, traditionally made in Los Angeles and New York, are now made in large numbers in Toronto and Vancouver.

Technological advances are not confined to the information and entertainment industry. Even milk production is undergoing a major technological change because of genetic engineering.

REVIEW QUIZ

- Describe the course of events in a competitive industry that follow a decrease in demand. What happens to output, price, and economic profit in the short run and in the long run? Explain how the presence of external economies and diseconomies influences the outcome.

- Describe the course of events in a competitive industry following an increase in demand. What happens to output, price, and economic profit in the short run and in the long run? Explain how the presence of external economies and diseconomies influences the outcome.

- Describe the course of events in a competitive industry following the adoption of a new technology. What happens to output, price, and economic profit in the short run and in the long run?

Competition and Efficiency

A COMPETITIVE INDUSTRY CAN ACHIEVE AN efficient use of resources. You studied efficiency in Chapter 6 using only the concepts of demand, supply, consumer surplus, and producer surplus. But now that you have learned what lies behind the demand and supply curves of a competitive market, you can gain a deeper understanding of how the competitive market achieves efficiency.

Efficient Use of Resources

Recall that resource use is efficient when we produce the goods and services that people value most highly (see Chapter 6, pp. 110–111). If someone can become better off without anyone else becoming worse off, resources are *not* being used efficiently. For example, suppose we produce a computer that no one uses and that no one will ever use. Suppose also that some people are clamouring for more video games. If we produce one less computer and reallocate the unused resources to produce more video games, some people will become better off and no one will be worse off. So the initial resource allocation was inefficient.

In the more technical language that you have learned, resource use is efficient when marginal benefit equals marginal cost. In the computer and video games example, the marginal benefit of video games exceeds the marginal cost. And the marginal cost of a computer exceeds its marginal benefit. So by producing fewer computers and more video games, we move resources towards a higher-value use.

Choices, Equilibrium, and Efficiency

We can use what you have learned about the decisions made by consumers and competitive firms and market equilibrium to describe an efficient use of resources.

Choices   Consumers allocate their budgets to get the most value possible out of them. And we derive a consumer's demand curve by finding how the best budget allocation changes as the price of a good changes. So consumers get the most value out of their resources at all points along their demand curves, which are also their marginal benefit curves.

Competitive firms produce the quantity that maximizes profit. And we derive the firm's supply curve by finding the profit-maximizing quantities at each price. So firms get the most value out of their resources at all points along their supply curves, which are also their marginal cost curves. (On their supply curves, firms are *technologically efficient*—they get the maximum possible output from given inputs—and *economically efficient*—they combine resources to minimize cost. See Chapter 10, pp. 205–206.)

Equilibrium   In competitive equilibrium, the quantity demanded equals the quantity supplied. So the price equals the consumers' marginal benefit and the producers' marginal cost. In this situation, the gains from trade between consumers and producers are maximized. These gains from trade are the consumer surplus plus the producer surplus.

The gains from trade for consumers are measured by *consumer surplus*, which is the area between the demand curve and the price paid. (See Chapter 6, p. 113.) The gains from trade for producers are measured by *producer surplus*, which is the area between the marginal cost curve and the price received. The total gains from trade are the sum of consumer surplus and producer surplus.

Efficiency   If the people who consume and produce a good or service are the only ones affected by it, and if the market for the good or service is in equilibrium, then resources are being used efficiently. They cannot be reallocated to increase their value.

In such a situation, there are no *external benefits* or *external costs*. **External benefits** are benefits that accrue to people other than the buyer of a good. For example, you might get a benefit from your neighbour's expenditure on her garden. Your neighbour buys the quantities of garden plants that make her as well off as possible, not her plus you.

In the absence of external benefits, the market demand curve measures marginal *social* benefit—the value that *everyone* places on one more unit of a good or service.

External costs are costs not borne by the producer of a good or service but by someone else. For example, a firm might lower its costs by polluting. The cost of pollution is an external cost. Firms produce the output level that maximizes their own profit and they do not count the cost of pollution as a charge against their profit.

In the absence of external costs, the market supply curve measures marginal *social* cost—the entire marginal cost that *anyone* bears to produce one more unit of a good or service.

An Efficient Allocation   Figure 12.12 shows an efficient allocation. Consumers are efficient at all points on the demand curve, D (which is also the marginal benefit curve MB). Producers are efficient at all points on the supply curve, S (which is also the marginal cost curve MC). Resources are used efficiently at the quantity Q^* and price P^*. Marginal benefit equals marginal cost, and the sum of producer surplus (blue area) and consumer surplus (green area) is maximized.

If output is Q_0, marginal cost is C_0 and marginal benefit is B_0. Producers can supply more of the good for a cost lower than the price consumers are willing to pay and everyone gains by increasing the quantity produced. If output is greater than Q^*, marginal cost exceeds marginal benefit. It costs producers more to supply the good than the price consumers are willing to pay and everyone gains by decreasing the quantity produced.

FIGURE 12.12
Efficiency of Competition

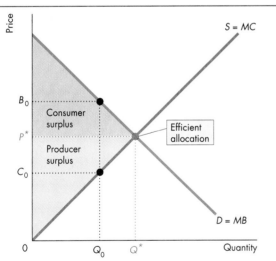

The efficient use of resources requires: consumers to be efficient, which occurs when they are on their demand curves; firms to be efficient, which occurs when they are on their supply curves; and the market to be in equilibrium with no external benefits or external costs. Resources are used efficiently at the quantity Q^* and the price P^*. With no external benefits or external costs, perfect competition achieves an efficient use of resources. If output is Q_0, the cost of producing one more unit, C_0, is less than its marginal benefit, B_0, and resources are not used efficiently.

Efficiency of Perfect Competition

Perfect competition achieves efficiency if there are no external benefits and external costs. In such a case, the benefits accrue to the buyers of the good and the costs are borne by its producer. In Fig. 12.12, the equilibrium quantity Q^* at the price P^* is efficient.

There are three main obstacles to efficiency:

1. Monopoly
2. Public goods
3. External costs and external benefits

Monopoly   Monopoly (Chapter 13) restricts output below its competitive level to raise price and increase profit. Government policies (Chapter 19) arise to limit such use of monopoly power.

Public goods   Goods such as national defence, the enforcement of law and order, the provision of clean drinking water, and the disposal of sewage and garbage are examples of public goods. Left to competitive markets, too small a quantity of them would be produced. Government institutions and policies (Chapter 18) help to overcome the problem of providing an efficient quantity of public goods.

External Costs and External Benefits   The production of steel and chemicals can generate air and water pollution and perfect competition might produce too large a quantity of these goods. Government policies (Chapter 20) attempt to cope with external costs and benefits.

◆ You've now completed your study of perfect competition. And *Reading Between the Lines* on pp. 262–263 gives you an opportunity to use what you have learned to understand recent events in the highly competitive Canadian retail services market with the exit from that market of Eaton's.

Although many markets approximate the model of perfect competition, many do not. Your next task is to study markets at the opposite extreme of market power—monopoly. Then, in Chapter 14, we'll study markets that lie between perfect competition and monopoly—monopolistic competition (competition with monopoly elements) and oligopoly (competition among a few producers). When you have completed this study, you'll have a toolkit that enables you to understand the variety of real-world markets.

Competition in Canadian Retailing

NATIONAL POST, AUGUST 21, 1999

130-year-old retailer winding down operations

By Zena Olijnyk

After a long and agonizing death watch, the once mighty department store retailer T. Eaton Co. Ltd. announced late last night that the end has come...

As a result, the livelihood of 13,000 employees—many who have made their life's career at the department store chain built by Irish immigrant Timothy Eaton in 1869—is threatened. ...

Trading in the retailer's shares was halted yesterday, having closed Thursday at 71 cents, a far cry from the $15 a share the company got when it went public in June, 1998. ...

But retail consultant Len Kubas said that the end of Eaton's is not all doom and gloom. "The $1-billion in sales rung up at Eaton's stores won't just disappear. That money will go to other retailers, who might end up stronger as a result," he said. "As for the workers, there is always a need for good, well-trained retail staff in the industry."

Essence of the Story

■ Eaton's, founded in 1869 by Irish immigrant Timothy Eaton, announced August 20, 1999, that it was closing down.

■ About 13,000 employees would lose their jobs.

■ Eaton's shares had fallen from $15 a share in June 1998 to 71 cents a share on August 19, 1999.

■ A retail consultant noted that Eaton's business will go to other retailers and most of Eaton's workers will find other jobs in the industry.

Economic Analysis

■ The retail market is highly competitive and we will assume that it is perfectly competitive.

■ Figure 1 shows the market in August 1999. The market in part (a) determines the price of retail services, which is Eaton's marginal revenue in part (b).

■ In part (b), Eaton's produces the quantity of services at which marginal revenue equals marginal cost, but incurs an economic loss shown by the red rectangle.

■ In Fig. 2, Eaton's liquidates its stock. Marginal cost falls from MC_0 to MC_1 because Eaton's does not now incur costs of buying new inventory to replace what it sells.

■ With a lower marginal cost at Eaton's, the industry supply increases and the price falls. Eaton's sells more, but during this period the profits of other retailers are squeezed.

■ Figure 3 shows the situation after Eaton's is gone. Another firm buys Eaton's assets, reorganizes them, and operates at a normal profit (zero economic profit). The retail market is now again in long-run equilibrium.

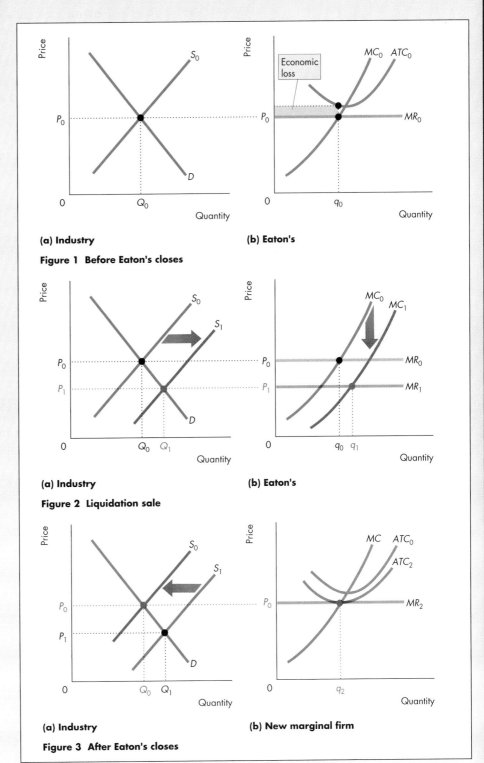

(a) Industry

(b) Eaton's

Figure 1 Before Eaton's closes

(a) Industry

(b) Eaton's

Figure 2 Liquidation sale

(a) Industry

(b) New marginal firm

Figure 3 After Eaton's closes

S U M M A R Y

Key Points

Competition (pp. 244–245)

- Perfect competition arises when demand is large relative to the efficient scale of production and when firms produce identical products.
- A perfectly competitive firm is a price taker.

The Firm's Decisions in Perfect Competition (pp. 246–251)

- The firm produces the output at which marginal revenue (price) equals marginal cost.
- In the short run, a firm can make an economic profit, incur an economic loss, or break even.
- If price is less than minimum average variable cost, the firm temporarily shuts down.
- A firm's supply curve is the upward-sloping part of its marginal cost curve above minimum average variable cost.
- An industry supply curve shows the sum of the quantities supplied by each firm at each price.

Output, Price, and Profit in Perfect Competition (pp. 252–255)

- Market demand and supply determine price.
- The firm produces the output at which price equals marginal cost.
- Economic profit induces entry. Economic loss induces exit.
- Entry and plant expansion increase supply and lower price and profit. Exit and plant contraction decrease supply and raise price and profit.
- In long-run equilibrium, economic profit is zero. There is no entry, exit, or change in plant size.

Changing Tastes and Advancing Technology (pp. 256–259)

- A permanent decrease in demand leads to a smaller industry output and a smaller number of firms.
- A permanent increase in demand leads to a larger industry output and a larger number of firms.

- The long-run effect of a change in demand on price depends on whether there are external economies (price falls) or external diseconomies (price rises) or neither (price remains constant).
- New technologies increase supply and in the long run lower the price and increase the quantity.

Competition and Efficiency (pp. 260–261)

- Resources are used efficiently when we produce goods and services in the quantities that people value most highly.
- When there are no external benefits and external costs, perfect competition achieves an efficient allocation. Marginal benefit equals marginal cost and the sum of consumer surplus and producer surplus is maximized.
- The existence of monopoly, public goods, and external costs and external benefits presents obstacles to efficiency.

Key Figures

Key Terms

PROBLEMS

*1. Quick Copy is one of the many copy shops near the campus. The figure shows Quick Copy's cost curves.

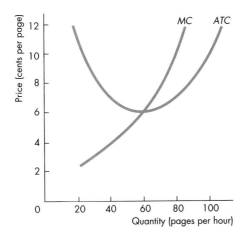

a. If the market price of copying one page is 10 cents, what is Quick Copy's profit-maximizing output?
b. Calculate Quick Copy's profit.
c. With no change in demand or technology, how will the price change in the long run?

2. Bob's is one of many burger stands along the beach. The figure shows Bob's cost curves.

a. If the market price of a burger is $4, what is Bob's profit-maximizing output?
b. Calculate the profit that Bob's makes.
c. With no change in demand or technology, how will the price change in the long run?

*3. Pat's Pizza Kitchen is a price taker. Pat's cost of producing pizza is:

Output (pizzas per hour)	Total cost (dollars per hour)
0	10
1	21
2	30
3	41
4	54
5	69

a. If a pizza sells for $14, what is Pat's profit-maximizing output?
b. What is Pat's shutdown point?
c. Derive Pat's supply curve.
d. Over what price range will Pat leave the pizza industry?
e. Over what price range will other firms with costs identical to Pat's enter the industry?
f. What is the price of a pizza in the long run?

4. Lucy's Lasagna is a price taker. Lucy's cost of producing lasagna is:

Output (plates per hour)	Total cost (dollars per hour)
0	5
1	20
2	26
3	35
4	46
5	59

a. If lasagna sells for $7.50 a plate, what is Lucy's profit-maximizing output?
b. What is Lucy's shutdown point?
c. Over what price range will Lucy leave the lasagna industry?
d. Over what price range will other firms with costs identical to Lucy's enter the industry?
e. What is the price of lasagna in the long run?

*5. The market demand schedule for cassettes is:

Price (dollars per cassette)	Quantity demanded (thousands of cassettes per week)
3.65	500
5.20	450
6.80	400
8.40	350
10.00	300
11.60	250
13.20	200
14.80	150

The market is perfectly competitive, and each firm has the following cost structure:

Output	Marginal cost	Average variable cost	Average total cost
(cassettes per week)	(dollars per additional cassette)	(dollars per cassette)	
150	6.00	8.80	15.47
200	6.40	7.80	12.80
250	7.00	7.00	11.00
300	7.65	7.10	10.43
350	8.40	7.20	10.06
400	10.00	7.50	10.00
450	12.40	8.00	10.22
500	12.70	9.00	11.00

There are 1,000 firms in the industry.
a. What is the market price?
b. What is the industry's output?
c. What is the output produced by each firm?
d. What is the economic profit made by each firm?
e. Do firms enter or exit the industry?
f. What is the number of firms in the long run?

6. The same demand conditions as those in problem 5 prevail, and there are 1,000 firms in the industry, but fixed costs increase by $980. What now are your answers to the questions in problem 5?

*7. In problem 5, the price of a compact disc decreases the demand for cassettes and the demand schedule becomes:

Price	Quantity demanded
(dollars per cassette)	(thousands of cassettes per week)
2.95	500
4.13	450
5.30	400
6.48	350
7.65	300
8.83	250
10.00	200
11.18	150

What now are your answers to the questions in problem 5?

8. In problem 6, the price of a compact disc decreases the demand for cassettes and the demand schedule becomes that given in the table in problem 7. What now are your answers to the questions in problem 6?

CRITICAL THINKING

 1. After you have studied *Reading Between the Lines* on pp. 262–263, answer the following questions.
a. Why is it reasonable to assume that retailing is a highly competitive (and perhaps perfectly competitive) industry?
b. What exactly do retailers produce? [Hint: Think about the services that they provide to you over and above the merchandise that you buy from them.]
c. What is the economic problem that Eaton's faced in the summer of 1999?
d. Use the link on the Parkin-Bade Web site and obtain information on Eaton's revenues and costs during 1998 and 1999.
e. What trends can you see in the company's revenues and costs?
f. How do you think the disappearance of Eaton's affects other retailers in Canada in both the short run and the long run?
g. What do you think will happen to Eaton's employees in the short run and in the long run? Use what you know about demand and supply to answer this question.
h. Can you think of some major changes in retailing technology that might have harmed Eaton's during the past few years?
i. Who are the winners and who are the losers from the exit of Eaton's?
j. Was the Canadian retail market efficient before the exit of Eaton's? Is it efficient now that Eaton's is gone?

 2. What has been the effect of an increase in world population on the wheat market and the individual wheat farmer? Explain your answer.

3. Visit the Parkin-Bade Web site and study the Web *Reading Between the Lines*, "Dumping Steel." Then answer the following questions.
a. What is the argument in the news article about limiting steel imports?
b. Do you agree with the argument? Why or why not?
c. Why do Canada and the United States claim that foreign steel is being dumped in North America?

13

Monopoly

You have been reading a lot in this book about firms that want to maximize profit. But perhaps you've been looking around at some of the places where you do business and wondering whether they are really so intent on profit. After all, don't you get a student's discount when you get a haircut? Don't museums and movie theatres give discounts to students, too? And what about the airline that gives a discount for buying a ticket in advance? Are your barber and movie theatre owner, as well as the museum and airline operators, simply generous folks to whom the model of profit-maximizing firms does not apply? Aren't they simply throwing profit away by cutting ticket prices and offering discounts? ◆ When you buy electric power, you don't shop around. You buy from your electric power utility, which is your only available supplier. If you live in the north of London, Ontario, and want cable TV service, you only have one option: buy from Rogers Cablesystems. These are examples of a single producer of a good or service controlling its supply. Such firms are obviously not like firms in perfectly competitive industries. They don't face a market-determined price. In practice, most monopolies are regulated. But to understand why they are regulated, we need to understand how an unregulated firm behaves. How does it choose the quantity to produce and the price at which to sell it? How does its behaviour compare with firms in perfectly competitive industries? Do such firms charge prices that are too high and that damage the interests of consumers? Do such firms bring any benefits? Finally, how are monopolies regulated?

◇ In this chapter, we study markets in which an individual firm can influence the quantity supplied and exert an influence on price. We also examine whether monopoly is as efficient as competition.

The Profits of Generosity

After studying this chapter, you will be able to:

- Explain how monopoly arises and distinguish between single-price monopoly and price-discriminating monopoly

- Explain how a single-price monopoly determines its output and price

- Compare the performance and efficiency of single-price monopoly and competition

- Define rent seeking and explain why it arises

- Explain how price discrimination increases profit

- Explain how monopoly regulation influences output, price, economic profit, and efficiency

Market Power

MARKET POWER AND COMPETITION ARE THE TWO forces that operate in most markets. **Market power** is the ability to influence the market, and in particular the market price, by influencing the total quantity offered for sale.

The firms in perfect competition that you studied in Chapter 12 have no market power. They face the force of raw competition and are price takers. The firms that we study in this chapter operate at the opposite extreme. They face no competition and exercise raw market power. We call this extreme *monopoly*. A **monopoly** is an industry that produces a good or service for which no close substitute exists and in which there is one supplier that is protected from competition by a barrier preventing the entry of new firms.

Examples of monopoly include natural gas distribution and the delivery of first-class mail, as well as DeBeers, the South African diamond producer, and Microsoft Corp., the software developer that created your computer's operating system.

How Monopoly Arises

Monopoly has two key features:

■ No close substitutes
■ Barriers to entry

No Close Substitutes If a good has a close substitute, even though only one firm produces it, that firm effectively faces competition from the producers of substitutes. Water supplied by a local public utility is an example of a good that does not have close substitutes. While it does have a close substitute for drinking—bottled spring water—it has no effective substitutes for showering or washing a car.

Monopolies are constantly under attack from new products and ideas that substitute for products produced by monopolies. For example, Federal Express, Purolator, and the fax machine have weakened the monopoly of Canada Post. Similarly, the satellite dish has weakened the monopoly of cable television companies.

But new products also are constantly creating monopolies. An example is Microsoft's monopoly in DOS during the 1980s and in the Windows operating system today.

Barriers to Entry Legal or natural constraints that protect a firm from potential competitors are called **barriers to entry**. A firm can sometimes create its own barrier to entry by acquiring a significant portion of a key resource. DeBeers, for example, controls more than 80 percent of the world's supply of natural diamonds. But most monopolies arise from two other types of barrier: legal barriers and natural barriers.

Legal Barriers to Entry Legal barriers to entry create legal monopoly. A **legal monopoly** is a market in which competition and entry are restricted by the granting of a public franchise, government licence, patent, or copyright.

A *public franchise* is an exclusive right granted to a firm to supply a good or service. An example is Canada Post, which has the exclusive right to carry first-class mail. A *government licence* controls entry into particular occupations, professions, and industries. Examples of this type of barrier to entry are medicine, law, dentistry, schoolteaching, architecture, and many other professional services. Licensing does not always create monopoly, but it does restrict competition.

A *patent* is an exclusive right granted to the inventor of a product or service. A *copyright* is an exclusive right granted to the author or composer of a literary, musical, dramatic, or artistic work. Patents and copyrights are valid for a limited time period that varies from country to country. In Canada, a patent is valid for 20 years. Patents encourage the *invention* of new products and production methods. They also stimulate *innovation*—the use of new inventions—by encouraging inventors to publicize their discoveries and offer them for use under licence. Patents have stimulated innovations in areas as diverse as soybean seeds, pharmaceuticals, memory chips, and video games.

Natural Barriers to Entry Natural barriers to entry create **natural monopoly**, which is an industry in which one firm can supply the entire market at a lower price than two or more firms can.

Figure 13.1 shows a natural monopoly in the distribution of electric power. Here, the demand curve for electric power is D and the average total cost curve is *ATC*. Because average total cost decreases as output increases, economies of scale prevail over the entire length of the *ATC* curve. One firm can produce 4 million kilowatt-hours at 5 cents a kilowatt-hour. At this price, the quantity demanded is 4 million kilowatt-hours. So if the price was 5 cents, one firm could supply the entire market. If two firms shared the market, it would cost each of them 10 cents a kilowatt-hour to produce a total of 4 million kilowatt-hours. If four firms shared the market, it would cost each of them 15 cents a kilowatt-hour to produce a total of 4 million kilowatt-hours. So in conditions like those shown in Fig. 13.1, one firm can supply the entire market at a lower cost than two or more firms can. The distribution of electric power is an example of natural monopoly. So is the distribution of water and gas.

Most monopolies are regulated in some way by government agencies. We will study such regulation at the end of this chapter. But for two reasons we'll first study unregulated monopoly. First, we can better understand why governments regulate monopolies and the effects of regulation if we also know how an unregulated monopoly behaves. Second, even in industries with more than one producer, firms often have a degree of monopoly power, and the theory of monopoly sheds light on the behaviour of such firms and industries.

A major difference between monopoly and competition is that a monopoly sets its own price. But in doing so, it faces a market constraint. Let's see how the market limits a monopoly's pricing choices.

Monopoly Price-Setting Strategies

All monopolies face a tradeoff between price and the quantity sold. To sell a larger quantity, the monopolist must charge a lower price. But there are two broad monopoly situations that create different tradeoffs. They are:

- Single price
- Price discrimination

Single Price DeBeers sells diamonds (of a given size and quality) for the same price to all its customers. If it tried to sell at a low price to some customers and at a higher price to others, only the low-price customers would buy from DeBeers. Others would buy from DeBeers' low-price customers.

DeBeers is a *single-price* monopoly. A **single-price monopoly** is a firm that must sell each unit of its output for the same price to all its customers.

Price Discrimination Many firms price discriminate, and most are *not* monopolies. Airlines offer a dizzying array of different prices for the same trip. Pizza producers charge one price for a single pizza and almost give away a second pizza. These are examples of *price discrimination*. **Price discrimination** is the practice of selling different units of a good or service for different prices. Different customers might pay different prices (like airline passengers) or one customer might pay different prices for different quantities bought (like the bargain price for a second pizza).

When a firm price discriminates, it looks as if it is doing its customers a favour. In fact, it is charging the highest possible price for each unit sold and making the largest possible profit.

Not all monopolies can price discriminate. The main obstacle to price discrimination is resale by customers who buy for a low price. Because of resale possibilities, price discrimination is limited to monopolies that sell services that cannot be resold.

We'll look first at single-price monopoly.

FIGURE 13.1
Natural Monopoly

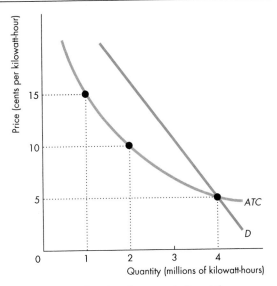

The demand curve for electric power is *D* and the average total cost curve is *ATC*. Economies of scale exist over the entire *ATC* curve. One firm can distribute 4 million kilowatt-hours at a cost of 5 cents a kilowatt-hour. This same total output costs 10 cents a kilowatt-hour with two firms and 15 cents a kilowatt-hour with four firms. So one firm can meet the market demand at a lower cost than two or more firms can, and the market is a natural monopoly.

A Single-Price Monopoly's Output and Price Decision

To understand how a single-price monopoly makes its output and price decision, we must first study the link between price and marginal revenue.

Price and Marginal Revenue

Because in a monopoly there is only one firm, the firm's demand curve is the market demand curve. Let's look at Bobbie's Barbershop, the only barbershop in Trout River, Newfoundland. The table in Fig. 13.2 shows the market demand schedule for haircuts in Trout River. At $20, Bobbie sells no haircuts. The lower the price, the more haircuts Bobbie can sell. For example, at $12 a haircut, consumers demand 4 haircuts per hour (row *e*).

Total revenue (*TR*) is the price (*P*) multiplied by the quantity sold (*Q*). For example, in row *d*, Bobbie sells 3 haircuts at $14 each, so total revenue is $42. *Marginal revenue* (*MR*) is the change in total revenue (*TR*) resulting from a one-unit increase in the quantity sold. For example, if the price falls from $16 (row *c*) to $14 (row *d*), the quantity sold increases from 2 to 3 haircuts. Total revenue rises from $32 to $42, so the change in total revenue is $10. Because the quantity sold increases by 1 haircut, marginal revenue equals the change in total revenue and is $10. Marginal revenue is placed between the two rows to emphasize that marginal revenue relates to the *change* in the quantity sold.

Figure 13.2 shows the market demand curve (*D*) and the marginal revenue curve (*MR*). It also illustrates the calculation we've just made. Notice that at each output, marginal revenue is less than price—the marginal revenue curve lies below the demand curve. Why is marginal revenue less than price? It is because when the price is lowered to sell one more unit, two opposing forces affect total revenue. The lower price results in a revenue loss, and the increased quantity sold results in a revenue gain. For example, at a price of $16, Bobbie sells 2 haircuts (point *c*). If she lowers the price to $14, she sells 3 haircuts and has a revenue gain of $14 on the third haircut. But she now receives only $14 on the first two—$2 less than before. As a result, she loses $4 of revenue on the first 2 haircuts. To calculate marginal revenue, she must deduct this amount from the revenue gain of $14. So her marginal revenue is $10, which is less than the price.

FIGURE 13.2

Demand and Marginal Revenue

	Price (P) (dollars per haircut)	Quantity demanded (Q) (haircuts per hour)	Total revenue (TR = P × Q) (dollars)	Marginal revenue (MR = ΔTR/ΔQ) (dollars per haircut)
a	20	0	0	
				18
b	18	1	18	
				14
c	16	2	32	
				10
d	14	3	42	
				6
e	12	4	48	
				2
f	10	5	50	

The table shows the demand schedule for haircuts. Total revenue (*TR*) is price multiplied by quantity sold. For example, in row *c* the price is $16 a haircut, Bobbie sells 2 haircuts and total revenue is $32. Marginal revenue (*MR*) is the change in total revenue that results from a one-unit increase in the quantity sold. For example, when the price falls from $16 to $14 a haircut, the quantity sold increases by 1 haircut and total revenue increases by $10. Marginal revenue is $10. The demand curve, *D*, and the marginal revenue curve, *MR*, are based on the numbers in the table and illustrate the calculation of marginal revenue when the price falls from $16 to $14.

Marginal Revenue and Elasticity

A single-price monopoly's marginal revenue is related to the *elasticity of demand* for its good. The demand for a good can be *elastic* (the elasticity of demand is greater than 1), *inelastic* (the elasticity of demand is less than 1), or *unit elastic* (the elasticity of demand is equal to 1). You know that a monopoly produces a good or service for which there is no close substitute. And you perhaps recall (see Chapter 5, p. 95 for a refresher) that the *closer* the substitutes for a good or service, the *more* elastic is the demand for it. So you might expect that the demand for what a monopoly produces is inelastic. It turns out that this conclusion is incorrect. A monopoly always operates where demand is elastic! Let's find out why.

If demand is elastic, a fall in price brings an increase in total revenue—the increase in revenue from the increase in quantity sold outweighs the decrease in revenue from the lower price—and marginal revenue is positive. If demand is inelastic, a fall in price brings a decrease in total revenue—the increase in revenue from the increase in quantity sold is outweighed by the decrease in revenue from the lower price—and marginal revenue is negative. If demand is unit elastic, total revenue does not change—the increase in revenue from the increase in quantity sold offsets the decrease in revenue from the lower price—and marginal revenue is zero (see Chapter 5, pp. 94–95).

Figure 13.3 illustrates the relationship between marginal revenue, total revenue, and elasticity. As the price of a haircut gradually falls from $20 to $10, the quantity of haircuts demanded increases from 0 to 5 an hour. Over this output range, marginal revenue is positive (part a), total revenue increases (part b), and the demand for haircuts is elastic. As the price falls from $10 to $0 a haircut, the quantity of haircuts demanded increases from 5 to 10 an hour. Over this output range, marginal revenue is negative (part a), total revenue decreases (part b), and the demand for haircuts is inelastic. When the price is $10 a haircut, marginal revenue is zero, total revenue is a maximum, and the demand for haircuts is unit elastic.

Monopoly Demand Is Always Elastic The relationship between marginal revenue and elasticity that you've just discovered implies that a profit-maximizing monopoly never produces an output in the inelastic range of its demand curve. If it did so, it could charge a higher price, produce a smaller quantity, and increase its profit. Let's now look more closely at a monopoly's output and price decision.

FIGURE 13.3
Marginal Revenue and Elasticity

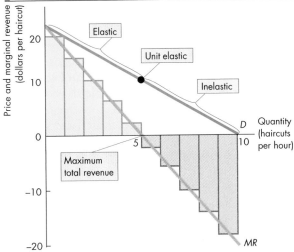

(a) Demand and marginal revenue curves

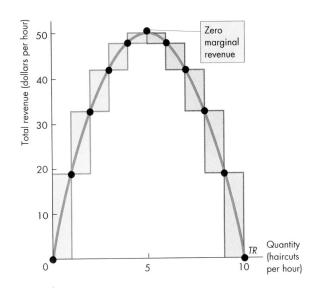

(b) Total revenue curve

In part (a), the demand curve is *D* and the marginal revenue curve is *MR*. In part (b), the total revenue curve is *TR*. Over the range from 0 to 5 haircuts an hour, a price cut increases total revenue so marginal revenue is positive, as shown by the blue bars. Demand is elastic. Over the range 5 to 10 haircuts an hour, a price cut decreases total revenue so marginal revenue is negative, as shown by the red bars. Demand is inelastic. At 5 haircuts an hour, total revenue is maximized, and marginal revenue is zero. Demand is unit elastic.

Output and Price Decision

To determine the output level and price that maximize a monopoly's profit, we need to study the behaviour of both revenue and costs as output varies. A monopoly and a competitive firm face the same types of technology and cost constraints. But they face different market constraints. The competitive firm is a price taker, whereas the monopoly's output decision influences the price it receives. Let's see how.

Bobbie's revenue, which we studied in Fig. 13.2, is shown again in Table 13.1. The table also contains information on Bobbie's costs and economic profit. Total cost (*TC*) rises as output increases, and so does total revenue (*TR*). Economic profit equals total revenue minus total cost. As you can see in the table, the maximum profit ($12) occurs when Bobbie sells 3 haircuts for $14 each. If she sells 2 haircuts for $16 each or 4 haircuts for $12 each, her economic profit will be only $8.

You can see why 3 haircuts is Bobbie's profit-maximizing output by looking at the marginal revenue and marginal cost columns. When Bobbie increases output from 2 to 3 haircuts, her marginal revenue is $10 and her marginal cost is $6. Profit increases by the difference—$4 an hour. If Bobbie increases output yet further, from 3 to 4 haircuts, her marginal revenue is $6 and her marginal cost is $10. In this case, marginal cost exceeds marginal revenue by $4, so profit decreases by $4 an hour. When marginal revenue exceeds marginal cost, profit increases if output increases. When marginal cost exceeds marginal revenue, profit increases if output decreases. When marginal cost and marginal revenue are equal, profit is maximized.

The information set out in Table 13.1 is shown graphically in Fig. 13.4. Part (a) shows Bobbie's total revenue curve (*TR*) and total cost curve (*TC*). Economic profit is the vertical distance between *TR* and *TC*. Bobbie maximizes her profit at 3 haircuts an hour—economic profit is $42 minus $30, or $12.

A monopoly, like a competitive firm, maximizes profit by producing the output at which marginal cost equals marginal revenue. Figure 13.4(b) shows Bobbie's demand curve (*D*) and marginal revenue curve (*MR*) along with her marginal cost curve (*MC*) and average total cost curve (*ATC*). Bobbie maximizes her profit by doing 3 haircuts an hour. But what price does she charge for a haircut? To set the price, the monopolist uses the demand curve and finds the highest price at which it can sell the profit-maximizing output. In Bobbie's case, the highest price at which she can sell 3 haircuts an hour is $14.

TABLE 13.1

A Monopoly's Output and Price Decision

Price (P) (dollars per haircut)	Quantity demanded (Q) (haircuts per hour)	Total revenue (TR = P × Q) (dollars)	Marginal revenue (MR = ΔTR/ΔQ) (dollars per haircut)	Total cost (TC) (dollars)	Marginal cost (MC = ΔTC/ΔQ) (dollars per haircut)	Profit (TR − TC) (dollars)
20	0	0		20		−20
			18		1	
18	1	18		21		−3
			14		3	
16	2	32		24		+8
			10		6	
14	3	42		30		+12
			6		10	
12	4	48		40		+8
			2		15	
10	5	50		55		−5

This table gives the information needed to find the profit-maximizing output and price. Total revenue (*TR*) equals price multiplied by the quantity sold. Profit equals total revenue minus total cost (*TC*). Profit is maximized when the price is $14 and 3 haircuts are sold. Total revenue is $42, total cost is $30, and economic profit is $12 ($42 − $30).

FIGURE 13.4

A Monopoly's Output and Price

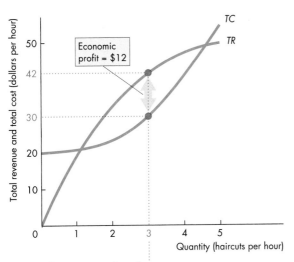

(a) Total revenue and total cost curves

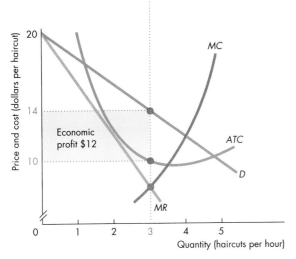

(b) Demand and marginal revenue and cost curves

In part (a), economic profit is the vertical distance between total revenue (*TR*) minus total cost (*TC*), and it is maximized at 3 haircuts an hour. In part (b), economic profit is maximized when marginal cost (*MC*) equals marginal revenue (*MR*). The price is determined by the demand curve (*D*) and is $14. Economic profit, the blue rectangle, is $12—the profit per haircut ($4) multiplied by 3 haircuts.

All firms maximize profit by producing the output at which marginal revenue equals marginal cost. For a competitive firm, price equals marginal revenue, so price also equals marginal cost. For a monopoly, price exceeds marginal revenue, so price also exceeds marginal cost.

A monopoly charges a price that exceeds marginal cost, but does it always make an economic profit? In Bobbie's case, when she produces 3 haircuts an hour, her average total cost is $10 (read from the *ATC* curve) and her price is $14 (read from the *D* curve). Her profit per haircut is $4 ($14 minus $10). Bobbie's economic profit is shown by the blue rectangle, which equals the profit per haircut ($4) multiplied by the number of haircuts (3), for a total of $12.

If firms in a perfectly competitive industry make a positive economic profit, new firms enter. That does not happen in monopoly. Barriers to entry prevent new firms from entering an industry in which there is a monopoly. So a monopoly can make a positive economic profit and continue to do so indefinitely. Sometimes that profit is large, as in the international diamond business.

Bobbie makes a positive economic profit. But suppose that the owner of the shop that Bobbie rents increases Bobbie's rent. If Bobbie pays an additional $12 an hour, her fixed cost increases by $12 an hour. Her marginal cost and marginal revenue don't change, so her profit-maximizing output remains at 3 haircuts an hour. Her profit decreases by $12 an hour to zero. If Bobbie pays more than an additional $12 an hour for her shop rent, she incurs an economic loss. If this situation were permanent, Bobbie would go out of business. But entrepreneurs are a hardy lot, and Bobbie might find another shop where the rent is less.

R E V I E W   Q U I Z

- What is the relationship between marginal cost and marginal revenue when a single-price monopoly maximizes profit?
- How does a single-price monopoly determine the price it will charge its customers?
- What is the relationship among price, marginal revenue, and marginal cost when a single-price monopoly is maximizing profit?
- Why can a monopoly make a positive economic profit even in the long run?

Single-Price Monopoly and Competition Compared

IMAGINE AN INDUSTRY THAT IS MADE UP OF MANY small firms operating in perfect competition. Then imagine that a single firm buys out all these small firms and creates a monopoly.

What will happen in this industry? Will the price rise or fall? Will the quantity produced increase or decrease? Will economic profit increase or decrease? Will either the original competitive situation or the new monopoly situation be efficient?

These are the questions we're now going to answer. First, we look at the effects of monopoly on the price and quantity produced. Then we turn to the questions about efficiency.

Comparing Output and Price

Figure 13.5 shows the market we'll study. The market demand curve is D. The demand curve is the same regardless of how the industry is organized. But the supply side and the equilibrium are different in monopoly and competition. First, let's look at the case of perfect competition.

Perfect Competition Initially, with many small perfectly competitive firms in the market, the market supply curve is S. This supply curve is obtained by summing the supply curves of all the individual firms in the market.

In perfect competition, equilibrium occurs where the supply curve and the demand curve intersect. The quantity produced by the industry is Q_C, and the price is P_C. Each firm takes the price P_C and maximizes its profit by producing the output at which its own marginal cost equals the price. Because each firm is a small part of the total industry, there is no incentive for any firm to try to manipulate the price by varying its output.

Monopoly Now suppose that this industry is taken over by a single firm. Consumers do not change so the market demand curve remains the same as in the case of perfect competition. But now, the monopoly recognizes this demand curve as a constraint on its sales. And the monopoly is confronted with the marginal revenue curve, MR.

The monopoly maximizes profit by producing the quantity at which marginal revenue equals marginal

cost. To find the monopoly's marginal cost curve, first recall that in perfect competition, the industry supply curve is the sum of the supply curves of the firms in the industry. Also recall that each firm's supply curve is its marginal cost curve (see Chapter 12, p. 250). So when the industry is taken over by a single firm, the competitive industry's supply curve becomes the monopoly's marginal cost curve. To remind you of this fact, the supply curve is also labelled MC.

The output at which marginal revenue equals marginal cost is Q_M. This output is smaller than the competitive output Q_C. And the monopoly charges the price P_M, which is higher than P_C. We have established that:

Compared to a perfectly competitive industry, a single-price monopoly restricts its output and charges a higher price.

We've seen how the output and price of a monopoly compare with those in a competitive industry. Let's now compare the efficiency of the two types of market.

FIGURE 13.5

Monopoly's Smaller Output and Higher Price

A competitive industry produces the quantity Q_C at price P_C. A single-price monopoly produces the quantity Q_M at which marginal revenue equals marginal cost and sells that quantity for the price P_M. Compared to perfect competition, a single-price monopoly restricts output and raises the price.

Efficiency Comparison

When we studied efficiency in perfect competition, (see Chapter 12, pp. 260–261), we discovered that if there are no external costs and benefits, perfect competition results in an efficient use of resources. Along the demand curve, consumers are efficient. Along the supply curve, producers are efficient. And where the curves intersect—the competitive equilibrium—both consumers and producers are efficient. Price equals marginal cost and the sum of consumer surplus and producer surplus is maximized.

Monopoly restricts output below the competitive level and is inefficient. If a monopoly's output was increased, marginal benefit would exceed marginal cost and resources would be used more efficiently.

Figure 13.6 illustrates the inefficiency of monopoly and shows the loss of consumer and producer surpluses in a monopoly. In perfect competition (part a), consumers pay P_C for each unit. The demand curve ($D = MB$) shows the maximum price that consumers are willing to pay for each unit. This price measures the value of the good to the consumer. Value minus price equals *consumer surplus*. (See Chapter 6, p. 113.) In Fig. 13.6(a), consumer surplus is shown by the green triangle.

The marginal cost of production (opportunity cost) in perfect competition is shown by the supply curve ($S = MC$). The amount received by the producer in excess of this marginal cost is *producer surplus*. In Fig. 13.6(a), the blue area shows producer surplus.

At the competitive equilibrium, the sum of consumer surplus and producer surplus is maximized and resources are used efficiently.

In Fig. 13.6(b), a monopoly restricts output to Q_M and sells that output for P_M. Consumer surplus decreases to the smaller green triangle. Consumers lose partly by having to pay more for the good and partly by getting less of it. Part of the original producer surplus is also lost. The total loss resulting from the smaller monopoly output (Q_M) is the grey triangle. The part of the grey triangle above P_C is the loss of consumer surplus, and the part of the triangle below P_C is a loss of producer surplus. The entire grey triangle measures the loss of consumer surplus plus producer surplus. This loss is called the *deadweight loss*. The smaller output and higher price drive a wedge between marginal benefit and marginal cost and eliminate the producer surplus and the consumer surplus on the output that a competitive industry would have produced but that the monopoly does not.

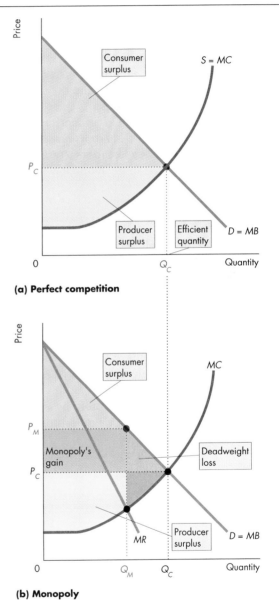

FIGURE 13.6

Inefficiency of Monopoly

(a) Perfect competition

(b) Monopoly

In perfect competition (part a), the quantity Q_C is sold at the price P_C. Consumer surplus is shown by the green triangle, and producer surplus is shown by the blue area. In long-run equilibrium, the sum of consumer surplus and producer surplus is maximized. A single-price monopoly (part b) restricts output to Q_M and increases the price to P_M. Consumer surplus is the smaller green triangle. The monopoly takes the blue rectangle and creates a deadweight loss (the grey triangle).

Redistribution of Surpluses

You've seen that monopoly is inefficient. The sum of consumer surplus and producer surplus is smaller with monopoly than with competition. There is a social loss. But monopoly also brings a *redistribution* of surpluses.

Some of the loss in consumer surplus goes to the monopoly. In Fig. 13.6, the monopoly gets the difference between the higher price, P_M, and the competitive price, P_C, on the quantity sold, Q_M. So the monopoly takes the part of the consumer surplus shown by the blue rectangle. This portion of the loss of consumer surplus is not a loss to society. It is redistribution from consumers to the monopoly producer.

Rent Seeking

You've seen that monopoly creates a deadweight loss and so is inefficient. But the social cost of monopoly exceeds the deadweight loss because of an activity called rent seeking. **Rent seeking** is the attempt to capture a consumer surplus, a producer surplus, or an economic profit. The activity is not confined to monopoly. But the attempt to make an economic profit is a major form of rent seeking.

You've seen that a monopoly makes its economic profit by diverting part of consumer surplus to itself. Thus the pursuit of an economic profit by a monopoly is rent seeking. It is the attempt to capture consumer surplus.

Rent seekers pursue their goals in two main ways. They might

■ Buy a monopoly
■ Create a monopoly

Buy a Monopoly　To rent seek by buying a monopoly, a person searches for a monopoly that is for sale at a lower price than the monopoly's economic profit. Trading taxicab licences is an example of this type of rent seeking. In some cities, taxicabs are regulated. The city restricts both the fares and the number of taxis that can operate so operating a taxi results in economic profit or rent. A person who wants to operate a taxi must buy a licence from someone who already has one. This type of rent seeking transfers rents from the buyer to the seller of the monopoly. The only person who ends up with rent is the one who created the monopoly in the first place. Even so, people rationally devote their time and effort to seeking out profitable

monopoly businesses to buy. In the process, they use up scarce resources that could otherwise have been employed producing goods and services.

Create a Monopoly　Rent seeking by creating a monopoly is mainly a political activity. It takes the form of lobbying and trying to influence the political process. Such influence might be sought by making campaign contributions in exchange for legislative support or by indirectly seeking to influence political outcomes through publicity in the media or more direct contacts with politicians and bureaucrats. An example of a monopoly right created in this way is the cable television monopoly created and regulated by the Canadian Radio-television and Telecommunications Commission (CRTC). Another is a regulation that restricts "split-run" magazines. These are regulations that restrict output and increase price.

This type of rent seeking is a costly activity that uses up scarce resources. Taken together, firms spend billions of dollars lobbying MPs, MPPs, and bureaucrats in the pursuit of licences and laws that create barriers to entry and establish a monopoly right. Everyone has an incentive to rent seek, and because there are no barriers to entry into the rent-seeking activity, there is a great deal of competition for new monopoly rights.

Rent-Seeking Equilibrium

Barriers to entry create monopoly. But there is no barrier to entry into rent seeking. Rent seeking is like perfect competition. If an economic profit is available, a new rent seeker will try to get some of it. And competition among rent seekers pushes up the price that must be paid for a monopoly right to the point at which only a normal profit can be made by operating the monopoly. For example, competition for the right to operate a taxi in Toronto leads to a price of more than $80,000 for a taxi licence, which is sufficiently high to eliminate economic profit for taxi operators and leave them with normal profit.

Figure 13.7 shows a rent-seeking equilibrium. The cost of rent seeking is a fixed cost that must be added to a monopoly's other costs. Rent seeking and rent-seeking costs increase to the point at which no economic profit is made. The average total cost curve, which includes the fixed cost of rent seeking, shifts upward until it just touches the demand curve. Economic profit (and producer surplus) are zero.

FIGURE 13.7
Rent-Seeking Equilibrium

With competitive rent seeking, a monopoly uses all its economic profit to prevent another firm from taking its economic rent. The firm's rent-seeking costs are fixed costs. They add to total fixed cost and to average total cost. The ATC curve shifts upward until, at the profit-maximizing price, the firm breaks even.

They have been lost in rent seeking. Consumer surplus is unaffected. But the deadweight loss of monopoly now includes the original deadweight loss triangle plus the lost producer surplus, shown by the enlarged grey area in the figure.

R E V I E W   Q U I Z

▦ Why does a single-price monopoly produce a smaller output and charge a higher price than what would prevail if the industry were perfectly competitive?

▦ Why is a single-price monopoly inefficient?

▦ What is rent seeking and how does it influence the inefficiency of monopoly?

So far, we've considered only a single-price monopoly. But many monopolies do not operate with a single price. Instead, they price discriminate. Let's now see how price-discriminating monopoly works.

Price Discrimination

PRICE DISCRIMINATION—SELLING A GOOD OR service at a number of different prices—is widespread. You encounter it when you travel, go to the movies, get your hair cut, buy pizza, or visit an art museum. Most price discriminators are *not* monopolies, but monopolies price discriminate when they can do so. To be able to price discriminate a monopoly must:

1. Identify and separate different buyer types
2. Sell a product that cannot be resold.

Price discrimination is charging different prices for a single good or service because of differences in buyers' willingness to pay and not because of differences in production costs. So not all price *differences* are price *discrimination*. Some goods that are similar but not identical have different prices because they have different production costs. For example, the cost of producing electricity depends on time of day. If an electric power company charges a higher price for consumption between 7:00 and 9:00 in the morning and between 4:00 and 7:00 in the evening than at other times of the day, it is not price discriminating.

At first sight, it appears that price discrimination contradicts the assumption of profit maximization. Why would a movie operator allow children to see movies at half price? Why would a hairdresser charge students and senior citizens less? Aren't these firms losing profit by being nice to their customers?

Deeper investigation shows that far from losing profit, price discriminators make a bigger profit than they would otherwise. So a monopoly has an incentive to find ways of discriminating and charging each buyer the highest possible price. Some people pay less with price discrimination, but others pay more.

Price Discrimination and Consumer Surplus

The key idea behind price discrimination is to convert consumer surplus into economic profit. Demand curves slope down because the value that people place on any good decreases as the quantity consumed of that good increases. When all the units consumed are sold for a single price, consumers benefit. The benefit is the value the consumers get from each unit of the good minus the price actually paid for it. We call this benefit *consumer surplus*. (If you need to refresh your understanding of consumer surplus, flip back to Chapter 6, page 113.) Price discrimination is an attempt by a monopoly to capture as much of the consumer surplus as possible for itself.

To extract every dollar of consumer surplus from every buyer, the monopoly would have to offer each individual customer a separate price schedule based on that customer's own willingness to pay. Clearly, such price discrimination cannot be carried out in practice because a firm does not have enough information about each consumer's demand curve.

But firms try to extract as much consumer surplus as possible and, to do so, they discriminate in two broad ways:

■ Among units of a good
■ Among groups of buyers

Discriminating Among Units of a Good One method of price discrimination charges each buyer a different price on each unit of a good bought. A discount for bulk buying is an example of this type of discrimination. The larger the order, the larger is the discount—and the lower is the price. (Note that some discounts for bulk arise from lower costs of production for greater bulk. In these cases, such discounts are not price discrimination.)

Discriminating Among Groups of Buyers Price discrimination often takes the form of discriminating between different groups of consumers on the basis of age, employment status, or some other easily distinguished characteristic. This type of price discrimination works when each group has a different average willingness to pay for the good or service.

For example, a face-to-face sales meeting with a customer might bring a large and profitable order. For salespeople and other business travellers, the marginal benefit from a trip is large and the price that such a traveller will pay for a trip is high. In contrast, for a vacation traveller, any of several different trips or even no vacation trip are options. So for vacation travellers, the marginal benefit of a trip is small and the price that such a traveller will pay for a trip is low. Because business travellers are willing to pay more than vacation travellers are, it is possible for an airline to profit by price discriminating between these two groups. Similarly, because students have a lower willingness to pay for a haircut than a working person does, it is possible for a hairdresser to profit by price discriminating between these two groups.

Let's see how an airline exploits the differences in demand by business and vacation travellers and increases its profit by price discriminating.

Profiting by Price Discriminating

Global Air has a monopoly on an exotic route. Figure 13.8 shows the demand curve (*D*) and the marginal revenue curve (*MR*) for travel on this route. It also shows Global Air's marginal cost curve (*MC*) and average total cost curve (*ATC*).

Initially, Global is a single-price monopoly and maximizes its profit by producing 8,000 trips a year (the quantity at which *MR* equals *MC*). The price is $1,200 per trip. The average total cost of a trip is $600, so economic profit is $600 a trip. On 8,000 trips, Global's economic profit is $4.8 million a year, shown by the blue rectangle. Global's customers enjoy a consumer surplus shown by the green triangle.

FIGURE 13.8

A Single Price of Air Travel

Global Air has a monopoly on an air route. The market demand curve is *D* and the marginal revenue curve is *MR*. Global Air's marginal cost curve is *MC* and its average total cost curve is *ATC*. As a single-price monopoly, Global maximizes profit by selling 8,000 trips a year at $1,200 a trip. Its profit is $4.8 million a year—the blue rectangle. Global's customers enjoy a consumer surplus—the green triangle.

Global is struck by the fact that many of its customers are business travellers and Global suspects they are willing to pay more than $1,200 a trip. So Global does some market research, which tells Global that some business travellers are willing to pay as much as $1,800 a trip. Also, these customers almost always change their travel plans at the last moment. Another group of business travellers is willing to pay $1,600. These customers know a week ahead when they will travel and they never want to stay over a weekend. Yet another group would pay up to $1,400 and these travellers know two weeks ahead when they will travel and don't want to stay away over a weekend.

So Global announces a new fare schedule. No restrictions, $1,800; 7-days advance purchase, no cancellation, $1,600; 14-days advance purchase, no cancellation, $1,400; 14-days advance purchase, must stay over weekend, $1,200.

Figure 13.9 shows the outcome with this new fare structure and also shows why Global is pleased with its new fares. It sells 2,000 seats at each of its four prices. Global's economic profit increases by the blue steps in Fig. 13.9. Its economic profit is now its original $4.8 million a year plus an additional $2.4 million from its new higher fares. Consumer surplus has shrunk to the smaller green area.

Perfect Price Discrimination

But Global reckons it can do even better. It plans to achieve **perfect price discrimination**, which extracts the entire consumer surplus. To do so, Global must come up with a host of additional fares ranging between $1,200 and $2,000, each one of which appeals to a small market segment of the business market and that extracts the entire consumer surplus from the business travellers.

With perfect price discrimination, something special happens to marginal revenue. For the perfect price discriminator, the demand curve becomes the marginal revenue curve. The reason is that when the price is cut to sell a larger quantity, the firm sells only the marginal unit at the lower price. All the other units continue to be sold for the highest price the buyers are willing to pay.

With marginal cost equal to price, Global can obtain yet greater profit by increasing output up to the point at which price (and marginal revenue) is equal to marginal cost.

So, Global now seeks additional travellers who will not pay as much as $1,200 a trip but who will pay more than marginal cost. More creative pricing comes up with vacation specials and other fares that have combinations of advance reservation, minimum-stay, and other restrictions that make these fares unattractive to its existing customers but attractive to a further group of travellers. With all these fares and specials, Global increases sales, extracts the entire consumer surplus, and maximizes economic profit.

Figure 13.10 shows the outcome with perfect price discrimination. The dozens of fares paid by the original travellers who are willing to pay between $1,200 and $2,000 has extracted the entire consumer surplus from this group and converted it into economic profit for Global.

The new fares between $900 and $1,200 have attracted 3,000 additional travellers but taken their entire consumer surplus also. Global is earning an economic profit of more than $9 million.

Real-world airlines are just as creative as Global as you can see in the cartoon!

FIGURE 13.9

Price Discrimination

Global revises its fare structure. No restrictions at $1,800; 7-days advance purchase at $1,600; 14-days advance purchase at $1,400; and must stay over weekend at $1,200. Global sells 2,000 units at each of its four new fares. Its economic profit increases by $2.4 million a year to $7.2 million a year, which is shown by the original blue rectangle plus the blue steps. Global's customers' consumer surplus shrinks.

FIGURE 13.10
Perfect Price Discrimination

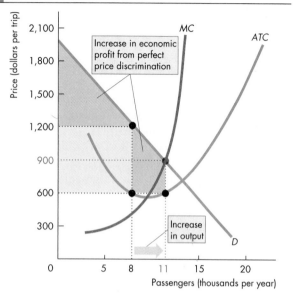

Dozens of fares discriminate among different types of business traveller, and many new low fares with restrictions appeal to vacation travellers. With perfect price discrimination, the demand curve becomes Global's marginal revenue curve. Economic profit is maximized when the lowest price equals marginal cost. Global sells 11,000 tickets between $2,000 and $900 each and makes an economic profit of $9.35 million a year.

Would it bother you to hear how little I paid for this flight?

From William Hamilton, "Voodoo Economics," ©1992 by The Chronicle Publishing Company, p. 3. Reprinted with permission of Chronicle Books.

Efficiency and Rent Seeking with Price Discrimination

With perfect price discrimination, output increases to the point at which price equals marginal cost—where the marginal cost curve intersects the demand curve. This output is identical to that of perfect competition. Perfect price discrimination pushes consumer surplus to zero but increases producer surplus to equal the sum of consumer surplus and producer surplus in perfect competition. Deadweight loss with perfect price discrimination is zero. So perfect price discrimination achieves efficiency.

The more perfectly the monopoly can price discriminate, the closer its output gets to the competitive output and the more efficient is the outcome.

But there are two differences between perfect competition and perfect price discrimination. First, the distribution of the surplus is different. It is shared by consumers and producers in perfect competition while the producer gets it all with perfect price discrimination. Second, because the producer grabs the surplus, rent seeking becomes profitable.

People use resources in pursuit of rents and the bigger the rents, the more resources get used pursuing them. With free entry into rent seeking, the long-run equilibrium outcome is that rent seekers use up the entire producer surplus.

REVIEW QUIZ

- What is price discrimination and how is it used to increase a monopoly's profit?
- What happens to consumer surplus when a monopoly price discriminates?
- What happens to consumer surplus, economic profit, and output if a monopoly perfectly price discriminates?
- What are some of the ways that real-world airlines use to price discriminate?

You've seen that monopoly is profitable for the producer but costly for other people. It results in inefficiency. Because of these features of monopoly, it is subject to policy debate and regulation. We'll now study the key monopoly policy issues.

Monopoly Policy Issues

THE COMPARISON OF MONOPOLY AND competition makes monopoly look bad. Monopoly is inefficient and it captures consumer surplus and converts it into producer surplus or pure waste in the form of rent-seeking costs. If monopoly is so bad, why do we put up with it? Why don't we have laws that crack down on monopoly so hard that it never rears its head? We do indeed have laws that limit monopoly power and regulate the prices that monopolies are permitted to charge. But monopoly also brings some benefits. We begin this review of monopoly policy issues by looking at the benefits of monopoly. We then look at monopoly regulation.

Gains from Monopoly

The main reason why monopoly exists is that it has potential advantages over a competitive alternative. These advantages arise from:

■ Economies of scale and economies of scope
■ Incentives to innovation

Economies of Scale and Scope   Economies of scale and scope can lead to *natural monopoly*. And as you saw at the beginning of this chapter, in a natural monopoly, a single firm can produce at a lower average cost than a larger number of smaller firms can.

A firm experiences *economies of scale* when an increase in its output of a good or service brings a decrease in the average total cost of producing it—see Chapter 11, p. 236. A firm experiences *economies of scope* when an increase in the *range of goods produced* brings a decrease in average total cost—see Chapter 10, p. 217. Economies of scope occur when different goods can share specialized (and usually costly) capital resources. For example, McDonald's can produce both hamburgers and french fries at a lower average total cost than can two separate firms—a burger firm and a french fries firm—because at McDonald's hamburgers and french fries share the use of specialized food storage and preparation facilities. A firm that produces a wide range of products can hire specialist computer programmers, designers, and marketing experts whose skills can be used across the product range, thereby spreading their costs and lowering the average total cost of production of each of the goods.

Large-scale firms that have control over supply and can influence price—and that therefore behave like the monopoly firm that you've studied in this chapter—can reap these economies of scale and scope. Small, competitive firms cannot. Consequently there are situations in which the comparison of monopoly and competition that we made earlier in this chapter is not valid. Recall that we imagined the takeover of a large number of competitive firms by a monopoly firm. But we also assumed that the monopoly would use exactly the same technology as the small firms and have the same costs. If one large firm can reap economies of scale and scope, its marginal cost curve will lie below the supply curve of a competitive industry made up of many small firms. It is possible for such economies of scale and scope to be so large as to result in a larger output and lower price under monopoly than a competitive industry would achieve.

Examples of industries in which economies of scale are so significant that they lead to a natural monopoly are becoming more rare. Public utilities such as gas, electric power, local telephone service, and garbage collection once were natural monopolies. But technological advances now enable us to separate the *production* of electric power and natural gas from their *distribution*. The provision of water, though, remains a natural monopoly. There are many examples in which a combination of economies of scale and economies of scope arise. Some examples are the brewing of beer, the manufacture of refrigerators and other household appliances, the manufacture of pharmaceuticals, and the refining of petroleum.

Where significant economies of scale and scope exist, it is usually worth putting up with monopoly and regulating its prices.

Incentives to Promote Innovation   Invention leads to a wave of innovation as new knowledge is applied to the production process. Innovation may take the form of developing a new product or a lower-cost way of making an existing product. Controversy rages over whether large firms with monopoly power or small competitive firms lacking such monopoly power are the most innovative. It is clear that some temporary monopoly power arises from innovation. A firm that develops a new product or process and patents it obtains an exclusive right to that product or process for the term of the patent.

But does the granting of a monopoly, even a temporary one, to an innovator increase the pace of innovation? One line of reasoning suggests that it does. Without protection, an innovator is not able to enjoy the profits from innovation for very long. Thus the incentive to innovate is weakened. A contrary argument is that monopolies can afford to be lazy while competitive firms cannot. Competitive firms must strive to innovate and cut costs even though they know that they cannot hang on to the benefits of their innovation for long. But that knowledge spurs them on to greater and faster innovation.

The evidence on whether monopoly leads to greater innovation than competition is mixed. Large firms do more research and development than do small firms. But measuring research and development is measuring the volume of inputs into the process of innovation. What matters is not input but output. Two measures of the output of research and development are the number of patents and the rate of productivity growth. On these measures, there is no clear evidence that big is better. But there is a clear pattern in the process of diffusion of technological knowledge. After innovation, a new process or product spreads gradually through the industry, with large firms jumping on the bandwagon more quickly than the remaining small firms. Thus large firms speed the process of diffusion of technological advances.

Regulating Natural Monopoly

Where demand and cost conditions create a natural monopoly, a government agency usually regulates the prices of the monopoly. By regulating a monopoly, some of the worst aspects of monopoly can be avoided, or at least made more moderate. One such natural monopoly is in the distribution of natural gas. Let's look at the regulation of this activity.

Fig. 13.11 shows the market demand curve *D* and the marginal revenue curve, *MR*, the average total cost curve *ATC*, and the marginal cost curve *MC* for a gas distribution company that is a natural monopoly.

The firm's marginal cost is constant at 10 cents per cubic metre. But average total cost decreases as output increases. The reason is that the natural gas company has a large investment in pipelines and so has high fixed costs. These fixed costs are part of the company's average total cost and so appear in the *ATC* curve. The average total cost curve slopes downward because as the number of cubic metres sold increases, the fixed cost is spread over a larger number of units. (If you need to refresh your memory on how the average total cost curve is calculated, take a quick look back at Chapter 11, pp. 230–231.)

This one firm can supply the entire market at a lower cost than two firms can because average total cost is falling even when the entire market is supplied. (Refer back to pp. 268–269 if you need a quick refresher on natural monopoly.)

Profit Maximization   First, suppose the natural gas company is not regulated and instead maximizes profit. Fig. 13.11 shows the outcome in this case. The company produces 2 million cubic metres a day, the quantity at which marginal cost equals marginal revenue. It prices this gas at 20 cents a cubic metre and makes an economic profit of 2 cents a cubic metre, or $40,000 a day.

This outcome is fine for the gas company, but it is inefficient. Price or marginal benefit is 20 cents a cubic metre when marginal cost is 10 cents a cubic metre. Also, the gas company is making a big profit. What can regulation do to improve this outcome?

The Efficient Regulation   If the monopoly regulator wants to achieve an efficient use of resources, it must require the gas monopoly to produce the quantity of gas that brings marginal benefit into equality with marginal cost. Marginal benefit is what the consumer is willing to pay and is shown by the market demand curve. Marginal cost is shown by the firm's marginal cost curve. You can see in Fig. 13.11 that this outcome occurs if the price is regulated at 10 cents per cubic metre and if 4 million cubic metres per day are produced. The regulation that produces this outcome is called a marginal cost pricing rule. A **marginal cost pricing rule** sets price equal to marginal cost. It maximizes total surplus in the regulated industry. In this example, that surplus is all consumer surplus and is the area of the triangle under the demand curve and above the marginal cost curve.

The marginal cost pricing rule is efficient. But it leaves the natural monopoly incurring an economic loss. Because average total cost is falling as output increases, marginal cost is below average total cost. And because price equals marginal cost, price is below average total cost. Average total cost minus price is the loss per unit produced. It's pretty obvious that a natural gas company that is required to use a marginal cost pricing rule will not stay in business for long. How can a company cover its costs and, at the same time, obey a marginal cost pricing rule?

One possibility is price discrimination. The company might charge a higher price to some customers but marginal cost to the customers who pay least. Another possibility is to use a two-part price (called a

FIGURE 13.11

Regulating a Natural Monopoly

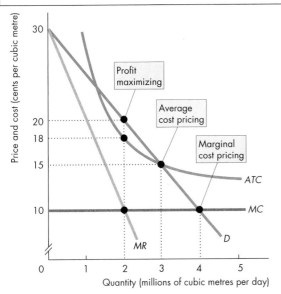

A natural monopoly is an industry in which average total cost is falling even when the entire market demand is satisfied. A natural gas producer faces the market demand curve D. The firm's marginal cost is constant at 10 cents per cubic metre, as shown by the curve labelled MC. Fixed costs are large, and the average total cost curve, which includes average fixed cost, is shown as ATC. A marginal cost pricing rule sets the price at 10 cents per cubic metre. The monopoly produces 4 million cubic metres per day and incurs an economic loss. An average cost pricing rule sets the price at 15 cents per cubic metre. The monopoly produces 3 million cubic metres a day and makes normal profit.

two-part tariff). For example, the gas company might charge a monthly fixed fee that covers its fixed cost and then charge for gas consumed at marginal cost.

But a natural monopoly cannot always cover its costs in these ways. If a natural monopoly cannot cover its total cost from its customers, and if the government wants it to follow a marginal cost pricing rule, the government must give the firm a subsidy. In such a case, the government raises the revenue for the subsidy by taxing some other activity. But as we saw in Chapter 7, taxes themselves generate deadweight loss. Thus the deadweight loss resulting from additional taxes must be subtracted from the efficiency

gained by forcing the natural monopoly to adopt a marginal cost pricing rule.

Average Cost Pricing Regulators almost never impose efficient pricing because of its consequences for the firm's profit. Instead, they compromise by permitting the firm to cover all its costs and to earn a normal profit. Normal profit, recall, is a cost of production and we include it along with the firm's other fixed costs in the average total cost curve. So pricing to cover cost and normal profit means setting price equal to average total cost—called an **average cost pricing rule**.

Figure 13.11 shows the average cost pricing outcome. The natural gas company charges 15 cents a cubic metre and sells 3 million cubic metres per day. This outcome is better for consumers than the unregulated profit-maximizing outcome. The price is 5 cents a cubic metre lower and the quantity consumed is 1 million cubic metres per day more. And the outcome is better for the producer than the marginal cost pricing rule outcome. The firm earns normal profit. The outcome is inefficient, but less so than the unregulated profit-maximizing outcome.

R E V I E W   Q U I Z

- What are the two main reasons why monopoly is worth tolerating?
- Can you provide some examples of economies of scale and economies of scope?
- Why might a monopoly have a greater incentive to innovate than a small competitive firm?
- What is the price that achieves an efficient outcome for a regulated monopoly? And what is the problem with this price?
- Compare the consumer surplus, producer surplus, and deadweight loss that arise from average cost pricing with those of profit-maximization pricing and marginal cost pricing.

◇ You've now studied two market structures: perfect competition and monopoly. *Reading Between the Lines* on pp. 284–285 looks at monopoly in action. In the next chapter, we're going to study the ground between monopoly and perfect competition. But you'll discover that the lessons you've learned from these two extreme market types are still relevant and help to understand how real-world markets work.

Telephone Monopoly

FINANCIAL POST, OCTOBER 2, 1998

Cheaper calls likely as Teleglobe loses monopoly

Average overseas calling rates could be halved with the end yesterday of Teleglobe Inc.'s monopoly over the routing of Canada's international phone traffic.

"A call to Europe that costs 90¢ a minute today could be 30¢ within a year or two," said Bernard Courtois, Bell Canada's group vice-president for regulatory issues.

Carriers including Bell and AT&T Long Distance Services Co. welcomed the end to Teleglobe's long-standing monopoly, and said regulations enacted yesterday to govern the overseas market are in line with expectations.

AT&T said eliminating all routing restrictions for Canadian telecom traffic will allow carriers to choose the cheapest and most efficient channels, with savings ultimately passed on to customers. ...

"International rates had been exceedingly high," said David Colville, vice-chairman of the Canadian Radio-television & Telecommunications Commission, which regulates telephone companies in Canada.

"I think you'll see dramatic reductions in the short term."

For more than 40 years, Montreal-based Teleglobe and its predecessor companies enjoyed a monopoly over facilities linking Canada to overseas destinations. All traffic had to move over Teleglobe's Canadian network. The business today is worth $1 billion a year to Teleglobe.

The monopoly came to a formal end yesterday as a result of international agreements, signed by more than 80 countries, aimed at increasing competition in global telecommunications services. Legislative and regulatory changes to open up Canada's international phone market also came into effect.

With Canada's domestic and international telecom markets now fully open, the CRTC said it expects to see a flurry of new entrants to the international calling business. ...

Essence of the Story

- Teleglobe Inc.'s monopoly over the routing of Canadian international phone traffic has ended.

- New entrants are expected in the international calling market.

- David Colville, vice-chairman of the CRTC, says that while the monopoly existed, prices were exceedingly high.

- Prices are now expected to fall.

- A call to Europe that cost 90¢ per minute under the monopoly could fall to 30¢ per minute within two years.

Economic Analysis

■ When Teleglobe Inc. has a monopoly over Canadian international phone traffic, the price of a call to Europe is 90¢ per minute.

■ When the international phone market becomes competitive, the price of a call to Europe is expected to fall.

■ Figure 1 compares the monopoly and a competitive market.

■ When Teleglobe Inc. is a monopoly, it maximizes profit by producing the quantity at which marginal revenue equals marginal cost. This quantity is Q_m in Fig. 1.

■ Teleglobe charges the highest price for which output Q_m can be sold. That price is 90¢ per minute, as seen on the demand curve, D, at point a.

■ In October 1998, Teleglobe's monopoly ended.

■ Initially, there is no change in cost. The industry supply curve, S, is the same as Teleglobe's marginal cost curve, MC.

■ The quantity produced by the industry and the price are determined by the intersection of the supply curve, S, and the demand curve, D, at point b.

■ The quantity bought and sold increases from Q_m under the monopoly to Q_c and the price falls from 90¢ per minute to 50¢ per minute.

■ When Teleglobe is a monopoly, output is restricted and the price is higher than in a competitive market.

■ In the long run, new entrants are expected in the international calling market.

■ Figure 2 shows that as supply increases, the supply curve shifts rightward from S_0 to S_1, the price falls further to 30¢ per minute, and the quantity of phone calls increases from Q_c to Q_1.

■ As the number of firms increases, the quantity of phone calls becomes even larger than in the monopoly market and the price falls even further.

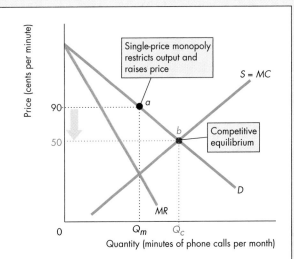

Figure 1 Market becomes competitive

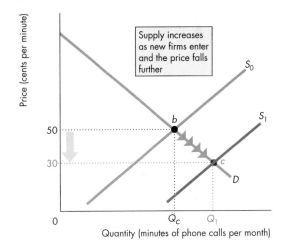

Figure 2 New firms enter the market

SUMMARY

Key Points

Market Power (pp. 268–269)

- A monopoly is an industry with a single supplier of a good or service that has no close substitutes and in which barriers to entry prevent competition.
- Barriers to entry may be legal (public franchise, licence, patent, copyright, firm owns control of a resource) or natural (created by economies of scale).
- A monopoly might be able to price discriminate when there is no resale possibility.
- Where resale is possible, a firm charges one price.

A Single-Price Monopoly's Output and Price Decision (pp. 270–273)

- The demand for a monopoly's output is the market demand curve and a single-price monopoly's marginal revenue is less than price.
- A monopoly maximizes profit by producing the output at which marginal revenue equals marginal cost and by charging the maximum price that consumers are willing to pay for that output.

Single-Price Monopoly and Competition Compared (pp. 274–277)

- A single-price monopoly charges a higher price and produces a smaller quantity than a perfectly competitive industry.
- A single-price monopoly restricts output and creates a deadweight loss.
- Monopoly imposes costs that equal its deadweight loss plus the cost of the resources devoted to rent seeking.

Price Discrimination (pp. 277–280)

- Price discrimination is an attempt by the monopoly to convert consumer surplus into economic profit.
- Perfect price discrimination extracts all the consumer surplus. Such a monopoly charges a different price for each unit sold and obtains the maximum price that each consumer is willing to pay for each unit bought.

- With perfect price discrimination, the monopoly produces the same output as would a perfectly competitive industry.
- Rent seeking with perfect price discrimination might eliminate the entire consumer surplus and producer surplus.

Monopoly Policy Issues (pp. 281–283)

- Monopolies with large economies of scale and scope can produce a larger quantity at a lower price than a competitive industry can achieve and monopoly might be more innovative than competition.
- Efficient regulation requires a monopoly to charge a price equal to marginal cost, but for a natural monopoly such a price is less than average total cost.
- Average cost pricing is a compromise pricing rule that covers a firm's costs and provides a normal profit but is not efficient. It is more efficient than unregulated profit maximization.

Key Figures and Table

Key Terms

PROBLEMS

*1. Minnie's Mineral Springs, a single-price monopoly, faces the market demand schedule:

Price (dollars per bottle)	Quantity demanded (bottles)
10	0
8	1
6	2
4	3
2	4
0	5

a. Calculate Minnie's total revenue schedule.
b. Calculate its marginal revenue schedule.

2. Dolly's Diamond Mines, a single-price monopoly, faces the market demand schedule:

Price (dollars per kilogram)	Quantity demanded (kilograms per day)
2,200	5
2,000	6
1,800	7
1,600	8
1,400	9
1,200	10

a. Calculate Dolly's total revenue schedule.
b. Calculate its marginal revenue schedule.

*3. Minnie's Mineral Springs in problem 1 has the following total cost:

Quantity produced (bottles)	Total cost (dollars)
0	1
1	3
2	7
3	13
4	21
5	31

Use a graph to calculate the profit-maximizing
a. Output
b. Price
c. Marginal cost
d. Marginal revenue
e. Economic profit
f. Does Minnie's use resources efficiently? Explain your answer.

4. Dolly's Diamond Mines in problem 2 has the following total cost:

Quantity produced (kilograms per day)	Total cost (dollars)
5	8,000
6	9,000
7	10,200
8	11,600
9	13,200
10	15,000

Use a graph to calculate the profit-maximizing
a. Output
b. Price
c. Marginal cost
d. Marginal revenue
e. Economic profit
f. Does Dolly's Mines use resources efficiently? Explain your answer.

*5. The figure illustrates the situation facing the publisher of the only newspaper containing local news in an isolated community.

a. What quantity of newspapers will maximize the publisher's profit?
b. What price will the publisher charge?
c. What is the publisher's daily total revenue?
d. At the price charged for a newspaper, is the demand elastic or inelastic? Why?

6. In problem 5, the publisher installs a new printing press that makes the marginal cost constant at 20 cents per copy.
a. What quantity of newspapers will maximize the publisher's profit?

b. What price will the publisher charge?

c. What is the publisher's daily total revenue?

d. At the price charged for a newspaper, is the demand elastic or inelastic? Why?

*7. In problem 5, what is:

a. The efficient quantity of newspapers to print each day? Explain your answer.

b. Consumer surplus?

c. Deadweight loss created by the publisher?

8. In problem 6, what is:

a. The efficient quantity of newspapers to print each day? Explain your answer.

b. Consumer surplus?

c. Deadweight loss created by the publisher?

*9. In problem 3, what is the maximum value of resources that will be used in rent seeking to acquire Minnie's monopoly? Considering this loss, what is the total social cost of Minnie's monopoly?

10. In problem 4, what is the maximum value of resources that will be used in rent seeking to acquire Dolly's monopoly? Considering this loss, what is the total social cost of Dolly's monopoly?

*11. The figure illustrates the situation facing a natural monopoly.

What quantity will be produced and what will the deadweight loss be if the firm is:

a. An unregulated profit-maximizer?

b. Regulated to earn only normal profit?

c. Regulated to be efficient?

12. What are the answers to the three questions in problem 11, if marginal cost falls by 50 percent?

CRITICAL THINKING

1. Study *Reading Between the Lines* on pp. 284–285 and then answer the following questions.

a. Was Teleglobe a natural monopoly or a legal monopoly?

b. Did Teleglobe operate efficiently? Explain.

c. With the end of Teleglobe's monopoly, what do you predict will happen to the price of international phone calls originating in Canada? What will happen to producer surplus, consumer surplus, and deadweight loss?

d. Is it necessary for the CRTC to regulate the providers of international telephone services? Why or why not?

e. If the market for international phone calls becomes competitive, will it then be efficient?

f. Suppose that some foreign firms enter the market for Canadian international phone calls. Will the market then be efficient or inefficient? Explain.

2. Use the links on the Parkin-Bade Web site to study the market for computer chips.

a. Is it correct to call Intel a monopoly? Why or why not?

b. How does Intel try to raise barriers to entry in this market?

3. Use the links on the Parkin-Bade Web site to obtain information about Microsoft. Then answer the following questions.

a. Is it correct to call Microsoft a monopoly?

b. How do you think Microsoft sets the price of Windows 98 and decides how many copies of the program to sell?

c. How would the arrival of a viable alternative operating system to Windows affect Microsoft?

d. How would you regulate the software industry to ensure that resources are used efficiently?

e. "Anyone is free to buy stock in Microsoft, so everyone is free to share in Microsoft's economic profit and the bigger that economic profit, the better for all." Evaluate this statement.

14

Monopolistic Competition and Oligopoly

Every week, we receive a newspaper stuffed with supermarket flyers describing this week's "specials," providing coupons and other enticements, all designed to grab our attention and persuade us that A&P, Zehr's, Safeway, Loblaws, and Miracle Mart have the best deals in town. One claims the lowest price, another the best brands, yet another the best value for money even if its prices are not the low-

Flyers and War Games

est. How do firms locked in fierce competition with other firms set their prices, pick their products, and choose the quantities to produce? How are the profits of such firms affected by the actions of other firms? ◆ Before 1994, only one firm made the chips that drive IBM and compatible PCs: Intel Corporation. During 1994, the prices of powerful personal computers based on Intel's fast Pentium chips collapsed. The reason: Intel suddenly faced competition from new chip producers such as Advanced Micro Devices Inc. and Cyrix Corp. The price of Intel's Pentium processor, set at more than $1,000 when it was launched in 1993, fell to less than $200 by spring 1996, and today you can buy a Pentium-based computer for less than $1,000. How did competition among a small number of chip makers bring such a rapid fall in the price of chips and computers?

◆ The theories of monopoly and perfect competition do not predict the kind of behaviour that we've just described. There are no flyers and coupons, best brands, or price wars in perfect competition because each firm produces an identical product and is a price taker. And there are none in monopoly because each monopoly firm has the entire market to itself. To understand coupons, flyers, and price wars, we need the richer models explained in this chapter.

After studying this chapter, you will be able to:

- Explain how output and price are determined in a monopolistically competitive industry
- Explain why advertising costs are high in a monopolistically competitive industry
- Explain why the price might be sticky in an oligopoly industry
- Explain how price and output are determined when an industry has one dominant firm and several small firms
- Use game theory to make predictions about price wars and competition among a small number of firms

Monopolistic Competition

You have studied two types of market structure: perfect competition and monopoly. In perfect competition, a large number of firms produce identical goods, there are no barriers to entry, and each firm is a price taker. In the long run, there is no economic profit. In monopoly, a single firm is protected from competition by barriers to entry and can make an economic profit, even in the long run.

Many real-world markets are competitive, but not as fiercely so as perfect competition. Firms in these markets possess some power to set their prices like monopolies do. We call this type of market *monopolistic competition*.

Monopolistic competition is a market structure in which:

- A large number of firms compete
- Each firm produces a differentiated product
- Firms compete on product quality, price, and marketing
- Firms are free to enter and exit.

Large Number of Firms

In monopolistic competition, as in perfect competition, the industry consists of a large number of firms. The presence of a large number of firms has three implications for the firms in the industry.

Small Market Share In monopolistic competition, each firm supplies a small part of the total industry output. Consequently, each firm has only limited power to influence the price of its product. Each firm's price can deviate from the average price of other firms by a relatively small amount.

Ignore Other Firms A firm in monopolistic competition must be sensitive to the average market price of the product. But it does not pay attention to any one individual competitor. Because all the firms are relatively small, no one firm can dictate market conditions so no one firm's actions directly affect the actions of the other firms.

Collusion Impossible Firms in monopolistic competition would like to be able to conspire to fix a higher price—called collusion. But because there are many firms, collusion is not possible.

Product Differentiation

A firm practises **product differentiation** if it makes a product that is slightly different from the products of competing firms. A differentiated product is one that is a close substitute but not a perfect substitute for the products of the other firms. Some people will pay more for one variety of the product, so when its price rises, the quantity demanded falls but it does not (necessarily) fall to zero. For example, Adidas, Asics, Diadora, Etonic, Fila, New Balance, Nike, Puma, and Reebok all make differentiated running shoes. Other things remaining the same, if the price of Adidas running shoes rises and the prices of the other shoes remain constant, Adidas sells fewer shoes and the other producers sell more. But Adidas shoes don't disappear unless the price rises by a large enough amount.

Competing on Quality, Price, and Marketing

Product differentiation enables a firm to compete with other firms in three areas: product quality, price, and marketing.

Quality The quality of a product is the physical attributes that make it different from the products of other firms. Quality includes design, reliability, the service provided to the buyer, and the buyer's ease of access to the product. Quality lies on a spectrum that runs from high to low. Some firms—Dell Computers is an example—offer high-quality products. They are well designed and reliable and the customer receives quick and efficient service. Other firms offer lower-quality products. These are less well designed and might not work perfectly, and the buyer might have to travel some distance to obtain them.

Price Because of product differentiation, a firm in monopolistic competition faces a downward-sloping demand curve. So, like a monopoly, the firm can set both its price and its output. But there is a tradeoff between the product's quality and price. A firm that makes a high-quality product can charge a higher price than a firm that makes a low-quality product.

Marketing Because of product differentiation, a firm in monopolistic competition must market its product. Marketing takes two main forms: advertising and packaging. A firm that produces a high-quality product wants to sell it for a suitably high price. To be able to do so, it must advertise and package its product in a way that convinces buyers that they are getting the higher quality for which they are paying a higher price. For example, drug companies advertise and package their brand-name drugs to persuade buyers that these items are superior to the lower-priced generic alternatives. Similarly, a low-quality producer uses advertising and packaging to persuade buyers that although the quality is low, the low price more than compensates for this fact.

Entry and Exit

In monopolistic competition, there is free entry and free exit. Consequently, a firm cannot make an economic profit in the long run. When firms make an economic profit, new firms enter the industry. This entry lowers prices and eventually eliminates economic profit. When economic losses are incurred, some firms leave the industry. This exit increases prices and profits and eventually eliminates the economic loss. In long-run equilibrium, firms neither enter nor leave the industry and the firms in the industry make zero economic profit.

Examples of Monopolistic Competition

Monopolistic competition is visible just about everywhere you look. Figure 14.1 shows eleven industries that are good examples. Even in the most concentrated of these industries, finance, the largest four firms receive less than 20 percent of industry total revenue. In the least concentrated, clothing, the largest four firms receive only 7 percent of industry total revenue. So these industries are very competitive, but the firms in them produce differentiated products.

R E V I E W   Q U I Z

- What are the distinguishing characteristics of monopolistic competition?
- How do firms in monopolistic competition compete?
- Provide some examples of industries located near your school that operate in monopolistic competition (other than the examples just given).

FIGURE 14.1

Examples of Monopolistic Competition

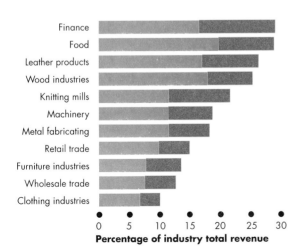

Percentage of industry total revenue

These industries operate in monopolistic competition. The blue bars show the percentage of industry total revenue received by the largest 4 firms. The red bars show the percentage of industry total revenue received by the next 4 firms. So the entire length of the red and blue bars combined shows the percentage of industry total revenue received by the largest 8 firms.

Source: *Annual Report of the Ministry of Industry, Science and Technology Under the Corporations and Labour Unions Returns Act*, March 1990, p. 94.

Output and Price in Monopolistic Competition

WE ARE NOW GOING TO LEARN HOW OUTPUT AND price are determined in monopolistic competition. First, we will suppose that the firm has already decided on the quality of its product and on its marketing program. For a given product and a given amount of marketing activity, the firm faces given costs and market conditions.

Figure 14.2 shows how a firm in monopolistic competition determines its price and output. Part (a) deals with the short run, and part (b) deals with the long run. We'll concentrate first on the short run.

Short Run: Economic Profit

The demand curve *D* shows the demand for the firm's product. It is the demand curve for Nautica jackets, not jackets in general. The curve labelled *MR* is the marginal revenue curve associated with the demand curve. It is derived just like the marginal revenue curve of a single-price monopoly that you studied in Chapter 13. The figure also shows the firm's average total cost (*ATC*) and marginal cost (*MC*). These curves are similar to the cost curves that you first encountered in Chapter 11.

Nautica maximizes profit by producing the output at which marginal revenue equals marginal cost. In Fig. 14.2, this output is 150 jackets a day. Nautica charges the maximum price that buyers are willing to pay for this quantity, which is determined by the demand curve. This price is $190 a jacket. When Nautica produces 150 jackets a day, the firm's average total cost is $140 a jacket, so it makes a short-run economic profit of $7,500 a day ($50 a jacket multiplied by 150 jackets a day). The blue rectangle shows this economic profit.

FIGURE 14.2

Output and Price in Monopolistic Competition

(a) Short run

(b) Long run

Part (a) shows the short-run outcome. Profit is maximized by producing 150 jackets per day and selling them for $190 per jacket. Average total cost is $140 per jacket, and the firm makes an economic profit (the blue rectangle) of $7,500 a day.

Economic profit encourages new entrants in the long run, and part (b) shows the long-run outcome. The entry of new firms decreases each firm's demand and shifts the demand curve and marginal revenue curve leftward. When the demand curve has shifted to *D'*, the marginal revenue curve is *MR'* and the firm is in long-run equilibrium. The output that maximizes profit is 50 jackets a day and the price is $145 per jacket. Average total cost is also $145 per jacket, so economic profit is zero.

So far, the firm in monopolistic competition looks just like a single-price monopoly. It produces the quantity at which marginal revenue equals marginal cost and then charges the highest price that buyers are willing to pay for that quantity, determined by the demand curve. The key difference between monopoly and monopolistic competition lies in what happens in the long run.

Long Run: Zero Economic Profit

There is no restriction on entry in monopolistic competition, so economic profit attracts new entrants. As new firms enter the industry, the firm's demand curve and marginal revenue curve start to shift leftward. At each point in time, the firm maximizes its short-run profit by producing the quantity at which marginal revenue equals marginal cost and by charging the highest price that buyers are willing to pay for this quantity. But as the demand curve shifts leftward, the profit-maximizing quantity and price fall.

Figure 14.2(b) shows the long-run equilibrium. Nautica's demand curve has shifted leftward to D', and its marginal revenue curve has shifted leftward to MR'. Nautica produces 50 jackets a day and sells them at a price of $145 each. At this output level, the firm's average total cost is also $145 a jacket. So Nautica is making zero economic profit.

When all the firms are making zero economic profit, there is no incentive for new firms to enter the industry.

If demand is so low relative to costs that firms are incurring economic losses, exit will occur. As firms leave an industry, the demand for the remaining firm's products increases and their demand curves shift rightward. The exit process ends when all the firms are making zero economic profit.

Monopolistic Competition and Efficiency

When we studied a perfectly competitive industry, we discovered that in some circumstances, such an industry allocates resources efficiently. A key feature of efficiency is that marginal benefit equals marginal cost. Price measures marginal benefit, so efficiency requires price to equal marginal cost. When we studied monopoly, we discovered that such a firm creates an inefficient use of resources because it restricts output to a level at which price exceeds marginal cost. In such

a situation, the marginal benefit exceeds marginal cost and production is less than its efficient level.

Monopolistic competition shares this feature of monopoly. Even though there is zero economic profit in long-run equilibrium, the monopolistically competitive industry produces an output at which price equals average total cost but exceeds marginal cost. This outcome means that firms in monopolistic competition always have excess capacity in long-run equilibrium.

Excess Capacity A firm's **capacity output** is the output at which average total cost is a minimum— the output at the minimum of the U-shaped *ATC* curve. This output is 100 jackets a day in Fig. 14.3. Firms in monopolistic competition always have *excess capacity*, in the long run. In Fig. 14.3, Nautica produces 50 jackets a day and has excess capacity of 50 jackets a day. That is, Nautica produces a smaller out-

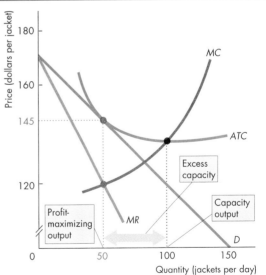

In the long run, entry decreases demand to the point at which the firm makes zero economic profit. Here the firm produces 50 jackets a day. The firm's capacity is the output at which average total cost is a minimum. Here, capacity output is 100 jackets a day. Because the demand curve in monopolistic competition slopes downward, the output that maximizes profit is always less than capacity output in long-run equilibrium. The firm operates with excess capacity in long-run equilibrium.

put than that which minimizes average total cost. Consequently, the consumer pays a price that exceeds minimum average total cost. This result arises from the fact that Nautica faces a downward-sloping demand curve. The demand curve slopes down because of product differentiation, so product differentiation creates excess capacity.

You can see the excess capacity in monopolistic competition all around you. Family restaurants (except for the truly outstanding ones) almost always have some empty tables. You can always get a pizza delivered in less than 30 minutes. It is rare that every pump at a gas station is in use with customers waiting in line. There is always an abundance of realtors ready to help find or sell a home.

These industries are all examples of monopolistic competition. The firms have excess capacity. They could sell more by cutting their prices. But they would then incur economic losses.

Because in monopolistic competition, price exceeds marginal cost, this market structure, like monopoly, is inefficient. The marginal cost of producing one more unit of output is less than the marginal benefit to the consumer, determined by the price the consumer is willing to pay. But the inefficiency of monopolistic competition arises from product differentiation—from product variety. Consumers value variety, but it is achievable only if firms make differentiated products. So the loss in efficiency that occurs in monopolistic competition must be weighed against the gain of greater product variety.

REVIEW QUIZ

- How does a firm in monopolistic competition decide how much to produce and at what price to offer its product for sale?
- Why can a firm in monopolistic competition earn an economic profit only in the short run?
- Is monopolistic competition efficient?
- Why do firms in monopolistic competition operate with excess capacity?

You've seen how the firm in monopolistic competition determines its output and price in the short run and the long run when it produces a given product and undertakes a *given* marketing effort. But how does the firm choose its product quality and marketing effort? We'll now study these decisions.

Product Development and Marketing

WHEN WE STUDIED A FIRM'S OUTPUT AND PRICE decision, we supposed that it had already made its product and marketing decisions. We're now going to study these decisions and the impact they have on the firm's output, price, and economic profit.

Innovation and Product Development

To enjoy economic profits, firms in monopolistic competition must be in a state of continuous product development. The reason is that wherever economic profits are earned, imitators emerge and set up business. So to maintain its economic profit, a firm must seek out new products that will provide it with a competitive edge, even if only temporarily. A firm that manages to introduce a new and differentiated variety will temporarily increase the demand for its product and will be able to temporarily increase its price. It will make an economic profit. Eventually, new firms that make close substitutes for the new product will enter and compete away the economic profit arising from this initial advantage. So to restore economic profit, the firm must again innovate.

The decision to innovate is based on the same type of profit-maximizing calculation that you've already studied. Innovation and product development are costly activities but they also bring in additional revenues. The firm must balance the cost and benefit at the margin. At a low level of product development, the marginal revenue from a better product exceeds the marginal cost. When the marginal dollar spent on product development brings in a dollar of revenue, the firm is spending the profit-maximizing amount on product development.

For example, when Eidos Interactive released Tomb Raider III, it was probably not the best game that Eidos could have created. Rather, it was the game that balanced the marginal benefit and willingness of the consumer to pay for further game enhancements against the marginal cost of these enhancements.

Efficiency and Product Innovation Is product innovation an efficient activity? Does it benefit the consumer? There are two views about these questions. One view is that monopolistic competition brings to market many improved products that bring great benefits to the consumer. Clothing, kitchen and other household appliances, computers, computer programs, cars, and many other products keep getting better every year and the consumer benefits from these improved products.

But many so-called improvements amount to little more than changing the appearance of a product. And sometimes, the improvement is restricted to a different look in the packaging. In these cases, there is little objective benefit to the consumer.

But regardless of whether a product improvement is real or imagined, its value to the consumer is its marginal benefit, which equals the amount the consumer is willing to pay. In other words, the value of product improvements is the increase in price that the consumer is willing to pay. The marginal benefit to the producer is marginal revenue, which equals marginal cost. Because price exceeds marginal cost in monopolistic competition, product development is not pushed to its efficient level.

Marketing

Some product differentiation is achieved by designing and developing products that are actually different from those of the other firms. But firms also attempt to create a consumer perception of product differentiation even when actual differences are small. Advertising and packaging are the principal means used by firms to achieve this end. An American Express card is a different product from a Visa card. But the actual differences are not the main ones that American Express emphasizes in its marketing. The deeper message is that if you use an American Express card, you can be like Tiger Woods (or some other high-profile successful person).

Marketing Expenditures Firms in monopolistic competition incur huge costs in order to persuade buyers to appreciate and value the differences between their own products and those of their competitors. So a large proportion of the prices that we pay cover the cost of selling a good. And this proportion is increasing. Advertising in newspapers and magazines and on radio and television is the main selling cost. But it is not the only one. Selling costs include the cost of shopping malls that look like movie sets; glossy catalogues and brochures; and the salaries, airfares, and hotel bills of salespeople.

A survey conducted by a commercial agency suggests that for cleaning supplies and toys, around

15 percent of the price of an item is spent on advertising. Figure 14.4 shows some estimates for other industries.

For the North American economy as a whole, there are more than 20,000 advertising agencies that employ more than 200,000 people and have sales of $45 billion. But these numbers are only part of the total cost of advertising because firms have their own internal advertising departments, the cost of which can only be guessed.

Advertising expenditures and other selling costs affect the profits of firms in two ways. They increase costs and they change demand. Let's look at these effects.

Selling Costs and Total Costs Selling costs such as advertising expenditures increase the costs of a monopolistically competitive firm above those of a competitive firm or a monopoly. Advertising costs and other selling costs are fixed costs. They do not vary as total output varies. So, just like fixed produc-

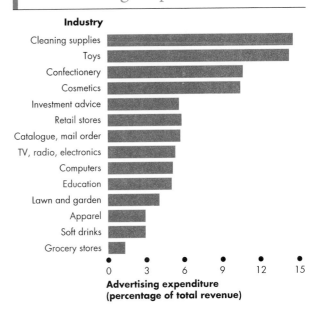

FIGURE 14.4

Advertising Expenditures

Advertising expenditures are a large part of total revenue for producers of cleaning supplies, toys, confectionery, and cosmetics.

Source: Schoenfeld & Associates, Lincolnwood, Illinois, reported at http://www.toolkit.cch.com/text/p03_7006.stm

tion costs, advertising costs per unit decrease as production increases.

Figure 14.5 shows how selling costs and advertising expenditures change a firm's average total cost. The blue curve shows the average total cost of production. The red curve shows the firm's average total cost of production plus advertising. The height of the red area between the two curves shows the average fixed cost of advertising. The *total* cost of advertising is fixed. But the *average* cost of advertising decreases as output increases.

The figure shows that if advertising increases the quantity sold by a large enough amount, it can lower average total cost. For example, if the quantity sold increases from 25 jackets a day with no advertising to 130 jackets a day with advertising, average total cost falls from $170 a jacket to $160 a jacket. The reason is that although the *total* fixed cost has increased, the greater fixed cost is spread over a greater output, so average total cost decreases.

FIGURE 14.5

Selling Costs and Total Cost

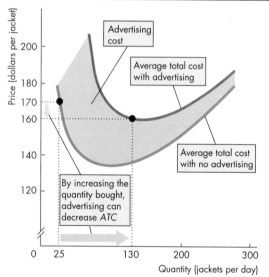

Selling costs such as the cost of advertising are fixed costs. When added to the average total cost of production, these costs increase average total cost (*ATC*) by a greater amount at small outputs than at large outputs. If advertising enables the quantity sold to increase from 25 jackets to 130 jackets a day, it *lowers* average total cost from $170 to $160 a jacket.

Selling Costs and Demand   Advertising and other selling efforts change the demand for a firm's product. But how? Does demand increase or does it decrease? The most natural answer is that advertising increases demand. By informing people about the quality of its products or by persuading people to switch from the products of other firms, a firm might expect to increase the demand for its own products.

But all firms in monopolistic competition advertise. And all seek to persuade customers that they have the best deal around. If advertising enables a firm to survive, it might increase the number of firms. And to the extent that it increases the number of firms, it *decreases* the demand faced by any one firm.

Efficiency: The Bottom Line   To the extent that selling costs provide consumers with services that they value and with information about the precise nature of the differentiation of products, they enable the consumer to make a better choice. But the opportunity cost of the additional services and information must be weighed against the gain to the consumer.

The bottom line on the question of efficiency of monopolistic competition is ambiguous. In some cases, the gains from extra product variety unquestionably offset the selling costs and the extra cost arising from excess capacity. The tremendous varieties of books and magazines, clothing, food, and drinks are examples of such gains. It is less easy to see the gains from being able to buy brand-name drugs that have a chemical composition identical to that of a generic alternative. But some people do willingly pay more for the brand-name alternative.

REVIEW QUIZ

- What are the two main ways other than by adjusting price in which a firm in monopolistic competition competes with other firms?
- Why might product innovation and development be efficient and why might it be inefficient?
- How do advertising expenditures influence a firm's cost curves? Do they increase or decrease average total cost?
- How do advertising expenditures influence a firm's demand curve? Do they increase or decrease demand?
- Why is it difficult to determine whether monopolistic competition is efficient or inefficient? What is your opinion about the bottom line and why?

Oligopoly

ANOTHER TYPE OF MARKET THAT STANDS between the extremes of perfect competition and monopoly is oligopoly. **Oligopoly** is a market structure in which a small number of firms compete.

In oligopoly, the quantity sold by any one firm depends on that firm's price *and* on the other firms' prices and quantities sold. To see why, suppose you run one of the three gas stations in a small town. If you cut your price and your two competitors don't cut theirs, your sales increase and the sales of the other two firms decrease. With lower sales, the other firms most likely cut their prices too. If they do cut their prices, your sales and profits take a tumble. So before deciding to cut your price, you must predict how the other firms will react and attempt to calculate the effects of those reactions on your own profit.

Several models have been developed to explain the prices and quantities in oligopoly. But no one theory has been found that can explain all the different types of behaviour that we observe in such markets. The models fall into two broad groups: traditional models and game theory models. We'll look at both types, starting with two traditional models.

The Kinked Demand Curve Model

The kinked demand curve model of oligopoly is based on the assumption that each firm believes that:

1. If it raises its price, others will not follow.
2. If it cuts its price, so will the other firms.

Figure 14.6 shows the demand curve (*D*) that a firm believes describes the demand for its product. The demand curve has a kink at the current price, *P*, and quantity, *Q*. A small price rise above *P* brings a big decrease in the quantity sold. The other firms hold their current price and the firm has the highest price, so it loses market share. Even a large price cut below *P* brings only a small increase in the quantity demanded. In this case, other firms match the price cut, so the firm gets no price advantage over its competitors.

The kink in the demand curve creates a break in the marginal revenue curve (*MR*). To maximize profit, the firm produces the quantity *Q* where the marginal cost curve passes through the gap *ab* in the marginal revenue curve. If marginal cost fluctuates between *a* and *b*, like the marginal cost curves MC_0 and MC_1,

FIGURE 14.6

The Kinked Demand Curve Model

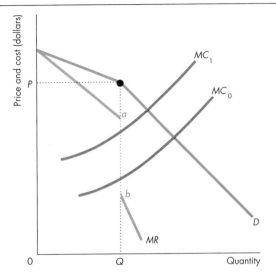

The price in an oligopoly market is *P*. Each firm believes the demand curve for its product is *D*. A small price rise above *P* brings a big decrease in the quantity sold because other firms do not raise their prices. Even a big price cut below *P* brings only a small increase in the quantity sold because other firms also cut their prices. Because the demand curve is kinked, the marginal revenue curve, *MR*, has a break *ab*. Profit is maximized by producing *Q*. The marginal cost curve passes through the break in the marginal revenue curve. Marginal cost changes inside the range *ab* leave the price and quantity unchanged.

the firm does not change its price or its output. Only if marginal cost fluctuates outside the range *ab* does the firm change its price and output. So the kinked demand curve model predicts that price and quantity are insensitive to small cost changes.

A problem with the kinked demand curve model is that the firms' beliefs about the demand curve are not always correct and firms can figure out that they are not correct. If marginal cost increases by enough to cause the firm to increase its price and if all firms experience the same increase in marginal cost, they all increase their prices together. The firm's beliefs that others will not join it in a price rise is incorrect. A firm that bases its actions on beliefs that are wrong does not maximize profit and might even end up incurring an economic loss.

Dominant Firm Oligopoly

A second traditional model explains a dominant firm oligopoly, which arises when one firm—the dominant firm—has a big cost advantage over the other firms and produces a large part of the industry output. The dominant firm sets the market price and the other firms are price takers. Examples of dominant firm oligopoly are a large gasoline retailer or a big video rental store that dominates its local market.

To see how a dominant firm oligopoly works, suppose that 11 firms operate gas stations in a city. Big-G is the dominant firm. Figure 14.7 shows the market for gas in this city. In part (a), the demand curve D tells us the total quantity of gas demanded in the city at each price. The supply curve S_{10} is the supply curve of the 10 small suppliers.

Part (b) shows the situation facing Big-G. Its marginal cost curve is MC. Big-G's demand curve is XD

and its marginal revenue curve is MR. Big-G's demand curve shows the excess demand not met by the 10 small firms. For example, at a price of $1 a litre, the quantity demanded is 20,000 litres, the quantity supplied by the 10 small firms is 10,000 litres, and the excess quantity demanded is 10,000, measured by the distance ab in both parts of the figure.

To maximize profit, Big-G operates like a monopoly. It sells 10,000 litres a week for a price of $1 a litre (point b). The 10 small firms take the price of $1 a litre. They behave just like firms in perfect competition. The quantity of gas demanded in the entire city at $1 a litre is 20,000 litres, as shown in part (a). Of this amount, Big-G sells 10,000 litres and the 10 small firms each sell 1,000 litres.

The traditional theories of oligopoly do not enable us to understand all oligopoly markets and, in recent years, economists have developed new models based on game theory. Let's now learn about game theory.

FIGURE 14.7

A Dominant Firm Oligopoly

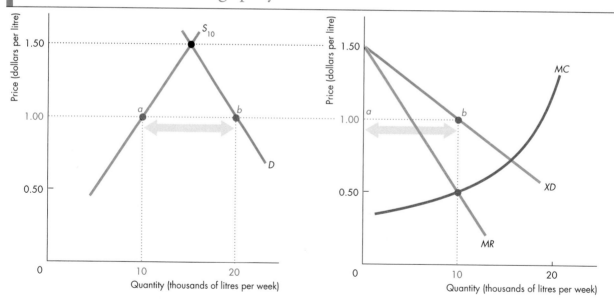

(a) Ten small firms and market demand

(b) Big-G's price and output decision

The demand curve for gas in a city is D in part (a). There are 10 small competitive firms that together have a supply curve of S_{10}. In addition, there is 1 large firm, Big-G, shown in part (b). Big-G faces the demand curve XD, determined as market demand D minus the supply of the other 10 firms S_{10}—the demand that is not satisfied by the small firms. Big-G's mar-

ginal revenue is MR, and marginal cost is MC. Big-G sets its output to maximize profit by equating marginal cost, MC, and marginal revenue, MR. This output is 10,000 litres per week. Big-G can sell this quantity at a price of $1 a litre (point b on XD). The other 10 firms take this price, and each firm sells 1,000 litres per week, point a in part (a).

Game Theory

THE MAIN TOOL THAT ECONOMISTS USE TO analyze *strategic behaviour*—behaviour that takes into account the expected behaviour of others and the mutual recognition of interdependence—is called **game theory**. Game theory was invented by John von Neumann in 1937 and extended by von Neumann and Oskar Morgenstern in 1944. Today, it is one of the major research fields in economics.

Game theory seeks to understand oligopoly as well all other forms of economic, political, social, and even biological rivalries by using a method of analysis specifically designed to understand games of all types, including the familiar games of everyday life. We will begin our study of game theory, and its application to the behaviour of firms, by thinking about familiar games.

What Is a Game?

What is a game? At first thought, the question seems silly. After all, there are many different games. There are ball games and parlour games, games of chance and games of skill. But what is it about all these different activities that make them games? What do all these games have in common? They share three features:

■ Rules
■ Strategies
■ Payoffs

Let's see how these common features of games apply to a game called "the prisoners' dilemma." This game, it turns out, captures some of the essential features of oligopoly, and it gives a good illustration of how game theory works and how it generates predictions.

The Prisoners' Dilemma

Art and Bob have been caught red-handed, stealing a car. Facing airtight cases, they will receive a sentence of 2 years each for their crime. During his interviews with the two prisoners, the Crown attorney begins to suspect that he has stumbled on the two people who were responsible for a multimillion-dollar bank robbery some months earlier. But this is just a suspicion. The Crown attorney has no evidence on which he can convict them of the greater crime unless he can get

them to confess. The Crown attorney decides to make the prisoners play a game with the following rules.

Rules Each prisoner (player) is placed in a separate room and cannot communicate with the other player. Each is told that he is suspected of having carried out the bank robbery and that:

If both of them confess to the larger crime, each will receive a sentence of 3 years for both crimes.

If he alone confesses and his accomplice does not, he will receive an even shorter sentence of 1 year while his accomplice will receive a 10-year sentence.

Strategies In game theory, **strategies** are all the possible actions of each player. Art and Bob each have two possible actions:

1. Confess to the bank robbery.
2. Deny having committed the bank robbery.

Payoffs Because there are two players, each with two strategies, there are four possible outcomes:

1. Both confess.
2. Both deny.
3. Art confesses and Bob denies.
4. Bob confesses and Art denies.

Each prisoner can work out exactly what happens to him—his *payoff*—in each of these four situations. We can tabulate the four possible payoffs for each of the prisoners in what is called a payoff matrix for the game. A **payoff matrix** is a table that shows the payoffs for every possible action by each player for every possible action by each other player.

Table 14.1 shows a payoff matrix for Art and Bob. The squares show the payoffs for each prisoner—the red triangle in each square shows Art's and the blue triangle shows Bob's. If both prisoners confess (top left), each gets a prison term of 3 years. If Bob confesses but Art denies (top right), Art gets a 10-year sentence and Bob gets a 1-year sentence. If Art confesses and Bob denies (bottom left), Art gets a 1-year sentence and Bob gets a 10-year sentence. Finally, if both of them deny (bottom right), neither can be convicted of the bank robbery charge but both are sentenced for the car theft—a 2-year sentence.

Equilibrium The equilibrium of a game occurs when each player takes the best possible action given the action of the other players. In the case of the prisoners' dilemma, the equilibrium occurs when Art makes his best choice given Bob's choice and when Bob makes his best choice given Art's choice. Let's find the equilibrium of the prisoners' dilemma game.

First, look at the situation from Art's point of view. If Bob confesses, it pays Art to confess because in that case, he is sentenced to 3 years rather than 10 years. If Bob does not confess, it still pays Art to confess because in that case he receives 1 year rather than 2 years. So Art's best action is to confess.

Second, look at the situation from Bob's point of view. If Art confesses, it pays Bob to confess because in that case, he is sentenced to 3 years rather than 10 years. If Art does not confess, it still pays Bob to confess because in that case he receives 1 year rather than 2 years. So Bob's best action is to confess.

Because each player's best action is to confess, each does confess, each gets a 3-year prison term, and the Crown attorney has solved the bank robbery. This is the equilibrium of the game.

Nash Equilibrium The equilibrium concept that we have used is called a **Nash equilibrium**; it is so named because it was first proposed by John Nash of Princeton University, who received the Nobel Prize for Economic Science in 1994.

The prisoners' dilemma has a special kind of Nash equilibrium called a dominant strategy equilibrium. A *dominant strategy* is a strategy that is the same regardless of the action taken by the other player. In other words, each player has a unique best action regardless of what the other player does. A **dominant strategy equilibrium** occurs when there is a dominant strategy for each player.

The Dilemma Now that you have found the outcome to the prisoners' dilemma, you can better see the dilemma. The dilemma arises as each prisoner contemplates the consequences of denying. Each prisoner knows that if both of them deny, they will receive only a 2-year sentence for stealing the car. But neither has any way of knowing that his accomplice will deny. Each poses the following questions: Should I deny and rely on my accomplice to deny so that we will both get only 2 years? Or should I confess in the hope of getting just 1 year (provided that my accomplice denies) knowing that if my accomplice does confess, we will both get 3 years in prison? The dilemma is resolved by finding the equilibrium of the game.

TABLE 14.1

Prisoners' Dilemma Payoff Matrix

Each square shows the payoffs for the two players, Art and Bob, for each possible pair of actions. In each square, the red triangle shows Art's payoff and the blue triangle shows Bob's. For example, if both confess, the payoffs are in the top left square. The equilibrium of the game is for both players to confess and each gets a 3-year sentence.

A Bad Outcome For the prisoners, the equilibrium of the game, with each confessing, is not the best outcome. If neither of them confesses, each gets only 2 years for the lesser crime. Isn't there some way in which this better outcome can be achieved? It seems that there is not, because the players cannot communicate with each other. Each player can put himself in the other player's place, and so each player can figure out that there is a dominant strategy for each of them. The prisoners are indeed in a dilemma. Each knows that he can serve 2 years only if he can trust the other to deny. But each prisoner also knows that it is not in the best interest of the other to deny. So each prisoner knows that he must confess, thereby delivering a bad outcome for both.

Let's now see how we can use the ideas we've just developed to understand a host of economic situations such as price fixing, price wars, and other aspects of the behaviour of firms in oligopoly.

An Oligopoly Price-Fixing Game

To understand how oligopolies fix prices, we're going to study a special case of oligopoly called duopoly. **Duopoly** is a market structure in which only two producers compete. You can probably find some examples of duopoly in your city. Many cities have only two local newspapers, two taxi companies, two car rental firms, two copy centres, or two campus bookstores. But the main reason for studying duopoly is not its realism. We study duopoly because it captures the essence of oligopoly and yet is more revealing.

Our goal is to predict the prices charged and the quantities produced by the two firms. To pursue that goal, we're going to study the duopoly game.

We will suppose that the two firms, Trick and Gear, enter into a collusive agreement. A **collusive agreement** is an agreement between two (or more) producers to restrict output in order to raise prices and profits. Such an agreement is illegal and is undertaken in secret. A group of firms that has entered into a collusive agreement to restrict output and increase prices and profits is called a **cartel**. The strategies that firms in a cartel can pursue are to:

- Comply
- Cheat

Complying simply means sticking to the agreement. Cheating means breaking the agreement in a manner designed to benefit the cheating firm.

Because each firm has two strategies, there are four possible combinations of actions for the two firms:

- Both firms comply.
- Both firms cheat.
- Trick complies and Gear cheats.
- Gear complies and Trick cheats.

We'll begin by describing the cost and demand conditions in a duopoly industry.

Cost and Demand Conditions

Trick and Gear face identical costs and Fig. 14.8(a) shows their average total cost curve (*ATC*) and marginal cost curve (*MC*). Figure 14.8(b) shows the market demand curve for switchgears (*D*). Each firm produces an identical product, so one firm's switchgear is a perfect substitute for the other's. The price of each firm's product, therefore, is identical. And the higher the price, the smaller is the quantity demanded.

This industry is a natural duopoly. Two firms can produce this good at a lower cost than either one firm or three firms can. For each firm, average total cost is at its minimum when production is 3,000 units a week. And when price equals minimum average total cost, the total quantity demanded is 6,000 units a week. So two firms can just supply that quantity.

FIGURE 14.8

Costs and Demand

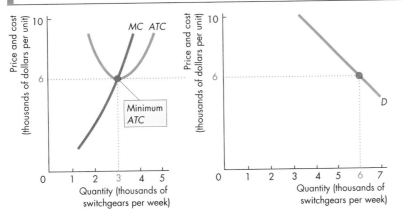

(a) Individual firm   **(b) Industry**

The average total cost curve for each firm is *ATC*, and the marginal cost curve is *MC* (part a). Minimum average total cost is at $6,000 a unit and it occurs at a production of 3,000 units a week. Part (b) shows the industry demand curve. At a price of $6,000, the quantity demanded is 6,000 units per week. The two firms can produce this output at the lowest possible average cost. If the market had one firm, it would be profitable for another to enter. If the market had three firms, one would exit. There is room for just two firms in this industry. It is a natural duopoly.

Colluding to Maximize Profits

Let's begin by working out the payoffs to the two firms if they collude to make the maximum industry profit by acting like a monopoly. The calculations that the two firms will perform are exactly the same calculations that a monopoly performs. (You can refresh your memory of these calculations by looking at Chapter 13, pp. 272–273.) The only thing that the duopolies must do that is additional to what a monopolist must do is to agree on how much of the total output each of them will produce.

Figure 14.9 shows the price and quantity that maximize industry profit for the duopolies. Part (a) shows the situation for each firm, and part (b) shows the situation for the industry as a whole. The curve labelled MR is the industry marginal revenue curve. This marginal revenue curve is exactly like that of a single-price monopoly. The curve labelled MC_I is the industry marginal cost curve if each firm produces the same level of output. That curve is constructed by adding together the outputs of the two firms at each level of marginal cost. That is, at each level of marginal cost, industry output is twice as much as the output of each individual firm. Thus the curve MC_I in part (b) is twice as far to the right as the curve MC in part (a).

To maximize industry profit, the duopolists agree to restrict output to the rate that makes the industry marginal cost and marginal revenue equal. That output rate, as shown in part (b), is 4,000 units a week.

The highest price for which the 4,000 switchgears can be sold is $9,000 each. This is the price that Trick and Gear agree to charge.

To hold the price at $9,000 a unit, production must be not exceed 4,000 units a week. So Trick and Gear must agree on production levels for each of them that totals 4,000 units a week. Let's suppose that they agree to split the market equally so that each firm produces 2,000 switchgears a week. Because the firms are identical, this division is the most likely.

The average total cost (ATC) of producing 2,000 switchgears a week is $8,000, so the profit per unit is $1,000 and economic profit is $2 million (2,000 units × $1,000 per unit). The economic profit of each firm is represented by the blue rectangle in Fig. 14.9(a).

We have just described one possible outcome for a duopoly game: The two firms collude to produce the monopoly profit-maximizing output and divide that output equally between themselves. From the industry point of view, this solution is identical to a monopoly. A duopoly that operates in this way is indistinguishable from a monopoly. The economic profit that is made by a monopoly is the maximum total profit that can be made by colluding duopolies.

But with price greater than marginal cost, either firm might think of trying to increase profit by cheating on the agreement and producing more than the agreed amount. Let's see what happens if one of the firms does cheat in this way.

FIGURE 14.9

Colluding to Make Monopoly Profits

(a) Individual firm   **(b) Industry**

The industry marginal cost curve, MC_I (part b) is the horizontal sum of the two firms' marginal cost curves, MC (part a). The industry marginal revenue curve is MR. To maximize profit, the firms produce 4,000 units a week (the quantity at which marginal revenue equals marginal cost). They sell that output for $9,000 a unit. Each firm produces 2,000 units a week. Average total cost is $8,000 a unit, so each firm makes an economic profit of $2 million (blue rectangle)— 2,000 units multiplied by $1,000 profit a unit.

One Firm Cheats on a Collusive Agreement

To set the stage for cheating on their agreement, Trick convinces Gear that demand has decreased and that it cannot sell 2,000 units a week. Trick tells Gear that it plans to cut its price in order to sell the agreed 2,000 units each week. Because the two firms produce an identical product, Gear matches Trick's price cut but still produces only 2,000 units a week.

In fact, there has been no decrease in demand. Trick plans to increase output, which it knows will lower the price, and Trick wants to ensure that Gear's output remains at the agreed level.

Figure 14.10 illustrates the consequences of Trick cheating. Suppose that Trick, the cheat, increases output to 3,000 units a week (part b). If Gear, the complier, sticks to the agreement to produce only 2,000 units a week (part a), total output is 5,000 a week, and given demand (part c), the price falls to $7,500 a unit.

Gear continues to produce 2,000 units a week at a cost of $8,000 a unit and incurs a loss of $500 a unit or $1 million a week. This economic loss is represented by the red rectangle in part (a). Trick produces 3,000 units a week at an average total cost of $6,000. With a price of $7,500, Trick makes a profit of $1,500 a unit and therefore an economic profit of $4.5 million. This economic profit is the blue rectangle in part (b).

We've now described a second possible outcome for the duopoly game: One of the firms cheats on the collusive agreement. In this case, the industry output is larger than the monopoly output and the industry price is lower than the monopoly price. The total economic profit made by the industry is less than the monopoly's economic profit. Trick (the cheat) makes an economic profit of $4.5 million, and Gear (the complier) incurs an economic loss of $1 million. The industry makes an economic profit of $3.5 million, which is $0.5 million less than the economic profit a monopoly would make. But the profit is distributed unevenly. Trick makes a bigger economic profit while Gear incurs an economic loss.

A similar outcome would arise if Gear cheated and Trick complied with the agreement. The industry profit and price would be the same, but in this case Gear (the cheat) would make an economic profit of $4.5 million and Trick (the complier) would incur an economic loss of $1 million.

Let's next see what happens if both firms cheat.

FIGURE 14.10

One Firm Cheats

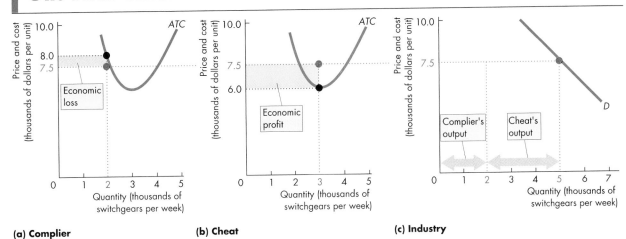

(a) Complier　　**(b) Cheat**　　**(c) Industry**

One firm, shown in part (a), complies with the agreement and produces 2,000 units. The other firm, shown in part (b), cheats on the agreement and increases its output to 3,000 units. Given the market demand curve, shown in part (c), and with a total production of 5,000 units a week, the price falls to $7,500. At this price, the complier in part (a) incurs an economic loss of $1 million ($500 per unit × 2,000 units) shown by the red rectangle. In part (b), the cheat makes an economic profit of $4.5 million ($1,500 per unit × 3,000 units), shown as the blue rectangle.

Both Firms Cheat

Suppose that instead of just one firm cheating on the collusive agreement, both firms cheat. In particular, suppose that each firm behaves in exactly the same way as the cheating firm that we have just analyzed. Each tells the other that it is unable to sell its output at the going price and that it plans to cut its price. But because both firms cheat, each will propose a successively lower price. As long as price exceeds marginal cost, each firm has an incentive to increase its production—to cheat. Only when price equals marginal cost is there no further incentive to cheat. This situation arises when the price has reached $6,000. At this price, marginal cost equals price. Also, price equals minimum average total cost. At a price less than $6,000, each firm incurs an economic loss. At a price of $6,000, each firm covers all its costs and makes zero economic profit (makes normal profit). Also, at a price of $6,000, each firm wants to produce 3,000 units a week, so the industry output is 6,000 units a week. Given the demand conditions, 6,000 units can be sold at a price of $6,000 each.

Figure 14.11 illustrates the situation just described. Each firm, shown in part (a), produces 3,000 units a week, and at this output level average total cost is a minimum ($6,000 per unit). The market as a whole, shown in part (b), operates at the point at which the demand curve (D) intersects the industry marginal cost curve. This marginal cost curve is constructed as the horizontal sum of the marginal cost curves of the two firms. Each firm has lowered its price and increased its output to try to gain an advantage over the other firm. Each has pushed this process as far as it can without incurring an economic loss.

We have now described a third possible outcome of this duopoly game: Both firms cheat. If both firms cheat on the collusive agreement, the output of each firm is 3,000 units a week and the price is $6,000. Each firm makes zero economic profit.

The Payoff Matrix

Now that we have described the strategies and payoffs in the duopoly game, let's summarize the strategies and the payoffs in the form of the game's payoff matrix and then calculate the equilibrium.

Table 14.2 sets out the payoff matrix for this game. It is constructed in exactly the same way as the payoff matrix for the prisoners' dilemma in Table 14.1. The squares show the payoffs for the two firms—Gear and Trick. In this case, the payoffs are profits. (In the case of the prisoners' dilemma, the payoffs were losses.)

The table shows that if both firms cheat (top left), they achieve the perfectly competitive outcome—each firm makes zero economic profit. If both firms comply (bottom right), the industry makes the monopoly profit and each firm earns an economic profit of $2 million. The top right and bottom left squares show what happens if one firm

---

FIGURE 14.11

Both Firms Cheat

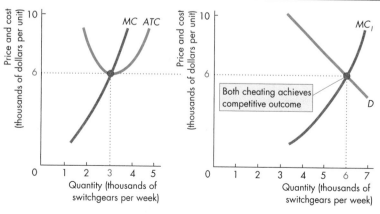

(a) Individual firm

(b) Industry

If both firms cheat by increasing production, the collusive agreement collapses. The limit to the collapse is the competitive equilibrium. Neither firm will cut price below $6,000, (minimum average total cost) for to do so results in losses. In part (a), both firms produce 3,000 units a week at an average total cost of $6,000 a unit. In part (b), with a total production of 6,000 units, the price falls to $6,000. Each firm now makes zero economic profit because price equals average total cost. This output and price are the ones that would prevail in a competitive industry.

TABLE 14.2

Duopoly Payoff Matrix

Gear's strategies

Cheat   Comply

Trick's strategies

Cheat

	Cheat	Comply
Cheat	$0 / $0	−$1.0m / +$4.5m
Comply	+$4.5m / −$1.0m	+$2m / +$2m

Each square shows the payoffs from a pair of actions. For example, if both firms comply with the collusive agreement, the payoffs are recorded in the bottom right square. The red triangle shows Gear's payoff, and the blue triangle shows Trick's. The equilibrium is a Nash equilibrium in which both firms cheat.

cheats while the other complies. The firm that cheats makes an economic profit of $4.5 million, and the firm that complies incurs a loss of $1 million.

This duopoly game is like the prisoners' dilemma that we examined earlier in this chapter; it is a duopolists' dilemma.

Equilibrium of the Duopolists' Dilemma

What do the firms do? Do they comply or cheat? To answer these questions, we must find the equilibrium of the duopoly dilemma.

Look at things from Gear's point of view. Gear reasons as follows: Suppose that Trick cheats. If I comply, I will incur an economic loss of $1 million. If I also cheat, I will make zero economic profit. Zero is better than *minus* $1 million, so I'm better off if I cheat. Now suppose Trick complies. If I cheat, I will make an economic profit of $4.5 million, and if I comply, I will make an economic profit of $2 mil-

lion. A $4.5 million profit is better than a $2 million profit, so I'm better off if I cheat. So regardless of whether Trick cheats or complies, it pays Gear to cheat. Cheating is Gear's dominant strategy.

Trick comes to the same conclusion as Gear because the two firms face an identical situation. So both firms cheat. The equilibrium of the duopoly game is that both firms cheat. And although the industry has only two firms, the price and quantity are the same as in a competitive industry and each firm makes zero economic profit.

Although we have done this analysis for only two firms, it would not make any difference (other than to increase the amount of arithmetic) if we were to play the game with three, four, or more firms. In other words, although we have analyzed duopoly, the game theory approach can also be used to analyze oligopoly. The analysis of oligopoly is much harder, but the essential ideas that we have learned also apply to oligopoly.

Repeated Games

The games we've studied are played just once. In contrast, most real-world games get played repeatedly. This fact suggests that real-world duopolies might find some way of learning to cooperate so that their efforts to collude are more effective.

If a game is played repeatedly, one player has the opportunity to penalize the other player for previous "bad" behaviour. If Gear cheats this week, perhaps Trick will cheat next week. Before Gear cheats this week, won't it take account of the possibility of Trick cheating next week? What is the equilibrium of this more complicated prisoners' dilemma game when it is repeated indefinitely?

Actually, there is more than one possibility. One is the Nash equilibrium that we have just analyzed. Both players cheat and each makes zero economic profit forever. In such a situation, it will never pay one of the players to start complying unilaterally; because to do so would result in a loss for that player and a profit for the other. The price and quantity remain at the competitive levels forever. But another equilibrium, called a cooperative equilibrium, is possible. A **cooperative equilibrium** is an equilibrium in which the players make and share the monopoly profit.

A cooperative equilibrium may occur if each player knows that the other player will punish cheating. There are two extremes of punishment. The smallest penalty that one player can impose on the other is what is called "tit for tat." A *tit-for-tat strategy* is one in which a player cooperates in the current period if the other player cooperated in the previous period but cheats in the current period if the other player cheated in the previous period. The most severe form of punishment that one player can impose on the other arises in what is called a trigger strategy. A *trigger strategy* is one in which a player cooperates if the other player cooperates but plays the Nash equilibrium strategy forever thereafter if the other player cheats.

In the duopoly game between Gear and Trick, a tit-for-tat strategy keeps both players cooperating and earning monopoly profits. Let's see why.

If both firms stick to the collusive agreement in period 1, each makes an economic profit of $2 million. Suppose that Trick contemplates cheating in period 2. The cheating produces a quick $4.5 million economic profit and inflicts a $1 million economic loss on Gear. Adding up the profits over two periods of play, Trick comes out ahead by cheating ($6.5 million compared with $4 million if it did not cheat). The next period, Gear punishes Trick with its tit-for-tat response and cheats. But Trick must cooperate to induce Gear to cooperate again in period 4. Gear now makes an economic profit of $4.5 million and Trick incurs an economic loss of $1 million. Adding up the profits over three periods of play, Trick would have made more profit by cooperating. In that case, its economic profit would have been $6 million compared with $5.5 million from cheating and generating Gear's tit-for-tat response.

What is true for Trick is also true for Gear. Because each firm makes a larger profit by sticking with the collusive agreement, both firms do so and the monopoly price, quantity, and profit prevail.

In reality, whether a cartel works like a one-play game or a repeated game depends primarily on the number of players and the ease of detecting and punishing cheating. The larger the number of players, the harder it is to maintain a cartel.

Games and Price Wars

The theory of price and output determination under duopoly can help us understand real-world behaviour and, in particular, price wars. Some price wars can be interpreted as the implementation of a tit-for-tat strategy. We've seen that with a tit-for-tat strategy in place, firms have an incentive to stick to the monop-

oly price. But fluctuations in demand lead to fluctuations in the monopoly price, and sometimes, when the price changes, it might seem to one of the firms that the price has fallen because the other has cheated. In this case, a price war will break out. The price war will end only when each firm has satisfied itself that the other is ready to cooperate again. There will be cycles of price wars and the restoration of collusive agreements. Fluctuations in the world price of oil can be interpreted in this way.

Some price wars arise from the entry of a small number of firms into an industry that had previously been a monopoly. Although the industry has a small number of firms, the firms are in a prisoners' dilemma, and they cannot impose effective penalties for price cutting. The behaviour of prices and outputs in the computer chip industry during 1995 and 1996 can be explained in this way. Until 1995, the market for Pentium chips for IBM-compatible computers was dominated by one firm, Intel Corporation, which was able to make maximum economic profit by producing the quantity of chips at which marginal cost equalled marginal revenue. The price of Intel's chips was set to ensure that the quantity demanded equalled the quantity produced. Then in 1995 and 1996, with the entry of a small number of new firms, the industry became an oligopoly. If the firms had maintained Intel's price and shared the market, together they could have made economic profits equal to Intel's profit. But the firms were in a prisoners' dilemma. So prices tumbled closer to competitive levels.

R E V I E W   Q U I Z

▪ Why does a collusive agreement to restrict output and raise price create a game like the prisoners' dilemma?

▪ What creates an incentive for firms in a collusive agreement to cheat and increase production?

▪ What is the equilibrium strategy for each firm in a prisoners' dilemma and why do the firms not collude?

▪ If a prisoners' dilemma game is played repeatedly, what punishment strategies might the players employ and how does playing the game repeatedly change the equilibrium?

The game theory approach can be extended to deal with a much wider range of choices that firms face. Let's look at some other oligopoly games.

Other Oligopoly Games

FIRMS MUST DECIDE WHETHER TO MOUNT expensive advertising campaigns; whether to modify their product; whether to make their product more reliable (the more reliable a product, usually, the more expensive it is to produce but the more are people willing to pay for it); whether to price discriminate and, if so, among which groups of customers and to what degree; whether to undertake a large research and development (R&D) effort aimed at lowering production costs; or whether to enter or leave an industry. All of these choices can be analyzed by using game theory. The basic method that you have studied can be applied to these problems by working out the payoff for each of the alternative strategies and then finding the equilibrium of the game.

We'll look at two examples: first an R&D game and second an entry-deterrence game.

An R&D Game

Disposable diapers were first marketed in 1966. The two market leaders from the start of this industry have been Procter & Gamble (maker of Pampers) and Kimberly-Clark (maker of Huggies). Procter & Gamble has about 40 percent of the total market, and Kimberly-Clark has about 33 percent. When the disposable diaper was first introduced in 1966, it had to be cost-effective in competition with reusable, laundered diapers. A costly research and development effort resulted in the development of machines that could make disposable diapers at a low enough cost to achieve that initial competitive edge. But as the industry has matured, a large number of firms have tried to get into the business and take market share away from the two industry leaders, and the industry leaders themselves have battled each other to maintain or increase their own market share.

During the early 1990s, Kimberly-Clark was the first to introduce Velcro closures. And in 1996, Procter & Gamble was the first to introduce "breathable" diapers into the North American market. The key to success in this industry (in any industry) is designing products that people value highly relative to the cost of producing them. The firm that develops the most highly valued product and also develops the least-cost technology for producing it gains a competitive edge, undercutting the rest of the market, increasing its market share, and increasing its

profit. But the research and development effort that must be undertaken to achieve product improvements and cost reductions is itself costly. This cost of research and development must be deducted from the profit resulting from the increased market share that lower costs achieve. If no firm does R&D, every firm can be better off, but if one firm initiates the R&D activity, all must follow.

Each firm is in a research and development dilemma situation that is similar to the game played by Art and Bob. Although the two firms play an ongoing game against each other, it has more in common with the one-play game than a repeated game. The reason is that research and development is a long-term process. Effort is repeated, but payoffs occur only infrequently and with uncertainty.

Table 14.3 illustrates the dilemma (with hypothetical numbers) for the R&D game that Kimberly-Clark and Procter & Gamble are playing. Each firm

TABLE 14.3

Pampers Versus Huggies: An R&D Game

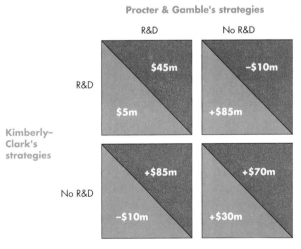

Procter & Gamble's strategies

	R&D	No R&D
R&D	$45m / $5m	−$10m / +$85m
No R&D	+$85m / −$10m	+$70m / +$30m

If both firms undertake R&D, their payoffs are those shown in the top left square. If neither firm undertakes R&D, their payoffs are in the bottom right square. When one firm undertakes R&D and the other one does not, their payoffs are in the top right and bottom left squares. The red triangle shows Procter & Gamble's payoff, and the blue triangle shows Kimberly-Clark's. The dominant strategy equilibrium for this game is for both firms to undertake R&D. The structure of this game is the same as that of the prisoners' dilemma.

has two strategies: to spend $25 million a year on R&D or to spend nothing on R&D. If neither firm spends on R&D, they make a joint profit of $100 million: $30 million for Kimberly-Clark and $70 million for Procter & Gamble (bottom right square of the payoff matrix). If each firm conducts R&D, market shares are maintained but each firm's profit is lower by the amount spent on R&D (top left square of the payoff matrix). If Kimberly-Clark pays for R&D but Procter & Gamble does not, Kimberly-Clark gains a large part of Procter & Gamble's market. Kimberly-Clark profits, and Procter & Gamble loses (top right square of the payoff matrix). Finally, if Procter & Gamble conducts R&D and Kimberly-Clark does not, Procter & Gamble gains market share from Kimberly-Clark, increasing its profit, while Kimberly-Clark incurs a loss (bottom left square).

Confronted with the payoff matrix in Table 14.3, the two firms calculate their best strategies. Kimberly-Clark reasons as follows: If Procter & Gamble does not undertake R&D, we will make $85 million if we do and $30 million if we do not; so it pays us to do R&D. If Procter & Gamble conducts R&D, we will lose $10 million if we don't and make $5 million if we do. Again, R&D pays off. Thus conducting R&D is a dominant strategy for Kimberly-Clark. It pays, regardless of Procter & Gamble's decision.

Procter & Gamble reasons similarly: If Kimberly-Clark does not undertake R&D, we will make $70 million if we follow suit and $85 million if we conduct R&D. It therefore pays to conduct R&D. If Kimberly-Clark does undertake R&D, we will make $45 million by doing the same and lose $10 million by not doing R&D. Again, it pays us to conduct R&D. So for Procter & Gamble, R&D is also a dominant strategy.

Because R&D is a dominant strategy for both players, it is the Nash equilibrium. The outcome of this game is that both firms conduct R&D. They make less profit than they would if they could collude to achieve the cooperative outcome of no R&D.

The real-world situation has more players than Kimberly-Clark and Procter & Gamble. There are a large number of other firms sharing a small portion of the market, all of them ready to eat into the market share of Procter & Gamble and Kimberly-Clark. So the R&D effort by these two firms not only serves the purpose of maintaining shares in their own battle, but also helps to keep barriers to entry high enough to preserve their joint market share.

Let's now study an entry-deterrence game in which a firm tries to prevent other firms from entering an industry. Such a game is played in a type of market called a contestable market.

Contestable Markets

A **contestable market** is a market in which one firm (or a small number of firms) operates but in which both entry and exit are free, so that the firm (or firms) in the market faces competition from *potential* entrants. Examples of contestable markets are routes served by airlines and by barge companies that operate on the major waterways. These markets are contestable because even though only one or a few firms actually operate on a particular air route or river, other firms could enter those markets if an opportunity for economic profit arose and could exit those markets if the opportunity for economic profit disappeared. The potential entrance prevents the firm (or few firms) from making an economic profit.

If the concentration ratio is used to determine the degree of competition, a contestable market appears to be uncompetitive. But a contestable market behaves as if it were perfectly competitive. To see why, let's look at a game that we'll call an entry-deterrence game.

Entry-Deterrence Game

In the entry-deterrence game we'll study, there are two players. One player is Agile Air, the only firm operating on a particular route. The other player is Wanabe Inc., a potential entrant that is making a normal profit in its current business. Agile Air must play first and can't react to Wanabe. Agile may set its price at the monopoly level or at the competitive level. When Agile has made its price decision, Wanabe decides whether to enter and undercut Agile's price or not to enter.

Table 14.4 shows the payoffs for the two firms. If Agile sets the monopoly price and Wanabe enters and undercuts Agile's price, Wanabe makes an economic profit and Agile incurs an economic loss. If Agile sets the monopoly price and Wanabe does not enter, Agile makes a monopoly profit and Wanabe earns normal profit. So if Agile sets a monopoly price, Wanabe enters. If Agile sets a competitive price and Wanabe enters and undercuts Agile's price, both firms incur an economic loss. But if Agile sets a competitive price and Wanabe does not enter, both firms earn a normal profit.

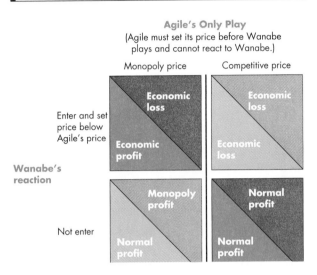

Agile's Only Play
(Agile must set its price before Wanabe plays and cannot react to Wanabe.)

Agile is the only firm in a contestable market. Agile must play first and can't react to Wanabe. If Agile sets the monopoly price, Wanabe earns an economic profit by entering and undercutting Agile's price or a normal profit by not entering. So if Agile sets the price at the monopoly level, Wanabe enters. If Agile sets the competitive price, Wanabe earns a normal profit if it does not enter or incurs an economic loss if it does enter. In this case, Wanabe will not enter. The Nash equilibrium of this game is for Agile to set the competitive price, for Wanabe not to enter, and for both firms to make normal profit.

The Nash equilibrium for this game is a competitive price at which Agile Air earns a normal profit and Wanabe does not enter. If Agile raised the price to the monopoly level, Wanabe would enter and by undercutting Agile's price would take all the business, leaving Agile with an economic loss equal to total cost. Agile avoids this outcome by setting a competitive price and deterring Wanabe from entering.

Limit Pricing The practice of charging a price below the monopoly profit-maximizing price and producing a quantity greater than that at which marginal revenue equals marginal cost in order to deter entry is called **limit pricing**. The game that we've just studied is an example of limit pricing but the practice is more general. For example, a firm can use limit pricing to try to convince potential entrants that its own costs are so low that new entrants will incur an economic loss if they enter the industry. To see how this works, let's go back to Agile and Wanabe.

Wanabe knows the current market price but does not know Agile's costs and profit. It can infer those costs though. Suppose Wanabe believes that marginal revenue is 50 percent of price. If the price is $100, then Wanabe estimates that marginal revenue is $50. Wanabe might assume that Agile is maximizing profit by setting marginal revenue equal to marginal cost. Given this assumption, Wanabe estimates Agile's marginal cost to be $50. If Wanabe's marginal cost is greater than $50, it can't compete with Agile, so it will drop the idea of entering this industry. But if its marginal cost is less than $50, it might be able to enter the industry and also to drive Agile out.

Recognizing that Wanabe (and other potential entrants) reason in this way, Agile might decide to use limit pricing to send a false but possibly believable signal to them. It might cut its price to (say) $80 to make Wanabe believe that its marginal cost is only $40 (50 percent of $80). The lower Wanabe believes Agile's marginal cost to be, the less likely is Wanabe to enter. The strategic use of limit pricing makes it possible, in some situations, for a firm (or group of firms) to maintain a monopoly or collusive oligopoly and limit entry.

◆ The two market structures you've studied in this chapter—monopolistic competition and oligopoly—are the most common ones you encounter in real-world markets. *Reading Between the Lines* on pp. 310–311 shows you monopolistic competition in action in the Canadian vacation travel market.

A key element in our study of markets for goods and services is the behaviour of firms' costs. Costs are determined by technology and by the prices of productive resources. We have treated resource prices as given. We are now going to see how resource prices are themselves determined. Resource prices interact with the goods market that we have just studied in two ways. First, they determine the firm's production costs. Second, they determine household incomes and therefore influence the demand for goods and services. Resource prices also affect the distribution of income. We study each of these interactions in the next three chapters.

Monopolistic Competition in the Vacation Travel Market

NATIONAL POST, AUGUST 18, 1999

Tour companies hit by overcapacity in Canada

BY SCHEHERAZADE DANESHKHU
AND EDWARD ALDEN

The cold climes of Canada have left Airtours and First Choice, the British-based package-holiday companies, hot and bothered recently.

Airtours said late last week it was looking at all the options for its North American operations after deepening losses in Canada. First Choice also recently reported losses in Canada for the first time in many years after one of the worst winters in the Canadian tour operating industry.

"It's a simple problem," said Tim Byrne, Airtours' finance director. "There is too much capacity."

Winter is high season in Canada, when people fly south to escape the chill, and the attractions of this counter-cyclical market for British tour operators are clear.

They can base some of their aircraft in Canada instead of leaving them idle in the winter. Peter Long, managing-director of First Choice, says that because Canadians travel in the winter, British tour operators can contract beds with

hotels year round and not just during the summer, thereby securing more favourable terms. ...

In 1995, for example, First Choice made an operating profit of £7.9-million ($18.7-million) in Canada and losses of £19.9-million in Britain.

First Choice, which entered the market before Airtours, says its Canadian operation is core to the company and it has no intention of selling it. ...

Airline overcapacity in the Canadian market last winter led to deep discounting on flights to such traditional holiday destinations as Florida, Hawaii and California.

The three largest charter operators are Air Transat, which also operates its own package tour company, Canada 3000 and Royal Aviation. ...

The problem of overcapacity is being addressed for this winter. Air Transat has taken two aircraft from its fleet; First Choice says it will take out its three aircraft and Skyservice, a smaller charter that flies exclusively for Airtours' Sunquest, has taken out another.

Financial Times August 14, 1999. Reprinted with permission.
Further reproduction prohibited.

Essence of the Story

■ Airtours and First Choice are participants in the Canadian winter tour market providing holidays in southern climates.

■ Both companies recorded losses in Canada in 1998.

■ This was the first loss in many years for First Choice.

■ Prices in 1998 for flights to Florida, Hawaii, and California were lower than in previous years.

■ Several tour companies will be flying fewer planes in 1999.

■ The tour industry in Canada is an example of monopolistic competition.

■ Figure 1 shows the average total cost curve, *ATC*, marginal cost curve, *MC*, demand curve, *D*, and marginal revenue curve, *MR*, of First Choice in 1995.

■ First Choice maximizes profit by selling Q_0 vacations at a price of P_0. Its average total cost is C_0 and the blue rectangle shows First Choice's economic profit.

■ Because First Choice and other firms were profitable, entry occurred.

■ By 1998, the demand curve for First Choice vacations had shifted leftward to D' and the marginal revenue curve had shifted to MR' in Fig. 2.

■ When the demand for First Choice vacations decreases, there is no change in the firm's cost. First Choice now maximizes profit by selling Q_1 vacations at a price of P_1. Its average total cost is C_1.

■ But because C_1 exceeds P_1, First Choice now incurs an economic loss.

■ First Choice now cuts costs by decreasing the size of its fleet of aircraft.

■ Figure 3 shows the effects of the new smaller aircraft fleet on cost, output, price, and profit.

■ The average total cost curve shifts downward to ATC_1 and the marginal cost curve shifts downward to MC_1. With lower costs but no change in demand, First Choice expands output to Q_2 vacations a year. Average total cost and price are equal ($C_2 = P_2$) and the firm makes normal profit.

■ The industry is in long-run equilibrium.

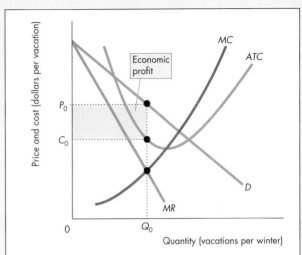

Figure 1 First Choice in 1995

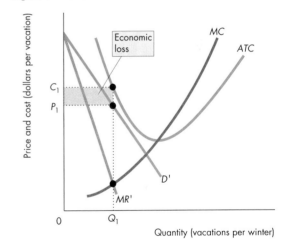

Figure 2 First Choice in 1998

Figure 3 First Choice grounds some aircraft

SUMMARY

Key Points

Monopolistic Competition (pp. 290–291)

- Monopolistic competition occurs when a large number of firms compete with each other on product quality, price, and marketing.

Output and Price in Monopolistic Competition (pp. 292–294)

- Firms in monopolistic competition face downward-sloping demand curves and produce the quantity at which marginal revenue equals marginal cost.
- Entry and exit result in zero economic profit and excess capacity in long-run equilibrium.

Product Development and Marketing (pp. 294–296)

- Firms in monopolistic competition innovate and develop new products to maintain economic profit.
- Advertising expenditures increase total cost but they might lower average total cost if they increase the quantity sold by enough.
- Advertising expenditures might increase demand but they might also decrease the demand facing a firm by increasing competition.
- Whether monopolistic competition is inefficient depends on the value we place on product variety.

Oligopoly (pp. 297–298)

- If rivals match price cuts but do not match price hikes, they face a kinked demand curve and change prices only when large cost changes occur.
- If one firm dominates a market, it acts like a monopoly and the small firms take its price as given and act like perfectly competitive firms.

Game Theory (pp. 299–300)

- Game theory is a method of analyzing strategic behaviour.
- In a prisoners' dilemma, two prisoners acting in their own interest harm their joint interest.

An Oligopoly Price-Fixing Game (pp. 301–306)

- An oligopoly (duopoly) price-fixing game is a prisoners' dilemma.
- The firms might collude, one firm might cheat, or both firms might cheat.
- In a one-play game, both firms cheat and output and price are the same as in perfect competition.
- In a repeated game, a punishment strategy can produce a cooperative equilibrium in which price and output are the same as in a monopoly.

Other Oligopoly Games (pp. 307–309)

- Firms' decisions about whether to enter or leave an industry; how much to spend selling the product; whether to modify the product; whether to undertake research and development can be studied by using game theory.

Key Figures and Table

Key Terms

P R O B L E M S

*1. The figure shows the situation facing Lite and Kool Inc., a producer of running shoes.

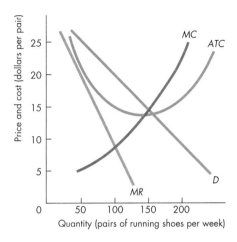

a. What quantity does Lite and Kool produce?
b. What does it charge?
c. How much profit does Lite and Kool make?

2. The figure shows the situation facing Well Done Inc., a producer of steak sauce.

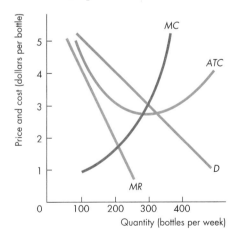

a. What quantity does Well Done produce?
b. What does it charge?
c. How much profit does Well Done make?

*3. A firm in monopolistic competition produces running shoes. If it spends nothing on advertising, it can sell no shoes at $100 a pair and, for each $10 cut in price, the quantity of shoes it can sell increases by 25 pairs a day so

that at $20 a pair, it can sell 200 pairs a day. The firm's total fixed cost is $4,000 a day. Its average variable cost and marginal cost is a constant $20 per pair. If the firm spends $3,000 a day on advertising, it can double the quantity of shoes sold at each price.
a. If the firm doesn't advertise, what is the quantity of shoes produced and what is the price per pair?
b. What is the firm's economic profit or economic loss?
c. If the firm does advertise, what is the quantity of shoes produced and what is the price per pair?
d. What is the firm's economic profit or economic loss?
e. Will the firm advertise or not? Why?

4. The firm in problem 3 has the same demand and costs as before if it does not advertise. But it hires a new advertising agency. If the firm spends $3,000 a day on advertising with the new agency, it can double the amount that consumers are willing to pay at each quantity demanded.
a. If the firm hires the new agency, what is the quantity of shoes produced and what is the price per pair?
b. What is the firm's economic profit or economic loss?
c. Will the firm advertise or not? Why?
d. What is the firm's economic profit in the long run?

*5. A firm with a kinked demand curve experiences an increase in its fixed costs. Explain the effects on the firm's price, output, and economic profit/loss.

6. A firm with a kinked demand curve experiences an increase in its variable cost. Explain the effects on the firm's price, output, and economic profit/loss.

*7. An industry with one very large firm and 100 very small firms experiences an increase in the demand for its product. Use the dominant firm model to explain the effects on the price, output, and economic profit of
a. The large firm
b. A typical small firm

8. An industry with one very large firm and 100 very small firms experiences an increase in total variable cost. Use the dominant firm

model to explain the effects on the price, output, and economic profit of

a. The large firm

b. A typical small firm

*9. Consider the following game: The game has two players, and each player is asked a question. The players can answer the question honestly or they can lie. If both answer honestly, each receives a payoff of $100. If one answers honestly and the other lies, the liar gains at the expense of the honest player. In that event, the liar receives a payoff of $500 and the honest player gets nothing. If both lie, then each receives a payoff of $50.

a. Describe this game in terms of its players, strategies, and payoffs.

b. Construct the payoff matrix.

c. What is the equilibrium for this game?

10. Describe the game known as the prisoners' dilemma. In describing the game:

a. Make up a story that motivates the game.

b. Work out a payoff matrix.

c. Describe how the equilibrium of the game is arrived at.

*11. Two firms, Soapy and Sudsies Inc., are the only producers of soap powder. They collude and agree to share the market equally. If neither firm cheats on the agreement, each makes $1 million economic profit. If either firm cheats, the cheater increases its economic profit to $1.5 million while the firm that abides by the agreement incurs an economic loss of $0.5 million. Neither firm has any way of policing the other's actions.

a. Describe the best strategy for each firm in a game that is played once.

b. What is the economic profit for each firm if both cheat?

c. Construct the payoff matrix of a game that is played just once.

d. What is the equilibrium if the game is played once?

e. If this duopoly game can be played many times, describe some of the strategies that each firm might adopt.

12. Two firms, Faster and Quicker, are the only two producers of sports cars on an island that has no contact with the outside world. The firms collude and agree to share the market equally. If neither firm cheats on the agreement, each firm makes $3 million economic profit. If either firm cheats, the cheater can increase its economic profit to $4.5 million, while the firm that abides by the agreement incurs an economic loss of $1 million. Neither firm has any way of policing the actions of the other.

a. What is the economic profit for each firm if they both cheat?

b. What is the payoff matrix of a game that is played just once?

c. What is the best strategy for each firm in a game that is played once?

d. What is the equilibrium if the game is played once?

e. If this game can be played many times, what are two strategies that could be adopted?

CRITICAL THINKING

1. After you have studied *Reading Between the Lines* on pp. 310–311, answer the following questions.

a. How would you characterize the Canadian tour industry in 1995: in long-run equilibrium, making economic profit, or incurring economic loss? What evidence enables you to reach your conclusion?

b. If the tour companies continue to incur economic losses through 2000, what do you predict will happen in the industry? Be specific about the quantity of companies, prices, and economic profits.

c. Suppose that people in Canada decide that during 2000 driving to their holiday destinations and making their own hotel reservations is better than using a tour company. What will happen to the price of a tour holiday and the number of tour companies?

d. Suppose that the decision made by the people of Canada in part (c) is permanent. Now what will happen to the price of a tour holiday and the number of tour companies?

2. Why do Molson and Labatt's spend huge amounts on advertising? Do they benefit? Does the consumer benefit? Explain your answer.

Understanding Firms and Markets

Our economy is constantly changing. Every year, new goods appear and old ones disappear. New firms are born and old ones die. This process of change is initiated and managed by firms operating in markets. When a new product is invented, just one or two firms sell it initially. For example, when the personal computer first became available, there was an Apple or an IBM. The IBM-PC had just one operating system, DOS, made by Microsoft. One firm, Intel, made the chip that ran the IBM-PC. These are examples of industries in which the producer has market power to determine the price of the product and the quantity produced. The extreme case of a single producer that cannot be challenged by new competitors is *monopoly*, which Chapter 13 explains. ◆ But not all industries with just one producer are monopolies. In many cases, the firm that is first to produce a new good faces severe competition from new rivals. One firm facing potential competition is the case of a *contestable market*. If demand increases and makes space for more than one firm, an industry becomes increasingly competitive. Even with just two rivals, the industry changes its face in a dramatic way. *Duopoly*—the case of just two producers—illustrates this dramatic change. The two firms must pay close attention to each other's production and prices and must predict the effects of their own actions on the actions of the other firm. We call this situation one of *strategic interdependence*. As the number of rivals

Managing Change

grows, the industry becomes an *oligopoly*, a market in which a small number of firms devise strategies and pay close attention to the strategies of their competitors. ◆ With the continued arrival of new firms in an industry, the market eventually becomes competitive. Competition might be limited because each firm produces its own special version or brand of a good. This case is called *monopolistic competition* because it has elements of both monopoly and competition. Chapter 14 explores the behaviour of firms in all of these types of markets that lie between monopoly at one extreme and perfect competition at the other. ◆ When competition is extreme—the case that we call *perfect competition*—the market changes again in a dramatic way. Now the firm is unable to influence price. Chapter 12 explains this case. ◆ Often, an industry that is competitive becomes less so as the bigger and more successful firms in the industry begin to swallow up the smaller firms, either by driving them out of business or by acquiring their assets. Through this process, an industry might return to oligopoly or even monopoly. You can see such a movement in the auto and banking industries today. ◆ By studying firms and markets, we gain a deeper understanding of the forces that allocate scarce resources and begin to see the anatomy of the invisible hand.

◇ Many economists have advanced our understanding of these forces and we'll now meet two of them: John von Neumann, who pioneered the idea of game theory, and Nancy Gallini, one of today's leading students of strategic behaviour.

Probing the Ideas

Market Power

John von Neumann *was one of the great minds of the twentieth century. Born in Budapest, Hungary, in 1903, Johnny, as he was known, showed early mathematical brilliance. His first mathematical publication was an article that grew out of a lesson with his tutor, which he wrote at the age of 18! But it was at the age of 25, in 1928, that von Neumann published the article that began a flood of research on game theory—a flood that has still not subsided today. In that article, he proved that in a zero-sum game (like sharing a pie), there exists a best strategy for each player.*

Von Neumann invented the computer and built the first modern practical computer, and he worked on the "Manhattan Project," which developed the atomic bomb at Los Alamos, New Mexico, during World War II.

Von Neumann believed that the social sciences would progress only if they used mathematical tools. But he believed they needed different tools from those developed from the physical sciences.

"Real life consists of bluffing, of little tactics of deception, of asking yourself what is the other man going to think I mean to do."

JOHN VON NEUMANN,
TOLD TO JACOB
BRONOWSKI (IN A LONDON
TAXI) AND REPORTED IN
THE ASCENT OF MAN

The Issues

It is not surprising that firms with market power will charge higher prices than those charged by competitive firms. But how much higher?

This question has puzzled generations of economists. Adam Smith said, "The price of a monopoly is upon every occasion the highest which can be got." But he was wrong. Antoine-Augustin Cournot (see p. 154) first worked out the price a monopoly will charge. It is not the "highest which can be got" but the price that maximizes profit. Cournot's work was not appreciated until almost a century later when Joan Robinson explained how a monopoly sets its price.

Questions about monopoly became urgent and practical during the 1870s, a time when rapid technological change and falling transportation costs enabled huge monopolies to emerge. Monopolies dominated oil, steel, railroads, tobacco, and even sugar. Industrial empires grew ever larger.

The success of the nineteenth century monopolies led to the creation of our anti-combine laws—laws that limit the use of monopoly power. Those laws have been used to prevent monopolies from being set up and to break up existing monopolies. They were used in the United States during the 1960s to end a conspiracy between General Electric, Westinghouse, and other firms when they colluded to fix their prices instead of competing with each other. The laws were used during the 1980s to bring greater competition to long-distance telecommunication. But in spite of anti-combine laws, near monopolies still exist. Among the most prominent today are those in computer chips and operating systems. Like their forerunners, today's near monopolies make huge profits. But unlike the situation in the nineteenth century, the technological change taking place today is strengthening the forces of competition. Today's information technologies are creating substitutes for services that previously had none. Direct satellite TV is competing with cable and new phone companies are competing with the traditional phone monopolies.

... and Now

In spite of anti-combine laws that regulate monopolies, they still exist. One is the monopoly in cable television. In many cities, one firm decides which channels viewers will receive and the price they will pay. During the 1980s, with the advent of satellite technology and specialist cable program producers such as CNN and HBO, the cable companies expanded their offerings. At the same time, they steadily increased prices and their businesses became very profitable. But the very technologies that made cable television profitable are now challenging its market position. Direct satellite TV services are eroding cable's monopoly and bringing greater competition to this market.

Then ...

Ruthless greed, exploitation of both workers and customers—these are the traditional images of monopolies and the effects of their power. These images appeared to be an accurate description during the 1880s, when monopolies were at their peak of power and influence. One monopolist, John D. Rockefeller, Sr., built his giant Standard Oil Company, which, by 1879, was refining 90 percent of the nation's oil and controlling its entire pipeline capacity.

Today, many economists who work on microeconomics use the ideas that John von Neumann pioneered. Game theory is the tool of choice. One economist who has made good use of this tool is Nancy Gallini of the University of Toronto, whom you can meet on the following pages.

Talking with
Nancy Gallini

Nancy T. Gallini *is Professor of Economics at the University of Toronto. Born in 1952, Professor Gallini was an undergraduate at the University of Missouri at Columbia and a graduate student at the University of California, Berkeley. She completed her Ph.D. and began her academic career at the University of Toronto in 1979. Professor Gallini studies the strategic behaviour of firms. Her work has covered a wide range of issues including the effects of patent laws on the efficiency of technological change and the reasons why in some markets a firm operates its own outlets and franchises others. Professor Gallini's work is an outstanding example of how technical (mathematical) economics helps us to understand the strategies that we see firms using in the marketplace.*

Robin Bade and Michael Parkin talked with Professor Gallini about her work and how economists are trying to better understand the complex world of competition and monopoly.

Why were you attracted to economics?
If you were to ask a random group of sixth graders about their career aspirations, chances are that "becoming an economist" would not appear on their top 10 list. This should come as no surprise. While many high schools have now introduced economics into their curriculum, the first encounter with this fascinating discipline for many is introductory economics in first-year university. For me, economics arrived even later, but when it did, I was instantly hooked. For three rather undirected years at university I had been taking 7:30 a.m. classes in mathematics and, while fascinated with these eye-opening sessions, I couldn't quite see myself proving mathematical theorems the rest of my life. So, I had one of those "What should I be when I grow up" conversations with a teaching assistant who was also a graduate student in economics. Next thing I knew I was working in a summer job as a research assistant for an economics prof, John Kuhlman. When Professor Kuhlman was not performing on stage for thousands of introductory economics students, he was performing on the stand as an expert witness in antitrust cases. With his latest price-fixing case as a backdrop, I learned how mathematics could be used to evaluate problems in game theory—in this case, rival firms devising ingenious methods for jointly agreeing to raise prices to consumers. Watching powerful companies succumb to the elegance of economic reasoning was the hook that turned my attention towards graduate school in economics. It didn't take long to find out that price fixing only touched the surface of the amazing world of economics.

Why is game theory a central tool for studying the wide range of economic questions that you work on?
The price-fixing case I just mentioned was analysed with game theory tools because it involved economic agents (firms in this case) whose actions (setting

318

prices) affected the payoffs or profits to other agents (competing firms).

Sounds like that applies to a lot of real-world situations?

Absolutely. Game theory is a remarkably useful tool for analysing and predicting outcomes in any situation in which agents (consumers, firms, governments, countries) interact with each other. Their interaction may be as common as selling products to customers or as complex as negotiating trade agreements or nuclear disarmament policies between countries.

Antitrust, one of my areas of research, studies the law and economics of the behaviour of firms that can reduce or deter competition in markets. This area involves heavy use of game theory. Many students will have heard about the recent Microsoft cases. Over the past years, Microsoft has engaged in a variety of practices that have attracted the attention of antitrust authorities—for example, "bundling" their operating system with an Internet browser or charging a royalty on each computer sold by retailers whether or not it included Microsoft's Windows system. We can use game theory models to analyse incentives for firms to engage in practices like this, asking whether they are anticompetitive with the effect of lessening competition or simply efficient ways of conducting business.

Do our current patent laws encourage the efficient amount and direction of innovation?

This is a very interesting question. It's the focus of lively debates in domestic and international arenas, especially regarding new complex technologies in the computer and biotechnology industries. Patents are property rights on inventions that give the inventor the exclusive right to use, make, or license her new product or process. By preventing the widespread copying of new inventions, patents give inventors the incentive to develop new technologies and to disclose information on those inventions so that others may build upon them after the patent has expired.

The downside of the patent system is that, because the owner has a monopoly on its invention, the use of the invention will not be efficient. This tradeoff between the dynamic benefits of innovation vs. the allocative costs in the use of the innovation is at the heart of the patent system. While the costs from suboptimal use of inventions is a concern, it is

now widely recognized that dynamic benefits from technological progress are at least as important to social welfare as is the elimination of the costs from non-competitive prices. The patent system may be only a second-best solution but it is a reasonably effective mechanism for encouraging the creation and diffusion of innovation.

Do patents create too much or too little temporary monopoly power?

The hardest part about implementing a patent system is getting the patent scope right. Patent scope refers to the extent of the patent coverage, the set of products or processes over which the patentee has exclusive rights. Patents that are weak will be easy to invent around; patents that are strong may deter others from developing subsequent improvements or related inventions. With the advent of new complex technologies, the debate on whether patents are too weak or strong has greatly intensified.

> *The downside of the patent system is that, because the owner has a monopoly on its invention, the use of the invention will not be efficient.*

Some scholars and practitioners worry that patents are too strong in at least two situations. The first occurs when innovations build upon each other. That is, a pioneer invention may be the foundation for later improvements or applications of the invention. For example, if patents are awarded on genetic material, then innovators of new drugs requiring that genetic material may have to pay large royalties for the right to bring the drug to market. If these royalties are large, then future research may be discouraged.

A second concern, especially among competition authorities, is awarding patents on inventions for which network externalities are important. Network externalities are present when the value of a particular invention depends on the number of users. A Macintosh computer may be more useful to you if more students with whom you work and share files also use that operating system. If an incumbent firm has amassed a large base of captured customers, then other customers will be less willing to sign on with a new entrant. Hence, strong patent protection in the presence of network externalities may be a significant barrier to entry.

These two features have the common result that early innovators may capture a secure hold on the market by blocking subsequent research or because network externalities tipped the customer base in their favour. While strong patents may delay subse-

> *Many clever practices for increasing profits are price discrimination schemes in disguise.*

quent innovation, one should not jump to conclusions that patents, therefore, should be weak in these instances. If they were, then the pioneer may not have the incentive to create the initial invention or disclose information on it in the first place! Moreover, vigorous competition may constrain the innovator's market power in these situations. There is no consensus on the level of protection that strikes the "right" balance between incentives to early and later inventors. What is clear, however, is that economic analysis can contribute immensely to this debate.

What are some of the truly clever ways in which firms try to extract consumer surplus, other than by standard price discrimination? How do they work?

Many clever practices for increasing profits are price discrimination schemes in disguise. For example, offering coupons on selected items, "tying" computer hardware with software and offering "no name" cereal brands are all ways for a single firm to extract surplus when consumers value the product differently. Firms may also work in concert with each other to extract surplus through clever devices, for example, the "most-favoured customer" (MFC) clause. You may have participated in an MFC arrangement if you pur-

chased a product from a retailer who guaranteed you a rebate if the price fell over some specified period of time, for example, the next six months. You may have thought such an offer sounded like a good deal. In fact, you may have been agreeing to a mechanism for the retailer to commit *not* to lower its prices! Think about what would happen if the firm were to lower its price. Under the MFC, it has committed to paying rebates to past customers. So, even if a rival lowers its prices, the retailer may not because the MFC makes price reductions very costly. That is, the MFC ties the retailer's hands from competing with its rival. This "good deal" to consumers may in fact be a clever scheme by firms to raise prices.

What is the case for majoring in economics today? What are the main benefits of an economic degree?

At a recent job-training session for our undergraduate students, Halina Kalita, who is a Ph.D. graduate from our department and now a successful economist at the Royal Bank, gave a superb presentation on how to prepare for the job market. She emphasized the importance of a solid training in economics. Essential to the job, she noted, is the ability to think through a wide range of complex problems, to simplify these problems to their most relevant features, and to be able to adjust to rapid changes in financial and international markets. Those are precisely the skills that a student of economics learns.

Just how much in demand are these skills? We set out to provide an informed response to the most frequently asked question from our prospective undergraduates: "What can I do with an economics degree?" We surveyed recently graduated students and their replies were encouraging: Nearly 80 percent had jobs within only a couple of months after graduating. They found jobs as economic analysts, accounting trainees, banking officers, and financial officers in a wide range of private and public sector organizations that include the large banks, consulting firms, accounting firms, and departments in the Ontario and federal governments. Of course, another fascinating career path for an economics student is graduate school. With a Ph.D. not only will you be able to push forward the frontiers of economic research but you will also have the opportunity to teach other bright students like yourself the wonders of this marvelous discipline.

Demand and Supply in Resource Markets

It may not be your birthday, and even if it is, chances are you are spending most of it working. But at the end of the week or month (or, if you're devoting all your time to university, when you graduate), you will receive the returns from your labour. Those *returns* vary a lot. Ed Jones, who spends his chilly winter days in a small container suspended from the top of Toronto's Bank of Montreal cleaning windows, makes a happy return of $12 an hour.

Many Happy Returns

Damon Stoudamire, who plays no more than 82 basketball games a year, makes a very happy return of $4.6 million over three years—including the gift of a Mercedes-Benz to his mother. Students working at what have been called McJobs—serving fast food or labouring in the fields of the Niagara Peninsula—earn just a few dollars an hour. Why aren't *all* jobs well paid? ◆ Most of us have little trouble spending our pay. But most of us do manage to save some of what we earn. What determines the amount of saving that people do and the returns they make on that saving? How do the returns on saving influence the allocation of savings across the many industries and activities that use our capital resources? ◆ Some people receive income from supplying land, but the amount earned varies enormously with the land's location and quality. For example, a hectare of farmland in Manitoba rents for about $1,000 a year, while a block in Toronto's Yorkville rents for several million dollars a year. What determines the rent that people are willing to pay for different blocks of land? Why are rents so enormously high in big cities and so relatively low in the great farming regions of the nation?

◆ In this chapter, we study the markets for productive resources—labour, capital, land, and entrepreneurship—and learn how their prices and people's incomes are determined.

After studying this chapter, you will be able to:

■ **Explain how firms choose the quantities of labour, capital, and natural resources to employ**

■ **Explain how people choose the quantities of labour, capital, and natural resources to supply**

■ **Explain how wages, interest, and natural resource prices are determined in competitive resource markets**

■ **Explain the concept of economic rent and distinguish between economic rent and opportunity cost**

Resource Prices and Incomes

GOODS AND SERVICES ARE PRODUCED BY USING the four economic resources—*labour, capital, land,* and *entrepreneurship*. (These resources are defined in Chapter 3, p. 38.) Incomes are determined by *resource prices*—the *wage* rate for labour, the *interest* rate for capital, the *rental* rate for land, and the rate of *normal profit* for entrepreneurship—and the quantities of resources used.

In addition to the four resource incomes, a residual income, *economic profit* (or *economic loss*) is paid to (or borne by) firms' owners. For a small firm, the owner is usually the entrepreneur. For a large corporation, the owners are the stockholders who supply capital.

An Overview of a Competitive Resource Market

We're going to learn how competitive resource markets determine the prices, quantities used, and incomes of productive resources. The tool that we use is the demand and supply model. The quantity demanded of a resource depends on its price, and the law of demand applies to resources just as it does to goods and services. The lower the price of a resource, other things remaining the same, the greater is the quantity demanded. Figure 15.1 shows the demand curve for a resource as the curve labelled *D*.

The quantity supplied of a resource also depends on its price. With a possible exception that we'll identify later in this chapter, the law of supply applies to resources. The higher the price of a resource, other things remaining the same, the greater is the quantity supplied of the resource. Figure 15.1 shows the supply curve of a resource as the curve labelled *S*.

The equilibrium is at the point of intersection of the demand and supply curves. In Fig. 15.1, the price is *PR* and the quantity used is *QR*.

The income earned by the resource is its price multiplied by the quantity used. In Fig. 15.1, the resource income equals the area of the blue rectangle. This income is the total income received by the resource. Each person who supplies the resource receives the resource price multiplied by the quantity supplied by that person. Changes in demand and supply change the equilibrium price and quantity and change income.

An increase in demand shifts the demand curve rightward and increases price, quantity, and income. An increase in supply shifts the supply curve rightward and decreases price. The quantity used increases, and the income of the resource can increase, decrease, or remain constant. The change in income that results from a change in supply depends on the elasticity of demand for the resource. If demand is elastic, income rises; if demand is inelastic, income falls; and if demand is unit elastic, income remains constant (see Chapter 5, pp. 94–95).

The rest of this chapter explores the influences on the demand for and supply of productive resources. It also studies the influences on the elasticities of supply and demand for resources. These elasticities have major effects on resource prices, quantities used, and incomes.

We begin with the market for labour. But most of what we learn about the labour market also applies to the other resource markets that we study later in the chapter.

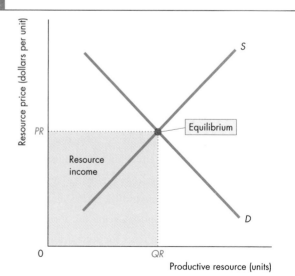

FIGURE 15.1

Demand and Supply in a Resource Market

The demand curve for a productive resource (*D*) slopes downward, and the supply curve (*S*) slopes upward. Where the demand and supply curves intersect, the resource price (*PR*) and the quantity of a resource used (*QR*) are determined. The resource income is the product of the resource price and the quantity of the resource, as represented by the blue rectangle.

Labour Markets

FOR MOST OF US, THE LABOUR MARKET IS OUR only source of income. And in recent years, many people have had a tough time. But over the years, both wage rates and the quantity of labour have moved steadily upward. Figure 15.2(a) shows the record since 1960. Using 1992 dollars to remove the effects of inflation, total compensation per hour of work almost doubled from $9 in 1960 to $17.50 in 1998. Over the same period, the quantity of labour employed exactly doubled from 12.5 billion hours in 1960 to 25 billion hours in 1998.

Figure 15.2(b) shows why these trends occurred. The demand increased from LD_{60} to LD_{98} and this increase was much larger than the increase in supply from LS_{60} to LS_{98}.

A lot of diversity lies behind the average wage rate and the aggregate quantity of labour. During the 1980s and 1990s, some wage rates have grown more rapidly than the average and others have fallen. To understand the trends in the labour market, we must probe the forces that influence the demand for labour and the supply of labour. This chapter studies these forces (and Chapter 16 takes a deeper look at them). We begin on the demand side of the labour market.

The Demand for Labour

The demand for labour is a derived demand. A **derived demand** is a demand for a productive resource, which is *derived* from the demand for the goods and services produced by the resource. The derived demand for labour (and the other resources demanded by firms) is driven by the firm's objective, which is to maximize profit.

You learned in Chapters 12, 13, and 14 that a profit-maximizing firm produces the output at which marginal cost equals marginal revenue. This principle holds true for all firms regardless of whether they operate in perfect competition, monopolistic competition, oligopoly, or monopoly.

A firm that maximizes profit hires the quantity of labour that can produce the profit-maximizing output. What is that quantity of labour? And how does it change as the wage rate changes? We can answer these questions by comparing the *marginal* revenue earned by hiring one more worker with the *marginal* cost of that worker. Let's look first at the marginal revenue side of this comparison.

FIGURE 15.2

Labour Market Trends in Canada

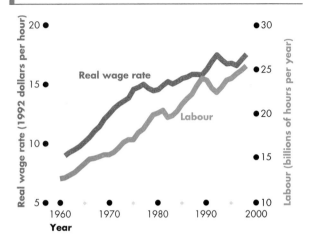

(a) Labour and wage rate

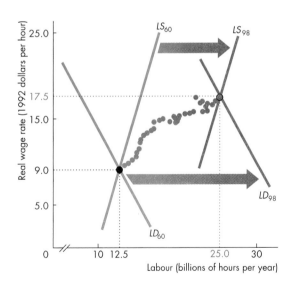

(b) Changes in demand and supply in the labour market

Between 1960 and 1998, the wage rate doubled and the quantity of labour employed almost doubled (part a). The demand for labour increased from LD_{60} to LD_{98} and the supply of labour increased from LS_{60} to LS_{98}. Demand increased by more than supply, so both the wage rate and the quantity of labour employed increased (part b).

Source: Statistics Canada, *StatCan: CANSIM Disc,* 1999, and authors' assumptions and calculations.

Marginal Revenue Product

The change in total revenue that results from employing one more unit of labour is called the **marginal revenue product** of labour. Table 15.1 shows you how to calculate marginal revenue product for a perfectly competitive firm.

The first two columns show the total product schedule for Max's Wash 'n' Wax car wash service. The numbers tell us how the number of car washes per hour varies as the quantity of labour varies. The third column shows the *marginal product of labour*—the change in total product that results from a one-unit increase in the quantity of labour employed. (Look back at p. 225 for a quick refresher on these concepts.)

The car wash market in which Max operates is perfectly competitive and he can sell as many washes as he chooses at $4 a wash, the (assumed) market price. So Max's *marginal revenue* is $4 a wash.

Given this information, we can now calculate *marginal revenue product* (fourth column). It equals marginal product multiplied by marginal revenue. For example, the marginal product of hiring a second worker is 4 car washes an hour and because marginal revenue is $4 a wash, the marginal revenue product of the second worker is $16 (4 washes at $4 each).

The last two columns of Table 15.1 show an alternative way to calculate the marginal revenue product of labour. Total revenue is equal to total product multiplied by price. For example, two workers produce 9 washes per hour and generate a total revenue of $36 (9 washes at $4 each). One worker produces 5 washes per hour and generates a total revenue of $20 (5 washes at $4 each). Marginal revenue product, in the sixth column, is the change in total revenue from hiring one more worker. When the second worker is hired, total revenue increases from $20 to $36, an increase of $16. So the marginal revenue product of the second worker is $16, which agrees with our previous calculation.

Diminishing Marginal Revenue Product As the quantity of labour increases, marginal revenue product diminishes. For a firm in perfect competition, marginal revenue product diminishes because marginal product diminishes. In monopoly (or in monopolistic competition) marginal revenue product diminishes for a second reason. When more labour is hired and total product increases, the firm must cut its price to sell the extra product. So marginal product *and* marginal revenue decrease, both of which bring decreasing marginal revenue product.

TABLE 15.1

Marginal Revenue Product at Max's Wash 'n' Wax

	Quantity of labour (L) (workers)	Total product (TP) (car washes per hour)	Marginal product (MP = ΔTP/ΔL) (washes per worker)	Marginal revenue product (MRP = MR × MP) (dollars per worker)	Total revenue (TR = P × TP) (dollars)	Marginal revenue product (MRP = ΔTR/ΔL) (dollars per worker)
a	0	0			0	
			5	20		20
b	1	5			20	
			4	16		16
c	2	9			36	
			3	12		12
d	3	12			48	
			2	8		8
e	4	14			56	
			1	4		4
f	5	15			60	

The car wash market is perfectly competitive and the price is $4 a wash. Marginal revenue is also $4 a wash. Marginal revenue product equals marginal product (column 3) multiplied by marginal revenue. For example, the marginal product of the second worker is 4 washes and marginal revenue is $4 a wash. So the marginal revenue product of the second worker (in column 4) is $16. Alternatively, if Max hires 1 worker (row b), total product is 5 washes an hour and total revenue is $20 (column 5). If he hires 2 workers (row c), total product is 9 washes an hour and total revenue is $36. By hiring the second worker, total revenue rises by $16—the marginal revenue product of labour is $16.

The Labour Demand Curve

Figure 15.3 shows how the labour demand curve is derived from the marginal revenue product curve. The *marginal revenue product curve* graphs the marginal revenue product of a resource at each quantity of the resource hired. Figure 15.3(a) illustrates the marginal revenue product curve for workers employed by Max. The horizontal axis measures the number of workers that Max hires, and the vertical axis measures the marginal revenue product of labour. The blue bars show the marginal revenue product of labour as Max employs more workers. These bars correspond to the numbers in Table 15.1. The curve labelled *MRP* is Max's marginal revenue product curve.

A firm's marginal revenue product curve is also its demand for labour curve. Figure 15.3(b) shows Max's demand for labour curve (*D*). The horizontal axis measures the number of workers hired—the same as in part (a). The vertical axis measures the wage rate in dollars per hour. In Fig. 15.3(a), when Max increases the quantity of labour employed from 2 workers an hour to 3 workers an hour, his marginal revenue product is $12 an hour. In Fig. 15.3(b), at a wage rate of $12 an hour, Max hires 3 workers an hour.

The marginal revenue product curve is also the demand for labour curve because the firm hires the profit-maximizing quantity of labour. If the wage rate is less than marginal revenue product, the firm can increase its profit by employing one more worker. Conversely, if the wage rate is greater than marginal revenue product, the firm can increase its profit by employing one fewer worker. But if the wage rate equals marginal revenue product, then the firm cannot increase its profit by changing the number of workers it employs. The firm is making the maximum possible profit. Thus the quantity of labour demanded by the firm is such that the wage rate equals the marginal revenue product of labour.

Because the marginal revenue product curve is also the demand curve, and because marginal revenue product diminishes as the quantity of labour employed increases, the demand for labour curve slopes downward. The lower the wage rate, other things remaining the same, the more workers a firm hires.

When we studied firms' output decisions, we discovered that a condition for maximum profit is that marginal revenue equals marginal cost. We've now discovered another condition for maximum profit: Marginal revenue product of a resource equals the resource's price. Let's study the connection between these two conditions.

FIGURE 15.3

The Demand for Labour at Max's Wash 'n' Wax

(a) Marginal revenue product

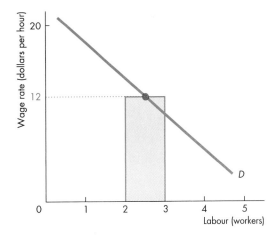

(b) Demand for labour

Max's Wash 'n' Wax operates in a perfectly competitive car wash market and can sell any quantity of washes at $4 a wash. The blue bars in part (a) represent the firm's marginal revenue product of labour. They are based on the numbers in Table 15.1. The orange line is the firm's marginal revenue product of labour curve. Part (b) shows Max's demand for labour curve. This curve is identical to Max's marginal revenue product curve. Max demands the quantity of labour that makes the wage rate equal to the marginal revenue product of labour. The demand for labour curve slopes downward because marginal revenue product diminishes as the quantity of labour employed increases.

Equivalence of Two Conditions for Profit Maximization

Profit is maximized when at the quantity of labour hired, *marginal revenue product* equals the wage rate and when, at the quantity produced, *marginal revenue* equals *marginal cost*. These two conditions for maximum profit are equivalent. The quantity of labour that maximizes profit produces the output that maximizes profit. To see the equivalence of the two conditions for maximum profit, first recall that

Marginal revenue product = Marginal revenue × Marginal product.

If we call marginal revenue product *MRP*, marginal revenue *MR*, and marginal product *MP*,

$$MRP = MR \times MP.$$

If we call the wage rate *W*, the first condition for maximum profit is

$$MRP = W.$$

But $MRP = MR \times MP$, so

$$MR \times MP = W.$$

This equation tells us that when profit is maximized, marginal revenue multiplied by marginal product equals the wage rate.

Divide the last equation by marginal product, *MP*, to obtain

$$MR = W \div MP.$$

This equation states that when profit is maximized, marginal revenue equals the wage rate divided by the marginal product of labour. The wage rate divided by the marginal product of labour equals marginal cost. It costs the firm *W* to hire one more hour of labour. But the labour produces *MP* units of output. So the cost of producing one of those units of output, which is marginal cost, is *W* divided by *MP*. If we call marginal cost *MC*, then

$$MR = MC,$$

which is the second condition for maximum profit.

Because the first condition for maximum profit implies the second condition, these two conditions are equivalent.

Table 15.2 summarizes the reasoning and calculations that show the equivalence between the two conditions for maximum profit.

TABLE 15.2

Two Conditions for Maximum Profit

Symbols

Marginal product	**MP**
Marginal revenue	**MR**
Marginal cost	**MC**
Marginal revenue product	**MRP**
Resource price	**PR**

Two Conditions for Maximum Profit

1. **MR = MC**   2. **MRP = PR**

Equivalence of Conditions

1. $MRP/MP =$ **MR** $=$ **MC** $= PR/MP$

Multiply by *MP* to give

$MRP = MR \times MP$ $MC \times MP = PR$

Flipping the equation over

2. $MR \times MP =$ **MRP** $=$ **PR** $= MC \times MP$

The two conditions for maximum profit are marginal revenue (*MR*) equals marginal cost (*MC*) and marginal revenue product (*MRP*) equals the price of the resource (*PR*). These two conditions are equivalent because marginal revenue product (*MRP*) equals marginal revenue (*MR*) multiplied by marginal product (*MP*), and the resource price (*PR*) equals marginal cost (*MC*) multiplied by marginal product (*MP*).

Max's Numbers   Check the numbers for Max's Wash 'n' Wax and confirm that the conditions you've just examined work. Max's profit-maximizing labour decision is to hire 3 workers if the wage rate is $12 an hour. When Max hires 3 hours of labour, marginal product is 3 washes per hour. Max sells the 3 washes an hour for a marginal revenue of $4 a wash. So marginal revenue product is 3 washes multiplied by $4 a wash, which equals $12 per hour. At a wage rate of $12 an hour, Max is maximizing profit.

Equivalently, Max's marginal cost is $12 an hour divided by 3 washes per hour, which equals $4 per wash. At a marginal revenue of $4 a wash, Max is maximizing profit.

You've discovered that the law of demand applies for labour just as it does for goods and services. Other things remaining the same, the lower the wage rate (the price of labour), the greater is the quantity of labour demanded.

Let's now study the influences that change the demand for labour and shift the demand for labour curve.

Changes in the Demand for Labour

The demand for labour depends on three factors:

1. The price of the firm's output
2. The prices of other productive resources
3. Technology

The higher the price of a firm's output, the greater is its demand for labour. The price of output affects the demand for labour through its influence on marginal revenue product. A higher price for the firm's output increases marginal revenue, which, in turn, increases the marginal revenue product of labour. A change in the price of a firm's output leads to a shift in the firm's demand for labour curve. If the price of the firm's output increases, the demand for labour increases, and the demand for labour curve shifts rightward.

The other two influences affect the *long-run demand for labour*, which is the relationship between the wage rate and the quantity of labour demanded when all resources can be varied. In contrast, the *short-run demand for labour* is the relationship between the wage rate and the quantity of labour demanded when the quantities of the other resources are fixed and labour is the only variable resource. A change in the relative price of productive resources— such as the relative price of labour and capital—leads to a substitution away from the resource whose relative price has increased and towards the resource whose relative price has decreased. So if the price of using capital decreases relative to that of using labour,

the firm substitutes capital for labour and increases the quantity of capital demanded.

But the demand for labour might increase or decrease. If the lower price of capital increases the scale of production by enough, the demand for labour increases. Otherwise the demand for labour decreases.

Finally, a new technology that changes the marginal product of labour changes the demand for labour. For example, the electronic telephone exchange has decreased the demand for telephone operators. This same new technology has increased the demand for telephone engineers. Again, these effects are felt in the long run when the firm adjusts all its resources and incorporates new technologies into its production process. Table 15.3 summarizes the influences on a firm's demand for labour.

We saw in Fig. 15.3 that the demand for labour has increased over time and the demand curve has shifted rightward. We can now give some of the reasons for this increase in demand. Advances in technology and investment in new capital increase the marginal product of labour and increase the demand for labour.

TABLE 15.3

A Firm's Demand for Labour

The Law of Demand

(Movements along the demand curve for labour)

The quantity of labour demanded by a firm

Decreases if:	*Increases if:*
■ The wage rate increases	■ The wage rate decreases

Changes in Demand

(Shifts in the demand curve for labour)

A firm's demand for labour

Decreases if:	*Increases if:*
■ The firm's output price decreases	■ The firm's output price increases
■ A new technology decreases the marginal product of labour	■ A new technology increases the marginal product of labour

(Changes in the prices of other resources have an ambiguous effect on the demand for labour.)

Market Demand

So far, we've studied the demand for labour by an individual firm. The market demand for labour is the total demand by all firms. By adding together the quantities demanded by all firms at each wage rate, we find the market demand for labour curve (just as we find the market demand curve for any good or service). Because a firm's demand for labour curve slopes downward, so does the market demand curve.

Elasticity of Demand for Labour

The demand for labour, on the average, is estimated to be about 3. This number means that the demand for labour is elastic. This fact is important because it means that an increase in the supply of labour, other things remaining the same, lowers the wage rate but increases labour income. If the demand for labour were inelastic, an increase in the supply of labour would decrease labour income. And if the demand for labour were unit elastic, an increase in the supply of labour would leave labour income unchanged.

Although the demand for labour is elastic on the average, there is variation across different types of labour. And the demand for labour is less elastic in the short run, when only labour can be varied, than in the long run, when labour and other resources can be varied. The elasticity of demand for a specific type of labour depends on:

■ The labour intensity of the production process
■ The elasticity of demand for the product
■ The substitutability of capital for labour

Labour Intensity   A labour-intensive production process is one that uses a lot of labour and little capital. Home building is an example. The greater the degree of labour intensity, the more elastic is the demand for labour. To see why, first suppose wages are 90 percent of total cost. A 10 percent increase in the wage rate increases total cost by 9 percent. Firms will be sensitive to such a large change in total cost, so if wages increase, firms will decrease the quantity of labour demanded by a relatively large amount. But if wages are 10 percent of total cost, a 10 percent increase in the wage rate increases total cost by only 1 percent. Firms will be less sensitive to this increase in cost, so if wages increase in this case, firms will decrease the quantity of labour demanded by a relatively small amount.

The Elasticity of Demand for the Product   The greater the elasticity of demand for the good, the larger is the elasticity of demand for the labour used to produce it. An increase in the wage rate increases marginal cost and decreases the supply of the good. The decrease in the supply of the good increases the price of the good and decreases the quantity demanded of the good and the quantities of the resources used to produce it. The greater the elasticity of demand for the good, the larger is the decrease in the quantity demanded of the good and so the larger is the decrease in the quantities of the productive resources used to produce it.

The Substitutability of Capital for Labour   The more easily capital can be used instead of labour in production, the more elastic is the long-run demand for labour. For example, it is easy to use robots rather than assembly line workers in car factories and grape-picking machines for labour in vineyards. So the long-run demand for these types of labour is elastic. At the other extreme, it is difficult (but possible) to substitute computers for newspaper reporters, bank loan officers, and teachers. So the long-run demand for these types of labour is less elastic.

Let's now turn from the demand side of the labour market to the supply side and examine the decisions that people make about how to allocate time between working and other activities.

The Supply of Labour

People can allocate their time to two broad activities—labour supply and leisure. (Leisure is a catch-all. It includes all activities other than supplying labour.) For most people, leisure is more enjoyable than supplying labour. We'll look at the labour supply decision of Amy, who is like most people. She enjoys her leisure time, and she would be pleased if she didn't have to spend her weekends working a supermarket checkout line.

But Amy has chosen to work weekends. The reason is that she is offered a wage rate that exceeds her *reservation wage*. Amy's reservation wage is the lowest wage at which she is willing to supply labour. If the wage rate exceeds her reservation wage, she supplies some labour. But how much labour does she supply? The quantity of labour that Amy is willing to supply depends on the wage rate.

Substitution Effect   Other things remaining the same, the higher the wage rate Amy is offered, at least over a range, the greater is the quantity of labour that she supplies. The reason is that Amy's wage rate is her *opportunity cost of leisure*. If she quits work an hour early to catch a movie, the cost of that extra hour of leisure is the wage rate that Amy forgoes. The higher the wage rate, the less willing is Amy to forgo the income and take the extra leisure time. This tendency for a higher wage rate to induce Amy to work longer hours is a *substitution effect*.

But there is also an *income effect* that works in the opposite direction to the substitution effect.

Income Effect   The higher Amy's wage rate, the higher is her income. A higher income, other things remaining the same, induces Amy to increase her demand for most goods. Leisure is one of those goods. Because an increase in income creates an increase in the demand for leisure, it also creates a decrease in the quantity of labour supplied.

Backward-Bending Supply of Labour Curve   As the wage rate rises, the substitution effect brings an increase in the quantity of labour supplied, while the income effect brings a decrease in the quantity of labour supplied. At low wage rates, the substitution

effect is larger than the income effect, so as the wage rate rises, people supply more labour. But as the wage rate continues to rise, the income effect eventually becomes larger than the substitution effect and the quantity of labour supplied decreases. The labour supply curve is *backward bending*.

Figure 15.4(a) shows the labour supply curves, for Amy, Jack, and Lisa. Each labour supply curve is backward bending but the three people have different reservation wage rates.

Market Supply   The market supply of labour curve is the sum of the individual supply curves. Figure 15.4(b) shows the market supply curve (S_M) derived from the supply curves of Amy, Jack, and Lisa (S_A, S_B, S_C) in Fig. 15.4(a). At wage rates of less than $1 an hour, no one supplies any labour. At a wage rate of $1 an hour, Amy works but Jack and Lisa don't. As the wage rate increases and reaches $7 an hour, all three of them work. The market supply curve S_M eventually bends backward but it has a long upward-sloping section.

Changes in the Supply of Labour   The supply of labour changes when influences other than the wage rate change. The key factors that change the supply of labour and that over the years have increased it are:

FIGURE 15.4

The Supply of Labour

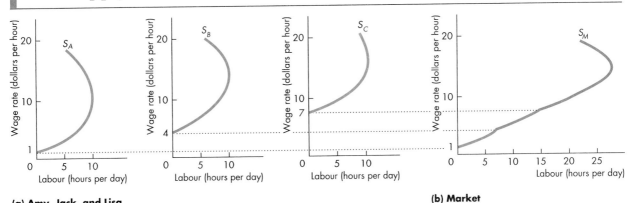

(a) Amy, Jack, and Lisa

(b) Market

Part (a) shows the labour supply curves of Amy (S_A), Jack (S_B), and Lisa (S_C). Each person has a reservation wage below which he or she will supply no labour. As the wage rises, the quantity of labour supplied increases to a maximum. If the wage continues to rise, the quantity of labour supplied begins to decrease.

Each person's supply curve eventually bends backward. Part (b) shows how, by adding the quantities of labour supplied by each person at each wage rate, we derive the market supply curve of labour (S_M). The market supply curve has a long upward-sloping region before it bends backward.

1. Adult population
2. Technological change and capital accumulation

An increase in the adult population increases the supply of labour. Also, an increase in capital in home production (of meals, laundry services, and cleaning services) increases the supply of labour. These factors that have increased the supply of labour have shifted the labour supply curve rightward.

Let's now build on what we've learned about the demand for labour and the supply of labour and study labour market equilibrium and the trends in wage rates and employment.

Labour Market Equilibrium

Wages and employment are determined by equilibrium in the labour market. You saw, in Fig. 15.2, that the wage rate and employment have both increased over the years. You can now explain why.

Trends in the Demand for Labour   The demand for labour has *increased* because of technological change and the accumulation of capital and the demand for labour curve has shifted rightward.

Many people are surprised that technological change and capital accumulation *increase* the demand for labour. They see new technologies *destroying jobs*, not creating them. Downsizing has become a catchword of the 1990s as the computer and information age has taken hold and eliminated millions of "good" jobs, even of managers. So how can it be that technological change *creates* jobs and increases the demand for labour?

Technological change destroys some jobs and creates others. But it creates more jobs than it destroys, and *on the average* the new jobs pay more than the old ones did. But to benefit from the advances in technology, people must acquire new skills and change their jobs. For example, during the past 15 years, the demand for typists has fallen almost to zero. But the demand for people who can type (on a computer rather than a typewriter) and do other things as well has increased. And the output of these people is worth more that that of a typist. So the demand for people with typing (and other) skills has increased.

Trends in the Supply of Labour   The supply of labour has increased because of population growth and technological change and capital accumulation in the home. The mechanization of home production of

fast-food preparation services (the freezer and the microwave oven) and laundry services (the automatic washer and dryer and drip dry clothing) has decreased the time spent on activities that once were full-time jobs and has led to a large increase in the supply of labour. As a result, the supply of labour curve has shifted steadily rightward, but at a slower pace than the shift in the demand curve.

Trends in Equilibrium   Because technological advances and capital accumulation have increased demand by more than population growth and technological change in home production has increased supply, both wages and employment have increased. But not everyone has shared in the advancing prosperity that comes from higher wage rates. Some groups have been left behind and some have even seen their wage rates fall. Why?

Two key reasons can be identified. First, technological change affects the marginal productivity of different groups in different ways. High-skilled computer-literate workers have benefited from the information revolution while low-skilled workers have suffered. The demand for the services of the first group has increased and the demand for the services of the second group has decreased. (Draw a supply and demand figure and you will see that these changes widen the wage difference between the two groups). Second, international competition has lowered the marginal revenue product of low-skilled workers and so decreased the demand for their labour. We look further at skill differences in Chapter 16 and at trends in the distribution of income in Chapter 17.

R E V I E W   Q U I Z

- Describe and explain the trends in wage rates and employment.
- Why do we call the demand for labour a *derived* demand? From what is it derived?
- What is the distinction between marginal revenue product and marginal revenue? Provide an example that illustrates the distinction.
- When a firm's marginal revenue product equals the wage rate, marginal revenue also equals marginal cost. Why? Provide a numerical example different from that in the text.
- What determines the amount of labour that households plan to supply?

Capital Markets

CAPITAL MARKETS ARE THE CHANNELS THROUGH which firms obtain *financial* resources to buy *physical* capital resources. These financial resources come from saving.

For most of us, the capital market is where we make our biggest ticket transactions. We borrow in the capital market to buy a home. And we lend in the capital market to build up a fund on which to live when we retire. Do the rates of return on capital increase like wage rates of labour increase?

Figure 15.5(a) answers this question by showing the record since 1965. We measure the rate of return on capital as the interest rate adjusted for the loss in the value of money that arises from inflation—the real interest rate. The real interest rate has fluctuated. It ranged between 2 percent a year and 3 percent a year during the late 1960s, became negative during the 1970s, climbed to 9 percent during the 1980s, and fell to average 5 percent a year during the 1990s. The quantity of capital employed increased steadily. In 1998, it stood at around \$3.2 trillion (1992 dollars), 3 times its 1965 level.

Figure 15.5(b) shows why these trends occurred. Demand increased from KD_{65} to KD_{98} and this increase was similar to the increase in supply from KS_{65} to KS_{98}. To understand the trends in the capital market, we must again probe the forces of demand and supply. Many of the ideas you've already met in your study of demand and supply in the labour market apply to the capital market as well. But there are some special features of capital. Its main special feature is that when people buy capital, they must compare *present* costs with *future* benefits. Let's discover how these comparisons are made by studying the demand for capital.

The Demand for Capital

A firm's demand for *financial* capital stems from its demand for *physical* capital, and the amount that a firm plans to borrow in a given time period is determined by its planned investment—purchases of new capital. This decision is driven by its attempt to maximize profit. As a firm increases the quantity of capital employed, other things remaining the same, the marginal revenue product of capital eventually diminishes. To maximize profit, a firm increases its plant size and uses more capital if the marginal

FIGURE 15.5

Capital Market Trends in Canada

(a) Capital stock and interest rate

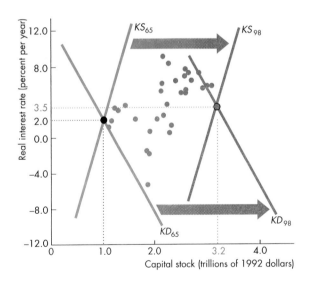

(b) Changes in demand and supply in the capital market

Between 1960 and 1998, the real interest rate fluctuated between *minus* 5 percent a year (in 1974) and 9 percent a year (in 1984). During the same period, the quantity of capital employed increased by 300 percent. The demand for capital increased from KD_{65} to KD_{98} and the supply of capital increased from KS_{65} to KS_{98}.

Source: Statistics Canada, StatCan: *CANSIM Disc*, 1999, and authors' assumptions and calculations.

revenue product of capital exceeds the cost of capital. But the marginal revenue product comes in the future and capital must be paid for in the present. So the firm must convert *future* marginal revenue products into a *present value* so that it can be compared with the price of a new piece of capital equipment.

To make this conversion, we use the technique of discounting.

Discounting and Present Value

Discounting is converting a future amount of money to a present value. And the **present value** of a future amount of money is the amount that, if invested today, will grow to be as large as that future amount when the interest that it will earn is taken into account.

The easiest way to understand discounting and present value is to begin with the relationship between an amount invested today, the interest that it earns, and the amount that it will grow to in the future. The future amount is equal to the present amount (present value) plus the interest it will accumulate in the future. That is:

Future amount = Present value + Interest income

The interest income is equal to the present value multiplied by the interest rate, r, so

Future amount = Present value + ($r \times$ Present value)

or

Future amount = Present value $\times$ (1 + r).

If you have $100 today and the interest rate is 10 percent a year ($r = 0.1$), one year from today you will have $110—the original $100 plus $10 interest. Check that the above formula delivers that answer: $100 $\times$ 1.1 = $110.

The formula that we have just used calculates a future amount one year from today from the present value and an interest rate. To calculate the present value, we just work backward. Instead of multiplying the present value by (1 + r), we divide the future amount by (1 + r). That is,

$$\text{Present value} = \frac{\text{Future amount}}{(1 + r)}.$$

You can use this formula to calculate present value. This calculation of present value is called discounting. Let's check that we can use the present value

formula by calculating the present value of $110 one year from now when the interest rate is 10 percent a year. You'll be able to guess that the answer is $100 because we just calculated that $100 invested today at 10 percent a year becomes $110 in one year. Thus it follows immediately that the present value of $110 in one year's time is $100. But let's use the formula. Putting the numbers into the above formula, we have

$$\text{Present value} = \frac{\$110}{(1 + 0.1)}$$

$$= \frac{\$110}{1.1} = \$100.$$

Calculating the present value of an amount of money one year from now is the easiest case. But we can also calculate the present value of an amount any number of years in the future. As an example, let's see how we calculate the present value of an amount of money that will be available two years from now.

Suppose that you invest $100 today for two years at an interest rate of 10 percent a year. The money will earn $10 in the first year, which means that by the end of the first year, you will have $110. If the interest of $10 is invested, then the interest earned in the second year will be a further $10 on the original $100 plus $1 on the $10 interest. Thus the total interest earned in the second year will be $11. The total interest earned overall will be $21 ($10 in the first year and $11 in the second year). After two years, you will have $121. From the definition of present value, you can see that the present value of $121 two years hence is $100. That is, $100 is the present amount that, if invested at an interest rate of 10 percent a year, will grow to $121 two years from now.

To calculate the present value of an amount of money two years in the future, we use the formula

$$\text{Present value} = \frac{\substack{\text{Amount of money} \\ \text{two years in future}}}{(1 + r)^2}.$$

Use this formula to calculate the present value of $121 two years from now at an interest rate of 10 percent a year. With these numbers the formula gives

$$\text{Present value} = \frac{\$121}{(1 + 0.1)^2}$$

$$= \frac{\$121}{(1.1)^2}$$

$$= \frac{\$121}{1.21}$$

$$= \$100.$$

We can calculate the present value of an amount of money any number of years in the future by using a formula based on the two that we've already used. The general formula is

$$\text{Present value} = \frac{\begin{array}{c}\text{Amount of money}\\ n \text{ in future}\end{array}}{(1 + r)^n}.$$

For example, if the interest rate is 10 percent a year, $100 to be received 10 years from now has a present value of $38.55. That is, if $38.55 is invested today at an interest rate of 10 percent, it will accumulate to $100 in 10 years. (You might check that calculation on your pocket calculator.)

You've seen how to calculate the present value of an amount of money one year in the future, two years in the future, and n years in the future. Most practical applications of present value calculate the present value of a sequence of future amounts of money that spread over several years. To calculate the present value of a sequence of amounts over several years, we use the formula you have learned and apply it to each year. We then sum the present values for each year to find the present value of the sequence of amounts.

For example, suppose that a firm expects to receive $100 a year for each of the next five years. And suppose that the interest rate is 10 percent per year (0.1 per year). The present value of these five payments of $100 each is calculated by using the following formula:

$$PV = \frac{\$100}{1.1} + \frac{\$100}{1.1^2} + \frac{\$100}{1.1^3} + \frac{\$100}{1.1^4} + \frac{\$100}{1.1^5}$$

which equals:

$$PV = \$90.91 + \$82.64 + \$75.13 + \$68.30 + \$62.09$$

$$= \$397.07.$$

You can see that the firm receives $500 over five years. But because the money arrives in the future, it is not worth $500 today. Its present value is only $397.07.

And the farther in the future it arrives, the smaller is its present value. The $100 received one year in the future is worth $90.91 today. And the $100 received five years in the future is worth only $68.30 today.

Let's now see how a firm uses the concept of present value to achieve an efficient use of capital.

The Present Value of a Computer We'll see how a firm decides how much capital to buy by calculating the present value of a new computer.

Tina runs Taxfile, Inc., a firm that sells advice to taxpayers. Tina is considering buying a new computer that costs $10,000. The computer has a life of two years, after which it will be worthless. If Tina buys the computer, she will pay $10,000 now and she expects to generate business that will bring in an additional $5,900 at the end of each of the next two years.

To calculate the present value, PV, of the marginal revenue product of a new computer, Tina calculates

$$PV = \frac{MRP_1}{(1 + r)} + \frac{MRP_2}{(1 + r)^2}.$$

Here, MRP_1 is the marginal revenue product received by Tina at the end of the first year. It is converted to a present value by dividing it by $(1 + r)$, where r is the interest rate (expressed as a proportion). The term MRP_2 is the marginal revenue product received at the end of the second year. It is converted to a present value by dividing it by $(1 + r)^2$.

If Tina can borrow or lend at an interest rate of 4 percent a year, the present value of her marginal revenue product is given by

$$PV = \frac{\$5,900}{(1 + 0.04)} + \frac{\$5,900}{(1 + 0.04)^2}$$

$$PV = \$5,673 + \$5,455$$

$$PV = \$11,128.$$

The present value of $5,900 one year in the future is $5,900 divided by 1.04 (4 percent as a proportion is 0.04). The present value of $5,900 two years in the future is $5,900 divided by $(1.04)^2$. Tina works out those two present values and then adds them to get the present value of the future flow of marginal revenue product, which is $11,128.

Table 15.4, parts (a) and (b), summarizes the data and the calculations we've just made. Review these calculations and make sure you understand them.

TABLE 15.4

Net Present Value of an Investment—Taxfile, Inc.

(a) Data

Price of computer	$10,000
Life of computer	2 years
Marginal revenue product	$5,900 at end of each year
Interest rate	4% a year

(b) Present value of the flow of marginal revenue product

$$PV = \frac{MRP_1}{(1 + r)} + \frac{MRP_2}{(1 + r)^2}$$

$$= \frac{\$5,900}{1.04} + \frac{\$5,900}{(1.04)^2}$$

$$= \$5,673 + \$5,455$$

$$= \$11,128$$

(c) Net present value of investment

$$NPV = PV \text{ of Marginal revenue product}$$
$$- \text{ Cost of computer}$$

$$= \$11,128 - \$10,000$$

$$= \$1,128$$

Tina's Decision to Buy Tina decides whether to buy the computer by comparing the present value of its future flow of marginal revenue product with its purchase price. She makes this comparison by calculating the net present value (*NPV*) of the computer. **Net present value** is the present value of the future flow of marginal revenue product generated by the capital minus the cost of the capital. If net present value is positive, the firm buys additional capital. If the net present value is negative, the firm does not buy additional capital. Table 15.4(c) shows the calculation of Tina's net present value of a computer. The net present value is $1,128—greater than zero—so Tina buys the computer.

Tina can buy any number of computers that cost $10,000 and have a life of two years. But like all other productive resources, capital is subject to diminishing

marginal returns. The greater the amount of capital employed, the smaller is its marginal revenue product. So if Tina buys a second computer or a third one, she gets successively smaller marginal revenue products from the additional machines.

Table 15.5(a) sets out Tina's marginal revenue products for one, two, and three computers. The marginal revenue product of one computer (the case just reviewed) is $5,900 a year. The marginal revenue product of a second computer is $5,600 a year, and the marginal revenue product of a third computer is $5,300 a year. Table 15.5(b) shows the calculations of the present values of the marginal revenue products of the first, second, and third computers.

You've seen that with an interest rate of 4 percent a year, the net present value of one computer is positive. At an interest rate of 4 percent a year, the present value of the marginal revenue product of a second computer is $10,562, which exceeds its price by $562. So Tina buys a second computer. But at an interest rate of 4 percent a year, the present value of the marginal revenue product of a third computer is $9,996, which is $4 less than the price of the computer. So Tina does not buy a third computer.

A Change in the Interest Rate We've seen that at an interest rate of 4 percent a year, Tina buys two computers but not three. Suppose that the interest rate is 8 percent a year. In this case, the present value of the first computer is $10,521 (see Table 15.5b), so Tina still buys one machine because it has a positive net present value. At an interest rate of 8 percent a year, the net present value of the second computer is $9,986, which is less than $10,000, the price of the computer. So, at an interest rate of 8 percent a year, Tina buys only one computer.

Suppose that the interest rate is even higher, at 12 percent a year. In this case, the present value of the marginal revenue product of one computer is $9,971 (see Table 15.5b). At this interest rate, Tina buys no computers.

These calculations trace Taxfile's demand schedule for capital, which shows the value of computers demanded by Taxfile at each interest rate. Other things remaining the same, as the interest rate rises, the quantity of capital demanded decreases. The higher the interest rate, the smaller is the quantity of *physical* capital demanded. But to finance the purchase of *physical* capital, firms demand *financial* capital. So the higher the interest rate, the smaller is the quantity of *financial* capital demanded.

TABLE 15.5

Taxfile's Investment Decision

(a) Data

Price of computer	$10,000
Life of computer	2 years
Marginal revenue product:	
Using 1 computer	$5,900 a year
Using 2 computers	$5,600 a year
Using 3 computers	$5,300 a year

(b) Present value of the flow of marginal revenue product

If r = 0.04 (4% a year):

Using 1 computer: $PV = \dfrac{\$5,900}{1.04} + \dfrac{\$5,900}{(1.04)^2} = \$11,128.$

Using 2 computers: $PV = \dfrac{\$5,600}{1.04} + \dfrac{\$5,600}{(1.04)^2} = \$10,562.$

Using 3 computers: $PV = \dfrac{\$5,300}{1.04} + \dfrac{\$5,300}{(1.04)^2} = \$9,996.$

If r = 0.08 (8% a year):

Using 1 computer: $PV = \dfrac{\$5,900}{1.08} + \dfrac{\$5,900}{(1.08)^2} = \$10,521.$

Using 2 computers: $PV = \dfrac{\$5,600}{1.08} + \dfrac{\$5,600}{(1.08)^2} = \$9,986.$

If r = 0.12 (12% a year):

Using 1 computer: $PV = \dfrac{\$5,900}{1.12} + \dfrac{\$5,900}{(1.12)^2} = \$9,971.$

Demand Curve for Capital

The quantity of capital demanded by a firm depends on the marginal revenue product of capital and the interest rate. A firm's demand curve for capital shows the relationship between the quantity of capital demanded by the firm and the interest rate, other things remaining the same. The market demand curve (as in Fig. 15.5) shows the relationship between the total quantity of capital demanded and the interest rate, other things remaining the same.

Changes in the Demand for Capital Figure 15.5 shows that the demand for capital has increased steadily over the years. The demand for capital changes when expectations about the future marginal revenue product of capital change. An increase in the expected marginal revenue product of capital increases the demand of capital. Two main factors that change the marginal revenue product of capital and bring changes in the demand for capital are:

1. Population growth
2. Technological change

An increase in the population increases the demand for all goods and services and so increases the demand for the capital that produces them. Advances in technology increase the demand for some types of capital and decrease the demand for other types. For example, the development of diesel engines for railroad transportation decreased the demand for steam engines and increased the demand for diesel engines. In this case, the railroad industry's overall demand for capital did not change much. In contrast, the development of desktop computers increased the demand for office computing equipment, decreased the demand for electric typewriters, and increased the overall demand for capital in the office.

Let's now turn to the supply side of the capital market.

The Supply of Capital

The quantity of capital supplied results from people's saving decisions. The main factors that determine saving are:

- Income
- Expected future income
- Interest rate

Income Saving is the act of converting *current* income into *future* consumption. Usually, the higher a person's income, the more he or she plans to consume both in the present and in the future. But to increase *future* consumption, the person must save. So, other things remaining the same, the higher a person's income, the more he or she saves. The relationship between saving and income is remarkably stable. Most people save a constant proportion of their income.

Expected Future Income Because a major reason for saving is to increase future consumption, the amount that a person saves depends not only on current income but also on *expected future income*. If a person's current income is high and expected future income is low, he or she will have a high level of saving. But if a person's current income is low and expected future income is high, he or she will have a low (perhaps even negative) level of saving.

Young people (especially students) usually have low current incomes compared with their expected future income. To smooth out consumption over their lifetime, young people consume more than they earn and incur debts. Such people have a negative amount of saving. In middle age, most people's incomes reach their peak. At this stage in life, saving is at its maximum. After retirement, people spend part of the wealth they have accumulated during their working lives.

Interest Rate A dollar saved today grows into a dollar plus interest tomorrow. The higher the interest rate, the greater is the amount that a dollar saved today becomes in the future. Thus the higher the interest rate, the greater is the opportunity cost of current consumption. With a higher opportunity cost of current consumption, people cut their consumption and increase their saving.

Supply Curve of Capital

The supply curve of capital (like that in Fig. 15.5) shows the relationship between the quantity of capital supplied and the interest rate, other things remaining the same. An increase in the interest rate brings an increase in the quantity of capital supplied and a movement along the supply curve. The supply curve is inelastic in the short run but probably quite elastic in the long run. The reason is that in any given year, the total amount of saving is small relative to the stock of capital in existence. So even a large change in the saving rate brings only a small change in the quantity of capital supplied.

Changes in the Supply of Capital The main influences on the supply of capital are the size and age distribution of the population and the level of income.

Other things remaining the same, an increase in the population or an increase in income brings an increase in the supply of capital. Also, other things remaining the same, the larger the proportion of middle-aged people, the higher is the saving rate. The reason is that middle-aged people do most of the saving as they build up a pension fund to provide a retirement income. Any one of the factors that increases the supply of capital shifts the supply curve of capital rightward.

Let's now use what we've learned about the demand for and supply of capital and see how the interest rate is determined.

The Interest Rate

Saving plans and investment plans are co-ordinated through capital markets and the interest rate adjusts to make these plans compatible.

Figure 15.6 shows the capital market. Initially, the demand for capital is KD_0 and the supply of capital is KS_0. The equilibrium interest rate is 6 percent a year and the quantity of capital is $2 trillion. If the interest rate exceeds 6 percent a year, the quantity of capital supplied exceeds the quantity of capital demanded and the interest rate falls. And if the interest rate is less than 6 percent a year, the quantity of capital demanded exceeds the quantity of capital supplied and the interest rate rises.

Over time, both the demand for capital and the supply of capital increase. The demand curve shifts rightward to KD_1 and the supply curve also shifts rightward to KS_1. Both curves shift because the same forces influence both. Population growth increases both demand and supply. Technological advances increase demand and bring higher incomes, which in turn increase supply. Because both demand and supply increase over time the quantity of capital trends upward and the interest rate has no trend.

Although the interest rate does not follow a rising or falling trend, it does fluctuate, as you can see in Fig. 15.5(a). The reason is that the demand for capital and the supply of capital do not change in lockstep. Sometimes rapid technological change brings an increase in the demand for capital *before* it brings rising incomes that increase the supply of capital. When this sequence of events occurs, the interest rate rises. The early 1980s appear to be such a time, as you can see in Fig. 15.5(a).

At other times, the demand for capital grows slowly or even decreases temporarily. In this situation, supply outgrows demand and the interest rate falls. Figure 15.5(a) shows that 1975 was one of these times.

FIGURE 15.6
Capital Market Equilibrium

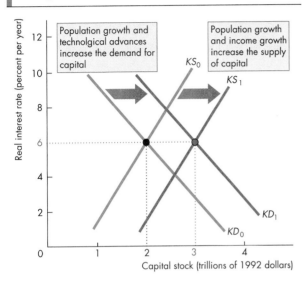

Initially, the demand for capital is KD_0 and the supply of capital is KS_0. The equilibrium interest rate is 6 percent a year and the capital stock is $2 trillion. Over time, both demand and supply increase to KD_1 and KS_1. The capital stock increases but the interest rate is constant. Demand and supply increase because they are influenced by common factors.

R E V I E W   Q U I Z

- What have been the main trends in the capital stock and interest rates since 1965?
- What is discounting and how is it used to calculate a present value? When might you want to calculate a present value to make a decision?
- How does a firm compare the future marginal revenue product of capital with the current cost of capital?
- What are the main influences on a firm's demand for capital?
- What are the main influences on the supply of capital?
- How can we explain the trends in the capital stock and interest rates?

The lessons that we've just learned about capital markets can be used to understand the prices of exhaustible natural resource prices. Let's see how.

Land and Exhaustible Natural Resource Markets

LAND IS THE QUANTITY OF NATURAL RESOURCES. All natural resources are called land and they fall into two categories:

- Nonexhaustible
- Exhaustible

A **nonexhaustible natural resource** is a natural resource that can be used repeatedly. Examples are land (in its everyday sense), rivers, lakes, rain, and sunshine.

An **exhaustible natural resource** is a natural resource that can be used only once and that cannot be replaced once it has been used. Examples are coal, natural gas, and oil—the so-called hydrocarbon fuels.

The demand for natural resources as inputs into production is based on the same principle of marginal revenue product as the demand for labour (and the demand for capital). But the supply of natural resources is special. Let's look first at the supply of nonexhaustible natural resources.

The Supply of Land (Nonexhaustible Natural Resource)

The quantity of land and other nonexhaustible natural resources available is fixed. The quantity supplied cannot be changed by individual decisions. People can vary the amount of land they own. But when one person buys some land, another person sells it. The aggregate quantity of land supplied of any particular type and in any particular location is fixed, regardless of the decisions of any individual. This fact means that the supply of each particular piece of land is perfectly inelastic. Figure 15.7 illustrates such a supply. Regardless of the rent available, the quantity of land supplied in Toronto's Yorkville is a fixed number of square metres.

Because the supply of land is fixed regardless of its price, price is determined by demand. The greater the demand for a specific block of land, the higher is its price.

Expensive land can be, and is, used more intensively than inexpensive land. For example, high-rise buildings enable land to be used more intensively. However, to use land more intensively, it has to be combined with another productive resource—capital.

FIGURE 15.7

The Supply of Land

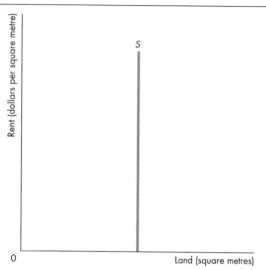

The supply of a given block of land is perfectly inelastic. No matter what the rent, no more land than the quantity that exists can be supplied.

An increase in the amount of capital on a block of land does not change the quantity of land itself.

Although the supply of each type of land is fixed and its supply is perfectly inelastic, each individual firm, operating in competitive land markets, faces an elastic supply of land. For example, Bloor Street in Toronto has a fixed amount of land, but Chapters, the bookstore, could rent some space from The Bay, the department store. Each firm can rent the quantity of land that it demands at the going rent, as determined in the marketplace. Thus provided that land markets are competitive, firms are price takers in these markets, just as they are in the markets for other productive resources.

The Supply of an Exhaustible Natural Resource

The *stock* of a natural resource is the quantity in existence at a given time. This quantity is fixed and is independent of the price of the resource. The *known* stock of a natural resource is the quantity that has been discovered. This quantity increases over time because advances in technology enable ever less accessible sources to be discovered. Both of these *stock* concepts influence the price of a natural resource. But the influence is indirect. The direct influence on price is the rate at which the resource is supplied for use in production—called the *flow* supply.

The flow supply of an exhaustible natural resource is *perfectly elastic* at a price that equals the present value of the expected price next period.

To see why, think about the economic choices of Saudi Arabia, a country that possesses a large inventory of oil. Saudi Arabia can sell an additional billion barrels of oil right now and use the income it receives to buy Canadian bonds. Or it can keep the billion barrels in the ground and sell them next year. If it sells the oil and buys Canadian bonds, it earns the interest rate on the bonds. If it keeps the oil and sells it next year, it earns the price increase or loses the price decrease between now and next year.

If Saudi Arabia expects the price to rise next year by a percentage that equals the current interest rate, the price that it expects next year equals $(1 + r)$ multiplied by this year's price. For example, if this year's price is $12 a barrel and the interest rate is 5 percent ($r = 0.5$), then next year's expected price is $1.05 \times \$12$, which equals $12.60 a barrel.

With the price expected to rise to $12.60 next year, Saudi Arabia is indifferent between selling now for $12 and not selling now but waiting until next year and selling for $12.60. It expects to make the same return either way. So, at $12 a barrel, Saudi Arabia will sell whatever quantity is demanded.

But if Saudi Arabia expects the price to rise next year by a percentage that exceeds the current interest rate, it expects to make a bigger return by hanging on to the oil than it can make from selling the oil and buying bonds. So it keeps the oil and sells none. And if it expects the price to rise next year by a percentage that is less than the current interest rate, the bond gives a bigger return than the oil so it sells as much oil as it can.

Recall the idea of discounting and present value. The minimum price at which Saudi Arabia is willing to sell oil is the present value of the expected future price. At this price, it will sell as much oil as buyers demand. So its supply is perfectly elastic.

Price and the Hotelling Principle

Figure 15.8 shows the equilibrium in a natural resource market. Because supply is perfectly elastic at the present value of next period's expected price, the

FIGURE 15.8
An Exhaustible Natural Resource Market

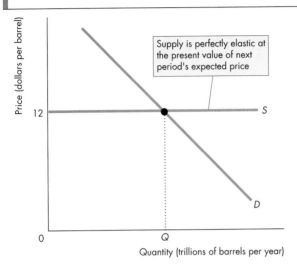

The supply of an exhaustible natural resource is perfectly elastic at the *present value* of next period's expected price. The demand for an exhaustible natural resource is determined by its marginal revenue product. The price is determined by supply and equals the *present value* of next period's expected price.

FIGURE 15.9
Falling Resource Prices

The prices of metals (here an average of the prices of aluminium, copper, iron ore, lead, manganese, nickel, silver, tin, and zinc) have tended to fall over time, not rise as predicted by the Hotelling Principle. The reason is that unanticipated advances in technology have decreased the cost of extracting resources and greatly increased the exploitable known reserves.

Source: International Financial Statistics, International Monetary Fund, Washington, D.C. (various issues).

actual price of the natural resource equals the present value of next period's expected price. Also, because the current price is the present value of the expected future price, the price of the resource is expected to rise at a rate equal to the interest rate.

The proposition that the price of a resource is expected to rise at a rate equal to the interest rate is called the *Hotelling Principle.* It was first realized by Harold Hotelling, a mathematician and economist at Columbia University. But as Fig. 15.9 shows, *actual* prices do not follow the path of *expected* prices predicted by the Hotelling Principle. Why do natural resource prices sometimes fall rather than follow their expected path and increase over time?

The key reason is that the future is unpredictable. Expected technological change is reflected in the price of a natural resource. But a previously unexpected new technology that leads to the discovery or the more efficient use of an exhaustible natural resource causes its price to fall. Over the years, as technology has advanced, we have become more efficient in our use of exhaustible resources. And we

haven't just become more efficient. We've become more efficient than we expected to.

R E V I E W   Q U I Z

- Why is the supply of a *nonexhaustible* natural resource such as land perfectly inelastic?
- At what price is the flow supply of an exhaustible natural resource perfectly elastic and why?
- Why is the price of an exhaustible natural resource expected to rise at a rate equal to the interest rate?
- Why do the prices of exhaustible resources not follow the path predicted by the Hotelling Principle?

People supply resources to earn an income. But some people earn enormous incomes. Are such incomes necessary to induce people to work and supply other resources? Let's now answer this question.

Income, Economic Rent, and Opportunity Cost

YOU'VE NOW SEEN HOW RESOURCE PRICES ARE determined by the interaction of demand and supply. And you've seen that demand is determined by marginal productivity and supply is determined by the resources available and by people's choices about their use. The interaction of demand and supply in resource markets determines who receives a large income and who receives a small income.

Large and Small Incomes

An NBA player earns $10 million a year because he has a high marginal revenue product—reflected in the demand for his services—and the supply of people with the combination of talents needed for this kind of job is small—reflected in the supply. Equilibrium occurs at a *high* wage rate and a *small* quantity employed. And if the demand for basketball players increases, their incomes increase by a large amount and the number of players barely changes.

People who do McJobs earn a low wage rate because they have a low marginal revenue product—reflected in the demand—and many people are able and willing to supply their labour for these jobs. Equilibrium occurs at a *low* wage rate and a *large* quantity employed. And if the demand for workers in McJobs increases, the number of people doing these jobs increases by a large amount and the wage rate barely changes.

Another difference between a basketball player and a fast-food cook is that if the basketball player was hit with a pay cut, he would probably still supply his services, but if a fast-food cook was hit with a pay cut, he would probably quit. This difference arises from the interesting distinction between economic rent and opportunity cost.

Economic Rent and Opportunity Cost

The total income of a productive resource is made up of its economic rent and its opportunity cost. **Economic rent** is the income received by the owner of a resource over and above the amount required to induce that owner to offer the resource for use. Any productive resource can receive an economic rent. The income required to induce the supply of a productive resource is the opportunity cost of using a productive resource—the value of the resource in its next best use.

Figure 15.10(a) illustrates the way in which a resource income has an economic rent and opportunity cost component. The figure shows the market for a productive resource. It could be *any* productive resource—labour, capital, or land—but we'll suppose it is labour. The demand curve is D, and its supply curve is S. The wage rate is W, and the quantity employed is C. The income earned is the sum of the yellow and green areas. The yellow area below the supply curve measures opportunity cost, and the green area above the supply curve but below the resource price measures economic rent.

To see why the area below the supply curve measures opportunity cost, recall that a supply curve can be interpreted in two different ways. It shows the quantity supplied at a given price and it shows the minimum price at which a given quantity is willingly supplied. If suppliers receive only the minimum amount required to induce them to supply each unit of the productive resource, they will be paid a different price for each unit. The prices will trace the supply curve, and the income received is entirely opportunity cost—the yellow area in Fig. 15.10(a).

The concept of economic rent is similar to the concepts of consumer surplus and producer surplus that you met in Chapter 6. Recall that consumer surplus is the maximum price someone is willing to pay, as indicated by the demand curve, minus the price paid. Producer surplus equals price minus opportunity cost. In a parallel sense, economic rent is the price a person receives for the use of a resource minus the minimum price at which a given quantity of the resource is willingly supplied.

Economic rent is not the same thing as the "rent" that a farmer pays for the use of some land or the "rent" that you pay for your apartment. Everyday "rent" is a price paid for the services of land or a building. *Economic rent* is a component of the income received by any productive resource.

The portion of the income of a productive resource that consists of economic rent depends on the elasticity of the supply of the productive resource. When the supply of a productive resource is perfectly inelastic, its entire income is economic rent. Most of Garth Brooks' and Pearl Jam's income is economic rent. Also, a large part of the income of a major league baseball player is economic rent. When the supply of a productive resource is perfectly elastic, none of its income is economic rent. Most of the income of a baby sitter is opportunity cost. In gener-

FIGURE 15.10
Economic Rent and Opportunity Cost

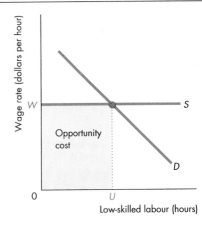

(a) General case

(b) All economic rent

(c) All opportunity cost

When a resource supply curve slopes upward—the general case—as in part (a), part of the resource income is economic rent (green) and part is opportunity cost (yellow).

When the supply of a productive resource is perfectly

inelastic (the supply curve is vertical), as in part (b), the entire resource income is economic rent. When the supply of the productive resource is perfectly elastic, as in part (c), the resource's entire income is opportunity cost.

---

al, when the supply curve is neither perfectly elastic nor perfectly inelastic, like that illustrated in Fig. 15.10(a), some part of the resource income is economic rent and the other part is opportunity cost.

Parts (b) and (c) of Fig. 15.10 show the other two possibilities. Part (b) shows the market for a particular block of land in Toronto. The quantity of land is fixed in size at *L* square metres. Therefore the supply curve of the land is vertical—perfectly inelastic. No matter what the rent on the land is, there is no way of increasing the quantity that can be supplied. Suppose that the demand curve in Fig. 15.10(b) shows the marginal revenue product of this block of land. Then it commands a rent of *R*. The entire income accruing to the owner of the land is the green area in the figure. This income is *economic rent*.

Figure 15.10(c) shows the market for a productive resource that is in perfectly elastic supply. An example of such a market might be that for low-skilled labour in a poor country such as India or China. In those countries, large amounts of labour flock to the cities and are available for work at the going wage rate (in this case, *W*). Thus in these situations, the supply of labour is almost perfectly elastic. The entire income earned by this labour is opportunity cost. They receive no economic rent.

R E V I E W   Q U I Z

- Why do basketball players earn larger incomes than do baby sitters?
- What is the distinction between an economic rent and an opportunity cost?
- Is the income that the Toronto Raptors pays to Charles Oakley an economic rent or compensation for his opportunity cost?
- Is a Big Mac more expensive in Toronto than in Brandon, Manitoba, because rents are higher in Toronto, or are rents higher in Toronto because people in Toronto are willing to pay more for a Big Mac?

◆ *Reading Between the Lines* on pp. 342–343 looks at the market for hockey players. The next chapter studies labour markets more closely and explains differences in wage rates among high-skilled and low-skilled workers and males and females. Chapter 17 looks at how the market economy distributes income and at efforts by governments to redistribute income and modify the market outcome.

Rents and Opportunity Costs on the Ice

THE GLOBE AND MAIL, JANUARY 19, 1999

NHL average salary climbs to $1.3-million

BY NEIL STEVENS

The return of Pavel Bure to the National Hockey League nudges the average annual player salary toward $1.3-million (U.S.) and lifts the Florida Panthers into the upper echelon of team payrolls.

The average salary was $1.17-million (U.S.) at the end of the 1997-98 season, and it shot up with the dozens of free-agent signings since the summer. With Bure's old $8 million (U.S.) contract with the Vancouver Canucks put into the mix, the average goes up to $1.3-million (U.S.).

But what Bure will make this season isn't precisely known. The Panthers, who acquired Bure in a trade with the Canucks, tore up the Vancouver contract and gave him a new one for the rest of the season, believed to be worth about $3 million (U.S.). ...

Bure, whose $8-million contract with Vancouver had put him fifth on the league-wide list, is expected to make his debut with Florida tomorrow in Uniondale, N.Y., against the Islanders.

Sergei Fedorov of the Detroit Red Wings is the top-paid NHL player this season, at $14-million (U.S.) from a front-loaded deal the Red Wings assumed in matching the free-agent offer Fedorov received from the Carolina Hurricanes last year.

Paul Kariya of the Anaheim Mighty Ducks and Eric Lindros of the Philadelphia Flyers are each receiving $8.5-million (U.S.) this season. Buffalo Sabres goaltender Dominik Hasek is getting $8-million (U.S.).

Bure slides in ahead of Mats Sundin of the Toronto Maple Leafs, whose rate is $6.3-million (U.S.). Wayne Gretzky of the New York Rangers, Doug Gilmour of the Chicago Blackhawks, Peter Forsberg of the Colorado Avalanche and Mark Messier of the Canucks are each getting $6-million (U.S.). ...

While Bure is at the high end of the salary scale, the least-paid of more than 620 players who have appeared in NHL games this season have been Stephen Leach of the Phoenix Coyotes ($150,000 Cdn.), backup Anaheim goalie Dominic Roussel ($160,000 U.S.) and Nashville goalie Tomas Vokoun ($275,000 Cdn.).

Essence of the Story

■ The average NHL salary in 1997–98 was $1.17 million (U.S.). In 1998–99, it was $1.3 million (U.S.).

■ Sergei Fedorov of the Detroit Red Wings is the highest-paid player, receiving $14 million (U.S.) per season.

■ Next on the highest-paid list are Paul Kariya and Eric Lindros at $8.5 million (U.S.) per season, and Dominik Hasek and Pavel Bure at $8 million (U.S.) per season.

■ The lowest-paid NHL player is Stephen Leach of the Phoenix Coyotes who receives $150,000 (Canadian) per season.

■ The marginal revenue product of players of the quality of Sergei Fedorov, Paul Kariya, and Eric Lindros is enormous.

■ These players fill arenas and generate huge revenues for their teams.

■ The supply of top-performing hockey players is limited. At a wage rate below the minimum industrial wage, no one would be willing to work and train to perform at the standard of these players. The quantity supplied would be zero.

■ At a wage rate similar to the average industrial wage, a large number of people are willing to work and train to play competition quality hockey. But few have the talent to perform at the level of a Fedorov, Kariya, or Lindros.

■ No matter by how much the wage rate rises above the average industrial wage, the quantity of top-performing hockey players does not increase. The supply is inelastic.

■ Figure 1 shows the supply of top-performing hockey players as the curve labelled S. The average industrial wage rate is a. As the wage rate for hockey increases above this wage rate, the quantity of star players supplied increases, but up to a maximum of Q_0. This quantity is limited by the available talent pool.

■ The demand for top-performing players is determined by their marginal revenue product and is the curve D.

■ Equilibrium in the market for top-performing hockey players occurs at an average wage rate of $1.3 million (U.S.) a year.

■ Most of their income is economic rent, which is shown as the green area. The rest, shown by the yellow area, is *opportunity cost*.

■ Figure 2 shows the situation facing an individual hockey team. The team faces a perfectly elastic supply of top-performing players shown by the curve S_i. The team's demand curve is D_i, and the team hires Q_i top-performing players.

■ If the teams could collude, they might be able to keep players' wages down. But competition for the best players means that each team must pay the going market wage for its talent.

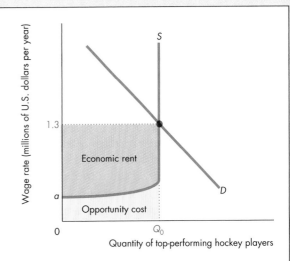

Figure 1 The market for hockey superstars

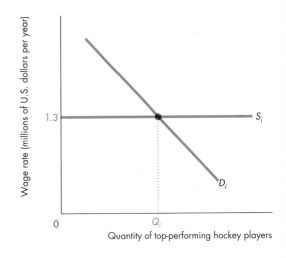

Figure 2 Florida Panthers

SUMMARY

Key Points

Resource Prices and Incomes (p. 322)

- An increase in the demand for a productive resource increases the resource's price and total income; a decrease in the demand for a productive resource decreases its price and total income.
- An increase in the supply of a productive resource increases the quantity used but decreases price and might increase or decrease its total income depending on whether demand is elastic or inelastic.

Labour Markets (pp. 323–330)

- The marginal revenue product of labour determines the demand for labour.
- The demand for labour increases if the price of the firm's output rises or if technological change and capital accumulation increase marginal product.
- The elasticity of demand for labour depends on the labour intensity of production, the elasticity of demand for the product, and on the ease with which labour can be substituted for capital.
- The quantity of labour supplied increases as the wage rate increases but, at high wage rates, the supply curve eventually bends backwards.
- An increase in population or an advance in home production technology increases the supply of labour.
- Real wages and employment increase because demand increases by more than supply.

Capital Markets (pp. 331–337)

- To make an investment decision, a firm compares the *present value* of the marginal revenue product of capital with the price of capital.
- Population growth and technological change increase the demand for capital.
- The higher the interest rate, the greater is the level of saving and the quantity of capital supplied.
- The supply of capital increases as incomes increase.
- Capital market equilibrium determines the real interest rate.

Land and Exhaustible Natural Resource Markets (pp. 337–339)

- The demand for natural resources is determined by marginal revenue product.
- The supply of land is inelastic.
- The supply of exhaustible natural resources is perfectly elastic at a price equal to the present value of the expected future price.
- The price of exhaustible natural resources is expected to rise at a rate equal to the interest rate, but it fluctuates and sometimes falls.

Income, Economic Rent, and Opportunity Cost (pp. 340–341)

- Economic rent is the income received by a resource owner over and above the amount needed to induce the owner to supply the productive resource for use.
- The rest of a resource's income is opportunity cost.
- When the supply of a resource is perfectly inelastic, its entire income is economic rent; and when supply is perfectly elastic, the entire income is opportunity cost.

Key Figures and Tables

Key Terms

P R O B L E M S

*1. The figure illustrates the market for blueberry pickers:

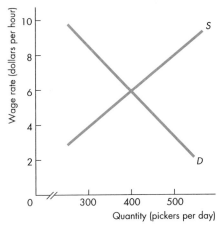

a. What is the wage rate paid to pickers?
b. How many blueberry pickers get hired?
c. What is the income received by pickers?

2. In problem 1, if the demand for blueberry pickers increases by 100 a day,
a. What is the new wage rate paid to the pickers?
b. How many additional pickers get hired?
c. What is the total income paid to pickers?

*3. The fish packing industry is competitive and Wanda owns a fish shop. She employs students to sort and pack the fish. Students can pack the following amounts of fish in an hour:

Number of students	Quantity of fish (kilograms)
1	20
2	50
3	90
4	120
5	145
6	165
7	180
8	190

The market price of fish is 50¢ a kilogram and the wage rate of packers is $7.50 an hour.
a. Calculate the marginal product of the students and draw the marginal product curve.
b. Calculate the marginal revenue product of the students and draw the marginal revenue product curve.
c. Find Wanda's demand for labour curve.
d. How many students does Wanda employ?

4. The party ice market is competitive and Barry makes party ice. He employs workers to bag the ice. The baggers can produce the following quantities in an hour:

Number of workers	Quantity of ice (bags)
1	40
2	100
3	180
4	240
5	290
6	330
7	360
8	380

The market price of ice is 25¢ a bag and the wage rate of a bagger is $5.00 an hour.
a. Calculate the marginal product of the workers and draw the marginal product curve.
b. Calculate the marginal revenue product of the workers and draw the marginal revenue product curve.
c. Find Barry's demand for labour curve.
d. How much ice does Barry sell?

*5. If, in problem 3, the price of fish falls to 33.33¢ a kilogram but fish packers' wages remain at $7.50 an hour, what happens to:
a. Wanda's marginal product?
b. Wanda's marginal revenue product?
c. Wanda's demand for labour curve?
d. the number of students Wanda employs?

6. If, in problem 4, the price of party ice falls to 10¢ a bag but baggers' wages remain at $5.00 an hour, what happens to:
a. Barry's marginal product?
b. Barry's marginal revenue product?
c. Barry's demand for labour curve?
d. the number of students Barry employs?

*7. Back at Wanda's fish shop described in problem 3, packers' wages increase to $10 an hour, but the price of fish remains at 50¢ a kilogram.
a. What happens to marginal revenue product?
b. What happens to Wanda's demand for

labour curve?

c. How many students does Wanda employ?

8. Back at Barry's party ice shop described in problem 4, baggers' wages increase to $10 an hour, but the price of ice remains at 25¢ a bag.
   a. What happens to marginal revenue product?
   b. What happens to Barry's demand for labour curve?
   c. How many baggers does Barry employ?

*9. Using the information in problem 3, calculate Wanda's marginal revenue, marginal cost, and marginal revenue product. Show that when Wanda is making maximum profit, marginal cost equals marginal revenue and marginal revenue product equals the wage rate.

10. Using the information in problem 4, calculate Barry's marginal revenue, marginal cost, and marginal revenue product. Show that when Barry is making maximum profit, marginal cost equals marginal revenue and marginal revenue product equals the wage rate.

*11. Venus makes Firecrackers, which she sells in December each year for New Year's celebrations. She must decide how many firecracker production lines to install. Each production line costs $1 million and operates for only two years, after which it must be replaced. With one production line, Venus expects to sell $590,000 worth of firecrackers a year. With two production lines, she expects to sell $1,150,000 worth of firecrackers each year. And with three production lines, she expects to sell $1,680,000 worth of firecrackers a year. The interest rate is 5 percent a year. How many production lines does Venus install? Explain your answer.

12. Vulcan Balloon Rides must decide how many balloons to operate. Each balloon costs $10,000 and must be replaced after three years of service. With one balloon, Vulcan expects to sell $5,900 worth of rides a year. With two balloons, it expects to sell $11,500 worth of rides each year. And with three balloons, it expects to sell $16,800 worth of rides a year. The interest rate is 8 percent a year. How many balloons does Vulcan operate? Explain your answer.

*13. Greg has found an oil well in his backyard. A geologist estimates that a total of 10 million barrels can be pumped for a pumping cost of a dollar a barrel. The price of oil is $20 a barrel. How much oil does Greg sell each year? If you can't predict how much he will sell, what extra information would you need to be able to do so?

14. Orley has a wine cellar in which he keeps choice wines from around the world. What does Orley expect to happen to the prices of the wines he keeps in his cellar? Explain your answer. How does Orley decide which wine to drink and when to drink it?

*15. Use the figure in problem 1, and show on the figure the blueberry pickers' economic rent and opportunity cost.

16. In the situation described in problem 2, show on the figure the blueberry pickers' economic rent and opportunity cost.

CRITICAL THINKING

1. Study *Reading Between the Lines* on pp. 342–343 and answer the following questions:
   a. What determines the demand for hockey players?
   b. What determines the supply of hockey players?
   c. What do you think Sergei Fedorov, Paul Kariya, and Eric Lindros would do if they didn't play hockey?
   d. What does your answer to (c) tell you about the opportunity cost of these players?
   e. What does your answer to (c) tell you about the economic rent received by these players?
   f. Why don't hockey players have contracts that give them their entire marginal revenue product?
   g. Why don't hockey teams negotiate contracts that pay the players their opportunity cost?

2. "We are running out of natural resources and must take urgent action to conserve our precious reserves." Do you agree? Why or why not?

3. Why do we keep finding new reserves of oil? Why don't we do once-and-for-all a big survey that catalogues the earth's entire inventory of natural resources?

Chapter 10

Labour Markets

As you well know, school is not just a party. Those exams and problem sets require a lot of time and effort. Are they worth the sweat that goes into them? What is the payoff? Is it sufficient to make up for the years of tuition, room and board, and lost wages? (You could, after all, be working for pay now instead of slogging through this economics course.) ◆ Many workers belong to labour unions. Usually, union workers earn a higher wage than nonunion workers in comparable jobs. Why? How are unions able to get higher wages for their members than the wages that nonunion workers are

The Sweat of Our Brows

paid? ◆ Among the most visible and persistent differences in earnings are those between men and women. Men, on the average, earn incomes that are one-third higher than the incomes earned by women. Certainly a lot of individuals defy the averages. But why do women so consistently earn less than men? Is it because of discrimination and exploitation? Or is it because of economic factors? Or is it a combination of the two? ◆ Equal pay laws have resulted in programs that try to ensure that jobs of equivalent value receive the same pay regardless of the pay set by the market. Can pay equity laws bring economic help to low-paid women? ◆ We've heard more and more during the past year about a Canadian brain drain—talented and well-educated Canadians migrating south to work in the United States. Is there a brain drain, and if there is, why does it occur?

◇ In this chapter, we answer questions such as these by continuing our study of labour markets. We begin by extending the competitive labour market model developed in Chapter 15 to study the effects of education and training on wages. We then study labour unions and the differences in union and nonunion wage rates. We also study differences in the wage rates of men and women, the effects of pay equity laws, and the source of the Canadian "brain drain."

After studying this chapter, you will be able to:

■ Explain why high-skilled workers earn more, on the average, than low-skilled workers

■ Explain why university and college graduates earn more, on the average, than high school graduates

■ Explain why union workers earn higher wages than nonunion workers

■ Explain why, on the average, men earn more than women

■ Predict the effects of pay equity laws

■ Explain why many well-educated Canadians are moving to the United States to work

Skill Differentials

EVERYONE IS SKILLED BUT THE VALUE THE market places on different types of skills varies a great deal so that differences in skills lead to large differences in earnings. For example, a clerk in a law firm earns less than a tenth of the earnings of the attorney he assists. An operating room assistant earns less than a tenth of the earnings of the surgeon she works with. Differences in skills arise partly from differences in education and partly from differences in on-the-job training. Differences in earnings between workers with varying levels of education and training can be explained by using a model of competitive labour markets. In the real world, there are many different levels and varieties of education and training. To keep our analysis as clear as possible, we'll study a model economy with two different skill levels and two types of labour: high-skilled labour and low-skilled labour. We'll study the demand for and supply of these two types of labour and see why there is a difference in their wages and what determines that difference. Let's begin by looking at the demand for the two types of labour.

The Demand for High-Skilled and Low-Skilled Labour

High-skilled workers can perform a variety of tasks that low-skilled workers would perform badly or perhaps could not even perform at all. Imagine an untrained, inexperienced person performing surgery or piloting an airplane. High-skilled workers have a higher marginal revenue product than do low-skilled workers. As we learned in Chapter 15, a firm's demand for labour curve is the same as the marginal revenue product of labour curve.

Figure 16.1(a) shows the demand curves for high-skilled (D_H) and low-skilled (D_L) labour. At any given level of employment, firms are willing to pay a higher wage rate to a high-skilled worker than to a low-skilled worker. The gap between the two wage rates measures the marginal revenue product of skill—for example, at an employment level of 2,000 hours, firms are willing to pay $12.50 for a high-skilled worker and only $5 for a low-skilled worker, a difference of $7.50 an hour. Thus the marginal revenue product of skill is $7.50 an hour.

The Supply of High-Skilled and Low-Skilled Labour

Skills are costly to acquire. Furthermore, a worker usually pays the cost of acquiring a skill before benefiting from a higher wage. For example, attending college usually leads to a higher income, but the higher income is not earned until after graduation. These facts imply that the acquisition of a skill is an investment. To emphasize the investment nature of acquiring a skill, we call that activity an investment in human capital. **Human capital** is the accumulated skill and knowledge of human beings.

The opportunity cost of acquiring a skill includes actual expenditures on such things as tuition and room and board and also costs in the form of lost or reduced earnings while the skill is being acquired. When a person goes to school full time, that cost is the total earnings forgone. However, some people acquire skills on the job. Such skill acquisition is called on-the-job training. Usually, a worker undergoing on-the-job training is paid a lower wage than one doing a comparable job but not undergoing training. In such a case, the cost of acquiring the skill is the difference between the wage paid to a person not being trained and that paid to a person being trained.

Supply Curves of High-Skilled and Low-Skilled Labour   The position of the supply curve of high-skilled workers reflects the cost of acquiring the skill. Figure 16.1(b) shows two supply curves: one for high-skilled workers and the other for low-skilled workers. The supply curve for high-skilled workers is S_H, and that for low-skilled workers is S_L.

The high-skilled workers' supply curve lies above the low-skilled workers' supply curve. The vertical distance between the two supply curves is the compensation that high-skilled workers require for the cost of acquiring the skill. For example, suppose that the quantity of low-skilled labour supplied is 2,000 hours at a wage rate of $5 an hour. This wage rate compensates the low-skilled workers mainly for their time on the job. Consider next the supply of high-skilled workers. To induce 2,000 hours of high-skilled labour to be supplied, firms must pay a wage rate of $8.50 an hour. This wage rate for high-skilled labour is higher than that for low-skilled labour because high-skilled labour must be compensated not only for the time on the job but also for the time and other costs of acquiring the skill.

FIGURE 16.1

Skill Differentials

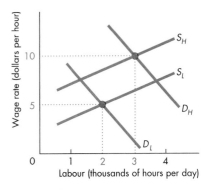

(a) Demand for high-skilled and low-skilled labour

(b) Supply of high-skilled and low-skilled labour

(c) Markets for high-skilled and low-skilled labour

Part (a) illustrates the marginal revenue product of skill. Low-skilled workers have a marginal revenue product that gives rise to the demand curve marked D_L. High-skilled workers have a higher marginal revenue product than low-skilled workers. Therefore the demand curve for high-skilled workers, D_H, lies to the right of D_L. The vertical distance between these two curves is the marginal revenue product of the skill.

Part (b) shows the effects of the cost of acquiring skills on the supply curves of labour. The supply curve for low-

skilled workers is S_L. The supply curve for high-skilled workers is S_H. The vertical distance between these two curves is the required compensation for the cost of acquiring a skill.

Part (c) shows the equilibrium employment and the wage differential. Low-skilled workers earn a wage rate of $5 an hour and 2,000 hours of low-skilled labour are employed. High-skilled workers earn a wage rate of $10 and 3,000 hours of high-skilled labour are employed. The wage rate for high-skilled workers always exceeds that for low-skilled workers.

Wage Rates of High-Skilled and Low-Skilled Labour

To work out the wage rates of high-skilled and low-skilled labour, we have to bring together the effects of skill on the demand and supply of labour.

Figure 16.1(c) shows the demand curves and the supply curves for high-skilled and low-skilled labour. These curves are exactly the same as those plotted in parts (a) and (b). Equilibrium occurs in the market for low-skilled labour where the supply and demand curves for low-skilled labour intersect. The equilibrium wage rate is $5 an hour, and the quantity of low-skilled labour employed is 2,000 hours. Equilibrium in the market for high-skilled workers occurs where the supply and demand curves for high-skilled workers intersect. The equilibrium wage rate is $10 an hour, and the quantity of high-skilled labour employed is 3,000 hours.

As you can see in part (c), the equilibrium wage rate of high-skilled labour is higher than that of low-skilled labour. This outcome occurs for two reasons: First, high-skilled labour has a higher marginal revenue product than low-skilled labour, so at a given wage rate, the quantity of high-skilled labour demanded exceeds that of low-skilled labour. Second, skills are costly to acquire, so at a given wage rate, the quantity of high-skilled labour supplied is less than that of low-skilled labour. The wage differential (in this case, $5 an hour) depends on both the marginal revenue product of the skill and the cost of acquiring it. The higher the marginal revenue product of the skill, the larger is the vertical distance between the demand curves. The more costly it is to acquire a skill, the larger is the vertical distance between the supply curves. The higher the marginal revenue product of the skill and the more costly it is to acquire, the larger is the wage differential between high-skilled and low-skilled workers.

Do Education and Training Pay?

There are large and persistent differences in earnings based on the degree of education and training. An indication of these differences is visible every day in the jobs columns of the newspaper. Take a few minutes and look at today's paper and see if you can find some examples. You'll almost certainly see lots of jobs for programmers and information systems managers that offer incomes greater than $50,000 a year. Look in *The Economist* weekly newsmagazine and you'll see jobs with income tags of $100,000 and more. All of these jobs seek applicants who have completed a university education in a relevant field and often seek relevant previous work experience.

Then look in the local newspaper at the types of jobs on offer for people with no special educational qualifications and limited work experience. You'll see such jobs on offer for incomes not much higher than the minimum wage.

Although the snapshot that you can get from newspaper advertisements is a useful one, it doesn't tell you directly about the lifetime experience of people with different levels of education. To obtain this information, we need to look at the kind of data that Statistics Canada collects. Figure 16.2 shows some of this data. The figure highlights two important sources of earnings differences:

1. Education
2. Work experience

The higher the level of education, other things remaining the same, the higher are a person's earnings. Work experience and the amount of on-the-job training a person has received is strongly correlated with age. Thus as a person gets older, up to middle age, earnings increase.

We can see from Fig. 16.2 that going through high school, postsecondary, and university education leads to higher incomes. But do they pay in the sense of yielding a higher income that compensates for the cost of education and for the delay in the start of earnings? For most people, postsecondary education does indeed pay. Rates of return have been estimated to be in the range of 5 to 10 percent after allowing for inflation, which suggests that a postsecondary degree is a better investment than almost any other that a person can undertake.

Education is an important source of earnings differences. But there are others. We next see how labour unions affect wages and why union wages tend to exceed nonunion wages.

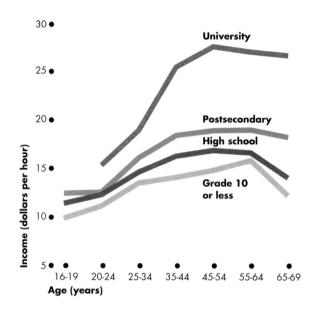

FIGURE 16.2

Education and Earnings

The figure shows the average earnings of employees at various ages and with varying levels of education. Earnings increase with length of education and also with age but only up to the mid-50s. Beyond that age, earnings decrease. These differences show the importance of experience and education in influencing skill differentials.

Source: Statistics Canada, *Survey of Consumer Finances*, 1997.*
*This analysis is based on a Statistics Canada microdata tape. All the computations on these microdata were performed by Audra J. Bowlus at the University of Western Ontario. The responsibility for the use and interpretation of these data is entirely that of the authors.

REVIEW QUIZ

- Why is the demand for high-skilled labour greater than the demand for low-skilled labour?
- Why is the supply of high-skilled labour less than the supply of low-skilled labour?
- How does education influence wage rates? Does education pay?
- How does work experience influence wage rates?

Let's now look at the influence of labour unions on the labour market.

Union–Nonunion Wage Differentials

WAGE DIFFERENTIALS CAN ARISE FROM monopoly power in the labour market. Just as a monopoly producer can restrict output and raise price, so a monopoly owner of a resource can restrict supply and raise the price of the resource.

The main source of monopoly power in the labour market is the labour union. A **labour union** is an organized group of workers whose purpose it is to increase the wage rate and influence other job conditions for its members. The union seeks to restrict competition and, as a result, increases the price at which labour is traded.

There are two main types of union: craft unions and industrial unions. A **craft union** is a group of workers who have a similar range of skills but work for many different firms in many different industries and regions. An example of a craft union is Glass, Molders, Pottery, Plastics and Allied Workers International Union. An **industrial union** is a group of workers who have a variety of skills and job types but work for the same firm or industry. The United Steelworkers Union and the United Paperworkers Union are examples of industrial unions.

Most unions are members of the Canadian Labour Congress (CLC). The CLC was created in 1956 when two labour organizations combined: the Labour Council of Canada (TLC), which was founded in 1883 to organize craft unions, and the Canadian Congress of Labour (CCL), founded in 1940 to organize industrial unions. The CLC often acts as the national voice of organized labour in the media and in the political arena.

Unions vary enormously in size. Craft unions are the smallest and industrial unions are the biggest. Figure 16.3 shows the six largest unions in Canada as measured by the number of members. Union strength peaked in1983 when 40 percent of the work force belonged to unions. That percentage has fallen slightly since then. Changes in union membership, however, have been uneven in the past several decades. Some unions have declined dramatically while others, especially those in the government sector, have increased in strength.

In some firms or plants where a union operates, all workers are required to be members of the union. Such a situation is known as a *closed shop*. A closed shop is an arrangement in which only union mem-

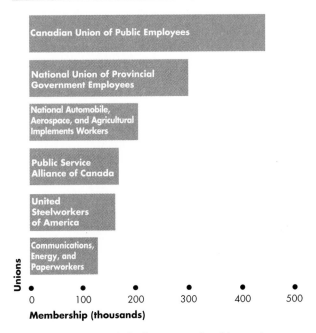

FIGURE 16.3

Unions with the Largest Membership

The labour unions with the largest membership are the two big public service unions. Together, they have almost 1 million members.

Source: Bureau of Labour Organization, *Directory of Labour Organizations*.

bers may be employed by a firm. There are other firms and plants in which a union negotiates the terms and conditions of employment but in which workers are not required to join the union. Nevertheless, in such situations, an arrangement called the Rand formula applies. The **Rand formula** is a rule (set out by Mr. Justice Ivan Rand in 1945) that makes it compulsory for all workers to contribute funds to the union whether or not they belong to the union.

Unions negotiate with employers or their representatives in a process called **collective bargaining**. The main weapons available to the union and the employer in collective bargaining are the strike and the lockout. A *strike* is a group decision to refuse to work under prevailing conditions. A *lockout* is a firm's refusal to operate its plant and employ its workers.

Each party uses the threat of a strike or a lockout to try to get an agreement in its own favour. Sometimes when the two parties in the collective bargaining process cannot agree on the wage rate or other conditions of employment, they agree to submit their disagreement to binding arbitration. *Binding arbitration* is a process in which a third party—an arbitrator—determines the wage rate and other employment conditions on behalf of the negotiating parties.

Although they are not labour unions in a legal sense, professional associations act in ways similar to labour unions. A *professional association* is an organized group of professional workers such as lawyers, dentists, or physicians (an example of which is the Ontario Medical Association—OMA).

The source of all monopoly power is a barrier to entry. Without a barrier to entry, even when there is only one supplier of a resource (or good or service) that supplier does not have monopoly power. Many professional associations know the importance of barriers to entry and they control entry into their professions by a system of licensing. Usually, the licensing takes the form of ensuring that members of the professional association meet some minimum standards of competence. This aspect of licensing brings clear benefits to consumers. But it also brings benefits to the members of the association by raising their level of income above what a competitive market would deliver.

Union's Objectives and Constraints

A union has three broad objectives that it strives to achieve for its members:

1. To increase compensation
2. To improve working conditions
3. To expand job opportunities

Each of these objectives contains a series of more detailed goals. For example, in seeking to increase members' compensation, a union operates on a variety of fronts: wage rates, fringe benefits, retirement pay, and such things as vacation allowances. In seeking to improve working conditions, a union is concerned with occupational health and safety as well as the environmental quality of the workplace. In seeking to expand job opportunities, a union tries to get greater job security for existing union members and to find ways of creating additional jobs for them.

A union's ability to pursue its objectives is restricted by two sets of constraints—one on the supply side of the labour market and the other on the demand side. On the supply side, the union's activities are limited by how well it can restrict nonunion workers from offering their labour in the same market as the union labour. The larger the fraction of the work force controlled by the union, the more effective the union can be in this regard. It is difficult for a union to operate in a market in which there is an abundant supply of willing nonunion labour. For example, the market for part-time checkout clerks is very tough for a union to organize because of the enormous rate of turnover of participants in that market. At the other extreme, unions in the construction industry can better pursue their goals because they can influence the number of people who can obtain skills as electricians, plasterers, and carpenters. The professional associations of dentists and physicians are best able to restrict the supply of dentists and physicians. These groups control the number of qualified workers by controlling either the examinations that new entrants must pass or entrance into professional degree programs.

On the demand side of the labour market, the union faces a tradeoff that arises from firms' profit-maximizing decisions. Because labour demand curves slope downward, anything a union does that increases the wage rate or other employment costs decreases the quantity of labour demanded.

Despite the difficulties they face, unions do operate in competitive labour markets. Let's see how they do so.

Unions in a Competitive Labour Market

When a union operates in an otherwise competitive labour market, it seeks to increase wages and other compensation and to limit employment reductions by increasing demand for the labour of its members. That is, the union tries to take actions that shift the demand curve for its members' labour rightward.

Figure 16.4 illustrates a competitive labour market that a union enters. The demand curve is D_C, and the supply curve is S_C. Before the union enters the market, the wage rate is $7 an hour and 100 hours of labour are employed.

Now suppose that a union is formed to organize the workers in this market. The union can attempt to increase the wage rate in this market in two ways. It

A Union in a Competitive Labour Market ◈

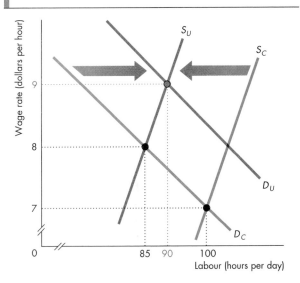

In a competitive labour market, the demand curve is D_C and the supply curve is S_C. Competitive equilibrium occurs at a wage rate of $7 an hour with 100 hours employed. By restricting employment below the competitive level, the union shifts the supply of labour to S_U. If the union can do no more than that, the wage rate will increase to $8 an hour, but employment will decrease to 85 hours. If the union can increase the demand for labour (by increasing the demand for the good produced by union members or by raising the price of substitute labour) and shift the demand curve to D_U, then it can increase the wage rate still higher, to $9 an hour, and achieve employment of 90 hours.

can try to restrict the supply of labour or it can try to stimulate the demand for labour. First, look at what happens if the union has sufficient control over the supply of labour to be able to artificially restrict that supply below its competitive level—to S_U. If that is all the union is able to do, employment falls to 85 hours of labour and the wage rate rises to $8 an hour. The union simply picks its preferred position along the demand curve that defines the tradeoff it faces between employment and the wage rate.

You can see that if the union can only restrict the supply of labour, it raises the wage rate but decreases the number of jobs available. Because of this outcome unions try to increase the demand for labour and

shift the demand curve rightward. Let's see what they might do to achieve this outcome.

How Unions Try to Change the Demand for Labour

Unless a union can take actions that change the demand for the labour that it represents, it has to accept the fact that a higher wage rate can be obtained only at the price of lower employment.

The union tries to operate on the demand for labour in two ways. First, it tries to make the demand for union labour less elastic. Second, it tries to increase the demand for union labour. Making the demand for labour less elastic does not eliminate the tradeoff between employment and wages. But it does make the tradeoff less unfavourable. If a union can make the demand for labour less elastic, it can increase the wage rate at a lower cost in terms of lost employment opportunities. But if the union can increase the demand for labour, it might even be able to increase both the wage rate and the employment opportunities of its members.

Some methods used by unions to change the demand for the labour of its members are to:

- Increase the marginal product of union members
- Encourage import restrictions
- Support minimum wage laws
- Support immigration restrictions
- Increase demand for the good produced

Unions try to increase the marginal product of their members, which in turn increases the demand for their labour, by organizing and sponsoring training schemes, by encouraging apprenticeship and other on-the-job training activities, and by professional certification.

One of the best examples of import restrictions is the support by the Canadian Auto Workers Union (CAW) for import restrictions on foreign cars.

Unions support minimum wage laws to increase the cost of employing low-skilled labour. An increase in the wage rate of low-skilled labour leads to a decrease in the quantity demanded of low-skilled labour and to an increase in demand for high-skilled union labour, a substitute for low-skilled labour.

Restrictive immigration laws decrease the supply and increase the wage rate of low-skilled workers. As a result, the demand for high-skilled union labour increases.

Because the demand for labour is a derived demand, an increase in the demand for the good produced increases the demand for union labour. The best examples of attempts by unions in this activity are in the textile and auto industries. The garment workers' union urges us to buy union-made clothes, and the CAW asks us to buy only North American cars made by union workers.

Figure 16.4 illustrates the effects of an increase in the demand for the labour of a union's members. If the union can also take steps that increase the demand for labour to D_U, it can achieve an even bigger increase in the wage rate with a smaller fall in employment. By maintaining the restricted labour supply at S_U, the union increases the wage rate to $9 an hour and achieves an employment level of 90 hours of labour.

Because a union restricts the supply of labour in the market in which it operates, its actions increase the supply of labour in nonunion markets. Workers who can't get union jobs must look elsewhere for work. This increase in supply in nonunion markets lowers the wage rate in those markets and further widens the union–nonunion differential.

The Scale of Union–Nonunion Wage Differentials

We have seen that unions can influence the wage rate by restricting the supply of labour and increasing the demand for labour. How much of a difference to wage rates do unions make in practice?

Union wage rates are, on the average, 30 percent higher than nonunion wage rates. In mining and financial services, union and nonunion wages are similar. In services, manufacturing, and transportation, the differential is between 11 and 19 percent. In wholesale and retail trades, the differential is 28 percent, and in construction it is 65 percent.

But these union–nonunion wage differentials don't give a true measure of the effects of unions. In some industries, union wages are higher than nonunion wages because union members do jobs that involve greater skill. Even without a union, those workers receive a higher wage. To calculate the effects of unions, we have to examine the wages of unionized and nonunionized workers who do nearly identical work. The evidence suggests that after allowing for skill differentials, the union–nonunion wage differential lies between 10 percent and 25 percent. For example, airline pilots who belong to the Air Line

Pilots' Union earn about 25 percent more than nonunion pilots with the same level of skill.

Let's now turn to the case in which employers have considerable influence in the labour market.

Monopsony

A **monopsony** is a market in which there is a single buyer. This market type is unusual but it does exist. With the growth of large-scale production over the last century, large manufacturing plants such as coal mines, steel and textile mills, and car manufacturers became the major employer in some regions, and in some places a single firm employed almost all the labour. Today, in Canada, the provincial health insurance plans are the major employer of physicians and other health-care professionals. These employers have monopsony power.

In monopsony, the employer determines the wage rate and pays the lowest wage at which it can attract the labour it plans to hire. A monopsony makes a bigger profit than a group of firms that compete with each other for their labour. Let's find out how they achieve this outcome.

Like all firms, a monopsony has a downward-sloping marginal revenue product curve, which is *MRP* in Fig. 16.5. This curve tells us the extra revenue the monopsony receives by selling the output produced by an extra hour of labour. The supply of labour curve is *S*. This curve tells us how many hours are supplied at each wage rate. It also tells us the minimum wage for which a given quantity of labour is willing to work.

A monopsony recognizes that to hire more labour, it must pay a higher wage rate; equivalently, by hiring less labour, it can pay a lower wage rate. Because a monopsony controls the wage rate, the marginal cost of labour exceeds the wage rate. The marginal cost of labour is shown by the curve *MCL*. The relationship between the marginal cost of labour curve and the supply curve is similar to the relationship between the marginal cost and average cost curves that you studied in Chapter 11. The supply curve is like the average cost of labour curve. In Fig. 16.5, the firm can hire 49 hours of labour for a wage rate of just below $4.90 an hour. The firm's total labour cost is $240. But suppose that the firm hires 50 hours of labour. It can hire the 50th hour of labour for $5 an hour. The total cost of labour is now $250 an hour. So, hiring the 50th hour of labour increases the cost of labour from $240 to $250,

A Monopsony Labour Market

A monopsony is a market structure in which there is a single buyer. A monopsony in the labour market has marginal revenue product curve MRP and faces a labour supply curve S. The marginal cost of labour curve is MCL. Making the marginal cost of labour equal to marginal revenue product maximizes profit. The monopsony hires 50 hours of labour and pays the lowest wage for which that labour will work, which is $5 an hour.

which is a $10 increase. The marginal cost of labour is $10 an hour. The curve MCL shows the $10 marginal cost of hiring the 50th hour of labour.

To calculate the profit-maximizing quantity of labour to hire, the firm sets the marginal cost of labour equal to the marginal revenue product of labour. That is, the firm wants the cost of the last worker hired to equal the extra total revenue brought in. In Fig. 16.5, this outcome occurs when the monopsony employs 50 hours of labour. What is the wage rate that the monopsony pays? To hire 50 hours of labour, the firm must pay $5 an hour, as shown by the supply of labour curve. So each worker is paid $5 an hour. But the marginal revenue product of labour is $10 an hour, which means that the firm makes an economic profit of $5 on the last hour of labour that it hires. Compare this outcome with that in a competitive labour market. If the labour market shown in Fig. 16.5 were competitive, equilibrium would occur at the point of intersection of the demand curve and the supply curve. The wage rate would be $7.50 an hour and 75 hours of labour a day would be

employed. So, compared with a competitive labour market, a monopsony decreases both the wage rate and the level of employment.

The ability of a monopsony to lower the wage rate and employment level and make an economic profit depends on the elasticity of labour supply. The more elastic the supply of labour, the less opportunity a monopsony has to cut the wage rate and employment and make an economic profit.

Monopsony Tendencies   Today, monopsony is rare. Workers can commute long distances to a job, so most people have more than one potential employer. But firms that are dominant employers in isolated communities do face an upward-sloping supply of labour curve and so have a marginal cost of labour that exceeds the wage rate. But in such situations, there is also, usually, a union. Let's see how unions and monopsonies interact.

Monopsony and Unions   When we studied monopoly in Chapter 13, we discovered that a single seller in a market is able to determine the price in that market. We have just studied monopsony—a market with a single buyer—and discovered that in such a market, the buyer is able to determine the price. Suppose that a union starts to operate in a monopsony labour market. A union is like a monopoly. It controls the supply of labour and acts like a single seller of labour. If the union (monopoly seller) faces a monopsony buyer, the situation is one of **bilateral monopoly**. In bilateral monopoly, the wage rate is determined by bargaining between the two sides. Let's study the bargaining process.

In Fig. 16.5, if the monopsony is free to determine the wage rate and the level of employment, it hires 50 hours of labour for a wage rate of $5 an hour. But suppose that a union represents the workers and can, if necessary, call a strike. Also suppose that the union agrees to maintain employment at 50 hours but seeks the highest wage rate the employer can be forced to pay. That wage rate is $10 an hour. That is, the wage rate equals the marginal revenue product of labour. It is unlikely that the union will get the wage rate up to $10 an hour. But it is also unlikely that the firm will keep the wage rate down to $5 an hour. The monopsony firm and the union bargain over the wage rate, and the result is an outcome between $10 an hour (the maximum that the union can achieve) and $5 an hour (the minimum that the firm can achieve).

The actual outcome of the bargaining depends on the costs that each party can inflict on the other as a result of a failure to agree on the wage rate. The firm can shut down the plant and lock out its workers, and the workers can shut down the plant by striking. Each party knows the other's strength and knows what it will lose if it does not agree to the other's demands. If the two parties are equally strong and they realize it, they will split the difference and agree to a wage rate of $7.50 an hour. If one party is stronger than the other—and both parties know that—the agreed wage will favour the stronger party. Usually, an agreement is reached without a strike or a lockout. The threat—knowledge that such an event can occur—is usually enough to bring the bargaining parties to an agreement. But when a strike or lockout does occur, it is often because one party has misjudged the costs each party can inflict on the other.

Minimum wage laws have interesting effects in monopsony labour markets. Let's study these effects.

Monopsony and the Minimum Wage

In a competitive labour market, a minimum wage that exceeds the equilibrium wage decreases employment (see Chapter 7, pp. 135–136). In a monopsony labour market, a minimum wage can *increase* both the wage rate and employment. Let's see how.

Figure 16.6 shows a monopsony labour market in which the wage rate is $5 an hour and 50 hours of labour are employed. A minimum wage law is passed that requires employers to pay at least $7.50 an hour. The monopsony in Fig. 16.6 now faces a perfectly elastic supply of labour at $7.50 an hour up to 75 hours. Above 75 hours, a wage that exceeds $7.50 an hour must be paid to hire additional hours of labour. Because the wage rate is a fixed $7.50 an hour up to 75 hours, the marginal cost of labour is also constant at $7.50 an hour up to 75 hours. Beyond 75 hours, the marginal cost of labour rises above $7.50 an hour. To maximize profit, the monopsony sets the marginal cost of labour equal to its marginal revenue product. That is, the monopsony hires 75 hours of labour at $7.50 an hour. The minimum wage law has made the supply of labour perfectly elastic and made the marginal cost of labour the same as the wage rate up to 75 hours. The law has not affected the supply of labour curve or the marginal cost of labour at employment levels above 75 hours. The minimum wage law has succeeded in raising the wage rate by $2.50 an hour and increasing the amount of labour employed by 25 hours.

FIGURE 16.6

Minimum Wage in Monopsony

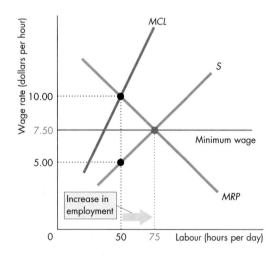

In a monopsony labour market, the wage rate is $5 an hour and 50 hours are hired. If a minimum wage law increases the wage rate to $7.50 an hour, employment increases to 75 hours.

REVIEW QUIZ

■ What are the main methods that labour unions use to increase the wage rates of their members above the levels of nonunion wage rates?

■ What are the main methods that professional associations use to increase the wage rates of their members above competitive market levels?

■ What is a monopsony and why is a monopsony able to pay a lower wage rate than a competitive firm?

■ What is the effect of a minimum wage in monopsony? What is the effect of a minimum wage in a competitive labour market? Why are the two effects different?

You now understand two sources of wage differentials: skill differentials and the actions of labour unions. These two sources of wage differentials are easy to see and to analyse. The third source of wage differentials, sex, is harder to explain but it is the most sensitive of the sources of income differentials.

Wage Differentials Between the Sexes

THE OBJECTIVE OF THIS SECTION IS TO SHOW YOU how to use economic analysis to address a controversial and emotionally charged issue: persistent earnings differentials between the sexes. Figure 16.7 gives a snapshot of these differences in 1991. For both part-time and full-time workers, Canadian women, on the average, earned 61.5 percent of Canadian men's earnings. For full-time workers, the earnings of women were 69.6 percent of men's earnings.

Why does this earnings differential exist? Does it arise because there is discrimination against women, or is there some other explanation? This controversial question generates an enormous amount of passion.

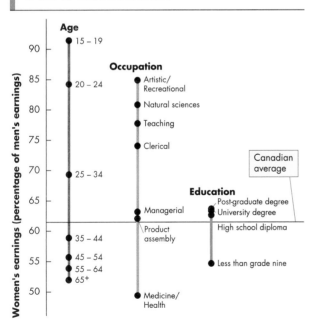

FIGURE 16.7

Sex Differentials

Women on the average earn about 61.5 percent of the amount earned by men. Much of this difference is accounted for by age—the incomes of younger women are much closer to those of men than are those of older women. The difference also arises from the fact that women predominate in lower-paid jobs. Education also plays a role.

Source: Statistics Canada, *Women in the Workplace*: 1993.

It is not our intention to make you angry, but that might happen as an unintended consequence of this discussion.

We are going to examine four possible explanations for earnings differences:

■ Job types
■ Discrimination
■ Differences in human capital
■ Differences in the degree of specialization

Job Types

Some of the difference in men's and women's wages arises from the fact that men and women do different jobs and, for the most part, men's jobs are better paid than women's jobs. But there are increasing numbers of women entering areas that were traditionally the preserve of men. This trend is particularly clear in professions such as architecture, medicine, economics, law, accounting, and pharmacology. The percentage of total enrolments in university courses in these subjects for women has increased from less than 20 percent in 1970 to approaching, and in some cases exceeding, 50 percent today. Women are also increasingly seen as bus drivers, police officers, and construction workers, all jobs that traditionally were done mainly by men.

But there are many situations in which women earn less than men, even when they do essentially the same job. One possible reason is that women are discriminated against. Let's see how discrimination might affect wage rates.

Discrimination

To see how discrimination can affect wage rates, let's look at an example—the market for investment advisors. Suppose that there are two groups of investment advisers who are identical in their skills at picking good investments. One group consists of females and the other of males. Figure 16.8 shows the supply curves of females, S_F, (in part a) and of males, S_M (in part b). The marginal revenue product of investment advisors, as shown by the two curves labelled *MRP* in parts (a) and (b), is the same for both groups.

If everyone is free of prejudice about sex, the market determines a wage rate of $40,000 a year for all investment advisors. But if the customers of investment houses are prejudiced against women, this prejudice is reflected in wage rates and employment.

FIGURE 16.8
Discrimination

(a) Women

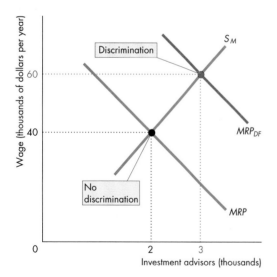

(b) Men

With no discrimination, the wage rate is $40,000 a year and 2,000 of each group are hired. With discrimination against women, the marginal revenue product curve in part (a) is MRP_{DA} and in part (b) MRP_{DF}. The wage rate for women falls to $20,000 a year, and only 1,000 are employed. The wage rate for men rises to $60,000 a year, and 3,000 are employed.

Suppose that the marginal revenue product of the females, when discriminated against, is MRP_{DA}, where DA stands for "discriminated against." Suppose that the marginal revenue product for males, the group discriminated in favour of, is MRP_{DF}, where DF stands for "discriminated in favour of." With these marginal revenue product curves, females earn $20,000 a year, and only 1,000 will work as investment advisors. Males earn $60,000 a year, and 3,000 of them will work as investment advisors.

Economists disagree about whether prejudice actually causes wage differentials, and one line of reasoning suggests that it does not. In the example you've just studied, customers who buy from men pay a higher service charge for investment advice than the customers who buy from women. This price difference acts as an incentive to encourage people who are prejudiced to buy from the people against whom they are prejudiced. This force could be so strong as to eliminate the effects of discrimination altogether. Suppose, as is true in manufacturing, that a firm's customers never meet its workers. If such a firm discriminates against women, it cannot compete with firms who hire women because its costs are higher than those of the non-prejudiced firms. So only those firms that do not discriminate survive in a competitive industry.

Let's now turn to the third source of wage differentials: human capital.

Differences in Human Capital

The more human capital a person possesses, the more that person earns, other things remaining the same. We measure human capital by using three indicators:

1. Years of schooling
2. Years of work experience
3. Number of job interruptions

In recent years, the median number of years in school for both sexes is almost equal at about 12 years.

Years of work experience and job interruptions are interrelated. For people of a given age and given amount of schooling, a person who has had fewer job interruptions has usually had more years of work experience. But interruptions to a career disrupt and reduce the effectiveness of job experience, slow down the accumulation of human capital, and even sometimes result in the depreciation of human capital through its lack of use. Historically and today, job interruptions are more serious for women than for men. Traditionally, women's careers have been interrupted for bearing and rearing children. This factor is a possible source of lower wages, on the average, for women. But just as education differences are virtually disappearing, so career interruptions for women are becoming less common. Maternity leave and day-care facilities are providing an increasing number of women with uninterrupted employment that makes their human capital accumulation more similar to that of men.

Thus it seems that human capital differences possibly can account for earnings differentials between women and men in the past and for some of the differentials that still remain. The trends, however, suggest that wage differentials from this source will eventually disappear.

There is one final source of wage differences that is likely to affect women's incomes adversely: the relative degree of specialization of women and men.

Differences in the Degree of Specialization

Families must choose how to allocate the time of their members between working for a wage and doing jobs in the home, such as cooking, cleaning, shopping, organizing vacations and, most importantly in terms of the time and commitment that it takes, in the bearing and rearing of children.

Let's look at the choices of Bob and Sue. Bob and Sue are both 35 years old. They both have masters degrees, Bob in programming and Sue in journalism. Both of them developed successful careers in their chosen fields and both earned about the same income until they decided to have children. Bob and Sue now have two pre-school children and they have made some tough choices.

To make these choices, they began by setting out the alternatives. As Bob and Sue saw things, they could organize their lives as parents in any of the following ways:

1. Bob specializes in earning an income and Sue diversifies by working shorter hours at her job and taking time off as needed to care for the children and the home.
2. Sue specializes in earning an income and Bob diversifies by working shorter hours at his job and taking time off as needed to care for the children and the home.

3. Both of them diversify between earning an income and working shorter hours, taking time off as needed to care for the children and the home and sharing household chores in the evenings and at the weekends.

The time allocation they choose depends on their preferences and on the earning potential of each of them. The choice of an increasing number of households is the third one. Each person diversifies between earning an income and doing some home chores.

But in most households, Bob specializes in earning an income and Sue diversifies between earning an income and taking care of the home. It seems likely that with this allocation, Bob will earn more than Sue. If Sue devotes time and effort to ensuring Bob's mental and physical well-being, the quality of Bob's market labour will be higher than if he were diversified. If the roles were reversed, Sue would be able to supply market labour that earns more than Bob.

To test whether the degree of specialization accounts for wage differentials between the sexes, economists have studied two groups: "never married" men and "never married" women. The available evidence suggests that, on the average, when they have the same amount of human capital—measured by years of schooling, work experience, and career interruptions—the wage rates of these two groups are not significantly different.

REVIEW QUIZ

- How important are differences in the types of jobs that men and women do in influencing their relative earnings?
- How important do you think discrimination is in influencing their relative earnings?
- How important are differences in the human capital of men and women in influencing their relative earnings?
- How might differences in the degree of specialization of men and women result in men earning higher wage rates than women?

Pay equity laws are designed to reduce the wage differences between the sexes. Do these laws work?

Pay Equity Laws

THE FEDERAL GOVERNMENT AND ALL PROVINCIAL governments have passed laws that require *equal pay for equal work without discrimination on the basis of sex*. Increasingly, attempts are being made to find ways of comparing jobs that are essentially different but require, on some criteria, similar degrees of skill. Such comparisons lead to a broader concept than "equal pay for equal work"; they call for equal pay for comparable work. Paying the same wage for different jobs that are judged to be comparable is called **pay equity**.

Advocates of pay equity laws argue that analysing the characteristics of jobs and determining their worth on objective grounds should determine wages. But such a method of determining wage rates does not achieve the objectives sought by supporters of wage equality. Let's see why.

Figure 16.9 shows how pay equity laws work. Part (a) shows the market for oil rig operators and part (b) the market for nurses. The marginal revenue product curves (MRP_R and MRP_N) and the supply curves (S_R and S_N) are shown for each type of labour. Competition generates a wage rate W_R for oil rig operators and W_N for nurses.

Suppose it is decided that these two jobs are comparable and that the courts enforce a wage rate of W_C for both groups. What happens? First, there is a shortage of oil rig operators. Oil rig companies are able to hire only S_R workers at the wage rate W_C. They cut back their production or build more expensive labour-saving oil rigs. Also the number of nurses employed decreases. But this decrease occurs because hospitals demand fewer nurses. At the higher wage W_C, hospitals demand only D_N nurses. The quantity of nurses supplied is S_N, and the difference between S_N and D_N is the number of unemployed nurses looking for jobs. These nurses eventually accept non-nursing jobs (which they don't like as much as nursing jobs), quite likely at a lower rate of pay than that of nurses.

FIGURE 16.9

The Problem with Pay Equity

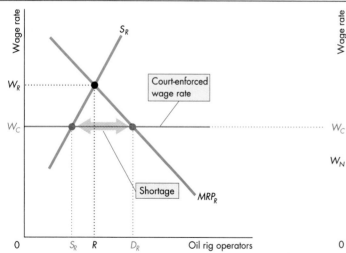

(a) Market for oil rig operators

(b) Market for nurses

Part (a) shows the demand for and supply of oil rig operators, MRP_R and S_R, and part (b) shows the demand for and supply of nurses, MRP_N and S_N. The competitive equilibrium wage rate for oil rig operators is W_R, and that for nurses is W_N. If an evaluation of the two jobs finds that they are comparable and pay equity rules that the wage rate W_C be paid to both types of workers, such a wage creates a shortage of oil rig operators and a surplus of nurses. Oil producers search for labour-saving ways of producing oil (that are more expensive), and nurses search for other jobs (that are less desirable to them and probably are less well paid)

Although pay equity laws can eliminate wage differences, they can only do so by incurring costly unintended consequences. They limit job opportunities and create unemployment among workers whose wage rate they raise. And they make it hard for employers to hire workers whose wage rate is held down. Only in the rare case of a monopsonistic labour market does equalizing wage rates not create permanent surpluses and shortages of skills. In this situation, a pay equity law works in a similar way to a minimum wage law.

Effective Wage Policies

We have now surveyed the major sources of wage differentials. Of the various possible sources of differences in wage rates, one stands out: the level of education. People with postgraduate degrees earn much more than college graduates, who in turn earn much more than high school graduates, who in turn earn more than people who have not completed high school. This source of wage differences is the main one on which an effective policy can operate.

By pursuing the most effective education available in grade school, high school, and college and university, people can equip themselves with human capital that brings significantly higher earnings. But in today's rapidly changing world, education and human capital accumulation must be an ongoing enterprise. The most successful workers are those who are able to repeatedly retool and actively embrace each new technological advance. The least successful are those who get locked into a particular technology and are unable or unwilling to adapt when that technology becomes redundant. So an effective wage policy is one that emphasizes the importance of ongoing education and training.

R E V I E W   Q U I Z

- What is a pay equity law and what does it seek to achieve?
- Do pay equity laws eliminate wage differences? What other effects do pay equity laws have that benefit or harm lower-paid workers?
- What is the most effective policy that can eliminate wage differentials among men and women?

We're now going to turn to the final topic of this chapter: migration.

Migration

SIXTY MILLION PEOPLE, OR ONE PERCENT OF THE world's current population and twice the population of Canada, have migrated from the country in which they were born. We'll study two questions about migration:

- How many people migrate into and out of Canada and where do they come from and go to?
- How does migration affect employment and wage rates of Canadians?

Scale and Origin of Migration Into Canada

About 100,000 immigrants arrive in Canada each year. This number seems large when compared with the population of metropolitan areas like Regina, Saskatchewan (199,000) or Saint John, New Brunswick (129,000). But it represents only one-third of one percent of the Canadian population, or 3 immigrants per 1,000 Canadians.

Figure 16.10 shows some interesting facts about the places of origin of Canadian immigrants. Before 1960, 90 percent of Canadian immigrants came from Europe. Fewer than 5 percent came from the United States and the rest of the American continent (which includes the Caribbean), and only 3 percent came from Asia. But gradually, over the decades, Asia replaced Europe as the main place of origin of new immigrants. By the 1990s, new migrants coming from Europe had fallen to 19 percent of the total and new migrants from Asia had increased to 57 percent of the total. Migration inside the American continent increased between 1960 and the 1970s and then decreased.

Scale and Destination of Migrating Canadians

Despite the enormous amount of publicity that surrounds the idea of a Canadian brain drain, the numbers of Canadians who leave to live in other countries is tiny. The main destination for Canadians is the United States. But the numbers are so small that the U.S. Census Department doesn't report them as a separate category in its summary tables of the origins of U.S. immigrants. The exact number of

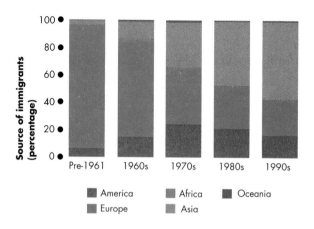

This figure shows that before 1960, almost all Canada's immigrants came from Europe. But over the years, Asia has replaced Europe as the main source of our new immigrants.

Canadians in the United States is not known, but it is fewer that 500,000.

Despite the small numbers, Canadian migration into the United States is significant in a number of highly visible areas. Canadian academics, journalists, movie stars and directors, doctors, musicians, computer scientists, architects, engineers, and business leaders feature prominently among the people who have left Canada over the years. So despite the small numbers involved, Canada does have a "brain drain."

How does migration influence the labour market? Let's study this question.

Immigrants and the Labour Market

Immigration increases the supply of labour. By so doing, it lowers the wage rates of existing workers. At the same time, it decreases the supply of labour and raises wage rates in the country the immigrants are leaving. Figure 16.11 shows these effects in the labour markets of Canada (part a) and Asia (part b). The demand for labour in Canada is LD_{CAN} and in Asia it is LD_A. Before immigration takes place,

25 million workers in Canada earn $15 an hour and 500 million workers in Asia earn $1 an hour. (The numbers are hypothetical.)

If the movement of people between Canada and Asia were entirely unrestricted, Asians would enter Canada, so long as by doing so they could increase their incomes. In this example, the labour force of Canada increases to 150 million and the wage rate falls to $8 an hour. In Asia, the labour force decreases to 375 million and the wage rate rises to $8 an hour. In the world equilibrium, there is no incentive for anyone to migrate between the two regions.

You can apply the analysis in Fig. 16.11 to the situation in Canada and the United States. Suppose the United States is the high-wage country and Canada is the low-wage country. Figure 16.11 can be interpreted as showing what would happen with a free border between Canada and the United States. The wage rate in Canada would rise and that in the United States would fall until wage rates in the two countries became equal.

The economic effects of migration that we've just studied apply not only to the movement of people between nations but also to the movement of people across the regions of a single country.

Again, you can use Fig. 16.11 to analyse migration among regions. Now suppose that Ontario is the high-wage region and Newfoundland is the low-wage region. With a higher wage rate in Toronto than in St. John's, some people decide to migrate from Newfoundland to Ontario. The decrease in the supply of labour in Newfoundland increases the wage rate there and the increase in the supply of labour in Ontario decreases its wage rate.

Does the outcome shown in Fig. 16.11 really occur? And are the effects large ones (like the ones in the example in Fig. 16.11)?

The outcome shown in Fig. 16.11 probably does not occur for at least three reasons. First, people are not willing to vote for an open-border immigration law. Instead, they vote for immigration laws that prevent the free movement of people and so prevent the outcome shown in Fig. 16.11.

Second, immigrants not only add to the supply of labour. They also add to the demand for goods and services and to the supply of capital.

Because immigrants bring a demand for goods and services, firms increase production and the demand for labour increases. This increase in the demand for labour limits the extent to which the wage rate falls.

FIGURE 16.11
Immigration and the Labour Market

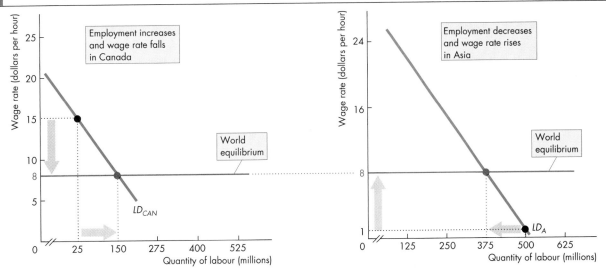

(a) The Canadian labour market

(b) The Asian labour market

Part (a) shows the labour market in Canada. The demand for labour is LD_{CAN} and with 25 million workers, the wage rate is $15 an hour. Part (b) shows the labour market in Asia. The demand for labour is LD_A and with 500 million workers, the wage rate is $1 an hour. With free movement of people between the two regions, people leave Asia and migrate to Canada. Employment increases and the wage rate falls in Canada and employment decreases and the wage rate rises in Asia. The world equilibrium occurs when the wage rate is equal in the two regions, at $8 an hour.

Because some immigrants bring capital with them, the additional capital is invested in businesses and the demand for labour increases.

Third, immigrants are not necessarily *substitutes* for domestic labour. They might be *complements* to it. For example, a shortage of low-skilled labour might cause a firm to close down and lay off its high-skilled workers. Immigration might restore the ability of the firm to operate profitably and enable it to hire again.

For these three reasons, the effects of immigration on wage rates are smaller than those shown in Fig. 16.11 and might even go in the opposite direction.

Immigration is a topic that creates a great deal of passion. It is important when studying its economic effects to stand back from the emotion that often attaches to the topic and try to analyse its effects dispassionately. Much less is known about the effects of immigration than can be supported by the rhetoric about it. And the numbers of people involved are so small that the economic effects are likely to be small.

REVIEW QUIZ

- Where do most of the immigrants into Canada come from? How has the number and place of origin of immigrants changed in recent years?
- How does immigration influence wage rates? Is the effect likely to be small or large?

◆ *Reading Between the Lines* on pages 364–365 returns to the Canadian labour market and looks at some recent data on the influence of education on jobs and earnings. It presents one more piece of evidence that the hard work that you are now doing will reap its reward.

In the next chapter, we're going to examine the distributions of income and wealth that result from the operation of labour markets and the markets for other productive resources.

POLICY WATCH

Investing in Human Capital

THE GLOBE AND MAIL, MARCH 1, 1999

The importance of being educated

BY BRUCE LITTLE

Something happened last year that hasn't occurred through the 1990s: Jobs were created in Canada for people who hadn't graduated from high school.

Just a handful, mind you, fewer than 2,000 across the whole country, ...

This is not a figure that should encourage would-be school drop-outs. If they've learned any math at all, they'll realize that 2,000 net new jobs don't go very far, not when there are about 437,000 people with similar qualifications seeking the kind of work that goes to people with little schooling.

When future scholars look back on the 1990s, they may see it as the decade when the labour market divided once and for all into the educational haves and have-nots. The latest annual figures from Statistics Canada's labour-force survey again drive home the brutal lesson that getting an education and getting a job go hand in hand.

All told, 386,000 jobs were added to the economy in 1998, the best showing of the decade. Of those, 298,000 went to people with either a university degree or some other postsecondary diploma or certificate. They accounted for 51 per cent of the labour force but got 77 per cent of the new jobs.

An additional 86,000 jobs went to people with at least a high-school diploma (and perhaps some post-secondary schooling, though no diploma). That group, comprising 30 per cent of the labour force, got 22 per cent of the new jobs.

The final 2,000 jobs (less than 1 per cent of the new jobs created) were picked up by the 19 per cent of the work force who are unschooled and presumably unskilled. ...

Through economic recession, recovery and expansion, this growing link between education and employment has been one of the overarching trends of the 1990s job market. ...

The very young (those 15 to 24) have a better chance to cope with employers' relentless drive to avoid the ill educated. They can look at the figures, examine the charts and come to the obvious conclusion: Stay in school. ...

Essence of the Story

■ One percent of the new jobs created in 1998 went to people with no high-school diploma.

■ Seventy-seven percent of the new jobs created in 1998 went to people with a university degree or a postsecondary diploma.

■ People with a university degree or postsecondary diploma account for 51 percent of the Canadian labour force and 77 percent of new jobs.

■ People without a high-school diploma account for 19 percent of the Canadian labour force and less than 1 percent of new jobs.

Economic Analysis

- Most people earn their income by working. And the income they earn depends on the demand for and supply of the skills they have to offer.

- The figure illustrates the market for two types of labour: those with a university degree or post-secondary diploma and those without a high-school diploma. We'll identify the groups as H for high education and L for low education.

- The demand for labour with a low education is D_L and the supply of labour with a low education is S_L.

- Equilibrium in the low-education labour market occurs at a wage rate of $13 an hour and a quantity of 3 million people employed (19 percent of the labour force).

- People with university degrees earn more than people with no high-school diploma for two reasons: Their marginal productivity is higher, so the demand for their labour is greater. And their training is costly so at a given wage rate, they are willing to supply less of their labour than are people without a high-school diploma.

- The figure shows the demand curve for high-education labour, D_H, is to the right of the demand curve for low-education labour, D_L.

- The vertical distance between the two demand curves is the marginal revenue product of the extra skills that university and postsecondary graduates possess.

- The supply of high-education labour is less than the supply of low-education labour.

- Education costs time and other resources, and to obtain the supply curve of high-education labour these costs must be added to the wage rate at which a low-education person is willing to work.

- In the figure, the supply curve of high-education labour, S_H, is to the left of the supply curve of low-education labour, S_L.

- The vertical distance between the two supply curves is the opportunity cost of education (converted to a rate per hour of work.)

- Equilibrium in the high-education labour market occurs at a wage rate of $30 an hour and a quantity of 8 million people employed (51 percent of the labour force).

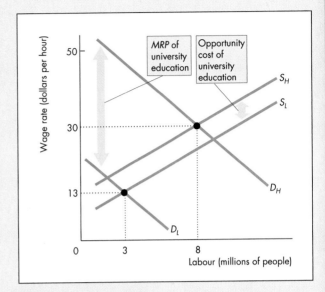

- Despite the fact that the supply of high-education labour is less than the supply of low-education labour, the productivity differential between the two types of labour is so large that the demand for and equilibrium quantity of high-education labour exceeds that of low-education labour.

You're The Voter

- Does the big payoff from education mean that the government should spend more on education?

- Or does it mean that because education leads to a higher income, the government should pay less for education and leave people to make their own choices based on likely personal payoff?

- Would you vote for more education dollars? Or would you vote for fewer education dollars and lower taxes through deductions for educational expenses?

S U M M A R Y

Key Points

Skill Differentials (pp. 348–350)

▪ Skill differentials arise from differences in marginal revenue products and because skills are costly to acquire.

▪ Wage rates of high-skilled and low-skilled labour are determined by demand and supply in the two labour markets.

Union–Nonunion Wage Differentials (pp. 351–356)

▪ Labour unions influence wages by controlling the supply of labour.

▪ In competitive labour markets, unions obtain higher wage rates only at the expense of lower employment but they try to influence the demand for labour.

▪ In a monopsony, a union can increase the wage rate without sacrificing employment.

▪ Bilateral monopoly occurs when a union confronts a single buyer of labour. The wage rate is determined by bargaining between the two parties.

▪ Union workers earn 10 to 25 percent more than comparable nonunion workers.

Wage Differentials Between the Sexes (pp. 357–359)

▪ Wage differentials between men and women arise from differences in types of jobs, discrimination, differences in human capital, and differences in degree of specialization.

▪ Well-paid jobs are more likely to be held by men than by women. But discrimination is hard to measure objectively.

▪ Historically, men have had more human capital than women, but human capital differences arising from schooling differences have been falling and have almost been eliminated.

▪ Differentials based on work experience have kept women's pay below that for men because women's careers have traditionally been interrupted more frequently than those of men. This difference is smaller today than in the past.

▪ Differentials arising from different degrees of specialization are probably important and might persist. Men have traditionally been more specialized in market activity, on the average, than women.

Pay Equity Laws (pp. 360–361)

▪ Pay equity laws determine wage rates by using objective characteristics rather than what the market will pay to assess the value of different types of jobs.

▪ Determining wage rates through pay equity will result in a decrease in the number of people employed in jobs on which the market places a lower value and a shortage of workers that the market values more highly.

Migration (pp. 361–363)

▪ About 100,000 people a year migrate into Canada and increasingly they come from Asia. Few Canadians leave, and most of those who do so earn high incomes in the United States.

▪ Immigration probably lowers wage rates only slightly.

Key Figures ◆

Key Terms

PROBLEMS

*1. The demand for and supply of low-skilled labour are given by the following figure:

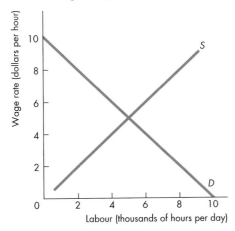

Workers can be trained—can obtain a skill—and their marginal productivity doubles. (The marginal product at each employment level is twice the marginal product of a low-skilled worker.) But the cost of acquiring the skill adds $2 an hour to the wage that must be offered to attract high-skilled labour. What is:
a. The wage rate of low-skilled labour?
b. The quantity of low-skilled labour employed?
c. The wage rate of high-skilled labour?
d. The quantity of high-skilled labour employed?

2. The demand for and supply of low-skilled labour are given by the following figure:

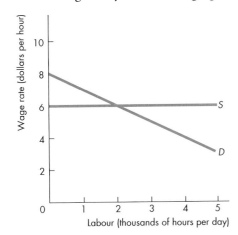

Workers can be trained—can obtain a skill—and their marginal productivity increases by $5 an hour. (The marginal product at each employment level is $5 greater than that of a low-skilled worker.) The cost of acquiring the skill adds $3 an hour to the wage that must be offered to attract high-skilled labour. What is:
a. The wage rate of low-skilled labour?
b. The quantity of low-skilled labour employed?
c. The wage rate of high-skilled labour?
d. The quantity of high-skilled labour employed?
e. Why does the wage rate increase by exactly the cost of acquiring the skill?

*3. Suppose in problem 1 that high-skilled workers become unionized and the union restricts the amount of high-skilled labour to 5,000 hours. What is:
a. The wage rate of high-skilled workers?
b. The wage differential between low- and high-skilled workers?

4. Suppose in problem 2 that high-skilled workers become unionized and the union restricts the amount of high-skilled labour to 2,000 hours. What is:
a. The wage rate of high-skilled workers?
b. The wage differential between low- and high-skilled workers?

*5. If in problem 1, the government introduces a minimum wage rate of $6 an hour for low-skilled workers
a. What is the wage rate paid to low-skilled workers?
b. How many hours of low-skilled labour gets hired each day?

6. If in problem 2, the government introduces a minimum wage rate of $8 an hour for low-skilled workers
a. What is the wage rate paid to low-skilled workers?
b. How many hours of low-skilled labour gets hired each day?

*7. A monopsony gold mining firm operates in an isolated part of the Amazon basin. The following table shows the labour supply schedule (columns 1 and 2) and the firm's total product schedule (columns 2 and 3). The price of gold is $1.40 per grain.

Wage rate (dollars per day)	Workers (number per day)	Quantity of gold produced (grains per day)
5	0	0
6	1	10
7	2	25
8	3	45
9	4	60
10	5	70
11	6	75

   a. What wage rate does the company pay?
   b. How many workers does the gold mine hire?
   c. What is the marginal revenue product at the quantity of labour employed?

8. A monopsony logging firm operates in an isolated part of the Rocky Mountains. The following table shows the firm's labour supply schedule (columns 1 and 2) and total product schedule (columns 2 and 3). The price of logs is $1.50 a tonne.

Wage rate (dollars per day)	Workers (number per day)	Quantity of logs produced (tonnes per day)
2.50	0	0
3.00	1	7
3.50	2	13
4.00	3	18
4.50	4	22
5.00	5	25
5.50	6	27

   a. What wage rate does the company pay?
   b. How many workers does the firm hire?
   c. What is the marginal revenue product at the quantity of labour employed?

*9. In problem 7, explain the effects of a court-enforced wage rate above the equilibrium wage rate on employment and unemployment.

10. In problem 8, explain the effects of the arrival of new immigrants on the demand for labour, the supply of labour, and the wage rate.

CRITICAL THINKING

1. Study *Reading Between the Lines* on pp. 364–365 and then answer the following questions:
   a. What are the broad facts about the job-market prospects of people who don't finish high school?
   b. How does a university degree influence a person's job-market prospects? Explain, using the analysis that you've learned in this chapter.
   c. Why do you think the Canadian economy created jobs for people with no high-school diploma in 1998?
   d. Why do you think the Canadian economy did *not* create jobs for people with no high-school diploma during the earlier 1990s?
   e. How do you think the job prospects of university graduates and high-school dropouts will evolve over the next few years?

2. Use the link on the Parkin-Bade Web site to visit the CLC and look at the "Don't Buy List." Choose an item on this list that interests you and explain why the CLC recommends a boycott of this item. Explain how not buying this item increases either the wage rate or employment of union members.

3. Use the link on the Parkin-Bade Web site to visit the Department of Labour, and obtain data for the past three months on usual weekly earnings and employment.
   a. What has happened to earnings and employment during the past three months?
   b. Try to explain the changes by using the tools of demand and supply.

4. "Wages should be determined on the basis of what is fair." Debate this proposition. Set out the cases for and against. Then determine and explain your verdict.

5. Suppose that all nations permitted free immigration. Which nations would be the biggest suppliers of immigrants and why? Which nations would attract most immigrants and why? Describe the world economy 10 years after the start of this process.

Inequality and Redistribution

Ken Thomson's family fortune, earned from the activities of the International Thomson Organization, is estimated as Canada's largest at more than $10 billion. Other billionaire Canadians are Charles Bronfman, owner of the Seagram Company, and Derek A. Price, owner of Starlaw Holdings, a massive Montreal firm that supplies investment and financial services. In stark contrast to these richest Canadians are the poorest, who can be seen any evening on the park benches of our major cities and in the hostels of the Salvation Army. Here are men and women who have no visible wealth at all other than their meagre clothes and a few possessions. ◆ Most Canadians are not as poor as those who seek help from the Salvation Army, but there is a large amount of relative poverty in our nation. One in ten families has an income that is so low that it spends close to half its income on rent. ◆ Why are some people exceedingly rich, while others are very poor and own almost nothing? Are the rich getting richer and the poor getting poorer? Does the information we have about the inequality of income and wealth in Canada paint an accurate picture or a misleading one? How do taxes, social security, and welfare programs influence economic inequality?

Riches and Rags

◆ In this chapter, we study economic inequality—its extent, its sources, and its potential remedies. We look at taxes and government programs that redistribute incomes and study their effects on economic inequality in Canada. Whether the inequality that the market economy generates is fair or unfair is a hard question to answer. We studied this question in Chapter 6 (see pp. 120–123). Here, our focus is on the amount of inequality, the reasons for it, and the effects of programs to reduce it. We'll begin by looking at some facts about economic inequality in Canada today and the recent trends.

After studying this chapter, you will be able to:

- ■ **Describe the inequality in income and wealth in Canada**
- ■ **Explain why wealth inequality is greater than income inequality**
- ■ **Explain how economic inequality arises**
- ■ **Explain the effects of taxes, social security, and welfare programs on economic inequality**

Economic Inequality in Canada

WE STUDY INEQUALITY BY LOOKING AT THE distribution of income and the distribution of wealth. A family's income is the amount that it receives in a given period. A family's wealth is the value of the things it owns at a point in time.

We measure income as the wages, interest, rent, and profit earned by a family in a year. In 1997, the average Canadian family income was $57,146. But there was considerable inequality around that average. The poorest 20 percent of families received 7.4 percent of total income. The next poorest 20 percent of families received 13.2 percent of total income. But the richest 20 percent of families received 36.4 percent of total income.

We measure wealth as the value of holdings of real estate plus financial assets minus financial liabilities. The most recent data available measure wealth in 1984. The median family wealth in 1984 was a little more than $40,000. The variation around this value was enormous. The distribution of wealth is much more unequal than the distribution of income. The poorest 40 percent of families owned only 2 percent of total wealth. The richest 10 percent owned more than 50 percent of total wealth. And the richest 1 percent owned 24 percent of total wealth.

Lorenz Curves

Figure 17.1 shows the distributions of income and wealth. The table divides families into five groups, called *quintiles*, that range from the lowest income (row *a*) to highest income (row *e*). It shows the percentages of income of each of these groups. For example, row *a* tells us that the lowest quintile of families receives 7.4 percent of total income. The table also shows the *cumulative* percentages of families and income. For example, row *b* tells us that the lowest two quintiles (lowest 40 percent) of families receive 20.6 percent of total income (7.4 percent for the lowest quintile and 13.2 percent for the next lowest). The data on cumulative income shares are illustrated by a Lorenz curve. A **Lorenz curve** graphs the cumulative percentage of income against the cumulative percentage of families.

If income were distributed equally to every family, the cumulative percentages of income received by the cumulative percentages of families would fall along

FIGURE 17.1

Lorenz Curves for Income and Wealth

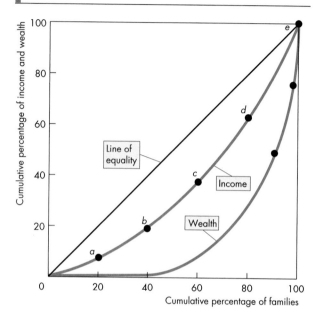

	Families		Income	
	Percentage	Cumulative percentage	Percentage	Cumulative percentage
a	Lowest 20	20	7.4	7.4
b	Second 20	40	13.2	20.6
c	Third 20	60	18.1	38.7
d	Fourth 20	80	24.9	63.6
e	Highest 20	100	36.4	100.0

The cumulative percentages of income and wealth are graphed against the cumulative percentage of families. If income and wealth were distributed equally, each 20 percent of families would have 20 percent of the income and wealth—the line of equality. Points *a* through *e* on the Lorenz curve for income correspond to the rows of the table. The Lorenz curve for wealth shows that wealth is more unequally distributed than income.

Sources: Income: Statistics Canada, *Income Distributions by Size in Canada*, 1997. Wealth: James B. Davies, "Distribution of Wealth in Canada," University of Western Ontario, mimeographed, March 1991, and Lars Osberg, "Canada's Economic Performance: Inequality, Poverty, and Growth," in *False Promises, The Failure of Conservative Economics* (Vancouver: New Start Books, 1992).

the straight line labelled "Line of equality." The actual distribution of income is shown by the Lorenz curve labelled "Income." The closer the Lorenz curve is to the line of equality, the more equal is the distribution.

The figure also shows a Lorenz curve for wealth. This curve is based on the distribution described above, in which total wealth is divided approximately equally between the top 1 percent, the next 9 percent, and the bottom 90 percent of families.

You can see from the two Lorenz curves in Fig. 17.1 that the Lorenz curve for wealth is much farther away from the line of equality than the Lorenz curve for income is, so the distribution of wealth is much more unequal than the distribution of income.

Inequality over Time

Figure 17.2 shows how the distribution of income has changed since 1980.

- The share of income received by the richest 20 percent of families has increased.
- The share of income received by the second and third poorest groups of families has decreased.

Despite a great deal of research on the topic, economists are still not sure why these trends in the distribution of income have occurred. The most promising explanation is that the highest-income group has gained because rapid technological change has increased the return to education. The lower-income groups have suffered for a variety of reasons. One of them is increased international mobility and competition that are keeping down the wages of low-skilled labour. Another is that the same technological trends that have increased the return to education have decreased the demand for and the wages of low-skilled labour.

Who Are the Poor and the Rich?

What are the characteristics of poor and rich families? The lowest-income family in Canada today is most likely to be a single-parent mother and her children. She is under 24 years old, has no job, and lives in Quebec. The highest-income family is a married couple with two full-time jobs. They are between 45 and 54 years old and live in Ontario.

These snapshot profiles are the extremes in Fig. 17.3. That figure illustrates the importance of source of income, family type, sex of the family head, age of the family head, labour force status, number of chil-

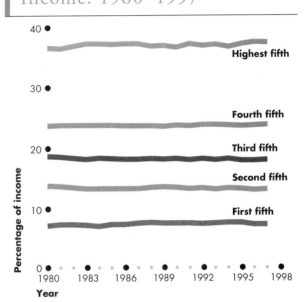

FIGURE 17.2

Trends in the Distribution of Income: 1980–1997

The distribution of income in Canada became less equal in the 1980s and 1990s. The fifth with the highest income gained the most and the fifths with the second and third highest incomes lost the most.

Source: Statistics Canada, *Income Distributions by Size in Canada*, 1997.

dren, education, and region of residence in influencing the likelihood that a family is living in poverty.

Poverty

Families at the low end of the income distribution are so poor that they are considered to be living in poverty. **Poverty** is a state in which a family's income is too low to be able to buy the quantities of food, shelter, and clothing that are deemed necessary. Poverty is a relative concept. Millions of people living in Africa and Asia survive on incomes of less than $400 a year. In Canada, poverty is measured in terms of a low-income cutoff. The **low-income cutoff** is the income level, determined separately for different types of families (for example, single persons, couples, one parent), that is selected such that families with incomes below that limit normally spend

FIGURE 17.3

The Incidence of Low Income by Family Characteristics

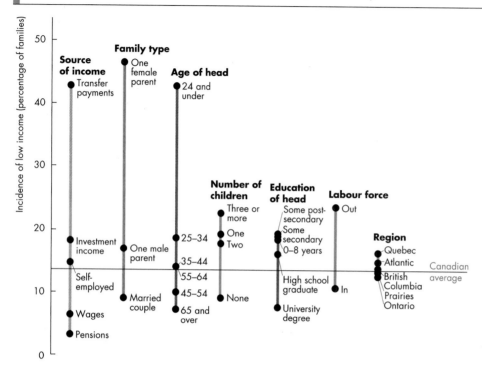

The vertical axis shows the incidence of low income—the percentage of families whose income falls below a low-income cutoff (the income level such that 54.7 percent of income is spent on food, shelter, and clothing). For Canada, on the average, in 1997 14 percent of families have incomes below the low-income cutoff. But that percentage varies depending on source of income, family type, sex and age of family head, number of children, education, and region of residence as indicated by the figure. Source of income, family type, and sex and age of family head are by far the most important factors influencing incidence of low income.

Source: Statistics Canada, *Income Distributions by Size in Canada*, 1997.

54.7 percent or more of their income on food, shelter, and clothing. The low-income cutoffs currently used by Statistics Canada are based on family expenditure data for 1992. Statistics Canada measures the incidence of low income as the percentage of families whose income falls below a low-income cutoff.

Figure 17.3 shows how the incidence of low income is related to other family characteristics. Poverty is heavily influenced by source of income and family status. More than 40 percent of families receiving transfer payments from the government are below the poverty line. About 46 percent of families in which the family head is a female and no husband is present are below the poverty level, while only 9 percent of married couples live in poverty. Almost 43 percent of families with the head 24 years or under live in poverty, while only 14 percent of families with the head 25 to 34 years do. More than 16 percent of families in Quebec live in poverty, while 12 percent of families in Ontario do. Almost 20 percent of

families in which the head has 8 or fewer years of education are below the poverty line, while only 8 percent of families in which the head is a university graduate are.

R E V I E W   Q U I Z

- Which is distributed more unequally: income or wealth?
- Has the distribution of income become more equal or more unequal?
- Which group of families has experienced the largest increase in income share during the past 20 years?
- The influences on a family's income are: age of family head, education of members, number of children, family type, labour force status, source of income, and region of residence. Rank the items in decreasing order of importance.

Comparing Like with Like

To determine the degree of inequality, we compare one person's economic situation with another person's. But what is the correct measure of a person's economic situation? Is it income or is it wealth? And is it *annual* income, the measure we've used so far in this chapter, or income over a longer time period—for example, over a family's lifetime?

Wealth Versus Income

Wealth is a stock of assets and income is the flow of earnings that results from the stock of wealth. Suppose that a person owns assets worth $1 million—has a wealth of $1 million. If the rate of return on assets is 5 percent a year, then this person receives an income of $50,000 a year from those assets. We can use either the wealth of $1 million or the income of $50,000 to describe this person's economic condition. When the rate of return is 5 percent a year, $1 million of wealth equals $50,000 of income in perpetuity. Wealth and income are simply different ways of looking at the same thing.

But in Fig. 17.1, the distribution of wealth is much more unequal than the distribution of income. Why? It is because the wealth data measure tangible assets and exclude the value of human capital, while the income data measure income from both tangible assets and human capital.

Table 17.1 illustrates the consequence of omitting human capital from the wealth data. Lee has twice the wealth and twice the income of Peter. But Lee's human capital is less than Peter's—$200,000 compared with $499,000. And Lee's income from human capital of $10,000 is less than Peter's income from human capital of $24,950. Lee's nonhuman capital is larger than Peter's—$800,000 compared with $1,000. And Lee's income from nonhuman capital of $40,000 is larger than Peter's income from nonhuman capital of $50.

The national wealth and income surveys record their incomes of $50,000 and $25,000 respectively, which indicates that Lee is twice as well off as Peter. And they record their tangible assets of $800,000 and $1,000 respectively, which indicates that Lee is 800 times as wealthy as Peter. Because the national survey of wealth excludes human capital, the income distribution is a more accurate measure of economic inequality than is the wealth distribution.

TABLE 17.1

Capital, Wealth, and Income

	Lee		Peter	
	Wealth	Income	Wealth	Income
Human capital	200,000	10,000	499,000	24,950
Nonhuman capital	800,000	40,000	1,000	50
Total	$1,000,000	$50,000	$500,000	$25,000

When wealth is measured to include the value of human capital as well as nonhuman capital, the distribution of income and the distribution of wealth display the same degree of inequality.

Annual or Lifetime Income and Wealth?

A typical family's income changes over time. It starts out low, grows to a peak when the family's workers reach retirement age, and then falls after retirement. Also, a typical family's wealth changes over time. Like income, it starts out low, grows to a peak at the point of retirement, and falls after retirement.

Suppose we look at three families that have identical lifetime incomes. One family is young, one is middle-aged, and one is retired. The middle-aged family has the highest income and wealth, the retired family has the lowest, and the young family falls in the middle. The distributions of annual income and wealth in a given year are unequal but the distributions of lifetime income and wealth are equal. So some of the measured inequality arises from the fact that different families are at different stages in the life cycle. Inequality of annual incomes overstates the degree of lifetime inequality.

R E V I E W   Q U I Z

- Which is the more accurate indicator of the degree of inequality: the distribution of income or the distribution of wealth? Why is one of these a better measure than the other?
- Which is the more accurate indicator of the degree of inequality: the distribution of lifetime income or the distribution of annual income? Why is one of these a better measure than the other?

Let's look at the sources of economic inequality.

Resource Prices, Endowments, and Choices

A FAMILY'S INCOME DEPENDS ON THREE THINGS:

- Resource prices
- Resource endowments
- Choices

The distribution of income depends on the distribution of these three things across the population. The first two are outside our individual control and are determined by market forces and by history. From the viewpoint of each one of us, they appear to be determined by luck. The last item is under individual control. We make choices that influence our incomes. Let's look at the three factors that influence incomes.

Resource Prices

Everyone faces the same interest rates in capital markets, but people face differing wage rates in the labour market. And the labour market is the biggest single source of income for most people. To what extent do variations in wage rates account for the unequal distribution of income? The answer is that they do to some extent, but wage differences cannot account for all the inequality. High-skilled workers earn about 4 times as much as low-skilled workers. High-paid professionals earn about 3 times as much as high-skilled workers. So high-paid professionals earn around 12 times what the least skilled earn.

Differences in resource endowments are another.

Resource Endowments

There is a large amount of variety in a family's endowments of capital and of human abilities. Differences in capital make a big contribution to differences in incomes. But so do differences in ability.

Physical and mental differences (some inherited, some learned) have a normal, or bell-shaped, distribution—like the distribution of heights or weights. The distribution of ability across individuals is a major source of inequality in income and wealth. But it is not the only source. If it were, the distributions of income and wealth would look like the bell-shaped curve that describes the distribution of heights. In fact, these distributions are skewed towards high incomes and look like the curve in Fig. 17.4. This

figure shows income on the horizontal axis and the percentage of families receiving each income on the vertical axis. In 1997, the median family income—the income that separates families into two groups of equal size—was $50,361. The most common income—called the mode income—is less than the median income. The mean income—also called the average income—is greater than the median income and in 1997 was $57,146. A skewed distribution like the one shown in Fig. 17.4 is one in which many more people have incomes below the average than above it, a large number of people have low incomes, and a small number of people have high incomes. The distribution of (nonhuman) wealth has a shape similar to that of the distribution of income but is even more skewed.

The skewed shape of the distribution of income cannot be explained by the bell-shaped distribution of individual abilities. It results from the choices that people make.

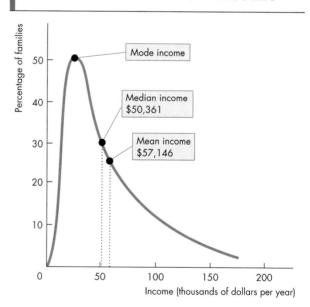

FIGURE 17.4

The Distribution of Income

The distribution of income is unequal and is not symmetric around the mean income. There are many more people with incomes below the mean income than above it. Also, the distribution has a long thin upper tail, which represents a small number of families that earn very large incomes.

Choices

While many poor families feel trapped and do not have many options open to them, a family's income and wealth depend partly on the choices that its members make. You are going to discover that the choices people make exaggerate the differences among them and make the distribution of income more unequal than the distribution of abilities, as well as make the distribution of income skewed.

Wages and the Supply of Labour Other things remaining the same, the quantity of labour that a person supplies usually increases as that person's wage rate increases. A person who has a low wage rate chooses to work fewer hours than a person who has a high wage rate.

Because the quantity of labour supplied increases as the wage rate increases, the distribution of income is more unequal than the distribution of hourly wages. It is also skewed, like the distribution shown in Fig. 17.4. People whose wage rates are below the average tend to work fewer hours than the average, and their incomes bunch together below the average. People whose wage rates are above the average tend to work more hours than the average, and their incomes stretch out above the average.

Saving and Bequests Another choice that results in unequal distributions in income and wealth is the decision to save and make bequests. A *bequest* is a gift from one generation to the next. The higher a family's income, the more that family tends to save and accumulate wealth across generations.

Saving and bequests are not inevitably a source of increased inequality. If a family saves to redistribute an uneven income over the life cycle and enable consumption to be constant, the act of saving decreases the degree of inequality. If a lucky generation that has a high income saves a large amount and makes a bequest to a generation that is unlucky, this act of saving also decreases the degree of inequality. But two features of bequests make intergenerational transfers of wealth a source of increased inequality:

- Debts cannot be bequeathed
- Mating is assortative

Debts Cannot Be Bequeathed Although a person may die with debts that exceed assets—with negative wealth—debts cannot be forced onto other family members. Because a zero inheritance is the smallest inheritance that anyone can receive, bequests can only add to future generations' wealth and income potential.

Most people inherit nothing or a very small amount. A few people inherit enormous fortunes. As a result, bequests make the distribution of income persistently more unequal than the distribution of ability and job skills. A family that is poor in one generation is more likely to be poor in the next. A family that is wealthy in one generation is likely to be wealthy in the next. But there is a tendency for income and wealth to converge, across generations, to the average. Although there can be long runs of good luck or bad luck, or good judgment or bad judgment, across the generations, such long runs are uncommon. But a feature of human behaviour that slows the convergence of wealth to the average and makes inequalities persist is assortative mating.

Assortative Mating *Assortative mating* is the tendency for people to marry within their own socioeconomic class. In the vernacular, "like attracts like." Although there is a good deal of folklore that "opposites attract," perhaps such Cinderella tales appeal to us because they are so rare in reality. Marriage partners tend to have similar socioeconomic characteristics. Wealthy individuals seek wealthy partners. The consequence of assortative mating is that inherited wealth becomes more concentrated in a small number of families and the distribution of wealth becomes more unequal.

REVIEW QUIZ

- What role do wage rates, endowments, and choices play in creating income inequality?
- What is the main reason that wage rates are unequal?
- If the distribution of endowments is bell shaped, what makes the distribution of income skewed?
- Which choices that people make generate the skew in the distribution of income?
- How do bequests and assortative mating make the distribution of wealth more unequal and skewed?

We've now examined why inequality exists. Next, we're going to see how taxes and government programs redistribute income and wealth.

Income Redistribution

THE THREE MAIN WAYS THAT GOVERNMENTS IN Canada redistribute income are:

■ Income taxes
■ Income maintenance programs
■ Subsidized services

Income Taxes

Income taxes may be progressive, regressive, or proportional. A **progressive income tax** is one that taxes income at a marginal rate that increases with the level of income. The term "marginal," applied to income tax rates, refers to the fraction of the last dollar earned that is paid in taxes. A **regressive income tax** is one that taxes income at a marginal rate that decreases with the level of income. A **proportional income tax** (also called a *flat-rate income tax*) is one that taxes income at a constant rate, regardless of the level of income.

The income tax rates that apply in Canada are composed of two parts: federal and provincial taxes. There is variety in the detailed tax arrangements in the individual provinces but the tax system, at both the federal and provincial levels, is progressive. The poorest families pay no income tax. Most Canadians who earn between $10,000 and $30,000 a year, except for those living in Quebec, pay around 25 percent of their taxable income. In Quebec, for the same income range, the marginal tax rates ranged from 30 to almost 40 percent. Canadians with incomes between $30,000 and $60,000 a year pay between 40 and 45 percent and those with incomes above $60,000 pay a marginal tax rate of 45 to 50 percent.

Income Maintenance Programs

Much of the revenue that the government receives from taxes is redistributed to individuals and families through a number of income maintenance programs. Three main government programs redistribute income by making direct payments (in cash, services, or vouchers) to individuals and families. They are:

■ Social security programs
■ Employment insurance system
■ Welfare programs

Social Security   Three programs, Old Age Security (OAS), Guaranteed Income Supplement (GIS), and Spouse Allowance (SPA) ensure a minimum level of income for the elderly. Monthly cash payments to retired or disabled workers or their surviving spouses are paid for by compulsory payroll taxes on both employers and employees. In 1999, the maximum OAS was $410.82 a month, the maximum GIS for a single person was $488.23 and for a married couple was $806.24, and the maximum SPA was $804.64.

Employment Insurance   To provide an income to unemployed workers, the federal government has established an unemployment compensation program. The Employment Insurance program is funded by employee and employer contributions, and after a qualifying period the worker is entitled to receive a benefit if the worker becomes unemployed. The maximum unemployment benefit is $413 a week or 55 percent of gross weekly earnings over the previous 20 weeks.

Welfare Programs   Other federal welfare programs provide income maintenance for families and persons. They are:

1. Canada Assistance Plan, a plan shared equally by the federal and provincial governments that gives financial assistance to families and individuals who are in need, regardless of the cause; the assistance includes food, shelter, fuel, utilities, family supplies, items required to carry on a trade, certain welfare services, and specified health and social services

2. Family Allowance and Child Tax Credit programs, designed to help families who have inadequate financial support

3. Canada/Quebec Pension Plans, funded equally by employee and employer contributions, provide retirement benefits, survivor benefits, disability benefits, and death benefits

4. Workers' Compensation, a provincial program funded by employers, designed to provide financial assistance as well as medical care and rehabilitation of workers injured at work

Subsidized Services

A great deal of redistribution takes place in Canada through the provision of subsidized services, which is the provision of goods and services by the government at prices below the cost of production. The taxpayers who consume these goods and services receive a transfer in kind from the taxpayers who do not consume them. The two most important areas in which this form of redistribution takes place are education—both kindergarten through grade 12 and college and university—and health care.

In 1998, Canadian students enrolled in the universities in Ontario paid annual tuition fees of around $3,500. The cost of one year's education at one of these universities in 1998 was about $17,500. Thus families with a member enrolled in these institutions received a benefit from the government of about $14,000 a year. Those with several college or university students received proportionately higher benefits.

Government provision of health care to all residents has brought high-quality and high-cost health care to millions of people who earn too little to buy such services themselves. As a result, this program has contributed a great deal to reducing inequality.

The Scale of Income Redistribution

A family's income in the absence of government redistribution is called *market income*. One way of measuring the scale of income redistribution is to calculate the percentage of market income paid in taxes and the percentage received in benefits at each income level. Making such a calculation in a way that takes into account the value of the services provided by the government is almost impossible. The only calculations available ignore this aspect of redistribution and focus on taxes and cash benefits.

Figure 17.5 shows how much redistribution in aggregate takes place in Canada. The income distribution that takes account of government policies is called the *distribution after taxes and benefits*. Figure 17.5 illustrates the amount of redistribution that takes place among the five income groups by comparing the Lorenz curves for the market distribution and the distribution after taxes and benefits. As you can see, there is considerable redistribution, especially to boost the incomes of the very poor. The poorest 20 percent of families receive more than 70 percent of their income from the government. The second poorest 20 percent receive 43 percent of their income from the government. In contrast, the richest 20 percent receive almost nothing from the government. But a great deal of inequality remains after the redistribution.

Income Redistribution

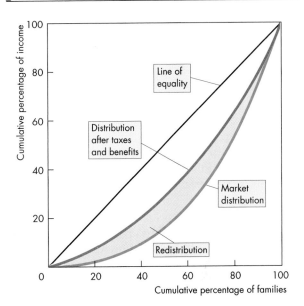

Taxes and income maintenance programs reduce the degree of inequality. In 1997, the 20 percent of families with the lowest incomes received net benefits that increased their share of total income from 1.6 percent to 7.4 percent. The 20 percent of families with the highest incomes paid taxes that decreased their share of total income from 46.4 percent to 36.4 percent of total income.

Source: Statistics Canada, *Income Distributions by Size in Canada,* 1997 and authors' assumptions and calculations.

The Big Tradeoff

The redistribution of income creates what has been called the **big tradeoff**, a tradeoff between equity and efficiency. The big tradeoff arises because redistribution uses scarce resources and weakens incentives.

A dollar collected from a rich person does not translate into a dollar received by a poor person. Some of it gets used up in the process of redistribution. Tax-collecting agencies such as Revenue Canada and welfare-administering agencies (as well as tax accountants and lawyers) use skilled labour, computers, and other scarce resources to do their work. The bigger the scale of redistribution, the greater is the opportunity cost of administering it.

But the cost of collecting taxes and making welfare payments is a small part of the total cost of redistribution. A bigger cost arises from the inefficiency—deadweight loss—of taxes and benefits. Greater equality can be achieved only by taxing productive activities such as work and saving. Taxing people's income from their work and saving lowers the after-tax income they receive. This lower income makes them work and save less, which in turn results in a smaller output and less consumption not only for the rich who pay the taxes but also for the poor who receive the benefits.

Both taxpayers and benefit recipients face weaker incentives. In fact, under our current welfare arrangements, some of the weakest incentives are those faced by families that benefit under programs such as Guaranteed Income Supplement. When a person in one of these families gets a job, benefits are withdrawn and the family in effect pays a tax of 100 percent on its marginal earnings. This marginal tax rate is higher than that paid by the wealthiest Canadians, and it helps lock poor families in a welfare trap.

So the scale and methods of income redistribution must pay close attention to the incentive effects of taxes and benefits.

A Major Welfare Challenge

The poorest people in Canada (see pp. 371–372) are young women who have not completed high school, have a child (or children), and live without a partner. But all single mothers present a major welfare challenge. First, their numbers are large. There are approximately one million single mothers in Canada today. Second, their economic plight and the economic prospects for their children are serious.

Janet Peterson and her four children aged between 3 and 13 are one example. Janet has a serious physical disability. She receives a social assistance cheque each month for $1,286, or $15,432 a year. The low-income cutoff for a family of five is $30,910. So Janet and her children live in severe poverty. She spends $625 a month on rent, $400 on food, and the rest on gas, hydro, the phone, and transportation. To provide Janet Peterson (and the other million single mothers) with an income that matches the low-income cutoff would cost more than $10 billion a year.

Janet Peterson has a physical disability that makes it unlikely that she could work. Many other single mothers are in this situation. But this is not the typical case. Most single mothers are physically fit and are capable of working. And some of them are well educated and therefore can earn a high wage rate. Even those single mothers who have not completed high school are capable of either attending school or getting a job.

For physically fit single mothers, the long-term solution to their problem is education and on-the-job training—acquiring human capital. The short-term solution is welfare. But welfare must be designed to minimize the disincentive to pursue the long-term goal. This is the challenge in designing an adequate welfare program. One possible program is the negative income tax, which we now describe.

Negative Income Tax

Negative income tax is *not* on the political agenda. But it is popular among economists and it is the subject of several real-world experiments.

A **negative income tax** gives every family a *guaranteed minimum annual income* and taxes *all* income above the guaranteed minimum at a fixed *marginal tax rate*. Suppose the guaranteed minimum annual income is $10,000 and the marginal tax rate is 25 percent. A family with no market income receives the $10,000 guaranteed minimum income from the government. This family "pays" income tax of *minus* $10,000, hence the name, *negative* income tax. A family with a market income of $40,000 also receives the $10,000 guaranteed minimum income from the government. But it also pays $10,000—25 percent of its market income—to the government. So this family pays no income tax. It has the break-even income. Families with a market income of between zero and $40,000 "pay" a negative income tax. They receive more than they pay. A family with a market income of $60,000 receives the $10,000 guaranteed minimum income from the government, but it pays $15,000—25 percent of its market income—to the government. So this family pays income tax of $5,000. All families with incomes greater than $40,000 pay income tax to the government.

Figure 17.6 illustrates a negative income tax and compares it with our current arrangements. In both parts of the figure, the horizontal axis measures *market income* and the vertical axis measures income *after* taxes are paid and benefits are received. The 45° line shows the hypothetical case of "no redistribution."

FIGURE 17.6

Comparing Traditional Programs and a Negative Income Tax

(a) Current redistribution arrangements

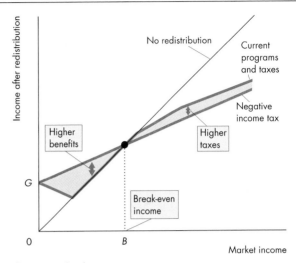

(b) A negative income tax

Part (a) shows traditional redistribution arrangements—the blue curve. Benefits of G are paid to those with no income. As incomes increase from zero to A, benefits are withdrawn, *lowering* income after redistribution below G and creating a welfare trap—the grey triangle. As incomes increase from A to C, there is no redistribution. As incomes increase above C, income taxes are paid at successively higher rates.

In part (b), a negative income tax gives a guaranteed annual income of G and decreases benefits at the same rate as the tax rate on incomes. The red line shows how market incomes translate into income after redistribution. Families with market incomes below B, the break-even income, receive net benefits. Those with market incomes above B pay net taxes.

Part (a) shows traditional redistribution arrangements—the blue curve. Benefits of G are paid to those with no income. As incomes increase from zero to A, benefits are withdrawn. This arrangement creates a *welfare trap* shown as the grey triangle. It does not pay a person to work if the income he or she can earn is less than A. Over the income range A to C, each additional dollar of market income increases income after redistribution by a dollar. At incomes greater than C, income taxes are paid and at successively higher rates, so income after redistribution is smaller than market income.

Part (b) shows the negative income tax. The guaranteed annual income is G, and the break-even income is B. Families with market incomes below B receive a net benefit (blue area), and those with incomes above B pay taxes (red area). A negative income tax removes the welfare trap and gives greater encouragement to low-income families to seek more employment, even at low wage rates. It also over-

comes many of the other problems arising from existing income maintenance programs.

R E V I E W   Q U I Z

- What are the methods that governments in Canada use to redistribute income?
- How large is the scale of redistribution in Canada?
- What is the major welfare challenge and how is it being tackled in Canada today?
- What problem is a negative income tax designed to solve? Why don't we have a negative income tax?

◆ *Reading Between the Lines* on pp. 380–381 takes another look at the trends in the distribution of income in Canada in recent years and of the anatomy of the changing distribution.

The Changing Income Distribution

THE GLOBE AND MAIL, MARCH 8, 1999

Poverty is single and she has a child

By Bruce Little

The headlines for the latest study of family incomes from Statistics Canada were predictable: The rich get richer and the poor get poorer. ...

Between 1970 and 1995, the top 30 per cent saw their share of all income increase 1.9 per cent... while the bottom 70 per cent saw their share fall 1.9 points...

What is most striking from the Statistics Canada study are the huge changes in the nature of families, and their income, over a quarter-century. Analyst Abdul Rashid's report appears in the agency's quarterly publication Perspectives on Labour and Income.

Using census data, Mr. Rashid took the total number of families, split them into 10 equal groups (called deciles) and ranked them according to income. In effect, he provides answers to the questions: Who's rich? Who's poor? ...

Begin with age. In 1970, fewer than 12 per cent of Canadians were 65 or older, yet they accounted for more than 26 per cent of the families in the bottom

decile. To a considerable degree, extreme poverty was a problem of the old, ...

By 1995, more than 15 per cent of all families were headed by someone 65 or older, but they constituted a mere 6 per cent of the bottom income group. The old had not grown rich by any stretch, but many had moved up the income scale; they accounted for 30 per cent of those in the third income decile, double their share in 1970.

In 1995, the bottom 10 per cent were still receiving about 1.5 per cent of all income, just as they had in 1970. But if the old have moved up the income ladder, who are today's poor?

Largely, they are single mothers. In 1970, they headed just over 7 per cent of all families; by 1995, the figure topped 12 per cent. ... Single mothers accounted for 24 per cent of those in the bottom decile in 1970 and a staggering 40 per cent in 1995.

What about the top end of the income scale, the best-off 10 per cent? ...

By 1995, both the husbands and wives were working in 81 per cent of those upper-income homes. ...

Reprinted with permission from The Globe and Mail.
Further reproduction prohibited.

Essence of the Story

- Between 1970 and 1995, the rich in Canada became richer and the poor became poorer.

- The composition of family types in the lowest income decile has changed.

- In 1970, less than 12 percent of Canadians were 65 or older and they composed 26 percent of the families in the lowest income decile.

- In 1995, 15 percent of Canadians were 65 or older and they composed 6 percent of the families in the lowest income decile.

- Between 1970 and 1995, the percentage of families headed by single mothers increased from 7 percent to 12 percent and their inclusion in the lowest income decile increased from 24 percent to 40 percent.

- 81 percent of upper-income homes contain two wage earners.

■ The lowest income decile includes all families that receive the lowest 10 percent of all income.

■ Between 1970 and 1995, the number of families headed by female single parents increased.

■ Because these families generally have low incomes, a disproportionate increase in the incidence of female single-parent families occurred in the lowest income decile.

■ Figure 1 shows the composition of the lowest income decile by the age of the head of the family in 1970 and Fig. 2 shows the composition in 1995.

■ The largest change comes in the 65-and-over age group, but there is also a significant increase in the 25-to-34 age group and the 35-to-44 age group.

■ Changes in social security payments including Old Age Security, the Guaranteed Income Supplement, and Canada and Quebec Pension Plans have helped elderly families move out of the lowest income decile.

■ Although the number of families headed by single mothers in the lowest income decile has increased from 24 percent to 40 percent, the 15-to-24 age group has increased from 9.8 percent to only 10.7 percent. So it appears that the largest percentage increase in single mothers in the lowest income decile is not occurring in the teenage years.

■ Figure 3 compares the composition of the lowest income decile and the highest income decile by family structure in 1995.

■ The female single-parent family, which comprises 40 percent of the lowest income decile, is only 1.4 percent of the highest income decile.

■ The highest income decile is dominated by the two-income family while the lowest income decile is dominated by the female single-parent family.

■ Family structure and spousal work patterns are significant influences on income determination.

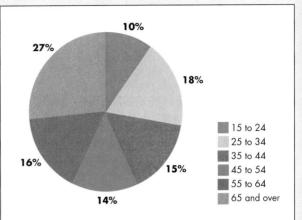

Figure 1 Distribution of family income by age in 1970

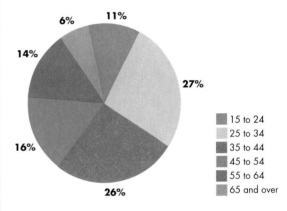

Figure 2 Distribution of family income by age in 1995

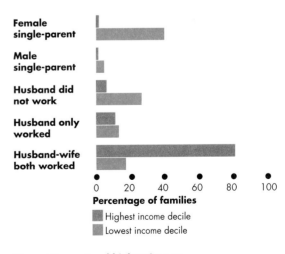

Figure 3 Lowest and highest income deciles by family structure

SUMMARY

Key Points

Economic Inequality in Canada (pp. 370–372)

■ The richest 1 percent of Canadians own 24 percent of the total wealth in the country.

■ Income is distributed less unevenly than wealth. Throughout the 1970s, 1980s, and 1990s, inequality increased.

■ The poorest people in Canada are single mothers with less than eight years of schooling and no job who live in Quebec. The richest people live in Ontario and are middle-aged couples with two full-time jobs.

Comparing Like with Like (p. 373)

■ The distribution of wealth exaggerates the degree of inequality because it excludes human capital.

■ The distributions of annual income and wealth exaggerate lifetime inequality because they do not take the life cycle into account.

Resource Prices, Endowments, and Choices (pp. 374–375)

■ Differences in income and wealth arise from differences in resource prices, endowments, and choices.

■ People who earn high wage rates generally work more hours than those who earn low wage rates, so the distribution of income becomes more unequal and more skewed than the distribution of wage rates.

Income Redistribution (pp. 376–379)

■ Governments redistribute income through income taxes, income maintenance programs, and provision of subsidized services.

■ Income taxes are progressive.

■ Redistribution creates a "big tradeoff" between equity and efficiency, which arises because the process of redistribution uses resources and weakens the incentives to work and save.

■ Traditional income maintenance programs create a welfare trap that discourages work, so poverty is persistent. Reforms seek to lessen the severity of the welfare trap. A more radical negative income tax reform would encourage those on welfare to find work.

Key Figures

Key Terms

PROBLEMS

*1. You are provided with the following information about income shares in an economy:

Percentage of families	Income shares (percent)
Lowest 20%	5
Second 20%	11
Third 20%	17
Fourth 20%	24
Highest 20%	43

a. Draw the Lorenz curve for income in this economy.
b. Compare the distributions of income in this economy with that in Canada. Is Canadian income distributed more equally or less equally than in the economy described in the table?

2. You are provided with the following information about wealth shares in an economy:

Percentage of families	Wealth shares (percent)
Lowest 20%	0
Second 20%	1
Third 20%	3
Fourth 20%	11
Highest 20%	85

a. Draw the Lorenz curve for wealth in this economy.
b. Compare the distribution of wealth in this economy with that in Canada. Is Canadian wealth distributed more equally or less equally than in the economy described in the table?
c. Explain which of the two variables—income in problem 1 or wealth in problem 2—is more unequally distributed.

*3. Imagine an economy with five people who are identical in all respects. Each lives for 70 years. For the first 14 of those years, they earn no income. For the next 35 years, they work and earn $30,000 a year from their work. For their remaining years, they are retired and have no income from labour. To make the arithmetic easy, let's suppose that the interest rate in this economy is zero; the individuals consume all their income during their lifetime and at a

constant annual rate. What are the distributions of income and wealth in this economy if the individuals have the following ages:
a. All are 45
b. 25, 35, 45, 55, 65
Does case (a) have greater inequality than case (b)?

4. In the economy described in problem 3, there is a "baby boom." Two people who were born in the same year are now 25. One person is 35, one 45, one 55, and no one is 65. What are the distributions of income and wealth:
a. This year?
b. 10 years in the future?
c. 20 years in the future?
d. 30 years in the future?
e. 40 years in the future?
f. Comment on and explain the changes in the distributions of income and wealth in this economy.

*5. An economy consists of 10 people, each of whom has the following labour supply schedule:

Wage rate (dollars per hour)	Hours worked per day
1	1
2	2
3	4
4	6
5	8

The people differ in ability and earn different wage rates. The distribution of *wage rates* is as follows:

Wage rate (dollars per hour)	Number of people
1	1
2	2
3	4
4	2
5	1

a. Calculate the average wage rate.
b. Calculate the ratio of the highest to the lowest wage rate.
c. Calculate the average daily income.
d. Calculate the ratio of the highest to the lowest daily income.
e. Sketch the distribution of hourly wage rates.

f. Sketch the distribution of daily incomes.

g. What important lesson is illustrated by this problem?

6. In the economy described in problem 5, the productivity of low-skilled labour falls and that of high-skilled labour rises. Consequently, the distribution of *wage rates* changes to the following:

Wage rate (dollars per hour)	Number of people
0	1
1	2
3	4
5	2
6	1

The labour supply schedule is the same as in problem 5. For this changed situation:

a. Calculate the average wage rate.

b. Calculate the ratio of the highest to the lowest wage rate.

c. Calculate the average daily income.

d. Calculate the ratio of the highest to the lowest daily income.

e. Sketch the distribution of hourly wage rates.

f. Sketch the distribution of daily incomes.

g. What important lesson is illustrated by comparing the economy in this problem with the one in problem 5?

*7. The table shows the distribution of market income in an economy.

Percentage of families	Income (millions of dollars)
Lowest 20%	5
Second 20%	10
Third 20%	18
Fourth 20%	28
Highest 20%	39

The government redistributes income with the taxes and benefits shown in the following table:

Percentage of families	Income taxes (percent of income)	Benefits (millions of dollars)
Lowest 20%	0	10
Second 20%	10	8
Third 20%	15	3
Fourth 20%	20	0
Highest 20%	30	0

a. Draw the Lorenz curve for this economy after taxes and benefits.

b. Is the scale of redistribution of income in this economy greater or smaller than in Canada?

8. In the economy described in problem 7, the government replaces its existing taxes and benefits with a negative income tax. What changes do you expect to occur in the economy?

CRITICAL THINKING

1. Study *Reading Between the Lines* on pp. 380–381, and then:

a. Describe the main facts about the distribution of income reported in the news article.

b. Explain how you think the tax system and the welfare system change the situation described in the news article.

c. How can we explain the trends reported in this news article? Are the trends inevitable or can we take measures to reverse them? Explain.

2. Use the link on the Parkin-Bade Web site to visit Statistics Canada to obtain information on average family income in the city in which you live. Also find the Statistics Canada data for London, Ontario. Then use the link on the Parkin-Bade Web site to visit the *London Free Press* poverty site. Review the information on poverty that you find there. Then:

a. Describe the main facts about poverty and the distribution of income in London, Ontario.

b. Do you think the situation described in London is similar, worse, or not as bad as that in your own home city?

c. Explain why you think your city is performing better or worse than London, Ontario and better or worse than the country as a whole.

Understanding Resource Markets

For Whom?

During the past 35 years, the rich have been getting richer and the poor poorer. This trend is new. From the end of World War II until 1965, the poor got richer at a faster pace than the rich and the gap between rich and poor narrowed a bit. What are the forces that generate these trends? The answer to this question is the interaction of the forces of supply and demand in resource markets. ◆ The three categories of resources are human, capital, and natural. Human resources include labour, human capital, and entrepreneurship. The income of labour and human capital depends on wage rates and employment levels, which are determined in labour markets. The income from capital depends on interest rates and the amount of capital, which are determined in capital markets. The income from natural resources depends on prices and quantities, which are determined in natural resource markets. Only the return to entrepreneurship is not determined directly in a market. That return is normal profit plus economic profit, and it depends on how successful each entrepreneur is in the business that he or she runs. ◆ The chapters in this part study the forces at play in resource markets and explain how those forces have led to changes in the distribution of income. ◆ In the overview of all the resource markets in Chapter 15, you learned how the demand for resources results from the profit-maximizing decisions of firms. You studied these decisions from a different angle in Chapters 10–14, where you learned how firms choose their profit-maximizing output. In Chapter 15, you learned how a firm's profit-maximizing output decision determines its demand for productive resources. You also learned how resource supply decisions are made and how equilibrium determines resource prices and the incomes of resource owners. ◆ You discovered that some of the biggest incomes earned by superstars are a surplus that we call *economic rent*. ◆ Chapter 15 uses the labour market as the main example. But you also learned in that chapter some special features of capital markets and natural resource markets. ◆ In Chapter 16, you took a closer look at the labour market and studied the main sources of differences among people's wages. ◆ Then, in Chapter 17, you studied the distribution of income. This chapter took you back to the fundamentals of economics and answered one of the big questions: Who gets to consume the goods and services that are produced?

◆ Many outstanding economists have advanced our understanding of resource markets and the role they play in helping to resolve the conflicts between the demands of humans and the resources available. One of them is Thomas Robert Malthus whom you can meet on the following page. Also, we will talk with Craig Riddell, a professor of economics at the University of British Columbia, who has made important contributions to our understanding of modern labour markets.

Probing the Ideas

Running Out of Resources?

The Economist

Thomas Robert Malthus

(1766–1834), an English clergyman and economist, was an extremely influential social scientist. In his best selling Essay on the Principle of Population, *published in 1798, he predicted that population growth would outstrip food production and said that wars, famine, and disease were inevitable unless population growth was held in check by what he called "moral restraint." By "moral restraint" he meant marrying at a late age and living a celibate life. He married at the age of 38 a wife of 27, marriage ages that he recommended for others. Malthus's ideas were regarded as too radical in their day. And they led Thomas Carlyle, a contemporary thinker, to dub economics the "dismal science." But the ideas of Malthus had a profound influence on Charles Darwin, who got the key idea that led him to the theory of natural selection from reading the* Essay on the Principle of Population. *And David Ricardo and the classical economists were strongly influenced by Malthus's ideas.*

"The passion between the sexes has appeared in every age to be so nearly the same, that it may always be considered, in algebraic language as a given quantity."

THOMAS ROBERT MALTHUS, *AN ESSAY ON THE PRINCIPLE OF POPULATION*

The Issues

Is there a limit to economic growth, or can we expand production and population without effective limit? Thomas Malthus gave one of the most influential answers to these questions in 1798. He reasoned that population, unchecked, would grow at a geometric rate—1, 2, 4, 8, 16 ...—while the food supply would grow at an arithmetic rate—1, 2, 3, 4, 5 ... To prevent the population from outstripping the available food supply, there would be periodic wars, famines, and plagues. In Malthus's view, only what he called moral restraint could prevent such periodic disasters.

As industrialization proceeded through the nineteenth century, Malthus's idea came to be applied to all natural resources, especially those that are exhaustible.

Modern-day Malthusians believe that his basic idea is correct and that it applies not only to food but also to every natural resource. These prophets of doom believe that in time, we will be reduced to the subsistence level that Malthus predicted. He was a few centuries out in his predictions but not dead wrong.

One modern-day Malthusian is ecologist Paul Ehrlich, who believes that we are sitting on a "population bomb." Governments must limit both population growth and the resources that may be used each year, says Ehrlich.

In 1931, Harold Hotelling developed a theory of natural resources with different predictions from those of Malthus. The Hotelling Principle is that the relative price of an exhaustible natural resource will steadily rise, bringing a decline in the quantity used and an increase in the use of substitute resources.

Julian Simon (who died in 1998) challenged both the Malthusian gloom and the Hotelling Principle. He believed that people are the "ultimate resource" and predicted that a rising population lessens the pressure on natural resources. A bigger population provides a larger number of resourceful people who can work out more efficient ways of using scarce resources. As these solutions are found, the prices of exhaustible resources actually fall. To demonstrate his point, in 1980, Simon bet Ehrlich that the prices of five metals—copper, chrome, nickel, tin, and tungsten—would fall during the 1980s. Simon won the bet!

... and Now

In Tokyo, the pressure on space is so great that in some residential neighbourhoods, a parking space costs $1,700 a month. To economize on this expensive space—and to lower the cost of car ownership and hence boost the sale of cars—Honda, Nissan, and Toyota, three of Japan's big car producers, have developed a parking machine that enables two cars to occupy the space of one. The most basic of these machines costs a mere $10,000—less than 6 months' parking fees.

Then ...

No matter whether it is agricultural land, an exhaustible natural resource, or the space in the centre of Winnipeg, and no matter whether it is 2000, or, as shown here, 1913, there is a limit to what is available, and we persistently push against that limit. Economists see urban congestion as a consequence of the value of doing business in the city centre relative to the cost. They see the price mechanism, bringing ever-higher rents and prices of raw materials, as the means of allocating and rationing scarce natural resources. Malthusians, in contrast, explain congestion as the consequence of population pressure, and they see population control as the solution.

Malthus developed his ideas about population growth in a world in which women played a limited role in the economy. Malthus did not consider the opportunity cost of women's time a factor to be considered in predicting trends in the birth rate and population growth. But today, the opportunity cost of women's time is a crucial factor because of the expanded role that women play in the labour force. One economist who has made significant contributions to our knowledge of labour markets is Craig Riddell. You can meet Professor Riddell on the following pages.

Talking with
Craig Riddell

labour economics and labour relations. Robin Bade and Michael Parkin talked to Craig Riddell about his work and the Canadian labour market.

Craig Riddell, *who was born in Toronto in 1946, is a Professor of Economics and former Head of the Department of Economics at the University of British Columbia. He was an undergraduate at the Royal Military College of Canada and a graduate student at Queen's University, where he obtained his Ph.D. in 1977. He began teaching at the University of Alberta in 1975 and moved to the University of British Columbia in 1979. Professor Riddell has acted as economic advisor and consultant to numerous federal and provincial government departments as well as international agencies. He is former Academic Co-Chair of the Canadian Employment Research Forum, an Associate of the Canadian Institute for Advanced Research, and past President of the Canadian Economics Association.*

Professor Riddell is a prolific researcher. In recent years he has examined a variety of issues in

How and why did you get into economics?

I started out in chemical engineering, but in the second year took an introductory course in economics. At the time I had little knowledge of what economics was—like many people, I confused the social science of economics with the professional program of business and commerce. Economics appealed to me for several reasons. Most of the subject matter was of immense social importance: What makes some countries rich and others poor? How should societies allocate their scarce resources in order to achieve the highest level of well-being for their citizens? What causes ups and downs of economics activity with the business cycle? and so on. I also liked the analytical rigour and the fact that the discipline seemed to have developed a set of tools that could be employed to address these "big questions"—as well as many smaller ones. Finally, the policy relevance of the subject was an attractive feature.

You have spent a lot of time in recent years studying unemployment. Why do you find this topic so absorbing?

One reason is the importance of the subject: unemployment may result in the underutilization of people's time and talents, reduce incomes and increase poverty. And persistent high unemployment raises questions in many observers' minds about the ability of the labour market to perform its key function of matching the demands of workers for jobs and of employers for workers. For these reasons, the unemployment rate is one of the most closely followed economic indicators.

Why in recent years has the Canadian unemployment rate remained so high compared with the U.S. unemployment rate?

At the outset, we need to recognize (or admit!) that we still don't fully understand the answer to this question, despite a fair amount of research. However, some important aspects are reasonably clear. First, it is important to distinguish between the 1980s and the 1990s. An unemployment rate gap of about 2 to 3 percentage points emerged beginning in the early 1980s, and this differential widened further in the 1990s. It is tempting to attribute the higher relative Canadian unemployment to weaker economic performance in Canada—that is, that the Canadian economy wasn't growing at a sufficiently rapid rate and wasn't creating enough jobs. This has been the case in the 1990s—both output growth and employment growth were lower in Canada than in the United States. The widening of the unemployment gap in the 1990s can largely be attributed to the weaker economic growth in Canada during the first half of that decade, much of which in turn appears to be due to the much more aggressive anti-inflation policy pursued in Canada during the late 1980s and early 1990s. However, this same story does not apply to the 1980s. During that decade, the performance of the Canadian economy did not deteriorate relative to the United States. Indeed, both overall growth in the production of goods and services and growth in employment were very similar in the two countries. Most of the unemployment gap during the 1980s can be attributed to the change in how Canadians spend their time when not employed relative to Americans, with Canadians becoming more likely to be engaged in job search, whereas Americans became more likely to drop out of the labour force when not employed. Understanding the causes of this change in behaviour is the key to understanding the emergence of the unemployment differential.

How does the Canadian labour market differ from that in the United States?

Relative to the differences that exist between most economies and societies, Canada and the United States are very similar. These similarities are evident in the labour market as well—for example, both countries have highly educated and skilled work forces, and similar industrial and occupational struc-

tures. But there are also a number of differences. Canadian labour market policies generally lie between the extremes of the more *laissez-faire* American approach and the more highly regulated European approach. The principal Canadian income support programs for the working-age population—unemployment insurance and welfare—cover a large fraction of the population and provide higher levels than their U.S. counterparts.

One of the principal conclusions of recent comparative Canada–U.S. labour research is that these differences in labour market and income support policies do influence outcomes and behaviour in the two societies—they are "small differences that matter" (borrowing a phrase that summed up the conclusions of one set of studies).

Can you give an example from your own work that illustrates this "small differences that matter" idea?

The divergence in the importance of unions in the two countries during the past three decades is a good

> *Most of the unemployment gap during the 1980s can be attributed to the change in how Canadians spend their time when not employed relative to Americans, ...*

illustration. The extent of unionization in Canada and the United States was very similar as recently as the mid-1960s, yet now union coverage in Canada is more than double that of the United States. A worker picked at random from either the public or the private sectors is more than twice as likely to be covered by a union contract in Canada than his or her counterpart in the United States.

A number of explanations have been offered for the decline of the unions in the United States and the emergence of a substantial Canada–U.S. unionization differential. These include: (i) changes in economic structure (decline of manufacturing employment, growth of service sector employment, growth of part-time work, growth of small firms, etc.); (ii) differences in social attitudes towards unions; (iii) greater demand for union coverage among Canadian workers; and (iv) differences between the two countries in labour laws relating to unionization and collective bargaining and in the administration and enforcement of these laws. My work on Canada–U.S. unionization finds very little support for the first three of these explanations, and points to the differences in the laws and their administration as the principal source of the differences in union coverage.

Another topic you have worked on is unemployment insurance. This has also been an area of considerable policy debate and reform in Canada. What role has the research played in this debate?
This case is a good illustration of progress in social science. In 1971, Canada made massive changes to its Unemployment Insurance program, including substantially increased coverage of the program, higher benefit levels, lower qualification requirements, and

> *Economics requires a diverse set of skills ... it's a mistake to concentrate mainly on highly technical and analytical subjects. Having a good "tool kit" is necessary, but not sufficient.*

other major changes. At the time relatively little was known about the labour market effects of Unemployment Insurance. Since then a substantial body of research on these effects—in Canada and elsewhere—has been built up. With hindsight, we now recognize that some of the 1971 changes were probably unwise. Recent reforms to the Unemployment Insurance program (now called "Employment Insurance") have had the advantage of a much greater base of information about the likely impacts of changes to the program. Indeed, the 1996 amendments to the Unemployment Insurance program had

more research input than any previous package of reforms.

What type of labour market research do you foresee having the greatest payoff in the future?
International comparative research, an area that has seen some growth recently, seems likely to be able to pay dividends for some time. There are a wide variety of labour market policies and institutions across countries, and this great variation provides much scope for a richer understanding of the impacts of these institutions and policies.

I also believe that there is great potential to learn from social experiments—that is, situations in which there is random assignment into "treatment" and "control" groups. Economics will remain a largely nonexperimental science for a long time, and random assignment is not practical or even feasible in all circumstances. Nonetheless, there are many labour market interventions whose impacts on behaviour could be determined with greater confidence than now exists through the use of social experiments. Policy makers need to take a long-term view—that such experiments add to society's stock of knowledge about the probable effects of policy interventions, thus making it more likely that future policies will achieve their desired effects and making it clearer what the unintended consequences of these policies will be.

What subjects would you advise a student to pursue if he or she wants to become a professional economist today?
Economics requires a diverse set of skills, making it a challenging but also very interesting profession. On the one hand, it's important to have a solid grounding in mathematics and statistics. I would stress the value of good empirical skills—the manipulation and interpretation of data—because I expect economics to continue to become an increasingly empirical science. On the other hand, it's important to have a good knowledge of instituitions and policy issues. Thus I believe it's a mistake to concentrate mainly on highly technical and analytical subjects. Having a good "tool kit" is necessary, but not sufficient. This argues for being exposed to a wide range of subjects father than focusing narrowly.

Chapter **18**

Market Failure and Public Choice

In 1998, the federal, provincial, and municipal governments in Canada employed 1.5 million people and spent 42 cents of every dollar earned by Canadians. Do we need this much government? Is government, as some conservatives and Reform Party members suggest, too big? Is government "the problem"? Or, despite its enormous size, is government too small to do all the things it must attend to? Is government, as some liberals and social democrats suggest, not contributing enough to eco-

Government— the Solution or the Problem?

nomic life? ◆ Government touches many aspects of our lives. It is present at our birth, paying for the hospitals in which we are born and training the doctors and nurses who deliver us. It is present throughout our education, paying for schools, colleges, and universities in which we study. It is present throughout our working lives, taxing our incomes, regulating our work environment, and paying us benefits when we are unemployed. It is present throughout our retirement, paying us a pension and, when we die, taxing our bequests. And government provides services such as the enforcement of law and order and the provision of national defence. But the government does not make all our choices. We decide what work to do, how much to save, and what to spend our income on. Why does the government participate in some aspects of our lives but not others? ◆ Almost everyone, from the poor, single mother to the wealthy taxpayer, grumbles about government services. Why is the bureaucracy so unpopular? And what determines the scale on which public services are provided?

◆ We begin our study of governments and markets by describing the government sector and explaining how, in the absence of a government, the market economy fails to achieve an efficient allocation of resources. We also explain how the scale of government is determined.

After studying this chapter, you will be able to:

- Explain how the economic role for government arises from market failure and inequity

- Distinguish between public goods and private goods and explain the free-rider problem

- Explain how the quantity of public goods is determined

- Explain why most of the government's revenue comes from income taxes and why income taxes are progressive

- Explain why some goods are taxed at a much higher rate than others

The Economic Theory of Government

THE ECONOMIC THEORY OF GOVERNMENT SEEKS to predict the economic actions that governments take and the consequences of those actions. Governments exist to help people cope with scarcity and provide a nonmarket mechanism for allocating scarce resources. Four economic problems that governments help people cope with are:

- Public goods
- Monopoly
- Externalities
- Economic inequality

Public Goods

Some goods and services are consumed either by everyone or by no one. Examples are national defence, law and order, and sewage and waste disposal services. National defence systems cannot isolate individuals and refuse to protect them. Airborne diseases from untreated sewage do not favour some people and hit others. A good or service that can be consumed simultaneously by everyone and from which no one can be excluded is called a **public good**.

The market economy fails to deliver the efficient quantity of public goods because of a free-rider problem. Everyone tries to free ride on everyone else because the good is available to all whether they pay for it or not. We'll study public goods and the free-rider problem later in this chapter.

Monopoly

Monopoly and *rent seeking* prevent the allocation of resources from being efficient. Every business tries to maximize profit. And when a monopoly exists, it can increase profit by restricting output and increasing price. Until fairly recently, for example, Bell Canada had a monopoly on long-distance telephone services, and the quantity of long-distance services was much smaller and the price much higher than they are today. Since the end of Bell's monopoly, the quantity of long-distance calls has exploded.

Some monopolies arise from *legal barriers to entry*—barriers to entry created by governments—but a major activity of government is to regulate monopoly and to enforce laws that prevent cartels and other restrictions on competition. We study these regulations and laws in Chapter 19.

Externalities

An **externality** is a cost or benefit that arises from an economic transaction and that falls on people who do not participate in that transaction. For example, when a chemical factory (legally) dumps its waste into a river and kills the fish, it imposes an external cost on the members of a fishing club who fish downstream. External costs and benefits are not usually taken into account by the people whose actions create them. For example, when the chemical factory decides whether to dump waste into the river, it does not take the fishing club's views into account. When a homeowner fills her garden with spring bulbs, she generates an external benefit for all the passers-by. In deciding how much to spend on this lavish display, she takes into account only the benefits accruing to herself. We study externalities in Chapter 20.

These three problems from which government economic activity arises create an *inefficient* use of resources, a situation called **market failure**. When market failure occurs, the market produces too many of some goods and services and too few of some others. In these cases, the cost of producing a good does not equal the value that people place on it. By reallocating resources, it is possible to make some people better off while making no one worse off. So some government activity is an attempt to modify the market outcome so as to moderate the effects of market failure.

Economic Inequality

Government economic activity also arises because an unregulated market economy delivers what most people regard as an unfair distribution of income. To lessen the degree of inequality, governments tax some people and pay benefits to others. You studied inequality and redistribution in Chapter 17. In this chapter, we'll look further at taxes and try to explain why the income tax is progressive and why some goods are taxed at extremely high rates.

Before we begin to study each of these problems from which government activity arises, let's look at the arena in which governments operate, the "political marketplace."

Public Choice and the Political Marketplace

Government is a complex organization made up of millions of individuals, each with his or her *own* economic objectives. Government policy is the outcome of the choices made by these individuals. To analyse these choices, economists have developed a *public choice theory* of the political marketplace. The actors in the political marketplace are:

- Voters
- Politicians
- Bureaucrats

Figure 18.1 illustrates the choices and interactions of these actors. Let's look at each in turn.

Voters Voters are the consumers in the political marketplace. In markets for goods and services, people express their preferences by their willingness to pay. In the political marketplace, they express their preferences by their votes, campaign contributions, and lobbying activity. Public choice theory assumes that people support the policies they believe will make them better off and oppose the policies they believe will make them worse off. It is voters' *perceptions* rather than reality that guide their choices.

Politicians Politicians are the entrepreneurs of the political marketplace. Public choice theory assumes that the objective of a politician is to get elected and to remain in office. Votes to a politician are like economic profit to a firm. To get enough votes, politicians propose policies that they expect will appeal to a majority of voters.

Bureaucrats Bureaucrats are the hired officials in government departments. They are the producers or firms in the political marketplace. Public choice theory assumes that bureaucrats aim to maximize their own utility and that to achieve this objective, they try to maximize the budget of their department.

The bigger the budget of a department, the greater is the prestige of its chief and the larger is the opportunity for promotion for people farther down the bureaucratic ladder. So all the members of a department have an interest in maximizing the department's budget. To maximize their budgets, bureaucrats devise programs that they expect will appeal to politicians and they help politicians to explain their programs to voters.

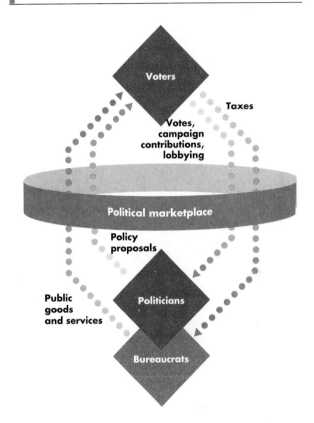

FIGURE 18.1

The Political Marketplace

Voters express their demands for policies by voting, making campaign contributions, and lobbying. Politicians propose policies to appeal to a majority of voters. Bureaucrats try to maximize the budgets of their departments. A political equilibrium emerges in which no group can improve its position by making a different choice.

Political Equilibrium

Voters, politicians, and bureaucrats make choices to best further their own objectives. But each group is constrained by the preferences of the other groups and by what is technologically feasible. The outcome that results from the choices of voters, politicians, and bureaucrats is a **political equilibrium**, which is a situation in which all their choices are compatible and in which no group can improve its position by making a different choice. Let's see how voters, politicians, and bureaucrats interact to determine the quantity of public goods.

Public Goods and the Free-Rider Problem

WHY DOES THE GOVERNMENT PROVIDE GOODS and services such as national defence and public health? Why don't we buy environmental protection from Arctic Ozone, Inc., a private firm that competes for our dollars in the marketplace in the same way that McDonald's and Coca-Cola do? The answer to these questions lies in the free-rider problem created by public goods. Let's explore this problem. We begin by looking at the nature of a public good.

Public Goods

A *public good* is a good or service that can be consumed simultaneously by everyone and from which no one can be excluded. The first feature of a public good is called nonrivalry. A good is *nonrival* if the consumption by one person does not decrease the consumption by another person. An example is watching a television show. The opposite of nonrival is rival. A good is *rival* if the consumption by one person decreases the consumption by another person. An example is eating a hotdog.

The second feature of a public good is that it is nonexcludable. A good is *nonexcludable* if it is impossible, or extremely costly, to prevent someone from benefiting from a good. An example is national defence. It would be difficult to exclude someone from being defended. The opposite of nonexcludable is excludable. A good is *excludable* if it is possible to prevent a person from enjoying the benefits of a good. An example is cable television. Cable companies can ensure that only those people who have paid the fee receive programs.

Figure 18.2 classifies goods according to these two criteria and gives examples of goods in each category. National defence is a *pure* public good. One person's consumption of the security provided by our national defence system does not decrease the security of someone else—defence is nonrival. And the military cannot select those whom it will protect and those whom it will leave exposed to threats—defence is nonexcludable.

Many goods have a public element but are not pure public goods. An example is a highway. A highway is nonrival until it becomes congested. One more car on a highway with plenty of space does not reduce anyone else's consumption of transportation

FIGURE 18.2
Public Goods and Private Goods

A pure public good (bottom right) is one for which consumption is nonrival and from which it is impossible to exclude a consumer. Pure public goods pose a free-rider problem. A pure private good (top left) is one for which consumption is rival and from which consumers can be excluded. Some goods are nonexcludable but are rival (bottom left), and some goods are nonrival but are excludable (top right).

Source: Adapted from and inspired by E. S. Savas, *Privatizing the Public Sector*, Chatham House Publishers, Inc., Chatham, NJ, 1982, p. 34.

services. But once the highway becomes congested, one extra vehicle lowers the quality of the service available to everyone else—it becomes rival like a private good. Also, users can be excluded from a highway by tollgates. Another example is fish in the ocean. Ocean fish are rival because a fish taken by one person is not available for anyone else. Ocean fish are also nonexcludable because it is difficult to prevent people from catching them.

The Free-Rider Problem

Public goods create a free-rider problem. A **free rider** is a person who consumes a good without paying for it. Public goods create a *free-rider problem* because the quantity of the good that a person is able to consume is not influenced by the amount the person pays for the good. So no one has an incentive to pay enough for a public good. Let's look more closely at the free-rider problem by studying an example.

The Benefit of a Public Good

Suppose that a device has been invented that makes it possible to eliminate acid rain. Let's call this device an acid-rain check. The benefit provided by an acid-rain check is the *value* of its services. The *value of a private* good is the maximum amount that a person is willing to pay for one more unit, which is shown by the person's demand curve. The value of a *public* good is the maximum amount that all the *people* are willing to pay for one more unit of it.

Total benefit is the dollar value that a person places on a given level of provision of a public good. The greater the quantity of a public good, the larger is a person's total benefit. *Marginal benefit* is the increase in total benefit that results from a one-unit increase in the quantity of a public good.

Figure 18.3 shows the marginal benefit that arises from acid-rain checks for a society with just two members, Lisa and Max. Lisa's and Max's marginal benefits are graphed as MB_L and MB_M, respectively, in parts (a) and (b) of the figure. The marginal benefit from a public good is similar to the marginal utility from a private good—its magnitude diminishes as the quantity of the good increases. For Lisa, the marginal benefit from the first acid-rain check is $80, and from the second it is $60. By the time 5 acid-rain checks are deployed, Lisa's marginal benefit is zero. For Max, the marginal utility from the first acid-rain check is $50, and from the second it is $40. By the time 5 acid-rain checks are installed, Max perceives only $10 worth of marginal benefit.

Part (c) shows the economy's marginal benefit curve, *MB*. An individual's marginal benefit curve for a public good is similar to the individual's demand curve for a private good. But the economy's marginal benefit curve for a public good is different from the market demand curve for a private good. To obtain the market demand curve for a *private* good, we sum the quantities demanded by all individuals at each price—we sum the individual demand curves *horizontally* (see Chapter 8, p. 169). But to find the economy's marginal benefit curve of a *public* good, we sum the marginal benefits of each individual at each quantity—we sum the individual marginal benefit curves *vertically*. The resulting marginal benefit for the economy made up of Lisa and Max is the economy's marginal benefit curve graphed in part (c)—the curve *MB*. Lisa's marginal benefit from the first acid-rain check gets added to Max's marginal benefit from the first acid-rain check because they *both* consume the first acid-rain check.

FIGURE 18.3

Benefits of a Public Good

(a) Lisa's marginal benefit

(b) Max's marginal benefit

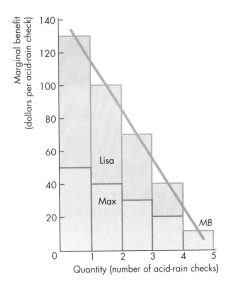

(c) Economy's marginal benefit

The marginal benefit to the economy at each quantity of the public good is the sum of the marginal benefits of all individuals. The marginal benefit curves are MB_L for Lisa, MB_M for Max, and *MB* for the economy.

The Efficient Quantity of a Public Good

An economy with two people would not buy any acid-rain checks—because the total benefit falls far short of the cost. But an economy with 25 million people might. To determine the efficient quantity, we need to take the cost as well as the benefit into account.

The cost of an acid-rain check is based on technology and the prices of the resources used to produce it (see Chapter 11).

Figure 18.4 shows the benefits and costs. The second and third columns of the table show the total and marginal benefits. The next two columns show the total and marginal cost of producing acid-rain checks. The final column shows net benefit. Part (a) graphs total benefit, *TB*, and total cost, *TC*.

The efficient quantity is the one that maximizes *net benefit*—total benefit minus total cost—and occurs when 2 acid-rain checks are provided.

The fundamental principles of marginal analysis that you have used to explain how consumers maximize utility and how firms maximize profit can also be used to calculate the efficient scale of provision of a public good. Figure 18.4(b) shows this alternative approach. The marginal benefit curve is *MB* and the marginal cost curve is *MC*. When marginal benefit exceeds marginal cost, net benefit increases if the quantity produced increases. When marginal cost exceeds marginal benefit, net benefit increases if the quantity produced decreases. Marginal benefit equals marginal cost with 2 acid-rain checks. So making marginal cost equal to marginal benefit maximizes net benefit and uses resources efficiently.

Private Provision

We have now worked out the quantity of acid-rain checks that maximizes net benefit. Would a private firm—Arctic Ozone, Inc.—deliver that quantity? It would not. To do so, it would have to collect $1.5 billion to cover its costs—or $60 from each of the 25 million people in the economy. But no one would have an incentive to buy his or her "share" of the acid-rain check system. Everyone would reason as follows: The number of acid-rain checks provided by Arctic Ozone, Inc., is not affected by my $60. But my own private consumption is greater if I free ride and do not pay my share of the cost of the acid-rain check system. If I do not pay, I enjoy the same quality of air and I can buy more private goods. Therefore I will spend my $60 on other goods and free ride on the public good. This is the free-rider problem.

If everyone reasons the same way, Arctic Ozone has zero revenue and so provides no acid-rain checks. Because two acid-rain checks is the efficient level, private provision is inefficient.

Public Provision

Suppose there are two political parties, the Greens and the Smokes, which agree with each other on all issues except for the quantity of acid-rain checks. The Greens would like to provide 4 acid-rain checks at a cost of $5 billion, with benefits of $5 billion and a net benefit of zero, as shown in Fig. 18.4. The Smokes would like to provide 1 acid-rain check at a cost of $0.5 billion, a benefit of $2 billion, and a net benefit of $1.5 billion—see Fig. 18.4.

Before deciding on their policy proposals, the two political parties do a "what-if" analysis. Each party reasons as follows. If each party offers the acid-rain check program it wants—Greens 4 acid-rain checks and Smokes 1 acid-rain check—the voters will see that they will get a net benefit of $1.5 billion from the Smokes and zero net benefit from the Greens, and the Smokes will win the election.

Contemplating this outcome, the Greens realize that their party is too "green" to get elected. They figure that they must scale back their proposal to 2 acid-rain checks. At this level of provision, total cost is $1.5 billion, total benefit is $3.5 billion, and net benefit is $2 billion. If the Smokes stick with 1 acid-rain check, the Greens will win the election.

But contemplating this outcome, the Smokes realize that they must match the Greens. They too propose to provide 2 acid-rain checks on exactly the same terms as the Greens. If the parties offer the same number of acid-rain checks, the voters are indifferent between them. They flip coins to decide their votes, and each party receives around 50 percent of the vote.

The result of the politicians' "what-if" analysis is that each party offers 2 acid-rain checks, so regardless of who wins the election, this is the quantity of acid-rain checks installed. And this quantity is efficient. It maximizes the perceived net benefit of the voters. Thus in this example, competition in the political marketplace results in the efficient provision of a public good. But for this outcome to occur, voters must be well informed and evaluate the alternatives. But as you will see below, they do not always have an incentive to achieve this outcome.

FIGURE 18.4

The Efficient Quantity of a Public Good

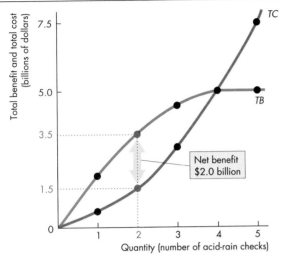

(a) Total benefit and total cost

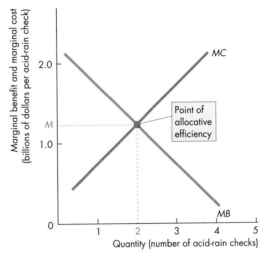

(b) Marginal benefit and marginal cost

Quantity (number of acid-rain checks)	Total benefit (billions of dollars)	Marginal benefit (billions of dollars per acid-rain check)	Total cost (billions of dollars)	Marginal cost (billions of dollars per acid-rain check)	Net benefit (billions of dollars)
0	0		0		0
		2.0		0.5	
1	2.0		0.5		1.5
		1.5		1.0	
2	3.5		1.5		2.0
		1.0		1.5	
3	4.5		3.0		1.5
		0.5		2.0	
4	5.0		5.0		0
		0		2.5	
5	5.0		7.5		−2.5

Net benefit—the vertical distance between total benefit, *TB*, and total cost, *TC*—is maximized when 2 acid-rain checks are installed (part a) and where marginal benefit, *MB*, equals marginal cost, *MC* (part b). The Smokes would like 1 acid-rain check, and the Greens would like 4. But each party recognizes that its only hope of being elected is to provide 2 acid-rain checks—the quantity that maximizes net benefit and so leaves no room for the other party to improve on.

The Principle of Minimum Differentiation   In the example we've just studied, both parties propose identical policies. This tendency towards identical policies is an example of the **principle of minimum differentiation**, which is the tendency for competitors to make themselves identical to appeal to the maximum number of clients or voters. This principle not only describes the behaviour of political parties but also explains why fast-food restaurants cluster in the same block, and even why new auto models share similar features. If McDonald's opens a restaurant in a new location, it is more likely that Burger King will open next door to McDonald's rather than a kilometre down the road. If Chrysler designs a new van with a sliding door on the driver's side, most likely Ford will too.

The Role of Bureaucrats

We have analysed the behaviour of politicians but not that of the bureaucrats who translate the choices of the politicians into programs and who control the day-to-day activities that deliver public goods. Let's now see how the economic choices of bureaucrats influence the political equilibrium.

To do so, we'll stick with the previous example. We've seen that competition between two political parties delivers the efficient quantity of acid-rain checks. But will the Department of the Environment (DOE) cooperate and accept this outcome?

Suppose the objective of the DOE is to maximize the environment budget. With 2 acid-rain checks being provided at minimum cost, the environment budget is $1.5 billion (see Fig. 18.4). To increase its budget, the DOE might do two things. First, it might try to persuade the politicians that 2 acid-rain checks cost more than $1.5 billion. As Fig. 18.5 shows, if possible, the DOE would like to convince Parliament that 2 acid-rain checks cost $3.5 billion—the entire benefit. Second, and pressing its position even more strongly, the DOE might argue for more acid-rain checks. It might press for 4 acid-rain checks and a budget of $5 billion. In this situation, total benefit and total cost are equal and net benefit is zero.

The DOE wants to maximize its budget, but won't the politicians prevent it from doing so because the DOE's preferred outcome costs votes? They will if voters are well informed and know what is best for them. But voters might be rationally ignorant. In this case, well-informed interest groups might enable the DOE to achieve its objective.

Rational Ignorance

A principle of public choice theory is that it is rational for a voter to be ignorant about an issue unless that issue has a perceptible effect on the voter's income. **Rational ignorance** is the decision *not* to acquire information because the cost of doing so exceeds the expected benefit. For example, each voter knows that he or she can make virtually no difference to the environment policy of the Canadian government. Each voter also knows that it would take an enormous amount of time and effort to become even moderately well informed about alternative technologies. So voters remain relatively uninformed about the technicalities of environment issues. (Though we are using

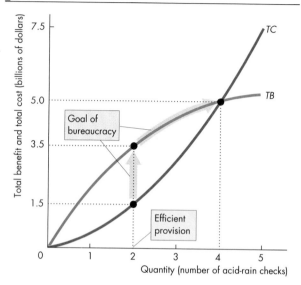

FIGURE 18.5

Bureaucratic Overprovision

The goal of a bureaucracy is to maximize its budget. A bureaucracy that maximizes its budget will seek to increase its budget so that its total cost equals total benefit and then to use its budget to expand output and expenditure. Here, the DOE tries to get $3.5 billion to provide 2 acid-rain checks. It would like to increase the quantity of acid-rain checks to 4 with a budget of $5 billion.

environment policy as an example, the same applies to all aspects of government economic activity.)

All voters are consumers of clean air. But not all voters are producers of the equipment to monitor air quality. Only a small number are in this category. Voters who own or work for firms that produce acid-rain checks have a direct personal interest in the environment because it affects their incomes. These voters have an incentive to become well informed about environment issues and to operate a political lobby aimed at furthering their own interests. In collaboration with the bureaucracy, these voters exert a larger influence than do the relatively uninformed voters who only consume this public good.

When the rationality of the uninformed voter and special interest groups are taken into account, the political equilibrium provides public goods in excess of the efficient quantity. So in the acid-rain check example, 3 or 4 acid-rain checks might be installed rather than the efficient quantity, which is 2 acid-rain checks.

Two Types of Political Equilibrium

We've seen that two types of political equilibrium are possible: efficient and inefficient. These two types of political equilibrium correspond to two theories of government:

■ Public interest theory
■ Public choice theory

Public Interest Theory Public interest theory predicts that governments make choices that achieve efficiency. This outcome occurs in a perfect political system in which voters are fully informed about the effects of policies and refuse to vote for outcomes that can be improved upon.

Public Choice Theory Public choice theory predicts that governments make choices that result in inefficiency. This outcome occurs in political markets in which voters are rationally ignorant and base their votes only on issues that they know affect their own net benefit. Voters pay more attention to their interests as producers than their interests as consumers, and public officials also act in their own best interest. The result is *government failure* that parallels market failure.

Why Government Is Large and Grows

Now that we know how the quantity of public goods is determined, we can explain part of the reason for the growth of government. Government grows, in part, because the demand for some public goods increases at a faster rate than the demand for private goods. There are two possible reasons for this growth:

■ Voter preferences
■ Inefficient overprovision

Voter Preferences The growth of government can be explained by voter preferences in the following way. As voters' incomes increase (as they usually do in most years), the demand for many public goods increases more quickly than income. (Technically, the *income elasticity of demand* for many public goods is greater than 1—see Chapter 5, pp. 98–99.) Many (and the most expensive) public goods are in this category. They include transportation systems such as highways, airports, and air-traffic control systems; public health; education; and national defence. If politicians did not support increases in expenditures on these items, they would not get elected.

Inefficient Overprovision Inefficient overprovision might explain the *size* of government, but not its *growth rate*. It (possibly) explains why government is *larger* than its efficient scale, but it does not explain why governments use an increasing proportion of total resources.

Voters Strike Back

If government grows too large, relative to what voters are willing to accept, there might be a voter backlash against government programs and a large bureaucracy. During the 1990s, the politicians of all parties embraced the idea of a smaller, leaner, and more efficient government.

Another way that voters—and politicians—can try to counter the tendency of bureaucrats to expand their budgets is to privatize the *production* of public goods. Government *provision* of a public good does not automatically imply that a government-operated bureau must *produce* the good. Garbage collection (public good) is often done by a private firm and in some countries experiments are being conducted with private fire departments and even private prisons.

R E V I E W   Q U I Z

- What is the free-rider problem and why does it make the private provision of a public good inefficient?
- Under what conditions will competition among politicians for votes result in an efficient quantity of a public good?
- How do rationally ignorant voters and budget maximizing bureaucrats prevent competition in the political marketplace from producing the efficient quantity of a public good? Do they result in too much or too little public provision of public goods?

We've now seen how voters, politicians, and bureaucrats interact to determine the quantity of a public good. But public goods are paid for with taxes. Taxes also redistribute income. How does the political marketplace determine the scale and variety of taxes that we pay?

Taxes

TAXES GENERATE THE FINANCIAL RESOURCES that provide voters with public goods and other benefits. Five groups of taxes are used:

- Income taxes
- Provincial sales taxes and the GST
- Property taxes
- Employment insurance taxes
- Excise taxes

Figure 18.6 shows the relative amounts raised by these five types of taxes in 1998. Income taxes are the biggest tax source and raised 56 percent of tax revenues in 1998. Provincial sales taxes and the GST are the next biggest revenue source and they raised 22 percent of total taxes in 1998. Property taxes raise about 11 percent of total taxes. Employment insurance taxes raise 7 percent of revenue. And finally, excise taxes raise 4 percent of government revenue. Although they raise a small amount of revenue, excise taxes have a big impact on some markets, as you'll discover later in this chapter. Let's take a closer look at each type of tax.

FIGURE 18.6

Government Tax Revenues

More than half of government revenues come from income taxes. About a third come from provincial sales tax, the GST, and property tax. Excise taxes bring in a small amount of revenue, but these taxes have big effects on a small number of markets.

Source: Statistics Canada, *StatsCan: Canada; CANSIM Disc,* March 1999.

Income Taxes

Income taxes are paid on personal incomes and corporate profits. In 1998, the personal income tax raised $73 billion for the federal government and another $46 billion for provincial governments. Corporate profits taxes raised $25 billion for the federal government and $15 billion for the provincial governments. We'll look first at the effects of personal income taxes and then at corporate profits taxes.

Personal Income Tax   The amount of income tax that a person pays depends on her or his *taxable income.* Taxable income equals total income minus expenses and other adjustments.

The *tax rate* (percent) depends on the income level and on the province of residence. Provincial income tax rates are defined as a percentage of the federal rate (except for Quebec) and range from 42.75 percent of the federal rate in Ontario to 69 percent of the federal rate in Newfoundland. But surtaxes at both the federal and provincial levels increase these rates. In Ontario, for a single person, and combining federal and provincial basic taxes and surtaxes, the tax rates increase according to the scale:

$0 to $29,590	24.8 percent
$29,591 to $46,747	37.9 percent
$46,748 to $57,184	40.1 percent
$57,185 to $59,180	41.7 percent
over $59,180	47.8 percent

The percentages in this list are marginal tax rates. A **marginal tax rate** is the percentage of an additional dollar of income that is paid in tax. For example if taxable income increases from $20,000 to $20,001, the additional tax paid is 24.8 cents and the marginal tax rate is 24.8 percent. If income increases from $60,000 to $60,001, the additional tax paid is 47.8 cents and the marginal tax rate is 47.8 percent.

The **average tax rate** is the percentage of income that is paid in tax. The average tax rate is less than the marginal tax rate. For example, a single person with a taxable income of $50,000 in 1998 pays $15,138 in income tax. This person's average tax rate is 30.3 percent. A person whose taxable income is $100,000 a year pays $38,366 in income tax, an average tax rate of 38.4 percent.

The average tax rate increases as income increases. When the average tax rate increases as income increases, the tax is called a **progressive tax**. A progressive tax contrasts with a **proportional tax**, which has the same average tax rate at all income levels, and a **regressive tax**, which has a decreasing average tax rate as income increases.

The Effect of Income Taxes Figure 18.7 shows how the income tax affects labour markets. Part (a) shows the market for low-wage workers and part (b) shows the market for high-wage workers. These labour markets are competitive and with no income taxes, they work just like all the other competitive markets you have studied. The demand curves are *LD* and the supply curves are *LS* (in both parts of the figure). Both groups work 40 hours a week. Low-wage workers earn $9 an hour and high-wage workers earn $170 an hour. What happens when an income tax is introduced?

If low-wage workers are willing to supply 40 hours a week for $9 an hour when there is no tax, then they are willing to supply that same quantity in

the face of a 25 percent tax only if the wage rises to $12 an hour. That is, they want to get the $9 an hour they received before plus the $3 (25 percent of $12) that they now must pay to the government. So the supply of labour decreases because the amount received from work is lowered by the amount of income tax paid. The acceptable wage rate at each level of employment rises by the amount of the tax that must be paid. For low-wage workers who face a tax rate of 25 percent, the supply curve shifts to *LS + tax*. The equilibrium wage rate rises to $10 an hour, but the after-tax wage rate falls to $7.50 an hour. Employment falls to 36 hours a week.

For high-wage workers who face a tax rate of 50 percent, the supply curve shifts to *LS + tax*. The equilibrium wage rate rises to $200 an hour, and the after-tax wage rate falls to $100 an hour. Employment decreases to 32 hours a week. The decrease in employment of high-wage workers is larger than that

---

FIGURE 18.7

The Effects of Income Taxes

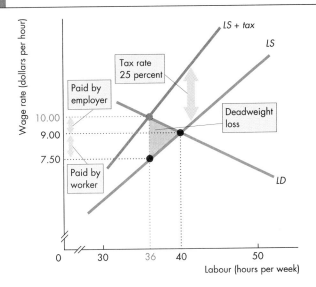

(a) Lowest income tax rate

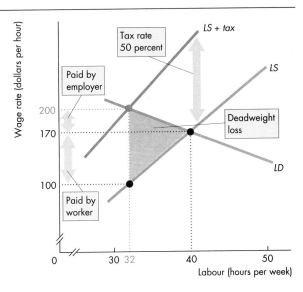

(b) Highest income tax rate

The demand for labour is *LD* and with no income taxes, the supply of labour is *LS* (both parts). In part (a), low-wage workers earn $9 an hour and each works 40 hours a week. In part (b), high-wage workers earn $170 an hour and each works 40 hours a week. An income tax decreases the supply of labour and the labour supply curve shifts leftward. For low-wage workers in part (a), whose marginal tax rate is 25 percent,

supply decreases to *LS + tax*. Employment decreases to 36 hours a week. For high-wage workers in part (b), whose marginal tax rate is 50 percent, supply decreases to *LS + tax*. Employment decreases to 32 hours a week. The deadweight loss from the high marginal tax rate on high-wage workers is much larger than that from the low marginal tax rate on low-wage workers.

of low-wage workers because of the differences in the marginal tax rates they each face.

Notice that both the employer and the worker pay the income tax. In the case of low-wage workers, the employer pays an extra $1 an hour and the worker pays $1.50 an hour. In the case of high-wage workers, employers pay an extra $30 an hour and workers pay $70 an hour. The split depends on the elasticities of demand and supply.

Notice also the difference in the *deadweight loss* for the two groups. (Check Chapter 6, pp. 118–119, if you need a refresher on the concept of deadweight loss.) The deadweight loss is much larger for the high-wage workers than for the low-wage workers.

Why Do We Have a Progressive Income Tax?

We have a progressive income tax because it is part of the political equilibrium. A majority of voters support it, so politicians who support it get elected.

The economic model that predicts progressive income taxes is called the *median voter* model. The core idea of the median voter model is that political parties pursue policies most likely to attract the support of the median voter. The median voter is the one in the middle—one-half of the population lies on one side and one-half on the other. Let's see how the median voter model predicts a progressive income tax.

Imagine that government programs benefit everyone equally and are paid for by a proportional income tax. Everyone pays the same percentage of his or her income. In this situation, there is redistribution from high-income voters to low-income voters. Everyone benefits equally but because they have higher incomes, the high-income voters pay a larger amount of taxes.

Is this situation the best one possible for the median voter? It is not. Suppose that instead of using a proportional tax, the marginal tax rate is lowered for low-income voters and increased for high-income voters—a progressive tax. Low-income voters are now better off and high-income voters are worse off. Low-income voters will support this change and high-income voters will oppose it. But there are many more low-income voters than high-income voters, so the low-income voters win.

The median voter is a low-income voter. In fact, because the distribution of income is skewed, the median voter has a smaller income than the average income (see Fig. 17.4). This fact raises an interesting question: why doesn't the median voter support taxes that skim off all income above the average and redistribute it to everyone with a below-average income? This tax would be so progressive that it would result in equal incomes after taxes and transfers were paid.

The answer is that high taxes discourage work and saving and the median voter would be worse off with such radical redistribution than under the arrangements that prevail today.

Let's now look at corporate profits taxes.

Corporate Profits Tax   In popular discussions of taxes, corporate profits taxes are seen as a free source of revenue for the government. Taxing people is bad but taxing corporations is just fine.

It turns out that taxing corporations is very inefficient. We use an inefficient tax because it redistributes income in favour of the median voter, just like the income tax. Let's see why taxing corporate profits is inefficient.

First, the tax is misnamed. It is only partly a tax on economic profit. It is mainly a tax on the income from capital. Taxing the income from capital works like taxing the income from labour except for two critical differences: The supply of capital is highly (perhaps perfectly) elastic, and the quantity of capital influences the productivity of labour and wage income. Because the supply of capital is highly elastic, the tax is fully borne by firms and the quantity of capital decreases. With a smaller capital stock than we would otherwise have, the productivity of labour and incomes are lower than they would otherwise be.

Provincial Sales Taxes and the GST

Provincial sales taxes and the GST are levied on a wide range of goods and services. We studied the effects of these taxes on prices, quantities traded, and tax revenue in Chapter 7.

Unlike the income tax, these taxes are *regressive*. The reason they are regressive is that saving increases with income and sales taxes are paid on only the part of income that is spent.

Suppose, for example, that combined provincial sales tax and GST is 15 percent. A family with an income of $20,000 that spends all its income pays $3,000 in sales tax. Its average tax rate is 15 percent. A family with an income of $100,000 that spends $60,000 and saves $40,000 pays sales taxes of $9,000 (15 percent of $60,000). So this family's average tax rate is 9 percent.

We explained the progressive income tax as the outcome of a voting system that places a large weight on the views of the median voter. If the sales tax is regressive, why does the median voter support it? It is the entire tax code that matters, not an individual tax. So a regressive sales tax is voted for only as part of an overall tax regime that is progressive.

Property Taxes

Property taxes are collected by local governments and are used to provide local public goods. A **local public good** is a public good that is consumed by all the people who live in a particular area. Examples of local public goods are parks, museums, and safe neighbourhoods. There is a much closer connection between property taxes paid and benefits received than in the case of federal and provincial taxes. This close connection makes property taxes similar to a price for local services. Because of this connection, property taxes change both the demand for and supply of property in a neighbourhood. A higher tax lowers supply, but improved local public goods increase demand. So some neighbourhoods have high taxes and high-quality local government services and other neighbourhoods have low taxes and low-quality services. Both can exist in the political equilibrium.

Employment Insurance Taxes

Employment insurance taxes are the contributions paid by employers and employees to provide unemployment compensation benefits.

Unions lobby to get employers to pay a bigger share of these taxes and employers' organizations lobby to get workers to pay a bigger share of them. But this lobbying effort is not worth much. For who *really* pays these taxes depends in no way on who writes the cheques. It depends on the elasticities of demand and supply for labour. Figure 18.8 shows you why.

In both parts of the figure, the demand curve LD and the supply curve LS are identical. With no employment insurance tax, the quantity of labour employed is QL^* and the wage rate is W^*.

An employment insurance tax is now introduced. In Fig. 18.8(a) the employment insurance tax is a payroll deduction; in Fig. 18.8(b) the tax is a charge on employers. When the tax is a payroll deduction, supply decreases and the supply of labour curve shifts leftward to $LS + tax$. The vertical distance between the supply curve LS and the new supply curve $LS + tax$ is the amount of the tax. The wage rate rises to WC, after-tax wage rate falls to WT, and employment decreases to QL_0.

When the employment insurance tax is a charge on employers (Fig. 18.8b), demand decreases and the demand for labour curve shifts leftward to $LD - tax$. The vertical distance between the curve LD and the new demand curve $LD - tax$ is the amount of the tax.

FIGURE 18.8
Employment Insurance Tax

(a) Tax on employees

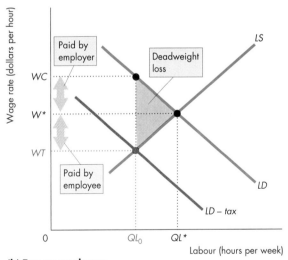

(b) Tax on employers

The labour demand curve is LD and the supply curve is LS. With no employment insurance tax, the quantity of labour employed is QL^* and the wage rate is W^* (in both parts). In part (a), the tax is a payroll deduction. Supply decreases and the supply of labour curve shifts leftward to $LS + tax$. The wage rate rises to WC, after-tax wage rate falls to WT, and employment decreases to QL_0. In part (b), the tax is a charge on employers. Demand decreases and the demand for labour curve shifts leftward to $LD - tax$. The wage rate falls to WT, but the cost of labour rises to WC and employment decreases to QL_0. The outcome is identical in both cases.

The wage rate falls to WT but the cost of labour rises to WC, and employment decreases to QL_0.

So regardless of which side of the market is taxed, the outcome is identical. If the demand for labour is perfectly inelastic or if the supply of labour is perfectly elastic, the employer pays the entire tax. And if the demand for labour is perfectly elastic or if the supply of labour is perfectly inelastic, the employee pays the entire tax. These cases are exactly like those for the sales tax that you studied in Chapter 7 on pp. 137–140.

Excise Taxes

An **excise tax** is a tax on the sale of a particular commodity. The total amount raised by these taxes is small, but they have a big impact on some markets. Let's study the effects of an excise tax by considering the tax on gasoline shown in Fig. 18.9. The demand curve for gasoline is D, and the supply curve is S. If there is no tax on gasoline, its price is 30¢ a litre and 400 million litres of gasoline a day are bought and sold.

Now suppose that a tax is imposed on gasoline at the rate of 30¢ a litre. As a result of the tax, the supply of gasoline decreases and the supply curve shifts leftward. The magnitude of the shift is such that the vertical distance between the original and the new supply curve is the amount of the tax. The new supply curve is the red curve, $S + tax$. The new supply curve intersects the demand curve at 300 million litres a day and 55¢ a litre. This situation is the new equilibrium after the imposition of the tax.

The excise tax creates a deadweight loss made up of the loss of consumer surplus and the loss of producer surplus. The dollar value of that loss is $30 million a day. Because 300 million litres of gasoline are sold each day and the tax is 30¢ a litre, total revenue from the gasoline tax is $90 million a day (300 million litres multiplied by 30¢ a litre). So to raise tax revenue of $90 million dollars a day by using the gasoline tax, a deadweight loss of $15 million a day—one-sixth of the tax revenue—is incurred.

One of the main influences on the deadweight loss arising from a tax is the elasticity of demand for the product. The demand for gasoline is fairly inelastic. As a consequence, when a tax is imposed, the quantity demanded falls by a smaller percentage than the percentage rise in price.

To see the importance of the elasticity of demand, let's consider a different commodity—orange juice. So that we can make a quick and direct comparison, let's assume that the orange juice market

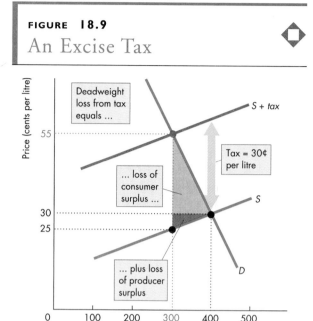

FIGURE 18.9

An Excise Tax

The demand curve for gasoline is D, and the supply curve is S. In the absence of any taxes, gasoline will sell for 30¢ a litre and 400 million litres a day will be bought and sold. When a tax of 30¢ a litre is imposed, the supply curve shifts leftward to become the curve $S + tax$. The new equilibrium price is 55¢ a litre, and 300 million litres a day are bought and sold. The excise tax creates a deadweight loss represented by the grey triangle. The tax revenue collected is 30¢ a litre on 300 million litres, which is $90 million a day. The deadweight loss from the tax is $30 million a day. That is, to raise tax revenue of $90 million a day, a deadweight loss of $15 million a day is incurred.

is exactly as big as the market for gasoline. Figure 18.10 illustrates this market. The demand curve for orange juice is D, and the supply curve is S. Orange juice is not taxed, and so the price of orange juice is 30¢ a litre—where the supply curve and the demand curve intersect—and the quantity of orange juice traded is 400 million litres a day.

Now suppose that the government contemplates abolishing the gasoline tax and taxing orange juice instead. The demand for orange juice is more elastic than the demand for gasoline. It has many good substitutes in the form of other fruit juices. The government wants to raise $90 million a day so that its total revenue is not affected by this tax change. The government's economists, armed with their statistical estimates of the demand and supply curves for orange

FIGURE 18.10

Why We Don't Tax Orange Juice

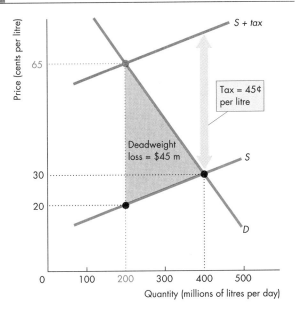

The demand curve for orange juice is D, and the supply curve is S. The equilibrium price is 30¢ a litre, and 400 million litres of juice a day are traded. To raise $90 million of tax revenue, a tax of 45¢ a litre will have to be imposed. The introduction of this tax shifts the supply curve to S + tax. The price rises to 65¢ a litre, and the quantity bought and sold falls to 200 million litres a day. The deadweight loss is represented by the grey triangle and equals $45 million a day. The deadweight loss from taxing orange juice is much larger than that from taxing gasoline (Fig. 18.9) because the demand for orange juice is much more elastic than the demand for gasoline. Items that have a low elasticity of demand are taxed more heavily than items that have a high elasticity of demand.

But what is the deadweight loss in this case? The grey triangle in Fig. 18.10 provides the answer. The magnitude of that deadweight loss is $45 million. Notice how much bigger the deadweight loss is from taxing orange juice than from taxing gasoline. In the case of orange juice, the deadweight loss is one-half the revenue raised, while in the case of gasoline, it is only one-sixth. What accounts for this difference? The supply curves are identical in each case, and the examples were also set up to ensure that the initial no-tax prices and quantities were identical. The difference between the two cases is the elasticity of demand: In the case of gasoline, the quantity demanded falls by only 25 percent when the price almost doubles. In the case of orange juice, the quantity demanded falls by 50 percent when the price only slightly more than doubles.

You can see why taxing orange juice is not on the political agenda of any of the major parties. Vote-seeking politicians seek out taxes that benefit the median voter. Other things remaining the same, this means that they try to minimize the deadweight loss of raising a given amount of revenue. Equivalently, they tax items with poor substitutes more heavily than items with close substitutes.

REVIEW QUIZ

- How do income taxes influence employment and efficiency? Why are income taxes progressive?
- Can Parliament make employers pay a larger share of the employment insurance tax?
- Why do some neighbourhoods have high taxes and high-quality services and others have low taxes and low-quality services?
- Why does the government impose excise taxes at high rates on goods that have a low elasticity of demand?

◆ *Reading Between the Lines* on pp. 406–407 looks at the way in which advancing technology changes the balance between public goods and private goods by examining the effect of the arrival of the GPS navigation technology and the public good role of the lighthouses.

In the next two chapters, we are going to look at government economic actions in the face of monopolies and externalities.

juice that appear in Fig. 18.10, work out that a tax of 45¢ a litre will do the job. With such a tax, the supply curve shifts leftward to become the curve labelled S + tax. This new supply curve intersects the demand curve at a price of 65¢ a litre and at a quantity of 200 million litres a day. The price at which suppliers are willing to produce 200 million litres a day is 20¢ a litre. The government collects a tax of 45¢ a litre on 200 million litres a day, so it collects a total revenue of $90 million dollars a day—exactly the amount that it requires.

Changing Public Goods

NATIONAL POST, MARCH 12, 1999

Lighthouse 'yard sale' coming, group fears

BY GRAEME HAMILTON

Maritime lighthouses that are beacons to mariners and tourists alike will be lost to neglect and foreign ownership if Ottawa doesn't act, a citizens' group warned yesterday.

At a news conference punctuated by the mournful blasts of a nearby fog horn, the group said the federal government is preparing for a "gigantic yard sale" of lighthouses that are no longer needed for navigation. ...

A debate over the future of the Maritime landmarks has simmered for years as many were rendered obsolete by modern navigational technology. ...

Now as the Coast Guard declares lighthouses surplus, they stand to be sold off at "fair market value," ... Some lighthouses in remote locations will be demolished, the group predicted, and others will be bought up by Americans and Europeans looking for oceanfront real estate.

"What would tourism in the Maritimes be without the lighthouses that are so much a part of our landscape, our culture, and our history," said David Curry, co-chairman of the newly formed Lighthouse Protection Act Committee.

The group wants Ottawa to introduce a Lighthouse Protection Act that would designate all lighthouses built before 1950 as heritage sites and allow community groups to lease them as trustees. Currently, fewer than 20 of the country's 580 lighthouses are protected as heritage structures. ...

Jim Calvesbert, regional director of marine programs for the Coast Guard, said budget cutbacks have made it impossible for the agency to continue looking after lighthouses that aren't needed for navigation. ...

Jim Guptill, who was the last keeper of the Chebucto Head lighthouse before it was automated, said he fears future generations could lose an important piece of Maritime history.

"I want these places to remain open to the public and to be maintained," ...

Economic Analysis

■ When lighthouses were installed along Canada's coastlines, they were public goods used as navigational aids.

■ The navigational service could be used simultaneously by everyone and no one could be excluded.

■ Figure 1 shows the marginal cost and marginal benefit of lighthouses.

■ The marginal cost curve is *MC*. When lighthouses were used for navigation, the marginal benefit curve was MB_0. The efficient quantity was 580 lighthouses.

■ Technological change has resulted in a new global public good for navigation, the Global Positioning System (GPS).

■ The GPS, funded and controlled by the U.S. Department of Defense, consists of 24 satellites used by millions of people worldwide.

■ The lighthouse as a navigational aid has become obsolete.

■ With obsolescence, the marginal benefit of lighthouses has decreased and the marginal benefit curve has shifted leftward to MB_1. The efficient quantity of lighthouses as a navigational aid is zero.

■ A lighthouse is no longer a public good.

■ By operating a lighthouse as a tourist site and charging admission, it is possible to prevent a person from enjoying all the benefits of the lighthouse. The lighthouse becomes an excludable good—a private good.

■ Figure 2 shows the emerging market for lighthouses as tourist sites.

■ The marginal cost curve is the same, regardless of the purpose for which the lighthouse is used. So the market supply curve *S* is the same as the marginal cost curve (*MC*) in Fig. 1. A private demand emerges, which is shown by the demand curve D_0. The competitive market determines some equilibrium quantity Q_0 (less than or equal to 580 lighthouses) and equilibrium price P_0.

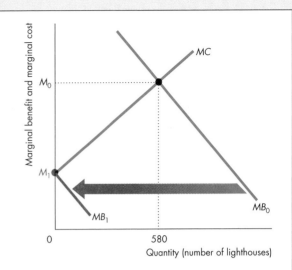

Figure 1 The disappearing lighthouse

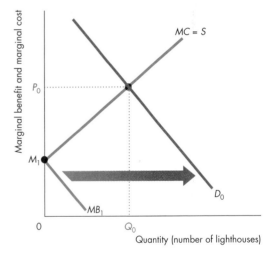

Figure 2 A tourist site market emerges

SUMMARY

Key Points

The Economic Theory of Government
(pp. 392–393)

- Government exists to provide public goods, regulate monopoly, cope with externalities, and reduce economic inequality.
- Public choice theory explains how voters, politicians, and bureaucrats interact in a political marketplace.

Public Goods and the Free-Rider Problem
(pp. 394–399)

- A public good is a good or service that is consumed by everyone and that is *nonrival* and *nonexcludable*.
- A public good creates a *free-rider* problem—no one has an incentive to pay his or her share of the cost of providing a public good.
- The efficient level of provision of a public good is that at which net benefit is maximized. Equivalently, it is the level at which marginal benefit equals marginal cost.
- Competition between political parties, each of which tries to appeal to the maximum number of voters, can lead to the efficient scale of provision of a public good and to both parties proposing the same policies—the principle of minimum differentiation.
- Bureaucrats try to maximize their budgets and if voters are rationally ignorant, producer interests might result in voting to support taxes that provide public goods in quantities that exceed those that maximize net benefit.

Taxes (pp. 400–405)

- Government revenue comes from income taxes, provincial sales taxes and the GST, property taxes, employment insurance taxes, and excise taxes.
- Income taxes decrease the level of employment and create a deadweight loss.

- Taxes can be progressive (the average tax rate rises with income), proportional (the average tax rate is constant), or regressive (the average tax rate falls with income).
- Income taxes are progressive because this arrangement is in the interest of the median voter.
- Property taxes change both demand and supply and can result in high taxes and high-quality service areas and low taxes and low-quality service areas.
- Employment insurance taxes are paid by the employer and the employee (and sales taxes are paid by the buyer and the seller) in amounts that depend on the elasticities of demand and supply.
- Excise taxes at high rates on gasoline, alcoholic beverages, and tobacco products create a smaller deadweight loss than would taxes on items with a more elastic demand.

Key Figures ◆

Key Terms

P R O B L E M S

*1. You are provided with the following information about a sewage disposal system that a city of 1 million people is considering installing:

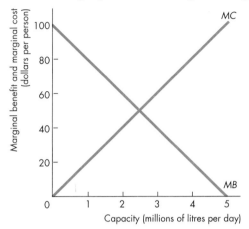

a. What is the capacity that achieves maximum net benefit?

b. How much will each person have to pay in taxes to pay for the efficient capacity level?

c. What is the political equilibrium if voters are well informed?

d. What is the political equilibrium if voters are rationally ignorant and bureaucrats achieve the highest attainable budget?

2. You are provided with the following information about a mosquito control program:

Quantity (square kilometres sprayed per day)	Marginal cost (dollars per day)	Marginal benefit (dollars per day)
0	0	0
1	1,000	5,000
2	2,000	4,000
3	3,000	3,000
4	4,000	2,000
5	5,000	1,000

a. What is the quantity of spraying that achieves maximum net benefit?

b. What is the total tax revenue needed to pay for the efficient quantity of spraying?

c. What is the political equilibrium if voters are well informed?

d. What is the political equilibrium if voters are rationally ignorant and bureaucrats achieve the highest attainable budget?

*3. An economy has two groups of people, A and B. The population consists of 80 percent A-types and 20 percent B-types. A-types have a perfectly elastic supply of labour at a wage rate of $10 an hour. B-types have a perfectly inelastic supply of labour and their equilibrium wage rate is $100 an hour.

a. What kinds of tax arrangements do you predict this economy will adopt?

b. Analyse the labour market in this economy and explain what will happen to the wage rates and employment levels of the two groups when the taxes you predict in your answer to part (a) are introduced.

4. Suppose that in the economy described in problem 3, the proportion of A-types was 20 percent and the proportion of B-types was 80 percent. Everything else remains the same.

a. Now what kinds of tax arrangements do you predict the economy will adopt?

b. Analyse the labour market in this economy and explain what will happen to the wage rates and employment levels of the two groups when the taxes you predict in your answer to part (a) are introduced.

c. Compare the economy in problem 3 with the economy in this problem. Which economy more closely resembles our actual economy?

*5. An economy has a competitive labour market, which is described by the following demand schedule and supply schedule:

Wage rate (dollars per hour)	Quantity demanded (hours per week)	Quantity supplied (hours per week)
20	0	50
16	15	40
12	30	30
8	45	20
4	60	10
0	75	0

a. What are the equilibrium wage rate and hours of work done?

b. If an employment insurance tax of $4 an hour is imposed on employers:
   (i) What is the new wage rate?
   (ii) How many hours are worked?
   (iii) What is the after-tax wage rate?
   (iv) What is the tax revenue?
   (v) What is the deadweight loss?

6. In the economy described in problem 5, the employment insurance tax on employers is eliminated and a new employment insurance tax of $4 an hour is imposed on employees.
   a. What is the new wage rate?
   b. How many hours are worked?
   c. What is the after-tax wage rate?
   d. What is the tax revenue?
   e. What is the deadweight loss?
   f. Compare the situation in problem 5 with that in this problem and explain the similarities and differences in the two situations.

*7. In a competitive market for cookies:

Price (dollars per kilogram)	Quantity demanded (kilograms per month)	Quantity supplied (kilograms per month)
10	0	28
8	4	24
6	8	20
4	12	16
2	16	12

a. What are the equilibrium price and the equilibrium quantity?
b. If cookies are taxed $2 a kilogram:
   (i) What is the new price of cookies?
   (ii) What is the new quantity bought?
   (iii) What is the tax revenue?
   (iv) What is the deadweight loss?

8. In the competitive market for cookies in problem 7, the government wants to change the tax on a kilogram of cookies so that it brings in the greatest possible amount of tax revenue.
   a. What is that tax on a kilogram of cookies?
   b. What is the new price of cookies?
   c. What is the new quantity bought?
   d. What is the tax revenue?
   e. What is the deadweight loss?

CRITICAL THINKING

 1. Study *Reading Between the Lines* on pp. 406–407, and then:
   a. Describe the events that have changed the public good status of the lighthouse.
   b. What is the new navigational public good and how is it provided?
   c. Do you think that the provision of GPS satellites is efficient? If not, what must be done to achieve the efficient level of provision?
   d. Use the links on the Parkin-Bade Web site and find out what has been happening to lighthouses. Do you think that the private market for lighthouses as tourist sites is efficient? Why or why not?

 2. Use the links on the Parkin-Bade Web site to obtain information about Ontario highways.
   a. Are highways 401 and 407 public goods, private goods, or a mixture of the two?
   b. Which highway, the 401 or the 407, is more public? Why?
   c. Is snow clearing and sanding and salting on highways 401 and 407 a public service or a private service, or a mixture of the two?
   d. Does Ontario have an efficient provision of highway services?

3. Your local city council believes that by installing computers to control the traffic signals, it can improve the speed of traffic flow. The bigger the computer the council buys, the better job it can do. The mayor and the other elected officials who are working on the proposal want to determine the scale of the system that will win them the most votes. The city bureaucrats want to maximize the budget. Suppose that you are an economist who is observing this public choice. Your job is to calculate the quantity of this public good that uses resources efficiently.
   a. What data would you need to reach your own conclusions?
   b. What does the public choice theory predict will be the quantity chosen?
   c. How could you, as an informed voter, attempt to influence the choice?
   d. What does the public interest theory predict will be the quantity chosen?

19

Competition Policy

When you consume water, electric power, natural gas, cable TV, or local telephone service, you buy from a regulated monopoly. Why do we regulate the industries that produce these goods and services? How do we regulate them? Does regulation work in the interests of consumers—the public interest—or does it serve the interests of producers—special interests? ◆ Regulation extends beyond monopoly to oligopoly. For example, until 1978 airline prices and routes were regulated. But

Public Interest or Special Interests?

in 1978, domestic air travel was deregulated and the airlines are free to choose their own routes and fares. Railways, interprovincial trucking, banking, and insurance were regulated in the past but in recent years they have been deregulated. Why do we regulate and then deregulate an industry? ◆ The government used its anti-combine laws to end Northern Telecom's monopoly on phone equipment and Bell Canada's monopoly on long-distance phone calls as well as the installation of phone lines. This action brought competition into all three markets. Now you can choose where to buy your phone equipment, which long-distance telephone service to use, and the company to install your phone line. What are the anti-combine laws? How have they evolved over the years? How are they used today? Do they serve the public interest of consumers or the special interests of producers?

◇ This chapter studies government regulation. It draws on your earlier study of how markets work and on your knowledge of consumer surplus and producer surplus. It shows how consumers and producers can redistribute the gains from trade in the political marketplace, and it identifies who stands to win and who stands to lose from government intervention.

After studying this chapter, you will be able to:

- **Define regulation, public ownership, and anti-combine law**

- **Distinguish between the public interest and capture theories of regulation**

- **Explain how regulation affects prices, outputs, profits, and the distribution of the gains from trade between consumers and producers**

- **Explain how public ownership affects prices, outputs, and allocative efficiency**

- **Explain how anti-combine law is used in Canada today**

Market Intervention

THE GOVERNMENT INTERVENES IN MONOPO-
listic and oligopolistic markets to influence what,
how, and for whom various goods and services are
produced in three main ways:

- Regulation
- Public ownership
- Anti-combine law

Regulation

Regulation consists of rules administered by a government agency to influence economic activity by
determining prices, product standards and types, and
the conditions under which new firms may enter an
industry. To implement its regulations, the government establishes agencies to oversee the regulations
and ensure their enforcement. The first such economic regulation in Canada was the Railway Act of
1888, which regulated railway rates. Since then and
up to the late 1970s, regulation spread to banking
and financial services, telecommunications, gas and
electric utilities, railways, trucking, airlines and buses,
and dozens of agricultural products. Since the early
1980s, there has been a tendency to deregulate the
Canadian economy.

Deregulation is the process of removing restrictions on prices, product standards and types, and
entry conditions. In recent years, deregulation has
occurred in domestic air transportation, telephone
service, interprovincial trucking, and banking and
financial services.

Public Ownership

In Canada, publicly owned firms are called **Crown
corporations**. The most important Crown corporations are Canada Post, the CBC, CN, VIA Rail, and
Atomic Energy of Canada. There are many provincial
Crown corporations, the most important of which
are the provincial hydro companies. Just as there has
been a tendency to deregulate the Canadian economy
in recent years, there has also been a tendency to privatize it. **Privatization** is the process of selling a publicly owned corporation to private shareholders.
Petro-Canada was privatized in 1991.

Anti-Combine Law

An **anti-combine law** is a law that regulates and prohibits certain kinds of market behaviour, such as
monopoly and monopolistic practices. The main
thrust of the anti-combine law is the prohibition of
monopoly practices and of restricting output in order
to achieve higher prices and profits. In Canada,
unlike the United States, the anti-combine law was,
until 1971, part of the Criminal Code. As a consequence, private lawsuits could not be filed. Also, the
test of guilt is much more stringent under the
Criminal Code than under civil law. As a result,
Canada's anti-combine laws have been used less vigorously than the parallel laws (called "anti-trust
laws") south of the border.

To understand why the government intervenes in
the markets for goods and services and to work out
the effects of its interventions, we need to identify the
gains and losses that government actions can create.
These gains and losses are the consumer surplus and
producer surplus associated with different outputs and
prices. We first study the economics of regulation.

Economic Theory of Regulation

THE ECONOMIC THEORY OF REGULATION IS PART
of the broader theory of public choice that is
explained in Chapter 18. Here, we apply public
choice theory to regulation. We'll examine the
demand for government actions, the supply of those
actions, and the political equilibrium that emerges.

Demand for Regulation

The demand for regulation is expressed through
political activity—voting, lobbying, and making
campaign contributions. But engaging in political
activity is costly and people demand political action
only if the benefit that they individually receive from
such action exceeds their individual costs in obtaining the action. The four main factors that affect the
demand for regulation are:

1. Consumer surplus per buyer

2. Number of buyers

3. Producer surplus per firm

4. Number of firms

The larger the consumer surplus per buyer resulting from regulation, the greater is the demand for regulation by buyers. Also, as the number of buyers increases, so does the demand for regulation. But numbers alone do not necessarily translate into an effective political force. The larger the number of buyers, the greater is the cost of organizing them, so the demand for regulation does not increase proportionately with the number of buyers.

The larger the producer surplus per firm that arises from a particular regulation, the larger is the demand for that regulation by firms. Also, as the number of firms that might benefit from some regulation increases, so does the demand for that regulation. But again, large numbers do not necessarily mean an effective political force. The larger the number of firms, the greater is the cost of organizing them.

For a given surplus, consumer or producer, the smaller the number of households or firms who share that surplus, the larger is the demand for the regulation that creates it.

Supply of Regulation

Politicians and bureaucrats supply regulation. According to public choice theory, politicians choose policies that appeal to a majority of voters, thereby enabling themselves to achieve and maintain office. Bureaucrats support policies that maximize their budgets (see Chapter 18, p. 398). Given these objectives of politicians and bureaucrats, the supply of regulation depends on the following three factors:

1. Consumer surplus per buyer
2. Producer surplus per firm
3. The number of persons affected

The larger the consumer surplus per buyer or producer surplus per firm generated by a regulation and the larger the number of persons affected by a regulation, the greater is the tendency for politicians to supply that regulation. Politicians are likely to supply regulation that benefits a large number of people by a large amount per person. They are also likely to supply regulation that benefits a *small* number of people when the benefit per person is large and the cost is spread widely and not easily identified. But they are unlikely to supply a regulation that brings a small benefit per person.

Political Equilibrium

In a political equilibrium, no interest group plans to use resources to press for changes and no group of politicians plans to offer different regulations. Being in a political equilibrium is not the same thing as everyone being in agreement. Lobby groups will devote resources to trying to change regulations that are already in place. And others will devote resources to maintaining the existing regulations. But no one will feel it is worthwhile to increase the resources they are devoting to such activities. Also, political parties might not agree with each other. Some support the existing regulations, and others propose different regulations. In equilibrium, no one wants to change the proposals that they are making.

What will a political equilibrium look like? The answer depends on whether the regulation serves the public interest or the interest of the producer. Let's look at these two possibilities.

Public Interest Theory The **public interest theory** is that regulations are supplied to satisfy the demand of consumers and producers to maximize total surplus—that is, to attain allocative efficiency. Public interest theory implies that the political process relentlessly seeks out deadweight loss and introduces regulations that eliminate it. For example, where monopoly practices exist, the political process will introduce price regulations to ensure that outputs increase and prices fall to their competitive levels.

Capture Theory The **capture theory** is that the regulations are supplied to satisfy the demand of producers to maximize producer surplus—that is, to maximize economic profit. The key idea of capture theory is that the cost of regulation is high and only those regulations that increase the surplus of small, easily identified groups and that have low organization costs are supplied by the political process. Consumers bear the cost of such regulation but the costs are spread thinly and widely so they do not lose votes.

The predictions of the capture theory are less clear-cut than the predictions of the public interest theory. According to the capture theory, regulations benefit cohesive interest groups by large and visible amounts and impose small costs on everyone else. But those costs are so small, in per person terms, that no one feels it is worthwhile to incur the cost of organizing an interest group to avoid them. To make these predictions concrete enough to be useful, the capture theory needs a model of the costs of political organization.

Whichever theory of regulation is correct, according to public choice theory, the political system delivers amounts and types of regulations that best further the electoral success of politicians. Because producer-oriented and consumer-oriented regulation are in conflict with each other, the political process can't satisfy both groups in any particular industry. Only one group can win. This makes the regulatory actions of government a bit like a unique product—for example, a painting by Emily Carr. There is only one original and it will be sold to just one buyer. Normally, a unique commodity is sold through an auction; the highest bidder takes the prize.

Equilibrium in the regulatory process can be thought of in much the same way: The suppliers of regulation will satisfy the demands of the higher bidder. If the producer demand offers a bigger return to the politicians, either directly through votes or indirectly through campaign contributions, then the regulation will serve the producers' interests. If the consumer demand translates into a larger number of votes, then the regulation will serve the consumers' interests.

REVIEW QUIZ

■ How do consumers and producers express their demand for regulation? What are their objectives? What are the costs of expressing a demand for regulation?

■ When politicians and bureaucrats supply regulation, what are they trying to achieve? Do politicians and bureaucrats have the same objectives?

■ What is a political equilibrium? When does the political equilibrium achieve economic efficiency? When does the political equilibrium serve the interests of producers? When do the bureaucrats win?

We have now completed our study of the *theory* of regulation in the marketplace. Let's turn our attention to the regulations that exist in our economy today. Which theory of regulation best explains these real-world regulations? Which of these regulations are in the public interest and which are in the interest of producers?

Regulation and Deregulation

THE PAST DECADE OR SO HAS SEEN DRAMATIC changes in the way in which the government has regulated the Canadian economy. We're going to examine some of these changes. To begin we'll look at what the government regulates and also at the scope of regulation. Then we'll turn to the regulatory process itself and examine how regulators control prices and other aspects of market behaviour. Finally, we'll tackle the more difficult and controversial questions: Why does the government regulate some things but not others? Who benefits from the regulation that we have—consumers or producers?

The Scope of Regulation

Regulation touches a wide range of economic activity in Canada. Table 19.1 sets out the major federal regulatory agencies, together with a brief statement of their responsibilities. As you can see by inspecting that table, the predominant sectors subject to regulation are agriculture, energy, transport, and telecommunications.

Provincial and municipal governments also establish regulations covering a wide range of economic activity. Some of these—for example, municipal regulation of the taxicab industry—have important direct effects on the marketplace. Our analysis of the regulatory process and the effects of regulation apply with equal force to price, output, and profit regulation at these other governmental levels.

What exactly do regulatory agencies do? How do they regulate?

The Regulatory Process

Though regulatory agencies vary in size and scope and in the detailed aspects of economic life that they control, there are certain features common to all agencies.

First, the government appoints the senior bureaucrats who are the key decision makers in a regulatory agency. In addition, all agencies have a permanent bureaucracy made up of experts in the industry being regulated and often recruited from the regulated firms. Agencies have financial resources,

TABLE 19.1

Federal Regulatory Agencies

Agency	Responsibility
Atomic Energy Control Board	Administers the Atomic Energy Control Act governing all uses of radioactive material.
Canadian Dairy Commission	Administers national dairy policy, which seeks to give producers an adequate return and keep the price to consumers low.
Canadian Radio-Television and Telecommunications Commission	Regulates all aspects of radio, television, and telecommunications.
Canadian Grain Commission	Regulates grain handling, establishes and maintains quality standards, audits grain stocks, and supervises future trading.
Canadian Wheat Board	Regulates exports of wheat and barley and domestic sales for human consumption.
National Energy Board	Regulates oil, gas, and electrical industries.
National Farm Products Marketing Council	Advises government on the establishment and operation of national agricultural marketing agencies and works with those agencies and provincial governments to promote marketing of farm products. Chicken, egg, and turkey agencies have been established under its aegis.
Canadian Transport Commission	Regulates transports under federal jurisdiction including rail, air, water, and pipeline and some interprovincial commercial motor transport.

Source: Statistics Canada, *Canada Year Book,* 1992.

voted by Parliament, to cover the costs of their operations.

Second, each agency adopts a set of practices or operating rules for controlling prices and other aspects of economic performance. These rules and practices are based on well-defined physical and financial accounting procedures that are relatively easy to administer and to monitor.

In a regulated industry, individual firms are usually free to determine the technology that they will use in production. But they are not free to determine the prices at which they will sell their output, the quantities that they will sell, or the markets that they will serve. The regulatory agency grants certification to a company to serve a particular market and with a particular line of products. The agency also determines the level and structure of prices that the company can charge. In some cases, the agency also determines the scale of output permitted.

To analyse the way in which regulation works, it is convenient to distinguish between the regulation of natural monopoly and the regulation of cartels. Let's begin with the regulation of natural monopoly.

Natural Monopoly

Natural monopoly was defined in Chapter 13 (p. 268) as an industry in which one firm can supply the entire market at a lower price than two or more firms can. As a consequence, natural monopoly experiences economies of scale, no matter how large an output rate it produces. Examples of natural monopolies include local distribution of cable television signals, electricity and gas, and urban rail services. It is much more expensive to have two or more competing sets of wires, pipes, and train lines serving every neighbourhood than it is to have a single set. (What is a natural monopoly changes over time as technology changes. With the introduction of fibre optic cables, both telephone companies and cable television companies will be able to compete with each other in both markets, so what is a natural monopoly will become a more competitive industry.)

Let's consider the example of cable TV, which is shown in Fig. 19.1. The demand curve for cable TV is *D*. The cable TV company's marginal cost curve is *MC*. That marginal cost curve is (assumed to be)

FIGURE 19.1

Natural Monopoly: Marginal Cost Pricing

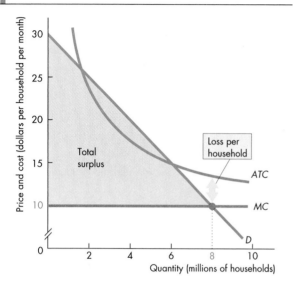

A natural monopoly is an industry in which average total cost is falling even when the entire market demand is satisfied. A cable TV operator faces the demand curve D. The firm's marginal cost is constant at $10 per household per month, as shown by the curve labelled MC. Fixed costs are large, and the average total cost curve, which includes average fixed cost, is shown as ATC. A marginal cost pricing rule that maximizes total surplus sets the price at $10 a month, with 8 million households being served. The resulting consumer surplus is shown as the green area. The firm incurs a loss on each household, indicated by the red arrow. To remain in business, the firm must price discriminate, use a two-part tariff, or receive a subsidy.

horizontal at $10 per household per month—that is, the cost of providing each additional household with a month of cable programming is $10. The cable company has a heavy investment in satellite receiving dishes, cables, and control equipment and so has high fixed costs. These fixed costs are part of the company's average total cost curve, shown as ATC. The average total cost curve slopes downward because as the number of households served increases, the fixed cost is spread over a larger number of households. (If you need to refresh your memory on how the average total cost curve is calculated, take a quick look back at Chapter 11, pp. 230–231.)

Regulation in the Public Interest How will cable TV be regulated according to the public interest theory? It will be regulated to maximize total surplus, which occurs if marginal cost equals price. As you can see in Fig. 19.1, that outcome occurs if the price is regulated at $10 per household per month and if 8 million households are served. Such a regulation is called a **marginal cost pricing rule**. A marginal cost pricing rule sets price equal to marginal cost. It maximizes total surplus in the regulated industry.

A natural monopoly that is regulated to set price equal to marginal cost incurs an economic loss. Because its average total cost curve is downward sloping, marginal cost is below average total cost. Because price equals marginal cost, price is below average total cost. Average total cost minus price is the loss per unit produced. It's pretty obvious that a cable TV company that is required to use a marginal cost pricing rule will not stay in business for long. How can a company cover its costs and, at the same time, obey a marginal cost pricing rule?

One possibility is price discrimination (see Chapter 13, pp. 277–280). Another is to use a two-part price (called a *two-part tariff*). For example, local telephone companies can charge consumers a monthly fee for being connected to the telephone system and then charge a price equal to marginal cost for each local call. A cable TV operator can charge a one-time connection fee that covers its fixed cost and then charge a monthly fee equal to marginal cost.

But a natural monopoly cannot always cover its costs in these ways. If a natural monopoly cannot cover its total cost from its customers, and if the government wants it to follow a marginal cost pricing rule, the government must give the firm a subsidy. In such a case, the government raises the revenue for the subsidy by taxing some other activity. But as we saw in Chapter 18, taxes themselves generate deadweight loss. Thus the deadweight loss resulting from additional taxes must be subtracted from the efficiency gained by forcing the natural monopoly to adopt a marginal cost pricing rule.

Deadweight loss might be minimized by making the natural monopoly cover its cost rather than by taxing another sector of the economy. When a monopoly covers its costs, it uses an average cost pricing rule. An **average cost pricing rule** sets price equal to average total cost. Figure 19.2 shows the average cost pricing solution. The cable TV operator charges $15 a month and serves 6 million households. A deadweight loss arises, which is shown by the grey triangle in the figure.

FIGURE 19.2

Natural Monopoly:
Average Cost Pricing

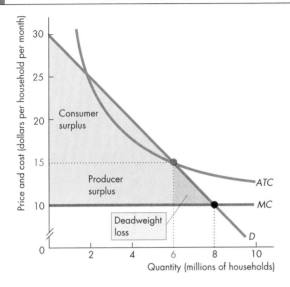

Average cost pricing sets price equal to average total cost. The cable TV operator charges $15 a month and serves 6 million households. In this situation, the firm breaks even—average total cost equals price. Deadweight loss, shown by the grey triangle, is generated. Consumer surplus is reduced to the green area.

FIGURE 19.3

Natural Monopoly:
Profit Maximization

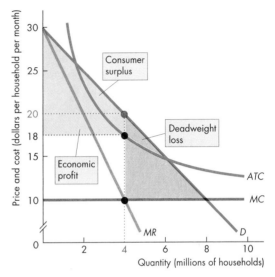

The cable TV operator would like to maximize profit. To do so, marginal revenue (*MR*) is made equal to marginal cost. At a price of $20 a month, 4 million households buy cable service. Consumer surplus is reduced to the green triangle. The deadweight loss increases to the grey triangle. The monopoly makes the profit shown by the blue rectangle. If the producer can capture the regulator, the outcome will be the situation shown here.

Capturing the Regulator   What does the capture theory predict about the regulation of this industry? According to the capture theory, the producer gets the regulator to set rules that work to serve the interest of the producer. But the producer interest is served by being able to operate at the same output and price as an unregulated monopoly. In Fig. 19.3, the monopoly's marginal revenue curve is the curve labelled *MR*. Marginal revenue equals marginal cost when output is 4 million households and the price is $20 a month. At this output and price, the producer makes the maximum profit. So regulation in the interest of the producer maintains the unregulated monopoly outcome.

But how can a producer go about capturing the regulator and obtaining regulation that results in this monopoly profit-maximizing outcome? To answer this question, we need to look at the way in which

agencies determine a regulated price. A key method used is called rate of return regulation.

Rate of Return Regulation   **Rate of return regulation** determines a regulated price by setting the price at a level that enables the regulated firm to earn a specified target percent return on its capital. The target rate of return is determined with reference to what is normal in competitive industries. This rate of return is part of the opportunity cost of the natural monopolist and is included in the firm's average total cost. By examining the firm's total cost, including the normal rate of return on capital, the regulator attempts to determine the price at which average total cost is covered. Thus rate of return regulation is equivalent to average cost pricing.

In Fig. 19.2, average cost pricing results in a regulated price of $15 a month with 6 million households being served. Thus rate of return regulation, based on a correct assessment of the producer's average total cost curve, results in a price that favours the consumer and does not enable the producer to maximize monopoly profit. The special interest group will have failed to capture the regulator, and the outcome will be closer to that predicted by the public interest theory of regulation.

But there is a feature of many real-world situations that the above analysis does not take into account: the ability of the monopoly firm to mislead the regulator about its true costs.

Inflating Costs The managers of a firm might be able to inflate the firm's costs by spending part of the firm's revenue on inputs that are not strictly required for the production of the good. By this device, the firm's apparent costs exceed the true costs. On-the-job luxury in the form of sumptuous office suites, limousines, free baseball tickets (disguised as public relations expenses), company jets, lavish international travel, and entertainment are all ways in which managers can inflate costs.

If the cable TV operator makes the regulator believe that its true cost is *ATC* (*inflated*) in Fig. 19.4, then the regulator will set the price at $20 a month. In this example, the price and quantity will be the same as those under unregulated monopoly. It might be impossible for firms to inflate their costs by as much as the amount shown in the figure. But to the extent that costs can be inflated, the apparent average total cost curve lies somewhere between the true average total cost curve and *ATC* (*inflated*). The greater the ability of the firm to pad its costs in this way, the more closely its profit (measured in economic terms) approaches the maximum possible. The shareholders of this firm don't receive this economic profit because it is used up in baseball tickets, luxury offices, and the other actions taken by the firm's managers to inflate the company's costs.

Public Interest or Capture?

It is not clear whether actual regulation produces prices and quantities that more closely correspond with the predictions of capture theory or with public interest theory. One thing is clear, however. Price regulation does not require natural monopolies to use the marginal cost pricing rule. If it did, most natural

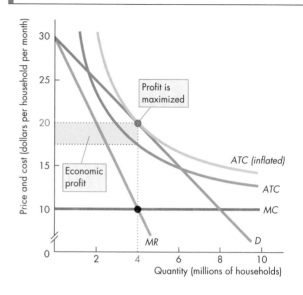

FIGURE 19.4

Natural Monopoly: Inflating Costs

If the cable TV operator is able to inflate its costs to *ATC* (*inflated*) and persuade the regulator that these are genuine minimum costs of production, rate of return regulation results in a price of $20 a month—the profit-maximizing price. To the extent that the producer can inflate costs above average total cost, the price rises, output decreases, and deadweight loss increases. The managers, not the shareholders (owners) of the firm, capture the profit.

monopolies would make losses and receive hefty government subsidies to enable them to remain in business. But there are even exceptions to this conclusion. For example, many local telephone companies do appear to use marginal cost pricing for local telephone calls. They cover their total cost by charging a flat fee each month for being connected to their telephone system but then permitting each call to be made at its marginal cost—zero or something very close to it.

We can test whether natural monopoly regulation is in the public interest or producer interest by comparing the rates of return in regulated natural monopolies with average returns. If regulated natural monopolies have rates of return significantly higher than those in the rest of the economy, then, to some degree, the regulator may have been captured by the producer. There is plenty of empirical evidence that many natural monopolies in Canada do earn higher rates of return than the economy average.

One recent striking example is cable television service; telephone service is another. The rates of return in these two industries exceed 10 percent a year, approaching double the economy average. Perhaps the most dramatic piece of evidence that regulation benefits the regulated firm is the profits of Bell Canada Enterprises (BCE), prior to deregulation of long-distance phone services. BCE is a conglomerate that produced *regulated* long-distance telephone services and *unregulated* phone equipment (Northern Telecom) and financial services (Montreal Trustco). In 1992, BCE made a total profit of $1.4 billion on total assets of $12.3 billion, a profit rate of 11.4 percent. But this total was made up of a profit of $0.9 billion on assets of $7 billion—a return of 12.9 percent—for the regulated Bell Canada and a profit of $0.5 billion on assets of $5.3 billion—9.4 percent—for all BCE's *unregulated* operation.

Until the early 1990s, long-distance telephone service was a natural monopoly, but technological advances in telecommunications have changed the situation. Today, the industry is an oligopoly. But oligopoly is also regulated. Let's examine regulation in oligopolistic industries—the regulation of cartels.

Cartel Regulation

A *cartel* is a collusive agreement among a number of firms that is designed to restrict output and achieve a higher profit for the cartel's members. Cartels are illegal in Canada and in most other countries. But international cartels can sometimes operate legally, such as the international cartel of oil producers known as OPEC (the Organization of Petroleum Exporting Countries).

Illegal cartels can arise in oligopolistic industries. An oligopoly is a market structure in which a small number of firms compete with each other. We studied oligopoly (and duopoly—two firms competing for a market) in Chapter 14. There we saw that if firms manage to collude and behave like a monopoly, they can set the same price and sell the same total quantity as a monopoly firm would. But we also discovered that in such a situation, each firm will be tempted to cheat, increasing its own output and profit at the expense of the other firms. The result of such cheating on the collusive agreement is the

unravelling of the monopoly equilibrium and the emergence of a competitive outcome with zero economic profit for producers. Such an outcome benefits consumers at the expense of producers.

How is oligopoly regulated? Does regulation prevent monopoly practices or does it encourage those practices?

According to the public interest theory, oligopoly is regulated to ensure a competitive outcome. Consider, for example, the market for trucking tomatoes from the fields of southwestern Ontario to a ketchup factory at Leamington, illustrated in Fig. 19.5. The demand curve for trips is *D*. The industry marginal cost curve—and the competitive supply curve—is *MC*. Public interest regulation will set the price of a trip at $20 and there will be 300 trips a week.

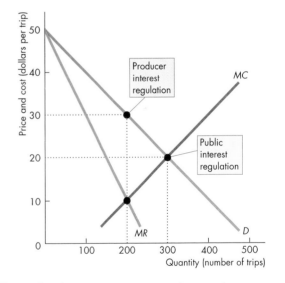

FIGURE 19.5
Collusive Oligopoly

Ten trucking firms transport tomatoes from southwestern Ontario to Leamington. The demand curve is *D*, and the industry marginal cost curve is *MC*. Under competition, the *MC* curve is the industry supply curve. If the industry is competitive, the price of a trip will be $20 and 300 trips will be made each week. Producers will demand regulation that restricts entry and limits output to 200 trips a week, where industry marginal revenue (*MR*) is equal to industry marginal cost (*MC*). This regulation raises the price to $30 a trip and results in each producer making maximum profit—as if it is a monopoly.

How would this industry be regulated according to the capture theory? Regulation that is in the interest of producers will maximize profit. To find the outcome in this case, we need to determine the price and quantity when marginal cost equals marginal revenue. The marginal revenue curve is *MR*. So, marginal revenue equals marginal cost at 200 trips a week. The price of a trip is $30.

One way of achieving this outcome is to place an output limit on each firm in the industry. If there are 10 trucking companies, an output limit of 20 trips per company ensures that the total number of trips in a week is 200. Penalties can be imposed to ensure that no single producer exceeds its output limit.

All the firms in the industry would support this type of regulation because it helps to prevent cheating and to maintain a monopoly outcome. Each firm knows that without effectively enforced production quotas, every firm has an incentive to increase output. (For each firm, price exceeds marginal cost, so a greater output brings a larger profit.) So each firm wants a method of preventing output from rising above the industry's profit-maximizing level, and the quotas enforced by regulation achieve this end. With this type of cartel regulation, the regulator enables a cartel to operate legally and in its own best interest.

What does cartel regulation do in practice? Although there is disagreement about the matter, the consensus view is that regulation tends to favour the producer. Trucking and airlines (when they were regulated by the Canadian Transport Commission) and taxicabs (regulated by cities) are specific examples in which profits of producers increased as a result of regulation. But the most dramatic examples of regulation favouring the producer are in agriculture. An Economic Council of Canada study, based on the situation prevailing in the early 1980s, estimated that regulation of the egg-producing and broiler chicken industries alone transferred more than $100 million a year to just 4,600 individual producers.[1]

Further evidence on cartel and oligopoly regulation can be obtained from the performance of prices and profit following deregulation. If, following deregulation, prices and profit fall, then, to some degree, the regulation must have been serving the interest of the producer. In contrast, if, following deregulation, prices and profits remain constant or increase, then

the regulation may be presumed to have been serving the public interest. Because there has been a substantial amount of deregulation in recent years, we may use this test of oligopoly regulation to see which of the two theories better fits the facts. The evidence is mixed, but in the cases of airlines, trucking, and long-distance phone calls, three oligopolies to be deregulated, prices fell and there was a large increase in the volume of business.

Making Predictions

Most industries have a few producers and many consumers. In these cases, public choice theory predicts that regulation will protect producers because a small number of people stand to gain a large amount and so they will be fairly easy to organize as a cohesive lobby. Under such circumstances, politicians will be rewarded with campaign contributions rather than votes. But there are situations in which the consumer interest is sufficiently strong and well organized and thus able to prevail. There are also cases in which the balance switches from producer to consumer, as seen in the deregulation process that began in the late 1970s.

Deregulation raises some hard questions for economists seeking to understand and make predictions about regulation. Why were the transportation and telecommunication sectors deregulated? If producers gained from regulation and if the producer lobby was strong enough to achieve regulation, what happened in the 1970s to change the equilibrium to one in which the consumer interest prevailed? We do not have a complete answer to this question at the present time. But regulation had become so costly to consumers, and the potential benefits to them from deregulation so great, that the cost of organizing the consumer voice became a price worth paying.

One factor that increased the cost of regulation borne by consumers and brought deregulation in the transportation sector was the large increase in energy prices in the 1970s. These price hikes made route regulation by the Canadian Transport Commission extremely costly and changed the balance in favour of consumers in the political equilibrium. Technological change was the main factor at work in the telecommunication sector. New satellite-based, computer-controlled long-distance technologies enabled smaller producers to offer low-cost services. These producers wanted a share of Bell Canada's business—and profit.

[1] J.D. Forbes, R.D. Hughes, and T.K. Warley, *Economic Intervention and Regulation in Canadian Agriculture* (Ottawa: Department of Supply and Services, 1982).

Furthermore, as communication technology improved, the cost of communication fell and the cost of organizing larger groups of consumers also fell. If this line of reasoning is correct, we can expect to see more consumer-oriented regulation in the future. In practice, more consumer-oriented regulation often means deregulation—removing the regulations that are already in place to serve the interests of producer groups.

R E V I E W   Q U I Z

- What are the main regulatory agencies in Canada?
- Why does natural monopoly need to be regulated?
- What pricing rule enables a natural monopoly to operate in the public interest?
- Why is a marginal cost pricing rule difficult to implement?
- What pricing rule is typically used to regulate a natural monopoly and what problems does it create?
- Why is it necessary to regulate a cartel?
- How might cartels be regulated in the public interest?

Let's now turn to the second method of intervention in markets—public ownership.

Public Ownership

CROWN CORPORATIONS HAVE A SIGNIFICANT AND historical presence in Canadian society. Before Confederation, Crown corporations were used for building canals and operating ports and harbours. The establishment of the Canadian nation involved a commitment to build an international railway to link New Brunswick and Nova Scotia to central Canada. Over the years, vast distances, a sparse population, the presence of a powerful neighbour, strong and distinct national interests, and the existence of two main cultural and linguistic groups nurtured the establishment of Crown corporations.

A Crown corporation is a corporation in which the government has 100 percent ownership. There are federal and provincial Crown corporations, and they are involved in many sectors of the economy,

including transportation; energy and resources; agriculture and fisheries; development and construction; government services; culture; financial intermediaries; telecommunications and broadcasting; provincial lotteries; housing; and alcoholic beverages. Examples of Crown corporations include the Business Development Bank of Canada, the Canadian Museum of Nature, and the Ontario Lottery Corporation.

Public ownership provides another way in which the government can influence the behaviour of natural monopoly. What are the effects of this method of natural monopoly control? How does a publicly owned corporation operate? Let's explore some alternative patterns of behaviour for such corporations.

Efficient Crown Corporations

One possibility is that a Crown corporation is operated in a manner that results in economic efficiency—maximization of total surplus. Let's consider the example of a railway. Figure 19.6(a) illustrates the demand for freight service and the railway's costs. The demand curve is D. The marginal cost curve is MC. Notice that the marginal cost curve is horizontal at $2 a tonne. The railway has a heavy investment in track, trains, and control equipment, so it has large fixed costs. These fixed costs feature in the company's average total cost curve ATC. The average total cost curve slopes downward because as the number of tonnes of freight carried increases, the fixed costs are spread over a larger number of tonnes. To be efficient, a Crown corporation obeys the rule:

Produce an output such that price equals marginal cost.

In this example, that output level is 8 billion tonnes a year at a price—and marginal cost—of $2 a tonne. To be able to operate in this manner, a publicly owned railway has to be subsidized; the subsidy on each unit of output must equal the difference between average total cost and marginal cost. And the subsidy has to be collected other than through the price of the good or service produced—in other words, by taxation. If the government taxes each household a fixed amount, the consumer surplus will shrink to the green triangle shown in Fig. 19.6(a), but consumer surplus will be at its maximum.

The situation depicted in Fig. 19.6(a) achieves an efficient outcome because consumer surplus is maximized. But it is not an outcome that is necessarily

FIGURE 19.6

Crown Corporation

(a) Efficient outcome

(b) Budget maximization

Part (a) shows a railway operated by a Crown corporation that produces the output at which price equals marginal cost. Its output is 8 billion tonnes a year and the price is $2 a tonne. The Crown corporation receives a subsidy that enables it to cover its total cost and that cost is the minimum possible cost of providing the efficient quantity.

Part (b) shows what happens if the managers of the Crown corporation pursue their own interest and maximize their budget by padding costs. Average total cost now increases to ATC (inflated). If the corporation is required to keep price equal to marginal cost, the quantity produced is efficient, but the managers divert the consumer surplus to themselves.

compatible with the interests of the managers of the Crown corporation. One model of the behaviour of managers is that suggested by the economic theory of bureaucracy. What does that alternative model predict about Crown corporation behaviour?

A Bureaucracy Model of Public Enterprise

The basic assumption of the economic theory of bureaucracy is that bureaucrats aim to maximize the budget of their bureau. The equivalent assumption for the managers of a Crown corporation is that they seek to maximize the budget of the Crown corporation. The effect of budget maximization by the managers of a Crown corporation depends on the pricing constraints under which the managers operate. We will consider two alternative cases:

■ Budget maximization with marginal cost pricing
■ Budget maximization at a zero price.

Budget Maximization with Marginal Cost Pricing If the bureau maximizes its budget but obeys the marginal cost pricing rule, it will produce the efficient outcome. It will produce 8 billion tonnes a year and it will sell its output for $2 a tonne, as Fig. 19.6(b) illustrates. But the corporation will not minimize its production cost. It will pad its costs and become inefficient. It will hire more workers than the number required to produce 8 billion tonnes a year, and its internal control mechanisms, which would ensure internal efficiency, as in a private profit-maximizing firm, will be weak. As a result, the average total cost of the corporation will rise to ATC (inflated).

What determines the limit on the extent to which the corporation can pad its costs? The answer is the maximum amount that the users of the output can be made to pay through taxation. That maximum is the total consumer surplus. That maximum consumer surplus is the area beneath the demand curve and above the marginal cost curve. You can work out how big it is by using the usual formula for the area of the triangle. The height of this triangle is $8 and its base is 8 billion tonnes a year, so the consumer surplus is $32 billion. This will be the upper limit that any government—in a political democracy—can extract from the taxpayer-consumers of the product of this corporation. Spread over 8 billion tonnes, $32 billion gives a subsidy of $4 a tonne, the amount shown in the figure.

Budget Maximization at Zero Price   What happens if a government bureau provides its goods or services free? Of course, it is improbable that a publicly owned railway would be able to persuade politicians and taxpayers that its activities should be expanded to the point of providing its services free. But there are several examples of publicly provided goods that are indeed free. Primary and secondary education and health care are two outstanding examples. For the sake of comparison, we'll continue with our railway, improbable though it is.

If in Fig. 19.6(b) the bureau increases output to the point at which the price that consumers are willing to pay for the last unit produced is zero, output rises to 10 billion tonnes a year. A deadweight loss is created because the marginal cost of production, $2 a tonne, is higher than the marginal benefit or willingness to pay, $0 per tonne. The bureau will be inefficient in its internal operations and inflate its costs. The subsidy will increase to the highest that the public will be willing to pay. The maximum subsidy will equal the consumer surplus. If the subsidy were higher, people would vote to shut down the Crown corporation because the subsidy would exceed the consumer surplus.

Compromise Outcome   There will be a tendency for the corporation to overproduce and to inflate its budget, but not to the extent shown in Fig. 19.6(b). There will be a tendency for consumer interest to have some influence, but not to the degree shown in Fig. 19.6(a). The basic prediction about the behaviour of a Crown corporation, then, is that it will overproduce and be less efficient than a private firm.

Crown Corporations in Reality

How do actual Crown corporations behave? Several studies have been directed to answering this question. One of the most fruitful ways of approaching the question is to compare public and private enterprises in which, as far as possible, other things are equal. There are two well-known and well-studied cases for which other things do seem to be fairly equal. One such comparison is of Canada's public and private railways—Canadian National (CN) and Canadian Pacific (CP). The other is from Australia, which has two domestic airlines, one private and the other public, that fly almost identical routes at almost identical times every day. Economists have studied the costs of these similar enterprises and concluded that each of the publicly owned enterprises operates with a cost structure that is significantly higher than that of the corresponding private firm. In the case of CN and CP, the estimated difference was 14 percent.[2]

Privatization

Largely because of an increasing understanding of how bureaucracies work and of the inefficiency of publicly operated enterprises, there has been a move to sell off publicly owned corporations. Since the mid-1980s, the federal government has sold a dozen companies, including Air Canada. Companies that are too unprofitable to sell, such as CN, are being savagely cut back.

REVIEW QUIZ

- How might a Crown corporation operate efficiently?
- What are the effects of budget maximization by the managers of a Crown corporation?
- What limits the maximum budget of a Crown corporation?

   Let's now turn to anti-combine law.

[2]W.S.W. Caves and Lauritis Christensen, "The Relative Efficiency of Public v. Private Firms in a Competitive Environment: the Case of Canada's Railroads," *Journal of Political Economy* 88, 5 (September–October 1980), 958–76.

Anti-Combine Law

ANTI-COMBINE LAW GIVES POWERS TO THE courts and to government agencies to influence markets. Like regulation, anti-combine law can work in the public interest to maximize total surplus or in private interests to maximize the surpluses of particular special interest groups such as producers. We'll describe Canada's anti-combine law and then examine some recent cases.

Canada's Anti-Combine Law

Canada's anti-combine law dates from 1889. At that time, monopoly was a major political issue and people were concerned about the absence of competition in industries as diverse as sugar and groceries, biscuits and confectionery, coal, binder twine, agricultural implements, stoves, coffins, eggs, and fire insurance.

Canada's anti-combine law today is defined in the Competition Act of 1986, which is described in Table 19.2. The Act established a Competition Bureau and a Competition Tribunal. The Competition Act distinguishes between practices that are:

1. Criminal
2. Non-criminal

Conspiracy to fix prices, bid-rigging, other anti-competitive price-fixing actions, and false advertising are criminal offences. The courts handle alleged offences, and the standard level of proof beyond a reasonable doubt must be established.

Mergers, abuse of a dominant market position, refusal to deal, and other actions designed to limit competition such as exclusive dealing are non-criminal offences. The Director of the Competition Bureau sends alleged violations of a non-criminal nature to the Competition Tribunal for examination.

Some Recent Anti-Combine Cases

Let's see how the Competition Act has been working by looking at some recent cases. The first case we'll examine is important because it confirms the Competition Tribunal's power to enforce its orders.

Chrysler In 1986, Chrysler stopped supplying auto parts to Richard Brunet, a Montreal auto dealer.

Chrysler also discouraged other dealers from supplying Brunet. The Competition Tribunal claimed that Chrysler wanted Brunet's business for itself and ordered Chrysler to resume doing business with Brunet. Chrysler did not resume sending supplies and the Tribunal cited Chrysler for contempt. Appeals against this ruling eventually reached the Supreme Court of Canada, which confirmed the Tribunal's power over contempt for its ruling. But the Tribunal subsequently dropped its contempt charge.

The second case we'll look at concerns aspartame, the sweetener in many soft drinks.

NutraSweet NutraSweet, the maker of aspartame, tried to gain a monopoly in aspartame. It did so by licensing the use of its "swirl" only on products for which it had an exclusive deal. The Competition Tribunal ruled that this action unduly limited competition and told NutraSweet that it may not enforce existing contracts, enter into new contracts in which it is the exclusive supplier, or give inducements to encourage the display of its "swirl." The result of this case was an increase in competition and a fall in the price of aspartame in Canada.

The third case we'll examine concerns a publication you use almost every day: the Yellow Pages.

Bell Canada Enterprises Two subsidiaries of Bell Canada Enterprises have a 90 percent share of the market for the publication of telephone directories in their territories. These companies tie the sale of advertising services to the sale of advertising space in the Yellow Pages. If you want to advertise in the Yellow Pages, you must buy the advertising services of one of these two companies. As a result, other advertising agencies cannot effectively compete for business in Yellow Pages advertising. The Director of the Competition Bureau applied for an order prohibiting the tied-sale practice of these two companies.

Other Recent Anti-Competitive Agreements During 1995 and 1996, the Competition Bureau took action against several anti-competitive agreements. Among such cases were driving schools in Sherbrooke, ready-mix concrete in the Saguenay-Lac St-Jean region, real estate dealing in Calgary, the importing of Australian mandarin oranges, wire for baling pulp, and ambulance services in Alberta.

The Competition Bureau is extremely active in reviewing and, in some cases, blocking mergers. The next cases we examine fall into this category.

TABLE 19.2

Canada's Anti-Combine Law: The Competition Act, 1986

Abuse of Dominant Position

79 (1) Where on application by the Director, the Tribunal finds that:

(a) one or more persons substantially or completely control, throughout Canada or any area thereof, a class or species of business,

(b) that person or those persons have engaged in or are engaging in a practice of anti-competitive acts, and

(c) the practice has had, is having or is likely to have the effect of preventing or lessening competition substantially in a market, the Tribunal may make an order prohibiting all or any of those persons from engaging in that practice.

Mergers

92 (1) Where on application by the Director, the Tribunal finds that a merger or proposed merger prevents or lessens, or is likely to prevent or lessen, competition substantially ... the Tribunal may ... [,] in the case of a completed merger, order any party to the merger

(i) to dissolve the merger ...

(ii) to dispose of assets and shares ...

[or]

in the case of a proposed merger, make an order directed against any party to the proposed merger

(i) ordering the person ... not to proceed with the merger

(ii) ordering the person not to proceed with part of the merger

---

Canada Packers and Labatt Canada Packers Inc. and John Labatt Ltd. proposed a merger of their flour milling operations that would have made them the biggest miller in Canada and the fifth biggest in North America. The Competition Tribunal stopped this merger saying that the Canadian flour milling business had been run too much like a cartel and that more, not less, competition was needed.

Banks and Airlines Some attempts to merge are so politically sensitive that they are decided at the highest political level. One example is the decision of the federal government to block an attempted merger by the Royal Bank and the Bank of Montreal. If Canada's two major airlines eventually merge, the sanction of the federal government will be needed.

Public or Special Interest?

The intent of anti-combine law is to protect the public interest and restrain the profit-seeking and anti-competitive actions of producers. On the whole, the overall thrust of the law and its enforcement has been in line with its intent and has served the public interest. Further, if the recent cases we have examined are setting a trend, we can expect a continuation of pro-consumer decisions from the courts and the Competition Tribunal in future cases.

R E V I E W   Q U I Z

■ What is the Act of Parliament that provides our anti-combine law?

■ What actions violate the anti-combine law?

■ Under what circumstances is a merger unlikely to be approved?

◆ In this chapter, we've seen how the government intervenes in markets to affect prices, quantities, consumer surplus, and producer surplus. *Reading Between the Lines* on pp. 426–427 looks at the recent debate about bank and airline mergers and provides an opportunity to think about that debate using the tools that you've learned and applied in this chapter.

Competition or Monopoly in Banking and Airlines

NATIONAL POST, DECEMBER 15, 1998

Bureau chides banks for not playing ball

By JILL VARDY

Paul Martin, the finance minister, said the resulting [Competition Bureau] reports are what convinced him to turn down the merger plans of Royal Bank of Canada with Bank of Montreal and Canadian Imperial Bank of Commerce with Toronto-Dominion Bank. ...

Unlike with conventional merger proposals, the competition bureau did not get the final say in this one.

Highlights of the Competition Bureau report include:

- The mergers ... would have lessened competition and caused higher prices, lower service levels, and less choice. ...
- More than half the markets in Canada would see competition between bank branches substantially reduced if the mergers were approved. ...

THE CALGARY HERALD, AUGUST 14, 1999

Ottawa opens loophole for airline rivals to talk

By ANNE CRAWFORD

The federal government has temporarily relaxed the rules of the competition law to allow Canada's two airlines to discuss a dramatic restructuring of the domestic industry, including a possible merger.

Transport Minister David Collenette and Industry Minister John Manley announced the relaxation of competition rules. "Sustaining a more viable air industry while preserving the interest of consumers is a priority for the government," Manley said.

"What we're trying to do is allow an unfettered reorganization of the airline industry," Collenette said. "The development of business proposals for restructuring will be undertaken entirely by the private sector, as ultimately these are business and marketplace decisions." ...

Essence of the Story

- Some Canadian banks proposed a merger that was not supported by Finance Minister Paul Martin and the Liberal government.

- The federal government has relaxed competition laws to allow Air Canada and Canadian Airlines to discuss a possible merger.

- The Canadian airline industry is facing the possibility of a monopoly.

■ A merger of either banks or airlines might:

1. Lower costs but not increase market power
2. Leave costs unchanged and increase market power, or
3. Lower costs *and* increase market power

■ Air transportation is a global business and world-wide competition among airlines is severe. It approaches perfect competition on busy international routes. For example Air Canada, British Airways, and a host of other airlines compete on the routes between Toronto and London.

■ Banking is also a global business and world-wide competition among banks approaches perfect competition in servicing large multinational corporations. The Canadian banking market includes the Canadian banks, foreign banks such as the Hong Kong Bank, and telephone and Internet banking services.

■ Airlines and banks have large fixed costs. They also have high marginal costs that might be lowered by merging and rationalizing two (or more) existing firms.

■ Figure 1 shows the effects of a merger of either airlines or banks, if the industry remains competitive and the merger lowers the marginal cost of delivering the service.

■ Initially, the demand curve D intersects the supply curve S_0 at a quantity Q_0 and a price P_0.

■ Then a marginal cost-cutting merger occurs. With a lower marginal cost, supply increases and the supply curve shifts rightward to S_1. The quantity increases to Q_1, the price falls to P_1, and consumer surplus increases.

■ The outcome in Fig. 1 is the one predicted by the Royal Bank and the Bank of Montreal and the supporters of an Air Canada–Canadian Airlines merger.

■ But airlines serve travellers who live in smaller communities and on many low-density routes, air transportation is a natural monopoly. Canada has many such air routes.

■ Similarly, banks serve customers who live in smaller communities, and in these communities, banking is a natural monopoly. Canada has many such communities.

■ Figure 2 shows the market for air travel from Vancouver to Penticton B.C., or the market for banking services in Penticton, B.C.

■ Again, initially, the demand curve D intersects the supply curve S at a quantity Q_0 and a price P_0.

Figure 1 Merger cuts costs

Price falls, quantity increases, and consumer surplus increases

Figure 2 Merger creates monopoly

Price increases, quantity decreases, and deadweight loss arises

■ Then a merger occurs that increases market power but has no effect on costs.

■ With market power, the newly merged firm has a marginal revenue curve MR. And with no change in marginal cost, the firm's marginal cost curve, MC, is the same as the supply curve of the initially competitive market.

■ The firm maximizes profit by decreasing the quantity to Q_2 and increasing the price to P_2. A deadweight loss now arises.

■ Paul Martin and the Liberal government predict the outcome in Fig. 2 in the case of banks but not in the case of airlines.

Key Points

Market Intervention (p. 412)

■ The federal government intervenes to regulate monopolistic and oligopolistic markets in three ways: regulation, public ownership, and anti-combine law.

Economic Theory of Regulation (pp. 412–414)

■ Consumers and producers express their demand for the regulation by voting, lobbying, and making campaign contributions.

■ The larger the surplus per person generated by a regulation, the greater the number of gainers, and the smaller the number of losers, the larger is the demand for the regulation.

■ Regulation is supplied by politicians who pursue their own best interest.

■ The larger the surplus per person generated and the larger the number of people affected by it, the larger is the supply of regulation.

■ Public interest theory predicts that regulation will maximize total surplus; capture theory predicts that producer surplus will be maximized.

Regulation and Deregulation (pp. 414–421)

■ Natural monopolies and cartels are regulated by agencies controlled by politically appointed bureaucrats and staffed by a permanent bureaucracy of experts.

■ Regulated firms must comply with rules about price, product quality, and output levels.

■ Regulation has not lowered the profit rates of regulated firms.

Public Ownership (pp. 421–423)

■ More than 100 Crown corporations produce such items as rail transport, hydroelectric power, and telecommunications.

■ The economic theory of bureaucracy is that managers maximize their budgets subject to political constraints.

■ Crown corporations tend to be inefficient: They overproduce and their costs are too high.

Anti-Combine Law (pp. 424–425)

■ Anti-combine law provides an alternative way for government to control monopoly and monopolistic practices.

■ The Competition Act of 1986 radically reformed anti-combine law and placed responsibility for enforcement with the Competition Tribunal.

Key Figures and Tables

Key Terms

Anti-combine law, 412
Average cost pricing rule, 416
Capture theory, 413
Crown corporations, 412
Marginal cost pricing rule, 416
Privatization, 412
Public interest theory, 413
Rate of return regulation, 417

P R O B L E M S

*1. Elixir Springs, Inc., is an unregulated natural monopoly that bottles Elixir, a unique health product with no substitutes. The total fixed cost incurred by Elixir Springs is $150,000, and its marginal cost is 10 cents a bottle. The figure illustrates the demand for Elixir.

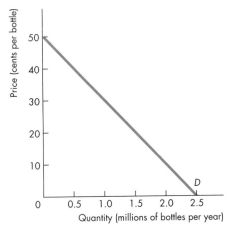

a. What is the price of a bottle of Elixir?
b. How many bottles does Elixir Springs sell?
c. Does Elixir Springs maximize total surplus or producer surplus?

2. Cascade Springs, Inc., is a natural monopoly that bottles water from a spring high in the Rocky Mountains. The total fixed cost that it incurs is $120,000, and its marginal cost is 20 cents a bottle. The figure illustrates the demand for Cascade Springs bottled water.

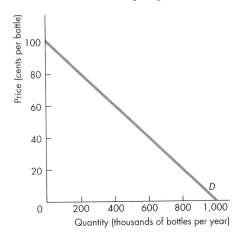

a. What is the price of Cascade Springs water?

b. How many bottles does Cascade Springs sell?
c. Does Cascade Springs maximize total surplus or producer surplus?

*3. The government regulates Elixir Springs in problem 1 by imposing a marginal cost pricing rule.
a. What is the price of a bottle of Elixir?
b. How many bottles does Elixir Springs sell?
c. What is Elixir Springs' economic profit?
d. What is the consumer surplus?
e. Is the regulation in the public interest? Explain.

4. The government regulates Cascade Springs in problem 2 by imposing a marginal cost pricing rule.
a. What is the price of Cascade Springs water?
b. How many bottles does Cascade Springs sell?
c. What is the economic profit?
d. What is the consumer surplus?
e. Is the regulation in the public interest? Explain.

*5. The government regulates Elixir Springs in problem 1 by imposing an average cost pricing rule.
a. What is the price of a bottle of Elixir?
b. How many bottles does Elixir Springs sell?
c. What is Elixir Springs' economic profit?
d. What is the consumer surplus?
e. Is the regulation in the public interest? Explain.

6. The government regulates Cascade Springs in problem 2 by imposing an average cost pricing rule.
a. What is the price of Cascade Springs water?
b. How many bottles does Cascade Springs sell?
c. What is Cascade Springs' economic profit?
d. What is the consumer surplus?
e. Is the regulation in the public interest? Explain.

*7. Two airlines share an international route. The figure shows the demand curve for trips on this route and the marginal cost curve that each firm faces. This air route is regulated.

a. What is the price of a trip and what is the number of trips per day if the regulation is in the public interest?

b. What is the price of a trip and what is the number of trips per day if the airlines capture the regulator?

c. What is the deadweight loss in part (b)?

8. Two telephone companies offer local calls in an area. The figure shows the market demand curve for calls and the marginal cost curve of each firm. These firms are regulated.

a. What is the price of a call and what is the number of calls per day if the regulation is in the public interest?

b. What is the price of a call and what is the number of calls per day if the telephone companies capture the regulator?

c. What is the deadweight loss in part (b)?

d. What do you need to know to predict whether the regulation will be in the public interest or the producer interest?

CRITICAL THINKING

1. After you have studied *Reading Between the Lines* on pp. 426–427, answer the following questions.

   a. Which parts of the business of an airline might be a natural monopoly and which parts are competitive?

   b. Which parts of the business of a bank might be a natural monopoly and which parts are competitive?

   c. If a merger of two of Canada's largest banks occurred, would there be an increase or a decrease in the efficiency of the banking industry? Who would benefit from and who would pay for the changes?

   d. If a merger of Canada's two major airlines occurred, would there be an increase or a decrease in the efficiency of the air transportation industry? Who would benefit from and who would pay for the changes?

   e. Critically evaluate the decision to block the merger of the Royal Bank and the Bank of Montreal.

2. The government of Canada regulates the production and sale of many goods and services. For example, it regulates the prices of local phone and cable TV services, the acreage that each wheat and cereal farmer can sow, the grain prices paid to these farmers and to whom they can sell the grain. The suppliers of local phone and cable TV services are monopolies, but there are many grain farmers. Why are grain farmers regulated? Is the regulation in the interest of grain farmers or consumers?

3. "Now that Canada has free trade with the United States, the government of Canada should not regulate monopolies in Canada because they are in direct competition with U.S. producers." Do you agree with this argument? If so, explain why. If not, explain why the argument is incorrect.

4. Use the link on the Parkin-Bade Web site to visit Competition Law Review. Look for cases of collusive agreement, abuse of dominant position, and mergers to restrict competition. In each case, describe the means cited as used to lessen competition.

Externalities, the Environment, and Knowledge

Greener and Smarter

We burn huge quantities of fossil fuels—coal, natural gas, and oil—that cause acid rain and possibly global warming. The persistent and large-scale use of chlorofluorocarbons (CFCs) may have caused irreparable damage to the earth's ozone layer, thereby exposing us to additional ultraviolet rays, which increase the incidence of skin cancer. We dump toxic waste into rivers, lakes, and oceans. These environmental issues are simultaneously everybody's problem and nobody's problem. What, if anything, can government do to protect our environment? How can government action help us to take account of the damage that we cause others every time we turn on our heating or air conditioning systems? ◆ Almost every day, we hear about a new discovery—in medicine, engineering, chemistry, physics, or even economics. The advance of knowledge seems boundless. And more and more people are learning more and more of what is already known. The stock of knowledge—what is known and how many people know it—is increasing, apparently without bounds. We are getting smarter. But is our stock of knowledge advancing fast enough? Are we spending enough on research and development? Do we spend enough on education? Do enough people remain in school for long enough? And do we work hard enough at school? Would we be better off if we spent more on research and education?

◇ In this chapter, we study the problems that arise because many of our actions create externalities. They affect other people, for ill or good, in ways that we do not usually take into account when we make our own economic choices. We study two big areas—the environment and the accumulation of knowledge—in which these problems are especially important. Externalities are a major source of *market failure*. When market failure occurs, we must either live with the inefficiency it creates or try to achieve greater efficiency by making some *public choices*. This chapter studies these choices. It begins by looking at external costs that affect the environment.

After studying this chapter, you will be able to:

- Explain how property rights can sometimes be used to overcome externalities

- Explain how emission charges, marketable permits, and taxes can be used to achieve efficiency in the face of external costs

- Explain how subsidies can be used to achieve efficiency in the face of external benefits

- Explain how scholarships, below-cost tuition, and research grants make the quantity of education and invention more efficient

- Explain how patents increase economic efficiency

Economics of the Environment

ENVIRONMENTAL PROBLEMS ARE NOT NEW, AND they are not restricted to rich industrial countries. Preindustrial towns and cities in Europe had severe sewage disposal problems that created cholera epidemics and plagues that killed tens of millions of people. Nor is the desire to find solutions to environmental problems new. The developments in the fourteenth century of pure water supplies and of garbage and sewage disposal are examples of early contributions to improving the quality of the environment.

Popular discussions of the environment usually pay little attention to economics. They focus on physical aspects of the environment, not costs and benefits. A common assumption is that if people's actions cause *any* environmental degradation, those actions must cease. In contrast, an economic study of the environment emphasizes costs and benefits. An economist talks about the efficient amount of pollution or environmental damage. This emphasis on costs and benefits does not mean that economists, as citizens, do not share the same goals as others and value a healthy environment. Nor does it mean that economists have the right answers and everyone else has the wrong ones (or vice versa). Economics provides a set of tools and principles that clarify the issues. It does not provide an agreed list of solutions. The starting point for an economic analysis of the environment is the demand for a healthy environment.

The Demand for Environmental Quality

The demand for a clean and healthy environment is greater today than it has ever been. We express our demand for a better environment in several ways. We join organizations that lobby for environmental regulations and policies. We vote for politicians who support the environmental policies that we want to see implemented. (All politicians at least pay lip service to the environment today.) We buy "green" products and avoid hazardous products, even if we pay a bit more to do so. And we pay higher housing costs and commuting costs to live in pleasant neighbourhoods.

The demand for a cleaner and healthier environment has grown for two main reasons. First, as our incomes increase, we demand a larger range of goods and services, and one of these "goods" is a high-quality environment. We value clean air, unspoiled natural scenery, and wildlife, and we are willing and able to pay for them.

Second, as our knowledge of the effects of our actions on the environment grows, so we are able to take measures that improve the environment. For example, now that we know how sulfur dioxide causes acid rain and how clearing rain forests destroys natural stores of carbon dioxide, we are able, in principle, to design measures that limit these problems.

Let's look at the range of environmental problems that have been identified and the actions that create those problems.

The Sources of Environmental Problems

Environmental problems arise from pollution of the air, water, and land, and these individual sources of pollution interact through the *ecosystem*.

Air Pollution   Figure 20.1(a) shows the five economic activities that create most of our air pollution. It also shows the relative contributions of each activity. More than two-thirds of air pollution comes from road transportation and industrial processes. Only one-sixth arises from electric power generation.

A common belief is that air pollution is getting worse. On many fronts, as we will see later in this chapter, *global* air pollution *is* getting worse. But air pollution in North America is becoming less severe for most substances. Figure 20.1(b) shows the trends in the concentrations of six air pollutants. While lead has been almost eliminated from our air and sulfur dioxide, carbon monoxide, and suspended particulates have been reduced substantially, levels of other pollutants have remained more stable.

While the facts about the sources and trends in air pollution are not in doubt, there is considerable disagreement in the scientific community about the *effects* of air pollution. The least controversial problem is *acid rain*, which is caused by sulfur dioxide and nitrogen oxide emissions from coal- and oil-fired generators of electric utilities. Acid rain begins with air pollution, and it leads to water pollution and damages vegetation.

More controversial are airborne substances (suspended particulates) such as lead from leaded gasoline. Some scientists believe that in sufficiently large

FIGURE **20.1**

Air Pollution

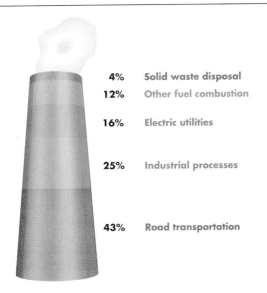

4%	Solid waste disposal
12%	Other fuel combustion
16%	Electric utilities
25%	Industrial processes
43%	Road transportation

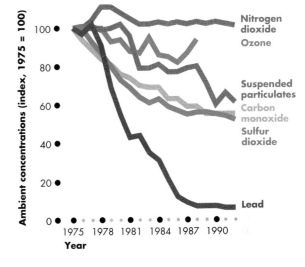

(a) Sources of emission

(b) Ambient concentrations

Part (a) shows that road transportation is the largest source of air pollution, followed by industrial processes and electric utilities. Part (b) shows that lead has almost been eliminated from our air and concentrations of carbon monoxide, sulfur dioxide, and suspended particulates have decreased. But nitrogen dioxide and ozone have persisted at close to their 1975 levels.

Source: U.S. Environmental Protection Agency, *National Air Quality and Emissions Trends Report*, 1996.

concentrations, these substances (189 of which have currently been identified) cause cancer and other life-threatening conditions.

Even more controversial is *global warming*, which some scientists say results from the carbon dioxide emissions of road transportation and electric utilities, from methane created by cows and other livestock, from nitrous oxide emissions of electric utilities and from fertilizers. The earth's average temperature has increased over the past 100 years, but most of the increase occurred *before* 1940. Determining what causes changes in the earth's temperature and isolating the effect of carbon dioxide is proving to be difficult.

Equally controversial is the problem of *ozone layer depletion*, which some scientists say results from chlorofluorocarbons (CFCs) used by refrigerators and (in the past) aerosols. There is no doubt that a hole in the ozone layer exists over Antarctica, and that the ozone layer protects us from cancer-causing ultravio-

let rays from the sun. But how industrial activity influences the ozone layer is not understood at this time.

One air pollution problem has almost been eliminated: lead from gasoline. In part, this happened because the cost of living without leaded gasoline, it turns out, is not high. But sulfur dioxide and the so-called greenhouse gases are a much tougher problem to tackle. Their alternatives are costly or have environmental problems of their own. The major sources of these pollutants are road vehicles and electric utilities. Road vehicles can be made "greener" in a variety of ways. One is with new fuels—some alternatives being investigated are alcohol, natural gas, propane and butane, and hydrogen. Another way of making cars and trucks "greener" is to change the chemistry of gasoline. Refiners are working on reformulations of gasoline that cut tailpipe emissions. Similarly, electric power can be generated in cleaner ways by harnessing solar power, tidal power, or geothermal power. Technically possible, these methods are more costly than conventional carbon-fuelled generators. Another alternative is nuclear power. This method is good for air pollution but bad for land and water pollution because there is no known safe method of disposing of spent nuclear fuel.

Water Pollution   The largest sources of water pollution are the dumping of industrial waste and treated sewage in lakes and rivers and the runoff from fertilizers. A more dramatic source is the accidental spilling of crude oil into the oceans, such as the *Exxon Valdez* spill in Alaska in 1989 and an even larger spill in the Russian Arctic in 1994. The most frightening is the dumping of nuclear waste into the ocean by the former Soviet Union.

There are two main alternatives to polluting the waterways and oceans. One is the chemical processing of waste to render it inert or biodegradable. The other, in wide use for nuclear waste, is to use land sites for storage in secure containers.

Land Pollution   Land pollution arises from dumping toxic waste products. Ordinary household garbage does not pose a pollution problem unless dumped garbage seeps into the water supply. This possibility increases as less suitable landfill sites are used. It is estimated that 80 percent of existing landfills will be full by 2010. Some regions (New York, New Jersey, and other East Coast U.S. states) and some countries (Japan and the Netherlands) are seeking less costly alternatives to landfill, such as recycling and incineration. Recycling is an apparently attractive alternative, but it requires an investment in new technologies to be effective. Incineration is a high-cost alternative to landfill, and it produces air pollution. But these alternatives are not free and they become efficient only when the cost of using landfill is high.

We've seen that the demand for a high-quality environment has grown, and we've described the range of environmental problems. Let's now look at the ways in which these problems can be handled. We'll begin by looking at property rights and how they relate to environmental externalities.

Absence of Property Rights and Environmental Externalities

Externalities arise because of an *absence* of property rights. **Property rights** are social arrangements that

govern the ownership, use, and disposal of productive resources, goods, and services. In modern societies, a property right is a legally established title that is enforceable in the courts.

Property rights are absent when externalities arise. No one owns the air, the rivers, and the oceans. So it is no one's private business to ensure that these resources are used in an efficient way. In fact, there is an incentive to use them more than if there were property rights.

Figure 20.2 shows an environmental externality in the absence of property rights. A chemical factory upstream from a fishing club must decide how to dispose of its waste.

The factory's marginal benefit curve, *MB*, tells us the benefit to the factory of an additional tonne of waste dumped into the river. The *MB* curve is also the firm's demand curve for the use of the river,

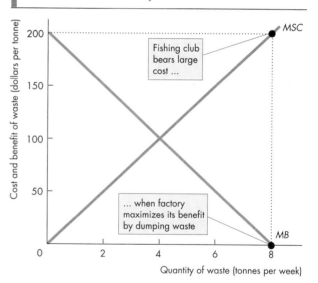

FIGURE 20.2

An Externality

A chemical factory's marginal benefit from dumping its waste into a river is *MB* and a fishing club's marginal cost of having waste dumped is *MSC*. With no property rights, the factory maximizes total benefit by dumping 8 tonnes a week, the quantity at which the marginal benefit of dumping equals the marginal cost (zero). With this quantity of waste, the fishing club bears a marginal cost of $200 per tonne. This outcome is inefficient because the marginal social cost exceeds the marginal benefit.

which is a productive resource. The demand for a resource slopes downward because of the law of diminishing returns (see Chapter 15, pp. 324–325).

Marginal social cost is the marginal cost incurred by the producer of a good—marginal private cost—plus the marginal cost imposed on others—the external cost. The factory bears no cost of dumping. All the costs are borne by the fishing club. The marginal social cost curve, *MSC*, tells us the cost borne by the club when one additional tonne of waste is dumped into the river. Marginal cost rises as the quantity dumped increases.

If no one owns the river, the factory dumps the amount of waste that maximizes *its own* total benefit. Its marginal cost is zero (along the *x*-axis) so it dumps 8 tonnes a week, the quantity that makes marginal benefit zero. The marginal social cost of the waste, which is borne by the fishing club, is $200 a tonne. Marginal cost exceeds marginal benefit, so the outcome is inefficient.

Property Rights and the Coase Theorem

Sometimes it is possible to correct an externality by establishing a property right where one does not currently exist. For example, suppose that the chemical factory owns the river. The fishing club must pay the factory for the right to fish in the river. But the price that the club is willing to pay depends on the number and quality of fish, which in turn depends on how much waste the factory dumps in the river. The greater the amount of pollution, the smaller is the amount the fishing club is willing to pay for the right to fish. The chemical factory is now confronted with the cost of its pollution decision. It might still decide to pollute, but if it does, it faces the opportunity cost of its actions—forgone revenue from the fishing club.

Alternatively, suppose that the fishing club owns the river. Now the factory must pay a fee to the fishing club for the right to dump its waste. The more waste it dumps (equivalently, the more fish it kills), the more it must pay. Again, the factory faces an opportunity cost for the pollution it creates.

Does it matter how property rights are assigned? Does it matter whether the polluter or the victim of the pollution owns the resource that might be polluted? At first thought, ownership seems crucial. And until 1960, that is what everyone thought—including economists who had thought about the problem for longer than a few minutes. But in 1960, Ronald

Coase had a remarkable insight, now called the Coase theorem. The **Coase theorem** is the proposition that if property rights exist and transactions costs are low, private transactions are efficient. Equivalently, with property rights and low transactions costs, there are no externalities. The transacting parties take all the costs and benefits into account. So it doesn't matter how the property rights are assigned.

Figure 20.3 illustrates the Coase theorem. As before, the demand curve for dumping waste is the factory's marginal benefit curve, *MB*. This curve tells us what the factory is willing to pay to dump. With property rights in place, the *MSC* curve is the fishing club's supply curve of river use to the firm. It tells us what the club's members must be paid if they are to put up with inferior fishing and supply the firm with a permit to dump.

The efficient level of waste is 4 tonnes a week. At

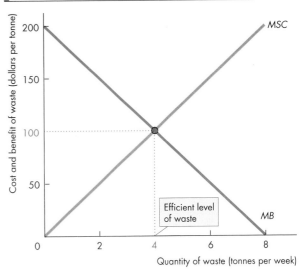

Pollution of a river imposes a marginal social cost, *MSC*, on the victim and provides a marginal benefit, *MB*, to the polluter. The efficient amount of pollution is the quantity that makes marginal benefit equal to marginal social cost—in this example, 4 tonnes per week. If the polluter owns the river, the victim will pay $400 a week ($100 a tonne × 4 tonnes a week) to the polluter for the assurance that pollution will not exceed 4 tonnes a week. If the victim owns the river, the polluter will pay $400 for pollution rights to dump 4 tonnes a week.

this level, the club bears a cost of $100 for the last tonne dumped into the river, and the factory gets a benefit of that amount. If waste disposal is restricted below 4 tonnes a week, an increase in waste disposal benefits the factory more than it costs the club. The factory can pay the club to put up with more waste disposal, and both the club and the factory can gain. If waste disposal exceeds 4 tonnes a week, an increase in waste disposal costs the club more than it benefits the factory. The club can now pay the factory to cut its waste disposal, and again, both the club and the factory can gain. Only when the level of waste disposal is 4 tonnes a week can neither party do any better. This is the efficient level of waste disposal.

The amount of waste disposal is the same regardless of who owns the river. If the factory owns it, the club pays $400 for fishing rights and for an agreement that waste disposal will not exceed 4 tonnes a week. If the club owns the river, the factory pays $400 for the right to dump 4 tonnes of waste a week. In both cases, the amount of waste disposal is the efficient amount.

Property rights work if transactions costs are low. The factory and the fishing club can negotiate the deal that produces the efficient outcome. But in many situations, transactions costs are high and property rights cannot be enforced. Imagine the transactions costs if the 50 million people who live in the northeastern part of Canada and the United States tried to negotiate an agreement with the 20,000 factories that emit sulfur dioxide and cause acid rain! In this type of case, governments use alternative methods of coping with externalities. They use:

1. Emission charges
2. Marketable permits
3. Taxes

In Canada, the federal government has established a government department, Environment Canada, to coordinate and administer the nation's environment policies. Let's look at the tools available to Environment Canada and see how they work.

Emission Charges

Emission charges are a method of using the market to achieve efficiency, even in the face of externalities. The government (or the regulatory agency established by the government) sets the emission charges, which are, in effect, a price per unit of pollution. The more

pollution a firm creates, the more it pays in emission charges. This method of dealing with environmental externalities has been used only modestly in North America, but it is common in Europe. For example, in France, Germany, and the Netherlands, water polluters pay a waste disposal charge.

To work out the emission charge that achieves efficiency, the regulator must determine the marginal social cost and marginal *social* benefit of pollution. **Marginal social benefit** is the marginal benefit received by the buyer—marginal private benefit—plus the marginal benefit to others—the external benefit. To achieve efficiency, the price per unit of pollution must be set to make the marginal social cost of the pollution equal to its marginal social benefit.

Figure 20.4 illustrates an efficient emission charge. The marginal benefit of pollution is *MB* and accrues to the polluters—there is no *external* benefit. The marginal social cost of pollution is *MSC* and is

FIGURE 20.4
Emission Charges

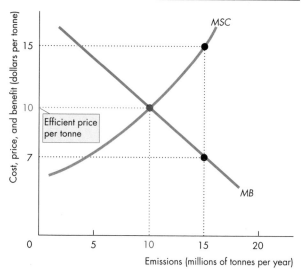

Electric utilities obtain marginal benefits from sulfur dioxide emissions of *MB*, and everyone else bears a marginal social cost of *MSC*. The efficient level of pollution—10 million tonnes a year in this example—is achieved by imposing an emission charge on the utilities of $10 a tonne. If the emission charge is set too low, at $7 a tonne, the resulting amount of pollution is greater than the efficient amount—at 15 million tonnes a year in this example. In this case, the marginal social cost is $15 a tonne, and it exceeds the marginal benefit of $7 a tonne.

entirely an external cost. The efficient level of sulfur dioxide emissions is 10 million tonnes a year, which is achieved with an emission charge of $10 per tonne. At this price, polluters do not find it worthwhile to buy the permission to pollute in excess of 10 million tonnes a year.

In practice, it is hard to determine the marginal benefit of pollution. And the people who are best informed about the marginal benefit, the polluters, have an incentive to mislead the regulators about the benefit. As a result, if a pollution charge is used, the most likely outcome is for the price to be set too low. For example, in Fig. 20.4, the price might be set at $7 per tonne. At this price, polluters find it worthwhile to pay for 15 million tonnes a year. At this level of pollution, the marginal social cost is $15 a tonne, and the amount of pollution exceeds the efficient level.

One way of overcoming excess pollution is to impose a quantitative limit. The most sophisticated way of doing this is with quantitative limits that firms can buy and sell—with marketable permits. Let's look at this alternative.

Marketable Permits

Instead of imposing emission charges on polluters, each potential polluter might be given a pollution limit. To achieve efficiency, marginal benefit and marginal cost must be assessed just as in the case of emission charges. Provided that these benefit-cost calculations are correct, the same efficient outcome can be achieved with quantitative limits as with charges. But in the case of quantitative limits, a cap must be set for each polluter. To set these caps at their efficient levels, the marginal benefit of *each* producer must be assessed. If firm H has a higher marginal benefit than firm L, an efficiency gain can be achieved by decreasing the cap of firm L and increasing that of firm H. It is virtually impossible to determine the marginal benefits of each firm, so in practice, quantitative restrictions cannot be allocated to each producer in an efficient way.

Marketable permits are a clever way of overcoming the need for the regulator to know every firm's marginal benefit schedule. Each firm can be allocated a permit to emit a certain amount of pollution, and firms may buy and sell such permits. Firms that have a low marginal benefit from sulfur dioxide emissions will be willing to sell their permits to other firms that have a high marginal benefit. If the market in permits is competitive, the price at which firms trade permits makes the marginal benefit of pollution equal for all firms. And if the correct number of permits has been allotted, the outcome can be efficient.

A Real-World Market for Emissions Environment Canada has not used marketable permits but the Environmental Protection Agency (the EPA) has. The EPA first implemented a marketable emission permit program following the passage of the Clean Air Act in 1970. Trading in lead pollution permits became common during the 1980s, and this marketable permit program has been rated a success. It enabled lead to be virtually eliminated from the atmosphere of the United States (see Figure 20.1b). But this success might not easily translate to other situations because lead pollution has some special features. First, most lead pollution came from a single source, leaded gasoline. Second, lead in gasoline is easily monitored. Third, the objective of the program was clear: eliminate lead in gasoline.

The EPA is now considering using marketable permits to promote efficiency in the control of chlorofluorocarbons, the gases that are believed to damage the ozone layer.

Taxes and External Costs

Taxes can be used to provide incentives for producers or consumers to cut back on an activity that creates external costs. To see how taxes work, consider the market for transportation services.

The costs borne by the producers of transportation services are not the only costs. External costs arise from the airborne particulates and greenhouse gases caused by vehicle emissions. Further, one person's decision to use a highway imposes congestion costs on others. These costs also are external costs. When all the external marginal costs are added to the marginal cost faced by the producer, we obtain the marginal social cost of transportation.

Figure 20.5 shows the market for transportation services. The demand curve, D, is also the marginal benefit curve, MB. This curve tells us how much consumers value each different quantity of transportation services. The curve MC measures the marginal *private* cost of producing transportation services—the costs directly incurred by the producers of these services. The curve MSC measures the marginal *social* cost, which adds the external costs to the private costs.

FIGURE 20.5

Taxes and Pollution

The demand curve for road transportation services is also the marginal benefit curve ($D = MB$). The marginal private cost curve is MC. If the market is competitive, output is Q_0 kilometres and the price is P_0 per kilometre. Marginal social cost is SC_0 per kilometre. Because of congestion and pollution, the marginal social cost exceeds the marginal private cost. Marginal social cost is shown by curve MSC. If the government imposes a tax so that producers of transportation services are confronted with the marginal social cost, the MSC curve becomes the relevant marginal cost curve for suppliers' decisions. The price increases to P_1 per kilometre, and the quantity decreases to Q_1 kilometres. The outcome is efficient.

If the transportation market is competitive and unregulated, road users will balance their own marginal cost, MC, against their own marginal benefit, MB, and travel Q_0 kilometres at a price (and cost) of P_0 per kilometre. At this scale of transportation services, the marginal social cost is SC_0. The marginal social cost minus the marginal private cost, $SC_0 - P_0$, is the marginal cost imposed on others—the marginal external cost.

Suppose the government taxes road transportation and that it sets the tax equal to the external marginal cost. By imposing such a tax, the government makes the suppliers of transportation services incur a marginal cost equal to the marginal social cost. That is, the marginal private cost plus the tax equals the

marginal social cost. The market supply curve is now the same as the MSC curve. The price rises to P_1 a kilometre, and at this price, people travel Q_1 kilometres. The marginal cost of the resources used in producing Q_1 kilometres is C_1, and the marginal external cost is P_1 minus C_1. That marginal external cost is paid by the consumer through the tax.

The situation at the price P_1 and the quantity Q_1 is efficient. At a quantity greater than Q_1, marginal social cost exceeds marginal benefit, so net benefit increases by decreasing the quantity of transportation services. At a quantity less than Q_1, marginal benefit exceeds marginal social cost, so net benefit increases by increasing the quantity of transportation services.

A Carbon Fuel Tax? A tax can be imposed on any activity that creates external costs. For example, we could tax *all* air-polluting activities. Because the carbon fuels that we use to power our vehicles and generate our electric power are a major source of pollution, why don't we have a broad-based tax on all activities that burn carbon fuel and set the tax rate high enough to give a large reduction in carbon emissions?

The question becomes even more pressing when we consider not only the current levels of greenhouse gases but also their projected future levels. In 1995, annual carbon emissions worldwide were a staggering 6 billion tonnes. By 2050, with current policies, that annual total is predicted to be 24 billion tonnes.

Uncertainty About Global Warming Part of the reason we do not have a high, broad-based, carbon fuel tax is that the scientific evidence that carbon emissions produce global warming is not accepted by everyone. Climatologists are uncertain about how carbon emissions translate into atmospheric concentrations—about how the *flow* of emissions translates into a *stock* of pollution. The main uncertainty arises because carbon drains from the atmosphere into the oceans and vegetation at a rate that is not well understood. Climatologists are also uncertain about the connection between carbon concentration and temperature. And economists are uncertain about how a temperature increase translates into economic costs and benefits. Some economists believe that the costs and benefits are almost zero, while others believe that a temperature increase of 3 degrees Celsius by 2090 will reduce the total output of goods and services by 20 percent.

Present Cost and Future Benefit Another factor weighing against a large change in fuel use is that the costs would be borne now, while the benefits, if any, would accrue many years in the future. To compare future benefits with current costs, we must use an interest rate. If the interest rate is 1 percent a year, a dollar today becomes $2.70 in 100 years. If the interest rate is 5 percent a year, a dollar today becomes more than $131.50 in 100 years. So at an interest rate of 1 percent a year, it is worth spending $1 million in 2000 on pollution control to avoid $2.7 million in environmental damage in 2100. At an interest rate of 5 percent a year, it is worth spending $1 million today only if this expenditure avoids $131.5 million in environmental damage in 2100.

Because large uncertain future benefits are needed to justify small current costs, a general tax on carbon fuels is not a high priority on the political agenda.

International Factors   A final factor against a large change in fuel use is the international pattern of the use of carbon fuels. Right now, carbon pollution comes in even doses from the industrial countries and the developing countries. But by 2050, three-quarters of the carbon pollution will come from the developing countries (if the trends persist).

One reason for the high pollution rate in some developing countries (notably China, Russia, and other Eastern European countries) is that their governments *subsidize* the use of coal or oil. These subsidies lower producers' marginal costs and encourage the use of fuels. The result is that the quantity of carbon fuels consumed exceeds the efficient quantity—and by a large amount. It is estimated that by 2050, these subsidies will induce annual global carbon emissions of some 10 billion tonnes—about two-fifths of total emissions. If the subsidies were removed, global emissions in 2050 would be 10 billion tonnes a year less.

A Global Warming Dilemma

With the high output rate of greenhouse gases in the developing world, Canada and the other industrial countries are faced with a global warming dilemma (like the prisoners' dilemma in Chapter 14, pp. 299–300). Decreasing pollution is costly and might bring benefits. But the benefits depend on all countries taking action to limit pollution. If one country acts alone, it bears the cost of limiting pollution and gets almost no benefits. So it is worthwhile taking steps to limit global pollution only if all nations act together.

Table 20.1 shows the global warming dilemma faced by industrial countries and developing countries. The numbers are hypothetical. Each country (we'll call each group of countries a country) has two possible policies: to control carbon emissions or to pollute. If each country pollutes, it receives a zero net return (by assumption), shown in the top left square in the table. If both countries control emissions, each bears the cost and gets the benefit. Each has a net return of $25 billion, as shown in the bottom right square of the table. If industrial countries control emissions but developing countries do not, industrial countries alone bear the cost and all countries enjoy a lower level of pollution. In this example, industrial countries pay $50 billion more than they benefit and developing countries benefit by $50 billion more than they pay, as shown in the top right corner of the table. Finally, if developing countries control emissions and industrial countries do not, developing countries bear the cost and industrial countries share

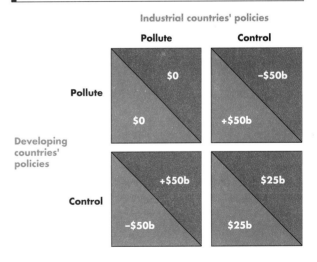

TABLE 20.1

A Global Warming Dilemma

If industrial countries and developing countries both pollute, their payoffs are those shown in the top left square. If both countries control pollution, the bottom right square shows their payoffs. When one group of countries pollutes and the other group does not, the top right and bottom left squares show their payoffs. The outcome of this game is for all countries to pollute. The structure of this game is the same as that of the prisoners' dilemma.

the gains. Developing countries lose $50 billion and industrial countries gain this amount, as shown in the bottom left corner of the table.

Confronted with these possible payoffs, industrial countries and developing countries decide their policies. Each country reasons as follows: If the other country does not control emissions, we break even if we pollute and we lose $50 billion if we control our emissions. Conclusion: Each country is better off individually by polluting. So no one controls emissions, and pollution continues unabated.

Treaties and International Agreements

To break the dilemma, international agreements—treaties—might be negotiated. But such treaties must have incentives for countries to comply with their agreements. Otherwise, even with a treaty, the situation remains as we've just described and illustrated in Table 20.1.

One such international agreement is the *climate convention* that came into effect on March 21, 1994. This convention is an agreement among 60 countries to limit their output of greenhouse gases. But the convention does not have economic teeth. The poorer countries are merely asked to list their sources of greenhouse gases. The rich countries must show how, by 2000, they will return to their 1990 emissions levels.

R E V I E W   Q U I Z

- Why do externalities prevent markets from being efficient?

- How can an externality be eliminated by assigning property rights? How does this method of coping with an externality work?

- How do emission charges and pollution limits work to deal with externalities? Is one preferred over the other?

- How do taxes help us to cope with externalities? At what level must a pollution tax be set if it is to induce firms to produce the efficient quantity of pollution?

- What are the problems that arise when an externality goes beyond the scope of one country?

Economics of Knowledge

KNOWLEDGE, THE THINGS PEOPLE KNOW AND understand, has a profound effect on the economy. The economics of knowledge is an attempt to understand that effect. It is also an attempt to understand the process of knowledge accumulation and the incentives people face to discover, to learn, and to pass on what they know to others. It is an economic analysis of the scientific and engineering processes that lead to the discovery and development of new technologies. And it is a study of the education process of teaching and learning.

You can think of knowledge as being both a consumer good and a productive resource. The demand for knowledge—the willingness to pay to acquire knowledge—depends on the marginal benefit it provides to its possessor. As a consumer good, knowledge provides utility, and this is one source of its marginal benefit. As a productive resource—part of the stock of capital—knowledge increases productivity, and this is another source of its marginal benefit.

Knowledge clearly creates benefits for its possessor. It might also create external benefits. When children learn the basics of reading, writing, and numbers in grade school, they are equipping themselves to be better citizens, better able to communicate and interact with each other. The process continues through high school, college, and university. But when people make decisions about how much schooling to undertake, they undervalue the external benefits that it creates.

External benefits also arise from research and development activities that lead to the creation of new knowledge. Once someone has worked out how to do something, others can copy the basic idea. They do have to work to copy an idea, so they face an opportunity cost. But they do not usually have to pay the person who made the discovery to use it. When Isaac Newton worked out the formulas for calculating the rate of response of one variable to another—calculus—everyone was free to use his method. When a spreadsheet program called VisiCalc was invented, others were free to copy the basic idea. Lotus Corporation developed its 1-2-3 and later Microsoft created Excel, and both became highly successful, but they did not pay for the key idea first used in VisiCalc. When the first shopping mall was built and found to be a successful way of arranging retailing, everyone was free to copy the idea, and malls spread like mushrooms.

When people make decisions about the quantity of education to undertake or the amount of research and development to do, they balance the *private* marginal costs against the private marginal benefits. They undervalue the external benefits. As a result, if we were to leave education and research and development to unregulated market forces, we would get too little of these activities. To deliver them in efficient quantities, we make public choices through governments to modify the market outcome.

Three devices that governments can use to achieve an efficient allocation of resources in the presence of the external benefits from education and research and development are:

- Subsidies
- Below-cost provision
- Patents and copyrights

Subsidies

A **subsidy** is a payment made by the government to producers that depends on the level of output. By subsidizing private activities, government can in principle encourage private decisions to be taken in the public interest. A government subsidy program might alternatively enable private producers to capture resources for themselves. Although subsidies cannot be guaranteed to work successfully, we'll study an example in which they do achieve their desired goal.

Figure 20.6 shows how subsidizing education can increase the amount of education undertaken and achieve an efficient quantity of education. Suppose that all schools are private and that the market for education is competitive. Suppose also that the marginal cost of producing education is a constant $20,000 per student-year. Assume that all these costs are borne by the schools and that there are no external costs. The marginal social cost is the same as the schools' marginal cost and is shown by the curve $MC = MSC$. The maximum price that students (or parents) are willing to pay for an additional year of education determines the marginal private benefit curve and the demand curve for education. That curve is $MB = D$. In this example, a competitive market in private education results in 20,000 students being enrolled with tuition at $20,000 a year.

Suppose that the external benefit—the benefit derived by people other than those who receive the

education—results in marginal social benefits described by the curve *MSB*. The efficient outcome occurs when marginal social cost equals marginal social benefit. In the example in Fig. 20.6, this equality occurs when 40,000 students are enrolled. One way of getting 40,000 students is to subsidize private schools. In the example, a subsidy of $15,000 per student per year does the job. With a subsidy of $15,000 and a marginal cost of $20,000, schools earn an economic profit if the annual tuition exceeds $5,000. Competition would drive the tuition down

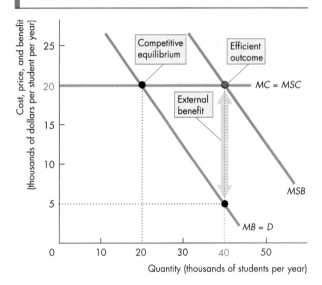

FIGURE 20.6

The Efficient Quantity of Education

The demand curve for education measures the marginal private benefit of education (*MB* = *D*). The curve *MC* shows the marginal cost of education—in this example, $20,000 per student-year. If education is provided in a competitive market, tuition is $20,000 a year and 20,000 students enrol. Education produces an external benefit, and adding the external benefit to the marginal private benefit gives marginal social benefit, *MSB*. Education has no external costs, so *MC* is also the marginal social cost of education, *MSC*. An efficient outcome is achieved if the government provides education services to 40,000 students a year, which is achieved by either subsidizing private schools or providing education below cost in public schools. In this example, students pay an annual tuition of $5,000 and the government pays a subsidy of $15,000.

to $5,000, and at this price, 40,000 students will enrol. So a subsidy can achieve an efficient outcome.

The lessons in this example can be applied to stimulating the rate of increase in the stock of knowledge—research and development. By subsidizing these activities, the government can move the allocation of resources towards a more efficient outcome. The mechanism that the government uses for this purpose is a research and development grant. In 1998, through agencies such as the National Science and Engineering Research Council, the Medical Research Council and the Social Sciences and Humanities Research Council, the government spent $620 million. A larger amount was spent in grants to industry.

Another way to achieve an efficient amount of education or research and development is through public provision below cost.

Below-Cost Provision

Instead of subsidizing private schools, the government can establish its own schools (public schools) that provide schooling below cost. And instead of subsidizing research and development in industry and the universities, the government can establish its own research facilities and make discoveries available to others. Let's see how this approach works by returning to the example in Fig. 20.6.

By establishing public schools with places for 40,000 students, the government can supply the efficient quantity of education. To ensure that this number of places is taken up, the public schools would charge a tuition, in this example, of $5,000 a student per year. The government provides this tuition below its marginal cost of $20,000 a student per year. At this price, the number of people who choose to attend school makes the marginal social benefit of education equal to its marginal social cost.

We've now looked at two examples of how government action can help market participants take account of the external benefits deriving from education to achieve an outcome different from that of a private unregulated market. In reality, governments use both methods of encouraging an efficient quantity of education. They subsidize private schools and universities, and they run their own institutions and sell their services at below cost. But in education, the public sector is by far the larger. In research and development, subsidies to the private sector are far larger than the government direct provision.

Patents and Copyrights

Knowledge may well be the only productive resource that does not display *diminishing marginal productivity*. More knowledge (about the right things) makes people more productive. And there seems to be no tendency for the additional productivity from additional knowledge to diminish.

For example, in just 15 years, advances in knowledge about microprocessors have given us a sequence of processor chips that has made our personal computers increasingly powerful. Each advance in knowledge about how to design and manufacture a processor chip has brought apparently ever-larger increments in performance and productivity. Similarly, each advance in knowledge about how to design and build an airplane has brought apparently ever larger increments in performance: Orville and Wilbur Wright's "Flyer 1" was a one-seat plane that could hop a farmer's field. The Lockheed Constellation was an airplane that could fly 120 passengers from New York to London, but with two refuelling stops in Newfoundland and Ireland. The latest version of the Boeing 747 can carry 400 people non-stop from Los Angeles to Sydney or Toronto to Tokyo (flights of 7,500 kilometres that take 13 1/2 hours). These examples can be repeated again and again in fields as diverse as agriculture, biogenetics, communications, engineering, entertainment, medicine, and publishing.

A key reason why the stock of knowledge increases without diminishing returns is the sheer number of different techniques that can in principle be tried. Paul Romer explains this fact with an amazing example. Suppose, says Romer,

> that to make a finished good, 20 different parts have to be attached to a frame, one at a time. A worker could proceed in numerical order, attaching part one first, then part two....Or the worker could proceed in some other order, starting with part 10, then adding part seven....With 20 parts, a standard (but incredible) calculation shows that there are about 10^{18} different sequences one can use for assembling the final good. This number is larger than the total number of seconds that have elapsed since the big bang created the universe, so we can be confident that in all activities, only a very small fraction of the possible sequences have ever been tried.[1]

Think about all the processes, all the products, and all the different bits and pieces that go into each, and you can see that we have only begun to scratch around the edges of what is possible.

Because knowledge is productive and creates external benefits, it is necessary to use public policies to ensure that those who develop new ideas face incentives that encourage an efficient level of effort. The main way of creating the right incentives is to provide the creators of knowledge with property rights in their discoveries—called **intellectual property rights**. The legal device for creating intellectual property rights is the patent or copyright. A **patent** or **copyright** is a government-sanctioned exclusive right granted to the inventor of a good, service, or productive process to produce, use, and sell the invention for a given number of years. A patent enables the developer of a new idea to prevent, for a limited number of years, others from benefiting freely from an invention. But to obtain the protection of the law, an inventor must make knowledge of the invention public.

Although patents encourage invention and innovation, they do so at an economic cost. While a patent is in place, its holder is a monopoly. And monopoly is another type of market failure. To maximize profit, a monopoly (patent holder) produces the quantity at which marginal cost equals marginal revenue. The monopoly sets the price above marginal cost and equal to the highest price at which the profit-maximizing quantity can be sold. In this situation, consumers value the good more highly (are willing to pay more for one more unit of it) than its marginal cost. So the quantity of the good available is less than the efficient quantity.

But without a patent, the effort to develop new goods, services, or processes is diminished and the flow of new inventions is slowed. So the efficient outcome is a compromise that balances the benefits of more inventions against the cost of temporary monopoly power in newly invented activities.

R E V I E W   Q U I Z

- What is special about knowledge as a consumer good and as a productive resource that creates external benefits?
- What are the external benefits that arise from education and from research and development?
- How might governments use subsidies, below-cost provision, and patents and copyrights to achieve an efficient amount of research and development?
- How might governments use subsidies or below-cost provision to deliver an efficient amount of education?
- Why might knowledge be special in *not* displaying diminishing returns?
- If patents and copyrights can stimulate research, why don't we just award unlimited patents and copyrights to inventors and other creators of new knowledge?

◆ *Reading Between the Lines* on pages 444–445 examines the externalities that arise in collecting and recycling garbage in Vancouver. As you study this topic, try to reflect on all the ideas you've learned in your study of *microeconomics*. You've learned how all economic problems arise from scarcity and involve an opportunity cost. Prices are opportunity costs and are determined by the interactions of buyers and sellers in markets. People choose what to buy and what resources to sell to maximize utility. Firms choose what to sell and what resources to buy to maximize profit. People and firms interact in markets. But the resulting equilibrium might be inefficient and might be viewed as creating too much inequality. By providing public goods, redistributing income, curbing monopoly power, and coping with externalities, public choice modifies the market outcome.

You've now completed your study of *micro*economics. What comes next depends on the type of course that you are taking. You might move from here to study *macro*economics, or you might study *international* economics next. Both will benefit from and draw on the microeconomics you've learned.

---

[1]From Paul Romer, "Ideas and Things," in *The Future Surveyed*, supplement to *The Economist*, 11 September, 1993, pp. 71–72. The "standard calculation" that Romer refers to is the number of ways of selecting and arranging in order 20 objects from 20 objects—also called the number of permutations of 20 objects 20 at a time. This number is *factorial* 20, or 20! = 20 × 19 × 18 × ... × 2 × 1 = $10^{18.4}$. A standard theory (challenged by observations made by the Hubbel space telescope in 1994) is that a big bang started the universe 15 billion years, or $10^{17.7}$ seconds, ago. Although $10^{18.4}$ and $10^{17.7}$ look similar, $10^{18.4}$ is *five* times as large as $10^{17.7}$, so if you started trying alternative sequences at the moment of the big bang and took only one second per trial, you would still have tried only one-fifth of the possibilities. Amazing?

The Market in Recyclables

VANCOUVER SUN, AUGUST 3, 1999

Recycling waste proves more costly than dumping

BY KEN MACQUEEN

Newspapers in blue bag? Check.

Mixed paper and cardboard in yellow bag? Check.

Plastic and metal containers washed and squashed? Check.

Labels removed from cans? Check.

Labels removed from glass. Arrgh! Not even with dynamite. ...

It's garbage day—or if you've got your act together, the night before—time for care and feeding of the blue box. It has become a shared national pastime.

A newly released survey by the Local Government Institute of the University of Victoria found an impressive 74 per cent national participation rate in recycling programs.

But the study also raises hard questions about the economics of the blue box program.

It costs almost three-times as much to recycle garbage as it does to chuck it into the dump, says a survey of the efficiency of recycling in 117 Canadian municipalities.

Garbage bound for dumps costs an average of $48.01 a tonne to collect, while the average net cost of recycling is $124.39 per tonne, ...

The survey raises the hackles of Pamela Nel, recycling coordinator for the Greater Vancouver regional district, who says local recycling programs are not only socially responsible but economically viable.

She said the survey takes a narrow view of the savings of recycling, and no consideration of the costs of stuffing landfills with wasted resources. ...

If grime doesn't pay, why do millions of Canadians stoop in common toil, sifting through their weekly garbage?

Nel of the GVRD said that public's motivation goes far beyond money, although she disputes the narrow way in which the municipal survey calculated costs and ignored benefits of recycling. ...

Residents in the region generated 667,765 tonnes of trash last year, and recycled 34 per cent of it or 228,400 tonnes.

Essence of the Story

- According to a recent survey, the Canadian participation rate in recycling programs is 74 percent.

- The survey states that the cost of collecting a tonne of garbage is $48.01 and the average net cost of recycling is $124.39 per tonne.

- Residents of the greater Vancouver region generated 667,765 tonnes of garbage last year of which 34 percent or 228,400 tonnes was recycled.

- Pamela Nel of the Greater Vancouver regional district says that recycling programs are socially responsible and economically viable.

- She says the survey does not take into consideration the costs of filling landfills with wasted resources and ignores the benefits of recycling.

Economic Analysis

■ Figure 1 shows the private marginal costs and benefits of garbage disposal in the greater Vancouver area.

■ The marginal private benefit curve is *MB*. When we set our garbage out for weekly pickup, the price we pay is zero. So the quantity of garbage disposal services demanded is 668,000 tonnes a week, where the *MB* curve touches the *x*-axis.

■ We'll assume that average cost and marginal cost are constant. With this assumption, marginal cost equals average cost and we can use the numbers in the news article as estimates of marginal cost.

■ The marginal private cost of dumping is $48 a tonne, which is shown by the MC_D curve in Fig. 1.

■ The marginal private cost of recycling is $124 a tonne. But only 34 percent of the greater Vancouver area's garbage is recycled. So the marginal cost of recycling 34 percent and dumping 66 percent is $74 a tonne, which is shown by the MC_R curve in Fig. 1. ($48 × 0.66 + $124 × 0.34 = $74.)

■ If the only benefits and costs of garbage disposal were those shown in Fig. 1, garbage disposal would be inefficient because marginal cost would exceed marginal benefit.

■ But garbage disposal has external benefits and external costs. The external benefit arises because everyone benefits from the hygienic disposal of other people's garbage. The external cost arises because dumping garbage in landfills creates environmental damage and imposes costs on other users of the adjacent areas.

■ Figure 2 shows the private and external costs and benefits of garbage disposal on the assumption that the greater Vancouver area has achieved an efficient use of resources.

■ In Fig. 2, the external benefit of garbage disposal is $74 a tonne. So the marginal social benefit curve, *MSB*, lies above the *MB* curve by that amount.

■ If the external cost of dumping is $26 a tonne and the external cost of recycling is zero, then the marginal social cost is $74 a tonne, shown by the *MSC* curve.

■ Marginal social cost equals marginal social benefit when 668,000 tonnes of garbage are disposed of each week, with 34 percent recycled.

Figure 1 Private costs and benefits

Figure 2 Efficient use of resources

■ If the external cost of landfill exceeds $26 a tonne, Vancouver can become more efficient by increasing the amount of recycling. If the external cost of landfill is less than $26 a tonne, Vancouver can become more efficient by *decreasing* the amount of recycling.

445

SUMMARY

Key Points

Economics of the Environment (pp. 432–440)

- Popular discussion of the environment frames the debate in terms of right and wrong, but economists emphasize costs and benefits and a need to find a way to balance the two.
- The demand for environmental policies has grown because incomes and awareness of the connection between actions and the environment have grown.
- Air pollution arises from road transportation, electric utilities, and industrial processes. In North America, the trends in most types of air pollution are downward.
- Externalities (environmental and others) arise when property rights are absent. Sometimes it is possible to overcome an externality by assigning a property right.
- The Coase theorem states that if property rights exist and transactions costs are low, private transactions are efficient—there are no externalities. In this case, the same efficient amount of pollution is achieved regardless of *who* has the property right: the polluter or the victim.
- When property rights cannot be assigned, governments might overcome environmental externalities by using emission charges, marketable permits, or taxes.
- Marketable permits were used successfully to virtually eliminate lead from our air.
- Global externalities, such as greenhouse gases and substances that deplete the earth's ozone layer, can be overcome only by international action. Each country acting alone has insufficient incentive to act in the interest of the world as a whole. But there is a great deal of scientific uncertainty and disagreement about the effects of greenhouse gases and ozone depletion, and in the face of this uncertainty, international resolve to act is weak.
- The world is locked in a type of prisoners' dilemma game, in which it is in every country's self-interest to let other countries carry the costs of environmental policies.

Economics of Knowledge (pp. 440–443)

- Knowledge is both a consumer good and a productive resource that creates external benefits.
- External benefits from education—passing on existing knowledge to others—arise because the basic reading, writing, and number skills equip people to interact and communicate more effectively.
- External benefits from research and development—creating and applying new knowledge—arise because once someone has worked out how to do something, others can copy the basic idea.
- To enable the efficient amount of education and innovation to take place, we make public choices through governments to modify the market outcome.
- Three devices are available to governments: subsidies, below-cost provision, and patents and copyrights.
- Subsidies to private schools or the provision of public education below cost can achieve an efficient provision of education.
- Patents and copyrights create intellectual property rights and increase the incentive to innovate. But they do so by creating a temporary monopoly, the cost of which must be balanced against the benefit of more inventive activity.

Key Figures

Key Terms

PROBLEMS

*1. A pesticide maker can dump waste into a lake or truck it to a safe storage place. The marginal cost of trucking is constant at $100 a tonne. A trout farm uses the lake and its profit, shown in the following table, depends on how much waste is dumped.

Quantity of waste (tonnes per week)	Trout farm profit (dollars per week)
0	1,000
1	950
2	875
3	775
4	650
5	500
6	325
7	125

a. What is the efficient amount of waste to be dumped into the lake?
b. If the trout farm owns the lake, how much waste is dumped and how much does the pesticide maker pay to the farmer per tonne?
c. If the pesticide maker owns the lake, how much waste is dumped and how much rent does the farmer pay the factory for the use of the lake?

2. A steel smelter is located at the edge of a residential area. The table shows the cost of cutting the pollution of the smelter. It also shows the property taxes that people are willing to pay at different levels of pollution.

Pollution cut (percentage)	Property taxes willingly paid (dollars per day)	Total cost of pollution cut (dollars per day)
0	0	0
10	150	10
20	285	25
30	405	45
40	510	70
50	600	100
60	675	135
70	735	175
80	780	220
90	810	270
100	825	325

Assume that the increase in property taxes that people are willing to pay measures the change in total benefit of cleaner air that results from a change in the percentage decrease in pollution.
a. What is the efficient percentage decrease in pollution?
b. With no regulation of pollution, how much pollution will there be?
c. If the city owns the smelter, how much pollution will there be?
d. If the city is a company town owned by the steel smelter, how much pollution will there be?

*3. Back at the pesticide plant and trout farm described in problem 1, suppose that no one owns the lake and that the government introduces a pollution tax.
a. What is the tax per tonne of waste dumped that will achieve an efficient outcome?
b. Explain the connection between the answer to part (a) and the answer to problem 1.

4. Back at the steel-smelting city in problem 2, suppose that the city government introduces a pollution tax.
a. What is the tax per percentage of waste dumped that will achieve an efficient outcome?
b. Explain the connection between the answer to part (a) and the answer to problem 2.

*5. Using the information provided in problem 1, suppose that no one owns the lake and that the government issues marketable pollution permits to both the farmer and the factory. Each may dump the same amount of waste in the lake, and the total that may be dumped is the efficient amount.
a. What is the quantity that may be dumped into the lake?
b. What is the market price of a permit? Who buys and who sells?
c. What is the connection between the answer to parts (a) and (b) and the answers to problems 1 and 2?

6. Using the information given in problem 2, suppose that the city government issues marketable pollution permits to citizens and the smelter. Each may pollute the air by the same percentage, and the total is the efficient amount.

a. What is the percentage of pollution?
b. What is the market price of a permit? Who buys and who sells?
c. What is the connection between the answer to parts (a) and (b) and the answers to problems 2 and 4?

*7. The marginal cost of educating a student is $4,000 a year and is constant. The figure shows the marginal private benefit curve.

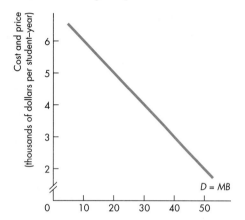

a. With no government involvement and if the schools are competitive, how many students are enrolled and what is the tuition?
b. The external benefit from education is $2,000 per student-year and is constant. If the government provides the efficient amount of education, how many school places does it offer and what is the tuition?

8. A technological advance cuts the marginal cost of educating a student to $2,000 a year and is constant. The marginal private benefit is the same as in problem 7. The external benefit from education increases to $4,000 per student-year and is constant.

a. With no government involvement and if the schools are competitive, how many students are enrolled and what is the tuition?
b. If the government provides the efficient amount of education, how many school places does it offer and what is the tuition?
c. Compare the outcomes in problem 8 with those in problem 7. Explain the differences between the two situations.

CRITICAL THINKING

1. After you have studied *Reading Between the Lines* on pp. 444–445, answer the following questions:
   a. What are the main external costs and external benefits that arise from garbage disposal?
   b. Could an unregulated market served by private garbage collectors and recyclers provide the efficient quantity of garbage disposal services? Why or why not?
   c. If we did leave garbage collection to private enterprise and unregulated markets, what types of property rights would we need to establish to get an efficient outcome?
   d. What are the pros and the cons of landfill versus recycling? Where do you stand on this issue and why?

2. Since its foundation 25 years ago, Greenpeace has fought for a cleaner and safer environment. What impact has Greenpeace had on the environment? Has pollution been eliminated? If not, why not?

3. To decrease the amount of over fishing in their territorial waters, the governments of Iceland and New Zealand have introduced private property rights with an allocation of Individual Transferable Quotas (ITQs). To check out the effects of this system, use the link on the Parkin-Bade Web site to visit the Fraser Institute in Vancouver. Then answer the following questions:
   a. Would the introduction of ITQs in Canada help to replenish Canadian fish stocks?
   b. Explain why ITQs give an incentive to not over fish.
   c. Who would oppose ITQs and why?

4. University tuition fees are rising and the federal government is permitting part of the tuition cost as a tax deduction.
   a. Why do you think tuition fees are rising?
   b. What effect will tax deductions for education costs have on the demand, supply, price, and quantity of education?
   c. What are the economic arguments in favour of tax incentives for education? What are the arguments against? Where do you come out on this issue and why?

Understanding Market Failure and Government

C reating a system of responsible democratic government is a huge enterprise and one that can easily go wrong. Creating a constitution that makes despotic and tyrannical rule impossible is relatively easy. And we have achieved such a constitution in Canada by using some sound economic ideas. We have designed a sophisticated system of incentives—of carrots and sticks—to make the government responsive to public opinion and to limit the ability of individual special interests to gain at the expense of the majority. But we have not managed to create a constitution that effectively blocks the ability of special interest groups to capture the consumer and producer surpluses that result from specialization and exchange.

Making the Rules

◆ We have created a system of government to deal with four economic problems. The market economy would produce too small a quantity of those public goods and services that we must consume together, such as national defence and air-traffic control. It enables monopoly to restrict production and charge too high a price. It produces too large a quantity of some goods and services, the production of which creates pollution. And it generates a distribution of income and wealth that most people believe is too unequal. So we need a government to help cope with these economic problems. But as the founding fathers knew would happen, when the government gets involved in the economy, people try to steer the government's actions in directions that bring personal gains at the expense of the general interest. ◆ The three chapters in this part explain the problems with which the market has a hard time coping. In Chapter 18, you previewed the entire range of problems and studied one of them, public goods, more deeply. In Chapter 19, you studied competition policy and the regulation of natural monopoly. And in Chapter 20, you studied externalities that arise from pollution (external costs) and from education and research (external benefits). You learned about some of the ways in which externalities can be dealt with. And you discovered that one way of coping with externalities is to strengthen the market and "internalize" the externalities rather than to intervene in the market.

◆ Many economists have thought long and hard about the issues discussed in this part. But none has had as profound an effect on our ideas in this area as Ronald Coase, whom you can meet on the following page. You can also meet Diane Francis, editor at large of the *National Post* and a provocative contemporary Canadian thinker and commentator on many of the issues that you have just studied.

Probing the Ideas

Externalities and Property Rights

Ronald Coase *(1910–), was born in England and educated at the London School of Economics, where he was deeply influenced by his teacher, Arnold Plant, and by the issues of his youth: communist central planning versus free markets. Professor Coase has lived in the United States since 1951. He first visited America as a 20-year-old on a travelling scholarship during the depths of the Great Depression. It was on this visit, and before he had completed his bachelor's degree, that he conceived the ideas that 60 years later were to earn him the 1991 Nobel Prize for Economic Science. He discovered and clarified the significance of transaction costs and property rights for the functioning of the economy. Ronald Coase has revolutionized the way we think about property rights and externalities and has opened up the growing field of law and economics.*

"The question to be decided is: is the value of fish lost greater or less than the value of the product which contamination of the stream makes possible?"

RONALD H. COASE, *THE PROBLEM OF SOCIAL COST*

The Issues

As knowledge accumulates, we are becoming more sensitive to environ-mental externalities. We are also developing more sensitive methods of dealing with them. But all the methods involve a public choice.

Urban smog, which is both unpleasant and dangerous to breathe, forms when sunlight reacts with emissions from the tailpipes of automobiles. Because of this external cost of auto exhaust, we set emission standards and tax gasoline. Emission standards increase the cost of a car, and gasoline taxes increase the cost of the marginal kilometre travelled. The higher costs decrease the quantity demanded of road transportation and so decrease the amount of pollution it creates. Is the value of cleaner urban air worth the higher cost of transportation? The public choices of voters, regulators, and lawmakers answer this question.

Acid rain, which imposes a cost on everyone who lives in its path, falls from sulfur-laden clouds produced by electric utility smokestacks. This external cost is being tackled with a market solution. This solution is marketable permits, the price and allocation of which are determined by the forces of supply and demand. Private choices determine the demand for pollution permits, but a public choice determines the supply.

As cars stream onto an urban highway at morning rush hour, the highway clogs and becomes an expensive parking lot. Each rush hour traveller imposes external costs on all the others. Today, road users bear private congestion costs but do not face a share of the external congestion costs they create. But a market solution to this problem is now technologically feasible. It is a solution that charges road users a fee similar to a toll that varies with time of day and degree of congestion. Confronted with the social marginal cost of their actions, each road user makes a choice and the market for highway space is efficient. Here, a public choice to use a market solution leaves the final decision about the degree of congestion to private choices.

... and Now

Today, Lake Erie supports a fishing industry, just as it did in the 1930s. No longer treated as a garbage dump for chemicals, the lake is regenerating its ecosystem. Fertilizers and insecticides are now recognized as products that have potential externalities, and their external effects are assessed by Environment Canada before new versions are put into widespread use. Dumping industrial waste into rivers and lakes is now subject to much more stringent regulations and penalties. Lake Erie's externalities have been dealt with by one of the methods available: government regulation.

Then ...

Chester Jackson, a Lake Erie fisherman, recalls that when he began fishing on the lake, boats didn't carry drinking water. Fishermen drank from the lake. Speaking after World War II, Jackson observed, "Can't do that today. Those chemicals in there would kill you." Farmers used chemicals, such as the insecticide DDT that got carried into the lake by runoff. Industrial waste and trash were also dumped in the lake in large quantities. As a result, Lake Erie became badly polluted during the 1940s and became incapable of sustaining a viable fish stock.

Many people are active participants in the search for better public economic policy and more effective and less intrusive government intervention in the economy. One of these people is Diane Francis, who you can meet on the following pages.

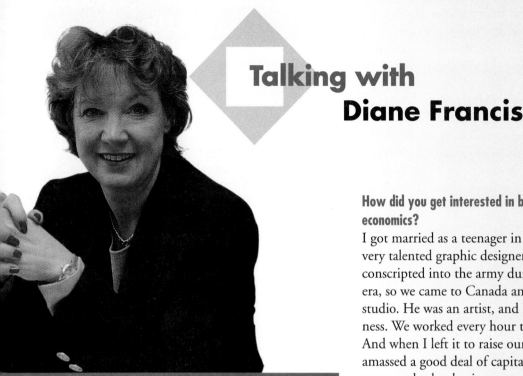

Talking with Diane Francis

Diane Francis *is editor-at-large of the*
National Post *and a well-known columnist, broad-caster, and author of best sellers such as* BRE-X:
The Inside Story, Fighting for Canada,
Underground Nation, Controlling Interest: Who
Owns Canada, Contrepreneurs, *and* A Matter of
Survival. *Self-taught and financially independent,
Francis began her journalism career in 1977 after
being a successful entrepreneur. She worked for
many publications and became Editor of* The
Financial Post *in 1991. Throughout the 1990s,
under her direction, the reputation and role of* The
Financial Post *reached new levels. Diane Francis is
a bold and provocative critic of anti-liberal and
anti-competitive forces. And her views on what
Canada must do to survive and prosper cannot be
ignored, either by her supporters or detractors.*

*Robin Bade and Michael Parkin talked with
Diane Francis about a wide range of political-economic issues that Canada faces today.*

How did you get interested in business, politics, and economics?

I got married as a teenager in the United States to a very talented graphic designer from Britain. He was conscripted into the army during the Vietnam War era, so we came to Canada and started our own art studio. He was an artist, and I was a natural at business. We worked every hour to build the business. And when I left it to raise our two kids we had amassed a good deal of capital so we invested in real estate and other businesses, sort of venture capital on a small scale. I just love business.

I started writing about politics and economics as they affect business. I understand the jargon of economics but not the nuances. I'm interested in business, free enterprise, and democracy. They are my theology!

Your writing is full of memorable phrases. An example: "Canadians are fed up with the red tape and rapacious taxation policies of successive governments." Can you elaborate and provide some examples?

Three examples of over-taxation are capital gains taxes, consumption taxes, and personal income taxes.

We have to compete against Americans whose capital gains taxes for investors are half our levels. They changed their capital gains tax some years ago in recognition of the fact that it was a disincentive. And ever since, their market has exploded because it encourages people to stay in markets and earn capital gains.

We pay bunches more on consumption taxes. Whether it's gasoline or so-called luxury taxes or sin taxes, we're paying two to three or four times as much for liquor, for cigarettes, for gasoline as the Americans do. And when it comes to regular consumption taxes on goods, we are paying routinely, except for Alberta, 7 to 9 percent provincial sales tax; whereas the top sales tax in the United States may be

6 percent and it doesn't apply to all goods. Then we also have the federal consumption tax, which is on services as well as goods, a flat tax of 7 percent everywhere. Americans do not tax services at all. So consumption taxes are onerous.

Then last and most important is personal income taxes, which are excessive at the high end and also at the low end. In most developed countries, income taxes kick in at $12,000 to $15,000. But we start at a much lower level. So at the low end, we tax people earlier and at 17 percent. At the other end, we consider $60,000 plus to be high-high earnings and the income tax rate at the $60,000 plus level is equivalent to what the Americans pay at the $225,000 plus level.

You've described the Canadian health care system and social benefits as being "the most generous but also the most comprehensively mismanaged in the world." Can you tell us what you have in mind?
I think there's an enormous amount of fraud. I did a series of articles on the social services—workmen's compensation, unemployment insurance, welfare, and health care—and discovered that all of these areas were eminently and easily defrauded. Then there's the underground economy that followed the GST—cash for everything.

But the health care stuff: an internal study, which was leaked to me, estimated that $1 out of every $17 was fraud. So $1 billion a year out of every $17 billion Ontario was spending was fraud.

One guy delivered three babies simultaneously in three cities. But the most memorable case was of a woman whose husband took her to an Ontario hospital for a Caesarean section on a Saturday night. Their regular physician was away. When he came back a few days later he said, "This can't be Mrs. So-and-so because I gave her a hysterectomy last year!" It turned out that the "husband" was in the business of smuggling in pregnant women from other countries because once they had a kid here they were entitled to stay. This was a multiple fraud.

Then I did a story about welfare. None of the computers in Ontario's welfare offices were linked. So you could actually get a cheque from every welfare office without one knowing that the other was issuing it to you. Same SIN number!

These programs are just badly engineered, loosely managed, and based on the honour system.

Let's talk about another area that you've written about, Canadian labour law. What's wrong and right with it?
I think the Rand formula, a decision in 1946 by Judge Rand that you don't have to join a union but you do have to pay dues if there's one there, has been a huge disservice to Canada. It has created powerful public sector unions that have been extremely good at getting what they want and has imposed a tax on four million Canadians who are unionized and streamed it into the coffers of a few dozen unions, who have in turn spent this money on political adventures and agenda setting. An elitist and powerful union movement has pulled the agenda towards social democracy European-style without any regard to the interest of the rank and file.

In *Controlling Interest: Who Owns Canada*, you say that 32 families and 5 conglomerates own one-third of Canada's corporate assets. Should we worry about the degree of concentration of ownership, and if we should, what should we do about it?
I think it is always a concern. But we have less reason to worry about it for three reasons. One is free trade with the Americans and another is a tougher Competition Act. We've got both of these in place. The third is just sheer economic growth given the existence of the other two.

> *…the Rand formula …that you don't have to join a union but you do have to pay dues if there's one there, has been a huge disservice to Canada.*

One of the things I said in the book was, if you don't have a referee on the ice, using the hockey metaphor, then only the goons will play and all the small talented players will be knocked off the ice. Every capitalist I've ever met wants to be a monopolist. Money destroys the system that made him what he was. So you have to have a referee—the cornerstone of a free and open society.

And this spills over into democracy too because

if you have a banana republic owned by three families and they start to own the politicians and the government too, then you lose your freedoms altogether—never mind economic freedom, but all freedom.

So financial feudalism has to be held at bay through the imposition of a very powerful referee who is acting hopefully in the public interest and enshrining competition. If you don't have competition, the cream will not rise to the top, there will not be opportunities, you will lose people or you will bury them, and basically it gets to the heart of the kind of society that you want to live in.

If you don't have a referee on the ice, ... then only the goons will play...

So to me it's part of a theology and you know you're putting a real big spin on it but I don't think it's accidental that the United States, which is unbelievably productive and good for the benefit of the majority of Americans, was the first to bring in very tough antitrust laws in the last century. Every time a company gets huge, whether it's Standard Oil, or AT&T, or Microsoft, they bust it up into little pieces and more opportunities result.

Less fossilization. You know that you just don't want what happened in Britain where the chinless wonders—third generation who were interested in fox hunting—end up with the factories and don't do a good job running them. The whole society suffers.

You've spoken approvingly about the Competition Act. What else has the Canadian federal government got right?

The system. One of the things that I like about the parliamentary system as opposed to an American system, which is the only other system I've lived under and know, is that it is more efficient. It can turn on a dime faster. So that's good.

Canada was faster off the mark in terms of redistributing wealth more fairly to those in need. I think public health care policy is enlightened. I think that it is as important for governments to provide basic health care as to provide basic education. The lower

10 or 15 percent of society has to be supported by the rest proportionately. And the Americans do that. I mean it's not a jungle! But Canada, I think, has done a better job.

To what extent do you think the media (not you, not the *National Post* or *The Financial Post* but the rest of the media!) are responsible for bad economic policy?

The Press is the Press. I think that one of the problems Canada has, vis-à-vis its policy-making process of which the media is a part, is that we're little and a bush league. I mean *60 Minutes*' budget is probably bigger than the CBC's for all of its prime-time programming. I'm just guessing, I'm pulling a figure out of the air. But you know television is an extremely expensive business and so how can you get the best minds, the best producers, the best visuals, the best information for your society unless you pay for it.

Now what's happening is that everything of a world-class or local nature is coming into our living room and people are able to pick and choose the information they need.

But I think that it has impeded decision making here. You know small media, incestuous, group think, drank and slept with the same people, married each other, and you know just hung out with the mandarins and the politicians and all of that—probably about 200 people who literally ran Canada for three generations.

It's changed and I don't want to blow my own horn but I'm an iconoclast and my paper was very iconoclastic. And I think that mixed it up. I think that made all the difference.

How does a student today become a successful economic journalist?

You've got to go journalism school. People are not hired anymore out of general liberal arts or post-graduate areas. The business has become pretty high-tech and capital intensive. If you think you want to become a journalist, get involved in a journalism course right away. You'll soon find out whether you like it or not or if it likes you. And if it doesn't like you, then don't stay in it. It is very important that anybody who gets into journalism is extremely interested in general knowledge of all kinds. Read a wide variety of things from sciences to religions to spirituality to politics to sports as well as current events.

Chapter 21

A First Look at Macroeconomics

During the past 100 years, the quantity of goods and services produced in the nation's farms, factories, shops, and offices has expanded more than twentyfold. As a result, we have a much higher living standard than our grandparents had. Will production always expand? Will your world be more prosperous than today's? ◆ For most of us, a high standard of living means finding a good job. What kind of job will you find when you graduate? Will you have lots of choice, or will you face a labour market with a high unemployment rate in which jobs are hard to find? ◆ A high

What Will Your World Be Like?

standard of living means being able to afford to buy life's necessities and some fun. If prices rise too quickly, some people get left behind and must trim what they buy. Prices have increased slowly over the past few years. But can we count on them rising slowly in the future? What will the dollar buy next year? What will it buy in 10 years

when you are paying off your student loan? And what will it buy in 50 years when you are spending your life's savings in retirement? ◆ Every year between 1972 and 1997, the federal government spent more than it raised in taxes. And most years, we spend more on imports from the rest of the world than we earn on our exports. We have experienced large and persistent government and international deficits. How will these deficits affect your future? ◆ To keep production expanding and prevent an economic slowdown, the federal government and the Bank of Canada— the nation's financial managers—take policy actions. What kinds of actions do they take? How do their actions influence production, jobs, prices, and the ability of Canadians to compete in the global marketplace?

◇ These are the questions of macroeconomics. The macroeconomic events through which we are now living are exciting. With what you learn in these chapters, you will be able to understand these events, the policy challenges they bring, and the political debate they stir. You will be able to prepare better for the economic world that you will enter when you graduate and in which you will earn your living.

After studying this chapter, you will be able to:

- Describe the origins and issues of macroeconomics
- Describe the trends and fluctuations in economic growth
- Describe the trends and fluctuations in jobs and unemployment
- Describe the trends and fluctuations in inflation
- Describe the trends and fluctuations in government and international surpluses and deficits
- Identify the macroeconomic policy challenges and describe the tools available for meeting them

Origins and Issues of Macroeconomics

ECONOMISTS BEGAN TO STUDY ECONOMIC growth, inflation, and international payments as long ago as the 1750s, and this work was the origin of macroeconomics. But modern macroeconomics did not emerge until the **Great Depression**, a decade (1929–1939) of high unemployment and stagnant production throughout the world economy. In the Depression's worst year, 1933, the production of Canada's farms, factories, shops, and offices was only 70 percent of its 1929 level, and 20 percent of the labour force was unemployed. These were years of human misery on a scale that is hard to imagine today. They were also years of extreme pessimism about the ability of the market economy to work properly. Many people believed that private ownership, free markets, and democratic political institutions could not survive.

The science of economics had no solutions to the Great Depression. The major alternative system of central planning and socialism seemed increasingly attractive to many people. It was in this climate of economic depression and political and intellectual turmoil that modern macroeconomics emerged with the publication in 1936 of John Maynard Keynes' *The General Theory of Employment, Interest, and Money* (see pp. 538–539).

Short-Term Versus Long-Term Goals

Keynes' theory was that depression and high unemployment result from insufficient private spending and that to cure these problems, the government must increase its spending. Keynes focused primarily on the *short term*. He wanted to cure an immediate problem almost regardless of the *long-term* consequences of the cure. "In the long run," said Keynes, "we're all dead."

But Keynes believed that after his cure for depression had restored the economy to a normal condition, the long-term problems of inflation and slow economic growth would return. And he suspected that his cure for depression, increased government spending, might trigger inflation and might lower the long-term growth rate of production. With a lower long-term growth rate, the economy would create fewer jobs. If this outcome did occur, a policy aimed at lowering unemployment in the short run might end up increasing it in the long run.

By the late 1960s and through the 1970s, Keynes' predictions became a reality. Inflation increased, economic growth slowed, and in some countries, unemployment became persistently high. The causes of these developments are complex. But they point to an inescapable conclusion: The long-term problems of inflation, slow growth, and persistent unemployment and the short-term problems of depression and economic fluctuations intertwine and are most usefully studied together. So although macroeconomics was reborn during the Great Depression, it has now returned to its older tradition. Today, macroeconomics is a subject that tries to understand long-term economic growth and inflation as well as short-term business fluctuations and unemployment.

The Road Ahead

There is no unique way to study macroeconomics. Because its rebirth was a product of depression, the common practice for many years was to pay most attention to short-term output fluctuations and unemployment, but to never completely lose sight of the long-term issues. When a rapid inflation emerged during the 1970s, this topic returned to prominence. During the 1980s, when long-term growth slowed in Canada and other rich industrial countries but exploded in East Asia, economists redirected their energy towards economic growth. During the 1990s, as information technologies further shrink the globe, the international dimension of macroeconomics has become more prominent. The result of these developments is that modern macroeconomics is a broad subject that studies all the issues we've just identified: economic growth and fluctuations, unemployment, inflation, and government and international deficits.

Over the past 40 years, economists have developed a clearer understanding of the forces that determine macroeconomic performance and have devised policies that they hope will improve this performance. Your main goal is to become familiar with the theories of macroeconomics and the policies that they make possible. To set you on your path towards this goal, we're going to take a first look at economic growth, unemployment, inflation, and deficits and learn why these macroeconomic phenomena merit our attention.

Economic Growth

YOUR PARENTS ARE RICHER THAN YOUR GRAND-parents were when they were young. But are you going to be richer than your parents are? And are your children going to be richer than you? The answers depend on the rate of economic growth.

Economic growth is the expansion of the economy's production possibilities. It can be pictured as an outward shift of the production possibility frontier (*PPF*)—see Chapter 3, pp. 45–46.

We measure economic growth by the increase in real gross domestic product. **Real gross domestic product** (also called **real GDP**) is the value of the total production of all the nation's farms, factories, shops, and offices measured in the prices of a single year. Real GDP in Canada is currently measured in the prices of 1992 (called 1992 dollars). We use the dollar prices of a single year to eliminate the influence of *inflation*—the increase in the average level of prices—and determine how much production has grown from one year to another. (Real GDP is explained more fully in Chapter 22 on pp. 481–484.)

Real GDP is not a perfect measure of total production because it does not include everything that is produced. It excludes the things we produce for ourselves at home (preparing meals, doing laundry, house painting, gardening, and so on). It also excludes production that people hide to avoid taxes or because the activity is illegal—the underground economy. But despite its shortcomings, real GDP is the best measure of total production available. Let's see what it tells us about economic growth.

Economic Growth in Canada

Figure 21.1 shows real GDP in Canada since 1960 and highlights two features of economic growth:

- The growth of potential GDP
- Fluctuations of real GDP around potential GDP

The Growth of Potential GDP When all the economy's labour, capital, land, and entrepreneurial ability are fully employed, the value of production is called **potential GDP**. Real GDP fluctuates around potential GDP and the rate of long-term economic growth is measured by the growth rate of potential GDP. It is shown by the steepness of the potential GDP line (the black line) in Fig. 21.1.

During the 1960s, real GDP grew at an unusually rapid rate of 5.5 percent a year. But the growth rate slowed during the 1970s and early 1980s. The growth rate of output per person sagged during these years in a phenomenon called the **productivity growth slowdown**. A more rapid growth trend might have returned during the 1990s, but it is too soon to be certain about this possibility.

Why did the productivity growth slowdown occur? This question is controversial. One possible cause is a sharp rise in the relative price of energy. We explore the causes of the productivity growth slowdown in Chapter 32 on p. 732. Whatever its cause, the slowdown means that we all have smaller incomes today than we would have had if the economy had continued to grow at its 1960s rate.

Let's now look at GDP fluctuations.

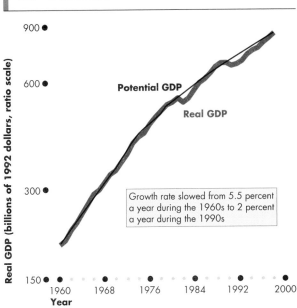

The long-term economic growth rate, measured by the growth of potential GDP, was 5.5 percent a year during the 1960s. Growth slowed during the 1970s, and during the past 20 years, real GDP growth has been only 1.6 percent a year. Real GDP fluctuates around potential GDP.

Source: Statistics Canada, *National Income and Expenditure Accounts*, catalogue 13020, Annual, 1998.

Fluctuations Around Potential GDP Real GDP fluctuates around potential GDP in a business cycle. A **business cycle** is the periodic but irregular up-and-down movement in production. It is measured by fluctuations in real GDP around potential GDP. When real GDP is less than potential GDP, some resources are underused. For example, some labour is unemployed and capital is underutilized. When real GDP is greater than potential GDP, resources are being overused. Many people work longer hours than they are willing to put up with in the long run, capital is worked so intensively that it is not maintained in prime working order, delivery times lengthen, bottlenecks occur, and backorders increase.

Business cycles are not regular, predictable, or repeating cycles like the phases of the moon. Their timing changes unpredictably. But cycles do have some things in common. Every business cycle has two phases:

1. A recession
2. An expansion

and two turning points:

1. A peak
2. A trough

Figure 21.2 shows these features of the most recent business cycle in Canada. A **recession** is a period during which real GDP decreases—the growth rate of real GDP is negative—for at least two successive quarters. The most recent recession, which is highlighted in the figure, began in the first quarter of 1990 and ended in the first quarter of 1991. This recession lasted for four quarters. An **expansion** is a period during which real GDP increases. The most recent expansion began in the second quarter of 1991. If it continues through 2000, it will become the longest expansion on record. An earlier expansion ended in the second quarter of 1990.

When a business cycle expansion ends and a recession begins, the turning point is called a *peak*. The most recent peak occurred in the third quarter of 1990. When a business cycle recession ends and a recovery begins, the turning point is called a *trough*. The most recent trough occurred in the first quarter of 1991.

FIGURE 21.2

The Most Recent Canadian Business Cycle

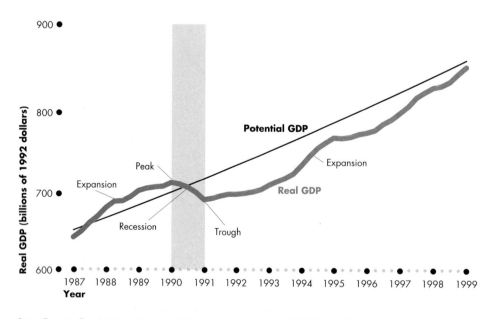

A business cycle has two phases: recession and expansion. The most recent recession (highlighted) ran from the first quarter of 1990 through the first quarter of 1991. Then a new expansion began in the second quarter of 1991.

A business cycle has two turning points, a peak and a trough. In the most recent business cycle, the peak occurred in the first quarter of 1990 and the trough occurred in the first quarter of 1991.

Source: Statistics Canada, *National Income and Expenditure Accounts*, catalogue 13020, Annual, 1998.

The Recent Recession in Historical Perspective

The recession of 1990–1991 seemed severe while we were passing through it, but compared with earlier recessions, it was mild. You can see how mild it was by looking at Fig. 21.3, which shows a longer history of Canadian economic growth. The biggest decrease in real GDP occurred during the Great Depression of the 1930s. A large decrease also occurred in 1946 and 1947, after a huge World War II expansion. A serious recession also occurred during the early 1980s, when the Bank of Canada and the Federal Reserve Board in the United States hiked interest rates to previously unimagined levels.

Each of these economic downturns was more severe than that in 1990–1991. But you can see that the Great Depression was much more severe than anything that followed it. This episode was so extreme that we don't call it a recession. We call it a *depression*.

This last truly great depression occurred before governments started taking policy actions to stabilize the economy. It also occurred before the birth of modern macroeconomics. Is the absence of another great depression a sign that macroeconomics has contributed to economic stability? Some people believe it is. Others doubt it. We'll evaluate these opinions on a number of occasions in this book.

We've looked at real GDP growth and fluctuations in Canada. But is the Canadian experience typical? Do other countries share our experience? Let's see.

Economic Growth Around the World

A country might have a rapid growth rate of real GDP, but it might also have a rapid population growth rate. To compare growth rates over time and across countries, we use the growth rate of real GDP *per person*. Real GDP per person is real GDP divided by the population. For example, Canadian real GDP in the first quarter of 1999 was $858 billion a year. The population of Canada was 30.3 million. So Canadian real GDP per person was $858 billion divided by 30.3 million, which equals $28,317.

Figure 21.4 shows real GDP per person between 1962 and 1998 for Canada alongside the world's

FIGURE 21.3
Long-Term Economic Growth in Canada

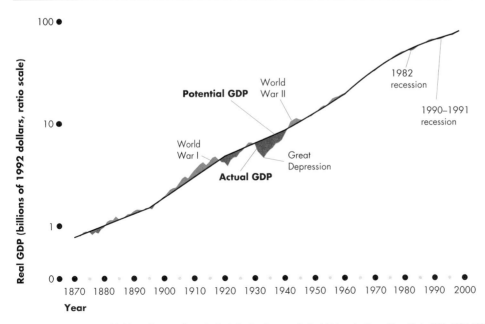

The thin black line shows potential GDP. Along this line, real GDP grew at an average rate of 3.7 percent a year between 1870 and 1998. The blue areas show when real GDP was above potential GDP, and the red areas show when it was below potential GDP. During some periods, such as World War II, real GDP expanded quickly. During other periods, such as the Great Depression and more recently in 1982 (following interest rate hikes) and 1990–1991, real GDP declined.

Sources: 1870-1925, Angus Maddison, *Dynamic Forces in Capitalist Development*, Oxford University Press, New York, 1991. 1926-1998, Statistics Canada, *Historical Statistics of Canada*, Series F 55, and *National Income and Expenditure Accounts*, catalogue 13020, Annual, 1998.

three largest economies: the United States, Japan, and Germany. In these countries, four features of the paths of real GDP per person stand out:

- Similar business cycles before 1990
- Different business cycles in the 1990s
- Similar 1970s growth slowdowns
- Different long-term growth trends

Similar Business Cycles Before 1990 Each of the three big economies had an expansion running from the early or mid-1960s through 1973, a recession from 1973 to 1975, an expansion through 1979, another recession in the early 1980s, and a long expansion through the rest of the 1980s.

Different Business Cycles in the 1990s The 1990s saw the United States in a strong business cycle expansion. But the decade brought severe recession in Japan and only moderate expansion in Germany. This divergence of business cycles is relatively uncommon and creates a concern that recession in Japan and the rest of Asia might spread.

Similar 1970s Growth Slowdowns Canadian real GDP per person grew at a rate of 3.8 percent a year from 1960 through 1973, but slowed to 2.5 percent a year between 1974 and 1988 and to only 0.2 percent a year after 1988. Growth in the United States slowed from 2.9 percent to 1.1 percent, in Germany from 3.5 percent to 1.6 percent and in Japan from 8.5 percent to 1.8 percent.

Different Long-Term Growth Trends In 1960, real GDP per person in Canada exceeded that in Germany and exceeded that of Japan by a large amount but was less than that in the United States.

During the 1960s, Japan's real GDP streaked upward like a rocket departing Cape Canaveral. Canada and Germany grew quickly too and all three countries closed the gap on the United States. Growth slowed in all four countries during the 1970s and Japan's growth rate more than halved. Even so, Japan's growth of real GDP per person equalled the U.S. rate *before* the slowdown. Because it achieved such a high growth rate, Japan narrowed the gap between its own level of real GDP per person and

---

FIGURE 21.4

Economic Growth in Canada and the Three Largest Economies

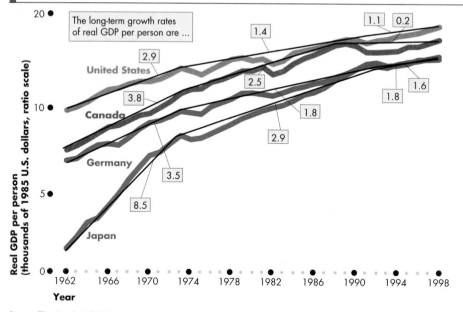

Economic growth in Canada and the three large economies (the United States, Germany, and Japan) was the most rapid during the 1960s. The growth rate in all four countries slowed during the 1970s, and each country has had similar business cycles. The United States has grown slowest and Canada has narrowed the gap on the United States. Japan has grown fastest, and Germany too has grown faster than the United States. But in recent years, growth in Canada and in Japan has slowed to a crawl.

Sources: The data for 1960 through 1992 are from "The Penn World Table," *Quarterly Journal of Economics,* May 1991, pp. 327–368. New computer disk supplement (Mark 5.6a). The data use comparable international relative prices converted to 1985 U.S. dollars. The data for 1993-1998 are from International Monetary Fund, *International Financial Statistics,* Washington, D.C., 1999.

those of Canada and the United States and overtook that of Germany.

During the 1990s, Japan's real GDP per person fell below Germany's and because the growth of Canada's real GDP per person slowed to a crawl, the gap between the level of real GDP per person in Canada and the United States widened.

Figure 21.5 compares the growth of the Canadian economy with that of several other countries and regions since 1980. Among the advanced economies (the red bars), the European Union has grown the slowest and the other advanced economies have grown fastest. Among the developing economies (the green bars) the most rapid growth has occurred in Asia, where the average growth rate has exceeded 7 percent a year. The slowest growing developing countries are in Africa and the Western Hemisphere (Central and South America). The transition economies (purple bars) have grown the slowest. These are countries such as Russia and the other countries of Central Europe that are making a transition from a state managed economy to a market economy. Production has been shrinking severely in these countries.

World average growth (the blue bar) has been just over 3 percent a year. The Canadian growth rate is slightly below the world average and much below the growth rates that the developing economies of Asia have achieved.

Benefits and Costs of Economic Growth

What are the benefits and costs of economic growth? Does it matter if the long-term growth rate slows as it did during the 1970s?

The main benefit of long-term economic growth is expanded consumption possibilities, including more health care for the poor and elderly, more cancer and AIDS research, more space research and exploration, better roads, and more and better housing. We can even have cleaner lakes, more trees, and cleaner air by devoting more resources to environmental problems.

When the long-term growth rate slows, some of these benefits are lost, and the loss can be large. For example, if long-term growth had not slowed in Canada during the 1970s, real GDP in 1998 would have been $1.1 trillion, or $36,400 per person. Instead, real GDP was $875 billion, or $28,900 per

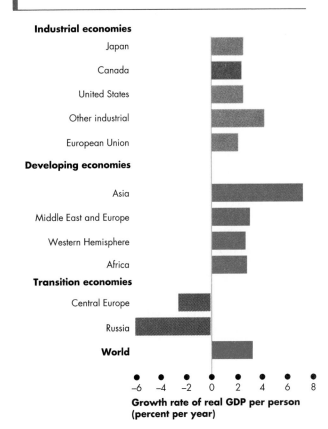

FIGURE 21.5

Growth Rates Around the World

Growth rate of real GDP per person (percent per year)

The growth of real GDP has been lower in Canada than in some other industrial economies. The developing economies of Asia have had the most rapid growth and those of Central Europe and Russia have had the slowest growth.

Source: International Monetary Fund, *World Economic Outlook*, Washington D.C., October 1998, p. 145.

person. So if the long-term trend of the 1960s had persisted, as a nation we would have had $225 billion more to spend. Each person (on the average) would have had $7,500 more each year. If the government had taken one-third of this extra income, it could have provided more health care, more education, more day-care services, and more and better highways. All these items could have been obtained with no cut in the provision of other goods and services. At the same time, you might have had another $7,500 a year to spend on whatever pleased you.

The main cost of economic growth is forgone consumption. To sustain a high growth rate, resources must be devoted to advancing technology and accumulating capital rather than to producing goods and services for current consumption. This cost cannot be avoided. But it brings the benefit of greater consumption in the future.

Two other possible costs of faster growth are a more rapid depletion of exhaustible natural resources, such as oil and natural gas, and increased pollution of the air, rivers, and oceans. But neither of these two costs is inevitable. The technological advances that bring economic growth help us to economize on natural resources and to clean up the environment. For example, more efficient auto engines cut gasoline use and tailpipe emissions.

A fourth possible cost of faster growth is more frequent job changes and more frequent moves from one region of the country to another. For example, during the 1990s, the economy of central Canada expanded and people migrated there from the Maritimes and the Prairies.

The pace of economic growth is determined by the choices that people make to balance the benefits and costs of economic growth. You'll study these choices and their consequences in Chapter 32.

R E V I E W   Q U I Z

- What is economic growth and how is the long-term economic growth rate measured?
- What is the distinction between real GDP and *potential* GDP?
- What is a business cycle and what are its phases?
- What is a *recession*?
- In what phase of the business cycle was the Canadian economy during 1998?
- What happened to productivity growth in Canada and other countries during the 1970s?
- What are the similarities and differences in growth among the major economies?
- What are the benefits and the costs of long-term economic growth?

We've seen that real GDP grows and that it fluctuates over the business cycle. The business cycle brings fluctuations in the number of jobs available and in unemployment. Let's now examine these core macroeconomic problems.

Jobs and Unemployment

WHAT KIND OF LABOUR MARKET WILL YOU ENTER when you graduate? Will there be plenty of good jobs to choose from, or will there be so much unemployment that you will be forced to take a low-paying job that doesn't use your education? The answer depends, to a large degree, on the total number of jobs available and on the unemployment rate.

Jobs

Finance Minister Paul Martin introduced the 1995 federal budget with what seemed an astonishing fact: "Canada is enjoying a period of strong economic growth and job creation. In the past year, 433,000 jobs have been created."

The Canadian economy is an incredible job-creating machine. In 1998, 14.3 million Canadians had jobs. That number is 1.5 million more than in 1988 and 3.4 million more than in 1978. But a year in which we create 433,000 new jobs is unusual. Every year, on the average, the Canadian economy creates almost 200,000 *additional* jobs.

The pace of job creation and destruction fluctuates over the business cycle. More jobs are destroyed than created during a recession, so the number of jobs decreases. But more jobs are created than destroyed during an expansion, so the number of jobs increases. For example, during the 1990–1991 recession, Canadian production shrank and 250,000 jobs disappeared. But through the expansion that followed, the number of jobs created expanded quickly.

Unemployment

Not everyone who wants a job can find one. On any one day in a normal or average year, more than 1 million people are unemployed, and during a recession or depression, unemployment rises above this level. For example, in November 1992, the worst month for unemployment in recent times, 1,740,000 people were looking for jobs.

Unemployment is defined as a state in which a person does not have a job but is available for work, willing to work, and has made some effort to find work within the previous four weeks. The total number of people who are employed and unemployed is called the **labour force**. The **unemployment rate** is the percentage of the people in the labour force who are unemployed. (The concepts of the labour force and unemployment are explained more fully in Chapter 23 on pp. 500–501.)

The unemployment rate is not a perfect measure of the underutilization of labour for two main reasons. First, it excludes discouraged workers. A **discouraged worker** is a person who does not have a job, is available for work, and willing to work but who has given up the effort to find work. Many people switch between the unemployment and discouraged worker categories in both directions every month. Second, the unemployment rate measures unemployed people rather than unemployed labour hours. As a result, the unemployment rate excludes part-time workers who want full-time jobs.

Despite these two limitations, the unemployment rate is the best available measure of underused labour resources. Let's look at some facts about unemployment.

Unemployment in Canada

Figure 21.6 shows the unemployment rate in Canada from 1926 through 1998. Three features stand out. First, during the Great Depression of the 1930s, the unemployment rate climbed to an all-time high of almost 20 percent during 1933 and remained high throughout the 1930s.

Second, the unemployment rate reached an all-time low of 1.2 percent during World War II.

Third, although in recent years we have not experienced anything as devastating as the Great Depression, we have seen some high unemployment rates during recessions. The figure highlights two of them—the 1982 recession and the 1990–1991 recession.

Fourth, unemployment never falls to zero. In the period since World War II, the average unemployment rate has been 6.7 percent.

How does Canadian unemployment compare with unemployment in other countries?

FIGURE 21.6
Unemployment in Canada

Unemployment is a persistent feature of economic life, but its rate varies. At its worst—during the Great Depression—almost 20 percent of the labour force was unemployed. Even in recent recessions, the unemployment rate climbed towards 12 percent. Between the late 1960s and 1982, there was a general tendency for the unemployment rate to increase. Since 1982, the unemployment rate has remained below its 1982 peak and has fallen during the 1990s.

Sources: Statistics Canada, Historical Statistics of Canada, 2nd edition, 1983 and Historical Labour Force Statistics, Catalogue 71-201.

Unemployment Around the World

Figure 21.7 compares the unemployment rate in Canada with those in Western Europe, Japan, and the United States. Over the period shown in this figure, Canadian unemployment averaged 9.6 percent, much higher than Japanese unemployment, which averaged 2.5 percent, and higher than U.S. unemployment, which averaged 7 percent, and European unemployment, which averaged 8.1 percent.

Canadian unemployment fluctuates over the business cycle. It increases during a recession and decreases during an expansion. Like Canadian unemployment, U.S. and European unemployment increase during recessions and decrease during expansions. The cycles in Canadian unemployment are similar to those in U.S. unemployment but the European cycle is out of phase with the North American cycle. Also, European unemployment was on a rising trend since 1980. In contrast with the other countries, Japanese unemployment was fairly steady during the 1980s, but drifted upward in recent years.

We've looked at some facts about unemployment in Canada and in other countries. Let's now look at some of the consequences of unemployment that make it the serious problem that it is.

Why Unemployment Is a Problem

Unemployment is a serious economic, social, and personal problem for two main reasons:

- Lost production and incomes
- Lost human capital

Lost Production and Incomes The loss of a job brings an immediate loss of income and production. These losses are devastating for the people who bear them and make unemployment a frightening prospect for everyone. Employment insurance creates a safety net, but it does not provide the same living standard that having a job provides.

Lost Human Capital Prolonged unemployment can permanently damage a person's job prospects. For example, a manager loses his job when his employer downsizes. Short of income, he becomes a taxi driver. After a year in this work, he discovers that he can't compete with new MBA graduates. He eventually gets hired as a manager but in a small firm and at a low wage. He has lost some of his human capital.

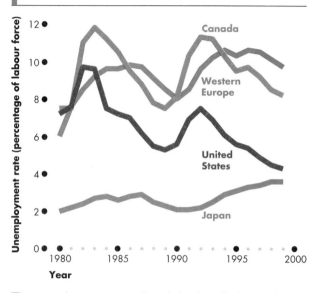

FIGURE 21.7

Unemployment in Industrial Economies

The unemployment rate in Canada has been higher, on the average, than the unemployment rates of the United States, Western Europe, and Japan. The cycles in Canadian unemployment are similar to those in the United States. Western European unemployment has a cycle that is out of phase with the Canadian unemployment cycle. Unemployment in Japan has drifted upward in recent years.

Source: International Monetary Fund, World Economic Outlook, October 1998, Washington, D.C., p. 149.

The costs of unemployment are spread unequally, which makes unemployment a highly charged political problem, as well as a serious economic problem.

R E V I E W   Q U I Z

- What is unemployment?
- What have been the main trends and cycles in the unemployment rate in Canada since 1926?
- Compare unemployment in Canada with that in the United States, Western Europe, and Japan.
- What are the main costs of unemployment that make it a serious problem?

Let's now turn to the third major macroeconomic issue: inflation.

Inflation

PRICES ON THE AVERAGE CAN BE RISING, FALLING, or stable. **Inflation** is a process of rising prices. We measure the *inflation rate* as the percentage change in the *average* level of prices or the **price level**. A common measure of the price level is the *Consumer Price Index* (CPI). The CPI tells us how the average price of all the goods and services bought by a typical urban household changes from month to month. (The CPI is explained in Chapter 22, p. 485).

So that you can see in a concrete way how the inflation rate is measured, let's do a calculation. In December 1997, the CPI was 107.7, and in December 1996, it was 106.9, so the inflation rate during 1997 was

$$\text{Inflation} = \frac{107.7 - 106.9}{106.9} \times 100$$

$$= 0.75 \text{ percent.}$$

Inflation in Canada

Figure 21.8 shows the Canadian inflation rate from 1960 through 1998. During the early 1960s, the inflation rate was low. It began to increase during the late 1960s at the time of the Vietnam War. But the largest increases occurred in 1974 and 1980, years in which the actions of the Organization of Petroleum Exporting Countries (OPEC) resulted in exceptionally large increases in the price of oil. Inflation was brought under control in the early 1980s when Bank of Canada Governor Gerald Bouey and U.S. Federal Reserve Chairman Paul Volcker pushed interest rates up and people cut back on their spending. Since 1983 inflation has been relatively mild, and during the 1990s its rate has fallen yet further.

The inflation rate rises and falls over the years, but it rarely becomes negative. If the inflation rate is negative, the price *level* is falling and we have **deflation**. Since the 1930s, the price level has generally increased—the inflation rate has been positive. Thus even when the inflation rate is low, as it was in 1994, the price level is rising.

FIGURE 21.8

Inflation in Canada

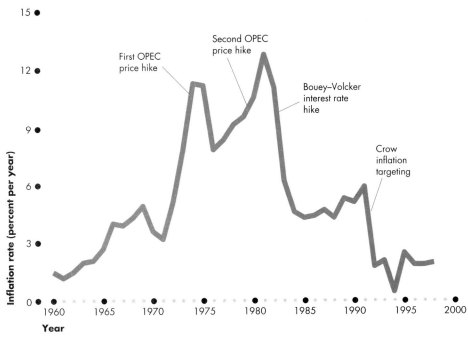

Inflation is a persistent feature of economic life in Canada. The inflation rate was low in the first half of the 1960s, but it increased during the late 1960s at the time of the Vietnam War. It increased further with the OPEC oil price hikes but eventually declined in the early 1980s because of policy actions taken by the Bank of Canada. Since 1983, inflation has been mild, and during the 1990s it has fallen further.

Source: Statistics Canada, *StatCan: CANSIM Disc,* 1999.

Inflation Around the World

Figure 21.9 shows inflation around the world since 1970. It also shows the Canadian inflation rate in a broader perspective. Part (a) shows that the other industrial countries shared Canada's burst of double-digit inflation during the 1970s and the decline in inflation during the 1980s and 1990s. But Canada has achieved a lower inflation rate than most countries. Part (b) shows that the average inflation rate of industrial countries has been very low compared with that of the developing counties. Among the developing countries, the most extreme inflation in recent times has occurred in the former Yugoslavia, where its rate has exceeded 6,000 percent per year.

Is Inflation a Problem?

If inflation were predictable, it would not be much of a problem. But inflation is not predictable. Unpredictable inflation makes the economy behave a bit like a casino in which some people gain and some lose and no one can predict where the gains and losses will fall. Gains and losses occur because of unpredictable changes in the value of money. Money is used as a measuring rod of value in the transactions that we undertake. Borrowers and lenders, workers and employers, all make contracts in terms of money. If the value of money varies unpredictably over time, then the amounts *really* paid and received—the quantity of goods that the money will buy—also fluctuate unpredictably. Measuring value with a measuring rod whose units vary is a bit like trying to measure a piece of cloth with an elastic ruler. The size of the cloth depends on how tightly the ruler is stretched.

In a period of rapid, unpredictable inflation, resources get diverted from productive activities to forecasting inflation. It becomes more profitable to forecast the inflation rate correctly than to invent a new product. Doctors, lawyers, accountants, farmers—just about everyone—can make themselves better off, not by specializing in the profession for which they have been trained but by spending more of their time dabbling as amateur economists and inflation forecasters and managing their investment portfolios.

From a social perspective, this diversion of talent resulting from inflation is like throwing scarce resources onto the garbage heap. This waste of resources is a cost of inflation.

FIGURE 21.9
Inflation Around the World

(a) Canada and other industrial countries

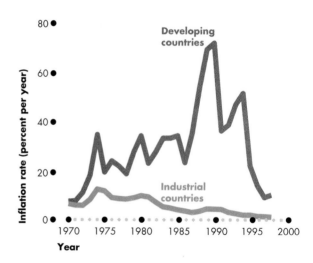

(b) Industrial countries and developing countries

Inflation in Canada is similar to that in the other industrial countries. Compared with the developing countries, inflation in Canada and the other industrial countries is low.

Source: International Monetary Fund, *International Financial Statistics Yearbook* 1998, Washington, D.C., 1998, and IMF, *World Economic Outlook*, May 1999, pp. 150–151.

The most serious type of inflation is called *hyper-inflation*— an inflation rate that exceeds 50 percent a month. At the height of a hyperinflation, workers are often paid twice a day because money loses its value so quickly. As soon as workers are paid, they rush out to spend their wages before they lose too much value.

Hyperinflation is rare but there have been some spectacular examples of it. Several European countries experienced hyperinflation during the 1920s after World War I and again during the 1940s after World War II. But hyperinflation is more than just a historical curiosity. It occurs in today's world. In 1994, the African nation of Zaire had a hyperinflation that peaked at a *monthly* inflation rate of 76 percent, which is 88,000 percent a year! Brazil has also been close to the hyperinflation stratosphere with a monthly inflation rate of 40 percent. A cup of coffee that cost 15 cruzeiros in 1980 cost 22 *billion* cruzeiros in 1994.

Inflation imposes costs, but getting rid of inflation is also costly. Policies that lower the inflation rate increase the unemployment rate. Most economists think the increase in the unemployment rate that accompanies a fall in the inflation rate is temporary. But some economists say that higher unemployment is a permanent cost of low inflation. The cost of lowering inflation must be evaluated when an anti-inflation policy is pursued. You will learn more about inflation and the costs of curing it in Chapter 30.

R E V I E W   Q U I Z

■ What is inflation and how does it influence the value of money?
■ How is inflation measured?
■ What has been Canada's inflation record since 1960?
■ How does inflation in Canada compare with inflation in other industrial countries and in developing countries?
■ What are some of the costs of inflation that make it a serious economic problem?

Now that you've studied economic growth and fluctuations, unemployment, and inflation, let's turn to the fourth macroeconomic issue: surpluses and deficits. What happens when a government spends more than it collects in taxes? And what happens when a nation buys more from other countries than it sells to them? Do governments and nations face the problem that you and I would face if we spent more than we earned? Do they run out of funds? Let's look at these questions.

Surpluses and Deficits

IN 1998, FOR THE FIRST TIME IN ALMOST 30 years, the federal government had a budget surplus. For 26 years, it had a deficit. And most years, Canada has an international deficit. What is the government budget surplus and deficit? What is an international deficit?

Government Budget Surplus and Deficit

If a government collects more in taxes than it spends, it has a surplus—a **government budget surplus**. If a government spends more than it collects in taxes, it has a deficit—a **government budget deficit**. The federal government had a surplus in 1998.

Figure 21.10(a) shows the federal government and total government budget surplus and deficit since 1970. (Total government is federal, provincial, and local government). So that we can compare the surplus or deficit in one year with that in another year, we measure it as a percentage of GDP. (The concept of GDP, which is explained more fully in Chapter 22, pp. 481-484, equals total income in the economy.) You can think of this measure as the number of cents of surplus or deficit per dollar of income earned by an average Canadian.

The government had a budget surplus in 1969 and again in 1998. In every year from 1970 through 1997, the government had a deficit that fluctuated and swelled during recessions. From 1980 through 1995, the deficit was never less than 2 percent of GDP.

Since 1992, the federal government deficit has been shrinking and a surplus emerged in 1998. In 1998, the federal government surplus was almost 1 percent of GDP and in 1999 and beyond, it is projected to become larger.

International Surplus and Deficit

When we import goods and services from the rest of the world, we make payments to foreigners. When we export goods and services to the rest of the world, we receive payments from foreigners. If our imports exceed our exports, we have an international deficit.

Figure 21.10(b) shows the history of Canada's international deficit since 1970. The figure shows the balance on the **current account**, which includes our

FIGURE 21.10

Government Budget and International Surpluses and Deficits

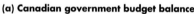

(a) Canadian government budget balance

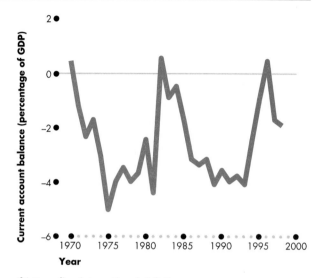

(b) Canadian international deficit

In part (a), the federal government has had a large and persistent deficit between 1974 and the mid-1990s. The provincial governments have had a large deficit during the 1980s and early 1990s. In part (b), the Canadian current account shows the balance of our exports minus our imports. In most years since 1970, Canada has had an international deficit. The deficit became large during the 1980s, and it has persisted at around 3 to 4 percent of GDP for much of the 1990s.

Sources: Statistics Canada, *National Income and Expenditure Accounts*, Catalogue 13-201, Annual, 1998 and *Canada's Balance of International Payments*, Catalogue 67-001, Annual, 1998.

exports minus our imports but also takes interest payments paid to and received from the rest of the world into account. To compare one year with another, the figure shows the current account as a percentage of GDP. The Canadian current account deficit has fluctuated and from 1986 to 1995 it was persistently around 3 percent to 4 percent of GDP. Our imports have exceeded our exports during these years. In 1996, we had a current account surplus.

Do Surpluses and Deficits Matter?

Why do deficits cause anxiety? What happens when a government cannot cover its spending with taxes or when a country buys more from other countries than it sells to them?

If you spend more than you earn, you have a deficit. And to cover your deficit, you go into debt. But when you borrow, you must pay interest on your debt. Just like you, if a government or a nation has a deficit, it must borrow. And like you, the government and the nation must pay interest on their debts.

Whether borrowing and paying out huge amounts of interest is a good idea depends on what the borrowed funds are used for. If you borrow to finance a vacation, you must eventually tighten your belt, cut spending, and repay your debt as well as pay interest on the debt. But if you borrow to invest in a business that earns a large profit, you might be able to repay your debt and pay the interest on it while continuing to increase your spending. It is the same with a government and a nation. A government or a nation that borrows to increase its consumption might be heading for trouble later. But a government or a nation that borrows to buy assets that earn a profit might be making a sound investment.

You will learn more about government budget deficits in Chapter 26 and about the international current account deficit in Chapter 36.

R E V I E W   Q U I Z

- What determines a government's budget deficit or budget surplus?
- How have the federal government deficit or surplus and provincial government deficits evolved since 1970?
- What is a country's international deficit?
- How has the Canadian international deficit changed since 1970?

Macroeconomic Policy Challenges and Tools

FROM THE TIME OF ADAM SMITH'S *Wealth of Nations* in 1776 until the publication of Keynes' *General Theory of Employment, Interest, and Money* in 1936, it was widely believed that the only economic role for government was to enforce property rights. The economy behaved best, it was believed, if the government left people free to pursue their own best interests. The macroeconomics of Keynes challenged this view. Keynes' central point was that the economy will not fix itself and that government actions are needed to achieve and maintain full employment. The Canadian government declared full employment as a policy goal soon after World War II ended.

Policy Challenges and Tools

Today, the five widely agreed challenges for macroeconomic policy are to:

1. Reduce unemployment
2. Boost economic growth
3. Stabilize the business cycle
4. Keep inflation low
5. Reduce government and international deficits

But how can we do all these things? What are the tools available to pursue the macroeconomic policy challenges? Macroeconomic policy tools are divided into two broad categories:

- Fiscal policy
- Monetary policy

Fiscal Policy   Making changes in tax rates and in government spending programs is called **fiscal policy**. This range of actions is under the control of the federal government. Fiscal policy can be used to try to boost long-term growth by creating incentives that encourage saving, investment, and technological change. Fiscal policy can also be used to try to smooth out the business cycle. When the economy is in a recession, the government might cut taxes or increase its spending. Conversely, when the economy is in a rapid expansion, the government might increase taxes or cut its spending in an attempt to slow real GDP growth and prevent inflation from increasing. Fiscal policy is discussed in Chapter 26.

Monetary Policy   Changing interest rates and changing the amount of money in the economy is called **monetary policy**. These actions are under the control of the Bank of Canada. The principal aim of monetary policy is to keep inflation in check. To achieve this objective, the Bank prevents the quantity of money from growing too rapidly. Monetary policy can also be used to smooth the business cycle. When the economy is in recession, the Bank might lower interest rates and inject money into the economy. When the economy is in a rapid expansion, the Bank might increase interest rates in an attempt to slow real GDP growth and prevent inflation from increasing. We study monetary policy in Chapters 27 and 28.

R E V I E W   Q U I Z

- What are the main challenges of macroeconomic policy?
- What are the main tools of macroeconomic policy?
- Can you distinguish between fiscal policy and monetary policy?

◆ In your study of macroeconomics, you will learn what is currently known about the causes of unemployment, economic growth, business cycles, inflation, and government and international deficits and about the policy choices and challenges the government and the Bank of Canada face. *Reading Between the Lines* on pp. 470–471 looks to Asia and examines the state of the Hong Kong macroeconomy in 1998. It looks at the long expansion that ended in 1998 with falling real GDP and rising unemployment.

The Economy of Hong Kong

FINANCIAL POST, AUGUST 4, 1998

Hong Kong's GDP fall a gloomy sign

HONG KONG — Hong Kong's economy shrank 2.8% in the first quarter as Asia's financial crisis took a heavy toll and the government said conditions had not improved.

The 2.8% fall in gross domestic product, the first official estimate for the first quarter, was worse than the government's rough guess of a 2% contraction announced May 29.

Until this year, Hong Kong had not experienced a quarter of negative growth since 1985. If GDP stays negative all year—and all indications are that it will—it will be Hong Kong's first recorded full-year economic contraction.

Hong Kong has been savaged by the Asian financial crisis, with hard hits to tourism, retail sales and employment. A falling Japanese yen has hit the local stock market, as have worries that some local banks would be hit by their exposure to troubled Asian countries.

With tourists spending their money elsewhere, Hong Kong's once vibrant retail sector has had a disastrous year. Retail sales were down 15% year over year in May after a 15% drop in April. Hong Kong's unemployment rate rose to 4.5% in the three months to June, a new 15-year high.

Essence of the Story

■ In the first quarter of 1998, Hong Kong's real GDP fell by 2.8 percent.

■ If real GDP growth is negative throughout 1998, Hong Kong will experience its first recorded full-year contraction.

■ In the second quarter of 1998, unemployment reached 4.5 percent, the highest in the past 15 years.

Economic Analysis

■ Real GDP is the value of total production.

■ Fig. 1 shows real GDP in Hong Kong, measured in 1990 Hong Kong dollars.

■ The figure shows that Hong Kong's real GDP has been on an upward trend. The average growth rate of real GDP has been 7.4 percent per year. With a growth rate this high, real GDP more than doubles every 10 years.

■ But Hong Kong's growth rate has fluctuated a great deal as Fig. 2 shows. The lowest growth rate, in 1974, was less than 1 percent. The highest growth rate, in 1976, was almost 15 percent.

■ Figure 3 looks more closely at Hong Kong's real GDP quarter by quarter from 1995 to the first quarter of 1998.

■ Hong Kong experiences a seasonal decrease in real GDP during the fourth quarter of the year.

■ The decrease during the fourth quarter of 1997 was smaller than usual.

■ It is unusual for Hong Kong to experience negative real GDP growth during the first quarter. But that is what happened in the first quarter of 1998.

■ Two consecutive quarters of negative real GDP growth is a recession. But the growth must be measured on a "seasonally adjusted" basis to count.

■ If real GDP decreases in the second quarter of 1998, then Hong Kong will be in a recession.

■ The news article also reports that Hong Kong's unemployment rate has increased sharply.

■ When the economy moves towards a recession, the unemployment rate usually increases.

■ In 1998, Hong Kong's chief concerns are shrinking real GDP and rising unemployment.

Figure 1 Hong Kong's real GDP, 1970–1997

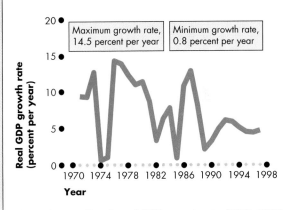

Figure 2 Hong Kong's real GDP growth rate, 1970–1997

Figure 3 Hong Kong's quarterly real GDP, 1995–1997

You're The Voter

■ Why do you think that the Asian economic slow-down might matter to Canadians?

■ What, if anything, do you think Canadians can do to protect themselves from the effects of an economic slowdown in another part of the world?

■ Would you support a proposal to use Canadian taxes to provide financial assistance to a country experiencing an economic slowdown?

471

SUMMARY

Key Points

Origins and Issues of Macroeconomics (p. 456)

- Macroeconomics studies economic growth and fluctuations, unemployment, inflation, and surpluses and deficits.

Economic Growth (pp. 457–462)

- Economic growth is the expansion of potential GDP. Real GDP fluctuates around potential GDP in a business cycle.
- Countries have similar productivity growth slowdowns and business cycles but different long-term trends in potential GDP.
- The main benefit of long-term economic growth is higher future consumption and the main cost is lower current consumption.

Jobs and Unemployment (pp. 462–464)

- The Canadian economy creates 200,000 jobs a year but unemployment persists.
- Canadian unemployment increases during a recession and decreases during an expansion. The Canadian unemployment rate is higher than that in the United States, Western Europe, and Japan.
- Unemployment can permanently damage a person's job prospects.

Inflation (pp. 465–467)

- Inflation, a process of rising prices, is measured by the percentage change in the CPI.
- Inflation is a problem because it lowers the value of money and makes money less useful as a measuring rod of value.

Surpluses and Deficits (pp. 467–469)

- When tax receipts exceed government spending, the government has a budget surplus. When government spending exceeds tax receipts, the government has a budget deficit.

- When imports exceed exports, a nation has an international deficit.
- Deficits are financed by borrowing.

Macroeconomic Policy Challenges and Tools (p. 469)

- The macroeconomic policy challenge is to use fiscal policy and monetary policy to boost long-term growth, stabilize the business cycle, lower unemployment, tame inflation, and prevent large deficits.

Key Figures

Key Terms

PROBLEMS

⌨ *1. Use Variable Graphing in Chapter 21 of *Economics in Action* to answer the following questions. In which country in 1992 was
   a. The growth rate of real GDP highest: Canada, France, Japan, or the United States?
   b. The unemployment rate highest: Canada, Japan, the United Kingdom, or the United States?
   c. The inflation rate lowest: Canada, Germany, the United Kingdom, or the United States?
   d. The government budget deficit (as a percentage of GDP) largest: Canada, Japan, the United Kingdom, or the United States?

⌨ 2. Use Variable Graphing in Chapter 21 in *Economics in Action* to answer the following questions. In which country in 1996 was
   a. The growth rate of real GDP highest: Canada, France, Japan, or the United States?
   b. The unemployment rate lowest: Canada, Japan, the United Kingdom, or the United States?
   c. The inflation rate lowest: Canada, Finland, Ireland, or the United States?
   d. The government budget deficit (as a percentage of GDP) smallest: Canada, Australia, Ireland, or the United States?
   e. Is it possible to say in which country consumption possibilities are growing faster? Why or why not?

*3. The figure shows real GDP growth rate in India and Pakistan from 1989 to 1996.

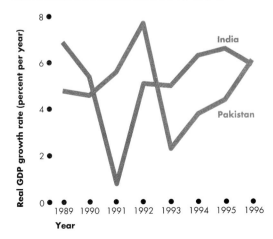

In which years did economic growth in
a. India increase? And in which year was growth the fastest?
b. Pakistan decrease? And in which year was growth the slowest?
c. Compare the paths of economic growth in India and Pakistan during this period.

4. The figure shows real GDP per person in Australia and Japan from 1989 to 1996.

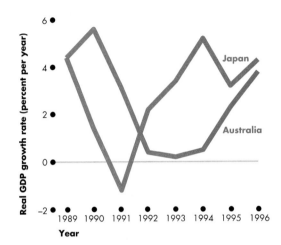

In which years did economic growth in
a. Australia increase? And in which year was growth the fastest?
b. Japan decrease? And in which year was growth the slowest?
c. Compare the paths of economic growth in Australia and Japan during this period.

*5. The figure shows real GDP in Germany from the first quarter of 1991 to the second quarter of 1994.

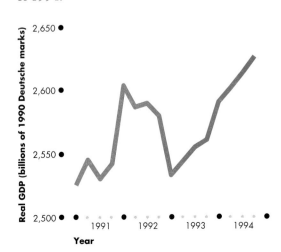

a. How many recessions did Germany experience during this period?

b. In which quarters, if any, did Germany experience a business cycle peak?

c. In which quarters, if any, did Germany experience a business cycle trough?

d. In which quarters, if any, did Germany experience an expansion?

6. Use the links on the Parkin-Bade Web site to obtain data on quarterly real GDP for Canada since the fourth quarter of 1998 and update Fig. 21.2. Use what you have discovered to answer the following questions:

a. Is the Canadian economy now in a recession or an expansion?

b. If the economy is still in an expansion, how long has the expansion lasted? If the economy is now in recession, how long has the economy been in recession?

c. During the last year, has the growth rate sped up or slowed down?

*7. Use Variable Graphing in Chapter 21 in *Economics in Action* to answer the following questions. Which country, in 1988, had

a. The largest budget deficit: Canada, Japan, the United Kingdom, or the United States?

b. A current account surplus: Canada, Japan, Germany, or the United States?

8. Use Variable Graphing in Chapter 21 in *Economics in Action* to answer the following questions. Which country, in 1988, had

a. The largest budget surplus: Canada, Japan, the United Kingdom, or the United States?

b. The largest current account deficit: Canada, Japan, Germany, or the United States?

*9. Use Variable Graphing in Chapter 21 in *Economics in Action* to make a scatter diagram of inflation and unemployment in Canada.

a. Describe the relationship.

b. Do you think that low unemployment brings an increase in the inflation rate?

10. Use Variable Graphing in Chapter 21 in *Economics in Action* to make a scatter diagram of the government budget deficit as a percentage of GDP and the unemployment rate in Canada.

a. Describe the relationship.

b. Do you think that low unemployment brings a decrease in the budget deficit?

CRITICAL THINKING

1. When you have studied *Reading Between the Lines* on pp. 470–471 on the state of the macroeconomy in Hong Kong:

a. Use the link on the Parkin-Bade Web site to get the latest data on the macroeconomy of Hong Kong.

b. Explain what is happening to real GDP growth and unemployment in Hong Kong.

c. Describe the phase of the business cycle through which Hong Kong is passing today.

d. Explain why the state of the Hong Kong economy is relevant for Canadians.

2. Use the links on the Parkin-Bade Web site to obtain the latest data on real GDP, unemployment, and inflation in Canada.

a. Update the figures on pages 458, 463, and 465.

b. What dangers does the Canadian economy face today?

c. What actions, if any, do you think might be needed to keep the economy strong?

3. Use the links on the Parkin-Bade Web site to obtain data on unemployment in your home province.

a. Compare unemployment in your home province with that in Canada as a whole.

b. Why do you think your province might have a higher or a lower unemployment rate than the Canadian average?

4. Use the links on the Parkin-Bade Web site to obtain data on the Consumer Price Index for the capital city in your home province.

a. Compare the inflation rate in your home province with that in Canada as a whole.

b. Compare the inflation rate in your home province with that of the capital cities in neighbouring provinces.

5. Use the links on the Parkin-Bade Web site to obtain data on each of the following variables for Canada for the most recent period. Describe how the variables have changed over the last year:

a. The unemployment rate

b. The inflation rate

c. The government budget surplus or deficit

d. The international deficit

22

Measuring GDP, Inflation, and Economic Growth

When Nortel contemplates spending $1 billion developing a wireless communications system in China, it pays close attention to forecasts of China's real GDP. When Bell Canada plans to expand its fibre optics network, it uses forecasts of long-term growth in the Canadian economy. The outcomes of many business decisions turn on the quality of forecasts of economic conditions. ◆ A key input for making economic forecasts is Gross Domestic Product, or GDP, which is like a barometer of a nation's economy. Economists pore over the numbers, looking at past trends and seeking patterns that might give a glimpse of the future. How do economic statisticians add up all the production of the country to arrive at the number called GDP? What exactly *is* GDP? ◆ Most of the time, our economy grows but sometimes it shrinks. To reveal the rate of growth (or shrinkage), we must remove the effects of inflation on GDP and assess how real GDP is changing. How do we remove the inflation component of GDP to reveal *real* GDP? ◆ From economists to homemakers, all types of people pay close attention to another economic barometer, the Consumer Price Index, or CPI. Statistics Canada publishes new figures each month, and analysts in newspapers and on TV quickly leap to conclusions about the causes of recent changes in prices and the prospects for future changes. How does the government determine the CPI? How well does it measure a consumer's living costs and the inflation rate? ◆ Some countries are rich while others are poor and only now are in the process of developing their industries and reaching their productive potential. How do we compare incomes in one country with incomes in another? How can we make international comparisons of GDP?

◇ In this chapter you are going to find out how economic statisticians measure real GDP and the price level. You are also going to learn how they use these measures to assess the economic growth rate and the inflation rate and to compare macroeconomic performance across countries.

Economic Barometers

After studying this chapter, you will be able to:

■ Distinguish between the *stocks* of capital and wealth and the *flows* of production, income, investment, and saving

■ Explain why for the economy as a whole income, expenditure, and the value of production are equal

■ Explain how GDP is measured

■ Explain how the Consumer Price Index (CPI) and the GDP deflator are measured

■ Explain the shortcomings of the CPI and the GDP deflator as measures of inflation

■ Explain how *real* GDP is measured

■ Explain the shortcomings of real GDP growth as a measure of improvements in living standards

Gross Domestic Product

WHAT EXACTLY IS GDP, HOW IS IT CALCULATED, what does it mean, and why do we care about it? You are going to discover the answers to these questions in this chapter. First, what *is* GDP? **GDP**, or **Gross Domestic Product**, is the value of the *aggregate* production of goods and services in a country during a given time period—usually a year. The GDP of Canada, which measures the value of aggregate production in Canada during a year, was more than $800 billion in 1998.

How is GDP calculated? In a nutshell, GDP is calculated by valuing everything that is produced and adding all the values together. But precisely what is valued and *how* is it valued? To answer these questions, you need to understand two fundamental principles of economic accounting:

■ The distinction between flows and stocks
■ The equality of income, expenditure, and the value of production

Flows and Stocks

To keep track of our personal economic transactions and the economic transactions of a country, we distinguish between flows and stocks. A **flow** is a quantity per unit of time. The water that is running from an open faucet into a bathtub is a flow. So are the number of CDs that you buy during a month and the amount of income that you earn during a month. GDP is a flow. It is the value of the goods and services produced in a country *during a given time period.*

A **stock** is a quantity that exists at a point in time. The water in a bathtub is a stock. So are the number of CDs that you own and the amount of money in your savings account.

Capital and Investment   The key macroeconomic stock is capital. **Capital** is the plant, equipment, buildings, and inventories of raw materials and semi-finished goods that are used to produce other goods and services. The amount of capital in the economy exerts a big influence on GDP. Two flows change the stock of capital: investment and depreciation.

Investment is the purchase of new capital including inventories. **Depreciation** is the decrease in the stock of capital that results from wear and tear

and obsolescence. Another name for depreciation is *capital consumption*. The total amount spent on adding to the stock of capital and on replacing depreciated capital is called **gross investment**. The amount spent on adding to the stock of capital is called **net investment**. Net investment equals gross investment minus depreciation.

Figure 22.1 illustrates these concepts. On January 1, 1999, Tom's Tapes, Inc. had 3 machines. This quantity was its initial capital. During 1999, Tom's scrapped an older machine. This quantity is its depreciation. After depreciation, Tom's stock of capital was down to 2 machines. But also during 1999, Tom's bought 2 new machines. This amount is its gross investment. By December 31, 1999, Tom's Tapes had 4 machines so its capital had increased by 1 machine. This amount is Tom's net investment.

FIGURE 22.1

Capital and Investment

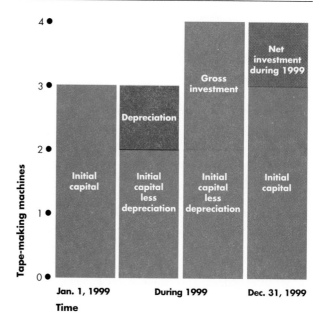

Tom's Tapes has a capital stock at the end of 1999 that equals its capital stock at the beginning of the year plus its net investment. Net investment is equal to gross investment less depreciation. Tom's gross investment is the 2 new machines bought during the year, and its depreciation is the 1 machine that Tom's scrapped during the year.

Tom's net investment equals its gross investment (the purchase of 2 new machines) minus its depreciation (1 machine scrapped).

The example of Tom's Tapes factory can be applied to the economy as a whole. The nation's capital stock decreases because capital depreciates and increases because of gross investment. The change in the nation's capital stock from one year to the next equals its net investment.

Wealth and Saving   Another macroeconomic stock is **wealth**, which is the value of all the things that people own. What people *own*, a stock, is related to what they *earn*, a flow. People *earn* an *income*, which is the amount they receive during a given time period from supplying the services of resources. Income can be either consumed or saved. **Consumption expenditure** is the amount spent on consumption goods and services. **Saving** is the amount of income remaining after meeting consumption expenditures. Saving adds to wealth, and dissaving (negative saving) decreases wealth.

For example, suppose that at the end of the school year you have $250 in a savings account and some textbooks that are worth $300. That's all you own. Your wealth is $550. Suppose that you take a summer job and earn an income of $5,000. You are extremely careful and spend only $1,000 through the summer on consumption goods and services. You save $4,000. Your saving of $4,000 equals your income of $5,000 minus your consumption expenditure of $1,000. At the end of the summer, when school starts again, your wealth is $4,550. Your wealth has increased by $4,000, which equals your saving of $4,000.

National wealth and national saving work just like this personal example. The wealth of a nation at the start of a year equals its wealth at the start of the previous year plus its saving during the year. Its saving equals its income minus its consumption expenditure.

We'll make the idea of the nation's income and consumption expenditure more precise a bit later in this chapter. Before doing so, let's see what the stocks and flows that we've just learned about imply for the recurring theme of macroeconomics: short-term fluctuations in actual real GDP and long-term growth in potential GDP.

The Short Term Meets the Long Term   You saw in Chapter 21 that potential GDP grows incessantly, year after year. You also saw that actual real GDP grows and fluctuates around potential GDP. The

stocks and flows that you've just studied influence *both* the long-term growth in potential GDP and the short-term fluctuations in actual GDP. One of the reasons why potential GDP grows is that the capital stock grows. One of the reasons that real GDP fluctuates is that investment fluctuates. So capital and investment as well as wealth and saving are part of the key to understanding the growth of potential GDP and fluctuations of real GDP around potential GDP.

The flows of investment and saving together with the flows of income and consumption expenditure interact in a circular flow of income and expenditure. In this circular flow, income equals expenditure, which also equals the value of production. This amazing equality is the foundation on which a nation's economic accounts are built and from which its GDP is measured.

Income, Expenditure, and the Value of Production

To see that for the economy as a whole income equals expenditure and also equals the value of production, we study the circular flow of income and expenditure.

Figure 22.2 illustrates the circular flow of income and expenditure. In the figure, the economy consists of four sectors: households, firms, governments, and the rest of the world (the blue diamonds). It has three types of markets: resource markets, goods (and services) markets, and financial markets. Focus first on households and firms.

Households and Firms   Households sell and firms buy the services of labour, capital, land, and entrepreneurship in resource markets. For these resource services, firms pay income to households: wages for labour services, interest for the use of capital, rent for the use of land, and profits for entrepreneurship. Firms' retained earnings—profits that are not distributed to households—are also part of the household sector's income. You can think of retained earnings as being income that households save and lend back to firms. Figure 22.2 shows the *aggregate income* received by all households in payment for the services of resources by the blue dots labelled *Y*.

Firms sell and households buy consumer goods and services—such as popcorn and pop, movies and chocolate bars, microwave ovens and inline skates, dental and dry cleaning services—in the markets for goods and services. The total payment that households make for these goods and services is *consump-*

FIGURE 22.2

The Circular Flow of Income and Expenditure

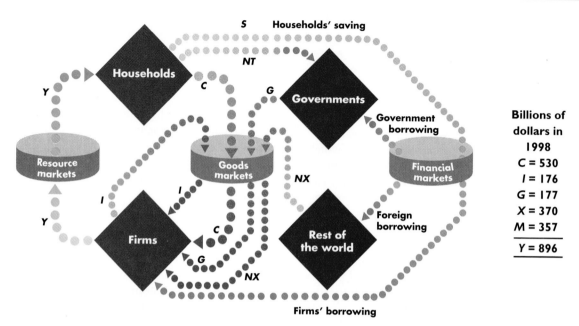

Billions of dollars in 1998
C = 530
I = 176
G = 177
X = 370
M = 357
Y = 896

In the circular flow of income and expenditure, households receive incomes (*Y*) from firms (blue flow) and make consumption expenditures (*C*); firms make investment expenditures (*I*); governments purchase goods and services (*G*); the rest of the world purchases net exports (*NX*)—(red flows). (*NX* equals exports, *X*, minus imports, *M*.) Aggregate income (blue flow) equals aggregate expenditure (red flows). Households' saving (*S*) and net taxes (*NT*) leak from the circular flow. Firms borrow to finance their investment expenditures, and governments and the rest of the world borrow to finance their deficits or lend their surpluses (green flows). The table shows the values of the flows in 1998.

Source: Statistics Canada, StatCan: CANSIM Disc, 1999.

---

tion expenditure. Figure 22.2 shows consumption expenditure by the red dots labelled *C*.

Firms buy and sell new capital equipment in the goods market. For example, IBM sells 1,000 PCs to General Motors, or Bombardier sells an airplane to Air Canada. Some of what firms produce might not be sold at all and is added to inventory. For example, if GM produces 1,000 cars and sells 950 of them, the other 50 cars remain unsold and GM's inventory of cars increases by 50. When a firm adds unsold output to inventory, we can think of the firm as buying goods from itself. The purchase of new plant, equipment, and buildings and the additions to inventories are *investment*.

Figure 22.2 shows investment by the red dots labelled *I*. Notice that in the figure, investment flows from firms through the goods markets and back to

firms. Some firms produce capital goods, and other firms buy them (and firms "buy" inventories from themselves).

Firms finance their investment by borrowing from households in financial markets. Households' saving flows into financial markets and firms' borrowing flows out of financial markets. Figure 22.2 shows these flows by the green dots labelled "Households' saving" or *S* and "Firms' borrowing." These flows are neither income nor expenditure. Income is a payment for the services of a resource, and expenditure is a payment for goods or services.

Governments Governments buy goods and services, called **government expenditures**, from firms. In Fig. 22.2 these government expenditures are shown as the red flow *G*. Governments use taxes to pay for their purchases. Figure 22.2 shows taxes as net taxes by the green dots labelled *NT*. **Net taxes** are equal to taxes paid to governments minus transfer payments received from governments. *Transfer payments* are cash transfers from governments to households and firms. They include social security benefits, unemployment compensation, subsidies, and interest payments on government debt.

When government expenditures (*G*) exceed net taxes (*NT*), the government has a budget deficit, which it finances by borrowing in financial markets (shown by the green dots labelled "Government borrowing.")

Rest of World Sector   Firms export goods and services to the rest of the world and import goods and services from the rest of the world. The value of exports minus the value of imports is called **net exports**. Figure 22.2 shows net exports by the red flow *NX*.

If the value of exports exceeds the value of imports, net exports are positive and flow from the rest of the world to firms. But if the value of exports is less than the value of imports, net exports are negative and flow from firms to the rest of the world.

If net exports are positive, the rest of the world is in deficit and we are in surplus. To finance its deficit, the rest of the world borrows from the domestic economy or sells domestic assets that it owns. For example, Comair, a commuter airline based in Ohio, can borrow in Toronto to finance the purchase of new airplanes from Bombardier. These transactions take place in financial markets and they are shown by the green flow labelled "Foreign borrowing."

If net exports are negative, we are in deficit and the rest of the world is in surplus. To finance our deficit, we borrow from the rest of the world or we sell foreign assets that we own. For example, an Ontario winemaker might borrow in Frankfurt, Germany, to finance the purchase of a German-made grape-picking machine. Again, these transactions take place in financial markets. To illustrate this case in Fig. 22.2, we would reverse the directions of the flows of net exports and foreign borrowing.

To help you keep track of the different types of flows that make up the circular flow of income and expenditure, the flows are colour-coded in Fig. 22.2. The red flows are expenditures on goods and services, the blue flow is income, and the green flows are financial transfers. The expenditure flows (red flows) are consumption expenditure, investment, government expenditures, and net exports. The income flow (blue flow) is aggregate income. The financial transfers (green flows) are saving, net taxes, government borrowing, foreign borrowing, and firms' borrowing.

Gross Domestic Product   Gross domestic product is the value of *aggregate production* in a country during a year. Production can be valued in two ways:

1. By what buyers pay for it
2. By what it costs producers to make it

From the viewpoint of buyers, goods are worth the prices paid for them. From the viewpoint of producers, goods are worth what it costs to make them. Fortunately, the value of production is the same regardless of which viewpoint we take. Let's see why.

Expenditure Equals Income   The total amount that buyers pay for the goods and services produced is *aggregate expenditure*. Figure 22.2 shows the expenditures on goods and services by the red flows. Firms' revenues from the sale of goods and services equal consumption expenditure (*C*) plus investment (*I*) plus government expenditures on goods and services (*G*) plus net exports (*NX*). The sum of these four flows is equal to aggregate expenditure on goods and services.

The total amount it costs producers to make goods and services is equal to the incomes paid for resource services. This amount is shown by the blue flow in Fig. 22.2.

The sum of the red flows equals the blue flow. The reason is that everything a firm receives from the sale of its output is paid out as incomes to the owners of the resources that it employs. That is,

$$Y = C + I + G + NX,$$

or aggregate income (*Y*) equals aggregate expenditure (*C* + *I* + *G* + *NX*).

The buyers of aggregate production pay an amount equal to aggregate expenditure, and the sellers of aggregate production pay an amount equal to aggregate income. Because aggregate expenditure equals aggregate income, these two methods of valuing aggregate production give the same answer. So

Aggregate production or GDP, equals aggregate expenditure and equals aggregate income.

We're now going to study two interesting facts that are implied by the circular flow. The first fact is that leakages from the flow equal injections into the flow. The second fact is that domestic saving and foreign borrowing finance investment.

Injections and Leakages

You can think of the circular flow of income and expenditure as pipes with liquid flowing through them. The flow of incomes equals the flow of expenditures. But some liquid is injected into the circular flow. An **injection** is an expenditure that does not originate with households. The injections are investment, government expenditures, and exports. For the pipes not to burst there must be some leakages. A **leakage** is income that is not spent on domestically produced goods and services. The leakages are saving, net taxes, and imports. You are going to see that injections equal leakages.

Start with the equality of aggregate income and the aggregate expenditure

$$Y = C + I + G + NX.$$

Net exports (NX) equals exports (X) minus imports (M). So we can write the above equation as

$$Y = C + I + G + X - M.$$

Now look at the flows into and out of households in Fig. 22.2. Aggregate income (Y) flows in and consumption expenditure (C), saving (S), and net taxes (NT) flow out. So

$$Y = C + S + NT.$$

Subtract the second equation from the first equation and you get

$$I + G + X - M - S - NT = 0.$$

Add saving (S), net taxes (NT), and imports (M) to both sides of this equation and you get

$$I + G + X = S + NT + M.$$

The left side of the equation is the sum of injections into the circular flow of income and expenditure and the right side is leakages from the circular flow. So

$$\text{Injections} = \text{Leakages}.$$

Let's next see how the circular flows of expenditure and income show us how investment is financed.

How Investment Is Financed

Investment, which adds to the stock of capital, is one of the determinants of the rate at which production grows. Investment is financed by

- National saving
- Borrowing from the rest of the world

National Saving The amount of saving by households and businesses plus government saving is called **national saving**. Saving by households and businesses is S. Government saving equals net taxes minus government expenditures, ($NT - G$). So

$$\text{National saving} = S + (NT - G).$$

If the government has a budget surplus, its saving is positive and if the government has a budget deficit, its saving is negative.

Borrowing from the Rest of the World Borrowing from the rest of the world bothers many people and is a source of concern in the media. In fact, foreign borrowing is a natural and normal way of financing investment when profitable investment opportunities exceed national savings.

Foreign borrowing equals imports, M, minus exports, X, and so equals $-NX$ (minus net exports).

If we spend more on foreign goods and services than the rest of the world spends on ours, we must borrow from the rest of the world to pay the balance. That is, if the value of our imports (M) exceeds the value of our exports (X), we must borrow from the rest of the world an amount equal to ($M - X$). In this case, part of the rest of the world's saving finances our negative net exports and frees up an equal amount of national saving to finance investment in Canada. Conversely, if foreigners spend more on Canadian-made goods and services than we spend on theirs, foreigners must borrow from us to pay the difference. That is, part of Canadian national saving flows to the rest of the world and is not available to finance Canadian investment.

Because the sum of national saving and borrowing from the rest of the world finance investment,

$$\text{Investment} = S + (NT - G) + (M - X).$$

In 1998, Canadian investment was $176 billion. National saving was $189 billion and $M - X$ was –$13 billion. Canada lent $13 billion of its national saving to the rest of the world.

- What is the distinction between a stock and a flow? What are the main macroeconomic stocks? What are the flows that change them?

- What are the components of aggregate expenditure?

- Why does aggregate income equal aggregate expenditure and the value of output (GDP)?

- What is the distinction between government expenditures of goods and services and transfer payments?

- What are injections, what are leakages, and why are they equal?

The circular flow of expenditure and income is the foundation for measuring GDP. Let's now see how Statistics Canada uses the circular flow to measure Canadian GDP.

Measuring Canadian GDP

To measure GDP, Statistics Canada uses two approaches:

- Expenditure approach
- Income approach

The Expenditure Approach

The *expenditure approach* measures GDP by using data on consumption expenditure, investment, government expenditures, and net exports. Table 22.1 shows this approach. The first column gives the terms used in the *National Income and Expenditure Accounts* (published by Statistics Canada). The next column gives the symbol we've used in our GDP equations. Using the expenditure approach, GDP is the sum of personal expenditure on consumer goods and services (C), business investment (I), government expenditures on goods and services (G), and net exports of goods and services (NX).

Personal expenditures on consumer goods and services are the expenditures by households on goods and services produced in Canada and in the rest of the world. They include goods such as CDs and books, and services such as banking and legal advice.

They do *not* include the purchase of new homes, which is counted as part of investment.

Business investment is expenditure on capital equipment and buildings by firms and expenditure on new homes by households. It also includes the change in business inventories.

Government expenditures on goods and services are the expenditures on goods and services by all levels of government. This item includes expenditures on national defence and garbage collection. But it does not include *transfer payments*. These payments, such as unemployment compensation and government pensions, are not purchases of goods and services. They are transfers of funds from government to households.

Net exports of goods and services are the value of exports minus the value of imports. Exports include telephone equipment that Nortel sells to AT&T in

---

TABLE 22.1

GDP: The Expenditure Approach

Item	Symbol	Amount in 1998 (billions of dollars)	Percentage of GDP
Personal expenditure on consumer goods and services	C	530	59.2
Business investment	I	176	19.6
Government expenditures on goods and services	G	177	19.8
Net exports of goods and services	NX	13	1.4
Gross domestic product	Y	896	100.0

The expenditure approach measures GDP by adding together personal expenditure on consumer goods and services (C), business investment (I), government expenditures on goods and services (G), and net exports (NX). In 1998, GDP measured by the expenditure approach was $896 billion. Almost 60 percent of aggregate expenditure is on personal consumer goods and services.

Source: Statistics Canada, *StatCan: CANSIM Disc*, March 1999.

the United States and imports include Mazda RX7s that your local dealer buys from Japan.

Table 22.1 shows the relative importance of the four items of aggregate expenditure. The largest component is personal expenditure on consumer goods and services, and the smallest is net exports.

Expenditures Not in GDP Aggregate expenditure, which equals GDP, does not include all the things that people and businesses buy. To distinguish total expenditure on GDP from other items of spending, we call the expenditure included in GDP *final expenditure*. Spending that is not part of final expenditure includes the purchase of:

■ Intermediate goods and services
■ Used goods
■ Financial assets

Intermediate goods and services are the goods and services that firms buy from each other and use as inputs in the goods and services that they eventually sell to final users. When Dell Corp. buys computer chips from Intel Corp., it buys an intermediate good. A Dell computer is a final good, but an Intel chip is an intermediate good. To count the expenditure on intermediate goods and services as well as the expenditure on the final good involves counting the same thing twice—called *double counting*.

A good can sometimes be an intermediate good and sometimes a final good. For example, the ice cream that you buy on a hot summer day is a final good, but the ice cream that a restaurant buys and uses to make sundaes is an intermediate good. Whether a good is intermediate or final depends on what it is used for, not on what it is.

Expenditure on *used goods* is not part of GDP because these goods were counted as part of GDP in the period in which they were produced and in which they were new goods. For example, a 1995 automobile was part of GDP in 1995. If the car is traded on the used car market in 1999, the amount paid for the car is not part of GDP in 1999.

Firms often sell *financial assets* such as bonds and stocks to finance purchases of newly produced capital goods. The expenditure on newly produced capital goods is part of GDP, but the expenditure on financial securities is not. GDP includes the amount spent on new capital, not the amount spent on pieces of paper.

Let's look at the second way of measuring GDP, the income approach.

The Income Approach

The *income approach* measures GDP by summing the incomes that firms pay households for the resources they hire—wages for labour, interest for capital, rent for land, and profits for entrepreneurship. Let's see how the income approach works.

The *National Income and Expenditure Accounts* divides incomes into five categories:

1. Wages, salaries, and supplementary labour income
2. Corporate profits
3. Interest and miscellaneous investment income
4. Farmers' income
5. Income from non-farm unincorporated businesses

Wages, salaries, and supplementary labour income are the total payments by firms for labour services. This item includes the net wages and salaries (called take-home pay) that workers receive plus taxes withheld on earnings plus fringe benefits such as social security and pension fund contributions.

Corporate profits are the total profits made by corporations. Some of these profits are paid to households in the form of dividends, and corporations retain some as undistributed profits.

Interest and miscellaneous investment income is the total interest payments received by households on loans made by them minus the interest payments made by households on their own borrowing. This item includes, on the plus side, payments of interest by firms to households on bonds, and on the minus side, households' interest payments on the outstanding balances on their credit cards. This item also includes payments for the use of land and other rented inputs. It includes payments for rented housing and imputed rent for owner-occupied housing. (Imputed rent is an estimate of what homeowners would pay to rent the housing they own and use themselves. By including this item in the national income accounts, we measure the total value of housing services, whether they are owned or rented.)

Farmers' income and income from non-farm unincorporated businesses are a mixture of the elements that we have just reviewed. A farmer or the proprietor of an owner-operated business supplies labour, capital, and perhaps land and buildings to the business. It is difficult to split up the income earned by an owner-operator into its component parts: compensation for labour, payment for the use of capital, rent payments for the use of land or buildings, and profit, so the national income accounts lump all these separate incomes into a single category.

Table 22.2 shows these five incomes and their relative magnitudes. Wages, salaries, and supplementary labour income is the largest item.

The sum of these five incomes is called *net domestic income at factor cost*. The term *factor cost* is used because *factor of production* is another name for a productive resource. But *net domestic income at factor cost* is not GDP. We must make two adjustments to get to GDP, one from *factor cost* to market prices and another from *net* product to *gross* product.

Factor Cost to Market Prices   When we add up all the incomes, we arrive at a total that is the value of production at *factor cost*. Production is valued at the prices of the resources used to produce goods and services. When we add up all the final expenditures on goods and services, we arrive at a value of production at *market prices*. Production is valued at the prices that people pay for the goods and services. If there were no government taxes or subsidies the factor cost and market price values would be the same. But the presence of indirect taxes and subsidies makes these two methods of valuation differ.

An *indirect tax* is a tax paid by consumers when they buy goods and services. (In contrast, a *direct tax* is a tax on income.) Provincial sales taxes, GST, and taxes on alcohol, gasoline, and tobacco products are indirect taxes. Because of indirect taxes, consumers pay more for some goods and services than producers receive. Market price exceeds factor cost. For example, if the sales tax is 7 percent, when you buy a $1 chocolate bar you pay $1.07. The factor cost of the chocolate bar including profit is $1. The market price is $1.07.

A *subsidy* is a payment by the government to a producer. Payments made to grain growers and dairy farmers are subsidies. Because of subsidies, consumers pay less for some goods and services than producers receive. Factor cost exceeds market price.

To get from factor cost to market price, we add indirect taxes and subtract subsidies. This adjustment brings us one step closer to GDP, but it does not quite get us there. We must make one further adjustment.

Net Domestic Product to Gross Domestic Product   *Gross* means *before* subtracting *depreciation*. *Net* means *after* subtracting depreciation. *Gross investment* is a component of aggregate expenditure. So total expenditure includes depreciation and is a gross measure. The *net profit* of businesses is profit *after*

TABLE 22.2

GDP: The Income Approach

Item	Amount in 1998 (billions of dollars)	Percentage of GDP
Wages, salaries, and supplementary labour income	472	52.7
Corporate profits	88	9.8
Interest and miscellaneous investment income	44	4.9
Farmers' income	2	0.2
Income of nonfarm unincorporated businesses	57	6.3
Indirect taxes *less* subsidies	120	13.5
Capital consumption (depreciation)	113	12.6
Gross domestic product	896	100.0

The sum of all incomes equals net domestic income. GDP equals net domestic income plus capital consumption (depreciation). In 1998, GDP measured by the income approach was $896 billion. Wages, salaries, and supplementary labour income was by far the largest part of aggregate income.

Source: Statistics Canada, StatCan: CANSIM disc, March 1999.

---

subtracting depreciation, so total income excludes depreciation and is a net measure. To get *gross* domestic product from the income approach, we must add depreciation to aggregate income.

Table 22.2 summarizes these calculations and shows how the income approach leads to the same estimate of GDP as the expenditure approach after making the adjustment that we've just described.

Valuing the Output of Industries

The methods used to measure GDP can also be used to measure the contribution that an industry makes to GDP. But to measure the value of production of an individual industry, we count only the value added by that industry. **Value added** is the value of a firm's production minus the value of the *intermediate goods* it buys from other firms. Equivalently, value added is the sum of the incomes (including profits) paid to the resources used by the firm.

Figure 22.3 illustrates value added by looking at the brief life of a loaf of bread. It starts with the farmer, who grows the wheat. The farmer hires labour, capital, and land and pays wages, interest, and rent for these resources. The farmer also earns a profit. The entire value of the wheat produced is the farmer's value added. The miller buys wheat from the farmer and turns it into flour. He hires labour and capital, pays wages and interest, and earns a profit. The miller has now added value to the wheat bought from the farmer. The baker buys flour from the miller. The price of the flour equals the value added by both the farmer and the miller. The baker adds more value by turning the flour into bread. The grocer buys the bread from the baker. The price paid by the grocer equals the value added by the farmer, the miller, and the baker. At this stage the value of the loaf is its *wholesale* value. The grocer adds further value by making the loaf available in a convenient place and time. The consumer buys the bread for a price— its *market price*—that equals the value added by the farmer, the miller, the baker, and the grocer.

Final Goods and Intermediate Goods   To value output, we count only value added because the sum of the *value added* at each stage of production equals expenditure on the *final good*. By using value added, we avoid double counting. In the above example the only thing that has been produced and consumed is a loaf of bread—shown by the green bar in Fig. 22.3. The red bars show the value added at each stage, and the sum of the red bars equals the green bar. The transactions involving intermediate goods, shown by the blue bars, are not part of value added and are not counted as part of the value of output or of GDP.

Aggregate Expenditure, Income, and GDP
Why does Statistics Canada use two approaches—the expenditure approach and income approach—to measure GDP when they are supposed to be the same? The answer is that although the two approaches are identical, the actual measurements, which are based on samples of information, give slightly different answers. The expenditure approach uses data from surveys of retail stores, house building and business investment, the accounts of the federal, provincial, and local governments, customs records, and many other sources. The income approach uses data supplied by Revenue Canada. None of these sources gives a complete coverage of all the items that make

FIGURE 22.3
Value Added and Final Expenditure

A consumer's expenditure on bread is equal to the sum of the value added at each stage in its production. Intermediate expenditure, for example the amount paid by the baker for the purchase of flour from the miller, equals the value added by the farmer and the miller. So to sum intermediate expenditure and final expenditure double counts some value added.

up aggregate expenditure and aggregate income. So by using the two approaches, Statistics Canada can check one aggregate against the other.

R E V I E W   Q U I Z

- Why does GDP measured by the expenditure approach equal GDP measured by the income approach?
- What is the distinction between expenditure on final goods and expenditure on intermediate goods?
- What is value added? How is it calculated?

So far we've been concerned with the *dollar value* of GDP. But the dollar value of GDP can change because either prices change or the volume of goods and services produced changes. Let's now see how we measure the price level and distinguish between the dollar value and the real value of GDP.

The Price Level, Inflation, and Real GDP

THE PRICE LEVEL IS THE AVERAGE LEVEL OF prices measured by a *price index*. The **inflation rate** is the percentage change in the price level from one year to the next. The two main price indexes that are used in Canada today are:

■ The Consumer Price Index
■ The GDP deflator

Let's see how the two price indexes are calculated.

The Consumer Price Index

The **Consumer Price Index (CPI)** measures the average level of prices of the goods and services that a typical urban Canadian family buys. Statistics Canada publishes the CPI every month.

To construct the CPI, Statistics Canada first selects a base period (currently 1992) and surveys consumers' spending patterns. Average spending during the base period determines the "basket" of 600 different goods and services used in the CPI.

Then, every month, Statistics Canada sends a team of observers to more than 64 urban centres across Canada to record the prices of the 600 items. The CPI is calculated by valuing the basket at the current month's prices and expressing its value as a percentage of the value of the same basket in the base period.

Table 22.3 shows an example of the CPI calculation. The basket contains 5 kilograms of oranges, 6 haircuts, and 100 bus rides. The table shows the prices in the base period and total expenditure. A typical consumer buys 100 bus rides at $1.40 each and spends $140 on bus rides. Expenditure on oranges and haircuts is worked out in the same way. Total expenditure is the sum of expenditures on the three goods, which is $210.

To calculate the CPI for the current period, we need only discover the prices of the goods in the current period. We do not need to know the quantities bought. Suppose that the prices are those shown in Table 22.3 under "Current period." We can now calculate the current period's value of the basket. For example, the current price of oranges is $1.20 per kilogram, so the current period's value of the oranges in the basket (5 kilograms) is 5 multiplied by $1.20, which is $6. The quantities of haircuts and bus rides are valued at this period's prices in a similar way. The total value of the basket in the current period is $231.

The CPI is the ratio of the current period's value of the basket to the base period's value, multiplied by 100. In Table 22.3, the CPI is 110 in the current period. The current period's price of the basket is 10 percent higher than it was in the base period.

TABLE 22.3
The CPI: A Simplified Calculation

Base-period basket	Base period Price	Base period Expenditure	Current period Price	Current period Expenditure
5 kilograms of oranges	$ 0.80/kilogram	$ 4	$ 1.20/kilogram	$ 6
6 haircuts	$11.00 each	$ 66	$12.50 each	$ 75
100 bus rides	$ 1.40 each	$140	$ 1.50 each	$150
Total expenditure		$210		$231
CPI	$\dfrac{\$210}{\$210} \times 100 = 100$		$\dfrac{\$231}{\$210} \times 100 = 110$	

A fixed basket of goods—5 kilograms of oranges, 6 haircuts, and 100 bus rides—is valued in the base period at $210. Prices change, and that same basket is valued at $231 in the current period. The CPI is equal to the current-period value of the basket divided by the base-period value of the basket, multiplied by 100. In the base period the CPI is 100, and in the current period the CPI is 110.

The GDP Deflator

The **GDP deflator** measures the average level of prices of all the goods and services that are included in GDP.

To calculate the GDP deflator, we use the formula

$$\text{GDP deflator} = \frac{\text{Nominal GDP}}{\text{Real GDP}} \times 100.$$

Nominal GDP is GDP valued in the current year's prices. It is the dollar value of GDP. **Real GDP** is GDP valued in the prices of the base year. Currently, the base year for the GDP deflator is 1992.

We are going to learn how to calculate the GDP deflator by studying an imaginary economy that produces just three final goods: a consumption good that households buy (oranges), a capital good that firms buy (computers), and a good that the government buys (red tape). Net exports are zero in this example. Table 22.4 summarizes the calculations of the GDP deflator in this economy.

To calculate nominal GDP, we'll use the expenditure approach. Table 22.4 shows the quantities of the final goods and their prices. The economy's current output is 4,240 kilograms of oranges, 5 computers, and 1,060 metres of red tape. To calculate nominal GDP, we work out the expenditure on each good and then total the three expenditures. Consumption expenditure (oranges) is $4,452, investment (computers) is $10,500, and government expenditure (red tape) is $1,060, so nominal GDP is $16,012.

Now let's calculate real GDP, the real value of the economy's current output. To do so, we value the current-period quantities at the base-period prices. Because the base year is 1992, we refer to the units in which real GDP is measured as "1992 dollars." Table 22.4 shows the prices for the base period. Real expenditure on oranges for the current period is 4,240 kilograms of oranges valued at $1 per kilogram, which is $4,240. If we perform the same types of calculations for computers and red tape and add up the real expenditures, we arrive at a real GDP of $15,300.

Let's put the numbers we've found into the formula for the GDP deflator. Nominal GDP is $16,012 and real GDP is $15,300, so

$$\text{GDP deflator} = \frac{\$16,012}{\$15,300} \times 100 = 104.7.$$

When the current period is also the base period, nominal GDP equals real GDP and the GDP deflator is 100. A GDP deflator of 104.7 tells us that the price level in the current period is 4.7 percent higher than it was in the base period.

You can think of nominal GDP as a balloon that

TABLE 22.4

Nominal GDP, Real GDP, and the GDP Deflator: Simplified Calculations

Current-year output	Current-period values		Base-period values	
	Price	**Expenditure**	**Price**	**Expenditure**
4,240 kilograms of oranges	$1.05/kilogram	$ 4,452	$1/kilogram	$ 4,240
5 computers	$2,100 each	$10,500	$2,000 each	$10,000
1,060 metres of red tape	$1/metre	$ 1,060	$1/metre	$ 1,060
	Nominal GDP	$16,012	**Real GDP**	$15,300
	GDP deflator $\frac{\$16,012}{\$15,300} \times 100 = 104.7$			

An imaginary economy produces only oranges, computers, and red tape. In the current period, nominal GDP is $16,012. If the current-period quantities are valued at the base-period prices, we obtain real GDP, which is $15,300. The GDP deflator is equal to nominal GDP divided by real GDP and multiplied by 100. Here, the GDP deflator is 104.7.

FIGURE 22.4

The Canadian GDP Balloon

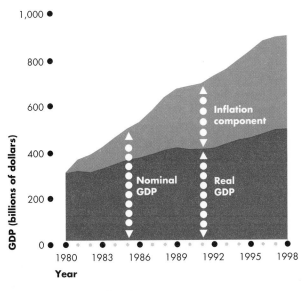

(a) Nominal GDP and real GDP

(b) Deflating nominal GDP

The increase in nominal GDP comes from inflation and from an increase in real GDP (part a). The GDP deflator lets the air out of the GDP balloon (part b) so that we can see real GDP and the extent to which it has expanded.

---

is being blown up by growing production and rising prices. Figure 22.5 illustrates this idea. In part (a), real GDP is measured by the height of the red area and nominal GDP by the height of the red area plus the green area. In part (b), the GDP deflator lets the inflation air—the contribution of rising prices—out of the nominal GDP balloon so that we can see what has happened to *real* GDP. The red balloon for 1980 shows real GDP in that year. The green balloon shows *nominal* GDP in 1998. The red balloon for 1998 shows real GDP in 1998. We've *deflated* nominal GDP using a GDP deflator with 1980 as the base year. By comparing the two red balloons we can see by how much real GDP has grown since 1980.

You now know how to calculate the CPI and the GDP deflator. There are two key differences between them. The first difference is the range of items covered. The CPI measures only consumer prices while the GDP deflator measures all final goods prices. The second difference is the period used for the quantities. The CPI uses base-year quantities while the GDP deflator uses current-year quantities.

REVIEW QUIZ

- What are the two main indexes used to measure the price level?
- How is the Consumer Price Index calculated?
- How is the GDP deflator calculated?
- What are the key differences between the CPI and the GDP deflator?

You now know how we calculate the price level and real GDP. In the closing sections of this chapter, you are going to learn about some of the limitations of these measures that we must keep in mind when we use them. In the next section, we look at some potential bias in the CPI as a measure of the price level. Then, in the final section of the chapter, we study the ways in which economists use real GDP and also discover the limitations of real GDP as a measure of production and economic wellbeing.

The Biased CPI

A MAJOR PURPOSE OF THE CPI IS TO MEASURE inflation and the measure is put to practical use. For example, it is used to determine cost of living adjustments to social insurance and welfare payments and changes in tax brackets—the income ranges over which different income tax rates apply. The data generated by the CPI survey are also used, along with other information, in the calculations of real GDP, nominal GDP, and the GDP deflator.

Measuring the inflation rate accurately is of crucial importance. It tells us how the value of money is changing, and it affects our assessment of changes in real GDP. A 1 percent upward bias in the estimated inflation rate translates into a 1 percent downward bias in the estimated growth rate of real GDP. A 1 percent a year bias sustained over ten years throws the estimate of real GDP off by more than 10 percent.

How good a measure of inflation is the CPI? Does a 2.7 percent increase in the CPI mean that the cost of living has increased by 2.7 percent? Does a 3 percent increase in the GDP deflator mean that the prices of the goods and services that make up real GDP have increased by 3 percent?

Despite the importance of getting the numbers right, the CPI and the GDP deflator give different views of the inflation rate, and neither index is a perfect measure. Figure 22.5 shows the difference in the two measures. The average inflation rate over the period shown is 4.9 percent a year for the CPI and 4.8 percent a year for the GDP deflator, but the fluctuations in the CPI are greater than the fluctuations in the GDP deflator.

Worse, *both* measures of inflation probably overstate the inflation rate. The main sources of bias in the CPI are:

- New goods bias
- Quality change bias
- Commodity substitution bias
- Outlet substitution bias

New Goods Bias New goods keep replacing old goods. For example, PCs have replaced typewriters. If you want to compare the price level in 1998 with that in 1978, you somehow have to compare the price of a computer today with that of a typewriter in 1978. Because PCs are more expensive than

FIGURE 22.5
Two Measures of Inflation

The CPI and the GDP deflator have similar averages over the period shown here—4.9 percent a year for the CPI and 4.8 percent a year for the GDP deflator—but the CPI fluctuates more than the GDP deflator, and both measures probably overstate the inflation rate.

Source: Statistics Canada, StatCan: CANSIM disc, March 1999.

typewriters, the arrival of these new goods puts an upward bias into the estimate of the price level.

Quality Change Bias Most goods undergo constant quality improvement. Cars, VCRs, computers, CD players, and even textbooks get better year after year. Improvements in quality sometimes bring higher prices. But such price increases are not inflation. For example, suppose that a 1998 car is 5 percent better and costs 5 percent more than a 1995 car. Adjusted for the quality change, the price of the car has been constant. But in calculating the CPI, the price of the car will be counted as having increased by 5 percent.

Commodity Substitution Bias A change in the CPI measures the percentage change in the price of a *fixed* basket of goods and services. But changes in relative prices lead consumers to seek less costly items and to substitute such items in place of items whose prices have increased. For example, if the price of beef rises and the price of chicken remains the same, consumers substitute chicken for beef—they increase their consumption of chicken and decrease their consumption of beef. They might consume the same number of calories, the same amount of protein, and get the same (or very similar) enjoyment from their food. The cost of the protein that people are actually buying has not changed, but the CPI records that it has increased because it does not take such a substitution into account.

Outlet Substitution Bias   People not only change the items they buy when relative prices change. They also change their shopping patterns. With higher prices, people use discount stores more frequently and convenience stores less frequently. This phenomenon is called *outlet substitution*. By being careful to find the least-cost outlets, consumers can cut the prices they pay. And when prices rise, the incentive to seek lower cost outlets increases. The CPI surveys do not monitor the outlet substitutions that people make.

Because of the four sources of bias, the CPI, which is based on a fixed basket, overstates the effects of a given price change on the inflation rate.

The Magnitude of the Bias

How big is the bias in the measurement of the CPI? The answer varies from country to country. In the United States, the bias is believed to range between 1 percent and 2 percent a year. But in Canada, it is believed to be at the most 1 percent a year and probably less than this amount.

To reduce the bias problems, Statistics Canada revises the basket used for calculating the CPI about every 10 years. Also, Statistics Canada tries to estimate the quantitative effects of the various sources of bias and eliminate them by statistical adjustments. It is these adjustments that make Canada's CPI a more reliable measure of the price level than the CPI in the United States is of the U.S. price level.

Is the GDP Deflator Biased?

The GDP deflator is calculated from nominal GDP and real GDP. In principle, real GDP includes new goods and quality improvements. It is also based on people's actual expenditures and so reflects substitutions of both commodities and retail outlets. So in principle, the GDP deflator is not subject to the biases of the CPI. But in practice, the GDP deflator suffers from some of the CPI's problems. To arrive at its estimate of real GDP, Statistics Canada does not directly measure the physical quantities produced. Instead, it estimates quantities by dividing expenditures by price indexes. And one of these price indexes is the CPI. So the biased CPI injects a bias into the GDP deflator.

Some Consequences of the Bias

The bias in the CPI has three main consequences. It

- Distorts private contracts
- Increases government outlays
- Biases estimates of real earnings

Many private agreements, such as wage contracts, are linked to the CPI. For example, a firm and its workers might agree to a three-year wage deal that increases the wage rate by 2 percent a year *plus* the percentage increase in the CPI. Such a deal ends up giving the workers more *real* income than the firm intended.

Close to a third of federal government outlays are linked directly to the CPI. And while a bias of 1 percent a year seems small, accumulated over a decade, it adds up to billions of dollars of additional expenditures.

Trade unions and businesses bargain over wages based in part on changes in the CPI. If the CPI is biased upwards, businesses might agree to wage increases that are larger than they would accept if the CPI was measured accurately.

REVIEW QUIZ

- What are the four main ways in which the CPI is an upward-biased measure of the price level?
- By how much is the CPI estimated to overstate the inflation rate? Is the amount the same in all countries?
- Why might the GDP deflator be a biased measure of the price level?
- What are the main problems that arise from a bias in the measurement of the price level?

Let's now look at limitations of the real GDP data.

The Limitations of Real GDP

ESTIMATES OF REAL GDP AND THE REAL GDP growth rate are used for three main purposes:

- Economic welfare comparisons
- International comparisons of GDP
- Business cycle assessment and forecasting

Although real GDP is used for these three purposes, it is not a perfect measure for any of them. We'll look at how real GDP is used and its limitations in each of the three cases.

Economic Welfare Comparisons

Economic welfare is a comprehensive measure of the general state of economic well-being. Real GDP growth is one indicator of an improvement in economic welfare. Today, with GDP per person in Canada of about $27,000, we are much better off than we were in 1960, when GDP per person (expressed in today's dollars) was $12,300. But are we more than twice as well off? Does real GDP give us a full and accurate measure of economic welfare? It does not. The reason is that economic welfare depends on many other factors that are not measured by real GDP (or that are not measured accurately by real GDP). Some of these factors are:

- Overadjustment for inflation
- Household production
- Underground economic activity
- Health and life expectancy
- Leisure time
- Environment quality
- Political freedom and social justice

Overadjustment for Inflation You've seen that the price indexes used to measure inflation give an upward-biased estimate of true inflation. They give a downward-biased estimate of the growth rate of real GDP. When car prices rise because cars have become better (safer, more fuel efficient, more comfortable), the CPI and the GDP deflator count the price increase as inflation. So what is really an increase in production is counted as an increase in price. The increase in real GDP is deflated away by the incorrectly measured higher price level. The magnitude of

this bias is less than the bias in the CPI (less than one-percentage point a year), but its exact magnitude is not known.

Household Production An enormous amount of production takes place every day in our homes. Changing a light bulb, cutting the grass, washing the car, and teaching a child to read are all examples of household production. These activities do not involve market transactions and are excluded from GDP.

Household production has become more capital intensive over the years. For example, a microwave meal that takes just a few minutes to prepare uses a great deal of capital and almost no labour. Because we use less labour and more capital in household production, it is not easy to work out whether household production has increased or decreased over time. But it is likely that market production counted in GDP has increasingly replaced household production. Two trends point in this direction. One is the trend in the number of people who hold jobs, which has increased from 58 percent in 1970 to 65 percent in 1998. The other is the trend in the purchase of traditionally home-produced goods and services in the market. For example, more and more families now eat in fast-food restaurants—one of the fastest-growing industries in Canada—and use day-care services. This trend means that an increasing proportion of food preparation and child care that used to be part of household production are now measured as part of GDP.

Statistics Canada is now attempting to estimate the value of some household production in its monthly Labour Force Survey.

Underground Economic Activity The *underground economy* is the part of the economy that is purposely hidden from the view of the government in order to avoid taxes and regulations or because the goods and services being produced are illegal. Because underground economic activity is unreported, it is omitted from GDP.

The underground economy is easy to describe, even if it is hard to measure. It includes the production and distribution of illegal drugs, production that uses illegal labour that is paid less than the minimum wage, and jobs done for cash to avoid paying income taxes. This last category might be quite large and includes tips earned by cab drivers, hairdressers, and hotel and restaurant workers.

Estimates of the scale of the underground economy range between 5 and 15 percent of GDP ($40 billion to $130 billion) in Canada and much more in some countries. It is particularly large in some Eastern European countries that are making a transition from communist economic planning to a market economy.

Provided that the underground economy is a reasonably stable proportion of the total economy, the growth rate of real GDP still gives a useful estimate of changes in economic welfare. But sometimes, production shifts from the underground to the rest of the economy, and sometimes it shifts the other way. The underground economy expands relative to the rest of the economy if taxes become especially high or if regulations become especially restrictive. And the underground economy shrinks relative to the rest of the economy if the burdens of taxes and regulations are eased. During the 1980s, when tax rates were cut, there was an increase in the reporting of previously hidden income, and tax revenues increased. So some part (but probably a very small part) of the expansion of real GDP during the 1980s represented a shift from the underground economy rather than an increase in production.

Health and Life Expectancy   Good health and a long life—the hopes of everyone—do not show up in real GDP, at least not directly. A higher real GDP does enable us to spend more on medical research, health care, a good diet, and exercise equipment. And as real GDP has increased, our life expectancy has lengthened—from 70 years at the end of World War II to approaching 80 years today. Infant deaths and death in childbirth, two fearful scourges of the nineteenth century, have almost been eliminated.

But we face new health and life expectancy problems every year. AIDS and drug abuse are taking young lives at a rate that causes serious concern. When we take these negative influences into account, we see that real GDP growth overstates the improvements in economic welfare.

Leisure Time   Leisure time is an economic good that adds to our economic welfare. Other things remaining the same, the more leisure we have, the better off we are. Our time spent working is valued as part of GDP, but our leisure time is not. Yet from the point of view of economic welfare, that leisure time must be at least as valuable to us as the wage that we earn on the last hour worked. If it was not, we would work instead of taking the leisure. Over the years, leisure time has steadily increased. The workweek has become shorter, more people take early retirement, and the number of vacation days has increased.

These improvements in economic wellbeing are not reflected in GDP.

Environment Quality   The quality of the environment is directly affected by economic activity. The burning of hydrocarbon fuels is the most visible activity that damages our environment. But it is not the only example. The depletion of exhaustible resources, the mass clearing of forests, and the pollution of lakes and rivers are other major environmental consequences of industrial production.

Resources that are used to protect the environment are valued as part of GDP. For example, the value of catalytic converters that help to protect the atmosphere from automobile emissions are part of GDP. But if we did not use such pieces of equipment and instead polluted the atmosphere, we would not count the deteriorating air that we were breathing as a negative part of GDP.

An industrial society possibly produces more atmospheric pollution than an agricultural society does. But such pollution does not always increase as we become wealthier. One of the things that wealthy people value is a clean environment, and they devote resources to protecting it. Compare the pollution that was discovered in East Germany in the late 1980s with pollution in Canada. East Germany, a relatively poor country, polluted its rivers, lakes, and atmosphere in a way that is unimaginable in Canada or in wealthy West Germany.

Political Freedom and Social Justice   Most people value political freedoms such as those provided by the Charter of Human Rights and the Constitution of Canada. And they value social justice or fairness—equality of opportunity and of access to social security safety nets that protect people from the extremes of misfortune.

A country might have a very large real GDP per person but have limited political freedom and equity. For example, a small elite might enjoy political liberty and extreme wealth while the vast majority are effectively enslaved and live in abject poverty. Such an economy would generally be regarded as having less economic welfare than one that had the same amount of real GDP but in which everyone enjoyed political freedoms. During the 1990s, China has had rapid real GDP growth but limited political freedoms, while Russia has had decreasing real GDP and an emerging democratic political system. Economists have no easy way to determine which of these countries is better off.

The Bottom Line   Do we get the wrong message about changes (or differences) in economic welfare by looking at changes (or differences) in real GDP? The influences omitted from real GDP are probably important and could be large. Developing countries have a larger underground economy and a larger amount of household production than do developed countries. So as an economy develops and grows, part of the apparent growth might reflect a switch from underground to regular production and from home production to market production. This measurement error overstates the rate of economic growth and the improvement in economic welfare.

Other influences on living standards include the amount of leisure time available, the quality of the environment, the security of jobs and homes, the safety of city streets, and so on. It is possible to construct broader measures that combine the many influences that contribute to human happiness. Real GDP will be one element in those broader measures, but it will by no means be the whole of them.

International Comparisons of GDP

All the problems we've just reviewed affect the economic welfare in every country, so to make international comparisons of economic welfare, factors additional to real GDP must be used. But real GDP comparisons are major components of international welfare comparisons and two special problems arise in making these comparisons. First, the real GDP of one country must be converted into the same currency units as the real GDP of the other country. Second, the same prices must be used to value the goods and services in the countries being compared. Let's look at these two problems by using a striking example, a comparison of China and Canada.

In 1992 (the most recent year for which we can make this comparison), real GDP per person in Canada was $25,453. The official Chinese statistics published by the International Monetary Fund (IMF) say that real GDP per person in China in 1992 was 2,028 yuan. (The yuan is the currency of China.) On the average, during 1992, a Canadian dollar was worth 4.768 yuan. If we use this exchange rate to convert Chinese yuan into dollars, we get a value of $425.

The official comparison of China and Canada makes China look extremely poor. In 1992, real GDP per person in Canada was 60 times that in China.

Figure 22.6 shows the official story of real GDP

FIGURE 22.6
Two Views of Real GDP in China

According to the official statistics of the International Monetary Fund (IMF) and the World Bank, China is a poor developing country. But according to an alternative view, Penn World Table (PWT), which is based on purchasing power prices, China has a real GDP more than 6 times the official view and has the world's third largest total production.

Sources: International Financial Statistics Yearbook, 1994, IMF, Washington, D.C.; World Development Report, 1994, World Bank, Washington, D.C.; "The Penn World Table (Mark 5.5): An Expanded Set of International Comparisons, 1950–1988," Quarterly Journal of Economics, May 1991, pp. 327–368; new computer diskette, Mark 5.5, June 15, 1993; and the authors' calculations.

---

in China between 1980 and 1998. But the figure also shows another story. It shows an estimate of real GDP per person in China that is much larger than the official measure. Let's see how this alternative measurement is made.

GDP in Canada is measured by using prices that prevail in Canada. China's GDP is measured by using prices that prevail in China. But the relative prices in the two countries are very different. Some goods that are expensive in Canada cost very little in China. These items get a small weight in China's real GDP. If, instead of using Canada's prices and China's prices, all the goods and services produced in Canada and China are valued at the same prices, we can make a more valid comparison of GDP in the two countries. Such a comparison uses prices called *purchasing power parity prices*.

Robert Summers and Alan Heston, economists in the Center for International Comparisons at the University of Pennsylvania, have used purchasing power parity prices to construct real GDP data for more than 100 countries. These data, which are published in the Penn World Table (PWT), tell a remarkable story about China.

The PWT data use 1985 as the base year and they use U.S. dollars, so they are measured in 1985 U.S. dollars. According to the Penn World Table, in 1992, real GDP per person was U.S.$16,362 in Canada. Real GDP per person was U.S.$1,493 in China. So, according to the PWT estimates, Canada's real GDP per person is 11 times that of China, not the 60 times shown in the official data.

Figure 22.6 shows the PWT view of China and compares it with the official view. The difference in the two views arises from the prices used. The official statistics use Chinese prices, while the PWT data use purchasing power parity prices.

Despite large differences in estimates of the level of China's real GDP, there is much less doubt about its growth rate. The economy of China is expanding at an extraordinary rate and it is for this reason that most businesses are paying a great deal of attention to the prospects of expanding their activities in China and the other Asian economies.

Canada's real GDP is measured quite reliably. But China's is not. So both of the alternative measures of China's real GDP are somewhat unreliable, and the truth about real GDP in China is not known.

Business Cycle Assessment and Forecasting

When the Bank of Canada decides to raise interest rates to slow an expansion that it believes is too strong, it looks at the latest estimates of real GDP and inflation. But we've seen that the inflation rate is biased. Does this bias hamper our ability to isolate the phases of the business cycle? It does not. The reason is that the bias in the CPI does not change over the business cycle. The CPI is inaccurate by a similar amount every year. So while inflation mismeasurement leads to wrong estimates of long-term real GDP growth, it does not cause a wrong assessment of the phase of the business cycle.

The fluctuations in economic activity measured by real GDP tell a reasonably accurate story about the phase of the business cycle that the economy is in. When real GDP grows, the economy is in a business cycle expansion; when real GDP shrinks (for two quarters), the economy is in a recession. Also, as real GDP fluctuates, so do employment and unemployment.

But real GDP fluctuations probably exaggerate or overstate the fluctuations in total production and economic welfare. The reason is that when business activity slows down in a recession, household production increases and so does leisure time. When business activity speeds up in an expansion, household production and leisure time decrease. Because household production and leisure time increase in a recession and decrease in an expansion, real GDP fluctuations tend to overstate the fluctuations in total production and in economic welfare. But the directions of change of real GDP, total production, and economic welfare are probably the same.

R E V I E W   Q U I Z

- Does real GDP measure economic welfare? If not, why not?
- Does real GDP measure total production of goods and services? If not, what are the main omissions?
- How can we make valid international comparisons of real GDP?
- Is the growth of real GDP a good measure of the growth of real economic activity?
- Do the fluctuations in real GDP measure the business cycle accurately? If not, why not?

◆ In Chapter 21 you studied the macroeconomic performance of Canada in recent years—the growth and fluctuations in real GDP, unemployment, inflation, and deficits. In this chapter, you have studied the methods used to measure the growth and fluctuations in real GDP and inflation.

Reading Between the Lines on pp. 494-495, applies one aspect of what you've learned in this chapter and explores the behaviour of the Canadian Consumer Price Index (CPI) during 1998. It also explains a common confusion that you'll frequently come across in the media. Study this feature before moving on to the next topic.

Our goal is to *explain* why real GDP grows and fluctuates and why inflation sometimes occurs. But before we begin this task, we study another aspect of macroeconomic measurement in the next chapter. We learn about a monthly survey of the labour market that tells us how Canadians allocate their time and how many people are employed and unemployed.

Inflation and the Consumer Price Index

VANCOUVER SUN, JUNE 20, 1998

Consensus absent on inflation impact

Inflation jumped to its highest level this year in May, but analysts can't agree on whether to blame the Asian crisis or credit it with keeping prices from rising even further.

They also disagree on whether the 0.3-point increase in consumer prices last month, which pushed the annual inflation rate to 1.1 per cent from 0.8 in April, will worry the Bank of Canada enough to start thinking again about increasing interest rates.

B.C. had the third-lowest inflation rate in Canada with an annual rate of just 0.3 per cent from May 1997 to May 1998.

Statistics Canada attributed B.C.'s low inflation to decreases in the price of new houses, mortgage interest costs and homeowner insurance rates. ...

(Scotiabank economist Randall)

Powley noted that prices for women's clothing have now fallen for two consecutive months.

"This has to be a reflection of lower Asian sourcing costs and heavy competition in the industry, since sales are relatively strong," he said. ...

Statistics Canada said higher hotel charges, in part due to the flood of Americans being lured here by the low dollar, and to a lesser extent due to higher prices for gasoline, fresh fruit and natural gas, pushed up its consumer price index during the month.

Lower prices for women's clothing, bakery products and transportation charges partially offset that upward push on the price index, composed of a basket of hundreds of commonly purchased goods and services.

Essence of the Story

■ The annual inflation rate in May 1998 was 1.1 percent, up from 0.8 percent in April.

■ Between May 1997 and May 1998, prices of women's clothing, bakery products, and transportation decreased and prices of hotel accommodation, gasoline, fresh fruit, and natural gas increased.

■ Scotiabank economist Randall Powley says that the fall in prices of women's clothing is attributable to lower costs in Asia.

■ British Columbia had the third-lowest inflation rate in Canada during May 1998.

Economic Analysis

- The Consumer Price Index (CPI) is reported each month by Statistics Canada.

- The CPI is obtained by comparing the price of a fixed basket of commodities purchased by Canadians over different time periods.

- The fixed basket includes food, shelter, household operations and furnishings, clothing and footwear, transportation, health and personal care, recreation, education and reading, and alcoholic beverages and tobacco products.

- Figure 1 shows the CPI for each month from January 1997 through May 1998.

- In April 1997, the CPI was 107.4, and in April 1998, it was 108.3.

- The inflation rate between April 1997 and April 1998 was 0.8 percent. This inflation rate equals

$$\frac{108.3 - 107.4}{107.4} \times 100 \ .$$

- In May 1997, the CPI was 107.5, and in May 1998, it was 108.7.

- The inflation rate between May 1997 and May 1998 was 1.1 percent. This inflation rate equals

$$\frac{108.7 - 107.5}{107.5} \times 100 \ .$$

- So the inflation rate increased from 0.8 percent in April to 1.1 percent in May.

- Figure 2 shows the percentage changes in the CPI for each month from January to May 1998 compared with the same month in 1997. The inflation rate decreased in February, March, and April and increased in May.

- Statistics Canada also reports a monthly index for each component of the CPI basket.

- Figure 3 shows the percentage changes in each component of the CPI basket between May 1997 and May 1998.

- These price changes tell us about *relative prices*. They do not tell us anything about inflation. Nor do they tell us *why* the inflation rate changed.

- It is a common mistake in the media to say that the inflation rate increased (or decreased) *because* a particular price increased (or decreased).

- The prices of women's clothing might have decreased because of the Asian crisis, as claimed in the article. But this change in relative prices provides no information about why the inflation rate changed.

Figure 1 Consumer Price Index

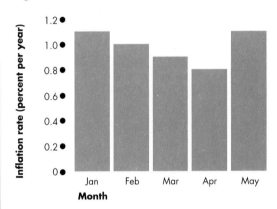

Figure 2 Inflation in 1998

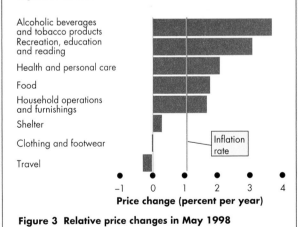

Figure 3 Relative price changes in May 1998

- Each month, Statistics Canada also reports a CPI for each province.

- In May 1997, the CPI for British Columbia was 110.0, and in May 1998, it was 110.3—an inflation rate of 0.3 percent a year.

495

S U M M A R Y

Key Points

Gross Domestic Product (pp. 476–481)

▨ Gross domestic product (GDP) is the value of total production in a country during a given period.

▨ GDP is calculated by using the circular flow of income and expenditure.

▨ Aggregate expenditure on goods and services equals aggregate income and GDP.

Measuring Canadian GDP (pp. 481–484)

▨ Because aggregate expenditure, aggregate income, and the value of aggregate production are equal, we can measure GDP by using the expenditure approach or the income approach.

▨ The expenditure approach sums consumption expenditure, investment, government expenditures on goods and services, and net exports.

▨ The income approach sums wages, interest, rent, and profit (and indirect taxes and depreciation).

The Price Level, Inflation, and Real GDP (pp. 485–487)

▨ Inflation is measured by the rate of change of the CPI or the GDP deflator.

▨ The price level is measured by the Consumer Price Index (CPI) and the GDP deflator.

▨ The CPI is based on the price of goods and services typically consumed by Canadian families.

▨ The GDP deflator is based on the prices of all the goods and services that make up GDP.

The Biased CPI (pp. 488–489)

▨ The CPI gives an upward-biased measure of inflation because some goods disappear and new goods become available, and the quality of goods and services change over time.

▨ The CPI is further biased because it ignores the fact that as relative prices change, consumers substitute less expensive items for more expensive items.

▨ Attempts are being made to limit the CPI bias.

The Limitations of Real GDP (pp. 490–493)

▨ Real GDP is not a perfect measure of aggregate production or economic welfare because it excludes quality improvements, household production, the underground economy, environmental damage, health and life expectancy, leisure time, political freedom, and social justice.

▨ The growth rate of real GDP gives a good indication of the phases of the business cycle.

Key Figures and Tables

Key Terms

PROBLEMS

*1. Martha owns a copy shop that has 5 copiers. One copier wears out each year and is replaced. In addition, this year Martha will expand her business to 7 copiers. Calculate Martha's initial capital stock, depreciation, gross investment, net investment, and final capital stock.

2. Wendy operates a weaving shop with 10 looms. One loom wears out each year and is replaced. But this year, Wendy will expand her business to 12 looms. Calculate Wendy's initial capital stock, depreciation, gross investment, net investment, and final capital stock.

*3. The figure at the bottom of the page shows the flows of income and expenditure on Lotus Island. During 1997: *A* was $10 million; *B* was $30 million: *C* was $12 million; *D* was $15 million; and *E* was $3 million.

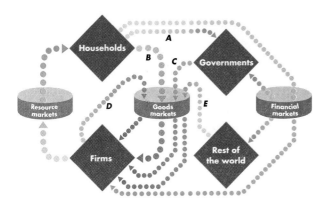

Calculate
a. Aggregate expenditure
b. Aggregate income
c. GDP
d. Government budget deficit
e. Household saving
f. Government saving
g. Foreign borrowing
h. National saving

4. In problem 3, during 1998: *A* was $10 million; *B* was $50 million: *C* was $15 million; *D* was $15 million; and *E* was –$5 million. Calculate the quantities in problem 3 during 1998.

*5. The transactions in Ecoland last year were:

Item	Dollars
Wages paid to labour	800,000
Consumption expenditure	600,000
Taxes	250,000
Transfer payments	50,000
Profits	200,000
Investment	250,000
Government expenditures	200,000
Exports	300,000
Saving	300,000
Imports	250,000

a. Calculate Ecoland's GDP.
b. Did you use the expenditure approach or the income approach to make this calculation?
c. Do injections equal leakages?

6. The transactions in Highland last year were:

Item	Dollars
Wages paid to labour	800,000
Consumption expenditure	650,000
Net taxes	200,000
Profits	250,000
Investment	300,000
Government expenditures	250,000
Exports	250,000
Saving	300,000
Imports	300,000

a. Calculate Highland's GDP.
b. What extra information do you need in order to calculate net domestic product?
c. Where does Highland get the funds to finance its investment?

*7. A typical family on Sandy Island consumes only juice and cloth. Last year, which was the base year, the family spent $40 on juice and $25 on cloth. In the base year, juice was $4 a bottle and cloth was $5 a length. In the current year, juice is $4 a bottle and cloth is $6 a length. Calculate
a. The basket used in the CPI.
b. The CPI in the current year.
c. The inflation rate in the current year.

8. A typical family on Lizard Island consumes only mangoes and nuts. Last year, which was the base year, the family spent $60 on nuts and $10 on mangoes. In the base year, mangoes were $1 each and nuts were $3 a bag. In the current year, mangoes are $1.50 each and nuts are $4 a bag. Calculate
   a. The basket used in the CPI
   b. The CPI in the current year
   c. The inflation rate in the current year

*9. Bananaland produces only bananas and sunscreen. The base year is 1997 and the tables give the quantities produced and the prices.

	Quantity	
Good	1997	1998
Bananas	1,000 bunches	1,100 bunches
Sunscreen	500 bottles	525 bottles

	Price	
Good	1997	1998
Bananas	$2 a bunch	$3 a bunch
Sunscreen	$10 a bottle	$8 a bottle

Calculate Bananaland's
a. GDP and real GDP in 1997 and 1998
b. Growth rate of real GDP in 1998
c. GDP deflator in 1998

10. Sea Island produces only lobsters and crabs. The base year is 1997 and the tables give the quantities produced and the prices.

	Quantity	
Good	1997	1998
Lobsters	1,000	1,100
Crabs	500	525

	Price	
Good	1997	1998
Lobsters	$20 each	$25 each
Crabs	$10 each	$12 each

Calculate Sea Island's
a. GDP and real GDP in 1997 and 1998
b. Growth rate of real GDP in 1998
c. GDP deflator in 1998

CRITICAL THINKING

1. Study *Reading Between the Lines* on pp. 494-495 and answer the following questions:
   a. Between January 1997 and May 1998, which month experienced the greatest change in the inflation rate?
   b. In May 1998, which items in the CPI basket had increasing prices? Which items in the CPI basket had decreasing prices?
   c. Think about different types of families: a single mother with a child, a single father with a child, a married couple with a child, and a married couple with no children. Do you think they will all be affected in the same way by inflation? Why or why not? [Hint: distinguish between inflation and relative price changes.]

2. Use the links on the Parkin-Bade Web site to obtain current data from the Statistics Canada Web site on the inflation rate measured by the CPI for Canada and for your province.
   a. Which items in the CPI basket have increasing prices and which items have decreasing prices?
   b. Draw a bar graph showing the change in current prices in your province for the categories composing the CPI.

3. Use the links on the Parkin-Bade Web site to obtain data for the two most recent years on real GDP, nominal GDP, and the GDP deflator.
   a. What was real GDP in the most recent year?
   b. What was real GDP in the previous year?
   c. What is the real GDP growth rate between these two years?
   d. What was nominal GDP in the most recent year?
   e. What was nominal GDP in the previous year?
   f. What was the GDP deflator in the most recent year?
   g. What was the GDP deflator in the previous year?
   h. Check that, for the data you have obtained, nominal GDP divided by real GDP equals the GDP deflator.
   i. What is the inflation rate as measured by the GDP deflator between these two years?

Measuring Employment and Unemployment

Vital Signs

Each month, we chart the course of the Canadian unemployment rate as a measure of economic health. How do we measure unemployment? What does it tell us? Is it a reliable vital sign for the economy? ◆ July 1993 was a month in which unemployment peaked at almost 1.7 million. How can such a large number of people be unemployed? How do people become unemployed? Do most of them get fired, or do most quit their jobs to look for better ones? How long do spells of unemployment last for most people—a week, two weeks, or several months? And how does the average length of unemployment spells vary over the business cycle? ◆ You probably know that unemployment is more common among young people than older people. Why don't all age groups share unemployment more equally? ◆ Each month, we also chart the number of people working. This number fluctuates as the unemployment rate fluctuates, but it also trends upward. In 1998, 14 million people in Canada had jobs. What does this vital sign tell us about the health of the Canadian economy? Does the number of jobs grow quickly enough to keep pace with increases in the population? ◆ Yet other signs of economic health are the hours people work and the wages they receive. Are work hours growing as quickly as the number of people with jobs? Are most of the new jobs full time or part time? Also, are most new jobs high-wage or low-wage jobs?

◇ These are the questions we study in this chapter. You will discover that a lot of ideas that people have about the Canadian labour market are just plain wrong. The economy has created millions of jobs and good jobs that pay high wages and provide good benefits. But most people have seen a slowdown in their rate of wage increase, and many have seen their wages fall. We begin by looking at the key labour market indicators and the way they are measured.

After studying this chapter, you will be able to:

- ■ Define the unemployment rate, the involuntary part-time rate, the labour force participation rate, the employment-to-population ratio, and aggregate hours

- ■ Describe the trends and fluctuations in the indicators of labour market performance

- ■ Describe the sources of unemployment, its duration, and the groups that are most affected by it

- ■ Describe the relationship between employment, unemployment, and real GDP

Employment and Wages

FOR MOST OF US, THE LABOUR MARKET IS THE source of almost all our income. We become concerned when jobs are hard to find. And we become more relaxed when jobs are plentiful. We also care about the kinds of jobs that are available. We want good jobs, which means we want well-paid and interesting jobs. In this chapter, we study the way that economists track the health of the labour market.

Population Survey

Every month, Statistics Canada surveys 59,000 households and asks questions about the age and job market status of its members. This survey is called the Labour Force Survey. Statistics Canada uses the answers to describe the anatomy of the labour force. This monthly report is a major source of information on the state of the economy.

Figure 23.1 shows the population categories used by Statistics Canada and the relationships among the categories. It divides the population into two groups: the working-age population and others who are too young to work. The **working-age population** is the total number of people aged 15 years and over. Statistics Canada divides the working-age population into two groups: those in the labour force and those not in the labour force. It also divides the labour force into two groups: the employed and the unemployed. So the **labour force** is the sum of the employed and the unemployed.

To be counted as employed in the Labour Force Survey, a person must have either a full-time job or a part-time job. To be counted as *un*employed, a person must be available for work and must be:

1. Without work, but actually looked for work within the previous four weeks
2. Waiting to be called back to a job from which he or she has been laid off
3. Waiting to start a new job within four weeks

Anyone surveyed who satisfies one of these three criteria is counted as unemployed. People in the working-age population who are neither employed nor unemployed are classified as not in the labour force.

In 1998, the population of Canada was 30 million. Six million people were under 15 years of age and the working-age population was 24 million. Of

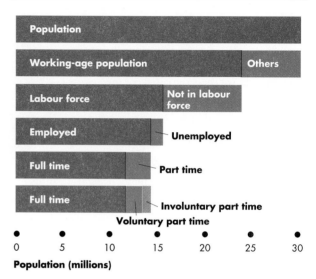

FIGURE 23.1

Population Labour Force Categories

Population (millions)

The population is divided into the working-age population and young people. The working-age population is divided into the labour force and those not in the labour force. The labour force is divided into those employed and those unemployed. The people employed are divided into those with full-time jobs and those with part-time jobs. And part-time workers are divided into voluntary and involuntary part-time workers.

Source: Statistics Canada, *StatCan: CANSIM Disc*, March 1999.

this number, 8.4 million were not in the labour force. These people were in full-time school or had chosen not to be in the labour force. The remaining 15.6 million people made up the Canadian labour force. Of these, 14.3 million were employed, 11.6 million full-time and 2.7 million part-time workers (850,000 involuntarily) and 1.3 million were unemployed.

Four Labour Market Indicators

Statistics Canada calculates four indicators of the state of the labour market:

■ The unemployment rate
■ The involuntary part-time rate
■ The labour force participation rate
■ The employment-to-population ratio

The Unemployment Rate   The amount of unemployment is an indicator of the extent to which people who want jobs can't find them. The **unemployment rate** is the percentage of the people in the labour force who are unemployed. That is,

$$\text{Unemployment rate} = \frac{\text{Number of people unemployed}}{\text{Labour force}} \times 100$$

and

Labour force = Number of people employed + Number of people unemployed.

In 1998, the number of people employed was 14.3 million and the number unemployed was 1.3 million. By using the above equations, you can verify that the labour force was 15.6 million (14.3 million plus 1.3 million) and the unemployment rate was 8.4 percent.

Figure 23.2 shows the unemployment rate (orange line) and three other labour market indicators between 1960 and 1998. The average unemployment rate has been 7.7 percent, and it reached peak values during the recessions of 1982 and 1990–1991.

The Involuntary Part-Time Rate   Part-time workers who want full-time work do not get counted as part of unemployment. To measure the extent of this type of underemployment, Statistics Canada counts the number of *involuntary part-time workers*— part-time workers who want full-time jobs. The **involuntary part-time rate** is the percentage of the people in the labour force who have part-time jobs and want full-time jobs. That is,

$$\text{Involuntary part-time rate} = \frac{\text{Number of involuntary part-time workers}}{\text{Labour force}} \times 100.$$

In 1998, the number of involuntary part-time workers was 850,000, the labour force was 15.6 million, and the involuntary part-time rate was 5.4 percent.

Figure 23.2 shows the involuntary part-time rate (plotted on the right-hand scale) from 1976 to 1995 and then a new definition after 1997. You can see that an increasing percentage of the labour force that wants full-time work is not able to get full-time work. You can also see that the fluctuations in the involuntary part-time rate are like those in the unemployment rate.

FIGURE 23.2

Employment, Unemployment, and the Labour Force: 1960–1998

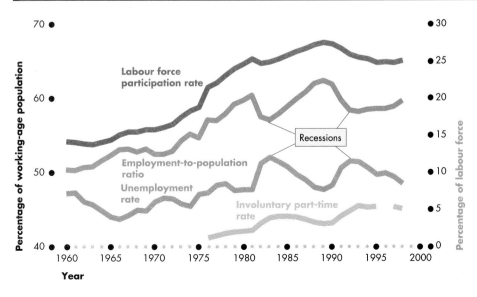

The unemployment rate and the involuntary part-time rate increase in recessions and decrease in expansions. The labour force participation rate and the employment-to-population ratio have upward trends and fluctuate with the business cycle. The employment-to-population ratio fluctuates and reflects cyclical fluctuations in the unemployment rate. The labour force participation rate fluctuates mainly because the number of discouraged workers fluctuates.

Source: Statistics Canada, *StatCan: CANSIM Disc*, March 1999.

The Labour Force Participation Rate   The number of people who join the labour force is an indicator of the willingness of people of working age to take jobs. The **labour force participation rate** is the percentage of working-age population who are members of the labour force. That is,

$$\text{Labour force participation rate} = \frac{\text{Labour force}}{\text{Working-age population}} \times 100.$$

In 1998, the labour force was 15.6 million and the working-age population was 24 million. By using the above equation, you can calculate the labour force participation rate. It was 65.2 percent—15.6 million divided by 24 million, multiplied by 100.

The labour force participation rate (graphed in red and plotted on the left scale) has followed an upward trend and has increased from 55 percent during the early 1960s to 65 percent during the 1990s. It has also had some mild fluctuations. They result from unsuccessful job seekers becoming discouraged workers. **Discouraged workers** are people who are available and willing to work, but have not made specific efforts to find a job within the previous four weeks. These workers often temporarily leave the labour force during a recession and re-enter during an expansion and become active job seekers.

The Employment-to-Population Ratio   The number of people of working age who have jobs is an indicator of both the availability of jobs and the degree of match between people's skills and jobs. The **employment-to-population ratio** is the percentage of people of working age who have jobs. That is,

$$\text{Employment-to-population ratio} = \frac{\text{Number of people employed}}{\text{Working-age population}} \times 100.$$

In 1998, employment was 14.3 million and the working-age population was 24 million. By using the above equation, you can calculate the employment-to-population ratio. It was 59.7 percent—14.3 million divided by 24 million, multiplied by 100.

The employment-to-population ratio (graphed in blue and plotted against the left scale) has increased from 50 percent during the early 1960s to almost 60 percent during the 1990s. The increase in the employment-to-population ratio means that the Canadian economy has created jobs at a faster rate than the working-age population has grown. This

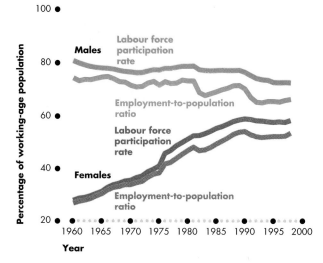

FIGURE   23.3

The Changing Face of the Labour Market

The upward trends in the labour force participation rate and the employment-to-population ratio are accounted for mainly by the increasing participation of women in the labour market. The male labour force participation rate and employment-to-population ratio have decreased.

Source: Statistics Canada, *StatCan: CANSIM Disc*, March 1999.

labour market indicator also fluctuates, and its fluctuations coincide with but are opposite to those in the unemployment rate. It falls during a recession and increases during an expansion.

Why have the labour force participation rate and the employment-to-population ratio increased? The main reason is an increase in the number of women in the labour force. Figure 23.3 shows this increase. Between 1960 and 1998, the female labour force participation rate increased from 27 percent to 52 percent. Shorter work hours, higher productivity, and an increased emphasis on white-collar jobs have expanded the job opportunities and wages available to women. At the same time, technological advances have increased productivity in the home and freed up women's time to take jobs outside the home.

Figure 23.3 also shows another remarkable trend in the Canadian labour force: The labour force participation rate and the employment-to-population ratio for men have *decreased*. Between 1960 and 1998, the male labour force participation rate decreased from 81 percent to 73 percent. It decreased because increasing numbers of men are remaining in school longer, working as homemakers, or retiring earlier.

Aggregate Hours

The four labour market indicators that we've just examined are useful signs of the health of the economy and directly measure what matters to most people: jobs. But they don't tell us the quantity of labour used to produce GDP and we cannot use them to calculate the productivity of labour. The productivity of labour is significant because it influences the wages that people earn.

The reason why the number of people employed does not measure the quantity of labour employed is that jobs are not all the same. People in part-time jobs might work just a few hours a week. People in full-time jobs work around 35 to 40 hours a week. And some people regularly work overtime. For example, a 7-11 convenience store might hire six students who work for three hours a day each. Another 7-11 store might hire two full-time workers who work nine hours a day each. The number of people employed in these two stores is eight, but the total hours worked by six of the eight is the same as the total hours worked by the other two. To determine the total amount of labour used to produce GDP, we measure labour in hours rather than in jobs. **Aggregate hours** are the total number of hours worked by all the people employed, both full time and part time, during a year.

Figure 23.4(a) shows aggregate hours in the Canadian economy from 1960 to 1998. Like the employment-to-population ratio, aggregate hours have an upward trend. But aggregate hours have not grown as quickly as have the number of people employed. Between 1960 and 1998, the number of people employed in the Canadian economy increased by 127 percent. During that same period, aggregate hours increased by only 93 percent. Why the difference? Because average hours per worker decreased.

Figure 23.4(b) shows average hours per worker. After hovering at almost 40 hours a week during the early 1960s, average hours per worker decreased to 34.5 hours a week during the 1990s. This shortening of the average workweek has arisen partly because the average hours worked by full-time workers decreased but mainly because the number of part-time jobs increased faster than the number of full-time jobs.

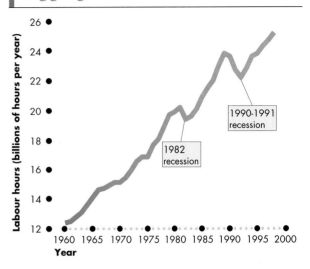

FIGURE 23.4

Aggregate Hours: 1960–1998

(a) Aggregate hours

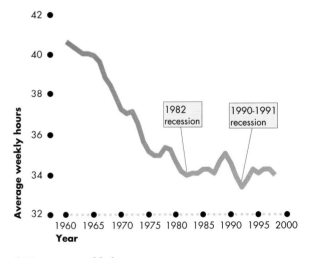

(b) Average weekly hours per person

Aggregate hours (part a) measure the total labour used to produce real GDP more accurately than does the number of people employed because an increasing proportion of jobs are part time. Between 1960 and 1998, aggregate hours increased by an average of almost 2 percent a year. Fluctuations in aggregate hours coincide with business cycle fluctuations. Aggregate hours have increased at a slower rate than the number of jobs because the average workweek has shortened (part b).

Source: Statistics Canada, *StatCan: CANSIM Disc*, March 1999, and the authors' calculations.

Fluctuations in aggregate hours and average hours per worker line up with the business cycle. Figure 23.4 highlights the past two recessions, during which aggregate hours decreased and average hours per worker decreased more quickly than their trend rate of decrease.

Wage Rates

The **real wage rate** is the quantity of goods and services that an hour's work can buy. It is equal to the money wage rate (dollars per hour) divided by the price level. The real wage is a significant economic variable because it measures the reward for labour. Figure 23.5 shows the broadest measure of the average hourly real wage rate in the Canadian economy.

The money wage rate is calculated from the national income accounts and aggregate hours. We know from the income side of the national income accounts the total amount of labour income. This total includes wages and salaries and all forms of supplementary labour income such as health and insurance benefits. It includes all labour income and not just that of people who are paid by the hour.

If we divide this total by aggregate hours, we arrive at an estimate of the economy-wide average money wage rate. This average includes all types of labour in all parts of the economy.

To calculate the real wage rate, we divide the money wage rate by the GDP deflator. Because the GDP deflator has a base of 100 in 1992, the real wage rate is expressed in 1992 dollars.

The real wage rate follows an upward path. But the trend growth rate slowed during the 1970s and early 1980s in the *productivity growth slowdown* that you saw in Chapter 21. This productivity slowdown is the main reason for this behaviour of average real wage rates.

The average real wage rate usually increases but you can see in Fig. 23.5 that it sometimes decreases. The real wage rate decreased during the late 1970s. And it decreased again during the 1990s.

FIGURE 23.5

Real Wage Rates: 1962–1998

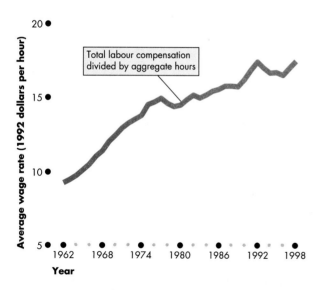

The average hourly real wage rate follows an upward trend. But the trend growth rate of real wages slowed during the 1970s. Occasionally, the real wage rate falls, as it did in the late 1970s and early 1990s.

Source: Statistics Canada, *StatCan: CANSIM Disc*, March 1999, and the authors' calculations and assumptions.

REVIEW QUIZ

- What are the trends in the unemployment rate, the involuntary part-time rate, the labour force participation rate, and the employment-to-population ratio?
- How do the unemployment rate, the involuntary part-time rate, the labour force participation rate, and the employment-to-population ratio fluctuate over the business cycle?
- Has the female labour force participation rate been similar to or different from the male labour force participation rate?
- How have aggregate hours changed?
- How have average hourly real wage rates changed since 1970?

Potential GDP depends on the full-employment quantity of labour. But at full employment, there is always some unemployment. Let's take a closer look at unemployment and see why it never disappears, even at full employment.

Unemployment and Full Employment

HOW DO PEOPLE BECOME UNEMPLOYED, HOW long do they remain unemployed, and who has the greatest risk of becoming unemployed? Let's answer these questions by looking at the anatomy of unemployment.

The Anatomy of Unemployment

People become unemployed if they:

1. Lose their jobs and search for another job
2. Leave their jobs and search for another job
3. Enter or re-enter the labour force to search for a job

People end a spell of unemployment if they:

1. Are hired or recalled
2. Withdraw from the labour force

People who are laid off, either permanently or temporarily, from their jobs are called **job losers**. Some job losers become unemployed but some immediately withdraw from the labour force.

People who voluntarily quit their jobs are called **job leavers**. Like job losers, some job leavers become unemployed and search for a better job, while others withdraw from the labour force temporarily or permanently retire from work.

People who enter or re-enter the labour force are called **entrants** and **re-entrants**. Entrants are mainly people who have just left school. Some entrants get a job right away and are never unemployed, but many spend time searching for their first job and, during this period, they are unemployed. Re-entrants are people who have previously withdrawn from the labour force. Most of these people are formerly discouraged workers. Figure 23.6 shows these labour market flows.

The Sources of Unemployment Figure 23.7 shows unemployment by reason for becoming unemployed. Job losers are the biggest source of unemployment. Also, their number fluctuates a great deal. In the recession of 1990–1991, on any given day, almost 1 million of the 1.6 million people unemployed were job losers. In contrast, in the peak year of 1989,

FIGURE 23.6
Labour Market Flows

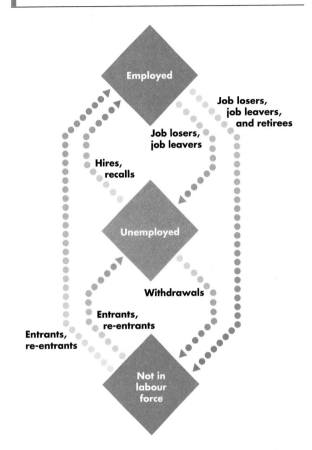

Unemployment results from employed people losing or leaving their jobs (job losers and job leavers) and from people entering the labour force (entrants and re-entrants). Unemployment ends because people get hired or recalled or because they withdraw from the labour force.

fewer than 500,000 of the 1 million people unemployed were job losers.

Entrants and re-entrants also are a large component of the unemployed and their number fluctuates mildly. On any given day, around 300,000 unemployed people are entrants and re-entrants.

Job leavers are the smallest and most stable source of unemployment. On any given day, around 200,000 people are unemployed because they are job leavers. The number of job leavers is relatively constant, although to the extent that it fluctuates, it does

FIGURE 23.7
Unemployment by Reasons

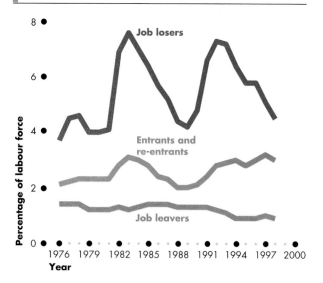

Everyone who is unemployed is either a job loser, a job leaver, or an entrant or re-entrant into the labour force. Most of the unemployment that exists results from job loss. The number of job losers fluctuates more closely with the business cycle than do the numbers of job leavers and entrants and re-entrants. Entrants and re-entrants are the second most commonly unemployed people. Their number fluctuates with the business cycle because of discouraged workers. Job leavers are the least commonly unemployed people.

Source: Statistics Canada, *StatCan: CANSIM Disc*, March 1999.

FIGURE 23.8
Unemployment by Duration

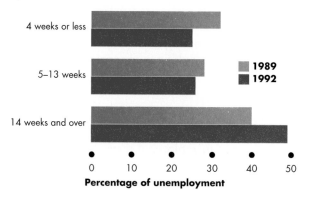

In the business cycle peak of 1989, when the unemployment rate was 7.5 percent, 32 percent of unemployment lasted 4 weeks or less, 28 percent lasted 5 to 13 weeks, and 40 percent lasted 14 weeks or more. In the business cycle trough of 1992, when the unemployment rate was 11 percent, 25 percent of unemployment lasted 4 weeks or less, 26 percent lasted 5 to 14 weeks, and 50 percent lasted 14 weeks or more.

Source: Statistics Canada, *StatCan: CANSIM Disc*, March 1999.

so in line with the business cycle: A slightly larger number of people leave their jobs in good times than in bad times.

The Duration of Unemployment Some people are unemployed for a week or two, and others are unemployed for periods of a year or more. The longer the spell of unemployment, the greater is the cost to the person unemployed. The average duration of unemployment varies over the business cycle. Figure 23.8 compares the duration of unemployment in a business cycle peak in 1989, when the unemployment rate was low, with that at the business cycle trough of 1992, when the unemployment rate was high. In 1989, when the unemployment rate hit a low of 7.5 percent, almost 32 percent of the unem-

ployed were in that state for 4 weeks or less and 40 percent of the unemployed were jobless for longer than 13 weeks. In 1992, when unemployment reached a high of 11 percent, only 25 percent of the unemployed found a new job in 4 weeks or less and 50 percent were unemployed for more than 13 weeks. At both low and high unemployment rates, about 27 percent of the unemployed take between 4 weeks and 13 weeks to find a job.

The Demographics of Unemployment Figure 23.9 shows unemployment for different demographic groups. The figure shows that high unemployment rates occur among young workers. In the business cycle trough in 1992, the unemployment rate of teenagers was 20 percent. Even at the business cycle peak in 1989, when the unemployment rate was 7.5 percent, the teenage unemployment rate was 13 percent.

Why are teenage unemployment rates so high? There are three reasons. First, young people are still in the process of discovering what they are good at

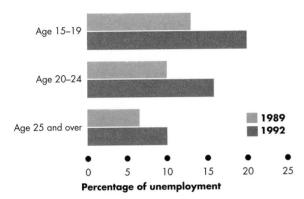

FIGURE 23.9
Unemployment by Demographic Group

Teenagers experience the highest unemployment rates. In 1992, at a business cycle trough (when unemployment was at its highest rate), the teenage unemployment rate was 20 percent. Even in a business cycle peak such as 1989 (when unemployment is at its lowest rate), 13 percent of the teenage labour force is unemployed.

Source: Statistics Canada, *StatCan: CANSIM Disc*, March 1999.

and trying different lines of work. So they leave their jobs more frequently than older workers do. Second, firms sometimes hire teenagers on a short-term trial basis. So the rate of job loss is higher for teenagers than for other people. Third, most teenagers are not in the labour force but are in school. This fact means that the percentage of the teenage population that is unemployed is much lower than the percentage of the teenage labour force that is unemployed.

Types of Unemployment

Unemployment is classified into four types that are based on its causes. They are:

- Frictional
- Structural
- Seasonal
- Cyclical

Frictional Unemployment   The unemployment that arises from normal labour turnover—from people entering and leaving the labour force and from the ongoing creation and destruction of jobs—is called **frictional unemployment**. This type of unemployment is a permanent and healthy phenomenon in a dynamic, growing economy.

The unending flow of people into and out of the labour force and the processes of job creation and job destruction create the need for people to search for jobs and for businesses to search for workers. Always there are businesses with unfilled jobs and people seeking jobs. Look in your local newspaper, and you will see that there are always some jobs being advertised. Businesses don't usually hire the first person who applies for a job, and unemployed people don't usually take the first job that comes their way. Instead, both firms and workers spend time searching out what they believe will be the best match available. By this process of search, people can match their own skills and interests with the available jobs and find a satisfying job and income. While these unemployed people are searching, they are frictionally unemployed.

The amount of frictional unemployment depends on the rate at which people enter and re-enter the labour force and on the rate at which jobs are created and destroyed. During the 1970s, the amount of frictional unemployment increased as a consequence of the post-war baby boom that began during the 1940s. By the late 1970s, the baby boom created a bulge in the number of people leaving school. As these people entered the labour force, the amount of frictional unemployment increased.

The amount of frictional unemployment is influenced by unemployment compensation. The greater the number of unemployed people covered by employment insurance and the more generous the unemployment benefit they receive, the longer is the average time taken in job search and the greater is the amount of frictional unemployment. Canadian employment insurance is among the most comprehensive and generous in the world. It is much more comprehensive than that in the United States. This factor is one reason why the Canadian unemployment rate has exceeded the U.S. unemployment rate since the early 1980s. But there are others. Canadian workers, especially young workers who make up the so-called Generation X, have shorter spells of employment and more frequent intervening spells of unemployment, supported by employment insurance, than do young U.S. workers.[1]

Structural Unemployment   The unemployment that arises when changes in technology or international competition change the skills needed to perform jobs or change the locations of jobs is called **structural unemployment**. This type of unemployment usually lasts longer than frictional unemployment because workers must retrain and possibly relocate to find a job. For example, when a steel plant in Hamilton, Ontario, is automated, some jobs in that city are destroyed. Meanwhile, new jobs for security guards, life-insurance salespeople, and retail clerks are created in the Ottawa valley and Vancouver. The unemployed former steelworkers remain unemployed for several months until they move, retrain, and get one of these jobs. Structural unemployment is painful, especially for older workers for whom the best available option might be to retire early but with a lower income than they had expected.

At some times the amount of structural unemployment is modest. At other times it is large, and at such times, structural unemployment can become a serious long-term problem. It was especially large during the late 1970s and early 1980s. During those years, oil price hikes and an increasingly competitive international environment destroyed jobs in traditional Canadian industries, such as auto and steel, and created jobs in new industries, such as electronics and bioengineering, as well as in banking and insurance. Structural unemployment was also present during the early 1990s as many businesses and governments "downsized."

Seasonal Unemployment   Many jobs are available only at certain times of the year. **Seasonal unemployment** is the unemployment that arises because the number of jobs available has decreased because of the season. Most seasonal unemployment in Canada occurs in the winter because construction and out-

door farming essentially close down for several months. But a few jobs, such as ski instructors and snow movers, are only available in winter.

In some regions, and especially the Atlantic Provinces, seasonal work is very hard to find in winter and the unemployment rate rises during the winter months. The seasonal swings in unemployment are largest in PEI. For example, in January through March, the worst months, PEI has an unemployment rate around 22 percent. In June, the best month, the rate falls to less than half its winter peak that fluctuates.

Cyclical Unemployment   The unemployment that fluctuates over the business cycle is called **cyclical unemployment**. This type of unemployment increases during a recession and decreases during an expansion. An autoworker who is laid off because the economy is in a recession and who gets rehired some months later when the expansion begins has experienced cyclical unemployment.

Full Employment

There is always *some* unemployment—someone looking for a job or laid off and waiting to be recalled. So what do we mean by *full employment*? **Full employment** occurs when the unemployment rate equals the natural rate of unemployment. And the **natural rate of unemployment** is the unemployment rate when there is no cyclical unemployment or, equivalently, when all the unemployment is frictional, structural, and seasonal.

There can be a lot of unemployment at full employment, and the term "full employment" is an example of a technical economic term that does not correspond with everyday language. The term "natural rate of unemployment" is another example of a technical economic term that does not correspond with everyday language. For most people—especially for unemployed workers—there is nothing *natural* about unemployment.

So, why do economists call a situation with a lot of unemployment one of full employment? And why is the unemployment at full employment "natural"?

The reason is that the complex machine that we call the Canadian economy undergoes constant changes in its players, structure, and direction. This process of change creates frictions and dislocations

---

[1]These conclusions are based on the work of David Card and Craig W. Riddell, "A Comparative Analysis of Unemployment in Canada and the United States," *Small Differences That Matter: Labour Markets and Income Maintenance in Canada and the United States*, edited by Richard Freeman and David Card, Chicago: University of Chicago Press and NBER, 1993, pp. 149–189, and Audra J. Bowlus, "What Generation X Can Tell Us About the U.S.-Canadian Unemployment Rate Gap," University of Western Ontario, 1996.

FIGURE 23.10

Unemployment and Real GDP

(a) Real GDP

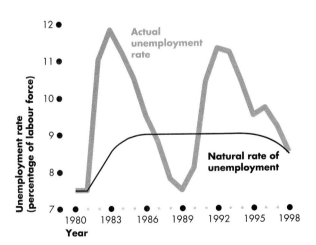

(b) Unemployment rate

As real GDP fluctuates around potential GDP (part a), the unemployment rate fluctuates around the natural rate of unemployment (part b). In the deep recession of 1982, unemployment reached almost 12 percent. In the slightly milder recession of 1990–1991, the unemployment rate peaked at about 11 percent. The natural rate of unemployment increased during the 1980s and decreased during the late 1990s.

Source: Statistics Canada, *StatCan: CANSIM Disc*, March 1999, and the authors' assumptions.

that are unavoidable. And they create unemployment. The amount of unemployment that arises from the frictions and structural changes is "natural" unemployment.

Figure 23.10 illustrates the natural unemployment rate along with actual and cyclical unemployment in Canada between 1980 and 1998. The divergence of the unemployment rate from the natural rate is cyclical unemployment.

The figure also shows the fluctuations of real GDP around potential GDP. Notice that the unemployment rate fluctuates around the natural rate of unemployment (part b) just as real GDP fluctuates around potential GDP (part a). When the unemployment rate equals the natural rate of unemployment, real GDP equals potential GDP. When the unemployment rate is less than the natural rate of unemployment, real GDP is greater than potential GDP. Note that in this case, cyclical unemployment is *negative*. Total unemployment is less than the sum of frictional, structural, and seasonal unemployment. When the unemployment rate is greater than the natural rate of unemployment, real GDP is less than potential GDP.

There is little controversy about the existence of a fluctuating natural rate of unemployment. But there is controversy about the magnitude of the natural rate of unemployment. In Fig. 23.10(b), the natural rate of unemployment rises to 9 percent during the1980s and falls during the late 1990s. This estimate of the natural rate of unemployment in Canada is one that many, but not all, economists would accept.

REVIEW QUIZ

- What are the categories of people who become unemployed?
- Define *frictional*, *structural*, *seasonal*, and *cyclical* unemployment and provide an example of each type of unemployment?
- What is the *natural rate of unemployment*?

◆ *Reading Between the Lines* on pp. 510–511 applies what you've learned in this chapter by examining unemployment in Canada in 1999.

You now know how we measure employment and unemployment and you understand the link between employment and real GDP. You are now ready to learn about the forces that make real GDP grow and fluctuate and that bring changes in the price level, wages, employment, and unemployment.

Jobs and Unemployment

NATIONAL POST, MAY 8, 1999

Jump in jobless rate signals surge in labour force: analysts

Canada's unemployment rate suffered its largest jump in nearly three years in April, rising to 8.3% from 7.8% in March, Statistics Canada said yesterday.

The news came as a shock to most observers, who were expecting to see the jobless rate hold steady, before taking a run toward 7.5% or even lower by the end of the year. ...

Despite the setback, however, analysts were quick to stress Canada's recent job creation boom has not gone up in smoke. In fact, they noted, the rate was dragged down by a flood of formerly discouraged workers returning to the workforce.

"Last month's employment picture was not nearly as bleak as the increase in the unemployment figures would suggest," said Marc Levesque, senior economist at Toronto-Dominion Bank. "The rise in the unemployment rate was entirely the result of a surge in the number of people looking for work, rather than a decline in the level of employment."

The labour force, which refers to the combined number of job seekers and employed, surged by more than 96,000—its largest monthly jump in five years.

Slightly more than half of those were youth, with adults making up the remainder. More than half of the increase to the national labour force took place in Ontario.

The increase in the size of the labour market was broadly interpreted as a positive turnaround for the economy, as workers who had given up their job search decided to renew their efforts.

"This suggests optimism on the part of job seekers," said John Johnston, chief economist for the Americas at RBC Dominion Securities Inc. ...

Essence of the Story

- Canada's unemployment rate increased from 7.8 percent in March 1999 to 8.3 percent in April 1999.

- Many observers were expecting the unemployment rate to fall.

- The unemployment rate increased because the labour force increased.

- The labour force increases when discouraged workers begin to seek employment.

Economic Analysis

■ Figure 1 shows the Canadian business cycle and the unemployment rate from 1980 to 1998.

■ As the economy moves out of recession and into expansion the unemployment rate falls.

■ In 1999, the Canadian economy is in an expansion, and the normal expectation is that the unemployment rate will fall.

■ The unemployment rate is the percentage of people in the labour force who are unemployed.

■ Discouraged workers are people who temporarily leave the labour force during a recession and re-enter during an expansion.

■ Figure 2 shows the change in the labour force and the change in the composition of the labour force from March to April 1999.

■ The labour force increased and the number of people employed increased, but the number of people unemployed increased by many more than the number of people employed.

■ The labour force increased in April 1999 partly because workers who were previously discouraged rejoined the labour force.

■ Discouraged workers can enter the labour force as either employed or unemployed.

■ Whenever the percentage increase in the number of unemployed exceeds the percentage increase in the labour force, the unemployment rate rises.

■ In April, the number of discouraged workers who entered the labour force as unemployed increased the number of people unemployed by a greater percentage than the increase in the labour force. As a result, the unemployment rate in April was greater than in March.

■ The April increase in the unemployment rate shows that it is possible for an economy to be growing but at the same time to experience a rise in the unemployment rate.

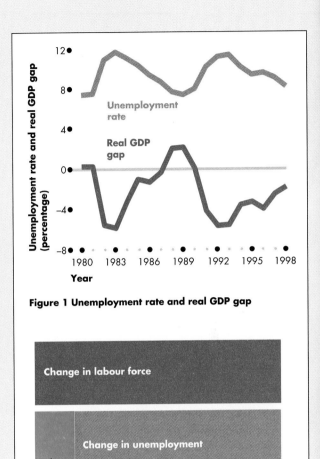

Figure 1 Unemployment rate and real GDP gap

Figure 2 Changes in the labour force composition

SUMMARY

Key Points

Employment and Wages (pp. 500–504)

- The unemployment rate and the involuntary part-time rate fluctuate with the business cycle.
- The labour force participation rate and the employment-to-population ratio have an upward trend and fluctuate with the business cycle.
- The labour force participation rate has increased for females and decreased for males.
- Aggregate hours have an upward trend, and they fluctuate with the business cycle.
- The growth rate of the real hourly wage rate slowed during the 1970s. In the late 1970s and 1990s, the real wage rate fell, but it usually increases.

Unemployment and Full Employment (pp. 505–509)

- People are constantly entering and leaving the state of unemployment.
- The duration of unemployment fluctuates over the business cycle. But the demographic patterns of unemployment are constant.
- Unemployment can be frictional, structural, seasonal, and cyclical.
- When all the unemployment is frictional, structural, and seasonal, unemployment is at its natural rate, and there is *full employment*. The natural rate of unemployment fluctuates because of fluctuations in frictional, structural, and seasonal unemployment.

Key Figures

Key Terms

PROBLEMS

⌨ *1. In 1995, Statistics Canada measured the labour force at 14,924,000, employment at 13,506,000, and the working-age population at 23,027,000. Calculate for 1995 the
   a. Unemployment rate
   b. Labour force participation rate
   c. Employment-to-population ratio

2. In 1997, Statistics Canada measured the labour force at 15,354,000, employment at 13,941,000, and the working-age population at 23,687,000. Calculate for 1997 the
   a. Unemployment rate
   b. Labour force participation rate
   c. Employment-to-population ratio

⌨ *3. During 1996, the working-age population increased by 325,000, employment increased by 170,000, and the labour force increased by 221,000. Use the data in problem 1 to calculate the change in unemployment and the change in the number of discouraged workers during 1996.

4. During 1998, the working-age population increased by 306,000, employment increased by 385,000, and the labour force increased by 269,000. Use the data in problem 2 to calculate the change in unemployment and the change in the number of discouraged workers during 1998.

⌨ *5. In August 1994, the unemployment rate was 10.1 percent. In August 1995, the unemployment rate was 9.6 percent. What do you predict happened between August 1994 and August 1995 to the numbers of
   a. Job losers and job leavers?
   b. Labour force entrants and re-entrants?

6. In January 1998, the unemployment rate was 8.8 percent. In January 1999, the unemployment rate was 7.8 percent. (These are seasonally adjusted rates that exclude the winter seasonal unemployment.) What do you predict happened in 1998 to the numbers of
   a. Job losers and job leavers?
   b. Labour force entrants and re-entrants?

*7. The figure shows the numbers of working-age people who were employed, unemployed, and not in the labour force in the nation of Labecon in July 1997 and the labour market flows during August 1997.

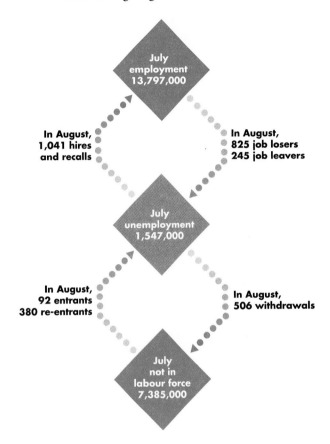

Calculate for July 1997:
a. The labour force
b. The unemployment rate
c. The working-age population
d. The employment-to-population ratio

Calculate for the end of August 1997:
e. The number of people unemployed
f. The number of people employed
g. The labour force
h. The unemployment rate
i. The employment-to-population ratio if the labour force participation rate is 65.5 percent

8. The figure shows the numbers of working-age people who were employed, unemployed, and not in the labour force in the nation of Ecolab in July 1998 and the labour market flows during August 1998.

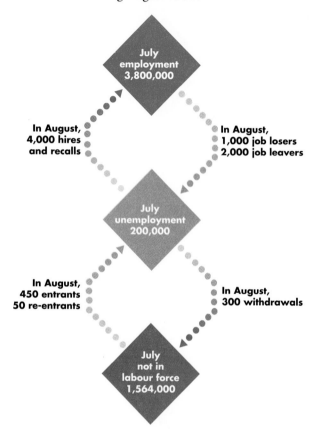

Calculate for July 1998:
a. The labour force
b. The unemployment rate
c. The working-age population
d. The employment-to-population ratio
Calculate for the end of August 1998:
e. The number of people unemployed
f. The number of people employed
g. The labour force
h. The unemployment rate
i. The employment-to-population ratio if the labour force participation rate is 60 percent

*9. Describe the main features of the labour market at the peak of the business cycle.

10. Describe the main features of the labour market at the trough of the business cycle.

CRITICAL THINKING

1. Study *Reading Between the Lines* on pp. 510–511 and then answer the following questions:
   a. What has been the trend in unemployment in Canada during the 1990s?
   b. Why did the Canadian unemployment rate increase during April 1999?
   c. What information would you need that is not supplied in the news article to determine to what extent the unemployment in Canada during 1999 was frictional, structural, seasonal, or cyclical?

2. Use the links on the Parkin-Bade Web site to find labour market data for your own province.
   a. What have been the trends in employment, part-time employment, unemployment, and labour force participation in your own province during the past two years?
   b. Based on what you know about your own region, how would you set about explaining its labour market trends?
   c. Based on what you know about your own region, how would you classify the unemployment among the categories of: frictional, structural, seasonal, and cyclical?
   d. Try to identify those industries that have expanded most and those that have shrunk.
   e. What are the problems with your own regional labour market that you think need provincial government action to resolve?
   f. Compare the labour market performance of your own province with that of the nation as a whole.
   g. If your province is performing better than the national average, to what do you attribute the success? If your province is performing worse than the national average, to what do you attribute its problems?

Aggregate Supply and Aggregate Demand

During the past 30 years, Canadian real GDP has more than doubled. In fact, a doubling of real GDP every 30 years has been routine. What forces drive our economy to grow? ◆ At the same time that real GDP has grown, we've experienced first a rise and then a fall in inflation. In 1965, Canadian prices were rising at a rate of 3 percent a year. In 1974, the peak inflation year, prices increased by 15 percent. Today, the inflation rate is close to zero. The result of all this past inflation is that you need $400 today to buy what $100 bought in 1965.

What Makes Our Garden Grow?

What causes inflation? And why did its rate explode during the 1970s? ◆ Our economy does not expand at a constant pace. Instead, it ebbs and flows over the business cycle. For example, we had a recession during 1990 and early 1991. For half a year, real GDP decreased. Then began a long period of expansion that was still in progress in 1998. What makes real GDP grow at an uneven pace? Why does growth sometimes speed up, and why does real GDP sometimes shrink? ◆ When economic growth speeds up in the rest of the world, we benefit because we sell more goods and services abroad. And when economic growth slows in Asia, we suffer because the demand for our goods and services decreases. But some influences on our economy are homemade and stem from the actions of the government and the Bank of Canada in Ottawa. How do events in the rest of the world and the policy actions of the government and the Bank of Canada affect production and prices?

◆ To answer these questions, we need a *model* of real GDP and the price level. Our main task in this chapter is to study such a model: the *aggregate supply–aggregate demand model*. Our second task is to use the aggregate supply-aggregate demand (or *AS-AD*) model to answer the questions we've just posed. You'll discover that this model enables us to understand the forces that make our economy expand, that bring inflation, and that cause business cycle fluctuations. You will also find that this model is a useful tool with which to organize your entire study of macroeconomics.

After studying this chapter, you will be able to:

- **Explain what determines aggregate supply**
- **Explain what determines aggregate demand**
- **Explain macroeconomic equilibrium**
- **Explain the effects of changes in aggregate supply and aggregate demand on economic growth, inflation, and business cycles**
- **Explain Canadian economic growth, inflation, and business cycles by using the *AS-AD* model**

Aggregate Supply

THE AGGREGATE SUPPLY-AGGREGATE DEMAND model enables us to understand three features of macroeconomic performance:

- Growth of potential GDP
- Inflation
- Business cycle fluctuations

The model uses the concepts of *aggregate* supply and *aggregate* demand to determine *real* GDP and the *price level* (the *GDP deflator*). We begin by looking at the limits to production that influence aggregate supply.

Aggregate Supply Fundamentals

The *quantity of real GDP supplied* (Y) depends on the quantity of labour employed and on productivity. The productivity of labour depends on the amount of capital per worker and the state of technology. So the quantity of real GDP supplied depends on:

1. The quantity of labour (L)
2. The quantity of capital (K)
3. The state of technology (T)

We describe the influence of these 3 factors on real GDP with the **aggregate production function**, which is written as the equation:

$$Y = F(L, K, T).$$

In words, the quantity of real GDP supplied is determined by (is a function F of) the quantities of labour and capital and of the state of technology. The larger is L, K, or T, the greater is Y.

At any given time, the quantity of capital and the state of technology are fixed. They depend on decisions that were made in the past. The population is also fixed. But the quantity of labour is not fixed. It depends on decisions made by people and firms about the supply of and demand for labour.

Firms demand labour only if it is profitable to do so. And the lower the wage rate, which is the cost of labour, the greater is the quantity of labour demanded. People supply labour only if doing so is the most valuable use of their time. And the higher the wage rate, which is the return to labour, the greater is the quantity of labour supplied. The wage rate that makes the quantity of labour demanded equal to the quantity of labour supplied is the equilibrium wage rate. At this wage rate there is **full employment**.

Even at full employment, there are always some people looking for jobs and some firms looking for people to hire. The reason is that there is constant turnover in the labour market. Every day, some jobs are destroyed as businesses reorganize or fail. Some jobs are created as new businesses start up or existing ones expand. Some workers decide, for any of a thousand personal reasons, to quit their jobs. And other people decide to start looking for a job. This constant churning in the labour market prevents unemployment from ever disappearing. At full employment, the unemployment rate is called the **natural rate of unemployment**. In 1998, the natural rate of unemployment was about 8 percent.

When unemployment is at its natural rate and there is full employment, the quantity of real GDP supplied is **potential GDP**. Potential GDP depends on the full-employment quantity of labour, the quantity of capital, and the state of technology.

Over the business cycle, employment fluctuates around full employment and real GDP fluctuates around potential GDP. You saw these fluctuations in Chapter 21, Figs. 21.2 and 21.3 on pp. 458–459.

To study the economy at full employment and over the business cycle, we distinguish two time frames for aggregate supply:

- Long-run aggregate supply
- Short-run aggregate supply

Long-Run Aggregate Supply

The economy is constantly bombarded by events that move real GDP away from potential GDP and, equivalently, that move the unemployment rate away from full employment. Following such an event, forces operate to take real GDP back towards potential GDP and restore full employment. The **macroeconomic long run** is a time frame that is sufficiently long for these forces to have done their work so that real GDP equals potential GDP and full employment prevails.

Long-run aggregate supply is the relationship between the quantity of real GDP supplied and the price level in the long run when real GDP equals potential GDP. The vertical curve *LAS* in Fig. 24.1 illustrates long-run aggregate supply. Along the long-run aggregate supply curve, as the price level changes, real GDP remains at potential GDP, which in Fig. 24.1 is $800 billion.

FIGURE 24.1

Long-Run Aggregate Supply

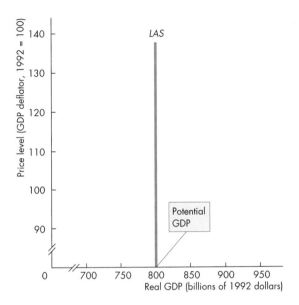

The long-run aggregate supply curve (*LAS*) shows the relationship between potential GDP and the price level. Potential GDP is independent of the price level, so the *LAS* curve is vertical at potential GDP.

The long-run aggregate supply curve is located at potential GDP. The *LAS* curve is vertical because potential GDP is independent of the price level. The reason for this independence is that a movement along the *LAS* curve is accompanied by a change in *two* sets of prices: the prices of goods and services—the price level—and the prices of productive resources. A 10 percent increase in the prices of goods and services is matched by a 10 percent increase in wage rates and other resource prices. That is, the price level, wage rate, and other resource prices all change by the same percentage and *relative prices* and the *real wage rate* remain constant. When the price level changes but relative prices and the real wage rate remain constant, real GDP also remains constant.

Production at a Pepsi Plant You can see why real GDP remains constant when prices and wage rates change by the same percentage by thinking about production decisions at a Pepsi bottling plant. For a given price of Pepsi and a given wage rate, the plant produces the quantity of Pepsi that maximizes profit. That quantity depends on the price of Pepsi *relative*

to the wage rate. If both the price of Pepsi and the wage rate increase by the same percentage, the price of Pepsi *relative* to the wage rate does not change. In this new situation, the quantity that maximizes profit is the same as before. So the firm doesn't change production.

Short-Run Aggregate Supply

The **macroeconomic short run** is a period during which real GDP has fallen below or risen above potential GDP. At the same time, the unemployment rate has risen above or fallen below the natural rate.

Short-run aggregate supply is the relationship between the quantity of real GDP supplied and the price level when the money wage rate, the prices of other resources, and potential GDP remain constant. The upward-sloping curve *SAS* in Fig. 24.2 illustrates short-run aggregate supply. This curve is based on the short-run aggregate supply schedule and each point on the aggregate supply curve corresponds to a row of the aggregate supply schedule. For example, point *a* on the short-run aggregate supply curve and row *a* of the schedule tell us that if the price level is 100, the quantity of real GDP supplied is $700 billion.

At point *c*, the price level is 110 and the quantity of real GDP supplied is $800 billion, which equals potential GDP. If the price level is higher than 110, the quantity of real GDP supplied exceeds potential GDP; if the price level is below 110, the quantity of real GDP supplied is less than potential GDP.

Back at the Pepsi Plant You can see why the short-run aggregate supply curve slopes upward by returning to the Pepsi plant. The plant produces the quantity that maximizes profit. If the price of Pepsi rises and the wage rate and other costs don't change, the firm has an incentive to increase its production. Why? If the firm increases production, it incurs a higher marginal cost. But the higher price of Pepsi covers the additional cost up to some new higher level of production. So the firm increases production.

Similarly, if the price of Pepsi falls and the wage rate and other costs don't change, the lower price is not sufficient to cover the marginal cost of Pepsi, so the firm decreases production.

Again, what's true for a Pepsi bottler is true for the producers of all goods and services. So when the price level rises and the money wage rate and other resource prices remain constant, the quantity of real GDP supplied increases.

FIGURE 24.2
Short-Run Aggregate Supply

	Price level (GDP deflator)	Real GDP (billions of 1992 dollars)
a	100	700
b	105	750
c	110	800
d	115	850
e	120	900

The short-run aggregate supply (SAS) curve shows the relationship between the quantity of real GDP supplied and the price level when the money wage rate, other resource prices, and potential GDP remain the same. The short-run aggregate supply curve SAS is based on the schedule in the table. The short-run aggregate supply curve is upward-sloping because firms' marginal costs increase as the rate of output increases, so a higher price is needed, relative to the prices of productive resources, to bring forth an increase in the quantity produced. On the SAS curve, when the price level is 110, real GDP equals potential GDP. If the price level is greater than 110, real GDP exceeds potential GDP; if the price level is below 110, real GDP is less than potential GDP.

Movements Along the *LAS* and *SAS* Curves

Figure 24.3 summarizes what you've just learned about the *LAS* and *SAS* curves. When the price level, the money wage rate, and other resource prices rise by the same percentage, relative prices remain constant and real GDP remains at potential GDP. There is a *movement along* the *LAS* curve.

When the price level rises but the money wage rate and other resource prices remain the same, the quantity of real GDP supplied increases and there is a *movement along* the *SAS* curve.

Let's next study the influences that bring changes in aggregate supply.

FIGURE 24.3
Movements Along the Aggregate Supply Curves

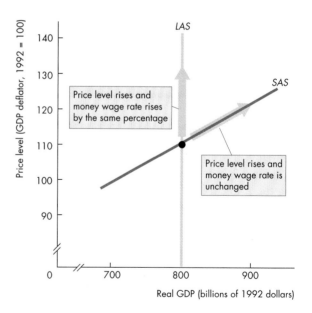

A rise in the price level with no change in the money wage rate and other resource prices brings an increase in the quantity of real GDP supplied and a movement along the short-run aggregate supply curve. A rise in the price level with equal percentage increases in the money wage rate and other resource prices keeps the quantity of real GDP supplied constant at potential GDP and brings a movement along the long-run aggregate supply curve.

Changes in Aggregate Supply

You've just seen that a change in the price level brings a movement along the aggregate supply curves but it does not change aggregate supply. Aggregate supply changes when influences on production plans other than the price level change. Let's begin by looking at factors that change potential GDP.

Changes in Potential GDP When potential GDP changes, both long-run aggregate supply and short-run aggregate supply change. Potential GDP changes for three reasons:

1. Change in the full-employment quantity of labour
2. Change in the quantity of capital
3. Advance in technology

An increase in the full-employment quantity of labour, an increase in the quantity of capital, or an advance in technology increases potential GDP. And an increase in potential GDP changes both the long-run aggregate supply and short-run aggregate supply.

Figure 24.4 shows these effects of a change in potential GDP. Initially, the long-run aggregate supply curve is LAS_0 and short-run aggregate supply curve is SAS_0. If an increase in the quantity of capital or a technological advance increases potential GDP to $900 billion, long-run aggregate supply increases and the long-run aggregate supply curve shifts rightward to LAS_1. Short-run aggregate supply also increases, and the short-run aggregate supply curve shifts rightward to SAS_1.

Let's look more closely at the influences on potential GDP and the aggregate supply curves.

A Change in the Full-Employment Quantity of Labour A Pepsi bottling plant that employs 100 workers bottles more Pepsi than an otherwise identical plant that employs 10 workers. The same is true for the economy as a whole. The larger the quantity of labour employed, the greater is real GDP.

Over time, potential GDP increases because the labour force increases. But (with constant capital and technology) *potential* GDP increases only if the full-employment quantity of labour increases. Fluctuations in employment over the business cycle bring fluctuations in real GDP. But these changes in real GDP are fluctuations around potential GDP. They are not changes in potential GDP and long-run aggregate supply.

FIGURE 24.4
A Change in Potential GDP

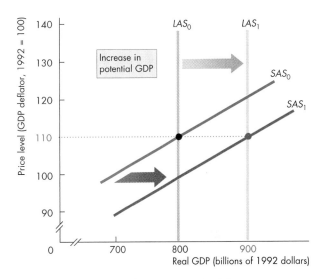

An increase in potential GDP increases both long-run aggregate supply and short-run aggregate supply and shifts both aggregate supply curves rightward from LAS_0 to LAS_1 and from SAS_0 to SAS_1.

A Change in the Quantity of Capital A Pepsi plant with two production lines bottles more Pepsi than an otherwise identical plant that has only one production line. For the economy, the larger the quantity of capital, the more productive is the labour force and the greater is its potential GDP. Potential GDP per person in the capital-rich Canada is vastly greater than that in capital-poor China and Russia.

Capital includes *human capital*. One Pepsi plant is managed by an economics major with an MBA and has a labour force with an average of 10 years experience. This plant produces a much larger output than an otherwise identical plant that is managed by someone with no business training or experience and that has a young labour force that is new to bottling. The first plant has a greater amount of human capital than the second. For the economy as a whole, the larger the quantity of *human capital*—the skills that people have acquired in school and through on-the-job training—the greater is potential GDP.

An Advance in Technology A Pepsi plant that has pre-computer age machines produces less than one that uses the latest robot technology. Technological change enables firms to produce more from any given amount of inputs. So even with fixed quantities of labour and capital, improvements in technology increase potential GDP.

Technological advances are by far the most important source of increased production over the past two centuries. Because of technological advances, one farmer in Canada today can feed 100 people, and one autoworker can produce almost 14 cars and trucks in a year.

Let's now look at the effects of changes in money wage rates.

Changes in Money Wage Rate and Other Resource Prices

When the money wage rate or the money prices of other resources such as the price of oil changes, short-run aggregate supply changes but long-run aggregate supply does not change.

Figure 24.5 shows the effect on aggregate supply of an increase in the money wage rate. Initially, the short-run aggregate supply curve is SAS_0. A rise in the money wage rate *decreases* short-run aggregate supply and shifts the short-run aggregate supply curve leftward to SAS_2.

Money wage rates (and resource prices) affect short-run aggregate supply because they change firms' costs. The higher the money wage rate, the higher are firms' costs and the smaller is the quantity that firms are willing to supply at each price level. So an increase in the money wage rate decreases short-run aggregate supply.

Changes in the money wage rate do not change long-run aggregate supply because on the *LAS* curve, a change in the money wage rate is accompanied by an equal percentage change in the price level. With no change in *relative* prices, firms have no incentive to change production and real GDP remains constant at potential GDP.

In Fig. 24.5, the vertical distance between the original *SAS* curve and the new *SAS* curve is determined by the percentage change in the money wage rate. That is, the percentage increase in the price level between point *a* and point *b* equals the percentage increase in the money wage rate.

Because potential GDP does not change when the money wage rate changes, long-run aggregate supply does not change. The long-run aggregate supply curve remains at *LAS*.

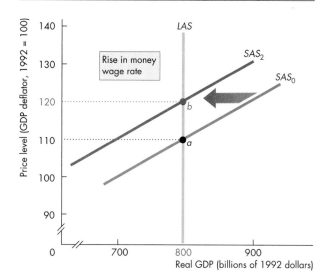

FIGURE 24.5

A Change in the Money Wage Rate

A rise in the money wage rate decreases short-run aggregate supply and shifts the short-run aggregate supply curve leftward from SAS_0 to SAS_2. A rise in the money wage rate does not change potential GDP, so the long-run aggregate supply curve does not shift.

R E V I E W   Q U I Z

■ If the price level rises and if the money wage rate also rises by the same percentage, what happens to the quantity of real GDP supplied? Along which aggregate supply curve does the economy move?

■ If the price level rises and the money wage rate remains constant, what happens to the quantity of real GDP supplied? Along which aggregate supply curve does the economy move?

■ If potential GDP increases, what happens to aggregate supply? Is there a shift of or a movement along the *LAS* curve and the *SAS* curve?

■ If the money wage rate rises and potential GDP remains the same, what happens to aggregate supply? Is there a shift of or a movement along the *LAS* curve and the *SAS* curve?

Aggregate Demand

THE QUANTITY OF REAL GDP DEMANDED IS THE sum of real consumption expenditure (*C*), investment (*I*), government expenditures (*G*), and exports (*X*) minus imports (*M*). That is,

$$Y = C + I + G + X - M.$$

The *quantity of real GDP demanded* is the total amount of final goods and services produced in Canada that people, businesses, governments, and foreigners plan to buy. What determines these buying plans?

These buying plans depend on many factors. Some of the main ones are:

- The price level
- Fiscal policy and monetary policy
- The world economy
- Expectations

We first focus on the relationship between the quantity of real GDP demanded and the price level, and to study this relationship, we keep all other influences on buying plans the same. We then ask: How does the quantity of real GDP demanded vary as the price level varies?

The Aggregate Demand Curve

Other things remaining the same, the higher the price level, the smaller is the quantity of real GDP demanded. This relationship between the quantity of real GDP demanded and the price level is called **aggregate demand**. Aggregate demand is described by an *aggregate demand schedule* and an *aggregate demand curve*.

Figure 24.6 shows an aggregate demand curve (*AD*) and an aggregate demand schedule. Each point on the *AD* curve corresponds to a row of the schedule. For example, point *c'* on the *AD* curve and row *c'* of the schedule tells us that if the price level is 110, the quantity of real GDP demanded is $800 billion.

The aggregate demand curve slopes downward for two reasons:

- Wealth effect
- Substitution effects

FIGURE 24.6

Aggregate Demand

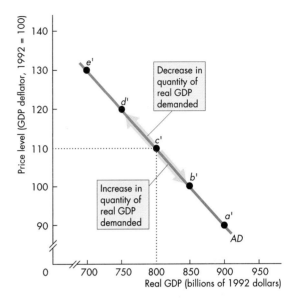

	Price level (GDP deflator)	Real GDP (billions of 1992 dollars)
a'	90	900
b'	100	850
c'	110	800
d'	120	750
e'	130	700

The aggregate demand curve (*AD*) shows the relationship between the quantity of real GDP demanded and the price level. The aggregate demand curve is based on the aggregate demand schedule in the table. Each point *a'* through *e'* on the curve corresponds to the row in the table identified by the same letter. Thus when the price level is 110, the quantity of real GDP demanded is $800 billion, shown by point *c'* in the figure.

Wealth Effect   When the price level rises but other things remain the same, *real* wealth decreases. Real wealth is the amount of money in the bank, bonds, stocks, and other assets that people own, measured not in dollars but in terms of the goods and services that this money, bonds, and stock will buy.

People save and hold money, bonds, and stocks for many reasons. One reason is to build up funds for education expenses or to meet possible medical or other big bills. But a bigger reason is to build up enough funds to provide a retirement income.

If the price level rises, real wealth decreases. People then try to restore their real wealth. To do so, they must decrease current consumption expenditure and increase saving. A decrease in consumption expenditure decreases the quantity of real GDP demanded.

Maria's Wealth Effect   You can see how the wealth effect works by thinking about Maria's buying plans. Maria lives in Moscow, Russia. She has worked hard all summer and saved 20,000 rubles (the ruble is the currency of Russia), which she plans to spend attending graduate school when she's finished her economics degree. So Maria's wealth is 20,000 rubles. Maria has a part-time job and her income from this job pays her current expenses. The price level in Russia rises by 100 percent, and now Maria needs 40,000 rubles to buy what 20,000 once bought. To try to make up some of the fall in value of her savings, Maria saves even more and cuts her current spending to the bare minimum.

Substitution Effects   When the price level rises and other things remain the same, interest rates rise. The reason is related to the wealth effect that you've just studied. A rise in the price level decreases the real value of the money in people's pockets and bank accounts. With a smaller amount of real money around, banks and other lenders can get a higher interest rate on loans. But faced with higher interest rates, people and businesses delay plans to buy new capital and consumer durable goods and cut back on spending.

This substitution effect involves substituting goods in the future for goods in the present and is called an *intertemporal* substitution effect—a substitution across time. Saving increases to increase future consumption.

To see this intertemporal substitution effect more clearly, think about your own plan to buy a new computer. At an interest rate of 5 percent a year, you might borrow $2,000 and buy the new machine you've been researching. But at an interest rate of 10 percent a year, you might decide the payments would be too high. You don't abandon your plan to buy the computer, but you decide to delay your purchase.

A second substitution effect works through inter-national prices. When the Canadian price level rises and other things remain the same, some of those other things are prices in other countries. So a rise in the Canadian price level makes Canadian-made goods and services more expensive relative to foreign-made goods and services. This change in relative prices encourages people to spend less on Canadian-made items. Suppose, for example, that the Canadian price level rises but the U.S. price level doesn't change. Americans buy fewer Canadian-made cars and Canadians buy more U.S.-made cars. Canadian exports decrease, imports increase, and the quantity of Canadian real GDP demanded decreases.

Maria's Substitution Effects   In Moscow, Maria makes some substitutions when the price level rises. She was planning on trading in her old motor scooter and getting a new one. But with a higher price level, and faced with higher interest rates, she decides to make her old scooter last one more year. Also, with the prices of Russian goods sharply increasing, Maria substitutes a low-cost dress made in Malaysia for the Russian-made dress she had originally planned to buy.

We've now seen how the quantity of real GDP demanded changes when the price level changes. How do other influences on buying plans affect aggregate demand?

Changes in Aggregate Demand

A change in any factor that influences buying plans other than the price level brings a change in aggregate demand. And when aggregate demand changes, the aggregate demand curve shifts. Figure 24.7 shows an increase and a decrease in aggregate demand. When aggregate demand increases the aggregate demand curve shifts rightward from AD_0 to AD_1. When aggregate demand decreases the aggregate demand curve shifts leftward from AD_0 to AD_2. The factors that change aggregate demand are:

- Fiscal policy and monetary policy
- The world economy
- Expectations

Fiscal Policy and Monetary Policy   The government's attempt to influence the economy by setting and changing taxes, transfer payments, and government expenditures is called **fiscal policy**. A tax cut or an increase in transfer payments—for example unemployment benefits or welfare payments—increases aggregate demand. Both of these influences operate by increasing households' *disposable* income.

Disposable income is aggregate income minus taxes plus transfer payments. The greater the disposable income, the greater is the quantity of consumption goods and services that households plan to buy and the greater is aggregate demand.

Government expenditures on goods and services are one component of aggregate demand. So if the government spends more on hospitals, schools, and highways, aggregate demand increases.

Monetary policy consists of changes in interest rates and in the quantity of money in the economy. The quantity of money is determined by the Bank of Canada and by the banks (in a process described in Chapters 27 and 28). An increase in the quantity of money in the economy increases aggregate demand. To see why money affects aggregate demand, imagine that the Bank of Canada borrows the army's helicopters, loads them with millions of new $10 bank notes, and sprinkles them like confetti across the nation. People gather the newly available money and plan to spend some of it. So the quantity of goods and services demanded increases. But people don't plan to spend all the new money. They plan to save some of it and lend it to others through the banks. Interest rates fall. And with lower interest rates, people plan to buy more consumer durables and firms plan to increase their investment.

The World Economy   Two main influences that the world economy has on aggregate demand are the foreign exchange rate and foreign income. The *foreign exchange rate* is the amount of a foreign currency that you can buy with a Canadian dollar. Other things remaining the same, a rise in the foreign exchange rate decreases aggregate demand. To see how the foreign exchange rate influences aggregate demand, suppose that $1 exchanges for 100 Japanese yen. A Fujitsu phone (made in Japan) costs 12,500 yen, and an equivalent Nortel phone (made in Canada) costs $110. In Canadian dollars, the Fujitsu phone costs $125, so people around the world buy the cheaper Canadian phone. Now suppose the exchange rate rises to 125 yen. At 125 yen per dollar, the Fujitsu phone costs $100 and is now cheaper than the Nortel phone. People will switch from the Canadian phone to the Japanese phone. Canadian exports will decrease and Canadian imports will increase, so Canadian aggregate demand will decrease.

FIGURE 24.7
Changes in Aggregate Demand

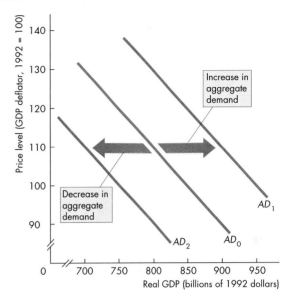

Aggregate demand

Decreases if

■ Fiscal policy decreases government expenditures, increases taxes, or decreases transfer payments

■ Monetary policy decreases the quantity of money and increases interest rates

■ The exchange rate increases or foreign income decreases

■ Expected future disposable income, inflation, or profits decrease

Increases if

■ Fiscal policy increases government expenditures, decreases taxes, or increases transfer payments

■ Monetary policy increases the quantity of money and decreases interest rates

■ The exchange rate decreases or foreign income increases

■ Expected future disposable income, inflation, or profits increase

An increase in foreign income increases Canadian exports and increases Canadian aggregate demand. For example, an increase in income in Japan and Germany increases Japanese and German consumers' and producers' planned expenditures on Canadian-made goods and services.

Expectations Expectations about future disposable income, future inflation, and future profits influence buying plans today. An increase in expected future disposable income increases the amount of consumption goods (especially big-ticket items like cars) that people plan to buy today and increases aggregate demand.

An increase in the expected future inflation rate increases aggregate demand because people decide to buy more goods and services at today's relatively lower prices. An increase in expected future profit increases the investment that firms plan to undertake today and increases aggregate demand.

Shifts of the Aggregate Demand Curve Figure 24.7, which shows an increase and a decrease in aggregate demand, summarizes the factors you've just been studying.

Aggregate demand increases and the aggregate demand curve shifts rightward from AD_0 to AD_1 when government expenditures on goods and services increase, taxes are cut, transfer payments increase, the quantity of money increases and interest rates fall, the foreign exchange rate falls, foreign income increases, or expected future disposable income, future inflation, or future profits increase.

Aggregate demand decreases and the aggregate demand curve shifts leftward from AD_0 to AD_2 when government expenditures on goods and services decrease, taxes increase, transfer payments decrease, the quantity of money decreases and interest rates rise, the foreign exchange rate rises, foreign income decreases, or expected future disposable income, future inflation, or future profits decrease.

R E V I E W   Q U I Z

- What does the aggregate demand curve show, and what factors change and what factors remain the same when there is a movement along the aggregate demand curve?
- Why does the aggregate demand curve slope downward? Explain your answer.
- How do changes in fiscal policy and monetary policy, changes in the world economy, and changes in expectations about the future change aggregate demand and shift the aggregate demand curve?

Macroeconomic Equilibrium

THE PURPOSE OF THE AGGREGATE SUPPLY— aggregate demand model is to explain changes in real GDP and the price level. To achieve this purpose, we combine aggregate supply and aggregate demand and determine macroeconomic equilibrium. There is a macroeconomic equilibrium for each of the time frames for aggregate supply: a long-run equilibrium and a short-run equilibrium. Long-run equilibrium is the state towards which the economy is heading. Short-run equilibrium is the normal state of the economy as it fluctuates around potential GDP.

We'll begin our study of macroeconomic equilibrium by looking first at the short run.

Short-Run Macroeconomic Equilibrium

The aggregate demand curve tells us the quantity of real GDP demanded at each price level, and the short-run aggregate supply curve tells us the quantity of real GDP supplied at each price level. **Short-run macroeconomic equilibrium** occurs when the quantity of real GDP demanded equals the quantity of real GDP supplied. That is, short-run macroeconomic equilibrium occurs at the point of intersection of the *AD* curve and the *SAS* curve. Figure 24.8 shows such an equilibrium at a price level of 110 and real GDP of $800 billion (points *c* and *c'*).

To see why this position is the equilibrium, think about what happens if the price level is something other than 110. Suppose, for example, that the price level is 120 and that real GDP is $900 billion (at point *e*) on the *SAS* curve. The quantity of real GDP demanded is less than $900 billion, so firms are unable to sell all their output. Unwanted inventories pile up, and firms cut both production and prices. Production and prices are cut until firms can sell all their output. This situation occurs only when real GDP is $800 billion and the price level is 110.

Now suppose the price level is 100 and real GDP is $700 billion (at point *a*) on the *SAS* curve. The quantity of real GDP demanded exceeds $700 billion, so firms are unable to meet the demand for their output. Inventories decrease, and customers clamour for goods and services. Firms respond by increasing production and raising prices. Production and prices increase until firms can meet demand. This situation

FIGURE 24.8

Short-Run Equilibrium

Short-run macroeconomic equilibrium occurs when real GDP demanded equals real GDP supplied—at the intersection of the aggregate demand curve (*AD*) and the short-run aggregate supply curve (*SAS*). Here, such an equilibrium occurs at points *c* and *c'* where the price level is 110 and real GDP is $800 billion. If the price level is 120 and real GDP is $900 billion (point *e*), firms will not be able to sell all their output. They will decrease production and cut prices. If the price level is 100 and real GDP is $700 billion (point *a*), people will not be able to buy all the goods and services they demand. Firms will increase production and raise their prices. Only when the price level is 110 and real GDP is $800 billion can firms sell all that they produce and people buy all that they demand. This is the short-run macroeconomic equilibrium.

occurs only when real GDP is $800 billion and the price level is 110.

In short-run macroeconomic equilibrium, the money wage rate is fixed. It does not adjust to bring full employment. So in the short run, real GDP can be greater than or less than potential GDP. But in the long run, the money wage rate does adjust and real GDP moves towards potential GDP. We are going to study this adjustment process. But first, let's look at the economy in long-run equilibrium.

Long-Run Macroeconomic Equilibrium

Long-run macroeconomic equilibrium occurs when real GDP equals potential GDP—equivalently, when the economy is on its *long-run* aggregate supply curve. Figure 24.9 shows long-run equilibrium, which occurs at the intersection of the aggregate demand curve and the long-run aggregate supply curve (the blue curves). Long-run equilibrium comes about because the money wage rate adjusts. Potential GDP and aggregate demand determine the price level, and the price level influences the money wage rate. In long-run equilibrium, the money wage rate has adjusted to put the (green) short-run aggregate supply curve through the long-run equilibrium point.

We'll look at this adjustment process later in this chapter. But first, let's use the *AS-AD* model to study economic growth and inflation.

FIGURE 24.9

Long-Run Equilibrium

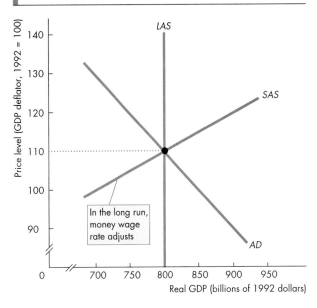

In long-run macroeconomic equilibrium, real GDP equals potential GDP. So long-run equilibrium occurs where the aggregate demand curve intersects the long-run aggregate demand curve. In the long run, aggregate demand determines the price level and has no effect on real GDP. The money wage rate adjusts in the long run so that the *SAS* curve intersects the *LAS* curve at the long-run equilibrium price level.

Economic Growth and Inflation

Economic growth occurs because, over time, the quantity of labour grows, capital is accumulated, and technology advances. These changes increase potential GDP and shift the long-run aggregate supply curve rightward. Figure 24.10 shows such a shift. The growth rate of potential GDP is determined by the pace at which labour grows, capital is accumulated, and technology advances.

Inflation occurs when, over time, aggregate demand increases by more than long-run aggregate supply. That is, inflation occurs if the aggregate demand curve shifts rightward by more than the rightward shift in the long-run aggregate supply curve. Figure 24.10 shows such shifts.

If aggregate demand increases at the same pace as long-run aggregate supply, we experience real GDP growth with no inflation.

In the long run, the main influence on aggregate demand is the growth rate of the quantity of money.

At times when the quantity of money increases rapidly, aggregate demand increases quickly and the inflation rate is high. When the growth rate of the quantity of money slows, other things remaining the same, the inflation rate eventually decreases.

Our economy experiences growth and inflation, like that shown in Fig. 24.10. But it does not experience *steady* growth and *steady* inflation. Real GDP fluctuates around potential GDP in a business cycle and inflation also fluctuates. When we study the business cycle, we ignore economic growth. By doing so, we can see the business cycle more clearly.

Business Cycles

The business cycle occurs because aggregate demand and short-run aggregate supply fluctuate but the money wage rate does not adjust quickly enough to keep real GDP at potential GDP. Figure 24.11 shows three types of short-run macroeconomic equilibrium.

In part (a) there is a below full-employment equilibrium. A **below full-employment equilibrium** is a short-run macroeconomic equilibrium in which potential GDP exceeds real GDP. The amount by which potential GDP exceeds real GDP is called a **recessionary gap**. This name reminds us that a gap has opened up between potential GDP and real GDP either because the economy has experienced a recession or because real GDP, while growing, has grown more slowly than potential GDP.

The below full-employment equilibrium shown in Fig. 24.11(a) occurs where the aggregate demand curve AD_0 intersects short-run aggregate supply curve SAS_0 at a real GDP of $780 billion and a price level of 110. The recessionary gap is $20 billion. The Canadian economy was in a situation similar to that shown in Fig. 24.11(a) during the early 1980s and again during the early 1990s. In those years, real GDP was less than potential GDP.

Figure 24.11(b) is an example of *long-run equilibrium* in which real GDP equals potential GDP. In this example, the equilibrium occurs where the aggregate demand curve AD_1 intersects the short-run aggregate supply curve SAS_1 at an actual and potential GDP of $800 billion. The Canadian economy was in a situation such as that shown in Fig. 24.11(b) in 1990.

Figure 24.11(c) shows an above full-employment equilibrium. An **above full-employment equilibrium** is a short-run macroeconomic equilibrium in which real GDP exceeds potential GDP. The amount

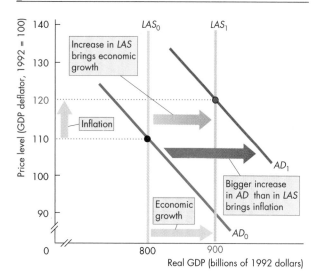

FIGURE 24.10

Economic Growth and Inflation

Economic growth is the persistent increase in potential GDP. Economic growth is shown as an ongoing rightward movement in the *LAS* curve. Inflation is the persistent rise in the price level. Inflation occurs when aggregate demand increases by more than the increase in long-run aggregate supply.

by which real GDP exceeds potential GDP is called an **inflationary gap**. This name reminds us that a gap has opened up between real GDP and potential GDP and that this gap creates inflationary pressure.

The above full-employment equilibrium shown in Fig. 24.11(c) occurs where the aggregate demand curve AD_2 intersects the short-run aggregate supply curve SAS_2 at a real GDP of $820 billion and a price level of 110. There is an inflationary gap of $20 billion. The Canadian economy was in a situation similar to that depicted in part (c) in 1988–1989.

The economy moves from one type of equilibrium to another as a result of fluctuations in aggregate demand and in short-run aggregate supply. These fluctuations produce fluctuations in real GDP and the price level. Figure 24.11(d) shows how real GDP fluctuates around potential GDP.

Let's now look at some of the sources of these fluctuations around potential GDP.

FIGURE 24.11

The Business Cycle

(a) Below full-employment equilibrium

(b) Long-run equilibrium

(c) Above full-employment equilibrium

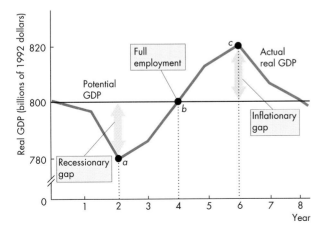

(d) Fluctuations in real GDP

Part (a) shows a below full-employment equilibrium; part (b) shows a long-run equilibrium; and part (c) shows an above full-employment equilibrium. Part (d) shows how real GDP fluctuates around potential GDP in a business cycle. In year 2, a recessionary gap exists and the economy is at point a (in parts a and d). In year 4, the economy is in long-run equilibrium and the economy is at point b (in parts b and d). In year 6, an inflationary gap exists and the economy is at point c (in parts c and d).

Fluctuations in Aggregate Demand

One reason real GDP fluctuates around potential GDP is that aggregate demand fluctuates. Let's see what happens when aggregate demand increases.

Figure 24.12(a) shows an economy in long-run equilibrium. The aggregate demand curve is AD_0, the short-run aggregate supply curve is SAS_0, and the long-run aggregate supply curve is LAS. Real GDP equals potential GDP at $800 billion, and the price level is 110.

Now suppose that the world economy expands and that the demand for Canadian-made goods increases in Japan and Europe. The increase in Canadian exports increases aggregate demand and the aggregate demand curve shifts rightward from AD_0 to AD_1 in Fig. 24.12(a).

Faced with an increase in demand, firms increase production and raise prices. Real GDP increases to $850 billion, and the price level rises to 115. The economy is now in an above-full employment equi-

librium. Real GDP exceeds potential GDP, and an inflationary gap exists.

The increase in aggregate demand has increased the prices of all goods and services. Faced with higher prices, firms have increased their output rates. At this stage, prices of goods and services have increased but money wage rates have not changed. (Recall that as we move along a short-run aggregate supply curve, the money wage rate is constant.)

The economy cannot produce in excess of potential GDP forever. Why not? What are the forces at work that bring real GDP back to potential GDP?

Because the price level has increased and the money wage rate is unchanged, workers have experienced a fall in the buying power of their wages and firms' profits have increased. In these circumstances, workers demand higher money wage rates and firms, anxious to maintain their employment and output levels, meet those demands. If firms do not raise money wage rates, they will either lose workers or have to hire less productive ones.

FIGURE 24.12

An Increase in Aggregate Demand

(a) Short-run effect

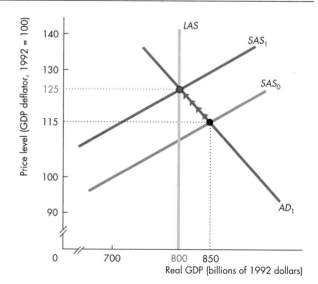

(b) Long-run effect

An increase in aggregate demand shifts the aggregate demand curve from AD_0 to AD_1. In short-run equilibrium, real GDP increases to $850 billion and the price level rises to 115 in part (a). In this situation, an inflationary gap exists. In the long run, the money wage rate rises, and the short-run aggregate

supply curve shifts leftward from SAS_0 to SAS_1 in part (b). As short-run aggregate supply decreases, the SAS curve shifts and intersects the aggregate demand curve AD_1 at higher price levels and real GDP decreases. Eventually, the price level rises to 125 and real GDP decreases to $800 billion—potential GDP.

As the money wage rate rises, the short-run aggregate supply curve shifts leftward from SAS_0 towards SAS_1 in Fig. 24.12(b). The leftward shift of the SAS curve produces a sequence of new equilibrium positions. The economy moves up along its aggregate demand curve as shown by the arrowheads in the figure as real GDP decreases and the price level rises.

Eventually, the money wage rate rises by the same percentage as the price level. At this time, the aggregate demand curve AD_1 intersects SAS_1 at a new long-run equilibrium. The price level has risen to 125, and real GDP is back where it started, at potential GDP.

A decrease in aggregate demand has similar but opposite effects to those that you've just seen. A decrease in aggregate demand shifts the aggregate demand curve leftward. Real GDP decreases to less than potential GDP and a recessionary gap emerges. Firms cut prices. The lower price level increases the purchasing power of wages and increases firms' costs relative to their output prices because the money wage rate remains unchanged. Eventually, the slack economy leads to a falling money wage rate and the short-run aggregate supply curve shifts rightward. But the money wage rate changes slowly, so real GDP only slowly returns to potential GDP.

Fluctuations in Aggregate Supply

Fluctuations in short-run aggregate supply can bring fluctuations in real GDP around potential GDP. Suppose that initially real GDP equals potential GDP. Then there is a large but temporary rise in the price of oil. What happens to real GDP and the price level?

Figure 24.13 answers this question. The aggregate demand curve is AD_0, the short-run aggregate supply curve is SAS_0, and the long-run aggregate supply curve is LAS. Equilibrium real GDP is $800 billion, which equals potential GDP, and the price level is 110. Then the price of oil rises. Faced with higher energy and transportation costs, firms decrease production. Short-run aggregate supply decreases, and the short-run aggregate supply curve shifts leftward to SAS_1. The price level rises to 120, and real GDP decreases to $750 billion. Because real GDP decreases, the economy experiences recession. Because the price level increases, the economy experiences inflation. A combination of recession and inflation, called *stagflation*, actually occurred in Canada in the mid-1970s and early 1980s. But events like this are not common.

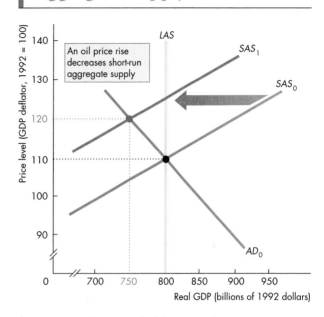

FIGURE 24.13

A Decrease in Aggregate Supply

An oil price rise decreases short-run aggregate supply

An increase in the price of oil decreases short-run aggregate supply and shifts the short-run aggregate supply curve from SAS_0 to SAS_1. Real GDP decreases from $800 billion to $750 billion, and the price level rises from 110 to 120. The economy experiences both recession and inflation—stagflation.

REVIEW QUIZ

▨ Does economic growth result from increases in aggregate demand, short-run aggregate supply, or long-run aggregate supply?

▨ Does inflation result from increases in aggregate demand, short-run aggregate supply, or long-run aggregate supply?

▨ Can you describe three types of short-run macroeconomic equilibrium?

▨ How do fluctuations in aggregate demand and short-run aggregate supply bring fluctuations in real GDP around potential GDP?

Let's put our new knowledge of aggregate supply and aggregate demand to work and see how we can explain recent Canadian macroeconomic performance.

Growth, Inflation, and Cycles in the Canadian Economy

THE ECONOMY IS CONTINUALLY CHANGING. If you imagine the economy as a video, then an aggregate supply–aggregate demand figure such as Fig. 24.13 is a freeze-frame. We're going to run the video—an instant replay—but keep our finger on the freeze-frame button and look at some important parts of the previous action. Let's run the video from 1971.

Figure 24.14 shows the state of the economy in 1971 at the point of intersection of its aggregate demand curve AD_{71} and short-run aggregate supply curve SAS_{71}. Real GDP was $359 billion, and the GDP deflator was 27.

By 1998, the economy had reached the point marked by the intersection of aggregate demand curve AD_{98} and short-run aggregate supply curve SAS_{98}. Real GDP was $838 billion, and the GDP deflator was 107. So, in1998, real GDP was more than twice its 1971 level and the GDP deflator was more than four times its 1971 level. The path traced by the blue and red dots shows three key features:

- Economic growth
- Inflation
- Business cycles

Economic Growth

Over the years, real GDP grows—shown in Fig. 24.14 by the rightward movement of the points. The faster real GDP grows, the larger is the horizontal distance between successive dots in the figure. The forces that generate economic growth are those that increase potential GDP. Potential GDP grows because the quantity of labour grows, we accumulate physical capital and human capital, and our technologies advance. These forces that bring economic growth were stronger during the early 1970s, mid-1980s, and late 1990s than at other times. During the mid 1970s, and early 1990s, real GDP growth was slow.

FIGURE 24.14

Aggregate Supply and Aggregate Demand: 1971–1998

Each point shows the value of the GDP deflator and real GDP in a given year. In 1971, these variables were determined by the intersection of aggregate demand curve AD_{71} and a short-run aggregate supply curve SAS_{71}. Each point is generated by the gradual shifting of the AD and SAS curves. By 1998, the curves were AD_{98} and SAS_{98}. Real GDP grew, and the price level increased. But growth and inflation did not proceed smoothly. Real GDP grew quickly during the early 1970s, mid 1980s, and late 1990s. In 1982 and 1990–1991, real GDP shrank in recession. Inflation was rapid during the 1970s, slowed after the 1982 recession, and almost vanished during the late 1990s.

Source: Statistics Canada, *StatCan: CANSIM Disc*, March 1999.

Inflation

The price level has risen over the years, but in 1998, the price level fell. Figure 24.14 shows the rise in the price level by the upward movement of the points. The larger the rise in the price level, the larger is the vertical distance between successive dots in the figure. The main force generating the persistent increase in the price level is a tendency for aggregate demand to increase at a faster pace than the increase in long-run aggregate supply. All of the factors that increase aggregate demand and shift the aggregate demand curve influence the pace of inflation. But one factor—the growth of the quantity of money—is the main source of *persistent* increases in aggregate demand and persistent inflation.

Business Cycles

Over the years, the economy grows and shrinks in cycles—shown in Fig. 24.14 by the wavelike pattern made by the points, with the recessions highlighted. Cycles arise because both the expansion of short-run aggregate supply and the growth of aggregate demand do not proceed at a fixed, steady pace. Although the economy has cycles, recessions do not usually follow quickly on the heels of their predecessors; "double-dip" recessions like the one in the cartoon are rare.

The Evolving Economy: 1971–1998

During the early 1970s, real GDP growth was rapid and inflation was low. This was a period of rapid increases in aggregate supply and of moderate increases in aggregate demand.

The mid-1970s were years of rapid inflation and recession—of stagflation. The major source of these developments was a series of massive oil price increases that decreased short-run aggregate supply and rapid increases in the quantity of money that increased aggregate demand curve. Recession occurred because the decrease in short-run aggregate supply occurred at a faster pace than the increase in aggregate demand.

The rest of the 1970s saw high inflation—the price level increased quickly—and only moderate growth in real GDP. By 1980, inflation was a major problem and the Bank of Canada decided to take strong action against it. It permitted interest rates to rise to previously unknown levels and aggregate demand decreased. By 1982, the decrease in aggregate demand put the economy in a deep recession.

"Please stand by for a series of tones. The first indicates the official end of the recession, the second indicates prosperity, and the third the return of the recession."

During the years 1983 to 1989, capital accumulation and steady technological advance resulted in a sustained increase in long-run aggregate supply. This increase in long-run aggregate supply also increased short-run aggregate supply. Increases in the money wage rate decreased short-run aggregate supply, but the rate of increase in the money wage rate was moderate, so short-run aggregate supply increased. Aggregate demand growth kept pace with the growth of aggregate supply. Sustained but steady growth in aggregate supply and aggregate demand kept real GDP growing and inflation steady. The economy moved from a recession with real GDP less than potential GDP in 1982 to above full-employment in 1989. It was in this condition when a decrease in aggregate demand led to the 1990–1991 recession. The economy again embarked on a path of expansion through 1998. The expansion took real GDP close to potential GDP and returned employment almost to full employment.

◆ The *AS–AD* model explains economic growth, inflation, and the business cycle. The model enables us to keep our eye on the big picture. But it lacks detail. It doesn't tell us what we need to know about the forces that lie behind aggregate supply and aggregate demand. The chapters that follow begin to fill in the details on aggregate demand. But before you embark on this next stage, take a look at *Reading Between the Lines* on pp. 532-533, which examines the economy of China in 1998.

Aggregate Supply and Aggregate Demand in Action

VANCOUVER SUN, JULY 18, 1998

China claims its growth target still within reach

China said Friday its economic growth target of eight per cent for the year is still within reach despite a slower first-half performance, but economists were dubious.

China's growth slowed to a year-on-year seven per cent in the first half as the country was battered by Asia's financial crisis and heavy summer rains, the State Statistical Bureau said.

Beijing says it needs to meet the eight-per-cent growth target to create new jobs for millions of workers to be laid off in a painful overhaul of state industry, long used to the comfortable cushion of central planning.

Despite the gloomy first-half performance, the bureau's chief economist, Qiu Xiaohua, said the pace of expansion will pick up in the second half as measures to spur domestic demand kicked in.

"We can predict that Chinese economic growth will continue to rise as all kinds of government measures come into effect," Qiu told reporters. ...

But other economists are pessimistic that the eight-per-cent goal is attainable. ...

Asia's financial troubles have cast a long shadow on China's ambitious economic goals by undermining two pillars of its growth—exports and foreign investment. ...

Foreign investors, wary of sinking money into Asia, have shied away from China. Direct foreign investment in China dropped a year-on-year 1.3 per cent in the first half to $20.5 billion, the statistics bureau said.

Moreover, reduced demand from Asia cut China's export growth in the first six months to a year-on-year 7.6 per cent from the sizzling 20.9 per cent growth for all of 1997, it said.

"Under the negative impact of the Asian financial crisis, China's exports have slowed significantly," Qiu said.

Torrential rainstorms caused flooding across much of southern and eastern China, trimming summer grain output by 11 per cent from last year, and shaving 0.4 of a percentage point off economic growth in the first half. ...

Essence of the Story

■ China's economic target for 1998 is an 8 per-cent increase in potential GDP.

■ During 1998, China was battered by the Asian financial crisis and by heavy summer rains.

■ The Asian financial crisis decreased foreign investment in China and slowed China's export growth.

■ The Chinese government says that an 8 per-cent increase in GDP is needed to provide jobs for workers who will be laid off in an overhaul of state-owned industry.

■ Throughout the 1990s, China experienced spectacular economic growth. The average growth rate of real GDP was 10.5 percent a year.

■ As you can see in Fig. 1, the growth rate increased through 1992 but then decreased. By 1998, it had fallen to 6 percent a year.

■ Between 1990 and 1994, China experienced rising inflation. After 1994, the inflation rate fell. By 1998 it was close to zero.

■ Figure 2 shows China's real GDP gap during the 1990s. At the start of the 1990s, there was a recessionary gap. By the mid-1990s, there was an inflationary gap. Then by 1998, a recessionary gap returned.

■ China was not in a recession in 1998 because real GDP had not decreased. But the growth rate of real GDP was less than the growth rate of potential GDP, so a recessionary gap emerged.

■ You can understand the economic growth and inflation that China has experienced during the 1990s by using the aggregate supply-aggregate demand model.

■ Figure 3 shows aggregate supply and aggregate demand in China in 1997 and 1998.

■ In 1997, potential GDP was 3.9 trillion yuan and the long-run aggregate supply curve was LAS_{97}. The short-run aggregate supply curve was SAS_{97}, and the aggregate demand curve is AD_{97}, Real GDP equalled potential GDP at 3.9 trillion yuan. The price level was 190.

■ During 1998, potential GDP grew by less than its normal pace because of heavy rains. The long-run aggregate supply curve shifted rightward to LAS_{98}.

■ When potential GDP increases, short-run aggregate supply also increases. If the money wage rate did not change, the SAS curve would shift rightward by the same amount as the shift in the LAS curve.

■ But the money wage rate increased, so the short-run aggregate supply curve shifted rightward by less than the shift in the LAS curve. It shifted from SAS_{97} to SAS_{98}.

■ Aggregate demand increased in 1998 but by much less than the increase in long-run aggregate supply.

■ The small growth in aggregate demand resulted from the broader Asian crisis and the slow growth of Japan, which decreased investment in China and slowed China's export growth.

Figure 1 Economic growth in China

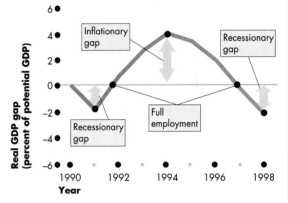

Figure 2 Real GDP gaps in China

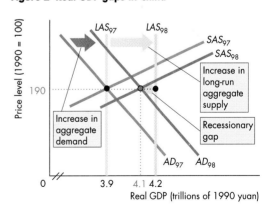

Figure 3 China in 1997-1998

■ The new equilibrium is at a real GDP of 4.1 trillion yuan and the price level remains at 190.

533

SUMMARY

Key Points

Aggregate Supply (pp. 516–520)

- In the long run, the quantity of real GDP supplied is potential GDP, which is independent of the price level. The long-run aggregate supply curve is vertical.

- In the short run, the money wage rate is constant, so a rise in the price level increases the quantity of real GDP supplied. The short-run aggregate supply curve is upward sloping.

- A change in potential GDP changes both long-run and short-run aggregate supply. A change in the money wage rate or resource prices changes only short-run aggregate supply.

Aggregate Demand (pp. 521–524)

- A rise in the price level decreases the quantity of real GDP demanded, other things remaining the same.

- The reason is that the higher price level decreases the quantity of *real* wealth, raises the interest rate, and raises the price of domestic goods compared with foreign goods.

- Changes in fiscal policy and monetary policy, changes in world real GDP and the foreign exchange rate, and changes in expected future disposable income, inflation, and profits change aggregate demand.

Macroeconomic Equilibrium (pp. 524–529)

- In the short run, real GDP and the price level are determined by aggregate demand and short-run aggregate supply.

- In the long run, real GDP equals potential GDP and aggregate demand determines the price level and the money wage rate.

- Economic growth occurs because potential GDP increases.

- Inflation occurs because aggregate demand grows more quickly than potential GDP.

- Business cycles occur because aggregate demand and aggregate supply fluctuate.

Growth, Inflation, and Cycles in the Canadian Economy (pp. 530–531)

- Canadian potential GDP grew fastest during the early 1970s, mid 1980s, and late 1990s and slowest during the late 1970s and early 1990s.

- Canadian inflation persists because aggregate demand grows faster than potential GDP.

- Canadian business cycles occur because aggregate supply and aggregate demand change at an uneven pace.

Key Figures

Key Terms

PROBLEMS

☐ *1. The following events occur that influence the economy of Toughtimes:
   (i) A deep recession hits the world economy
   (ii) Oil prices rise sharply
   (iii) Businesses expect huge losses in the near future.
   a. Explain the separate effects of each of these events on real GDP and the price level in Toughtimes, starting from a position of long-run equilibrium.
   b. Explain the combined effects of these events on real GDP and the price level in Toughtimes, starting from a position of long-run equilibrium.
   c. Explain what the Toughtimes government and central bank can do to overcome the problems faced by the economy.

2. The following events occur that influence the economy of Coolland:
   (i) A strong expansion in the world economy
   (ii) Businesses expect huge profits in the near future
   (iii) The Coolland government cuts its expenditure
   a. Explain the separate effects of each of these events on real GDP and the price level in Coolland, starting from a position of long-run equilibrium.
   b. Explain the combined effects of these events on real GDP and the price level in Coolland, starting from a position of long-run equilibrium.
   c. Explain why the Coolland government or central bank might want to take action to influence the Coolland economy.

☐ *3. The economy of Mainland has the following aggregate demand and supply schedules:

Price level	Real GDP demanded	Real GDP supplied in the short run
	(billions of 1992 dollars)	
90	450	350
100	400	400
110	350	450
120	300	500
130	250	550
140	200	600

a. In a figure, plot the aggregate demand curve and short-run aggregate supply curve.
   b. What are the values of real GDP and the price level in Mainland in a short-run macroeconomic equilibrium?
   c. Mainland's potential GDP is $500 billion. Plot the long-run aggregate supply curve in the same figure in which you answered part (a).

4. The economy of Miniland has the following aggregate demand and supply schedules:

Price level	Real GDP demanded	Real GDP supplied in the short run
	(billions of 1992 dollars)	
90	600	150
100	500	200
110	400	250
120	300	300
130	200	350
140	100	400

a. In a figure, plot the aggregate demand curve and short-run aggregate supply curve.
   b. What are the values of real GDP and the price level in Miniland in a short-run macroeconomic equilibrium?
   c. Miniland's potential GDP is $250 billion. Plot the long-run aggregate supply curve in the same figure in which you answered part (a).

☐ *5. In problem 3, aggregate demand is increased by $100 billion. How do real GDP and the price level change in the short run?

6. In problem 4, aggregate demand is decreased by $150 billion. How do real GDP and the price level change in the short run?

☐ *7. In problem 3, aggregate supply decreases by $100 billion. What now is the short-run macroeconomic equilibrium?

8. In problem 4, aggregate supply increases by $150 billion. What now is the short-run macroeconomic equilibrium?

*9. In the economy shown in the figure (next page), initially the short-run aggregate supply is SAS_0 and aggregate demand is AD_0. Then some events change aggregate demand and the aggregate demand curve shifts rightward to AD_1. Later, some other events change aggregate supply and shift the short-run aggregate supply curve leftward to SAS_1.

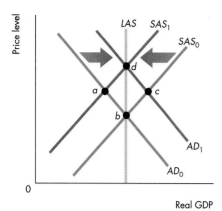

a. What is the equilibrium point after the change in aggregate demand?

b. What is the equilibrium point after the change in aggregate supply?

c. What events could have changed aggregate demand from AD_0 to AD_1?

d. What events could have changed aggregate supply from SAS_0 to SAS_1?

10. In the economy shown in the figure, initially long-run aggregate supply is LAS_0, short-run aggregate supply is SAS_0, and aggregate demand is AD. Then some events change aggregate supply and the aggregate supply curves shift rightward to LAS_1 and SAS_1.

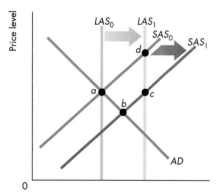

a. What is the equilibrium point after the change in aggregate supply?

b. What events could have changed long-run aggregate supply from LAS_0 to LAS_1?

c. What events could have changed short-run aggregate supply from SAS_0 to SAS_1?

d. After the increase in aggregate supply, is real GDP greater than or less than potential GDP?

e. What change in aggregate demand will make real GDP equal to potential GDP?

CRITICAL THINKING

1. After you have studied the account of the Chinese economy during the 1990s in *Reading Between the Lines* on pp. 532–533:

   a. Describe the main features of Chinese economic growth during the 1990s.

   b. In which periods did China have a recessionary gap and in which did it have an inflationary gap?

   c. Use the *AS-AD* model to show the effects in 1999 of fiscal policies and monetary policies that are designed to achieve full employment.

2. Use the links on the Parkin-Bade Web site to obtain the latest data on Canadian real GDP and the price level. Then:

   a. Create a figure similar to those on p. 533 to interpret the latest numbers.

   b. In light of the events that occurred during 1999, do you think that the Canadian economy is at full employment, above full employment, or below full employment? Explain.

3. You are the Finance Minister's economic advisor and have the following forecasts of aggregate demand and aggregate supply for next year:

Price level	Real GDP demanded	Real GDP supplied	Potential GDP
		(billions of 1992 dollars)	
100	930	630	800
105	880	730	800
110	830	830	800
115	780	930	800

This year, real GDP is $838 billion, potential GDP is around $850 billion and the price level is 107. The Minister wants answers to the following questions:

a. What is your forecast of next year's real GDP?

b. What is your forecast of next year's price level?

c. What is your forecast of the inflation rate?

d. What is your forecast of the growth rate of real GDP?

e. What is your forecast of the growth rate of potential GDP?

f. Will there be a recessionary gap or an inflationary gap? By how much?

Understanding the Issues of Macroeconomics

Macroeconomics is a large and controversial subject that is interlaced with political ideological disputes. And it is a field in which charlatans as well as serious thinkers have much to say. This page is a map that looks back at the road you've just travelled and forward at the path you will take from here.

◆ You began your study of macroeconomics with the core questions of the subject. What are the causes of:

- Economic growth?
- Business cycles?
- Unemployment?
- Inflation?

The Big Picture

In Chapter 21, you took your first look at each of these questions. You learned some facts about economic growth, business cycles, unemployment, and inflation in Canada and around the world. ◆ In Chapter 22, you learned how we measure the economy's output and prices. These measures are used to calculate the rate of economic growth, business cycle fluctuations, and inflation. You discovered that making these measurements is not straightforward and that small measurement errors can have a big effect on our perceptions about how we are doing. ◆ In Chapter 23, you learned how we measure the state of the labour market—the levels of employment and unemployment and wages. And in Chapter 24, you studied the macroeconomic version of supply and demand—

aggregate supply and *aggregate demand*. You saw that the *AS–AD* model is the big picture model. It explains both the long-term trends in economic growth and inflation and the short-term business cycle fluctuations in production, jobs, and inflation.

◆ The chapters that lie ahead of you look behind aggregate supply and aggregate demand, beginning on the demand side. In Chapters 25 through 30, you will study aggregate demand, inflation, and deflation and learn about the macroeconomics that Keynes developed as a response to the Great Depression. And you will learn about the effects of monetary and fiscal policies on aggregate demand. ◆ Then, in Chapters 31 through 34, you will study aggregate supply, economic growth and fluctuations, and policy challenges that we face in stabilizing our economy and speeding its growth. Here, you learn today's answer to the question posed by Adam Smith—what are the causes of differences in the wealth of nations? In Chapter 31, you study the economy at full employment and the forces that change potential GDP. In Chapter 32, you study the roles of saving, investment, and technological change in the process of economic growth. In Chapter 33, you study the business cycle and in Chapter 34, the policy challenges.

◇ Before continuing your study of macroeconomics, spend a few minutes with John Maynard Keynes and Jean-Baptiste Say, the leading scholars who developed this subject. And spend a few minutes with today's leading macroeconomist, Robert E. Lucas, Jr. of the University of Chicago.

Probing the Ideas

Macroeconomic Revolutions

John Maynard Keynes,
born in England in 1883, was one of the outstanding minds of the twentieth century. He wrote on probability as well as economics, represented Britain at the Versailles peace conference at the end of World War I, was a master speculator on international financial markets (an activity he conducted from bed every morning and which made and lost him several fortunes), and played a prominent role in creating the International Monetary Fund. He was a member of the Bloomsbury Group, a circle of outstanding artists and writers that included E. M. Forster, Bertrand Russell, and Virginia Woolf. Keynes was a controversial and quick-witted figure. A critic once complained that Keynes had changed his opinion on some matter, to which Keynes retorted: "When I discover I am wrong, I change my mind. What do you do?"

"...The ideas of economists and political philosophers, both when they are right and when they are wrong, are more powerful than is commonly understood. Indeed the world is ruled by little else."

JOHN MAYNARD KEYNES,
THE GENERAL THEORY OF EMPLOYMENT, INTEREST, AND MONEY

538

The Issues

During the Industrial Revolution, as technological change created new jobs and destroyed old ones, people began to wonder whether the economy could create enough jobs and sufficient demand to buy all the things that the new industrial economy could produce.

Jean-Baptiste Say argued that production creates incomes that are suffi-cient to buy everything that is produced—supply creates its own demand—an idea that came to be called *Say's Law*.

Say and Keynes would have had a lot to disagree about. Jean-Baptiste Say, born in Lyon, France, in 1767 (he was 9 years old when Adam Smith's *Wealth of Nations* was published), suffered the wrath of Napoleon for his views on government and the economy. In today's world, Say would be leading a radical conservative charge for a smaller and leaner government. Say was the most famous economist of his era on both sides of the Atlantic. His book, *Traité d'économie politique (A Treatise in Political Economy)*, published in 1803, became a best-selling university economics textbook in both Europe and North America.

As the Great Depression of the 1930s became more severe and more prolonged, Say's Law looked less and less relevant. John Maynard Keynes revolutionized macroeconomic thinking by turning Say's Law on its head, arguing that production does not depend on supply. Instead, it depends on what people are willing to buy—on demand. Or as Keynes put it, production depends on *effective demand*. It is possible, argued Keynes, for people to refuse to spend all of their incomes. If businesses fail to spend on new capital the amount that people plan to save, demand might be less than supply. In this situation, resources might go unemployed and remain unemployed indefinitely.

The influence of Keynes persists even today, more than 60 years after the publication of his main work. But during the past 20 years, Nobel Laureate Robert E. Lucas, Jr., with significant contributions from a list of outstanding macroeconomists too long to name, has further revolutionized macroeconomics. Today, we know a lot about economic growth, unemployment, inflation, and business cycles. And we know how to use fiscal policy and monetary policy to improve macroeconomic performance. But we don't yet have all the answers. Macroeconomics remains a field of lively controversy and exciting research.

Then ...

In 1776, James Hargreaves, an English weaver and carpenter, developed a simple hand-operated machine called a spinning jenny (pictured here). Using this machine, a person could spin 80 threads at once. Thousands of hand-wheel spinners, operators of machines that could spin only one thread, lost their jobs. They protested by wrecking spinning jennies. In the long run, the displaced hand-wheel spinners found work, often in factories that manufactured the machines that had destroyed their previous jobs. From the earliest days of the Industrial Revolution to the present day, people have lost their jobs as new technologies have automated what human effort had previously been needed to accomplish.

... and Now

Advances in computer technology have made it possible for us to dial our own telephone calls to any part of the world and get connected in a flash. A task that was once performed by telephone operators, who made connections along copper wires, is now performed faster and more reliably by computers along fibre-optic cables. Just as the Industrial Revolution transformed the textile industry, so today's Information Revolution is transforming the telecommunications industry. In the process, the mix of jobs is changing. There are fewer jobs for telephone operators but more jobs for telephone systems designers, builders, managers, and marketers. In the long run, as people spend the income they earn in their changing jobs, supply creates its own demand, just as Say predicted. But does supply create its own demand in the short run, when displaced workers are unemployed?

Keynes and Robert E. Lucas, Jr. would have had plenty of disagreements too. Lucas, of the University of Chicago, has led a revolution in macroeconomics that has enabled economists to build model (artificial) economies that display properties similar to those of the actual economy and to use these models to study the effects of alternative policies on macroeconomic performance. But Lucas, like Say, believes that it is easier for government intervention to do harm than good. Said Lucas, "I don't want to manage the economy. And I don't think anybody else should take the job either." You can meet Professor Lucas on the following pages.

Talking with
Robert E. Lucas, Jr.

Robert E. Lucas, Jr. *is a professor of economics at the University of Chicago, a position he has held since 1975. Professor Lucas was born in Yakima, Washington, in 1937. He earned his B.A. and his Ph.D. from the University of Chicago in 1959 and 1963, respectively.*

In 1995, Professor Lucas received the Nobel Prize for Economic Science for his work on developing the theory of rational expectations. Challenging the Keynesian theories of economic fluctuations, this new macroeconomic theory is based on the hypothesis that people and businesses make rational decisions based on rational expectations and markets reconcile individual decisions by balancing supply and demand, even in a recession.

Robin Bade and Michael Parkin spoke with Professor Lucas about rational expectations macroeconomics, his views of economic policy, and the legacy of Keynes.

Why are you an economist?
I grew up in a family where everyone talked about politics and economics every night at dinner. So I've been concerned with social questions as long as I can remember. My experience as an undergraduate history major confirmed my belief in the importance of economic forces.

You applied the idea of rational expectations to macroeconomics and to expectations about inflation. How has that hypothesis changed the way we think about things?
It ties down a loose end that shouldn't have been there. Any important economic decision depends on what you think about the future. Rational expectations is a way of dealing with that.

What do you see as the chief criticism of the rational expectations hypothesis?
Here's the genuine difficulty people have with the idea. You would never discover the idea of rational expectations by introspection. Rational expectations describes something that has to be true of the outcome of a much more complicated underlying process. But it doesn't describe the actual thought process people use in trying to figure out the future. Our behaviour is adaptive. We try some mode of behaviour. If it's successful, we do it again. If not, we try something else. Rational expectations describes the situation when you've got it right.

Can you give an example?
In economics, we're mostly concerned about repetitive events and decisions of some consequence. Our capitalist economy has been operating under pretty much the same laws for 200 years now. People aren't reacting to every monetary contraction as if it's the first time it ever happened: That is just inconceivable. I think people have developed certain ways of living with regular events as best they can.

One of the most significant developments in macroeconomics in recent years has been real business cycle theory. How do you evaluate this approach?

Real business cycle theory asks what the time path of the economy's GDP or employment would be under the best possible macroeconomic policy. The early authors of this approach asked themselves what fraction of the actual variation in GDP you could account for if you restricted yourself to the fluctuations in the rate of technological change. Their initial answer was: All of it, that there is nothing left over for traditional macroeconomic theory to account for. I don't think that can be right.

For example, you can't account for something like the events of 1929 to 1933, when real output fell by a quarter in four years, as if it resulted from the changes in the rate at which technology was decaying. The Great Depression didn't occur because production techniques got worse. But real business cycle theory has shown us that real forces are much more important than we had thought and that the questions addressed by traditional macroeconomics are not as important as we once thought. That's the important message.

How can we introduce monetary forces into a macroeconomic model that at the same time pays serious attention to real forces, one that shows fluctuations in price as well as in output?

This question is the subject of my Nobel Lecture, "Monetary Neutrality." I think it is the central question of macroeconomics, but it remains unresolved today, as it did when David Hume first addressed it in the eighteenth century.

Your early work focussed primarily on short-term macroeconomic problems. For the past 10 years, you've increasingly devoted your life to thinking about long-term growth. Why has your work changed in that direction?

When I began taking economics courses in the early 1960s, the Great Depression of the 1930s was a key topic of discussion for all my professors. The study of macroeconomics was, at that time, the study of how to prevent depressions and how to get out of them. The United States has not had a serious depression since the 1930s, and we should not be surprised that macroeconomic study has switched from a depression focus to a growth focus. If you ask what determines our income today relative to what it

was in the 1960s, 99 percent of the answer is economic growth.

What can we bring to the study of growth today that Smith couldn't bring to it when he tried to figure out what caused the wealth of nations?

When Adam Smith wrote about the wealth of nations, he was thinking about a world in which no country had ever experienced sustained growth in living standards. Some countries had higher *levels* of income than others, and Smith was interested in understanding why those differences existed. But Smith never observed or imagined a country where production could grow at 3 percent per year for a century and more. Smith also lacked good data, by modern standards. We now have tremendous data sets on income and the growth of income for the richest and poorest countries. During the past 15 years, growth theory has evolved from being the study of the United States, Canada, the United Kingdom, and a few other very wealthy economies

People aren't reacting to every monetary contractions as if it's the first time it ever happened.

to being the comparative study of rich and poor economies. The hope is that the same general theoretical principles will apply to both.

There's about a 25 to 1 difference between the United States and India in per capita production. How do you explain that difference?

Only a small fraction can be explained by the differences in physical capital. U.S. workers have better equipment than Indian workers, and that's certainly a factor in making them more productive, but a much more important factor is human capital. The level of education and training of the U.S. worker is much higher than the typical Indian worker. Once human capital is introduced—and placed at the centre of growth theory—a lot of things start falling into place and it becomes much easier to understand the enormous differences in incomes.

541

How do you explain the astonishing growth rates of per capita incomes in East Asia compared with the 1 to 2 percent growth rates of North America?

The countries of East Asia are catching up with those of Europe and North America. The Industrial Revolution has opened them up to trade with the more advanced countries of the world. East Asia is experiencing annual growth rates of 6 to 8 percent. Nothing like that ever occurred in the United States or the United Kingdom, the countries that were leaders from the start of the Industrial Revolution. East Asian countries are rapidly learning technology that took decades to produce.

You were a student of Milton Friedman, the architect of the movement called monetarism. How do you distinguish this approach from the kind of macroeconomics that you are responsible for creating?

I'm not that big on the distinction. I think of myself as a monetarist. But the term does refer to several different things. One aspect of what people call monetarism is just an emphasis on the quantity of some money as a determinant of prices and of economic activity. In some ways, I think that revolution has been so successful that it doesn't seem like a revolu-

Economics is a great major…. economics is a good pre-almost anything major.

tion any more. In this day and age, no one talks about the price level, exchange rates, or interest rates without talking about the quantity of money. In that sense, we're all monetarists. The second aspect of monetarism is a hostility towards the government's continual management of the economy. The role of government, in a monetarist perspective, is to make its own behaviour on fiscal or monetary policy simple and predictable and then just to let the system operate without fine tuning. That view, I think, is absolutely right.

Until recently, the United States has experienced the biggest peacetime government budget deficit ever. How have you viewed the deficit over the years?

I was a deficit alarmist in the early years of the Reagan administration because I thought the deficits would be inflationary. Well, that just hasn't happened. I've become more sympathetic to people like Larry Kotlikoff, who argued that the deficit just doesn't measure anything we care about, since things like future social security liabilities are arbitrarily excluded.

What for you is the legacy of Keynes?

Keynes' influence was almost entirely political. He wrote *The General Theory* in the 1930s at a time when many of the major countries were in the process of moving away from liberal democracy and capitalism towards fascism in Germany and Italy and towards Communism in Russia. These countries appeared to deal better with the depression of the 1930s than countries like ours that stayed with liberal institutions. Keynes' message in *The General Theory* is that we can deal with depressions within the framework of a basically capitalistic economy and liberal democratic institutions. This is an important message to get across.

The intellectual forefathers of modern macroeconomics are, for me, the classical economists, Smith and Ricardo, the neoclassical work of Marshall, and the generation of our teachers, Arrow, Friedman, and Samuelson.

Would you advise undergraduates to major in economics?

Economics is a great major. I feel economics is a good pre-almost anything major. Most of the economics majors at the University of Chicago will go to law school, professional school, or work for a while. Our students have a lot of electives to choose from; they have a broad, liberal arts education.

Chapter 25

Expenditure Multipliers

In Toronto's Molson Amphitheatre, Alanis Morissette sings into a microphone in a barely audible whisper. Moving to a louder passage, she increases the volume of her voice and now, through the magic of electronic amplification, booms across the amphitheatre, drowning out every other sound. ◆ Gary Doer, Premier of Manitoba, is being driven to a business meeting along a bumpy Winnipeg street. The car's wheels are bouncing and vibrating over potholes, but Doer is completely undisturbed and writes notes without a ripple, thanks to the car's efficient shock absorbers. ◆ Investment and exports fluctuate like the volume of Alanis Morissette's voice and the uneven surface of a Winnipeg street. How does the economy react to those fluctuations? Does it react like Gary Doer's car, absorbing the shocks and providing a smooth ride for the economy's passengers? Or does it behave like Alanis Morissette's amplifier, blowing up the fluctuations and spreading them out to affect the many millions of participants in an economic rock concert?

Economic Amplifier or Shock Absorber?

◆ You will explore these questions in this chapter. You will learn how a recession or a recovery begins when a change in investment or exports triggers a larger change in *aggregate* expenditure and real GDP—like Alanis Morissette's amplifier. You will also learn how imports and income taxes have lowered the power of the amplifier. Finally, you will discover that in contrast to the initial amplification effect, the economy's shock absorbers, which are price and wage changes, pull real GDP back towards potential GDP. ◆ To achieve these objectives, we use a model called the *aggregate expenditure model*. This model explains changes in aggregate expenditure in a very short time frame during which prices do not change.

After studying this chapter, you will be able to:

- Explain how expenditure plans are determined
- Explain how real GDP is determined when the price level is fixed
- Explain the expenditure multiplier
- Explain how imports and taxes influence the multiplier
- Explain how recessions and expansions begin
- Explain the relationship between aggregate expenditure and aggregate demand
- Explain how the multiplier gets smaller as the price level changes

Expenditure Plans and GDP

THE COMPONENTS OF AGGREGATE EXPENDITURE, consumption expenditure (C), investment (I), government expenditures on goods and services (G), and net exports—exports (X) *minus* imports (M)—sum to real GDP (Y). (See Chapter 22, p. 479.) That is,

$$Y = C + I + G + X - M.$$

Two of these components, consumption expenditure and imports, depend on the level of real GDP. Because real GDP influences consumption expenditure and imports, and because consumption expenditure and imports are components of aggregate expenditure, there is a feedback loop between aggregate expenditure and GDP. You are going to learn how this feedback loop determines real GDP at a given price level.

The starting point is to consider the first piece of the feedback loop: the influence of real GDP on planned consumption expenditure and saving.

Consumption and Saving Plans

Consumption expenditure and saving are influenced by several factors. The most direct influence, especially in the short term, is **disposable income**, which is real GDP or aggregate income (Y) minus net taxes (NT)—taxes minus transfer payments. The equation for disposable income (YD) is:

$$YD = Y - NT.$$

Disposable income either is spent on consumption goods and services—consumption expenditure (C)—or is saved—saving (S). So planned consumption expenditure plus planned saving equals disposable income. That is,

$$YD = C + S.$$

The table in Fig. 25.1 shows some examples of planned consumption expenditure and planned saving at different levels of disposable income. The greater the disposable income, the greater is consumption expenditure and the greater is saving. Also, at each level of disposable income, consumption expenditure plus saving equals disposable income.

The relationship between consumption expenditure and disposable income, with other things remaining the same, is called the **consumption function**. The relationship between saving and disposable income, with other things remaining the same, is called the **saving function**. Let's look at the consumption function and the saving function in Fig. 25.1.

Consumption Function Figure 25.1(a) shows a consumption function. The x-axis measures disposable income and the y-axis measures consumption expenditure. Along the consumption function, the points labelled a through f correspond to the rows of the table. For example, point e shows that when disposable income is $400 billion, consumption expenditure is $375 billion. Along the consumption function, as disposable income increases, consumption expenditure also increases.

At point a on the consumption function, consumption expenditure is $75 billion even though disposable income is zero. This consumption expenditure is called *autonomous consumption expenditure* and it is the amount of consumption expenditure that would take place even if people had no income. You can think of this amount as the expenditure on vital necessities of life.

When consumption expenditure exceeds disposable income, past savings are used to pay for current consumption. Such a situation cannot last forever but it can occur temporarily.

Consumption expenditure in excess of autonomous consumption is called *induced consumption expenditure*—expenditure that is induced by an increase in disposable income.

Saving Function Figure 25.1(b) shows a saving function. The x-axis is the same as that in part (a). The y-axis measures saving. Again, the points marked a through f correspond to the rows of the table. For example, point e shows that when disposable income is $400 billion, saving is $25 billion. Along the saving function, as disposable income increases, saving also increases. If disposable income is less than $300 billion (point d), saving is negative. Negative saving is called *dissaving*. If disposable income is greater than $300 billion, saving is positive, and if disposable income is $300 billion, saving is zero.

45° Line Figure 25.1(a) also contains a 45° line, the height of which measures disposable income. At each point on this line, consumption expenditure equals disposable income. In the range over which

FIGURE 25.1

Consumption Function and Saving Function

(a) Consumption function

(b) Saving function

	Disposable income	Planned consumption expenditure	Planned saving
	(billions of 1992 dollars per year)		
a	0	75	−75
b	100	150	−50
c	200	225	−25
d	300	300	0
e	400	375	25
f	500	450	50

The table shows consumption expenditure and saving plans at various levels of disposable income. Part (a) of the figure shows the relationship between consumption expenditure and disposable income (the consumption function). The height of the consumption function measures consumption expenditure at each level of disposable income. Part (b) shows the relationship between saving and disposable income (the saving function). The height of the saving function measures saving at each level of disposable income. Points *a* through *f* on the consumption and saving functions correspond to the rows in the table. The height of the 45° line in part (a) measures disposable income. So along the 45° line, consumption expenditure equals disposable income. Consumption expenditure plus saving equals disposable income. When the consumption function is above the 45° line, saving is negative (dissaving occurs). When the consumption function is below the 45° line, saving is positive. At the point where the consumption function intersects the 45° line, all disposable income is consumed and saving is zero.

the consumption function is above the 45° line—between *a* and *d*—consumption expenditure exceeds disposable income. In the range over which the consumption function is below the 45° line—between *d* and *f*—consumption expenditure is less than disposable income. And at a point at which the consumption function intersects the 45° line—at point *d*—

consumption expenditure equals disposable income. When the consumption function is above the 45° line in part (a), saving is negative in part (b). When the consumption function is below the 45° line in part (a), saving is positive in part (b). And when the consumption function intersects the 45° line in part (a), saving is zero in part (b).

Marginal Propensity to Consume

The amount by which consumption expenditure changes when disposable income changes depends on the marginal propensity to consume. The **marginal propensity to consume** (*MPC*) is the fraction of a *change* in disposable income that is consumed. It is calculated as the *change* in consumption expenditure (Δ*C*) divided by the *change* in disposable income (Δ*YD*) that brought it about. That is,

$$MPC = \frac{\Delta C}{\Delta YD}.$$

In the table in Fig. 25.1, when disposable income increases from $300 billion to $400 billion, consumption expenditure increases from $300 billion to $375 billion. The $100 billion increase in disposable income increases consumption expenditure by $75 billion. The *MPC* is $75 billion divided by $100 billion, which equals 0.75.

The marginal propensity to consume is the slope of the consumption function. You can check this fact out in Fig. 25.2(a). Here, a $100 billion increase in disposable income from $300 billion to $400 billion is the base of the red triangle. The increase in consumption expenditure that results from this increase in income is $75 billion and is the height of the triangle. The slope of the consumption function is given by the formula "slope equals rise over run" and is $75 billion divided by $100 billion, which equals 0.75—the *MPC* that you calculated by using the numbers in the table in Fig. 25.1.

Marginal Propensity to Save

The amount by which saving changes when disposable income changes depends on the marginal propensity to save. The **marginal propensity to save** (*MPS*) is the fraction of a *change* in disposable income that is saved. It is calculated as the *change* in saving (Δ*S*) divided by the *change* in disposable income (Δ*YD*) that brought it about. That is,

$$MPS = \frac{\Delta S}{\Delta YD}.$$

In the table in Fig. 25.1, an increase in disposable income from $300 billion to $400 billion increases saving from zero to $25 billion. The $100 billion increase in disposable income increases saving by $25 billion. The *MPS* is $25 billion divided by $100 billion, which equals 0.25.

FIGURE 25.2

Marginal Propensities to Consume and Save

(a) Consumption function

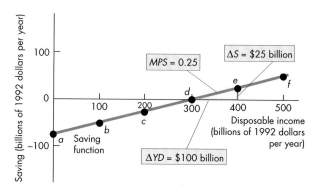

(b) Saving function

The marginal propensity to consume, *MPC*, is equal to the change in consumption expenditure divided by the change in disposable income, other things remaining the same. It is measured by the slope of the consumption function. In part (a), the *MPC* is 0.75. The marginal propensity to save, *MPS*, is equal to the change in saving divided by the change in disposable income, other things remaining the same. It is measured by the slope of the saving function. In part (b), the *MPS* is 0.25.

The marginal propensity to save is the slope of the saving function. You can check this fact out in Fig. 25.2(b). Here, a $100 billion increase in disposable income from $300 billion to $400 billion (the base of the red triangle) increases saving by $25 billion (the height of the triangle). The slope of the saving function is $25 billion divided by $100 billion, which equals 0.25—the *MPS* that you calculated by using the numbers in the table in Fig. 25.1.

The marginal propensity to consume plus the marginal propensity to save always equals 1. They sum to 1 because consumption expenditure and saving exhaust disposable income. Part of each additional dollar of disposable income is consumed, and the remaining part is saved. You can see that these two marginal propensities sum to 1 by using the equation

$$\Delta C + \Delta S = \Delta YD.$$

Divide both sides of the equation by the change in disposable income to obtain

$$\frac{\Delta C}{\Delta YD} + \frac{\Delta S}{\Delta YD} = 1.$$

$\Delta C/\Delta YD$ is the *marginal propensity to consume* (*MPC*), and $\Delta S/\Delta YD$ is the *marginal propensity to save* (*MPS*), so

$$MPC + MPS = 1.$$

Other Influences on Consumption Expenditure and Saving

Changes in disposable income change consumption expenditure and saving and bring a movement along the consumption function and the saving function. Changes in any other influence on consumption expenditure and saving shift the consumption function and the saving function as shown in Fig. 25.3. The main other influences are

1. Expected future disposable income
2. Interest rates
3. Wealth

An increase in expected future disposable income makes people feel better off and leads to an increase in current consumption expenditure and a decrease in saving. A fall in interest rates, other things remaining the same, encourages an increase in borrowing and consumption expenditure and a decrease in

FIGURE 25.3

Shifts in the Consumption and Saving Functions

(a) Consumption function

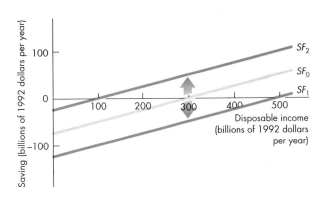

(b) Saving function

An increase in expected future disposable income, a fall in interest rates, or an increase in wealth increases consumption expenditure and decreases saving. The consumption function shifts upward from CF_0 to CF_1 and the saving function shifts downward from SF_0 to SF_1. A decrease in expected future disposable income, a rise in interest rates, or a decrease in wealth shifts the consumption function downward from CF_0 to CF_2 and shifts the saving function upward from SF_0 to SF_2.

saving. And an increase in wealth, other things remaining the same, stimulates consumption expenditure and decreases saving.

When expected future disposable income increases, interest rates fall, or wealth increases, consumption expenditure increases and saving decreases. In Fig. 25.3, the consumption function shifts upward from CF_0 to CF_1, and the saving function shifts downward from SF_0 to SF_1. When expected future disposable income decreases, interest rates rise, or wealth decreases, consumption expenditure decreases and saving increases. The consumption function shifts downward from CF_0 to CF_2, and the saving function shifts upward from SF_0 to SF_2.

Shifts in the consumption function and saving function occur over the business cycle. When an expansion begins, expected future disposable income increases so the consumption function shifts upward. When a recession begins, expected future disposable income decreases so the consumption function shifts downward. Let's look more closely at the Canadian consumption function.

Canadian Consumption Function

Figure 25.4 shows the Canadian consumption function. Each dot represents consumption expenditure and disposable income for a particular year from 1978 to 1998, and the dots for even numbered years are identified in the figure. The line CF_0 is an estimate of the Canadian consumption function in 1978 and the line CF_1 is an estimate of the Canadian consumption function in 1998.

The slope of the consumption function in Fig. 25.4 is 0.65, which means that a $100 billion increase in disposable income brings a $65 billion increase in consumption expenditure. This slope, which is an estimate of the marginal propensity to consume, is an assumption that is in the middle of the range of values that economists have estimated for the Canadian marginal propensity to consume.

The consumption function shifts upward over time as other influences on consumption expenditure change. Interest rates, wealth, and expected future disposable income fluctuate and so bring upward *and* downward shifts in the consumption function. Rising wealth and rising expected future disposable incomes bring a steady upward shift in the consumption function.

FIGURE 25.4

The Canadian Consumption Function

Each blue dot shows consumption expenditure and disposable income for a particular year. The lines CF_0 and CF_1 are estimates of the Canadian consumption function in 1978 and 1998 respectively. Here, the (assumed) marginal propensity to consume is 0.65.

Consumption As a Function of Real GDP

Consumption expenditure changes when disposable income changes. And disposable income changes when either real GDP changes or when net taxes change. But net taxes—taxes minus transfer payments—are themselves related to real GDP. When real GDP increases, taxes increase and transfer payments decrease. Because net taxes depend on real GDP, disposable income depends on real GDP and consumption expenditure depends on real GDP. We use this link between consumption expenditure and real GDP to determine equilibrium expenditure. But before we do so, we need to look at one other component of aggregate expenditure: imports. Like consumption expenditure, imports are influenced by real GDP.

Import Function

Canadian imports are determined by many factors but the dominant factor in the short run is Canadian real GDP. Other things remaining the same, the greater the Canadian real GDP, the larger is the quantity of Canadian imports.

The relationship between imports and real GDP is determined by the marginal propensity to import. The **marginal propensity to import** is the fraction of an increase in real GDP that is spent on imports when all other influences on imports remain the same. For example, if a $100 billion increase in real GDP increases imports by $25 billion, the marginal propensity to import is 0.25.

Since the North American Free Trade Agreement was implemented, Canadian imports have surged. For example, between 1990 and 1998, real GDP increased by $111 billion and imports increased by $126 billion. We cannot conclude from these numbers that the Canadian marginal propensity to import exceeds one. If the marginal propensity to import did exceed one, as real GDP increases, we would not only spend more on foreign-produced goods and services but also spend less on Canadian-produced goods and services. Canadian imports have increased by more than real GDP during the 1990s because other factors have had a big influence on imports.

R E V I E W   Q U I Z

▦ Which components of aggregate planned expenditure are influenced by real GDP?
▦ Define the marginal propensity to consume.
▦ What is your estimate of your own marginal propensity to consume? After you graduate and begin work, will your marginal propensity to consume change? Why or why not?
▦ How do we calculate the effects of real GDP on consumption expenditure and imports?

Real GDP influences consumption expenditure and imports. But consumption expenditure and imports along with investment, government expenditures, and exports influence real GDP. Your next task is to study this second part of the feedback loop between aggregate expenditure and real GDP and see how all the components of aggregate planned expenditure interact to determine real GDP.

Equilibrium Expenditure at a Fixed Price Level

MOST FIRMS ARE LIKE YOUR LOCAL SUPERMARKET. They set their prices, advertise their products, and sell the quantities their customers are willing to buy. If firms persistently sell more than they plan to and are constantly running out of inventory, they eventually raise their prices. And if firms persistently sell less than they plan to and have inventories piling up, they eventually cut their prices. But for a period that might run from a few days to a few months, their prices are fixed. Firms hold the prices they have set, and the quantities they sell depend on demand, not supply.

The Aggregate Implications of Fixed Prices

Fixed prices have two immediate implications for the economy as a whole:

1. Because each firm's price is fixed, the *price level* is fixed.
2. Because demand determines the quantities that each firm sells, *aggregate demand* determines the aggregate quantity of goods and services sold, which equals real GDP.

So to understand how real GDP is determined when the price level is fixed, we must understand how aggregate demand is determined. Aggregate demand is determined by aggregate expenditure plans. We define **aggregate planned expenditure** as *planned* consumption expenditure plus *planned* investment plus *planned* government expenditures plus *planned* exports minus *planned* imports.

You've just studied planned consumption expenditure and planned imports and seen that these two components of aggregate planned expenditure are influenced by real GDP. The other components of aggregate planned expenditure—investment, government expenditures, and exports—are not influenced by real GDP. They fluctuate for many reasons but they do not fluctuate because of fluctuations in real GDP.

You are now going to study a model called the *aggregate expenditure model* that explains how consumption expenditure, imports, and real GDP are *simultaneously* determined by a feedback loop between expenditure plans and real GDP.

The Aggregate Expenditure Model

You are now going to discover how aggregate expenditure plans interact to determine real GDP when the price level is fixed. First, we study the relationship between aggregate planned expenditure and real GDP. Second, we learn about the key distinction between *planned* expenditure and *actual* expenditure.

And third, we study equilibrium expenditure.

The relationship between aggregate planned expenditure and real GDP can be described by either an aggregate expenditure schedule or an aggregate expenditure curve. The *aggregate expenditure schedule* lists aggregate planned expenditure generated at each level of real GDP. The *aggregate expenditure curve* is a graph of the aggregate expenditure schedule.

FIGURE 25.5

Aggregate Planned Expenditure

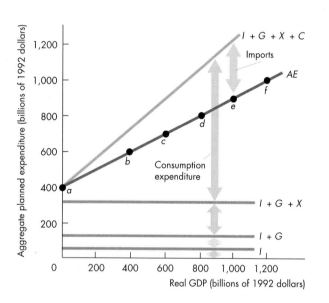

The aggregate expenditure schedule shows the relationship between aggregate planned expenditure and real GDP. Aggregate planned expenditure is the sum of planned consumption expenditure, investment, government expenditures, and exports minus imports. For example, in row *b* of the table, when real GDP is $400 billion, planned consumption expenditure is $375 billion, planned investment is $50 billion, planned government expenditures are $75 billion, planned exports are $200 billion, and planned imports are $100 billion. Thus when real GDP is $400 billion, aggregate planned expenditure is $600 billion ($375 + $50 + $75 + $200 − $100). The schedule shows that aggregate planned expenditure increases as real GDP increases. This relationship is graphed as the aggregate expenditure curve *AE*, the line *af*. The components of aggregate expenditure that increase with real GDP are consumption expenditure and imports. The other components—investment, government expenditures, and exports—do not vary with real GDP.

	Real GDP (Y)	Consumption expenditure (C)	Investment (I)	Government expenditures (G)	Exports (X)	Imports (M)	Aggregate planned expenditure (AE = C + I + G + X – M)
				(billions of 1992 dollars)			
a	0	75	50	75	200	0	400
b	400	375	50	75	200	100	600
c	600	525	50	75	200	150	700
d	800	675	50	75	200	200	800
e	1,000	825	50	75	200	250	900
f	1,200	975	50	75	200	300	1,000

Aggregate Planned Expenditure and Real GDP

The table in Fig. 25.5 sets out an aggregate expenditure schedule together with the components of aggregate planned expenditure. To calculate aggregate planned expenditure at a given real GDP, we add the various components together. The first column of the table shows real GDP, and the second column shows the consumption expenditure generated by each level of real GDP. A $400 billion increase in real GDP generates a $300 billion increase in consumption expenditure—the MPC is 0.75.

The next two columns show investment and government expenditures on goods and services. Investment depends on such factors as interest rates and the expected future profit. But at a given point in time, these factors generate a particular level of investment. Suppose this level of investment is $50 billion. Also, suppose that government expenditures on goods and services are $75 billion.

The next two columns show exports and imports. Exports are influenced by events in the rest of the world, prices of foreign-made goods and services relative to the prices of similar Canadian-made goods and services, and foreign exchange rates. But exports are not directly affected by real GDP in Canada. Exports are a constant $200 billion no matter what real GDP in Canada is. Imports increase as real GDP increases. A $200 billion increase in real GDP generates a $50 billion increase in imports—the marginal propensity to import is 0.25.

The final column shows aggregate planned expenditure—the sum of planned consumption expenditure, investment, government expenditures on goods and services, and exports minus imports.

Figure 25.5 plots an aggregate expenditure curve. Real GDP is shown on the x-axis, and aggregate planned expenditure is shown on the y-axis. The aggregate expenditure curve is the red line AE. Points a through f on that curve correspond to the rows of the table. The AE curve is a graph of aggregate planned expenditure (the last column) plotted against real GDP (the first column).

Figure 25.5 also shows the components of aggregate expenditure. The constant components—investment (I), government expenditures on goods and services (G), and exports (X)—are shown by the horizontal lines in the figure. Consumption expenditure (C) is the vertical gap between the lines labelled I + G + X and I + G + X + C.

To construct the AE curve, subtract imports (M) from the I + G + X + C line. Aggregate expenditure is expenditure on Canadian-made goods and services. But the components of aggregate expenditure—C, I, and G—include expenditure on imported goods and services. For example, a student's purchase of a new motor bike is part of consumption expenditure. But if that motor bike is a Honda made in Japan, expenditure on it must be subtracted from consumption expenditure to find out how much is spent on goods and services produced in Canada—on Canadian real GDP. Money paid to Honda for motor bike imports from Japan does not add to aggregate expenditure on Canadian-made goods and services.

Figure 25.5 shows that aggregate planned expenditure increases as real GDP increases. But as real GDP increases, only some of the components of aggregate planned expenditure increase. These components are consumption expenditure and imports. The sum of the components of aggregate expenditure that vary with real GDP is called **induced expenditure**. The sum of the components of aggregate expenditure that are not influenced by real GDP is called **autonomous expenditure**. The components of autonomous expenditure are investment, government expenditures, exports, and autonomous consumption expenditure—that part of consumption expenditure that does not vary with real GDP. That is, autonomous expenditure is equal to the level of aggregate planned expenditure when real GDP is zero. In Fig. 25.5, autonomous expenditure is $400 billion. And as real GDP increases from zero to $400 billion, aggregate planned expenditure increases from $400 billion to $600 billion. Induced expenditure is $200 billion—$600 billion minus $400 billion.

The aggregate expenditure curve summarizes the relationship between aggregate *planned* expenditure and real GDP. But what determines the point on the aggregate expenditure curve at which the economy operates? What determines *actual* aggregate expenditure?

Actual Expenditure, Planned Expenditure, and Real GDP

Actual aggregate expenditure is always equal to real GDP, as we saw in Chapter 22 (p. 479). But aggregate *planned* expenditure is not necessarily equal to actual aggregate expenditure and therefore is not necessarily equal to real GDP. How can actual expenditure and planned expenditure differ from each other? Why don't expenditure plans get implemented? The main reason is that firms might end up with more inventories than planned or with less inventories than planned. People carry out their consumption expenditure plans, the government implements its planned expenditures on goods and services, and net exports are as planned. Firms carry out their plans to purchase new buildings, plant, and equipment. But one component of investment is the change in firms' inventories of goods. If aggregate planned expenditure is less than real GDP, firms don't sell all the goods they produce and they end up with inventories they hadn't planned. If aggregate planned expenditure exceeds real GDP, firms sell more than they produce and inventories decrease below the level that firms had planned.

FIGURE 25.6

Equilibrium Expenditure

(a) Equilibrium expenditure

(b) Unplanned inventory changes

	Real GDP (Y)	Aggregate planned expenditure (AE)	Unplanned inventory change (Y – AE)
		(billions of 1992 dollars)	
a	0	400	–400
b	400	600	–200
c	600	700	–100
d	800	800	0
e	1,000	900	100
f	1,200	1,000	200

The table shows expenditure plans at different levels of real GDP. When real GDP is $800 billion, aggregate planned expenditure equals real GDP.

Part (a) of the figure illustrates equilibrium expenditure, which occurs when aggregate planned expenditure equals real GDP at the intersection of the 45° line and the AE curve. Part (b) of the figure shows the forces that bring about equilibrium expenditure. When aggregate planned expenditure exceeds real GDP, inventories decrease—for example, point b in both parts of the figure. Firms increase production and real GDP increases.

When aggregate planned expenditure is less than real GDP, inventories increase—for example, point f in both parts of the figure. Firms decrease production and real GDP decreases. When aggregate planned expenditure equals real GDP, there are no unplanned inventory changes and real GDP remains constant at equilibrium expenditure.

Equilibrium Expenditure

Equilibrium expenditure is the level of aggregate expenditure that occurs when aggregate *planned* expenditure equals real GDP. It is a level of aggregate expenditure and real GDP at which everyone's spending plans are fulfilled. When the price level is fixed, equilibrium expenditure determines real GDP. When aggregate planned expenditure and actual aggregate expenditure are unequal, a process of convergence towards equilibrium expenditure occurs. And throughout this convergence process, real GDP adjusts. Let's examine equilibrium expenditure and the process that brings it about.

Figure 25.6(a) illustrates equilibrium expenditure. The table sets out aggregate planned expenditure at various levels of real GDP. These values are plotted as points *a* through *f* along the *AE* curve. The 45° line shows all the points at which aggregate planned expenditure equals real GDP. Thus where the *AE* curve is above the 45° line, aggregate planned expenditure exceeds real GDP; where the *AE* curve is below the 45° line, aggregate planned expenditure is less than real GDP; and where the *AE* curve intersects the 45° line, aggregate planned expenditure equals real GDP. Point *d* illustrates equilibrium expenditure. At this point, real GDP is $800 billion.

Convergence to Equilibrium

What are the forces that move aggregate expenditure towards its equilibrium level? To answer this question, we must look at a situation in which aggregate expenditure is away from its equilibrium level. Suppose that in Fig. 25.6, real GDP is $400 billion. With real GDP at $400 billion, actual aggregate expenditure is also $400 billion. But aggregate *planned* expenditure is $600 billion (point *b* in Fig. 25.6a). Aggregate planned expenditure exceeds *actual* expenditure. When people spend $600 billion and firms produce goods and services worth $400 billion, firms' inventories fall by $200 billion (point *b* in Fig. 25.6b). Because the change in inventories is part of investment, *actual* investment is $200 billion less than *planned* investment.

Real GDP doesn't remain at $400 billion for very long. Firms have a target level for inventories and when they fall below target, firms increase production to restore inventories to the target level. To increase inventories, firms hire additional labour and increase production. Suppose that they increase pro-

duction in the next period by $200 billion. Real GDP increases by $200 billion to $600 billion. But again, aggregate planned expenditure exceeds real GDP. When real GDP is $600 billion, aggregate planned expenditure is $700 billion (point *c* in Fig. 25.6a). Again, inventories decrease, but this time by less than before. With real GDP of $600 billion and aggregate planned expenditure of $700 billion, inventories decrease by $100 billion (point *c* in Fig. 25.6b). Again, firms hire additional labour, and production increases; real GDP increases yet further.

The process that we have just described— planned expenditure exceeds real GDP, inventories decrease, and production increases to restore the level of inventories—ends when real GDP has reached $800 billion. At this real GDP, there is an equilibrium. There are no unplanned inventory changes, and firms do not change their production.

You can do an experiment similar to the one we've just done but starting with a level of real GDP greater than equilibrium expenditure. In this case, planned expenditure is less than actual expenditure, inventories pile up, and firms cut production. As before, real GDP keeps on changing (decreasing this time) until it reaches its equilibrium level of $800 billion.

R E V I E W   Q U I Z

- Explain the relationship between aggregate planned expenditure and real GDP.
- What is the relationship between aggregate planned expenditure and real GDP at equilibrium expenditure?
- What adjustments occur to bring aggregate planned expenditure to equality with actual expenditure?
- If real GDP and aggregate expenditure are less than their equilibrium levels, what happens to unplanned inventories, production, and real GDP?
- If real GDP and aggregate expenditure exceed their equilibrium levels, what happens to unplanned inventories, production, and real GDP?

You've learned that when the price level is fixed, real GDP is determined by equilibrium expenditure. And you have seen how unplanned changes in inventories and the production response they generate bring a convergence towards equilibrium. You're now going to study *changes* in equilibrium and discover an economic amplifier called the *multiplier*.

The Multiplier

INVESTMENT AND EXPORTS CAN CHANGE FOR many reasons. Recession in Japan and the rest of Asia might lead Canadian firms to decrease their planned investment and might decrease Canadian exports. These are examples of a decrease in autonomous expenditure. An economic boom in Western Europe might induce firms to increase their planned investment and might also increase Canadian exports. These are examples of increases in autonomous expenditure. We'll study the effects of an increase in autonomous expenditure.

When autonomous expenditure increases, aggregate expenditure increases, and so does equilibrium expenditure and real GDP. But the increase in real GDP is *larger* than the change in autonomous expenditure. The **multiplier** is the amount by which a change in autonomous expenditure is magnified or multiplied to determine the change in equilibrium expenditure and real GDP.

It is easiest to get the basic idea of the multiplier if we work with an example economy in which there are no income taxes and no imports. So we'll first assume that these factors are absent. Then, when you understand the basic idea, we'll bring these factors back into play and see what difference they make to the multiplier.

The Basic Idea of the Multiplier

Suppose that investment increases. The additional expenditure by businesses means that aggregate expenditure and real GDP increase. The increase in real GDP increases disposable income and with no income taxes, real GDP and disposable income increase by the same amount. The increase in disposable income brings an increase in consumption expenditure. And the increased consumption expenditure adds even more to aggregate expenditure. Real GDP and disposable income increase further, and so does consumption expenditure. The initial increase in investment brings an even bigger increase in aggregate expenditure because it induces an increase in consumption expenditure. The magnitude of the increase in aggregate expenditure that results from an increase in autonomous expenditure is determined by the *multiplier*.

The table in Fig. 25.7 shows an aggregate planned expenditure schedule. When real GDP is $700 billion, aggregate planned expenditure is $725 billion. For each $100 billion increase in real GDP, aggregate planned expenditure increases by $75 billion. This aggregate expenditure schedule is shown in the figure as the aggregate expenditure curve AE_0. Initially, equilibrium expenditure is $800 billion. You can see this equilibrium in row b of the table and in the figure where the curve AE_0 intersects the 45° line at the point marked b.

Now suppose that autonomous expenditure increases by $50 billion. What happens to equilibrium expenditure? You can see the answer in Fig. 25.7. When this increase in autonomous expenditure is added to the original aggregate planned expenditure, aggregate planned expenditure increases by $50 billion at each level of real GDP. The new aggregate expenditure curve is AE_1. The new equilibrium expenditure, highlighted in the table (row d'), occurs where AE_1 intersects the 45° line and is $1,000 billion (point d'). At this real GDP, aggregate planned expenditure equals real GDP.

Notice that an initial increase in expenditure of $50 billion has increased real GDP by $200 billion. So aggregate expenditure has increased by four times the initial increase. The multiplier is 4. A change in autonomous expenditure leads, like Alanis Morissette's music-making equipment, to an amplified change in equilibrium expenditure.

The multiplier works for both an increase and a decrease in autonomous expenditure. In Fig. 25.7, a decrease in autonomous expenditure of $50 billion that shifts the aggregate expenditure curve downward by $50 billion from AE_1 to AE_0 decreases equilibrium expenditure from $1,000 billion to $800 billion. The decrease in equilibrium expenditure is four times the decrease in autonomous expenditure—again, the multiplier is 4.

Some Intuition—A Campus Multiplier A campus president gets a bright idea. She commissions student artists to create murals and other works of art to brighten up the campus buildings. She pays the artists a total of $100,000 for their work.

Soon after the artists have been paid, the campus begins to feel the multiplier effect of this increase in expenditure. The student artists start buying books, computer equipment and software, and snacks and drinks, all from campus-operated stores. To keep up with the new level of spending, the campus bookstore, computer store, and snack bars all begin to hire more help—student help. And so the incomes of yet more students increase. These students join in the

Why Is the Multiplier Greater Than 1?

FIGURE 25.7

The Multiplier

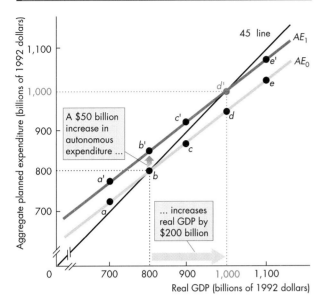

Real GDP (Y)	Aggregate planned expenditure			
	Original (AE₀)			New (AE₁)

Real GDP (Y)		Original (AE_0)		New (AE_1)
		(billions of 1992 dollars)		
700	a	725	a'	775
800	b	800	b'	850
900	c	875	c'	925
1,000	d	950	d'	1,000
1,100	e	1,025	e'	1,075

A $50 billion increase in autonomous expenditure shifts the AE curve upward by $50 billion from AE_0 to AE_1. Equilibrium expenditure increases by $200 billion from $800 billion to $1,000 billion. The increase in equilibrium expenditure is 4 times the increase in autonomous expenditure, so the multiplier is 4.

increased spending and add to the initial increase from the student artists.

Total expenditure on the campus increases by more than $200,000. And the campus president is delighted that the profits from campus enterprises have gone a long way to paying for her initial investment of $100,000.

Why Is the Multiplier Greater Than 1?

We've seen that equilibrium expenditure increases by more than the increase in autonomous expenditure and so the multiplier is greater than 1. Why does equilibrium expenditure increase by more than the increase in autonomous expenditure?

Expenditure increases by more than the increase in autonomous expenditure because induced expenditure increases—an increase in autonomous expenditure *induces* further increases in expenditure. If Rogers Cablesystems spends $10 million on a new pay-per-view system, aggregate expenditure and real GDP immediately increase by $10 million. But that is not the end of the story. Video systems designers and computer producers now have more income, and they spend part of the extra income on cars, microwave ovens, vacations, and a host of other goods and services. Real GDP now rises by the initial $10 million plus the extra consumption expenditure induced by the $10 million increase in income. The producers of cars, microwave ovens, vacations, and other goods now have increased incomes, and they, in turn, spend part of the increase in their incomes on consumption goods and services. Additional income induces additional expenditure, which creates additional income.

How big is the multiplier effect?

The Size of the Multiplier

The *multiplier* is the amount by which a change in autonomous expenditure is multiplied to determine the change in equilibrium expenditure that it generates. To calculate the multiplier, we divide the change in equilibrium expenditure by the change in autonomous expenditure. Let's calculate the multiplier for the example in Fig. 25.7. Initially, equilibrium expenditure is $800 billion. Then autonomous expenditure increases by $50 billion, and equilibrium expenditure increases by $200 billion to $1,000 billion.

The multiplier is

$$\text{Multiplier} = \frac{\text{Change in equilibrium expenditure}}{\text{Change in autonomous expenditure}}$$

$$= \frac{\$200 \text{ billion}}{\$50 \text{ billion}} = 4.$$

The Multiplier and the Slope of the AE Curve

What determines the magnitude of the multiplier? The answer is the slope of the AE curve. The steeper the AE curve, the larger is the multiplier. To see why, think about what the slope of the AE curve tells you. It tells you by how much induced expenditure increases when real GDP increases. The steeper the AE curve, the greater is the increase in induced expenditure that results from a given increase in real GDP. Let's do a calculation to show the relationship between the slope of the AE curve and the multiplier.

The change in real GDP (ΔY) equals the change in induced expenditure (ΔN) plus the change in autonomous expenditure (ΔA). That is,

$$\Delta Y = \Delta N + \Delta A.$$

The slope of the AE curve equals the "rise," ΔN, divided by the "run," ΔY. That is,

$$\text{Slope of } AE \text{ curve} = \Delta N \div \Delta Y.$$

So,

$$\Delta N = \text{Slope of } AE \text{ curve} \times \Delta Y.$$

Now use this equation to replace ΔN in the first equation above to give

$$\Delta Y = (\text{Slope of } AE \text{ curve} \times \Delta Y) + \Delta A.$$

Now, solve for ΔY as

$$(1 - \text{Slope of } AE \text{ curve}) \times \Delta Y = \Delta A.$$

and rearranging,

$$\Delta Y = \frac{\Delta A}{1 - \text{Slope of } AE \text{ curve}}.$$

The multiplier that we want to calculate is

$$\text{Multiplier} = \frac{\Delta Y}{\Delta A}.$$

so divide both sides of the previous equation by ΔA to give

$$\text{Multiplier} = \frac{\Delta Y}{\Delta A} = \frac{1}{1 - \text{Slope of } AE \text{ curve}}.$$

With the numbers from Fig. 25.7, the slope of the AE curve is 0.75 so the multiplier is

$$\text{Multiplier} = \frac{1}{1 - 0.75} = \frac{1}{0.25} = 4.$$

When there are no income taxes and no imports, the slope of the AE curve equals the marginal propensity to consume (MPC). So the multiplier is

$$\text{Multiplier} = \frac{1}{1 - MPC}.$$

There is another formula for the multiplier in this special case. Because the marginal propensity to consume (MPC) and the marginal propensity to save (MPS) sum to 1, the term $(1 - MPC)$ equals MPS. Therefore, another formula for the multiplier is

$$\text{Multiplier} = \frac{1}{MPS}.$$

Because the marginal propensity to save (MPS) lies between 0 and 1, the multiplier exceeds 1.

Figure 25.8 illustrates the multiplier process. In round 1, autonomous expenditure increases by $50 billion (shown by the green bar). At this time, induced expenditure does not change, so aggregate expenditure and real GDP increase by $50 billion. In round 2, the larger real GDP induces more consumption expenditure. Induced expenditure increases by 0.75 times the increase in real GDP, so the increase in real GDP of $50 billion induces a further increase in expenditure of $37.5 billion. This change in induced expenditure (the green bar in round 2), when added to the previous increase in expenditure (the blue bar in round 2), increases aggregate expenditure and real GDP by $87.5 billion. The round 2 increase in real GDP induces a round 3 increase in expenditure. The process repeats through successive rounds. Each increase in real GDP is 0.75 times the previous increase. The cumulative increase in real GDP gradually approaches $200 billion.

So far, we've ignored imports and income taxes. Let's now see how these two factors influence the multiplier.

Imports and Income Taxes

The multiplier is determined, in general, not only by the marginal propensity to consume but also by the marginal tax rate and by the marginal propensity to import.

Income taxes make the AE curve less steep and the multiplier smaller than it otherwise would be. To see why, think about what happens following an

FIGURE 25.8

The Multiplier Process

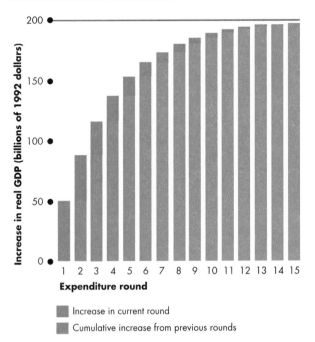

■ Increase in current round
■ Cumulative increase from previous rounds

Autonomous expenditure increases in round 1 by $50 billion. As a result, real GDP increases by the same amount. Each additional dollar of real GDP induces an additional 0.75 of a dollar of aggregate expenditure, so the round 1 increase in real GDP induces an increase in consumption expenditure of $37.5 billion in round 2. At the end of round 2, real GDP has increased by $87.5 billion. The extra $37.5 billion of real GDP in round 2 induces a further increase in consumption expenditure of $28.125 billion in round 3. Real GDP increases yet further to $105.625 billion. This process continues with real GDP increasing by ever-smaller amounts. When the process comes to an end, real GDP has increased by a total of $200 billion.

to see why think about what happens following an increase in autonomous expenditure. An increase in autonomous expenditure increases real GDP, which in turn increases consumption expenditure. But part of the increase in expenditure is on imported goods and services, not Canadian-produced goods and services. Only expenditure on Canadian-produced goods and services increases Canadian real GDP. The larger the marginal propensity to import, the smaller is the change in Canadian real GDP.

The marginal propensity to import and the marginal tax rate together with the marginal propensity to consume determine the multiplier. And their combined influence depends on the slope of the AE curve. The multiplier is equal to 1 divided by 1 minus the slope of the AE curve. Figure 25.9 compares two situations. In Fig. 25.9(a), there are no imports and no income taxes. The slope of the AE curve equals the marginal propensity to consume, which is 0.75 and the multiplier is 4. In Fig. 25.9(b), imports and income taxes decrease the slope of the AE curve to 0.5. In this case, the multiplier is 2. So, anything that decreases the slope of the AE curve—a lower MPC, a higher marginal tax rate, or a higher marginal propensity to import—decreases the size of the multiplier.

Over time, the value of the multiplier changes as marginal tax rates change and as the marginal propensity to consume and the marginal propensity to import change. These ongoing changes make the multiplier hard to predict. But they do not change the fundamental fact that an initial change in autonomous expenditure leads to a magnified change in aggregate expenditure and real GDP.

The multiplier that you've just studied plays a powerful role at business cycle turning points, as you will now discover.

Business Cycle Turning Points

At business cycle turning points, the economy moves from expansion to recession or from recession to expansion. Economists understand these turning points like seismologists understand earthquakes. They know quite a lot about the forces and mechanisms that produce them but they can't predict them. The forces that bring business cycle turning points are the swings in autonomous expenditure such as investment and exports. The mechanism that gives momentum to the economy's new direction is the multiplier. Let's use what we've now learned to examine these turning points.

increase in autonomous expenditure. An increase in autonomous expenditure increases real GDP. But the increase in real GDP means that income and income taxes increase. So disposable income increases by less than the increase in real GDP. Consequently, consumption expenditure increases by less than it would do if taxes had not changed. The larger is the marginal tax rate, the smaller is the change in disposable income and real GDP.

Imports make the AE curve less steep and the multiplier smaller than it otherwise would be. Again,

FIGURE 25.9

The Multiplier and the Slope of the *AE* Curve

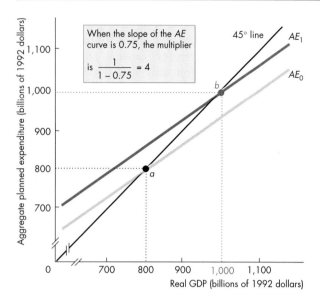

When the slope of the *AE* curve is 0.75, the multiplier is $\dfrac{1}{1-0.75} = 4$

(a) Multiplier is 4

When the slope of the *AE* curve is 0.5, the multiplier is $\dfrac{1}{1-0.5} = 2$

(b) Multiplier is 2

Imports and income taxes make the *AE* curve less steep and reduce the value of the multiplier. In part (a) with no imports and income taxes, the slope of the *AE* curve is 0.75 (the marginal propensity to consume) and the multiplier is 4. But with imports and income taxes, the slope of the *AE* curve is less than the marginal propensity to consume. In part (b), the slope of the *AE* curve is 0.5. In this case, the multiplier is 2.

An Expansion Begins An expansion is triggered by an increase in autonomous expenditure that increases aggregate planned expenditure. At the moment the economy turns the corner into expansion, aggregate planned expenditure exceeds real GDP. In this situation, firms see their inventories taking an unplanned dive. The expansion now begins. To meet their inventory targets, firms increase production, and real GDP begins to increase. This initial increase in real GDP brings higher incomes that stimulate consumption expenditure. The multiplier process kicks in, and the expansion picks up speed.

A Recession Begins The process we've just described works in reverse at a business cycle peak. A recession is triggered by a decrease in autonomous expenditure that decreases aggregate planned expenditure. At the moment the economy turns the corner into recession, real GDP exceeds aggregate planned expenditure. In this situation, firms see unplanned inventories piling up. The recession now begins. To lower their inventories, firms cut production, and real GDP begins to decrease. This initial decrease in real GDP brings lower incomes that cut consumption expenditure. The multiplier process reinforces the initial cut in autonomous expenditure, and the recession takes hold.

The Next Canadian Recession? Since 1991, the Canadian economy has been in a business cycle expansion. The last real GDP trough was in the first quarter of 1991. The science of macroeconomics cannot predict when the next recession will begin. A recession seemed possible in 1998 following a rapid buildup of inventories during 1997. But firms planned this inventory buildup. At the beginning of 1999, there was still no immediate prospect of the next recession. But it will surely come. And when it does, the mechanism you've just studied will operate.

- What is the multiplier? What does it determine?
- Why does the multiplier matter?
- How do the marginal propensity to consume, the marginal tax rate, and the marginal propensity to import influence the multiplier?
- If autonomous expenditure decreases, which phase of the business cycle does the economy enter?

The economy's potholes are changes in investment and exports. And the economy does not operate like the shock absorbers on Gary Doer's car. While the price level is fixed, the effects of the economic potholes are not smoothed out. Instead, they are amplified like Alanis Morissette's voice. But we've considered only the adjustments in spending that occur when the price level is fixed. What happens after a long enough time lapse for the price level to change? Let's answer this question.

The Multiplier and the Price Level

WHEN FIRMS CAN'T KEEP UP WITH SALES AND their inventories fall below target, they increase production, but at some point they raise their prices. Similarly, when firms find unwanted inventories piling up, they decrease production, but eventually they cut their prices. So far, we've studied the macroeconomic consequences of firms changing their production levels when their sales change, but we haven't looked at the effects of price changes. When individual firms change their prices, the economy's price level changes.

To study the simultaneous determination of real GDP and the price level, we use the *aggregate supply –aggregate demand model*, which is explained in Chapter 24. But to understand how aggregate demand adjusts, we need to work out the connection between the aggregate supply–aggregate demand model and the aggregate expenditure model that we've used in this chapter.

The key to understanding the relationship between these two models is the distinction between the aggregate *expenditure* and aggregate *demand* and the related distinction between the aggregate *expenditure curve* and the aggregate *demand curve*.

Aggregate Expenditure and Aggregate Demand

The aggregate expenditure curve is the relationship between the aggregate planned expenditure and real GDP, all other influences on aggregate planned expenditure remaining the same. The aggregate demand curve is the relationship between the aggregate quantity of goods and services demanded and the price level when all other influences remain the same. Let's explore the links between these two relationships.

Aggregate Expenditure and the Price Level

When the price level changes, aggregate planned expenditure changes and the quantity of real GDP demanded changes. The aggregate demand curve slopes downward. Why? There are two main reasons:

- Wealth effect
- Substitution effect

Wealth Effect   Other things remaining the same, the higher the price level, the smaller is people's wealth. For example, suppose you have $100 in the bank and the price level is 110. If the price level rises to 130, your $100 buys fewer goods and services. You are less wealthy. With less wealth, you will probably want to try to spend a bit less and save a bit more. Aggregate planned expenditure is less, the higher the price level, other things remaining the same.

Substitution Effects   A rise in the price level today, other things remaining the same, makes current goods and services more costly relative to future goods and services and results in a delay in purchases—an *intertemporal substitution*. A rise in the price level, other things remaining the same, makes Canadian-produced goods more expensive relative to foreign-produced goods and services and increases imports and decreases exports—an *international substitution*.

When the price level rises, each of these effects reduces aggregate planned expenditure at each level of real GDP. As a result, when the price level rises, the aggregate expenditure curve shifts downward. A fall in the price level has the opposite effect. When the price level falls, the aggregate expenditure curve shifts upward.

Figure 25.10(a) shows the shifts of the *AE* curve. When the price level is 110, the aggregate expenditure curve is AE_0, which intersects the 45° line at point *b*. Equilibrium expenditure is $800 billion. If the price level rises to 130, the aggregate expenditure curve shifts downward to AE_1, which intersects the 45° line at point *a*. Equilibrium expenditure decreases to $700 billion. If the price level falls to 90, the aggregate expenditure curve shifts upward to AE_2, which intersects the 45° line at point *c*. Equilibrium expenditure increases to $900 billion.

When the price level changes and other things remain the same, the *AE* curve shifts and equilibrium expenditure changes. And when the price level changes and other things remain the same, there is a movement along the aggregate demand curve. Figure 25.10(b) shows these movements. At a price level of 110, the aggregate quantity of goods and services demanded is $800 billion—point *b* on the aggregate demand curve *AD*. If the price level rises to 130, the aggregate quantity of goods and services demanded decreases to $700 billion. There is a movement along the aggregate demand curve to point *a*. If the price level falls to 90, the aggregate quantity of goods and services demanded increases to $900 billion. There is a movement along the aggregate demand curve to point *c*.

Each point on the aggregate demand curve corresponds to a point of equilibrium expenditure. The equilibrium expenditure points *a*, *b*, and *c* in Fig. 25.10(a) correspond to the points *a*, *b*, and *c* on the aggregate demand curve in Fig. 25.10(b).

When the price level changes, other things remaining the same, the aggregate expenditure curve shifts and there is a movement along the aggregate demand curve. When any other influence on aggregate planned expenditure changes, *both* the aggregate expenditure curve and the aggregate demand curve shift. For example, an increase in investment or in exports increases both aggregate planned expenditure and aggregate demand and shifts both the *AE* curve and the *AD* curve. Figure 25.11 illustrates the effect of such an increase.

Initially, the aggregate expenditure curve is AE_0 in part (a) and the aggregate demand curve is AD_0 in part (b). The price level is 110, real GDP is $800 billion, and the economy is at point *a* in both parts of the figure. Now suppose that autonomous expenditure increases by $100 billion. At a constant price level of 110, the aggregate expenditure curve shifts upward to AE_1. This curve intersects the 45° line at an equilibrium expenditure of $1,000 billion (point *b*).

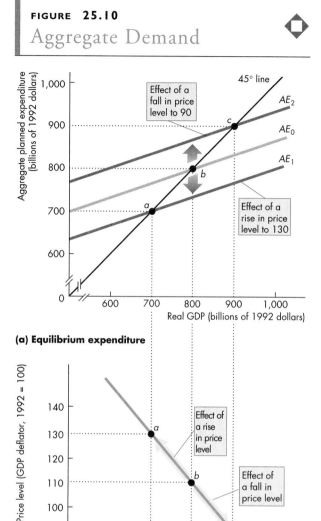

FIGURE 25.10

Aggregate Demand

(a) Equilibrium expenditure

(b) Aggregate demand

A change in the price level shifts the *AE* curve and results in a *movement along* the *AD* curve. When the price level is 110, the *AE* curve is AE_0, and equilibrium expenditure is $800 billion at point *b*. When the price level rises to 130, the *AE* curve shifts downward to AE_1, and equilibrium expenditure is $700 billion at point *a*. When the price level falls to 90, the *AE* curve shifts upward to AE_2, and equilibrium expenditure is $900 billion at point *c*. Points *a*, *b*, and *c* on the *AD* curve in part (b) correspond to the equilibrium expenditure points *a*, *b*, and *c* in part (a).

FIGURE 25.11

A Change in
Aggregate Demand

(a) Aggregate expenditure

(b) Aggregate demand

The price level is 110. When the aggregate expenditure curve is AE_0 (part a), the aggregate demand curve is AD_0 (part b). An increase in autonomous expenditure shifts the AE curve upward to AE_1 and equilibrium real GDP is $1,000 billion (at b). Because the quantity of real GDP demanded at a price level of 110 increases to $1,000 billion, the AD curve shifts rightward to AD_1.

This equilibrium expenditure of $1,000 billion is the aggregate quantity of goods and services demanded at a price level of 110, as shown by point b in part (b). Point b lies on a new aggregate demand curve. The aggregate demand curve has shifted rightward to AD_1.

But how do we know by how much the AD curve shifts? The multiplier determines the answer.

$$\begin{matrix} AD \text{ curve} \\ \text{shift} \end{matrix} = \begin{matrix} \text{Change in} \\ \text{autonomous} \\ \text{expenditure} \end{matrix} \times \text{Multiplier}$$

In this example, the multiplier is 2. A $100 billion increase in autonomous expenditure produces a $200 billion increase in the aggregate quantity of goods and services demanded at each price level. That is, a $100 billion increase in autonomous expenditure shifts the AD curve rightward by $200 billion.

A decrease in autonomous expenditure shifts the aggregate expenditure curve downward and shifts the aggregate demand curve leftward. You can see these effects by reversing the change that we've just studied. Suppose that the economy is initially at point b on the aggregate expenditure curve AE_1 and the aggregate demand curve AD_1. A decrease in autonomous expenditure shifts the aggregate planned expenditure curve downward to AE_0. The aggregate quantity of goods and services demanded falls from $1,000 billion to $800 billion, and the aggregate demand curve shifts leftward to AD_0.

Let's summarize what we have just discovered:

If some factor other than a change in the price level increases autonomous expenditure, the AE curve shifts upward and the AD curve shifts rightward.

The size of the AD curve shift depends on the change in autonomous expenditure and the multiplier.

Equilibrium GDP and the Price Level

In Chapter 24, we learned that aggregate demand and short-run aggregate supply determine equilibrium real GDP and the price level. We've now put aggregate demand under a more powerful microscope and discovered that a change in investment (or in any component of autonomous expenditure) changes aggregate demand and shifts the aggregate demand curve. The magnitude of the shift depends on the multiplier. But whether a change in autonomous expenditure results ultimately in a change in real GDP, a change in the price level, or a combination of the two depends on aggregate supply. There are two time frames to consider: the short run and the long run. First we'll see what happens in the short run.

An Increase in Aggregate Demand in the Short Run Figure 25.12 describes the economy. In part (a), the aggregate expenditure curve is AE_0, and equilibrium expenditure is $800 billion—point *a*. In part (b), aggregate demand is AD_0, and the short-run aggregate supply curve is *SAS*. (Look at Chapter 24 if you need to refresh your understanding of this curve.) Equilibrium is at point *a*, where the aggregate demand and short-run aggregate supply curves intersect. The price level is 110, and real GDP is $800 billion.

Now suppose that autonomous expenditure increases by $100 billion. With the price level fixed at 110, the aggregate expenditure curve shifts upward to AE_1. Equilibrium expenditure increases to $1,000 billion—point *b* in part (a). In part (b), the aggregate demand curve shifts rightward by $200 billion, from AD_0 to AD_1. How far the aggregate demand curve shifts is determined by the multiplier when the price level is fixed. But with this new aggregate demand curve, the price level does not remain fixed. The price level rises, and as it does so the aggregate expenditure curve shifts downward. The short-run equilibrium occurs when the aggregate expenditure curve has shifted downward to AE_2 and the new aggregate demand curve, AD_1, intersects the short-run aggregate supply curve. Real GDP is $960 billion and the price level is 116 (at point *c*).

When price level effects are taken into account, the increase in autonomous expenditure still has a multiplier effect on real GDP, but the effect is smaller than it would be if the price level were fixed. The steeper the slope of the short-run aggregate supply curve, the larger is the increase in the price level and the smaller is the multiplier effect on real GDP.

An Increase in Aggregate Demand in the Long Run Figure 25.13 illustrates the long-run effect of an increase in aggregate demand. In the long run, real GDP equals potential GDP and there is full employment. Potential GDP is $800 billion, and the long-run aggregate supply curve is *LAS*. Initially, the economy is at point *a* (parts a and b).

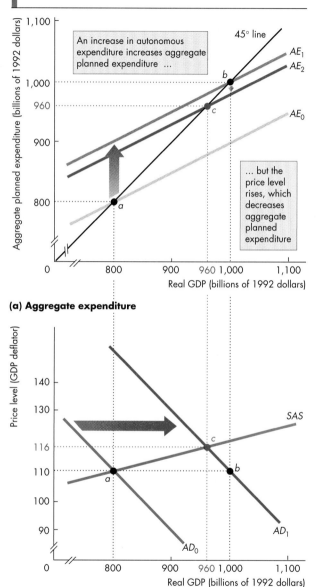

FIGURE 25.12

The Multiplier in the Short Run

(a) Aggregate expenditure

(b) Aggregate demand

An increase in autonomous expenditure shifts the *AE* curve from AE_0 to AE_1 (part a) and shifts the *AD* curve from AD_0 to AD_1 (part b). The price level does not remain at 110 but rises, and the higher price level shifts the *AE* curve downward from AE_1 to AE_2. The economy moves to point *c* in both parts. In the short run, when prices are flexible, the multiplier effect is smaller than when the price level is fixed.

FIGURE 25.13

The Multiplier
in the Long Run

(a) Aggregate expenditure

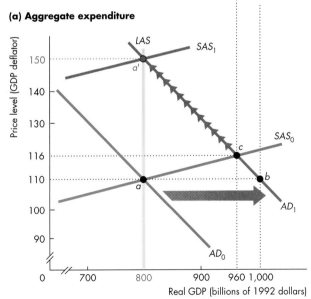

(b) Aggregate demand

Starting from point *a*, an increase in autonomous expenditure shifts the *AE* curve to AE_1 and shifts the *AD* curve to AD_1. In the short run, the economy moves to point *c*. In the long run, the money wage rate rises, the *SAS* curve shifts to SAS_1, the *AE* curve shifts back to AE_0, the price level rises, and real GDP decreases. The economy moves to point *a'*. In the long run, the multiplier is zero.

Autonomous expenditure increases by $100 billion. The aggregate expenditure curve shifts upward to AE_1 and the aggregate demand curve shifts rightward to AD_1. With no change in the price level, the economy would move to point *b* and real GDP would increase to $1,000 billion. But in the short run, the price level rises to 116 and real GDP increases to only $960 billion. With the higher price level, the *AE* curve shifts from AE_1 to AE_2. The economy is now in a short-run equilibrium at point *c*. Real GDP exceeds potential GDP and the money wage rate starts to rise. The higher money wage rate increases costs, which decreases short-run aggregate supply and the *SAS* curve starts to shift leftward towards SAS_1. The price level rises further. There is a movement along AD_1, and the *AE* curve shifts downward from AE_2 towards AE_0. Real GDP decreases. When the money wage rate and the price level have increased by the same percentage, real GDP is again equal to potential GDP and the economy is at point *a'*. In the long run, the multiplier is zero.

R E V I E W   Q U I Z

- How does a change in the price level influence the *AE* curve and the *AD* curve?
- If autonomous expenditure changes with no change in the price level, what happens to the *AE* curve and the *AD* curve? Which curve shifts by an amount determined by the multiplier and why?
- How does real GDP change in the short run when autonomous expenditure increases? Does real GDP change by the same amount as the change in aggregate demand? Why or why not?
- How does real GDP change in the long run when autonomous expenditure increases? Does real GDP change by the same amount as the change in aggregate demand? Why or why not?

◆ You are now ready to build on what you've learned and study the roles of fiscal policy and monetary policy in smoothing the business cycle. In Chapter 26, we study fiscal policy—government expenditures, taxes, and budget deficits and surpluses—and in Chapter 28, we study monetary policy—interest rates and the quantity of money. But before you leave the current topic, look at *Reading Between the Lines* on pages 564–565 and see the model you've studied in this chapter in action in the Canadian economy.

Recession Watch

FINANCIAL POST, AUGUST 5, 1998

Sunny economic outlook, but clouds on horizon

There is enough strength in the economy for it to keep creating jobs at a strong clip through 1999, the Conference Board of Canada says in its summer outlook report.

A buildup of inventories will slow economic growth over the next year, but there is enough momentum to drop the unemployment rate as low as 7.7% next year, the board forecast yesterday. ...

Gross domestic product is expected to grow 3.1% this year, up slightly from the board's call for 2.9% growth in April.

This year's expansion may run even higher, stealing from 1999's growth, if businesses continue to build inventory in the face of slowing demand, said Paul Darby, the board's director of economic services.

"A large-scale inventory buildup generally triggers a serious slowdown as inventory levels are corrected," the summer report said. "The result would be stronger growth in 1998, but a sharp pause next year, reminiscent of the Canadian experience in 1996 when growth was only 1.2%."

At this point, the board is calling for 2.9% expansion in GDP in 1999.

Other than ballooning inventories, the board identified additional risks to the economy, including the failure of Asian markets to rebound from recessions this year. ...

Essence of the Story

■ The Conference Board of Canada reports that a buildup of inventories will slow economic growth in 1999.

■ GDP is expected to grow 3.1 percent in 1998 and 2.9 percent in 1999.

■ Although demand is decreasing, GDP growth could be even higher in 1998 if businesses continue to increase their inventories.

■ An increase in GDP growth in 1998 and an increase in inventories could diminish GDP growth in 1999.

Economic Analysis

■ Inventory investment fluctuates, and when a recession begins, an unplanned inventory buildup occurs.

■ Not all increases in inventories are unplanned.

■ Planned inventory changes are part of planned investment and so are part of aggregate planned expenditure.

■ Two possible scenarios exist for the economy in 1999.

■ In the first scenario, the increase in inventories is planned.

■ In Fig. 1 aggregate planned expenditure increases from AE_{98} to AE_{99} because firms plan to increase their inventories.

■ With real GDP at $840 billion, the economy is at point a and aggregate planned expenditure on AE_{99} exceeds real GDP.

■ Because aggregate planned expenditure exceeds real GDP and despite the fact that firms plan an increase in inventories, they end up selling more than they had planned and there is an unplanned decrease in inventories.

■ As firms scramble to make up the inventory deficit, they increase production. Real GDP increases to $900 billion (in this example).

■ In Fig. 2 aggregate planned expenditure decreases from AE_{98} to AE_{99}. The reason for the decrease in aggregate planned expenditure is not important.

■ With real GDP at $840 billion, the economy is at point b and real GDP exceeds aggregate planned expenditure on AE_{99}.

■ Because real GDP exceeds aggregate planned expenditure, firms sell less than they had planned and there is an unplanned increase in inventories.

■ As firms try to work off the unwanted excess inventories, they decrease production. Real GDP decreases to $800 billion (in this example).

■ When the increase in inventories is planned, real GDP increases and the economy experiences growth.

■ When the increase in inventories is unplanned, real GDP exceeds aggregate planned expenditure and real GDP shrinks.

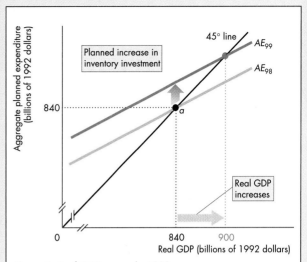

Figure 1 Real GDP grows in 1999

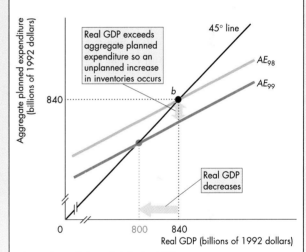

Figure 2 Real GDP shrinks in 1999

MATHEMATICAL NOTE: THE ALGEBRA OF THE MULTIPLIER

THIS NOTE EXPLAINS THE MULTIPLIER IN GREATER detail than that presented on p. 556. We begin by defining the symbols we need:

- Aggregate planned expenditure, AE
- Real GDP, Y
- Consumption expenditure, C
- Investment, I
- Government expenditures, G
- Exports, X
- Imports, M
- Net taxes, NT
- Disposable income, YD
- Autonomous consumption expenditure, a
- Marginal propensity to consume, b
- Marginal propensity to import, m
- Marginal tax rate, t
- Autonomous expenditure, A

Aggregate Expenditure

Aggregate planned expenditure (AE) is the sum of the planned amounts of consumption expenditure (C), investment (I), government expenditures (G), and exports (X) minus the planned amount of imports (M). That is

$$AE = C + I + G + X - M.$$

Consumption Function Consumption expenditure (C) depends on disposable income (YD) and we write the consumption function as

$$C = a + bYD.$$

Disposable income (YD) equals real GDP minus net taxes ($Y - NT$). So replacing YD with ($Y - NT$), the consumption function becomes

$$C = a + b(Y - NT).$$

Net taxes equal real GDP (Y) multiplied by the marginal tax rate (t). That is,

$$NT = tY.$$

Use this equation in the previous one to obtain

$$C = a + b(1 - t)Y.$$

This equation describes consumption expenditure as a function of real GDP.

Import Function Imports depend on real GDP and the import function is

$$M = mY.$$

Aggregate Expenditure Curve Use the consumption function and the import function to replace C and M in the aggregate planned expenditure equation. That is,

$$AE = a + b(1 - t)Y + I + G + X - mY.$$

Collect the terms on the right-side of the equation that involve Y to obtain

$$AE = [a + I + G + X] + [b(1 - t) - m]Y.$$

Autonomous expenditure (A) is $[a + I + G + X]$, and the slope of the AE curve is $[b(1 - t) - m]$. So the equation for the AE curve, which is shown in Fig. 1, is

$$AE = A + [b(1 - t) - m]Y.$$

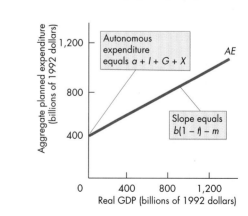

Figure 1 The *AE* curve

Equilibrium Expenditure

Equilibrium expenditure occurs when aggregate planned expenditure (AE) equals real GDP (Y). That is,

$$AE = Y.$$

In Fig. 2, the scales of the x-axis (real GDP) and the y-axis (aggregate planned expenditure) are identical, so the 45° line shows the points at which aggregate planned expenditure equals real GDP. That is, along the 45° line, AE equals Y.

The figure shows the point of equilibrium expenditure at the intersection of the AE curve and the 45° line.

To calculate equilibrium expenditure and real GDP, we solve the equations for the AE curve and the 45° line for the two unknown quantities AE and Y. So, starting with

$$AE = A + [b(1 - t) - m]Y$$

$$AE = Y,$$

replace AE with Y in the AE equation to obtain:

$$Y = A + [b(1 - t) - m]Y.$$

The solution for Y is

$$Y = \frac{1}{1 - [b(1 - t) - m]} A.$$

The Multiplier

The multiplier equals the change in equilibrium expenditure and real GDP (Y) that results from a change in autonomous expenditure (A) divided by the change in autonomous expenditure. A change in autonomous expenditure (A) changes equilibrium expenditure and real GDP (Y) by

$$\Delta Y = \frac{1}{1 - [b(1 - t) - m]} \Delta A.$$

$$\text{Multiplier} = \frac{1}{1 - [b(1 - t) - m]}.$$

The slope of the AE curve is $b(1 - t) - m$, so the

$$\text{Multiplier} = \frac{1}{1 - \text{Slope of the } AE \text{ curve}}.$$

The size of the multiplier depends on the slope of the AE curve and the larger the slope, the larger is the multiplier. So the multiplier is larger,

- The greater the marginal propensity to consume (b)
- The smaller the marginal tax rate (t)
- The smaller the marginal propensity to import (m)

An economy with no imports and no marginal taxes has $m = 0$ and $t = 0$. In this case, the multiplier equals $1/(1 - b)$. If b is 0.75, then the multiplier is 4 as shown in Fig. 3. In an economy with $b = 0.75$, $t = 0.2$, and $m = 0.1$, the slope of the AE curve is $[0.75(1 - 0.2) - 0.1]$, which equals 0.5 and the multiplier is 2. Make up some more examples to show the effects of b, t, and m on the multiplier.

Figure 2 Equilibrium expenditure

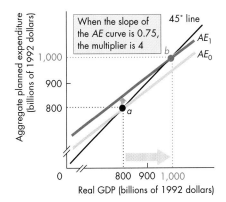

Figure 3 The multiplier

568

SUMMARY

Key Points

Expenditure Plans and GDP (pp. 544–549)

■ When the price level is fixed, expenditure plans determine real GDP.

■ Consumption expenditure is determined by disposable income, and the marginal propensity to consume (*MPC*) determines the change in consumption expenditure brought about by a change in disposable income. Real GDP is the main influence on disposable income.

■ Imports are determined by real GDP, and the marginal propensity to import determines the change in imports brought about by a change in real GDP.

Equilibrium Expenditure at a Fixed Price Level (pp. 549–553)

■ Aggregate *planned* expenditure depends on real GDP.

■ Equilibrium expenditure occurs when aggregate planned expenditure equals actual expenditure and real GDP.

The Multiplier (pp. 554–559)

■ The multiplier is the magnified effect of a change in autonomous expenditure on real GDP.

■ The multiplier equals 1 divided by 1 minus the slope of the *AE* curve.

■ The multiplier is influenced by the marginal propensity to consume, the marginal income tax rate, and the marginal propensity to import.

The Multiplier and the Price Level (pp. 559–563)

■ The aggregate demand curve is the relationship between the quantity of real GDP demanded and the price level, other things remaining the same.

■ The aggregate expenditure curve is the relationship between aggregate planned expenditure and real GDP, other things remaining the same.

■ At a given price level, there is a given aggregate expenditure curve. A change in the price level changes aggregate planned expenditure and shifts the aggregate expenditure curve. A change in the price level also creates a movement along the aggregate demand curve.

■ A change in autonomous expenditure that is not caused by a change in the price level shifts the aggregate expenditure curve and shifts the aggregate demand curve. The magnitude of the shift of the aggregate demand curve depends on the multiplier and on the change in autonomous expenditure.

■ The multiplier decreases as the price level changes and the multiplier in the long-run is zero.

Key Figures ◆

Key Terms

PROBLEMS

*1. You are given the following information about the economy of Heron Island:

Disposable income	Consumption expenditure
(millions of dollars per year)	
0	5
10	10
20	15
30	20
40	25

Calculate Heron Island's
a. Marginal propensity to consume.
b. Saving at each level of disposable income.
c. Marginal propensity to save.

2. You are given the following information about the economy of Spendthrift Island:

Disposable income	Saving
(millions of dollars per year)	
0	−100
500	−50
1,000	0
1,500	50
2,000	100
2,500	150
3,000	200

Calculate Spendthrift Island's
a. Marginal propensity to save.
b. Consumption expenditure at each level of disposable income.
c. Marginal propensity to consume.

*3. Turtle Island has no imports or exports, the people of Turtle Island pay no income taxes, and the price level is fixed. The figure illustrates the components of aggregate planned expenditure on Turtle Island.
On Turtle Island, what is:
a. Autonomous expenditure?
b. The marginal propensity to consume?
c. Equilibrium expenditure?
d. Happening to inventories if real GDP is $4 billion?
e. Happening to inventories if real GDP is $6 billion?
f. The multiplier?

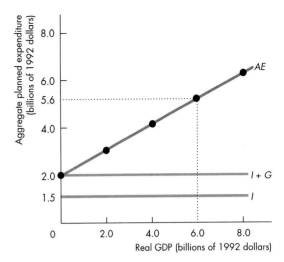

4. The spreadsheet lists the components of aggregate planned expenditure in Spice Bay. The numbers are in billions of cloves, the currency of the Bay.

	A	B	C	D	E	F	G
1		Y	C	I	G	X	M
2	a	100	110	50	60	60	15
3	b	200	170	50	60	60	30
4	c	300	230	50	60	60	45
5	d	400	290	50	60	60	60
6	e	500	350	50	60	60	75
7	f	600	410	50	60	60	90

In Spice Bay, what is:
a. Autonomous expenditure?
b. The marginal propensity to consume?
c. Aggregate planned expenditure when real GDP is 200 billion cloves?
d. Happening to inventories if real GDP is 200 billion cloves?
e. Happening to inventories if real GDP is 500 billion cloves?
f. The multiplier in Spice Bay?

*5. In the economy of Zee, autonomous consumption expenditure is $100 billion and the marginal propensity to consume is 0.9. Investment is $460 billion, government expenditures on goods and services are $400 billion, and net taxes are $400 billion and do not vary with income. Zee has no imports or exports.
a. What is the consumption function?
b. What is the equation that describes the aggregate expenditure curve?
c. Calculate equilibrium expenditure.

d. If investment decreases to $360 billion, what is the change in equilibrium expenditure and what is the size of the multiplier?

6. In the economy of Antarctica: Autonomous consumption expenditure is $1 billion, and the marginal propensity to consume is 0.95. Investment is $4 billion, government expenditures on goods and services are $4 billion, and net taxes are a constant $4 billion—they do not vary with income.
   a. What is the consumption function?
   b. What is the equation that describes the aggregate expenditure curve?
   c. Calculate equilibrium expenditure.
   d. If investment decreases to $3 billion, what is the change in equilibrium expenditure and what is the size of the multiplier?

*7. Suppose that in problem 5 the price level is 100 and real GDP equals potential GDP. If investment increases by $100 billion,
   a. What is the change in the quantity of real GDP demanded?
   b. In the short run, does equilibrium real GDP increase by more than, less than, or the same amount as the increase in the quantity of real GDP demanded?
   c. In the long run, does equilibrium real GDP increase by more than, less than, or the same amount as the increase in the quantity of real GDP demanded?
   d. In the short run, does the price level in Zee rise, fall, or remain unchanged?
   e. In the long run, does the price level in Zee rise, fall, or remain unchanged?

8. Suppose that in problem 6 the price level is 100 and real GDP equals potential GDP. If investment increases by $1 billion,
   a. What is the change in the quantity of real GDP demanded?
   b. In the short run, does equilibrium real GDP increase by more than, less than, or the same amount as the increase in the quantity of real GDP demanded?
   c. In the long run, does equilibrium real GDP increase by more than, less than, or the same amount as the increase in the quantity of real GDP demanded?
   d. In the short run, does the price level in Antarctica rise, fall, or remain unchanged?
   e. In the long run, does the price level in Antarctica rise, fall, or remain unchanged?

CRITICAL THINKING

1. Study *Reading Between the Lines* on pp. 564–565 and then answer the following questions.
   a. What is the relationship between an unplanned increase in inventories and the change in real GDP?
   b. What is the relationship between an unplanned decrease in inventories and the change in real GDP?
   c. Are there any indicators in the economy that would tell you if the buildup of inventories was planned or unplanned?
   d. If unemployment is decreasing and inventories are increasing, what would you predict is happening to real GDP growth?

2. Use the links on the Parkin-Bade Web site to access the Penn World Table and obtain data on real GDP per person and consumption as a percentage of real GDP for Canada, China, South Africa, and Mexico from 1960 to the latest year available.
   a. In a spreadsheet, calculate consumption expenditure per person. Hint: multiply real GDP per person by consumption as a percentage of GDP and divide by 100.
   b. Use the real GDP data and consumption data that you have calculated and make graphs to show the relationship between consumption expenditure and real GDP for these four countries.
   c. On the basis of the numbers you've obtained, in which country do you expect the multiplier to be largest (other things remaining the same)?
   d. What other data would you need to be able to calculate the multipliers for these countries?

3. You are a research assistant in the office of the Minister of Finance. You've been asked to draft a note for the Minister that explains the power and limitations of the multiplier. The Minister wants only 250 words of crisp, clear, jargon-free explanation together with a lively example.

Fiscal Policy

The federal government spends close to 20 cents of every dollar that Canadians earn. Some of this spending is on goods and services and some is the transfer of cash to individuals, businesses, and provincial governments. What are the effects of government spending on the economy? Does it create jobs? Or does it destroy them? And does a dollar spent by the government on goods and services have the same effect as a dollar spent by someone else? ◆ In 1998, at the same time that it planned to spend 20 cents of every dollar earned, the federal government also planned to tax us by that amount. What are the effects of taxes on the economy? Do taxes harm employment and economic growth? ◆ The plan to have tax revenues equal expenditures is new on Parliament Hill. For the 23 years between 1974 and 1997, the federal government ran a budget deficit. During those years, the federal government's debt increased from $20 billion to $550 billion—a *27-fold increase*. If these numbers are too big to visualize, divide them by the population of Canada to find *your* share of the total. Government debt per person has grown from $950 in 1974 to more than $20,000 in 1998. What are the effects of accumulating government debt? Does it slow economic growth? Does it impose a burden on future generations—on you and your children? ◆ Two people who think that governments spend too much are Paul Martin, the Federal Minister of Finance and Ernie Eves, the Ontario Treasurer. In recent budgets, these ministers have lopped billions of dollars off government spending. Will these actions bring economic growth or will they create yet more unemployment?

◆ These are the fiscal policy issues you will explore in this chapter. We'll begin by describing the budgets of the federal and provincial governments. We'll then use the multiplier analysis of Chapter 25 and the aggregate supply–aggregate demand model of Chapter 24 to study the effects of the budget on the economy.

Balancing Acts on Parliament Hill

After studying this chapter, you will be able to:

■ Describe how federal and provincial budgets are created

■ Describe the recent history of federal and provincial expenditures, tax revenues, and budget deficits

■ Distinguish between automatic and discretionary fiscal policy

■ Define and explain the fiscal policy multipliers

■ Explain the effects of fiscal policy in both the short run and the long run

■ Distinguish between and explain the demand-side and the supply-side effects of fiscal policy

Government Budgets

THE ANNUAL STATEMENT OF THE EXPENDITURES and tax revenues of the government of Canada together with the laws and regulations that approve and support those expenditures and taxes makes up the **federal budget**. Similarly, a **provincial budget** is an annual statement of the revenues and outlays of a provincial government together with the laws and regulations that approve or support those revenues and outlays.

Before World War II, the federal budget had no purpose other than to finance the business of government. But since the late 1940s, the federal budget has assumed a second purpose, which is to pursue the government's fiscal policy. **Fiscal policy** is the use of the federal budget to achieve macroeconomic objectives such as full employment, sustained long-term economic growth, and price level stability. Our focus is this second purpose.

Budget Making

The federal government and Parliament make fiscal policy. The process begins with long drawn-out consultations between the Minister of Finance and Department of Finance officials and their counterparts in the provincial governments. These discussions deal with programs that are funded and operated jointly by the two levels of government.

The Minister also consults with business and consumer groups on a wide range of issues. After all these consultations, the Minister develops a set of proposals, which are discussed in Cabinet and which become government policy. The Minister finally presents a budget plan to Parliament, which debates the plan and enacts the laws necessary to implement it.

Highlights of the 1999 Budget

Table 26.1 shows the main items in the federal budget and the projected amounts for the fiscal year beginning on April 1, 1999. The main items are

- Revenues
- Outlays
- Budget balance

TABLE 26.1

The Federal Budget in 1999–2000

Item		Projections (billions of dollars)
Revenues	**157**	
Personal income taxes		93
Corporate income taxes		21
Indirect taxes		35
Investment income		8
Outlays	**154**	
Transfer payments		76
Expenditures on goods and services		35
Debt interest		43
Budget balance	**+3**	

Source: Department of Finance *Budget Plan* 1999.

Revenues   Revenues are the federal government's receipts, which in the 1999 budget were projected at $157 billion. These revenues come from four sources:

1. Personal income taxes
2. Corporate income taxes
3. Indirect taxes
4. Investment income

The largest revenue source is *personal income taxes*, which in 1999 were projected to be $93 billion. These are the taxes paid by individuals on their incomes. The second largest source of revenue is *indirect taxes*, which in 1999 were projected to be $35 billion. These taxes include the Goods and Services Tax or GST and taxes on the sale of gasoline, alcoholic drinks, and a few other items. The smallest revenue sources are *corporate income taxes*, which are the taxes paid by companies on their profits, and *investment income*, which is the income from government enterprises and investments. In 1999, corporate income taxes were projected to raise $21 billion and investment income was projected at $8 billion. Total federal government revenue in 1999 was projected at $157 billion.

Outlays Outlays are classified in three categories:

1. Transfer payments
2. Expenditures on goods and services
3. Debt interest

The largest outlay, and by a big margin, is *transfer payments*. Transfer payments are payments to individuals, businesses, other levels of government, and the rest of the world. In 1999, this item was $76 billion. It includes unemployment cheques and welfare payments to individuals, farm subsidies, grants to provincial and local governments, aid to developing countries, and dues to international organizations such as the United Nations.

Expenditures on goods and services are expenditures on final goods and services, and in 1999 this item totalled $35 billion. These expenditures include those on national defence, computers for Revenue Canada, government cars, and highways. This component of the federal budget is *government expenditures on goods and services* that appears in the circular flow of expenditure and income and in the national income and product accounts (see Chapter 22, pp. 478–479).

Debt interest is the interest on the government debt. In 1999, this item was $43 billion—more than government expenditures on goods and services. This interest payment is large because the government has a large debt—$584 billion. This large debt has arisen because, until recently, the federal government has had a large and persistent budget deficit.

Budget Balance The government's budget balance is equal to its revenues minus its outlays. That is,

$$\text{Budget balance} = \text{Revenues} - \text{Outlays}.$$

If revenues exceed outlays, the government has a **budget surplus**. If outlays exceed revenues, the government has a **budget deficit**. If revenues equal outlays, the government has a **balanced budget**. In 1999, with projected outlays of $153 billion and revenues of $157 billion, the government projected a budget surplus of $3 billion.

How typical is the federal budget of 1999? Let's look at its recent history.

The Budget in Historical Perspective

Figure 26.1 shows the government's revenues, outlays, and budget balance since 1970. To get a better sense of the magnitudes of these items, they are shown as percentages of GDP. Expressing them in

---

FIGURE 26.1
Revenues, Outlays, and the Budget Balance

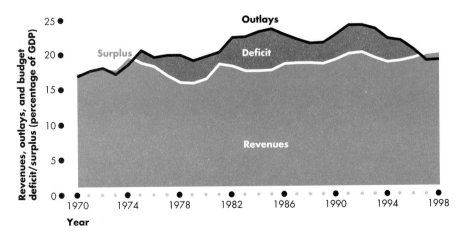

The figure records the federal government's revenues, outlays, and budget balance as percentages of GDP from 1970 to 1998. During the late 1970s, the budget deficit was small and decreasing, but during the 1980s, it became large and persisted. The budget deficit arose because revenues decreased and outlays increased as percentages of GDP. The deficit was eliminated in 1997. In 1998, the federal government had a budget surplus.

Source: Statistics Canada, *StatCan: CANSIM Disc*, March 1999.

this way lets us see how large government is relative to the size of the economy and also helps us to study *changes* in the scale of government over time. You can think of the percentages of GDP as telling you how many cents of each dollar that Canadians earn get paid to and spent by the government.

In 23 of the 29 years shown in Fig. 26.1, the federal budget has been in deficit and the average deficit over these years was 2.4 percent of GDP. The deficit climbed to a peak of 5.8 percent of GDP in 1985. It then decreased through the rest of the 1980s. During the recession of 1991–1992, the deficit increased again, and it remained above 3 percent of GDP for most of the 1980s and early 1990s. Only in 1997 did the federal government finally eradicate its deficit. And it did this by cutting outlays, especially transfer payments to provincial governments.

Why did the government deficit grow during the early 1980s and remain high through the early 1990s? The immediate answer is that outlays increased while revenues remained relatively constant. But which components of outlays increased? And did all the sources of revenues remain constant?

To answer these questions, we need to examine each of the sources of revenues and outlays in detail. We'll begin by looking at the sources of revenue.

Revenues   Figure 26.2 shows the components of government revenues (as percentages of GDP) since 1970. Total revenues have an upward trend. Throughout the 1980s and 1990s, total government revenues as a percentage of GDP have been increasing. The main source of this increase is an increase in personal income taxes. Corporate income taxes and indirect taxes have decreased as a percentage of GDP.

The increase in income taxes has resulted from increases in tax rates in successive budgets throughout the 1980s and 1990s. The decrease in indirect taxes is mainly the result of replacing an old Federal Sales Tax with the current GST. This switch was intended to maintain revenues at a constant level, but this outcome was not realized. The decrease in corporate taxes has resulted from incentives to businesses.

Outlays   Figure 26.3 shows the components of government outlays (as percentages of GDP) since 1970. Total outlays have been cyclical. They were on a rising trend during the 1970s, and they increased just before the tax cuts that you've just seen. The main source of increasing outlays is transfer payments. Expenditures on goods and services as a percentage of GDP have decreased. The item that has increased most persistently is debt interest.

FIGURE   26.2

Federal Government Revenues

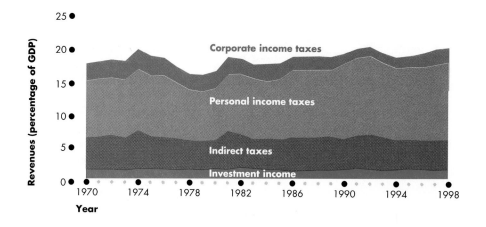

The figure shows the four components of government revenues: personal income taxes, corporate income taxes, indirect taxes, and investment income. Revenues from personal income taxes decreased during the late 1970s but trended upward during the 1980s and 1990s. Corporate income taxes decreased slightly. The other two components of revenues remained steady.

Source: Statistics Canada, *StatCan: CANSIM Disc,* March 1999.

FIGURE 26.3
Federal Government Outlays

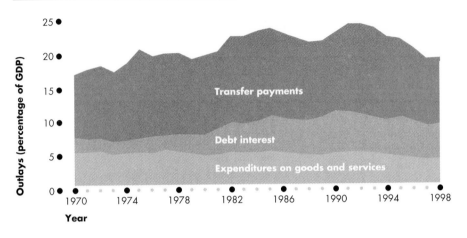

The figure shows three components of government outlays: expenditures on goods and services, debt interest, and transfer payments. Since 1970, expenditures on goods and services have fluctuated but they have not increased. Transfer payments have fluctuated the most and have increased, especially during the early 1980s. Debt interest increased steadily during the 1980s as the budget deficit fed on itself.

Source: Statistics Canada, StatCan: CANSIM Disc, March 1999.

To understand why debt interest has persistently increased, we need to see the connection between the budget deficit and government debt.

Deficit and Debt   The government borrows to finance its deficit. And **government debt** is the total amount of government borrowing. It is the sum of past deficits minus the sum of past surpluses. When the government has a deficit, its debt increases. Once a persistent deficit emerged during the 1980s, the deficit began to feed on itself. The deficit led to increased borrowing; increased borrowing led to larger debt and larger interest payments; and larger interest payments led to a larger deficit and yet larger debt. That is the story of the increasing deficit of the 1980s.

Figure 26.4 shows the history of government debt since 1946. At the end of World War II, debt (as a percentage of GDP) was at an all-time high of 113 percent. Huge wartime deficits had increased debt to the point that it exceeded GDP. Post-war budget surpluses lowered the debt to GDP ratio through 1974, by which time it stood at 14 percent, its lowest point since World War II. Small deficits increased the debt to GDP ratio slightly through the 1970s, and large deficits increased it dramatically between 1981 and 1986. During the late 1980s, the ratio continued to increase but at a more moderate rate. It grew quickly

FIGURE 26.4
Federal Government Debt

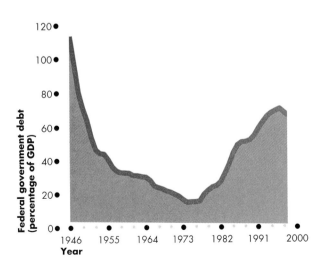

Federal government debt as a percentage of GDP decreased from 1946 through 1974 but then increased through 1997.

Source: Statistics Canada, StatCan: CANSIM Disc, March 1999.

again during the 1990–1991 recession, but its growth rate slowed when the economy recovered during 1993 and 1995.

Debt and Capital When individuals and businesses incur debts, they usually do so to buy capital—assets that yield a return. In fact, the main point of debt is to enable people to buy assets that will earn a return that exceeds the interest paid on the debt. The government is similar to individuals and businesses in this regard. Some government expenditure is investment—the purchase of public capital that yields a return. Highways, major irrigation schemes, public schools and universities, public libraries, and the stock of national defence capital all yield a social rate of return that probably far exceeds the interest rate the government pays on its debt.

But total government debt, which is $584 billion, is much larger than the value of the public capital stock. This fact means that some government debt has been incurred to finance public consumption expenditure.

Provincial and Local Government Budgets

The *total government* sector of Canada includes provincial and local governments as well as the federal government. In 1996, when federal government outlays were $170 billion, provincial and local government outlays were $235 billion and total government outlays were $405 billion. Most provincial and local government outlays are on public hospitals and public schools, colleges, and universities.

Provincial government outlays and revenue sources vary a great deal across the provinces. Figure 26.5 shows the range of variation. Part (a) shows outlays as a percentage of provincial GDP. You can see that the outlays of Atlantic governments are the greatest and those of the governments of Alberta, Ontario, and Saskatchewan are the least. Part (b) shows the sources of provincial revenues as a percentage of total outlays. The Atlantic provinces receive the largest transfers from the federal government, while British Columbia, Alberta, and Ontario receive the least.

Figure 26.6 shows the revenues, outlays, and deficits of the federal government and of total government between 1970 and 1998.

You can see that federal government outlays and revenues and total government outlays and revenues

FIGURE 26.5

Provincial Government Budgets

(a) Outlays

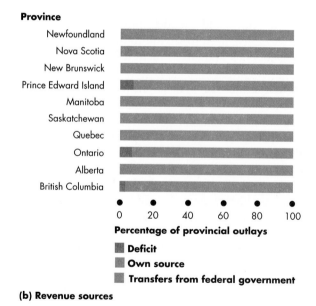

(b) Revenue sources

Provincial government budgets vary a lot across the provinces. As a percentage of provincial GDP, outlays (part a) are highest in Atlantic Canada and lowest in Alberta, Ontario, and Saskatchewan. The Atlantic provinces receive the largest share of revenue from the federal government (part b) while British Columbia, Alberta, and Ontario receive the least.

Source: Statistics Canada, *StatCan: CANSIM Disc*, March 1999.

Total Government Budgets

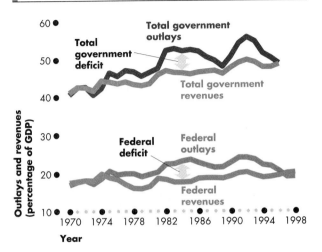

Total government is the sum of the federal, provincial, and local governments. The total government deficit fluctuates more than does the federal government deficit because provincial government deficits are large and have increased. But the fluctuations in provincial revenues, outlays, and deficit are in similar directions as those of the federal government.

Source: Statistics Canada, *StatCan: CANSIM Disc*, March 1999.

fluctuate in similar ways, but the total government is much larger than the federal government. In other words, the provincial and local governments are a large component of total government. You can also see that total government outlays fluctuate more than federal government outlays.

How does the Canadian government budget balance compare with budgets in other countries?

The Budget Surplus in Global Perspective

Is Canada unusual in having eliminated its budget deficit and now running a budget surplus? Do other countries have budget surpluses or do they have budget deficits? Figure 26.7 answers these questions. In today's world, almost all countries have budget deficits. To compare countries, we measure the budget surplus or deficit as percentages of GDP. The biggest deficit relative to GDP is found in Japan, where the

Government Deficits Around the World in 1998

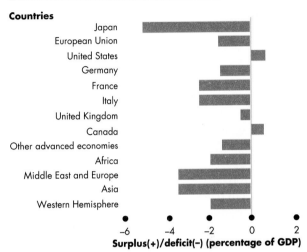

Governments in most countries have budget deficits. The largest ones are in Japan followed by the Middle East and the rest of Asia. Canada and the United States (and a few other countries not shown) have surpluses.

Source: World Economic Outlook, October 1998, International Monetary Fund, Washington, D.C., Tables A15 and A20.

deficit exceeds 5 percent of GDP. The rest of Asia and the Middle East also have large deficits. The smallest deficit relative to GDP is found in the United Kingdom. Canada and the United States (and a small group of other countries not shown in Fig. 26.7) are relatively unusual in having budget surpluses.

REVIEW QUIZ

- What are the main items of government revenues and outlays?
- Under what circumstances does the government have a budget surplus?
- Explain the connection between a government deficit and a government debt.

Your next task is to study the effects of the government's budget on the economy and learn about fiscal policy multipliers.

Fiscal Policy Multipliers

FISCAL POLICY ACTIONS CAN BE EITHER discretionary or automatic. **Discretionary fiscal policy** is a policy action that is initiated by an act of Parliament. It requires a change in tax laws or in some spending program. For example, an increase in the income tax rate and an increase in defence spending are discretionary fiscal policy actions. That is, discretionary fiscal policy is a deliberate policy action. **Automatic fiscal policy** is a change in fiscal policy that is triggered by the state of the economy. For example, an increase in unemployment triggers an *automatic* increase in payments to the unemployed. A fall in incomes triggers an *automatic* decrease in tax receipts. That is, this type of fiscal policy adjusts automatically.

We begin by studying the effects of *discretionary* changes in government spending and taxes. To focus on the essentials, we'll initially study a model economy that is simpler than the one in which we live. In our model economy, there is no international trade and the taxes are autonomous. **Autonomous taxes** are taxes that do not vary with real GDP. The government fixes them, and they change when the government changes them. But they do not vary automatically with the state of the economy.

The main example of an autonomous tax is the *property tax*. This tax varies across individuals and depends on the value of the property a person occupies. But unlike the income tax, it does not change simply because a person's income changes.

We use autonomous taxes in our model economy because they make the principles we are studying easier to understand. Once we've grasped the principles, we'll explore our real economy with its international trade and income taxes—taxes that *do* vary with real GDP.

Spending fluctuations bombard the model economy that we study just like they bombard our real economy. Business investment in new building, plant and equipment, and inventories fluctuates because of swings in profit expectations and interest rates. These fluctuations set up multiplier effects that begin a recession or an expansion. If a recession takes hold, unemployment increases and incomes fall. If an expansion becomes too strong, inflationary pressures build up. To minimize the effects of these swings in spending, the government might change either its expenditures on goods and services or taxes. By changing either of these items, the government can influence aggregate expenditure and real GDP. But it

also changes its budget deficit or surplus. An alternative fiscal policy action is to change both expenditures and taxes together so that the budget balance does not change. We are first going to study the effects of these discretionary fiscal policy actions when the price level is fixed. Later in the chapter we'll study their effects when the price level adjusts. Each of these fiscal policy actions creates a multiplier effect on real GDP. These multipliers are:

- The government expenditures multiplier
- The autonomous tax multiplier

The Government Expenditures Multiplier

The **government expenditures multiplier** is the magnification effect of a change in government expenditures on goods and services on equilibrium expenditure and real GDP.

Government expenditures are a component of autonomous expenditure. So when government expenditures change, aggregate expenditure and real GDP change. The change in real GDP induces a change in consumption expenditure, which brings a further change in aggregate expenditure. A multiplier process ensues. This multiplier process is identical to the one described in Chapter 25 (pp. 554–558). Let's look at an example.

A Y2K Multiplier The Government of Canada has spent many millions of tax dollars to ensure that Canada's communications and defence systems are immune to the Y2K bug. The injection of these millions of dollars of public funds to build parallel communications systems and to test and reprogram tens of thousands of computers created many new jobs for programmers and electronic engineers. These newly employed workers saved some of what they earned, but they spent most of it and consumption expenditure increased. Retail stores, airlines, and hotels and restaurants expanded their businesses and hired yet more people and, in the process, created yet bigger incomes. Most of these incomes were also spent, so expenditure and incomes rose still further.

The Size of the Multiplier Table 26.2 illustrates the government expenditures multiplier with a numerical example. The first column lists various possible levels of real GDP. Our task is to find equilibrium expenditure and the change in real GDP when government expenditures change.

TABLE 26.2
The Government Expenditures Multiplier

	Real GDP (Y)	Taxes (T)	Disposable income (Y − T)	Consumption expenditure (C)	Investment (I)	Initial government expenditures (G)	Initial aggregate planned expenditure (C + I + G)	Increase in government expenditures (ΔG)	New aggregate planned expenditure (C + I + G + ΔG)
					(trillions of dollars)				
a	700	100	600	450	150	125	725	50	775
b	800	100	700	525	150	125	800	50	850
c	900	100	800	600	150	125	875	50	925
d	1,000	100	900	675	150	125	950	50	1,000
e	1,100	100	1,000	750	150	125	1,025	50	1,075

The second column shows taxes. They are fixed at $100 billion, regardless of the level of real GDP. (This is an assumption that keeps your attention on the key idea and makes the calculations easier to do.)

The third column calculates disposable income. Because taxes are autonomous, disposable income equals real GDP minus the $100 billion of taxes. For example, in row *b*, real GDP is $800 billion and disposable income is $700 billion.

The next column shows consumption expenditure. In this example, the *marginal propensity to consume* is 0.75. That is, a $1 increase in disposable income brings a 75 cent increase in consumption expenditure. Check this fact by calculating the increase in consumption expenditure when disposable income increases by $100 billion from row *b* to row *c*. Consumption expenditure increases by $75 billion.

The next column shows investment, which is a constant of $150 billion. The next column shows the initial level of government expenditures, which is $125 billion. Aggregate planned expenditure is the sum of consumption expenditure, investment, and government expenditures.

Equilibrium expenditure and real GDP occur when aggregate planned expenditure equals actual expenditure. In this example, equilibrium expenditure is $800 billion (highlighted in row *b* of the table).

The final two columns of the table show what happens when government expenditures increase by $50 billion. Aggregate planned expenditure increases by $50 billion at each level of real GDP. At the initial real GDP of $800 billion (row *b*), aggregate planned expenditure increases to $850 billion.

Because aggregate planned expenditure now exceeds real GDP, inventories decrease and firms increase production. Output, incomes, and expenditure increase. Increased incomes induce a further increase in expenditure. But the induced increase in aggregate planned expenditure is less than the increase in income, and eventually a new equilibrium is reached. The new equilibrium is at a real GDP of $1,000 billion (highlighted in row *d*).

A $50 billion increase in government expenditures has increased equilibrium expenditure and real GDP by $200 billion. Therefore the government expenditures multiplier is 4. The size of the multiplier depends on the marginal propensity to consume, which in this example is 0.75. The following formula shows the connection between the government expenditures multiplier and the marginal propensity to consume (*MPC*):

$$\text{Government expenditures multiplier} = \frac{1}{1 - MPC}.$$

Let's check this formula by using the numbers in the above example. The marginal propensity to consume is 0.75, so the government expenditures multiplier is $1 \div 0.25$, which equals 4.

Figure 26.8 illustrates the government expenditures multiplier. Initially, aggregate planned expenditure is shown by the curve labelled AE_0. The points on this curve, labelled *a* through *e*, correspond with the rows of Table 26.2. This aggregate expenditure curve intersects the 45° line at an equilibrium level of real GDP of $800 billion.

FIGURE 26.8
The Government Expenditures Multiplier

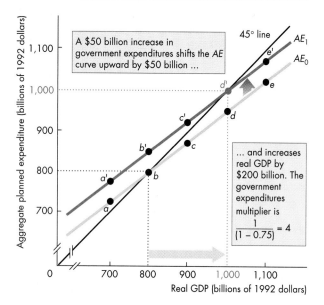

Initially, the aggregate expenditure curve is AE_0, and real GDP is $800 billion (at point b). An increase in government expenditures of $50 billion increases aggregate planned expenditure at each level of real GDP by $50 billion. The aggregate expenditure curve shifts upward from AE_0 to AE_1—a parallel shift. At the initial real GDP of $800 billion, aggregate planned expenditure is now $850 billion. Because aggregate planned expenditure is greater than real GDP, real GDP increases. The new equilibrium is reached when real GDP is $1,000 billion— the point at which the AE_1 curve intersects the 45° line (at d'). In this example, the government expenditures multiplier is 4.

When government expenditures increase by $50 billion, the aggregate expenditure curve shifts upward by that amount to AE_1. With this new aggregate expenditure curve, equilibrium real GDP increases to $1,000 billion. The increase in real GDP is 4 times the increase in government expenditures. The government expenditures multiplier is 4.

You've seen that when the price level is fixed, an increase in government expenditures increases real GDP. But to produce more output, more people must be employed, so when the price level is fixed, an increase in government expenditures can create jobs.

Changing its expenditures on goods and services is one way in which the government can try to influence real GDP. A second way in which the government might act to influence real GDP is by changing autonomous taxes. Let's see how this action works.

The Autonomous Tax Multiplier

The **autonomous tax multiplier** is the magnification effect of a change in autonomous taxes on equilibrium aggregate expenditure and real GDP. An *increase* in taxes *decreases* disposable income, which *decreases* consumption expenditure. The amount by which consumption expenditure initially changes is determined by the marginal propensity to consume. In our example the marginal propensity to consume is 0.75, so a $1 increase in taxes decreases disposable income by $1 and decreases aggregate expenditure initially by 75 cents.

This initial change in aggregate expenditure has a multiplier just like the government expenditures multiplier. We've seen that the government expenditures multiplier is $1/(1 - MPC)$. Because a tax *increase* leads to a *decrease* in expenditure, the autonomous tax multiplier is *negative*. And because a change in autonomous taxes changes aggregate expenditure initially by only MPC multiplied by the tax change, the autonomous tax multiplier is equal to

$$\text{Autonomous tax multiplier} = \frac{-MPC}{1 - MPC}.$$

In our example, the marginal propensity to consume is 0.75, so the autonomous tax multiplier is

$$\text{Autonomous tax multiplier} = \frac{-0.75}{1 - 0.75} = -3.$$

Figure 26.9 illustrates the autonomous tax multiplier. Initially, the aggregate expenditure curve is AE_0, and equilibrium expenditure is $1,000 billion. Taxes increase by $100 billion, and disposable income decreases by that amount. With a marginal propensity to consume of 0.75, aggregate expenditure decreases initially by $75 billion and the aggregate expenditure curve shifts downward by that amount to AE_1. Equilibrium expenditure and real GDP decrease by $300 billion to $700 billion. The autonomous tax multiplier is –3.

You've just seen that a tax increase leads to a decrease in real GDP. So to increase real GDP, the government might *decrease* autonomous taxes.

FIGURE 26.9

The Autonomous Tax Multiplier

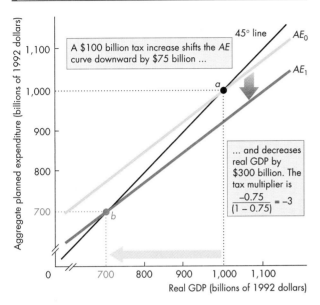

Initially, the aggregate expenditure curve is AE_0 and equilibrium expenditure is \$1,000 billion. The marginal propensity to consume is 0.75. Autonomous taxes increase by \$100 billion, so disposable income falls by \$100 billion. The decrease in aggregate expenditure is found by multiplying this change in disposable income by the marginal propensity to consume, which is \$100 billion × 0.75 = \$75 billion. The aggregate expenditure curve shifts *downward* by this amount to AE_1. Equilibrium expenditure decreases by \$300 billion, from \$1,000 billion to \$700 billion. The autonomous tax multiplier is −3.

Autonomous Transfer Payments   The autonomous tax multiplier also tells us the effects of a change in autonomous transfer payments. Transfer payments are like negative taxes, so an increase in transfer payments works like a decrease in taxes. Because the tax multiplier is negative, a decrease in taxes increases aggregate expenditure. An increase in transfer payments also increases aggregate expenditure. So the autonomous transfer payments multiplier is positive. It is

$$\text{Autonomous transfer} \atop \text{payments multiplier} = \frac{MPC}{1 - MPC}.$$

Automatic Stabilizers

So far, we've studied *discretionary* fiscal policy. Let's now study *automatic* stabilizers. An **automatic stabilizer** is a mechanism that dampens the fluctuations in real GDP without an explicit policy action by the government. The name is borrowed from engineering and conjures up images of a shock absorber that makes a car ride smoothly over a bumpy road, or a thermostat that maintains a comfortable temperature in a home, or a gyroscope that keeps a ship steady in a turbulent sea. Automatic economic stabilizers work by decreasing the multiplier effect of fluctuations in investment and exports. Two features of the economy create an automatic stabilizer. They are:

- Induced taxes and transfer payments
- Imports

Induced Taxes and Transfer Payments

You've seen that a change in *autonomous* taxes or a change in *autonomous* transfer payments has a multiplier effect on real GDP. But most changes in taxes and transfer payments are not autonomous. They are *induced* by the state of the economy. Taxes that vary with real GDP are called **induced taxes**.

On the revenue side of the budget, tax laws define tax *rates* to be paid, not tax *dollars* to be paid. Tax *dollars* paid depend on tax *rates* and incomes. But incomes vary with real GDP, so tax *revenues* depend on real GDP. When the economy expands, induced taxes increase because real GDP increases. When the economy is in a recession, induced taxes decrease because real GDP decreases.

On the outlay side of the budget, the government creates programs that entitle suitably qualified people and businesses to receive benefits. The spending on such programs is not fixed in dollars. Instead, it results in transfer payments that depend on the economic state of individual citizens and businesses. When the economy is in a recession, unemployment is high, the number of people experiencing economic hardship increases, and a larger number of firms and farms experience hard times. Transfer payments increase. When the economy expands, transfer payments decrease.

Induced taxes and transfer payments have two interesting consequences: they act as automatic stabilizers and they decrease the size of the multiplier.

Automatic Stabilization Effect   The automatic fluctuations in induced taxes and transfer payments act as an automatic stabilizer. The automatic stabilizing effect arises because of the influence of induced taxes and transfer payments on disposable income. When investment or exports fluctuate, real GDP fluctuates by a magnified (or multiplied) amount because a change in real GDP changes incomes, which induces a change in consumption expenditure. But the change in consumption expenditure depends not on the change in real GDP but on the change in disposable income. And induced taxes and transfer payments make the fluctuations in disposable income smaller than those in real GDP. By decreasing the swings in disposable income and consumption expenditure, induced taxes and transfer payments slow expansions and moderate recessions.

You can get a sense of the automatic stabilizing power of induced taxes by looking at Fig. 26.10, which shows the fluctuations of real GDP around potential GDP (part a) and the federal government's budget balance (part b). By comparing the two parts of this figure, you can see that during the recessions of the 1980s and 1990s (shaded) as induced taxes decreased and induced transfer payments increased the budget deficit became larger. During the expansion of the late 1990s as induced taxes increased and induced transfer payments decreased, the budget deficit decreased and turned to a surplus.

Smaller Multiplier Effect   Because induced taxes and transfer payments weaken the link between real GDP and disposable income and decrease the effect of a change in real GDP on consumption expenditure, they decrease the multiplier effects of changes in autonomous expenditure.

The extent to which induced taxes and transfer payments decrease the multiplier depends on the marginal tax rate. The **marginal tax rate** is the proportion of an additional dollar of real GDP that flows to the government in net taxes (taxes minus transfer payments). The higher the marginal tax rate, the larger is the proportion of an additional dollar of real GDP that is paid to the government and the smaller is the induced change in consumption expenditure. The smaller the change in consumption expenditure induced by a change in real GDP, the smaller is the multiplier effect of a change in autonomous expenditure, including the multiplier effects of a change in government expenditures or autonomous taxes.

FIGURE   26.10

The Business Cycle and the Budget Balance

(a) Growth and recessions

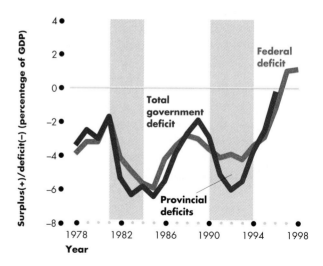

(b) Deficits and surpluses

As real GDP fluctuates around potential GDP (part a), the budget deficit fluctuates (part b). During a recession (shaded years), tax revenues decrease, transfer payments increase, and the budget deficit increases.

Source: Statistics Canada, *StatCan: CANSIM Disc*, March 1999, and the authors' calculations.

Imports

Imports act like induced taxes and transfer payments to reduce the multiplier and help to automatically stabilize real GDP fluctuations. You studied the effects of imports on the autonomous expenditure multiplier in Chapter 25, (see pp. 556–557). The proportion of an additional dollar of real GDP that is spent on imports is determined by the *marginal propensity to import.* Expenditure by Canadians on imports does not generate Canadian real GDP and does not lead to an increase in Canadian consumption expenditure. The larger the marginal propensity to import, the smaller is the increase in expenditure on Canadian-made goods and services that is induced by an increase in real GDP and so the smaller is the autonomous expenditure multiplier and the smaller are the fluctuations in real GDP.

The Cyclically Adjusted Deficit

Because the government budget balance fluctuates with the business cycle, we need a method of measuring the balance that tells us whether it is a temporary cyclical phenomenon or a persistent phenomenon. A temporary and cyclical surplus or deficit vanishes when full employment returns. A persistent surplus or deficit requires government action to remove it.

To determine whether the budget balance is temporary and cyclical or persistent, economists have developed the concepts of the structural budget balance and the cyclical budget balance. The **structural surplus or deficit** is the budget balance that would occur if the economy were at full employment and real GDP equalled potential GDP. The **cyclical surplus or deficit** is the actual surplus or deficit minus the structural surplus or deficit. That is, the cyclical surplus or deficit is the part of the budget balance that arises purely because real GDP does not equal potential GDP.

For example, suppose there is a budget deficit of $10 billion. And suppose that economists have determined that there is a structural deficit of $2 billion. Then there is a cyclical deficit of $8 billion.

Figure 26.11 illustrates the concepts of the cyclical surplus or deficit and the structural surplus or deficit. The blue curve shows government outlays. The outlays curve slopes downward because the bigger the level of real GDP, the smaller is the level of transfer payments so the smaller is the level of gov-

FIGURE 26.11

Cyclical and Structural Surpluses and Deficits

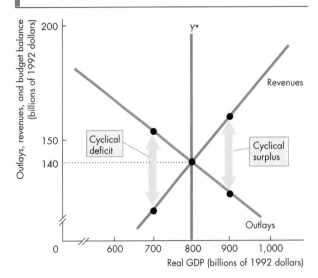

(a) Cyclical deficit and cyclical surplus

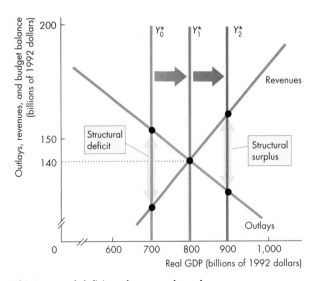

(b) Structural deficit and structural surplus

In part (a), potential GDP is $800 billion. When real GDP is less than potential GDP, the budget is in a *cyclical deficit.* When real GDP exceeds potential GDP, the budget is in a *cyclical surplus.* The government has a *balanced budget* when real GDP equals potential GDP. In part (b), when potential GDP is $700 billion, there is a *structural deficit.* But when potential GDP is $900 billion, there is a *structural surplus.*

ernment outlays. The green curve shows revenues. The revenues curve slopes upward because most components of revenues increase as incomes and real GDP increase.

In Fig. 26.11(a), potential GDP is $800 billion. If real GDP equals potential GDP, the government has a *balanced budget*. Outlays and revenues each equal $140 billion. If real GDP is less than potential GDP, outlays exceed revenues and there is a *cyclical deficit*. If real GDP is greater than potential GDP, outlays are less than revenues and there is a *cyclical surplus*.

In Fig. 26.11(b), potential GDP grows but the revenues curve and the outlays curve do not change. When potential GDP is $700 billion, there is a *structural deficit*. When potential GDP is $800 billion, there is a *structural balance* of zero (neither a deficit nor a surplus). And when potential GDP is $900 billion, there is a *structural surplus*.

The Canadian federal budget was in a structural deficit starting in the mid-1970s and through the mid-1990s. That is, even if the economy had been at full employment, the budget would have been in deficit. Worse, the structural deficit was so large that even at the peak of a business cycle, the budget was in deficit. At the end of the 1990s, a budget surplus has emerged. And it is probable that this surplus is structural because the economy is close to full employment.

REVIEW QUIZ

- Why, when the price level is fixed, does a change in government expenditures or autonomous taxes have a multiplier effect on real GDP?
- Which multiplier effect is larger: the multiplier effect of a change in government expenditures or of a change in autonomous taxes? Explain why.
- How do income taxes and imports influence the fiscal policy multipliers?
- Why do income taxes and transfer payments work as automatic stabilizers to dampen the business cycle?
- How do we tell whether a budget deficit needs government action to remove it?

Your next task is to see how, with the passage of more time and with some price level adjustments, these multiplier effects change.

Fiscal Policy Multipliers and the Price Level

WE'VE SEEN HOW REAL GDP RESPONDS TO changes in fiscal policy when the price level is fixed and all the adjustments that take place are in spending, income, and production. The period over which this response occurs is very short. Once production starts to change, regardless of whether it increases or decreases, prices also start to change. The price level and real GDP change together and the economy moves to a new short-run equilibrium.

To study the simultaneous changes in real GDP and the price level that result from fiscal policy, we use the aggregate supply–aggregate demand model of Chapter 24. In the long run, both the price level and the money wage rate respond to fiscal policy. As these further changes take place, the economy gradually moves toward a new long-run equilibrium. We also use the aggregate supply–aggregate demand model to study these adjustments.

We begin by looking at the effects of fiscal policy on aggregate demand and the aggregate demand curve.

Fiscal Policy and Aggregate Demand

You learned about the relationship between aggregate demand, aggregate expenditure, and equilibrium expenditure in Chapter 25. You are now going to use what you learned there to work out what happens to aggregate demand, the price level, real GDP, and jobs when fiscal policy changes. We'll start by looking at the effects of a change in fiscal policy on aggregate demand.

Figure 26.12 shows the effects of an increase in government expenditures on aggregate demand. Initially, the aggregate expenditure curve is AE_0 in part (a), and the aggregate demand curve is AD_0 in part (b). The price level is 110, real GDP is $800 billion, and the economy is at point a in both parts of the figure. Now suppose that government expenditures increase by $50 billion. At a constant price level of 110, the AE curve shifts upward to AE_1. This curve intersects the 45° line at an equilibrium expenditure of $1,000 billion at point b. This amount is the aggregate quantity of goods and services demanded at a price level of 110, as shown by point b in part (b). Point b lies on a new aggregate demand curve. The aggregate demand curve has shifted rightward to AD_1.

The government expenditures multiplier determines the distance by which the aggregate demand curve shifts rightward. The larger the multiplier, the larger is the shift in the aggregate demand curve resulting from a given change in government expenditures. In this example, a $50 billion increase in government expenditures produces a $200 billion increase in the aggregate quantity of goods and services demanded at each price level. The multiplier is 4. So the $50 billion increase in government expenditures shifts the aggregate demand curve rightward by $200 billion.

Figure 26.12 shows the effects of an increase in government expenditures. But a similar effect occurs for *any* expansionary fiscal policy. An **expansionary fiscal policy** is an increase in government expenditures or a decrease in taxes. But the distance of the *AD* curve shift is smaller for a tax cut than for a government expenditures increase of the same size.

Figure 26.12 can also be used to illustrate the effects of a **contractionary fiscal policy**—a decrease in government expenditures or an increase in taxes. Start at point *b* in each part of the figure and decrease government expenditures or increase taxes. The aggregate expenditure curve shifts downwards, aggregate demand decreases, and the aggregate demand curve shifts leftward from AD_1 to AD_0.

Equilibrium GDP and the Price Level in the Short Run We've seen how an increase in government expenditures increases aggregate demand. Let's now see how it changes real GDP and the price level. Figure 26.13(a) describes the economy. Aggregate demand is AD_0, and the short-run aggregate supply curve is *SAS*. (Check back to Chapter 24 if you need to refresh your understanding of the *SAS* curve.) Equilibrium is at point *a*, where the aggregate demand and short-run aggregate supply curves intersect. The price level is 110, and real GDP is $800 billion.

An increase in government expenditures of $50 billion shifts the aggregate demand curve rightward from AD_0 to AD_1. While the price level is fixed at 110, the economy moves towards point *b* and real GDP increases towards $1,000 billion. But during the adjustment process, the price level does not remain constant. It gradually rises and the economy moves along the short-run aggregate supply curve to the point of intersection of the short-run aggregate supply curve and the new aggregate demand curve—point *c*. The price level rises to 126 and real GDP increases to only $960 billion.

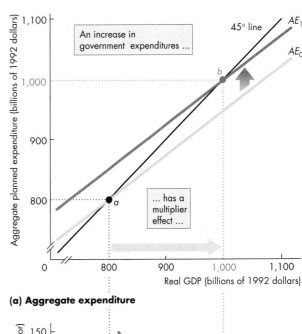

FIGURE 26.12

Government Expenditures and Aggregate Demand

(a) Aggregate expenditure

(b) Aggregate demand

The price level is 110, aggregate planned expenditure is AE_0 (part a), and aggregate demand is AD_0 (part b). An increase in government expenditures shifts the AE curve to AE_1 and equilibrium real GDP increases to $1,000 billion. The aggregate demand curve shifts rightward to AD_1.

FIGURE 26.13

Fiscal Policy, Real GDP, and the Price Level

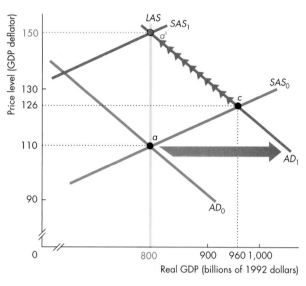

(a) Fiscal policy with unemployment

An increase in government expenditures shifts the *AD* curve from AD_0 to AD_1. With a fixed price level, the economy would have moved to point *b*. But the price level rises, and in the short run, the economy moves to point *c*. The price level increases to 126, and real GDP increases to $960 billion.

(b) Fiscal policy with full employment

At point *c*, real GDP exceeds potential GDP. In the long run, the wage rate rises and short-run aggregate supply decreases. The *SAS* curve shifts leftward to SAS_1 and the economy moves to point *a'*. The price level rises to 150, and real GDP returns to $800 billion.

When we take the price level effect into account, the increase in government expenditures still has a multiplier effect on real GDP, but the effect is smaller than it would be if the price level remained constant. Also, the steeper the slope of the short-run aggregate supply curve, the larger is the increase in the price level, the smaller is the increase in real GDP, and the smaller is the government expenditures multiplier. But the multiplier is not zero.

In the long run, real GDP equals potential GDP—the economy is at full-employment equilibrium. When real GDP equals potential GDP, an increase in aggregate demand has the same short-run effect as we've just worked out, but its long-run effect is different. The increase in aggregate demand raises the price level but it leaves real GDP unchanged at potential GDP.

To study this case, let's see what happens if the government embarks on an expansionary fiscal policy when real GDP equals potential GDP.

Fiscal Expansion at Potential GDP

Suppose that real GDP is equal to potential GDP, which means that unemployment is equal to the natural rate of unemployment. But suppose also that the unemployment rate and the natural rate are high and that most people, including the government, mistakenly think that unemployment is above the natural rate. In this situation, the government tries to lower the unemployment rate by using an expansionary fiscal policy.

Figure 26.13(b) shows the effect of an expansionary fiscal policy when real GDP equals potential GDP. In this example, potential GDP is $800 billion. Aggregate demand increases and the aggregate demand curve shifts rightward from AD_0 to AD_1. The short-run equilibrium, point *c*, is an above full-employment equilibrium. The labour force is more than fully employed, and there are shortages of labour. Wage rates begin to increase. Higher wage rates increase costs, and short-run aggregate supply decreases. The *SAS* curve begins to shift leftward from SAS_0 to SAS_1. The economy moves up the aggregate demand curve AD_1 towards point a'.

Eventually, when all adjustments to wage rates have been made, the price level is 150 and real GDP is again at potential GDP of $800 billion. The multiplier in the long run is zero. There has been a temporary decrease in the unemployment rate during the process you've just looked at, but not a permanent decrease. But the rise in the price level is permanent.

Limitations of Fiscal Policy

Because the short-run fiscal policy multipliers are not zero, expansionary fiscal policy can be used to increase real GDP and decrease the unemployment rate in a recession. Contractionary fiscal policy can also be used if the economy is overheating to decrease real GDP and help to keep inflation in check. But the use of fiscal policy is limited by two factors.

First, the legislative process is slow, which means that it is difficult to take fiscal policy actions in a timely way. The economy might be able to benefit from fiscal stimulation right now, but it will take Parliament many months and perhaps more than a year to act. By the time the action is taken, the economy might need an entirely different fiscal medicine.

Second, it is not always easy to tell whether real GDP is below (or above) potential GDP. A change in aggregate demand can move real GDP away from potential GDP or a change in aggregate supply can change real GDP and change potential GDP. This difficulty is a serious one because, as you've seen, fiscal stimulation at full employment leads to a rise in the price level and has no long-run effect on real GDP.

R E V I E W   Q U I Z

- How do changes in the price level influence the multiplier effects of fiscal policy on real GDP?
- What is the long-run effect of fiscal policy on real GDP?

So far, we have ignored any potential effects of fiscal policy on aggregate supply. Let's now study the supply-side effects of fiscal policy.

Fiscal Policy and Aggregate Supply

TAX CUTS INCREASE DISPOSABLE INCOME AND increase aggregate demand. But tax cuts also strengthen incentives and increase aggregate supply. The strength of the supply-side effects of tax cuts is not known with certainty. Some economists believe that the supply-side effects are large and exceed the demand-side effects. Other economists, while agreeing that supply-side effects are present, believe that they are relatively small.

The controversy over the size of the effects of taxes on aggregate supply is a political controversy. Generally, people on the conservative or right wing of the political debate believe that supply-side effects are powerful and people on the liberal or left wing of the political debate view supply-side effects as being small.

Regardless of which view is correct, we can study the supply-side effects of tax cuts by using the *AS–AD* model. Let's study the effects of taxes on potential GDP and then see how the supply-side effects and demand-side effects together influence real GDP and the price level.

Fiscal Policy and Potential GDP

Potential GDP depends on the full-employment quantity of labour, the quantity of capital, and the state of technology. Taxes can influence all three of these factors. The main tax to consider is the income tax. By taxing the incomes people earn when they work or save, the government weakens the incentives to work and save. The result is a smaller quantity of labour and capital and a smaller potential GDP. Also, the income tax weakens the incentive to develop new technologies that increase income. So the pace of technological change might be slowed, which slows the growth rate of potential GDP. Let's look at the effect of the income tax on both the quantity of labour and the quantity of capital.

Labour Market Taxes   The quantity of labour employed is determined in the labour market (see Chapter 4, pp. 74–75 and Chapter 31, pp. 699–704). Figure 26.14(a) shows a labour market. The demand for labour is *LD* and the supply is *LS*. The equilibrium real wage rate is $15 an hour and 230 billion hours of labour per year are employed.

FIGURE 26.14

Supply-Side Effects of the Income Tax

(a) The labour market

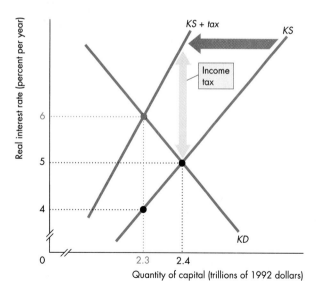

(b) The capital market

In part (a), an income tax decreases the supply of labour from *LS* to *LS + tax* and a payroll tax decreases the demand for labour from *LD* to *LD – tax*. The quantity of labour decreases. In part (b), the income tax decreases the supply of capital from *KS* to *KS + tax*. The quantity of capital decreases. With less labour and less capital, potential GDP decreases.

Now suppose that two taxes are introduced. An income tax weakens the incentive to work and decreases the supply of labour. The supply curve shifts leftward to *LS + tax*. A payroll tax makes it more costly to employ labour and decreases the demand for labour. The demand curve shifts leftward to *LD – tax*. With the new lower supply and demand, the quantity of labour employed decreases to 210 billion hours a year. The *before-tax* real wage rate remains at $15 an hour (but it might rise or fall depending on whether demand or supply decreases more). The *after-tax* real wage rate falls to $13 an hour, and the cost of hiring labour rises to $16 an hour.

Capital and the Income Tax The quantity of capital is determined by demand and supply in the capital market. Figure 26.14(b) shows the capital market. The demand for capital is *KD* and the supply is *KS*. The equilibrium real interest rate is 5 percent a year and the quantity of capital is $2.4 trillion.

A tax on the income from capital weakens the incentive to save and decreases the supply of capital. The supply curve shifts leftward to *KS + tax*. With the new decreased supply, the quantity of capital decreases to $2.3 trillion. The *before-tax* interest rate rises to 6 percent a year and the *after-tax* interest rate falls to 4 percent a year.

Potential GDP and *LAS* Because the income tax decreases the equilibrium quantities of labour and capital, it also decreases potential GDP. But potential GDP determines long-run aggregate supply. So the income tax decreases long-run aggregate supply and shifts the *LAS* curve leftward.

Supply Effects and Demand Effects

Let's now bring the supply-side effects and demand-side effects of fiscal policy together. Figure 26.15(a) shows the most likely effects of a tax cut. The tax cut increases aggregate demand and shifts the *AD* curve rightward, just as before. But a tax cut that increases the incentive to work and save also increases aggregate supply. It shifts the long-run and short-run aggregate supply curves rightward. Here we focus on the short run and show the effect on the *SAS* curve, which shifts rightward to *SAS₁*. In this example, the tax cut has a large effect on aggregate demand and a small effect on aggregate supply. The aggregate demand curve shifts rightward by a larger amount than the rightward shift in the short-run aggregate

FIGURE 26.15

Two Views of the Supply-Side Effects of Fiscal Policy

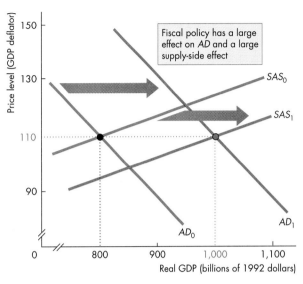

(a) The traditional view

A tax cut increases aggregate demand and shifts the *AD* curve rightward from AD_0 to AD_1 (both parts). Such a policy change also has a supply-side effect. If the supply-side effect is small, the *SAS* curve shifts rightward from SAS_0 to SAS_1 in part (a). The demand-side effect dominates the supply-side effect, real GDP increases, and the price level rises.

(b) The supply-side view

If the supply-side effect of a tax cut is large, the *SAS* curve shifts to SAS_1 in part (b). In this case, the supply-side effect is as large as the demand-side effect. Real GDP increases, and the price level remains constant. But if the supply-side effect were larger than the demand-side effect, the price level would actually fall.

supply curve. The outcome is a rise in the price level and an increase in real GDP. But notice that the price level rises by *less* and real GDP increases by *more* than would occur if there were no supply-side effects.

Figure 26.15(b) shows the effects that supply-siders believe to occur. A tax cut still has a large effect on aggregate demand, but it has a similarly large effect on aggregate supply. The aggregate demand curve and the short-run aggregate supply curve shift rightward by similar amounts. In this particular case, the price level remains constant and real GDP increases. A slightly larger increase in aggregate supply would have brought a fall in the price level, a possibility that some supply-siders believe could occur.

The general point that everyone agrees with is that a tax cut that strengthens incentives increases real GDP by more and is less inflationary than an equal-sized expansionary fiscal policy that does not change incentives or that weakens them.

REVIEW QUIZ

▨ How do income taxes and payroll taxes influence the supply of and demand for labour and how would a cut in these taxes influence real GDP?

▨ How would an income tax cut influence aggregate supply and aggregate demand? How would an income tax cut influence real GDP and the price level?

◆ You've seen how fiscal policy influences the way real GDP fluctuates around its trend and how it influences potential GDP. *Reading Between the Lines* on pp. 590–591 looks further at the 1999 budget and Finance Minister Paul Martin's fiscal policy. Your next task is to study the other main arm of macroeconomic policy: monetary policy.

Lower Taxes or Increase Spending?

TORONTO STAR, JULY 29, 1998

Reduce taxes to ease Asia fallout: Manning

SHANGHAI—The damage caused by Asia's financial crisis is proof that Canada must start looking seriously at cutting taxes and reducing government debt, Opposition Leader Preston Manning says.

"Canada must get its financial house in order if we want to withstand Asian competition," Manning told about 35 business people yesterday during a luncheon at an exclusive hotel in China's largest city. ...

The lessons Canada must learn from the crisis, according to Manning, come straight from the Reform party's platform.

Canada must cut taxes to levels more comparable to the United States and the federal government must focus on reducing the debt instead of increasing spending.

"The lesson from the Asian downturn is that you must get your fundamentals right when you have relative strength and growth," he said during a speech that quickly turned into a town-hall style discussion.

Manning mocked government leaders who have suggested that the declining Canadian dollar is not a huge problem and could make the country's exports more competitive.

"If we are relying on that to compensate for low productivity and high taxes, we are kidding ourselves," he said. ...

Essence of the Story

■ Reform Party Leader Preston Manning says that Canada must cut taxes and reduce government debt.

■ Manning believes that Canada must not increase government spending.

■ Manning says we must not rely on the low value of the Canadian dollar to keep exports and GDP growth up.

If the supply-side effects of a cut in the marginal tax rate are large, it is possible that a decrease in the tax *rate* could increase tax *revenue*. But this case would be unusual. The typical case is that a cut in the tax rate decreases tax revenue.

Preston Manning is a "supply-sider." He believes that by cutting tax rates, tax revenue will increase, government debt will decrease, and economic growth will increase.

Figure 1(a) shows the effects of a tax cut on aggregate planned expenditure. Aggregate planned expenditure increases and the *AE* curve shifts upward from AE_0 to AE_1.

Equilibrium expenditure increases from $818 billion to $845 billion (assumed numbers).

Figure 1(b) shows the effects of the same tax cut on aggregate demand. The tax cut increases aggregate demand and shifts the *AD* curve rightward from AD_0 to AD_1. With no change in the price level, real GDP increases to $845 billion.

But the price level rises as the economy moves along its *SAS* curve to point *a*, where the price level is 111.

In Fig. 1(a) with a higher price level, aggregate planned expenditure decreases and the *AE* curve shifts downward to AE_2.

Equilibrium expenditure is $840 billion.

The tax cut has increased real GDP and raised the price level.

But supply-siders believe that a tax cut increases aggregate supply. Figure 2 shows such an effect. When taxes are cut, the incentive to work improves and aggregate supply increases. The *SAS* curve shifts rightward from SAS_0 to SAS_1.

Now, equilibrium real GDP increases to $845 billion and the price level remains constant.

The outcome shown in Fig. 2 is just one of many possible outcomes. There, the increase in aggregate supply is the same as the increase in aggregate demand. Either could increase by more than the other.

The tax cut we've studied is a discretionary fiscal policy. The changes in real GDP and the price level create some automatic fiscal policy responses.

Because real GDP has increased, real incomes have increased. So transfer payments automatically decrease, taxes increase, and the deficit decreases.

If the supply-side effects of the tax multiplier are large enough, the tax cut will actually reduce the budget deficit. But this outcome is unlikely.

(a) Aggregate expenditure

(b) Aggregate demand

Figure 1 A tax cut

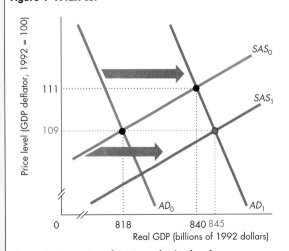

Figure 2 Tax cut, real GDP, and price level

MATHEMATICAL NOTE: THE ALGEBRA OF THE FISCAL POLICY MULTIPLIERS

THIS MATHEMATICAL NOTE DERIVES FORMULAS for the fiscal policy multipliers. We begin by defining the symbols we need:

- Aggregate planned expenditure, AE
- Real GDP, Y
- Consumption expenditure, C
- Investment, I
- Government expenditures, G
- Exports, X
- Imports, M
- Net taxes, NT
- Autonomous consumption expenditure, a
- Autonomous taxes, T_a
- Autonomous transfer payments, T_r
- Autonomous expenditure, A
- Marginal propensity to consume, b
- Marginal propensity to import, m
- Marginal tax rate, t

Equilibrium Expenditure

Aggregate planned expenditure is

$$AE = C + I + G + X - M.$$

The consumption function is

$$C = a + b(Y - NT).$$

Net taxes equals autonomous taxes minus autonomous transfer payments plus induced taxes, which is

$$NT = T_a - T_r + tY.$$

Use the last equation in the consumption function to give consumption expenditure as a function of GDP:

$$C = a - bT_a + bT_r + b(1 - t)Y.$$

The import function is

$$M = mY.$$

Use the consumption function and the import function to replace C and M in the aggregate planned expenditure equation to obtain

$$AE = a - bT_a + bT_r + b(1 - t)Y + I + G + X - mY.$$

Collect the terms on the right side of the equation that involve Y to obtain

$$AE = [a - bT_a + bT_r + I + G + X] + [b(1 - t) - m]Y.$$

Autonomous expenditure (A) is given by

$$A = a - bT_a + bT_r + I + G + X.$$

so

$$AE = A + [b(1 - t) - m]Y.$$

Equilibrium expenditure occurs when aggregate planned expenditure (AE) equals real GDP (Y). That is,

$$AE = Y.$$

To calculate equilibrium expenditure, we solve the equation

$$Y = A + [b(1 - t) - m]Y$$

to obtain

$$Y = \frac{1}{1 - [b(1 - t) - m]} A.$$

Government Expenditures Multiplier

The government expenditures multiplier equals the change in equilibrium expenditure (Y) that results from a change in government expenditures (G) divided by the change in government expenditures. Because autonomous expenditure is

$$A = a - bT_a + bT_r + I + G + X,$$

the change in autonomous expenditure equals the change in government expenditures. That is,

$$\Delta A = \Delta G.$$

The government expenditures multiplier is found by working out the change in Y that results from the change in A. You can see from the solution for Y that

$$\Delta Y = \frac{1}{1 - [b(1 - t) - m]} \Delta G.$$

The government expenditures multiplier equals

$$\frac{1}{1 - [b(1 - t) - m]}.$$

In an economy in which $t = 0$ and $m = 0$, the government expenditures multiplier is $1/(1 - b)$. With $b = 0.75$, the government expenditures multiplier equals 4, as part (a) of the figure shows. Make up some examples and use the above formula to show how b, m, and t influence the government expenditures multiplier.

Autonomous Tax Multiplier

The autonomous tax multiplier equals the change in equilibrium expenditure (Y) that results from a change in autonomous taxes (T_a) divided by the change in autonomous taxes. Because autonomous expenditure is

$$A = a - bT_a + bT_r + I + G + X,$$

the change in autonomous expenditure equals *minus* b multiplied by the change in autonomous taxes. That is,

$$\Delta A = -b\Delta T_a.$$

You can see from the solution for Y that

$$\Delta Y = \frac{-b}{1 - [b(1-t) - m]}\Delta T_a.$$

The autonomous tax multiplier equals

$$\frac{-b}{1 - [b(1-t) - m]}.$$

In an economy in which $t = 0$ and $m = 0$, the autonomous tax multiplier is $-b/(1-b)$. With $b = 0.75$, the autonomous tax multiplier equals -3, as part (b) of the figure shows. Make up some examples and use

the above formula to show how b, m, and t influence the autonomous tax multiplier.

Autonomous Transfer Payments Multiplier

The autonomous transfer payments multiplier equals the change in equilibrium expenditure (Y) that results from a change in autonomous transfer payments (T_r) divided by the change in autonomous transfer payments. Because autonomous expenditure is

$$A = a - bT_a + bT_r + I + G + X,$$

the change in autonomous transfer payments changes autonomous expenditure such that

$$\Delta A = b\Delta T_r.$$

Because transfer payments are like negative taxes, the autonomous transfer payments multiplier equals minus the autonomous tax multiplier. The autonomous transfer payments multiplier equals

$$\frac{b}{1 - [b(1-t) - m]}.$$

In an economy in which $t = 0$ and $m = 0$, the autonomous transfer payments multiplier is $b/(1-b)$. With $b = 0.75$, the autonomous transfer payments multiplier equals 3, as part (c) of the figure shows. Make up some examples and use the above formula to show how b, m, and t influence the autonomous transfer payments multiplier.

(a) Government expenditures multiplier

(b) Autonomous tax multiplier

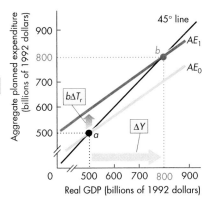

(c) Autonomous transfer payments multiplier

| S U M M A R Y |

Key Points

Government Budgets (pp. 572–577)

- The federal budget finances the activities of the government and is used to stabilize real GDP.
- Federal revenues come from personal income taxes, corporate income taxes, indirect taxes, and investment income. Federal expenditures include transfer payments, expenditures on goods and services, and debt interest.
- When the government's revenues exceed its outlays, the government has a budget surplus.

Fiscal Policy Multipliers (pp. 578–584)

- Fiscal policy actions are discretionary or automatic.
- The government expenditures multiplier equals $1/(1 - MPC)$. The autonomous tax multiplier equals $-MPC/(1 - MPC)$.
- The transfer payments multiplier is equal in magnitude to the autonomous tax multiplier but is positive.
- Induced taxes and transfer payments and imports make the fiscal policy multipliers smaller.
- Income taxes and transfer payments bring fluctuations in government revenues and outlays over the business cycle and act as automatic stabilizers.

Fiscal Policy Multipliers and the Price Level (pp. 584–587)

- An expansionary fiscal policy increases aggregate demand and shifts the aggregate demand curve rightward. It increases real GDP and raises the price level. (A contractionary fiscal policy has the opposite effects.)
- Price level changes dampen fiscal policy multiplier effects.
- At potential GDP, an expansionary fiscal policy raises the price level and in the long run leaves real GDP unchanged. The fiscal policy multipliers are zero in the long run.

Fiscal Policy and Aggregate Supply (pp. 587–589)

- Fiscal policy has supply-side effects because the increases in taxes weaken the incentives to work and save.
- A tax cut increases both aggregate demand and aggregate supply. It increases real GDP but has an ambiguous effect on the price level.

Key Figures

Key Terms

PROBLEMS

*1. In the economy of Zap, the marginal propensity to consume is 0.9. Investment is $50 billion, government expenditures on goods and services are $40 billion, and autonomous taxes are $40 billion. Zap has no exports, no imports, and no income taxes.
   a. The government cuts its expenditures on goods and services to $30 billion. What is the change in equilibrium expenditure?
   b. What is the value of the government expenditures multiplier?
   c. The government continues to buy $40 billion worth of goods and services and cuts autonomous taxes to $30 billion. What is the change in equilibrium expenditure?
   d. What is the value of the tax multiplier?
   e. The government simultaneously cuts both its expenditures on goods and services and taxes to $30 billion. What is the change in equilibrium expenditure? Why does equilibrium expenditure decrease?

2. In the economy of Zip, the marginal propensity to consume is 0.8. Investment is $60 billion, government expenditures on goods and services are $50 billion, and autonomous taxes are $60 billion. Zip has no exports, no imports, and no income taxes.
   a. The government increases its expenditures on goods and services to $60 billion. What is the change in equilibrium expenditure?
   b. What is the value of the government expenditures multiplier?
   c. The government continues to purchase $60 billion worth of goods and services and increases autonomous taxes to $70 billion. What is the change in equilibrium expenditure?
   d. What is the value of the tax multiplier?
   e. The government simultaneously increases both its expenditures on goods and services and taxes by $10 billion. What is the change in equilibrium expenditure? Why does equilibrium expenditure increase?

*3. Suppose that the price level in the economy of Zap as described in problem 1 is 100. The economy is also at full employment.
   a. If the government of Zap increases its expenditures on goods and services by $10 billion, what happens to the quantity of real GDP demanded?
   b. How does Zap's aggregate demand curve change? Draw a two-part diagram that is similar to Fig. 26.12 to illustrate the change in both the AE curve and the AD curve.
   c. In the short run, does equilibrium real GDP increase by more than, less than, or the same amount as the increase in the quantity of real GDP demanded?
   d. In the long run, does equilibrium real GDP increase by more than, less than, or the same amount as the increase in the quantity of real GDP demanded?
   e. In the short run, does the price level in Zap rise, fall, or remain unchanged?
   f. In the long run, does the price level in Zap rise, fall, or remain unchanged?

4. Suppose that the price level in the economy of Zip, as described in problem 2, is 100. The economy is also at full employment.
   a. If the government of Zip decreases its expenditures on goods and services by $5 billion, what happens to the quantity of real GDP demanded?
   b. How does Zip's aggregate demand curve change? Draw a two-part diagram that is similar to Fig. 26.12 to illustrate the change in both the AE curve and the AD curve.
   c. In the short run, does equilibrium real GDP decrease by more than, less than, or the same amount as the decrease in the quantity of real GDP demanded?
   d. In the short run, does the price level in Zip rise, fall, or remain unchanged?
   e. Why does real GDP in the short run decrease by a smaller amount than the decrease in aggregate demand?

*5. The figure shows revenues and outlays of the government of Dreamland. Potential GDP is $40 million.

a. What is the government's budget balance if real GDP is $40 million?

b. Does Dreamland have a structural surplus or deficit if its real GDP is $40 million? What is its size? Explain why.

c. What is the government's budget balance if real GDP is $30 million?

d. If Dreamland's real GDP is $30 million, does Dreamland have a structural surplus or deficit? What is its size? Explain why.

e. If Dreamland's real GDP is $50 million, does Dreamland have a structural surplus or deficit? What is its size? Explain why.

6. In problem 5, if Dreamland's real GDP is $40 million:

a. What is the government's budget balance?

b. If potential GDP is $30 million, does Dreamland have a cyclical surplus or deficit? What is its size? Explain why.

c. If potential GDP is $40 million, does Dreamland have a cyclical surplus or deficit? What is its size? Explain why.

d. If potential GDP is $50 million, does Dreamland have a cyclical surplus or deficit? What is its size? Explain why.

e. How can the Dreamland government eliminate a structural deficit/surplus and avoid a cyclical deficit/surplus if potential GDP is $40 million?

CRITICAL THINKING

1. Study *Reading Between the Lines* on pp. 590–591 and then answer the following questions.

a. What are the advantages to Canadians if the government reduces the government's debt?

b. Do you think it is possible to decrease taxes and still maintain a government budget surplus?

c. What fiscal policy would you suggest to eventually eliminate the government debt and at the same time promote an increase in real GDP?

d. Why do you think Mr. Manning is proposing that Canada cut taxes to levels more comparable to the United States?

2. Thinking about the supply-side effects of tax cuts:

a. What would be the main effects of lower income tax rates on the level of potential GDP?

b. How would lower income taxes influence the real wage rate and the real interest rate?

c. What are the main costs of lower income taxes?

3. Use the link on the Parkin-Bade Web site to visit the Department of Finance and obtain data on the current federal budget. Use the information that you find together with the fiscal policy multiplier analysis that you've learned about in this chapter to predict the effects of the Canadian budget on real GDP and the price level. Explain the reasons for your predictions.

4. Use the link on the Parkin-Bade Web site to visit Statistics Canada and obtain the most recent data you can find on the revenues, outlays, and budget surplus or deficit for Canada and for the province in which you live.

a. What are the main features of the two sets of budget data?

b. What are the main trends in the budget data?

c. Predict the effects of your province's budget on provincial GDP.

Money, Banking, and Interest Rates

Money, like fire and the wheel, has been around for a very long time. An incredible array of items has served as money. Wampum (beads made from shells) was used by the First Nations of North America, whale's teeth were used by Fijians, and tobacco was used by early American colonists. Cakes of salt served as money in Ethiopia and Tibet. Today, when we want to buy something, we use coins or bills, write a cheque, or present a credit card. Tomorrow, we'll use a "smart card" that keeps track of spending and that our pocket computer can read. Are all these things money?

Money Makes the World Go Around

◆ When we deposit some coins or notes into a bank, is that still money? And what happens when the bank lends the money in our deposit account to someone else? How can we get our money back if it's been lent out? Does lending by banks create money—out of thin air? ◆ In the 1970s, you had either a savings deposit that earned interest or a demand deposit that didn't. Today, there's an array of accounts that provide the convenience of a demand deposit and the income of a savings deposit. ◆ There is enough currency—coins and Bank of Canada notes—circulating in Canada today for every person to have a wallet stuffed with $1,000. In addition, there is enough money deposited in banks and other financial institutions for every Canadian to have a deposit of $21,000. What determines the amount of currency and bank deposits in existence? And why do we hold such a large amount of money? Between 1988 and 1990, Canadian interest rates increased by more than 50 percent—up from 8 percent to 12 percent. Since 1990, interest rates have fallen. What determines interest rates?

◇ In this chapter you'll study that useful invention: money. You will learn about its functions, its different forms, and the way it is defined and measured in Canada today. You will also learn how banks and other financial institutions create money. Finally, you will learn how interest rates are determined.

After studying this chapter, you will be able to:

■ Define money and describe its functions

■ Explain the economic functions of banks and other depository institutions

■ Describe the financial innovations of the 1980s and 1990s

■ Explain how banks create money

■ Explain what determines the demand for money

■ Explain how interest rates are determined

■ Explain how interest rates influence expenditure plans

What Is Money?

WHAT DO WAMPUM, TOBACCO, AND NICKELS AND dimes have in common? Why are they all examples of money? To answer these questions, we need a definition of money. **Money** is any commodity or token that is generally acceptable as the means of payment. A **means of payment** is a method of settling a debt. When a payment has been made, there is no remaining obligation between the parties to a transaction. So what wampum, tobacco, and nickels and dimes have in common is that they have served (or still do serve) as the means of payment. But money has three other functions:

■ Medium of exchange
■ Unit of account
■ Store of value

Medium of Exchange

A *medium of exchange* is an object that is generally accepted in exchange for goods and services. Money acts as such a medium. Without money, it would be necessary to exchange goods and services directly for other goods and services—an exchange called **barter**. For example, if you want to buy a hamburger, you offer the paperback novel you've just finished reading in exchange for it. Barter requires a *double coincidence of wants*, a situation that occurs when Erika wants to buy what Kazia wants to sell and Kazia wants to buy what Erika wants to sell. To get your hamburger, you must find someone who's selling hamburgers and who wants your paperback novel. Money guarantees that there is a double coincidence of wants because people with something to sell will always accept money in exchange for it. Money acts as a lubricant that smoothes the mechanism of exchange.

Unit of Account

A *unit of account* is an agreed measure for stating the prices of goods and services. To get the most out of your budget, you have to figure out whether seeing one more movie is worth its opportunity cost. But that cost is not dollars and cents. It is the number of ice-cream cones, pops, and phone calls that you must give up. It's easy to do such calculations when all these goods have prices in terms of dollars and cents (see

Table 27.1). If a movie costs $6 and a six-pack of pop costs $3, you know right away that seeing one more movie costs you 2 six-packs of pop. If jelly beans are 50¢ a pack, one more movie costs 12 packs of jelly beans. You need only one calculation to figure out the opportunity cost of any pair of goods and services.

But imagine how troublesome it would be if your local movie theatre posted its price as 2 six-packs of pop, and if the convenience store posted the price of a six-pack of pop as 2 ice-cream cones, and if the ice-cream shop posted the price of a cone as 3 packs of jelly beans, and if the candy store priced a pack of jelly beans as 2 local phone calls! Now how much running around and calculating would you have to do to figure out how much that movie is going to cost you in terms of the pop, ice cream, jelly beans, or phone calls that you must give up to see it? You get the answer for pop right away from the sign posted

TABLE 27.1

The Unit of Account Function of Money Simplifies Price Comparisons

Good	Price in money units	Price in units of another good
Movie	$6.00 each	2 six-packs of pop
Pop	$3.00 per six-pack	2 ice-cream cones
Ice cream	$1.50 per cone	3 packs of jelly beans
Jelly beans	$0.50 per pack	2 local phone calls
Phone call	$0.25 per call	1 local phone call

Money as a unit of account: The price of a movie is $6 and the price of a local phone call is 25¢, so the opportunity cost of a movie is 24 local phone calls ($6.00 ÷ 25¢ = 24).

No unit of account: You go to a movie theatre and learn that the price of a movie is 2 six-packs of pop. You go to a candy store and learn that a pack of jelly beans costs 2 local phone calls. But how many phone calls does seeing a movie cost you? To answer that question, you go to the convenience store and find that a six-pack of pop costs 2 ice-cream cones. Now you head for the ice-cream shop, where an ice-cream cone costs 3 packs of jelly beans. Now you get out your pocket calculator: 1 movie costs 2 six-packs of pop, or 4 ice-cream cones, or 12 packs of jelly beans, or 24 phone calls!

on the movie theatre. But for all the other goods you'd have to visit many different stores to establish the price of each commodity in terms of another and then calculate prices in units that are relevant for your own decision. Cover up the column labelled "price in money units" in Table 27.1 and see how hard it is to figure out the number of local phone calls it costs to see one movie. It's enough to make a person swear off movies! How much simpler it is if all the prices are expressed in dollars and cents.

Store of Value

Any commodity or token that can be held and exchanged later for goods and services is called a *store of value*. Money acts as a store of value. If it did not, it would not be acceptable in exchange for goods and services. The more stable the value of a commodity or token, the better it can act as a store of value and the more useful it is as money. No store of value is completely safe. The value of a physical object, such as a house, a car, or a work of art, fluctuates over time. The values of commodities and tokens used as money also fluctuate, and when there is inflation, they persistently fall in value.

Money in Canada Today

In Canada today, money consists of:

■ Currency
■ Deposits at banks and other financial institutions

Currency   The coins and Bank of Canada notes that we use today are known as **currency**. Currency is money because the government declares it to be so. Look at a Bank of Canada note and notice the words

"CE BILLET A COURS LÉGAL—THIS NOTE IS LEGAL TENDER."

Currency is the most convenient type of money for settling small debts and buying low-priced items.

Deposits   Deposits at banks and trust companies are also money. Deposits are money because they can be converted into currency and because they are used to settle debts. When you write a cheque or use a debit card, you are telling your bank to transfer money from your account to the account of the person from whom you are buying. Bank deposits are the most convenient type of money for settling large debts and buying big-ticket items.

Deposits Are Money but Cheques Are Not   In defining money, we include, along with currency, deposits at banks and other financial institutions. But we do not count the cheques that people write as money. Why are deposits money and cheques not?

To see why deposits are money but cheques are not, think about what happens when Colleen buys some inline skates for $200 from Rocky's Rollers. When Colleen goes to Rocky's shop, she has $500 in her deposit account at the Laser Bank. Rocky has $1,000 in his deposit account—at the same bank, as it happens. The total deposits of these two people are $1,500. Colleen writes a cheque for $200. Rocky takes the cheque to the bank right away and deposits it. Rocky's bank balance rises from $1,000 to $1,200 and Colleen's balance falls from $500 to $300. The total deposits of Colleen and Rocky are still the same as before: $1,500. Rocky now has $200 more and Colleen has $200 less than before.

This transaction has transferred money from Colleen to Rocky. The cheque itself was never money. There wasn't an extra $200 worth of money while the cheque was in circulation. The cheque instructs the bank to transfer money from Colleen to Rocky.

In the example, Colleen and Rocky use the same bank. The same story, but with additional steps, describes what happens if Colleen and Rocky use different banks. Rocky's bank credits the cheque to Rocky's account and then takes the cheque to a cheque-clearing centre. The cheque is then sent to Colleen's bank, which pays Rocky's bank $200 and then debits Colleen's account $200. This process can take a few days, but the principles are the same as when two people use the same bank.

Debit Cards Are Not Money   So cheques are not money. But what about debit cards? Isn't presenting a debit card to pay for your inline skates the same thing as using money? Why aren't debit cards counted as part of the quantity of money?

A debit card works just like a cheque—an electronic cheque—and it is not money. When you use a debit card, money leaves your bank account and is deposited into the account of the person from whom you are buying at the instant of the transaction.

Credit Cards Are Not Money   Sometimes you need ID and you pull out your driver's licence. Your credit card is another type of ID card. A credit card is a special ID card that enables you to take a loan at the instant you buy something. When you sign a credit card sales slip, you are saying: "I agree to pay for these goods when the credit card company bills me." Once you get your statement from the credit card company, you must make the minimum payment due (or clear your balance). To make that payment you need money—currency or a bank deposit. So although you use a credit card when you buy something, the credit card is not the *means of payment*, and it is not money.

Official Measures of Money   There is no unique measure of money. The two main measures used in Canada today are M1 and M2+. Figure 27.1 shows

---

FIGURE 27.1

Two Measures of Money

	$ billions in Dec 1998
M2+	**642**
Comprises all in M1, plus...	
Deposits at other financial institutions	85
Deposits at credit unions and caisses populaires	95
Deposits at trust and mortgage loan companies	49
Nonpersonal notice deposits at chartered banks	37
Personal savings deposits at chartered banks	288
M1	**88**
Currency	31
Demand deposits	57

M1   ■ Currency held outside banks
　　　■ Demand deposits at chartered banks that are owned by individuals and businesses

M2+   ■ M1
　　　■ Personal savings deposits at chartered banks
　　　■ Nonpersonal notice deposits at chartered banks
　　　■ Deposits at trust and mortgage companies
　　　■ Deposits at credit unions and caisses populaires
　　　■ Deposits at other financial institutions

Source: Bank of Canada Review, Summer, 1999.

---

the items that make up these two measures. **M1** consists of currency held outside the banks plus demand deposits at chartered banks that are owned by individuals and businesses. M1 does *not* include currency held by banks, and it does not include currency and bank deposits owned by the government of Canada. **M2+** consists of M1 plus personal savings deposits and nonpersonal notice deposits at chartered banks plus all types of deposits at trust and mortgage companies, credit unions, caisses populaires, and other financial institutions.

Are M1 and M2+ Really Money?   Money is the means of payment. So if an item is money it must serve as a means of payment. Currency passes the test. But what about deposits? Deposit accounts on which cheques can be written are money because they can be transferred from one person to another by writing a cheque. Transferring a deposit is equivalent to handing over currency. Because M1 consists of currency plus demand deposits and each of these is a means of payment, M1 *is money*.

But what about M2+? Some of the savings deposits in M2+ are means of payment. You can use the ATM at the grocery store checkout or gas station and transfer funds directly from your savings account to pay for your purchase. But other savings deposits are not means of payment. These deposits are known as *liquid assets*. **Liquidity** is the property of being instantly convertible into a means of payment with little loss in value. Because most of the deposits in M2+ are quickly and easily converted into currency or demand deposits, they are operationally similar to M1, but they are not means of payment.

REVIEW QUIZ

▥ What is the distinguishing feature of money and what are the functions that money performs?
▥ What has served as money in Canada in the past and what serves as money in Canada today?
▥ What is the distinction between M1 and M2+ and what are the largest components of money circulating in Canada today?
▥ Why are cheques, debit cards, and credit cards not counted as money?

We've seen that the main component of money in Canada is deposits at banks and other financial institutions. Let's take a closer look at these institutions.

Depository Institutions

A FIRM THAT TAKES DEPOSITS FROM HOUSEHOLDS and firms and makes loans to other households and firms is called a **depository institution**. The deposits of three types of depository institution make up the nation's money:

- Chartered banks
- Credit unions and caisses populaires
- Trust and mortgage loan companies

Chartered Banks

A **chartered bank** is a private firm, chartered under the Bank Act of 1992 to receive deposits and make loans. In 1998, there were 11 Canadian-owned banks and 43 foreign-owned banks chartered by Parliament. In 1998, total deposits at chartered banks were almost $500 billion. A chartered bank's business is summarized in its balance sheet.

A bank's *balance sheet* lists its assets, liabilities, and net worth. *Assets* are what the bank *owns*, *liabilities* are what the bank *owes*, and *net worth*, which is equal to assets minus liabilities, is the value of the bank to its stockholders—its owners. A bank's balance sheet is described by the equation

Liabilities + Net worth = Assets.

Among a bank's liabilities are the deposits that are part of the nation's money. Your deposit at the bank is a liability to your bank (and an asset to you) because the bank must repay your deposit (and sometimes the interest on it too) whenever you decide to take your money out of the bank.

Profit and Prudence: A Balancing Act   The aim of a bank is to maximize the net worth of its stockholders. To achieve this objective, the interest rate at which a bank lends exceeds the interest rate at which it borrows. But a bank must perform a delicate balancing act. Lending is risky, and the more a bank ties up its deposits in high-risk, high-interest rate loans, the bigger is its chance of not being able to repay its depositors. And if depositors perceive a high risk of not being repaid, they withdraw their funds and create a crisis for the bank. So a bank must be prudent in the way it uses its deposits, balancing security for the depositors against profit for its stockholders.

Reserves and Loans   To achieve security for its depositors, a bank divides its funds into two parts: reserves and loans. **Reserves** are cash in a bank's vault plus its deposits at the Bank of Canada. (We'll study the Bank of Canada in Chapter 28.) The cash in a bank's vaults is a reserve to meet its depositor's demand for currency. It keeps the ATM replenished every time you and your friends have raided it for cash for a midnight pizza. The account of a bank at the Bank of Canada is similar to your own bank account. Chartered banks use these accounts to receive and make payments. A chartered bank deposits cash into or draws cash out of its account at the Bank of Canada and writes cheques on that account to settle debts with other banks.

If a bank kept all its deposits as reserves, it wouldn't make any profit. In fact, it keeps only a small fraction of its funds in reserves and lends the rest. A bank has three types of assets. They are:

1. *Liquid assets* are Canadian government Treasury bills and commercial bills. These assets are the banks' first line of defence if they need cash. They can be sold and instantly converted into cash with virtually no risk of loss. Because liquid assets are virtually risk free, they have a low interest rate.

2. *Investment securities* are longer-term Canadian government bonds and other bonds. These assets can be sold quickly and converted into cash but at prices that fluctuate. Because their prices fluctuate, these assets are riskier than liquid assets but they have a higher interest rate.

3. *Loans* are commitments of fixed amounts of money for agreed-upon periods of time. Most banks' loans are made to corporations to finance the purchase of capital equipment and inventories and to households—personal loans—to finance consumer durable goods, such as cars or boats. The outstanding balances on credit card accounts are also bank loans. Loans are the riskiest assets of a bank because they cannot be converted into cash until they are due to be repaid. And some borrowers default and never repay. Because they are the riskiest of a bank's assets, they also carry the highest interest rate.

Chartered bank deposits are one component of the nation's money. But other depository institutions also take deposits that form part—an increasing part—of the nation's money. The largest of these other depository institutions are the credit unions and caisses populaires.

Credit Unions and Caisses Populaires

A **credit union** is a cooperative organization that operates under the Co-operative Credit Association Act of 1992 and that receives deposits from and makes loans to its members. A caisse populaire is a similar type of institution that operates in Quebec. In 1998, the deposits in these institutions were $95 billion.

Trust and Mortgage Companies

A **trust and mortgage company** is a privately owned depository institution that operates under the Trust and Loan Companies Act of 1992. It receives deposits and makes loans and in addition acts as a trustee for pension funds and for estates. In 1998, trust and mortgage loan companies' deposits included in M2+ were $49 billion.

Financial Legislation

Canada has historically made a sharp legal distinction between banks and other depository institutions. But the economic functions of all depository institutions have grown increasingly similar. This fact is recognized in laws governing these institutions that became effective in 1992. Today, the deposits in other depository institutions approach the same magnitude as those of the chartered banks. For example, the deposits in depository institutions such as trust and mortgage loan companies, credit unions, and caisses populaires were 31 percent of the M2+ definition of money in 1970 but 40 percent in 1998.

The 1999 Reform Proposals   In 1999, the government announced a new policy framework for Canada's depository institutions, foreign banks, and insurance companies. The new policy framework, outlined in *Reforming Canada's Financial Services Sector: A Framework for the Future*, is based on four principles: flexibility, competition, consumer protection, and reduced regulation.

Chartered banks will be permitted to form joint ventures and strategic alliances, broaden their investments, and face more streamlined regulation. In addition, the process for reviewing bank mergers will become more open. But chartered banks will face tougher competition from trust companies, credit unions, and foreign banks, all of which will face less stringent restrictions and regulation.

The Economic Functions of Depository Institutions

All depository institutions make a profit from the spread between the interest rate they pay on deposits and the interest rate at which they lend. Why can depository institutions get deposits at a low interest rate and lend at a higher one? What services do they perform that makes their depositors willing to put up with a low interest rate and their borrowers willing to pay a higher one?

Depository institutions provide four main services that people are willing to pay for:

■ Creating liquidity
■ Minimizing the cost of borrowing
■ Minimizing the cost of monitoring borrowers
■ Pooling risk

Creating Liquidity   Depository institutions create liquidity. *Liquid* assets are those that are easily and with certainty convertible into money. Some of the liabilities of depository institutions are themselves money; others are highly liquid assets.

Depository institutions create liquidity by borrowing short and lending long. Borrowing short means taking deposits but standing ready to repay them on short notice (and on even no notice in the case of demand deposits). Lending long means making loan commitments for a prearranged, and often quite long, period of time. For example, when a person makes a deposit with a trust company, that deposit can be withdrawn at any time. But the trust company makes a lending commitment for perhaps more than 20 years to a homebuyer.

Minimizing the Cost of Borrowing   Finding someone from whom to borrow can be a costly business. Imagine how troublesome it would be if there were no depository institutions. A firm that was looking for $1 million to buy a new production plant would probably have to hunt around for several dozen people from whom to borrow in order to acquire enough funds for its capital project. Depository institutions lower those costs. The firm that needs $1 million can go to a single depository institution to obtain those funds. The depository institution has to borrow from a large number of people, but it's not doing that just for this one firm and the $1 million that it wants to borrow. The depository institution can establish an organization that is capable of raising funds from a large number of depositors and can spread the cost of this activity over a large number of borrowers.

Minimizing the Cost of Monitoring Borrowers

Lending money is a risky business. There is always a danger that the borrower may not repay. Firms are the biggest borrowers. And they borrow to invest in projects that they hope will return a profit. But sometimes those hopes are not fulfilled. Monitoring the activities of a borrower and ensuring that the best possible decisions are being taken to make a profit and to avoid a loss are costly and specialized activities. Imagine how costly it would be if each household that lent money to a firm had to incur the costs of monitoring that firm directly. By depositing funds with a depository institution, households avoid those costs. The depository institution performs the monitoring activity by using specialized resources that have a much lower cost than what each household would incur if it had to undertake the activity individually.

Pooling Risk   As we noted above, lending money is risky. There is always a chance of not being repaid—of default. Lending to a large number of different individuals can reduce the risk of default. In such a situation, if one person defaults on a loan, it is a nuisance but not a disaster. In contrast, if only one person borrows and that person defaults on the loan, the entire loan is a write-off. Depository institutions enable people to pool risk in an efficient way. Thousands of people lend money to any one depository institution, and, in turn, the depository institution re-lends the money to hundreds, perhaps thousands, of individual firms. If any one firm defaults on its loan, that default is spread across all the depositors and no individual depositor is left exposed to a high degree of risk.

R E V I E W   Q U I Z

- What are the main types of depository institutions in Canada?
- Why don't banks keep all the money that people place on deposit in their vaults?
- What are the main economic functions of depository institutions?
- How do depository institutions create liquidity?

How Banks Create Money

BANKS CREATE MONEY.[1] BUT THIS DOESN'T MEAN that they have smoke-filled back rooms in which counterfeiters are busily working. Remember, most money is deposits, not currency. What banks create is deposits, and they do so by making loans. But the amount of deposits they can create is limited by their reserves.

Reserves: Actual and Desired

We've seen that banks don't have $100 in bills for every $100 that people have deposited with them. In fact, a typical bank today has reserves of $1.90 for every $100 of deposits. No need for panic. These reserve levels are adequate for ordinary business needs.

The fraction of a bank's total deposits that are held in reserves is called the **reserve ratio**. The reserve ratio changes when a bank's customers make a deposit or withdrawal. Making a deposit increases the reserve ratio, and making a withdrawal decreases the reserve ratio.

The **desired reserve ratio** is the ratio of reserves to deposits that banks wish to hold. A bank's *desired reserves* are equal to its deposits multiplied by the desired reserve ratio. Actual reserves minus desired reserves are **excess reserves**. Whenever banks have excess reserves, they are able to create money.

To see how banks create money, we'll look at two model banking systems. In the first, there is only one bank; in the second, there are many banks.

Creating Deposits by Making Loans in a One-Bank Economy

In the model banking system that we'll study first, there is only one bank, and its desired reserve ratio is 25 percent. That is, for each dollar deposited, the bank keeps 25¢ in reserves and lends the rest. The balance sheet of One-and-Only Bank is shown in Fig. 27.2(a). On January 1, its deposits are $400 million and its reserves are 25 percent of this amount— $100 million. Its loans are equal to deposits minus reserves and are $300 million.

---

[1]In this section, we'll use the term *bank* to refer to any type of depository institution whose deposits are part of the money supplied—chartered banks, credit unions, caisses populaires, and trust and mortgage companies.

The story begins when Darth Vader retires and begins his quiet life in Winnipeg. He has been holding all his money in currency and has $1 million in Canadian money. On January 2, Darth puts his $1 million on deposit at the One-and-Only Bank. On the day that Darth makes his deposit, the One-and-Only Bank's balance sheet changes. The new situation is shown in Fig. 27.2(b). The bank now has $101 million in reserves and $401 million in deposits. It still has loans of $300 million.

FIGURE 27.2

Creating Money at the One-and-Only Bank

(a) Balance sheet on January 1

Assets (millions of dollars)		Liabilities (millions of dollars)	
Reserves	$100	Deposits	$400
Loans	$300		
Total	$400	Total	$400

(b) Balance sheet on January 2

Assets (millions of dollars)		Liabilities (millions of dollars)	
Reserves	$101	Deposits	$401
Loans	$300		
Total	$401	Total	$401

(c) Balance sheet on January 3

Assets (millions of dollars)		Liabilities (millions of dollars)	
Reserves	$101	Deposits	$404
Loans	$303		
Total	$404	Total	$404

In part (a) the One-and-Only Bank has deposits of $400 million, loans of $300 million, and reserves of $100 million. The bank's desired reserve ratio is 25 percent. When the bank receives a deposit of $1 million (part b), it has excess reserves. It lends $3 million and creates a further $3 million of deposits. Deposits increase by $3 million, and loans increase by $3 million (in part c). The bank has no excess reserves.

The bank now has *excess reserves*. With reserves of $101 million and a desired reserve ratio of 25 percent, the bank would like to have deposits of $404 million. Because the One-and-Only Bank is the only bank, the manager knows that the reserves will remain at $101 million. That is, she knows that when she makes a loan and creates a deposit, the amount lent remains on deposit at the One-and-Only Bank. She knows, for example, that all the suppliers of Sky's-the-Limit Construction are also depositors of One-and-Only. So she knows that if she makes the loan that Sky's-the-Limit has just requested, the deposit she creates will never leave One-and-Only. When Sky's-the-Limit uses part of its new loan to pay $100,000 to I-Dig-It Excavating Company for some excavations, the One-and-Only Bank simply moves the funds from Sky's-the-Limit's account to I-Dig-It's account.

So on January 3, the manager of One-and-Only calls Sky's-the-Limit's accountant and offers to lend the maximum that she can. How much does she lend? She lends $3 million. By lending $3 million, One-and-Only's balance sheet changes to the one shown in Fig. 27.2(c). Loans increase by $3 million to $303 million. The loan shows up in Sky's-the-Limit's deposit initially, and total deposits increase to $404 million—$400 million plus Darth Vader's deposit of $1 million plus the newly created deposit of $3 million. The bank now has no excess reserves and has reached the limit of its ability to create money.

The Deposit Multiplier

The **deposit multiplier** is the amount by which an increase in bank reserves is multiplied to calculate the increase in bank deposits. That is,

$$\text{Deposit multiplier} = \frac{\text{Change in deposits}}{\text{Change in reserves}}.$$

In the example we've just worked through, the deposit multiplier is 4. The $1 million increase in reserves created a $4 million increase in deposits. The deposit multiplier is linked to the desired reserve ratio by the following equation:

$$\text{Deposit multiplier} = \frac{1}{\text{Desired reserve ratio}}.$$

In the example, the desired reserve ratio is 25 percent, or 0.25. That is,

$$\text{Deposit multiplier} = \frac{1}{0.25} = 4.$$

Creating Deposits by Making Loans with Many Banks

If you told the loans officer at your own bank that she creates money, she wouldn't believe you. Bankers see themselves as lending the money they receive from others, not creating money. But in fact, even though each bank lends only what it receives, the banking *system* creates money. To see how, let's look at another example.

Figure 27.3 is going to keep track of what is happening in the process of money creation by a banking system in which each bank has a desired reserve ratio of 25 percent. The process begins when Art decides to decrease his currency holding and put $100,000 on deposit. Now Art's bank has $100,000 of new deposits and $100,000 of additional reserves. With a desired reserve ratio of 25 percent, the bank keeps $25,000 in reserves and lends $75,000 to Amy. Amy writes a cheque for $75,000 to buy a copy-shop franchise from Barb. At this point, Art's bank has a new deposit of $100,000, new loans of $75,000, and new reserves of $25,000. You can see this situation in Fig. 27.3 as the first row of the "running tally."

For Art's bank, that is the end of the story. But it's not the end of the story for the entire banking system. Barb deposits her cheque for $75,000 in another bank and its deposits and reserves increase by $75,000. This bank keeps 25 percent of its increase in deposits ($18,750) in reserves and lends $56,250 to Bob. And Bob writes a cheque to Carl to pay off a business loan. The current state of play is seen in Fig. 27.3. Now total bank reserves have increased by $43,750 ($25,000 plus $18,750), total loans have increased by $131,250 ($75,000 plus $56,250), and total deposits have increased by $175,000 ($100,000 plus $75,000).

When Carl takes his cheque to his bank, its deposits and reserves increase by $56,250, $14,063 of which it keeps in reserve and $42,187 of which it lends. This process continues until there are no excess reserves in the banking system. But the process takes a lot of further steps. One additional step is shown in Fig. 27.3. The figure also shows the final tallies—reserves increase by $100,000, loans increase by $300,000, and deposits increase by $400,000.

The sequence in Fig. 27.3 is the first four stages of the process. To figure out the entire process, look closely at the numbers in the figure. At each stage, the loan is 75 percent (0.75) of the previous loan and the deposit is 0.75 of the previous deposit. Call that proportion L ($L = 0.75$). The complete sequence is

$$1 + L + L^2 + L^3 + \dots .$$

Remember, L is a fraction, so at each stage in this sequence the amount of new loans gets smaller. The total number of loans made at the end of the process is the above sum, which is[2]

$$\frac{1}{(1 - L)}.$$

If we use the numbers from the example, the total increase in deposits is

$$\$100,000 + 75,000 + 56,250 + 42,187 + \dots$$
$$= \$100,000 \,(1 + 0.75 + 0.5625 + 0.42187 + \dots)$$
$$= \$100,000 \,(1 + 0.75 + 0.75^2 + 0.75^3 + \dots)$$

$$= \$100,000 \times \frac{1}{(1 - 0.75)}$$

$$= \$100,000 \times \frac{1}{(0.25)}$$

$$= \$100,000 \times 4$$

$$= \$400,000.$$

By using the same method, you can check that the totals for reserves and loans are the ones shown in Fig. 27.3.

---

[2]Both here and in the expenditure multiplier process in Chapter 25, the sequence of values is called a convergent geometric series. To find the sum of a series such as this, begin by calling the sum S. Then write the sum as

$$S = 1 + L + L^2 + L^3 + \dots$$

Multiply by L to get

$$LS = L + L^2 + L^3 + \dots$$

and then subtract the second equation from the first to get

$$S(1 - L) = 1$$

or

$$S = \frac{1}{(1 - L)}.$$

FIGURE 27.3

The Multiple Creation of Bank Deposits

The sequence

Deposit $100,000

Reserve $25,000	Loan $75,000

Deposit $75,000

Reserve $18,750	Loan $56,250

Deposit $56,250

Reserve $14,063	Loan $42,187

Deposit $42,187

Reserve $10,547	Loan $31,640

and so on ...

The running tally

Reserves	Loans	Deposits
$25,000	$75,000	$100,000
$43,750	$131,250	$175,000
$57,813	$173,437	$231,250
$68,360	$205,077	$273,437
•	•	•
•	•	•
▼	▼	▼
$100,000	$300,000	$400,000

When a bank receives a deposit, it keeps 25 percent of it in reserves and lends the other 75 percent. The amount lent becomes a new deposit at another bank. The next bank in the sequence keeps 25 percent and lends 75 percent, and the process continues until the banking system has created enough deposits to eliminate its excess reserves. The running tally tells us the amounts of deposits and loans created at each stage. At the end of the process, an additional $100,000 of reserves creates an additional $400,000 of deposits.

So even though each bank lends only part of the money it receives, the banking system creates money by making loans. The amount created is exactly the same in a multibank system as in a one-bank system.

The Deposit Multiplier in Canada The deposit multiplier in Canada works like the deposit multiplier we've just worked out for a model economy. But the deposit multiplier in Canada differs from the one we've just calculated for two reasons. First, the desired reserve ratio of Canadian banks is smaller than the 25 percent we used here. Second, not all the loans made by banks return to them in the form of reserves. Some of the loans remain outside the banks and are held as currency. The smaller desired reserve ratio makes the Canadian multiplier larger than the multiplier in the above example. But the other factor makes the Canadian multiplier smaller.

REVIEW QUIZ

■ Explain how banks create deposits and how their reserves and the desired reserve ratio determine the amount they can create.

■ When a bank makes a loan, what happens to deposits and desired reserves at other banks?

■ Explain what limits the ability of a bank to create money.

■ What is the magnitude of the deposit multiplier and how is it related to the desired reserve ratio?

We've now seen what money is and how banks create it. Money has a powerful influence on the economy and this influence begins with interest rates. To understand how money influences interest rates, we must study the demand for money.

The Demand for Money

THE AMOUNT OF MONEY WE RECEIVE EACH WEEK in payment for our labour is income—a flow. The amount of money that we hold in our wallet or in a deposit account at the bank is an inventory—a stock. There is no limit to how much income we would like to receive each week. But there is a limit to how big an inventory of money each of us would like to hold on to and not spend.

The Influences on Money Holding

The quantity of money that people choose to hold depends on four main factors:

■ The price level
■ The interest rate
■ Real GDP
■ Financial innovation

Let's look at each of them.

The Price Level The quantity of money measured in dollars is called the quantity of *nominal money*. The quantity of nominal money demanded is proportional to the price level, other things remaining the same. That is, if the price level (GDP deflator) increases by 10 percent, people will want to hold 10 percent more nominal money than before, other things remaining the same. What matters is not the number of dollars that you hold but their buying power. If you hold $20 to buy your weekly movies and pop, you will increase your money holding to $22 if the prices of movies and pop—and your wage rate—increase by 10 percent.

The quantity of money measured in constant dollars (for example, in 1992 dollars) is called *real money*. Real money is equal to nominal money divided by the price level. It is the quantity of money measured in terms of what it will buy. In the above example, when the price level rises by 10 percent and you increase the amount of money that you hold by 10 percent, you keep your *real* money constant. Your $22 at the new price level buys the same quantity of goods and is the same quantity of *real money* as your $20 at the original price level. The quantity of real money held does not depend on the price level.

The Interest Rate A fundamental principle of economics is that as the opportunity cost of something increases, people try to find substitutes for it. Money is no exception. The higher the opportunity cost of holding money, other things remaining the same, the lower is the quantity of real money demanded. But what is the opportunity cost of holding money? It is the interest rate that you must forgo on other assets that you could hold instead of money minus the interest rate that you can earn by holding money.

The interest rate that you earn on currency and demand deposits is zero. So the opportunity cost of holding these items is the interest rate on other assets such as a savings bond or Treasury bill. By holding money instead, you forgo the interest that you otherwise would have received. This forgone interest is the opportunity cost of holding money.

Money loses value because of inflation. So why isn't the inflation rate part of the cost of holding money? It is: Other things remaining the same, the higher the expected inflation rate, the higher are all interest rates (see Chapter 30, pp. 682–683.) Therefore the higher the inflation rate, the higher is the opportunity cost of holding money.

Real GDP The quantity of money that households and firms plan to hold depends on the amount they are spending, and the quantity of money demanded in the economy as a whole depends on aggregate expenditure—real GDP.

Again, suppose that you hold an average of $20 to finance your weekly purchases of movies and pop. Now imagine that the prices of these goods and of all other goods remain constant but that your income increases. As a consequence you now spend more, and you also keep a larger amount of money on hand to finance your higher volume of expenditure.

Financial Innovation Technological change and the arrival of new financial products change the quantity of money held. The major financial innovations are the widespread use of:

1. Daily interest deposits
2. Automatic transfers between demand deposits and savings deposits
3. Automatic teller machines
4. Credit cards and debit cards

These innovations have occurred because the development of computing power has lowered the cost of calculations and record keeping.

The Demand for Money Curve

We summarize the effects of the influences on money holding by using the demand for money curve. The **demand for money** is the relationship between the quantity of real money demanded and the interest rate, when all other influences on the amount of money that people wish to hold remain the same.

Figure 27.4 shows a demand for money curve, MD. When the interest rate rises, everything else remaining the same, the opportunity cost of holding money rises and the quantity of real money demanded decreases—there is a movement upward along the demand for money curve. Similarly, when the interest rate falls, the opportunity cost of holding money falls, and the quantity of real money demanded increases—there is a movement downward along the demand for money curve.

Other influences on the amount of money that people plan to hold change the demand for money.

Shifts in the Demand for Money Curve

A change in real GDP or financial innovation changes the demand for money and shifts the demand for money curve. Figure 27.5 illustrates the change in the demand for money. A decrease in real GDP decreases the demand for money and shifts the demand curve leftward from MD_0 to MD_1. An increase in real GDP has the opposite effect. It increases the demand for money and shifts the demand curve rightward from MD_0 to MD_2.

The influence of financial innovation on the demand for money curve is more complicated. It might increase the demand for some types of deposits, decrease the demand for others, and decrease the demand for currency. We'll look at the effects of financial innovation by studying the demand for money in Canada.

FIGURE 27.4
The Demand for Money

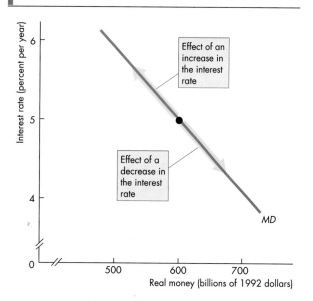

The demand for money curve, MD, shows the relationship between the quantity of real money that people plan to hold and the interest rate, other things remaining the same. The interest rate is the opportunity cost of holding money. A change in the interest rate brings a movement along the demand curve.

FIGURE 27.5
Changes in the Demand for Money

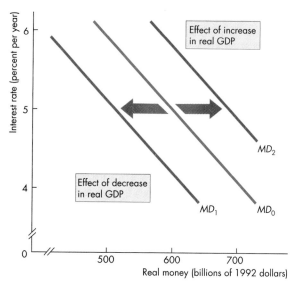

A decrease in real GDP decreases the demand for money and shifts the demand curve leftward from MD_0 to MD_1. An increase in real GDP increases the demand for money and shifts the demand curve rightward from MD_0 to MD_2. Financial innovation decreases the demand for some forms of money and increases the demand for other forms of money.

The Demand for Money in Canada

Figure 27.6 shows the relationship between the interest rate and the quantity of real money demanded in Canada between 1970 and 1998. Each dot shows the interest rate and the amount of real money held in a given year. In part (a), the measure of money is M1 and in part (b), it is M2+.

In 1970, the demand for M1 (in part a) was MD_{70}. During the 1970s, real GDP increased by $200 billion, and this increase in real GDP increased the demand for M1 and shifted the demand for M1 curve rightward to MD_{80}. During the 1980s, real GDP increased by $170 billion, but the demand for

M1 did not change. The reason is that during the 1980s the increased use of credit cards decreased the demand for M1. The increase in real GDP increased the demand for M1 and financial innovation decreased the demand for M1, so during the 1980s, the demand for M1 did not change. During the 1990s, real GDP increased by $130 billion and the demand for M1 increased again. The demand for M1 curve shifted rightward to MD_{98}.

In 1970, the demand for M2+ (in part b) was MD_{70}. The $200 billion increase in real GDP that occurred during the 1970s increased the demand for M2+ and the demand curve shifted rightward to MD_{80}. The $170 billion increase in real GDP that

---

FIGURE 27.6

The Demand for Money in Canada

(a) Demand for M1

(b) Demand for M2+

The dots show the quantity of real money and the interest rate in each year between 1970 and 1998. In 1970, the demand for M1 was MD_{70} in part (a). During the 1970s, real GDP grew and the demand for M1 increased. The demand curve shifted rightward to MD_{80}. The demand for M1 did not increase during the 1980s because financial innovation (mainly the increased use of credit cards) offset the effects of real GDP growth. The demand for M1 increased again during the 1990s.

In 1970, the demand for M2+ curve was MD_{70} in part (b). The growth of real GDP increased the demand for M2+ and by 1980 the demand curve had shifted rightward to MD_{80}. Real GDP growth and the development of interest-bearing accounts with cheque facilities further increased the demand for M2+ during the 1990s and the demand for M2+ curve shifted rightward to MD_{98}.

Source: Statistics Canada, *StatCan: CANSIM Disc*, March 1999, and the authors' calculations and assumptions.

occurred during the 1980s increased the demand for M2+ and the demand curve shifted rightward. The further $130 billion increase in real GDP that occurred during the 1990s increased the demand for M2+ yet again. By 1998, the demand curve for M2+ had shifted rightward to MD_{98}.

You can see by comparing the two parts of Fig. 27.6 that the financial innovation that decreased the demand for M1 during the 1980s did not slow the growth of M2+. Because M1 is a component of M2+, the increased use of credit cards had the same effect on M2+ as it did on M1. But the development of new types of savings deposits with cheque facilities and the payment of more competitive interest rates on savings accounts increased the demand for M2+.

The opportunity cost of holding money is the interest forgone by not holding some other type of asset. But what is forgone depends partly on the interest that is paid on money itself. The interest rate on currency and demand deposits is zero. So for these components of money, the opportunity cost of holding money is the interest rate on non-money assets. But savings deposits and other types of deposits that are included in M2+ earn interest. So the opportunity cost of holding these forms of money is the interest rate on non-money assets minus the interest rate on these deposits.

R E V I E W   Q U I Z

▦ What are the main influences on the quantity of real money that people and businesses plan to hold?

▦ What does the demand for money curve show?

▦ How does an increase in the interest rate change the quantity of money demanded and how would you use the demand for money curve to show the effects?

▦ How does an increase in real GDP change the demand for money and how would you use the demand for money curve to show the effects?

▦ How have financial innovations changed the demand for M1 and M2+?

We now know what determines the demand for money. And we've seen that a key factor is the interest rate—the opportunity cost of holding money. But what determines the interest rate? Let's find out.

Interest Rate Determination

AN INTEREST RATE IS THE PERCENTAGE YIELD ON a financial security such as a *bond* or a *stock*. The **interest rate** is the amount received by a lender and paid by a borrower expressed as a percentage of the amount of the loan.

A bond is a promise to make a sequence of future payments. There are many different possible sequences but the simplest one is the case of a bond called perpetuity. A *perpetuity* is a bond that promises to pay a specified fixed amount of money each year forever. The issuer of such a bond will never buy the bond back (redeem it); the bond will remain outstanding forever and will earn a fixed dollar payment each year. Because the payment each year is a fixed dollar amount, the interest rate on a bond varies as the price of the bond varies. In the case of a perpetuity, the formula that links the interest rate to the price of the bond is a particularly simple one. That formula is:

$$\text{Interest rate} = \frac{\text{Dollar payment per year}}{\text{Price of bond}} \times 100.$$

This formula states that the higher the price of a bond, other things remaining the same, the lower is the interest rate. An example will make this relationship clear. Suppose the government of Canada sells a bond that promises to pay $10 a year. If the price of the bond is $100, the interest rate is 10 percent a year—$10 is 10 percent of $100. If the price of the bond is $50, the interest rate is 20 percent a year—$10 is 20 percent of $50. If the price of the bond is $200, the interest rate is 5 percent a year—$10 is 5 percent of $200.

You've just seen the link between the price of a bond and the interest rate. Because of this link, fluctuations in the interest rate bring fluctuations in the price of a bond. People try to anticipate these fluctuations and avoid holding bonds when they expect the price of a bond to fall. But they spread their risks. To do so, they divide their wealth between bonds (and other interest-bearing financial assets) and money, and the amount they hold as money depends on the interest rate. We can study the forces that determine the interest rate in either the market for bonds or the market for money. Because the Bank of Canada can influence the *supply* of money (which we study in Chapter 28), we focus on the market for money.

Money Market Equilibrium

The supply of and the demand for money determine the interest rate. The actions of the Bank of Canada and the banking system determine the quantity of money supplied. On any given day, the quantity of money supplied is fixed. The quantity of *real* money supplied is equal to the nominal quantity supplied divided by the price level. At a given moment in time, there is a particular price level, and so the quantity of real money supplied is also a fixed amount. In Fig. 27.7, the quantity of real money supplied is $600 billion and the vertical line labelled *MS* is the supply of money curve.

On any given day, all the influences on the demand for money except for the interest rate are constant. But the lower the interest rate, the greater

---

FIGURE 27.7
Money Market Equilibrium

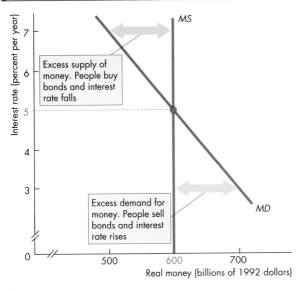

Money market equilibrium occurs when the interest rate has adjusted to make the quantity of money demanded equal to the quantity supplied. Here, equilibrium occurs at an interest rate of 5 percent a year. At interest rates above 5 percent a year, the quantity of money demanded is less than the quantity supplied, so people buy bonds, and the interest rate falls. At interest rates below 5 percent a year, the quantity of real money demanded exceeds the quantity supplied, so people sell bonds and the interest rate rises. Only at 5 percent a year is the quantity of real money in existence willingly held.

---

is the quantity of money demanded. Figure 27.7 shows a demand for money curve, *MD*.

Equilibrium   When the quantity of money supplied equals the quantity of money demanded, the money market is in equilibrium. Figure 27.7 illustrates equilibrium in the money market. Equilibrium is achieved by changes in the interest rate. If the interest rate is too high, people demand a smaller quantity of money than the quantity supplied. They are holding too much money. In this situation, they try to get rid of money by buying bonds. As they do so, the price of a bond rises and the interest rate falls to the equilibrium rate. Conversely, if the interest rate is too low, people demand a larger quantity of money than the quantity supplied. They are holding too little money. In this situation, they try to get more money by selling bonds. As they do so, the price of a bond falls and the interest rate rises to the equilibrium rate. Only when the interest rate is at the level at which people are holding the quantity of money supplied do they willingly hold the money and take no actions that change the interest rate.

Influencing the Interest Rate

Imagine that the economy is slowing down and the Bank of Canada wants to increase aggregate demand. To do so, it wants to lower interest rates and encourage more borrowing and more expenditure on goods and services. What does the Bank of Canada do? How does it fiddle with the knobs to achieve lower interest rates?

The answer is that the Bank of Canada changes the quantity of money in the economy. Chapter 28 (pp. 627–631) explains *how* the Bank of Canada changes the quantity of money. Here, we study the *effects* of a change in the quantity of money.

Suppose that initially, the quantity of real money is $600 billion. In Fig. 27.8, the supply of money curve is MS_0. With the demand for money given by the curve *MD*, the equilibrium interest rate is 5 percent a year.

Now suppose that the quantity of real money increases to $700 billion. The supply of money curve shifts rightward from MS_0 to MS_1. At an interest rate of 5 percent a year, people are now holding more money than they would like to hold. They attempt to decrease their money holding by buying bonds. As they do so, the price of a bond rises and the interest rate falls. When the interest rate has fallen to

3 percent a year, people are willing to hold the greater $700 billion quantity of real money.

Conversely, suppose that the economy is overheating and the Bank of Canada fears inflation. The Bank decides to take action to decrease aggregate demand. In this case, the Bank decreases the quantity of real money. Suppose that the Bank decreases the quantity of real money from the initial quantity of $600 billion to $500 billion. Now, in Fig. 27.8, the supply of money curve shifts leftward from MS_0 to MS_2. At an interest rate of 5 percent a year, people are now holding less money than they would like to hold. They attempt to increase their money holding by selling bonds. As they do so, the price of a bond falls and the interest rate rises. When the interest rate has risen to 7 percent, people are willing to hold the smaller $500 billion quantity of real money.

FIGURE 27.8
Interest Rate Changes

Initially, the quantity of real money is $600 billion and the interest rate is 5 percent a year. When the Bank of Canada increases the quantity of real money to $700 billion, the supply of money curve shifts rightward to MS_1 and the interest rate falls to 3 percent a year. When the Bank of Canada decreases the quantity of real money to $500 billion, the supply of money curve shifts leftward to MS_2 and the interest rate rises to 7 percent a year.

Influencing the Exchange Rate

The **exchange rate** is the price at which the Canadian dollar exchanges for another currency. For example, in July 1999, a Canadian dollar cost 67 U.S. cents. So the exchange rate at that time was 67 U.S. cents per Canadian dollar. The exchange rate is the price of the Canadian dollar determined by demand and supply in the global foreign exchange market. This market is described and studied in detail in Chapter 36 on pp. 831–839. Here, we'll look only at the influence of the interest rates on the exchange rate.

The interest rate that can be earned by moving funds into Canada is a key influence on the demand for Canadian dollars. People are constantly seeking the highest interest rate available, and when the interest rate that can be earned in one country rises with all other interest rates remaining the same, people move funds into that country. But to move funds into Canada, people must buy Canadian dollars in the foreign exchange market. And if more funds are moving into Canada, the demand for Canadian dollars increases.

An increase in the demand for Canadian dollars in the foreign exchange market raises the exchange rate. That is, the price of a Canadian dollar rises. So monetary policy actions that change the interest rate also change the exchange rate and in the same direction. Other things remaining the same, a rise in interest rates brings a rise in the exchange rate and a fall in interest rates brings a fall in the exchange rate.

REVIEW QUIZ

■ What is a bond and what is the relationship between the price of a bond and the interest rate?

■ How is the interest rate determined?

■ What do people do if they are holding *less* money than they plan to hold and what happens to the interest rate?

■ What do people do if they are holding *more* money than they plan to hold and what happens to the interest rate?

■ What happens to the interest rate and the exchange rate if the quantity of money increases or decreases?

Your final task in this chapter is to study the influence of the interest rate on expenditure plans.

The Interest Rate and Expenditure Plans

YOU'VE SEEN THAT THE INTEREST RATE AFFECTS the quantity of money that people plan to hold. The interest rate also influences people's spending decisions. The reason is the same in both cases. The interest rate is an opportunity cost. But the interest rate that is relevant for the money holding decision is not quite the same as the interest rate that is relevant for a spending decision. Let's find out why.

Nominal Interest and Real Interest

We distinguish between two interest rates: the nominal interest rate and the real interest rate. The **nominal interest rate** is the percentage return on an asset such as a bond expressed in terms of money. It is the interest rate that is quoted in everyday transactions and news reports. The **real interest rate** is the percentage return on an asset expressed in terms of what money will buy. It is the nominal interest rate adjusted for inflation and is approximately equal to the nominal interest rate minus the inflation rate.

Suppose that the nominal interest rate is 10 percent a year and the inflation rate is 4 percent a year. The real interest rate is 6 percent a year—10 percent minus 4 percent.[3]

To see why the real interest rate is 6 percent, think about the following example. Jackie lends Joe $1,000 for one year. At the end of the year, Joe repays Jackie the $1,000 plus interest. At 10 percent a year, the interest is $100, so Jackie receives $1,100 from Joe.

Because of inflation, the money that Joe uses to repay Jackie is worth less than the money that Jackie originally loaned to Joe. At an inflation rate of 4 percent a year, Jackie needs an extra $40 a year to compensate her for the fall in the value of money. So when Joe repays the loan, Jackie needs $1,040 to buy the same items that she could have bought for $1,000 when she made the loan. Because Joe pays Jackie $1,100, the interest that she *really* earns is $60, which is 6 percent of the $1,000 that she lent to Joe.

---

[3]The exact calculation allows for the change in the purchasing power of the interest as well as the amount of the loan. The *exact* formula is: *real interest rate = nominal interest rate − inflation rate* divided by (1 + *inflation rate*/100). If the nominal interest rate is 10 percent and the inflation rate is 4 percent, the real interest rate is $(10 − 4) \div (1 + 0.4) = 5.77$ percent.

Interest Rate and Opportunity Cost

Now that you understand the distinction between the nominal interest rate and the real interest rate, let's think about the effects of interest rates on decisions.

The interest rate influences decisions because it is an opportunity cost. *The nominal interest rate is the opportunity cost of holding money.* And it is the nominal interest rate that is determined by the demand for real money and the supply of real money in the money market. To see why the nominal interest rate is the opportunity cost of holding money, think about the *real* interest rate on money compared with the real interest rate on other financial assets. Money loses value at the inflation rate. So the real interest rate on money equals *minus* the inflation rate. The real interest rate on other financial assets equals the nominal interest rate minus the inflation rate. So the difference between the real interest rate on money and the real interest rate on other financial assets is the nominal interest rate. By holding money rather than some other financial asset, we incur a real opportunity cost equal to the nominal interest rate.

The real interest rate is the opportunity cost of spending. Spending more today means spending less in the future. But spending one additional dollar today means cutting future spending by more than a dollar. And the real amount by which future spending must be cut is determined by the *real* interest rate.

A change in the real interest rate changes the opportunity cost of two components of aggregate expenditure:

■ Consumption expenditure
■ Investment

Consumption Expenditure

Other things remaining the same, the lower the real interest rate, the greater is the amount of consumption expenditure and the smaller is the amount of saving.

You can see why the real interest rate influences consumption expenditure and saving by thinking about the effect of the interest rate on a student loan. If the real interest rate on a student loan fell to 1 percent a year, students would be happy to take larger loans and spend more. But if the real interest rate on a student loan jumped to 20 percent a year, students would cut their expenditure, buying cheaper food and finding lower-rent accommodation for example, to pay off their loans as quickly as possible.

The effect of the real interest rate on consumption expenditure is probably not large. And it is certainly not as powerful as the effect of disposable income that we studied in Chapter 25 (pp. 544–547). You can think of the real interest rate as influencing *autonomous consumption expenditure* (p. 551). The lower the real interest rate, the greater is autonomous consumption expenditure.

Investment

Other things remaining the same, the lower the real interest rate, the greater is the amount of investment.

The funds used to finance investment might be borrowed, or they might be the financial resources of the firm's owners (the firm's retained earnings). But regardless of the source of the funds, the opportunity cost of the funds is the real interest rate. The real interest paid on borrowed funds is an obvious cost. The real interest rate is also the cost of using retained earnings because these funds could be loaned to another firm. The real interest rate forgone is the opportunity cost of using retained earnings to finance an investment project.

To decide whether to invest in new capital, firms compare the real interest rate with the expected profit rate from the investment. For example, suppose that Chrysler expects to earn 20 percent a year from a new car assembly plant. It is profitable for Chrysler to invest in this new plant as long as the real interest rate is less than 20 percent a year. That is, at a real interest rate below 20 percent a year, Chrysler will build this assembly line, and at a real interest rate in excess of 20 percent a year, it will not. Some projects are profitable at a high real interest rate, but other projects are profitable only at a low real interest rate. So the higher the real interest rate, the smaller is the number of projects that are worth undertaking and the smaller is the amount of investment.

The interest rate has another effect on expenditure plans. It changes net exports. Let's find out why.

Net Exports and the Interest Rate

Net exports change when the interest rate changes because, other things remaining the same, a change in the interest rate changes the exchange rate.

Net Exports and the Exchange Rate Let's first see why the exchange rate influences exports and imports. When a Canadian buys a Dell PC that is shipped from Texas, the price of the PC equals the U.S. dollar price converted into Canadian dollars. If the PC price is U.S.\$2,000, and if the exchange rate is 66.67 U.S. cents per Canadian dollar, the PC price in Canada is \$3,000. If the Canadian dollar rises to 75 U.S. cents per Canadian dollar, the PC price in Canada falls to \$2,666.67. When the price of a U.S. PC falls, Canadians import more PCs.

Similarly, when a U.S. company buys a Nortel telephone system that is shipped from Ontario the price of the system equals the Canadian dollar price converted into U.S. dollars. If the price of the telephone system is \$6,000, and if the exchange rate is 66.67 U.S. cents per Canadian dollar, the price in the United States is U.S.\$4,000. If the Canadian dollar rises to 75 U.S. cents per Canadian dollar, the price of the telephone system in the United States *rises* to \$4,500. When the price of a Canadian telephone system rises, Americans buy fewer of them and Canada's exports decrease.

So when the Canadian dollar rises, imports increase, exports decrease, and net exports decrease. Similarly, when the Canadian dollar falls, imports decrease, exports increase, and net exports increase.

The Interest Rate and the Exchange Rate
When the interest rate in Canada rises, and other things remain the same, the Canadian dollar exchange rate rises. The reason is that more people move funds into Canada to take advantage of the higher interest rate. But when money flows into Canada, the demand for Canadian dollars increases, so the Canadian dollar exchange rate (the price) rises. And when the interest rate in Canada falls, and other things remain the same, the Canadian dollar exchange rate falls.

Because the interest rate influences the exchange rate, it also influences net exports. A rise in the interest rate decreases net exports and a fall in the interest rate increases net exports, other things remaining the same.

The Interest-Sensitive Expenditure Curve

Figure 27.9 illustrates the effects of the real interest rate on expenditure plans and summarizes those effects in the interest-sensitive expenditure curve. The **interest-sensitive expenditure curve** (the *IE* curve) shows the relationship between aggregate expenditure plans and the real interest rate when all other influences on expenditure plans remain the same.

FIGURE 27.9

The Interest Rate and Expenditure Plans

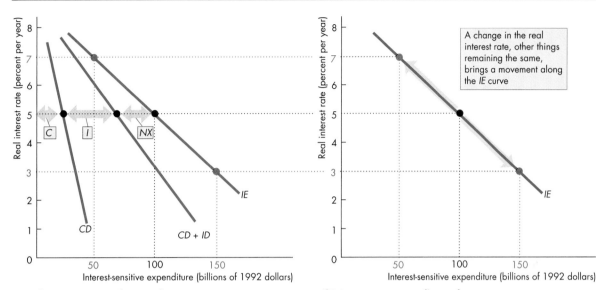

(a) The components of expenditure

(b) Aggregate expenditure plans

In part (a), when the real interest rate is 5 percent a year, autonomous consumption expenditure is $20 billion on the *CD* curve, investment is $50 billion so *CD + ID* is $70 billion, and net exports are $30 billion, so interest-sensitive expenditure is $100 billion on the *IE* curve.

In part (b), other things remaining the same, when the real interest rate falls to 3 percent a year, interest-sensitive expenditure increases to $150 billion a year and when the interest rate rises to 7 percent a year, interest-sensitive expenditure decreases to $50 billion a year.

Figure 27.9(a) shows the components of interest-sensitive expenditure: autonomous consumption expenditure, investment, and net exports. When the real interest rate is 5 percent a year, autonomous consumption expenditure is $20 billion on the curve *CD*. Investment is $50 billion, so when we add investment and autonomous consumption expenditure together, we get $70 billion on the curve *CD + ID*. Net exports are $30 billion, so when we add this amount to $70 billion, we obtain the sum of all the interest-sensitive components of aggregate expenditure, which is $100 billion on the *IE* curve.

In Fig. 27.9(b), as the real interest rate changes, interest-sensitive expenditure changes along the *IE* curve. Other things remaining the same, when the real interest rate falls to 3 percent a year, interest-sensitive expenditure increases to $150 billion. And when the real interest rate rises to 7 percent a year, interest-sensitive expenditure decreases to $50 billion.

REVIEW QUIZ

- What is the real interest rate and how does it differ from the nominal interest rate?
- Which interest rate influences the quantity of money that people plan to hold and why?
- Which interest rate influences expenditure decisions and why?
- How does the interest rate influence net exports?

◆ Take a look at some recent trends in the way we use money in Canada in *Reading Between the Lines* on pp. 616–617. You've now seen how the quantity of money influences the interest rate and how the interest rate influences expenditure plans. In the next chapter, we're going to discover how the Bank of Canada can change the quantity of money and interest rates. Then, in Chapter 29, we see how fiscal policy and monetary policy interact to influence the course of the economy.

The Demand for Money in Canada

TORONTO STAR, DECEMBER 12, 1998

Oh, how we love our debit cards

Canadians love to swipe the stripe.

After just four years, the Interac direct-payment system, which deducts purchases straight from bank accounts, has grown to more than a billion transactions a year. Canadians swiped the stripe an average of 32 times a second every hour of every day last year. ...

A 1997 survey conducted by Strategic Counsel Inc. found... debit transactions are rising at the expense of other payment methods, particularly cheques, ...

In 1995, 58 per cent said they preferred to pay with cash, 16 per cent credit cards, 12 per cent cheques and only 9 per cent debit transactions. This year cash is still the Number 1 preference, but at only 45 per cent. Direct payment is second at 31 per cent, followed by credit cards at 18 per cent and cheques at 5 per cent.

"Debit is replacing cheques," said Jim Okamura, a retail consultant at J.C. Williams Groups Ltd. in Toronto. ...

Data from the Canadian Bankers Association also suggest cheques may be going the way of the DoDo bird. The number of cheques written for less than $50,000 actually dropped last year by 7.36 per cent. ...

The 1 billion direct-payment transactions last year surpassed credit-card transactions, which totalled 949 million. But unlike cheques, credit-card transactions continue to grow by 10 to 12 per cent a year. ...

Debit cards are used mostly at supermarkets, department stores and various other retail outlets. But the marketplace is changing as different sectors of the Canadian economy adopt the Interac direct-payment system. People can now use their debit cards to pay the renewal fees on drivers' licences, pay for dental appointments, even to cover taxi fares. ...

Will Canada ever be cashless? Will the world become totally dependent on debit cards?

"I doubt it," said Okamura. "Cash will always have its place."

Essence of the Story

■ Debit card transactions are increasing and the use of cheques is decreasing.

■ Credit card transactions are also increasing.

■ The number of sectors in the economy accepting debit cards for payment is growing.

■ According to a 1997 survey, most people still prefer to pay with cash, but the percentage of those who do use cash is falling.

Economic Analysis

■ Figure 1 shows the amount of currency in circulation in Canada as a percentage of GDP since 1970. This percentage decreased during the 1970s and 1980s but increased during the 1990s.

■ The news article emphasizes reasons why the amount of currency in circulation might have *decreased*. But why did currency in circulation increase during the 1990s?

■ Currency is one component of money, and the demand for money increases when real GDP increases.

■ But Fig. 1 graphs currency as a percentage of GDP. So, even holding real GDP constant, currency in circulation has increased during the 1990s.

■ The reason for the increase in currency in circulation is that the interest rate, which is the opportunity cost of holding currency, decreased during the 1990s.

■ Figure 2 shows the relationship between currency in circulation (as a percentage of GDP) against the interest rate. You can see that, as the theory of the demand for money predicts, the lower the interest rate, the greater is the quantity of currency in circulation.

■ So what is left of the message in the news article? Are we using less currency as we switch increasingly to the use of debit cards?

■ Figure 3 provides an answer to this question. It shows that since 1996, composition of M1 has changed.

■ The percentage of M1 held as currency has fallen from 42 percent to 35 percent.

■ Debit cards make it possible to pay for purchases directly from bank accounts and the need to carry cash decreases.

■ The biggest decrease in currency (as a percentage of M1) occurred during 1996. Since then, the rate of decrease has been small.

■ As the number of businesses that accept debit cards and the number of debit card transactions increase, people require less cash and keep more money as demand deposits.

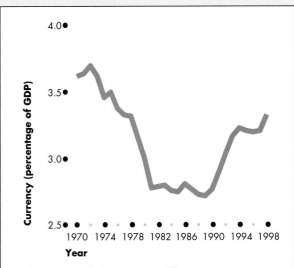

Figure 1 Trends in currency holding

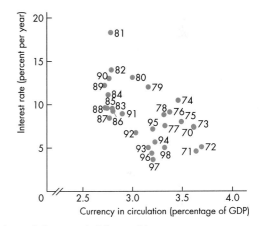

Figure 2 Currency holding and interest rates

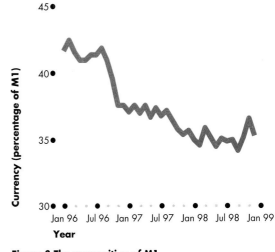

Figure 3 The composition of M1

S U M M A R Y

Key Points

What Is Money? (pp. 598–600)

■ Money is the means of payment, a medium of exchange, a unit of account, and a store of value.

■ M1 consists of currency and households' and businesses' demand deposits at chartered banks; M2+ consists of M1 plus savings deposits and other deposits at all types of depository institutions.

Depository Institutions (pp. 601–603)

■ The depository institutions are the chartered banks, credit unions and caisses populaires, and trust and mortgage companies.

■ Depository institutions provide four main economic services: They create liquidity, minimize the cost of obtaining funds, minimize the cost of monitoring borrowers, and pool risks.

How Banks Create Money (pp. 603–606)

■ Banks create money by making loans.

■ The total quantity of deposits that can be supported by a given amount of reserves (the deposit multiplier) is determined by the desired reserve ratio.

The Demand for Money (pp. 607–610)

■ The quantity of money demanded is the amount of money that people plan to hold.

■ The quantity of real money equals the quantity of nominal money divided by the price level.

■ The quantity of real money demanded depends on the interest rate and real GDP. As the interest rate rises, the quantity of real money demanded decreases.

Interest Rate Determination (pp. 610–612)

■ The interest rate adjusts to achieve equilibrium in the markets for money and financial assets.

■ Money market equilibrium achieves an interest rate (and an asset price) that makes the quantity of real money available willingly held.

■ If the quantity of real money increases, the interest rate falls and the prices of financial assets rise.

The Interest Rate and Expenditure Plans (pp. 613–615)

■ The real interest rate (approximately) equals the nominal interest rate minus the inflation rate.

■ The nominal interest rate is the opportunity cost of holding money. The real interest rate is the opportunity cost of consumption expenditure and investment.

■ A fall in the interest rate increases interest-sensitive expenditure.

Key Figures

Key Terms

P R O B L E M S

*1. Which of the following items are money?
   a. Bank of Canada notes in the Bank of Montreal's cash machines
   b. Your Visa card
   c. The quarters inside public phones
   d. Canadian dollar bills in your wallet
   e. The cheque you have just written to pay for your rent
   f. The loan you took out last August to pay for your school fees

2. Which of the following items are money? Which are deposit money?
   a. Demand deposits at the CIBC
   b. Bell Canada stock held by individuals
   c. A "loonie"
   d. Canadian government securities

*3. Sara withdraws $1,000 from her savings account at the Lucky Trust and Mortgage Company, keeps $50 in cash, and deposits the balance in her demand deposit account at the Bank of Montreal. What is the immediate change in M1 and M2+?

4. Monica takes $10,000 from her demand deposit account at the CIBC and puts it into her savings account at Canada Trust. What is the immediate change in M1 and M2+?

*5. The banks in Zap have:

Reserves	$250 million
Loans	$1,000 million
Deposits	$2,000 million
Total assets	$2,500 million

   a. Construct the banks' balance sheet. If you are missing any assets or liabilities, call them "other assets" and "other liabilities."
   b. Calculate the banks' reserve ratio.
   c. If banks hold no excess reserves, calculate the deposit multiplier.

6. The banks in Zip have:

Reserves	$125 million
Loans	$1,875 million
Deposits	$2,000 million
Total assets	$2,100 million

   a. Construct the banks' balance sheet. If you are missing any assets or liabilities, call them "other assets" and "other liabilities."
   b. Calculate the banks' reserve ratio.
   c. If banks hold no excess reserves, calculate the deposit multiplier.

*7. The spreadsheet provides information about the demand for money in Minland. Column A is the interest rate, R. Columns B, C, and D show the quantity of money demanded at three different levels of real GDP: Y_0 is $10 billion, Y_1 is $20 billion, and Y_2 is $30 billion.

	A	B	C	D
1	R	Y_0	Y_1	Y_2
2	7	1.0	1.5	2.0
3	6	1.5	2.0	2.5
4	5	2.0	2.5	3.0
5	4	2.5	3.0	3.5
6	3	3.0	3.5	4.0
7	2	3.5	4.0	4.5
8	1	4.0	4.5	5.0

   The quantity of money supplied by the Minland central bank is $3.0 billion. Initially, real GDP is $20 billion. What happens in Minland if the interest rate:
   a. Exceeds 4 percent a year?
   b. Is less than 4 percent a year?
   c. Equals 4 percent a year?

8. In problem 7, Minland experiences a severe recession. Real GDP falls to $10 billion. The Minland central bank takes no actions to change the quantity of money.
   a. What happens in Minland if the interest rate is 4 percent a year?
   b. What is the equilibrium interest rate?
   c. Compared with the situation in problem 7, does the interest rate in Minland rise or fall? Why?

*9. In problem 7, Minland experiences a severe business cycle. Real GDP rises to $30 billion and then falls to $10 billion. The Minland central bank takes no actions to change the quantity of money. What happens to the interest rate in Minland during the:
   a. Expansion phase of the cycle?
   b. Recession phase of the cycle?

10. In problem 7, a financial innovation changes the demand for money. People plan to hold $0.5 billion less than the numbers in the spreadsheet.
   a. What happens to the interest rate if the Minland central bank takes no actions?
   b. What happens to the interest rate if the Minland central bank decreases the quantity of money by $0.5 billion? Explain.

*11. The figure shows the demand for real money in Upland.

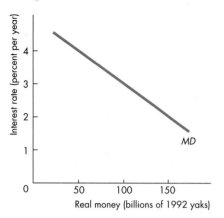

a. Draw the supply of money curve if the interest rate is 3 percent a year.
b. If the Upland central bank wants to lower the interest rate by 1 percentage point, by how much must it change the quantity of real money?

12. In problem 11, a new smart card replaces currency and the demand for money changes. Also, the new smart card causes business to boom and real GDP increases.
a. Use the figure for problem 11 and draw a new demand for money curve that is consistent with the events just described.
b. If the Upland central bank wants to prevent the interest rate from changing, what must it do to the supply of money?

*13. In problem 9, when Minland experiences a severe business cycle, what happens to autonomous consumption expenditure, investment, the exchange rate, and net exports during the:
a. Expansion phase of the cycle?
b. Recession phase of the cycle?

14. In problem 10, when Minland experiences a financial innovation that changes the demand for money:
a. What happens to autonomous consumption expenditure, investment, the exchange rate, and net exports if the Minland central bank takes no actions?
b. What happens to autonomous consumption expenditure, investment, the exchange rate, and net exports if the Minland central bank decreases the quantity of money by $0.5 billion? Explain.

CRITICAL THINKING

1. Study *Reading Between the Lines* on pp. 616–617 and then answer the following questions:
a. What changes in the payments technology are described in the news article?
b. What does the news article imply has happened to currency in circulation?
c. What are the trends in currency use?
d. Why did the use of currency increase during the 1990s?
e. Does the increased use of currency during the 1990s contradict the news article?
f. What do you expect the future trends in currency use to be and why?

2. Rapid inflation in Brazil caused the cruzeiro, the currency of Brazil, to lose its ability to function as money. People were unwilling to accept it because it lost value too fast. Which of the following commodities do you think would be most likely to take the place of the cruzeiro and act as money in the Brazilian economy?
a. Tractor parts
b. Packs of cigarettes
c. Loaves of bread
d. Impressionist paintings
e. Baseball trading cards

3. Use the link on the Parkin-Bade Web site to visit Mark Bernkopf's Central Banking Resource Centre and read the article on Electronic Cash. Also read "The End of Cash" by James Gleick (first published in the *New York Times Magazine* 16 June 1996). Then answer the following questions:
a. What is e-cash?
b. Mark Bernkopf asks: "Will 'e-cash' enable private currencies to overturn the ability of governments to make monetary policy?" Will it?
c. When you buy an item on the Internet and pay by using a form of e-cash, are you using money? Explain why or why not.
d. In your opinion, is the concern about e-cash a real concern or hype?

28

Monetary Policy

The year is 1982. A student has just found the ideal car and would like to buy it. But the interest rate on car loans has just jumped to 22 percent a year. Amid much gnashing of teeth, she puts off her purchase until the interest rate falls and makes a car affordable. What determines interest rates? Do forces of nature determine them? Or is somebody fiddling with the knobs somewhere? ◆ You suspect that someone is indeed fiddling with the knobs. For you've just read in your newspaper: "Bank of Canada nudging interest rates down to spark recovery." And a few months earlier, you had read: "The Bank

Fiddling with the Knobs

of Canada doesn't plan to push interest rates higher unless it sees further rebound of inflation." What *is* the Bank of Canada? Why would the Bank of Canada want to change interest rates—especially upward? And how can the Bank of Canada influence interest rates? ◆ During the 1970s, the quantity of money in Canada grew quickly. But during the 1980s and 1990s, the pace of money creation slowed. What makes the quantity of money increase quickly at some times and more slowly at others? What role does the Bank of Canada play in changing the quantity of money? And how does the quantity of money in existence influence interest rates? ◆ How do interest rates influence the economy? Can the Bank of Canada speed up economic growth and lower unemployment by lowering interest rates? And can the Bank of Canada keep inflation in check by raising interest rates?

◆ In this chapter, you will learn about the Bank of Canada and monetary policy. You will learn how the Bank of Canada influences interest rates and how interest rates influence the economy. You'll discover that interest rates depend, in part, on the amount of money in existence. You will also discover how the Bank of Canada changes the quantity of money to influence interest rates as it attempts to smooth the business cycle and keep inflation in check.

After studying this chapter, you will be able to:

- **Describe the structure of the Bank of Canada**
- **Describe the tools used by the Bank of Canada to conduct monetary policy**
- **Explain what an open market operation is and how it works**
- **Explain how the Bank of Canada changes the quantity of money**
- **Explain how the Bank of Canada influences interest rates**
- **Explain how the Bank of Canada influences the economy**

The Bank of Canada

THE BANK OF CANADA IS CANADA'S CENTRAL bank. A **central bank** is a public authority that supervises financial institutions and markets and conducts monetary policy. **Monetary policy** is the attempt to control inflation and moderate the business cycle by changing the quantity of money in circulation and adjusting interest rates and the exchange rate.

The **Bank of Canada** was created by the Bank of Canada Act of 1935 (revised in 1967) and a Governor, who is appointed by the government of Canada, directs its operations. Six people have served as governor of the Bank of Canada. They are

- 1934–1954, Graham Towers
- 1955–1961, James Coyne
- 1961–1973, Louis Rasminsky
- 1973–1987, Gerald Bouey
- 1987–1994, John Crow
- 1994– , Gordon Thiessen

Both the Bank of Canada and the government of Canada play a role in determining Canada's monetary policy. And the Bank of Canada Act regulates the balance between these two power centres. The Act embodies the practices that have evolved over 60 years of experience. There are two possible models for the relationship between a country's central bank and its central government, and Canada has evolved from one model to the other. The two models are

- Independent central bank
- Subordinate central bank

Independent Central Bank An independent central bank is one that determines the nation's monetary policy without interference from the government. Public servants and politicians might comment on monetary policy but the Bank has no obligation to pay attention to these opinions.

The argument for an independent central bank is that it can pursue the long-term goal of price stability and can prevent monetary policy from being used for short-term, political advantage. This argument becomes more powerful when the government is running a budget deficit. One way of covering a deficit is for the central bank to buy government securities. But this action increases the quantity of money and creates inflation (see Chapter 29, p. 659 and Chapter 30, pp. 672–673). Another way of financing a government budget deficit is by selling securities to the general public. By taking a firm stand and being unwilling to print new money to pay for the government budget deficit, the central bank can force the government to face the higher interest rates that it brings upon itself by running a deficit.

Countries that have independent central banks today are Germany, the United States, and Switzerland. When the Bank of Canada was founded, in 1935, it too was established as an independent central bank. Governors Towers and Coyne enjoyed substantial autonomy from the government of Canada. But in 1961, Governor James Coyne and Prime Minister John Diefenbaker clashed over who was in charge of monetary policy. Coyne resigned and for some time it was not clear whether the Bank of Canada was indeed independent as the act that established it proclaimed or subordinate to the government as the outcome of the Coyne–Diefenbaker clash seemed to imply.

The issue was resolved in 1967 when an amendment to the Bank of Canada Act redefined the relationship between the Bank and the government and made the Bank subordinate to the government.

Subordinate Central Bank Many central banks are subordinate to their governments. In the event of a difference of opinion between the central bank and government, the government carries the day and, if necessary, the central bank governor resigns if he or she is unwilling to implement the policies directed by the government. The argument for a subordinate central bank is that monetary policy affects the lives of everyone and so must be subject to democratic control.

Although the government (through the minister of finance) has final responsibility for Canada's monetary policy, this fact does not mean that the Bank of Canada is impotent. Because of its expertise and authority in the field and because of the quality of the analysis done by the Bank's staff of senior economists and advisors, the Bank (through the governor) has considerable power. Only a sharp, deep, and wide-ranging disagreement would bring a government to the point of forcing a governor's resignation. Also, there are times when a government wants to pursue unpopular monetary policies and, at such times, it is convenient for the government to hide behind the authority of the Bank of Canada.

We are now going to study the policy actions the Bank of Canada takes. To understand these actions, we first must describe the Bank's balance sheet.

Bank of Canada's Balance Sheet

Table 28.1 shows the balance sheet of the Bank of Canada. The numbers are for March 1999. The assets on the left side are what the Bank of Canada owns and the liabilities on the right side are what it owes. Most of the Bank of Canada's assets are government of Canada securities. A small asset item is loans to chartered banks.

The most significant aspect of the Bank of Canada's balance sheet is on the liabilities side. The largest liability is Bank of Canada notes outside the Bank. These are the bank notes that we use in our daily transactions. Some of these bank notes are held by households and firms and others are in the tills and vaults of banks and other financial institutions.

The other economically significant but numerically small liability of the Bank of Canada is the deposits by chartered banks. These deposits are reserves of the chartered banks. The liabilities of the Bank of Canada are the largest component of the monetary base. The **monetary base** is the sum of Bank of Canada notes outside the Bank, chartered banks' deposits at the Bank of Canada, and coins held by households, firms, and banks. The government of Canada issues coins, so they do not appear as a liability of the Bank of Canada. The government of Canada also has deposits with the Bank of Canada.

You now know what the Bank of Canada is and you can describe the Bank's assets and liabilities. Your next task is to learn how the Bank goes about its work of making monetary policy.

TABLE 28.1
The Bank of Canada's Balance Sheet, March 1999

Assets (billions of dollars)		Liabilities (billions of dollars)	
Government securities	30	Bank of Canada notes	31
Loans to banks	1	Banks' deposits	1
		Government deposits	0
Other assets (net)	1		
Total assets	32	Total liabilities	32

[All the items are shown rounded to the nearest $1 billion.]
Source: Statistics Canada, *StatCan CANSIM Disc*, series B3418, B54401, and B14001, March 1999.

Making Monetary Policy

Making monetary policy is like driving a very strange car. The car has an accelerator (lower interest rates) and a brake (higher interest rates). The accelerator and the brake work, but not very predictably. The driver (the Bank of Canada) cannot be sure how strong or how delayed the response to its actions will be. Also, to make the ride more interesting, the driver has only a rear view. The road just travelled can be seen, but the road ahead is invisible.

The objective is to drive the car at a constant speed over a terrain that alternates between uphill (tough economic times with a falling real GDP growth rate and rising unemployment) and downhill (easy economic times with a rising real GDP growth rate and falling unemployment). So sometimes the accelerator must be applied, sometimes the brake, and sometimes neither. You can see that to have a smooth ride, the driver must read the current situation and try to predict what lies ahead.

So to make monetary policy, the Bank of Canada must anticipate the future course of the economy and it must try to read that course from current economic conditions. To study the Bank's challenging task, economists break the monetary policy process into three pieces:

- Monetary policy objectives
- Monetary policy indicators
- Monetary policy tools

Monetary Policy Objectives

The objectives of monetary policy are ultimately political, and they stem from the mandate of the Bank that is set out in the Bank of Canada Act. These objectives are to

> regulate credit and currency in the best interests of the economic life of the nation ... and to mitigate by its influence fluctuations in the general level of production, trade, prices and employment, so far as may be possible within the scope of monetary action...[1]

In simple language, these words have come to mean that the Bank's job is to control the quantity of money and interest rates in order to avoid inflation and, when possible, prevent excessive swings in real

[1]This quotation is from the preamble of the Bank of Canada Act, 1935.

GDP growth and unemployment. In terms of the car analogy, the Bank sees its job as being cautious in applying the accelerator and more aggressive in applying the brake.

This modern interpretation of the Bank's objectives is controversial. Some people believe that the emphasis is wrong and that the Bank should pay less attention to inflation and use its influence to avoid low real GDP growth and high unemployment. Or, the Bank should put more pressure on the gas pedal and less on the brake.

Monetary Policy Indicators

If inflation is raging too rapidly or unemployment is too high, there is nothing the Bank of Canada can do that will bring immediate relief. Furthermore, if the Bank is doing a good job, it will already have taken the actions it believes are the best available for dealing with *today's* situation. The actions the Bank takes today are designed to influence the economy many months into the future. **Monetary policy indicators** are the *current* features of the economy that the Bank looks at to determine whether it needs to apply the brake or the accelerator to the economy to influence its *future* real GDP growth, unemployment, and inflation.

The best monetary policy indicators are variables that the Bank of Canada can observe accurately and frequently, that are good predictors of the future course of real GDP growth, unemployment, and inflation (the objectives of policy), and that the Bank can control quickly.

The Bank of Canada's monetary policy indicators change as more research is done and the Bank learns more about which indicators work well and which are faulty. Today, the main monetary policy indicator is an interest rate called the overnight loans rate. The **overnight loans rate** is the interest rate on large-scale loans that chartered banks make to each other and to dealers in financial markets. The Bank of Canada sets a range for the overnight loans rate of half a percentage point and takes actions to keep the rate inside its desired range.[2] The overnight loans rate is like the cruise control on the Bank's strange car.

Figure 28.1 shows the overnight loans rate. This interest rate climbed steeply after 1975 and reached a peak of almost 19 percent in 1981. At this time, Governor Gerald Bouey was wrestling with double-digit inflation. Since 1981, the overnight loans rate has fluctuated, but it has generally followed a downward trend. This downward trend was interrupted during the late 1980s when Governor John Crow pursued a vigorous policy of low inflation.

Monetary Policy Tools

The Bank of Canada controls the overnight loans rate by adjusting the reserves of the banks. These adjustments then spread through the banks to change the quantity of money, other interest rates, and the

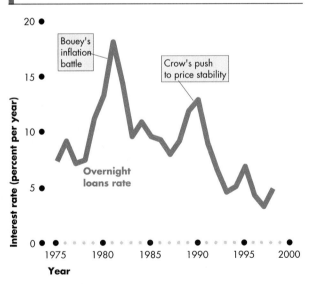

FIGURE 28.1

The Main Monetary Policy Indicator: The Overnight Loans Rates

The Bank of Canada sets a target range for the overnight loans rate and then takes actions to keep this monetary policy indicator inside its target range. When the Bank wants to slow inflation, it takes actions that raise the overnight loans rate. When the Bank wants to increase real GDP, it takes actions that lower the overnight loans rate.

Source: Statistics Canada, *StatCan: CANSIM Disc,* March 1999.

---

[2]Half a percentage point is sometimes called 50 *basis points.* A basis point is one-hundredth of one percentage point. For example, the Bank might set the range at 3.5 to 4.0 percent or from 7.1 to 7.6 percent. In each case, the range is half a percentage point or 50 basis points.

exchange rate. Four policy tools impact on bank reserves and the quantity of money:

- Required reserve ratio
- Bank rate and bankers' deposit rate
- Open market operations
- Government deposit shifting

Required Reserve Ratio   Banks hold reserves in the form of currency and deposits at the Bank of Canada so that they can meet the demands of their customers. If the Bank of Canada chooses to do so, it can require the chartered banks to hold larger reserves than the banks themselves desire. Since 1992, banks in Canada have not been required to hold reserves. *The required reserve ratio is zero.* Before 1992, the Bank imposed reserve requirements on the banks. Required reserves were 8 percent of deposits before 1967. They then decreased steadily through the 1970s and 1980s and were finally abolished in 1992.

By changing the required reserve ratio, the Bank of Canada changes the amount of lending the banks can do and therefore changes the quantity of money. It also changes the magnitude of the deposit multiplier. The higher the reserve ratio, the smaller is the deposit multiplier (see Chapter 27, p. 604).

Required reserves act like a tax on the banks. When banks are required to hold either currency or deposits at the Bank of Canada, the banks earn no interest on either of these assets. So the banks are taxed by the Bank of Canada by an amount equal to the interest that they could have earned by lending these funds rather than by holding them as reserves. The *opportunity cost* of reserves is the loan interest forgone. By abolishing required reserves, the Bank of Canada has made the banks more profitable.

Bank Rate and Bankers' Deposit Rate   The chartered banks hold tiny reserves relative to their deposits. The reason the banks can manage with such small reserves is that the Bank of Canada stands ready to lend reserves to them to ensure that they can always meet their depositors' demands for currency. The **bank rate** is the interest rate that the Bank charges the chartered banks on the reserves it lends them.

The Bank of Canada sets the bank rate. At one time, the Bank linked the bank rate to the interest rate on 3-month government of Canada Treasury bills. But today, it is set as the upper end of the Bank's target range for the overnight loans rate. Because the Bank is willing to lend funds to the chartered banks at this interest rate, the bank rate acts as a

cap on the overnight loans rate. If the chartered banks can borrow from the Bank of Canada at the bank rate, they will not borrow from another bank unless the rate is lower than or equal to the bank rate.

The Bank of Canada pays the chartered banks interest at the *bankers' deposit rate* on their deposits at the Bank. The Bank sets this interest rate at the bank rate minus half a percentage point, which also equals the low end of the Bank's target range for the overnight loans rate. If chartered banks can earn the bank rate minus half a percentage point from the Bank, they will not make overnight loans to other banks unless they earn a higher interest rate than what the Bank is paying.

You can see now that the Bank can always make the overnight loans rate hit its target range by its setting of the bank rate and the bankers' deposit rate. But the Bank usually wants to keep the overnight loans rate inside its target range, not at one end of it. The other two policy tools are used to move the overnight loans rate around inside its target range.

Open Market Operations   An **open market operation** is the purchase or sale of government of Canada securities—Treasury bills and government bonds—by the Bank of Canada from or to a chartered bank or the public. When the Bank of Canada buys securities, it pays for them with newly created monetary base. Its payment for the securities increases the chartered banks' deposits at the Bank of Canada. With extra reserves, the banks make new loans, the quantity of money increases, and interest rates fall. When the Bank of Canada sells securities, it receives payments that decrease the monetary base. Banks' reserves decrease, the banks cut lending, the quantity of money decreases, and interest rates rise.

Open market operations are the main method of controlling bank reserves and the money supply, and they are undertaken on a huge scale. For example, during 1998 the Bank of Canada bought or sold government securities valued at an average of $600 million a week. In some weeks, the Bank buys or sells more than $2 billion of government securities. Some of these transactions occur to cope with seasonal fluctuations in the demand for money that arise from factors such as the timing of tax payments and Christmas shopping. Others occur because the Bank of Canada wants to raise or lower the overnight interest rate. Because open market operations are the main tool for controlling the quantity of money and influencing other interest rates, we study them in more detail later in this chapter (on pp. 627–631).

Government Deposit Shifting The government of Canada has deposits in accounts at chartered banks and the Bank of Canada. On a typical day, the government has about $2.5 billion in the bank and most of this money is on deposit at chartered banks. The government's deposit at the Bank of Canada is usually around $20 million (less than 1 percent of its total bank deposits).

Government deposit shifting is the transfer of government funds by the Bank of Canada from the government's account at the Bank of Canada to its accounts at the chartered banks or from the government's accounts at the chartered banks to its account at the Bank of Canada. When the Bank of Canada shifts government funds from itself to the chartered banks, it increases chartered bank deposits and reserves. When the Bank shifts government funds from the chartered banks to itself, it decreases chartered bank deposits and reserves.

Table 28.2 shows the effects of government deposit shifting. Suppose the Bank of Canada writes cheques on a government of Canada account totalling $10 million and deposits those cheques into government of Canada accounts at the chartered banks. (To avoid benefiting or hurting an individual bank, these operations are spread across the banks according to an agreed formula.)

Two sets of transactions now occur. First, government deposits increase at the chartered banks and decrease at the Bank of Canada. This transaction appears as a +$10 million in government deposits in chartered banks' liabilities and a –$10 million in government deposits in Bank of Canada liabilities. Second, chartered banks' reserves increase. This transaction appears as a +$10 million in chartered banks' assets and a +$10 million in Bank of Canada liabilities. The chartered banks have $10 million more assets and $10 million more liabilities, and the Bank of Canada has no net additional liabilities.

The money supply has not changed because government deposits are not counted as money. But bank reserves have increased, so the banks can now increase their loans. And, when banks make loans they create money. The quantity of money increases. By doing the transactions you've just seen in reverse, the Bank of Canada can decrease bank reserves and cause a contraction of loans, and the quantity of money decreases.

Government deposit shifting is done on a very small scale and is a way of fine-tuning the quantity of bank reserves from one day to another. On the aver-

---

TABLE 28.2

The Effects of Government Deposit Shifting

Chartered Banks' Balance Sheet

Change in assets		Change in liabilities	
Reserves (deposits at the Bank of Canada)	+$10 million	Government deposits	+$10 million
Total assets	+$10 million	Total liabilities	+$10 million

Bank of Canada's Balance Sheet

Change in assets		Change in liabilities	
		Government deposits	–$10 million
		Chartered bank deposits	+$10 million
Total assets	$0	Total liabilities	$0 million

---

age, during 1998, only $2 million a week was shifted and the largest weekly shifting has never exceeded $10 million. Compared with open market operations, these transactions are small change.

R E V I E W   Q U I Z

- What is the central bank of Canada?
- What functions does a central bank perform?
- What are the Bank of Canada's monetary policy objectives?
- Why does the Bank of Canada need a monetary policy indicator and what is its main indicator?
- What are the four policy tools that the Bank of Canada can use to attempt to achieve its monetary policy objectives?

We're now going to look in greater detail at the way the Bank of Canada influences the quantity of money and interest rates by using its main tool, the open market operation. We'll first see how the Bank changes the monetary base and second see how the monetary base influences the quantity of money. We'll then see how the quantity of money influences interest rates and the exchange rate.

Controlling the Money Supply

THE BANK OF CANADA CONSTANTLY MONITORS and adjusts the quantity of money in the economy. When the Bank of Canada *buys* securities in an open market operation, the monetary base *increases*, banks increase their lending, and the quantity of money *increases*. When the Bank of Canada *sells* securities in an open market operation, the monetary base *decreases*, banks decrease their lending, and the quantity of money *decreases*.

Let's study these changes in the quantity of money, beginning with the effects of open market operations on the monetary base.

How an Open Market Operation Works

When the Bank of Canada conducts an open market operation, the reserves of the banking system, a part of the monetary base, change. To see why this outcome occurs, we'll trace the effects of an open market operation when the Bank of Canada buys securities.

Suppose the Bank of Canada buys $100 million of government securities in the open market. There are two cases to consider: when the Bank of Canada buys from a chartered bank and when it buys from the public (a person or business that is not a chartered bank). The outcome is essentially the same in either case, but you need to be convinced of this fact. We'll start with the simpler case: the Bank of Canada buys securities from a chartered bank.

Buy from a Chartered Bank   When the Bank of Canada buys $100 million of securities from the Toronto Dominion Bank, two things happen:

1. The Toronto Dominion Bank has $100 million less securities, and the Bank of Canada has $100 million more securities.
2. The Bank of Canada pays for the securities by crediting the Toronto Dominion Bank's deposit account at the Bank of Canada with $100 million.

Figure 28.2(a) shows the effects of these actions on the balance sheets of the Bank of Canada and the Toronto Dominion Bank. Ownership of the securities passes from the chartered bank to the Bank of Canada, so the Toronto Dominion Bank's assets decrease by $100 million and the Bank of Canada's

FIGURE 28.2
Bank of Canada Buys Securities in the Open Market

(a) The Bank of Canada buys securities from a chartered bank

(b) The Bank of Canada buys securities from the public

assets increase by $100 million, as shown by the blue arrow running from the Toronto Dominion Bank to the Bank of Canada. The Bank of Canada pays for the securities by crediting the Toronto Dominion Bank's deposit account—its reserves—at the Bank of Canada with $100 million, as shown by the green arrow running from the Bank of Canada to the Toronto Dominion Bank. This action increases the monetary base and increases the reserves of the banking system.

The Bank of Canada's assets increase by $100 million, and its liabilities also increase by $100 million. The chartered bank's total assets remain constant but their composition changes. Its deposit at the Bank of Canada increases by $100 million, and its holding of government securities decreases by $100 million. So the bank has additional reserves, which it can use to make loans.

We've just seen that when the Bank of Canada buys government securities from a bank, the bank's reserves increase. But what happens if the Bank of Canada buys government securities from the public—say from London Life, an insurance company?

Buy from the Public When the Bank of Canada buys $100 million of securities from London Life, three things happen:

1. London Life has $100 million less securities, and the Bank of Canada has $100 million more securities.
2. The Bank of Canada pays for the securities with a cheque for $100 million drawn on itself, which London Life deposits in its account at the Toronto Dominion Bank.
3. The Toronto Dominion Bank collects payment of this cheque from the Bank of Canada, and $100 million is deposited in Toronto Dominion's deposit account at the Bank of Canada.

Figure 28.2(b) shows the effects of these actions on the balance sheets of the Bank of Canada, London Life, and the Toronto Dominion Bank. Ownership of the securities passes from London Life to the Bank of Canada, so London Life's assets decrease by $100 million and the Bank of Canada's assets increase by $100 million, as shown by the blue arrow running from London Life to the Bank of Canada. The Bank of Canada pays for the securities with a cheque payable to London Life, which London Life deposits in the Toronto Dominion Bank. This transaction increases London Life's deposit at the Toronto Dominion Bank by $100 million, as shown by the red arrow running from the Toronto Dominion Bank to London Life.

This transaction also increases Toronto Dominion's reserves by $100 million, as shown by the green arrow running from the Bank of Canada to the Toronto Dominion Bank. Just as when the Bank of Canada buys securities from a bank, this action increases the monetary base and increases the reserves of the banking system.

Again, the Bank of Canada's assets increase by $100 million, and its liabilities also increase by $100 million. London Life has the same total assets as before, but their composition has changed. It now has more money and less securities. The Toronto Dominion Bank's total assets increase, and so do its liabilities. Its deposit at the Bank of Canada—its reserves—increases by $100 million, and its deposit liability to London Life increases by $100 million. Because its reserves have increased by the same amount as its deposits, the bank has excess reserves, which it can use to make loans.

We've now studied what happens when the Bank of Canada buys government securities either from a bank or from the public. If the Bank of Canada sells securities, all the events that you've just studied occur in reverse. Reserves decrease, and the banks are short of reserves.

The effects of an open market operation on the balance sheets of the Bank of Canada and the banks that we've just described are not the end of the story—they are just the beginning. With an increase in their reserves, the banks are able to make more loans, which increases the quantity of money. With a decrease in reserves, the banks must cut back on their loans, which decreases the quantity of money.

You learned how loans create deposits in Chapter 27. Here, we build on that basic idea but instead of studying the link between *bank reserves* and *bank deposits*, we examine the related broader link between the *monetary base* and the *quantity of money*.

Monetary Base and Bank Reserves

We've defined the monetary base as the sum of Bank of Canada notes outside the Bank, banks' deposits at the Bank of Canada, and coins held by households, firms, and banks. The monetary base is held either by banks as reserves or by households and firms as currency. When the monetary base increases, both bank reserves and currency held by households and firms increase. Only the increase in bank reserves can be used by banks to make loans and create additional money. An increase in currency held by households and firms is called a **currency drain**. A currency drain reduces the amount of additional money that can be created from a given increase in the monetary base.

The **money multiplier** is the amount by which a change in the monetary base is multiplied to determine the resulting change in the quantity of money. That is, the money multiplier is equal to the change in the quantity of money (*M*) divided by the change in the monetary base (*MB*):

$$\text{Money Multiplier} = \frac{\Delta M}{\Delta MB}.$$

The money multiplier is related to but differs from the *deposit multiplier* that we studied in Chapter 27. The deposit multiplier is the amount by which a change in bank reserves is multiplied to determine the change in the bank deposits.

Let's now look at the money multiplier.

The Money Multiplier

Let's work out the money multiplier by studying the case in which the Bank of Canada *buys securities from the banks*. Figure 28.3 shows the events that follow this open market purchase by the Bank of Canada. These events are:

1. Banks have excess reserves.
2. Banks lend excess reserves.
3. Bank deposits increase.
4. The quantity of money increases.
5. New money is used to make payments.
6. Some of the new money remains on deposit.
7. Some of the new money is a *currency drain*.
8. Desired reserves increase because deposits have increased.
9. Excess reserves decrease, but remain positive.

FIGURE 28.3

A Round in the Multiplier Process Following an Open Market Operation

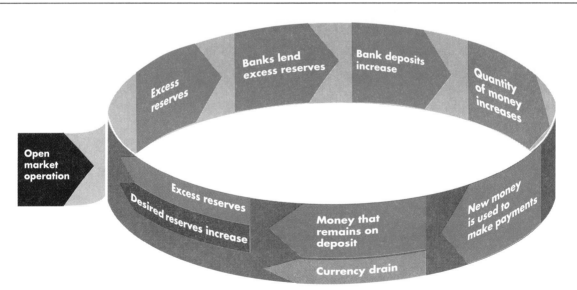

An open market operation increases bank reserves and creates excess reserves. Banks lend the excess reserves, new deposits are created, and the quantity of money increases. New money is used to make payments. Households and firms receiving payments keep some of the receipts as currency—a currency drain—and place the rest on deposit in banks. The increase in bank deposits increases banks' reserves but also increases banks' desired reserves. Desired reserves increase by less than actual reserves, so the banks still have some excess reserves, though less than before. The process repeats until excess reserves have been eliminated.

The sequence repeats in a series of rounds, but each round begins with a smaller quantity of excess reserves than did the previous one. The process continues until excess reserves have finally been eliminated.

You've seen that an open market operation creates excess reserves for the banks and that the reaction of the banks to this situation increases the quantity of money. But you've not yet seen the magnitude of the increase in the quantity of money.

Figure 28.4 illustrates the series of rounds and keeps track of the magnitudes of the increases in reserves, loans, deposits, currency, and money that result from an open market purchase of $100,000. In this figure, the *currency drain* is 33.33 percent of money and the *desired reserve ratio* is 10 percent of deposits.

The Bank of Canada buys $100,000 of securities from the banks. The banks' reserves increase by this amount, but deposits do not change. The banks have excess reserves of $100,000, and they lend those reserves. When the banks lend $100,000 of excess reserves, $66,667 remains in the banks as deposits and $33,333 drains off and is held outside the banks as currency. The quantity of money has now increased by $100,000—the increase in deposits plus the increase in currency holdings.

The increased bank deposits of $66,667 generate an increase in desired reserves of 10 percent of that amount, which is $6,667. Actual reserves have increased by the same amount as the increase in deposits—$66,667. So the banks now have excess reserves of $60,000. At this stage, we have gone around the circle shown in Fig. 28.3 once. The process we've just described repeats but begins with excess reserves of $60,000. Figure 28.4 shows the next two rounds. When the process comes to an end, the quantity of money has increased by $250,000.

FIGURE 28.4

The Multiplier Effect of an Open Market Operation

The Sequence

					The Running Tally			
					Reserves	Deposits	Currency	Money
Open market operation $100,000								
Loan $100,000								
Currency $33,333	Deposit $66,667					$66,667	$33,333	$100,000
Reserve $6,667	Loan $60,000							
Currency $20,000	Deposit $40,000				$6,667	$106,667	$53,333	$160,000
Reserve $4,000	Loan $36,000							
Currency $12,000	Deposit $24,000				$10,667	$130,667	$65,333	$196,000
and so on ...					• • ▼	• • ▼	• • ▼	• • ▼
					$16,667	$166,667	$83,333	$250,000

When a Bank of Canada open market operation gives the banks an additional $100,000 of reserves, the banks lend those reserves. Of the amount lent, $33,333 (33.33 percent) leaves the banks in a currency drain and $66,667 remains on deposit. With additional deposits, desired reserves increase by $6,667 (10 percent desired reserve ratio) and the banks lend $60,000. Of this amount, $20,000 leaves the banks in a currency drain and $40,000 remains on deposit. The process repeats until the banks have created enough deposits to eliminate their excess reserves. An additional $100,000 of reserves creates $250,000 of money.

The Canadian Money Multiplier

In the example you've just worked through, a $100,000 open market purchase increases the quantity of money by $250,000. The money multiplier is 2.5. What is the magnitude of the Canadian money multiplier? Let's look at some numbers.

The Canadian money multiplier is the change in the quantity of money divided by the change in the monetary base. Because there are two main definitions of money, there are two money multipliers: one for M1 and one for M2+. The M1 multiplier is about 2.2, and the M2+ multiplier is about 10. That is, a $1 million increase in the monetary base brings (approximately) a $2.2 million increase in M1 and a $10 million increase in M2+. These multipliers are based on a desired reserve ratio for M1 of 0.12 (12 percent) and for M2+ of 0.01 (1 percent). That is, a $100 increase in M1 increases desired reserves by $12, while a $100 increase in M2+ brings an increase in desired reserves of only $1. These multipliers are also based on a currency drain of 0.36 (or 36 percent) for M1 and 0.08 (or 8 percent) for M2+. That is, a $100 increase in M1 increases currency held by households and firms by $36, while a $100 increase in M2+ increases currency held by households and firms by $8.

R E V I E W   Q U I Z

- What happens when the Bank of Canada buys securities in the open market?
- What happens when the Bank of Canada sells securities in the open market?
- What do the banks do when they have excess reserves and how do their actions influence the quantity of money?
- What do the banks do when they are short of reserves and how do their actions influence the quantity of money?

The Bank of Canada's objective in changing the quantity of money is to influence the course of the economy—especially unemployment, real GDP growth, and inflation. The immediate effects of a change in the quantity of money are changes in the interest rate and the exchange rate. These changes create ripple effects that ultimately change the course of the economy. Let's now study these ripple effects.

Ripple Effects of Monetary Policy

YOU'VE SEEN HOW THE BANK OF CANADA CAN use its power in financial markets to change the quantity of money. And you learned in Chapter 27 that a change in the quantity of money changes the interest rate and the exchange rate.

We're now going to study the consequences of these changes in the interest rate and the exchange rate as they ripple through the economy.

When the Bank of Canada sells securities on the open market and decreases the monetary base, the quantity of money decreases, and the interest rate and the exchange rate rise. The higher interest rate decreases consumption expenditure and investment. And the higher exchange rate makes Canadian exports more expensive and imports cheaper. So net exports decrease. Tighter bank credit brings fewer loans, which reinforce the effects of higher interest rates on consumption expenditure and investment.

Similarly, when the Bank of Canada buys securities on the open market and increases the monetary base, the quantity of money increases, and the interest rate and the exchange rate fall. The lower interest rate increases consumption expenditure and investment. And the lower exchange rate makes Canadian exports cheaper and imports more costly. So net exports increase. Easier bank credit brings an expansion of loans, which reinforce the effects of lower interest rates on consumption expenditure and investment.

Figure 28.5 provides a schematic summary of these ripple effects. We're going to look at each stage in the transmission process. But before we do so, and so that we keep our eye on the ultimate objectives of monetary policy, we'll first use the *AD–AS* model and refresh our understanding of how a change in the quantity of money influences real GDP and the price level.

Monetary Policy to Lower Unemployment

Figure 28.6 shows an economy that is experiencing unemployment. Potential GDP is $800 billion, but actual real GDP is only $750 billion, at the intersection of the aggregate demand curve AD_0 and the short-run aggregate supply curve *SAS*. The price level is 105. With a large amount of unemployment,

FIGURE 28.5

The Channels for the Ripple Effects of Monetary Policy

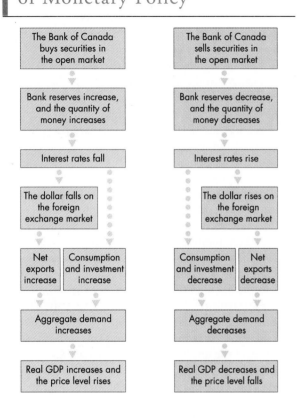

FIGURE 28.6

Monetary Policy to Lower Unemployment

The aggregate demand curve is AD_0 and the short-run aggregate supply curve is SAS. The price level is 105, and real GDP is $750 billion. Long-run aggregate supply is LAS, and the economy is at a below full-employment equilibrium. An increase in the quantity of money shifts the AD curve rightward to AD_1. The price level rises to 110, and real GDP increases to $800 billion. Full employment is restored.

the money wage rate will eventually fall. As a result, the SAS curve will shift rightward, the price level will fall, and real GDP will increase, restoring full employment. But this automatic adjustment process is extremely slow.

To bring the economy to full employment more quickly, the Bank of Canada increases the quantity of money by conducting an open market operation in which it purchases government securities. Flush with excess reserves, banks make loans and the loans create money. With more money in their bank accounts, people increase their expenditure and aggregate demand increases. The aggregate demand curve shifts rightward to become AD_1. The new equilibrium is at the intersection point of AD_1 and SAS. The price level rises to 110 and real GDP increases to $800 billion. The economy is now at full employment.

Monetary Policy to Lower Inflation

Figure 28.7 shows an economy in which real GDP exceeds potential GDP and in which inflation is about to break out. Potential GDP is $800 billion and the long-run aggregate supply curve is LAS. Initially, the short-run aggregate supply curve is SAS_0, and the aggregate demand curve is AD_0. The price level is 115 and real GDP is $850 billion.

If the Bank of Canada does not take action, the money wage rate will begin to rise and the SAS curve will shift leftward to SAS_1. The price will rise to 125, and inflation will occur.

The Bank of Canada can prevent inflation by decreasing the quantity of money. By conducting an open market operation in which it sells securities, the Bank of Canada can decrease the quantity of money and shift the aggregate demand curve leftward to

The economy is at an above full-employment equilibrium. The price level is 115, and real GDP is $850 billion. With no change in aggregate demand, the money wage rate rises and the short-run aggregate supply curve shifts to SAS_1. The price level rises to 125, and inflation occurs. If before the money wage rate rises, the Bank of Canada decreases the quantity of money so that the aggregate demand curve shifts to AD_1, the price level falls to 110 and the economy returns to full employment.

AD_1. If the Bank takes this action before the money wage rate has increased, the new equilibrium is at the intersection point of AD_1 and SAS_0. The price level falls to 110 and real GDP decreases to $800 billion. Inflation is avoided.

Time Lags in the Adjustment Process

To achieve its goal of full employment and the absence of inflation, the Bank of Canada needs a combination of good judgment and good luck. Too large an injection of money into an underemployed economy can bring inflation, as it did during the 1970s. And too large a decrease in the quantity of money in an inflationary economy can create unemployment, as it did in 1991.

The Bank is especially handicapped by the fact that the ripple effects of its policy actions are long drawn out. Also, the economy does not always respond in exactly the same way to policy. Further, many factors other than policy are constantly changing and bringing a new situation for policy to respond to.

We'll look at each stage in the transmission process of monetary policy and see some of the problems that confront the Bank.

Interest Rate Fluctuations

The first effect of monetary policy is a change in the interest rate. This effect occurs quickly and relatively predictably. Figure 28.8 shows the fluctuations in three interest rates: the overnight loans rate, the 3-month Treasury bill rate, and the 10-year government bond rate (which is similar to the rate paid by big

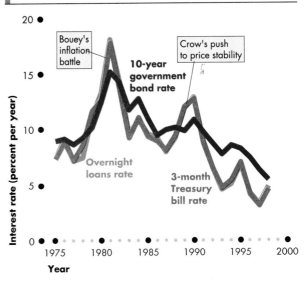

The short-term interest rates—the overnight loans rate and the 3-month Treasury bill rate—move closely together. The 10-year government bond rate moves in the same direction but fluctuates less. The overnight loans rate climbed during the 1970s and peaked at 19 percent a year in 1981. The rate fell during the 1980s, but it increased again to peak at 13 percent a year in 1990. It then fell again through the 1990s.

Source: Statistics Canada, StatCan: CANSIM Disc, March 1999.

corporations). The overnight loans rate is the one that the Bank of Canada targets directly and influences most closely. But notice how closely the 3-month Treasury bill rate follows the overnight loans rate. The 3-month Treasury bill rate is similar to the interest rate paid by Canadian businesses on short-term funds. These are short-term interest rates.

Notice also how the 10-year government bond rate moves with the short-term rates. It does not fluctuate as much as the short-term rates but its direction of change is the same.

Do the Bank of Canada's own actions make interest rates fluctuate? The answer is "yes." Figure 28.9 shows the relationship between the 3-month Treasury bill rate and the monetary base. Over time, the monetary base increases because the economy grows. So what matters for interest rates is not the absolute amount of monetary base, but the amount relative to GDP. The x-axis measures the monetary base as a percentage of GDP. During the 1970s, the Bank decreased the monetary base relative to GDP and interest rates rose. You can see the Bank at work as the movement up the line labelled MB_0. During the 1990s, the Bank increased the monetary base relative to GDP and interest rates fell. You can see the Bank at work as the movement down the line labelled MB_1.

But the relationship between monetary base and interest rates is not completely predictable. During the 1980s, the monetary base decreased relative to GDP and interest rates fell. The normal relationship broke down mainly because of ongoing decreases in the required reserve ratio.

Money Supply Target Versus Interest Rate Target

Because the demand for money fluctuates, the Bank of Canada prefers to target the interest rate rather than the quantity of money. To pursue a target interest rate, the Bank changes the quantity of money supplied in response to changes in the demand for money. If the Bank chose instead to target the quantity of money, the interest rate would fluctuate in response to changes in the demand for money.

Figure 28.10 illustrates the difference between money supply targeting and interest rate targeting. In part (a), the Bank targets the money supply and keeps it at $600 billion with money supply curve MS. The demand for money fluctuates around an average level of MD_A to a high of MD_H and a low of MD_L. As the demand for money fluctuates, so does the interest rate. In this example, the interest rate is 5 percent

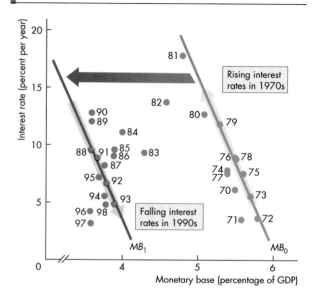

FIGURE 28.9

Monetary Base and the Interest Rate

To increase interest rates during the 1970s, the Bank of Canada decreased the monetary base relative to GDP. To decrease interest rates during the 1990s, the Bank increased the monetary base relative to GDP. During the 1980s, the relationship between the monetary base and the interest rate changed as reserve requirements and other factors changed.

Source: Statistics Canada, *StatCan: CANSIM Disc*, March 1999.

a year on the average but fluctuates between 4 percent when the demand for money is MD_L to 6 percent when the demand for money is MD_H.

In Fig. 28.10(b), the Bank sets an interest rate target. The supply of money is MS_A *on the average.* But the Bank changes the quantity of money when the demand for money changes to hold the interest rate at 5 percent a year. When the demand for money increases to MD_H, the supply of money increases to MS_H. And when the demand for money decreases to MD_L, the supply of money decreases to MS_L.

The decision by the Bank of Canada to target the interest rate does not mean that the Bank has abandoned control of the money supply. The Bank controls the money supply to achieve its interest rate target. If the Bank wants to raise the interest rate, it must decrease the *average* quantity of money by decreasing bank reserves. Short of reserves, banks will

FIGURE 28.10
Money Target Versus Interest Rate Target

(a) Money supply target

(b) Interest rate target

The demand for money fluctuates between MD_L and MD_H and on the average is MD_A. If the Bank of Canada targets the money supply and keeps the quantity of money at MS, the interest rate fluctuates between 4 percent a year and 6 percent a year and averages 5 percent a year (part a). If the Bank targets the interest rate, it must permit the supply of money to fluctuate between MS_L and MS_H and on the average be MS_A. The interest rate is stable at 5 percent a year (part b).

decrease the quantity of loans and bank deposits. And if the Bank wants to lower the interest rate, it must increase the *average* quantity of money by increasing bank reserves. Flush with excess reserves, the banks will increase the quantity of loans and bank deposits.

The Exchange Rate

The exchange rate responds to changes in the interest rate in Canada relative to the interest rates in other countries. But other factors are also at work that make the exchange rate hard to control and even harder to predict. The red line in Fig. 28.11 shows the gap between the Canadian and U.S. short-term

FIGURE 28.11
The Interest Rate and the Dollar

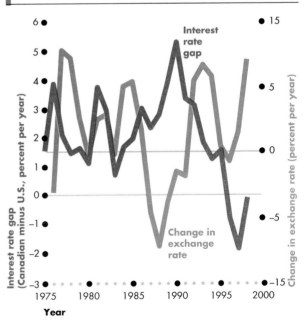

Other things remaining the same, when the gap between Canadian and U.S. short-term interest rates widens, the Canadian dollar rises in value or its value falls less quickly, and when the gap between Canadian and U.S. short-term interest rates narrows, the Canadian dollar falls in value or its value rises less quickly. Most of the time, other things do not remain the same, so the relationship between the interest rate gap and the exchange rate is weak.

Source: Statistics Canada, StatCan: CANSIM Disc, March 1999.

interest rate. And the blue line shows the change in the Canadian dollar against the U.S. dollar. You can see that sometimes when the interest rate gap widens (when Canadian interest rates rise relative to U.S. rates), the Canadian dollar rises or falls less quickly. Also, sometimes, when the interest rate gap narrows (when Canadian interest rates fall relative to U.S. rates), the Canadian dollar falls or rises less quickly. But the relationship between the interest rate gap and the exchange rate is weak. The exchange rate often changes independently of the interest rate gap.

Interest Rates, Aggregate Demand, and Real GDP Fluctuations

You've seen that the Bank of Canada's actions influence interest rates and the exchange rate. And you know that according to the *AS-AD* model, changes in the quantity of money, interest rates, and the exchange rate change aggregate demand and lead to changes in real GDP and the price level. But how powerful are the influences of money on real GDP? And how long does it take for these influences to occur?

Figure 28.12 answers these questions. The blue line in this figure shows the short-term interest rate minus the long-term interest rate. The short-term interest rate is influenced by the Bank of Canada in the way that you studied earlier in this chapter. And changes in the short-term interest rate have some effect on the long-term interest rate. But this effect is small. The long-term interest rate is also influenced by saving and investment plans and by inflation expectations.

The red line in Fig. 28.12 is the real GDP growth rate *one year later*. You can see that when the short-term interest rate rises or the long-term interest rate falls, the real GDP growth rate slows in the following year. The long-term interest rate fluctuates less than the short-term rate, so when the short-term rate rises above the long-term rate, it is because the Bank of Canada has pushed the short-term rate up. And when the short-term rate falls below the long-term rate, it is because the Bank has pushed the short-term rate down. So when the Bank stimulates aggregate demand (pushes the short-term rate down), the GDP growth rate speeds up, and when the Bank lowers aggregate demand (pushes the short-term rate up), the real GDP growth rate slows. The inflation rate also increases and decreases in sympathy with these fluctuations in the real GDP growth rate. But the effects on the inflation rate take even longer.

FIGURE 28.12

Interest Rates and Real GDP Growth

When the short-term interest rate rises relative to the long-term interest rate, the real GDP growth usually slows about one year later. Similarly, when the short-term interest rate falls relative to the long-term interest rate, the real GDP growth rate speeds up about one year later.

Source: Statistics Canada, *StatCan: CANSIM Disc,* March 1999.

R E V I E W   Q U I Z

■ Describe the channels by which monetary policy ripples through the economy and explain why each channel operates.

■ Do interest rates fluctuate in response to the Bank of Canada's actions?

■ What change has occurred in the relationship between the monetary base and the interest rate?

■ How do the Bank of Canada's actions influence the exchange rate?

■ How do the Bank of Canada's actions influence real GDP and how long does it take for real GDP to respond to the Bank's policy actions?

We now look at the Bank of Canada in action.

The Bank of Canada in Action

YOU HAVE NOW LEARNED A GREAT DEAL ABOUT the Bank of Canada, the monetary policy actions it can take, and the effects of those actions on short-term interest rates. But you are possibly thinking: All this sounds nice in theory, but does it really happen? Does the Bank of Canada actually do the things we've learned about in this chapter? Indeed, it does happen, sometimes with dramatic effect. Let's look at two episodes in the life of the Bank of Canada.

Gerald Bouey's Fight Against Inflation

Bank of Canada Governor Gerald Bouey eradicated a near double-digit inflation during the early 1980s. He did so by forcing interest rates sharply upward.

You know that to increase interest rates, the Bank must decrease the quantity of real money. In practice, because the economy is growing and because prices are rising, a slowdown in the growth rate of nominal money is enough to decrease the quantity of real money and increase interest rates.

In 1982, the quantity of money was held in check relative to the demand for money and interest rates increased sharply. The Treasury bill rate increased from 13 percent a year in 1980 to 18 percent a year in 1981. Mortgage rates—the rate at which house buyers borrow—increased to more than 20 percent a year. The economy went into severe recession. Real GDP shrank and the inflation rate slowed.

John Crow and Gordon Thiessen

John Crow became governor of the Bank of Canada on February 1, 1987. Like his predecessor, Crow was a fierce inflation fighter and intent on holding the growth rate of money steady. But in October 1987, he was faced with one of the most severe crises that any central banker can be faced with—a stock market crash. The Bank of Canada, in the company of other central banks around the world, feared the recession potential that might be signalled by the stock market crash. So to avoid any hint of financial tightness that might exacerbate a recessionary situation, the Bank of Canada permitted the quantity of money to grow quickly and short-term interest rates fell.

As the months passed, fears of recession were replaced by fears of a re-emergence of inflation. Seeking to avoid such an event, the Bank of Canada again slowed the growth rate of money, just as Gerald Bouey had done eight years earlier, forcing interest rates upward again. The Bank's operations were targeted towards creating a shortage of bank reserves to slow the growth rate of the money supply. As a consequence, during 1988, the growth rates of all the monetary aggregates were substantially below what they had been in 1987.

The Bank of Canada continued to keep a tight rein on the growth rate of money through 1990 as it increasingly focused on achieving price stability at the cost of a severe recession in 1991.

As the 1990–1991 recession intensified, the Bank eased off the monetary policy brakes and moved interest rates down to unusually low levels. But as the global economic expansion of 1993 and 1994 began, fears of renewed inflation emerged and the Bank pushed interest rates up again.

This move to higher interest rates during 1994 kept inflation in check but at the price of persistently high unemployment.

Gordon Thiessen succeeded John Crow as governor of the Bank of Canada in 1994. Through 1995 and 1996, persistently high unemployment and slow economic growth combined with low inflation encouraged the Bank of Canada to lower interest rates. The lower interest rates eventually (but only modestly) lowered the unemployment rate and speeded real GDP growth. Inflation remained in check.

REVIEW QUIZ

- What was the policy challenge that Gerald Bouey faced and how did he respond to it?
- What was John Crow's first challenge and how did he respond to it?
- What were the challenges that faced Gordon Thiessen during the 1990s, and how did he respond to them?

◈ In the next chapter, we're going to learn how monetary policy and fiscal policy interact. But first, take a look at *Reading Between the Lines* on pages 638–639, which examines the Bank of Canada in action during 1999.

Monetary Policy in Action

THE GLOBE AND MAIL, MAY 5, 1999

Bank of Canada trims rates; to boost 1999 growth forecast

Canada's low inflation and stable financial markets paved the way for the Bank of Canada to trim interest rates yesterday by one-quarter of a percentage point and to boost its growth forecast for this year.

At a speech in Sherbrooke, Que., Bank of Canada Governor Gordon Thiessen painted an upbeat picture of an improving economy, with robust job growth and a more accommodative monetary policy setting the stage for stronger consumer and investment spending.

Mr. Thiessen said the bank will release a more optimistic outlook in its monetary policy report on May 19; its previous forecast called for growth of 2.25 to 3.25 per cent this year.

"It's great to be able to influence your own forecast," said Peter Drake, deputy chief economist at Toronto-Dominion Bank. "By lowering interest rates, the bank is increasing the amount of growth that will take place."

The latest rate reduction lowered the bank rate to 4.75 per cent, triggering a quarter-point cut in the prime lending rate to 6.25 per cent, the lowest since January of 1998.

Prime is the rate chartered banks charge for loans to their most credit-worthy customers, and is the benchmark for most consumer and business lending rates. Some banks lowered short-term mortgage rates tied to prime.

Mr. Thiessen said the bank made the cut to ensure that inflation is "comfortably" within the target band of 1 to 3 per cent looking ahead to 2000. ...

The central bank's announcement made no mention of the sharp appreciation in the Canadian dollar, which has risen by 3 cents since the last rate cut on March 31, Mr. Drake said. Such a sharp rise has the same effect on the economy as a one-percentage-point increase in interest rates. ...

Essence of the Story

■ The Bank of Canada lowered the bank rate in May 1999 and major banks followed by lowering the prime rate.

■ The bank rate in May 1999 was the lowest since January 1998.

■ Gordon Thiessen, governor of the Bank of Canada, said that the cut in the interest rate was made to keep annual inflation between 1 and 3 percent.

■ One economist said that the 3-cent rise in the Canadian dollar exchange rate between March 31, 1999, and May 5, 1999, has the same effect on the economy as a 1-percentage-point rise in interest rates.

■ The Bank of Canada cut interest rates to boost its growth forecast.

Economic Analysis

■ Figure I shows the state of the economy in 1998. Real GDP was $838 billion (1992 dollars) and the price level was 107, at the intersection of the aggregate demand curve AD_{98} and the short-run aggregate supply curve SAS_{98}.

■ No one knows for sure what potential GDP was in 1998, but it was probably greater than actual GDP. The long-run aggregate supply curve LAS_{98} is based on the *assumption* that potential GDP was $850 billion and the *recessionary* gap in 1998 was $12 billion.

■ The Bank of Canada tries to keep the inflation rate between 1 and 3 percent a year.

■ The Bank of Canada also wants to avoid low real GDP growth.

■ Faced with negative inflation, the Bank of Canada took actions to lower interest rates. Figure 2 shows these actions. The bank increased the quantity of real M2+ from $589 billion at the beginning of 1998 to $603 billion in mid-1999.

■ This increase in the real quantity of money brought lower interest rates. And lower interest rates boost spending.

■ No one knows by how much spending increases when the interest rate falls. Figure 3 shows the hoped-for effect.

■ If the fall in interest rates results in the aggregate demand curve shifting rightward from AD_{98} to AD_{99}, then the recessionary gap will be eliminated, real GDP will grow by 3.5 percent, and the inflation rate will be 2 percent a year.

■ In the news article, economist Peter Drake says that a rise of 3 cents in the Canadian dollar exchange rate is equivalent in effect to a 1 percentage point rise in interest rates.

■ If this statement is correct, then the fall in the bank rate from 5.00 percent to 4.75 percent a year would not be enough to counter the effect of the change in the exchange rate.

■ The news article implies that the Bank of Canada can cut the interest rate and increase the real GDP growth rate.

■ But the time lags in the operation of monetary policy make it very unlikely that growth in 1999 will be influenced by an interest rate cut in May 1999.

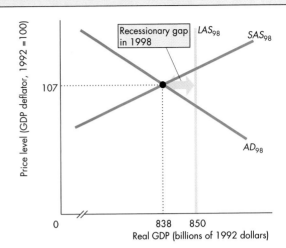

Figure 1 The economy in 1998

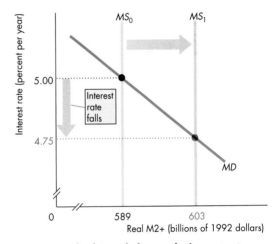

Figure 2 Bank of Canada lowers the interest rate

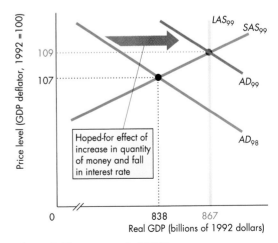

Figure 3 The economy in 1999?

SUMMARY

Key Points

The Bank of Canada (pp. 622–626)

- The Bank of Canada is the central bank of Canada.
- The Bank of Canada's goals are to achieve low inflation and, as far as possible, moderate the business cycle.
- The Bank of Canada influences the economy by setting the required reserve ratio for banks, by setting the bank rate and the bankers' deposit rate, by open market operations, and by government deposit shifting.

Controlling the Money Supply (pp. 627–631)

- By buying government securities in the open market (an open market purchase), the Bank of Canada is able to increase the monetary base and the reserves available to banks.
- The increase in bank reserves leads to an expansion of bank lending and the quantity of money increases.
- By selling government securities in the open market, the Bank of Canada is able to decrease the monetary base and bank reserves and decrease the quantity of money.

Ripple Effects of Monetary Policy (pp. 631–636)

- An increase in the quantity of money lowers the interest rate and the exchange rate, increases aggregate demand, and eventually increases real GDP and the price level.
- An increase in the quantity of money can fight unemployment and a decrease in the quantity of money can fight inflation.
- The Bank of Canada targets the short-term interest rate, but to change the interest rate, the Bank must change the quantity of money.
- Changes in the short-term interest rate change real GDP about one year later and change the inflation rate with an even longer time lag.

The Bank of Canada in Action (p. 637)

- Since the early 1980s the Bank of Canada has been fighting inflation.
- Under Governor Gerald Bouey, the Bank increased the interest rate to a record level in 1981 and lowered the inflation rate but at the cost of a severe recession.
- Under Governor John Crow, the Bank increased the interest rate during the early 1990s and almost eliminated inflation but again at the cost of a severe recession.
- During the mid-1990s, the Bank of Canada lowered the interest rate and stimulated the economy.

Key Figures

Key Terms

P R O B L E M S

⌨ *1. You are given the following information about the economy of Nocoin: The banks have deposits of $300 billion. Their reserves are $15 billion, two-thirds of which is in deposits with the central bank. There are $30 billion notes outside the banks. There are no coins!
   a. Calculate the monetary base.
   b. Calculate the quantity of money.
   c. Calculate the banks' reserve ratio.
   d. Calculate the currency drain as a percentage of the quantity of money.

2. You are given the following information about the economy of Freezone: The people and businesses in Freezone have bank deposits of $500 billion and hold $100 billion in notes and coin. The banks hold deposits at the Freezone central bank of $5 billion and they keep $5 billion in notes and coin in their vaults and ATM machines.
   a. Calculate the monetary base.
   b. Calculate the quantity of money.
   c. Calculate the banks' reserve ratio.
   d. Calculate the currency drain as a percentage of the quantity of money.

⌨ *3. In problem 1, suppose that the Bank of Nocoin, the central bank, undertakes an open market purchase of securities of $1 billion. What happens to the money supply? Explain why the change in the money supply is not equal to the change in the monetary base.

4. In problem 2, suppose that the Freezone central bank undertakes an open market sale of securities of $1 billion. What happens to the money supply? Explain why the change in the money supply is not equal to the change in the monetary base.

*5. The figure shows the economy of Freezone. The aggregate demand curve is *AD* and the short-run aggregate supply curve is *SAS_A*. Potential GDP is $300 billion.
   a. What is the price level and real GDP in Freezone?
   b. Does Freezone have an unemployment problem or an inflation problem? Why?
   c. What do you predict will happen in Freezone if the central bank takes no monetary policy actions?

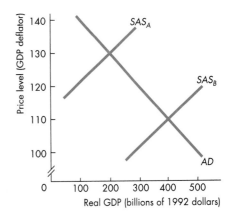

   d. What monetary policy action would you advise the central bank to take and what do you predict the effect of that action will be?

6. In Freezone, shown in the figure in problem 5, the aggregate demand curve is *AD* and potential GDP is $300 billion but the short-run aggregate supply curve is *SAS_B*.
   a. What is the price level and real GDP in Freezone?
   b. Does Freezone have an unemployment problem or an inflation problem? Why?
   c. What do you predict will happen in Freezone if the central bank takes no monetary policy actions?
   d. What monetary policy action would you advise the central bank to take and what do you predict the effect of that action will be?

*7. Suppose that in Freezone in problem 5, the short-run aggregate supply curve increases to *SAS_B* and potential GDP increases to $350 billion.
   a. What happens in Freezone if the central bank buys securities on the open market?
   b. What happens in Freezone if the central bank sells securities on the open market?
   c. Do you recommend that the central bank buy securities or sell securities? Why?

8. Suppose that in Freezone in problem 6, the short-run aggregate supply curve decreases to *SAS_A* and a drought decreases potential GDP to $250 billion.
   a. What happens in Freezone if the central bank buys securities on the open market?
   b. What happens in Freezone if the central bank sells securities on the open market?

c. Do you recommend that the central bank buy securities or sell securities? Why?

*9. For a given real GDP, the demand for money in Minland fluctuates between MD_B and MD_C and on the average is MD_A.

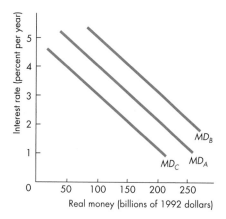

If the Bank of Minland (the central bank) fixes the quantity of money at $150 billion,

a. What is the interest rate in Minland on the average?

b. What is the range of interest rates in Minland?

c. What do you expect to happen to aggregate demand, real GDP, and the price level, when the demand for money changes but the quantity of money remains fixed?

10. In Minland, in problem 9, if the central bank pegs the interest rate at 3 percent a year,

a. How does the Bank of Minland prevent the interest rate from rising when the demand for money increases to MD_B?

b. How does the Bank of Minland prevent the interest rate from falling when the demand for money decreases to MD_C?

c. Suppose that potential GDP decreases in Minland. Do you think that the Bank of Minland will maintain the 3 percent a year interest rate target? If not, do you think the Bank will try to raise the interest rate or lower it? What actions would the Bank have to take to change the interest rate?

d. If inflation breaks out in Minland, do you think that the Bank of Minland will maintain its interest rate target?

CRITICAL THINKING

1. Study *Reading Between the Lines* on pp. 638–639 and then answer the following questions:

a. Why did the Bank of Canada cut the interest rate in May 1999?

b. What does the Bank of Canada look at when it is deciding whether to change interest rates?

c. What are the risks from the Bank of Canada lowering interest rates and from not lowering interest rates? Which is the more risky in your opinion and why?

d. When the Bank of Canada lowers the interest rate, what actions does it take?

2. Could the Bank of Canada have brought inflation under control during the early 1990s without creating a recession? If you think the answer is "no," do you think it was wise to lower inflation? If you think the answer is "yes," what would the Bank of Canada have had to do differently?

3. Use the link on the Parkin-Bade Web site to visit the Web site of the Bank of Canada and obtain the latest data on M1, M2+, and some short-term interest rates. Then answer the following questions.

a. Is the Bank of Canada trying to slow the economy or speed it up? How can you tell which?

b. What open market operations do you think the Bank of Canada has undertaken during the past month?

c. In the light of the Bank of Canada's recent actions, what ripple effects do you expect over the coming months?

d. What do you think the effects of the Bank of Canada's recent actions will be on bond prices and stock prices?

4. Use the link on the Parkin-Bade Web site to visit the Web site of Statistics Canada and look at the current economic conditions. On the basis of the current state of the Canadian economy, do you predict that the Bank of Canada will raise interest rates, lower interest rates, or hold interest rates steady? Write a brief summary of your predictions and reasons.

Fiscal and Monetary Interactions

In 1998, the federal Parliament and provincial and local legislatures approved budgets that put tax revenues and outlays at more than $400 billion—close to one-half of GDP. Not far from Parliament Hill, on Sparks Street, the Bank of Canada pulls the nation's monetary policy levers that influence interest rates and the exchange rate. How does the government's fiscal policy interact with the Bank of Canada's monetary policy to influence interest rates, the exchange rate, and real GDP?

Sparks Fly in Ottawa

◆ Sometimes, fiscal policy and monetary policy are in harmony with each other. At other times, they come into conflict—creating sparks on Sparks Street! Do fiscal and monetary policies need to be coordinated? Are they equivalent to each other? ◆ If a recession is looming on the horizon, is an interest rate cut by the Bank of Canada just as good as a tax cut by Parliament? Or is one of these actions likely to have more desirable effects than the other? ◆ If the economy is overheating, is an interest rate hike by the Bank of Canada just as good as a tax increase by Parliament? Or again, is one of these actions likely to have more desirable effects than the other? ◆ When the government has a large budget deficit, must interest rates rise? Can the Bank of Canada simply give the government some newly created money so that it can increase spending without putting stress on capital markets and raising interest rates?

◇ We are going to answer these questions in this chapter. You already know a lot about the effects of fiscal policy and monetary policy. And you know that their ultimate effects work through their influences on both aggregate demand and aggregate supply. This chapter gives you a deeper understanding of the aggregate demand side of the economy and how the combined actions of the federal government and the Bank of Canada affect aggregate demand.

After studying this chapter, you will be able to:

- Explain how fiscal policy and monetary policy interact to influence interest rates and aggregate demand

- Explain the relative effectiveness of fiscal policy and monetary policy

- Describe the Keynesian–monetarist controversy about policy and explain how the controversy was settled

- Explain fiscal and monetary policies at full employment

- Explain how fiscal and monetary policy influence real GDP and the price level

Macroeconomic Equilibrium

OUR GOAL IN THIS CHAPTER IS TO LEARN HOW changes in government expenditure and changes in the quantity of money interact to change real GDP, the price level, and the interest rate. But before we study the effects of *changes* in these policy variables, we must describe the state of the economy with a given level of government expenditure and a given quantity of money.

The Basic Idea

Aggregate demand and short-run aggregate supply determine real GDP and the price level. And the demand for and supply of real money determine the interest rate. But aggregate demand and the money market are linked together.

Other things remaining the same, the greater the level of aggregate demand, the higher are real GDP and the price level. A higher real GDP means a greater demand for money; a higher price level means a smaller supply of real money; so a greater level of aggregate demand means a higher interest rate.

And aggregate demand depends on the interest rate. The reason is that consumption expenditure, investment, and net exports are influenced by the interest rate (see Chapter 27, pp. 613-615). So, other things remaining the same, the lower the interest rate, the greater is aggregate demand.

Only one level of aggregate demand and one interest rate are consistent with each other in macro-economic equilibrium. Figure 29.1 describes this unique equilibrium.

AS–AD Equilibrium

In Fig. 29.1(a) the intersection of the aggregate demand curve, *AD*, and the short-run aggregate supply curve, *SAS*, determines real GDP at $800 billion and the price level at 110.

The equilibrium amounts of consumption expenditure, investment, government expenditures, and net exports lie behind the *AD* curve. But some components of these expenditures are influenced by the interest rate. And the interest rate, in turn, is determined by equilibrium in the money market. Assume that interest-sensitive expenditures total $100 billion, government expenditure is $100 billion, and the rest of real GDP totals $600 billion.

Money Market Equilibrium and Interest-Sensitive Expenditure

In Fig. 29.1(b) the intersection of the demand for money curve, *MD*, and the supply of money curve, *MS*, determines the interest rate at 5 percent a year.

The position of the *MD* curve depends on the level of real GDP. Suppose that the demand for money curve shown in the figure describes the demand for money when real GDP is $800 billion, which is equilibrium real GDP in Fig. 29.1(a).

The position of the *MS* curve depends on the quantity of nominal money and the price level. Suppose that the supply of money curve shown in the figure describes the supply of real money when the price level is 110, which is the equilibrium price level in Fig. 29.1(a).

In Fig. 29.1(c), the *IE* curve determines the level of interest-sensitive expenditure at the equilibrium interest rate of 5 percent a year. Interest-sensitive expenditure is $100 billion, which is the level of this expenditure that lies behind the aggregate demand curve *AD* in Fig. 29.1(a).

Check the Equilibrium

The *AS–AD* equilibrium in Fig. 29.1(a), the money market equilibrium in Fig. 29.1(b), and interest-sensitive expenditure in Fig. 29.1(c) are consistent with each other. And there is no other equilibrium.

To check this claim, assume that aggregate demand is less than *AD* in Fig. 29.1(a) so that real GDP is less than $800 billion. If this assumption is correct, the demand for money curve lies to the left of *MD* in Fig. 29.1(b) and the equilibrium interest rate is less than 5 percent a year. With an interest rate less than 5 percent a year, interest-sensitive expenditure exceeds the $100 billion in Fig. 29.1(c). If interest-sensitive expenditure exceeds $100 billion, the *AD* curve lies to the right of the one we assumed and equilibrium real GDP exceeds $800 billion. Thus if we assume a real GDP of less than $800 billion, equilibrium real GDP is greater than $800 billion. There is an inconsistency. The assumed equilibrium real GDP is too small.

Now assume that aggregate demand is greater than *AD* in Fig. 29.1(a) so that real GDP exceeds $800 billion. If this assumption is correct, the demand for money curve lies to the right of *MD* in Fig. 29.1(b) and the equilibrium interest rate exceeds 5 percent a year. With an interest rate above

FIGURE 29.1

Equilibrium Real GDP, Price Level, Interest Rate, and Expenditure

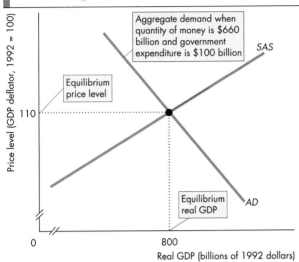

(a) Aggregate supply and aggregate demand

In part (a), the intersection of the aggregate demand curve, *AD*, and the short-run aggregate supply curve, *SAS*, determines real GDP at $800 billion and the price level at 110. Behind the *AD* curve, interest-sensitive expenditure is $100 billion, government expenditure is $100 billion, and the rest of real GDP is $600 billion. In part (b), when real GDP is $800 billion, the demand for money is *MD* and when the price level is 110, the supply of (real) money is *MS*. The intersection of the demand for money curve, *MD*, and the supply of money curve, *MS*, determines the interest rate at 5 percent a year. In part (c), on the *IE* curve, interest-sensitive expenditure is $100 billion at the equilibrium interest rate of 5 percent a year.

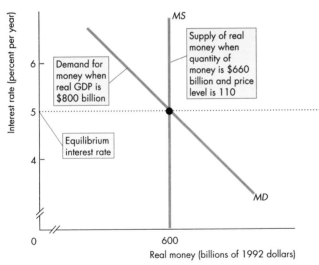

(b) Money and the interest rate

(c) Expenditure and the interest rate

5 percent a year, interest-sensitive expenditure is less than the $100 billion in Fig. 29.1(c), in which case the *AD* curve must lie to the left of the one we assumed and equilibrium real GDP must be smaller than $800 billion. Thus if we assume that real GDP exceeds $800 billion, equilibrium real GDP is less than $800 billion. There is another inconsistency. The assumed equilibrium real GDP is too large.

Only one level of aggregate demand delivers the same money market equilibrium and *AS–AD* equili-

brium. In this example, it is the aggregate demand curve *AD* in Fig. 29.1(a). Assuming this level of aggregate demand implies this level of aggregate demand. Assuming a lower level of aggregate demand implies a higher level. And assuming a higher level of aggregate demand implies a lower level.

Now that you understand how aggregate demand and the interest rate are simultaneously determined, let's study the effects of a change in government expenditures.

Fiscal Policy in the Short Run

REAL GDP GROWTH IS SLOWING, AND THE
Finance Minister is concerned that a recession is
likely. So the government decides to try to head off
the recession by using fiscal policy to stimulate aggregate demand. A fiscal policy that increases aggregate
demand is called an *expansionary fiscal policy*.

The effects of an expansionary fiscal policy are
similar to those of throwing a pebble into a pond.
There's an initial splash followed by a series of ripples
that become ever smaller. The initial splash is the
"first round effect" of the fiscal policy action. The
ripples are the "second round effects." You've already
met the first round effects in Chapter 26, so here is a
refresher.

First Round Effects of Fiscal Policy

The economy starts out in the position shown in
Fig. 29.1. Real GDP is $800 billion, the price level is
110, the interest rate is 5 percent a year, and interest-
sensitive expenditure is $100 billion. The govern-
ment now increases its expenditures on goods and
services by $100 billion.

Figure 29.2 shows the first round effects of this
action. The increase in government expenditures has a
multiplier effect because it induces an increase in consumption expenditure. (You can refresh your memory
about the government expenditures multiplier on
pp. 578-583.) Let's assume that the multiplier is 2, so
a $100 billion increase in government expenditure
increases aggregate demand at a given price level by
$200 billion. The aggregate demand curve shifts
rightward from AD_0 to AD_1. At a price level of 110,
the quantity of real GDP demanded increases from
$800 billion to $1,000 billion.

Real GDP now starts to increase and the price
level starts to rise. These are the first round effects of
expansionary fiscal policy.

Second Round Effects of Fiscal Policy

Through the second round, real GDP increases and
the price level rises until a new macroeconomic equilibrium is reached. But to find that equilibrium and
to describe the changes that result from the initial

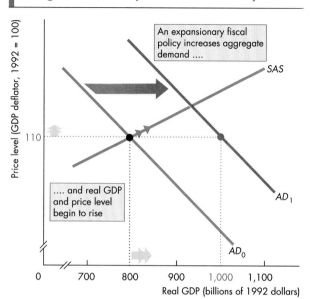

FIGURE 29.2

First Round Effects of an Expansionary Fiscal Policy

Initially, the aggregate demand curve is AD_0, real GDP is
$800 billion, and the price level is 110. A $100 billion increase
in government expenditures on goods and services has a multiplier effect and increases aggregate demand by $200 billion.
The aggregate demand curve shifts rightward to AD_1. Real GDP
begins to increase and the price level begins to rise. These are
the first round effects of an expansionary fiscal policy.

increase in government expenditures, we must keep
track of further changes in the money market and in
expenditure plans.

It is easier to keep track of the second round
effects if we split them into two parts, one that results
from the increasing real GDP and the other that
results from the rising price level. We follow these
effects in Fig. 29.3.

First, the increasing real GDP increases the
demand for money. In Fig. 29.3(b), the demand for
money curve shifts rightward. Eventually, it shifts to
MD_1 and the interest rate rises to 6 percent a year. At
this interest rate, interest-sensitive expenditure
decreases to $75 billion in Fig. 29.3(c). The decrease
in planned expenditure decreases aggregate demand
and the aggregate demand curve shifts leftward from
AD_1 to AD_2 in Fig. 29.3(a).

FIGURE 29.3
Second Round Effects of an Expansionary Fiscal Policy

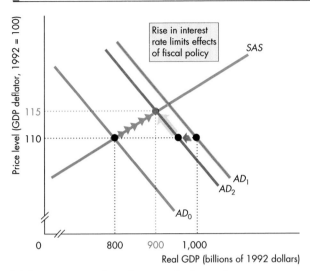

(a) Aggregate supply and aggregate demand

Initially, (part b) the demand curve for money is MD_0, the supply of real money is MS_0, and the interest rate is 5 percent a year. With an interest rate of 5 percent a year, interest-sensitive expenditure is \$100 billion on the curve IE (part c). With the increased level of government expenditures, the aggregate demand curve is AD_1 (part a). Real GDP is increasing, and the price level is rising. The increasing real GDP increases the demand for money and the demand for money curve shifts rightward to MD_1. The higher interest rate decreases interest-sensitive expenditure, which decreases aggregate demand to AD_2. The rising price level brings a movement along the new AD curve. It does so because it decreases the supply of real money to MS_1, which in turn raises the interest rate further and decreases expenditure. The new equilibrium occurs when real GDP has increased to \$900 billion and the price level has risen to 115.

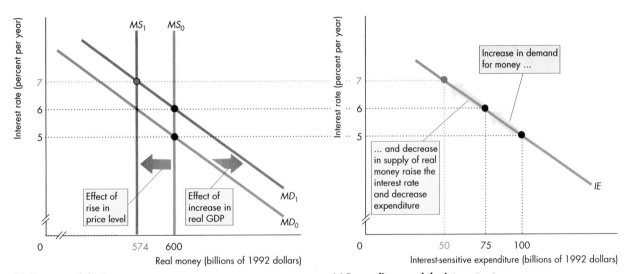

(b) Money and the interest rate

(c) Expenditure and the interest rate

Second, with a given quantity of nominal money, the rising price level decreases the quantity of real money. In Fig. 29.3(b), the money supply curve shifts leftward to MS_1. The decrease in the quantity of real money raises the interest rate further to 7 percent a year. In Fig. 29.3(c), the higher interest rate decreases interest-sensitive expenditure to \$50 billion. Because this decrease in spending plans is induced by a rise in the price level, it decreases the quantity of real GDP

demanded and is shown as a movement along the aggregate demand curve AD_2 in Fig. 29.3(a).

During this second round process, real GDP is increasing and the price level is rising in a gradual movement up along the short-run aggregate supply curve as indicated by the arrows. In the new equilibrium, real GDP is \$900 billion, the price level is 115, the interest rate is 7 percent a year, and interest-sensitive expenditure is \$50 billion.

FIGURE 29.4
How the Economy Adjusts to an Expansionary Fiscal Policy

(a) First round effect of expansionary fiscal policy

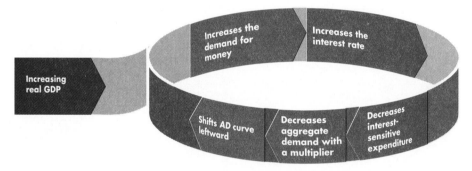

(b) Second round real GDP effect

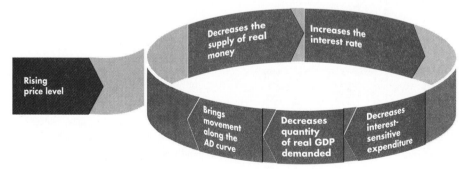

(c) Second round price level effect

Just as the initial equilibrium in Fig. 29.1 was consistent, so the new equilibrium is consistent. The *AS–AD* equilibrium in Fig. 29.3(a), the money market equilibrium in Fig. 29.3(b), and interest-sensitive expenditure in Fig. 29.3(c) are all consis-tent with each other. And there is no other equilib-rium.

Figure 29.4 summarizes the first round and the two parts of the second round adjustments as the economy responds to an expansionary fiscal action.

Other Fiscal Policies

A change in government expenditures is only one possible fiscal policy action. Others are a change in transfer payments, such as an increase in unemployment compensation or an increase in social benefits and a change in taxes. All fiscal policy actions work by changing expenditure. But the magnitude of the initial change in expenditure differs for different fiscal actions. For example, changes in taxes and transfer payments change expenditure by smaller amounts than does a change in government expenditures on goods and services. But fiscal policies that change autonomous expenditure by a given amount and in a given direction have similar effects on equilibrium real GDP, the price level, and the interest rate regardless of the initial fiscal action. Let's take a closer look at the effect of the rise in the interest rate.

Crowding Out and Crowding In

Because an expansionary fiscal policy increases the interest rate, it decreases all the interest-sensitive components of aggregate expenditure. One of these components is investment and the decrease in investment that results from an expansionary fiscal action is called **crowding out**.

Crowding out may be partial or complete. Partial crowding out occurs when the decrease in investment is less than the increase in government expenditures. This is the normal case—and the case we've just seen.

Complete crowding out occurs if the decrease in investment equals the initial increase in government expenditures. For complete crowding out to occur, a small change in the demand for real money must lead to a large change in the interest rate, and the change in the interest rate must lead to a large change in investment.

But another potential influence of government expenditures on investment works in the opposite direction to the crowding-out effect and is called "crowding in." **Crowding in** is the tendency for expansionary fiscal policy to *increase* investment. This effect works in three ways.

First, in a recession, an expansionary fiscal policy might create expectations of a more speedy recovery and bring an increase in expected profits. Higher expected profits might increase investment despite a higher interest rate.

Second, government expenditures might be productive and lead to more profitable business opportu-

nities. For example, a new government-built highway might cut the cost of transporting a farmer's produce to a market and induce the farmer to invest in a new fleet of refrigerated trucks.

Third, if an expansionary fiscal policy takes the form of a cut in taxes on business profits, firms' after-tax profits increase and investment might increase.

The Exchange Rate and International Crowding Out

We've seen that an expansionary fiscal policy leads to higher interest rates. But a change in interest rates also affects the exchange rate. Higher interest rates make the dollar rise in value against other currencies. With interest rates higher in Canada than in the rest of the world, funds flow into Canada and people around the world demand more Canadian dollars. As the dollar rises in value, foreigners find Canadian-produced goods and services more expensive and Canadians find imports less expensive. Exports decrease and imports increase—net exports decrease. The tendency for an expansionary fiscal policy to decrease net exports is called **international crowding out**. The decrease in net exports offsets, to some degree, the initial increase in aggregate expenditure brought about by an expansionary fiscal policy.

REVIEW QUIZ

- Describe macroeconomic equilibrium. What conditions are met in such an equilibrium? What are the links between aggregate demand, the money market, and investment?
- What is an expansionary fiscal policy and what are its first round effects? What is happening at the end of the first round?
- What are the second round effects of an expansionary fiscal policy action? Describe the forces at work and the changes that occur in the interest rate, investment, real GDP, and the price level.
- What is crowding out? What is crowding in? How do they influence the outcome of a fiscal policy action?
- How does an expansionary fiscal policy affect the exchange rate? What happens to imports and exports?

Monetary Policy in the Short Run

TO STUDY THE EFFECTS OF AN EXPANSIONARY monetary policy, we look at the first round effects and the second round effects, just as we did for fiscal policy. Figure 29.5 describes the economy, which is initially in the situation that we studied in Fig. 29.1. The quantity of money is $660 billion, the interest rate is 5 percent a year, interest-sensitive expenditure is $100 billion, real GDP is $800 billion, and the price level is 110.

The Bank of Canada now increases the money supply so that the quantity of money increases to $1,155 billion. With a price level of 110, the quantity of real money increases to $1,050 billion. Figure 29.5(a) shows the immediate effect. The real money supply curve shifts rightward from MS_0 to MS_1, and the interest rate falls from 5 percent to 1 percent a year. The lower interest rate increases interest-sensitive

---

FIGURE **29.5**

First Round Effects of an Expansionary Monetary Policy

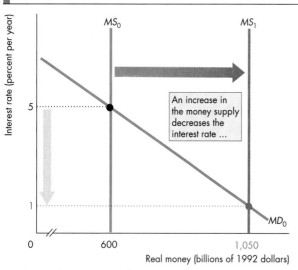

(a) Change in money supply

(b) Change in expenditure

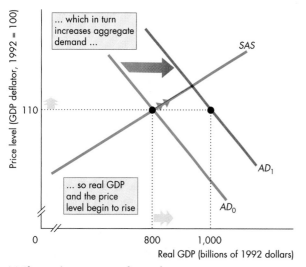

(c) Change in aggregate demand

Initially, the demand curve for real money is MD_0, the real money supply is MS_0, and the interest rate is 5 percent a year (part a). With an interest rate of 5 percent a year, interest-sensitive expenditure is $100 billion on the IE curve (part b). The aggregate demand curve is AD_0 and equilibrium real GDP $800 billion and the price level is 110 (part c). An increase in the quantity of money shifts the money supply curve rightward to MS_1 (part a). The increased money supply lowers the interest rate to 1 percent a year and interest-sensitive expenditure increases to $200 billion (part b). The increase in expenditure increases aggregate demand to AD_1 (in part c). Real GDP begins to increase and the price level begins to rise.

expenditure to $200 billion (part b). The increase in interest-sensitive expenditure increases aggregate demand and shifts the AD curve rightward from AD_0 to AD_1 (part c). The increase in aggregate demand sets off a multiplier process in which real GDP and the price level begin to increase towards their equilibrium levels.

These are the first round effects of an expansionary monetary policy. An increase in the money supply lowers the interest rate and increases aggregate demand. Real GDP and the price level begin to increase.

Let's now look at the second round effects.

Second Round Effects

The increasing real GDP and rising price level set off the second round, which Fig. 29.6(b) illustrates. And as in the case of fiscal policy, it is best to break the second round into two parts: the consequence of increasing real GDP and the consequence of the rising price level.

FIGURE 29.6

Second Round Effects of an Expansionary Monetary Policy

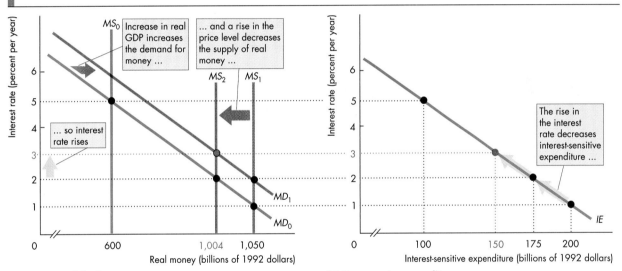

(a) Money and the interest rate

(b) Decrease in expenditure

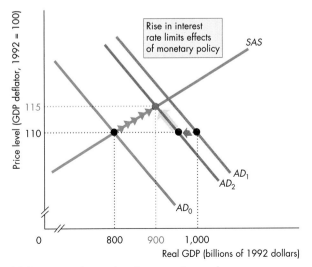

(c) Aggregate demand and aggregate supply

At the start of the second round, the demand curve for money is still MD_0 (part a), the supply of real money is MS_1, and the interest rate is 1 percent a year. With an interest rate of 1 percent a year, interest-sensitive expenditure is $200 billion on the curve IE (part b). With the increased quantity of money and expenditure level, the aggregate demand curve is AD_1 (part c). Real GDP is increasing, and the price level is rising. The increasing real GDP increases the demand for money and the demand for money curve shifts rightward to MD_1. The higher interest rate decreases interest-sensitive expenditure, which decreases aggregate demand to AD_2. The rising price level brings a movement along the new AD curve. It does so because the rising price level decreases the supply of real money to MS_2, which in turn raises the interest rate further and decreases expenditure. The new equilibrium occurs when real GDP has increased to $900 billion and the price level has risen to 115.

The increasing real GDP increases the demand for money from MD_0 to MD_1 in Fig. 29.6(a). The increased demand for money raises the interest rate to 2 percent a year. The higher interest rate brings a decrease in interest-sensitive expenditure from $200 billion to $175 billion in Fig. 29.6(b). And the lower level of expenditure decreases aggregate demand and shifts the aggregate demand curve leftward from AD_1 to AD_2 in Fig. 29.6(c).

The rising price level brings a movement along the new aggregate demand curve in Fig. 29.6(c). This movement occurs because the rising price level decreases the real money supply. As the price level rises, the real money supply decreases to $1,004 billion and the money supply curve shifts leftward from MS_1 to MS_2 (part a). The interest rate rises further to 3 percent a year. And interest-sensitive expenditure decreases to $150 billion (part b).

FIGURE 29.7

How the Economy Adjusts to an Expansionary Monetary Policy

(a) First round effect of expansionary monetary policy

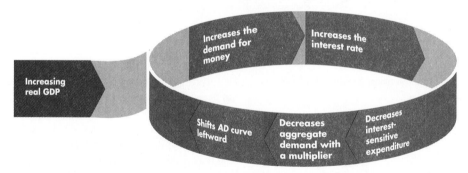

(b) Second round real GDP effect

(c) Second round price level effect

In the new short-run equilibrium, real GDP has increased to $900 billion, and the price level has risen to 115, where aggregate demand curve AD_2 intersects the short-run aggregate supply curve SAS.

The demand for money is MD_1, the supply of (real) money is MS_2, and the interest rate is 3 percent a year in part (a). With an interest rate of 3 percent a year, interest-sensitive expenditure is $150 billion (part b).

The new equilibrium is the only consistent one and is like that of Fig. 29.1. Figure 29.7 summarizes the adjustments that occur to bring the economy to this new equilibrium.

Money and the Exchange Rate

An increase in the money supply lowers the interest rate. If the interest rate falls in Canada but does not fall in the United States, Japan, and Western Europe, international investors buy the now higher yielding foreign assets and sell the relatively lower yielding Canadian assets. As they make these transactions, they sell Canadian dollars. So the dollar depreciates against other currencies. (This mechanism is explained in greater detail in Chapter 28, pp. 635–636.)

As the Canadian dollar depreciates, foreigners face lower prices for Canadian-produced goods and services and Canadians face higher prices for foreign-produced goods and services. Foreigners increase their imports from Canada, and Canadians decrease their imports from the rest of the world. Canadian net exports increase, and real GDP and the price level increase further.

R E V I E W   Q U I Z

- What are the first round effects of an expansionary monetary policy? What happens to the interest rate, interest-sensitive expenditure, aggregate demand, the demand for money, real GDP, and the price level in the first round?
- What are the second round effects of an expansionary monetary policy? What happens to the interest rate, interest-sensitive expenditure, aggregate demand, the demand for money, real GDP, and the price level in the second round?
- How does an expansionary monetary policy influence the exchange rate, imports, and exports?

Relative Effectiveness of Policies

WE'VE SEEN THAT AGGREGATE DEMAND AND REAL GDP are influenced by both fiscal and monetary policy. But which policy is the more potent? This question was once at the centre of a controversy among macroeconomists. Later in this section we'll look at that controversy and see how it was settled. But we begin by discovering what determines the effectiveness of fiscal policy.

Effectiveness of Fiscal Policy

The effectiveness of fiscal policy is measured by the magnitude of the increase in aggregate demand that results from a given increase in government expenditures (or decrease in taxes). The effectiveness of fiscal policy depends on the strength of the crowding-out effect. Fiscal policy is most powerful if no crowding out occurs. Fiscal policy is impotent if there is complete crowding out. And the strength of the crowding-out effect depends on two things:

- The responsiveness of expenditure to the interest rate
- The responsiveness of the quantity of money demanded to the interest rate

If expenditure is not very responsive to a change in the interest rate, the crowding-out effect is small. But if expenditure is highly responsive to a change in the interest rate, the crowding-out effect is large. Other things remaining the same, the smaller the responsiveness of expenditure to the interest rate, the smaller is the crowding-out effect and the more effective is fiscal policy.

The responsiveness of the quantity of money demanded to the interest rate also affects the size of the crowding-out effect. An increase in real GDP increases the demand for money and with no change in the supply of money, the interest rate rises. But the extent to which the interest rate rises depends on the responsiveness of the quantity of money demanded to the interest rate. Other things remaining the same, the greater the responsiveness of the quantity of money demanded to the interest rate, the smaller is the rise in the interest rate, the smaller is the crowding-out effect and the more effective is fiscal policy.

Effectiveness of Monetary Policy

The effectiveness of monetary policy is measured by the magnitude of the increase in aggregate demand that results from a given increase in the money supply. The effectiveness of monetary policy depends on the same two factors that influence the effectiveness of fiscal policy:

■ The responsiveness of the quantity of money demanded to the interest rate
■ The responsiveness of expenditure to the interest rate

The starting point for monetary policy is a change in the quantity of money that changes the interest rate. A given change in the quantity of money might bring a small change or a large change in the interest rate. The less responsive the quantity of money demanded to the interest rate, the greater is the change in the interest rate. So other things remaining the same, the larger the initial change in the interest rate, the more effective is monetary policy.

But effectiveness of monetary policy also depends on how much expenditure changes. If expenditure is not very responsive to a change in the interest rate, monetary actions do not have much effect on expenditure. But if expenditure is highly responsive to a change in the interest rate, monetary actions have a large effect on aggregate expenditure. The greater the responsiveness of expenditure to the interest rate, the more effective is monetary policy.

The effectiveness of fiscal policy and monetary policy that you've just studied were once controversial. During the 1950s and 1960s, this issue lay at the heart of what was called the Keynesian–monetarist controversy. Let's look at the dispute and see how it was resolved.

The Keynesian–Monetarist Controversy

The Keynesian–monetarist controversy was an ongoing dispute in macroeconomics between two broad groups of economists. A **Keynesian** is a macroeconomist whose view about the functioning of the economy is based on the theories of John Maynard Keynes, published in Keynes' *General Theory* (see pp. 538–539). Keynesians regard the economy as being inherently unstable and as requiring active government intervention to achieve stability. Traditionally they assigned a low degree of importance to monetary policy and a high degree of

importance to fiscal policy. Modern Keynesians assign a high degree of importance to both types of policy. A **monetarist** is a macroeconomist whose view about the functioning of the economy is based on theories most forcefully set forth by Milton Friedman (see pp. 690–691). Monetarists regard the economy as being inherently stable and as requiring no active government intervention. Monetarists believe that most macroeconomic fluctuations are caused by fluctuations in the quantity of money. Traditionally they assigned a low degree of importance to fiscal policy. But modern monetarists, like modern Keynesians, assign a high degree of importance to both types of policy.

The nature of the Keynesian–monetarist debate has changed over the years. During the 1950s and 1960s, it was a debate about the relative effectiveness of fiscal policy and monetary policy in changing aggregate demand. We can see the essence of that debate by distinguishing three views:

■ Extreme Keynesianism
■ Extreme monetarism
■ Intermediate position

Extreme Keynesianism   The extreme Keynesian hypothesis is that a change in the money supply has no effect on aggregate demand and a change in government expenditures on goods and services or in taxes has a large effect on aggregate demand. The two circumstances in which a change in the money supply has no effect on aggregate demand are

1. Expenditure is completely insensitive to the interest rate
2. The quantity of money demanded is highly sensitive to the interest rate

If expenditure is completely insensitive to the interest rate (if the *IE* curve is vertical), a change in the money supply changes the interest rate, but the change does not affect aggregate planned expenditure. Monetary policy is impotent.

If the quantity of money demanded is highly sensitive to the interest rate (if the *MD* curve is horizontal), people are willing to hold any amount of money at a given interest rate—a situation called a *liquidity trap*. With a liquidity trap, a change in the money supply affects only the amount of money held. It does not affect the interest rate. With an unchanged interest rate, expenditure remains constant. Monetary policy is impotent. Some people believe that Japan was in a liquidity trap during the late 1990s.

Extreme Monetarism   The extreme monetarist hypothesis is that a change in government expenditures on goods and services or in taxes has no effect on aggregate demand and that a change in the money supply has a large effect on aggregate demand. Two circumstances give rise to these predictions:

1. Expenditure is highly sensitive to the interest rate
2. The quantity of money demanded is completely insensitive to the interest rate

If an increase in government expenditures on goods and services induces an increase in the interest rate that is sufficiently large to reduce expenditure by the same amount as the initial increase in government expenditures, then fiscal policy has no effect on aggregate demand. This outcome is complete crowding out. For this result to occur, either the quantity of money demanded must be insensitive to the interest rate—a fixed amount of money is held regardless of the interest rate—or expenditure must be highly sensitive to the interest rate—any amount of expenditure will be undertaken at a given interest rate.

The Intermediate Position   The intermediate position is that both fiscal and monetary policy affect aggregate demand. Crowding out is not complete, so fiscal policy does have an effect. There is no liquidity trap and expenditure responds to the interest rate, so monetary policy does indeed affect aggregate demand. This position is the one that now appears to be correct and is the one that we've spent most of this chapter exploring. Let's see how economists came to this conclusion.

Sorting Out the Competing Claims

The dispute between monetarists, Keynesians, and those taking an intermediate position was essentially a disagreement about the magnitudes of two economic parameters:

1. The responsiveness of expenditure to the interest rate
2. The responsiveness of the demand for real money to the interest rate

If expenditure is highly sensitive to the interest rate or the demand for real money is barely sensitive to the interest rate, then monetary policy is powerful and fiscal policy relatively ineffective. In this case, the world looks similar to the claims of extreme monetarists. If expenditure is very insensitive to the interest rate, or the demand for real money is highly sensitive, then fiscal policy is powerful and monetary policy is relatively ineffective. In this case, the world looks similar to the claims of the extreme Keynesians.

By using statistical methods to study the demand for real money and expenditure and by using data from a wide variety of historical and national experiences, economists were able to settle this dispute. Neither extreme position turned out to be supported by the evidence and the intermediate position won. The demand curve for real money slopes downward. And expenditure *is* interest sensitive. Neither demand curve is vertical nor horizontal, so the extreme Keynesian and extreme monetarist hypotheses are rejected.

Interest Rate and Exchange Rate Effectiveness

Although fiscal policy and monetary policy are alternative ways of changing aggregate demand, they have opposing effects on the interest rate and the exchange rate. A fiscal policy action that increases aggregate demand raises the interest rate and increases the exchange rate. A monetary policy action that increases aggregate demand lowers the interest rate and decreases the exchange rate. Because of these opposing effects on interest rates and the exchange rate, if the two policies are combined to increase aggregate demand, their separate effects on the interest rate and the exchange rate can be minimized.

R E V I E W   Q U I Z

- What two macroeconomic parameters influence the relative effectiveness of fiscal policy and monetary policy?
- Under what circumstances is the Keynesian view correct and under what circumstances is the monetarist view correct?
- How can fiscal policy and monetary policy be combined to increase aggregate demand yet at the same time keep the interest rate constant?

We're now going to look at expansionary fiscal and monetary policy at full employment.

Policy Actions at Full Employment

AN EXPANSIONARY FISCAL POLICY OR MONETARY policy can bring the economy to full employment. But it is often difficult to determine whether the economy is below full employment. So an expansionary fiscal policy or monetary policy might be undertaken when the economy is at full employment. What happens then? Let's answer this question starting with an expansionary fiscal policy.

Expansionary Fiscal Policy at Full Employment

Suppose the economy is at full employment and the government increases expenditure. All the effects that we worked out earlier in this chapter occur. Except that these effects determine only a *short-run equilibrium*. That is, the first round and second round effects of policy both occur in the short run. There is a third round, which is the long-run adjustment.

Starting out at full employment, an expansionary fiscal policy will create an above full-employment equilibrium in which there is an *inflationary gap*. The money wage rate begins to rise, short-run aggregate supply decreases, and a long-run adjustment occurs in which real GDP decreases to potential GDP and the price level rises.

Figure 29.8 illustrates the combined first and second round short-run effects and the third round long-run adjustment.

In Fig. 29.8, potential GDP is $800 billion. Real GDP equals potential GDP on aggregate demand curve AD_0 and short-run aggregate supply curve SAS_0. An expansionary fiscal action increases aggregate demand. The combined first round and second round effect increases aggregate demand to AD_1. Real GDP increases to $900 billion and the price level rises to 120. There is an inflationary gap of $100 billion.

With the economy above full employment, a shortage of labour puts upward pressure on the money wage rate, which now begins to rise. And a third round of adjustment begins. The rising money wage rate decreases short-run aggregate supply and the *SAS* curve starts moving leftward towards SAS_1.

As short-run aggregate supply decreases, real GDP decreases and the price level rises. This process

FIGURE 29.8

Fiscal Policy at Full Employment

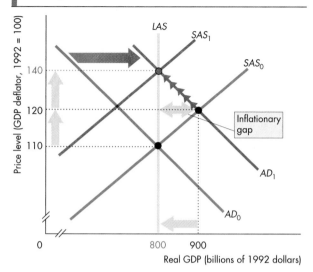

The long-run aggregate supply curve is *LAS* and initially the aggregate demand curve is AD_0 and the short-run aggregate supply curve is SAS_0. Real GDP is $800 billion and the price level is 110. Fiscal and monetary policy changes shift the aggregate demand curve to AD_1. At the new short-run equilibrium, real GDP is $900 billion and the price level is 120. Because real GDP exceeds potential GDP, the money wage rate begins to rise and the short-run aggregate supply curve begins to shift leftward to SAS_1. At the new long-run equilibrium, the price level is 140 and real GDP is back at its original level.

continues until the inflationary gap has been eliminated at full employment. At long-run equilibrium, real GDP is $800 billion, which is potential GDP, and the price level is 140.

Crowding Out at Full Employment

You've just seen that when government expenditures increase at full employment, the long-run change in real GDP is zero. The entire effect of the increase in aggregate demand is to increase the price level. This outcome implies that at full employment, an increase in government expenditures either *completely crowds out private expenditure,* or *creates an international (net exports) deficit,* or results in a combination of the two.

The easiest way to see why is to recall that aggregate expenditure, which equals consumption expenditure, C, plus investment, I, plus government expenditures, G, plus net exports, NX, equals real GDP. That is:

$$Y = C + I + G + NX.$$

If we compare the initial situation with the outcome, real GDP has not changed. So aggregate expenditure, $C + I + G + NX$, is constant between the two situations.

But government expenditures have increased, so the sum of consumption expenditure, investment, and net exports must have decreased. If net exports don't change, consumption expenditure plus investment decreases by the full amount of the increase in government expenditures. If consumption expenditure and investment don't change, net exports decrease by an amount equal to the increase in government expenditures. A decrease in net exports is an increase in our international deficit.

You've now seen that the effects of expansionary fiscal policy are extremely sensitive to the state of the economy when the policy action is taken. At less than full employment, an expansionary fiscal policy can move the economy towards full employment. At full employment, an expansionary fiscal policy raises the price level, crowds out private expenditure, and creates an international deficit.

Expansionary Monetary Policy at Full Employment

Now suppose the economy is at full employment and the Bank of Canada increases the money supply. Again, all the effects that we worked out earlier in this chapter occur. But again, these effects determine only a *short-run equilibrium*. That is, the first round and second round effects of monetary policy both occur in the short run. And again, there is a third round, which is the long-run adjustment.

Starting out at full employment, an expansionary monetary policy will create an above full-employment equilibrium in which there is an *inflationary gap*. The money wage rate begins to rise, short-run aggregate supply decreases, and a long-run adjustment occurs in which real GDP decreases to potential GDP and the price level rises.

Figure 29.8, which illustrates the effects of an expansionary fiscal policy at full employment also illustrates the effects of an expansionary monetary policy at full employment.

In the short run, an expansionary monetary policy increases real GDP and the price level. But in the long run, it increases only the price level and leaves real GDP unchanged at potential GDP.

Long-Run Neutrality

In the long run, a change in the quantity of money changes only the price level and leaves real GDP unchanged. The independence of real GDP from the quantity of money is an example of the long-run neutrality of money.

But long-run neutrality applies not only to real GDP but also to all real variables. The so-called **long-run neutrality** proposition is that in the long run, a change in the quantity of money changes the price level and leaves all real variables unchanged.

You can see this outcome in the case of real GDP in Fig. 29.8. With no change in real GDP, the demand for money does not change. The price level rises by the same percentage as the increase in the quantity of money, so the supply of real money does not change. With no change in the demand for money and no change in the supply of real money, the interest rate does not change. And with no change in the interest rate, expenditure remains the same. Finally, with no change in real GDP or the interest rate, consumption expenditure, investment, government expenditures, and net exports are unchanged.

R E V I E W Q U I Z

- Contrast the short-run effects of an expansionary fiscal policy on real GDP and the price level with its long-run effects when the policy action occurs at full employment.
- Contrast the short-run effects of an expansionary monetary policy on real GDP and the price level with its long-run effects when the policy action occurs at full employment.
- Explain crowding out at full employment.
- Explain the long-run neutrality of money.

Policy Coordination and Conflict

SO FAR, WE'VE STUDIED FISCAL POLICY AND monetary policy in isolation from each other. We are now going to consider what happens if the two branches of policy are coordinated and if they come into conflict.

Policy coordination occurs when the government and the Bank of Canada work together to achieve a common set of goals. **Policy conflict** occurs when the government and the Bank of Canada pursue different goals and the actions of one make it harder (perhaps impossible) for the other to achieve its goals.

Policy Coordination

The basis for policy coordination is the fact that either fiscal policy or monetary policy can be used to increase aggregate demand. Starting from a position of *unemployment equilibrium*, an increase in aggregate demand increases real GDP and decreases unemployment. If the size of the policy action is well judged, it can restore full employment. Similarly, starting from a position of *above full-employment equilibrium*, a decrease in aggregate demand decreases real GDP and can, if the size of the policy action is well judged, eliminate an *inflationary gap*. Because either a fiscal policy or a monetary policy action can achieve these objectives, the two policies can (in principle) be combined to also achieve the same outcome.

If either or both policies can restore full employment and eliminate inflation, why does it matter which policy is used? It matters because the two policies have different side effects—different effects on other variables about which people care. These side effects work through the influence of policy on two key variables:

■ The interest rate
■ The exchange rate

Interest Rate Effects   An expansionary fiscal policy *raises* the interest rate while an expansionary monetary policy *lowers* the interest rate. When the interest rate changes, investment changes, so an expansionary fiscal policy lowers investment (crowding out) while an expansionary monetary policy

increases investment. So if an expansionary fiscal policy increases aggregate demand, consumption expenditure increases and investment decreases. But if an expansionary monetary policy increases aggregate demand, consumption expenditure and investment increase.

By coordinating fiscal policy and monetary policy and increasing aggregate demand with an appropriate combination of the two, it is possible to increase real GDP and lower unemployment with either no change in the interest rate or any desired change in the interest rate. A big dose of fiscal expansion and a small dose of monetary expansion raises the interest rate and decreases investment, while a small dose of fiscal expansion and a big dose of monetary expansion lowers the interest rate and increases investment.

The interest rate affects our long-term growth prospects because the growth rate of potential GDP depends on the level of investment. The connection between investment, capital, and growth is explained in Chapters 31 and 32.

Exchange Rate Effects   An expansionary fiscal policy raises not only the interest rate but also the exchange rate. In contrast, an expansionary monetary policy *lowers* the exchange rate. When the exchange rate changes, net exports change. An expansionary fiscal policy lowers net exports (international crowding out) while an expansionary monetary policy increases net exports. So if full employment is restored by expansionary policy, net exports decrease with fiscal expansion and increase with monetary expansion.

Policy Conflict

Policy conflicts are not planned. But they sometimes happen. When they arise, it is usually because of a divergence of the political priorities of the government and the objectives of the Bank of Canada.

Governments (both federal and provincial) pay a lot of attention to employment and production over a short time horizon. They look for policies that make their re-election chances high. The Bank of Canada pays a lot of attention to price level stability and has a long time horizon. It doesn't have an election to worry about.

So a situation might arise in which the government wants the Bank to pursue an expansionary monetary policy but the Bank wants to keep its foot on the monetary brake. The government says that an increase in the money supply is essential to lower interest rates and the exchange rate and to boost investment and exports. The Bank says that the problem is with fiscal policy. Spending is too high and revenues too low. With fiscal policy too expansionary, interest rates and the exchange rate are high and they cannot be lowered permanently by monetary policy. To lower interest rates and give investment and exports a boost, fiscal policy must become contractionary. Only then can an expansionary monetary policy be pursued.

A further potential conflict between the government and the Bank of Canada concerns the financing of the government deficit. A government deficit can be financed either by borrowing from the general public or by borrowing from the Bank. If the government borrows from the general public, it must pay interest on its debt. If it borrows from the Bank, it pays interest to the Bank. But the government owns the Bank, so the interest comes back to the government. Financing a deficit by selling debt to the central bank costs the government no interest. So the temptation to sell debt to the central bank is strong.

But when the Bank of Canada buys government debt, it pays for the debt with newly created monetary base. The money supply increases. And such finance leads to inflation. In many countries, for example in Eastern Europe, Latin America, and Africa, government deficits are financed by the central bank. In Canada, they are not. Despite huge government deficits, the Bank has stood firm in its purchase of government debt. Only tiny amounts have been bought by the Bank to keep the monetary base growing at a rate that keeps up with real GDP growth and sustains a modest inflation. Figure 29.9 shows the Bank's contribution to financing the federal government's deficits since they emerged in 1975. You can see that the Bank has been able to pursue its primary objective of price level stability despite the huge debts incurred by the government.

REVIEW QUIZ

- What are the main things that can be achieved by coordinating fiscal policy and monetary policy?
- What are the main sources of conflict in policy between the Bank of Canada and the government of Canada?
- What are the main consequences of the government and the Bank of Canada pursuing conflicting policies? Are all the consequences bad?

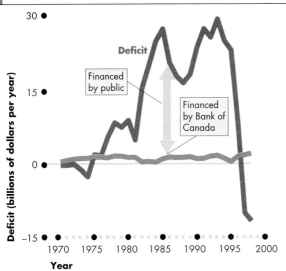

FIGURE 29.9

Debt Financing

The federal government's budget deficit mushroomed after 1975. The deficit was financed mostly by selling bonds to the public. The Bank of Canada's monetary policy has created little new money to finance the deficit.

Source: Statistics Canada, StatCan: CANSIM Disc, 1999.

◆ You have now studied the interaction of fiscal policy and monetary policy. *Reading Between the Lines* on pages 660–661 takes a further look at the way these two sets of policies interact by studying the policy actions of 1998. You've seen that these policies are alternative ways of changing aggregate demand and real GDP. But they have different effects on the interest rate and the exchange rate. You've seen what determines the relative effectiveness of fiscal and monetary policies and how the mix of these policies can influence the composition of aggregate expenditure. But you've also seen that the ultimate effects of these policies on real GDP and the price level depend not only on the behaviour of aggregate demand but also on aggregate supply and the state of the labour market. You will turn to the aggregate supply side of the economy in the next part. But first, in Chapter 30, we complete our study of aggregate demand by learning about inflation.

Fiscal and Monetary Policy in Action

THE GLOBE AND MAIL, AUGUST 11, 1999

20% tax cut is feasible in five years, report says

BY BRUCE LITTLE

The federal government's surplus is rising so fast that Ottawa could cut personal income taxes by 20 per cent within five years without reducing spending on programs, according to a new report by the Royal Bank of Canada.

In a study to be released today, the bank says the surplus could reach $25.9-billion by the 2004–05 fiscal year. Even if Ottawa set aside $7-billion of that as a cushion against unexpected financial reverses, it would still leave an $18.9-billion fiscal windfall for tax cuts, new spending or for paying down the federal debt.

Applying the entire $18.9-billion for personal income-tax cuts would relieve Canadians of about one-fifth of the personal-tax burden projected for that year, Royal Bank chief economist John McCallum said in an interview. ...

In Canada, the debate over tax cuts has intensified in recent months as Ottawa's surplus continues to build. In his

February budget, federal Finance Minister Paul Martin cut some taxes effective July 1, notably the 3-per-cent general surtax. But he used most of the extra cash handed to him by economic growth and burgeoning revenues to increase spending so that he would not run a surplus bigger than the one he had planned a year earlier. ...

In his report, Mr. McCallum examines three options for the government:

- A series of tax cuts uses up all the $18.9 billion. It could all be plowed into personal-tax reductions, but some could also be used to reduce unemployment-insurance premiums and business taxes.

- Half is used to finance tax cuts and the other half to pay down some of Ottawa's $577-billion debt.

- Half goes to tax cuts and half to finance higher spending on programs. ...

Mr. McCallum said that if Ottawa decides to use its fiscal dividend to cut taxes, it would probably reduce unemployment-insurance premiums and perhaps business taxes as well as personal taxes. ...

Reprinted with permission from *The Globe and Mail*.
Further reproduction prohibited.

Essence of the Story

- The federal government has a budget surplus.

- According to a Royal Bank of Canada report, Ottawa can cut income taxes by 20 percent without reducing spending on programs.

- The federal government cut taxes on July 1 and increased spending.

- John McCallum, chief economist of the Royal Bank, says that the federal government can use the surplus entirely for tax reduction, a combination of tax reduction and debt reduction, or a combination of tax reduction and increased program spending.

Economic Analysis

■ A tax cut has both supply-side and demand-side effects. Here, we look only at the demand-side effects. Throughout, we use numbers that are reasonable conjectures about the Canadian economy in 2000.

■ In 2000, with no tax cut, the aggregate demand curve is AD_0. Short-run aggregate supply is SAS. Real GDP is $900 billion and the price level is 107. (Fig. 1.)

■ In 2000, M2+ is $680 billion. With no tax cut and a price level of 107, real M2+ is $635 billion and the money supply curve is MS_0. With real GDP at $900 billion, the demand for money curve is MD_0 and the interest rate is 5 percent a year. (Fig. 2.)

■ With an interest rate of 5 percent a year, interest-sensitive expenditure is $200 billion. (Fig. 3.)

■ A tax cut increases aggregate demand. In Fig. 1, the AD curve shifts rightward to AD_1. Real GDP and the price level begin to rise. These are the first round effects of the tax cut.

■ Increasing real GDP increases the demand for money. The demand for money curve shifts rightward from MD_0 to MD_1 and the interest rate rises. (Fig. 2.)

■ The rise in the interest rate decreases interest-sensitive expenditure. In Fig. 3, there is a movement along the IE curve and in Fig. 1, aggregate demand decreases from AD_1 to AD_2.

■ The rising price level decreases the supply of real money. At a price level of 109, the real money supply decreases to $624 billion. The money supply curve shifts leftward from MS_0 to MS_1 in Fig. 2 and the interest rate rises. Interest-sensitive expenditure decreases and in Fig. 3, there is a movement along the IE curve.

■ In Fig.1, the rising price level decreases the quantity of real GDP demanded—a movement along the AD curve.

■ So a tax cut increases real GDP, raises the price level and the interest rate, and decreases investment and other components of interest-sensitive expenditure.

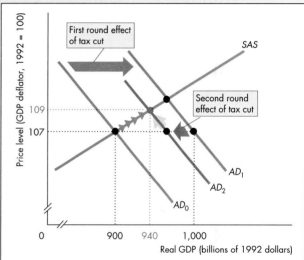

Figure 1 Aggregate demand and aggregate supply

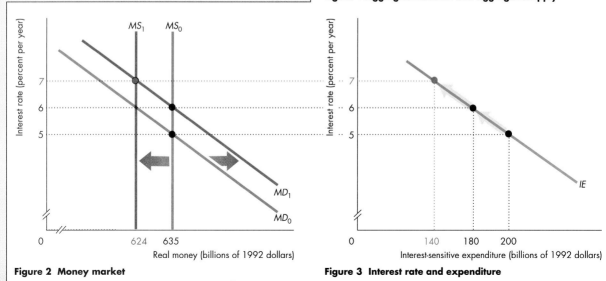

Figure 2 Money market

Figure 3 Interest rate and expenditure

S U M M A R Y

Key Points

Macroeconomic Equilibrium (pp. 644–645)

▪ Equilibrium real GDP, the price level, and the interest rate are determined simultaneously by equilibrium in the money market and equality of aggregate demand and aggregate supply.

Fiscal Policy in the Short Run (pp. 646–649)

▪ The first round effects of an expansionary fiscal policy are an increase in aggregate demand, an increasing real GDP, and a rising price level.

▪ The second round effects are an increasing demand for money and a decreasing supply of (real) money that limit the increase in real GDP and the rise in the price level.

▪ Interest-sensitive expenditure, which includes investment and net exports, decreases.

Monetary Policy in the Short Run (pp. 650–653)

▪ The first round effects of an expansionary monetary policy are a fall in the interest rate, an increase in aggregate demand, an increasing real GDP, and a rising price level.

▪ The second round effects are an increasing demand for money and a decreasing supply of (real) money that limit the increase in real GDP and the rise in the price level.

▪ Interest-sensitive expenditure, which includes investment and net exports, increases.

Relative Effectiveness of Policies (pp. 653–655)

▪ The relative effectiveness of fiscal and monetary policy depends on the interest-sensitivity of expenditure and the quantity of money demanded.

▪ The extreme Keynesian position is that only fiscal policy affects aggregate demand. The extreme monetarist position is that only monetary policy affects aggregate demand. Neither extreme is correct.

▪ The mix of fiscal and monetary policy influences the composition of aggregate demand.

Policy Actions at Full Employment (pp. 656–657)

▪ An expansionary fiscal policy at full employment increases real GDP and the price level in the short run but increases only the price level in the long run. Complete crowding out of private expenditure occurs or the international deficit increases.

▪ An expansionary monetary policy at full employment increases real GDP and the price level in the short run but increases only the price level in the long run. Money is neutral—has no real effects—in the long run.

Policy Coordination and Conflict (pp. 658–659)

▪ Policy coordination can make changes in the interest rate and the exchange rate small.

▪ Policy conflict can avoid inflation in the face of a government deficit.

Key Figures ◆

Key Terms

P R O B L E M S

*1. In the economy described in Fig. 29.1, suppose the government decreases its expenditures on goods and services.
   a. Work out the first round effects.
   b. Explain how real GDP and the interest rate change.
   c. Explain the second round effects that take the economy to a new equilibrium.

2. In the economy described in Fig. 29.1, suppose the government increases its expenditures on goods and services by $25 billion.
   a. Work out the first round effects.
   b. Explain how real GDP and the interest rate change.
   c. Explain the second round effects that take the economy to a new equilibrium.
   d. Compare the equilibrium in this case with the one described in the chapter on pp. 646–647. In which case does real GDP change by most? In which case does the interest rate change by most? Why?

*3. In the economy described in Fig. 29.1, suppose the Bank of Canada decreases the money supply.
   a. Work out the first round effects.
   b. Explain how real GDP and the interest rate change.
   c. Explain the second round effects that take the economy to a new equilibrium.

4. In the economy described in Fig. 29.1, suppose the Bank of Canada increases the money supply by $250 billion.
   a. Work out the first round effects.
   b. Explain how real GDP and the interest rate change.
   c. Explain the second round effects that take the economy to a new equilibrium.
   d. Compare the equilibrium in this case with the one described in the chapter on pp. 650–652. In which case does real GDP change by most? In which case does the interest rate change by most? Why?

*5. The economies of two countries, Alpha and Beta, are identical in every way except the following: in Alpha, a change in the interest rate of 1 percentage point (for example, from 5 percent to 6 percent) results in a $1 billion change

in the quantity of real money demanded. In Beta, a change in the interest rate of 1 percentage point results in a $0.1 billion change in the quantity of real money demanded.
   a. In which economy does an increase in government expenditures on goods and services have a larger effect on real GDP?
   b. In which economy is the crowding-out effect weaker?
   c. In which economy does a change in the money supply have a larger effect on equilibrium real GDP?
   d. Which economy, if either, is closer to the Keynesian extreme and which is closer to the monetarist extreme?

6. The economies of two countries, Gamma and Delta, are identical in every way except the following: in Gamma, a change in the interest rate of 1 percentage point (for example, from 5 percent to 6 percent) results in a $0.1 billion change in interest-sensitive expenditure. In Delta, a change in the interest rate of 1 percentage point results in a $10 billion change in interest-sensitive expenditure.
   a. In which economy does an increase in government expenditures on goods and services have a larger effect on real GDP?
   b. In which economy is the crowding-out effect weaker?
   c. In which economy does a change in the money supply have a larger effect on equilibrium real GDP?
   d. Which economy, if either, is closer to the Keynesian extreme and which is closer to the monetarist extreme?

*7. The economy is in a recession and the government wants to increase aggregate demand, stimulate exports, and increase investment. It has three policy options: increase government expenditures on goods and services, decrease taxes, and increase the money supply.
   a. Explain the mechanisms at work under each alternative policy.
   b. What is the effect of each policy on the composition of aggregate demand?
   c. What are the short-run effects of each policy on real GDP and the price level?
   d. Which policy would you recommend that the government adopt? Why?

8. The economy has an inflationary gap and the government wants to decrease aggregate demand, cut exports, and decrease investment. It has three policy options: decrease government expenditures on goods and services, increase taxes, and decrease the money supply.
   a. Explain the mechanisms at work under each alternative policy.
   b. What is the effect of each policy on the composition of aggregate demand?
   c. What are the short-run effects of each policy on real GDP and the price level?
   d. Which policy would you recommend that the government adopt? Why?

*9. The economy is at full employment, but the government is disappointed with the growth rate of real GDP. It wants to increase real GDP growth by stimulating investment. At the same time, it wants to avoid an increase in the price level.
   a. Suggest a combination of fiscal and monetary policies that will achieve the government's objective.
   b. Explain the mechanisms at work under your suggested policy.
   c. What is the effect of your suggested policy on the composition of aggregate demand?
   d. What are the short-run and long-run effects of your suggested policy on real GDP and the price level?

10. The economy is at full employment, and the government is worried that the growth rate of real GDP is too high because it is depleting the country's natural resources. The government wants to lower real GDP growth by lowering investment. At the same time it wants to avoid a fall in the price level.
   a. Suggest a combination of fiscal and monetary policies that will achieve the government's objective.
   b. Explain the mechanisms at work under your suggested policy.
   c. What is the effect of your suggested policy on the composition of aggregate demand?
   d. What are the short-run and long-run effects of your suggested policy on real GDP and the price level?

CRITICAL THINKING

1. Study *Reading Between the Lines* on pp. 660–661 and then answer the following questions:
   a. Why is the Minister of Finance planning to cut taxes?
   b. What are your predictions about the effects of a major tax cut on real GDP, the price level, interest rates, investment, the exchange rate, and net exports?
   c. What actions do you think that the Bank of Canada needs to take to ensure that tax cuts deliver a good outcome?
   d. What would happen if the Bank of Canada decided to raise interest rates at the same time that the government cut taxes? Explain the likely effects on real GDP, the price level, investment, the exchange rate, and net exports.

2. Use the link on the Parkin-Bade Web site to visit the Web site of Statistics Canada and look at the current economic conditions. On the basis of the current state of the Canadian economy, and in the light of what you now know about fiscal and monetary policy interaction, what do you predict would happen to real GDP and the price level:
   a. If the Bank of Canada conducted an expansionary monetary policy?
   b. If the Bank of Canada conducted a contractionary monetary policy?
   c. If the government of Canada conducted an expansionary fiscal policy?
   d. If the government of Canada conducted a contractionary fiscal policy?
   e. If the Bank of Canada conducted an expansionary monetary policy and the government of Canada conducted a contractionary fiscal policy?
   f. If the Bank of Canada conducted a contractionary monetary policy and the government of Canada conducted an expansionary fiscal policy?

3. What do you think the government of Canada should do with its fiscal surplus? Should it cut taxes, increase spending, or do some of both? How would your recommended actions influence real GDP, the price level, the interest rate, the exchange rate, and net exports?

Inflation

At the end of the third century A.D., Roman Emperor Diocletian struggled to contain an inflation that raised prices by more than 300 percent a year. At the end of the twentieth century, Russian President Boris Yeltsin struggled to contain a severe inflation that raised prices at a rate of close to 1,000 percent a year. But the most rapid recent inflations have been in Brazil, where the inflation rate hit 40 percent *per month* in 1994, and in Zaire, which had an inflation rate of 75 percent *per month*. What causes rapid inflation? ◆ In comparison with the cases just described, Canada has had remarkable price stability. Nevertheless, during the 1970s the Canadian price level more than doubled—an inflation of more

From Rome to Russia

than 100 percent over the decade. Today, along with the other rich industrial countries, Canada has a low inflation rate of less than 2 percent a year. Why do some countries have a low inflation rate? And why did

a more serious inflation break out in Canada during the 1970s? ◆ Most of life's big economic decisions—whether to buy or rent a home, whether to save more for retirement—turn on what is going to happen to inflation. Will inflation increase so our savings buy less? Will inflation decrease so our debts are harder to repay? To make good decisions, we need good forecasts of inflation, and not just for next year but for many years into the future. How do people try to forecast inflation? And how do expectations of inflation influence the economy? ◆ As the inflation rate rises and falls, the unemployment rate and interest rates fluctuate. What are the links between inflation and the economy that make unemployment and interest rates fluctuate when inflation fluctuates?

◆ In this chapter, you will study the causes of inflation and the effects of inflation on the unemployment rate and the interest rate. You will pull together several of the threads you have been following through your study of macroeconomics. In particular, you will use the *AS-AD* model of Chapter 24 and the analysis of the money market of Chapters 27 and 28. But first, let's recall what inflation is and how it is measured.

After studying this chapter, you will be able to:

- **Distinguish between inflation and a one-time rise in the price level**

- **Explain the different ways in which inflation can be generated**

- **Explain the quantity theory of money**

- **Describe the effects of inflation on the labour market and the capital market**

- **Explain the relationship between inflation and unemployment**

- **Explain the relationship between inflation and interest rates**

Inflation and the Price Level

WHEN THE PRICE LEVEL IS RISING AND MONEY IS losing value, we are experiencing **inflation**. If the price level rises persistently, then people need more and more money to make transactions. Incomes rise, so firms must pay out more in wages and other payments to resource owners. And prices rise, so consumers must take more money with them when they go shopping. But the value of money falls.

A change in one single price is not inflation. For example, if the price of a hot dog jumps to $25 and all other money prices fall slightly so that the price level remains constant, there is no inflation. Instead, the relative price of a hot dog has increased. If the price of a hot dog and all other prices rise by a similar percentage, there is inflation.

But a one-time jump in the price level is not inflation either. Inflation is an ongoing *process*. Figure 30.1 illustrates this distinction. The red line shows the price level rising continuously. That is inflation. The blue line shows a one-time jump in the price level. This economy is not experiencing inflation. Its price level is constant most of the time.

Inflation is a serious problem and preventing inflation is the main task of monetary policy and the actions of the Bank of Canada. We are going to learn how inflation arises and see how we can avoid the situation shown in the cartoon. But first, let's see how we calculate the inflation rate.

To measure the inflation *rate*, we calculate the annual percentage change in the price level. For

"I told you the Fed should have tightened."

FIGURE 30.1

Inflation Versus a One-Time Rise in the Price Level

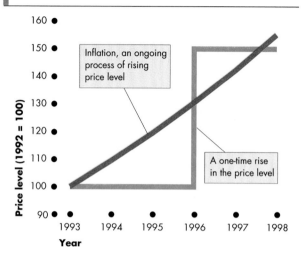

Along the red line, an economy experiences inflation because the price level is rising persistently. Along the blue line, an economy experiences a one-time rise in the price level.

example, if this year's price level is 126 and last year's price level was 120, the inflation rate is 5 percent per year. That is,

$$\text{Inflation rate} = \frac{126 - 120}{120} \times 100$$

$$= 5 \text{ percent per year.}$$

This equation shows the connection between the *inflation rate* and the *price level*. For a given price level last year, the higher the price level in the current year, the higher is the inflation rate. If the price level is *rising*, the inflation rate is *positive*. If the price level rises at a *faster* rate, the inflation rate *increases*. Also, the higher the new price level, the lower is the value of money, and the higher the inflation rate.

Inflation can result from either an increase in aggregate demand or a decrease in aggregate supply. These two sources of impulses that can get inflation started are called:

1. Demand pull
2. Cost push

We'll first study a demand-pull inflation.

Demand-Pull Inflation

AN INFLATION THAT RESULTS FROM AN INITIAL increase in aggregate demand is called **demand-pull inflation**. Such an inflation can arise from any factor that increases aggregate demand such as an:

1. Increase in the money supply
2. Increase in government expenditures
3. Increase in exports

Initial Effect of an Increase in Aggregate Demand

Suppose that last year the price level was 110 and real GDP was $800 billion. Potential GDP was also $800 billion. Figure 30.2(a) illustrates this situation. The aggregate demand curve is AD_0, the short-run

aggregate supply curve is SAS_0, and the long-run aggregate supply curve is LAS.

In the current year, aggregate demand increases to AD_1. Such a situation arises if, for example, the Bank of Canada loosens its grip on the money supply, or the government increases its expenditures on goods and services, or exports increase.

With no change in potential GDP, and with no change in the money wage rate, the long-run aggregate supply curve and the short-run aggregate supply curve remain at LAS and SAS_0.

The price level and real GDP are determined at the point where the aggregate demand curve AD_1 intersects the short-run aggregate supply curve. The price level rises to 113, and real GDP increases above potential GDP to $850 billion. The economy experiences a 2.7 percent rise in the price level (a price level of 113 compared with 110 in the previous year) and a rapid expansion of real GDP. Unemployment falls below the natural rate. The next step in the unfolding story is a rise in the money wage rate.

FIGURE 30.2

A Demand-Pull Rise in the Price Level

(a) Initial effect

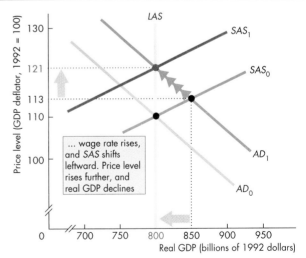

(b) Wages adjust

In part (a) the aggregate demand curve is AD_0, the short-run aggregate supply curve is SAS_0, and the long-run aggregate supply curve is LAS. The price level is 110, and real GDP is $800 billion. Potential GDP is $800 billion. Aggregate demand increases to AD_1 (because the Bank of Canada increases the money supply or the government increases its expenditures or exports

increase). The new equilibrium occurs where AD_1 intersects SAS_0. The price level rises to 113, and real GDP increases to $850 billion. In part (b), starting from above full employment, the money wage rate begins to rise and the short-run aggregate supply curve shifts leftward towards SAS_1. The price level rises further, and real GDP returns to potential GDP.

Wage Response

Real GDP cannot remain above potential GDP forever. With unemployment below its natural rate, there is a shortage of labour. In this situation, the money wage rate begins to rise. As it does, short-run aggregate supply decreases and the *SAS* curve starts to shift leftward. The price level rises further, and real GDP begins to decrease.

With no further change in aggregate demand— the aggregate demand curve remains at AD_1—this process ends when the short-run aggregate supply curve has shifted to SAS_1 in Fig. 30.2(b). At this time, the price level has increased to 121 and real GDP has returned to potential GDP of $800 billion, the level from which it started.

A Demand-Pull Inflation Process

The process we've just studied eventually ends when, for a given increase in aggregate demand, the money wage rate has adjusted enough to restore the real wage rate to its full-employment level. We've studied a one-time rise in the price level like that described in Fig. 30.1(b). For inflation to proceed, aggregate demand must persistently increase.

The only way in which aggregate demand can persistently increase is if the quantity of money persistently increases. Suppose the government has a large budget deficit that it finances by selling bonds to the Bank of Canada. When the Bank of Canada buys these bonds, it creates more money. In this situation, aggregate demand increases year after year. The aggregate demand curve keeps shifting rightward. This persistent increase in aggregate demand puts continual upward pressure on the price level. The economy now experiences demand-pull inflation.

Figure 30.3 illustrates the process of demand-pull inflation. The starting point is the same as that shown in Fig. 30.2. The aggregate demand curve is AD_0, the short-run aggregate supply curve is SAS_0, and the long-run aggregate supply curve is LAS. Real GDP is $800 billion, and the price level is 110. Aggregate demand increases, shifting the aggregate demand curve to AD_1. Real GDP increases to $850 billion, and the price level rises to 113. The economy is at an above full-employment equilibrium. There is a shortage of labour and the money wage rate rises, shifting the short-run aggregate supply curve to SAS_1. The price level rises to 121, and real GDP returns to potential GDP.

FIGURE 30.3

A Demand-Pull Inflation Spiral

Each time the money supply increases, aggregate demand increases, and the aggregate demand curve shifts rightward from AD_0 to AD_1 to AD_2, and so on. Each time real GDP goes above potential GDP and unemployment goes below the natural rate, the money wage rate rises and the short-run aggregate supply curve shifts leftward from SAS_0 to SAS_1 to SAS_2, and so on. As aggregate demand continues to increase, the price level rises from 110 through 113, 121, 125, to 133, and so on. There is a perpetual demand-pull inflation. Real GDP fluctuates between $800 billion and $850 billion.

But the money supply increases again, and aggregate demand continues to increase. The aggregate demand curve shifts rightward to AD_2. The price level rises further to 125, and real GDP again exceeds potential GDP at $850 billion. Again, the money wage rate rises and short-run aggregate supply decreases. The *SAS* curve shifts to SAS_2 and the price level rises to 133. As the money supply continues to grow, aggregate demand increases and the price level rises in an ongoing demand-pull inflation process.

The process you have just studied generates inflation—an ongoing process of a rising price level.

Demand-Pull Inflation in Chatham   You may better understand the inflation process that we've just described by considering what is going on in an individual part of the economy, such as a Chatham ketchup plant. Initially, when aggregate demand increases, the demand for ketchup increases and the price of ketchup rises. Faced with a higher price, the ketchup plant works overtime and increases production. Conditions are good for workers in Chatham, and the ketchup factory finds it hard to hang onto its best people. To do so, it has to offer higher wages. As wages increase, so do the ketchup factory's costs.

What happens next depends on what happens to aggregate demand. If aggregate demand remains constant (as in Fig. 30.2b), the firm's costs are increasing, but the price of ketchup is not increasing as quickly as its costs. Production is scaled back. Eventually, wages and costs increase by the same percentage as the price of ketchup. In real terms, the ketchup factory is in the same situation as initially—before the increase in aggregate demand. The plant produces the same amount of ketchup and employs the same amount of labour as it did before the increase in demand.

But if aggregate demand continues to increase, so does the demand for ketchup, and the price of ketchup rises at the same rate as wages. The ketchup factory continues to operate above full employment, and there is a persistent shortage of labour. Prices and wages chase each other upward in an unending spiral.

Demand-Pull Inflation in Canada A demand-pull inflation like the one you've just studied occurred in Canada during the late 1960s and early 1970s. In 1960, inflation was less than 2 percent a year, but its rate increased slowly to 3 percent a year by 1966. Then, between 1966 and 1969, inflation surged to more than 4 percent a year. It dipped back to 3 percent a year during 1970 and 1971 but then took off again and by 1973, its rate was approaching 6 percent a year. These increases in the inflation rate resulted from increases in aggregate demand that had two main sources. The first was from the United States, where large increases in government expenditures and in the money supply increased aggregate demand in the entire world economy. The second source was an increase in Canadian government expenditures and money supply.

With the economy above full employment, the money wage rate started to rise more quickly and the short-run aggregate supply curve shifted leftward. The Bank of Canada responded with a further increase in the money supply growth rate and a demand-pull inflation spiral unfolded. By 1974, the inflation rate had reached double digits.

R E V I E W   Q U I Z

- How does demand-pull inflation begin? What are the initial effects of demand-pull inflation on real GDP and the price level?
- When real GDP moves above potential GDP, what happens to the money wage rate and short-run aggregate supply? How do real GDP and the price level respond?
- What must happen to create a demand-pull inflation spiral?

Next, let's see how shocks to aggregate supply can create cost-push inflation.

Cost-Push Inflation

AN INFLATION THAT RESULTS FROM AN INITIAL increase in costs is called **cost-push inflation**. The two main sources of increases in costs are:

1. An increase in the money wage rate
2. An increase in the money price of raw materials

At a given price level, the higher the cost of production, the smaller is the amount that firms are willing to produce. So if the money wage rate rises or if the price of raw materials (for example, oil) rises, firms decrease their supply of goods and services. Aggregate supply decreases, and the short-run aggregate supply curve shifts leftward.[1] Let's trace the effects of such a decrease in short-run aggregate supply on the price level and real GDP.

Initial Effect of a Decrease in Aggregate Supply

Suppose that last year the price level was 110 and real GDP was $800 billion. Potential real GDP was also $800 billion. Figure 30.4 illustrates this situation. The aggregate demand curve was AD_0, the short-run aggregate supply curve was SAS_0, and the long-run aggregate supply curve was LAS. In the

---

[1] Some cost-push forces, such as a rise in the price of oil accompanied by a decrease in the availability of oil, can also decrease long-run aggregate supply. We'll ignore such effects here and examine cost-push factors that change only short-run aggregate supply.

FIGURE 30.4

A Cost-Push Rise in the Price Level

Initially, the aggregate demand curve is AD_0, the short-run aggregate supply curve is SAS_0, and the long-run aggregate supply curve is LAS. A decrease in aggregate supply (for example, resulting from an increase in the world price of oil) shifts the short-run aggregate supply curve to SAS_1. The economy moves to the point where the short-run aggregate supply curve SAS_1 intersects the aggregate demand curve AD_0. The price level rises from 110 to 117, and real GDP decreases from $800 billion to $750 billion. The economy experiences inflation and a contraction of real GDP—*stagflation*.

current year, the world's oil producers form a price fixing organization that strengthens their market power and increases the relative price of oil. They raise the nominal price of oil and this action decreases short-run aggregate supply. The short-run aggregate supply curve shifts leftward to SAS_1. The price level rises to 117, and real GDP decreases to $750 billion. The combination of a rise in the price level and a decrease in real GDP is called **stagflation**.

This event is a one-time rise in the price level like that in Fig. 30.1. It is not inflation. In fact, a supply shock on its own cannot cause inflation. Something more must happen to enable a one-time supply shock to be converted into a process of money supply growth and ongoing inflation. The money supply must persistently increase. And it often does increase, as you will now see.

Aggregate Demand Response

When real GDP decreases, the unemployment rate rises above the natural rate. In such a situation, there is usually an outcry of concern and a call for action to restore full employment. Suppose that the Bank of Canada increases the money supply. Aggregate demand increases. In Fig. 30.5 the aggregate demand curve shifts rightward to AD_1. The increase in aggregate demand has restored full employment. But the price level rises to 121, a 10 percent increase over the initial price level.

A Cost-Push Inflation Process

The oil producers now see the prices of everything that they buy increase by 10 percent. So they increase the price of oil again to restore its new high relative price. Figure 30.6 continues the story.

FIGURE 30.5

Aggregate Demand Response to Cost Push

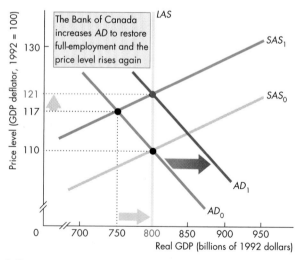

Following a cost-push increase in the price level, real GDP is below potential GDP and unemployment is above the natural rate. If the Bank of Canada responds by increasing aggregate demand to restore full employment, the aggregate demand curve shifts rightward to AD_1. The economy returns to full employment but at the expense of more inflation. The price level rises from 117 to 121.

The short-run aggregate supply curve now shifts to SAS_2, and another bout of stagflation ensues. The price level rises further to 129, and real GDP decreases to $750 billion. Unemployment increases above its natural rate. If the Bank of Canada responds yet again with an increase in the money supply, aggregate demand increases and the aggregate demand curve shifts to AD_2. The price level rises even higher—to 133—and full employment is again restored. A cost-push inflation spiral results. But if the Bank of Canada does not respond, the economy remains below full employment.

You can see that the Bank has a dilemma. If it increases the money supply to restore full employment, it invites another oil price hike that will call forth yet a further increase in the money supply. Inflation will rage along at a rate decided by the oil-exporting nations. If the Bank of Canada keeps the lid on money supply growth, the economy operates with a high level of unemployment.

Cost-Push Inflation in Chatham What is going on in the Chatham ketchup plant when the economy is experiencing cost-push inflation? When the oil price increases, so do the fuel costs of a ketchup plant. These higher costs decrease the supply of ketchup, increasing its price and decreasing the quantity produced. The ketchup plant lays off some workers. This situation will persist until either the Bank of Canada increases aggregate demand or the price of oil falls. If the Bank of Canada increases aggregate demand, as it did in the mid-1970s, the demand for ketchup increases and so does its price. The higher price of ketchup brings higher profits, and the ketchup plant increases its production. The ketchup factory rehires the laid-off workers.

Cost-Push Inflation in Canada A cost-push inflation like the one you've just studied occurred in Canada during the 1970s. It began in 1974 when the Organization for Petroleum Exporting Countries (OPEC) raised the price of oil fourfold. The higher oil price decreased aggregate supply, which caused the price level to rise more quickly and real GDP to shrink. The Bank of Canada then faced a dilemma. Would it increase the quantity of money and accommodate the cost-push forces or would it keep aggregate demand growth in check by limiting money growth? In 1975, 1976, and 1977, the Bank of Canada repeatedly allowed the money supply to grow quickly and inflation proceeded at a rapid rate. In 1979 and 1980, OPEC was again able to push oil prices higher. On that occasion the Bank of Canada along with the U.S. Federal Reserve and many other central banks decided not to respond to the oil price hike with an increase in the money supply. The result was a recession but also, eventually, a fall in inflation.

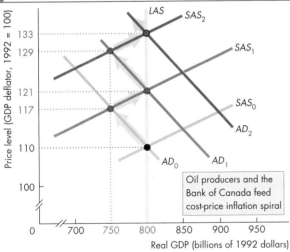

FIGURE 30.6

A Cost-Push Inflation Spiral

When a cost increase (for example, a rise in the world oil price) decreases short-run aggregate supply from SAS_0 to SAS_1, the price level rises to 117 and real GDP decreases to $750 billion. The Bank of Canada responds with an increase in the money supply that shifts the aggregate demand curve from AD_0 to AD_1. The price level rises to 121, and real GDP returns to $800 billion. A further cost increase occurs, which shifts the short-run aggregate supply curve to SAS_2. Stagflation is repeated, and the price level now rises to 129. The Bank of Canada responds again, and the cost-push inflation spiral continues.

R E V I E W Q U I Z

- How does cost-push inflation begin? What are its initial effects on real GDP and the price level?
- What is *stagflation* and why does cost-push inflation cause stagflation?
- What must the Bank of Canada do to convert a one-time rise in the price level into a freewheeling cost-push inflation?

The Quantity Theory of Money

YOU'VE SEEN THAT REGARDLESS OF WHETHER IT originates in a demand pull or a cost push, to convert a one-time rise in the price level into an ongoing inflation, aggregate demand must increase. And although many factors can and do influence aggregate demand, only one factor can persistently increase in the long run: the quantity of money. This special place of money gives rise to a special long-run theory of inflation, called the quantity theory of money.

The **quantity theory of money** is the proposition that in the long run, an increase in the quantity of money brings an equal percentage increase in the price level. The basis of the quantity theory of money is a concept known as *the velocity of circulation* and an equation called *the equation of exchange*.

The **velocity of circulation** is the average number of times a dollar of money is used annually to buy the goods and services that make up GDP. GDP equals the price level (P) multiplied by real GDP (Y); that is,

$$GDP = PY.$$

Call the quantity of money M. The velocity of circulation, V, is determined by the equation

$$V = PY/M.$$

For example, if GDP is $800 billion ($PY$ = $800) and the quantity of money is $200 billion, the velocity of circulation is 4 ($800 divided by $200 equals 4).

The **equation of exchange** states that the quantity of money (M) multiplied by the velocity of circulation (V) equals GDP, or

$$MV = PY.$$

Given the definition of the velocity of circulation, this equation is *always* true—it is true by definition. With M equal to $200 billion and V equal to 4, MV is equal to $800 billion, the value of GDP.

The equation of exchange becomes the quantity theory of money by making two assumptions:

1. The velocity of circulation is not influenced by the quantity of money.
2. Potential GDP is not influenced by the quantity of money.

If these two assumptions are true, then the equation of exchange tells us that a change in the quantity of money brings about an equal proportional change in the price level. You can see why by solving the equation of exchange for the price level. Dividing both sides of the equation by real GDP (Y) gives

$$P = (V/Y) \times M.$$

In the long run, real GDP (Y) equals potential GDP. So if potential GDP and velocity are not influenced by the quantity of money, then the relationship between the change in the price level (ΔP) and the change in the quantity of money (ΔM) is

$$\Delta P = (V/Y) \times \Delta M.$$

Divide this equation by $P = (V/Y) \times M$, and multiply by 100 to get

$$\Delta P/P \times 100 = \Delta M/M \times 100.$$

($\Delta P/P$) $\times$ 100 is the inflation rate and ($\Delta M/M$) $\times$ 100 is the growth rate of the money supply. So this equation is the quantity theory of money: The percentage increases in the price level and the quantity of money are equal.

Evidence on the Quantity Theory

Figure 30.7 summarizes some Canadian evidence on the quantity theory of money. The figure reveals that:

1. On the average, the money growth rate exceeds the inflation rate.
2. The money growth rate is correlated with the inflation rate.

Money growth exceeds inflation because real GDP grows. Money growth that matches real GDP growth does not create inflation. But money growth in excess of real GDP growth does create inflation.

Money growth and inflation are correlated—move up and down together. For example, the rise in the inflation rate during the 1970s and the slight rebound in inflation during the late 1980s were accompanied by a rise in the money growth rate. The decreases in the inflation rate during the 1980s and 1990s were accompanied by decreases in the money growth rate. But the correlation is not perfect. Nor does it tell us that money growth *causes* inflation. Money growth might cause inflation; inflation might cause money growth; or some third variable might simultaneously cause inflation and money growth.

Figure 30.8 summarizes some international evidence on the quantity theory of money. It shows the inflation rate and the money growth rate for 60 countries. There is a clear tendency for high money

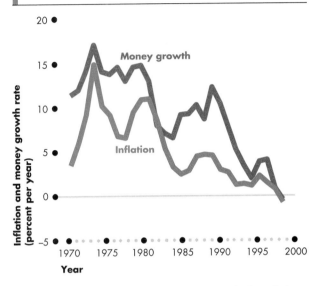

FIGURE 30.7

Money Growth and Inflation in Canada

On the average, the money growth rate exceeds the inflation rate because real GDP grows. Money growth and inflation are correlated—they rise and fall together.

Source: Statistics Canada, *StatCan: CANSIM Disc,* March 1999.

growth to be associated with high inflation. The evidence is strongest for the high-inflation countries shown in Fig. 30.8 (a), but it is also present for low-inflation countries, which are shown in Fig. 30.8 (b).

R E V I E W   Q U I Z

- What is the quantity theory of money?
- What is the velocity of circulation of money and how is it calculated?
- What is the equation of exchange? Can the equation of exchange be wrong?
- What does the long-run historical evidence and international evidence on the relationship between money growth and inflation tell us about the quantity theory of money?

We next turn to an examination of the effects of inflation.

FIGURE 30.8

Money Growth and Inflation in the World Economy

(a) All countries

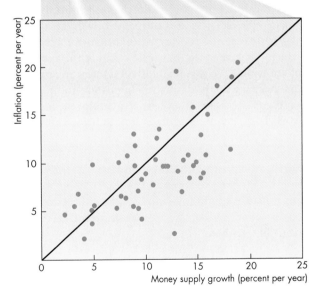

(b) Low-inflation countries

Inflation and money growth in 60 countries (in part a) and low-inflation countries (in part b) show a clear positive relationship between money growth and inflation.

Source: Federal Reserve Bank of St. Louis, *Review,* May/June 1988, p. 15.

Effects of Inflation

REGARDLESS OF WHETHER INFLATION IS demand-pull or cost-push, the failure to correctly *anticipate* it results in unintended consequences. These unintended consequences impose costs in both labour markets and capital markets. Let's examine these costs.

Unanticipated Inflation in the Labour Market

Unanticipated inflation has two main consequences for the operation of the labour market:

- Redistribution of income
- Departure from full employment

Redistribution of Income Unanticipated inflation redistributes income between employers and workers. Sometimes employers gain at the expense of workers, and sometimes they lose. If an unexpected increase in aggregate demand increases the inflation rate, then the money wage rate has not been set high enough. Profits will be higher than expected, and the money wage rate will buy fewer goods than expected. In this case, employers gain at the expense of workers. But if aggregate demand is expected to increase at a rapid rate and it fails to do so, workers gain at the expense of employers. With a high inflation rate anticipated, the money wage rate is set too high and profits are squeezed. Redistribution between employers and workers creates an incentive for both firms and workers to try to forecast inflation correctly.

Departure from Full Employment Redistribution brings gains to some and losses to others. But any departure from full employment imposes costs on everyone. To see why, let's return to the ketchup plant in Chatham.

If the ketchup plant and its workers do not anticipate inflation, but inflation occurs, the money wage rate does not rise to keep up with inflation. The real wage rate falls, and the firm tries to hire more labour and increase production. But because the real wage rate has fallen, the firm has a hard time attracting the labour it wants to employ. It pays overtime rates to its existing work force, and because it runs its plant at a faster pace, it incurs higher plant maintenance and parts replacement costs. But also, because the real wage rate has fallen, workers begin to quit the

ketchup plant to find jobs that pay a real wage rate that is closer to one prevailing before the outbreak of inflation. This labour turnover imposes additional costs on the firm. So even though its production increases, the firm incurs additional costs, and its profits do not increase as much as they otherwise would. The workers incur additional costs of job search, and those who remain at the ketchup plant wind up feeling cheated. They've worked overtime to produce the extra output, and when they come to spend their incomes, they discover that prices have increased, so their incomes buy a smaller quantity of goods and services than expected.

If the ketchup plant and its workers anticipate a high inflation rate that does not occur, they increase the money wage rate by too much and the real wage rate rises. At the higher real wage rate, the firm lays off some workers and the unemployment rate increases. Those workers who keep their jobs gain, but those who become unemployed lose. Also, the ketchup plant loses because its output and profits fall.

Unanticipated Inflation in the Capital Market

Unanticipated inflation has two consequences for the operation of the capital market. They are:

- Redistribution of income
- Too much or too little borrowing and lending

Redistribution of Income Unanticipated inflation redistributes income between borrowers and lenders. Sometimes borrowers gain at the expense of lenders and sometimes they lose. When inflation is unexpected, the interest rate is not set high enough to compensate lenders for the falling value of money. In this case, borrowers gain at the expense of lenders. But if inflation is expected and then fails to occur, the interest rate is set too high. In this case, lenders gain at the expense of borrowers. Redistributions of income between borrowers and lenders create an incentive for both groups to try to forecast inflation correctly.

Too Much or Too Little Borrowing and Lending If the inflation rate turns out to be either higher or lower than expected, the interest rate does not incorporate a correct allowance for the fall in the value of money and the real interest rate is either lower or higher than it otherwise would be. When the real interest rate turns out to be too low, which occurs when inflation is *higher* than expected, borrowers wish they had borrowed more and lenders wish they had lent less. Both groups would have made different borrowing and lending decisions with greater foresight about the inflation rate. When the real interest rate turns out to be too high, which occurs when inflation is *lower* than expected, borrowers wish they had borrowed less and lenders wish they had lent more. Again, both groups would have made different borrowing and lending decisions with greater foresight about the inflation rate.

So unanticipated inflation imposes costs regardless of whether the inflation turns out to be higher or lower than anticipated. The presence of these costs gives everyone an incentive to forecast inflation correctly. Let's see how people go about this task.

Forecasting Inflation

Inflation is difficult to forecast for two reasons. First, there are several sources of inflation—the demand-pull and cost-push sources you've just studied. Second, the speed with which a change in either aggregate demand or aggregate supply translates into a change in the price level varies. This speed of response also depends, as you will see below, on the extent to which the inflation is anticipated.

Because inflation is costly and difficult to forecast, people devote considerable resources to improving inflation forecasts. Some people specialize in forecasting, and others buy forecasts from specialists. The specialist forecasters are economists who work for public and private macroeconomic forecasting agencies and for banks, insurance companies, labour unions, and large corporations. The returns these specialists make depend on the quality of their forecasts, so they have a strong incentive to forecast as accurately as possible. The most accurate forecast possible is the one that is based on all the relevant information and is called a **rational expectation**.

A rational expectation is not a correct forecast. It is simply the best forecast available. It will often turn out to be wrong, but no other forecast that could have been made with the information available could be predicted to be better.

You've seen the effects of inflation when people fail to anticipate it. And you've seen why it pays to try to anticipate inflation. Let's now see what happens if inflation is correctly anticipated.

Anticipated Inflation

In the demand-pull and cost-push inflations that we studied earlier in this chapter, the money wage rate is sticky. When aggregate demand increases, either to set off a demand-pull inflation or to accommodate cost-push inflation, the money wage rate does not change immediately. But if people correctly anticipate increases in aggregate demand, they will adjust money wage rates so as to keep up with anticipated inflation.

In this case, inflation proceeds with real GDP equal to potential GDP and unemployment equal to the natural rate. Figure 30.9 explains why. Suppose that last year the price level was 110 and real GDP was $800 billion, which is also potential GDP. The aggregate demand curve was AD_0, the short-run aggregate supply curve was SAS_0, and the long-run aggregate supply curve was LAS.

Suppose that potential GDP does not change, so the LAS curve does not shift. Also suppose that aggregate demand is expected to increase and that the expected aggregate demand curve for this year is AD_1. In anticipation of this increase in aggregate demand, money wage rate rises and the short-run aggregate supply curve shifts leftward. If the money wage rate rises by the same percentage as the price level rises, the short-run aggregate supply curve for next year is SAS_1.

If aggregate demand turns out to be the same as expected, the aggregate demand curve AD_1 and the short-run aggregate supply curve SAS_1 determine the actual price level at 121. Between last year and this year, the price level increased from 110 to 121 and the economy experienced an inflation rate of 10 percent, the same as the inflation rate that was anticipated. If this anticipated inflation is ongoing, in the following year aggregate demand increases (as anticipated) and the aggregate demand curve shifts to AD_2. The money wage rate rises to reflect the anticipated inflation and the short-run aggregate supply curve shifts to SAS_2. The price level rises by a further 10 percent to 133.

What has caused this inflation? The immediate answer is that because people expected inflation, the money wage rate was increased and prices increased. But the expectation was correct. Aggregate demand was expected to increase, and it did increase. Because aggregate demand was *expected* to increase from AD_0 to AD_1, the short-run aggregate supply curve shifted from SAS_0 to SAS_1. Because aggregate demand actually did increase by the amount that was expected, the actual aggregate demand curve shifted from AD_0 to AD_1. The

FIGURE 30.9

Anticipated Inflation

Potential real GDP is $800 billion. Last year, aggregate demand was AD_0, and the short-run aggregate supply curve was SAS_0. The actual price level was the same as the expected price level—110. This year, aggregate demand is expected to increase to AD_1. The rational expectation of the price level changes from 110 to 121. As a result, the money wage rate rises and the short-run aggregate supply curve shifts to SAS_1. If aggregate demand actually increases as expected, the actual aggregate demand curve AD_1 is the same as the expected aggregate demand curve. Equilibrium occurs at a real GDP of $800 billion and an actual price level of 121. The inflation is correctly anticipated. Next year the process continues with aggregate demand increasing as expected to AD_2 and the money wage rate rising to shift the short-run aggregate supply curve to SAS_2. Again, real GDP remains at $800 billion and the price level rises, as anticipated, to 133.

combination of the anticipated and actual shifts of the aggregate demand curve rightward produced an increase in the price level that was anticipated.

Only if the forecast of aggregate demand growth is correct does the economy follow the course described in Fig. 30.9.

Unanticipated Inflation

When aggregate demand increases by *more* than expected, there is some unanticipated inflation that looks just like the demand-pull inflation that you studied earlier. Some inflation is expected, and the money wage rate is set to reflect that expectation. The *SAS* curve intersects the *LAS* curve at the expected price level. Aggregate demand then increases, but by more than expected. So the *AD* curve intersects the *SAS* curve at a level of real GDP that exceeds potential GDP. With real GDP above potential GDP and unemployment below the natural rate, the money wage rate rises. So the price level rises further. If aggregate demand increases again, a demand-pull inflation spiral unwinds.

When aggregate demand increases by *less* than expected, there is some unanticipated inflation that looks like the cost-push inflation that you studied earlier. Again, some inflation is expected, and the money wage rate is set to reflect that expectation. The *SAS* curve intersects the *LAS* curve at the expected price level. Aggregate demand then increases, but by less than expected. So the *AD* curve intersects the *SAS* curve at a level of real GDP below potential GDP. Aggregate demand increases to restore full employment. But if aggregate demand is expected to increase by more than it actually does, the money wage rate again rises, short-run aggregate supply again decreases, and a cost-push inflation spiral unwinds.

We've seen that only when inflation is unanticipated does real GDP depart from potential GDP. When inflation is anticipated, real GDP remains at potential GDP. Does this mean that an anticipated inflation has no costs?

The Costs of Anticipated Inflation

The costs of an anticipated inflation depend on its rate. At a moderate rate of 2 or 3 percent a year, the cost is probably small. But as the anticipated inflation rate rises, so does its costs and an anticipated inflation at a rapid rate can be extremely costly.

Anticipated inflation decreases potential GDP and slows economic growth. These adverse consequences arise for three major reasons:

■ Transactions costs
■ Tax effects
■ Increased uncertainty

Transactions Costs The first transactions costs are known as the "boot leather costs." These are costs that arise from an increase in the velocity of circulation of money and an increase in the amount of running around that people do to try to avoid incurring losses from the falling value of money.

When money loses value at a rapid anticipated rate, it does not function well as a store of value and people try to avoid holding money. They spend their incomes as soon as they receive them, and firms pay out incomes—wages and dividends—as soon as they receive revenue from their sales. The velocity of circulation increases. During the 1920s when inflation in Germany reached *hyperinflation* levels (rates more than 50 percent a month), wages were paid and spent twice in a single day!

The range of estimates of the boot leather costs is large. Some economists put the cost at close to zero. Others estimate it to be as much as 2 percent of GDP for a 10 percent inflation. For a rapid inflation, these costs are much more.

The boot leather costs of inflation are just one of several transactions costs that are influenced by the inflation rate. At high anticipated inflation rates, people seek alternatives to money as a means of payment and use tokens and commodities or even barter, all of which are less efficient than money as a means of payment. For example, in Russia during the 1990s, when inflation reached 1,000 percent a year, the U.S. dollar started to replace the increasingly worthless Russian ruble. Consequently, people had to keep track of the exchange rate between the ruble and the dollar hour by hour and had to engage in many additional and costly transactions in the foreign exchange market.

Because anticipated inflation increases transactions costs, it diverts resources from producing goods and services and it decreases potential GDP. The faster the anticipated inflation rate, the greater is the decrease in potential GDP and the further leftward does the *LAS* curve shift.

Tax Effects Anticipated inflation interacts with the tax system and creates serious distortions in incentives. Its major effect is on the real interest rate.

Anticipated inflation swells the dollar returns on investments. But dollar returns are taxed, so the effective tax rate rises. This effect becomes serious at even modest inflation rates. Let's consider an example.

Suppose the real interest rate is 4 percent a year and the tax rate is 50 percent. With no inflation, the nominal interest rate is also 4 percent a year and 50 percent of this rate is taxable. The real *after-tax* interest rate is 2 percent a year (50 percent of 4 percent). Now suppose the inflation rate is 4 percent a year so

the nominal interest rate is 8 percent a year. The *after-tax* nominal rate is 4 percent a year (50 percent of 8 percent). Now subtract the 4 percent inflation rate from this amount and you see that the *after-tax real interest rate* is zero! The true tax rate on interest income is 100 percent.

The higher the inflation rate, the higher is the effective tax rate on income from capital. And the higher the tax rate, the higher is the interest rate paid by borrowers and the lower is the after-tax interest rate received by lenders (see Chapter 26, p. 588).

With a low after-tax real interest rate, the incentive to save is weakened and the saving rate falls. With a high cost of borrowing the amount of investment decreases. And with a fall in saving and investment, the pace of capital accumulation slows and so does the long-term growth rate of real GDP.

Increased Uncertainty When the inflation rate is high, there is increased uncertainty about the long-term inflation rate. Will inflation remain high for a long time or will price stability be restored? This increased uncertainty makes long-term planning difficult and gives people a shorter-term focus. Investment falls and so the growth rate slows.

But this increased uncertainty also misallocates resources. Instead of concentrating on the activities at which they have a comparative advantage, people find it more profitable to search for ways of avoiding the losses that inflation inflicts. As a result, inventive talent that might otherwise work on productive innovations works on finding ways of profiting from the inflation instead.

The implications of inflation for economic growth have been estimated to be enormous. Canadian economist Peter Howitt, now working at Ohio State University, estimates that the costs of inflation that we've just described are very high. Building on and extending work by Robert Barro of Harvard University, Howitt has estimated that if inflation is lowered from 3 percent a year to zero, the growth rate of real GDP will rise by between 0.06 and 0.09 percentage points a year. These numbers might seem small. But they are growth rates. After 30 years, real GDP would be 2.3 percent higher and the present value of all the future output would be 85 percent of current GDP—about $700 billion! In the rapid anticipated inflations of Brazil and Russia, the costs are much greater than the numbers given here. The implication is that inflation is very costly.

- What is a *rational expectation*? Are people who form rational expectations ever wrong?
- Why do people forecast inflation and what information do they use to do so?
- How does anticipated inflation occur?
- What are the effects of a rapid anticipated inflation? Does anticipated inflation bring an increase in real GDP?

You've seen that an increase in aggregate demand that is not fully anticipated increases both the price level and real GDP. It also decreases unemployment. Similarly, a decrease in aggregate demand that is not fully anticipated decreases the price level and real GDP. It also increases unemployment. Do these relationships mean that there is a tradeoff between inflation and unemployment? That is, does low unemployment always bring inflation and does low inflation bring high unemployment? We explore these questions next.

Inflation and Unemployment: The Phillips Curve

THE AGGREGATE SUPPLY–AGGREGATE DEMAND model focuses on the price level and real GDP. Knowing how these two variables change, we can work out what happens to the inflation rate and the unemployment rate. But the model does not place inflation and unemployment at the centre of the stage.

A more direct way of studying inflation and unemployment uses a relationship called the Phillips curve. The Phillips curve approach uses the same basic ideas as the *AS–AD* model, but it focuses directly on inflation and unemployment. The Phillips curve is so named because New Zealand economist A.W. Phillips popularized it. A **Phillips curve** is a curve that shows a relationship between inflation and unemployment. There are two time frames for Phillips curves:

- The short-run Phillips curve
- The long-run Phillips curve

The Short-Run Phillips Curve

The **short-run Phillips curve** is a curve that shows the tradeoff between inflation and unemployment, holding constant:

1. The expected inflation rate
2. The natural unemployment rate

You've just seen what determines the expected inflation rate. The natural rate of unemployment and the factors that influence it are explained in Chapters 23 and 31 on pp. 508–509 and pp. 709–11.

Figure 30.10 shows a short-run Phillips curve, *SRPC*. Suppose that the expected inflation rate is 10 percent a year and the natural unemployment rate

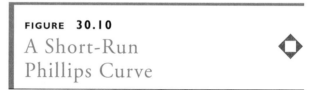

FIGURE 30.10

A Short-Run Phillips Curve

The short-run Phillips curve (*SRPC*) shows the relationship between inflation and unemployment at a given expected inflation rate and given natural unemployment rate. With an expected inflation rate of 10 percent a year and a natural unemployment rate of 6 percent, the short-run Phillips curve passes through point *a*. If aggregate demand increases by more than expected, unemployment decreases and inflation increases—a movement up the short-run Phillips curve. If aggregate demand increases by less than expected, unemployment increases and inflation decreases—a movement down the short-run Phillips curve.

is 6 percent, point *a* in the figure. A short-run Phillips curve passes through this point. If inflation rises above its expected rate, unemployment falls below its natural rate. This joint movement in the inflation rate and the unemployment rate is illustrated as a movement up the short-run Phillips curve from point *a* to point *b* in the figure. Similarly, if inflation falls below its expected rate, unemployment rises above the natural rate. In this case there is movement down the short-run Phillips curve from point *a* to point *c*.

This negative relationship between inflation and unemployment along the short-run Phillips curve is explained by the aggregate supply–aggregate demand model. Figure 30.11 shows the connection between the two approaches. Initially, the aggregate demand curve is AD_0, the short-run aggregate supply curve is SAS_0, and the long-run aggregate supply curve is *LAS*. Real GDP is $800 billion and the price level is 100. Aggregate demand is expected to increase and the aggregate demand curve is expected to shift rightward to AD_1. Anticipating this increase in aggregate demand, the money wage rate rises, which shifts the short-run aggregate supply curve to SAS_1. What happens to actual inflation and real GDP depends on the *actual* change in aggregate demand.

First, suppose that aggregate demand actually increases by the amount expected so the aggregate demand curve shifts to AD_1. The price level rises from 100 to 110 and the inflation rate is an anticipated 10 percent a year. Real GDP remains at potential GDP and unemployment remains at the natural rate. The economy moves to point *a* in Fig. 30.11 and it can equivalently be described as being at point *a* on the short-run Phillips curve in Fig. 30.10.

Alternatively, suppose that aggregate demand is expected to increase to AD_1 but actually increases by more than expected to AD_2. The price level now rises to 113, a 13 percent inflation rate. Real GDP increases above potential GDP and unemployment falls below the natural rate. We can now describe the economy as moving to point *b* in Fig. 30.11 or at point *b* on the short-run Phillips curve in Fig. 30.10.

Finally, suppose that aggregate demand is expected to increase to AD_1 but actually remains at AD_0. The price level now rises to 107, a 7 percent inflation rate. Real GDP decreases below potential GDP and unemployment rises above the natural rate. We can now describe the economy as moving to point *c* in Fig. 30.11 or at point *c* on the short-run Phillips curve in Fig. 30.10.

AS–AD and the Short-Run Phillips Curve

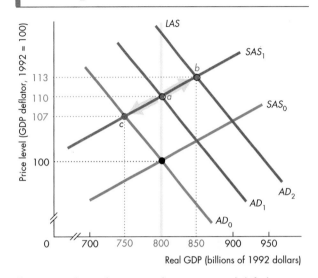

If aggregate demand is expected to increase and shift the aggregate demand curve from AD_0 to AD_1, then the money wage rate rises by an amount that shifts the short-run aggregate supply curve from SAS_0 to SAS_1. The price level rises to 110, a 10 percent rise, and the economy is at point *a* in this figure and at point *a* on the short-run Phillips curve in Fig. 30.10. If, with the same expectations, aggregate demand increases and shifts the aggregate demand curve from AD_0 to AD_2, the price level rises to 113, a 13 percent rise, and the economy is at point *b* in this figure and at point *b* on the short-run Phillips curve in Fig. 30.10. If, with the same expectations, aggregate demand does not change, the price level rises to 107, a 7 percent rise, and the economy is at point *c* in this figure and at point *c* on the short-run Phillips curve in Fig. 30.10.

The short-run Phillips curve is like the short-run aggregate supply curve. A movement along the *SAS* curve that brings a higher price level and an increase in real GDP is equivalent to a movement along the short-run Phillips curve that brings an increase in the inflation rate and a decrease in the unemployment rate. (Similarly, a movement along the *SAS* curve that brings a lower price level and a decrease in real GDP is equivalent to a movement along the short-run Phillips curve that brings a decrease in the inflation rate and an increase in the unemployment rate.)

The Long-Run Phillips Curve

The **long-run Phillips curve** shows the relationship between inflation and unemployment when the actual inflation rate equals the expected inflation rate. The long-run Phillips curve is vertical at the natural unemployment rate. In Fig. 30.12, it is the vertical line *LRPC*. The long-run Phillips curve tells us that any anticipated inflation rate is possible at the natural unemployment rate. This proposition is consistent with the *AS–AD* model, which predicts that when inflation is anticipated, real GDP equals potential GDP and unemployment is at the natural rate.

When the expected inflation rate changes, the short-run Phillips curve shifts but the long-run Phillips curve does not shift. If the expected inflation rate is 10 percent a year, the short-run Phillips curve

is $SRPC_0$ in Fig. 30.12. If the expected inflation rate falls to 7 percent a year, the short-run Phillips curve shifts downward to $SRPC_1$. The distance by which the short-run Phillips curve shifts downward is equal to the change in the expected inflation rate.

To see why the short-run Phillips curve shifts when the expected inflation rate changes, let's do a thought experiment. There is full employment and a 10 percent a year anticipated inflation is raging. The Bank of Canada now begins an attack on inflation by slowing money supply growth. Aggregate demand growth slows and the inflation rate falls to 7 percent a year. At first, the decrease in inflation is *un*anticipated, so the money wage rate continues to rise at its original rate. The short-run aggregate supply curve shifts leftward at the same pace as before. Real GDP decreases, and unemployment increases. In Fig. 30.12, the economy moves from point *a* to point *c* on $SRPC_0$.

If the actual inflation rate remains steady at 7 percent a year, this rate eventually comes to be expected. As this happens, wage growth slows and the short-run aggregate supply curve shifts leftward less quickly. Eventually, it shifts leftward at the same pace at which the aggregate demand curve is shifting rightward. The actual inflation rate equals the expected inflation rate, and full employment is restored. Unemployment is back at its natural rate. In Fig. 30.12, the short-run Phillips curve has shifted from $SRPC_0$ to $SRPC_1$ and the economy is at point *d*.

An increase in the expected inflation rate has the opposite effect to that shown in Fig. 30.12. Another important source of shifts in the Phillips curve is a change in the natural rate of unemployment.

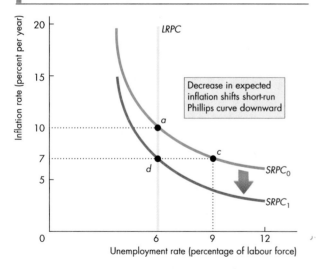

FIGURE 30.12

Short-Run and Long-Run Phillips Curves

The long-run Phillips curve is *LRPC*, a vertical line at the natural unemployment rate. A fall in expected inflation shifts the short-run Phillips curve downward. For example, when the expected inflation rate falls from 10 percent a year to 7 percent a year, the short-run Phillips curve shifts downward from $SRPC_0$ and $SRPC_1$. The new short-run Phillips curve intersects the long-run Phillips curve at the new expected inflation rate—point *d*. With the original expected inflation rate (of 10 percent), an actual inflation rate of 7 percent a year would occur at an unemployment rate of 9 percent, at point *c*.

Changes in the Natural Unemployment Rate

The natural unemployment rate changes for many reasons. (See Chapter 31, pp. 709–711.) A change in the natural unemployment rate shifts both the short-run and long-run Phillips curves. Figure 30.13 illustrates such shifts. If the natural unemployment rate increases from 6 percent to 9 percent, the long-run Phillips curve shifts from $LRPC_0$ to $LRPC_1$, and if expected inflation is constant at 10 percent a year, the short-run Phillips curve shifts from $SRPC_0$ to $SRPC_1$. Because the expected inflation rate is constant, the short-run Phillips curve $SRPC_1$ intersects the long-run curve $LRPC_1$ (point *e*) at the same inflation rate at which the short-run Phillips curve $SRPC_0$ intersects the long-run curve $LRPC_0$ (point *a*).

FIGURE 30.13

A Change in the Natural Unemployment Rate

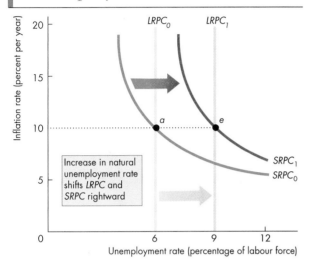

A change in the natural unemployment rate shifts both the short-run and long-run Phillips curves. Here the natural unemployment rate increases from 6 percent to 9 percent, and the two Phillips curves shift right to *SRPC₁* and *LRPC₁*. The new long-run Phillips curve intersects the new short-run Phillips curve at the expected inflation rate—point e.

The Canadian Phillips Curve

Figure 30.14(a) is a scatter diagram of inflation and unemployment since 1960. We can interpret the data in terms of a shifting long-run and short-run Phillips curve as in Fig. 30.14(b). In 1960, the natural rate of unemployment was 5 percent so the long-run Phillips curve was $LRPC_1$. The expected inflation rate was 3 percent a year so the short-run Phillips curve, which intersects the long-run Phillips curve at point *a*, was $SRPC_1$. During the 1970s and through 1982, the expected inflation rate and the natural unemployment rate increased. The long-run Phillips curve shifted rightward to $LRPC_2$ and the short-run Phillips curve shifted rightward to $SRPC_2$. During the 1980s and 1990s, the expected inflation rate and the natural unemployment rate decreased. The long-run Phillips curve shifted leftward to $LRPC_3$ and the short-run Phillips curve shifted leftward back to $SRPC_1$. The SRPC of 1998 is the same as that of 1960, but in 1998, the natural rate of unemployment is higher and the expected inflation rate is lower than in 1960.

FIGURE 30.14

Phillips Curves in Canada

(a) The time sequence

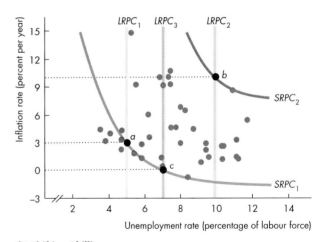

(b) Shifting Phillips curves

In part (a), each dot represents the combination of inflation and unemployment for a particular year in Canada. There is no clear relationship between the two variables. Part (b) interprets the data with shifting Phillips curves. During the 1960s, the natural rate was 5 percent and the expected inflation rate was 3 percent a year. The Phillips curves were $SRPC_1$ and $LRPC_1$ (which intersect at *a*). The curves were $SRPC_2$ and $LRPC_2$ (intersecting at *b*) by 1982, and $SRPC_1$ and $LRPC_3$ (intersecting at *c*) by the late 1990s.

Source: Statistics Canada, *StatCan: CANSIM Disc,* March 1999, and the authors' calculations and assumptions.

■ How would you illustrate an unanticipated change in the inflation rate by using the Phillips curve?

■ What are the effects of an unanticipated increase in the inflation rate on the unemployment rate?

■ If the expected inflation rate increased by 10 percentage points, how would the short-run Phillips curve change and how would the long-run Phillips curve change?

■ If the natural unemployment rate increases, what happens to the short-run Phillips curve? What happens to the long-run Phillips curve? What happens to the expected inflation rate?

■ Does Canada have a short-run Phillips curve? Has the Canadian short-run Phillips curve remained stable?

■ Does Canada have a stable long-run Phillips curve?

So far, we've studied the effects of inflation on real GDP, real wages, employment, and unemployment. But inflation lowers the value of money and changes the real value of the amounts borrowed and repaid. As a result, the interest rate is influenced by inflation. Let's see how.

Interest Rates and Inflation

TODAY, BUSINESSES IN CANADA CAN BORROW AT interest rates of around 6 percent a year. Businesses in Russia pay interest rates of 60 percent a year and in Turkey, 80 percent a year. Although Canadian interest rates have never been as high as these two cases, during the 1980s, Canadian businesses faced interest rates of 20 percent a year or higher. Why do interest rates vary so much both across countries and over time? Part of the answer is because risk differences make *real interest rates* vary across countries. But another part of the answer is that the inflation rate varies.

You can see in Fig. 30.15 that the higher the inflation rate, the higher is the nominal interest rate. This proposition is true for Canada over time (Fig. 30.15a) and it is true for the world at a given time (Fig. 30.15b).

FIGURE 30.15
Inflation and the Interest Rate

(a) Canada

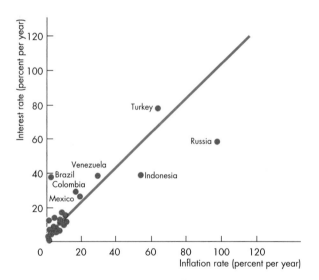

(b) Around the world

Other things remaining the same, the higher the inflation rate, the higher is the nominal interest rate. Part (a) shows this relationship between nominal interest rates and the inflation rate in Canada and part (b) shows the relationship across a number of countries in 1999.

Source: Statistics Canada, *StatCan: CANSIM Disc*, March 1999; *The Economist*, March 6, 1999; and the authors' calculations and assumptions.

How Interest Rates Are Determined

The *real* interest rate is determined by investment demand and saving supply in the global capital market. Investment demand and saving supply depend on the real interest rate. And the real interest rate adjusts to make investment plans and saving plans equal. You can think of the forces that determine the equilibrium real interest rate by using the standard demand and supply model. National real interest rates vary around the world-average real interest rate because of national differences in risk.

A *nominal* interest rate is determined by the demand for money and the supply of money in each nation's money market. The demand for money depends on the nominal interest rate and the supply of money is determined by the central bank's monetary policy—the Bank of Canada's monetary policy in Canada. And the nominal interest rate adjusts to make the quantity of money demanded equal to the quantity supplied. (Chapter 27, p. 611 explains the forces that determine the equilibrium nominal interest rate.)

Why Inflation Influences the Nominal Interest Rate

Because the real interest rate is determined in the global capital market and nominal interest rates are determined in each nation's money market, there is no tight and mechanical link between the two interest rates. But on the average, and other things remaining the same, a 1 percentage point rise in the inflation rate leads to a 1 percentage point rise in the nominal interest rate. Why? The answer is that the capital market and the money market are closely interconnected. The investment, saving, and demand for money decisions that people make are connected and the result is that the equilibrium nominal interest rate approximately equals the real interest rate plus the expected inflation rate.

To see why this relationship between the real interest rate and the nominal interest rate arises, think about the investment, saving, and demand for money decisions that people make. Imagine first that there is no inflation. Investment equals saving at a real interest rate of 6 percent a year. The demand for money equals the supply of money at a nominal interest rate of 6 percent a year. Teleglobe Canada is willing to pay an interest rate of 6 percent a year to get the funds it needs to pay for its global investment in new satellites. Sue and thousands of people like her

are willing to save and lend Teleglobe Canada the amount it needs to buy its satellites if they can get a *real* return of 6 percent a year. (Sue is saving to buy a new car.) And Teleglobe Canada, Sue, and everyone else are willingly holding the quantity of (real) money supplied by the Bank of Canada.

Now imagine the inflation rate is a steady and expected 4 percent a year. All dollar amounts, including satellite service profits and car prices are rising by 4 percent a year. If Teleglobe Canada was willing to pay a 6 percent interest rate when there was no inflation, it is now willing to pay 10 percent interest. Its profits are rising by 4 percent a year, so it is *really* paying only 6 percent. Similarly, if Sue was willing to lend at a 6 percent interest rate when there was no inflation, she is now willing to lend only if she gets 10 percent interest. The price of the car Sue is planning on buying is rising by 4 percent a year, so she is *really* getting only a 6 percent interest rate.

Because borrowers are willing to pay the higher rate and lenders are willing to lend only if they receive the higher rate when inflation is anticipated, the *nominal interest rate* increases by an amount equal to the expected inflation rate. The *real interest rate* remains constant.

At a nominal interest rate of 10 percent a year, people are willingly holding the quantity of (real) money supplied by the Bank of Canada. This quantity is less than with zero inflation. The price level rises by more than the quantity of money and the real quantity of money decreases because of the increase in inflation.

R E V I E W   Q U I Z

◼ What is the relationship between the real interest rate, the nominal interest rate, and the inflation rate?

◼ Why does inflation change the nominal interest rate?

◆ *Reading Between the Lines* on pages 684–685 looks at the current low inflation in Canada and the Bank of Canada's actions to keep it that way.

You have now completed your study of the aggregate demand side of the economy. Your task in the following chapters is to probe more deeply the supply side. We study the forces that determine aggregate supply in the short run and the long run and that bring economic growth and cycles.

Reading Between the Lines

**POLICY
WATCH**

Is Inflation Dead in Canada?

THE GLOBE AND MAIL, AUGUST 19, 1999

Central bank sees strong growth

By Marian Stinson

The Bank of Canada yesterday forecast strong economic growth with controlled inflation, and economists predicted the central bank would be able to hold down interest rates despite an anticipated hike by the U.S. Federal Reserve Board.

Indeed, the only blip on the inflation front came from gasoline prices, which jumped 4.1 per cent in July and pushed the annual inflation rate up to 1.8 per cent from 1.6 per cent in June, in line with economists' forecasts. ...

Even with the recent price increases, the central bank sees inflation remaining in the lower half of its target range of 1 to 3 per cent this year, while the economy is poised to grow near the upper end of its forecast of 2.75 to 3.75 per cent, the Bank of Canada said. ...

After dipping to a recent low in February of 0.8 per cent, core prices have been trending higher in recent months, so that "inflation has ostensibly moved from below the Bank of Canada's target band and closer to the midpoint," said Bank of Montreal economist Paul Ferley. ...

"With the Canadian economy continuing to operate below capacity, the greater risk to the inflation outlook remains that it could fall below rather than move above the target band," Mr. Ferley said. "This weighs in favour of the Bank of Canada continuing to resist raising interest rates even in the face of a likely tightening by the U.S. Federal Reserve next week." ...

Canada can look forward to solid growth with little inflationary pressure for the rest of this year ... [and] an unemployment rate close to 8 per cent in Canada means that wage pressure is not seen as an immediate threat to inflation as it was a decade ago.

*Reprinted with permission from The Globe and Mail.
Further reproduction prohibited.*

Essence of the Story

■ In July 1999, the annual inflation rate in Canada was 1.8 percent.

■ The Bank of Canada anticipates that the inflation rate will remain in the lower half of the target range of 1 to 3 percent a year during 1999 and that the economy will grow near the upper end of the forecast of 2.75 to 3.75 percent.

■ Because the inflation outlook is in the bottom half of the target range, the Bank of Canada is likely to resist raising interest rates.

■ With the Canadian economy operating below capacity (real GDP less than potential GDP), inflation could fall below the lower target band.

■ With the unemployment rate close to 8 percent, wage pressure is not seen as a threat to inflation.

684

Economic Analysis

■ Inflation is low in Canada because the Bank of Canada has slowed the money supply growth rate on three occasions.

■ Figure 1 shows these episodes in the years 1980–1983, 1989–1994, and 1996–1997.

■ Figure 1 also shows (during the shaded years) that when the money supply growth rate is slowed, the inflation rate falls.

■ Since 1992, the inflation rate has been within the target zone of the Bank of Canada—between 1 and 3 percent a year.

■ When the Bank of Canada wants to slow inflation, it slows money growth and raises interest rates.

■ With the inflation rate within the Bank of Canada's target range, an interest rate hike is unlikely.

■ During February 1999, the inflation rate actually fell below the target range.

■ To return inflation to the target range, the Bank of Canada could have increased the growth rate of the money supply and lowered the interest rate. But if the Bank had adopted such a policy, inflation would have increased.

■ If the economy is operating below potential GDP (as the news article implies), there is no inflationary gap and no wage pressure to increase the inflation rate.

■ Figure 2 shows part of the cost of lowering the inflation rate. Generally, when money growth is slowed and the inflation rate falls, the unemployment rate increases and the real GDP growth rate decreases. Output and incomes are lost. But these costs are temporary, while the benefits of low inflation are permanent.

■ With the Bank of Canada holding the inflation rate steady, the Canadian economy is likely to continue to grow.

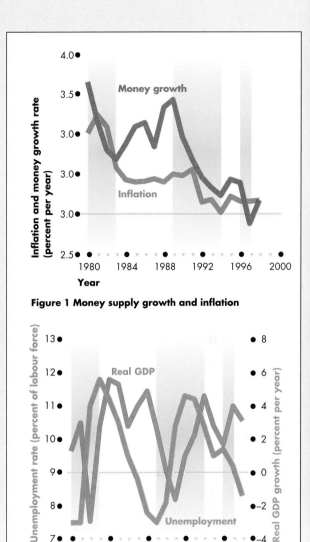

Figure 1 Money supply growth and inflation

Figure 2 Real GDP growth and unemployment

685

SUMMARY

Key Points

Inflation and the Price Level (p. 666)

▨ Inflation is a process of persistently rising prices and falling value of money.

Demand-Pull Inflation (pp. 667–669)

▨ Demand-pull inflation arises from increasing aggregate demand.

▨ Its main sources are increases in the money supply or in government expenditures.

Cost-Push Inflation (pp. 669–671)

▨ Cost-push inflation can result from any factor that decreases aggregate supply.

▨ Its main sources are increasing wage rates and increasing prices of key raw materials.

The Quantity Theory of Money (pp. 672–673)

▨ The quantity theory of money is the proposition that money growth and inflation move up and down together in the long run.

▨ The Canadian and international evidence is consistent with the quantity theory on the average.

Effects of Inflation (pp. 674–678)

▨ Inflation is costly when it is unanticipated because it creates inefficiencies and redistributes income and wealth.

▨ People try to anticipate inflation to avoid its costs.

▨ Forecasts of inflation based on all the available relevant information are called rational expectations.

▨ A moderate anticipated inflation has a small cost. But a rapid anticipated inflation is costly because it decreases potential GDP and slows growth.

Inflation and Unemployment: The Phillips Curve (pp. 678–682)

▨ The short-run Phillips curve is a tradeoff between inflation and unemployment, given the expected inflation rate and the natural unemployment rate.

▨ The long-run Phillips curve is vertical at the natural unemployment rate.

▨ Unexpected changes in the inflation rate bring movements along the short-run Phillips curve.

▨ Changes in expected inflation shift the short-run Phillips curve.

▨ Changes in the natural unemployment rate shift both the short-run and long-run Phillips curves.

Interest Rates and Inflation (pp. 682–683)

▨ The higher the expected inflation rate, the higher is the nominal interest rate.

▨ As the anticipated inflation rate rises, borrowers willingly pay a higher interest rate and lenders successfully demand a higher interest rate.

▨ The nominal interest rate adjusts to equal the real interest rate plus the expected inflation rate.

Key Figures ◆

Key Terms

PROBLEMS

*1. The figure shows an economy's long-run aggregate supply curve, *LAS*, three aggregate demand curves AD_0, AD_1, and AD_2, and three short-run aggregate supply curves SAS_0, SAS_1, and SAS_2. The economy starts out on the curves AD_0 and SAS_0. Some events then occur that generate a demand-pull inflation.

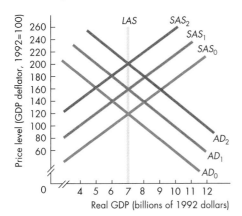

a. List the events that might cause demand-pull inflation.
b. Using the figure, describe the initial effects of demand-pull inflation.
c. Using the figure, describe what happens as a demand-pull inflation spiral unwinds.

2. In the economy described in problem 1, some events then occur that generate a cost-push inflation.
a. List the events that might cause cost-push inflation.
b. Using the figure, describe the initial effects of cost-push inflation.
c. Using the figure, describe what happens as a cost-push inflation spiral unwinds.

*3. Quantecon is a country in which the quantity theory of money operates. The country has a constant population, capital stock, and technology. In year 1, real GDP was $400 million, the price level was 200, and the velocity of circulation of money was 20. In year 2, the quantity of money was 20 percent higher than in year 1.
a. What was the quantity of money in year 1?
b. What was the quantity of money in year 2?
c. What was the price level in year 2?

d. What was the level of real GDP in year 2?
e. What was the velocity of circulation in year 2?

4. In Quantecon described in problem 3, in year 3, the quantity of money falls to one-fifth of its year 2 level.
a. What is the quantity of money in year 3?
b. What is the price level in year 3?
c. What is the level of real GDP in year 3?
d. What is the velocity of circulation in year 3?
e. If it takes more than one year for the full quantity theory effect to occur, what do you predict happens in Quantecon in year 3 to real GDP? Why?

*5. In the economy described in problem 1, some events then occur that generate a perfectly anticipated inflation.
a. List the events that might cause a perfectly anticipated inflation.
b. Using the figure, describe the initial effects of anticipated inflation.
c. Using the figure, describe what happens as anticipated inflation proceeds.

6. In the economy described in problem 1, suppose that people anticipate deflation (a falling price level) but aggregate demand turns out to not change.
a. What happens to the short-run and long-run aggregate supply curves? (Draw some new curves if you need to.)
b. Using the figure, describe the initial effects of anticipated deflation.
c. Using the figure, describe what happens as it becomes obvious to everyone that the anticipated deflation is not going to occur.

*7. An economy with a natural unemployment rate of 4 percent and an expected inflation rate of 6 percent a year has the following inflation and unemployment history:

Year	Inflation rate (percent per year)	Unemployment rate (percent)
1999	10	2
2000	8	3
2001	6	4
2002	4	5
2003	2	6

a. Draw a diagram of the economy's short-run and long-run Phillips curves.

b. If the actual inflation rate rises from 6 percent a year to 8 percent a year, what is the change in the unemployment rate? Explain why it occurs.

8. For the economy described in problem 7, the natural unemployment rate rises to 5 percent and the expected inflation rate falls to 5 percent a year. Draw the new short-run and long-run Phillips curves in a diagram.

*9. An economy has an unemployment rate of 4 percent and an inflation rate of 5 percent a year at point *a* in the figure. Some events then occur that move the economy to point *d*.

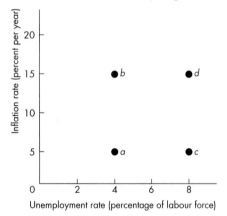

a. Describe the events that could move the economy from point *a* to point *d*.

b. Draw in the diagram the economy's short-run and long-run Phillips curves when the economy is at point *a*.

c. Draw in the diagram the economy's short-run and long-run Phillips curves when the economy is at point *d*.

10. In the economy described in problem 9, some events occur that move the economy from point *b* to point *c*.

a. Describe the events that could move the economy from point *b* to point *c*.

b. Draw in the diagram the economy's short-run and long-run Phillips curves when the economy is at point *b*.

c. Draw in the diagram the economy's short-run and long-run Phillips curves when the economy is at point *c*.

CRITICAL THINKING

 1. Study *Reading Between the Lines* on pp. 684–685 and then answer the following questions:

a. What does the governor of the Bank of Canada say about the likelihood of inflation increasing?

b. Is the news article describing a cost-push inflation or a demand-pull inflation or an anticipated inflation? Provide detailed reasons.

c. If the Bank of Canada tightens money and raises interest rates, how do you think that action will influence inflation and unemployment in the short run?

d. Use the links on the Parkin-Bade Web site and obtain information on the Bank of Canada's interest rate changes since the news article was written. Did the Bank resist raising interest rates as predicted in the article? Did the Canadian economy behave as foreseen in the news article?

2. In the light of what you have learned in this chapter, what do you think the Bank of Canada should do during 2000 to keep inflation in check? Use the links on the Parkin-Bade Web site and find out what actions the Bank has been taking.

3. If inflation rates of 10 percent a year (like we had during the 1970s) returned in Canada, who would benefit and who would lose?

4. "The Phillips curve is a menu from which the government must choose how much inflation and how much unemployment to buy." Evaluate this statement. Under what conditions is it true? Under what conditions is it false?

5. If the Bank of Canada aimed to use monetary policy to lower the unemployment rate to 3 percent, what do you predict would happen to:

a. Unemployment in the short run?

b. Unemployment in the long run?

c. Inflation in the short run?

d. Inflation in the long run?

e. The short-run Phillips curve?

f. The long-run Phillips curve?

g. Potential GDP?

h. The growth rate of potential GDP?

Understanding Aggregate Demand and Inflation

Aggregate demand fluctuations bring recessions and expansions. If aggregate demand expands more rapidly than long-run aggregate supply, we get inflation. So understanding the forces that determine aggregate demand helps us to understand both the business cycle and inflation. ◆ It took economists a long time to achieve this knowledge, and we still don't know enough about aggregate demand to be able to forecast it more than a few months ahead. But we do know the basic factors that influence aggregate demand. And we know a lot about how those factors interact to send shock waves rippling through the economy. ◆ Fundamentally, aggregate demand is a monetary phenomenon. The quantity of money is the single most significant influence on aggregate demand. This insight was first outlined more than 200 years ago by David Hume, a Scottish philosopher and close friend of Adam Smith. Said Hume, "In every Kingdom into which money begins to flow in greater abundance than formerly, every thing takes a new face: labour and industry gain life; the merchant becomes more enterprising, the manufacturer more diligent and skilful, and even the farmer follows his plough with greater alacrity and attention." Milton Friedman and other economists known as *monetarists* also emphasize the central role of money. Money lies at the centre of Keynes' theory of aggregate demand as well. But Keynes also called attention to the power of independent changes in government expenditures,

Money Chasing Goods

taxes, and business investment to influence aggregate demand. In the modern world, we also recognize the effect of changes in exports on aggregate demand.
◆ The chapters in this part explain the factors that influence aggregate demand and help you to understand how they interact to bring multiplier effects on aggregate expenditure. Chapter 25 explains the effects of changes in business investment and the multiplier effect it has on consumption expenditure and aggregate expenditure. This chapter also explains how changes in business inventories trigger changes in production and incomes. Chapter 26 looks at fiscal policy and applies the model of Chapter 25 to study the effects of changes in government expenditures and taxes. Chapter 27 brings money into the picture and explains what money is, how banks create it, and what determines the interest rate. Chapter 28 shows you how the Bank of Canada controls the quantity of money and influences interest rates and expenditure. Chapter 29 returns to the aggregate supply–aggregate demand model and explains how fiscal policy and monetary policy interact. Chapter 30 explains inflation and shows how the trend in the money supply determines the trend in inflation and how fluctuations in aggregate demand bring fluctuations in inflation, employment, and unemployment.

◇ Many economists have developed the insights that you've learned in these chapters. One of the truly outstanding ones is Milton Friedman, whom you can meet on the next page. You can also meet one of today's leading macroeconomists, David Laidler of the University of Western Ontario.

Probing the Ideas

Money and Inflation

"Inflation is always and everywhere a monetary phenomenon."

MILTON FRIEDMAN, *THE COUNTER-REVOLUTION IN MONETARY THEORY.*

Milton Friedman *was born into a poor immigrant family in New York City in 1912. He was an undergraduate at Rutgers and a graduate student at Columbia University during the Great Depression. Today, Professor Friedman is a Senior Fellow at the Hoover Institution at Stanford University. But his reputation was built between 1946 and 1983, when he was a leading member of the "Chicago School," an approach to economics developed at the University of Chicago and based on the views that free markets allocate resources efficiently and that stable and low money supply growth delivers macroeconomic stability.*

Friedman has advanced our understanding of the forces that determine aggregate demand and clarified the effects of the quantity of money. And for this work, he was awarded the (much overdue in the opinion of his many admirers) 1977 Nobel Prize for Economic Science.

By reasoning from basic economic principles, Friedman predicted that persistent demand stimulation would not increase output but would cause inflation. When output growth slowed and inflation broke out in the 1970s, Friedman seemed like a prophet and, for a time, his policy prescription, known as "monetarism," was embraced around the world.

The Issues

The combination of history and economics has taught us a lot about the causes of inflation. Severe inflation—hyperinflation—arises from a breakdown of the normal fiscal policy processes at times of war or political upheaval. Tax revenues fall short of government spending, and newly printed money fills the gap between them. As inflation increases, the quantity of money needed to make payments increases, and a shortage of money can even result. So the rate of money growth increases yet further, and prices rise yet faster. Eventually, the monetary system collapses. Such was the experience of Germany during the 1920s and Brazil during the 1990s.

In earlier times, when commodities were used as money, inflation resulted from the discovery of new sources of money. The most recent occurrence of this type of inflation was at the end of the nineteenth century when gold, then used as money, was discovered in Australia, the Klondike, and South Africa.

In modern times, inflation has resulted from increases in the money supply that has accommodated increases in costs. The most dramatic of such inflations occurred during the 1970s when the Bank of Canada, the Federal Reserve, and other central banks around the world accommodated oil price increases.

To avoid inflation, money supply growth must be held in check. But at times of severe cost pressure, central banks feel a strong tug in the direction of avoiding recession and accommodating the cost pressure.

Yet some countries have avoided inflation more effectively than others have. One source of success is central bank independence. In low-inflation countries, such as Germany and Japan, the central bank decides how much money to create and at what level to set interest rates, and does not take instructions from the government. In high-inflation countries, such as the United Kingdom and Italy, the central bank takes direct orders from the government about interest rates and money supply growth. The architects of a new monetary system for the European Community have noticed this connection between central bank independence and inflation, and they are modelling the European Central Bank on Germany's Bundesbank.

Then ...

When inflation is especially rapid, as it was in Germany in 1923, money becomes almost worthless. In Germany at that time, bank notes were more valuable as fire kindling than as money, and the sight of people burning Reichmarks was a common one. To avoid having to hold money for too long, wages were paid and spent twice a day. Banks took deposits and made loans, but at interest rates that compensated both depositors and the bank for the falling value of money—interest rates that could exceed 100 percent a month. The price of a dinner would increase during the course of an evening, making lingering over coffee a very expensive pastime.

... and Now

In 1994, Brazil had a computer-age hyperinflation, an inflation rate that was close to 50 percent a month. Banks installed ATMs on almost every street corner and refilled them several times an hour. Brazilians tried to avoid holding currency. As soon as they were paid, they went shopping and bought enough food to get them through to the next payday. Some shoppers filled as many as six carts on a single monthly trip to the supermarket. Also, instead of using currency, Brazilians used credit cards whenever possible. But they paid their card balances off quickly because the interest rate on unpaid balances was 50 percent a month. Only at such a high interest rate did it pay banks to lend to cardholders, because banks themselves were paying interest rates of 40 percent a month to induce depositors to keep their money in the bank.

Many contemporary economists have contributed to our understanding of the forces that influence aggregate demand and inflation. David Laidler, whom you can meet on the following pages, is one of these economists.

Talking with David Laidler

David Laidler, *Professor of Economics at the University of Western Ontario, is one of Canada's most distinguished economists. Born in Tynemouth, England, in 1938, Professor Laidler was an undergraduate at the London School of Economics and a graduate student at Syracuse University and the University of Chicago. He has taught at the University of California, Berkeley, the Universities of Essex and Manchester, and been a visiting professor or guest lecturer in many other universities around the world. During 1998–99, he served as Special Advisor to the Bank of Canada. A past president of the Canadian Economics Association, Professor Laidler is the author of numerous books and articles on a wide range of topics that include the history of monetary theory and macroeconomics, money and inflation, and Canadian economic policy. His most recent book,* Fabricating the Keynesian Revolution, *(Cambridge University*

Press, 1999) is a meticulous account of economists' efforts to understand money, the business cycle, and inflation during the 1920s and 1930s.

Robin Bade and Michael Parkin talked with David Laidler about Canada's present fiscal policy and monetary policy challenges and about the lessons to be learned from the turbulent episodes of the past.

Why and how did you get into economics?

During my last three years in high school, I took a course in the economic history of modern Britain. Unlike anything else I had studied, this was about places I knew and about events that had been relevant to shaping the lives of the people around me. I applied to the London School of Economics under the impression that economics would be like economic history. It was not, of course, and the abstract nature of economic theory came as quite a shock; but after about two years I began to understand how I could use that theory to develop a richer understanding of the history that had attracted me to the subject in the first place. After that, I was hooked.

What can we learn from episodes of extreme inflation, like that of Germany during the 1920s, and extreme deflation, like the Great Depression of the1930s?

The most obvious lesson, and not just for economists, is just how socially divisive and destructive monetary instability can be. The monetary system is an extraordinarily important institution that permits people to get on with their own economic lives in their own way in a decentralized economy. But it functions because people who do not really understand the system nevertheless trust it. When it malfunctions, they feel cheated and start looking for simple solutions. For example, the Weimar hyperinflation weakened democracy's newly established foothold in German society, and, before it had fully recovered, the Depression, which spread to Germany from the United States, created a crisis of confidence in liberal institutions that brought the Nazis to power.

It's only a small consolation that extreme episodes like these generate the nearest thing that economists have to controlled experiments, where they can observe fundamental forces at work in ways that remain hidden in normal times. Economics is one of those subjects where we learn the most from mistakes.

Has economics progressed? Do we now know enough to avoid extremes of inflation and depression?

Yes, but . . . at the time there were people around who knew well enough that the burden of reparations on Germany after World War I was insupportable and capable of forcing the authorities into continuing the ruinous programme of money creation that had started during the war. Keynes was one of them. And in the 1930s, there were those who warned that Federal Reserve policy was much tighter than it looked and that it would lead to serious trouble. But in both cases, the sensible people lost the policy debate.

One has to hope that we can do better now. Most important of all perhaps, in countries like Canada, the level of economic literacy is much higher these days and is much more widespread among the general population. Large numbers of people have taken economics in school, college, and university. And the widespread wealth-holding gives large numbers of people a strong incentive to keep themselves well informed about economic policy.

Even so, though they aren't influential just at the moment, there are still economists who will argue that money creation is a consequence but not a cause of inflation, and they might just gain the upper hand in policy circles. It's only 20 or 30 years since this view did have the upper hand and did an enormous amount of damage to western economies. As to depression, the recent policies of the Bank of Japan have been disturbingly like those of the Fed in the early 1930s, and the rationalization offered has been more or less the same too. So I don't think we'll ever be quite out of the wood. Our best hope of staying out of trouble is a well-informed and economically literate electorate.

Why do you think Canada, along with most other countries, operated with a persistent and at times large federal fiscal deficit during the years between 1975 and 1997? Is the public debt that we built up during the deficit years a problem?

Partly it was because, in the 1970s, economics itself didn't pay much attention to the problems that public debt can cause in the real world. Right now, interest on the federal debt in Canada is running at more than twice the revenue collected by the GST, but in the 1970s, I don't recall any textbooks that paid attention to the problems of servicing a large debt. But clearly the taxes that are needed to service debt on the scale that we now have put an enormous deadweight load on the economy and cripple our ability to undertake other policies that we might like: tax cuts if we are right of centre or new social spending programmes if we veer to the left.

Canadian taxes are too high for comfort in the longer run, both on average and on the margin.

Now that we have a federal surplus, how should fiscal policy change?

I would go very slowly on the changes right now. The federal budget is indeed in surplus, but the debt is still huge, so I'd concentrate on getting it down for a year or so more. Though I'm told that we could now get through a mild downturn, the public finances are still very vulnerable to another recession on the scale of the last two, which would drive up spending and drive down revenues pretty quickly.

Are federal taxes too high on the average? Are marginal tax rates too high?

Yes, I'd agree that Canadian taxes are too high for comfort in the longer run, both on average and on the margin. If we're going to keep a welfare state in Canada, taxes will always be higher than those in the United States, but that doesn't mean that we can ignore the advantages that the U.S. private sector gets from its lower tax burden. Canada must remain competitive with the United States, but if average tax rates get too high here, some corporations and some individuals will migrate to the United States.

Marginal tax rates are a more subtle problem. The issue here is the way in which they distort incentives and lower productivity. Two factors are at stake here. You need to lower marginal tax rates on income across the board to encourage people to work harder, but you also need to even rates out across different activities and sectors of the economy to make sure that people don't devote their efforts to low productivity activities where tax breaks are available. Remember, it's after-tax income that individuals are pursuing.

Bank of Canada would have done better to keep its eyes more firmly on achieving low inflation and to avoid the distraction of trying to prop up the exchange rate

Why do you think Canada has had such a high unemployment rate compared with the United States?
Well, there are some measurement differences, but they only account for a percentage point or so of the difference. Canadian unemployment started moving up in the 1970s, and I'm inclined to put a lot of that down to ill-advised "reforms" of the UI system, introduced in 1972. These gave large hidden subsidies to seasonal industries, which generate a lot of unemployment at particular times of the year, and, by making benefits more generous in high unemployment areas, they also discouraged people from leaving to look for work elsewhere, where they were more likely to find it. If I'm right, we should now be seeing some improvement in the wake of the changes to unemployment benefits introduced in 1995.

Canada has achieved low inflation, but at a high cost. Was the cost worth paying?
The Canadian economy of the late 1980s was certainly in need of some pretty basic adjustments, including in the monetary policy area, and it got them. The effects were enormously painful because the adjustments had been put off for far too long. But the deep and drawn-out recession of the early 1990s wasn't solely caused by monetary policy geared to reducing inflation. To get a complete picture, you also have to consider the

effects of the restructuring that the Free Trade agreement brought about at the beginning of the period and of government spending cutbacks later in the decade.

But could we have lowered inflation at a lower cost?
I have long thought that the Bank of Canada would have done better to keep its eyes more firmly on achieving low inflation and to avoid the distraction of trying to prop up the exchange rate from time to time. In 1990 and 1995, concerns about the dollar surely caused monetary policy to be tighter than was needed for purely domestic reasons, and maybe in 1992–3 as well. Again, the last couple of years have been more encouraging. The Bank did raise interest rates sharply in August 1998 to prop up the dollar as it had done on earlier occasions. That was a difficult judgement call at the time. But it's worth noting that Australia, which was under similar pressure at the time, got through without an interest rate increase. Nevertheless, the Bank of Canada unwound its increase much more rapidly than on past occasions, and when the Fed tightened in 1999, the Bank didn't follow, thus giving a very public signal to foreign exchange market participants that medium-term inflation goals are now dominating policy.

How would you advise a student on the range of subjects to combine with economics if the goal is to pursue a career as an economist?
First and foremost, I would have to say mathematics. That is not because economics is mathematics, but rather because mathematics makes economic theory clearer and more precise. Take demand theory for example. It's all based on the assumption that households try to make the best use of their incomes. But that down-to-earth idea can be reformulated mathematically as "maximum satisfaction subject to not exceeding the household budget." Calculus, such as you might learn in grade 12 or first year university, yields results that you cannot obtain through common sense alone. Mathematics also enables us to develop better statistical techniques for analysing data.

But I think that students should study some history as well. It is platitudinous, but true, that history is the source of all our economic data; and if we want our economic theory to be empirically relevant we must continuously test it against those data. To do that intelligently, we must understand the sources of the data.

Chapter 31

The Economy at Full Employment

In 1943, at the height of World War II, total production in Canada was a staggering 61 percent higher than it had been just four years earlier. How could production increase by such a large amount in such a short time? ◆ Over longer periods, we gradually become more productive and our incomes grow. On the average, each hour that we worked in 1998 earned us 70 percent more than it did in 1960. Despite setbacks during the past few years, the economies of Japan and China have expanded more rapidly than ours has and incomes in these countries have grown more quickly than ours. What makes production and incomes grow over the years? ◆ What are the forces that determine employment, wage rates, and real GDP when our economy is at full employment? ◆ Our population grows every year. Some of this population growth comes from immigration. What effect does population size have on employment, wage rates, and potential GDP? ◆ We also hear a lot about the importance of increasing our national saving to invest in new capital, about the importance of education, and about the need to support science and technology. How do capital accumulation, education, and advances in technology influence employment, wage rates, and potential GDP? ◆ When we talk about full employment, we don't mean there is *no* unemployment. What determines the amount of unemployment when the economy is at full employment?

Production and Jobs

◇ In this chapter, we study the economy at full employment. We'll study the relationship between production and employment and learn about the forces that determine the quantity of employment. We'll also discover how changes in population, capital, and technology influence employment and incomes. And we'll learn about the forces that create unemployment when the economy is at full employment.

After studying this chapter, you will be able to:

- Describe the relationship between the quantity of labour employed and real GDP

- Explain what determines the demand for labour and the supply of labour

- Explain how labour market equilibrium determines employment, the real wage rate, and potential GDP

- Explain the influences on employment, the real wage rate, and potential GDP of an increase in the population, an increase in capital, and an advance in technology

- Explain what determines unemployment when the economy is at full employment

Real GDP and Employment

To PRODUCE MORE OUTPUT, WE MUST USE MORE inputs. We can increase real GDP by employing more labour, increasing the quantity of capital, or developing technologies that are more productive. In the short term, the quantity of capital and the state of technology are fixed. So to increase real GDP in the short term, we must increase the quantity of labour employed. Let's look at the relationship between real GDP and the quantity of labour employed.

Production Possibilities

When you studied the limits to production in Chapter 3 (see p. 39), you learned about the **production possibility frontier**, which is the boundary between those combinations of goods and services that can be produced and those that cannot. We can think about the production possibility frontier for any pair of goods or services when we hold the quantities of all other goods and services constant. Let's think about the production possibility frontier between two special items—real GDP and the quantity of leisure time.

Real GDP is a measure of the final goods and services produced in the economy in a given time period (see Chapter 22, pp. 476–479). We measure real GDP as a number of 1992 dollars but the measure is a *real* one. Real GDP is not a pile of dollars. It is a pile of goods and services. Think of it as a number of big shopping carts filled with goods and services. Each cart contains some of each of different goods and services produced, and one cartload of items costs $1 billion. To say that real GDP is $700 billion means that real GDP is 700 big shopping carts of goods and services.

The quantity of leisure time is the number of hours we spend not working. It is the time we spend doing sports, seeing movies, and hanging out with friends. Leisure time is a special type of good or service.

Each hour that we spent pursuing fun could have been an hour that we spent at work. So when the quantity of leisure time increases by one hour, the quantity of labour employed decreases by one hour. If we spent all our time having fun rather than working, we would not produce anything. Real GDP would be zero. The more leisure time we forgo to work, the greater is the quantity of labour employed and the greater is real GDP.

The relationship between leisure time and real GDP is a *production possibility frontier*. Figure 31.1(a) shows an example of this frontier. Here, an economy has 45 billion hours of leisure time available. If people use all these hours to pursue leisure, no labour is employed and real GDP is zero. As people forgo leisure and work more, real GDP increases. If people took 20 billion hours in leisure and spent 25 billion hours working, real GDP would be $800 billion at point *a*. If people spent all the available hours working, real GDP would be $1,000 billion.

The bowed-out *PPF* displays increasing opportunity cost. In this case, the opportunity cost of a given amount of real GDP is the amount of leisure time forgone to produce the real GDP. The additional hours of leisure forgone to produce a given additional amount of real GDP increases as real GDP increases. The reason is that we use the most productive labour first and, as we use more labour, we use increasingly less productive labour.

The Production Function

The **production function** is the relationship between real GDP and the quantity of labour employed when all other influences on production remain the same. The production function shows how real GDP varies as the quantity of labour employed varies, other things remaining the same.

Because one more hour of labour employed means one less hour of leisure, the production function is like a mirror image of the leisure time-real GDP *PPF*. Figure 31.1(b) shows the production function for the economy whose *PPF* is shown in Fig. 31.1(a). You can see that when the quantity of labour employed is zero, real GDP is also zero. And as the quantity of labour employed increases, so does real GDP. When 25 billion labour hours are employed, real GDP is $800 billion (at point *a*).

A decrease in leisure hours and the corresponding increases in the quantity of labour employed and real GDP bring a movement along the production possibility frontier and along the production function. The arrows along the *PPF* and production function in Fig. 31.1 show these movements. Such movements occurred when employment and real GDP surged during the first four years of World War II.

But the increase in real GDP during World War II changed for an additional reason. Labour became more productive. Let's study the influences on the productivity of labour.

FIGURE 31.1

Production Possibilities and the Production Function

(a) Production possibility frontier

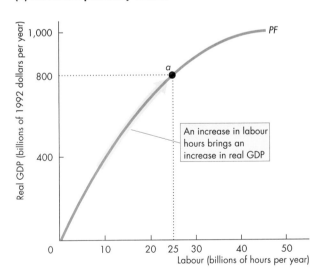

(b) Production function

On the production possibility frontier in part (a), if we enjoy 45 billion hours of leisure, we produce no real GDP. If we forgo 25 billion hours of leisure time and spend only 20 billion hours of leisure, we produce a real GDP of $800 billion, at point *a*.

The production function in part (b) is like a mirror image of the *PPF*. At point *a* on the production function, we use 25 billion hours of labour to produce $800 billion of real GDP.

Changes in Productivity

When we talk about *productivity*, we usually mean the labour productivity. **Labour productivity** is real GDP per hour of labour. Three factors influence labour productivity:

- Physical capital
- Human capital
- Technology

Physical Capital A farm worker equipped with only a stick and primitive tools can cultivate almost no land and grow barely enough food to feed a single family. One equipped with a steel plough pulled by an animal can cultivate more land and produce enough food to feed a small village. One equipped with high-yield seeds, a modern tractor, plough, and harvester can cultivate thousands of acres and produce enough food to feed hundreds of people.

By using physical capital on our farms and in our factories, shops, and offices, we enormously increase labour productivity. And the more physical capital we use, the greater is our labour productivity, other things remaining the same.

Human Capital An economy's **human capital** is the knowledge and skill that people have obtained from education and on-the-job training.

The average university graduate has a greater amount of human capital than the average high school graduate possesses. Consequently, the university graduate is able to perform some tasks that are beyond the ability of the high school graduate. The university graduate is more productive. For the nation as a whole, the greater the amount of schooling completed by its citizens, the greater is its real GDP, other things remaining the same.

Regardless of how much schooling a person has completed, on the first day at work, not much production is accomplished. Learning about the new work environment consumes the newly hired worker. But as time passes and experience accumulates, the worker becomes more productive. We call this activity of on-the-job education **learning-by-doing**.

Learning-by-doing can bring incredible increases in labour productivity. The more experienced the work force, the greater is its labour productivity, and, other things remaining the same, the greater is real GDP.

World War II provides a carefully documented example of the importance of this source of increase

FIGURE 31.2

An Increase in Labour Productivity

(a) An increase in labour productivity

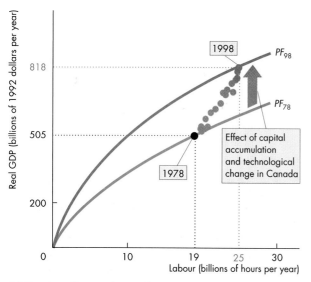

(b) The Canadian production function

The production function is initially PF_0 and 25 billion labour hours produces a real GDP of $800 billion (point a). An increase in capital or an advance in technology that increases labour productivity shifts the production function upward to PF_1 and 25 billion labour hours can now produce a real GDP of $1,030 billion (point b). Canadian real GDP (part b) has increased because labour has become more productive and the quantity of labour employed has increased.

in labour productivity. In the shipyards that produced transport vessels called *Liberty Ships*, labour productivity increased by an astonishing 30 percent purely as a result of learning-by-doing.

Technology A student equipped with a pen can complete a readable page of writing in perhaps 10 minutes. This same task takes 5 minutes with a typewriter and 2 minutes with a computer. Travelling on foot from Toronto to Vancouver takes a person (a fit person!) more than 100 days. In a car, the trip takes a comfortable 5 days. And in an airplane, the trip takes 5 hours. These are examples of the enormous impact of technology on productivity. Imagine the profound effect of these advances in technology on the productivity of a business executive who works in Toronto and Vancouver!

Shift in the Production Function

Any influence on production that increases the labour productivity of a given quantity of labour shifts the production function upward (and shifts the *PPF* outward). Real GDP increases at each level of labour hours. In Fig. 31.2(a), the production function is initially PF_0. Then an increase in physical capital and human capital and an advance in technology occurs. The production function shifts upward to PF_1.

At each quantity of labour employed, real GDP is greater on the new production function than it was on the original one. For example, at 25 billion hours, real GDP increases from $800 billion (point a) to $1,030 billion (point b).

Figure 31.2(b) shows how the Canadian production function has shifted upward between 1978 and 1998. Along PF_{98}, labour productivity is 35 percent greater than on PF_{78}. Labour productivity in Canada increases by about 1.5 percent a year.

REVIEW QUIZ

- What is the relationship between the production function and the leisure hours–real GDP *PPF*?
- What does the bowed-out shape of the leisure hours–real GDP *PPF* imply about the opportunity cost of real GDP and why is the *PPF* bowed out?
- Why does the production function shift upward when capital increases and technology advances?

The Labour Market and Aggregate Supply

YOU'VE SEEN THAT IN A GIVEN YEAR, WITH A given amount of physical and human capital and given technology, real GDP depends on the quantity of labour hours employed. To produce more real GDP, we must employ more labour hours. The labour market determines the quantity of labour hours employed and the quantity of real GDP supplied. We'll learn how by studying:

- The demand for labour
- The supply of labour
- Labour market equilibrium
- Aggregate supply

The Demand for Labour

The **quantity of labour demanded** is the labour hours hired by all the firms in the economy. The **demand for labour** is the relationship between the quantity of labour demanded and the real wage rate when all other influences on firms' hiring plans remain the same. The **real wage rate** is the quantity of goods and services that an hour of labour earns. In contrast, the **money wage rate** is the number of dollars that an hour of labour earns. A real wage rate is equal to a money wage rate divided by the price of a good. For the economy as a whole, the average real wage rate equals the average money wage rate divided by the price level multiplied by 100. So we measure the real wage rate in constant dollars. (Today, we measure this real wage rate in 1992 dollars.)

The *real* wage rate influences the quantity of labour demanded because what matters to firms is not the number of dollars they pay (money wage) but how much output they must sell to earn those dollars.

We can represent the demand for labour as either a demand schedule or a demand curve. The table in Fig. 31.3 shows part of a demand for labour schedule. It tells us the quantity of labour demanded at three different real wage rates. For example, if the real wage rate falls from $25 an hour to $20 an hour, the quantity of labour demanded increases from 20 billion hours a year to 25 billion hours a year. (You can find these numbers in rows *a* and *b* of the table.)

The demand for labour curve is *LD*. Points *a*, *b*, and *c* on the curve correspond to rows *a*, *b*, and *c* of the demand schedule.

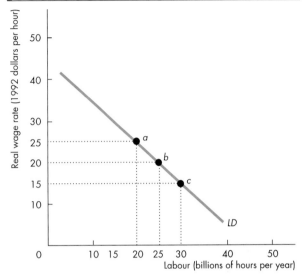

FIGURE 31.3

The Demand for Labour

	Real wage rate (1992 dollars per hour)	Quantity of labour demanded (billions of hours per year)
a	25	20
b	20	25
c	15	30

The table shows part of a demand for labour schedule. Points *a*, *b*, and *c* on the demand for labour curve correspond to the rows of the table. The lower the real wage rate, the greater is the quantity of labour demanded.

Why does the quantity of labour demanded *increase* as the real wage rate *decreases*? That is, why does the demand for labour curve slope downward? To answer these questions, we must first return to the production function and learn about the marginal product of labour.

The Marginal Product of Labour The **marginal product of labour** is the additional real GDP produced by an additional hour of labour when all other influences on production remain the same. We calculate the marginal product of labour as the change in real GDP divided by the change in the quantity of labour employed. Figure 31.4(a) shows some marginal product calculations and Fig. 31.4(b) shows the marginal product curve.

In Fig. 31.4(a), when the quantity of labour employed increases from 10 billion hours to 20 billion hours, an increase of 10 billion hours, real GDP increases from $388 billion to $688 billion, an increase of $300 billion. The marginal product of labour equals the increase in real GDP ($300 billion) divided by the increase in the quantity of labour employed (10 billion hours), which is $30 an hour.

When the quantity of labour employed increases from 20 billion hours to 30 billion hours, an increase of 10 billion hours, real GDP increases from $688 billion to $888 billion, an increase of $200 billion. The marginal product of labour equals the increase in real GDP ($200 billion) divided by the increase in the quantity of labour employed (10 billion hours), which is $20 an hour.

In Fig. 31.4(b), as the quantity of labour employed increases, the marginal product of labour diminishes. Between 10 billion and 20 billion (at 15 billion), marginal product is $30 an hour. And between 20 billion and 30 billion (at 25 billion), marginal product is $20 an hour.

Diminishing Marginal Product The marginal product of labour diminishes as the quantity of labour employed increases because all the labour, both the old and the new, works with the same fixed amount of physical capital and given technology. As more labour hours are hired, the physical capital is worked more intensively, and more breakdowns and bottlenecks arise. Eventually, as more labour hours are hired, workers get in each other's way and output increases barely at all.

The diminishing marginal product of labour limits the demand for labour.

Diminishing Marginal Product and the Demand for Labour Firms are in business to maximize profits. Each hour of labour that a firm hires increases output and adds to costs. Initially, an extra hour of labour produces more output than the real wage that the labour costs. Marginal product exceeds the real wage rate. But each additional hour of labour produces less additional output than the previous hour—the marginal product of labour diminishes.

As a firm hires more labour, eventually the extra output from an extra hour of labour is exactly what that hour of labour costs. At this point, marginal product equals the real wage rate. Hire one less hour and marginal product exceeds the real wage rate. Hire one more hour and the real wage rate exceeds the marginal product. In either case, profit is less.

FIGURE 31.4

The Marginal Product and the Demand for Labour

(a) Calculating marginal product

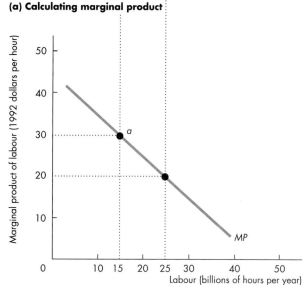

(b) The marginal product curve

An increase in labour from 10 billion to 20 billion hours increases real GDP by $300 billion. The marginal product of labour is $30 an hour. An increase in labour from 20 billion to 30 billion hours increases real GDP by $200 billion. The marginal product of labour is $20 an hour. At point *a* on the *MP* curve, the marginal product of labour is $30 an hour at 15 billion hours (midpoint between 10 billion and 20 billion). The *MP* curve is the demand for labour curve.

Because marginal product diminishes as the quantity of labour employed increases, the lower the real wage rate, the greater is the quantity of labour that a firm can profitably hire. The marginal product curve is the same as the demand for labour curve.

You might gain a clearer understanding of the demand for labour by looking at an example.

The Demand for Labour in a Ketchup Factory

Suppose that when a ketchup factory employs one additional hour of labour, output increases by 11 bottles. Marginal product is 11 bottles an hour. If the money wage rate is $5.50 an hour and if ketchup sells for 50¢ a bottle, the real wage rate is 11 bottles an hour. (We calculate the real wage rate as the money wage rate of $5.50 an hour divided by a price of 50¢ a bottle, which equals a real wage rate of 11 bottles an hour.) Because marginal product diminishes, we know that if the firm did not hire this hour of labour, marginal product would exceed 11 bottles. Because the firm can hire the hour of labour for a real wage rate of 11 bottles, it pays it to do so.

If the price of ketchup remains at 50¢ a bottle, and the money wage rate falls to $5.00 an hour, the real wage rate falls to 10 bottles an hour, and the firm increases the quantity of labour demanded.

Similarly, if the money wage rate remains at $5.50 an hour and the price of ketchup rises to 55¢ a bottle, the real wage rate falls to 10 bottles an hour, and the firm increases the quantity of labour demanded.

When the firm pays a real wage rate equal to the marginal product of labour, it is maximizing profit.

Changes in the Demand for Labour

When the marginal product of labour changes, the demand for labour changes and the demand curve for labour shifts. You've seen that an increase in capital (both physical and human) and an advance in technology that increase productivity shifts the production function upward. These same forces increase the demand for labour and shift the demand for labour curve rightward.

The Supply of Labour

The **quantity of labour supplied** is the number of labour hours that all the households in the economy plan to work. The **supply of labour** is the relationship between the quantity of labour supplied and the real wage rate when all other influences on work plans remain the same.

We can represent the supply of labour as either a supply schedule or a supply curve. The table in Fig. 31.5 shows a supply of labour schedule. It tells us the quantity of labour supplied at three different real wage rates. For example, if the real wage rate rises from $13 an hour (row *a*) to $20 an hour (row *b*), the quantity of labour supplied increases from 20 billion to 25 billion hours a year. The curve *LS* is a supply of labour curve. Points *a*, *b*, and *c* on the curve correspond to rows *a*, *b*, and *c* of the supply schedule.

The *real* wage rate influences the quantity of labour supplied because what matters to people is not the number of dollars they earn (the money wage rate) but what those dollars will buy.

FIGURE 31.5

The Supply of Labour

The table shows part of a supply of labour schedule. Points *a*, *b*, and *c* on the supply of labour curve correspond to the rows of the table. The higher the real wage rate, the greater is the quantity of labour supplied.

	Real wage rate (1992 dollars per hour)	**Quantity of labour supplied** (billions of hours per year)
a	13	20
b	20	25
c	30	30

The quantity of labour supplied increases as the real wage rate increases for two reasons:

■ Hours per person increase.
■ Labour force participation increases.

Hours per Person   In choosing how many hours to work, a household considers the opportunity cost of not working. This opportunity cost is the real wage rate. The higher the real wage rate, the greater is the opportunity cost of taking leisure and not working. And as the opportunity cost of taking leisure rises, other things remaining the same, the more the household chooses to work.

But other things don't remain the same. The higher the real wage rate, the greater is the household's income. And the higher the household's income, the more it wants to consume. One item that it wants to consume more of is leisure.

So a rise in the real wage rate has two opposing effects. By increasing the opportunity cost of leisure, it makes the household want to consume less leisure and to work more. And by increasing the household's income, it makes the household want to consume more leisure and to work fewer hours. For most households, the opportunity cost effect is stronger than the income effect. So the higher the real wage rate, the greater is the amount of work that the household chooses to do.

Labour Force Participation   Some people have productive opportunities outside the labour force. These people choose to work only if the real wage rate exceeds the value of these other productive activities. For example, a parent might spend time caring for her or his child. The alternative is day care. The parent will choose to work only if he or she can earn enough per hour to pay the cost of childcare and have enough left to make the work effort worthwhile. The higher the real wage rate, the more likely it is that a parent will choose to work and so the greater is the labour force participation rate.

Labour Supply Response   The quantity of labour supplied increases as the real wage rate rises. But the quantity of labour supplied is not highly responsive to the real wage rate. A large percentage change in the real wage rate brings a small percentage change in the quantity of labour supplied.

Let's now see how the labour market determines employment, the real wage rate, and potential GDP.

Labour Market Equilibrium and Potential GDP

The forces of supply and demand operate in labour markets just as they do in the markets for goods and services. The price of labour is the real wage rate. A rise in the real wage rate eliminates a shortage of labour by decreasing the quantity demanded and increasing the quantity supplied. A fall in the real wage rate eliminates a surplus of labour by increasing the quantity demanded and decreasing the quantity supplied. If there is neither a shortage nor a surplus, the labour market is in equilibrium.

In macroeconomics, we study the economy-wide labour market to determine the total quantity of labour employed and the average real wage rate.

Labour Market Equilibrium   Figure 31.6(a) shows a labour market in equilibrium. The demand curve *LD* and the supply curve *LS* are the same as those in Fig. 31.3 and Fig. 31.5.

If the real wage rate exceeds $20 an hour, the quantity of labour supplied exceeds the quantity demanded and there is a surplus of labour. In this situation, the real wage rate falls.

If the real wage rate is less than $20 an hour, the quantity of labour demanded exceeds the quantity supplied and there is a shortage of labour. In this situation, the real wage rate rises.

If the real wage rate is $20 an hour, the quantity of labour demanded equals the quantity supplied and there is neither a shortage nor a surplus of labour. In this situation, the labour market is in equilibrium and the real wage rate remains constant. The equilibrium level of employment is 25 billion hours a year. This equilibrium is *full-employment equilibrium*.

Potential GDP   You've seen that the quantity of real GDP depends on the quantity of labour employed. The production function tells us how much real GDP a given amount of employment can produce. At the labour market equilibrium, employment is at its full-employment level. And the quantity of real GDP produced by the full-employment quantity of labour is **potential GDP**.

Figure 31.6(b) shows potential GDP. The equilibrium level of employment in part (a) of Fig. 31.6 is 25 billion hours. The production function in part (b) tells us that 25 billion hours of labour can produce a real GDP of $800 billion. This amount is potential GDP.

FIGURE 31.6

The Labour Market
and Potential GDP

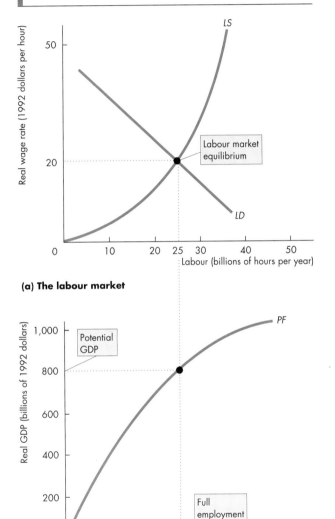

(a) The labour market

(b) Potential GDP

Labour market equilibrium occurs (in part a) when the quantity of labour demanded equals the quantity of labour supplied. The equilibrium real wage rate is $20 an hour. Equilibrium employment, which is full employment, is 25 billion hours a year.

Part (b) shows how potential GDP is determined. It is the quantity of real GDP determined by the production function and the full-employment quantity of labour.

Aggregate Supply

The **long-run aggregate supply curve** is the relationship between the quantity of real GDP supplied and the price level when real GDP equals potential GDP. Figure 31.7 shows this relationship as the vertical *LAS* curve. Along the long-run aggregate supply curve, as the price level changes, the money wage rate also changes to keep the real wage rate at the full-employment equilibrium level in Fig. 31.6(a). With no change in the real wage rate and no change in employment, real GDP remains at potential GDP.

The **short-run aggregate supply curve** is the relationship between the quantity of real GDP supplied and the price level when the money wage rate and potential GDP remain constant. Figure 31.7 shows a short-run aggregate supply curve as the

FIGURE 31.7

The Aggregate Supply
Curves

A rise in the price level accompanied by a rise in the money wage rate that keeps the real wage rate at its full-employment equilibrium level keeps the quantity of real GDP supplied at potential GDP—a movement along the long-run aggregate supply curve. A rise in the price level with no change in the money wage rate lowers the real wage rate and increases employment and the quantity of real GDP supplied—a movement along the short-run aggregate supply curve.

upward-sloping *SAS* curve. Along the short-run aggregate supply curve, as the price level rises, the money wage rate remains fixed so the real wage rate *falls*. In Fig. 31.6, when the real wage rate falls, the quantity of labour demanded increases and real GDP increases.

When the economy is on its short-run aggregate supply curve above potential GDP, the real wage rate is below the full-employment equilibrium level. And when the economy is on the short-run aggregate supply curve below potential GDP, the real wage rate is above the full-employment equilibrium level. In both cases, the quantity of labour employed, which is chosen by firms, differs from the quantity that households would supply if they could choose their work hours.

Production is efficient in the sense that firms operate on their production functions. But the allocation of time is inefficient. In an above full-employment equilibrium, people do more work and produce more real GDP than they would if they could choose their work hours. And in below full-employment equilibrium, people do less work and produce less real GDP than they would if they could choose their work hours.

When the real wage rate departs from its full-employment equilibrium level, the resulting shortage or surplus of labour brings market forces into play that move the real wage rate and quantity of labour employed back towards their full-employment levels.

The appendix to this chapter (pp. 714–719) explains in detail how to derive the long-run and short-run aggregate supply curves.

R E V I E W   Q U I Z

- Why does a rise in the real wage rate bring a decrease in the quantity of labour demanded, other things remaining the same?
- Why does a rise in the real wage rate bring an increase in the quantity of labour supplied, other things remaining the same?
- What happens in the labour market if the real wage rate is above or below the full-employment level?
- How is potential GDP determined?
- What is the relationship between full-employment equilibrium in the labour market and long-run aggregate supply?
- What is the relationship between the labour market and short-run aggregate supply?

Let's now study *changes* in potential GDP.

Changes in Potential GDP

REAL GDP WILL INCREASE IF:

1. The economy recovers from recession
2. Potential GDP increases

Recovery from recession means the economy moves along the real GDP–leisure *PPF* from a point at which real GDP is less than potential GDP. Equivalently, the economy moves along the short-run aggregate supply curve. Economists have a lot to say about such a move. And Chapters 25–29 explain this type of short-term change in real GDP.

Increasing potential GDP means expanding production possibilities. We're going to study such an expansion in the rest of this chapter and in Chapter 32. We begin this process here by examining two influences on potential GDP:

- An increase in population
- An increase in labour productivity

An Increase in Population

As the population increases and additional people reach working age, the supply of labour increases. With more labour available, and with capital and technology remaining the same, production possibilities expand. But does the expansion of production possibilities mean that potential GDP increases? And does it mean that potential GDP *per person* increases?

The answers to these questions have intrigued economists for many years. And they cause heated political debate today. In China, for example, families are under enormous pressure to limit the number of children they have. In other countries, an example of which is France, the government encourages large families. We can study the effects of an increase in population by using the model of the full-employment economy in Fig. 31.8.

In Fig. 31.8(a), the demand for labour is *LD* and initially the supply of labour is LS_0. At full employment, the real wage rate is $20 an hour and employment is 25 billion hours a year. In Fig. 31.8 (b), the production function (*PF*) shows that with 25 billion hours of labour employed, potential GDP is $800 billion. We're now going to work out what happens when the population increases.

An Increase in Population

(a) The labour market

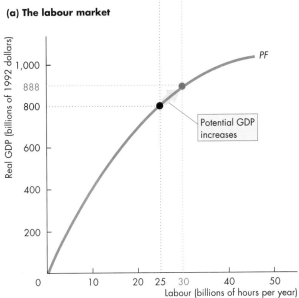

(b) Potential GDP

An increase in population increases the supply of labour and shifts the supply curve rightward (in part a). The real wage rate falls and the quantity of labour employed at full employment increases. In part (b), the increase in full-employment equilibrium employment increases potential GDP. Because the marginal product of labour diminishes, the increased population produces a greater potential GDP but a smaller potential GDP per hour of work.

An increase in the working-age population increases the supply of labour. In Fig. 31.8, the labour supply curve shifts rightward to LS_1. At a real wage rate of $20 an hour, there is now a surplus of labour. So the real wage rate falls. In this example, it falls until it reaches $15 an hour. At $15 an hour, the quantity of labour demanded equals the quantity of labour supplied. Equilibrium employment increases to 30 billion hours a year.

Figure 31.8(b) shows the effect of the increase in equilibrium employment on real GDP. As the full-employment quantity of labour increases from 25 billion hours to 30 billion hours, potential GDP increases from $800 billion to $888 billion.

So at full employment, an increase in population increases employment, increases potential GDP, and lowers the real wage rate.

An increase in population also decreases potential GDP per hour of work. You can see this decrease by dividing potential GDP by total labour hours. Initially, with potential GDP at $800 billion and labour hours at 25 billion, potential GDP per hour of work was $32. With the increase in population, potential GDP is $888 billion and labour hours are 30 billion. Potential GDP per hour of work is $29.60. Diminishing returns is the source of the decrease in potential GDP per hour of work.

You've seen that an increase in population increases potential GDP and decreases potential GDP per work hour. Some people challenge this conclusion and argue that people are the ultimate economic resource. They claim that a larger population brings forth a greater amount of scientific discovery and technological advance. Consequently, these people argue that an increase in population never takes place in isolation. It is always accompanied by an increase in labour productivity. Let's now look at the effects of this influence on potential GDP.

An Increase in Labour Productivity

We've seen that three factors increase labour productivity:

- An increase in physical capital
- An increase in human capital
- An advance in technology.

The quantity of physical capital increases over time because of saving and investment. Human capital increases because of education and on-the-job training and experience. And technology advances because of research and development efforts. We study the way all these forces interact to determine the growth rate of potential GDP in Chapter 32.

Here, we study the *effects* of an increase in physical capital, or an increase in human capital, or an advance in technology on the labour market and potential GDP. We'll see how the real wage rate, employment, and potential GDP change when any of these three influences on labour productivity changes.

An Increase in Physical Capital If the quantity of physical capital increases, labour productivity increases. With labour being more productive, the economy's production possibilities expand. How does such an expansion of production possibilities change the equilibrium real wage rate, employment, and potential GDP?

The additional capital increases the real GDP that each quantity of labour can produce. It also increases the marginal product of labour and so increases the demand for labour. Some physical capital replaces some types of labour. So the demand for those types of labour decreases when capital increases. But an increase in physical capital creates a demand for those types of labour that build, sell, and maintain the additional capital. The increases in demand for labour are always larger than the decreases in demand and the economy-wide demand for labour increases.

With an increase in the economy-wide demand for labour, the real wage rate rises and the quantity of labour supplied increases. Equilibrium employment increases.

Potential GDP now increases for two reasons. First, a given level of employment produces more real GDP. Second, equilibrium employment increases.

An Increase in Human Capital If the quantity of human capital increases, labour productivity increases. Again, with labour being more productive, the economy's production possibilities expand. And this expansion of production possibilities changes the equilibrium real wage rate, employment, and potential GDP in a similar manner to the effects of a change in physical capital.

An Advance in Technology As technology advances, labour productivity increases. And exactly as in the case of an increase in capital, the economy's production possibilities expand. Again, just as in the case of an increase in capital, the new technology increases the real GDP that each quantity of labour can produce and increases the marginal product of labour and the demand for labour.

With an increase in the demand for labour, the real wage rate rises, the quantity of labour supplied increases, and equilibrium employment increases. And again, potential GDP increases because a given level of employment produces more real GDP and because equilibrium employment increases.

Illustrating the Effects of an Increase in Labour Productivity Figure 31.9 shows the effects of an increase in labour productivity that results from an increase in capital or an advance in technology. In part (a), the demand for labour initially is LD_0 and the supply of labour is LS. The real wage rate is $20 an hour, and full employment is 25 billion hours a year.

In part (b), the production function initially is PF_0. With 25 billion hours of labour employed, potential GDP is $800 billion.

Now an increase in capital or an advance in technology increases the productivity of labour. In Fig. 31.9(a), the demand for labour increases and the demand curve shifts rightward to LD_1. In Fig. 31.9(b), the productivity of labour increases, and the production function shifts upward to PF_1.

In Fig. 31.9(a), at the original real wage rate of $20 an hour, there is now a shortage of labour. So the real wage rate rises. In this example, it keeps rising until it reaches $30 an hour. At $30 an hour, the quantity of labour demanded equals the quantity of labour supplied and full employment increases to 30 billion hours a year.

Figure 31.9(b) shows the effects of the increase in full employment combined with the new production function on potential GDP. As employment increases from 25 billion hours to 30 billion hours, potential GDP increases from $800 billion to $1,140 billion.

Potential GDP per hour of work also increases. You can see this increase by dividing potential GDP by total labour hours. Initially, with potential GDP at $800 billion and labour hours at 25 billion, potential GDP per hour of work was $32. With the increase in labour productivity, potential GDP is $1,140 billion and labour hours are 30 billion, so potential GDP per hour of work is $38.

We've just studied the effects of a change in population and an increase in labour productivity separately. In reality, these changes occur together. We can see the combined effects by examining an episode in the life of the Canadian economy.

FIGURE 31.9

An Increase in Labour Productivity

(a) The labour market

(b) Potential GDP

An increase in labour productivity shifts the demand for labour curve rightward from LD_0 to LD_1 (part a) and the production function upward from PF_0 to PF_1 (part b). The real wage rate rises from $20 to $30 an hour, and full employment increases from 25 billion to 30 billion hours. Potential GDP increases from $800 billion to $1,140 billion. Potential GDP increases because labour becomes more productive and full employment increases.

Population and Productivity in Canada

To study the changes in population and productivity in Canada, we'll compare 1998 with 1980. In both of these years, the Canadian economy was at, or close to, full employment. (The unemployment in these years is assumed to be frictional, structural, or seasonal rather than cyclical.)

In 1980, real GDP in Canada was $535 billion, employment was 20 billion hours, and the real wage rate was $14.50 an hour. (We are using 1992 dollars.)

By 1998, real GDP had increased to $818 billion, labour hours had increased to 25 billion, and the real wage rate had risen to $17.50 an hour. (Again, we are using 1992 dollars.)

The factors that you've just studied—an increase in population, an increase in physical and human capital, and advances in technology—brought these changes.

Population Increase   In 1980, the working-age population of Canada was 18.7 million. By 1998, this number had increased to 23.2 million. The 1998 working-age population was 24 percent greater than the 1980 population. Recall that labour hours were 20 billion in 1980. A 24 percent increase would take labour hours in 1998 to 24.8 billion. But labour hours actually increased to 25 billion. Why? The answer is that an increase in capital and advances in technology increased labour productivity, which increased the employment-to-population ratio slightly.

Capital Increase   In 1980, the Canadian capital stock was probably around $1.6 trillion (1992 dollars). By 1998, the capital stock had increased to around $2.4 trillion. This increase in capital increased labour productivity. But the increase in capital was not the only influence on labour productivity. Technological advances also occurred.

Technological Advances   In 1980, we were just getting into the information revolution. Personal computers had just entered the scene, but they were slow, had little memory, and had no hard drive. The Internet existed as a tool used by academic researchers for e-mail and file transfers, but no one had imagined the World Wide Web. Telephones couldn't remember numbers and record messages. Communication was slower and more costly than it was to become by 1998.

Production processes were beginning to be com-

FIGURE 31.10

Full Employment in Canada: 1980 and 1998

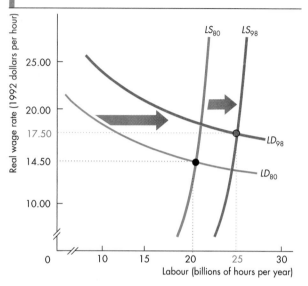

(a) The Canadian labour market in 1980 and 1998

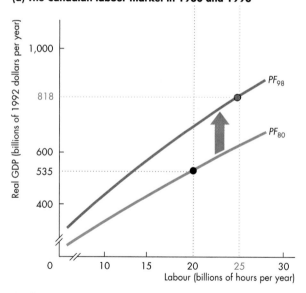

(b) The Canadian production function in 1980 and 1998

In 1980, the real wage rate was \$14.50 an hour and the quantity of labour employed was 20 billion hours at the intersection of LD_{80} and LS_{80} (part a). Potential GDP was \$535 billion on PF_{80} (part b). By 1998, the real wage rate increased to \$17.50 an hour and the quantity of labour employed increased to 25 billion hours at the intersection of LD_{98} and LS_{98} (part a). Potential GDP increased to \$818 billion on PF_{98} (part b).

puterized but on a limited scale. Banks equipped with ATMs were in the future. Supermarkets with laser scanners were only a dream. Robots in car factories and coal mines were still unknown. The biotechnology sector had still to be developed. The combined effects of capital accumulation and technological advance have made our farms and factories, shops and offices more productive.

Figure 31.10 shows their effects along with the effects of the increase in population that occurred. In 1980, the demand for labour curve was LD_{80}, the supply of labour curve was LS_{80}, the full-employment real wage rate was \$14.50 an hour, and 20 billion hours of labour were employed. The production function in 1980 was PF_{80}, so 20 billion hours of labour produced a real GDP (and potential GDP) of \$535 billion.

By 1998, the increase in population had increased the working-age population by 24 percent. This increase in population increased the supply of labour and shifted the labour supply curve rightward to LS_{98}.

The accumulation of capital and advances in technology increased labour productivity. The demand for labour increased and the demand for labour curve shifted rightward to LD_{98}. And the production function shifted upward to PF_{98}.

The real wage rate increased to \$17.50 an hour and employment increased to 25 billion hours. At this quantity of labour, real GDP (and potential GDP) increased to \$818 billion.

So in Canada, the effects of an increase in capital and advances in technology have been larger than the effects of increases in population. The forces that increase labour productivity have been sufficiently strong to overcome the effects of an increase in population.

R E V I E W   Q U I Z

■ When the population increases but nothing else changes, why does real GDP per hour of work decrease?

■ How does an increase in capital change the real wage rate, full employment, and potential GDP?

■ How do advances in technology change the real wage rate, full employment, and potential GDP?

■ If, as some people suggest, capital accumulation and technological change always accompany an increase in population, is it possible for potential GDP per hour of work to decrease?

Unemployment at Full Employment

SO FAR, WE'VE FOCUSED ON THE FORCES THAT determine the real wage rate, the quantity of labour employed, and potential GDP. And we've studied the effects of changes in population, capital, and technology on these variables. We're now going to bring unemployment into the picture.

In Chapter 23 (pp. 500–509), we learned how unemployment is measured. We *described* how people become unemployed—they lose jobs, leave jobs, and enter or reenter the labour force—and we *classified* unemployment—it can be frictional, structural, seasonal, and cyclical. We also learned that we call the unemployment rate at full employment the **natural rate of unemployment**.

But measuring, describing, and classifying unemployment does not *explain* it. Why is there always some unemployment? Why does its rate fluctuate? Why was the unemployment rate lower during the 1960s and the late 1990s than during the 1980s and early 1990s?

The forces that make the unemployment rate fluctuate around the natural rate take some time to explain and we study these forces in Chapters 29–35. Here, we look at the churning economy and the reasons why we have unemployment at full employment.

Unemployment is ever present for two broad reasons:

- Job search
- Job rationing

Job Search

Job search is the activity of looking for an acceptable vacant job. There are always some people who have not yet found a suitable job and who are actively searching for one. The reason is that the labour market is in a constant state of change. The failure of existing businesses destroys jobs. The expansion of existing businesses and the startup of new businesses that use new technologies and develop new markets create jobs. As people pass through different stages of life, some enter or reenter the labour market. Still others leave their jobs to look for better ones, and others retire. This constant churning in the labour market means that

there are always some people looking for jobs and these people are the unemployed.

The amount of job search depends on a number of factors, one of which is the real wage rate. In Figure 31.11, when the real wage rate is $20 an hour, the economy is at a full-employment equilibrium. The amount of job search that takes place at this wage rate generates unemployment at the natural rate. If the real wage rate is above the full-employment equilibrium, for example at $30 an hour, there is a surplus of labour. At this higher real wage rate, more job search takes place and the unemployment rate rises above the natural rate. If the real wage rate is below the full-employment equilibrium, for example at $10 an hour, there is a shortage of labour. At this real wage rate, less job search takes place and the unemployment rate falls below the natural rate.

The market forces of supply and demand move the real wage rate towards the full-employment

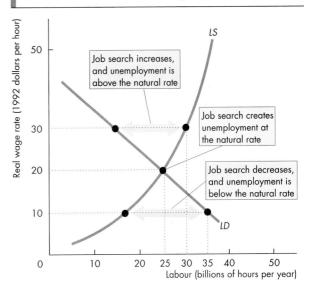

FIGURE 31.11

Job Search Unemployment

When the real wage rate is at its full-employment level—$20 an hour in this example—job search puts unemployment at the natural rate. If the real wage rate is above the full-employment level, there is a surplus of labour. Job search increases and unemployment rises above the natural rate. If the real wage rate is below the full-employment level, there is a shortage of labour. Job search decreases and unemployment falls below the natural rate.

equilibrium. And these same forces move the amount of job search towards the level that creates unemployment at the natural rate.

But other influences on the amount of job search bring changes, over time, in the natural rate of unemployment. The main sources of these changes are:

- Demographic change
- Unemployment compensation
- Structural change

Demographic Change   An increase in the proportion of the population that is of working age increases the entry rate into the labour force and increases the unemployment rate. This factor has been important in the Canadian labour market in recent years. The bulge in the birth rate during the late 1940s and early 1950s increased the proportion of new entrants into the labour force during the 1970s and increased the unemployment rate.

As the birth rate declined, the bulge moved into higher age groups and the proportion of new entrants declined during the 1980s. During this period, the natural rate of unemployment decreased.

Another demographic trend is an increase in the number of households with two paid workers. When unemployment comes to one of these workers, it is possible, with income still flowing in, to take longer to find a new job. This factor might have increased the amount of frictional unemployment.

Unemployment Compensation   The length of time that an unemployed person spends searching for a job depends, in part, on the opportunity cost of job search. An unemployed person who receives no unemployment benefits faces a high opportunity cost of job search. In this situation, search is likely to be short and the person is likely to accept a less attractive job rather than continue a costly search process. An unemployed person who receives generous unemployment benefits faces a low opportunity cost of job search. In this situation, search is likely to be prolonged. The unemployed worker will continue to search for an ideal job.

The extension of unemployment benefits to larger groups of workers during the late 1960s and 1970s lowered the opportunity cost of job search. Consequently, the amount of job search and the natural rate of unemployment increased during those years.

Structural Change   Labour market flows and unemployment are influenced by the pace and direction of technological change. Sometimes, technological change brings a *structural slump*, a condition in which some industries die and some regions suffer while other industries are born and other regions flourish. When these events occur, labour turnover is high—the flows between employment and unemployment increase and the number of people unemployed increases. The decline of industries in the Maritimes and the rapid expansion of industries in the Ottawa Valley illustrate the effects of technological change and were a source of the increase in unemployment during the 1970s and early 1980s. While these changes were taking place, the natural rate of unemployment increased.

Job Rationing

You've learned that markets *allocate* scarce resources by adjusting the market price to make buying plans and selling plans agree. Another word that has a similar meaning to "allocate" is "ration." Markets *ration* scarce resources by adjusting prices. In the labour market, the real wage rate rations employment and therefore rations jobs. Changes in the real wage rate keep the number of people seeking work and the number of jobs available in balance.

But the real wage rate is not the only possible instrument for rationing jobs. And in some industries, the real wage rate is set above the market equilibrium level. **Job rationing** is the practice of paying a real wage rate above the equilibrium level and then rationing jobs by some method.

Two reasons why the real wage rate might be set above the equilibrium level are:

- Efficiency wage
- Minimum wage

Efficiency Wage   It is costly for a firm to pay its workers more than the market wage rate. But to do so also brings benefits. An **efficiency wage** is a real wage rate that is set above the full-employment equilibrium wage rate and that balances the costs and benefits of this higher wage rate to maximize the firm's profit.

The cost of paying a higher wage is direct. It is the addition to the firm's wage bill. The benefits of paying a higher wage rate are indirect.

First, a firm that pays a high wage rate can attract the most productive workers. Second, the firm can get greater productivity from its work force if it threatens to fire those who do not perform at the desired standard. The threat of losing a well-paid job stimulates greater work effort. Third, workers are less likely to quit their jobs, so the firm faces a lower rate of labour turnover and lower training costs. Fourth, the firm's recruiting costs are lower. The firm always faces a steady stream of available new workers.

Faced with benefits and costs, a firm offers a wage rate that balances productivity gains from the higher wage rate against its additional cost. This wage rate maximizes the firm's profit and is the efficiency wage.

The Minimum Wage A **minimum wage** law determines the lowest wage rate at which a firm may legally hire labour. If the minimum wage is set *below* the equilibrium wage, the minimum wage has no effect. The minimum wage law and market forces are not in conflict. But if a minimum wage is set *above* the equilibrium wage, the minimum wage is in conflict with the market forces and does have some effects on the labour market.

Minimum wages in Canada are set by the provincial governments. In 1999, the minimum wage rate ranged from a low of $5.25 an hour in Newfoundland to a high of $7.20 an hour in Yukon. The minimum wage increases from time to time and fluctuates relative to the average wage of all workers.

Job Rationing and Unemployment

Regardless of the reason, if the real wage rate is set above the equilibrium level, the natural rate of unemployment increases. The above-equilibrium real wage rate decreases the quantity of labour demanded and increases the quantity of labour supplied. So even at full employment, the quantity of labour supplied exceeds the quantity of labour demanded.

The surplus of labour is an addition to the amount of unemployment. The unemployment that results from a non-market wage rate and job rationing increases the natural rate of unemployment because it is added to the job search that takes place at full-employment equilibrium.

Economists broadly agree that efficiency wages can create persistent unemployment. Most economists believe that the minimum wage contributes to unemployment, especially among low-skilled young workers. But David Card of the University of California at Berkeley, and Alan Krueger of Princeton University have challenged this view. And the challenge has been rebutted.

Card and Krueger say that an increase in the minimum wage works like an efficiency wage. It makes workers more productive and less likely to quit. Most economists remain skeptical about this suggestion. If higher wages make workers more productive and reduce labour turnover, why don't firms freely pay the wage rates that encourage the correct work habits? Daniel Hamermesh of the University of Texas at Austin says that firms anticipate increases in the minimum wage and cut employment *before* they occur. Looking for the effects of an increase in the minimum wage *after* it has occurred misses its effects. Finis Welch of Texas A&M University and Kevin Murphy of the University of Chicago say that regional differences in economic growth, not changes in the minimum wage, explain the facts that Card and Krueger found.

R E V I E W   Q U I Z

- Why does the economy experience unemployment at full employment?
- Why does the natural rate of unemployment fluctuate?
- What is job rationing and why does it occur?
- How does an efficiency wage influence the real wage rate, employment, and unemployment?
- How does the minimum wage create unemployment?

◆ In this chapter, you've seen how the economy operates at full employment. *Reading Between the Lines* on pp. 712–713 looks at some interesting differences between employment in Canada and the United States. In the next chapter, we study the rate of growth of the full-employment economy. We study the implications of decisions by firms to increase the amount of capital they employ and the decisions by households about the amount to save to finance capital accumulation. We also study the interactions of capital accumulation, technological change, and population growth in the process of economic growth.

Productivity in Canada

NATIONAL POST, SEPTEMBER 6, 1999

Canadians spend less time at work than Americans

BY ERIC BEAUCHESNE

Canadian workers, and those in most other industrial countries, are putting in less time on the job than their American counterparts. ...

"Currently, the U.S. worker works more hours than his or her counterpart in other industrial countries, and he or she also leads the way in terms of productivity," said Lawrence Jeff Johnson, an ILO economist, ...

Mr. Johnson said it's not known precisely why Americans are working longer hours, or why they are more productive than most of their counterparts in the rest of the world. ...

American workers, on average, clocked 1,951 hours, while Canadians put in 1,732, or 5 1/2 work-weeks less on the job in 1996, the last year for which the study has comparable figures on hours worked in the two countries.

U.S. workers added another 16 hours on the job in 1997, 77 hours, or about two work weeks, more than the traditionally hardworking Japanese, and produced $9 an hour more worth of goods or services.

In 1997, the value added per hour—the value of a worker's output—in the United States was $30.66, in Canada $25.33 and in Japan $21.19.

"If you look at the value added per hour of work, you've had an increase of 23% [since 1980], so you're becoming more efficient by using technology and capital," Mr. Johnson said. "The U.S. is doing the same thing, but the value added per hour of work rose only 20%."...

Essence of the Story

■ Productivity in the United States exceeds that in other developed countries.

■ In 1996, the number of hours worked per person was greater in the United States than in Canada.

■ In 1997, the value of a worker's output (real GDP per hour of work) was greater in the United States than in Canada.

■ Figure 1 shows the U.S. and Canadian production functions and Fig. 2 shows the labour markets in Canada and the United States. To compare the two countries, we measure labour as hours per person per year (*x*-axis in both figures), real GDP per hour of work (*y*-axis of Fig. 1), and the real wage rate (*y*-axis of Fig. 2) as 1992 U.S. dollars per hour.

■ With more capital per worker and with more productive technologies, the U.S. production function, PF_{US}, is higher than the Canadian production function, PF_C.

■ We assume that the supply of labour curve *LS* is the same for both countries.

■ Because the U.S. production function is higher than the Canadian production function at each quantity of labour, the marginal product of labour in the United States exceeds that in Canada and the U.S. demand for labour curve, LD_{US}, lies to the right of the Canadian demand for labour curve, LD_C.

■ Equilibrium in the U.S. labour market occurs at an employment level of 1,250 hours per person and a real wage rate of $19 an hour. (On average, employed Americans work 1,951 hours a year. The employment-to-population ratio in the United States is 64.1 percent, so the number of hours worked per person per year in the working-age population is 1,250.)

■ Equilibrium in the Canadian labour market occurs at an employment level of 1,032 hours per person and a real wage rate of $12 an hour. (On average, employed Canadians work 1,732 hours a year. The employment-to-population ratio in Canada is 59.6 percent, so the number of hours worked per person per year in the working-age population is 1,032.)

■ The greater demand for labour in the United States with the same supply of labour in the two countries results in the U.S. real wage rate and employment level exceeding that of Canada.

■ At the equilibrium level of employment in the United States, real GDP per hour of work is $27.50 in Fig. 1. (This amount equals the $30.66 in the news article converted to 1992 dollars.)

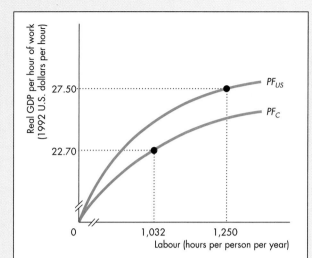

Figure 1 Canadian and U.S. production functions

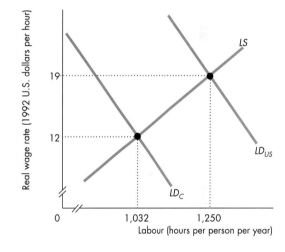

Figure 2 Canadian and U.S. labour markets

■ At the equilibrium level of employment in Canada, real GDP per hour of work is $22.70 in Fig. 1. (This amount equals the $25.33 in the news article converted to 1992 dollars.)

■ Countries with greater labour productivity work more hours because the higher real wage rate induces a greater amount of work.

Appendix

Deriving the Aggregate Supply Curves

THIS APPENDIX EXPLAINS HOW TO DERIVE THE long-run aggregate supply curve and the short-run aggregate supply curve. It shows the links between the labour market, the production function, and the aggregate supply curves and fills in the steps from Figure 31.6 to Figure 31.7 on p. 703 in this chapter.

Deriving the Long-Run Aggregate Supply Curve

FIGURE A31.1 SHOWS HOW TO DERIVE THE LONG-run aggregate supply curve. Part (a) shows the labour market. The demand and supply curves shown are similar to those in Fig. 31.6(a) on p. 703. The equilibrium, a real wage of $20 an hour and employment of 25 billion hours, is exactly the same equilibrium that was determined in that figure.

Figure A31.1(b) shows the production function. This production function is similar to that in Fig. 31.1(b) on p. 697. We know from the labour market (part a) that 25 billion hours of labour are employed. Part (b) tells us that when 25 million hours of labour are employed, real GDP is $800 billion.

Figure A31.1(c) shows the long-run aggregate supply curve. That curve tells us that real GDP is $800 billion regardless of the price level. To see why, look at what happens when the price level changes.

Start with a GDP deflator of 100. The economy is at point j in part (c) of the figure. That is, the GDP deflator is 100 and real GDP is $800 billion. We've determined, in part (a), that the real wage rate is $20 an hour. With a GDP deflator of 100, the money wage rate (the wage rate in current dollars) is also $20 an hour.

What happens to real GDP if the GDP deflator falls from 100 to 80 (a 20 percent decrease in the price level)? If the money wage rate remains at $20 an hour, the real wage rate rises and the quantity of labour supplied exceeds the quantity demanded. In the long run, the money wage rate will fall. It falls to $16 an hour. With a money wage rate of $16 an hour and a GDP deflator of 80, the real wage rate is still $20 an hour ($16 divided by 80 and multiplied by 100 equals $20). With the lower money wage rate but a constant real wage rate, employment remains at 25 billion hours and real GDP remains at $800 billion. The economy is at point k in Fig. A31.1(c).

What happens to real GDP if the GDP deflator rises from 100 to 120 (a 20 percent increase in the price level)? If the money wage rate stays at $20 an hour, the real wage rate falls and the quantity of labour demanded exceeds the quantity supplied. In the long run, the money wage rate rises. It keeps rising until it reaches $24 an hour. At that money wage rate, the real wage rate is $20 an hour ($24 divided by 120 and multiplied by 100 equals $20) and the quantity of labour demanded equals the quantity supplied. Employment remains at 25 billion hours and real GDP remains at $800 billion. The economy is at point *l* in Fig. A31.1(c).

Points *j*, *k*, and *l* in part (c) all lie on the long-run aggregate supply curve. We have considered only three price levels. We can consider any price level and we will reach the same conclusion: a change in the price level generates a proportionate change in the money

wage rate and leaves the real wage rate unchanged. Employment and real GDP are also unchanged.

Because in the long run the price level *and the money wage rate* adjust to achieve full employment, the real wage rate, employment, and real GDP remain constant as the price level changes. In the long run, one level of real GDP—potential GDP—occurs at any price level and the *LAS* curve is vertical.

FIGURE A31.1

The Labour Market and Long-Run Aggregate Supply

(a) The labour market

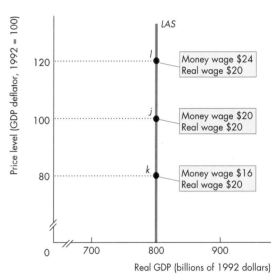

(c) Long-run aggregate supply curve

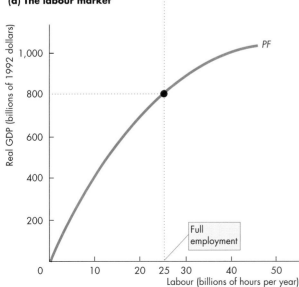

(b) Potential GDP

Equilibrium in the labour market determines the real wage rate and employment. The demand for labour curve (*LD*) intersects the supply of labour curve (*LS*) at a real wage rate of $20 an hour and 25 billion hours of employment (part a). The production function (*PF*) and employment of 25 billion hours determine real GDP at $800 billion (part b). Potential GDP is $800 billion and in the long run, real GDP supplied is $800 billion regardless of the price level. The long-run aggregate supply curve (*LAS*) is the vertical line in part (c). If the GDP deflator is 100, the economy is at point *j*. If the GDP deflator is 120, the money wage rate rises to keep the real wage rate constant at $20 an hour, employment remains at 25 billion hours, and real GDP is $800 billion. The economy is at point *l*. If the GDP deflator is 80, the money wage rate falls to keep the real wage rate constant at $20 an hour, employment remains at 25 billion hours, and real GDP is $800 billion. The economy is at point *k*.

Changes in Long-Run Aggregate Supply

Long-run aggregate supply can change for two reasons:

- Change in labour supply
- Change in labour productivity

Change in Labour Supply The supply of labour can change for many reasons, but the biggest one is a change in the population. Over time, the population grows and the supply of labour increases.

We study and illustrate the effects of these labour market changes and their effects on potential GDP on pp. 704–705. An increase in the supply of labour means the supply of labour curve shifts rightward. The real wage rate falls and the full-employment level of employment increases. Potential GDP increases.

Now that we've derived the long-run aggregate supply curve, you can see when potential GDP changes, long-run aggregate supply also changes and the long-run aggregate supply curve shifts. Because an increase in the supply of labour increases potential GDP, it also increases long-run aggregate supply and shifts the long-run aggregate supply curve rightward. The new (vertical) long-run aggregate supply curve is located at the increased level of potential GDP.

Change in Labour Productivity An increase in labour productivity means that a given amount of labour can produce a larger quantity of real GDP. The production function shifts upward and the demand for labour curve shifts rightward. The real wage rate rises; the full-employment level of employment increases. Potential GDP increases.

We study and illustrate the effects of an increase in productivity on the quantity of labour, the real wage rate, and potential GDP on pp. 705–707.

Again, because an increase in labour productivity increases potential GDP, it also increases long-run aggregate supply and shifts the long-run aggregate supply curve rightward. The new (vertical) long-run aggregate supply curve is located at the increased level of potential GDP.

Whether the real wage rate increases when long-run aggregate supply increases depends on the source of the increase in potential GDP. If the source is an increase in the supply of labour, the real wage rate falls. If the source is an increase in labour productivity, the real wage rate rises.

Short-Run Aggregate Supply

SHORT-RUN AGGREGATE SUPPLY IS THE RELATION-ship between the quantity of real GDP supplied and the price level when the money wage rate and all other influences on production plans remain the same. We are now going to learn about the connection between short-run aggregate supply and the labour market. Before we can derive the short-run aggregate supply curve, we must understand how the labour market works when the money wage rate is fixed.

Short-Run Equilibrium in the Labour Market

When the money wage rate is fixed, a change in the price level changes the real wage rate. Suppose the money wage rate is $20 an hour and the GDP deflator is 100. Then the real wage rate is also $20 an hour.

Now suppose that the money wage rate remains at $20 an hour but the GDP deflator rises to 133.3. In this case, the real wage rate falls to $15 an hour. A money wage rate of $20 an hour and a GDP deflator of 133.3 enables people to buy the same goods and services that a money wage rate of $15 an hour buys when the GDP deflator is 100.

Alternatively, suppose that the GDP deflator falls to 80. In this case, the real wage rate rises to $25 an hour. A money wage rate of $20 an hour with a GDP deflator of 80 buys the same quantity of goods and services that a money wage rate of $25 an hour buys when the GDP deflator is 100.

Figure A31.2 shows the labour market in the short run at the three different price levels we've just considered. As before, the demand for labour is *LD* and the supply of labour is *LS*. The money wage rate is constant at $20 an hour and the higher the price level, the lower is the real wage rate. The three points *b*, *c*, and *d* in Fig. A31.2 tell us the quantities of labour demanded at the three different real wage rates. If the price level is 80, the real wage rate is $25 an hour and the quantity of labour demanded is 20 billion hours a year (indicated by point *b*). If the price level is 100, the real wage rate is $20 an hour and the quantity of labour demanded is 25 billion hours a year (indicated by point *c*). And if the price level is 133.3, the real wage rate is $15 an hour and the quantity of labour demanded is 30 billion hours a year (indicated by point *d*).

FIGURE **A31.2**

The Labour Market in the Short Run

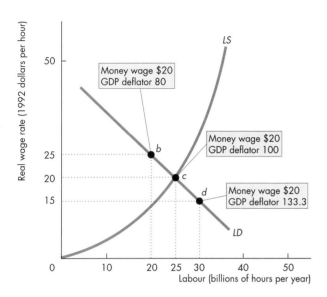

The labour demand curve is *LD* and the labour supply curve is *LS*. The money wage rate is fixed at $20 an hour. If the GDP deflator is 100, the *real* wage rate is $20 an hour and 25 billion hours of labour are employed. The economy operates at point *c*. If the GDP deflator is 80, the real wage rate is $25 an hour and 20 billion hours of labour are employed. The economy operates at point *b*. If the GDP deflator is 133.3, the real wage rate is $15 an hour and 30 billion hours of labour are employed. The economy operates at point *d*.

You can see that when the money wage rate is fixed and the price level rises, the real wage rate falls, and the quantity of labour *demanded* increases. But what determines the quantity of labour *employed*?

Employment with Sticky Wages   When the real wage rate is not at its long-run equilibrium level, there are many possible ways in which the level of employment could be determined. It is assumed that when the labour market is not at full employment, firms decide the level of employment and households supply whatever quantity firms demand. Provided that firms pay the agreed money wage rate, households supply whatever quantity of labour firms

demand. In the short run, households are willing to be "off" their labour supply curves.

In Fig. A31.2, with a money wage rate of $20 an hour and a price level of 80 (point *b* in the figure) the actual level of employment is 20 billion hours. In this situation, people supply less labour than they would like to. If the GDP deflator is 133.3, the real wage rate is $15 an hour and employment is 30 billion hours (point *d* in the figure). In this case, people supply more labour than they would like to.

It is easy to understand why people might supply less labour than they would like to. But why would someone supply *more* labour than they would like to? In the long run, they would not. But in the short run, during the life of an existing wage contract, it is quite likely that people will agree to supply whatever quantity of labour their employer demands. The employer gives the employee an "all-or-nothing" choice. The employee must either work the hours requested or find another job.

Deriving the Short-Run Aggregate Supply Curve

The short-run aggregate supply curve is the relationship between the quantity of real GDP supplied and the price level when the money wage rate and all other influences on production plans remain the same. Along the short-run aggregate supply curve, when the price level changes, the *real wage rate also changes*, which means that employment and real GDP also change. The short-run aggregate supply curve is upward sloping.

Figure A31.3 shows the derivation of the short-run aggregate supply curve. Part (a) shows the aggregate labour market. The demand and supply curves are the same as those in Fig. A31.2. The long-run equilibrium, a real wage of $20 an hour and employment of 25 billion hours, is exactly the same equilibrium that was determined in that figure.

Focus first on part (a). It shows the three short-run equilibrium levels of the real wage rate and employment that we discovered in Fig. A31.2. The money wage rate is fixed at $20 an hour. If the price level is 100, the real wage rate is also $20 an hour and 25 billion hours of labour are employed—point *c*. If the price level is 80, the real wage rate is $25 an hour and employment is 20 billion hours—point *b*. If the price level is 133.3, the real wage rate is $15 an hour and employment is 30 billion hours—point *d*.

FIGURE **A31.3**

The Labour Market and Short-Run Aggregate Supply

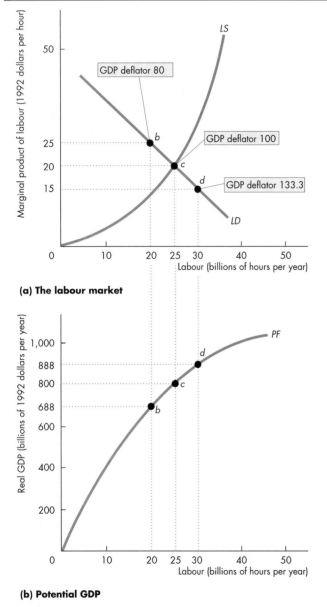

(a) The labour market

(b) Potential GDP

(c) Aggregate supply curves

The money wage rate is fixed at $20 an hour. In part (a), the demand for labour curve (*LD*) intersects the supply of labour curve (*LS*) at a real wage rate of $20 an hour and 25 billion hours of employment. If the GDP deflator is 100, the economy operates at point *c*. In part (b), the production function (*PF*) determines real GDP at $800 billion. This is long-run aggregate supply (*LAS*) in part (c). If the GDP deflator is 80, the real wage rate is $25 an hour and the economy is at point *b*. Employment is 20 billion hours (part a) and real GDP is $688 billion (part b). The economy is at point *b* on its short-run aggregate supply curve (*SAS*) in part (c). If the GDP deflator is 133.3, the real wage rate is $15 an hour and the economy is at point *d*. Employment is 30 billion hours (part a) and real GDP is $888 billion (part b). The economy is at point *d* on its short-run aggregate supply curve in part (c).

Figure A31.3(b) shows the production function. We know from the labour market (part a) that at different price levels, different quantities of labour are employed. Part (b) shows the real GDP produced by these employment levels. For example, when employment is 20 billion hours, real GDP is $688 billion— point *b*. When employment is 25 billion hours, real GDP is $800 billion—point *c*. And when employment is 30 billion hours, real GDP is $888 billion—point *d*.

Figure A31.3(c) shows the short-run aggregate supply curve. It also shows the long-run aggregate supply curve, *LAS*, that we derived in Fig. A31.1. The short-run aggregate supply curve, *SAS*, is derived from the labour market and production function. To see how, first focus on point *b* in all three parts of the figure. At point *b*, the price level is 80. From the labour market (part a) we know that when the price level is 80, the real wage is $25 an hour, and 20 billion hours of labour are employed. At this employment level, we know from the production function (part b) that real GDP is $688 billion. That's what point *b* on the *SAS* curve in part (c) tells us—when the price level is 80, the quantity of real GDP supplied is $688 billion. The other two points on the *SAS* curve, *c* and *d*, are derived in the same way. At point *d*, the price level is 133.3 so the real wage rate is $15 an hour and 30 billion hours of labour are employed (part a). This employment level produces a real GDP of $888 billion (part b).

The short-run aggregate supply curve intersects the long-run aggregate supply curve at the price level that delivers the equilibrium real wage rate in the labour market. In this example, that price level is 100. At labour market equilibrium, the economy is at full employment and real GDP equals potential GDP. At price levels above 100, the quantity of real GDP supplied in the short run exceeds potential GDP; at price levels below 100, the quantity of real GDP supplied in the short run falls short of potential GDP.

Changes in Short-Run Aggregate Supply

Short-run aggregate supply can change for two reasons:

- Change in long-run aggregate supply
- Change in money wage rate

Change in Long-Run Aggregate Supply   Anything that changes long-run aggregate supply also changes short-run aggregate supply. That is, anything that increases potential GDP increases the quantity of real GDP supplied at each and every price level. Both long-run aggregate supply and short-run aggregate supply increase and both curves shift rightward.

A key feature of the *SAS* curve is that it intersects the *LAS* curve at the price level that puts the real wage rate at its full-employment level. That is, the real wage rate at which the labour market is in equilibrium. So if long-run aggregate supply changes and the *LAS* curve shifts, the short-run aggregate supply curve also shifts. And the new *SAS* curve intersects the new *LAS* curve at the price level that makes the real wage rate equal to its *new* full-employment level.

Change in Money Wage Rate   Short-run aggregate supply changes and long-run aggregate supply remains unchanged if the money wage rate changes and all other influences on production plans remain the same. A rise in the money wage rate with a given price level means that the real wage rate has increased. Faced with a higher real wage rate, firms decrease the quantity of labour demanded. Employment decreases and firms produce less output, so the quantity of real GDP supplied decreases.

But the changes that we've just described would occur at any given price level. So short-run aggregate supply decreases. The *SAS* curve shifts leftward.

Short-Run Changes in the Quantity of Real GDP Supplied

Even if short-run aggregate supply does not change, real GDP can change in the short run. The reason is that there can be a *change in the quantity of real GDP supplied*, which appears as a *movement along the SAS curve*. These changes in real GDP are brought about by changes in aggregate demand. All the factors that can change aggregate demand result in a shift of the aggregate demand curve and movement along the *SAS* curve. Real GDP changes and the price level also changes, and they both change in the same direction. An increase in aggregate demand brings an increase in real GDP and a rise in the price level; a decrease in aggregate demand brings a decrease in real GDP and a fall in the price level.

The Shape of the Short-Run Aggregate Supply Curve

The short-run aggregate supply curve that we've derived in Fig. A31.3(c) is *curved*. Along this *SAS* curve, as the price level rises, real GDP increases. But for given increments in the price level, the increments in real GDP become successively smaller. In contrast, the *SAS* in Fig. 31.7 on p. 703, like that in Chapter 24, is linear—a curve that graphs as a straight line. Along a linear *SAS* curve, as the price level rises, real GDP increases. You can regard the linear *SAS* curve as an approximation over a small range of real GDP in the neighbourhood of potential GDP. The farther the economy moves away from potential GDP, the less close is the approximation.

S U M M A R Y

Key Points

Real GDP and Employment (pp. 696–698)

- To produce real GDP, we must forgo leisure time.
- As the quantity of labour increases, real GDP increases.
- Labour productivity increases if capital or human capital increases or if technology advances.

The Labour Market and Aggregate Supply (pp. 699–704)

- The quantity of labour demanded increases as the real wage rate falls, other things remaining the same.
- The diminishing marginal product of labour is the reason the quantity of labour demanded increases as the real wage rate falls.
- The quantity of labour supplied increases as the real wage rate rises, other things remaining the same.
- At full-employment equilibrium, the quantity of labour demanded equals the quantity of labour supplied.
- Potential GDP is real GDP produced by the full-employment quantity of labour.
- Along the long-run aggregate supply curve, the real wage rate is constant at its full-employment level. Along the short-run aggregate supply curve, the real wage rate, employment, and real GDP change.

Changes in Potential GDP (pp. 704–708)

- An increase in population increases the supply of labour, lowers the real wage rate, increases the quantity of labour employed, and increases potential GDP. It decreases potential GDP per hour of work.
- An increase in capital or an advance in technology increases labour productivity. It shifts the production function upward and the demand for labour curve rightward. The real wage rate rises, the quantity of labour employed increases, and potential GDP increases.

Unemployment at Full Employment (pp. 709–711)

- The unemployment rate at full employment is the natural rate of unemployment.
- Unemployment is ever present because of job search and job rationing.
- Job-search unemployment is influenced by demographic change, unemployment compensation, and structural change.
- Job-rationing unemployment arises from efficiency wages and the minimum wage.

Key Figures

Key Terms

PROBLEMS

*1. Robinson Crusoe lives on a desert island on the equator. He has 12 hours of daylight every day to allocate between leisure and work. The table shows seven alternative combinations of leisure and real GDP in the economy of Crusoe:

Possibility	Leisure (hours per day)	Real GDP ($ per day)
a	12	0
b	10	10
c	8	18
d	6	24
e	4	28
f	2	30
g	0	30

a. Make a graph of Crusoe's PPF for leisure and real GDP.
b. Make a table and a graph of Crusoe's production function.
c. Find Crusoe's marginal product of labour at different quantities of labour.

2. The people of Nautica have 100 hours every day to allocate between leisure and work. The table shows the opportunity cost of real GDP in terms of leisure time forgone in the economy of Nautica:

Possibility	Leisure (hours per day)	Opportunity cost of leisure ($ of real GDP per hour)
a	0	0
b	20	5
c	40	10
d	60	15
e	80	20
f	100	25

a. Make a table and a graph of Nautica's PPF for leisure and real GDP.
b. Make a table and a graph of Nautica's production function.
c. Find Nautica's marginal product of labour at different quantities of labour.

*3. Use the information provided in problem 1 about the economy of Crusoe. Also, use the information that Crusoe must earn $4.50 an hour. If he earns less than this amount, he does not have enough food on which to live. He has no interest in earning more than $4.50 an hour. At a real wage rate of $4.50 an hour he is willing to work any number of hours between zero and the total available to him.

a. Make a table that shows Crusoe's demand for labour schedule and draw Crusoe's demand for labour curve.
b. Make a table that shows Crusoe's supply of labour schedule and draw Crusoe's supply of labour curve.
c. What is the full-employment equilibrium real wage rate and quantity of labour in Crusoe's economy?
d. Find Crusoe's potential GDP.

4. Use the information provided in problem 2 about the economy of Nautica. Also, use the information that the people of Nautica are willing to work 20 hours a day for a real wage rate of $10 an hour. And for each 50¢ an hour *increase* in the real wage, they are willing to work an *additional* hour a day.

a. Make a table that shows Nautica's demand for labour schedule and draw Nautica's demand for labour curve.
b. Make a table that shows Nautica's supply of labour schedule and draw Nautica's supply of labour curve.
c. Find the full-employment equilibrium real wage rate and quantity of labour in Nautica's economy.
d. Find Nautica's potential GDP.

*5. Crusoe, whose economy is described in problems 1 and 3, gets a bright idea. He diverts a stream and increases his food production by 50 percent. That is, each hour that he works produces 50 percent more real GDP than before.

a. Make a table that shows Crusoe's new production function and new demand for labour schedule.
b. Find the new full-employment equilibrium real wage rate and quantity of labour in Crusoe's economy.
c. Find Crusoe's new potential GDP.
d. Explain and interpret the results you have obtained in parts (a), (b), and (c).

6. Nautica's economy, described in problems 2 and 4, experiences a surge in its population. The supply of labour increases and 50 percent more hours are supplied at each real wage rate.
   a. Make a table that shows Nautica's new supply of labour schedule.
   b. Find the new full-employment equilibrium real wage rate and quantity of labour in Nautica's economy.
   c. Find Nautica's new potential GDP.
   d. Explain and interpret the results you have obtained in parts (a), (b), and (c).

*7. The figure describes the labour market in Cocoa Island. In addition (not shown in the figure) a survey tells us that when Cocoa Island is at full employment, people spend 1,000 hours a day in job search.

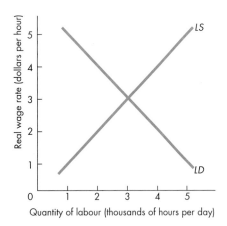

a. Find the full-employment equilibrium real wage rate and quantity of labour employed.
b. Find potential GDP in Cocoa Island. [Hint: the demand for labour curve tells you the *marginal* product of labour. How do we calculate the marginal product of labour?]
c. Calculate the natural rate of unemployment in Cocoa Island.

8. In problem 7, the government of Cocoa Island introduces a minimum real wage of $4 an hour.
   a. Find the new equilibrium real wage rate and quantity of labour employed.
   b. What now is potential GDP in Cocoa Island?
   c. Calculate the new natural rate of unemployment in Cocoa Island.
   d. How much of the unemployment results from the minimum wage?

CRITICAL THINKING

1. Study the news article about Canadian employment in *Reading Between the Lines* on pp. 712–713 and then answer the following questions:
   a. What is the claim in the news article about the major difference in work hours between Canada and the United States?
   b. Why might productivity differences exist between Canada and the United States?
   c. Some people claim that there is a brain drain from Canada to the United States. If there is, how will the real wage rate, employment, and potential GDP change in the two countries as a result of the movement of people?
   d. Do you think it matters how much people work? Why or why not?

2. Visit the Parkin-Bade Web site and use the links provided there to obtain information about the economy of Russia during the 1990s. Try to figure out what has happened to the production possibility frontier and production function and to the demand for labour and supply of labour in Russia during the 1990s. Tell a story about the Russian economy during these years using only the concepts and tools that you have learned about in this chapter.

3. Visit the Parkin-Bade Web site and use the links provided there to obtain information about the economy of China during the 1990s. Try to figure out what has happened to the production possibility frontier and production function and to the demand for labour and supply of labour in China during the 1990s. Tell a story about the Chinese economy during these years using only the concepts and tools that you have learned about in this chapter.

4. You are working for the Finance Minister's office and must write a memo for the minister that provides a checklist of policy initiatives that will increase potential GDP. Be as imaginative as possible but justify each of your suggestions with reference to the concepts and tools that you have learned about in this chapter. Visit the Parkin-Bade Web site for information on current Canadian policy.

Chapter 32

Economic Growth

Real GDP *per person* in Canada more than doubled between 1960 and 1998. If you live in a dorm, chances are it was built during the 1960s and equipped with two electricity outlets, one for a desk lamp and one for a bedside lamp. Today, with the help of a power bar (or two), your room bulges with a television and VCR, CD player, microwave, refrigerator, coffee maker, toaster, and computer—the list goes on. What has brought about this growth in production and incomes? What can be done to speed up economic growth? ◆ We

Transforming People's Lives

see greater extremes of economic growth if we look at modern Asia. On the banks of the Li River in Southern China, Songman Yang breeds cormorants, amazing birds that he trains to fish and to deliver their catch to a basket on his simple bamboo raft. Songman's work, the capital equipment and technology he uses, and the income he earns are similar to those of his ancestors going back some 2,000 years. Yet all around Songman, in China's bustling villages, towns, and cities, people are participating in an economic miracle. They are creating businesses, investing in new technologies, developing local and global markets, and experiencing income growth of more than 6 percent a year. Despite a slowdown in 1998, similar rapid economic growth has taken place in Hong Kong, South Korea, and Taiwan. In these countries, real GDP doubled *three times*—an eightfold increase—between 1960 and 1998. Why have incomes in these Asian economies grown so rapidly? What makes an economic miracle?

◇ In this chapter, we study the forces that make real GDP grow, that make some countries grow faster than others, and that make our own growth rate sometimes slow down and sometimes speed up. We'll also look at policies for achieving faster economic growth.

After studying this chapter, you will be able to:

- Describe the long-term growth trends in Canada and other countries and regions
- Identify the main sources of long-term growth of real GDP
- Explain the productivity growth slowdown in Canada during the 1970s
- Explain the rapid economic growth rates being achieved in East Asia
- Explain the theories of economic growth
- Describe the policies that might be used to speed up economic growth

Long-Term Growth Trends

THE LONG-TERM GROWTH TRENDS THAT WE study in this chapter are the trends in *potential GDP*. We are interested in long-term growth primarily because it brings rising incomes *per person*. So we begin by looking at some facts about the level and the growth rate of real GDP per person in Canada and around the world. Let's look first at real GDP per person in Canada over the past hundred years.

Growth in the Canadian Economy

Figure 32.1 shows real GDP *per person* in Canada for the hundred years from 1898 to 1998. The average growth rate over this period is 2.2 percent a year.

The growth rate was high during the 1920s, when it averaged 4.8 percent a year, during the first decade of the century, when it was almost 4 percent a year,

and during the 1960s, when it was 3.4 percent a year.

The growth rate was close to zero during the 1910s and the 1930s. The average growth rate during the 1970s, 1980s, and 1990s was 1.6 percent a year. But through these years, the growth rate has been slowing.

The middle of the graph is dominated by two extraordinary events: the Great Depression of the 1930s and World War II of the 1940s. The fall in real GDP during the depression and the bulge during the war obscure the changes in the long-term growth trend that occurred within these years. But growth was very slow during the 1930s and between 1930 and 1950, averaging out the depression and the war, the long-term growth rate was close to its 100-year average at 2 percent a year.

A major goal of this chapter is to explain why our economy grows and why the long-term growth rate varies. But growth rates vary not only over time but also across countries. So a related goal is to explain why growth rates vary across countries. Let's look at some facts about these variations.

FIGURE 32.1

A Hundred Years of Economic Growth in Canada

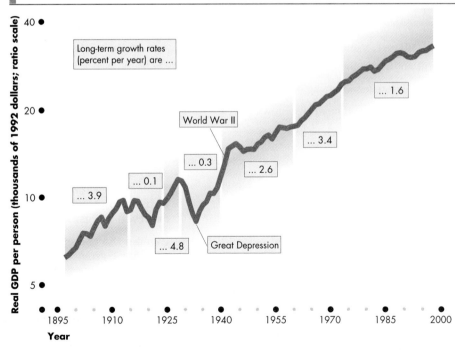

During the 100 years from 1898 to 1998, real GDP per person in Canada grew by an average of 2.2 percent a year. The growth rate was the most rapid during the early part of the century and during the 1920s and 1960s. Growth was slowest during the 1910s, 1930s, and 1990s.

Sources: 1898–1926: Morris Altman, "Revised Real Canadian GNP Estimates and Canadian Economic Growth, 1870-1926," *Review of Income and Wealth*, series 38, number 4, December 1992, pp. 455–474; 1927–1949: F.H. Leacy (ed.), *Historical Statistics of Canada*, 2nd ed., series F 55, Statistics Canada, Ottawa, 1983; 1950–1998: *StatCan: CANSIM Disk*, 1999.

Real GDP Growth in the World Economy

Figure 32.2 shows real GDP per person in Canada and in other countries between 1960 and 1998. (The data shown in this figure are in 1985 U.S. dollars.) Part (a) looks at the richest countries. The United States has the highest real GDP per person.

In 1998, Canada had the second highest real GDP per person and Japan the third highest. Before the 1990s, both of these countries grew faster than the United States and were catching up. Japan also grew faster than the Europe Big 4 (France, Germany, Italy, and the United Kingdom) and overtook them in the mid-1980s. The Europe Big 4 grew faster than the United States but only by a small margin.

Not all countries are growing faster than, and

catching up with, Canada. Figure 32.2(b) looks at some of these. Western Europe (other than the Big 4) grew faster than Canada before 1975, slowed to the Canadian growth rate during the 1980s, and has fallen behind during the 1990s. After a brief period of catch-up, the former Communist countries of Central Europe have fallen increasingly behind Canada and by 1998, they were as far behind as they had been thirty years earlier.

Africa and Central and South America have persistently grown more slowly than Canada. Real GDP per person in Central and South America has slipped from a comparative high of 30 percent of the Canadian level of real GDP per person in 1980 to 23 percent in 1998. Africa has slipped from 8 percent of the Canadian level of real GDP per person in 1960 to 6 percent in 1998.

FIGURE 32.2

Economic Growth Around the World: Catch-Up or Not?

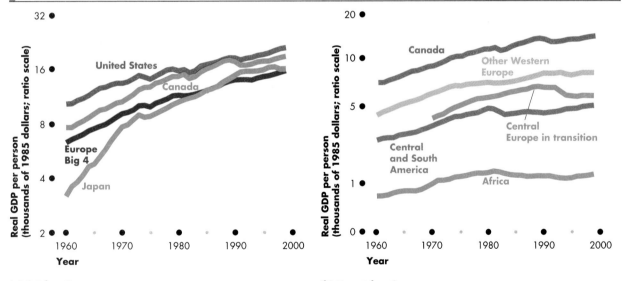

(a) Catch up?

(b) No catch up?

Real GDP per person has grown throughout the world economy. Among the rich industrial countries (part a), real GDP growth has been faster in Canada, the Europe Big 4 (France, Germany, Italy, and the United Kingdom), and Japan than in the United States, and they are catching up. The most spectacular growth was in Japan during the 1960s. Real GDP per person in

Canada has also become closest to the U.S. real GDP per person. Among a wider range of countries (part b), there is little sign of catch-up. The gaps between the levels of real GDP per person in Canada, other Western European countries, Central Europe, Central and South America, and Africa have remained remarkably constant.

Sources: 1960-1992, Robert Summers and Alan Heston, New Computer Diskette (Mark 5.6a), January 15, 1995, distributed by the National Bureau of Economic Research to update "The Penn World Table: An Expanded Set of International Comparisons, 1950–1988" *Quarterly Journal of Economics*, May 1991, 327–368. 1993-1998, *World Economic Outlook*, International Monetary Fund, Washington D.C., October 1998.

Taking both parts of Fig. 32.2 together, we can see that the catch-up in real GDP per person that is visible in part (a) is not a global phenomenon.

Hong Kong, Korea, Singapore, and Taiwan were in the headlines in 1998 because, along with some other Asian countries, they experienced a recession. But as Fig. 32.3 shows, their long-term growth has been spectacular. In 1960, these countries had levels of real GDP per person that ranged from one-tenth to one-quarter that in Canada. By 1998, two of them (Hong Kong and Singapore) had caught Canada and the other two were close behind.

Figure 32.3 also shows that China is catching up, but more slowly and from a very long way behind. In 1960, China's real GDP per person was one-twentieth that of Canada, but by 1998 it was one-eighth.

The four small Asian countries shown in Fig. 32.3 are like fast trains running on the same track at similar speeds and with a roughly constant gap between them. Hong Kong is the lead train and runs about 10 years in front of Korea, which is the last train. Real GDP per person in Korea in 1990 was similar to that in Hong Kong in 1980, ten years earlier. Between 1960 and 1999, Hong Kong transformed itself from a poor developing country into one of the world's richest countries.

China is now doing what Hong Kong has done. If China continues its rapid growth, the world economy will become a dramatically different place because China is equivalent to more than 200 countries the size of Hong Kong. Whether China will continue on its current path of rapid growth is impossible to predict.

FIGURE 32.3
Catch-Up in Asia

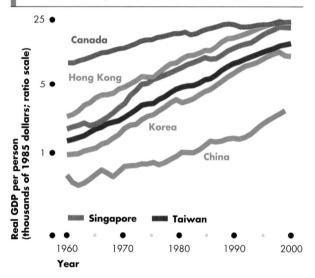

The clearest examples of catch-up have occurred in five economies in Asia. After starting out in 1960 with real GDP per person as little as one-tenth of that in Canada, Hong Kong, Singapore, Taiwan, and Korea have substantially narrowed the gap on Canada. And although China was a very poor developing country in 1960, its real GDP per person now exceeds that of Hong Kong in 1960. China is growing at a rate that is enabling it to continue to catch up with Canada.

Sources: 1960-1992, Robert Summers and Alan Heston, New Computer Diskette (Mark 5.5), June 15 1993, distributed by the National Bureau of Economic Research to update "The Penn World Table (Mark 5): An Expanded Set of International Comparisons, 1950–1988" *Quarterly Journal of Economics*, May 1991, 327–368. 1993–1998, *World Economic Outlook*, International Monetary Fund, Washington D.C., (October, 1998).

R E V I E W   Q U I Z

■ What is the average rate of economic growth in Canada over the past one hundred years? In which periods was growth the most rapid and in which was it the slowest?

■ Describe the gaps between the levels of real GDP per person in Canada and other countries. For which countries are the gaps narrowing? For which countries are the gaps widening? And for which countries are the gaps remaining unchanged?

■ Compare the growth rates and levels of real GDP per person in Hong Kong, Singapore, Taiwan, Korea, China, and Canada. How far is China behind the other Asian economies?

The facts about economic growth in Canada and around the world raise some big questions that we're now going to answer. We'll study the causes of economic growth in three stages. First, we'll look at the social foundations for growth and the activities that sustain it. Second, we'll learn how economists measure the relative contributions of the sources of growth—an activity called *growth accounting*. And third, we'll study three theories of economic growth that seek to explain how the influences on growth interact to determine the growth rate. Let's take our first look at the causes of economic growth.

The Causes of Economic Growth: A First Look

MOST HUMAN SOCIETIES HAVE LIVED FOR centuries and even thousands of years, like Songman Yang, with no economic growth. The key reason is that they have lacked some fundamental social institutions and arrangements that are the foundations on which economic growth occurs. Let's see what these foundations are.

Foundations of Economic Growth

The most basic foundation for economic growth is an appropriate *incentive* system. Three institutions are crucial to the creation of incentives. They are:

1. Markets
2. Property rights
3. Monetary exchange

Markets enable buyers and sellers to get information and to do business with each other, and market prices send signals to buyers and sellers that create incentives to increase or decrease the quantities demanded and supplied. Markets enable people to specialize and trade and to save and invest. But markets need property rights and monetary exchange.

Property rights are the social arrangements that govern the ownership, use, and disposal of productive resources and goods and services. They include the rights to physical property (land, buildings, and capital equipment), to financial property (claims by one person against another), and to intellectual property (such as inventions). Clearly established and enforced property rights give people an assurance that a capricious government will not confiscate their income or their savings.

Monetary exchange facilitates transactions of all kinds, including the orderly transfer of private property from one person to another. Property rights and monetary exchange create incentives for people to specialize and trade, to save and invest, and to discover new technologies.

No unique political system is necessary to deliver the foundations for economic growth. Liberal democracy, founded on the fundamental principle of the rule of law, is the system that does the best job. It provides a solid base on which property rights can be established and enforced. But authoritarian political systems have sometimes provided an environment in which economic growth has occurred.

Early human societies, based on hunting and gathering, did not experience economic growth because they lacked these foundations. Economic growth began when societies evolved the three key institutions that create incentives. But the presence of an incentive system and the institutions that create it does not guarantee that economic growth will occur. It permits economic growth but does not make that growth inevitable.

The simplest way in which growth happens when the appropriate incentive system exists is that people begin to specialize in the activities at which they have a comparative advantage and trade with each other. You saw in Chapter 3 how everyone can gain from such activity. By specializing and trading, everyone can acquire goods and services at the lowest possible cost. Equivalently, people can obtain a greater volume of goods and services from their labour.

As an economy moves from one with little specialization to one that reaps the gains from specialization and exchange, its production and consumption grows. Real GDP per person increases and the standard of living rises.

But for growth to be persistent, people must face incentives that encourage them to pursue three activities that generate ongoing economic growth. These activities are:

- Saving and investment in new capital
- Investment in human capital
- Discovery of new technologies

These three sources of growth, which interact with each other, are the primary sources of the extraordinary growth in productivity during the past 200 years. Let's look at each in turn.

Saving and Investment in New Capital

Saving and investment in new capital increase the amount of capital per worker and increase real GDP per hour of labour—labour productivity. Labour productivity took the most dramatic upturn when the amount of capital per worker increased during the Industrial Revolution. Production processes that use hand tools can create beautiful objects, but production methods that use large amounts of capital per worker, such as auto plant assembly lines, are much more productive. The accumulation of capital on farms, in textile factories, in iron foundries and steel mills, in coal mines, on building sites, in chemical plants, in auto plants, in banks and insurance companies, and in shopping malls has added incredibly to the productivity of our economy. The next time you see a movie set in the Old West, look carefully at the small amount of capital around. Try to imagine how productive you would be in such circumstances compared with your productivity today.

Investment in Human Capital

Human capital—the accumulated skill and knowledge of human beings—is the most fundamental source of economic growth. It is a source of both increased productivity and technological advance.

The development of one of the most basic human skills—writing—was the source of some of the earliest major gains in productivity. The ability to keep written records made it possible to reap ever-larger gains from specialization and exchange. Imagine how hard it would be to do any kind of business if all the accounts, invoices, and agreements existed only in people's memories.

Later, the development of mathematics laid the foundation for the eventual extension of knowledge about physical forces and chemical and biological processes. This base of scientific knowledge was the foundation for the technological advances of the Industrial Revolution 200 years ago and of today's Information Revolution.

But much human capital that is extremely productive is much more humble. It takes the form of millions of individuals learning and repetitively doing simple production tasks and becoming remarkably more productive in the tasks.

One carefully studied example illustrates the importance of this kind of human capital. Between 1941 and 1944 (during World War II), U.S. shipyards produced some 2,500 units of a cargo ship, called the Liberty Ship, to a standardized design. In 1941 it took 1.2 million person-hours to build a ship. By 1942, it took 600,000, and by 1943, it took only 500,000. Not much change occurred in the capital employed during these years. But an enormous amount of human capital was accumulated. Thousands of workers and managers learned from experience and accumulated human capital that more than doubled their productivity in two years.

Discovery of New Technologies

Saving and investment in new capital and the accumulation of human capital have made a large contribution to economic growth. But the contribution of technological change—of the discovery and the application of new technologies and new goods—has made an even greater contribution.

People are many times more productive today than they were a hundred years ago. We are not more productive because we have more steam engines per person and more horse-drawn carriages per person. Rather, it is because we have the engines and transportation equipment that use technologies that were unknown a hundred years ago and that are more productive than the old technologies were. Technological change makes an enormous contribution to our increased productivity. It arises from formal research and development programs and from informal trial and error, and it involves discovering new ways of getting more out of our resources.

To reap the benefits of technological change, capital must increase. Some of the most powerful and far-reaching fundamental technologies are embodied in human capital—for example, language, writing, and mathematics. But most technologies are embodied in physical capital. For example, to reap the benefits of the internal combustion engine, millions of horse-drawn carriages and horses had to be replaced by automobiles; more recently, to reap the benefits of computerized word processing, millions of typewriters had to be replaced by PCs and printers.

REVIEW QUIZ

- How do markets, property rights, and monetary exchange facilitate economic growth? What are the economic activities that they make possible that lead to economic growth?
- What are the roles of saving and investment in new capital, the growth of human capital, and the discovery of new technologies in economic growth?
- Provide some examples of how human capital has created new technologies that are embodied in both human and physical capital.

What is the quantitative contribution of the sources of economic growth? To answer this question, economists use growth accounting.

Growth Accounting

THE QUANTITY OF REAL GDP SUPPLIED (Y) depends on three factors:

1. The quantity of labour (L)

2. The quantity of capital (K)

3. The state of technology (T)

The purpose of **growth accounting** is to calculate how much real GDP growth results from growth of labour and capital and how much is attributable to technological change.

The key tool of growth accounting is the **aggregate production function**, which is written as the equation:

$$Y = F(L, K, T).$$

In words, the quantity of real GDP supplied is determined by (is a function F of) the quantities of labour and capital and by the state of technology. The larger are L, K, or T, the greater is Y. And the faster L and K grow and the faster T advances, the faster does Y grow.

So understanding what makes labour and capital grow and technology advance is the key to understanding economic growth. Labour growth depends primarily on population growth. And the growth rate of capital and the pace of technological advance determine the growth rate of labour productivity.

Labour Productivity

Labour productivity is real GDP per hour of work. It is calculated by dividing real GDP by aggregate labour hours. That is, labour productivity equals Y divided by L.

Labour productivity determines how much income an hour of labour generates. Figure 32.4 shows labour productivity for the period 1965–1998. You can see in this figure that productivity growth was most rapid before 1973. During these years, labour productivity grew by 3 percent a year. But after 1973, the average growth rate was 1.2 percent a year.

Why did productivity grow fastest before 1973? Why did it slow down after 1973? Growth accounting answers these questions by dividing the growth of

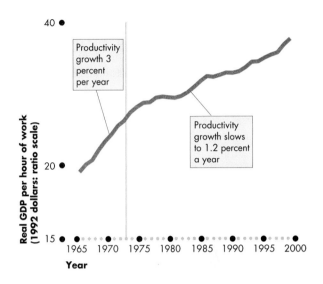

FIGURE 32.4

Real GDP per Hour of Work

Real GDP divided by aggregate hours equals real GDP per hour of work, which is a broad measure of productivity. During the 1960s, the productivity growth rate in Canada was high. During the 1970s, 1980s, and 1990s, it slowed.

Sources: Statistics Canada, *StatCan: CANSIM Disc*, March 1999, and authors' calculations.

labour productivity into two components and then measuring the contribution of each. The components are:

■ Growth in capital per hour of labour

■ Technological change

Technological change includes everything that contributes to labour productivity growth that is not included in growth in capital per hour. In particular, it includes human capital growth. Human capital growth and technological change are intimately related. Technology advances because knowledge advances. And knowledge is part of human capital. So "technological change" is a broad catchall concept.

The analytical engine of growth accounting is a relationship called the productivity function. Let's learn about this relationship and see how it is used.

The Productivity Function

The **productivity function** is a relationship that shows how real GDP per hour of labour changes as the amount of capital per hour of labour changes with a given state of technology. Figure 32.5 illustrates the productivity function. Capital per hour of work is measured on the *x*-axis and real GDP per hour of work is measured on the *y*-axis. The figure shows *two* productivity functions. One is the curve labelled PF_0 and the other is the curve labelled PF_1.

An increase in the quantity of capital per hour of labour increases real GDP per hour of labour, which is shown by a movement along a productivity function. For example, on PF_0, when capital per hour of labour is $30, real GDP per hour of labour is $20. If capital per hour of labour increases to $60, real GDP per hour of labour increases to $25.

Technological change increases the amount of GDP per hour of labour that can be produced by a given amount of capital per hour of labour. It is shown by an upward shift of the productivity function. For example, if capital per hour of work is $30 and a technological change increases real GDP per hour of work from $20 to $25, the productivity function shifts upward from PF_0 to PF_1 in Fig. 32.5. Similarly, if capital per hour of work is $60, the same technological change increases real GDP per hour of work from $25 to $32 and shifts the productivity function upward from PF_0 to PF_1.

To calculate the contributions of capital growth and technological change to productivity growth, we need to know the shape and slope of the productivity function. The shape of the productivity function reflects a fundamental economic law—the law of diminishing returns. The **law of diminishing returns** states that as the quantity of one input increases with the quantities of all other inputs remaining the same, output increases but by ever smaller increments. For example, in a factory that has a given amount of capital, as more labour is hired, production increases. But each *additional* hour of labour produces less *additional* output than the previous hour produced. Two people working with one computer key in fewer than twice as many pages per day as one person working with one computer.

Applied to capital, the law of diminishing returns states that if a given number of hours of labour use more capital (with the same technology), the *additional* output that results from the *additional* capital gets smaller as the amount of capital increases. One person working with two computers keys in fewer than twice as many pages per day as one person

FIGURE 32.5
How Productivity Grows

Productivity is measured by real GDP per hour of work, and it can grow for two reasons: (1) Capital per hour of work increases, and (2) technological advances occur. The productivity function, PF_0, shows the effects of an increase in capital per hour of work on productivity. Here, when capital per hour of work increases from $30 to $60, real GDP per hour of work increases from $20 to $25 along the blue productivity curve PF_0. Technological advance shifts the productivity function upward. Here, an advance in technology shifts the productivity function from PF_0 to PF_1. With this technological advance, real GDP per hour of work, when there is $60 of capital per hour of work, increases from $25 to $32.

working with one computer. More generally, one hour of labour working with $40 of capital produces less than twice the output of one hour of labour working with $20 of capital. But how much less? The answer is given by the *one-third rule*.

The One-Third Rule Robert Solow of MIT estimated a production function from U.S. data. He discovered that on the average, with no change in technology, a one percent increase in capital per hour of labour brings a *one-third of one percent* increase in real GDP per hour of labour. This one-third rule is used to calculate the contributions of an increase in capital per hour of work and technological change to the growth of real GDP. Let's do such a calculation.

Suppose that capital per hour of work grows by 3 percent a year and real GDP per hour of work grows by 2.5 percent a year. The one-third rule tells us that capital growth has contributed one-third of 3 percent, which is 1 percent. The rest of the 2.5 percent growth of real GDP comes from technological change. That is, technological change has contributed 1.5 percent, which is the 2.5 percent growth of real GDP per hour of work minus the estimated 1 percent contribution of capital growth.

Accounting for the Productivity Growth Slowdown

We can use the one-third rule to study Canadian productivity growth and the productivity growth slowdown. Figure 32.6 tells the story, starting in 1965.

1965 to 1973 In 1965, capital per hour of work was $74 and real GDP per hour of work was $19.60 at the point marked 65 on PF_{65}. During the next 8 years, real GDP per hour of work expanded by 27 percent to $25. At the same time, capital per hour of work increased by 42 percent to $105. With no change in technology, the economy would have moved to point a on PF_{65} in Fig. 32.6, where real GDP per hour of work has increased by 14 percent (1/3 of the 42 percent increase in capital per hour of work). But rapid technological change shifted the productivity curve upward to PF_{73} and the economy moved to the point marked 73 on that curve.

1973 to 1998 During the 25 years from 1973 to 1998, real GDP per hour of work expanded by 34 percent to $33.60. At the same time, capital per hour of work increased by 21 percent to $127. With no change in technology, the economy would have moved to point b on PF_{73} in Fig. 32.6, where real GDP per hour of work has increased by 7 percent (1/3 of the 21 percent increase in capital per hour of work). But a technological change shifted the productivity curve upward to PF_{98} and the economy moved to the point marked 98 on that curve.

Because the two periods, 1965 to 1973 and 1973 to 1998, are of different lengths, let's translate the changes that we've just described into annual averages. The growth rate of real GDP per hour of work was 3.4 percent a year between 1965 and 1973 and 1.4 percent a year between 1973 and 1998. The growth rate of capital per hour of work was 4.5 per-

FIGURE 32.6

Growth Accounting and the Productivity Growth Slowdown

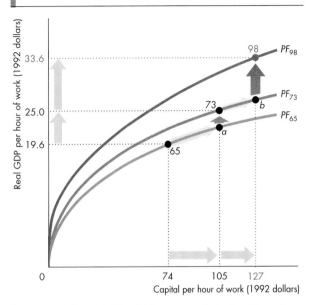

Between 1965 and 1973, which was a period of rapid productivity growth, capital per hour of work increased from $74 to $105 and technological progress shifted the productivity function upward from PF_{65} to PF_{73}. Between 1973 and 1998, capital per hour of work increased from $105 to $127 and technological progress shifted the productivity function upward from PF_{73} to PF_{98}. The annual productivity growth rate slowed from 3.4 percent before 1973 to 1.4 percent after 1973.

Sources: Statistics Canada, *StatCan: CANSIM Disc,* March 1999, and authors' calculations.

cent a year before 1973 and less than 0.8 percent a year after 1973. And the growth rate of real GDP per hour of work attributed to technological change was 1.4 percent a year before 1973 and 0.9 percent a year after 1973. So, after 1973, the growth rate of capital per hour of work fell to less than one-fifth of its pre-1973 rate of increase, and the contribution of technological change fell to a little more than one-half its pre-1973 contribution.

You've seen how growth accounting can be used to decompose the sources of productivity growth. But growth accounting does not tell us the deeper reasons for the productivity growth slowdown. Let's now look at these reasons.

Deeper Sources of Growth Slowdown

The productivity slowdown occurred because capital accumulation and the effects of technological change slowed down. Two of the deeper causes of these slowdowns were:

- Energy price shocks
- Environment concerns

Energy Price Shocks   Energy price increases that occurred in 1973–1974 diverted research efforts and capital accumulation towards saving energy rather than increasing productivity. Airplanes became more fuel efficient, but they didn't operate with smaller crews. Real GDP per litre of fuel increased faster but real GDP per hour of labour increased more slowly.

Environment Concerns   The 1970s saw an increased effort to protect the environment and improve the quality of the workplace. The benefits of these actions—cleaner air and water and safer factories—are not included in real GDP. So the growth of these benefits is not measured as productivity growth.

Achieving Faster Growth

Growth accounting tells us that to achieve faster economic growth, we must either increase the growth rate of capital per hour of work or increase the pace of technological advance (which includes improving human capital). The main suggestions for achieving these objectives are:

- Stimulate saving
- Stimulate research and development
- Target high-technology industries
- Encourage international trade
- Improve the quality of education

Stimulate Saving   Saving finances investment, which brings capital accumulation. So stimulating saving can stimulate economic growth. The East Asian economies have the highest growth rates and saving rates. Some African economies have the lowest growth rates and saving rates.

Tax incentives can increase saving. Registered Retirement Saving Plans (RRSPs) are an example of a tax incentive to save. Economists claim that a tax on consumption rather than on income provides the best saving incentive.

Stimulate Research and Development   Everyone can use the fruits of *basic* research and development efforts. For example, all biotechnology firms can use advances in gene splicing technology. Because basic inventions can be copied, the inventor's profit is limited, and the market allocates too few resources to this activity.

Governments can direct public funds towards financing basic research but this solution is not foolproof. It requires a mechanism for allocating the public funds to their highest-value use. The Natural Sciences and Engineering Research Council of Canada is one possibly efficient channel for allocating public funds to the universities to finance and stimulate basic research.

Target High-Technology Industries   Some people say that by providing public funds to high-technology firms and industries, a country can become the first to exploit a new technology and can earn above-average profits for a period while others are busy catching up. This strategy is risky and just as likely to use resources inefficiently as to speed growth.

Encourage International Trade   Free international trade stimulates growth by extracting all the available gains from specialization and exchange. The fastest growing nations today are those with the fastest growing exports and imports.

Improve the Quality of Education   Because education brings benefits beyond those valued by the people who receive it, the free market does not produce enough education services. By funding basic education and by ensuring high standards in basic skills such as language, mathematics, and science, governments can contribute to a nation's growth potential. Education can also be stimulated and improved by using tax incentives to encourage improved private provision.

REVIEW QUIZ

- Explain the *one-third rule* and explain how the rule is used in growth accounting to isolate the contributions of capital growth and technological change to productivity growth.
- Explain how growth accounting can be used to provide information about the factors that contributed to the productivity growth slowdown.

Growth Theories

WE'VE SEEN THAT REAL GDP GROWS WHEN THE quantities of labour and capital (which includes human capital) grow and when technology advances. Does this mean that the growth of labour and capital and technological advances *cause* economic growth? It might. But there are other possibilities. *One* of these factors might be the cause of real GDP growth and the others the *effect*. We must try to discover how the influences on economic growth interact with each other to make some economies grow quickly and others grow slowly. And we must probe the reasons why a country's long-term growth rate sometimes speeds up and sometimes slows.

Growth theories are designed to study the interactions among the several factors that contribute to growth and to disentangle cause and effect. They are also designed to enable us to study the way the different factors influence each other.

Growth theories are also designed to be universal. They are not theories about the growth of poor countries only or rich countries only. They are theories about why and how poor countries become rich and rich countries continue to get richer.

We're going to study three theories of economic growth, each of which gives some insights about the process of economic growth. But none provides a definite answer to the basic questions: what causes economic growth and why do growth rates vary? Economics has some way to go before it can provide a definite answer to these most important of questions. The three growth theories we study are:

- Classical growth theory
- Neoclassical growth theory
- New growth theory

Classical Growth Theory

Classical growth theory is the view that real GDP growth is temporary and that when real GDP per person rises above the subsistence level, a population explosion eventually brings real GDP per person back to the subsistence level. Adam Smith, Thomas Robert Malthus, and David Ricardo, the leading economists of the late eighteenth century and early nineteenth century, proposed this theory, but the view is most closely associated with the name of Malthus and is sometimes called the *Malthusian theory*.

Many people today are Malthusians! They say that if today's global population of 5 billion explodes to 11 billion by 2200, we will run out of resources and return to a primitive standard of living. We must act, say the Malthusians, to contain the population growth.

The Basic Idea To understand the basic idea of classical growth theory, let's transport ourselves back to the world of 1776, when Adam Smith is first explaining the idea. Most of the 2.5 million people who live in the newly emerging nations of North America work on farms or on their own land and perform their tasks using simple tools and animal power. They earn an average of 2 shillings (a bit less than $12 in today's money) for working a ten-hour day.

Then advances in farming technology bring new types of ploughs and seeds that increase farm productivity. As farm productivity increases, farm production increases and some farm workers move from the land to the cities, where they get work producing and selling the expanding range of farm equipment. Incomes rise and the people seem to be prospering. But will the prosperity last? Classical growth theory says it will not.

Advances in technology—in both agriculture and industry—lead to an investment in new capital, which makes labour more productive. More and more businesses start up and hire the now more productive labour. The greater demand for labour raises the real wage rate and increases employment.

At this stage, economic growth has occurred and everyone has benefited from it. Real GDP has increased and the real wage rate has increased. But the classical economists believe that this new situation can't last because it will induce a population explosion.

Classical Theory of Population Growth When the classical economists were developing their ideas about population growth, an unprecedented population explosion was under way. In Britain and other Western European countries, improvements in diet and hygiene had lowered the death rate while the birth rate remained high. For several decades, population growth was extremely rapid. For example, after being relatively stable for several centuries, the population of Britain increased by 40 percent between 1750 and 1800 and by a further 50 percent between 1800 and 1830. At the same time, an estimated one million people (about 20 percent of the 1750 population) left Britain for North America and

Australia before 1800, and outward migration continued on a similar scale through the nineteenth century. These facts are the empirical basis for the classical theory of population growth.

To explain the high rate of population growth, the classical economists used the idea of a **subsistence real wage rate**, which is the minimum real wage rate needed to maintain life. If the actual real wage rate is less than the subsistence real wage rate, some people cannot survive and the population decreases. In classical theory, when the real wage rate exceeds the subsistence real wage rate, the population grows. But a rising population brings diminishing returns to labour. So labour productivity eventually decreases. This dismal implication led to economics being called the *dismal science*. The dismal implication is that no matter how much technological change occurs, real wage rates are always pushed back towards the subsistence level.

Figure 32.7 illustrates the classical growth theory. Part (a) shows the situation before growth begins. The labour demand curve is LD_0 and the labour supply curve is LS_0. There is equilibrium in the labour market: The quantity of labour demanded equals the quantity supplied at a real wage rate of 2 shillings a day and 2 million people are employed. (We will use constant 1776 prices in this example to keep it in its historical context.)

Figure 32.7(a) also shows what happens when growth begins. Technological change and investment in new capital that make labour more productive increase the demand for labour and the demand curve shifts rightward to LD_1. With this greater demand for labour, the real wage rate rises to 4 shillings a day, and this higher wage rate brings an increase in the quantity of labour supplied (a movement along the labour supply curve). Now, 3 million people are employed.

Figure 32.7(b) shows what happens next according to the Malthusians. Here, the subsistence real wage rate is (by assumption) 2 shillings a day. The actual real wage rate, at the intersection of LS_0 and LD_1, is now 4 shillings a day. Because the actual real wage rate exceeds the subsistence real wage rate, the population grows and the labour supply increases. The labour supply curve shifts rightward to LS_1. As it does so, the real wage rate falls and the quantity of labour demanded increases. Eventually, in the absence of further technological change, the economy comes to rest at the subsistence real wage rate of 2 shillings a day and 5 million people are employed.

FIGURE 32.7

Classical Growth Theory

(a) Growth begins

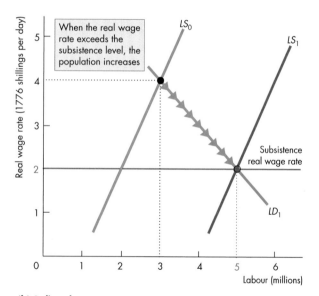

(b) A dismal outcome

Initially, 2 million people employed earn 2 shillings (1776 shillings) a day. The demand for labour increases to LD_1. The real wage rate rises to 4 shillings a day, and 3 million people are employed. With an above-subsistence real wage rate, the population increases and the labour supply curve shifts rightward to LS_1. The real wage rate falls and the quantity of labour employed increases. Population growth stops when the subsistence real wage rate returns.

The economy has grown, real GDP has increased, but a larger population is earning only the subsistence real wage rate.

The classical growth theory, with its focus on the labour market and population, makes technological change and capital accumulation the engines of growth. But the classical theory ignores any influences that real GDP growth might have on the capital stock, investment, saving, and interest rates. The neoclassical theory corrects this omission. It demotes the labour market and places it in the background. Instead, it puts capital, investment, saving, and the interest rate at centre stage. It explores the interactions among these capital market variables and the level and growth rate of real GDP. Let's now study neoclassical growth theory.

Neoclassical Growth Theory

Neoclassical growth theory is the proposition that real GDP per person grows because technological change induces a level of saving and investment that makes capital per person grow. Growth ends if technological change stops.

Robert Solow of MIT suggested the most popular version of neoclassical growth theory during the 1950s. But Frank Ramsey of Cambridge University in England first developed this theory during the 1920s.

Neoclassical theory's big break with its classical predecessor is its view about population growth. So we'll begin our account of neoclassical theory by examining its views about population growth.

The Neoclassical Economics of Population Growth

The population explosion of eighteenth century Europe that created the classical theory of population eventually ended. The birth rate fell, and while the population continued to increase, its rate of increase became moderate. This slowdown in population growth seemed to make the classical theory increasingly less relevant. It also eventually led to the development of a modern economic theory of population growth.

The modern view is that although the population growth rate is influenced by economic factors, the influence is not a simple and mechanical one like that proposed by the classical economists. Key among the economic influences on population growth is the opportunity cost of a woman's time. As women's wage rates increase and their job opportunities expand, the opportunity cost of having children increases. Faced with a higher opportunity cost, families choose to have a smaller number of children and the birth rate falls.

A second economic influence works on the death rate. The technological advance that brings increased productivity and increased incomes brings advances in health care that extend lives.

So two opposing economic forces influence population growth. As incomes increase, the birth rate decreases and the death rate decreases. It turns out that these opposing forces are almost offsetting, so to a good approximation, the rate of population growth is independent of the rate of economic growth.

This modern view of population growth and the historical trends that support it contradict the views of the classical economists. It also calls into question the modern doomsday conclusion that one day we will be swamped with too many people for the planet to feed.

Neoclassical growth theory adopts this modern view of population growth. Forces other than real GDP and its growth rate determine population growth.

Technological Change   In the neoclassical theory, the rate of technological change influences the rate of economic growth, but economic growth does not influence the pace of technological change. It is assumed that technological change results from chance. When we get lucky, we have rapid technological change; and when bad luck strikes, the pace of technological advance slows.

The Basic Idea   To understand the basic idea of neoclassical growth theory, imagine the world of the mid-1950s, when Robert Solow is explaining his idea. Canadians are enjoying post–World War II prosperity. Income per person is around $12,000 a year in today's money. The population is growing at about 1 percent a year. People are saving and investing about 20 percent of their incomes. But income per person is not growing much.

Then technology begins to advance at a more rapid pace across a range of activities. The transistor revolutionizes an emerging electronics industry. New plastics revolutionize the manufacture of household appliances. Jet airliners start to replace piston-engine airplanes and speed transportation. Elvis revolutionizes popular music!

These technological advances bring new profit opportunities. Businesses expand and new businesses are created to exploit the newly available profitable technologies. Investment and saving increase. The economy enjoys new levels of prosperity and growth. But will the prosperity last? And will the growth last? Neoclassical growth theory says the prosperity will last but the growth will not unless technology keeps advancing.

According to the neoclassical growth theory, the prosperity will persist because there is no classical population growth induced to lower wages.

But growth will stop if technology stops advancing for two related reasons. First, high profit rates that result from technological change bring increased saving and capital accumulation. But second, capital accumulation eventually results in diminishing returns that lower the return on capital. Eventually, the return on capital falls to a level at which saving and capital accumulation stop.

Figure 32.8 illustrates neoclassical growth theory. Think of the economy as today's global economy. In part (a), the curve ID_0 tells us how investment is influenced by the real interest rate. And the curve SS tells us how saving responds to the real interest rate. Equilibrium occurs at a real interest rate of 4 percent a year where saving and investment are equal at $1 trillion. Suppose that this amount of investment is sufficient to replace depreciated capital. Net investment is zero and the capital stock is constant. Real GDP per person is also constant.

Now a technological advance increases the productivity of capital and increases the expected profit rate. So investment demand increases and the investment demand curve shifts rightward to ID_1. The real interest rate rises to 6 percent a year and saving and investment increases to $1.5 trillion. Net investment is now positive, the capital stock is increasing, and real GDP is growing.

Now that real GDP is growing, rising disposable income and an increasing capital stock induce changes in saving and investment—the saving supply curve and the investment demand curve shift. We cannot keep track of all these changes by using the investment demand–saving supply figure. Instead, we look at two related demand and supply curves, the demand for and the supply of the *stock* of capital.

Investment demand is the demand for *newly produced* capital during a given time period. The demand for the *stock* of capital is the quantity of capital that people and businesses would like to have available for use at the end of a period. It is equal to the capital stock at the beginning of a period *plus* investment demand during the period.

Similarly, saving supply is the supply of funds to buy newly produced capital in a given time period. And

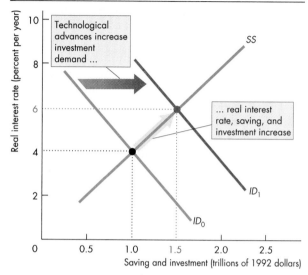

FIGURE 32.8

Neoclassical Growth Theory

(a) Growth begins

(b) Growth ends

Initially, investment is $1 trillion a year, the real interest rate is 4 percent a year, and the capital stock is $10 trillion. A technological advance increases investment demand to ID_1 and increases the demand for capital to KD_1. The real interest rate rises to 6 percent a year, investment increases to $1.5 trillion (part a) and the capital stock grows (part b). The KS curve shifts rightward towards KS_1 and the real interest rate falls. When the real interest rate equals the target rate, the capital stock is $15 trillion and growth ends.

the supply of the *stock* of capital is the quantity of funds (wealth) that people and businesses plan to own at the end of a period. It is equal to the quantity at the beginning of a period *plus* saving supply during the period.

Figure 32.8(b) shows the demand for the stock of capital KD_0. The lower the real interest rate, the greater is the quantity of capital demanded. This demand curve slopes downward for the same reason that the investment demand curve slopes downward.

At a given moment, the quantity of capital is given. It is the vertical line KS_0. In the long run, the supply of capital depends on the saving decision.

Target Rate and Long-Run Saving The neoclassical theory holds that if the real interest rate exceeds a *target rate*, the supply of capital increases; if the real interest rate is less than a target rate, the supply of capital decreases; and if the real interest rate equals a target rate, the supply of capital is constant. In Fig. 32.8, the target real interest rate is 4 percent a year and the long-run capital supply curve is LKS. If the real interest rate exceeds 4 percent a year, saving is positive, and the quantity of capital supplied increases. And if the real interest rate is less than 4 percent a year, saving is negative, and the quantity of capital supplied decreases. (Negative saving occurs and capital decreases when capital is not replaced as it wears out.)

Initially, equilibrium is at point *a*, where KD_0 and KS_0 intersect and where the real interest rate is 4 percent a year—its target rate. The capital stock is $10 trillion. Neoclassical growth begins from this point.

A technological advance now increases the productivity of capital and the demand for capital curve shifts rightward to KD_1. The expected rate of profit increases. As a result, investment increases (shown in Fig. 32.8a). With greater investment, the supply of capital increases and the supply of capital curve begins to shift rightward. As it does so, the real interest rate falls.

The capital stock continues to increase and the real interest rate continues to fall until the economy reaches point *b* in Fig. 32.8(b). Here, the real interest rate is back at its target rate of 4 percent a year and the capital stock has grown to $15 trillion. With no further growth of the capital stock, real GDP stops growing and, in the absence of another technological advance, growth ends.

Throughout the process you've just studied, real GDP grows but the growth rate gradually decreases and eventually ends. Ongoing technology advances are constantly increasing the demand for capital, raising the real interest rate, and inducing the saving that increases the capital stock. The process repeats as long as technology advances and creates ongoing long-term economic growth. The growth rate fluctuates because technological progress occurs at a variable rate.

A Problem with Neoclassical Growth Theory
All economies have access to the same technologies, and capital is free to roam the globe, seeking the highest available real interest rate. So neoclassical growth theory implies that growth rates and income levels per person around the globe will converge. While there is some sign of convergence among the rich countries (shown in Fig. 32.2a), convergence is slow and it does not appear to be imminent for all countries (as we saw in Fig. 32.2b).

New growth theory attempts to overcome this shortcoming of neoclassical growth theory and explain why convergence might never occur. But the major purpose of new growth theory is to explain differences in the rate of technological change both over time and among countries.

New Growth Theory

New growth theory holds that real GDP per person grows because of the choices people make in the pursuit of profit and that growth can persist indefinitely. Paul Romer of Stanford University developed this theory during the 1980s but the ideas go back to work by Joseph Schumpeter during the 1930s and 1940s.

The theory begins with two facts about market economies:

■ Discoveries result from choices.
■ Discoveries bring profit and competition destroys profit.

Discoveries and Choices When people discover a new product or technique, they think of themselves as being lucky. They are right. But the pace at which new discoveries are made—and at which technology advances—is not determined by chance. It depends on how many people are looking for a new technology and how intensively they are looking.

Discoveries and Profits Profit is the spur to technological change. The forces of competition squeeze profits, so to increase profit, people constantly seek either lower-cost methods of production or new and better products for which people are willing to pay a higher price. Inventors can maintain a profit for several years by taking out a patent or copyright. But eventually, a new discovery is copied, and profits disappear.

Two further facts play a key role in the new growth theory. They are:

- Discoveries can be used by many people at the same time.
- Physical activities can be replicated.

Discoveries Used by All Once a profitable new discovery has been made, everyone can use it. And one person's use of a new discovery does not prevent others from using it. This fact means that as the benefits of a new discovery spread, free resources become available. These resources are free because nothing is given up when they are used. They have a zero opportunity cost.

Replicating Activities Production activities can be replicated. For example, there might be two, three, or fifty-three identical firms making fibre-optic cable using an identical assembly line and production technique. If one firm increases its capital and output, that firm experiences diminishing returns. But the economy can increase its capital and output by adding another identical fibre cable factory and the economy does not experience diminishing returns.

The assumption that capital does *not* experience diminishing returns is the central novel proposition of the new growth theory. And the implication of this simple and appealing idea is astonishing. In the neoclassical theory, with its diminishing returns to capital, as capital is accumulated, the real interest rate gradually falls until it equals the target real interest rate. At this point, growth stops. But the new growth theory has no such growth-stopping mechanism. As capital accumulates, the real interest rate is unaffected. It can remain above the target real interest rate indefinitely. Real GDP per person grows indefinitely as long as people can undertake research and development that yields a higher real interest rate than the target rate.

New growth theory sees the economy as a kind of perpetual motion mechanism. Economic growth is driven by our insatiable wants, which lead us to pursue profit and innovate. The result of this process is new and better products. But new and better products result in new firms starting up and old firms going out of business. In this process, jobs are created and destroyed. The outcome is new and better jobs, more leisure, and more consumption. But our insatiable wants are still there, so the process continues, going round and round a circle of wants, profits, innovation, and new products.

The growth rate depends on people's ability to innovate and the real interest rate. Over the years, this ability has changed. The invention of language and writing (the two most basic human capital tools), and later the development of the scientific method and the establishment of universities and research institutions, brought a huge increase in the return to capital. Today, a deeper understanding of genes is bringing profit in a growing biotechnology industry. And astonishing advances in computer technology are creating an explosion of profit opportunities in a wide range of new information age industries.

Figure 32.9 illustrates new growth theory. Like Fig. 32.8(b), it shows the demand for and supply of the *stock* of capital. But unlike Fig. 32.8(b), here the marginal product of capital does not diminish as the quantity of capital increases. The demand curve for capital is horizontal at the real interest rate equal to the expected rate of profit. This expected profit rate does not change as the stock of capital changes. The horizontal demand for capital curve captures the special feature of the new growth theory that produces its novel prediction.

The supply of capital is fixed in the short run and is shown by a vertical supply curve such as KS_0. The long-run capital supply curve is horizontal at the target real interest rate and is LKS.

Initially, the real interest rate is 2 percent a year, and the line KD_0 in Fig. 32.9 shows the demand for capital. This real interest rate is below the target rate so no one has an incentive to save. The economy is stuck at point *a*.

The development of basic human capital tools such as mathematics and physics increases the return to capital and innovation and the demand for capital curve shifts upward to KD_1. The real interest rate now exceeds the target rate and there is an incentive to save and invest. So investment and saving increase and the quantity of capital grows. As it does so, the supply of capital curve shifts rightward through KS_0, KS_1, KS_2, KS_3, and so on. The capital stock grows, real GDP grows, and because there are no diminishing returns to capital, the real interest rate remains constant. Economic growth continues indefinitely as long as the real interest rate exceeds the target rate.

Figure 32.9 shows the process we've just described. The target rate is 4 percent a year, and the real interest rate is 6 percent a year. With positive saving, the capital supply curve shifts rightward indefinitely. The speed with which it shifts rightward depends on the extent to which the real interest rate exceeds the target rate. The higher the real interest rate, the more it exceeds that target rate, and the faster the capital supply curve shifts rightward. So the faster the economy grows.

FIGURE 32.9

New Growth Theory

In new growth theory, economic growth results from incentives to innovate and from capital that does not experience diminishing returns. Initially, the real interest rate is 2 percent a year and the demand for capital is KD_0. The stock of capital is zero and the economy is stuck at point a. The development of the scientific method increases the real interest rate to 6 percent a year and the demand for capital increases to KD_1. With a real interest rate greater than the target rate, saving increases and the supply of capital increases. The capital supply curve shifts rightward successively through KS_0, KS_1, KS_2, KS_3, and so on. As capital grows, real GDP grows but the real interest rate does not fall because there are no diminishing returns. Real GDP growth continues indefinitely.

Sorting Out the Theories

Which theory is correct? Probably none is exactly correct. But they all teach us something of value. The classical theory reminds us that our physical resources are limited and that with no advances in technology, we must eventually hit diminishing returns. Neoclassical theory reaches essentially the same conclusion, but not because of a population explosion. Instead, it emphasizes potentially diminishing returns to capital and reminds us that we cannot necessarily keep growth going just by accumulating capital. New growth theory emphasizes the possible capacity of human resources to innovate at a pace that offsets diminishing returns.

REVIEW QUIZ

- What is the central idea of classical growth theory that leads to the dismal outcome?
- Explain the mechanism at work in the classical growth theory and describe the role played by diminishing returns.
- What, according to the neoclassical growth theory, is the fundamental cause of economic growth?
- What is the key proposition of the new growth theory that makes growth persist? Is the proposition believable? Is the conclusion believable?

◆ Economic growth is the single most decisive factor that influences a country's living standard, but it is not the only one. Another is the extent to which the country fully employs its scarce resources, especially its labour. In recent years, Canada has enjoyed full employment and steady growth. But the business cycle is almost certainly not dead. And unemployment has become a severe problem for many countries.

In the next chapter, we study the fluctuations of real GDP and employment and unemployment around their long-term trends—the business cycle. But before embarking on this topic, take a look at *Reading Between the Lines* on pages 740–741, which compares Canada's economic growth with that of the other major industrial countries and also compares the economic growth performance of the Canadian provinces from Newfoundland to British Columbia.

Growth in the Canadian Economy

NATIONAL POST, AUGUST 5, 1999

Canada to lead G7 countries in growth, forecast says

BY GREG CRONE

Canada is poised to overtake the U.S. and become the number one G7 economy in terms of growth, a forecast issued by the Canadian Imperial Bank of Commerce says.

Canada's real gross domestic product (GDP) will grow about 3.5% in 1999 and 2.7% in 2000, the forecast says. This far outstrips the expected average growth rate of 2.4% for 1999 and 2% in 2000 for the G7 top industrialized countries.

Canada's growth rate should come close to the 3.8% expected for the U.S. in 1999 and should actually outperform the 2.4% projected for the U.S. in 2000.

"Canada will do better than the U.S. in 2000," said Alister Smith, CIBC's deputy chief economist. "Next year we will be on top of the heap in the G7." ...

Gradual improving of the economies of countries in the rest of the world will help to pull up commodity prices which will assist Canada's rate of growth, Mr. Smith said. ...

The CIBC outlook is in line with another forecast issued by Bank of Montreal yesterday, which predicts the growth in Canada's economy to accelerate to 3.4% this year, before easing slightly to 3% in 2000.

The strongest economic growth will be in Newfoundland and Ontario, the Bank of Montreal says.

Newfoundland's economy will grow 5.5% in 1999, fuelled by rising production in the Hibernia oil field. Newfoundland's unemployment rate will decline slightly from 17.9% in 1998 to 16% in 2000, but will still be the highest in Canada.

Among provinces with diversified economies, Ontario will lead with 4.6% growth this year and 3.5% growth in 2000.

British Columbia will experience the slowest growth in the country. There will be little improvement in 1999 and growth will edge up to 1.8% in 2000.

The sharp recovery in crude oil prices and continuing improvement in natural gas prices will assist Alberta, which is expected to have 2.8% growth in 1999 and 3.3% growth in 2000.

Essence of the Story

■ According to a CIBC report, Canada will become the fastest growing economy in the G7 in 2000.

■ An improvement in economies in the rest of the world will raise commodity prices. The increase in commodity prices will boost Canada's growth rate.

■ Ontario and Newfoundland will experience the fastest economic growth.

■ British Columbia will have the slowest economic growth.

■ The increases in crude oil prices and natural gas prices will aid economic growth in Alberta.

Economic Analysis

■ The G7 is the seven industrial countries: Canada, France, Germany, Italy, Japan, the United Kingdom, and the United States.

■ The Canadian Imperial Bank of Commerce (CIBC) says that Canada will become the fastest growing G7 economy in 2000. That is, Canada's growth rate of real GDP will be the greatest in the G7.

■ Most news articles on economic growth (including this one) do not distinguish between short-term growth of real GDP at different phases of the business cycle and the growth rate of *potential* GDP, which excludes the effects of the business cycle.

■ The prediction that Canada will be the fastest-growing G7 economy in 2000 is a prediction that Canada's current business cycle expansion will remain strong, while other economies will begin to slow.

■ The ranking of countries in the growth league table depends on the time period over which we measure growth.

■ Figure 1 shows the growth rate of real GDP in the G7 countries between 1970 and 2000. (The data for 1999 and 2000 are forecasts by the International Monetary Fund.)

■ Over this thirty-year period, Canada and Japan have grown the most and the United Kingdom the least.

■ The U.S. growth rate is almost as high as that of Canada and Japan. Before hitting a severe period of stagnation during the 1990s, Japan was out-growing all the other G7 countries.

■ Figure 2 shows growth during the 1990s. Over this period, the United States tops the table and Canada comes second. Now, Japan comes in last.

■ Figure 3 looks at the International Monetary Fund (IMF) growth forecast for 2000. Over this very short period, France and Germany lead the pack, with Canada coming third and Japan last. The IMF and the CIBC forecasts differ.

■ Growth rates differ across countries because of differences in saving rates and differences in the pace of technological change.

■ Growth rates differ across regions for the same reasons. For example, Newfoundland is expected to have a strong growth rate during 1999 and 2000 because of a big investment in the Hibernia oil field.

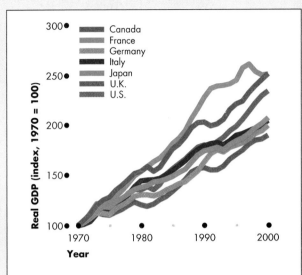

Figure 1 Growth since 1970

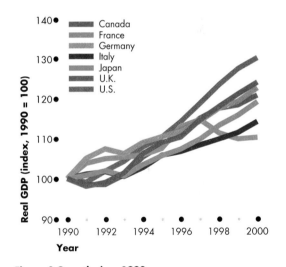

Figure 2 Growth since 1990

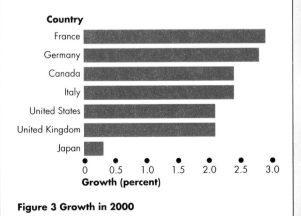

Figure 3 Growth in 2000

S U M M A R Y

Key Points

Long-Term Growth Trends (pp. 724–726)

▨ Between 1898 to 1998, real GDP per person in Canada grew at an average rate of 2.2 percent a year. Growth was fastest during the first decade of this century, the 1920s, and the 1960s.

▨ The real GDP gaps between Canada and Africa as well as Central and South America have widened. The gaps between Canada and Hong Kong, Taiwan, Korea, and China have narrowed.

The Causes of Economic Growth: A First Look (pp. 727–728)

▨ Economic growth requires an *incentive* system created by markets, property rights, and monetary exchange.

▨ Economic growth occurs when people save, invest in physical and human capital, and discover new technologies.

Growth Accounting (pp. 729–732)

▨ Growth accounting measures the contributions of capital accumulation and technological change to productivity growth.

▨ Growth accounting uses the productivity function and the *one-third rule*: a one percent increase in capital per hour of work brings a one-third percent increase in real GDP per hour of work.

▨ During the productivity growth slowdown of the 1970s, technological change made no contribution to real GDP growth.

▨ It might be possible to achieve faster growth by stimulating saving, subsidizing research and development, targeting (and possibly subsidizing) high-technology industries, and encouraging more international trade.

Growth Theories (pp. 733–739)

▨ In classical theory, when technological advances increase real GDP per person above the *subsistence* level, a population explosion brings diminishing returns to labour and real GDP per person returns to the subsistence level.

▨ In neoclassical growth theory, when technological advances increase saving and investment, an increase in the capital stock brings diminishing returns to capital and eventually, without further technological change, the capital stock and real GDP per person stop growing.

▨ In new growth theory, when technological advances increase saving and investment, an increase in the capital stock *does not* bring diminishing returns to capital and growth persists indefinitely.

Key Figures ◆

Key Terms

PROBLEMS

☐ *1. The following information has been discovered about the economy of Longland: The economy's productivity function is:

Capital per hour of work (1992 dollars per hour)	Real GDP per hour of work (1992 dollars per hour)
10	3.80
20	5.70
30	7.13
40	8.31
50	9.35
60	10.29
70	11.14
80	11.94

Does this economy conform to the one-third rule? If so, explain why. If not, explain why not and explain what rule, if any, it does conform to. Explain how you would do the growth accounting for this economy.

2. The following information has been discovered about the economy of Flatland: The economy's productivity function is:

Capital per hour of work (1992 dollars per hour)	Real GDP per hour of work (1992 dollars per hour)
10	3.00
20	3.75
30	4.22
40	4.57
50	4.86
60	5.10
70	5.31
80	5.50

Does this economy conform to the one-third rule? If so, explain why. If not, explain why not and explain what rule, if any, it does conform to. Explain how you would do the growth accounting for this economy.

☐ *3. In Longland, described in problem 1, capital per hour of work in 1999 was $40 and real GDP per hour of work was $8.31. In 2001, capital per hour of work had increased to $50 and real GDP per hour of work had increased to $10.29 an hour.

a. Does Longland experience diminishing returns? Explain why or why not.

b. Use growth accounting to find the contribution of the change in capital between 1999 and 2001 to the growth of productivity in Longland.

c. Use growth accounting to find the contribution of technological change between 1999 and 2001 to the growth of productivity in Longland.

4. In Flatland, described in problem 2, capital per hour of work in 1999 was $30 and real GDP per hour of work was $4.22. In 2001, capital per hour of work had increased to $60 and real GDP per hour of work had increased to $6.37 an hour.

a. Does Flatland experience diminishing returns? Explain why or why not.

b. Use growth accounting to find the contribution of the change in capital between 1999 and 2001 to the growth of productivity in Flatland.

c. Use growth accounting to find the contribution of technological change between 1999 and 2001 to the growth of productivity in Flatland.

☐ *5. The following information has been discovered about the economy of Cape Despair. The subsistence real wage rate is $7 an hour. Whenever the real wage rate rises above this level the population grows, and when the real wage rate falls below this level the population decreases. With its current population, the demand and supply schedules for labour in Cape Despair are:

Real wage rate (1992 dollars per hour)	Quantity of labour demanded (billions of hours per year)	Quantity of labour supplied (billions of hours per year)
3	8	4
5	7	5
7	6	6
9	5	7
11	4	8
13	3	9
15	2	10
17	1	11

Initially, the labour force of Cape Despair is constant, and the real wage is at its subsistence level. Then a technological advance increases the amount that firms are willing to pay for labour by $2 at each level of employment.

a. What is the initial level of employment and real wage rate in Cape Despair?

b. What happens to the real wage rate immediately following the technological advance?

c. What happens to the population growth rate following the technological advance?

d. What is the employment level when Cape Despair returns to a long-run equilibrium?

6. Martha's Island is an economy that behaves according to the neoclassical growth model. The economy is in long-run equilibrium and is described in the following table.

Real interest rate (percent per year)	Quantity of capital demanded (billions of dollars)	Quantity of capital (billions of dollars)
1	9	7
2	8	7
3	7	7
4	6	7
5	5	7
6	4	7
7	3	7
8	2	7

a. What is the initial real interest rate on Martha's Island?

b. What is the target rate?

A technological advance increases the demand for capital $2 billion at each real interest rate.

c. What is the real interest rate immediately following the technological advance?

d. What is the real interest rate and quantity of capital when Martha's Island returns to a long-run equilibrium?

*7. Romeria is a country that behaves according to the predictions of new growth theory. The target rate is 3 percent a year. A technological advance increases the demand for capital and raises the real interest rate to 5 percent a year. Describe the events that happen in Romeria and contrast them with the events in Martha's Island in problem 6.

8. Suppose that in Romeria, which is described in problem 7, technological advance slows and the real interest rate falls to 3 percent a year. Describe what happens in Romeria.

CRITICAL THINKING

1. After studying *Reading Between the Lines* on pp. 740–741, answer the following questions:

a. How quickly is the Canadian economy growing compared with the growth of the other large industrial countries?

b. How would you account for the differences in national growth rates?

c. What are the main differences in growth rates across the Canadian provinces? Which provinces grow fastest, and which grow slowest?

d. How would you account for differences in provincial growth rates?

e. Which of the three economic growth theories—classical, neoclassical, and new—does the author of the news article seem to believe is relevant in Canada today? If none, what theory does the author of the article seem to use?

2. Visit the Penn World Table Web site (linked from the Parkin-Bade Web site) and obtain data on real GDP per person for Canada, China, South Africa, and Mexico from 1960 to the latest year available.

a. Draw a graph of the data.

b. Which country has the lowest real GDP per person and which has the highest?

c. Which country has experienced the fastest growth rate since 1960 and which the slowest?

d. Explain why the growth rates in these four countries are ranked in the order you have discovered.

e. Return to the Penn World Table Web site and obtain data for any four other countries that interest you. Describe and explain the patterns that you find for these countries.

3. Write a memo to your Member of Parliament in which you set out the policies you believe the Canadian government must follow to speed up the growth rate of real GDP in Canada.

4. Is faster economic growth always a good thing? Argue the case for faster growth and for slower growth and then reach a conclusion on whether growth should be increased or decreased.

The Business Cycle

The 1920s were years of unprecedented prosperity for Canadians. After the horrors of World War I (1914–1918), the economic machine was back at work, producing such techno-logical marvels as cars and airplanes, telephones and vacuum cleaners. Houses and apartments were being built at a frantic pace. Then, almost without warning, in October 1929, came a devastating stock market crash. Overnight, the values of stocks trading on Wall Street and Bay Street fell by 30 percent. During the four succeeding years, there followed

Must What Goes Up Always Come Down?

the most severe economic contrac-tion in recorded history. By 1933, real GDP had fallen by 30 percent and unemployment had increased to 20 per-cent of the labour force. What caused the Great Depression? ◆ By the standard of the Great Depression, recent recessions have been mild. But recessions have not gone away. Our economy has experienced 15 recessions since 1920, 10 of which have occurred since the end of World War II in 1945. In 1981, real GDP fell by 3.2 percent. It fell again in 1990 and 1991 by more than 2 percent. It was not until mid-1992 that real GDP returned to its 1989 level. Since the 1990–1991 recession, real GDP has soared. By the end of 1998, it was some 22 per-cent higher than it had been in the 1990–1991 recession and 18 percent higher than its peak before the 1990–1991 recession. What causes a repeating sequence of recessions and expansions in our economy? Must what goes up always come down? Will we have another recession? When?

◇ In this chapter, we are going to explore the business cycle. You will see how all the strands of macroeconomics that you've been following come together and weave a complete picture of the forces and mechanisms that generate economic growth and fluctuations in production, employment and unemployment, and inflation.

After studying this chapter, you will be able to:

- Distinguish among the different theories of the business cycle
- Explain the Keynesian and monetarist theories of the business cycle
- Explain the new classical and new Keynesian theories of the business cycle
- Explain real business cycle theory
- Describe the origins of and the mechanisms at work during recessions and expansions during the 1990s
- Describe the origins of and the mechanisms at work during the Great Depression

Cycle Patterns, Impulses, and Mechanisms

CYCLES ARE A WIDESPREAD PHYSICAL PHENOMEnon. In a tennis match, the ball cycles from one side of the court to the other and back again. Every day, the earth cycles from day to night and back to day. A child on a rocking horse creates a cycle as the horse swings back and forth.

The tennis ball cycle is the simplest. It is caused by the actions of the players. Each time the ball changes direction (at each turning point), the racket (an outside force) is applied. The day-night-day cycle is the most subtle. This cycle is caused by the rotation of the earth. No new force is applied each day to make the sun rise and set. It happens because of the design of the objects that interact to create the cycle. Nothing happens at a turning point (sunrise and sunset) that is any different from what is happening at other points except that the sun comes into or goes out of view. The child's rocking horse cycle is a combination of these two cases. To start the horse rocking, some outside force must be exerted (as in the tennis ball cycle). But once the horse is rocking, the to-and-fro cycle continues for some time with no further force being applied (as in the day-night-day cycle). The rocking horse cycle eventually dies out unless the horse is pushed again, and each time the horse is pushed, the cycle temporarily becomes more severe.

The economy is a bit like all three of these examples. It can be hit by shocks (like a tennis ball) that send it in one direction or another, it can cycle indefinitely (like the turning of day into night), and it can cycle in swings that get milder until another shock sets off a new burst of bigger swings (like a rocking horse). While none of these analogies is perfect, they all contain some insights into the business cycle. Different theories of the cycle emphasize different impulses (different tennis rackets) and different cycle mechanisms (different solar system and rocking horse designs).

Although there are several different theories of the business cycle, they all agree about one aspect of the cycle: the central role played by investment and the accumulation of capital.

The Role of Investment and Capital

Whatever the shocks are that hit the economy, they hit one crucial variable: investment. Recessions begin when investment in new capital slows down, and they turn into expansions when investment speeds up. Investment and capital interact like the spinning earth and the sun to create an ongoing cycle.

In an expansion, investment proceeds at a rapid rate and the capital stock grows quickly. But rapid capital growth means that the amount of capital per hour of labour is growing. Equipped with more capital, labour becomes more productive. But the *law of diminishing returns* begins to operate. The law of diminishing returns states that as the quantity of capital increases, with the quantity of labour remaining the same, the gain in productivity from the additional units of capital eventually diminishes. Diminishing returns to capital bring a fall in the profit rate and with a lower profit rate, the incentive to invest weakens. As a result, investment eventually falls. When it falls by a large amount, recession begins.

In a recession, investment is low and the capital stock grows slowly. In a deep recession, the capital stock might actually fall. Slow capital growth (or even a falling capital stock) means that the amount of capital per hour of labour is falling. With a low amount of capital per hour of labour, businesses begin to see opportunities for profitable investment and the pace of investment eventually picks up. As it does so, recession turns into expansion.

The AS–AD Model

Investment and capital are a crucial part of the business cycle mechanism but they are just one part. To study the broader business cycle mechanism, we need a broader framework. That framework is the *AS–AD* model of Chapter 24. All the theories of the business cycle can be described in terms of the *AS–AD* model. Theories differ both in what they identify as the impulse and in the cycle mechanism. But all theories can be thought of as making assumptions about the factors that make either aggregate supply or aggregate demand fluctuate and assumptions about how they interact with each other to create a business cycle. Business cycle impulses can affect either the supply side or the demand side of the economy or both. But there are no pure supply-side theories. We will classify all theories of the business cycle as either:

1. Aggregate demand theories
2. Real business cycle theory

We'll study the aggregate demand theories first. Then we'll study real business cycle theory, which is a more recent approach that isolates a shock that has both aggregate supply and aggregate demand effects.

Aggregate Demand Theories of the Business Cycle

THREE TYPES OF AGGREGATE DEMAND THEORY OF the business cycle have been proposed. They are:

■ Keynesian theory
■ Monetarist theory
■ Rational expectations theories

Keynesian Theory

The **Keynesian theory of the business cycle** regards volatile expectations as the main source of economic fluctuations. This theory is distilled from Keynes' *General Theory of Employment, Interest, and Money*. We'll explore the Keynesian theory by looking at its main impulse and the mechanism that converts that impulse into a real GDP cycle.

Keynesian Impulse The *impulse* in the Keynesian theory of the business cycle is *expected future sales and profits*. A change in expected future sales and profits changes the demand for new capital and changes the level of investment.

Keynes reasoned that profit expectations would be volatile because most of the events that shape the future are unknown and impossible to forecast. So, he reasoned, news or even rumours about future influences on profit (such as tax rate changes, interest rate changes, advances in technology, global economic and political events, or any other of the thousands of relevant factors) have large effects on the expected profit rate.

To emphasize the volatility and diversity of sources of changes in expected sales and profits, Keynes described these expectations as *animal spirits*.

Keynesian Cycle Mechanism In the Keynesian theory, once a change in animal spirits has changed investment, a cycle mechanism begins to operate that has two key elements. First, the initial change in investment has a multiplier effect. The change in investment changes *aggregate* expenditure, real GDP, and disposable income. The change in disposable income changes consumption expenditure, and aggregate demand changes by a multiple of the initial change in investment. (This mechanism is described in detail in Chapter 25, p. 554 and pp. 560–561.)

The aggregate demand curve shifts leftward in a recession and rightward in an expansion.

The second element of the Keynesian cycle mechanism is a sticky money wage rate together with a horizontal short-run aggregate supply curve. With a horizontal *SAS* curve, swings in aggregate demand translate into swings in real GDP with no changes in the price level.

Figure 33.1 illustrates the Keynesian cycle. The long-run aggregate supply curve is *LAS*, the short-run aggregate supply curve is *SAS*, and the aggregate demand curve is AD_F. Initially, the economy is at full employment (point *a*) with real GDP at $800 billion and the price level at 110.

A fall in animal spirits decreases investment and a multiplier process decreases aggregate demand. The aggregate demand curve shifts leftward to AD_R. With

FIGURE 33.1

The Keynesian Cycle

The economy is operating at point *a* at the intersection of the long-run aggregate supply curve (*LAS*), the short-run aggregate supply curve (*SAS*), and the aggregate demand curve (AD_F). A Keynesian recession begins when a fall in animal spirits causes investment demand to decrease. Aggregate demand decreases and the *AD* curve shifts leftward to AD_R. With a sticky money wage rate, real GDP decreases to $700 billion and the price level does not change. The economy moves to point *b*. An increase in animal spirits has the opposite effect and takes the economy back to point *a*. The economy cycles by bouncing between point *a* and point *b*.

a fixed money wage rate, real GDP decreases to $700 billion and the economy moves to point *b*.

Unemployment has increased and there is a surplus of labour, but the money wage rate does not fall and the economy remains at point *b* until some force moves it away.

That force is a rise in animal spirits, which increases investment. The multiplier process kicks in again and aggregate demand increases. The *AD* curve shifts back to AD_F and real GDP increases in an expansion to $800 billion again.

As long as real GDP remains below potential GDP ($800 billion in this example), the money wage rate and the price level remain constant. And real GDP cycles between points *a* and *b*.

Keynesian Inflation If animal spirits increase investment at full employment, an inflationary gap arises. Real GDP increases temporarily, but soon returns to potential GDP at a higher price level. Figure 33.2 shows this case.

Starting from full employment, at point *a*, an increase in aggregate demand shifts the aggregate demand curve rightward from AD_0 to AD_1. Real GDP increases to $900 billion at point *c*. There is now an inflationary gap. Once real GDP exceeds potential GDP and unemployment falls below the natural rate, the money wage rate begins to rise. As it does so, the short-run aggregate supply curve begins to shift from SAS_0 towards SAS_1. Real GDP now begins to decrease and the price level rises. The economy follows the arrows from point *c* to point *d*, the eventual long-run equilibrium.

The Keynesian business cycle is like a tennis match. It is caused by outside forces—animal spirits—that change direction and set off a process that ends at an equilibrium that must be hit again by the outside forces to disturb it.

On the downside, when aggregate demand decreases and unemployment rises, the money wage rate does not change. It is completely rigid in the down direction. With a decrease in aggregate demand and no change in the money wage rate, the economy gets stuck in an unemployment equilibrium. There are no natural forces operating to restore full employment. The economy remains in that situation until animal spirits are lifted and investment increases again.

On the upside, if an increase in aggregate demand creates an inflationary gap, the money wage rate rises and the price level also rises. Real GDP returns to potential GDP.

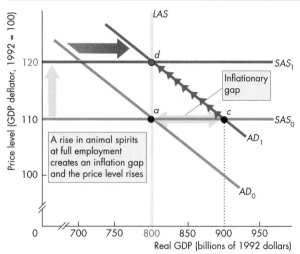

Starting at point *a*, a Keynesian expansion begins when a rise in animal spirits causes investment demand to increase. Aggregate demand increases and the *AD* curve shifts rightward to AD_1. With a sticky money wage rate, real GDP increases to $900 billion at point *c*. There is now an inflationary gap. The money wage rate rises and the *SAS* curve shifts from SAS_0 towards SAS_1. Real GDP decreases and the price level rises as the economy heads towards point *d*.

Monetarist Theory

The **monetarist theory of the business cycle** regards fluctuations in the money stock as the main source of economic fluctuations. This theory is distilled from the writings of Milton Friedman and several other economists. We'll explore the monetarist theory as we did the Keynesian theory, by looking first at its main impulse and second at the mechanism that creates a cycle in real GDP.

Monetarist Impulse The *impulse* in the monetarist theory of the business cycle is the *growth rate of the quantity of money*. A speedup in money growth brings expansion, and a slowdown in money growth brings recession. The source of the change in the growth rate of the quantity of money is the monetary policy actions of the Bank of Canada.

Monetarist Cycle Mechanism In the monetarist theory, once the Bank of Canada has changed the money growth rate, a cycle mechanism begins to operate that, like the Keynesian mechanism, first affects aggregate demand. When the money growth rate increases, the quantity of real money in the economy increases. Interest rates fall, and real money balances increase. The foreign exchange rate also falls—the dollar loses value on the foreign exchange market. These initial financial market effects begin to spill over into other markets. Investment demand and exports increase, and consumers spend more on durable goods. These initial changes in expenditure have a multiplier effect, just as investment has in the Keynesian theory. Through these mechanisms a speedup in money growth shifts the aggregate demand curve rightward and brings an expansion. Similarly, a slowdown in money growth shifts the aggregate demand curve leftward and brings a recession.

The second element of the monetarist cycle mechanism is the response of aggregate supply to a change in aggregate demand. The short-run aggregate supply curve is upward-sloping. With an upward-sloping SAS curve, swings in aggregate demand translate into swings in both real GDP and the price level. But monetarists believe that real GDP deviations from full employment are temporary.

In monetarist theory, the money wage rate is only *temporarily sticky*. When aggregate demand decreases and unemployment rises, the money wage rate eventually begins to fall. As the money wage rate falls, so does the price level and after a period of adjustment, real GDP returns to potential GDP, the unemployment rate returns to the natural rate and full employment is restored. When aggregate demand increases and unemployment falls below the natural rate, the money wage rate begins to rise. As the money wage rate rises, so does the price level. And through a period of adjustment, real GDP returns to potential GDP and the unemployment rate returns to the natural rate.

Figure 33.3 illustrates a monetarist recession and recovery. The economy is initially at full employment (point *a*) on the long-run aggregate supply curve (LAS), the aggregate demand curve (AD_0), and the short-run aggregate supply curve (SAS_0). A slowdown in the money growth rate decreases aggregate demand, and the aggregate demand curve shifts leftward to AD_1. Real GDP decreases to $750 billion, and the economy goes into recession (point *b*).

Unemployment increases and there is a surplus of labour. The money wage rate begins to fall. As the money wage rate falls, the short-run aggregate supply curve starts to shift rightward towards SAS_1. The price level falls, and real GDP begins to expand as the economy moves to point *c*, its new full-employment equilibrium.

The monetarist business cycle is like a rocking horse. It needs an outside force to get it going, but once going, it rocks back and forth (but just once). When the money supply decreases (or its growth rate slows) like you've just studied, the economy cycles with a recession followed by expansion. But if the money supply increases (or its growth rate speeds) the economy also cycles but with an expansion followed by recession.

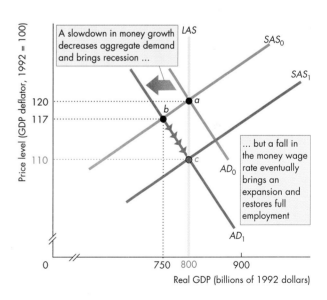

FIGURE 33.3

A Monetarist Recession

A monetarist recession begins when a slowdown in money growth decreases aggregate demand. The *AD* curve shifts leftward from AD_0 to AD_1. With a sticky money wage rate, real GDP decreases to $750 billion and the price level falls to 117 as the economy moves from point *a* to point *b*. With a surplus of labour, the money wage rate falls and the *SAS* curve shifts rightward to SAS_1. The price level falls further, and real GDP returns to potential GDP at point *c*.

Figure 33.4 shows the effects of this opposite case in which the money supply increases. Here, starting out at point *c*, an increase in the quantity of money increases aggregate demand and shifts the *AD* curve to *AD₂*. Both real GDP and the price level increase as the economy moves to point *d*, where *SAS₁* and *AD₂* intersect. With real GDP above potential GDP and unemployment below the natural rate, the money wage rate begins to rise and the *SAS* curve starts to shift leftward towards *SAS₂*. As the money wage rate rises, the price level also rises and real GDP decreases. The economy moves from point *d* to point *e*, its new full-employment equilibrium.

Although monetarists think that the money wage rate will fall when real GDP is less than potential GDP—when there is a recessionary gap—they do not see this process as being a rapid one.

FIGURE 33.4
A Monetarist Expansion

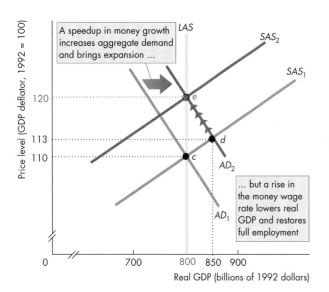

Starting at point *c*, a monetarist expansion begins when an increase in money growth increases aggregate demand and shifts the *AD* curve rightward to *AD₂*. With a sticky money wage rate, real GDP rises to $850 billion, the price level rises to 113, and the economy moves to point *d*. With a shortage of labour, the money wage rate rises and the *SAS* curve shifts towards *SAS₂*. The price level rises and real GDP decreases to potential GDP as the economy heads towards point *e*.

Rational Expectations Theories

A **rational expectation** is a forecast that is based on all the available relevant information. Rational expectations theories of the business cycle are theories based on the view that the money wage rate is determined by a rational expectation of the price level. Two distinctly different rational expectations theories of the cycle have been proposed. A **new classical theory of the business cycle** regards *unanticipated* fluctuations in aggregate demand as the main source of economic fluctuations. This theory is based on the work of Robert E. Lucas, Jr., (see pp. 540–542) and several other economists, including Thomas J. Sargent and Robert J. Barro. A different **new Keynesian theory of the business cycle** also regards *unanticipated* fluctuations in aggregate demand as the main source of economic fluctuations but also leaves room for *anticipated* demand fluctuations to play a role. We'll explore these theories as we did the Keynesian and monetarist theories, by looking first at the main impulse and second at the cycle mechanism.

Rational Expectations Impulse   The *impulse* that distinguishes the rational expectations theories from the other aggregate demand theories of the business cycle is the *unanticipated change in aggregate demand*. A larger than anticipated increase in aggregate demand brings an expansion and a smaller than anticipated increase in aggregate demand brings a recession. Any factor that influences aggregate demand—for example, fiscal policy, monetary policy, or developments in the world economy that influence exports—whose change is not anticipated, can bring a change in real GDP.

Rational Expectations Cycle Mechanisms   To describe the rational expectations cycle mechanisms, we'll deal first with the new classical version. When aggregate demand decreases, if the money wage rate doesn't change, short-run aggregate supply remains unchanged, so real GDP and the price level both decrease. The fall in the price level increases the *real* wage rate, and employment decreases and unemployment rises. In the new classical theory, these events occur only if the decrease in aggregate demand is not anticipated. If the decrease in aggregate demand *is* anticipated, the price level is expected to fall and both firms and workers will agree to a lower money wage rate. By doing so, they can prevent the real wage from rising and avoid a rise in the unemployment rate.

Similarly, if firms and workers anticipate an increase in aggregate demand, they expect the price level to rise and will agree to a higher money wage rate. By doing so, they can prevent the real wage rate from falling and avoid a fall in the unemployment rate below the natural rate.

Only fluctuations in aggregate demand that are unanticipated and not taken into account in wage agreements bring changes in real GDP. *Anticipated* changes in aggregate demand change the price level but they leave real GDP and unemployment unchanged and do not create a business cycle.

New Keynesian economists, like new classical economists, believe that the money wage rate is influenced by rational expectations of the price level. But new Keynesians emphasize the long-term nature of most wage contracts. They say that *today's* money wage rate is influenced by *yesterday's* rational expectations. These expectations, which were formed in the past, are based on old information that might now be known to be incorrect. After they have made a long-term wage agreement, both firms and workers might anticipate a change in aggregate demand, which they expect will change the price level. But because they are locked into their agreement, they are unable to change the money wage rate. So the money wage rate is sticky in the new Keynesian theory and with a sticky money wage rate, even an *anticipated* change in aggregate demand changes real GDP.

New classical economists believe that long-term contracts are renegotiated when conditions change to make them outdated. So they do not regard long-term contracts as an obstacle to money wage flexibility, provided both parties to an agreement recognize the changed conditions. If both firms and workers expect the price level to change, they will change the agreed money wage rate to reflect that shared expectation. In this situation, anticipated changes in aggregate demand change the money wage rate and the price level and leave real GDP unchanged.

The distinctive feature of both versions of the rational expectations theory of the business cycle is the role of unanticipated changes in aggregate demand and Fig. 33.5 illustrates its effect on real GDP and the price level.

Potential GDP is $800 billion and the long-run aggregate supply curve is *LAS*. Aggregate demand is expected to be *EAD*. Given potential GDP and *EAD*, the money wage rate is set at the level that is expected to bring full employment. At this money wage rate, the short-run aggregate supply curve is *SAS*. Imagine

that initially aggregate demand equals expected aggregate demand, so there is full employment. Real GDP is $800 billion and the price level is 110. Then, unexpectedly, aggregate demand turns out to be less than expected and the aggregate demand curve shifts leftward to AD_0. Many different aggregate demand shocks, such as a slowdown in the money growth rate or a collapse of exports, could have caused this shift. A recession begins. But aggregate demand is expected to be at *EAD* so the money wage rate doesn't change and the short-run aggregate supply curve remains at *SAS*. Real GDP decreases to $750 billion and the price level falls to 107. The economy moves to point *b*. Unemployment increases and there is a surplus of labour. The recession ends when aggregate demand increases again to its expected level.

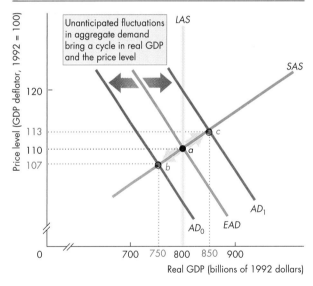

FIGURE 33.5

A Rational Expectations Business Cycle

The economy is expected to be at point *a*. As long as aggregate demand is expected to be *EAD*, there is no change in the money wage rate and the *SAS* curve does not shift. A rational expectations recession begins when an unanticipated fall in aggregate demand shifts the *AD* curve leftward to AD_0. Real GDP decreases to $750 billion and the price level falls to 107, at point *b*. A rational expectations expansion begins when an unanticipated increase in aggregate demand shifts the *AD* curve rightward to AD_1. Real GDP increases to $850 billion and the price level rises to 113 at point *c*.

A shock that takes aggregate demand to a level that exceeds *EAD* brings an expansion. The aggregate demand curve shifts rightward to AD_1. Such an increase in aggregate demand might be caused by a speedup in the money growth rate or an export boom. But aggregate demand is expected to be at *EAD* so the money wage rate doesn't change and the short-run aggregate supply curve remains at *SAS*. Real GDP now increases to $850 billion and the price level rises to 113. The economy moves to point *c*. Unemployment is now below the natural rate.

Fluctuations in aggregate demand between AD_0 and AD_1 around expected aggregate demand *EAD* bring fluctuations in real GDP and the price level between points *b* and *c*.

The two versions of the rational expectations theory differ in their predictions about the effects of a change in expected aggregate demand. The new classical theory predicts that as soon as expected aggregate demand changes, the money wage rate also changes so the *SAS* curve shifts. The new Keynesian theory predicts that the money wage rate changes only gradually when new contracts are made so that the *SAS* curve moves only slowly. This difference between the two theories is crucial for policy. According to the new classical theory, anticipated policy actions change the price level only and have no effect on real GDP and unemployment. The reason is that when policy is expected to change, the money wage rate changes so the *SAS* curve shifts and offsets the effects of the policy action on real GDP. In contrast, in the new Keynesian theory, because the money wage rate changes only when new contracts are made, even anticipated policy actions change real GDP and can be used in an attempt to stabilize the cycle.

Like the monetarist business cycle, these rational expectations cycles are similar to rocking horses. They need an outside force to get going, but once going the economy rocks around its full-employment point. The new classical horse rocks faster and comes to rest more quickly than the new Keynesian horse.

AS–AD General Theory

All the theories of the business cycle that we've considered can be viewed as particular cases of the more general *AS–AD* theory. In this more general theory, the impulses of both the Keynesian and monetarist theories can change aggregate demand. A multiplier effect makes aggregate demand change by more than any initial change in one of its components. The money wage rate can be viewed as responding to changes in the expected price level. Even if the money wage rate is flexible, it will change only to the extent that price level expectations change. As a result, the money wage rate will adjust gradually.

Although in all three business cycle theories that we've considered, the cycle is caused by fluctuations in aggregate demand, the possibility that an occasional aggregate supply shock might occur is not ruled out by the aggregate demand theories.

A recession could occur because aggregate supply decreases. For example, a widespread drought that cuts agricultural production could cause a recession in an economy that has a large agricultural sector. But these aggregate demand theories of the business cycle regard aggregate supply shocks as rare rather than normal events. Aggregate demand fluctuations are the normal ongoing sources of fluctuations.

REVIEW QUIZ

▨ What, according to Keynesian theory, is the main business cycle impulse?

▨ What, according to Keynesian theory, are the main business cycle mechanisms? Describe the roles of *animal spirits*, the multiplier, and a sticky money wage rate in this theory.

▨ What, according to monetarist theory, is the main business cycle impulse?

▨ What, according to monetarist theory, are the business cycle mechanisms? Describe the roles of the Bank of Canada and the money supply in this theory.

▨ What, according to new classical theory and new Keynesian theory, causes the business cycle? What are the roles of rational expectations and unanticipated fluctuations in aggregate demand in these theories?

▨ What are the differences between the new classical theory and the new Keynesian theory concerning the money wage rate over the business cycle?

A new theory of the business cycle challenges the mainstream and traditional aggregate demand theories that you've just studied. It is called the real business cycle theory. Let's look at this new cycle theory.

Real Business Cycle Theory

THE NEWEST THEORY OF THE BUSINESS CYCLE, known as **real business cycle theory** (or RBC theory), regards random fluctuations in productivity as the main source of economic fluctuations. These productivity fluctuations are assumed to result mainly from fluctuations in the pace of technological change, but they might also have other sources such as international disturbances, climate fluctuations, or natural disasters. The origins of real business cycle theory can be traced to the rational expectations revolution set off by Robert E. Lucas, Jr., but the first demonstration of the power of this theory was given by Edward Prescott and Finn Kydland and by John Long and Charles Plosser. Today, real business cycle theory is part of a broad research agenda called *dynamic general equilibrium analysis*, and hundreds of young macroeconomists do research on this topic.

Like our study of the aggregate demand theories, we'll explore RBC theory by looking first at its impulse and second at the mechanism that converts that impulse into a cycle in real GDP.

The RBC Impulse

The *impulse* in RBC theory is the *growth rate of productivity that results from technological change*. RBC theorists believe this impulse to be generated mainly by the process of research and development that leads to the creation and use of new technologies.

Most of the time, technological change is steady and productivity grows at a moderate pace. But sometimes productivity growth speeds up and occasionally productivity *decreases*—labour becomes less productive, on the average.

A period of rapid productivity growth brings a strong business cycle expansion and a *decrease* in productivity triggers a recession.

It is easy to understand why technological change brings productivity growth. But how does it *decrease* productivity? All technological change eventually increases productivity. But if, initially, technological change makes a sufficient amount of existing capital, especially human capital, obsolete, productivity temporarily decreases. At such a time, more jobs are destroyed than created and more businesses fail than start up.

FIGURE 33.6

The Real Business Cycle Impulse

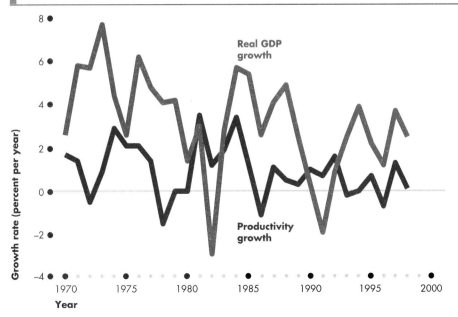

The real business cycle is caused by changes in technology that bring fluctuations in the growth rate of productivity. The fluctuations in productivity growth shown here are calculated by using growth accounting (the one-third rule) to remove the contribution of capital accumulation to productivity growth. Productivity fluctuations are correlated with real GDP fluctuations. Economists are not sure what the productivity variable actually measures or what causes it to fluctuate.

Source: Statistics Canada, *StatCan: CANSIM Disc*, March 1999 and the authors' calculations.

To isolate the RBC theory impulse, economists use growth accounting, which is explained in Chapter 32, pp. 729–732. Figure 33.6 shows the RBC impulse for Canada from 1970 to 1998. You can see that fluctuations in productivity growth are correlated with real GDP fluctuations. But this RBC impulse variable is a catch-all and no one knows what it actually measures or what causes it to fluctuate.

The RBC Mechanism

According to RBC theory, two immediate effects follow from a change in productivity that get an expansion or a contraction going:

1. Investment demand changes.
2. The demand for labour changes.

We'll study these effects and their consequences during a recession. In an expansion, they work in the direction opposite to what is described here.

Technological change makes some existing capital obsolete and temporarily decreases productivity. Firms expect the future profits to fall and see their labour productivity falling. With lower profit expectations, they cut back their purchases of new capital, and with lower labour productivity, they plan to lay off some workers. So the initial effect of a temporary fall in productivity is a decrease in investment demand and a decrease in the demand for labour.

Figure 33.7 illustrates these two initial effects of a decrease in productivity. Part (a) shows investment demand, ID, and saving supply, SS. (In real business cycle theory, saving depends on the real interest rate.) Initially, investment demand is ID_0, and the equilibrium investment and saving are $100 billion at a real interest rate of 6 percent a year. A decrease in productivity decreases investment demand and the ID curve shifts leftward to ID_1. The real interest rate falls to 4 percent a year, and investment and saving decrease to $70 billion.

Part (b) shows the demand for labour, LD, and the supply of labour, LS (which are explained in Chapter 31, pp. 699–701). Initially, the demand for labour is LD_0, and equilibrium employment is 20 billion hours a year at a real wage rate of $15 an hour. The decrease in productivity decreases the demand for labour, and the LD curve shifts leftward to LD_1.

Before we can determine the new level of employment and real wage rate, we need to take a ripple effect into account—the key ripple effect in RBC theory.

The Key Decision: When to Work? According to RBC theory, people decide *when* to work by doing a cost-benefit calculation. They compare the return from working in the current period with the *expected* return from working in a later period. You make such a comparison every day in school. Suppose your goal in this course is to get an A. To achieve this goal, you work pretty hard most of the time. But during the few days before the midterm and final exams, you work especially hard. Why? Because you believe that the return from studying close to the exam is greater than the return from studying when the exam is a long time away. So during the term, you take time off for the movies and other leisure pursuits, but at exam time, you work every evening and weekend.

Real business cycle theory says that workers behave like you. They work fewer hours, sometimes zero hours, when the real wage rate is temporarily low, and they work more hours when the real wage rate is temporarily high. But to properly compare the current wage rate with the expected future wage rate, workers must use the real interest rate. If the real interest rate is 6 percent a year, a real wage of $1 an hour earned this week will become $1.06 a year from now. If the real wage rate is expected to be $1.05 an hour next year, today's real wage of $1 looks good. By working longer hours now and shorter hours a year from now, a person can get a 1 percent higher real wage. But suppose the real interest rate is 4 percent a year. In this case, $1 earned now is worth $1.04 next year. Working fewer hours now and more next year is the way to get a 1 percent higher real wage.

So the when-to-work decision depends on the real interest rate. The lower the real interest rate, other things remaining the same, the smaller is the supply of labour. Many economists believe this *intertemporal substitution* effect to be of negligible size. RBC theorists believe that the effect is large, and it is the key element in the RBC mechanism.

You've seen in Fig. 33.7(a) that the decrease in investment demand lowers the real interest rate. This fall in the real interest rate lowers the return to current work and decreases the supply of labour. In Fig. 33.7(b) the labour supply curve shifts leftward to LS_1. The effect of a productivity shock on the demand for labour is larger than the effect of the fall in the real interest rate on the supply of labour. That is, the LD curve shifts farther leftward than does the LS curve. As a result, the real wage rate falls to $14.50 an hour and the level of employment decreases to 19.5 billion hours. A recession has begun and is intensifying.

FIGURE 33.7
Capital and Labour Markets in a Real Business Cycle

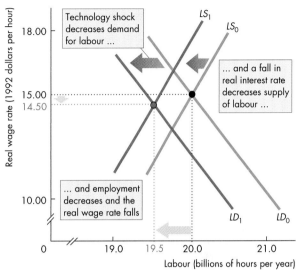

(a) Investment, saving, and interest rate

(b) Labour and wage rate

Saving supply is *SS* and, initially, investment demand is *ID₀* (part a). The real interest rate is 6 percent a year, and saving and investment are $100 billion. In the labour market (part b) the demand for labour is *LD₀* and the supply of labour is *LS₀*. The real wage rate is $15 an hour, and employment is 20 billion hours. A technological change temporarily decreases productivity, and both investment demand and the demand for labour

decrease. The two demand curves shift leftward to *ID₁* and *LD₁*. In part (a), the real interest rate falls to 4 percent a year and investment and saving decrease. In part (b), the fall in the real interest rate decreases the supply of labour (the when-to-work decision) and the supply curve shifts leftward to *LS₁*. Employment decreases to 19.5 billion hours, and the real wage rate falls to $14.50 an hour. A recession is underway.

Real GDP and the Price Level   The next part of the RBC story traces the consequences of the changes you've just seen for real GDP and the price level. With a decrease in employment, aggregate supply decreases, and with a decrease in investment demand, aggregate demand decreases. Figure 33.8 illustrates these effects, using the *AS–AD* framework. Initially, the long-run aggregate supply curve is *LAS₀*, and the aggregate demand curve is *AD₀*. The price level is 110, and real GDP is $800 billion. There is no short-run aggregate supply curve in this figure because the *SAS* curve has no meaning in RBC theory. The labour market moves relentlessly towards its equilibrium, and the money wage rate adjusts freely (either upward or downward) to ensure that the real wage rate keeps the quantity of labour demanded equal to the quantity supplied. In RBC theory, unemploy-

ment is always at the natural rate, and the natural rate fluctuates over the business cycle because the amount of job search fluctuates.

The decrease in employment decreases total production, and aggregate supply decreases. The *LAS* curve shifts leftward to *LAS₁*. The decrease in investment demand decreases aggregate demand, and the *AD* curve shifts leftward to *AD₁*. The price level falls to 107, and real GDP decreases to $750 billion. The economy has gone into a recession.

What Happened to Money?   The name *real* business cycle theory is no accident. It reflects the central prediction of the theory. Real things, not nominal or monetary things, cause the business cycle. If the quantity of money changes, aggregate demand changes. But if there is no real change—with no

FIGURE 33.8

AS–AD in a Real
Business Cycle

Initially, the long-run aggregate supply curve is *LAS₀* and the
aggregate demand curve is *AD₀*. Real GDP is $800 billion
(which equals potential GDP), and the price level is 110. There
is no *SAS* curve in the real business cycle theory because the
money wage rate is flexible. The technological change
described in Fig. 33.7 temporarily decreases potential GDP, and
the *LAS* curve shifts leftward to *LAS₁*. The fall in investment
demand decreases aggregate demand, and the *AD* curve shifts
leftward to *AD₁*. Real GDP decreases to $750 billion, and the
price level falls to 107. The economy has gone into recession.

change in the use of resources and no change in
potential GDP—the change in money changes only
the price level. In real business cycle theory, this outcome occurs because the aggregate supply curve is the
LAS curve, which pins real GDP down at potential
GDP. So when *AD* changes, only the price level
changes.

Cycles and Growth The shock that drives the
business cycle of RBC theory is the same as the force
that generates economic growth: technological
change. On the average, as technology advances, productivity grows. But it grows at an uneven pace. You
saw this fact when you studied growth accounting in

Chapter 32. There, we focused on slow-changing
trends in productivity growth. Real business cycle
theory uses the same idea but says that there are
frequent shocks to productivity that are mostly
positive but that are occasionally negative.

Criticisms of Real Business Cycle Theory

RBC theory is controversial, and when economists
discuss it, they often generate more heat than light.
Its detractors claim that its basic assumptions are just
too incredible. The money wage rate *is* sticky, they
claim, so to assume otherwise is at odds with a clear
fact. Intertemporal substitution is too weak, they say,
to account for large fluctuations in labour supply and
employment with small changes in the real wage rate.

But what really kills the RBC story, say most
economists, is an implausible impulse. Technology
shocks are not capable of creating the swings in productivity that growth accounting reveals. These
swings in productivity are caused by something, they
concede, but they are as likely to be caused by *changes
in aggregate demand* as by technology. If the fluctuations in productivity are caused by aggregate demand
fluctuations, then the traditional demand theories are
needed to explain them. Fluctuations in productivity
do not cause the cycle but are caused by it!

Building on this theme, the critics point out that
the so-called productivity fluctuations that growth
accounting measures are correlated with changes in
the growth rate of money and other indicators of
changes in aggregate demand.

Defence of Real Business Cycle Theory

The defenders of RBC theory claim that the theory
works. It explains the macroeconomic facts about the
business cycle and is consistent with the facts about
economic growth. In effect, a single theory explains
both growth and cycles. The growth accounting exercise that explains slowly changing trends also explains
the more frequent business cycle swings. Its defenders
also claim that RBC theory is consistent with a wide
range of *micro*economic evidence about labour supply decisions, labour demand and investment
demand decisions, and information on the distribution of income between labour and capital.

RBC theorists acknowledge that money and the business cycle are correlated. That is, rapid money growth and expansion go together, and slow money growth and recession go together. But, they argue, causation does not run from money to real GDP as the traditional aggregate demand theories state. Instead, they view causation as running from real GDP to money—so-called reverse causation. In a recession, the initial fall in investment demand that lowers the interest rate decreases the demand for bank loans and lowers the profitability of banking. So banks increase their reserves and decrease their loans. The quantity of bank deposits and hence the quantity of money decreases. This reverse causation is responsible for the correlation between money growth and real GDP according to real business cycle theory.

Its defenders also argue that the RBC view is significant because it at least raises the possibility that the business cycle is efficient. The business cycle does not signal an economy that is misbehaving; it is business as usual. If this view is correct, it means that policy designed to smooth the cycle is misguided. Only by taking out the peaks can the troughs be smoothed out. But peaks are bursts of investment to take advantage of new technologies in a timely way. So smoothing the cycle means delaying the benefits of new technologies.

R E V I E W   Q U I Z

- What, according to real business cycle theory, causes the business cycle? What is the role of fluctuations in the rate of technological change?
- How, according to real business cycle theory, does a fall in productivity growth influence investment demand, the real interest rate, the demand for labour, the supply of labour, employment, and the real wage rate?
- How, according to real business cycle theory, does a fall in productivity growth influence long-run aggregate supply, aggregate demand, real GDP, and the price level?

You've now reviewed the main theories of the business cycle. Your next task is to examine some actual business cycles. In pursuing this task, we'll focus on two episodes of recession during the 1990s and on the Great Depression of the 1930s.

Recessions During the 1990s

THE 1990S HAVE BROUGHT SOME INTERESTING business cycle experience. In Canada, we had a recession during 1990–1991 followed by a period of sustained expansion. In contrast, Japan has experienced a decade of slow growth and has ended the decade in serious recession. In 1999, while the three-fifths of the global economy that includes Canada, the United States, and Western Europe continued to expand vigorously, the other two-fifths that includes Japan, some other East Asian countries, and Central Europe were in recession.

In the theories of the business cycle that you've studied, recessions and expansions can be triggered by a variety of forces, some on the aggregate demand side and some on the aggregate supply side. We'll study the shocks that triggered some of these 1990s episodes and the processes at work during them. We'll focus on two cases:

- The recession of 1990–1991
- The Japanese recession of the 1990s

The Recession of 1990–1991

Three forces were at work in Canada during 1990 that appear to have contributed to the recession and subsequent sluggish growth. They are:

- The Bank of Canada's anti-inflation policy
- A slowdown in economic expansion in the United States
- The Canada–United States Free Trade Agreement

The Bank of Canada's Anti-Inflation Policy The Bank of Canada began to pursue low inflation targets in 1988. But because of the time lags involved in the operation of monetary policy, the policy began to bite in 1989 and to bite hard in 1990. The best evidence available suggests that the long-term effects of price stability will be extremely beneficial to Canadians. But its short-term effects are costly.

To achieve price stability, the Bank of Canada must slow the growth rate of the money supply. The extent to which the Bank did slow money growth can be seen in Fig. 33.9. The growth rate of the narrow definition of money, M1, slowed in 1989 to almost zero during 1990. The growth rate of the M2+ definition of money also slowed, but more gently.

FIGURE 33.9

Money Supply Growth 1989–1995

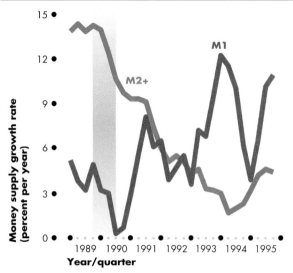

The Bank of Canada began to pursue the goal of low inflation in 1988 and the growth rate of the M2+ money supply began to slow during 1989. It slowed even further during 1990. The narrow definition of money, M1, barely grew during 1990.

Source: Bank of Canada, M1 is *CANSIM* series B1629 and M2+ is *CANSIM* series B1633.

FIGURE 33.10

U.S. and Canadian Real GDP Growth 1989–1995

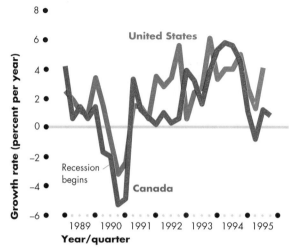

The United States had a recession in 1990, but Canada's recession preceded that in the United States by one quarter. The Canadian recession was deeper than the U.S. recession and with the exception of the first quarter of 1991, Canadian real GDP growth rate has remained below that of the United States.

Source: Statistics Canada, *StatCan: CANSIM Disc*, 1999 and *Economic Report of the President*, 1993, Table B-3, p. 350.

A Slowdown in Economic Expansion in the United States After its longest ever period of peace-time expansion, U.S. real GDP growth began to slow in 1989 and 1990 and the United States went into recession in mid-1990, a quarter of a year behind Canada. You can see the performance of real GDP growth in the United States (and Canada) by looking at Fig. 33.10. You can see that the U.S. recession not only lagged behind Canada's recession but also was less severe than Canada's. Also, the U.S. recovery during 1991 and 1992 was more rapid than Canada's.

The slowdown of the U.S. economy brought slower growth in the demand for Canada's exports and resulted in lower export prices and smaller export volumes.

The Canada–United States Free Trade Agreement The first tariff cuts under the Free Trade Agreement with the United States occurred on January 1, 1989, and the second phase of cuts came a

year later. The gradual elimination of tariffs on most of Canada's trade with the United States will result in a rationalization of production activities on both sides of the border. The long-term effects of this rationalization are expected to be beneficial to Canada (and the United States). But like the Bank of Canada's price stability policy, tariff cuts impose costs in the short term. These costs arise because initially, tariff cuts destroy more jobs than they create. Production cutbacks in sectors that must contract precede production increases in sectors that must expand. The result is a temporary decrease in both short-run and long-run aggregate supply as structural unemployment increases.

The elimination of tariffs changes the profitability of businesses, bringing gains to some industries and firms and losses to others. It is easy to see who the immediate winners and losers are. But it is difficult to predict where the gains and losses will ultimately be when the new tariff structure has been in place for some time. As a result, tariff cuts bring an increase in uncertainty that decreases investment in new buildings, plant, and equipment. This decrease in investment decreases aggregate demand.

Let's see how the events we've just described influenced the Canadian economy in 1990.

Aggregate Demand and Aggregate Supply in the 1990–1991 Recession The Canadian economy in the first quarter of 1990, on the eve of the 1990–1991 recession, is shown in Fig. 33.11. The aggregate demand curve was AD_0, the short-run aggregate supply curve was SAS_0, real GDP was \$711 billion, and the price level was 96.

The 1990–1991 recession was caused by a decrease in both aggregate demand and aggregate supply. Aggregate demand decreased, initially, because of the slowdown in the growth rate of the

quantity of money. This initial source was soon reinforced by the slowdown in the U.S. economy that brought a decline in the growth of exports. These two factors together with increased uncertainty arising from tariff cuts triggered a massive decline in investment. The resulting decrease in aggregate demand is shown in Fig. 33.11 by the shift of the aggregate demand curve leftward to AD_1. Aggregate supply decreased partly because of the effects of the Free Trade Agreement and partly because the money wage rate continued to increase throughout 1990 at a rate similar to that in 1989. This decrease in aggregate supply is shown as the shift in the short-run aggregate supply curve leftward to SAS_1. (The figure does not show the long-run aggregate supply curve.)

The combined effect of the decreases in aggregate supply and aggregate demand was a decrease in real GDP to \$687 billion—a 3.5 percent decrease—and a rise in the price level to 99—a 3.5 percent rise.

What happened in the labour market during this recession?

The Labour Market in the 1990s The unemployment rate increased persistently from the beginning of 1990 to the end of 1992. Figure 33.12 shows two

FIGURE **33.11**

The 1990–1991 Recession

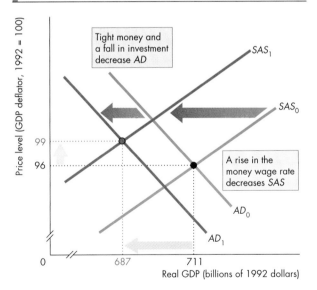

At the beginning of 1990, real GDP was \$711 billion and the GDP deflator was 96. Sectoral reallocations resulting from the Canada–U.S. Free Trade Agreement together with increases in the money wage rate decreased aggregate supply and the short-run aggregate supply curve shifted leftward to SAS_1. Tight monetary policy, a slowdown in the U.S. economy, and increased uncertainty and lowered profit expectations shifted the aggregate demand curve leftward to AD_1. Real GDP decreased to \$687 billion, and the economy went into recession.

FIGURE **33.12**

Employment and Real Wages

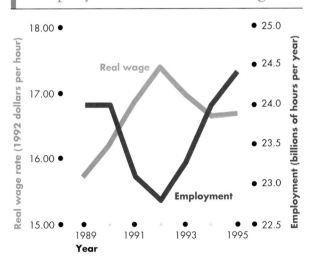

During 1990–1991, the economy was in a recession. Employment decreased and the real wage rate increased. During the expansion that followed, employment increased and the real wage rate decreased.

other facts about the labour market during this period—facts about employment and the real wage rate. As employment decreased through 1990 and 1991, the real wage rate increased. During the recovery, employment increased and the real wage rate decreased. These movements in employment and the real wage rate suggest that the forces of supply and demand do not operate smoothly in the labour market. The money wage rate rose because people didn't anticipate the slowdown in inflation. When inflation did slow down, the real wage increased and the quantity of labour demanded decreased.

The Japanese Recession of the 1990s

Between 1992 and 1998, when real GDP in the United States expanded by more than 20 percent, Japan's real GDP expanded by a mere 6 percent—a growth rate of only 0.7 percent per year. By 1999, real GDP in Japan was shrinking at a near 5 percent annual rate.

Why has Japan experienced such a low rate of economic growth during the 1990s and a recession in 1998? Several factors seem to have combined to produce Japan's problems. And these factors together with the fiscal policies and monetary policies that Japan has pursued provide valuable information about the validity of the alternative theories of the business cycle that you studied earlier in this chapter.

The main factors that have contributed to Japan's weak economy and ultimate recession are:

■ Collapse of asset prices
■ Fiscal policy
■ Monetary policy
■ Structural rigidities

Collapse of Asset Prices During the second half of the 1980s, land prices and stock prices in Japan increased *threefold*. This increase was much larger than that in the United States and Europe. Asset prices increased for three main reasons.

First, investors believed Japan's medium-term and long-term prospects were bright. Second, financial deregulation brought an increase of foreign investment into Japan. Japan's banks expanded loans to finance the purchase of assets whose prices were rising. Third, the Bank of Japan (the nation's central bank) lowered interest rates between 1985 and 1987 and permitted a rapid growth rate of money. The motivation for rapid monetary expansion was to pre-

vent the yen from rising and the U.S. dollar from falling in the foreign exchange market. (See Chapter 36, pp. 838–839 for an explanation of how monetary policy influences the foreign exchange rate.)

Asset prices collapsed in 1990. And the collapse created a wealth effect. Saving and consumption were not much affected by the decrease in wealth. But investment expenditure decreased sharply and so did aggregate demand. And with a lower investment rate, the capital stock and potential GDP grew more slowly.

Fiscal Policy From 1991 through 1996, Japan pursued ambitious and substantial fiscal policies to stimulate the economy. In 1991, the government of Japan had a budget surplus equal to 3 percent of GDP. By 1996, this surplus had been transformed into a deficit equal to more than 7 percent of GDP. Six major *discretionary* actions occurred, which are detailed in Table 33.1, that added 12.9 percent to aggregate expenditure. With its associated multiplier effects, this represents an enormous increase in aggregate demand relative to what it would have been in the absence of stimulation. But the stimulation was not persistent during the 1990s.

The removal of temporary tax cuts and cuts in government investment expenditures *lowered* aggregate expenditure by 3 percent of real GDP in 1996–1997. This fiscal policy tightening decreased aggregate demand and contributed to the recession of 1998.

Monetary Policy The Bank of Japan lowered its official interest rate (called the official discount rate or ODR) from 6 percent in 1991 to 1.75 percent by the end of 1993 and to 0.5 percent by 1995. The ODR has remained at this level since 1995. Despite

---

TABLE 33.1

Fiscal Stimulation in Japan

Date proposed	Total stimulation (percent of GDP)
August 1992	2.3
April 1993	2.8
September 1993	1.3
February 1994	3.2
September 1995	3.0
Mid-1996–mid-1997	−3.0
April 1998	3.3
Total	12.9

FIGURE 33.13

Japan's Sliding Growth Rate

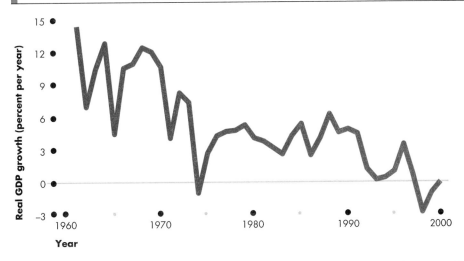

Japan's economic growth rate has been on a slide for many years. Growth of 10 percent a year during the 1960s was followed by growth of 4 percent a year during the 1970s and 1980s and by less than 1 percent a year during the 1990s.

Source: The Penn World Table: An Expanded Set of International Comparisons, 1950–1988, *Quarterly Journal of Economics*, May 1991, 327–368. 1993–1998, International Monetary Fund, *World Economic Outlook*, Washington D.C., October 1998.

these large cuts in interest rates, a lower inflation rate meant that the real interest rate did not fall as much and so did not act as a stimulus to investment. Also, a strong yen limited the growth of export demand.

Since 1996, a weaker yen and lower real short-term interest rates have had a small but positive effect on aggregate demand in Japan.

Structural Rigidities   Market distortions in agriculture, transportation, retail and wholesale trades, and construction that protect inefficient farms and firms create a lack of competition and low productivity growth. Rich countries such as the United States, Canada, and those in Western Europe have experienced a process of de-industrialization as manufacturing processes have migrated to poorer countries and have been replaced by rapid expansion in the service sector. Japan has not shared this experience.

Japan's structural rigidities are real, supply-side problems. These problems have brought a gradually falling rate of growth of real GDP over many years. Figure 33.13 shows this steadily falling growth rate.

This aspect of Japan's business cycle is an example of the real business cycle. It is a slowdown in productivity growth that slows the rate of increase in long-run aggregate supply. Slower productivity

growth works through the real business cycle mechanism described earlier in this chapter. It lowers the demand for capital and labour and decreases potential GDP.

If this explanation for Japan's problems is the correct one, no amount of fiscal and monetary demand stimulation will end the recession.

R E V I E W   Q U I Z

- What events triggered Canada's 1990–1991 recession?
- What role was played by external shocks and by policy?
- What mechanisms translated the shocks into a recession?
- What factors contributed to the slow growth and eventual recession in Japan during the 1990s?

You've now seen how business cycle theory can be used to interpret Canada's recession of 1990–1991 and Japan's persistent recession of the 1990s. We're now going to use business cycle theory to explain the greatest of recessions—the Great Depression that engulfed the global economy during the 1930s.

The Great Depression

THE LATE 1920S WERE YEARS OF ECONOMIC BOOM. New houses and apartments were built on an unprecedented scale, new firms were created, and the capital stock of the nation expanded. At the beginning of 1929, Canadian real GDP equalled potential GDP and the unemployment rate was only 2.9 percent.

But as that eventful year unfolded, increasing signs of economic weakness began to appear. The most dramatic events occurred in October when the stock market collapsed. Stocks lost more than one-third of their value in two weeks. The four years that followed were a period of monstrous economic depression.

We'll describe the recession by using the aggregate supply–aggregate demand model and identify the forces that made aggregate demand and aggregate supply change.

Figure 33.14 shows the dimensions of the Great Depression and the changes in aggregate demand and aggregate supply that occurred. On the eve of the Great Depression in 1929, the economy was on aggregate demand curve AD_{29} and short-run aggregate supply curve SAS_{29}. Real GDP was $81 billion (1992 dollars) and the GDP deflator was 7.7.

In 1930, there was a widespread expectation that the price level would fall, and the money wage rate fell. With a lower money wage rate, short-run aggregate supply increased. But increased pessimism and uncertainty decreased investment and the demand for consumer durables. Aggregate demand decreased. In 1930, the economy went into recession as real GDP decreased by about 7 percent. The price level also fell by a similar amount.

In a normal recession, the economy might have remained below full employment for a year or so and then started an expansion. But the recession of 1930 was not a normal one. In 1930 and for the next two years, the economy was further bombarded with huge negative aggregate demand shocks (the sources of which we'll look at in a moment). The aggregate demand curve shifted leftward all the way to AD_{33}. With a depressed economy, the price level was expected to fall and the money wage rate fell in line with those expectations. As a result, the aggregate supply curve shifted to SAS_{33}. But the size of the shift of the short-run aggregate supply curve was much less than the decrease in aggregate demand. As a result, the aggregate demand curve and the short-run aggregate supply curve intersected in 1933 at a real

FIGURE 33.14

The Great Depression

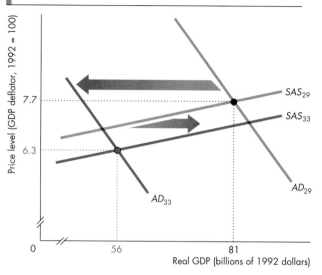

In 1929, real GDP was $81 billion and the GDP deflator was 7.7—at the intersection of AD_{29} and SAS_{29}. In 1930, increased pessimism and uncertainty resulted in a drop in investment, which led to a decrease in aggregate demand. To some degree, this decrease was reflected in the labour market and the money wage rate fell, so short-run aggregate supply decreased. Real GDP decreased and the price level fell. In the next three years, decreases in the money supply and investment decreased aggregate demand, shifting the aggregate demand curve to AD_{33}. Again, to some degree, the decrease in aggregate demand was reflected in a lower money wage rate so the short-run aggregate supply curve shifted to SAS_{33}. By 1933, real GDP had decreased to $56 billion (71 percent of its 1929 level) and the GDP deflator had fallen to 6.3 (80 percent of its 1929 level).

GDP of $56 billion (a decrease of 31 percent from 1929) and a GDP deflator of 6.3 (a fall of 19 percent from 1929).

Although the Great Depression brought enormous hardship, the distribution of that hardship was uneven. Twenty percent of the work force had no jobs at all. Also at that time, there were virtually no organized social assistance and unemployment programs in place. So many families had virtually no income. But the pocketbooks of those who kept their jobs barely noticed the Great Depression. It is true that the money wage rate fell. But at the same time, the price level fell by almost exactly the same percentage, so the real wage rate remained constant. Thus those who had jobs continued to be paid a wage rate that had roughly the same buying power at the depth of the Great Depression as in 1929.

You can begin to appreciate the magnitude of the Great Depression if you compare it with the 1990–1991 recession. In 1990, real GDP fell by 3.7 percent. In comparison, from 1929 to 1933, it fell by 31 percent. A 1999 Great Depression of the same magnitude would lower income per person to its level of more than 20 years earlier.

Why the Great Depression Happened

The late 1920s were years of economic boom, but they were also years of increasing uncertainty. The main source of increased uncertainty was international. The world economy was going through tumultuous times. The patterns of world trade were changing as Britain, the traditional economic powerhouse of the world, began its period of relative economic decline and new economic powers such as Japan began to emerge. International currency fluctuations and the introduction of restrictive trade policies by many countries (see Chapter 35) further increased the uncertainty faced by firms. There was also domestic uncertainty arising from the fact that there had been such a strong boom in recent years, especially in the capital goods sector and housing. No one believed that this boom could continue, but there was great uncertainty as to when it would end and how the pattern of demand would change.

This environment of uncertainty led to a slowdown in consumer spending, especially on new homes and household appliances. By the fall of 1929, the uncertainty had reached a critical level and contributed to the stock market crash. The stock market crash, in turn, heightened people's fears about economic prospects in the foreseeable future. Fear fed fear. Investment collapsed. The building industry almost disappeared. An industry that had been operating flat out just two years earlier was now building virtually no new houses and apartments. It was this drop in investment and a drop in consumer spending on durables that led to the initial decrease in aggregate demand.

At this stage, what became the Great Depression was no worse than many previous recessions had been. What distinguishes the Great Depression from previous recessions are the events that followed between 1930 and 1933. But economists, even to this day, have not come to agreement on how to interpret those events. One view, argued by Peter Temin, is that spending continued to fall for a wide variety of reasons—including a continuation of increasing pessimism and uncertainty.[1] According to Temin's view, the continued contraction resulted from a collapse of expenditure that was independent of the decrease in the quantity of money. The investment demand curve shifted leftward. Milton Friedman and Anna J. Schwartz have argued that the continuation of the contraction was almost exclusively the result of the subsequent worsening of financial and monetary conditions in the United States.[2] According to Friedman and Schwartz, it was a severe cut in the U.S. money supply that lowered aggregate demand in that country and that prolonged the contraction and deepened the depression. Recently, Ben Bernanke, Barry Eichengreen, and James Hamilton have added further to our understanding of the Great Depression by explaining how it was transmitted among countries by the attempts of central banks to increase their gold reserves.[3]

As a result of these recent efforts to probe more deeply into the causes of the Great Depression, the range of disagreement has narrowed. Everyone now agrees that increased pessimism and uncertainty lowered investment demand, and that there was a massive contraction of the real money supply. Temin and his supporters assign primary importance to the fall in autonomous expenditure and secondary importance to the fall in the money supply. Friedman and Schwartz and their supporters assign primary responsibility to the money supply and regard the other factors as being of limited importance.

Let's look at the contraction of the U.S. money supply a bit more closely. Between 1929 and 1933, the nominal money supply in the United States decreased by 20 percent. This decrease in the money supply was not directly induced by the Federal Reserve's actions. The *monetary base* (currency in circulation and bank reserves) hardly fell at all. But the bank deposits component of the money supply suffered an enormous collapse. It did so primarily because a large number of banks failed. Before the

---

[1]Peter Temin, *Did Monetary Forces Cause the Great Depression?* (New York: W.W. Norton, 1976).
[2]This explanation was developed by Milton Friedman and Anna J. Schwartz in *A Monetary History of the United States 1867–1960* (Princeton: Princeton University Press, 1963), Chapter 7.
[3]Ben Bernanke, "The Macroeconomics of the Great Depression: A Comparative Approach," *Journal of Money, Credit, and Banking,* 28 (1995), pp. 1–28; Barry Eichengreen, *Golden Fetters: The Gold Standard and the Great Depression, 1919–1939* (New York: Oxford University Press, 1992); and James Hamilton, "The Role of the International Gold Standard in Propagating the Great Depression," *Contemporary Policy Issues,* 6 (1988), pp. 67–89.

Great Depression, fuelled by increasing stock prices and booming business conditions, bank loans expanded. But after the stock market crash and the downturn, many borrowers found themselves in hard economic times. They could not pay the interest on their loans, and they could not meet the agreed repayment schedules. Banks had deposits that exceeded the realistic value of the loans that they had made. When depositors withdrew funds from the banks, the banks lost reserves and many of them simply couldn't meet their depositors' demands to be repaid.

Bank failures feed on themselves and create additional failures. Seeing banks fail, people become anxious to protect themselves and so take their money out of the banks. Such were the events in the United States in 1930. The quantity of notes and coins in circulation increased and the volume of bank deposits declined. But the very action of taking money out of the bank to protect one's wealth accentuated the process of banking failure. Banks were increasingly short of cash and unable to meet their obligations.

Monetary contraction also occurred in Canada, although on a less serious scale than in the United States. The Canadian money supply declined in each of the contraction years of the Great Depression, but at a steady 5 percent a year in contrast to the whopping 20 percent in the United States. Also, we had much less severe problems with bank failures than they did in the United States.

What role did the stock market crash of 1929 play in producing the Great Depression? It certainly created an atmosphere of fear and panic, and probably also contributed to the overall air of uncertainty that dampened investment spending. It also reduced the wealth of stockholders, encouraging them to cut back on their consumption spending. But the direct effect of the stock market crash on consumption, although a contributory factor to the Great Depression, was not the major source of the drop in aggregate demand. It was the collapse in investment arising from increased uncertainty that brought the 1930 decline in aggregate demand.

But the stock market crash was a predictor of severe recession. It reflected the expectations of stockholders concerning future profit prospects. As those expectations became pessimistic, people sold their stocks. There were more sellers than buyers and the prices of stocks were bid lower and lower. That is, the behaviour of the stock market was a consequence of expectations about future profitability and those expectations were lowered as a result of increased uncertainty.

Can It Happen Again?

Since, even today, we have an incomplete understanding of the causes of the Great Depression, we are not able to predict such an event or to be sure that it cannot occur again. But there are some significant differences between the economy of the 1990s and that of the 1930s that make a severe depression much less likely today than it was 60 years ago. The most significant features of the economy that make severe depression less likely today are as follows:

■ Deposit insurance
■ The Bank of Canada's role as lender of last resort
■ Taxes and government spending
■ Multi-income families

Let's examine these in turn.

Bank Deposit Insurance   In 1967, the government of Canada established the Canada Deposit Insurance Corporation (CDIC). The CDIC insures bank deposits for up to $60,000 per deposit so that most depositors need no longer fear bank failure. If a bank fails, the CDIC pays the deposit holders.

Similar arrangements have been introduced in the United States, where deposits up to $100,000 are insured by the Federal Deposit Insurance Corporation. With government-insured bank deposits, the key event that turned a fairly ordinary recession into the Great Depression is most unlikely to occur. It was the fear of bank failure that caused people to withdraw their deposits from banks. The aggregate consequence of these individually rational acts was to cause the very bank failures that were feared. With deposit insurance, most depositors have nothing to lose if a bank fails and so have no incentive to take actions that are likely to give rise to that failure.

Although bank failure was not a severe problem in Canada during the Great Depression, it clearly was an important factor in intensifying the depression in the United States. And the severity of the U.S. recession certainly had an impact on Canada and the rest of the world.

Lender of Last Resort   The Bank of Canada is the lender of last resort in the Canadian economy. If a single bank is short of reserves, it can borrow reserves from other banks. If the entire banking system is short of reserves, banks can borrow from the Bank of Canada. By making reserves available (at a suitable interest rate), the Bank of Canada is able to make the quantity of reserves in the banking system respond flexibly to the demand for those reserves. Bank failure can be prevented, or at least contained, to cases where bad management practices are the source of the problem. Widespread failures of the type that occurred in the Great Depression can be prevented.

It is interesting to note, in this regard, that during the weeks following the October 1987 stock market crash, Bank of Canada Governor John Crow and Federal Reserve Chairman Alan Greenspan used every opportunity available to remind the world banking and financial community of their ability and readiness to maintain calm financial conditions and to supply sufficient reserves to ensure that the banking system did not begin to contract.

Taxes and Government Spending The government sector was a much smaller part of the economy in 1929 than it has become today. On the eve of that earlier recession, government expenditures on goods and services were less than 11 percent of GDP. Today, government expenditures on goods and services exceed 20 percent of GDP. Government transfer payments were about 5 percent of GDP in 1929. Today, they are 20 percent of GDP.

A larger level of government expenditures on goods and services means that when recession hits, a large component of aggregate demand does not decline. But it is government transfer payments that are the most sensitive economic stabilizer. When the economy goes into recession and depression, more people qualify for unemployment insurance and social assistance. As a consequence, although disposable income decreases, the extent of the decrease is moderated by the existence of such programs. Consumption expenditure, in turn, does not decline by as much as it would in the absence of such government programs. The limited decline in consumption spending further limits the overall decrease in aggregate expenditure, thereby limiting the magnitude of an economic downturn.

Multi-Income Families At the time of the Great Depression, families with more than one wage earner were much less common than they are today. The labour force participation rate in 1929 was around 55 percent. Today, it is 67 percent. Thus even if the unemployment rate increased to around 20 percent today, close to 54 percent of the adult population would actually have jobs. During the Great Depression,

only 44 percent of the adult population had work. Multi-income families have greater security than single-income families. The chance of both (or all) income earners in a family losing their jobs simultaneously is much lower than the chance of a single earner losing work. With greater family income security, family consumption is likely to be less sensitive to fluctuations in family income that are seen as temporary. Thus when aggregate income falls, it does not induce a cut in consumption. For example, during the 1982 and 1990–1991 recessions, as real GDP fell personal consumption expenditure actually increased.

For the four reasons we have just reviewed, it appears the economy has better shock-absorbing characteristics today than it had in the 1920s and 1930s. Even if there is a collapse of confidence leading to a decrease in investment, the recession mechanism that is now in place will not translate that initial shock into the large and prolonged decrease in real GDP and increase in unemployment that occurred more than 60 years ago.

Because the economy is now more immune to severe recession than it was in the 1930s, even a stock market crash of the magnitude that occurred in 1987 had barely noticeable effects on spending. A crash of a similar magnitude in 1929 resulted in the near collapse of housing investment and consumer durable purchases. In the period following the 1987 stock market crash, investment and spending on durable goods hardly changed.

None of this is to say that there might not be a deep recession or even a Great Depression in the future. But it would take a very severe shock to trigger one.

◈ We have now completed our study of the business cycle. During an expansion, analysts use the theories you have studied to try to forecast the strength of an expansion. You can see an example of this activity in *Reading Between the Lines* on pp. 766–767.

We have also completed our study of the science of macroeconomics and learned about the influences on long-term economic growth and inflation as well as the business cycle. We have discovered that these issues pose huge policy challenges. How can we speed up the rate of economic growth while at the same time keeping inflation low and avoiding big swings of the business cycle? Our task in the next chapter is to study these macroeconomic policy challenges.

Will the Canadian Economic Expansion Continue?

VANCOUVER SUN, JUNE 11, 1999

Canada's economy shines with few clouds in sight

BY PHILIP DEMONT

Canada continued to show its ability to defy economic gravity as the country's gross domestic product grew by one per cent during the first three months of 1999, according to Statistics Canada.

That means Canada's national income is on track to expand by 4.2 per cent for the entire year with no end to the good times in sight, the agency reported Thursday. ...

Higher consumer spending, housing construction and foreign exports led the expansion. Prices also crept up in the quarter, but not enough to make people worry about higher inflation.

Canada grew by 3.2 per cent when comparing the first three months of 1999 to the first three months of 1998. ...

The strength of the national economy in the first quarter prompted the Bank of Montreal to revise its 1999 GDP growth target Thursday to 3.4 per cent, up from 3.2 per cent.

Canada's first-quarter pace is slightly slower than the blistering 4.8 per cent the country experienced in the final three months of 1998. ...

And, even as Canada expands, the threat of an outbreak of inflation remains remote, analysts said.

Prices rose 2.6 per cent, on a yearly basis, in the first quarter, which is higher than in the fourth quarter last year.

With Canada's unemployment rate standing at 8.1 per cent, however, the country is unlikely to see wages start rising any time soon.

Essence of the Story

- Canada's GDP grew one percent during the first three months of 1999.

- If the economy continues to grow at this rate, GDP will increase by 4.2 percent over the entire year.

- The expansion is led by higher consumption expenditure, housing construction, and exports.

- The Bank of Montreal has revised its GDP growth target upward.

- An inflationary period is not expected.

- Canada's unemployment rate is 8.1 percent and it is unlikely that wages will start rising in the near future.

■ Between the first quarter of 1998 and the first quarter of 1999, real GDP grew by 3.4 percent.

■ A reasonable assumption is that potential GDP in 1999 is $875 billion (1992 dollars). Actual real GDP in 1998 was $838 billion. So for the economy to get to potential GDP in 1999, a growth rate of 4.5 percent is needed.

■ Figure 1 shows the economy in 1998 and 1999. Aggregate demand in 1998 was AD_{98} and short-run aggregate supply was SAS.

■ Consumer spending, housing construction, and exports increased in 1999. The aggregate demand curve shifted rightward towards AD_{99}.

■ Canada's unemployment rate was 8.1 percent and wages were not expected to rise.

■ For Canada to return to full employment, consumer spending, housing construction, and exports must continue to increase.

■ In the scenario in Fig. 1, the growth rate picks up to 4.5 percent a year and the inflation rate is less than 3 percent a year.

■ Figure 2 shows what will happen if aggregate demand growth is stronger than expected. This might occur if consumption expenditure increases and continued growth in the United States increases Canadian exports.

■ In this scenario, Canada's real GDP will grow by more than 4.5 percent and an inflationary gap will emerge.

■ The money wage rate will begin to rise and short-run aggregate supply will decrease. The SAS curve will shift leftward until the economy returns to potential GDP.

■ Either scenario might occur in the Canadian economy. Or growth in 1999 might be insufficient to reach potential GDP and restore full employment.

■ Although the Bank of Montreal revised upward its growth prediction, the business cycle is impossible to predict. Unforeseen changes in aggregate demand and aggregate supply can throw any forecast off.

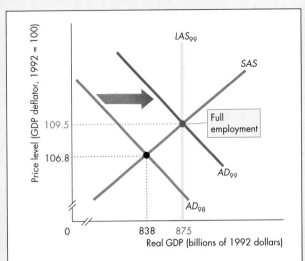

Figure 1 Canada returns to full employment?

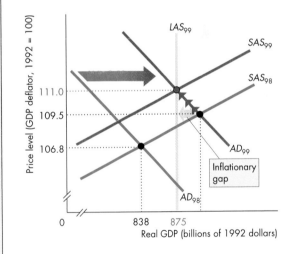

Figure 2 Canadian growth stronger than expected?

767

SUMMARY

Key Points

Cycle Patterns, Impulses, and Mechanisms (p. 746)

▨ The economy can be hit (like a tennis ball), cycle indefinitely (like the turning of day into night), and cycle in swings that get milder until another shock hits (like a rocking horse).

Aggregate Demand Theories of the Business Cycle (pp. 747–752)

▨ Keynesian business cycle theory identifies volatile expectations about future sales and profits as the main source of economic fluctuations.

▨ Monetarist business cycle theory identifies fluctuations in the quantity of money as the main source of economic fluctuations.

▨ Rational expectations theory identifies unanticipated fluctuations in aggregate demand as the main source of economic fluctuations.

Real Business Cycle Theory (pp. 753–757)

▨ In real business cycle (RBC) theory, economic fluctuations are caused by fluctuations in the influence of technological change on productivity growth.

▨ A temporary slowdown in the pace of technological change decreases investment demand and both the demand for labour and supply of labour.

Recessions During the 1990s (pp. 757–761)

▨ The 1990–1991 recession resulted from tight monetary policy, a slowdown in the United States, and adjustments to the Canada–United States Free Trade Agreement.

▨ The Japanese slowdown and recession of the 1990s was triggered by an asset price collapse combined with structural problems. Policy stimulation occurred but it was not sufficient to prevent recession and a tightening of fiscal policy in 1996 and 1997 contributed to the 1998 recession.

The Great Depression (pp. 762–765)

▨ The Great Depression started with increased uncertainty, which brought a decrease in investment (especially in housing) and spending on consumer durables.

▨ There then followed a near total collapse of the financial system. Banks failed and the money supply decreased, resulting in a continued decrease in aggregate demand.

▨ The Great Depression itself produced a series of reforms that make a repeat of such a depression much less likely.

Key Figuress ◆

Key Terms

PROBLEMS

Use the figure for all the problems.

*1. The figure shows the economy of Virtual Reality. When the economy is in a long-run equilibrium, it is at points *b*, *f*, and *j*. When a recession occurs in Virtual Reality, the economy moves away from these points to one of the three other points identified in each part of the figure.

  a. If the Keynesian theory is the correct explanation for the recession, to which points does the economy move?

  b. If the monetarist theory is the correct explanation for the recession, to which points does the economy move?

  c. If the new classical rational expectations theory is the correct explanation for the recession, to which points does the economy move?

  d. If the new Keynesian rational expectations theory is the correct explanation for the recession, to which points does the economy move?

  e. If real business cycle theory is the correct explanation for the recession, to which points does the economy move?

2. The figure shows the economy of Vital Signs. When the economy is in a long-run equilibrium, it is at points *a*, *e*, and *i*. When an expansion occurs in Vital Signs, the economy moves away from these points to one of the three other points identified in each part of the figure.

  a. If the Keynesian theory is the correct explanation for the recession, to which points does the economy move?

  b. If the monetarist theory is the correct explanation for the recession, to which points does the economy move?

  c. If the new classical rational expectations theory is the correct explanation for the recession, to which points does the economy move?

  d. If the new Keynesian rational expectations theory is the correct explanation for the recession, to which points does the economy move?

  e. If real business cycle theory is the correct explanation for the recession, to which points does the economy move?

(a) Labour market

(b) AS-AD

(c) Investment

*3. Suppose that when the recession occurs in Virtual Reality, the economy moves to *d*, *g*, and *k*. Which theory of the business cycle, if any, explains this outcome?

4. Suppose that when the expansion occurs in Vital Signs, the economy moves to *d*, *h*, and *l*. Which theory of the business cycle, if any, explains this outcome?

*5. Suppose that when the recession occurs in Virtual Reality, the economy moves to *c*, *g*, and *k*. Which theory of the business cycle, if any, explains this outcome?

6. Suppose that when the expansion occurs in Vital Signs, the economy moves to *c*, *h*, and *l*. Which theory of the business cycle, if any, explains this outcome?

*7. Suppose that when the recession occurs in Virtual Reality, the economy moves to *d*, *h*, and *k*. Which theory of the business cycle, if any, explains this outcome?

8. Suppose that when the expansion occurs in Vital Signs, the economy moves to *d*, *g*, and *l*. Which theory of the business cycle, if any, explains this outcome?

*9. Suppose that when the recession occurs in Virtual Reality, the economy moves to *c*, *h*, and *k*. Which theory of the business cycle, if any, explains this outcome?

10. Suppose that when the expansion occurs in Vital Signs, the economy moves to *c*, *g*, and *l*. Which theory of the business cycle, if any, explains this outcome?

*11. Suppose that when the recession occurs in Virtual Reality, the economy moves to *d*, *g*, and *l*. Which theory of the business cycle, if any, explains this outcome?

12. Suppose that when the expansion occurs in Vital Signs, the economy moves to *c*, *h*, and *k*. Which theory of the business cycle, if any, explains this outcome?

*13. Suppose that when the recession occurs in Virtual Reality, the economy moves to *c*, *g*, and *l*. Which theory of the business cycle, if any, explains this outcome?

14. Suppose that when the expansion occurs in Vital Signs, the economy moves to *d*, *h*, and *k*. Which theory of the business cycle, if any, explains this outcome?

CRITICAL THINKING

1. Study *Reading Between the Lines* on pp. 766–767 and then answer the following questions:
   a. What does this news article foresee for the Canadian economy in the year it is forecasting?
   b. What does the author of the article regard as positive signs that point to continued expansion?
   c. Why does the author of the article say that it is unlikely that wages will rise?
   d. Can you detect any clues in the news article to tell you whether the author is a Keynesian, monetarist, new classical, new Keynesian, or real business cycle supporter?
   e. What policy actions, if any, do you think the Bank of Canada or Parliament of Canada needs to take in 1999 and 2000 to keep the economy growing and to prevent a new recession?
   f. What is the main danger facing Canada in 2000, inflation or recession?

2. Describe the changes in real GDP, employment and unemployment, and the price level that occurred during the Great Depression years of 1929–1933.

3. Use the links on the Parkin-Bade Web site to obtain information about the current state of the Canadian economy. Then:
   a. List all of the features of the economy during the current year that you can think of that are consistent with a pessimistic outlook for the next two years.
   b. List all of the features of the economy during the current year that you can think of that are consistent with an optimistic outlook for the next two years.
   c. Drawing on the pessimistic and optimistic factors that you have listed in the previous two parts and on your knowledge of macroeconomic theory, explain how you think the Canadian economy is going to evolve over the next year or two.

34

Macroeconomic Policy Challenges

The Canadian economy has performed with mixed results during the past twenty years. Real GDP has expanded and the inflation rate has been lowered but unemployment remains persistently high. Canada was not alone in achieving economic growth. Real GDP in the United States expanded by more than ours has and in the developing countries of Asia, growth has averaged 8 percent a year. But not all countries and regions shared in this solid growth. Japan's real GDP expanded by a lacklustre 1 percent, and in Russia, real GDP shrank for five successive years to less than two-thirds its 1990 level. ◆ There are clouds, even in the North American economic sky. Real interest rates remain relatively high and the international deficit stubbornly persists. Also, there are questions about how fast Canada's real GDP can grow over the longer term. Has the potential GDP growth rate increased? Has the natural rate of unemployment increased? Or is real GDP now above potential GDP? Is the economy overheating again? If it is overheating, is inflation about to increase? And when is the next recession coming? ◆ The variety of macroeconomic performance raises questions about macroeconomic policy. Can policy improve performance? Specifically, can the federal government use its fiscal policy to speed up long-term growth, keep inflation in check, and maintain a low unemployment rate? Can the Bank of Canada use its monetary policy to achieve any of these ends? Are some policy goals better achieved by fiscal policy and some by monetary policy? What specific policy actions do the best job? Are some ways of conducting policy better than others?

◆ In this chapter, we're going to study the challenges of achieving the highest sustainable long-term growth rate and low unemployment while avoiding inflation. At the end of the chapter, you will have a deeper understanding of the macroeconomic policy problems facing Canada today and of the debates that surround us concerning those problems.

What Can Policy Do?

After studying this chapter, you will be able to:

- Describe the goals of macroeconomic policy

- Describe the main features of fiscal policy and monetary policy since the 1970s

- Explain how fiscal policy and monetary policy influence long-term economic growth

- Evaluate fixed-rule and feedback-rule policies to stabilize the business cycle

- Explain how fiscal policy influences the natural unemployment rate

- Explain why lowering inflation usually brings recession

Policy Goals

MACROECONOMIC POLICY GOALS FALL INTO TWO big categories: domestic and international. We study international macroeconomic policy issues in Chapters 35 and 36. Here, we focus on domestic policy. The four main domestic macroeconomic policy goals are to:

- Achieve the highest sustainable rate of potential GDP growth
- Smooth out avoidable business cycle fluctuations
- Maintain low unemployment
- Maintain low inflation

Potential GDP Growth

Sustained real GDP growth since the industrial revolution of the mid-eighteenth century has made a profound contribution to economic well-being. But some countries have grown faster than others and a small difference in the annual growth rate accumulates to a huge difference in living standards. With a growth rate of 2 percent a year, it takes more than 30 years for production to double. With a growth rate of 5 percent a year, production more than doubles in just 15 years. And with a growth rate of 10 percent a year, like some Asian countries are achieving, production doubles in just 7 years. The limits to *sustainable* growth are determined by the availability of natural resources and by the willingness of people to save and invest in human and physical capital and new technologies rather than consume everything they produce.

How fast can the economy grow over the long term? Between 1988 and 1995, through one complete business cycle, potential GDP grew at a rate of 2.9 percent a year. But the Canadian population grows at about 1.5 percent a year, so the growth rate of real GDP per person was 1.4 percent a year, which means that output per person doubles every 50 years. Most economists believe that the Canadian economy can maintain a long-term growth rate of potential GDP of about 3 percent a year. This growth rate would double output per person every 48 years. A few economists believe that with the right policies, sustainable growth of 5 percent a year is possible. This growth rate would double output per person every 18 years, increase it more than sixfold over 48 years, and increase it more than twelvefold in 70 years. So increasing the long-term growth rate is of critical importance.

The Business Cycle

Potential GDP probably does not grow at a constant rate. Fluctuations in the pace of technological advance and in the pace of investment in new capital bring fluctuations in potential GDP. So some fluctuations in real GDP represent fluctuations in potential GDP. But when real GDP grows less quickly than potential GDP, output is lost, and when real GDP grows more quickly than potential GDP, bottlenecks arise. Keeping real GDP growth steady and equal to potential GDP growth avoids these problems.

It is not known how smooth real GDP growth can be made. Real business cycle theory regards all the fluctuations in real GDP as fluctuations in potential GDP. The aggregate demand theories regard most of the fluctuations in real GDP as being avoidable deviations from potential GDP.

Unemployment

When real GDP growth slows, unemployment rises above the natural rate of unemployment. The higher the unemployment rate, the longer is the time taken by unemployed people to find jobs. Productive labour is wasted, and there is a slowdown in the accumulation of human capital. If high unemployment persists, serious psychological and social problems arise for the unemployed workers and their families.

When real GDP growth speeds up, unemployment decreases and falls below the natural rate of unemployment. The lower the unemployment rate, the harder it becomes for expanding industries to hire the labour they need to keep growing. If extremely low unemployment persists, serious bottlenecks and production dislocations occur.

Keeping unemployment at the natural rate avoids both of these problems. But just what is the natural rate of unemployment? Assessments vary. The actual average unemployment rate over the decade 1988–1998, which is also a complete business cycle, was 9.4 percent. Some economists think the natural unemployment rate is around 8 or 9 percent. But most economists would put the natural rate at around 6 percent. Real business cycle theorists believe the natural rate fluctuates and always equals the actual unemployment rate.

If the natural rate of unemployment is high, then a goal of policy becomes lowering the natural rate itself. This goal is independent of smoothing the business cycle.

Inflation

When inflation fluctuates unpredictably, money becomes less useful as a measuring rod for conducting transactions. In extreme cases, it becomes useless and is abandoned as the means of payment. Borrowers and lenders and employers and workers must take on extra risks. Keeping the inflation rate steady and predictable avoids these problems.

What is the most desirable inflation rate? Some economists say that the *rate* of inflation doesn't matter much as long as the rate is *predictable*. But most economists believe that price stability, which they translate as an inflation rate of between 0 and 3 percent a year, is desirable. The reason why zero is not the target is that some price increases are due to quality improvements—a measurement bias in the price index—so a *measured* inflation rate of between 0 and 3 percent a year is equivalent to price stability.

The Two Core Policy Indicators: Real GDP Growth and Inflation

Although macroeconomic policy pursues the four goals we've just considered, the goals are not independent ones. Three of these goals—increasing the real GDP growth rate, smoothing the business cycle, and maintaining low unemployment—are linked together. Real GDP growth tells us directly about the long-term goal of high sustainable growth and the business cycle. It also has a strong link to unemployment. If growth becomes too rapid, unemployment falls below the natural rate; and if growth becomes too slow, unemployment rises above the natural rate. So keeping real GDP growing steadily at its maximum sustainable rate is equivalent to avoiding business fluctuations and keeping unemployment at the natural rate.

There are some connections between real GDP growth and inflation, but over the long run, these two variables are largely independent. So two variables, real GDP growth and inflation, are the core policy targets.

Policy performance, judged by the two core policy targets—real GDP growth and inflation—is shown in Fig. 34.1. Here the red line shows real GDP growth. Real GDP growth averaged 5.4 percent a year between 1970 and 1973 but then gradually fell. Between 1988 and 1998, real GDP growth fluctuated between a high of 3.9 percent in 1994 and a low of −1.9 percent in 1991 and averaged only 2.1 percent a year. The height of the green shaded area shows inflation. The inflation rate was low in 1970, exploded during the 1970s, and then fell through the 1980s and almost vanished during the 1990s.

FIGURE 34.1

Macroeconomic Performance: Real GDP and Inflation

Real GDP growth and inflation fluctuate a great deal. During the 1970s, inflation mushroomed (the height of the green shaded area) and real GDP growth slowed. This macroeconomic performance falls far short of the goals of a high and stable real GDP growth rate and low and predictable inflation.

Source: Statistics Canada, StatCan: CANSIM Disc, March 1999.

R E V I E W   Q U I Z

- Why does macroeconomic stabilization policy try to achieve the highest sustainable rate of potential GDP growth, small business cycle fluctuations, low unemployment, and low inflation?
- Can stabilization policy keep the unemployment rate below the natural rate?
- Why are real GDP growth and inflation the two core policy indicators?

We've examined the policy goals. Let's now look at the policy tools and the way they have been used.

Policy Tools and Performance

THE TOOLS THAT ARE USED TO TRY TO ACHIEVE macroeconomic performance objectives are fiscal policy and monetary policy. **Fiscal policy**, which is described in Chapter 26, is the use of the federal budget to achieve macroeconomic objectives. The detailed fiscal policy tools are tax rates, benefit rates, and government expenditures on goods and services. These tools work by influencing aggregate supply and aggregate demand in the ways explained in Chapter 24. **Monetary policy**, which is described in Chapter 28, is the adjustment of the quantity of money in circulation and interest rates by the Bank of Canada to achieve macroeconomic objectives. These tools work by changing aggregate demand.

Fiscal policy and monetary policy interact in the ways described in Chapter 29 and the outcome depends on how the tools are combined. How have the tools actually been used in Canada? Let's answer this question by summarizing the main directions of fiscal and monetary policy over recent years.

Fiscal Policy Since 1970

Figure 34.2 gives a broad summary of fiscal policy since 1970. It shows the levels of government revenues and outlays and the budget balance (each as a percentage of GDP). So that you can see the political context of fiscal policy, the figure also shows the election years and the names of the incumbent prime ministers.

Fiscal policy was neutral during the early 1970s, when Pierre Trudeau was prime minister. It then became expansionary before the 1976 election. Trudeau won that election and during his next term as prime minister, spending exploded and so did the deficit. At this time, fiscal policy was strongly expansionary.

The Progressive Conservatives replaced the Liberals, and Brian Mulroney became prime minister in 1983. The Mulroney years were a period of spending cuts and modest tax increases and overall fiscal policy was contractionary during these years.

The Liberals returned to power in the election of 1993 and during 1994 through 1998, Prime Minister Jean Chrétien and Finance Minister Paul Martin cut

FIGURE 34.2

The Fiscal Policy Record: A Summary

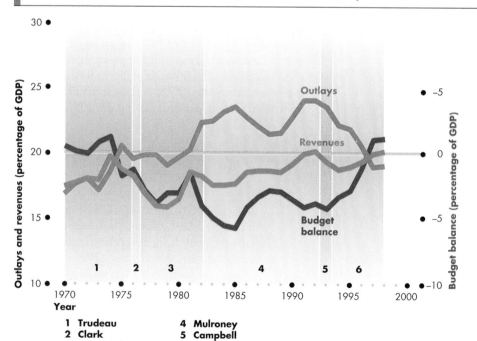

Fiscal policy is summarized here by the performance of government outlays, revenues, and the budget balance. Outlays have been on an upward trend and have persistently exceeded revenues, resulting in a budget deficit. Cycles in outlays and revenues have resulted in cycles in the budget balance.

1 Trudeau
2 Clark
3 Trudeau/Turner
4 Mulroney
5 Campbell
6 Chrétien

Source: Statistics Canada, *StatCan: CANSIM Disc*, March 1999, and the authors' calculations.

outlays and lowered the deficit. By 1998, aided by strong real GDP growth, the deficit was finally eliminated and a surplus was achieved for the first time since 1974.

Recall that the Canadian economy experienced a recession during 1982 and again during 1990–1991. You can see, in Fig. 34.2, that in these two recessions, outlays increased, revenues decreased, and the deficit increased. But when the economy expanded after the recessions, outlays decreased, revenues increased, and the deficit decreased.

Let's now look at monetary policy.

Monetary Policy Since 1975

Figure 34.3 shows three measures of monetary policy. They are the growth rate of M2+, the interest rate on overnight loans, and the *real* interest rate on overnight loans.

The M2+ growth rate provides a broad indication of the influence of monetary policy on aggregate demand.

The **overnight loans rate** is the interest rate on large-scale loans that chartered banks make to each other and to dealers in financial markets. The Bank of Canada sets a target range for the overnight loans rate and takes actions to keep the rate inside its target range (see Chapter 28, p. 624). Movements in the overnight loans rate tell us how the Bank is acting to change money growth. When the overnight loans rate rises, the Bank is tightening; and when it falls, the Bank is loosening its grip on money growth.

The real overnight loans rate tells us how the Bank of Canada's actions eventually ripple through the economy to influence spending plans. It is the real interest rate, not the nominal rate, to which expenditure plans respond.

Figure 34.3 also identifies the election years, the prime ministers, and the Bank of Canada governors. The Bank has had three governors during this period. Notice that the term of a governor does not coincide with the term of a government and the governor's term extends across the terms of several governments.

There are four distinct phases of monetary policy. In the first phase, between 1975 and 1980, inflation was rapid and so was money supply growth.

The Monetary Policy Record: A Summary

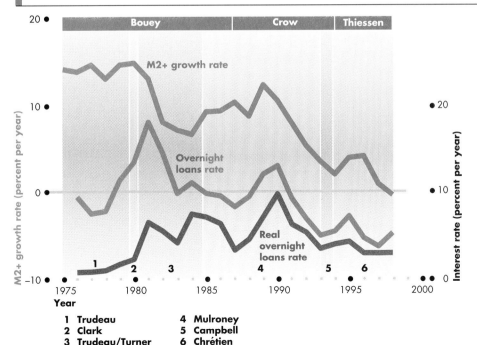

The monetary policy record is summarized here by the growth rate of M2+ and by the overnight loans rate. The M2+ growth rate slowed during the Trudeau years when fiscal policy was expansionary, sped up during Mulroney's first term when fiscal policy was contractionary, and became severely tight during Mulroney's second term when fiscal policy became expansionary again. There is no sign that monetary policy has been used to stimulate the economy to influence the outcome of a federal election.

1 Trudeau	4 Mulroney
2 Clark	5 Campbell
3 Trudeau/Turner	6 Chrétien

Source: Statistics Canada, *StatCan: CANSIM Disc*, March 1999, and the authors' calculations.

During this period, the nominal interest rate was not much higher than the inflation rate, so the real interest rate was close to zero.

In the second phase, during the early 1980s, Bank of Canada governor Gerald Bouey embarked on a concerted anti-inflation policy. The money supply growth rate fell and interest rates increased. As a result of these actions, the inflation rate fell from around 10 percent a year to less than 5 percent a year.

In the third phase, which began in 1989 when John Crow was governor of the Bank of Canada, a further attack on inflation was launched to achieve price stability. The money supply growth rate fell again and interest rates increased.

In the fourth phase, which began in 1994 when Gordon Thiessen became governor of the Bank of Canada, the challenge was to keep inflation at its new low level but to pursue a monetary policy that permits the economy to expand and to bring lower unemployment. The M2+ growth rate continued to decrease, but the Bank lowered the nominal interest rate through 1997. The real interest rate has been remarkably steady during the past three years.

You can see that monetary policy has had a long-term anti-inflation focus rather than a short-term business cycle focus. You can also see that there is no tendency for monetary policy to be linked to the timing of elections. The Bank of Canada has pursued its monetary policy to achieve its economic objectives and has been immune from political pressures to change the course of monetary policy for short-term political gains.

R E V I E W   Q U I Z

■ What were the main features and effects of fiscal policy during the terms of the various prime ministers during the 1980s and 1990s? What problems did fiscal policy respond to during the late 1960s and the 1970s?

■ What were the main features and effects of monetary policy during the 1980s and 1990s? In which periods was monetary policy inflationary? In which periods was it used to fight inflation?

You've now studied the goals of policy and seen the broad trends and cycles in fiscal and monetary policy. Let's now study the ways in which policy might be used better to achieve its goals. We'll begin by looking at long-term growth policy.

Long-Term Growth Policy

THE SOURCES OF THE LONG-TERM GROWTH OF potential GDP, which are explained in Chapter 32 (pp. 727–732), are the accumulation of physical and human capital and the advance of technology. Chapter 32 also briefly examines the range of policies to achieve faster growth. Here, we probe more deeply into the problem of boosting the long-term growth rate.

Monetary policy can contribute to long-term growth by keeping the inflation rate low. (Chapter 30, pp. 676–678, explains some connections between inflation and growth.) Fiscal policy and other policies can also contribute to growth by influencing the private decisions on which long-term growth depends in three areas. All growth policies increase:

■ National saving
■ Investment in human capital
■ Investment in new technologies

National Saving

National saving equals private saving plus government saving (see Chapter 22, p. 480). Figure 34.4 shows national saving and its private and government components since 1970. Between 1970 and 1998, national saving (green line) fluctuated around an average of 20 percent of GDP. It ranged between a low of 16 percent in 1975 and a high of 22 percent in 1998.

Private saving (blue line) increased as a percentage of GDP between 1974 and 1985, when it peaked at 25 percent of GDP. Government saving (the vertical gap between the blue line and the green line) was positive before 1975, became increasingly negative (government dissaving) during the 1980s, and returned to a positive number in the late 1990s.

The data you have just examined are for *gross* saving. Each year, national wealth grows by the amount of *net* saving, which equals gross saving minus the value of capital that is scrapped during the year. Figure 34.4 also shows *net* national saving as a percentage of GDP (the red line). Net national saving has fluctuated but does not have an upward or a downward trend. Gross national saving minus net national saving averages 12 percent of GDP. This amount is the average depreciation of capital, which has ranged from a low of

11 percent of GDP in 1973 to a high of 13 percent of GDP in 1998. Because depreciation is so constant, the fluctuations in net national saving are very similar to those in gross national saving.

Canadian investment, which is one of the engines of real GDP growth, is not limited by Canadian saving. The reason is that Canadians can borrow abroad to finance domestic investment. And foreigners can invest some of their saving directly in Canadian businesses. Either way, the foreign saving boosts Canadian real GDP growth. Also, because all investment, regardless of how it is financed, creates jobs, the boost in Canadian incomes leads to an increase in national saving. Further, by using foreign saving along with domestic saving, Canadians can invest in a wider range of potentially profitable business enterprises and can better spread their risks across traditional and high-return new technologies. How can national saving be increased? The two points of attack are:

■ Increasing government saving
■ Increasing private saving

Increasing Government Saving   Government saving has been negative since 1974 and its average, during the 1990s has been –2.4 percent of GDP. Increasing government saving means increasing the federal surplus and bringing the budgets of the larger provinces such as Ontario and Quebec into surplus. But achieving a substantial government surplus will be hard work and will only be achieved by cuts in sensitive social, educational, and health-care programs.

Increasing Private Saving   Private saving in Canada has remained steady, but it could be even larger. The main way that government actions can boost private saving is by increasing the after-tax rate of return on saving. This is what government policy has sought to do, but on only one type of asset, registered retirement saving plan (RRSP) accounts and pension funds. By putting their savings into an RRSP or pension fund, people can avoid income tax on their interest income and on the part of the income that they shelter in this way. But they cannot use their RRSPs (without a tax penalty) until they retire. Also, there are limits to the amount that can be accumulated tax-free in an RRSP and a pension fund each year.

Private saving probably could be stimulated more effectively by cutting taxes on interest income across the board and replacing the government revenue lost from such a tax cut with an increase in the Goods and Services Tax or an increase in the tax on labour income. But such a move would be regarded as inequitable and probably not politically feasible. So governments are limited to making minor changes to the taxation of interest income, and these changes will have negligible effects on the saving rate.

Private Saving and Inflation   Inflation erodes the value of money and other financial assets, and uncertainty about inflation discourages saving. So a monetary policy that preserves stable prices and minimizes uncertainty about the future value of money stimulates saving. With a higher saving rate, real GDP grows more rapidly (see Chapter 30, pp. 676–677).

FIGURE   34.4

Saving Rates in Canada: 1970–1998

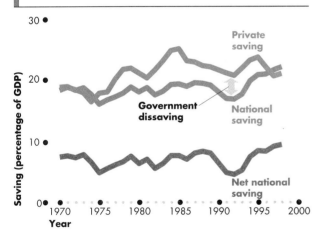

Gross national saving (green line) ranged between 16 percent in 1975 and 22 percent in 1998. Private saving (blue line) increased between 1974 and 1985 and peaked at 25 percent of GDP. Government saving (the vertical gap between the blue line and the green line) was positive before 1975, became increasingly negative during the 1980s, and became positive again in the late 1990s. Net national saving (red line) has fluctuated but has no trend.

Source: Statistics Canada, *StatCan: CANSIM Disc*, March 1999, and the authors' calculations.

Investment in Human Capital

The accumulation of human capital plays a crucial role in economic growth, and three areas are relevant: education, on-the-job experience, and health care. Economic research shows that education, on-the-job training, and good health yield high rates of return.

On the average, the greater the number of years a person remains in school, the higher are that person's earnings. A university graduate earns more, on the average, than does a college graduate, who in turn earns more than does a high school graduate. Again on the average, a person with ten years of work experience earns more than an otherwise identical person who has no work experience. Similarly, and again on the average, the better a person's health, the more productive is that person.

So, by providing subsidized education, governments can increase the rate of investment in human capital and boost the rate of real GDP growth. By maintaining a low level of unemployment, government can increase the number of people who have work experience and again increase the rate of investment in human capital. And by providing comprehensive high-quality health-care services, governments can help to build a more productive labour force.

But if education, on-the-job experience, and good health yield higher earnings, why, you might be wondering, does the government need a policy that increases the rate of investment in human capital? Why can't people simply be left to get on with making their own decisions about how much human capital to acquire?

The answer is that the *social* returns to human capital probably exceed the *private* returns. Some of the productivity of human capital comes from the *interactions* of people who are well endowed with human capital. The greater the number of well-educated, experienced, and healthy people, the greater is the productivity of each person. The design and production of just about every good and service benefits from team efforts.

When each person makes a decision about how much education or on-the-job training to get, the benefits that will accrue to others are ignored. So, left to ourselves, we would probably accumulate too little human capital. For this reason, free schooling and heavily subsidized college and university education is efficient. Tax deductibility of interest on student loans is also efficient. Countries that provide a good basic education and health care for everyone have a better economic growth performance, on the average, than countries that do not.

Investment in New Technologies

Investment in new technologies is the third area in which policy can influence economic growth. As Chapter 32 explains, investment in new technologies is special for two reasons. First, it appears not to run into the problem of diminishing returns that plagues all other productive resources. Second, the benefits of new technologies spill over to influence all parts of the economy, not just the firms undertaking the investment. For these reasons, increasing the rate of investment in new technologies appears to be a particularly promising way of boosting long-term growth. But how can government policy influence the pace of technological change?

Governments can fund and provide tax incentives for research and development activities. Through the Natural Sciences Research Council, the universities, and various research establishments, governments fund a large amount of basic research.

Considering the payoff from faster growth and the payoff, therefore, from improved knowledge about the forces that create growth, it is surprising that more is not spent, both on research and development and on economic research on the causes of growth.

REVIEW QUIZ

- Why do long-term growth policies focus on increasing saving and increasing investment in human capital and new technologies?
- What have been the trends in the Canadian net saving rate in recent years?
- What actions can the government take that might increase the saving rate?
- What actions can the government take that might increase the rate of investment in human capital?
- What actions can the government take that might increase investment in new technologies?

We've seen how government might use its fiscal and monetary policies to influence long-term growth. How can it influence the business cycle and unemployment? Let's now address this question.

Business Cycle and Unemployment Policy

MANY DIFFERENT FISCAL AND MONETARY policies can be pursued to stabilize the business cycle and cyclical unemployment. But all these polices fall into three broad categories:

- Fixed-rule policies
- Feedback-rule policies
- Discretionary policies

Fixed-Rule Policies

A **fixed-rule policy** specifies an action to be pursued independently of the state of the economy. An everyday life example of a fixed rule is a stop sign. It says, "Stop regardless of the state of the road ahead—even if no other vehicle is trying to use the road." One fixed-rule policy, proposed by Milton Friedman, is to keep the quantity of money growing at a constant rate year in and year out, regardless of the state of the economy, to make the *average* inflation rate zero. Another fixed-rule policy is to balance the federal budget. Fixed rules are rarely followed in practice, but they have some merits in principle, and later in this chapter, we will study how they would work if they were pursued.

Feedback-Rule Policies

A **feedback-rule policy** specifies how policy actions respond to changes in the state of the economy. A yield sign is an everyday feedback rule. It says, "Stop if another vehicle is attempting to use the road ahead, but otherwise, proceed." A macroeconomic feedback-rule policy is one that changes the money supply, interest rates, or even tax rates in response to the state of the economy. Some feedback rules guide the actions of policy makers. For example, the Bank of Canada used a feedback rule when it kept pushing interest rates ever higher through 1994 in response to persistently falling unemployment and strong real GDP growth. Other feedback-rule policies are automatic. Examples are the automatic increase in tax revenues and decrease in transfer payments during an expansion and the automatic decrease in tax revenues and increase in transfer payments during a recession.

Discretionary Policies

A **discretionary policy** responds to the state of the economy in a possibly unique way that uses all the information available, including perceived lessons from past "mistakes." An everyday discretionary policy occurs at an unmarked intersection. Each driver uses discretion in deciding whether to stop and how slowly to approach the intersection. Most macroeconomic policy actions have an element of discretion because every situation is to some degree unique. For example, through 1994 the Bank of Canada increased interest rates several times but by small increments. It might have delayed increasing rates until it was more sure that higher rates were needed and then increased them in a larger increment. The Bank used discretion based on lessons it had learned from earlier expansions. But despite the fact that all policy actions have an element of discretion, they can be regarded as modifications of a basic feedback-rule policy.

We'll study the effects of business cycle policy by comparing the performance of real GDP and the price level under a fixed rule and a feedback rule. Because the business cycle can result from demand shocks or supply shocks, we need to consider these two cases. We'll begin by studying demand shocks.

Stabilizing Aggregate Demand Shocks

We'll study an economy that starts out at full employment and has no inflation. Figure 34.5 illustrates this situation. The economy is on aggregate demand curve AD_0 and short-run aggregate supply curve *SAS*. These curves intersect at a point on the long-run aggregate supply curve, *LAS*. The GDP deflator is 110, and real GDP is $800 billion. Now suppose that there is an unexpected and temporary decrease in aggregate demand. Let's see what happens.

Perhaps investment decreases because of a wave of pessimism about the future, or perhaps exports decrease because of a recession in the rest of the world. Regardless of the origin of the decrease in aggregate demand, the aggregate demand curve shifts leftward, to AD_1 in Fig. 34.5. Aggregate demand curve AD_1 intersects the short-run aggregate supply curve, *SAS*, at a GDP deflator of 105 and a real GDP of $750 billion. The economy is in a recession. Real GDP is less than potential GDP, and unemployment is above its natural rate.

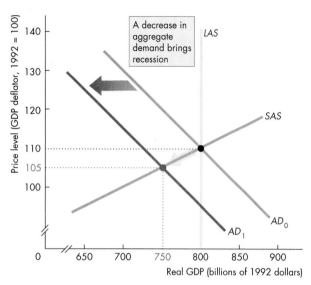

FIGURE 34.5

A Decrease in Aggregate Demand

A decrease in aggregate demand brings recession

The economy starts out at full employment on aggregate demand curve AD_0 and short-run aggregate supply curve SAS, the two curves intersecting on the long-run aggregate supply curve, LAS. Real GDP is $800 billion, and the GDP deflator is 110. A decrease in aggregate demand (due to pessimism about future profits, for example) unexpectedly shifts the aggregate demand curve to AD_1. Real GDP decreases to $750 billion, and the GDP deflator falls to 105. The economy is in a recession.

Suppose that the decrease in aggregate demand from AD_0 to AD_1 is temporary. As confidence in the future improves, firms' investment picks up, or as economic expansion proceeds in the rest of the world, exports gradually increase. As a result, the aggregate demand curve gradually returns to AD_0, but it takes some time to do so.

We are going to work out how the economy responds under two alternative policies during the period in which aggregate demand gradually increases to its original level: a fixed rule and a feedback rule.

Fixed Rule: Monetarism The fixed rule that we'll study here is one in which government expenditures on goods and services, taxes, and the money supply remain constant. Neither fiscal policy nor monetary policy responds to the depressed economy. This is the

rule advocated by monetarists. A **monetarist** is an economist who believes that fluctuations in the money stock are the main source of economic fluctuations—the monetarist theory of the business cycle (see Chapter 33, p. 748–750).

Figure 34.6(a) illustrates the response of the economy under a fixed rule when the decrease in aggregate demand to AD_1 is *temporary*. Gradually, aggregate demand returns to its original level and the aggregate demand curve shifts rightward to AD_0. As it does so, real GDP and the GDP deflator gradually increase. The GDP deflator gradually returns to 110 and real GDP to $800 billion, as shown in Fig. 34.6(a). Throughout this process, the economy experiences more rapid growth than usual but beginning from a state in which real GDP is less than potential GDP. Also throughout the adjustment, unemployment remains above the natural rate.

Figure 34.6(b) illustrates the response of the economy under a fixed rule when the decrease in aggregate demand to AD_1 is *permanent*. Gradually, with unemployment above the natural rate, the money wage rate falls and the short-run aggregate supply curve shifts rightward to SAS_1. As it does so, real GDP gradually increases and the GDP deflator falls. Real GDP gradually returns to potential GDP of $800 billion and the GDP deflator gradually falls to 95, as shown in Fig. 34.6(b). Again, throughout the adjustment, real GDP is less than potential GDP and unemployment exceeds the natural rate.

Let's contrast the adjustment under a fixed rule with that under a feedback-rule policy.

Feedback Rule: Keynesian Activism The feedback rule that we'll study is one in which government expenditures on goods and services increase, tax rates decrease, and the money supply increases when real GDP decreases below potential GDP. In other words, both fiscal policy and monetary policy become expansionary when real GDP is less than potential GDP. When real GDP exceeds potential GDP, both policies operate in reverse, becoming contractionary. This rule is advocated by Keynesian activists. A **Keynesian activist** is an economist who believes that fluctuations in aggregate demand combined with sticky money wage rates (and/or sticky price levels) are the main source of economic fluctuations—the Keynesian and new Keynesian theories of the business cycle (see Chapter 33, pp. 747–748).

Figure 34.6(c) illustrates the response of the economy under this feedback rule policy. When aggregate

FIGURE 34.6
Two Stabilization Policies: Aggregate Demand Shock

  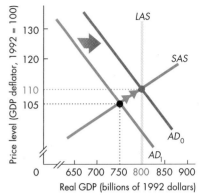

(a) Fixed rule: temporary demand shock   **(b) Fixed rule: permanent demand shock**   **(c) Feedback rule**

Aggregate demand has decreased from AD_0 to AD_1 and the economy is in a recession. Real GDP has decreased to $750 billion and the GDP deflator has fallen to 105. A fixed-rule stabilization policy (parts a and b) leaves aggregate demand at AD_1, so real GDP remains at $750 billion and the GDP deflator remains at 105. If the aggregate demand shock is temporary (part a), aggregate demand subsequently returns to its original level and the aggregate demand curve shifts back to AD_0. As it does, real GDP increases back to $800 billion and the GDP deflator increases to 110. If the demand shock is

permanent (part b), aggregate demand remains at AD_1. Eventually, because unemployment is above the natural rate, the money wage rate falls and the SAS curve shifts to SAS_1. The price level falls further (to a GDP deflator of 95) and real GDP returns to $800 billion. Part (c) shows a feedback rule. With the economy in recession, expansionary fiscal and monetary policies increase aggregate demand and shift the aggregate demand curve from AD_1 to AD_0. Real GDP returns to $800 billion and the GDP deflator returns to 110.

demand decreases to AD_1, the expansionary fiscal and monetary policies increase aggregate demand, shifting the aggregate demand curve immediately to AD_0. As other influences begin to increase aggregate demand, fiscal and monetary policies become contractionary and hold the aggregate demand curve steady at AD_0. Real GDP is held steady at $800 billion, and the GDP deflator remains at 110.

The Two Rules Compared   Under a fixed-rule policy the economy goes into a recession and stays there for as long as it takes for aggregate demand to increase again under its own steam. Only gradually does the aggregate demand curve return to its original position and the recession come to an end.

Under a feedback-rule policy, the economy is pulled out of its recession by the policy action. Once back at potential GDP, real GDP is held there by a gradual, policy-induced decrease in aggregate demand that exactly offsets the increase in aggregate demand coming from private spending decisions.

The price level and real GDP decrease and increase by the same amounts under the two policies, but real GDP stays below potential GDP for longer with a fixed rule than it does with a feedback rule.

The Bank's Feedback Rule: 1992–1996   The Bank tries to operate a feedback rule like the one you've just studied. At the end of 1992, real GDP was below potential GDP and unemployment was above the natural rate. Through 1992, the Bank gradually lowered interest rates and increased the money growth rate. The economy expanded. By 1994, real GDP was close to potential GDP and was growing faster than potential GDP. To prevent an outbreak of inflation, the Bank increased interest rates and slowed money growth. As the economy slowed, during 1995, the Bank lowered interest rates and increased the money growth rate. Real GDP growth again speeded up in 1996. And again, in early 1997, the Bank applied the monetary brake.

Is a Feedback Rule Better?

Is a feedback rule better than a fixed rule? Can the government and the Bank use feedback rules to keep the economy close to full employment with a stable price level? Of course, unforecasted events, such as a collapse in business confidence, will hit the economy from time to time. But by responding with a change in tax rates, spending, interest rates, and money supply, can't the government and the Bank minimize the damage from such a shock?

Despite the apparent superiority of a feedback rule, many economists are convinced that a fixed rule stabilizes aggregate demand more effectively than a feedback rule does. These economists assert that fixed rules are better than feedback rules because:

- Potential GDP is not known.
- Policy lags are longer than the forecast horizon.
- Feedback-rule policies are less predictable than fixed-rule policies.

Knowledge of Potential GDP   To decide whether a feedback policy needs to stimulate or retard aggregate demand, it is necessary to determine whether real GDP is currently above or below potential GDP. But potential GDP is not known with certainty. It depends on a large number of factors, one of which is the level of employment when unemployment is at its natural rate. But uncertainty and disagreement exist about how the labour market works, so we can only estimate the natural rate of unemployment. As a result, there is uncertainty about the *direction* in which a feedback policy should be pushing the level of aggregate demand.

Policy Lags and the Forecast Horizon   The effects of policy actions taken today are spread out over the following two years or even more. But we can't forecast accurately that far ahead. The forecast horizon of the policy makers is less than one year. Further, it is not possible to predict the precise timing and magnitude of the effects of policy actions. Thus feedback policies that react to today's economy may be inappropriate for the state of the economy at that uncertain future date when the policy's effects are felt.

For example, suppose that today the economy is in recession. The Bank reacts with an increase in the money supply growth rate. When the Bank puts on the monetary accelerator, the first reaction is a fall in interest rates. Some time later, lower interest rates produce an increase in investment and expenditures on consumer durable goods. Some time still later, this increase in expenditure increases income; higher income in turn induces more consumption expenditure. Later yet, the higher expenditure increases the demand for labour, and, eventually, wages and prices rise. The industries and regions in which spending increases occur vary, and so does the impact on employment. It can take from nine months to two years for an initial action by the Bank to cause a change in real GDP, employment, and the inflation rate.

By the time the Bank's actions are having their maximum effect, the economy has moved on to a new situation. Perhaps a world economic slowdown has added a new negative effect on aggregate demand that is offsetting the Bank's expansionary actions. Or perhaps a boost in business confidence has increased aggregate demand yet further, adding to the Bank's own expansionary policy. Whatever the situation, the Bank can take the appropriate actions today only if it can forecast those future shocks to aggregate demand.

Thus to smooth the fluctuations in aggregate demand, the Bank needs to take actions today, based on a forecast of what will be happening over a period stretching two or more years into the future. It is no use taking actions a year from today to influence the situation that then prevails. By then it will be too late.

If the Bank of Canada is good at economic forecasting and bases its policy actions on its forecasts, then it can deliver the type of aggregate-demand-smoothing performance that we assumed in the model economy that we studied earlier in this chapter. But if the Bank takes policy actions that are based on today's economy rather than on the forecasted economy a year into the future, then those actions will often be inappropriate ones.

When unemployment is high and the Bank of Canada puts its foot on the accelerator, it speeds the economy back to full employment. But the Bank might not be able to see far enough ahead to know when to ease off the accelerator and gently tap the brake, holding the economy at its full-employment point. Usually, the Bank keeps its foot on the accelerator for too long. And after the Bank has taken its foot off the accelerator pedal, the economy races through the full-employment point and starts to experience shortages and inflationary pressures. Eventually, when inflation increases and unemployment falls below its natural rate, the Bank steps on the brake, pushing the economy back below full employment.

According to advocates of fixed rules, the Bank's own reactions to the current state of the economy is one of the major sources of fluctuations in aggregate demand and the major factor that people have to forecast to make their own economic choices.

During 1994, the Bank tried hard to avoid the problems just described. It increased interest rates early in the expansion and by small increments. In 1995, after real GDP growth slowed but before any serious signs of recession were on the horizon, it began to cut interest rates. And in 1997, before inflation turned seriously upward, the Bank squeezed the monetary brake. Whether the Bank now knows enough to avoid some of the mistakes of the past is too early to tell. But its actions during 1992–1996 were gentler and better timed than in previous cycles.

The problems for fiscal policy feedback rules are more severe than those for monetary policy because of the lags in the implementation of fiscal policy. The Bank of Canada can take actions relatively quickly. But before a fiscal policy action can be taken, the entire legislative process must be completed. Thus even before a fiscal policy action is implemented, the economy might have moved on to a new situation that calls for a different feedback policy from the one that is in the legislative pipeline.

Predictability of Policies   To make decisions about long-term contracts for employment (wage contracts) and for borrowing and lending, people have to anticipate the future course of prices—the future inflation rate. To forecast the inflation rate, it is necessary to forecast aggregate demand. And to forecast aggregate demand, it is necessary to forecast the policy actions of the government and the Bank.

If the government and the Bank stick to rock-steady, fixed rules for tax rates, spending programs, and money supply growth, then policy itself cannot be a contributor to unexpected fluctuations in aggregate demand.

In contrast, when a feedback rule is being pursued, there is more scope for the policy actions to be unpredictable. The main reason is that feedback rules are not written down for all to see. Rather, they have to be inferred from the behaviour of the government and the Bank.

Thus with a feedback policy it is necessary to predict the variables to which the government and Bank react and the extent to which they react. Consequently, a feedback rule for fiscal and monetary policies can create more unpredictable fluctuations in aggregate demand than a fixed rule can.

Economists disagree about whether those bigger fluctuations offset the potential stabilizing influence of the predictable changes the Bank makes. No agreed measurements have been made to settle this dispute. Nevertheless, the unpredictability of the Bank in its pursuit of feedback policies is an important fact of economic life. And the Bank does not always go out of its way to make its reactions clear. Even in Parliamentary testimony, Bank of Canada governors are reluctant to make the Bank's actions and intentions entirely plain. Rather, they like to create a degree of mystery about what they are doing and place a smokescreen between themselves and the rest of the government economic policy-making machine.

It is not surprising that the Bank seeks to keep *some* of its actions behind a smokescreen. First, the Bank wants to maintain as much freedom of action as possible and so does not want to state with too great a precision the feedback rules that it will follow in any given circumstances. Second, the Bank is part of a political process and, although legally independent of the federal government, is not immune to subtle influence. For at least these two reasons, the Bank does not specify feedback rules as precisely as the one we've analysed in this chapter. As a result, the Bank cannot deliver an economic performance that has the stability that we generated in the model economy.

To the extent that the Bank's actions are discretionary and unpredictable, they lead to unpredictable fluctuations in aggregate demand. These fluctuations, in turn, produce fluctuations in real GDP, employment, and unemployment.

If it is difficult for the Bank to pursue a predictable feedback stabilization policy, it is probably impossible for Parliament to do so. The stabilization policy of Parliament is formulated in terms of spending programs and tax laws. Because these programs and laws are the outcome of a political process that is constrained only by the Constitution, there can be no effective way in which a predictable feedback fiscal policy can be adhered to.

We reviewed three reasons why feedback-rule policies might not be more effective than fixed-rule policies in controlling aggregate demand. But there is a fourth reason why some economists prefer fixed rules: Not all shocks to the economy are on the demand side. Most advocates of feedback rules believe that most fluctuations do come from aggregate demand. Some advocates of fixed rules believe that aggregate supply fluctuations are the dominant ones. Let's now see how aggregate supply fluctuations affect the economy under a fixed rule and a feedback rule. We will also see why those economists who believe that aggregate supply fluctuations are the dominant ones also favour a fixed rule rather than a feedback rule.

Stabilizing Aggregate Supply Shocks

Real business cycle theorists believe that fluctuations in real GDP (and in employment and unemployment) are caused not by fluctuations in aggregate demand but by fluctuations in productivity growth. According to real business cycle theory, there is no useful distinction between long-run aggregate supply and short-run aggregate supply. Because the money wage rate is flexible, the labour market is always in equilibrium and unemployment is always at its natural rate. The vertical long-run aggregate supply curve is also the short-run aggregate supply curve. Fluctuations occur because of shifts in the long-run aggregate supply curve. Normally, the long-run aggregate supply curve shifts rightward—the economy expands. But the pace at which the long-run aggregate supply curve shifts rightward varies. Also, on occasion, the long-run aggregate supply curve shifts leftward, bringing a decrease in aggregate supply and a decrease in real GDP.

If the real business cycle theory is correct, economic policy that influences the aggregate demand curve has no effect on real GDP. But it does affect the price level. If a feedback-rule policy is used to increase aggregate demand every time real GDP decreases, and if the real business cycle theory is correct, the feedback-rule policy will make price level fluctuations more severe than they otherwise would be. To see why, consider Fig. 34.7.

Imagine that the economy starts out on aggregate demand curve AD_0 and long-run aggregate supply curve LAS_0 at a GDP deflator of 110 and with real GDP equal to \$800 billion. Now suppose that the long-run aggregate supply curve shifts to LAS_1. An actual decrease in long-run aggregate supply can occur as a result of a severe drought or other natural catastrophe or perhaps as the result of a disruption of international trade such as the OPEC embargo of the 1970s.

Fixed Rule With a fixed rule, the decrease in long-run aggregate supply has no effect on the policies of the Bank of Canada or the government and no effect on aggregate demand. The aggregate demand curve

FIGURE 34.7

Responding to a Productivity Growth Slowdown

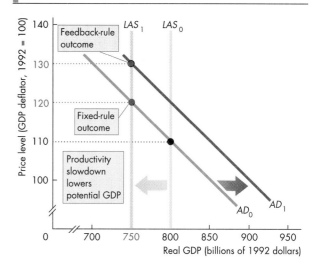

A productivity growth slowdown shifts the long-run aggregate supply curve from LAS_0 to LAS_1. Real GDP decreases to \$750 billion, and the GDP deflator rises to 120. With a fixed rule, there is no change in the money supply, taxes, or government spending; aggregate demand stays at AD_0; and that is the end of the matter. With a feedback rule, the Bank of Canada increases the money supply and Parliament cuts taxes or increases spending, intending to increase real GDP. Aggregate demand shifts to AD_1, but the result is an increase in the price level—the GDP deflator rises to 130—with no change in real GDP.

remains AD_0. Real GDP decreases to \$750 billion, and the GDP deflator increases to 120.

Feedback Rule Now suppose that the Bank of Canada and the government use feedback rules. In particular, suppose that when real GDP decreases, the Bank increases the money supply and Parliament enacts a tax cut to increase aggregate demand. In this example, the increase in the money supply and the tax cut shift the aggregate demand curve to AD_1. The policy goal is to bring real GDP back to \$800 billion. But the long-run aggregate supply curve has shifted, and so potential GDP has decreased to \$750 billion. The increase in aggregate demand cannot bring forth an increase in output if the economy does not have the capacity to produce that output. So real GDP stays at $750 billion and the price level rises further—the GDP deflator goes to 130. You can see that in this case the attempt to stabilize real GDP using a feedback-rule policy has no effect on real GDP but generates a substantial price level increase.

We've now seen some of the shortcomings of using feedback rules for stabilization policy. Some economists believe that these shortcomings are serious and want to constrain Parliament and the Bank so that they use fixed rules. Others, regarding the potential advantages of feedback rules as greater than their costs, advocate the continued use of such policies but with an important modification that we'll now look at.

Nominal GDP Targeting

Nominal GDP targeting is an attempt to keep the growth rate of nominal GDP steady. This policy target was first proposed by a leading Keynesian activist, James Tobin of Yale University. It is a policy that recognizes the strengths of a fixed rule but that regards the monetarist fixed rule as inappropriate. Instead, nominal GDP targeting uses feedback rules for fiscal and monetary policy to hit a fixed nominal GDP growth target.

Because nominal GDP growth equals the real GDP growth rate plus the inflation rate, keeping nominal GDP growth steady does not directly target either real GDP growth or inflation. But nominal GDP usually grows quickly because the inflation rate is high. And nominal GDP usually grows slowly because real GDP growth is negative—the economy is in recession. So the idea is that, by keeping nominal GDP growth steady, both excessive inflation and severe recession might be avoided.

Nominal GDP targeting uses feedback rules. Expansionary fiscal and/or monetary actions increase aggregate demand when nominal GDP is below target; and contractionary fiscal and/or monetary actions decrease aggregate demand when nominal GDP is above target. The main problem with nominal GDP targeting is that there are long and variable time lags between the identification of a need to change aggregate demand and the effects of the policy actions that are taken.

Natural Rate Policies

The business cycle and unemployment policies we've considered have been directed at smoothing the business cycle and minimizing *cyclical unemployment*. It is also possible to pursue policies aimed at lowering the natural rate of unemployment. But there are no costless ways of lowering the natural rate of unemployment. Let's look at two possible ways.

One policy tool is unemployment compensation. To lower the natural rate of unemployment, the government might lower the unemployment compensation rate, or shorten the period for which compensation is paid, or restrict compensation to people who undertake training programs that increase the likelihood of their finding jobs. With lower compensation, an unemployed person would spend less time looking for a job and would accept a job even if it was not a good match for the person's skills. But such a policy might create hardship and have a cost that exceeds the cost of a high natural rate of unemployment.

The government might lower the minimum real wage rate. It could achieve a cut in the minimum wage either by holding the minimum money wage rate constant and letting inflation cut the minimum real wage rate or by cutting the minimum money wage rate. A lower minimum real wage rate increases the quantity of labour demanded and lowers unemployment. The government faces the tradeoff between the real wage rate and the unemployment rate.

R E V I E W   Q U I Z

- What is a fixed-rule fiscal policy and a fixed-rule monetary policy?
- Can you provide two examples of fixed rules in everyday life (other than those in the text)?
- What is a feedback fiscal policy and a feedback monetary policy?
- When might a feedback policy be used? Can you provide two examples of feedback rules in everyday life (other than those in the text)?
- Why do some economists say that feedback rules do not necessarily deliver a better macroeconomic performance than fixed rules? Do you agree or disagree with them? Why?

We've studied growth policy and business cycle and unemployment policy. Let's now study inflation policy.

Inflation Policy

THERE ARE TWO INFLATION POLICY PROBLEMS. In times of price level stability, the problem is to prevent inflation from breaking out. In times of inflation, the problem is to reduce its rate and restore price stability. Preventing inflation from breaking out means avoiding both demand-pull and cost-push forces. Avoiding demand-pull inflation is the flip side of avoiding demand-driven recession and is achieved by stabilizing aggregate demand. So the business cycle and unemployment policy we've just studied is also an anti-inflation policy. But avoiding cost-push inflation raises some special issues that we need to consider. So we will look at two issues for inflation policy:

■ Avoiding cost-push inflation
■ Slowing inflation

Avoiding Cost-Push Inflation

Cost-push inflation is inflation that has its origins in cost increases. In 1973–1974 and again in 1979, the world oil price exploded. Cost shocks such as these become inflationary if they are accommodated by an increase in the quantity of money. Such an increase in the quantity of money can occur if a monetary policy feedback rule is used. A fixed-rule policy for the money stock makes cost-push inflation impossible. Let's see why.

Figure 34.8 shows the economy at full employment. Aggregate demand is AD_0, short-run aggregate supply is SAS_0, and long-run aggregate supply is LAS. Real GDP is $800 billion, and the GDP deflator is 110. Now suppose that OPEC tries to gain a temporary advantage by increasing the price of oil. The short-run aggregate supply curve shifts leftward from SAS_0 to SAS_1.

FIGURE 34.8
Responding to an OPEC Oil Price Increase

(a) Fixed rule

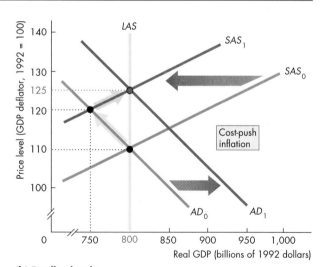

(b) Feedback rule

The economy starts out on AD_0 and SAS_0, with a GDP deflator of 110 and real GDP of $800 billion. OPEC forces up the price of oil, and the short-run aggregate supply curve shifts to SAS_1. Real GDP decreases to $750 billion, and the GDP deflator increases to 120. With a fixed-rule policy (part a), the Bank of Canada makes no change to aggregate demand. The economy

stays in a recession until the price of oil falls again and the economy returns to its original position. With a feedback-rule policy (part b), the Bank injects additional money and the aggregate demand curve shifts to AD_1. Real GDP returns to $800 billion (potential GDP), but the GDP deflator increases to 125. The economy is set for another round of cost-push inflation.

Monetarist Fixed Rule   Figure 34.8(a) shows what happens if the Bank of Canada follows a fixed rule for monetary policy and the government follows a fixed rule for fiscal policy. Suppose that the fixed rule is for zero money growth and no change in taxes or government expenditures on goods and services. With these fixed rules, the Bank and the government pay no attention to the fact that there has been an increase in the price of oil. No policy actions are taken. The short-run aggregate supply curve has shifted to SAS_1, but the aggregate demand curve remains at AD_0. The GDP deflator rises to 120, and real GDP decreases to $750 billion. The economy has experienced *stagflation*. With unemployment above the natural rate, the money wage rate will eventually fall. The low level of real GDP and low sales will probably also bring a fall in the price of oil. These events shift the short-run aggregate supply curve back to SAS_0. The GDP deflator will fall to 110 and real GDP will increase to $800 billion. But this adjustment might take a long time.

Keynesian Feedback Rule   Figure 34.8(b) shows what happens if the Bank of Canada and government operate a feedback rule. The starting point is the same as before—the economy is on SAS_0 and AD_0 with a GDP deflator of 110 and real GDP of $800 billion. OPEC raises the price of oil, and the short-run aggregate supply curve shifts to SAS_1. Real GDP decreases to $750 billion, and the price level rises to 120.

A feedback rule is followed. With potential GDP perceived to be $800 billion and with actual real GDP at $750 billion, the Bank pumps money into the economy and the government increases its spending and lowers taxes. Aggregate demand increases and the aggregate demand curve shifts rightward to AD_1. The price level rises to 125 and real GDP returns to $800 billion. The economy moves back to full employment but at a higher price level. The economy has experienced *cost-push inflation*.

The Bank of Canada responded in the way we've just described to the first wave of OPEC price increases in the mid-1970s. OPEC sees the same advantage in forcing up the price of oil again. A new rise in the price of oil decreases aggregate supply, and the short-run aggregate supply curve shifts leftward once more. The Bank chases it with an increase in aggregate demand, and the economy is in a free-wheeling inflation. Realizing this danger, the Bank did *not* respond to the second wave of OPEC price increases in the early 1980s as it had done before. Instead, the Bank held firm and even slowed the growth of aggregate demand to further dampen the inflation consequences of OPEC's actions.

Incentives to Push Up Costs   You can see that there are no checks on the incentives to push up *nominal* costs if the Bank of Canada accommodates price hikes. If some group sees a temporary gain from pushing up the price at which they are selling their resources and if the Bank always accommodates the increase to prevent unemployment and slack business conditions from emerging, then cost-push elements will have a free rein. But when the Bank pursues a fixed-rule policy, the incentive to attempt to steal a temporary advantage from a price increase is severely weakened. The cost of higher unemployment and lower output is a consequence that each group will have to face and recognize.

Thus a fixed rule can deliver steady inflation, while a feedback rule, in the face of cost-push pressures, leaves inflation free to rise and fall at the whim of whichever group believes a temporary advantage to be available from pushing up its price.

Slowing Inflation

So far, we've concentrated on *avoiding* inflation. But often the problem is not to avoid inflation but to tame it. Canada was in such a situation during the late 1970s and early 1980s. How can inflation, once it has set in, be cured? We'll look at two cases:

■ A surprise inflation reduction
■ A credible announced inflation reduction

A Surprise Inflation Reduction   We'll use two equivalent approaches to study the problem of lowering inflation: the *AS–AD* model and the Phillips curve. The *AS–AD* model tells us about real GDP and the price level, while the Phillips curve, which is explained in Chapter 30 (pp. 678–682), lets us keep track of inflation and unemployment.

Figure 34.9 illustrates the economy at full employment with inflation raging at 10 percent a year. In part (a), the economy is on aggregate demand curve AD_0 and short-run aggregate supply curve SAS_0. Real GDP is $800 billion, and the GDP deflator is 110. The economy is on its *LAS* curve, so real GDP equals potential GDP and the economy is at full employment. Equivalently, in part (b), the economy is on its long-run Phillips curve, *LRPC*, and short-run Phillips curve, $SRPC_0$. The inflation rate of 10 percent a year is anticipated, so unemployment is

788

CHAPTER 34 MACROECONOMIC POLICY CHALLENGES

FIGURE 34.9

Lowering Inflation

(a) Aggregate demand and aggregate supply

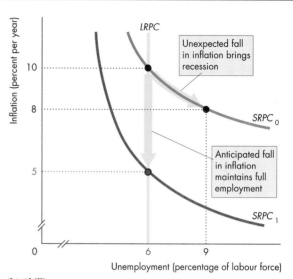

(b) Phillips curves

In part (a), aggregate demand is AD_0, short-run aggregate sup-ply is SAS_0, and real GDP and potential GDP are $800 billion. The aggregate demand curve is expected to shift and actually shifts to AD_1. The short-run aggregate supply curve shifts to SAS_1. The GDP deflator rises to 121 but real GDP remains at $800 billion. Inflation is proceeding at 10 percent a year, and this inflation rate is anticipated. In part (b), which shows this same situation, the economy is on the short-run Phillips curve $SRPC_0$ and on the long-run Phillips curve $LRPC$. Unemployment is at the natural rate of 6 percent and inflation is 10 percent a year. An unexpected slowdown in aggregate demand growth

means that the aggregate demand curve shifts from AD_0 to AD_2, real GDP decreases to $750 billion, and inflation slows to 8 percent (GDP deflator is 118.8). Unemployment rises to 9 percent as the economy slides down $SRPC_0$. An anticipated, credible, announced slowdown in aggregate demand growth means that when the aggregate demand curve shifts from AD_0 to AD_2, the short-run aggregate supply curve shifts from SAS_0, to SAS_2. The short-run Phillips curve shifts to $SRPC_1$. Inflation slows to 5 percent, real GDP remains at $800 billion, and unemployment remains at its natural rate of 6 percent.

at its natural rate, 6 percent of the labour force.

Next year, aggregate demand is *expected* to increase and the aggregate demand curve in Fig. 34.9(a) is expected to shift rightward from AD_0 to AD_1. In expectation of this increase in aggregate demand, the money wage rate rises and shifts the short-run aggregate supply curve from SAS_0 to SAS_1. If expectations are fulfilled, the GDP deflator rises to 121—a 10 percent inflation—and real GDP remains at potential GDP. In part (b) the economy remains at its original position—unemployment is at the natural rate and the inflation rate is 10 percent a year.

Now suppose that no one is expecting the Bank to change its policy, but it actually tries to slow infla-tion. It raises interest rates and slows money growth.

Aggregate demand growth slows, and the aggregate demand curve (in part a) shifts rightward from AD_0 not to AD_1, as people expect, but only to AD_2.

With no change in the expected inflation rate, the money wage rate rises by the same amount as before and the short-run aggregate supply curve shifts leftward from SAS_0 to SAS_1. Real GDP decreases to $750 billion, and the GDP deflator rises to 118.8—an inflation rate of 8 percent a year. In Fig. 34.9(b) the economy moves along the short-run Phillips curve $SRPC_0$ as unemployment rises to 9 percent and inflation falls to 8 percent a year. The Bank's policy has succeeded in slowing inflation but at the cost of recession. Real GDP is below potential GDP, and unemployment is above its natural rate.

A Credible Announced Inflation Reduction

Suppose that instead of simply slowing down the growth of aggregate demand, the Bank of Canada announces its intention ahead of its action and in a credible and convincing way so that its announcement is believed. That is, the Bank's policy is anticipated. Because the lower level of aggregate demand is expected, the money wage rate increases at a pace consistent with the lower level of aggregate demand. The short-run aggregate supply curve (in Fig. 34.9a) shifts leftward from SAS_0 but only to SAS_2. Aggregate demand increases by the amount expected, and the aggregate demand curve shifts from AD_0 to AD_2. The GDP deflator rises to 115.5—an inflation rate of 5 percent a year—and real GDP remains at potential GDP.

In Fig. 34.9(b) the lower expected inflation rate shifts the short-run Phillips curve downward to $SRPC_1$, and inflation falls to 5 percent a year while unemployment remains at its natural rate of 6 percent.

A credible announced inflation reduction lowers inflation but with no accompanying loss of output or increase in unemployment.

Inflation Reduction in Practice

When the Bank of Canada in fact slowed inflation in 1981, we paid a high price. The Bank's policy action was unpredicted. It occurred in the face of a money wage rate that had been set at too high a level to be consistent with the growth of aggregate demand that the Bank subsequently allowed. The consequence was recession—a decrease in real GDP and a rise in unemployment. Could the Bank have lowered inflation without causing recession by telling people far enough ahead of time that it did indeed plan to lower inflation?

The answer appears to be no. The main reason is that people expect the Bank to behave in line with its record, not with its stated intentions. How many times have you told yourself that it is your firm intention to take off five unwanted kilograms or to keep within your budget and put a few dollars away for a rainy day, only to discover that, despite your very best intentions, your old habits win out in the end?

To form expectations of the Bank's actions, people look at the Bank's past *actions*, not its stated intentions. Based on such observations—called Bank-watching—they try to work out what the Bank's policy is, to forecast its future actions, and to forecast the effects of those actions on aggregate demand and inflation. The Bank of Canada now has a solid reputation for being anti-inflationary. That reputation is

valuable because it helps the Bank of Canada to contain inflation and lowers the cost of eliminating inflation if it temporarily returns. The reason is that with a low expected inflation rate, the short-run Phillips curve is in a favourable position (like $SRPC_1$ in Fig. 34.9b). The Bank's actions during the 1990s have been designed to keep inflation expectations low and prevent the gains made during the 1980s recession from being eroded.

A Truly Independent Bank

A radical suggestion for strengthening the Bank's reputation as the guardian of price stability is to make the Bank more independent of government and to charge it with the single responsibility of achieving and maintaining price level stability. Some central banks are more independent than the Bank of Canada. The German and Swiss central banks are the best examples. Another example is the New Zealand central bank. All these central banks have the responsibility of stabilizing prices but not real GDP and of pursuing their objective without interference from the government. Recent research on central bank performance has strengthened the view that a more independent central bank can deliver a lower average inflation rate without creating either a higher unemployment rate or a lower real GDP growth rate.

R E V I E W   Q U I Z

- Why does a fixed rule provide more effective protection against a cost-push inflation than a feedback rule?
- Why does a recession usually result as inflation is being tamed?
- How does establishing a reputation of being an inflation fighter improve the ability of the Bank to maintain low inflation and to lower the cost of fighting inflation?

◆ *Reading Between the Lines* on pages 790–791 looks at the challenges the Bank of Canada faced in 1999 as it sought to keep the economy expanding, lowering unemployment, but avoiding renewed inflation.

You've now completed your study of macroeconomics. In the remaining chapters, we shift our focus to the international economy.

Unemployment and the Bank of Canada

THE GLOBE AND MAIL, APRIL 10, 1999

Stalled unemployment rate prompts talk of an interest rate cut

BY SHAWN MCCARTHY

Canada's employment market shifted into reverse in March, fueling speculation among some economists that the Bank of Canada may soon cut interest rates again.

Nationally, the country dropped 29,200 jobs in March, although the unemployment rate remained steady at 7.8 per cent because fewer people were actively looking for work.

The job losses were in part-time, private sector jobs and were concentrated among 15- to 24-year-olds. Full-time employment actually grew by 14,000 positions in March, and is up 3.4 per cent or 393,000 jobs since March, 1998.

Economists don't expect the downturn to continue, however, predicting more job gains in the months to come. Since last June, the last time employment fell, the Canadian economy has added 384,000 jobs.

"There is a lot more strength than the report suggests," said Sherry Cooper, chief economist at Nesbitt Burns Inc.

She noted that the country continued to add full-time jobs, and that the slowdown in retail and construction was related to nasty winter weather in early March.

Still, Ms. Cooper said she believes the central bank will cut rates at least two more times before the end of the year, and yesterday's employment report will do nothing to dissuade it. ...

Marc Lévesque, economist with Toronto-Dominion Bank, said financial markets had expected the Bank of Canada to move as early as yesterday, after the Japanese and several European banks cut rates.

"The weak tone of the March employment report should be enough to keep the markets' perception of a bias towards easier monetary policy firmly intact," he said.

Last week, the Bank of Canada cut its trend-setting bank rate for overnight loans to financial institutions to 5 per cent, sparking a similar move in the prime lending rate to 6.5 per cent. Prime is the rate charged the most creditworthy customers for business and consumer loans.

Royal Bank of Canada chief economist John McCallum argued that the central bank may not ease monetary policy any further since the combination of low interest rates and a low dollar already amount to highly stimulative conditions. ...

Essence of the Story

■ Canada's unemployment rate in March 1999 remained unchanged at 7.8 percent.

■ Economists differ in how they expect monetary policy to respond to the steady unemployment rate.

■ Economist Sherry Cooper of Nesbitt Burns Inc. believes that the Bank of Canada will cut interest rates at least twice before year end.

■ Economist Marc Lévesque of Toronto-Dominion Bank says that the March unemployment report encourages easier monetary policy.

■ Economist John McCallum of the Royal Bank of Canada disagrees. He believes that low interest rates are already stimulating the Canadian economy sufficiently.

Economic Analysis

- Since 1988, the primary goal of the Bank of Canada has been to keep Canada's inflation rate between 1 and 3 percent a year.

- During this period, the Bank's actions have looked more like a fixed-rule policy than a feedback-rule policy.

- Because the Bank of Canada has pursued a fixed-rule policy, we can gain some insight into how such a policy works by studying the performance of money growth, inflation, and unemployment during the years since 1988.

- Figure 1 shows the relationship between the growth rate of M2+, the broadest indicator of monetary policy in Canada, and the inflation rate since 1988.

- The overall trend of M2+ growth has been downward and the overall trend of inflation has also been downward.

- You can see that when the M2+ growth rate temporarily increased in 1989 and 1995, the inflation rate also temporarily increased.

- Following negative M2+ growth in 1997, the Bank of Canada increased the growth rate of money in 1998, but the inflation rate continued to fall.

- When the Bank of Canada decreases the growth rate of M2+, the growth rate of aggregate demand decreases. And when the growth rate of aggregate demand decreases, the growth rate of real GDP decreases and the unemployment rate *increases*.

- Figure 2 shows the M2+ growth rate and the unemployment rate since 1988. You can see that between 1989 and 1992, as the M2+ growth rate decreased, the unemployment rate increased.

- But after 1992, despite a continued decrease in the M2+ growth rate, the unemployment rate began to decrease. Why?

- The reason is that aggregate demand and short-run aggregate supply *together* determine real GDP and the unemployment rate.

- The more the Bank of Canada persisted in its focus on low inflation, the more people came to expect the lower growth rate of aggregate demand. Consequently, the rate of increase in the money wage rate slowed.

Figure 1 Money growth and inflation

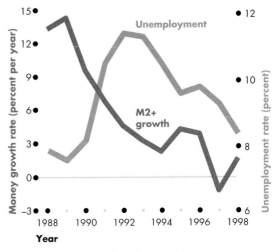

Figure 2 Money growth and unemployment

- With a lower rate of increase in the money wage rate, the growth rate of short-run aggregate supply increased. Inflation continued to slow, but the growth rate of real GDP increased and the unemployment rate decreased.

- It seems likely that the unemployment rate in 1999 is getting close to the natural rate and if a further decrease in unemployment is to be achieved, measures will be needed to lower the natural rate rather than to stimulate aggregate demand.

S U M M A R Y

Key Points

Policy Goals (pp. 772–773)

- The goals of macroeconomic policy are to achieve the highest sustainable rate of long-term real GDP growth, smooth the business cycle, maintain low unemployment, and avoid inflation.

Policy Tools and Performance (pp. 774–776)

- Fiscal policy was expansionary during the Trudeau–Turner years and contractionary during the Mulroney and Chrétien years.
- There have been four phases of monetary policy since 1975: (1) permit inflation to rise, (2) bring inflation down, (3) eliminate inflation, and (4) keep inflation low and encourage expansion.

Long-Term Growth Policy (pp. 776–778)

- Policies to increase the long-term growth rate focus on increasing saving and investment in human capital and new technologies.
- To increase the saving rate, government saving must increase or incentives for private saving must be strengthened by increasing after-tax returns.
- Human capital investment might be increased with improved education and by improving on-the-job training programs.
- Investment in new technologies can be encouraged by tax incentives.

Business Cycle and Unemployment Policy (pp. 779–785)

- In the face of an aggregate demand shock, a fixed-rule policy takes no action. Real GDP and the price level fluctuate.
- In the face of an aggregate demand shock, a feedback-rule policy takes offsetting fiscal and monetary action. An ideal feedback rule keeps the economy at full employment, with stable prices.
- Feedback rules create fluctuations because policy lags extend beyond our forecast horizon.

- In the face of a productivity growth slowdown, both rules have the same effect on output. A feedback rule brings a higher inflation rate than does a fixed rule.
- Nominal GDP targeting might avoid the extremes of inflation and recession.

Inflation Policy (pp. 786–789)

- A fixed rule minimizes the threat of cost-push inflation. A feedback rule validates cost-push inflation and leaves the price level and inflation rate free to move to wherever they are pushed.
- Inflation can be tamed, at little or no cost in terms of lost output or excessive unemployment, by slowing the growth of aggregate demand in a credible and predictable way. But usually, when inflation is slowed down, a recession occurs.

Key Figures ◆

Key Terms

PROBLEMS

*1. A productivity growth slowdown has occurred. Explain its possible origins and describe a policy package that is designed to speed up growth again.

2. A nation is experiencing a falling saving rate. Explain its possible origins and describe a policy package that is designed to increase the saving rate.

*3. The economy shown in the figure is initially on aggregate demand curve AD_0 and short-run aggregate supply curve SAS. Then aggregate demand decreases and the aggregate demand curve shifts leftward to AD_1.

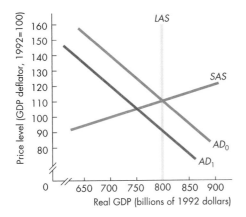

a. What is the initial equilibrium real GDP and price level?
b. If the decrease in aggregate demand is temporary and the government follows a fixed-rule fiscal policy, what happens to real GDP and the price level? Trace the immediate effects and the adjustment as aggregate demand returns to its original level.
c. If the decrease in aggregate demand is temporary and the government follows a feedback-rule fiscal policy, what happens to real GDP and the price level? Trace the immediate effects and the adjustment as aggregate demand returns to its original level.
d. If the decrease in aggregate demand is permanent and the government follows a fixed-rule fiscal policy, what happens to real GDP and the price level?

e. If the decrease in aggregate demand is permanent and the government follows a feedback-rule fiscal policy, what happens to real GDP and the price level?

4. The economy shown in the figure is initially on aggregate demand curve AD and short-run aggregate supply curve SAS_0. Then short-run aggregate supply decreases and the short-run aggregate supply curve shifts leftward to SAS_1.

a. What is the initial equilibrium real GDP and price level?
b. What type of event could have caused the decrease in short-run aggregate supply?
c. If the government follows a fixed-rule monetary policy, what happens to real GDP and the price level? Trace the immediate effects and the adjustment as short-run aggregate supply returns to its original level.
d. If the government follows a feedback-rule monetary policy, what happens to real GDP and the price level? Trace the immediate effects and the adjustment as aggregate demand and short-run aggregate supply respond to the policy action.

*5. The economy is experiencing 10 percent inflation and 7 percent unemployment. Real GDP growth has sagged to 1 percent a year. The stock market has crashed.

a. Explain how the economy might have gotten into its current state.
b. Set out policies for the Bank of Canada and the government to pursue that will lower inflation, lower unemployment, and speed real GDP growth.

c. Explain how and why your proposed policies will work.

6. The inflation rate has fallen to 1 percent a year but the unemployment rate is stubborn and has not fallen much. Real GDP is growing at more than 3 percent a year. The stock market is at a record high.

  a. Explain how the economy might have gotten into its current state.

  b. Set out policies for the Bank of Canada and the government to pursue that will keep inflation low, lower unemployment, and maintain a high real GDP growth rate.

  c. Explain how and why your proposed policies will work.

*7. When the economies of Indonesia, Korea, Thailand, Malaysia, and the Philippines entered into recession in 1997, the International Monetary Fund (IMF) made loans but only on condition that the recipients of the loans increased interest rates, raised taxes, and cut government expenditures.

  a. Would you describe the IMF prescription as a feedback-rule policy or a fixed-rule policy?

  b. What do you predict the effects of the IMF policies would be?

  c. Do you have any criticisms of the IMF policies? What would you have required these countries to do? Why?

8. As the Canadian economy continued to expand and its stock market soared to new record levels during 1998, the Bank of Canada cut interest rates.

  a. Would you describe the Bank of Canada's actions as a feedback-rule policy or a fixed-rule policy?

  b. What do you predict the effects of the Bank of Canada's policies would be?

  c. Do you have any criticisms of the Bank of Canada's policies? What monetary policy would you have pursued? Why?

CRITICAL THINKING

1. Study *Reading Between the Lines* on pp. 790–791 and then:

  a. Describe the dilemma faced by the Bank of Canada and explain why the dilemma was particularly acute during 1999.

  b. What is the short-run relationship between inflation and unemployment?

  c. What signs do you look for to determine whether the economy is in a "danger zone" in which inflation is likely to take off?

  d. What, in your opinion, does the Bank of Canada's dilemma of 1999 tell us about the relative merits of a fixed-rule monetary policy and a feedback-rule monetary policy?

2. The economy is booming, and inflation is beginning to rise, but it is widely agreed that a massive recession is just around the corner. Weigh the advantages and disadvantages of Parliament pursuing a fixed-rule and a feedback-rule for *fiscal* policy.

3. The economy is in a recession, and inflation is falling. It is widely agreed that a strong recovery is just around the corner. Weigh the advantages and disadvantages of the Bank of Canada pursuing a fixed-rule and a feedback-rule for *monetary* policy.

4. You have been hired to draw up an economic plan that will maximize the chance of the government being re-elected.

  a. What are the macroeconomic stabilization policy elements in that plan?

  b. What do you have to make the economy do in an election year?

  c. What policy actions would help the prime minister achieve re-election?

  (In dealing with this problem, be careful to take into account the effects of your proposed policy on expectations and the effects of those expectations on actual economic performance.)

5. Use the links on the Parkin-Bade Web site to visit the Finance Department and Bank of Canada Web sites. Obtain information on the current state of the economy and of policy. Write a summary and critique of what you discover.

Understanding Aggregate Supply and Economic Growth

Economics is about how we cope with scarcity. We cope by making choices that balance marginal benefits and marginal costs so that we use our scarce resources efficiently. ◆ These choices determine how much work we do; how hard we work at school to learn the mental skills that form our human capital and that determine the kinds of jobs we get and the incomes we earn; and how much we save for future big ticket expenditures. These choices also determine how much businesses and governments spend on new capital—on auto assembly lines, computers and fibre

Expanding the Frontier

cables for improved Internet services, shopping malls, highways, bridges, and tunnels; how intensively existing capital and natural resources are used and therefore how quickly they wear out or are used up. And most significant of all, these choices determine the problems that scientists, engineers, and other inventors work on to develop new technologies. ◆ All the choices we've just described determine two vital measures of economic performance:

■ Real GDP

■ Economic growth

Real GDP is determined by the quantity of labour, the quantity of capital, and the state of technological knowledge. And economic growth—the growth rate of real GDP—is determined by growth in the quantity of labour, by capital accumulation, and by technological advances. ◆ Economic growth, maintained at a steady rate over a number of decades, is the single most powerful influence on any society. It brings a transformation that continues to amaze thoughtful people. Economic growth, maintained at a rapid rate, can transform a society in years, not decades. Such transformations are taking place right now in many Asian countries. These transformations are economic miracles. ◆ The four chapters in this part study the miracle of rapid economic growth, the forces that shape our capacity to produce goods and services, and the forces that from time to time interrupt the growth process. ◆ Chapter 31 explains how labour market equilibrium determines potential GDP. Chapter 32 studies the process of economic growth in the fast-growing economies of Asia and Canada. It explains how growth is influenced by technological change and the incentives that stimulate it. Chapter 33 studies the business cycle that interrupts growth, and Chapter 34 reviews the policy debate and looks at alternative approaches to speeding growth, smoothing the business cycle, and containing inflation.

◇ Modern ideas about economic growth and fluctuations owe much to two economists, Joseph Schumpeter and Paul Romer, whom you can meet on the following pages.

The Economist

Joseph Schumpeter, *the son of a textile factory owner, was born in Austria in 1883. He moved from Austria to Germany during the tumultuous 1920s when those two countries experienced hyperinflation. And in 1932, in the depths of the Great Depression, he left Europe for the United States and became a professor of economics at Harvard University.*

This creative economic thinker wrote on economic growth and development, business cycles, political systems, and economic biography. He was a person of strong opinions who expressed them skilfully and forcefully and delighted in verbal battles.

Schumpeter has become the unwitting founder of modern growth theory. He saw the development and diffusion of new technologies by profit-seeking entrepreneurs as the source of economic progress. But he saw economic progress as a process of creative destruction—the creation of new profit opportunities and the destruction of currently profitable businesses. For Schumpeter, economic growth and the business cycle were a single phenomenon.

When Schumpeter died, in 1950, he had achieved his self-expressed life ambition: He was regarded as the world's greatest economist.

"Economic progress, in capitalist society, means turmoil. "

JOSEPH SCHUMPETER,
CAPITALISM, SOCIALISM,
AND DEMOCRACY

The Issues

Technological change, capital accumulation, and population growth all interact to produce economic growth. But what is cause and what is effect and can we expect productivity and income per person to keep growing?

The classical economists of the eighteenth and nineteenth centuries believed that technological advances and capital accumulation were the engines of growth. But they also believed that no matter how successful people were at inventing more productive technologies and investing in new capital, they were destined to live at the subsistence level. These economists based their conclusion on the belief that productivity growth causes population growth, which in turn causes productivity to decline. These classical economists believed that whenever economic growth raises incomes above the subsistence level, the population will increase. They went on to reason that the increase in population brings diminishing returns that lower productivity. As a result, incomes must always return to the subsistence level. Only when incomes are at the subsistence level is population growth held in check.

A new approach, called neoclassical growth theory, was developed by Robert Solow of MIT during the 1950s. Solow, who was one of

Schumpeter's students, received the Nobel Prize for Economic Science for this work.

Solow challenged the conclusions of the classical economists. But the new theories of economic growth developed during the 1980s and 1990s went further. They stand the classical belief on its head. Today's theory of population growth is that rising income slows the population growth rate because it increases the opportunity cost of having children and lowers the opportunity cost of investing in children and equipping them with more human capital, which makes them more productive. Productivity and income grow because technology advances and the scope for further productivity growth, which is stimulated by the search for profit, is practically unlimited.

Then ...

In 1830, a strong and experienced farm worker could harvest three acres of wheat in a day. The only capital employed was a scythe to cut the wheat, which had been used since Roman times, and a cradle on which the stalks were laid, which had been invented by Flemish farmers in the fifteenth century. With newly developed horse-drawn ploughs, harrows, and planters, farmers could plant more wheat than they could harvest. But despite big efforts, no one had been able to make a machine that could replicate the swing of a scythe. Then in 1831, the 22-year-old Cyrus McCormick built a machine that worked. It scared the horse that pulled it, but it did in a matter of hours what three men could accomplish in a day. Technological change has increased productivity on farms and brought economic growth. Do the facts about productivity growth mean that the classical economists, who believed that diminishing returns would push us relentlessly back to a subsistence living standard, were wrong?

... and Now

Today's technologies are expanding our horizons beyond the confines of our planet and are expanding our minds. Geosynchronous satellites bring us global television, voice and data communication, and more accurate weather forecasts, which incidentally increase agricultural productivity. In the foreseeable future, we might have superconductors that revolutionize the use of electric power, virtual reality theme parks and training facilities, pollution-free hydrogen cars, wristwatch telephones, and optical computers that we can talk to. Equipped with these new technologies, our ability to create yet more dazzling technologies increases. Technological change begets technological change in an (apparently) unending process and makes us ever more productive and brings ever higher incomes.

Today's revolution in the way economists think about economic growth has been led by Paul Romer, a professor of economics at Stanford University, whom you can meet on the following pages.

797

Talking with
Paul Romer

Paul Romer is *Professor of Economics at the Graduate School of Business at Stanford University and the Royal Bank Fellow of the Canadian Institute for Advanced Research. Born in 1955 in Denver, Colorado, he earned his B.S. in Mathematics (1977) and his Ph.D. in Economics (1983) from the University of Chicago.*

Professor Romer has transformed the way economists think about economic growth. He believes that sustained economic growth arises from competition among firms. Firms try to increase their profits by devoting resources to creating new products and developing new ways of making existing products.

Robin Bade and Michael Parkin talked with Professor Romer about his work, how he was influenced by Joseph Schumpeter and Robert Solow, and the insights economic growth offers us.

Professor Romer, why did you decide to become an economist?

As an undergraduate, I studied math and physics and was interested in becoming a cosmologist. During my senior year, I concluded that job prospects in physics were not very promising, so I decided to go to law school. I was an undergraduate at the University of Chicago, where the law and economics movement first emerged. In the fall of my senior year, I took my first economics course to prepare for law school. My economics professor, Sam Peltzman, presented a simple piece of economic analysis that changed my life. He argued that the demand for economists was likely to grow for decades. The government, which employs economists, would grow in size. Businesses that deal with the government would want their own economists. The legal profession that serves businesses would also need more economists. Because of all these demands, many students would want to take economics courses. This meant that there would be many job openings for economists at universities. Moreover, he claimed, being a professor of economics was a lot like being a cosmologist and far more fun than being a lawyer. I could take fragmentary bits of evidence and try to make sense of them using mathematical equations. So I tore up my law school applications, applied to graduate school in economics, and never looked back.

What are the truly important lessons about the causes of economic growth?

As a physics major, I felt that the description economists used for growth violated a basic law of physics: the conservation of mass. Economists seemed to be saying that GDP, the output of a nation, was a bunch of stuff that was "produced" and that the quantity of stuff produced has grown steadily over time and will continue to do so. But this can't be right. We have the same amount of stuff, or elements from the periodic table, that we had 100,000 years ago because there are many more people now. In terms of kilograms of matter per person, we know that we are vastly poorer than our ancestors were 100,000 years ago. Yet we clearly have a higher standard of living. How could this be? This basic question indicates that thinking about growth as a production process that generates stuff is a dead-end. Instead, economic growth has to be about rearranging the fixed amount of matter that we have to work with and making new combinations that seem a lot more valuable. The key insight is that economic growth comes from increases in value, not increases in the amount of matter.

Can you give us an example of an increase in value?

For tens of thousands of years, we treated iron oxide, ordinary rust, like dirt. When we lived in caves, we learned how to use it as a pigment for decorating cave walls. We took the low-value dirt and put it to the higher-valued use of making cave paintings. Later, we learned how to extract the iron from iron ore to make bridges and rails. Later still, we learned how to arrange the iron atoms together with carbon atoms and make steel. Recently, we learned how to take iron oxide and put it on magnetic tape and use it to store sound and pictures. The iron, oxygen, and carbon atoms have always been here. We have a higher standard of living because we have learned how to arrange these atoms in ways that we find more valuable.

What kind of policy implications does this kind of thinking lead to?

Policy makers must encourage institutions to become more efficient at discovering new recipes to rearrange matter. Consider the transistor as an example. We take silicon and mix it with a few impurities and some metal in just the right way, and we get a computer chip worth thousands of times what the raw ingredients were worth. Research grants, subsidies for education, and institutions like the nonprofit private university encourage the production of new recipes or ideas. But so do venture capitalists who help new-technology startups, competitive markets that allow the firms with better instructions or ideas to quickly displace existing firms, and labour laws that let inefficient firms lay off workers when more efficient new firms come on the scene. We must let firms like Digital Electronics or Wang Computers shrink, maybe even fail, if we want to make room for new firms like Intel to enter the scene and thrive.

Were the classical economists wrong in their view that population growth and diminishing returns are the dominant long-term influences on production and incomes? Or is the current global population explosion part of a process that will ultimately prove them correct?

Classical economists like Malthus and Ricardo were right when they argued that we have a fixed amount of natural resources to work with. Malthus pointed out that resource scarcity will lead to falling standards of living if we continue to work with the same set of recipes or instructions for using our resources. Where he went wrong was in assuming that there was little scope for us to find new recipes for taking resources such as land, water, carbon dioxide, nitrogen, and sunshine and converting them into carbohydrates and proteins that we can eat.

The classical economists got half of the story right. We do live in a world with scarce resources. They missed the other half. There is an incomprehensibly large number of different formulas we can use to recombine these scarce resources into things we value, such as protein or entertainment.

We take silicon and mix it with a few impurities and some metal in just the right way, and we get a computer chip worth thousands of times what the raw ingredients were worth.

Scarcity is a very important part of economics and our lives. For example, we know that there is an absolute limit on the number of people who can live on the earth. One way or another, we know that the rate of population growth will slow down. It's only a question of how and when. But will this ultimately lead to a period when standards of living fall as Malthus predicted? I doubt it. As countries get rich, population growth slows. As a larger fraction of the worldwide population becomes educated, these people will help us to discover new things, like plants that are more efficient at taking carbon dioxide out of the atmosphere, and more efficient distribution systems. Thus standards of living for all humans will continue to improve.

Despite the recession of the late 1990s, China and several other economies in East Asia have experienced rapid, unheralded growth rates. Why?

These countries took some of the recipes, formulas, and instructions for generating value that already existed in the advanced countries of the world and put them to use within their borders. It's the same process that the Japanese followed after the Meiji restoration at the end of the last century. These countries noticed that other people in the world knew a lot about how to create value and realized that by trading with these people, they could share in the gains.

> *If you can learn how to write readable prose and use the basic tools of mathematics, you can do almost anything.*

What lessons from East Asia can, in principle, be applied in Africa and Central Europe?

The basic insight is that there are huge potential gains from trade. Poor countries can supply their natural and human resources. Rich countries can supply their know-how. When these are combined, everyone can be better off. The challenge is for a country to arrange its laws and institutions so that both sides can profitably engage in trade. If there are barriers to trade or if the government cannot protect basic property rights and prevent crime, trade can't take place. For example, the Japanese have been able to borrow many ideas about manufacturing and design and even to improve on some of these ideas. But because they have barriers that limit entry of foreign firms into the retail sector, they still waste vast quantities of resources on a very inefficient distribution system.

What does today's thinking about economic growth owe to Joseph Schumpeter and Robert Solow?

Schumpeter worked at a time before most economists had learned to work with equations. He coined the phrase "creative destruction," which describes the process by which companies like Wang shrink or go out of business when new firms come in. He also described in words how important monopoly profits are in the process of innovation. There were many other economists, including Alfred Marshall, who described these same issues in verbal terms and also struggled to express these ideas in terms of equations.

Robert Solow was part of the post-World War II generation of economists who truly mastered the use of equations and wrote eloquently using both words and equations. As a result, his ideas have been far more influential than Schumpeter's. Many economists in the 1950s were trying to get a grasp on the economic effects of knowledge, formulas, recipes, and instructions. Solow called these things "technology" and gave us a wonderfully concise and workable way to think about how technology interacts with other economic inputs such as capital and labour. He also linked the methods that he and several economists were using to measure technology with this framework for thinking about the behaviour of the economy as a whole. His work on growth was a masterful piece of invention, synthesis, and exposition.

Recent economists have taken Solow's mathematical framework and extended it to bring in some of the elements that Schumpeter described in words, like creative destruction and monopoly power. One of the great things about ideas is that they build on each other. In Isaac Newton's famous phrase, those of us working on growth today are "able to see farther because we stand on the shoulders of giants." Newton was another person who was pretty good with equations and could turn a good phrase.

Is economics a worthwhile subject to major in? What can one do with an economics degree?

Economics is an excellent training ground for developing mathematical and verbal skills. But students should supplement the courses in economics with courses in mathematics and science that force them to practise working with equations, graphs, and numbers. There is no substitute for such practice. Innate ability is far less important than most students think.

They should also take courses that force them to write, revise, and edit. I took an English course in college that taught me the basics of how to edit, and it is one of the best investments I made. You can't tell what you will end up doing or what skills you will need later in life. But if you can learn how to write readable prose and use the basic tools of mathematics, you can do almost anything.

Chapter 35

Trading with the World

Since ancient times, people have expanded their trading as far as technology allowed. Marco Polo opened up the silk route between Europe and China in the thirteenth century. Today, container ships laden with cars and machines and Boeing 747s stuffed with farm-fresh foods ply sea and air routes, carrying billions of dollars' worth of goods. Why do people go to such great lengths to trade with those in other nations? ◆ Low-wage Mexico has entered into a free trade agreement with high-wage

Silk Routes and Sucking Sounds

Canada and the United States—the North American Free Trade Agreement, or NAFTA. According to Texas billionaire Ross Perot, this agreement has caused a "giant sucking sound" and transferred jobs from Michigan and Ontario to Mexico. Is Perot right? Can we compete with a country that pays its workers a fraction of Canadian wages? Are there any industries, besides perhaps software and movies, in which we have an advantage? ◆ Tariffs—taxes on goods imported from other countries—have been a source of government revenue in Canada since before Confederation and were the centrepiece of Sir John A. Macdonald's national policy of the 1870s. After World War II, a process of trade liberalization brought about a gradual reduction of tariffs. What are the effects of tariffs on international trade? Why don't we have completely unrestricted international trade?

◇ In this chapter, we're going to learn about international trade. We'll discover how *all* nations can gain by specializing in producing the goods and services in which they have a comparative advantage and trading with other countries. We'll discover that *all* countries can compete, no matter how high their wages. We'll also explain why, despite the fact that international trade brings benefits to all, countries restrict trade.

After studying this chapter, you will be able to:

- ■ Describe the patterns in international trade

- ■ Explain comparative advantage and explain why all countries can gain from international trade

- ■ Explain how economies of scale and diversity of taste lead to gains from trade

- ■ Explain why trade restrictions reduce our imports, exports, and consumption possibilities

- ■ Explain the arguments used to justify trade restrictions and show how they are flawed

- ■ Explain why we have trade restrictions

Patterns and Trends in International Trade

THE GOODS AND SERVICES THAT WE BUY FROM people in other countries are called **imports**. The goods and services that we sell to people in other countries are called **exports**. What are the most important things that we import and export? Most people would probably guess that a rich nation such as Canada imports raw materials and exports manufactured goods. Although that is one feature of Canadian international trade, it is not its most important feature. The vast bulk of our exports *and* imports are manufactured goods. We sell foreigners earth-moving equipment, airplanes, and telecommunication and scientific equipment. We buy televisions, VCRs, blue jeans, and T-shirts from foreigners. Also, we are a major exporter of agricultural products and raw materials. We also import and export a huge volume of services.

Trade in Goods

Manufactured goods account for 50 percent of our exports and 70 percent of our imports. Industrial materials (raw materials and semi-manufactured items) account for 40 percent of our exports and 15 percent of our imports, and agricultural products account for only 5 percent of our exports and 2 percent of our imports. Our largest individual export and import items are capital goods and autos.

But goods account for only 80 percent of our exports and imports. The rest of our international trade is in services.

Trade in Services

You may be wondering how a country can "export" and "import" services. Here are some examples.

If you take a vacation in France and travel there on an Air France flight from Montreal, you import transportation services from France. The money you spend in France on hotel bills and restaurant meals is also classified as a Canadian import. Similarly, the vacation taken by a French student in Quebec counts as a Canadian export to France.

When we import TV sets from South Korea, the owner of the ship that transports them might be Greek and the company that insures them might be British.

The payments that we make for the transportation and insurance are imports of services. Similarly, when a Canadian shipping company transports timber from British Columbia to Tokyo, the transportation cost is an export of a service to Japan. Our international trade in these types of services is large and growing.

Geographical Patterns

Canada has trading links with every part of the world, but the United States is our biggest trading partner for both exports and imports. We buy 77 percent of our imports from the United States and sell Americans 84 percent of our exports. Japan, China, Hong Kong, South Korea, and Taiwan along with Europe and Latin America are our other big trading partners.

Trends in the Volume of Trade

In 1978, we exported 22 percent of total output and imported 20 percent of the goods and services that we bought. In 1998, we exported 36 percent of total output and imported 34 percent of the goods and services that we bought.

On the export side, automobiles, capital goods, and raw materials have remained large items and held a roughly constant share of total exports. But the composition of imports has changed. Food and raw material imports have fallen steadily. Imports of fuel increased during the 1970s but decreased during the 1980s. Imports of equipment and machinery have grown and today are 30 percent of total imports.

Balance of Trade and International Borrowing

The value of exports minus the value of imports is called the **balance of trade**. In 1998, the Canadian balance of trade was a positive $13 billion. Our exports were $13 billion more than our imports. When we export more than we import, as we did in 1998, we lend to foreigners or buy more foreign assets. When we import more than we export, we borrow from foreigners or sell some of our assets to foreigners.

In this chapter, our goal is to understand the factors that influence the *volume* and the *direction* of international trade rather than the *balance* of international trade. And the key to this understanding is the concept of comparative advantage.

Comparative Advantage and International Trade

THE FUNDAMENTAL FORCE THAT GENERATES international trade is *comparative advantage*. And the basis of comparative advantage is divergent *opportunity costs*. You met these ideas in Chapter 3, when we learned about the gains from specialization and exchange between Tom and Nancy.

Tom and Nancy each specialize in producing just one good and then trade with each other. Most nations do not go to the extreme of specializing in a single good and importing everything else. Nonetheless, nations can increase the consumption of all goods if they redirect their scarce resources towards the production of those goods and services in which they have a comparative advantage.

To see how this outcome occurs, we'll apply the same basic ideas we learned in the case of Tom and Nancy to trade among nations. We'll begin by recalling how we can use the production possibility frontier to measure opportunity cost. Then we'll see how divergent opportunity costs bring comparative advantage and gains from trade for countries as well as for individuals, even though no country completely specializes in the production of just one good.

Opportunity Cost in Farmland

Farmland (a fictitious country) can produce grain and cars at any point inside or along its production possibility frontier, *PPF*, shown in Fig. 35.1. (We're holding constant the output of all the other goods that Farmland produces.) The Farmers (the people of Farmland) are consuming all the grain and cars that they produce, and they are operating at point *a* in the figure. That is, Farmland is producing and consuming 15 million tonnes of grain and 8 million cars each year. What is the opportunity cost of a car in Farmland?

We can answer that question by calculating the slope of the production possibility frontier at point *a*. The magnitude of the slope of the frontier measures the opportunity cost of one good in terms of the other. To measure the slope of the frontier at point *a*, place a straight line tangential to the frontier at point *a* and calculate the slope of that straight line. Recall that the formula for the slope of a line is the change in the value of the variable measured on the *y*-axis divided by the change in the value of the variable

measured on the *x*-axis as we move along the line. Here, the variable measured on the *y*-axis is millions of tonnes of grain, and the variable measured on the *x*-axis is millions of cars. So the slope is the change in the number of tonnes of grain divided by the change in the number of cars.

As you can see from the red triangle at point *a* in the figure, if the number of cars produced increases by 2 million, grain production decreases by 18 million tonnes. Therefore the magnitude of the slope is 18 million divided by 2 million, which equals 9. To get one more car, the people of Farmland must give up 9 tonnes of grain. Thus the opportunity cost of 1 car is 9 tonnes of grain. Equivalently, 9 tonnes of grain cost 1 car. For the people of Farmland, these opportunity costs are the prices they face. The price of a car is 9 tonnes of grain, and the price of 9 tonnes of grain is 1 car.

FIGURE 35.1

Opportunity Cost in Farmland

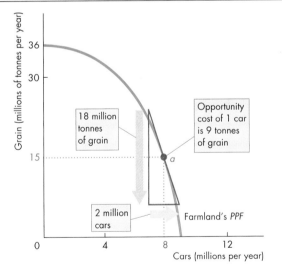

Farmland produces and consumes 15 million tonnes of grain and 8 million cars a year. That is, it produces and consumes at point *a* on its production possibility frontier. Opportunity cost is equal to the magnitude of the slope of the production possibility frontier. The red triangle tells us that at point *a*, 18 million tonnes of grain must be forgone to get 2 million cars. That is, at point *a*, 2 million cars cost 18 million tonnes of grain. Equivalently, 1 car costs 9 tonnes of grain or 9 tonnes cost 1 car.

Opportunity Cost in Mobilia

Figure 35.2 illustrates the production possibility frontier of Mobilia (another fictitious country). Like the Farmers, the Mobilians consume all the grain and cars that they produce. Mobilia consumes 18 million tonnes of grain a year and 4 million cars, at point a'.

Let's calculate the opportunity costs in Mobilia. At point a', the opportunity cost of a car is equal to the magnitude of the slope of the red line tangential to the production possibility frontier, *PPF*. You can see from the red triangle that the magnitude of the slope of Mobilia's production possibility frontier is 6 million tonnes of grain divided by 6 million cars, which equals 1 tonne of grain per car. To get one more car, the Mobilians must give up 1 tonne of grain. Thus the opportunity cost of 1 car is 1 tonne of grain, or, equivalently, the opportunity cost of 1 tonne of grain is 1 car. These are the prices faced in Mobilia.

FIGURE 35.2

Opportunity Cost in Mobilia

Mobilia produces and consumes 18 million tonnes of grain and 4 million cars a year. That is, it produces and consumes at point a' on its production possibility frontier. Opportunity cost is equal to the magnitude of the slope of the production possibility frontier. The red triangle tells us that at point a', 6 million tonnes of grain must be forgone to get 6 million cars. That is, at point a', 6 million cars cost 6 million tonnes of grain. Equivalently, 1 car costs 1 tonne of grain or 1 tonne of grain costs 1 car.

Comparative Advantage

Cars are cheaper in Mobilia than in Farmland. One car costs 9 tonnes of grain in Farmland but only 1 tonne of grain in Mobilia. But grain is cheaper in Farmland than in Mobilia—9 tonnes of grain costs only 1 car in Farmland, while that same amount of grain costs 9 cars in Mobilia.

Mobilia has a comparative advantage in car production. Farmland has a comparative advantage in grain production. A country has a **comparative advantage** in producing a good if it can produce that good at a lower opportunity cost than any other country.

Let's see how opportunity cost differences and comparative advantage generates gains from international trade.

Gains from Trade

IF MOBILIA BOUGHT GRAIN FOR WHAT IT COSTS Farmland to produce it, then Mobilia could buy 9 tonnes of grain for 1 car. That is much lower than the cost of growing grain in Mobilia, for there it costs 9 cars to produce 9 tonnes of grain. If the Mobilians can buy grain at the low Farmland price, they will reap some gains.

If the Farmers can buy cars for what it costs Mobilia to produce them, they will be able to obtain a car for 1 tonne of grain. Because it costs 9 tonnes of grain to produce a car in Farmland, the Farmers would gain from such an opportunity.

In this situation, it makes sense for Mobilians to buy their grain from Farmers and for Farmers to buy their cars from Mobilians. But at what price will Farmland and Mobilia trade?

The Terms of Trade

The quantity of grain that Farmland must pay Mobilia for a car is Farmland's **terms of trade** with Mobilia. Because Canada exports and imports many different goods and services, we measure the terms of trade in the real world as an index number that averages the terms of trade over all the items we trade.

The forces of international supply and demand determine the terms of trade. Figure 35.3 illustrates these forces in the Farmland–Mobilia international

FIGURE 35.3

International Trade in Cars

As the price of a car falls, the quantity of imports demanded by Farmland increases—Farmland's import demand curve for cars is downward sloping. As the price of a car rises, the quantity of cars supplied by Mobilia for export increases—Mobilia's export supply curve of cars is upward sloping. Without international trade, the price of a car is 9 tonnes of grain in Farmland (point *a*) and 1 tonne of grain in Mobilia (point *a'*).

With free international trade, the price (terms of trade) is determined where the export supply curve intersects the import demand curve—3 tonnes of grain per car. At that price, 4 million cars a year are imported by Farmland and exported by Mobilia. The value of grain exported by Farmland and imported by Mobilia is 12 million tonnes a year, the quantity required to pay for the cars imported.

car market. The quantity of cars *traded internationally* is measured on the *x*-axis. On the *y*-axis, we measure the price of a car. This price is expressed as the *terms of trade*—tonnes of grain per car. If no international trade takes place, the price of a car in Farmland is 9 tonnes of grain, its opportunity cost, indicated by point *a*. Again, if no trade takes place, the price of a car in Mobilia is 1 tonne of grain, its opportunity cost, indicated by point *a'*. The no-trade points *a* and *a'* correspond to the points identified by those same letters in Figs. 35.1 and 35.2. The lower the price of a car (terms of trade), the greater is the

quantity of cars that the Farmers are willing to import from the Mobilians. This fact is illustrated by the downward-sloping curve, which shows Farmland's import demand for cars.

The Mobilians respond in the opposite direction. The higher the price of a car (terms of trade), the greater is the quantity of cars that Mobilians are willing to export to Farmers. This fact is reflected in Mobilia's export supply of cars—the upward-sloping line in Fig. 35.3.

The international market in cars determines the equilibrium price (terms of trade) and quantity traded. This equilibrium occurs where the import demand curve intersects the export supply curve. In this case, the equilibrium price is 3 tonnes of grain per car. Mobilia exports and Farmland imports 4 million cars a year. Notice that the price with trade is lower than the initial price in Farmland but higher than the initial price in Mobilia.

Balanced Trade

The number of cars exported by Mobilia—4 million a year—is exactly equal to the number of cars imported by Farmland. How does Farmland pay for its cars? It pays by exporting grain. How much grain does Farmland export? You can find the answer by noticing that for 1 car, Farmland has to pay 3 tonnes of grain. Hence, for 4 million cars, Farmland has to pay 12 million tonnes of grain. Thus Farmland's exports are 12 million tonnes of grain a year. Mobilia imports this same quantity of grain.

Mobilia is exchanging 4 million cars for 12 million tonnes of grain each year, and Farmland is doing the opposite, exchanging 12 million tonnes of grain for 4 million cars. Trade is balanced between these two countries. The value received from exports equals the value paid out for imports.

Changes in Production and Consumption

We've seen that international trade makes it possible for Farmers to buy cars at a lower price than that at which they can produce them for themselves. Equivalently, Farmers can sell their grain for a higher price. International trade also enables Mobilians to sell their cars for a higher price. Equivalently, Mobilians can buy grain for a lower price. Thus everybody gains. How is it possible for *everyone* to gain? What are the changes in production and consumption that accompany these gains?

An economy that does not trade with other economies has identical production and consumption possibilities. Without trade, the economy can consume only what it produces. But with international trade, an economy can consume different quantities of goods from those that it produces. The production possibility frontier describes the limit of what a country can produce, but it does not describe the limits to what it can consume. Figure 35.4 will help you to see the distinction between production possibilities and consumption possibilities when a country trades with other countries.

First of all, notice that the figure has two parts, part (a) for Farmland and part (b) for Mobilia. The production possibility frontiers that you saw in Figs. 35.1 and 35.2 are reproduced here. The slopes of the two black lines in the figure represent the opportunity costs in the two countries when there is no international trade. Farmland produces and consumes at point a, and Mobilia produces and consumes at a'. A car costs 9 tonnes of grain in Farmland and 1 tonne of grain in Mobilia.

Consumption Possibilities   The red line in each part of Fig. 35.4 shows the country's consumption possibilities with international trade. These two red lines have the same slope, and the magnitude of that slope is the opportunity cost of a car in terms of grain on the world market—3 tonnes per car. The *slope* of the consumption possibilities line is common to both countries because its magnitude equals the *terms of trade*. But the position of a country's consumption possibilities line depends on the country's production possibilities. A country cannot produce outside its production possibility curve, so its consumption possibility curve touches its production possibility curve. Thus Farmland could choose to consume at point b with no international trade or, with international trade, at any point on its red consumption possibilities line.

Free Trade Equilibrium   With international trade, the producers of cars in Mobilia can get a higher price for their output. As a result, they increase the quantity of car production. At the same time, grain producers in Mobilia get a lower price for their grain, and so they reduce production. Producers in Mobilia adjust their output by moving along their production possibility frontier until the opportunity cost in

Mobilia equals the terms of trade (the opportunity cost in the world market). This situation arises when Mobilia is producing at point b' in Fig. 35.4(b).

But the Mobilians do not consume at point b'. That is, they do not increase their consumption of cars and decrease their consumption of grain. Instead, they sell some of their car production to Farmland in exchange for some of Farmland's grain. They trade internationally. But to see how that works out, we first need to check in with Farmland to see what's happening there.

In Farmland, producers of cars now get a lower price and producers of grain get a higher price. As a consequence, producers in Farmland decrease car production and increase grain production. They adjust their outputs by moving along the production possibility frontier until the opportunity cost of a car in terms of grain equals the terms of trade (the opportunity cost on the world market). They move to point b in part (a). But the Farmers don't consume at point b. They trade some of their additional grain production for the now cheaper cars from Mobilia.

Figure 35.4 shows the quantities consumed in the two countries. We saw in Fig. 35.3 that Mobilia exports 4 million cars a year to Farmland and Farmland exports 12 million tonnes of grain a year to Mobilia. So Farmland consumes 12 million tonnes a year less grain than it produces, and it consumes 4 million more cars a year more than it produces. Farmland consumes at point c in Fig. 35.4(a). And Mobilia consumes 12 million tonnes of grain more than it produces and 4 million cars fewer than it produces. Mobilia consumes at c' in Fig. 35.4(b).

Calculating the Gains from Trade

You can now literally see the gains from trade in Fig. 35.4. Without trade, Farmers produce and consume at point a in part (a)—a point on Farmland's production possibility frontier. With international trade, Farmers consume at point c—a point *outside* the production possibility frontier. At point c, Farmers are consuming 3 million tonnes of grain a year and 1 million cars a year more than before. These increases in consumption of both cars and grain, beyond the limits of the production possibility frontier, are the gains from international trade. Mobilians also gain. Without trade, they consume at point a' in part (b)—a point on Mobilia's production possibility frontier. With international trade, they consume at point c'—a point outside

FIGURE 35.4

Expanding Consumption Possibilities

(a) Farmland

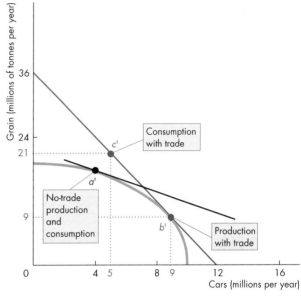

(b) Mobilia

With no international trade, Farmers produce and consume at point *a* and the opportunity cost of a car is 9 tonnes of grain (the slope of the black line in part a). Also, with no international trade, Mobilians produce and consume at point *a'* and the opportunity cost of 1 tonne of grain is 1 car (the slope of the black line in part b). Goods can be exchanged internationally at a price of 3 tonnes of grain for 1 car along the red line in each part of the figure. In part (a), Farmland decreases its production of cars and increases its production of grain, mov-

ing from *a* to *b*. It exports grain and imports cars, and it consumes at point *c*. Farmers have more of both cars and grain than they would if they produced all their own consumption goods—at point *a*. In part (b), Mobilia increases car production and decreases grain production, moving from *a'* to *b'*. Mobilia exports cars and imports grain, and it consumes at point *c'*. Mobilians have more of both cars and grain than they would if they produced all their own consumption goods—at point *a'*.

the production possibility frontier. Mobilia consumes 3 million tonnes of grain a year and 1 million cars a year more than without trade. These are the gains from international trade for Mobilia.

Gains for All

Trade between the Farmers and the Mobilians does not create winners and losers. Everyone wins. Sellers add the net demand of foreigners to their domestic demand and so their market expands. Buyers are faced with domestic supply plus net foreign supply and so have a larger supply available to them.

R E V I E W Q U I Z

- In what circumstances can countries gain from international trade?
- What determines the goods and services that a country will export? What determines the goods and services that a country will import?
- What is a comparative advantage and what role does it play in determining the amount and type of international trade that occurs?
- How can it be that all countries gain from international trade and that there are no losers?

Gains from Trade in Reality

THE GAINS FROM TRADE THAT WE HAVE JUST studied between Farmland and Mobilia in grain and cars occur in a model economy—in a world economy that we have imagined. But these same phenomena occur every day in the real global economy.

Comparative Advantage in the Global Economy

We buy TVs and VCRs from Korea, machinery from Europe, and fashion goods from Hong Kong. In exchange, we sell machinery, grain and lumber, airplanes, computers, and financial services. All this international trade is generated by comparative advantage, just like the international trade between Farmland and Mobilia in our model economy. All international trade arises from comparative advantage, even when trade is in similar goods such as tools and machines. At first thought, it seems puzzling that countries exchange manufactured goods. Why doesn't each developed country produce all the manufactured goods its citizens want to buy?

Trade in Similar Goods

Why does Canada produce automobiles for export and at the same time import cars from the United States, Japan, Korea, and Western Europe? Wouldn't it make more sense to produce all the cars that we buy here in Canada? After all, we have access to the best technology available for producing cars. Autoworkers in Canada are surely as productive as their fellow workers in the United States, Western Europe, and Asian countries. So why does Canada have a comparative advantage in some types of cars and Japan and Europe in others?

Diversity of Taste and Economies of Scale

The first part of the answer is that people have a tremendous diversity of taste. Let's stick with the example of cars. Some people prefer a sports car, some prefer a limousine, some prefer a regular, full-size car, and some prefer a minivan. In addition to size and type of car, there are many other dimensions in which cars vary. Some have low fuel consumption, some have high performance, some are spacious and comfortable, some have a large trunk, some have four-wheel drive, some have front-wheel drive, some have a radiator grill that looks like a Greek temple, others look like a wedge. People's preferences across these many dimensions vary. The tremendous diversity in tastes for cars means that people value variety and are willing to pay for it in the marketplace.

The second part of the answer to the puzzle is *economies of scale*—the tendency for the average cost to be lower, the larger the scale of production. In such situations, larger and larger production runs lead to ever lower average costs. Many goods, including cars, experience economies of scale. For example, if a car producer makes only a few hundred (or perhaps a few thousand) cars of a particular type and design, the producer must use production techniques that are much more labour-intensive and much less automated than those employed to make hundreds of thousands of cars in a particular model. With short production runs and labour-intensive production techniques, costs are high. With very large production runs and automated assembly lines, production costs are much lower. But to obtain lower costs, the automated assembly lines have to produce a large number of cars.

It is the combination of diversity of taste and economies of scale that determines opportunity cost, produces comparative advantages, and generates such a large amount of international trade in similar commodities. With international trade, each car manufacturer has the whole world market to serve. Each producer can specialize in a limited range of products and then sell its output to the entire world market. This arrangement enables large production runs on the most popular cars and feasible production runs even on the most customized cars demanded by only a handful of people in each country.

The situation in the market for cars is also present in many other industries, especially those producing specialized equipment and parts. For example, Canada exports illustration software but imports database software, exports telecommunications systems but imports PCs, exports specialized video equipment but imports VCRs. Thus international exchange of similar but slightly differentiated manufactured products is a highly profitable activity.

Let's next see what happens when governments restrict international trade. We'll see that free trade brings the greatest possible benefits. We'll also see why, in spite of the benefits of free trade, governments sometimes restrict trade.

Trade Restrictions

GOVERNMENTS RESTRICT INTERNATIONAL TRADE to protect domestic industries from foreign competition. Governments use two main tools:

1. Tariffs
2. Nontariff barriers

A **tariff** is a tax that is imposed by the importing country when an imported good crosses its international boundary. A **nontariff barrier** is any action other than a tariff that restricts international trade. Examples of nontariff barriers are quantitative restrictions and licensing regulations limiting imports. First, let's look at tariffs.

The History of Tariffs

The Canadian economy has always been protected by a tariff. Figure 35.5 shows the history of that tariff, from Confederation through 1998. The figure shows tariffs as a percentage of total imports—the average tariff. As you can see, the average tariff rate climbed

from the early 1870s to exceed 20 percent by the late 1890s. The rate fluctuated but gradually decreased through the early 1920s. It increased again during the Great Depression years of the early 1930s. During these years, most countries increased their tariff rates in what became a "beggar-my-neighbour" policy. The average tariff then decreased through the late 1930s and continued its decrease throughout the years after World War II. Today, the average tariff rate is less than 1 percent.

The reduction in tariffs since World War II followed the signing in 1947 of the **General Agreement on Tariffs and Trade** (GATT). Since its formation, the GATT has organized several rounds of negotiations that have resulted in tariff reductions. One of these, the Kennedy Round that began in the early 1960s, resulted in large tariff cuts starting in 1967. Another, the Tokyo Round, resulted in further tariff cuts in 1979. The most recent, the Uruguay Round, which started in 1986 and was completed in 1994, was the most ambitious and comprehensive of the rounds and led to the creation of a new **World Trade Organization** (WTO). Membership of the WTO brings greater obligations on countries to observe the GATT rules.

FIGURE 35.5

The Canadian Tariff: 1867–1998

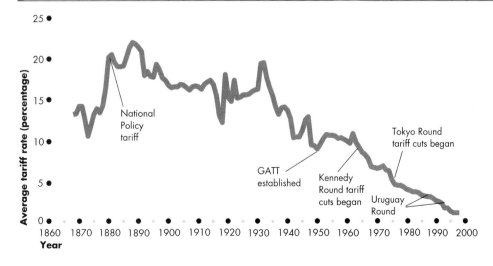

Canadian tariffs were in place before Confederation. Tariffs increased sharply in the 1870s and remained high until the 1930s. Since the establishment of the GATT in 1947, tariffs have steadily decreased in a series of "rounds." The most significant "rounds" are identified in the figure. Tariffs are now lower than they have ever been.

Sources: Statistics Canada, *Historical Statistics of Canada*, Series G485, and *StatCan: CANSIM Disc*, March 1999.

In addition to the agreements under the GATT and the WTO, Canada is a party to the **North American Free Trade Agreement** (NAFTA), which became effective on January 1, 1994, and under which barriers to international trade between Canada, the United States, and Mexico will be virtually eliminated after a 15-year phasing-in period.

In other parts of the world, trade barriers have virtually been eliminated among the member countries of the European Union, which has created the largest unified tariff-free market in the world. In 1994, discussions among the Asia-Pacific Economic group (APEC) led to an agreement in principle to work towards a free-trade area that embraces China, all the economies of East Asia and the South Pacific, Canada, and the United States. These countries include the fastest-growing economies and hold the promise of heralding a global free-trade area. But the Asia crisis of 1997 and other problems with China make it unlikely that free trade will come to APEC in the near term.

The effort to achieve freer trade underlines the fact that trade in some goods is still subject to extremely high tariffs. The highest tariffs faced by Canadian buyers are those on textiles and footwear. A tariff of more than 10 percent (on the average) is imposed on almost all our imports of textiles and footwear. For example, when you buy a pair of blue jeans for $20, you pay about $5 more than you would if there were no tariffs on textiles. Other goods protected by tariffs are agricultural products, energy and chemicals, minerals, and metals. Meat, cheese, and sugar cost more because of protection than they would with free international trade.

The temptation on governments to impose tariffs is a strong one. First, tariffs provide revenue to the government. Second, they enable the government to satisfy special interest groups in import-competing industries. But, as we'll see, free international trade brings enormous benefits that are reduced when tariffs are imposed. Let's see how.

How Tariffs Work

To analyse how tariffs work, let's return to the example of trade between Farmland and Mobilia. Figure 35.6 shows the international market for cars in which these two countries are the only traders. The volume of trade and the price of a car are determined at the point of intersection of Mobilia's export

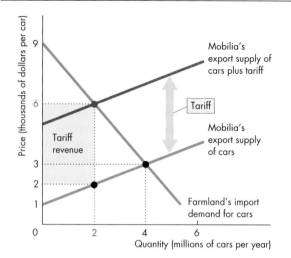

FIGURE 35.6

The Effects of a Tariff

Farmland imposes a tariff on car imports from Mobilia. The tariff increases the price that Farmers have to pay for cars. It shifts the supply curve of cars in Farmland leftward. The vertical distance between the original supply curve and the new one is the amount of the tariff, $4,000 per car. The price of a car in Farmland increases, and the quantity of cars imported decreases. The government of Farmland collects a tariff revenue of $4,000 per car—a total of $8 billion on the 2 million cars imported. Farmland's exports of grain decrease because Mobilia now has a lower income from its exports of cars.

supply curve of cars and Farmland's import demand curve for cars.

In Fig. 35.6, these two countries trade cars and grain in exactly the same way that we saw in Fig. 35.3. Mobilia exports cars, and Farmland exports grain. The volume of car imports into Farmland is 4 million a year, and the world market price of a car is 3 tonnes of grain. Fig. 35.6 expresses prices in dollars rather than in units of grain and is based on a money price of grain of $1,000 a tonne. With grain costing $1,000 a tonne, the money price of a car is $3,000.

Now suppose that the government of Farmland, perhaps under pressure from car producers, decides to impose a tariff on imported cars. In particular, suppose that a tariff of $4,000 per car is imposed. (This is a huge tariff, but the car producers of Farmland are pretty fed up with competition from Mobilia.) What happens?

■ The supply of cars in Farmland decreases.

■ The price of cars in Farmland rises.

■ The quantity of cars imported by Farmland decreases.

■ The government of Farmland collects the tariff revenue.

■ Resource use is inefficient.

■ The *value* of exports changes by the same amount as the *value* of imports and trade remains balanced.

Change in the Supply of Cars   Farmland cannot buy cars at Mobilia's export supply price. It must pay that price plus the $4,000 tariff. So the supply curve in Farmland shifts leftward. The new supply curve is that labelled "Mobilia's export supply of cars plus tariff." The vertical distance between Mobilia's export supply curve and the new supply curve is the tariff of $4,000 a car.

Rise in Price of Cars   A new equilibrium occurs where the new supply curve intersects Farmland's import demand curve for cars. That equilibrium is at a price of $6,000 a car, up from $3,000 with free trade.

Fall in Imports   Car imports decrease from 4 million to 2 million cars a year. At the higher price of $6,000 a car, domestic car producers in Farmland increase their production. Domestic grain production decreases as resources are moved into the expanding car industry.

Tariff Revenue   Total expenditure on imported cars by the Farmers is $6,000 a car multiplied by the 2 million cars imported ($12 billion). But not all of that money goes to the Mobilians. They receive $2,000 a car, or $4 billion for the 2 million cars. The difference—$4,000 a car, or a total of $8 billion for the 2 million cars—is collected by the government of Farmland as tariff revenue.

Inefficiency   The people of Farmland are willing to pay $6,000 for the marginal car imported. But the opportunity cost of that car is $2,000. So there is a gain from trading an extra car. In fact, there are gains—willingness to pay exceeds opportunity cost—all the way up to 4 million cars a year. Only when 4 million cars are being traded is the maximum price that a Farmer is willing to pay equal to the minimum price that is acceptable to a Mobilian. Thus restricting trade reduces the gains from trade.

Trade Remains Balanced   With free trade, Farmland was paying $3,000 a car and buying 4 million cars a year from Mobilia. Thus the total amount paid to Mobilia for imports was $12 billion a year. With a tariff, Farmland's imports have been cut to 2 million cars a year and the price paid to Mobilia has also been cut to only $2,000 a car. Thus the total amount paid to Mobilia for imports has been cut to $4 billion a year. Doesn't this fact mean that Farmland now has a balance of trade surplus?

It does not. The price of a car in Mobilia has fallen. But the price of grain remains at $1,000 a tonne. So the relative price of cars has fallen, and the relative price of grain has increased. With free trade, the Mobilians could buy 3,000 tonnes of grain for one car. Now they can buy only 2,000 tonnes for a car. With a higher relative price of grain, the quantity demanded by the Mobilians decreases and Mobilia imports less grain. But because Mobilia imports less grain, Farmland exports less grain. In fact, Farmland's grain industry suffers from two sources. First, there is a decrease in the quantity of grain sold to Mobilia. Second, there is increased competition for inputs from the now expanded car industry. Thus the tariff leads to a contraction in the scale of the grain industry in Farmland.

It seems paradoxical at first that a country imposing a tariff on imports of cars hurts its own export industry, decreasing its exports of grain. It might help to think of it this way: Mobilians buy grain with the money they make from exporting cars to Farmland. If they export fewer cars, they cannot afford to buy as much grain. In fact, in the absence of any international borrowing and lending, Mobilia must cut its imports of grain by exactly the same amount as the loss in revenue from its export of cars. Grain imports into Mobilia are cut back to a value of $4 billion, the amount that can be paid for by the new lower revenue from Mobilia's car exports. Thus trade is still balanced. The tariff cuts imports and exports by the same amount. The tariff has no effect on the *balance* of trade but it reduces the *volume* of trade.

The result that we have just derived is perhaps one of the most misunderstood aspects of international economics. On countless occasions, politicians and others call for tariffs to remove a balance of trade deficit or argue that lowering tariffs would produce a balance of trade deficit. They reach this conclusion by failing to work out all the implications of a tariff.

Let's now turn our attention to the other tool for restricting trade: nontariff barriers.

Nontariff Barriers

The two main forms of nontariff barrier are:

1. Quotas
2. Voluntary export restraints

A **quota** is a quantitative restriction on the import of a particular good, which specifies the maximum amount of the good that may be imported in a given period of time. A **voluntary export restraint** (VER) is an agreement between two governments in which the government of the exporting country agrees to restrain the volume of its own exports.

Quotas are especially prominent in textiles and agriculture. Voluntary export restraints are used to regulate trade between Japan and Canada.

How Quotas and VERs Work

To see how a quota works, suppose that Farmland imposes a quota that restricts its car imports to 2 million cars a year. Figure 35.7 shows the effects of this action. The quota is shown by the vertical red line at 2 million cars a year. Because it is illegal to exceed the quota, car importers buy only that quantity from Mobilia, for which they pay $2,000 a car. But because the quantity of imported cars is restricted to 2 million cars a year, people are willing to pay $6,000 per car. This is the price of a car in Farmland.

The value of imports falls to $4 million, exactly the same as in the case of the tariff. So with lower incomes from car exports and with a higher relative price of grain, Mobilians cut back on their imports of grain in exactly the same way that they did under a tariff.

The key difference between a quota and a tariff lies in who collects the gap between the import supply price and the domestic price. In the case of a tariff, it is the government of the importing country. In the case of a quota, it goes to the person who has the right to import under the import quota regulations.

A voluntary export restraint is like a quota arrangement in which quotas are allocated to each exporting country. The effects of voluntary export restraints are similar to those of quotas but differ from them in that the gap between the domestic price and the export price is captured not by domestic importers but by the foreign exporter. The government of the exporting country has to establish procedures for allocating the restricted volume of exports among its producers.

FIGURE 35.7
The Effects of a Quota

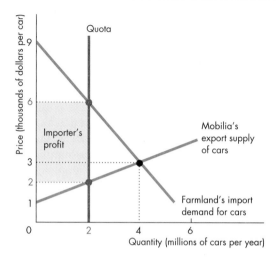

Farmland imposes a quota of 2 million cars a year on car imports from Mobilia. That quantity appears as the vertical line labelled "Quota." Because the quantity of cars supplied by Mobilia is restricted to 2 million, the price at which those cars will be traded increases to $6,000. Importing cars is profitable because Mobilia is willing to supply cars at $2,000 each. There is competition for import quotas.

- What happens to a country's consumption possibilities when it opens itself up to international trade and trades freely at world market prices?
- What do trade restrictions do to the gains from international trade?
- What is best for a country: restricted trade, no trade, or free trade?
- What does a tariff on imports do to the volume of imports and the volume of exports?
- In the absence of international borrowing and lending, how do tariffs and other trade restrictions influence the total value of imports and exports and the balance of trade—the value of exports minus the value of imports?

Let's now look at some commonly heard arguments for restricting international trade.

The Case Against Protection

FOR AS LONG AS NATIONS AND INTERNATIONAL trade have existed, people have debated whether a country is better off with free international trade or with protection from foreign competition. The debate continues, but for most economists, a verdict has been delivered and is the one you have just seen. Free trade promotes prosperity for all; protection is inefficient. We've seen the most powerful case for free trade in the example of how Farmland and Mobilia both benefit from their comparative advantage. But there is a broader range of issues in the free trade versus protection debate. Let's review these issues.

Three arguments for restricting international trade are:

- The national security argument
- The infant industry argument
- The dumping argument

Let's look at each in turn.

The National Security Argument

The national security argument for protection is that a country must protect industries that produce defence equipment and armaments and those on which the defence industries rely for their raw materials and other intermediate inputs. This argument for protection does not withstand close scrutiny.

First, it is an argument for international isolation, for in a time of war, there is no industry that does not contribute to national defence. Second, if the case is made for boosting the output of a strategic industry, it is more efficient to achieve this outcome with a subsidy to the firms in the industry financed out of taxes. Such a subsidy would keep the industry operating at the scale judged appropriate, and free international trade would keep the prices faced by consumers at their world market levels.

The Infant Industry Argument

The so-called **infant industry argument** for protection is that it is necessary to protect a new industry to enable it to grow into a mature industry that can compete in world markets. The argument is based on the idea of *dynamic comparative advantage*, which can arise from *learning-by-doing* (see Chapter 3).

Learning-by-doing is a powerful engine of productivity growth, and comparative advantage evolves and changes because of on-the-job experience. But these facts do not justify protection.

First, the infant industry argument is valid only if the benefits of learning-by-doing *not only* accrue to the owners and workers of the firms in the infant industry but also *spill over* to other industries and parts of the economy. For example, there are huge productivity gains from learning-by-doing in the manufacture of telecommunication equipment. But almost all of these gains benefit the stockholders and workers of Northern Telecom and other producers. Because the people making the decisions, bearing the risk, and doing the work are the ones who benefit, they take the dynamic gains into account when they decide on the scale of their activities. In this case, almost no benefits spill over to other parts of the economy, so there is no need for government assistance to achieve an efficient outcome.

Second, even if the case is made for protecting an infant industry, it is more efficient to do so by a subsidy to the firms in the industry, with the subsidy financed out of taxes.

The Dumping Argument

Dumping occurs when a foreign firm sells its exports at a lower price than its cost of production. Dumping might be used by a firm that wants to gain a global monopoly. In this case, the foreign firm sells its output at a price below its cost to drive domestic firms out of business. When the domestic firms have gone, the foreign firm takes advantage of its monopoly position and charges a higher price for its product. Dumping is usually regarded as a justification for temporary countervailing tariffs.

But there are powerful reasons to resist the dumping argument for protection. First, it is virtually impossible to detect dumping because it is hard to determine a firm's costs. As a result, the test for dumping is whether a firm's export price is below its domestic price. But this test is a weak one because it can be rational for a firm to charge a low price in markets in which the quantity demanded is highly sensitive to price and a higher price in a market in which demand is less sensitive to price.

Second, it is hard to think of a good that is produced by a natural *global* monopoly. So even if all the domestic firms in some industry were driven out of business, it would always be possible to find several and usually many alternative foreign sources of supply and to buy at prices determined in competitive markets.

Third, if a good or service were a truly global natural monopoly, the best way of dealing with it would be by regulation—just as in the case of domestic monopolies. Such regulation would require international cooperation.

The three arguments for protection that we've just examined have an element of credibility. The counter-arguments are in general stronger, so these arguments do not make the case for protection. But they are not the only arguments that you might encounter. The many other arguments that are commonly heard are quite simply wrong. They are fatally flawed. The most common of them are that protection:

- Saves jobs
- Allows us to compete with cheap foreign labour
- Brings diversity and stability
- Penalizes lax environmental standards
- Protects national culture
- Prevents rich countries from exploiting developing countries

Saves Jobs

The argument is: When we buy shoes from Brazil or shirts from Taiwan, Canadian workers lose their jobs. With no earnings and poor prospects, these workers become a drain on welfare and spend less, causing a ripple effect of further job losses. The proposed solution to this problem is to ban imports of cheap foreign goods and protect Canadian jobs. The proposal is flawed for the following reasons.

First, free trade does cost some jobs, but it also creates other jobs. It brings about a global rationalization of labour and allocates labour resources to their highest-value activities. Because of international trade in textiles, tens of thousands of workers in Canada have lost jobs because textile mills and other factories have closed. But tens of thousands of workers in other countries have gotten jobs because textile mills have opened there. And tens of thousands of Canadian workers have gotten better-paying jobs than textile workers because other export industries have expanded and created more jobs than have been destroyed.

Second, imports create jobs. They create jobs for retailers that sell imported goods and firms that service those goods. They also create jobs by creating incomes in the rest of the world, some of which are spent on imports of Canadian-made goods and services.

Although protection does save particular jobs, it does so at inordinate cost. A striking example of the cost of quotas is that of quotas on the import of textiles. Quotas imposed under an international agreement called the Multifibre Arrangement (that is now being phased out) have protected textile jobs, especially in the United States. It has been estimated that because of the quotas, 72,000 jobs existed in textiles in the United States that would otherwise have disappeared. But each textile job saved cost more than $300,000 a year in added clothing costs!

Allows Us to Compete with Cheap Foreign Labour

With the removal of protective tariffs in Canadian and U.S. trade with Mexico, Texan entrepreneur Ross Perot said he would hear a "giant sucking sound" of jobs rushing to Mexico (one of which is shown in the cartoon). Let's see what's wrong with this view.

The labour cost of a unit of output equals the wage rate divided by labour productivity. For example, if a Canadian auto worker earns $30 an hour

"I don't know what the hell happened—one minute I'm at work in Flint, Michigan, then there's a giant sucking sound and suddenly here I am in Mexico."

and produces 15 units of output an hour, the average labour cost of a unit of output is $2. If a Mexican auto assembly worker earns $3 an hour and produces 1 unit of output an hour, the average labour cost of a unit of output is $3. Other things remaining the same, the higher a worker's productivity, the higher is the worker's wage rate. High-wage workers have high productivity. Low-wage workers have low productivity.

Although high-wage Canadian workers are more productive, on the average, than low-wage Mexican workers, there are differences across industries. Canadian labour is relatively more productive in some activities than in others. For example, the productivity of Canadian workers in producing financial services and telephone systems is relatively higher than in the production of metals and some standardized machine parts. The activities in which Canadian workers are relatively more productive than their Mexican counterparts are those in which Canada has a *comparative advantage*. By engaging in free trade, increasing our production and exports of the goods and services in which we have a comparative advantage and decreasing our production and increasing our imports of the goods and services in which our trading partners have a comparative advantage, we can make ourselves and the citizens of other countries better off.

Brings Diversity and Stability

A diversified investment portfolio is less risky than one that has all the eggs in one basket. The same is true for an economy's production. A diversified economy fluctuates less than an economy that produces only one or two goods.

But a big, rich, diversified economy like that of Canada does not have this type of problem. Even a country like Saudi Arabia that produces almost only one good (oil) can benefit from specializing in the activity at which it has a comparative advantage and then investing in a wide range of other countries to bring greater stability to its income and consumption.

Penalizes Lax Environmental Standards

A new argument for protection is that many poorer countries, such as Mexico, do not have the same

environment policies that we have and, because they are willing to pollute and we are not, we cannot compete with them without tariffs. So if they want free trade with the richer and "greener" countries, they must clean up their environments to our standards.

This argument for trade restrictions is weak. First, not all poorer countries have significantly lower environmental standards than Canada has. Many poor countries and the former communist countries of Eastern Europe do have bad environment records. But some countries enforce strict laws. Second, a poor country cannot afford to be as concerned about its environment as a rich country can. The best hope for a better environment in Mexico and in other developing countries is rapid income growth through free trade. As their incomes grow, developing countries will have the *means* to match their desires to improve their environment. Third, poor countries have a comparative advantage at doing "dirty" work, which helps rich countries achieve higher environment standards than they otherwise could.

Protects National Culture

The national culture argument for protection is one of the most often heard in Canada and Europe and just about everywhere else except for the United States.

The expressed fear is that free trade in books, magazines, movies, and television programs means U.S. domination and the end of local culture. So, the reasoning continues, it is necessary to protect domestic "culture" industries from free international trade to ensure the survival of a national cultural identity.

Protection of these industries is common and takes the form of nontariff barriers. For example, local content regulations on radio and television broadcasting and in magazines are often required.

The cultural identity argument for protection has no merit and it is one more example of "rent-seeking" (see Chapter 13, p. 276). Writers, publishers, and broadcasters want to limit foreign competition so that they can earn larger economic profits. There is no actual danger to national culture. In fact, many of the creators of so-called American cultural products are not Americans, but the talented citizens of other countries, ensuring the survival of their national cultural identities in Hollywood! Also, if national culture is in danger, there is no surer way of helping it on its way out than by impoverishing the nation whose culture it is. And protection is an effective way of doing just that.

Prevents Rich Countries from Exploiting Developing Countries

Another new argument for protection is that international trade must be restricted to prevent the people of the rich industrial world from exploiting the poorer people of the developing countries, forcing them to work for slave wages.

Wage rates in some developing countries are indeed very low. But by trading with developing countries, we increase the demand for the goods that these countries produce, and, more significantly, we increase the demand for their labour. When the demand for labour in developing countries increases, the wage rate also increases. So, far from exploiting people in developing countries, trade improves their opportunities and increases their incomes.

We have reviewed the arguments that are commonly heard in favour of protection and the counter-arguments against them. There is one counter-argument to protection that is general and quite overwhelming. Protection invites retaliation and can trigger a trade war. The best example of a trade war occurred during the Great Depression of the 1930s when the United States, Canada, and European countries erected high trade barriers. Country after country retaliated with its yet higher tariff, and in a short period, world trade had almost disappeared. The costs to all countries were large and led to a renewed international resolve to avoid such self-defeating moves in the future. They also led to the creation of GATT and are the impetus behind the WTO, NAFTA, APEC, and the European Union.

R E V I E W   Q U I Z

- Is there any merit to the view that we should restrict international trade to achieve national security goals, to stimulate the growth of new industries, or to restrain foreign monopoly?
- Is there any merit to the view that we should restrict international trade to save jobs, compensate for low foreign wages, make the economy more diversified, compensate for costly environmental policies, protect national culture, or protect developing countries from being exploited?
- Is there any merit to the view that we should restrict international trade for any reason? What is the main argument against trade restrictions?

Why Is International Trade Restricted?

WHY, DESPITE ALL THE ARGUMENTS AGAINST protection, is trade restricted? There are two key reasons:

- Tariff revenue
- Rent seeking

Tariff Revenue

Government revenue is costly to collect. In the developed countries such as Canada, a well-organized tax-collection system is in place that can generate billions of dollars of income tax and sales tax revenues. This tax-collecting system is made possible by the fact that firms that must keep audited financial accounts do most of the economic transactions. Without reliable accounts, the revenue collection agencies (Revenue Canada in Canada) would be severely hampered in their work. Even with audited financial accounts, some proportion of potential tax revenue is lost. Nonetheless, for the industrialized countries, the income tax and sales taxes are the major sources of revenue and the tariff plays a very small role.

But governments in developing countries have a difficult time collecting taxes from their citizens. Much economic activity takes place in an informal economy with few financial records. So only a small amount of revenue is collected from income taxes and sales taxes in these countries. The one area in which economic transactions are well recorded and audited is in international trade. So this activity is an attractive base for tax collection in these countries and is used much more extensively than in the developed countries.

Rent Seeking

The major reason why international trade is restricted is because of rent seeking. Free trade increases consumption possibilities *on the average* but not everyone shares in the gain and some people even lose. Free trade brings benefits to some and imposes costs on others, with total benefits exceeding total costs. It is the uneven distribution of costs and benefits that is the principal source of impediment to achieving more liberal international trade.

Returning to our example of trade in cars and grain between Farmland and Mobilia, the benefits to Farmland from free trade accrue to all the producers of grain and those producers of cars who would not have to bear the costs of adjusting to a smaller car industry. These costs are transition costs, not permanent costs. The costs of moving to free trade are borne by those car producers and their employees who have to become grain producers. The number of people who gain will, in general, be enormous compared with the number who lose. The gain per person will therefore be rather small. The loss per person to those who bear the loss will be large. Because the loss that falls on those who bear it is large, it will pay those people to incur considerable expense to lobby against free trade. On the other hand, it will not pay those who gain to organize to achieve free trade. The gain from trade for any one individual is too small for that individual to spend much time or money on a political organization to achieve free trade. The loss from free trade will be seen as being so great by those bearing that loss that they *will* find it profitable to join a political organization to prevent free trade. Each group is optimizing—weighing benefits against costs and choosing the best action for themselves. The anti-free-trade group will, however, undertake a larger quantity of political lobbying than will the pro-free-trade group.

Compensating Losers

If, in total, the gains from free international trade exceed the losses, why don't those who stand to gain from free trade offer to compensate those who stand to lose so that everyone votes for free trade?

The main answer is that there are serious obstacles to providing direct and correctly calculated compensation. First, the cost of identifying the losers from free trade and of estimating the value of their losses would be enormous.

Second, it would never be clear whether a person who has fallen on hard times is suffering because of free trade or for other reasons, perhaps reasons that are largely under the control of the individual.

Third, some people who look like losers at one point in time may, in fact, end up gaining. The young autoworker that loses her job in Windsor and becomes a computer assembly worker in Ottawa resents the loss of work and the need to move. But a year or two later, looking back on events, she counts herself fortunate. She has made a move that has increased her income and given her greater job security.

Despite the absence of explicit compensation, those who lose from a change in protection do receive some compensation. But compensation is not restricted to the losers from changes in trade policy. In Canada (and in all the other rich industrial countries) elaborate schemes are in place to ensure that people who suffer from economic change receive help during their transition to new activities.

Two major forms of compensation in Canada arise from inter-provincial fiscal transfers and employment insurance. Inter-provincial fiscal transfers result in tax dollars collected in the rich and expanding regions of the country being spent in the poorer regions. Employment insurance provides substantial compensation for workers who lose their jobs regardless of the reason for the job loss. Jobs lost because of changes in international protection are included among those for which benefits are paid.

But because we do not explicitly compensate the losers from free international trade, protectionism remains a popular and permanent feature of our national economic and political life.

Compensating Losers from Protection

There is no general presumption that it is the ones who lose from a tariff cut that should be compensated. Protection brings losses to the consumer and the view might be taken that the winners from protection should compensate the losers from protection. When this perspective is taken, the removal of protection would mean the removal of the compensation of the losers by the winners and there would be no further adjustments needed. What is fair is a tricky matter (as we explain in Chapter 6, pp. 120–123.)

R E V I E W   Q U I Z

■ What are the two main reasons for imposing tariffs on imports?

■ What type of country benefits most from the revenue from tariffs? Does Canada need to use tariffs to raise revenue for the government?

■ If trade restrictions are costly, why do we use them? Why don't the people who gain from trade organize a political force that is strong enough to ensure their interests are protected?

The North American Free Trade Agreement

THE NORTH AMERICAN FREE TRADE AGREEMENT came into effect on January 1, 1994. It was the outgrowth of an earlier Canada–United States Free Trade Agreement, which was signed in October 1987. Both agreements were struck only after several years of intense negotiations and, on the Canadian side of the border, an intense political debate. First, let's look at the terms of the Canada–United States agreement of 1987 and at the progress made in achieving freer trade between two of the world's largest trading partners.

The Terms of the Canada–United States Agreement

The main terms of the Canada–United States Free Trade Agreement are:

- Tariffs to be phased out through 1999
- Nontariff barriers to be reduced
- Free trade in energy products, with energy resource sharing in times of national shortage
- More freedom of trade in services
- Future negotiations to eliminate subsidies
- Creation of dispute-settling mechanisms

Removal of Tariffs   Scheduled tariff cuts began on January 1, 1989 and were completed on January 1, 1998. But tariff protection remains in place and an atmosphere of tension prevails in many areas. Agriculture remains effectively protected with new tariffs that have replaced old quotas. And a series of so-called *countervailing duties* have been introduced to offset the effects of domestic subsidies. Further, several so-called *antidumping duties* have also been introduced in cases in which it is alleged that products are being exported at a price below the cost of production.

Nontariff Barriers   Nontariff barriers such as government procurement policies of buying local products are removed by the agreement. Subsequent to entering into the free trade agreement, Canada and the United States took on additional obligations as members of the WTO, which require the removal of agricultural quotas. So many agricultural quotas have been removed but they have been replaced with tariffs. So despite the free trade agreement, we remain a long way from achieving free trade in agricultural products.

Energy Products   Free trade in energy products existed before the free trade agreement but the agreement ratified the intent to maintain that arrangement. The agreement that scarce energy resources will be shared in times of national shortage became a controversial one. In effect, what the energy sharing clause amounts to is an agreement that governments will not intervene in energy markets to prevent firms from selling their energy to the other country.

Trade in Services   International trade in services has been expanding more quickly than trade in manufactured goods in recent years. The free trade agreement, recognizing this factor and seeking to facilitate further expansion of trade in services between the United States and Canada, incorporates two principles: the *right of establishment* and *national treatment*. The right of establishment means that American firms have the right to set up branches in Canada and Canadian firms have the right to set up operations in the United States. National treatment means that each country will treat the goods and firms and investors of the other country as if they were operating within its own borders.

Future Negotiations on Subsidies   In both the United States and Canada, there are many subsidies, especially on agricultural products. The presence of subsidies causes problems and makes it legitimate under the agreement for the country importing subsidized goods to impose countervailing duties. As we have just noted, several such duties have been imposed.

Dispute-Settling Mechanisms   The Free Trade Agreement included two dispute-settling mechanisms: one to settle disputes relating to all aspects of the agreement and the other to deal with applications of countervailing duties and antidumping laws in either country. For example, the United States has applied for and received permission to impose countervailing duties on Canadian exports of Durum wheat, lumber products, poultry, and live hogs. In each case, the United States accuses Canada of subsidizing these industries unfairly so that Canadian exports are cheaper than U.S. producers can supply them.

The Extension of the Agreement: NAFTA

The North American Free Trade Agreement (NAFTA) is an agreement between Canada, the United States and Mexico that has six objectives. They are to:

- Eliminate trade barriers
- Promote conditions of fair competition
- Increase investment opportunities
- Protect intellectual property rights
- Create an effective dispute resolution mechanism
- Establish a framework for the expansion of the agreement to include other nations in the hemisphere

Effects of the Free Trade Agreement

Working out the effects of an agreement as complex as NAFTA is difficult, and there is no general consensus on what the effects have been. The theory that you have studied in this chapter predicts that the removal of tariffs will produce an increase in the volume of international trade. That is, the theory predicts that Canadians will increasingly specialize in those activities at which they have a comparative advantage and Mexicans and Americans will specialize in a different range of activities and that the three countries will exchange a larger volume of goods and services.

As predicted, trade between the three countries has increased. During the first five years of NAFTA, Canada's trade with the United States increased by 80 percent and Canada's trade with Mexico doubled.

The trade expansion that followed the entry of Mexico in 1995 was especially dramatic. Mexico's exports increased by 31 percent (in U.S. dollar value) in 1995 and by 21 percent in 1996 compared with increases that averaged less than 15 percent a year during the two years before the agreement. But trade expansion with Mexico has not been in one direction. Mexico's imports also increased following the agreement by 23 percent in both 1996 and 1997.

During the 1990s, Canada's exports have expanded from less than 30 percent of total production to 36 percent of production and Canada's imports have increased from 27 percent to 34 percent of total expenditure.

Canada greatly increased its exports of advertising services, office and telecommunication equipment, paper, and transportation services. And its imports of meat and dairy products, communications services, clothing, furniture, and processed foods and beverages also increased by a large percentage.

These huge changes in exports and imports brought gains from increased specialization and exchange. But they also brought a heavy toll of adjustment. Thousands of jobs were lost in the declining sectors and new jobs were created in the expanding sectors. The amount of job destruction in the years following the free trade agreement was historically high and the unemployment rate rose for three successive years. Only during the Great Depression did the rate of job destruction exceed that in the late 1980s and early 1990s. To what extent a high rate of labour market turnover was caused by the free trade agreement is unclear and controversial. But the net outcome of NAFTA appears to be strongly positive. More than a million new Canadian jobs were created between 1994 and 1999.

REVIEW QUIZ

- By when, under the Canada–United States Free Trade Agreement, were all tariffs on trade between Canada and the United States intended to be phase out? What progress and setbacks have we experienced?
- What effect has NAFTA had on nontariff barriers?
- What effect has NAFTA had on trade in services?
- How has the volume of trade among Canada, the United States, and Mexico changed during the period since NAFTA was established?

You've now seen how free international trade enables all nations to gain from specialization and trade. By producing goods in which we have a comparative advantage and trading some of our production for that of others, we expand our consumption possibilities. Placing impediments on that trade restricts the extent to which we can gain from specialization and trade. By opening our country up to free international trade, the market for the things that we sell expands and the relative price rises. The market for the things that we buy also expands and the relative price falls. *Reading Between the Lines* on pp. 820–821 looks at Canada's international trade experience during 1999 and at the astonishing increases in trade that have occurred under NAFTA.

Net Exports Surplus

NATIONAL POST, AUGUST 20, 1999

Canada's trade surplus continues to rise

Canada's June trade surplus climbed to $2.808-billion, exceeding expectations, as booming U.S. demand for machinery drove exports to their highest level ever, Statistics Canada said yesterday.

Economists had expected a $2.5-billion surplus. May's surplus was revised lower to $2.348-billion from the $2.444-billion reported earlier, StatsCan said. ...

June's surplus reflected an 8% jump in machinery and equipment exports as shipments of aircraft and plane parts increased, the bulk headed to the United States, which takes about 85% of Canada's exports and is completing a decade of economic expansion. ...

June's exports climbed 1.9% to $29.418-billion, topping the May record of $28.880-billion. Exports to the United States exceeded imports by $5.023-billion, up from $4.258-billion in May and surpassing the previous benchmark of $4.594-billion set in March.

Exports to the U.S. surged 2.4% to a record $25.255-billion. ...

Imports, meanwhile, gained 0.3% to $26.610-billion from $26.532-billion, as increased energy and machinery imports were partly offset by lower agricultural and industrial imports.

The trade surplus bolstered expectations that economic growth in Canada is picking up. Yesterday, the Bank of Canada said it expects the economy to expand at a 3.75% pace this year, with little inflation. Earlier this year the central bank forecast growth of closer to 3.25%. ...

Essence of the Story

■ Statistics Canada reported that Canada's trade surplus in June was $2.8 billion. Exports increased 1.9 percent to $29.4 billion and imports grew 0.3 percent to $26.6 billion.

■ June exports are the highest ever.

■ The United States buys 85 percent of Canada's exports.

■ The United States is completing a decade of economic growth.

■ The trade surplus increased expectations that economic growth in Canada is increasing. The Bank of Canada expects the Canadian economy to expand 3.75 percent in 1999.

■ Canada's biggest trading partner is the United States. So Canadian exports are strongly influenced by U.S. imports. And U.S. imports are strongly influenced by U.S. real GDP.

■ Figure 1 shows the relationship between U.S. real GDP and Canadian exports to the United States. You can see a strong positive relationship between these two variables.

■ As the United States has experienced real GDP growth throughout the last decade, Canadian exports to the United States have increased.

■ You can also see in Fig. 1 that Canadian exports became more responsive to U.S. real GDP during the 1990s after the Free Trade Agreement came into effect.

■ Canadian imports are determined primarily by Canadian real GDP. Figure 2 shows the relationship between these two variables. You can see a similar pattern to that in Fig. 1. There is a strong positive relationship between Canadian imports and real GDP, and imports became more responsive to real GDP during the 1990s.

■ Figure 3 shows real GDP growth in Canada and the United States. In 1998, U.S. real GDP grew at a faster rate than did Canadian real GDP. The relative growth rates, in part, contribute to the faster growth of Canadian exports than of Canadian imports and lead to the big trade surplus.

■ Because an increase in exports results in an increase in real GDP, other things remaining the same, the article is correct when it states that an increase in the trade surplus raises expectations that Canada's economic growth rate is increasing.

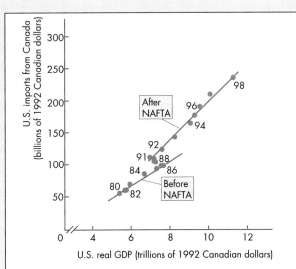

Figure 1 Canadian exports to the United States

Figure 2 Canadian imports

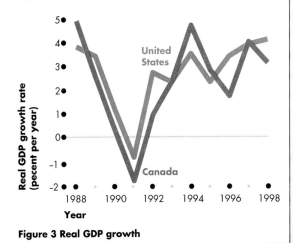

Figure 3 Real GDP growth

S U M M A R Y

Key Points

Patterns and Trends in International Trade (p. 802)

- Large flows of trade take place between countries, most of which is in manufactured goods exchanged among rich industrialized countries.
- Between 1978 and 1998, the volume of Canadian trade increased from one-fifth to more than one-third of total production.

Comparative Advantage and International Trade (pp. 803–804)

- When opportunity costs between countries diverge, comparative advantage enables countries to gain from international trade.

Gains from Trade (pp. 804–807)

- By increasing the production of the goods in which a country has a comparative advantage and then trading some of the increased output, the country can consume at points outside its production possibility frontier.
- In the absence of international borrowing and lending, trade is balanced as prices adjust to reflect the international supply of and demand for goods.
- The terms of trade balance the production and consumption plans of the trading parties. At the equilibrium price, trade is balanced.

Gains from Trade in Reality (p. 808)

- Comparative advantage explains the international trade that takes place in the real world.
- But trade in similar goods arises from economies of scale in the face of diversified tastes.

Trade Restrictions (pp. 809–812)

- Countries restrict international trade by imposing tariffs, nontariff barriers, and quotas.
- Trade restrictions raise the domestic price of imported goods, decrease the volume of imports, and reduce the total value of imports.
- Trade restrictions reduce the total value of exports by the same amount as the reduction in the value of imports.

The Case Against Protection (pp. 813–816)

- Arguments that protection is necessary for security, infant industries, and to prevent dumping are weak.
- Arguments that protection saves jobs, allows us to compete with cheap foreign labour, makes the economy diversified and stable, protects national culture, and is needed to offset the costs of environmental policies are fatally flawed.

Why Is International Trade Restricted? (pp. 816–817)

- Trade is restricted because tariffs raise government revenue and because protection brings a small loss to a large number of people and a large gain per person to a small number of people.

The North American Free Trade Agreement (pp. 818–819)

- NAFTA is an agreement between Canada, the United States, and Mexico, which began in 1995 and grew from a previous Canada–U.S. agreement.
- Under NAFTA, trade has expanded more rapidly than before the agreement.

Key Figures ◆

Key Terms

P R O B L E M S

*1. The table provides information about Virtual Reality's production possibilities.

TV sets (per day)		Computers (per day)
0	and	36
10	and	35
20	and	33
30	and	30
40	and	26
50	and	21
60	and	15
70	and	8
80	and	0

  a. Calculate Virtual Reality's opportunity cost of a TV set when it produces 10 sets a day.
  b. Calculate Virtual Reality's opportunity cost of a TV set when it produces 40 sets a day.
  c. Calculate Virtual Reality's opportunity cost of a TV set when it produces 70 sets a day.
  d. Using the answers to parts (a), (b), and (c), graph the relationship between the opportunity cost of a TV set and the quantity of TV sets produced in Virtual Reality.

2. The table provides information about Vital Signs' production possibilities.

TV sets (per day)		Computers (per day)
0	and	18.0
10	and	17.5
20	and	16.5
30	and	15.0
40	and	13.0
50	and	10.5
60	and	7.5
70	and	4.0
80	and	0

  a. Calculate Vital Signs' opportunity cost of a TV set when it produces 10 sets a day.
  b. Calculate Vital Signs' opportunity cost of a TV set when it produces 40 sets a day.
  c. Calculate Vital Signs' opportunity cost of a TV set when it produces 70 sets a day.
  d. Using the answers to parts (a), (b), and (c), sketch the relationship between the opportunity cost of a TV set and the quantity of TV sets produced in Vital Signs.

*3. Suppose that with no international trade, Virtual Reality in problem 1 produces and consumes 10 TV sets a day and Vital Signs produces and consumes 60 TV sets a day. Now suppose that the two countries begin to trade with each other.
  a. Which country exports TV sets?
  b. What adjustments are made to the amount of each good produced by each country?
  c. What adjustments are made to the amount of each good consumed by each country?
  d. What can you say about the terms of trade (the price of a TV set expressed as computers per TV set) under free trade?

4. Suppose that with no international trade, Virtual Reality in problem 1 produces and consumes 50 TV sets a day and Vital Signs produces and consumes 20 TV sets a day. Now suppose that the two countries begin to trade with each other.
  a. Which country exports TV sets?
  b. What adjustments are made to the amount of each good produced by each country?
  c. What adjustments are made to the amount of each good consumed by each country?
  d. What can you say about the terms of trade (the price of a TV set expressed as computers per TV set) under free trade?

*5. Compare the total quantities of each good produced in problems 1 and 2 with the total quantities of each good produced in problems 3 and 4.
  a. Does free trade increase or decrease the total quantities of TV sets and computers produced in both cases? Why or why not?
  b. What happens to the price of a TV set in Virtual Reality in the two cases? Why does it rise in one case and fall in the other?
  c. What happens to the price of a computer in Vital Signs in the two cases? Why does it rise in one case and fall in the other?

6. Compare the international trade in problem 3 with that in problem 4.
  a. Why does Virtual Reality export TV sets in one of the cases and import them in the other case?
  b. Do the TV producers or the computer producers gain in each case?
  c. Do consumers gain in each case?

*7. The figure depicts the international market for soybeans.

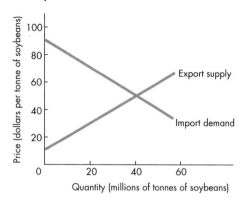

a. If the two countries did not engage in international trade, what would be the prices of soybeans in the two countries?
b. What are the terms of trade if there is free trade between these countries?
c. What quantities of soybeans are exported and imported?
d. What is the balance of trade?

8. If the soybean importing country in problem 7 imposes a tariff of $2 per tonne, what are the terms of trade and what quantity of soybeans gets traded internationally? What is the price of soybeans in the importing country? Calculate the tariff revenue.

*9. If the soybean importing country in problem 7 imposes a quota of 30 million tonnes on imports of soybeans,
a. What is the price of soybeans in the importing country?
b. What is the revenue from the quota?
c. Who gets this revenue?

10. If the soybean exporting country in problem 7 imposes a VER of 30 million tonnes on its exports of soybeans,
a. What are the terms of trade now?
b. What is the revenue of soybean growers in the exporting country?
c. Which country gains from the VER?

CRITICAL THINKING

1. Study *Reading Between the Lines* on pp. 820–821, and then answer the following questions:
a. Why are Canada's exports influenced by the performance of the U.S. economy?
b. Does the U.S. economy exert a powerful influence or a weak influence on Canadian exports? Explain?
c. What effect, if any, does NAFTA appear to have had on Canadian exports and on the U.S. influence on those exports?
d. Why do you think that Canada's exports have expanded more than its imports?
e. Does the performance of the Canadian economy influence U.S. exports?
f. Does the Canadian economy exert a powerful influence or a weak influence on U.S. exports? Explain.

2. Visit the Parkin-Bade Web site and study the *Web Reading Between the Lines* on steel dumping. Then answer the following questions:
a. What is the argument in the news article for limiting steel imports?
b. Evaluate the argument. Is it correct or incorrect in your opinion? Why?
c. Would you vote to limit steel imports? Why or why not?
d. Would you vote differently if you lived in another steel-producing country? Why or why not?

3. Use the links on the Parkin-Bade Web site to visit the Department of Foreign Affairs and International Trade and the Public Citizen Global Trade. Study "Five Years of NAFTA: A Scorecard" and "School of Real-Life Results Report Card." Then answer the following questions.
a. What is the picture painted by the Department of Foreign Affairs?
b. What is the picture painted by the Public Citizen?
c. Whose picture do you think is correct and why?
d. Would you vote to maintain NAFTA? Why or why not?
e. Would you vote to expand NAFTA to include other countries? Why or why not?

International Finance

Yes! The yen (¥), the euro (€), and the dollar ($) are the world's three big currencies. The yen (the currency of Japan) and the dollar (the currency of the United States) have been around for a long time. The euro is new. It was launched on January 1, 1999 as the fledgling currency of 11 members of the European Union, and it will not be used for ordinary transactions until 2002. But it is already an international currency. Most of the world's international trade and finance is conducted using these three currencies. ◆ Currencies fluctuate in value. In 1976, an American needed 1.01 U.S. dollars to buy a Canadian dollar. But in 1999, 67 U.S. cents was sufficient to buy a Canadian dollar. Many currencies have fallen by much more than the Canadian dollar. In 1997 and 1998, during the Asian financial crisis, the currency of Indonesia fell against our dollar to less than one-third of its pre-crisis value. ◆ Why do currency values fluctuate? Is there anything we can do or should do to stabilize the value of the dollar? In 1998, Canadian payments to the rest of the world for imports and debt interest exceeded the amount received by Canadians for exports by $16 billion. During the past five years, imports and debt interest exceeded exports by a staggering $50 billion. Through these years, foreigners bought Canadian assets on a grand scale. Cadbury Schweppes (a British firm) bought George Weston's chocolate company and foreign companies now own Canada's four biggest makers of chocolate bars. Campbell Soup Co. (a U.S. firm) now owns Canadian beer giant John Labatt Ltd. By 1999, foreigners owned more than $630 billion of Canadian assets, up from $300 billion a decade earlier. In 1999, our net interest payments to foreigners were $30 billion—almost 4 cents for every dollar we earned. Why have foreigners bought so many Canadian businesses?

◇ We're going to discover what determines the amount of international borrowing and lending, and why the Canadian dollar fluctuates against other currencies.

¥€ $!

After studying this chapter, you will be able to:

- **Explain how international trade is financed**
- **Describe a country's balance of payments accounts**
- **Explain what determines the amount of international borrowing and lending**
- **Explain why Canada is an international borrower**
- **Explain how the foreign exchange value of the dollar is determined**
- **Explain why the foreign exchange value of the dollar fluctuates**

Financing International Trade

WHEN A SONY STORE IN CANADA IMPORTS CD players from Japan, it does not pay for them with Canadian dollars—it uses Japanese yen. And when an Irish railroad company buys a locomotive from GM in London Ontario, it pays in Canadian dollars. Whenever we buy things from another country, we use the currency of that country to make the transaction. It doesn't make any difference what the item being traded is; it might be a consumption good or a capital good, a building, or even a firm.

We're going to study the markets in which money—different types of currency—is bought and sold. But first we're going to look at the scale of international trading and borrowing and lending and at the way in which we keep our records of these transactions. Such records are called the balance of payments accounts.

Balance of Payments Accounts

A country's **balance of payments accounts** records its international trading, borrowing, and lending. There are in fact three balance of payments accounts:

1. Current account
2. Capital account
3. Official settlements account

The **current account** records payments for imports of goods and services from abroad, receipts from exports of goods and services sold abroad, net interest paid abroad, and net transfers (such as foreign aid payments). The *current account balance* equals exports minus imports, net interest payments, and net transfers. The **capital account** records foreign investment in Canada minus Canadian investment abroad. The **official settlements account** records the change in official Canadian reserves. **Official Canadian reserves** are the government's holdings of foreign currency. If Canadian official reserves increase, the *official settlements account balance* is negative. The reason is that holding foreign money is like investing abroad. Canadian investment abroad is a minus item in the capital account and in the official settlements account. (By the same reasoning, if official Canadian reserves decrease, the *official settlements account balance* is positive.)

The sum of the balances on the three accounts always equals zero. That is, to pay for our current account deficit, we must either borrow more from abroad than we lend abroad or our official reserves must decrease to cover the shortfall.

Table 36.1 shows the Canadian balance of payments accounts in 1998. Items in the current account and capital account that provide foreign currency to Canada have a plus sign; items that cost Canada foreign currency have a minus sign. The table shows that in 1998, imports plus net interest payments exceeded exports plus net transfers and the current account had a deficit of $16 billion. How do we pay for our current account deficit? We pay by borrowing from the rest of the world. The capital account tells us by how much. We borrowed $66 billion (foreign investment in Canada) but made loans of $44 billion (Canadian investment abroad). Thus our net foreign borrowing was $22 billion. A statistical discrepancy arises because of illegal and hidden transactions, which in 1998 was $1 billion.

TABLE 36.1

Canadian Balance of Payments Accounts in 1998

	Billions of dollars
Current account	
Imports of goods and services	−356
Exports of goods and services	+368
Net interest payments	−29
Net transfers	+1
Current account balance	−16
Capital account	
Foreign investment in Canada	+66
Canadian investment abroad	−44
Capital account balance	+22
Statistical discrepancy	+1
Official settlements account	
Increase in official Canadian reserves	−7

Source: Bank of Canada, *Banking and Financial Statistics*, August 1999.

Our net borrowing from abroad minus our current account deficit is the change in official Canadian reserves. In 1998, reserves increased because of net foreign borrowing of $22 billion plus the statistical discrepancy of $1 billion exceeded our current account deficit of $16 billion by $7 billion. When our reserves change, we record an increase in reserves as a negative number in our international accounts. Why? Because an increase in our reserves is like making a loan to the rest of the world.

The numbers in Table 36.1 give a snapshot of the balance of payments accounts in 1998. Figure 36.1 puts that snapshot into perspective by showing the balance of payments between 1980 and 1998. Because the economy grows and the price level rises, changes in the dollar value of the balance of payments do not convey much information. To remove the influences of growth and inflation, Fig. 36.1 shows the balance of payments as a percentage of nominal GDP.

As you can see, the capital account balance is almost a mirror image of the current account balance. The official settlements balance is very small in comparison with the balances on these other two accounts. A large current account deficit (and capital account surplus) emerged during the 1980s but declined from 1993 to 1996. Since then it has increased again.

You will perhaps obtain a better understanding of the balance of payments accounts and the way in which they are linked together if you consider the income and expenditure, borrowing and lending, and bank account of an individual.

Individual Analogy An individual's current account records the income from supplying the services of productive resources and the expenditure on goods and services. Consider, for example, Joanne. She worked in 1998 and earned an income of $25,000. Joanne has $10,000 worth of investments that earned her an interest income of $1,000. Joanne's current account shows an income of $26,000. Joanne spent $18,000 buying goods and services for consumption. She also bought a new house, which cost her $60,000. So Joanne's total expenditure was $78,000. The difference between her expenditure and income

FIGURE 36.1

The Balance of Payments: 1980–1998

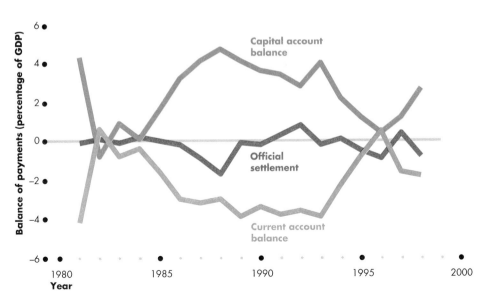

During the 1980s, a large current account deficit arose. That deficit decreased between 1993 and 1996 but then increased again. The capital account balance mirrors the current account balance. When the current account balance is negative, the capital account balance is positive—we borrow from the rest of the world. Fluctuations in the official settlements balance are small in comparison with fluctuations in the current account balance and the capital account balance.

Source: Bank of Canada, *Banking and Financial Statistics*, August 1999.

is $52,000 ($78,000 minus $26,000). This amount is Joanne's current account deficit.

To pay for expenditure of $52,000 in excess of her income, Joanne has to use the money that she has in the bank or has to take out a loan. In fact, Joanne took a mortgage of $50,000 to help buy her house. This mortgage was the only borrowing that Joanne did, so her capital account surplus was $50,000. With a current account deficit of $52,000 and a capital account surplus of $50,000, Joanne is still $2,000 short. She got that $2,000 from her own bank account. Her cash holdings decreased by $2,000.

Joanne's income from her work is analogous to a country's income from its exports. Her income from her investments is analogous to a country's interest income from foreigners. Her purchases of goods and services, including her purchase of a house, are analogous to a country's imports. Joanne's mortgage—borrowing from someone else—is analogous to a country's borrowing from the rest of the world. The change in her own bank account is analogous to the change in the country's official reserves.

Borrowers and Lenders, Debtors and Creditors

A country that has a current account deficit and that borrows more from the rest of the world than it lends to it is called a **net borrower**. Similarly, a **net lender** is a country that lends more to the rest of the world than it borrows from it.

Canada is a net borrower and has been so for most of the past 50 years. During the 54 years between the end of World War II and 1998, Canada was a net lender in only 12 years, and most of those were in the 1940s. During the 1990s alone, Canada has borrowed $150 billion (net) from the rest of the world. Canada's cumulative borrowing since the end of World War II is $236 billion. Only in the deep recession of the early 1980s and briefly in 1996 has Canada been a net lender in recent memory. The year of greatest foreign borrowing was 1993 when Canada borrowed (net) almost $30 billion from the rest of the world.

Most countries are net borrowers like Canada. But a small number of countries, including Japan and oil-rich Saudi Arabia, are net lenders. And for the world as a whole, net foreign borrowing equals net foreign lending.

A net borrower might be going deeper into debt or might simply be reducing its net assets held in the rest of the world. The total stock of foreign invest-

ment determines whether a country is a debtor or creditor. A **debtor nation** is a country that during its entire history has borrowed more from the rest of the world than it has lent to it. It has a stock of outstanding debt to the rest of the world that exceeds the stock of its own claims on the rest of the world. A **creditor nation** is a country that has invested more in the rest of the world than other countries have invested in it.

At the heart of the distinction between a net borrower/net lender and a debtor/creditor nation is the distinction between flows and stocks, which you have encountered many times in your study of macroeconomics. Borrowing and lending are flows—amounts borrowed or lent per unit of time. Debts are stocks—amounts owed at a point in time. The flow of borrowing and lending changes the stock of debt. But the outstanding stock of debt depends mainly on past flows of borrowing and lending, not on the current period's flows. The current period's flows determine the change in the stock of debt outstanding.

Canada is a debtor nation. In 1998, the net international debt of Canadians was $324 billion. To put this number in perspective, it is $11,000 per person, or 36 percent of total income. Almost one-half of this debt has been accumulated during the 1990s. Other debtor nations are a diverse group. They include the United States as well as the poor capital-hungry nations of the developing regions of Central and South America, Asia, and Africa. The international debt of the developing countries grew from less than a third to more than a half of their gross domestic product during the 1980s and 1990s and has created what was called the "Third World debt crisis."

Should we be concerned that Canada is a net borrower and debtor nation? The answer to this question depends on what we do with the funds that we borrow. If borrowing finances investment that in turn generates economic growth and higher income, borrowing is not a problem. If borrowing finances consumption, then higher interest payments are being incurred, and as a consequence, consumption will eventually have to be reduced. In this case, the more the borrowing and the longer it goes on, the greater is the reduction in consumption that will eventually be necessary.

Is Canada Borrowing for Consumption or Investment?

In 1998, our current account deficit was $16 billion and we borrowed this amount from abroad. Did we borrow for consumption or investment? In 1998, private investment in buildings, plant, and equipment was $176 billion. Government investment in a wide range of public buildings and structures such as highways was around $20 billion. All this investment added to the nation's capital and much of it increased productivity. Government also spends on education and health-care services, which increase *human capital*. Our international borrowing is financing private and public investment, not consumption.

Current Account Balance

What determines a country's current account balance and net foreign borrowing? You've seen that net exports (*NX*) is the main item in the current account. We can define the current account balance (*CAB*) as:

$$CAB = NX + \text{Net interest income} + \text{Net transfers.}$$

Fluctuations in net exports are the main source of fluctuations in the current account balance. The other two items have trends but they do not fluctuate much. So we can study the current account balance by looking at what determines net exports.

Net Exports

Net exports are determined by the government budget and private saving and investment. To see how net exports are determined, we need to recall some of the things that we learned about the National Income Accounts in Chapter 22. Table 36.2 will refresh your memory and summarize some calculations.

Part (a) lists the national income variables that are needed, with their symbols. Part (b) defines three surpluses and deficits. **Net exports** is exports of goods and services minus imports of goods and services.

The **government sector surplus or deficit** is equal to net taxes minus government expenditures on goods and services. If that number is positive, a government sector surplus is lent to other sectors; if that number is negative, a government deficit must be financed by borrowing from other sectors. The government sector deficit is the sum of the deficits of the federal, provincial, and municipal governments.

The **private sector surplus or deficit** is saving minus investment. If saving exceeds investment, a private sector surplus is lent to other sectors. If investment exceeds saving, borrowing from other sectors finances a private sector deficit.

Part (b) also shows the values of these deficits and surpluses for Canada in 1998. As you can see, net

---

TABLE 36.2

Net Exports, the Government Budget, Saving, and Investment

	Symbols and equations	Canada in 1998 (billions of dollars)
(a) Variables		
Exports*	X	370
Imports*	M	357
Government expenditures	G	177
Net taxes	NT	187
Investment	I	176
Saving	S	179
(b) Surpluses and deficits		
Net exports	X – M	370 – 357 = 13
Government sector	NT – G	187 – 177 = 10
Private sector	S – I	179 – 176 = 3

(c) Relation among surpluses and deficits

National accounts	$Y = C + I + G + X - M$	
	$= C + S + NT$	
Rearranging:	$X - M = S - I + NT - G$	
Net exports	X – M	13
Equals:		
Government sector	NT – G	10
Plus		
Private sector	S – I	3

Source: Statistics Canada StatCan: CANSIM Disc, March 1999.

*The national income accounts' measures of exports and imports are different from the balance of payments accounts' measures by small amounts.

exports were $13 billion, a surplus of $13 billion. The government sector's revenue from net taxes was $187 billion and it purchased $177 billion worth of goods and services. The government sector surplus was $10 billion. The private sector saved $179 billion and invested $176 billion, so it had a surplus of $3 billion.

Part (c) shows the relationship among the three surpluses. From the national income accounts, we know that real GDP (Y) is the sum of consumption expenditure (C), investment (I), government expenditures (G), and net exports ($X - M$). It also equals the sum of consumption expenditure (C), saving (S), and net taxes (NT). Rearranging these equations tells us that net exports ($X - M$) is the sum of the government sector surplus ($NT - G$) and the private sector surplus ($S - I$). In Canada in 1998, the government sector had a surplus of $10 billion and the private sector had a surplus of $3 billion. The government sector surplus plus the private sector surplus equals net exports of $13 billion.

The Twin Deficits

You've seen that net exports equals the sum of the government surplus and the private surplus. And net exports plus debt interest (and other small transfers) equals the current account balance. What is the relationship over time between the current account balance and the government budget balance? How do these balances fluctuate over time? Figure 36.2 answers this question. It shows the government budget (the red line) and the current account balance (the blue line).

You can see that with an important exception during the early 1980s, there is a tendency for the current account to go into a deeper deficit when the government budget goes into a deeper deficit. Because of the tendency for the government budget deficit and the current account deficit to move in the same direction they have been called the **twin deficits**.

Why are the two deficits linked? They are linked because capital is highly mobile in today's world. If the Canadian government increases expenditure or lowers taxes, total spending in Canada rises. But with the economy at or near to full employment, the extra goods and services demanded are sucked in from the rest of the world. Imports increase. Capital flows in to pay for those imports. Saving and investment don't change. This relationship broke down during the early 1980s because we were in recession and investment decreased relative to saving.

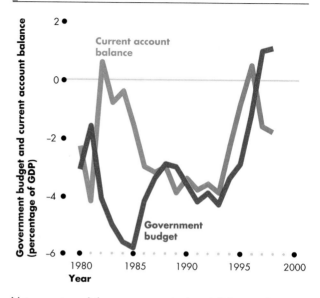

FIGURE 36.2

The Twin Deficits

Net exports and the government budget deficit move in similar ways and look like twin deficits. But this relationship broke down during the early 1980s when the private sector surplus swelled.

Source: Statistics Canada StatCan: CANSIM Disc, March 1999.

REVIEW QUIZ

■ When a Canadian art dealer buys a painting from a French gallery, which currency gets used to make the transaction?

■ When a German car maker buys parts from a Windsor car maker, which currency gets used to make the transaction?

■ What types of transactions do we record in the balance of payments accounts?

■ What transactions does the current account record? What transactions does the capital account record? What transactions does the official settlements account record?

■ How are the current account deficit, the government sector deficit, and the private sector surplus related?

The Exchange Rate

WHEN WE BUY FOREIGN GOODS OR INVEST IN another country, we have to obtain some of that country's currency to make the transaction. When foreigners buy Canadian-produced goods or invest in Canada, they have to obtain some Canadian dollars. We get foreign currency, and foreigners get Canadian dollars in the foreign exchange market. The **foreign exchange market** is the market in which the currency of one country is exchanged for the currency of another. The foreign exchange market is not a place like a downtown flea market or produce market. The market is made up of thousands of people—importers and exporters, banks, and specialists in the buying and selling of foreign exchange, called foreign exchange brokers. The foreign exchange market opens on Monday morning in Hong Kong, which is still Sunday evening in Montreal and Toronto. As the day advances, markets open in Singapore, Tokyo, Bahrain, Frankfurt, London, New York, Montreal, Toronto, and Vancouver. As the West Coast markets close, Hong Kong is only an hour away from opening for the next day of business. The sun barely sets on the foreign exchange market. Dealers around the world are in continual contact by telephone and on a typical day in 1999, $1.4 trillion changed hands.

The price at which one currency exchanges for another is called a **foreign exchange rate**. For example, in October 1999, one Canadian dollar bought 68 U.S. cents. The exchange rate was 68 U.S. cents per dollar.

Figure 36.3 shows the exchange rate of the Canadian dollar in terms of the U.S. dollar between 1968 and 1998. On the average, the Canadian dollar has fallen in value against the U.S. dollar.

A fall in the value of one currency in terms of another currency is called **currency depreciation**. For example when the Canadian dollar fell from 101 U.S. cents in 1976 to 94 U.S. cents in 1977, the Canadian dollar depreciated by 7 percent.

The opposite of currency depreciation is **currency appreciation**, which is the rise in the value of one currency in terms of another currency. From 1968 to 1976, and again from 1986 to 1991, the value of the Canadian dollar increased against the U.S. dollar—the Canadian dollar appreciated.

We've just expressed the value of the Canadian dollar in terms of the U.S. dollar. But we can express the value of the dollar in terms of any currency. Also,

FIGURE 36.3

The Exchange Rate

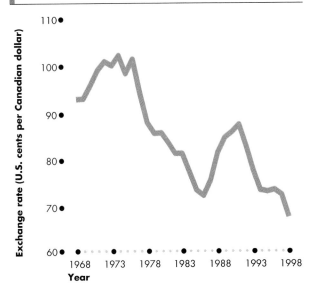

The Canadian dollar exchange rate, expressed as U.S. cents per dollar, shows that the dollar fell in value—depreciated—against the U.S. dollar from 1976 through 1986. It rose in value—appreciated—from 1986 through 1991 and then depreciated again.

Source: Bank of Canada *Bank of Canada Review*, Summer 1999.

we can express the exchange rate of the U.S. dollar in terms of the Canadian dollar as a number of Canadian dollars per U.S. dollar.

When the Canadian dollar depreciates against the U.S. dollar, the U.S. dollar appreciates against the Canadian dollar.

Why does the Canadian dollar fluctuate in value? Why does it sometimes depreciate and sometimes appreciate? What happened between 1976 and 1986 and again between 1992 and 1998 to make the Canadian dollar depreciate? And what happened during the late 1960s and between 1986 and 1991 to make it appreciate against the U.S. dollar? To answer these questions, we need to understand the forces that determine the exchange rate.

The exchange rate is the price of one country's money in terms of another country's money. And like all prices, the exchange rate is determined by demand and supply.

Demand in the Foreign Exchange Market

The quantity of Canadian dollars demanded in the foreign exchange market is the amount that traders plan to buy during a given time period at a given exchange rate. This quantity depends on many factors but the main ones are:

■ The exchange rate
■ Interest rates in Canada and other countries
■ The expected future exchange rate

Let's look first at the relationship between the quantity of Canadian dollars demanded in the foreign exchange market and the exchange rate.

The Law of Demand for Foreign Exchange

People do not buy dollars because they enjoy them. The demand for dollars is a *derived demand*. People demand Canadian dollars so that they can buy Canadian-made goods and services (Canadian exports). They also demand dollars so they can buy Canadian assets such as bank accounts, bonds, stocks, businesses, and real estate. Nevertheless, the law of demand applies to dollars just as it does to anything else that people value.

Other things remaining the same, the higher the exchange rate, the smaller is the quantity of Canadian dollars demanded in the foreign exchange market. For example, if the price of the Canadian dollar rose from 68 U.S. cents to 75 U.S. cents but nothing else changed, the quantity of Canadian dollars that people plan to buy in the foreign exchange market would decrease. The exchange rate influences the quantity of dollars demanded for two reasons:

■ Exports effect
■ Expected profit effect

Exports Effect   The larger the value of Canadian exports, the larger is the quantity of Canadian dollars demanded on the foreign exchange market. But the value of Canadian exports depends on the exchange rate. The lower the exchange rate, with other things remaining the same, the cheaper are Canadian-produced goods and services and the more Canada exports. So the quantity of Canadian dollars demanded on the foreign exchange market increases.

Expected Profit Effect   The larger the expected profit from holding Canadian dollars, the greater is the quantity of Canadian dollars demanded. But expected profit depends on the exchange rate. The lower the exchange rate, other things remaining the same, the larger is the expected profit from buying Canadian dollars and the greater is the quantity of Canadian dollars demanded.

To understand this effect, suppose that today, a Canadian dollar costs 68 U.S. cents. Tina thinks the dollar will be worth 70 U.S. cents by the end of the month and Jack thinks it will be worth 67 U.S. cents. In this situation, Tina buys Canadian dollars but Jack does not. Now suppose that expectations remain the same, but that today a Canadian dollar costs 65 U.S. cents. Now both Tina and Jack buy Canadian dollars. So the quantity of dollars demanded increases.

For the two reasons we've just reviewed, other things remaining the same, when the foreign exchange rate rises, the quantity of Canadian dollars demanded decreases and when the foreign exchange rate falls, the quantity of Canadian dollars demanded increases.

Figure 36.4 shows the demand curve for Canadian dollars in the foreign exchange market. In this figure, when the foreign exchange rate rises, other things remaining the same, there is a decrease in the quantity of Canadian dollars demanded and a movement upward along the demand curve as shown by the arrow. When the exchange rate falls, other things remaining the same, there is an increase in the quantity of Canadian dollars demanded and a movement downward along the demand curve as shown by the arrow.

Changes in the Demand for Dollars

A change in any other influence on the quantity of Canadian dollars that people plan to buy brings a change in the demand for dollars and a shift in the demand curve for dollars. Demand either increases or decreases. These other influences are:

■ Interest rates in Canada and other countries
■ The expected future exchange rate

Interest Rates in Canada and Other Countries
People and businesses buy financial assets to make a return. The higher the interest rate that people can make on Canadian assets compared with foreign assets, the more Canadian assets they buy. What matters is not the level of Canadian interest rates, but the

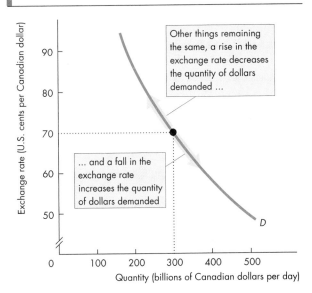

FIGURE 36.4

The Demand for Dollars

Other things remaining the same, a rise in the exchange rate decreases the quantity of dollars demanded ...

... and a fall in the exchange rate increases the quantity of dollars demanded

The quantity of Canadian dollars that people plan to buy depends on the exchange rate. Other things remaining the same, if the exchange rate rises, the quantity of dollars demanded decreases and there is a movement up along the demand curve for dollars. If the exchange rate falls, the quantity of dollars demanded increases and there is a movement down along the demand curve for dollars.

Canadian interest rate minus the foreign interest rate, a gap that is called the **Canadian interest rate differential**. If the Canadian interest rate rises and the foreign interest rate remains constant, the Canadian interest rate differential increases. The larger the Canadian interest rate differential, the greater is the demand for Canadian assets and the greater is the demand for Canadian dollars on the foreign exchange market.

The Expected Future Exchange Rate Other things remaining the same, the higher the expected future exchange rate, the greater is the demand for Canadian dollars. To see why, suppose you are American Express's finance manager. The exchange rate is 70 U.S cents per dollar and you think that by the end of the month, it will be 75 U.S. cents per dollar. You spend $U.S.700,000 today and buy $C1,000,000. At the end of the month, the Canadian

dollar is 75 U.S. cents, as you predicted it would be, and you sell the $C1,000,000. You get $U.S.750,000. You've made a profit of $U.S.50,000. The higher the expected future exchange rate, other things remaining the same, the greater is the expected profit and the greater is the demand for Canadian dollars.

Figure 36.5 summarizes the influences on the demand for dollars. A rise in the Canadian interest differential or a rise in the expected future exchange rate increases the demand for Canadian dollars and shifts the demand curve rightward from D_0 to D_1. A fall in the Canadian interest differential or a fall in the expected future exchange rate decreases the demand for Canadian dollars and shifts the demand curve leftward from D_0 to D_2.

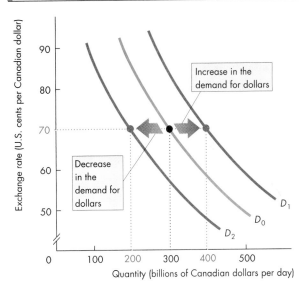

FIGURE 36.5

Changes in the Demand for Dollars

Increase in the demand for dollars

Decrease in the demand for dollars

A change in any influence on the quantity of Canadian dollars that people plan to buy, other than today's exchange rate, brings a change in the demand for Canadian dollars.

The demand for Canadian dollars:

Increases if:
- The Canadian interest rate differential increases
- The expected future exchange rate rises

Decreases if:
- The Canadian interest rate differential decreases
- The expected future exchange rate falls

Supply in the Foreign Exchange Market

The quantity of Canadian dollars supplied in the foreign exchange market is the amount that traders plan to sell during a given time period at a given exchange rate. This quantity depends on many factors but the main ones are:

- The exchange rate
- Interest rates in Canada and other countries
- The expected future exchange rate

Let's look first at the relationship between the quantity of Canadian dollars supplied in the foreign exchange market and the exchange rate.

The Law of Supply for Foreign Exchange

People supply dollars in the foreign exchange market when they buy other currencies. And they buy other currencies so they can buy foreign-made goods and services (Canadian imports). People also supply dollars and buy foreign currencies so they can buy foreign assets such as bank accounts, bonds, stocks, businesses, and real estate. The law of supply applies to dollars just as it does to anything else that people plan to sell.

Other things remaining the same, the higher the exchange rate, the greater is the quantity of dollars supplied in the foreign exchange market. For example, if the price of the Canadian dollar rose from 68 U.S. cents to 75 U.S. cents but nothing else changed, the quantity of Canadian dollars that people plan to sell in the foreign exchange market would increase. The exchange rate influences the quantity of dollars supplied for two reasons:

- Imports effect
- Expected profit effect

Imports Effect The larger the value of Canadian imports, the larger is the quantity of foreign currency demanded to pay for these imports. And when people buy foreign currency, they supply Canadian dollars. So the larger the value of Canadian imports, the greater is the quantity of Canadian dollars supplied on the foreign exchange market. But the value of Canadian imports depends on the exchange rate. The

higher the exchange rate, with other things remaining the same, the cheaper are foreign-produced goods and services to Canadians, and the more Canada imports. So the greater is the quantity of Canadian dollars supplied.

Expected Profit Effect The larger the expected profit from holding a foreign currency, the greater is the quantity of that currency demanded and the greater is the quantity of Canadian dollars supplied in the foreign exchange market. But the expected profit from holding a foreign currency depends on the exchange rate. The higher the exchange rate, other things remaining the same, the larger is the expected profit from selling Canadian dollars and the greater is the quantity of Canadian dollars supplied.

For the two reasons we've just reviewed, other things remaining the same, when the foreign exchange

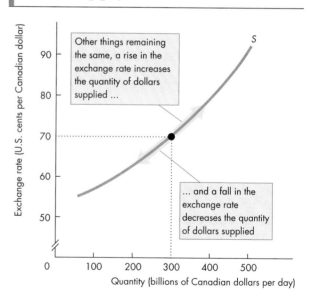

FIGURE 36.6
The Supply of Dollars

The quantity of Canadian dollars that people plan to sell depends on the exchange rate. Other things remaining the same, if the exchange rate rises, the quantity of Canadian dollars supplied increases and there is a movement up along the supply curve for dollars. If the exchange rate falls, the quantity of Canadian dollars supplied decreases and there is a movement down along the supply curve for dollars.

rate rises, the quantity of dollars supplied increases and when the foreign exchange rate falls, the quantity of Canadian dollars supplied decreases. Figure 36.6 shows the supply curve for Canadian dollars in the foreign exchange market. In this figure, when the foreign exchange rate rises, other things remaining the same, there is an increase in the quantity of Canadian dollars supplied and a movement upward along the supply curve as shown by the arrow. When the exchange rate falls, other things remaining the same, there is a decrease in the quantity of Canadian dollars supplied and a movement downward along the supply curve as shown by the arrow.

Changes in the Supply of Dollars

A change in any other influence on the quantity of Canadian dollars that people plan to sell in the foreign exchange market brings a change in the supply of dollars and a shift in the supply curve for dollars. Supply either increases or decreases. These other influences parallel the other influences on demand but have exactly the opposite effects. These influences are:

- Interest rates in Canada and other countries
- The expected future exchange rate

Interest Rates in Canada and Other Countries
The larger the Canadian interest rate differential, the smaller is the demand for foreign assets, and the smaller is the supply of Canadian dollars on the foreign exchange market.

The Expected Future Exchange Rate Other things remaining the same, the higher the expected future exchange rate, the smaller is the supply of dollars. To see why, suppose the Canadian dollar is trading at 70 U.S. cents per dollar today and you think that by the end of the month, the dollar will be worth 75 U.S. cents per dollar. You were planning on selling Canadian dollars today, but you decide to hold off and wait until the end of the month. If you supply dollars today, you get only 70 U.S. cents. But at the end of the month, if the dollar is worth 75 U.S. cents as you predict, you'll get 75 U.S. cents for each dollar you supply. You'll make a profit of 5 U.S. cents per dollar. So the higher the expected future exchange rate, other things remaining the same, the smaller is the expected profit from selling Canadian dollars

today and the smaller is the supply of Canadian dollars today.

Figure 36.7 summarizes the influences on the supply of Canadian dollars. A rise in the Canadian interest rate differential or a rise in the expected future exchange rate decreases the supply of Canadian dollars and shifts the supply curve leftward from S_0 to S_1. A fall in the Canadian interest rate differential or a fall in the expected future exchange rate increases the supply of Canadian dollars and shifts the supply curve rightward from S_0 to S_2.

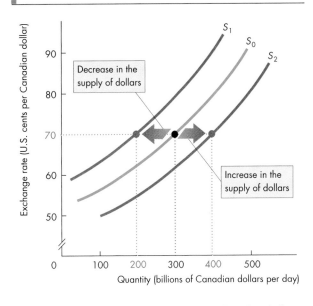

FIGURE 36.7

Changes in the Supply of Dollars

A change in any influence on the quantity of Canadian dollars that people plan to sell, other than today's exchange rate, brings a change in the supply of Canadian dollars.

The supply of Canadian dollars:

Increases if:
- The Canadian interest rate differential decreases
- The expected future exchange rate falls

Decreases if:
- The Canadian interest rate differential increases
- The expected future exchange rate rises

Market Equilibrium

Figure 36.8 shows how demand and supply in the foreign exchange market determine the exchange rate. The demand curve is *D* and the supply curve is *S*. As in other markets you've studied, price (the exchange rate) acts as a regulator. If the exchange rate is too high, there is a surplus—the quantity supplied exceeds the quantity demanded. For example, in Fig. 36.8, if the exchange rate is 80 U.S. cents per Canadian dollar, there is a surplus of Canadian dollars.

If the exchange rate is too low, there is a shortage—the quantity supplied is less than the quantity demanded. For example, in Fig. 36.8, if the exchange rate is 60 U.S. cents per Canadian dollar, there is a shortage of Canadian dollars.

At the equilibrium exchange rate, there is neither a shortage nor a surplus. The quantity supplied equals the quantity demanded. In Fig. 36.8, the equilibrium exchange rate is 70 U.S. cents per Canadian dollar. At this exchange rate, the quantity demanded and the quantity supplied are each $300 billion a day.

The foreign exchange market is constantly pulled to its equilibrium by the forces of supply and demand. Foreign exchange dealers are constantly looking for the best price they can get. If they are selling, they want the highest price available. If they are buying, they want the lowest price available. Information flows from dealer to dealer through the worldwide computer network and the price adjusts second by second to keep buying plans and selling plans in balance. That is, price adjusts minute by minute to keep the market at its equilibrium.

Changes in the Exchange Rate

If the demand for dollars increases and the supply of dollars does not change, the exchange rate rises. If the demand for dollars decreases and the supply of dollars does not change, the exchange rate falls. Similarly, if the supply of dollars decreases and the demand for dollars does not change, the exchange rate rises. If the supply of dollars increases and the demand for dollars does not change, the exchange rate falls.

These predictions about the effects of changes in demand and supply are exactly the same as for any other market.

Why the Exchange Rate is Volatile   Sometimes the dollar depreciates and at other times it appreciates but the quantity of dollars traded each day barely changes. Why? The main reason is that supply and demand are not independent of each other in the foreign exchange market.

When we studied the demand for dollars and the supply of dollars, we saw that the demand side and the supply side of the market have some common influences. A change in the expected future exchange rate or a change in the Canadian interest rate differential changes both demand and supply and in opposite directions. These common influences explain why the exchange rate can be volatile at times even though the quantity of dollars traded does not change.

Everyone in the market is potentially either a demander or a supplier. Each has a price above which he or she will sell and below which he or she will buy. Let's see how these common supply and demand effects work by looking at two episodes: one in which the dollar appreciated and one in which it depreciated.

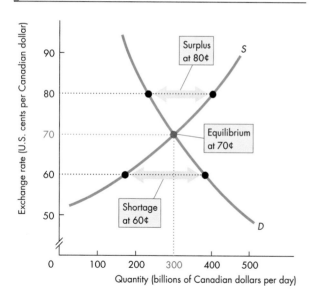

FIGURE 36.8
Equilibrium Exchange Rate

The demand curve for dollars is *D* and the supply curve is *S*. If the exchange rate is 80 U.S. cents per dollar, there is a surplus of dollars and the exchange rate falls. If the exchange rate is 60 U.S. cents per dollar, there is a shortage of dollars and the exchange rate rises. If the exchange rate is 70 U.S. cents per dollar, there is neither a shortage nor a surplus of dollars and the exchange rate remains constant. The market is in equilibrium.

An Appreciating Dollar: 1986–1991   Between 1986 and 1991 the Canadian dollar appreciated. It rose from 72 U.S. cents in 1986 to 87 U.S. cents in 1991. Figure 36.9(a) explains why this happened. In 1986, the demand and supply curves were those labelled D_{86} and S_{86}. The exchange rate was 72 U.S. cents—where the supply and demand curves intersect. During the next five years, people expected the Canadian dollar to appreciate. They expected a higher future exchange rate. As a result, the demand for dollars increased and the supply of dollars decreased. The demand curve shifted from D_{86} to D_{91} and the supply curve shifted from S_{86} to S_{91}. These two shifts reinforced each other and the exchange rate increased to 87 U.S. cents per dollar.

A Depreciating Dollar: 1991–1998   Between 1991 and the fall of 1998, the dollar fell from 87 U.S. cents to 68 U.S. cents per dollar. Figure 36.9(b) explains this fall. In 1991, the demand and supply curves were those labelled D_{91} and S_{91}. The exchange

rate was 87 U.S. cents per dollar. During the 1990s, traders expected the Canadian dollar to depreciate. They expected a lower exchange rate. As a result, the demand for dollars decreased and the supply of dollars increased. The demand curve shifted leftward to D_{98} and the supply curve shifted rightward to S_{98}. The exchange rate fell to 68 U.S. cents per dollar.

Exchange Rate Expectations

The changes in the exchange rate that we've just examined occurred mainly because the exchange rate was expected to change. This explanation sounds a bit like a self-fulfilling forecast. But what makes expectations change? The answer is new information about the deeper forces that influence the value of money. Two such forces are:

- Purchasing power parity
- Interest rate parity

FIGURE 36.9

Exchange Rate Fluctuations

(a) 1986 to 1991

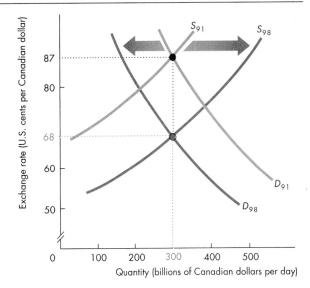

(b) 1991 to 1998

The exchange rate fluctuates because changes in demand and supply are not independent of each other. Between 1986 and 1991 (part a), the dollar appreciated from 72 U.S. cents to 87 U.S. cents per dollar. This appreciation occurred because an increase in the expected future exchange rate increased the

demand for dollars and decreased the supply. Between 1991 and 1998 (in part b), the exchange rate fell from 87 U.S. cents to 68 U.S. cents per dollar. This depreciation occurred because a decrease in the expected future exchange rate decreased the demand for dollars and increased the supply.

Purchasing Power Parity   Money is worth what it will buy. But two kinds of money, Canadian dollars and U.S. dollars for example, might buy different amounts of goods and services. Suppose a Big Mac costs $4 (Canadian) in Toronto and $3 (U.S.) in New York. If the Canadian dollar exchange rate is 75 U.S. cents per Canadian dollar, the two monies have the same value. You can buy a Big Mac in either Toronto or New York for either $4 Canadian or $3 U.S.

The situation we've just described is called **purchasing power parity**, which means *equal value of money*. If purchasing power parity does not prevail, some powerful forces go to work. To understand these forces, let's suppose that the price of a Big Mac in New York rises to $4 U.S. but in Toronto it remains at $4 Canadian. Suppose the exchange rate remains at 75 U.S. cents per Canadian dollar. In this case, a Big Mac in Toronto still costs $4 Canadian or $3 U.S. But in New York, it costs $4 U.S. or $5.33 Canadian. Money buys more in Canada than in the United States. Money is not of equal value in both countries.

If all (or most) prices have increased in the United States and have not increased in Canada, then people will generally expect that the value of the Canadian dollar on the foreign exchange market must rise. In this situation, the exchange rate is expected to rise. The demand for Canadian dollars increases and the supply of Canadian dollars decreases. The exchange rate rises, as expected. If the exchange rate rises to $1.00 U.S. per Canadian dollar and there are no further price changes, purchasing power parity is restored. A Big Mac now costs $4 in either Canadian or U.S. dollars in both New York and Toronto.

If prices increase in Canada but remain constant in other countries, then people will generally expect that the value of the Canadian dollar on the foreign exchange market is too high and that it is going to fall. In this situation, the exchange rate is expected to fall. The demand for Canadian dollars decreases and the supply of Canadian dollars increases. The exchange rate falls, as expected.

Ultimately, the value of money is determined by the price level, which in turn is determined by aggregate supply and aggregate demand (see Chapter 24, pp. 524–525.) So the deeper forces that influence the exchange rate have tentacles that spread throughout the economy. If the price level rises faster in Canada than in other countries, the exchange rate falls. And if the price level rises slower in Canada than in other countries, the exchange rate rises.

Interest Rate Parity   Money is worth what it can earn. Again two kinds of money, Canadian dollars and U.S. dollars for example, might earn different amounts. For example, suppose a Canadian dollar bank deposit in Toronto earns 4 percent a year and a U.S. dollar bank deposit in New York earns 5 percent a year. In this situation, why does anyone deposit money in Toronto? Why doesn't all the money flow to New York? The answer is: because of exchange rate expectations. Suppose people expect the Canadian dollar to appreciate by 1 percent a year. This 1 percent appreciation must be added to the 4 percent interest to obtain a return of 5 percent a year that an American can earn by depositing funds in a Toronto bank. The two returns are equal. This situation is one of **interest rate parity**, which means *equal rates of return*.

Adjusted for risk, interest rate parity always prevails. Funds move to get the highest return available. If for a few seconds a higher return is available in New York than in Toronto, the demand for Canadian dollars rises and the exchange rate rises until the expected rates of return are equal.

The Bank of Canada in the Foreign Exchange Market

Interest rates in Canada are determined by the demand for and supply of money (see Chapter 27, pp. 610–612). But the Bank of Canada influences the supply of money, so, ultimately, the exchange rate is influenced by monetary policy. When interest rates in Canada rise relative to those in other countries, the demand for Canadian dollars increases, the supply decreases, and the exchange rate rises. (Similarly, when interest rates in Canada fall relative to those in other countries, the demand for Canadian dollars decreases, the supply increases, and the exchange rate falls.)

But the Bank of Canada can intervene directly in the foreign exchange market. It can buy or sell dollars and try to smooth out fluctuations in the exchange rate. Let's look at the foreign exchange interventions that the Bank can make.

Suppose the Bank of Canada wants the exchange rate to be steady at 70 U.S. cents per dollar. If the exchange rate rises above 70 U.S. cents, the Bank sells dollars. If the exchange rate falls below 70 U.S. cents, the Bank buys dollars. By these actions, it changes the supply of dollars and keeps the exchange rate close to its target rate of 70 U.S. cents per Canadian dollar.

Figure 36.10 shows the Bank of Canada's intervention in the foreign exchange market. The supply of dollars is S and initially the demand for dollars is D_0. The equilibrium exchange rate is 70 U.S. cents per dollar. This exchange rate is the Bank's target rate, shown by the horizontal red line.

When the demand for dollars increases and the demand curve shifts rightward to D_1, the Bank sells $100 billion. This action increases the supply of dollars by $100 billion and prevents the exchange rate from rising. When the demand for dollars decreases and the demand curve shifts leftward to D_2, the Bank buys $100 billion. This action decreases the supply of dollars by $100 billion and prevents the exchange rate from falling.

If the demand for dollars fluctuates between D_1 and D_2 and on the average is to D_0, the Bank can repeatedly intervene in the way we've just seen.

Sometimes the Bank of Canada buys and sometimes it sells but, on the average, it neither buys nor sells.

But suppose the demand for dollars increases permanently from D_0 to D_1. The Bank cannot now maintain the exchange rate at 70 U.S. cents indefinitely. For to do so, the Bank would have to sell Canadian dollars every day. When the Bank sells dollars in the foreign exchange market, it buys foreign currency. So the Bank would be piling up foreign currency.

Now suppose the demand for dollars decreases permanently from D_0 to D_2. Again the Bank cannot maintain the exchange rate at 70 U.S. cents indefinitely. In this situation, to hold the exchange rate at 70 U.S. cents per dollar the Bank would have to buy Canadian dollars every day. When the Bank buys dollars in the foreign exchange market, it uses its holdings of foreign currency. So the Bank would be losing foreign currency. Eventually, it would run out of foreign currency and would then have to abandon its attempt to fix the exchange rate.

FIGURE 36.10

Foreign Exchange Market Intervention

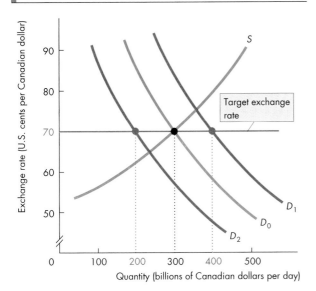

Initially, the demand for dollars is D_0, the supply of dollars is S, and the exchange rate is 70 U.S. cents per dollar. The Bank of Canada can intervene in the foreign exchange market to keep the exchange rate close to its target rate (70 U.S. cents in this example). If demand increases from D_0 to D_1, the Bank sells dollars to increase supply. If demand decreases from D_0 to D_2, the Bank buys dollars to decrease supply. Persistent intervention on one side of the market cannot be sustained.

REVIEW QUIZ

- What is the exchange rate and how is it determined?
- What are the influences of interest rates and the expected future exchange rate on the demand for and supply of dollars in the foreign exchange market?
- How do changes in the expected future exchange rate influence the actual exchange rate?
- How do purchasing power parity and interest rate parity affect exchange rate expectations?
- How can the Bank of Canada influence the foreign exchange market?

Reading Between the Lines on pages 840–841 looks at the Canadian dollar in 1999.

You have now reached the end of your economics course. Go back to the big ideas that define the way of economic thinking (on pp. 6–11) and see how much more they mean to you now than they did when you first read them. We hope that your instructor and we have helped open your eyes and shown you a new way of seeing the world. If we have, you can now do your own "reading between the lines" every day. Keep your economics text handy. Use it to refresh your memory of the economic principles that help you make sense of your world.

The Fluctuating Dollar

THE GLOBE AND MAIL, SEPTEMBER 21, 1999

Dollar tumbles to 67.63 cents (U.S.)

BY MARIAN STINSON

The dollar fell one-third of a cent yesterday as markets braced for the possibility that Bank of Canada Governor Gordon Thiessen will give a hint about his policies in a speech later this week.

The dollar ended the day at 67.63 cents (U.S.) down 0.33 cents from Friday.

"Mr. Thiessen might use the opportunity to clarify policy and prepare us for the semi-annual monetary policy report in November," said Harvinder Kalirai, a New York-based analyst with Idea Inc. Mr. Thiessen's speech Thursday to the Regina Chamber of Commerce will discuss Canada's economy as 2000 approaches.

Recent Bank of Canada statements indicate that growth is strong, which could mean higher interest rates in the months ahead to dampen future inflation.

"The bank should take its foot off the monetary accelerator" because it is probably satisfied with the economy's performance, which is approaching full capacity, Mr. Kalirai said.

With inflation rising, it's prudent to start raising interest rates to head off price pressure in the months ahead, he added.

Market players also will be scrutinizing speeches by several U.S. Federal Reserve Board officials this week for clues about U.S. policy.

With the Fed's Oct. 5 policy meeting fast approaching, there will be few opportunities after this week to get a reading on the current thinking of the central bank governors. Currency markets have been watching for clues about another U.S. interest rate hike, which would make returns on U.S. fixed-income products even more attractive than on Canadian holdings.

Increasingly, analysts expect the Fed to hold rates steady at the meeting, after raising them by one-quarter of a percentage point at each of the past two meetings. The Bank of Canada did not match those moves. ...

Market players also are watching for news from Japan this morning, to see if the Japanese central bank cuts interest rates to weaken the yen. Such a move could weaken the dollar.

Essence of the Story

■ The Canadian dollar fell slightly against the U.S. dollar in September 1999.

■ At the same time, the Bank of Canada saw sustained economic growth, which might mean a rise in the interest rate to avoid future inflation.

■ If the U.S. Federal Reserve raises the U.S. interest rate, people will be able to earn more by moving their funds from Canada to the United States.

■ If the Bank of Japan cuts interest rates, the yen exchange rate will fall and the Canadian dollar could weaken against the U.S. dollar.

■ Figure 1 shows the Canadian dollar exchange rate expressed in U.S. cents from August 1998 to August 1999.

■ Throughout this period, the Canadian dollar shows an *upward* trend.

■ Figure 2 shows the gap between the U.S. federal funds rate and the Canadian overnight loans rate, the short-term interest rates that are used as policy indicators by the two central banks.

■ Figure 2 also shows the change in the exchange rate from one month to the next month.

■ In the short run, there is no relationship between the Canadian interest rate differential and changes in the exchange rate. Changes in the exchange rate are much more volatile than movements in the interest rate differential.

■ In the short run, the exchange rate cannot be predicted by movements in short-term interest rate differential.

■ The exchange rate is determined by expectations. The higher the expected future exchange rate, the smaller is the supply of dollars and the larger is the demand for dollars, so the exchange rate rises. Similarly, the lower the expected future exchange rate, the larger is the supply of dollars and the smaller is the demand for dollars, so the exchange rate falls.

■ Figure 3 shows the changes in the Canadian dollar versus the Japanese yen and the changes in the Canadian dollar versus the U.S. dollar.

■ When the change in the number of Japanese yen per Canadian dollar increases, the Japanese yen is depreciating.

■ Figure 3 shows that when the Japanese yen depreciates against the Canadian dollar, the Canadian dollar sometimes appreciates against the U.S. dollar and sometimes it depreciates. There is no exact relationship.

■ According to the article, if the Bank of Japan cuts interest rates, the yen will weaken and the Canadian dollar might weaken as a result.

■ This prediction seems to be incorrect. Other things remaining the same, a lower Japanese interest rate will make the yen fall against both the Canadian dollar and the U.S. dollar and have no effect on the Canadian–U.S. dollar exchange rate.

Figure 1 The Canadian-U.S dollar exchange rate

Figure 2 The interest rate and the exchange rate

Figure 3 Changes in U.S. dollar and Japanese yen exchange rates

SUMMARY

Key Points

Financing International Trade (pp. 826–830)

- International trade, borrowing, and lending are financed by using foreign currency.
- A country's international transactions are recorded in its balance of payments accounts.
- Canada is a net borrower and a net debtor.
- The net exports surplus is equal to the government sector surplus plus the private sector surplus.

The Exchange Rate (pp. 831–839)

- Foreign currency is obtained in exchange for domestic currency in the foreign exchange market.
- The exchange rate is determined by demand and supply in the foreign exchange market.
- The lower the exchange rate, the greater is the quantity of dollars demanded. A change in the exchange rate brings a movement along the demand curve for dollars.
- Changes in the Canadian interest differential and the expected future exchange rate change the demand for Canadian dollars and shift the demand curve.
- The lower the exchange rate, the smaller is the quantity of dollars supplied. A change in the exchange rate brings a movement along the supply curve for dollars.
- Changes in the Canadian interest rate differential and the expected future exchange rate change the supply of dollars and shift the supply curve.
- Fluctuations in the exchange rate result from fluctuations in the demand for and supply of dollars.
- The Bank of Canada can intervene in the foreign exchange market to smooth fluctuations in the dollar.

Key Figures and Table

Key Terms

PROBLEMS

*1. Silecon, whose currency is the grain, conducted the following transactions in 1999:

Item	Billions of grains
Imports of goods and services	350
Exports of goods and services	500
Borrowing from the rest of the world	60
Lending to the rest of the world	200
Increase in official holdings of foreign currency	10

a. Set out the three balance of payments accounts for Silecon.
b. Does the Silecon central bank intervene in the foreign exchange market?

2. Spin, whose currency is the wheel, conducted the following transactions in 1999:

Item	Billions of wheels
Imports of goods and services	50
Exports of goods and services	60
Borrowing from the rest of the world	2
Lending to the rest of the world	12
Increase in official holdings of foreign currency	0

a. Set out the three balance of payments accounts for Spin.

b. Does the Spin central bank intervene in the foreign exchange market?

*3. The figure below shows the flows of income and expenditure in Dream Land in 2000. The amounts are in millions of dollars. GDP in Dream Land is $60 million.
a. Calculate Dream Land's net exports.
b. Calculate saving in Dream Land.
c. How is Dream Land's investment financed?

4. The figure below shows the flows of income and expenditure in Dream Land in 2001. The amounts are in millions of dollars. Dream Land's GDP has increased to $65 million but all the other items whose values are provided in the figure remain the same as they were in 2000.
a. Calculate Dream Land's net exports in 2001.
b. Calculate saving in Dream Land in 2001.
c. How is Dream Land's investment financed?

*5. The following tables (next page) tell you about Ecflex, whose currency is the band.

Calculate the following for Ecflex:
a. Imports of goods and services
b. Current account balance
c. Capital account balance
d. Net taxes
e. Private sector surplus

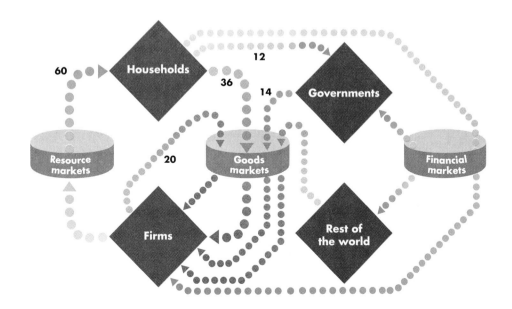

Item	Billions of bands
GDP	100
Consumption expenditure	60
Government expenditures on goods and services	24

Item	Billions of bands
Investment	22
Exports of goods and services	20
Government budget deficit	4

6. The following table tells you about Ecfix, whose currency is the rock:

Item	Billions of rocks
GDP	200
Consumption expenditure	120
Government expenditures on goods and services	50
Investment	50
Exports of goods and services	40
Saving	45

Calculate the following for Ecfix:
a. Imports of goods and services
b. Current account balance
c. Capital account balance
d. Net taxes
e. Private sector surplus
f. Government deficit or surplus

*7. A country's currency appreciates, and its official holdings of foreign currency increase. What can you say about:
a. Intervention in the foreign exchange market by the country's central bank?
b. The possible central bank sources of the currency appreciation?
c. The possible private actions behind the appreciation?

8. A country's currency depreciates, and its official holdings of foreign currency decrease. What can you say about:
a. Intervention in the foreign exchange market by the country's central bank?
b. The possible sources of the depreciation?
c. The possible private actions behind the depreciation?

CRITICAL THINKING

1. Study *Reading Between the Lines* on pp. 840–841 and then answer the following questions.
   a. What was the state of expectations about the growth of real GDP in Canada in September 1999?
   b. What was the state of expectations about the Bank of Canada's future interest rate changes?
   c. How would an increase in the U.S. interest rate with no change in the Canadian interest rate influence the exchange rate?
   d. What does the news article say about the likely effects of a decrease in the Japanese interest rate on the yen and the dollar?
   e. Do you agree or disagree with the last sentence of the news article? Explain your reasons.

2. Use the link on the Parkin-Bade Web site to visit Statistics Canada and find data on the exchange rate and international trade.
   a. When did Canada last have a current account surplus?
   b. When did official Canadian reserves last increase?
   c. Does Canada have a surplus or a deficit in its trade in services?
   d. What has happened to foreign investment in Canada during the past ten years?
   e. Do you think that Canada's balance of payments record is a matter for concern? Why or why not?

3. Use the link on the Parkin-Bade Web site to get recent data on the exchange rate of the Canadian dollar against two other currencies that interest you over the past month. Then:
   a. Explain the changes (or lack of change) in the exchange rate over the past month.
   b. What specific events might have changed exchange rate expectations?
   c. What forces might have prevented the exchange rates from changing?
   d. What information would you need to be able to determine whether intervention by the Bank of Canada or the central bank of the other country has prevented the exchange rate from changing by as much as it otherwise would have?

Understanding the Global Economy

The scale of international trade, borrowing, and lending, both in absolute dollar terms and as a percentage of total world production expands every year. One country, Singapore, imports and exports goods and services in a volume that exceeds its gross domestic product. The world's largest nation, China, returned to the international economic stage during the 1980s and is now a major producer of manufactured goods. ◆ International economic activity is large because today's economic world is small and because communication is so incredibly fast. But today's world is not a new world. From the beginning of recorded history, people have traded over large and steadily increasing distances. The great Western civilizations of Greece and Rome traded not only around the Mediterranean but also into the Gulf of Arabia. The great Eastern civilizations traded around the Indian Ocean. By the Middle Ages, the East and the West were trading routinely overland on routes pioneered by Venetian traders and explorers such as Marco Polo. When, in 1497, Vasco da Gama opened a sea route between the Atlantic and Indian Oceans around Africa, a new trade between East and West began, which brought tumbling prices of Eastern goods in Western markets. ◆ The European discovery of America and the subsequent opening up of Atlantic trade continued the process of steady globalization. So the developments of the 1990s, amazing though many of them

It's a Small World

were, represent a continuation of an ongoing expansion of human horizons. ◆ The two chapters in this final part study the interaction of nations in today's global economy. ◆ In Chapter 35, you learned about international trade in goods and services. Here, you came face to face with one of the biggest policy issues of all ages, free trade versus protection. You learned how all nations can benefit from free international trade. And you saw how protection from competition brings big benefits to a few and small losses to the many. The total gains from protection are dwarfed by the losses, but because the losses are spread thinly and the gains thickly, protectionism always has its supporters and political backers. ◆ In Chapter 36, you learned about international borrowing and lending and the exchange rate. You discovered that the size of a nation's international deficit depends not on how efficient it is, but on how much its citizens save relative to how much they invest. Nations with low saving rates, everything else being the same, have international deficits. ◆ You also discovered why foreign exchange rates fluctuate so much.

◇ The global economy is a big news source these days. And it has always attracted attention. On the next page, you can meet the economist who first explained the fundamental idea of comparative advantage: David Ricardo. And you can meet one of today's leading international economists, Stanley Fischer, formerly a professor at MIT and now Deputy Managing Director of the International Monetary Fund.

Probing the Ideas

The Gains from International Trade

David Ricardo *(1772-1832) was a highly successful 27-year-old stockbroker when he stumbled on a copy of Adam Smith's* Wealth of Nations *(see p. 58) on a weekend visit to the country. He was immediately hooked and went on to become the most celebrated economist of his age and one of the all-time great economists. One of his many contributions was to develop the principle of comparative advantage, the foundation on which the modern theory of international trade is built. The example he used to illustrate this principle was the trade between England and Portugal in cloth and wine.*

The General Agreement on Tariffs and Trade was established as a reaction against the devastation wrought by beggar-my-neighbour tariffs imposed during the 1930s. But it is also a triumph for the logic first worked out by Smith and Ricardo.

"Under a system of perfectly free commerce, each country naturally devotes its capital and labour to such employments as are most beneficial to each."

DAVID RICARDO, *THE PRINCIPLES OF POLITICAL ECONOMY AND TAXATION,* 1817.

The Issues

Until the mid-eighteenth century, it was generally believed that the purpose of international trade was to keep exports greater than imports and pile up gold. If gold was accumulated, it was believed, the nation would prosper; and if gold was lost through an international deficit, the nation would be drained of money and impoverished. These beliefs are called *mercantilism,* and the *mercantilists* were pamphleteers who advocated with missionary fervour the pursuit of an international surplus. If exports did not exceed imports, the mercantilists wanted imports restricted.

In the 1740s, David Hume explained that as the quantity of money (gold) changes, so also does the price level, and the nation's *real* wealth is unaffected. In the 1770s, Adam Smith argued that import restrictions would lower the gains from specialization and make a nation poorer. Thirty years later, David Ricardo proved the law of comparative advantage and demonstrated the superiority of free trade. Mercantilism was intellectually bankrupt but remained politically powerful.

Gradually, through the nineteenth century, the mercantilist influence waned and North America and Western Europe prospered in an environment of increasingly free international trade. But despite remarkable advances in economic understanding, mercantilism never quite died. It had a brief and devastating revival in the 1920s and 1930s when tariff hikes brought about the collapse of international trade and accentuated the Great Depression. It subsided again after World War II with the establishment of the General Agreement on Tariffs and Trade.

But mercantilism lingers on. Many Canadians fear that NAFTA will bring economic ruin to Canada and this belief is a modern manifestation of mercantilism. It would be interesting to have David Hume, Adam Smith, and David Ricardo commenting on these views. But we know what they would say—the same things that they said to the eighteenth century mercantilists. And they would still be right today.

... and Now

The container ship has revolutionized international trade and contributed to its continued expansion. Today, most goods cross the oceans in "containers"—metal boxes—packed into and piled on top of ships like this one. Container technology has cut the cost of ocean shipping by economizing on handling and by making cargoes harder to steal, which has reduced insurance costs. It is unlikely that there would be much international trade in goods such as television sets and VCRs without this technology. High-value and perishable cargoes such as flowers and fresh foods, as well as urgent courier packages, travel by air. Every day, dozens of cargo-laden 747s fly between major Canadian cities and destinations across the Atlantic and Pacific oceans.

Then ...

In the eighteenth century, when mercantilists and economists were debating the pros and cons of free international exchange, the transportation technology available limited the gains from international trade. Sailing ships with tiny cargo holds took close to a month to cross the Atlantic Ocean. But the potential gains were large and so was the incentive to cut shipping costs. By the 1850s, the clipper ship had been developed cutting the journey from Halifax to Liverpool to only 12 days. Half a century later, 10,000-tonne steamships were sailing between Canada and England in just 4 days. As sailing times and costs declined, the gains from international trade increased and the volume of trade expanded.

As the world economy has become more integrated, new international institutions have evolved. One of these institutions is the International Monetary Fund, or IMF. Let's talk with one of today's outstanding economists who now plays a leading role at the IMF, and who became a household name during the Asian financial crisis, Stanley Fischer.

Talking with
Stanley Fischer

Stanley Fischer *has served as the First Deputy Managing Director of the International Monetary Fund (The IMF) since 1994. Born in Zambia in 1943, he received a B.S. and an M.S. from the London School of Economics in 1965 and 1966, respectively, and a Ph.D. from MIT in 1969. Professor Fischer has taught at the University of Chicago and MIT. He served as Vice President of Development Economics and Chief Economist at the World bank from 1988 to 1992.*

Robin Bade and Michael Parkin talked with Stanley Fischer about his work at the IMF, the goals of that institution, and the lessons that we've learned from the Asian financial crisis.

How did you get into economics?

I was at high school in Zimbabwe (then Rhodesia) and in the sixth form I began to specialize in physics, chemistry, and math. Then I heard about economics. I switched one of my science courses to economics and I loved it.

This was the perfect field, one that provided an analytic way of understanding an important part of how societies work and also one in which I could use my quantitative skills. I went to the London School of Economics for my bachelor's and master's degrees and then to MIT for my Ph.D. My first appointment was at the University of Chicago at a time when Milton Friedman was still the dominant influence there.

Can we talk first about the amazing liberalization and growth of the world trade during the post-World War II years? Has this growth of world trade brought economic growth for all countries? Or have some gained more than others?

If you were to look at what has happened in the postwar period to the industrialized countries—which, despite some slowing since the 1960s, have grown faster, more consistently, and with less disruption than in any period of similar length in history—you would have to say that the architecture of the postwar economy has been very successful. And then if you look at the developing countries, you will find that, on the average, they have grown faster yet. In the most populous part of the globe, namely, East Asia, China, and, to some extent, India, we have had absolutely unprecedented growth. Every one of the successful East Asian countries has succeeded by integrating with the world economy, by promoting exports and increasing imports, especially of capital and intermediate goods. This process of opening up and using world markets for exports and imports has been absolutely critical. This outcome is what most economists from Adam Smith and David Ricardo on would have predicted.

The one part of the world where progress has, on the average, been most disappointing, is Africa. But there are countries in Africa that have done well. The countries that have been serious about trying to trade in the global economy and about implementing market-friendly policies have done better on the whole. We have seen significant growth in per capita income in Africa in the last few years. The prospects for South Africa look good, and that could be very important for a large part of the continent. In addition, countries such as Mozambique and Uganda have begun growing very fast after terrible civil wars, and Botswana has been one of the fastest-growing economies in the world for the past two decades.

What is the role of the IMF and what are the main problems that it seeks to address?

The IMF has several main functions. The first is *surveillance:* It is an institution in which countries discuss problems of the international economy, as well as each other's economies. Twice a year, the Fund staff presents its survey of the world economy, the *World Economic Outlook.*

In addition, Fund staff presents an annual report—the Article IV report—on the economy of each member country. The Article IV reports are based on the staff's analysis and discussions with the economic policy makers in each country.

Another function of the Fund is to *make loans to countries* in economic trouble. These loans typically provide balance of payments support to countries in crisis and countries to which the private capital markets are reluctant to lend.

One such crisis began in 1997—the financial crisis of Asia, Russia, Brazil, and other countries. What was its central feature?

Financial system weakness was a feature of almost all the crisis countries except Brazil. All the crises were driven and worsened by rapid international movements of capital. Investors pushed money into the crisis countries and then pulled out, very rapidly, as the crisis approached its peak. The crisis featured *contagion,* spreading fast from one country to another.

What are the lessons of this episode of financial crisis?

The main lesson is that individual countries and the international financial system must adapt to the new circumstances of globally integrated financial markets. We must reduce the volatility of international capital flows and improve the capacity of financial systems and economies to cope with the shifts in market confidence and investor sentiment that will inevitably occur in future.

Work is now under way in the emerging market economies, industrialized countries and international institutions, to identify the policies and reforms that are needed.

For the *emerging market countries,* the list of items that need attention is a long one. Efforts must focus on sound macroeconomic policies, which include avoiding operating fixed exchange rate systems, which have been crisis-prone. Banking systems must be restructured, and the supervision and regulation of banks must be improved. Better economic

> *Every one of the successful East Asian countries has succeeded by integrating with the world economy.*

and financial information on private and public sector activities must be provided. Business financial practices and bankruptcy laws must be improved. And these countries need to find ways of dealing with rapid and large reversals in international capital flows.

Countries need to think carefully about how fast and in what order to free capital account transactions and to make sure their borrowing is not too short term. They also need adequate reserves and, possibly, lines of credit that will give them access to liquidity when they need it.

The *advanced industrialized countries* need to pursue macroeconomic policies that bring sustainable growth. When these countries are not expanding, developing countries, too, find it difficult to grow. The advanced countries also need to maintain healthy financial systems and to regulate their own financial institutions to minimize potential disruptive capital flows to emerging market countries.

The *international financial institutions,* the IMF among them, must act as well. One example of an important initiative is the design and adoption of

849

international standards for bank operation and supervision and for reporting fiscal and monetary data. Another is the effort to encourage the provision of better economic and financial data to the public by emerging market economies. A third is the effort to strengthen *surveillance* by the IMF. The IMF reports regularly on each country's economy, assessing its policies and practices, thereby encouraging the country to do better. Fourth, IMF member countries are gradually coming to the view that IMF reports, the Article IV reports, should be published so that the general public and investors can share information

---

…Countries and the international financial system must adapt to the new circumstances of globally integrated financial markets.

---

that so far has been available only to governments. Fifth, we are finding ways of making sure that private investors do their share in solving crises. One important criticism of IMF programs has been that the official sector bails out the private sector, providing loans so that the private sector can take its money out of a country in trouble. This is a very complicated issue, but we are definitely making progress on what is known as "bailing in" the private sector, finding ways of discouraging the private sector from taking its money out when a crisis hits.

What big conclusions should we draw from the special features of Russia's economic and financial condition?

A key question that has been asked since the onset of Russia's crisis in 1999 is: Was the reform strategy of the previous Russian government wrong? My conclusion is, fundamentally, no. The problem was not that the basic strategy was wrong, but that it was not pursued vigorously or deeply enough. What has been necessary in Russia for some time has been a comprehensive strategy for moving boldly to tackle a large fiscal imbalance and to deal with important structural problems related to the way its economy operates—in particular, the nonpayment problem. Such a strat-

egy was at the heart of the July 1998 program agreed on with the IMF. But by then, the financial situation and market confidence were too precarious and vulnerable to any missteps in implementation, which indeed happened and quickly led to the August collapse.

Put differently, the conclusion is that stabilization is not enough. Russia stabilized its economy extremely successfully from about the middle of 1995, with an appropriate degree of monetary discipline accompanied by a fixed exchange rate regime, which stabilizes inflationary expectations following a prolonged period of high inflation. However, the fiscal adjustment needed was not forthcoming, so there was a massive and rapid buildup in public debt. Ultimately, the government was not able to service its debt out of its own resources and could not convince investors to continue financing its ongoing deficit. This led to both the devaluation of the ruble and the government default on its treasury bills in August 1998.

Moreover, a critical reason why the fiscal adjustment could not be implemented was the lack of progress in industrial restructuring and other structural reforms; thus the stabilization was not sustainable. A very large part of the Russian economy remains unreformed, has not been part of the monetary economy, and is conducting its operations largely through barter—not only literally barter of goods against goods, but in many cases barter through very sophisticated financial mechanisms that do not involve the use of money. This situation has arisen because of a vast number of factors, including poor enforcement of tax obligations, an unfair tax system, weak bankruptcy laws, poor lending practices by banks, and corrupt business practices. Thus, much of the productive sector was either losing money in real terms or not paying a fair share of taxes. So the failure of structural reforms underlies the fiscal problem in Russia. Without these reforms, the budget will not balance, growth will not materialize, and eventually financial stability will be compromised.

Why do you believe that the IMF can play a role as the lender of last resort?

The IMF already is increasingly playing that role, both as crisis lender and as crisis manager. As crisis lender, the IMF, whose financial structure is similar to that of a credit union, has access to a pool of resources. As crisis manager, it has been taking the lead in negotiating with its member countries that are experiencing a financial crisis. It also has played an important coordinating and advisory role in arranging financing packages to help countries work out their debt problems with their foreign creditors.

Some have asked whether the IMF has enough resources to act as crisis lender. While the resources available have grown less than the size of the world economy since the IMF's inception in 1945, the IMF can still assemble a sizable financial package in response to a crisis, including, in special circumstances, by borrowing from members' central banks and by creating additional reserves for its members through the issuance of Special Drawing Rights (SDRs).

Should the IMF function as an international lender of last resort?

I believe that there is a need for an agency that will act as such a lender to countries facing a crisis. The need arises because international capital flows are both extremely volatile and contagious, exhibiting the classic signs of financial panics, and an international lender of last resort can help to mitigate the effects of this instability and perhaps even help prevent the instability itself. Again, the IMF has already been acting in many ways as such a lender, and there is ongoing work to help make the IMF more effective in that capacity.

Of the main criticisms leveled at the IMF during the Asian crisis, which are the easiest to dismiss, and which, if any, should we take more seriously?

This is a complex question that cannot be easily answered in a few words. While I will try, I should say that the IMF has taken all the criticisms seriously and indeed has produced a comprehensive study of the experience in Indonesia, Korea, and Thailand, which I would encourage those interested to read.

The programs in the Asian crisis countries supported by the IMF sought to restore macroeconomic stability and the conditions for growth while addressing deep-rooted structural weaknesses that lay at the heart of the crisis in each country. These programs have been attacked from a number of angles, but here again I believe that, particularly in the highly fluid and uncertain circumstances, the approach taken and choices made were basically correct.

A frequent criticism is that the policy of high interest rates worsened financial problems being experienced by corporations and therefore made the recessions worse in these countries. However, their currencies were collapsing, and it was critical to avoid a depreciation-inflation spiral. Indeed, the critics fail to recognize that in addition to the well-known negative effects on growth of high inflation, in a situation where companies and banks had borrowed heavily abroad, the further depreciations implied by lower interest rates would have exacerbated financial problems by increasing the burden of servicing dollar-denominated debts.

Another criticism is that the programs entailed unduly contractionary fiscal policies. The original programs in these countries, formulated in the initial stages of the crisis, included some degree of fiscal adjustment to lessen the burden that might be placed on the private sector in the face of the large adjustment in the current account of the balance of payments that was needed. The truth is that, even then, the fiscal adjustment that was planned was rather

Should the IMF function as an international lender of last resort? I believe that there is a need for an agency that will act as such a lender to countries facing a crisis.

small in both Korea and Indonesia and was substantial only in Thailand, where the initial fiscal imbalance was larger. Moreover, as economic activity deteriorated over the course of the programs, fiscal policy was progressively allowed to become more expansionary. In fact, our study concluded that fiscal policy was not a major factor accounting for the output decline in these countries.

The inclusion of structural measures in our programs also has drawn criticism. Financial and corporate sector inefficiencies were at the heart of these crises, and it was clear from the start that the restoration of durable growth required financial and corporate restructuring. Still, some argued that these reforms, while sensible over the medium term, impose large costs in the short term, and therefore it was a mistake to put them in place when economic activity was already so weak. While this is a valid concern, I think that attempting to stabilize the situation without attempting to address the underlying causes of the crisis would have been akin to treating the symptom without addressing the real cause of the disease. And delay does not make the structural problem any easier to deal with; indeed, as the problem of the Japanese banking sector in the 1990s clearly demonstrates, it makes it worse.

All this said, why did the programs work less well than we all hoped? Why was the economic downturn worse than initially foreseen? Clearly, the projections embodied in the original programs were somewhat more optimistic than the consensus view. However, very few observers foresaw the severity of the downturn—neither the governments, private forecasters, nor academic observers. A number of factors conspired to make matters worse than foreseen. First, the external environment for the crisis countries worsened markedly. In particular, the Japanese recession has been deeper and more prolonged than anticipated, hurting the exports of the crisis countries. Second, several factors—an initial reluctance by governments to implement the programs, political uncertainties, and lack of public support for the programs—made it much more difficult for market confidence to be restored than had been assumed. This led to greater capital outflows and put additional upward pressure on interest rates and downward pressure on exchange rates, and forced a larger downward adjustment of domestic demand.

While I believe the basic approach of the programs was right, that doesn't mean that we shouldn't try to do better. As I already discussed, the recent financial crises have revealed weaknesses in the inter-national financial system that we must try to deal with. As briefly described above, the IMF and other international institutions are doing their part to help in that endeavor.

What kinds of jobs do economics graduates get in organizations such as the IMF and the World Bank? What should students be doing as undergraduates to prepare themselves for such positions?

People who want to work in the Fund and the Bank should take courses in macroeconomics, international trade and finance, development, monetary economics, and public finance. From the viewpoint of the Bank, it would also be useful to study micro-oriented policy issues. The Fund and the Bank have entry programs for people who may be destined for their professional ranks. The World Bank's is called Young Professionals, and the IMF's is called the Economist Program.

The IMF and the World Bank are terrific places to work. You use your analytic skills all the time, in the real world. You have to decide what really matters, you have to be sure that what you're recommending will improve the lives of people. Then if you work in the operational parts of the Fund or Bank, you have to persuade the countries with which you're working that you're right. If you are right and you succeed, you have the satisfaction of having done something useful.

In the process, you'll have had the benefit of learning some diplomacy. You are also likely to learn some humility—for you will realize that the really hard work of implementing policies is done by the politicians and officials of the countries that undertake them. Your job is to help them do their own jobs better, always bearing in mind that the benefits or costs are borne by their people.

Canadian
Economy
Database

Canadian Economy Database

The following data tables provide a description of some of the main features of the Canadian economy from 1926 to 1998.

You can make graphs of these data by using your *Economics in Action* CD. To do so, open the table of contents page for *any* chapter, click on Variable Graphing and then click on Canada Historical.

These data are updated annually on the Parkin-Bade Web site.

Sources

CANSIM series: Statistics Canada, Ottawa

HSC series: Statistics Canada, *Historical Statistics of Canada*, Second Edition, F. H. Leacy (ed.), Ottawa, 1983.

HSC(1) series: The MacMillan Company of Canada Limited, *Historical Statistics of Canada*, M.C. Urquhart (ed.), Toronto, 1965.

A break in a series is indicated by *b*.

Variables

1. Real GDP
HSC series F55 and CANSIM series D15721: The data for 1926–1960 are F55 multiplied by the 1961 ratio of D15721 to F55.

2. Real consumption expenditure
HSC series F33 and CANSIM series D15691: The data for 1926–1960 are F33 multiplied by the 1961 ratio of D15691 to F33 and multiplied by the ratio of real GDP to aggregate expenditure.

3. Real investment
HSC the sum of series F55, F32, F33, F51, F52, F34 and the sum of CANSIM series D15697, D15721, D15691, D15711, D15715: The data for 1926–1960 are *HSC* multiplied by the 1961 ratio of CANSIM to *HSC* and multiplied by the ratio of real GDP to aggregate expenditure.

4. Real government expenditure
HSC series F34 and CANSIM series D15697: The data for 1926–1960 are F34 multiplied by the 1961 ratio of D15697 to F34 and multiplied by the ratio of real GDP to aggregate expenditure.

5. Real exports
HSC series F51 and CANSIM series D15711: The data for 1926–1960 are F51 multiplied by the 1961 ratio of D15711 to F51 and multiplied by the ratio of real GDP to aggregate expenditure.

6. Real imports
HSC series F52 and CANSIM series D15715: The data for 1926–1960 are F51 multiplied by the 1961 ratio of D15715 to F52 and multiplied by the ratio of real GDP to aggregate expenditure.

7. Real net exports
Real exports *minus* real imports.

8. Potential GDP
Real GDP trends and authors' assumptions and calculations.

9. Fluctuations around potential GDP
Percentage deviation of real GDP from potential GDP.

10. Real GDP growth rate
Annual percentage change in real GDP.

11. GDP deflator
HSC series K172 and CANSIM series D23203: The data for 1926–1960 are K172 multiplied by the 1961 ratio of D23203 to K172.

12. CPI:
Statistics Canada, CANSIM series P200000.

13. Inflation rate
Annual percentage change in the GDP deflator.

14. Inflation rate
Annual percentage change in the CPI.

15. Labour force
CANSIM series D31254 and D980048.

16. Labour force participation rate
CANSIM series D31254, D41983, and D980466.

17. Average weekly hours
HSC series E128, E129, E130, E131, E132, E133, E134, E135; Statistics Canada, CANSIM series D980120 and authors' calculations and assumptions.

18. Unemployment rate
HSC series D127, D132, and D491 and CANSIM series D44950 and D980404.

19. Long-term interest rate
HSC(1) series H605, *HSC* series J475, and CANSIM series B14013.

20. Short-term interest rate
HSC series J471 and CANSIM series B14060.

21. Federal government revenues
HSC series H18 and CANSIM series D18355.

22. Federal government outlays
HSC series H34 and CANSIM series D18386.

23. Federal government surplus(+)/deficit(-)
HSC series H18 and H34 and CANSIM series D 18355 and D18386.

24. Gross federal debt
CANSIM series D469409.

25. M1
CANSIM series B2033.

26. M2+
CANSIM series B2037.

27. M1 velocity
Series 1 multiplied by series 11 divided by series 25.

28. M2+ velocity
Series 1 multiplied by series 11 divided by series 26.

29. Exchange rate
HSC series J562 and CANSIM series B3400.

30. Current account
855 series G83 and CANSIM series D59832.

Year		1926	1927	1928	1929	1930	1931	1932	1933	1934	1935
Real GDP (billions of 1992 dollars)	1	56.8	62.2	67.9	68.1	65.2	56.9	51.0	47.6	53.4	57.6
Real consumption expenditure (billions of 1992 dollars)	2	33.9	37.9	41.6	43.3	41.1	37.9	34.4	33.6	36.0	38.0
Real investment (billions of 1992 dollars)	3	10.5	12.2	13.6	12.8	11.6	5.5	3.1	2.1	4.0	5.1
Real government expenditures (billions of 1992 dollars)	4	9.7	10.2	10.3	11.4	12.4	12.6	12.1	10.2	11.0	11.6
Real exports (billions of 1992 dollars)	5	10.8	10.8	12.3	11.3	9.8	8.5	7.7	7.8	9.0	10.0
Real imports (billions of 1992 dollars)	6	8.0	8.9	10.0	10.7	9.7	7.5	6.3	6.0	6.6	7.1
Real net exports (billions of 1992 dollars)	7	2.7	1.9	2.3	0.6	0.1	1.0	1.4	1.8	2.5	2.9
Potential GDP (billions of 1992 dollars)	8	58.0	60.0	62.0	64.0	66.0	68.0	70.0	72.0	74.0	76.0
Fluctuations around potential GDP (percentage)	9	−2.0	3.7	9.5	6.5	−1.1	−16.3	−27.1	−33.8	−27.8	−24.2
Real GDP growth rate (percent per year)	10	—	9.5	9.1	0.4	−4.3	−12.7	−10.4	−6.7	12.1	7.8
GDP deflator (1992 = 100)	11	9.4	9.3	9.3	9.4	9.1	8.6	7.8	7.6	7.7	7.8
CPI (1992 = 100)	12	10.9	10.8	10.8	11.0	10.9	9.8	8.9	8.5	8.6	8.7
Inflation rate (GDP deflator percent per year)	13	—	−1.1	−0.6	1.1	−2.5	−6.2	−9.3	−1.7	1.4	0.3
Inflation rate (CPI percent per year)	14	0	−0.9	0	1.9	−0.9	−10.1	−9.2	−4.5	1.2	1.2
Labour force (millions)	15	3.7	3.8	3.9	4.0	4.1	4.2	4.2	4.3	4.3	4.4
Labour force participation rate (percentage)	16	57.8	57.9	58.0	58.1	58.2	58.3	58.2	58.0	57.9	57.8
Average weekly hours (hours per week)	17	—	—	—	—	—	—	—	—	—	—
Unemployment rate (percentage)	18	2.9	1.8	1.7	2.9	9.1	11.6	17.6	19.3	14.5	14.2
Long–term interest rate (percent per year)	19	4.9	4.6	4.5	4.9	4.7	4.6	5.1	4.6	4.0	3.6
Short–term interest rate (percent per year)	20	—	—	—	—	—	—	—	—	2.5	1.5
Federal government revenues (billions of dollars)	21	0.4	0.4	0.5	0.5	0.4	0.3	0.3	0.3	0.4	0.4
Federal government outlays (billions of dollars)	22	0.4	0.4	0.4	0.4	0.4	0.4	0.5	0.5	0.5	0.5
Federal government surplus (+)/deficit(−) (billions of dollars)	23	0	0.1	0.1	0	−0.1	−0.1	−0.2	−0.1	−0.1	−0.2
Gross federal debt (billions of dollars)	24	2.8	2.8	2.7	2.7	2.6	2.7	2.9	3.1	3.2	3.5
M1 (billions of dollars)	25	—	—	—	—	—	—	—	—	—	—
M2+ (billions of dollars)	26	—	—	—	—	—	—	—	—	—	—
M1 velocity (GDP/M1)	27	—	—	—	—	—	—	—	—	—	—
M2+ velocity (GDP/M2+)	28	—	—	—	—	—	—	—	—	—	—
Exchange rate (U.S. dollars per Canadian dollar)	29	1.00	1.00	1.00	1.00	1.00	0.96	0.88	0.92	1.01	0.99
Current account balance (billions of dollars)	30	0.1	0	0	−0.3	−0.3	−0.2	−0.1	0	0.1	0.1

1936	1937	1938	1939	1940	1941	1942	1943	1944	1945	1946	1947	1948	1949	
60.2	66.2	66.7	71.7	81.8	93.6	110.9	115.4	120.0	117.3	114.1	119.0	121.9	126.6	1
39.7	42.8	42.1	43.7	45.3	47.1	44.0	44.5	46.1	54.9	67.5	74.2	73.8	77.5	2
4.9	8.0	8.4	10.2	8.1	5.4	−2.2	−6.5	−8.1	−2.6	11.1	17.6	19.6	19.9	3
11.6	11.9	13.4	14.3	24.4	34.4	65.5	70.3	78.1	58.1	30.4	23.5	22.7	25.0	4
12.0	12.5	11.3	12.5	13.8	17.6	14.4	19.6	18.3	19.3	17.9	18.3	19.2	18.0	5
8.0	9.0	8.4	9.1	9.8	11.0	10.8	12.6	14.4	12.4	12.7	14.7	13.5	13.7	6
4.0	3.5	2.9	3.5	4.0	6.6	3.6	7.0	3.9	6.9	5.2	3.6	5.8	4.2	7
79.0	81.0	83.0	86.0	88.0	92.0	95.0	99.0	103.0	107.0	112.0	116.0	121.0	126.0	8
−23.9	−18.3	−19.6	−16.6	−7.1	1.7	16.8	16.5	16.5	9.6	1.9	2.6	0.8	0.5	9
4.4	10.0	0.8	7.4	14.1	14.4	18.6	4.0	4.0	−2.2	−2.7	4.3	2.5	3.8	10
8.0	8.2	8.2	8.2	8.5	9.2	9.6	10.0	10.3	10.5	10.8	11.8	13.3	13.8	11
8.8	9.1	9.2	9.2	9.5	10.1	10.5	10.7	10.8	10.9	11.2	12.3	14.0	14.5	12
3.3	2.6	0	−0.9	4.7	7.9	4.5	3.5	3.1	2.5	2.9	8.8	12.3	4.3	13
1.1	3.4	1.1	0	3.3	6.3	4.0	1.9	0.9	0.9	2.8	9.8	13.8	3.6	14
4.5	4.5	4.6	4.6	4.6	4.5	4.6	4.6	4.5	4.5	4.8	4.9	5.0	5.2	15
57.6	57.5	57.4	57.2	56.6	55.4	56.5	58.0	57.4	56.2	55.0	54.9	54.6	54.4	16
—	—	—	—	—	—	—	—	—	44.1	42.7	42.5	42.3	42.2	17
12.8	9.1	11.4	11.4	9.0	4.1	2.7	1.4	1.2	1.4	[b]3.4	2.2	2.3	2.8	18
[b]3.0	3.2	3.1	3.2	3.3	3.1	3.1	3.0	3.0	2.9	2.6	2.6	2.9	2.8	19
0.9	0.7	0.6	0.7	0.7	0.6	0.5	0.5	0.4	0.4	0.4	0.4	0.4	0.5	20
0.5	0.5	0.5	0.6	0.9	1.5	2.3	2.8	2.7	3.0	3.0	2.9	2.8	2.6	21
0.5	0.5	0.6	0.7	1.3	1.9	4.4	5.3	5.2	5.1	2.6	2.2	2.2	2.4	22
−0.1	0	−0.1	−0.1	−0.4	−0.4	−2.1	−2.6	−2.6	−2.1	0.4	0.7	0.6	0.1	23
3.5	3.6	3.6	3.7	4.0	5.0	6.6	8.8	11.8	14.9	17.9	17.7	17.2	16.9	24
—	—	—	—	—	—	—	—	—	—	—	—	—	—	25
—	—	—	—	—	—	—	—	—	—	—	—	—	—	26
—	—	—	—	—	—	—	—	—	—	—	—	—	—	27
—	—	—	—	—	—	—	—	—	—	—	—	—	—	28
1.00	1.00	0.99	0.96	0.90	0.90	0.90	0.90	0.90	0.91	1.00	1.00	1.00	0.97	29
0.2	0.2	0.1	0.1	0.2	0.5	0.1	0.7	0.1	0.7	[b]0.08	0	0.1	0	30

Year		1950	1951	1952	1953	1954	1955	1956	1957	1958	1959
Real GDP (billions of 1992 dollars)	1	136.2	143.0	155.8	163.8	161.8	177.0	192.0	196.5	201.1	208.7
Real consumption expenditure (billions of 1992 dollars)	2	82.7	82.1	86.9	92.9	95.9	105.0	113.5	118.1	122.2	129.0
Real investment (billions of 1992 dollars)	3	23.6	23.7	22.4	24.8	21.6	27.3	33.9	34.0	31.5	34.1
Real government expenditures (billions of 1992 dollars)	4	27.0	34.6	42.2	43.5	41.6	42.9	44.3	43.6	44.9	44.5
Real exports (billions of 1992 dollars)	5	17.9	19.3	21.2	21.0	20.1	21.8	23.6	23.9	23.8	24.7
Real imports (billions of 1992 dollars)	6	15.0	16.6	17.0	18.4	17.4	19.9	23.3	23.1	21.4	23.6
Real net exports (billions of 1992 dollars)	7	2.9	2.7	4.2	2.6	2.7	1.9	0.4	0.8	2.4	1.1
Potential GDP (billions of 1992 dollars)	8	131.0	137.0	143.0	149.0	155.0	162.0	169.0	177.0	184.0	193.0
Fluctuations around potential GDP (percentage)	9	4.0	4.4	8.9	9.9	4.4	9.3	13.6	11.0	9.3	8.1
Real GDP growth rate (percent per year)	10	7.6	5.0	8.9	5.1	−1.2	9.4	8.4	2.4	2.3	3.8
GDP deflator (1992 = 100)	11	14.2	15.8	16.5	16.4	16.7	16.8	17.4	17.8	18.0	18.4
CPI (1992 = 100)	12	14.9	16.4	16.9	16.7	16.8	16.8	17.1	17.6	18.0	18.3
Inflation rate (GDP deflator percent per year)	13	2.4	11.3	4.4	−0.2	1.6	0.6	3.7	2.1	1.5	2.0
Inflation rate (CPI percent per year)	14	2.8	10.1	3.0	−1.2	0.6	0	1.8	2.9	2.3	1.7
Labour force (millions)	15	5.2	5.2	5.3	5.4	5.5	5.6	5.8	6.0	6.1	6.2
Labour force participation rate (percentage)	16	53.7	53.7	53.5	53.1	52.9	52.9	53.5	54.0	53.9	53.8
Average weekly hours (hours per week)	17	42.3	41.7	41.5	41.3	40.7	41.0	41.0	40.4	40.2	40.7
Unemployment rate (percentage)	18	3.6	2.4	2.9	3.0	4.6	4.4	3.4	4.6	7.0	6.0
Long-term interest rate (percent per year)	19	2.8	3.2	3.6	3.7	3.1	3.1	3.6	4.2	4.5	5.0
Short-term interest rate (percent per year)	20	0.6	0.8	1.1	1.7	1.4	1.6	2.9	3.8	2.3	4.8
Federal government revenues (billions of dollars)	21	3.1	4.0	4.6	4.7	4.4	4.7	5.5	5.4	5.1	5.8
Federal government outlays (billions of dollars)	22	2.9	3.8	4.6	4.7	4.7	4.8	5.2	5.5	6.0	6.3
Federal government surplus (+)/deficit(−) (billions of dollars)	23	0.2	0.2	−0.1	0	−0.2	−0.1	0.3	−0.1	−0.8	−0.4
Gross federal debt (billions of dollars)	24	16.7	16.7	16.8	17.4	17.6	17.6	18.7	18.0	18.0	19.7
M1 (billions of dollars)	25	—	—	—	4.2	4.4	4.8	4.8	4.8	5.4	5.2
M2+ (billions of dollars)	26	—	—	—	—	—	—	—	—	—	—
M1 velocity (GDP/M1)	27	—	—	—	6.4	6.1	6.2	7.0	7.3	6.7	7.3
M2+ velocity (GDP/M2+)	28	—	—	—	—	—	—	—	—	—	—
Exchange rate (U.S. dollars per Canadian dollar)	29	[b]0.95	0.95	1.02	1.02	1.03	1.01	1.02	1.04	1.03	1.04
Current account balance (billions of dollars)	30	−0.1	−0.1	0	−0.1	−0.1	−0.2	−0.3	−0.4	−0.3	−0.4

1960	1961	1962	1963	1964	1965	1966	1967	1968	1969	1970	1971	1972	1973	
214.7	220.8	235.9	247.9	264.2	281.2	299.7	308.6	325.1	342.5	351.4	370.9	390.7	418.8	1
133.5	134.0	140.9	146.7	154.5	163.5	171.7	178.1	186.0	195.0	198.4	210.3	224.8	240.0	2
33.5	31.6	36.8	39.0	43.4	50.9	55.0	49.2	51.0	57.1	49.5	53.7	57.7	66.5	3
45.6	51.6	53.9	55.8	58.7	61.4	66.8	72.6	77.4	80.8	87.9	91.5	94.3	98.8	4
25.8	27.5	28.8	31.3	35.6	37.3	42.3	46.8	52.7	57.0	62.3	65.3	71.0	78.5	5
23.6	23.9	24.5	24.9	28.0	31.8	36.1	38.1	42.0	47.4	46.6	50.0	57.1	65.5	6
2.2	3.6	4.3	6.5	7.6	5.4	6.2	8.7	10.7	9.5	15.7	15.4	13.8	13.0	7
200.0	213.0	227.0	241.0	255.0	270.0	285.0	301.0	317.0	333.0	350.0	367.0	384.0	402.0	8
7.4	3.7	3.9	2.9	3.6	4.2	5.2	2.5	2.6	2.8	0.4	1.1	1.7	4.2	9
2.9	2.8	6.8	5.1	6.5	6.5	6.6	3.0	5.3	5.3	2.6	5.5	5.4	7.2	10
18.6	18.7	19.0	19.4	19.9	20.6	21.7	22.6	23.5	24.5	25.7	26.6	28.2	30.8	11
18.5	18.7	18.9	19.2	19.6	20.0	20.8	21.5	22.4	23.4	24.2	24.9	26.1	28.1	12
1.3	0.4	1.6	2.1	2.6	3.5	5.3	4.1	4.0	4.3	4.9	3.5	6.0	9.2	13
1.1	1.1	1.1	1.6	2.1	2.0	4.0	3.4	4.2	4.5	3.4	2.9	4.8	7.7	14
6.4	6.5	6.6	6.7	6.9	7.1	7.4	7.7	7.9	8.2	8.4	8.6	8.9	9.3	15
54.2	54.1	53.9	53.8	54.1	54.4	55.1	55.5	55.5	55.8	57.8	58.1	58.6	59.7	16
40.7	40.5	40.3	40.2	40.2	40.1	39.8	39.1	38.7	38.1	37.5	37.4	37.4	36.8	17
7.0	7.1	5.9	5.5	4.7	3.9	[b]3.3	3.8	4.5	4.4	5.7	6.2	6.2	5.6	18
5.1	5.0	5.1	5.1	5.1	5.3	5.7	6.0	6.7	7.6	7.9	7.0	7.2	7.6	19
3.2	2.8	4.1	3.6	3.8	4.0	5.0	4.6	6.3	7.2	6.0	3.5	3.6	5.5	20
6.2	[b]6.9	7.1	7.4	8.4	9.2	10.1	11.1	12.4	14.7	15.8	17.6	19.9	23.2	21
6.6	[b]7.2	7.6	7.8	8.2	8.7	9.9	11.2	12.4	13.4	15.3	17.5	20.0	22.2	22
−0.3	[b]−0.2	−0.6	−0.4	0.2	0.5	0.2	0	0.1	1.3	0.5	0.1	−0.1	1.12	23
20.4	20.9	22.8	24.5	26.2	26.8	27.7	29.8	32.0	34.4	35.8	39.9	43.8	46.2	24
5.5	5.9	6.1	6.3	6.7	7.1	7.7	8.4	8.9	9.2	9.8	11.5	13.2	14.6	25
—	—	—	—	—	—	—	—	34.0	37.2	41.0	46.3	53.4	63.6	26
7.3	[b]7.1	7.4	7.6	7.9	8.1	8.4	8.4	8.6	9.1	9.3	8.6	8.4	8.8	27
—	—	—	—	—	—	—	—	2.2	2.3	2.2	2.1	2.1	2.0	28
1.03	0.99	0.94	0.93	0.93	0.93	0.93	0.93	0.93	0.93	0.96	0.99	1.01	1.00	29
−0.3	−0.3	−0.3	−0.2	−0.1	−0.4	−0.4	−0.3	−0.3	−0.5	0.1	−0.3	−0.6	−0.5	30

Year		1974	1975	1976	1977	1978	1979	1980	1981	1982	1983
Real GDP (billions of 1992 dollars)	1	436.2	445.8	470.3	486.6	506.4	527.7	535.0	551.3	535.1	549.8
Real consumption expenditure (billions of 1992 dollars)	2	252.9	263.4	277.6	285.9	295.6	303.9	309.9	314.7	306.9	315.7
Real investment (billions of 1992 dollars)	3	74.4	70.0	76.1	73.3	76.5	91.5	91.3	107.0	80.8	87.5
Real government expenditures (billions of 1992 dollars)	4	105.1	112.1	114.2	119.6	121.7	123.0	127.2	129.2	131.9	134.1
Real exports (billions of 1992 dollars)	5	76.5	71.5	79.2	85.4	94.6	98.1	99.9	103.6	102.3	108.8
Real imports (billions of 1992 dollars)	6	72.7	71.2	76.8	77.6	82.0	88.8	93.3	103.1	86.9	96.2
Real net exports (billions of 1992 dollars)	7	3.8	0.4	2.4	7.8	12.6	9.3	6.6	0.4	15.4	12.6
Potential GDP (billions of 1992 dollars)	8	420.0	437.0	455.0	473.0	491.0	509.0	527.0	545.0	563.0	580.0
Fluctuations around potential GDP (percentage)	9	3.8	2.0	3.4	2.9	3.1	3.7	1.5	1.2	−5.0	−5.2
Real GDP growth rate (percent per year)	10	4.1	2.2	5.5	3.5	4.1	4.2	1.4	3.0	−2.9	2.8
GDP deflator (1992 = 100)	11	35.4	39.0	42.6	45.5	48.5	53.1	58.9	65.4	71.0	74.8
CPI (1992 = 100)	12	31.1	34.5	37.1	40.0	43.6	47.6	52.4	58.9	65.3	69.1
Inflation rate (GDP deflator percent per year)	13	14.9	10.2	9.2	6.8	6.6	9.5	10.9	11.0	8.6	5.4
Inflation rate (CPI percent per year)	14	10.7	10.9	7.5	7.8	9.0	9.2	10.1	12.4	10.9	5.8
Labour force (millions)	15	9.6	10.0	10.5	10.9	11.3	11.6	12.0	12.3	12.4	12.6
Labour force participation rate (percentage)	16	60.5	61.1	61.5	62.1	63.1	64.0	64.6	65.3	64.6	64.9
Average weekly hours (hours per week)	17	36.0	35.5	35.4	35.4	35.7	35.8	35.2	34.7	34.5	34.5
Unemployment rate (percentage)	18	5.3	6.9	b7.2	8.1	8.4	7.5	7.5	7.6	11.0	12.0
Long-term interest rate (percent per year)	19	8.9	9.0	9.2	8.7	9.3	10.2	12.5	15.2	14.3	11.8
Short-term interest rate (percent per year)	20	7.8	7.4	8.9	7.3	8.7	11.7	12.7	17.8	13.7	9.3
Federal government revenues (billions of dollars)	21	30.6	32.7	36.6	37.7	39.3	44.7	52.1	67.2	69.5	72.3
Federal government outlays (billions of dollars)	22	28.7	35.8	39.2	44.1	49.0	53.4	62.0	73.0	85.1	92.7
Federal government surplus (+)/deficit(−) (billions of dollars)	23	1.8	−3.1	−2.6	−6.4	−9.7	−8.7	−9.9	−5.8	−15.6	−20.4
Gross federal debt (billions of dollars)	24	49.1	55.1	61.9	69.7	82.4	100.5	110.6	127.7	144.5	173.1
M1 (billions of dollars)	25	15.5	19.0	19.4	21.7	23.6	24.6	27.3	27.4	28.5	30.8
M2+ (billions of dollars)	26	73.9	87.5	102.2	118.1	137.0	161.2	187.9	209.9	226.7	242.0
M1 velocity (GDP/M1)	27	10.0	9.2	10.3	10.2	10.4	11.4	11.6	13.1	13.3	13.4
M2+ velocity (GDP/M2+)	28	2.1	2.0	2.0	1.9	1.8	1.7	1.7	1.7	1.7	1.7
Exchange rate (U.S. dollars per Canadian dollar)	29	1.02	0.98	1.01	0.94	0.88	0.85	0.86	0.83	0.81	0.81
Current account balance (billions of dollars)	30	−1.1	−2.1	−1.9	−1.9	−2.3	−2.5	−1.8	−3.7	0.6	−0.8

1984	1985	1986	1987	1988	1989	1990	1991	1992	1993	1994	1995	1996	1997	1998	
581.0	612.4	628.6	654.4	686.2	703.6	705.5	692.2	698.5	714.6	748.4	769.1	782.1	813.0	838.3	1
329.9	347.0	360.7	375.7	392.1	406.0	411.3	405.8	412.9	420.4	433.6	442.9	454.0	472.9	485.9	2
100.1	111.5	114.6	126.3	140.4	147.7	134.7	124.1	119.0	120.8	133.0	137.7	140.4	166.8	168.4	3
135.7	141.5	144.2	146.2	152.9	157.2	162.9	167.5	169.3	169.4	167.3	166.4	164.5	163.7	166.4	4
129.1	136.2	143.4	148.1	162.2	164.2	172.0	175.9	189.8	210.5	238.1	259.7	274.6	297.8	322.3	5
113.7	123.8	134.3	141.9	161.4	171.6	175.5	181.1	192.4	206.6	223.7	237.6	251.4	288.1	304.8	6
15.4	12.5	9.0	6.2	0.8	−7.4	−3.5	−5.2	−2.6	4.0	14.4	22.1	23.2	9.7	17.5	7
598.0	614.0	631.0	647.0	663.0	680.0	690.0	710.0	720.0	740.0	760.0	780.0	800.0	820.0	840.0	8
−2.8	−0.3	−0.4	1.1	3.5	3.5	2.2	−2.5	−3.0	−3.4	−1.5	−1.4	−2.2	−0.8	−0.2	9
5.7	5.4	2.6	4.1	4.9	2.5	0.3	−1.9	0.9	2.3	4.7	2.8	1.7	4.0	3.1	10
77.3	79.2	81.4	85.3	89.2	93.3	96.1	98.7	100.0	101.5	102.6	104.9	106.6	107.5	106.9	11
72.1	75.0	78.1	81.5	84.8	89.0	93.3	98.5	100.0	101.8	102.0	104.2	105.9	107.6	108.6	12
3.3	2.5	2.8	4.8	4.6	4.6	3.0	2.7	1.3	1.5	1.1	2.2	1.6	0.8	−0.6	13
4.3	4.0	4.1	4.4	4.0	5.0	4.8	5.6	1.5	1.8	0.2	2.2	1.6	1.6	0.9	14
12.9	13.1	13.4	13.6	13.9	14.2	14.3	14.4	14.5	14.7	14.8	14.9	15.1	15.4	15.6	15
65.3	65.9	66.3	66.7	67.2	67.5	67.4	66.7	65.9	65.5	65.3	64.8	64.9	64.8	65.2	16
34.6	34.8	34.8	34.7	35.3	35.7	35.2	34.5	34.0	34.5	34.9	34.6	34.4	34.0	33.3	17
11.3	10.5	9.6	8.9	7.8	7.5	8.1	10.4	11.3	11.2	10.4	9.5	9.7	9.2	8.3	18
12.8	11.0	9.5	10.0	10.2	9.9	10.9	9.8	8.8	7.8	8.6	8.3	7.5	6.4	5.5	19
11.1	9.4	9.0	8.2	9.5	12.1	12.8	8.8	6.6	4.8	5.5	7.1	4.2	3.2	4.7	20
78.9	86.1	95.0	104.3	114.2	122.0	130.1	136.4	141.2	140.3	144.2	153.7	161.8	175.1	180.7	21
104.1	114.4	116.7	123.1	131.7	141.5	154.6	164.8	168.3	171.3	170.2	177.1	171.5	166.4	170.7	22
−25.2	−28.3	−21.7	−18.8	−17.5	−19.4	−24.6	−28.4	−27.1	−31.0	−26.0	−23.4	−9.6	8.7	10.0	23
209.3	250.5	284.0	318.3	349.9	380.0	406.6	444.6	476.1	514.4	557.6	595.9	634.9	651.1	646.1	24
31.0	34.2	36.5	39.7	42.5	44.0	43.5	45.6	48.5	55.7	59.5	63.2	74.0	81.6	89.0	25
263.1	291.6	325.0	352.4	399.4	456.5	500.3	535.0	559.6	577.8	591.0	616.5	640.4	632.7	643.3	26
14.5	14.2	14.0	14.1	14.4	14.9	15.6	15.0	14.4	13.0	12.9	12.8	11.3	10.7	10.1	27
1.7	1.7	1.6	1.6	1.5	1.4	1.4	1.3	1.2	1.3	1.3	1.3	1.3	1.4	1.4	28
0.77	0.73	0.72	0.75	0.81	0.84	0.86	0.87	0.83	0.78	0.73	0.73	0.73	0.72	0.67	29
−0.4	−2.0	−3.9	−4.5	−4.6	−6.5	−5.8	−6.4	−6.3	−7.0	−4.4	−1.5	1.1	−3.6	−4.1	30

Glossary

Glossary

Above full-employment equilibrium A short-run macroeconomic equilibrium in which real GDP exceeds potential GDP.

Absolute advantage A person has an absolute advantage in the production of two goods if that person can produce more of both goods than another person; a country has an absolute advantage if its output per unit of inputs of all goods is larger than that of another country.

Aggregate demand The relationship between the quantity of real GDP demanded and the price level.

Aggregate hours The total number of hours worked by all the people employed, both full time and part time, during a year.

Aggregate planned expenditure The sum of planned consumption expenditure, planned investment, planned government expenditures, and planned exports minus planned imports.

Aggregate production function The relationship between the quantity of real GDP supplied and the quantities of labour and capital and the state of technology.

Anti-combine law A law that regulates and prohibits certain kinds of market behaviour, such as monopoly and monopolistic practices.

Automatic fiscal policy A change in fiscal policy that is triggered by the state of the economy.

Automatic stabilizer A mechanism that dampens the fluctuations in real GDP without an explicit policy action by the government.

Autonomous expenditure The sum of those components of aggregate planned expenditure that are not influenced by real GDP.

Autonomous tax multiplier The magnification effect of a change in autonomous taxes on equilibrium aggregate expenditure and real GDP.

Autonomous taxes Taxes that do not vary with real GDP.

Average cost pricing rule A rule that sets price equal to average total cost.

Average fixed cost Total fixed cost per unit of output.

Average product The average product of a resource. It equals total product divided by the quantity of the resource employed.

Average tax rate The percentage of income that is paid in tax.

Average total cost Total cost per unit of output.

Average variable cost Total variable cost per unit of output.

Balanced budget A government budget in which revenues and outlays are equal.

Balance of payments accounts A country's record of international trading, borrowing, and lending.

Balance of trade The value of exports minus the value of imports.

Bank of Canada Canada's central bank, created by the Bank of Canada Act of 1935 (revised in 1967).

Bank rate The interest rate that the Bank of Canada charges the chartered banks on the reserves it lends them.

Barriers to entry Legal or natural constraints that protect a firm from potential competitors.

Barter The direct exchange of one good or service for other goods and services.

Below full-employment equilibrium A short-run macroeconomic equilibrium in which potential GDP exceeds real GDP.

Big tradeoff The conflict between equity and efficiency.

Bilateral monopoly A situation in which there is a single seller (a monopoly) and a single buyer (a monopsony).

Black market An illegal trading arrangement in which the price exceeds the legally imposed price ceiling.

Budget deficit A government's budget balance that is negative—outlays exceed revenues.

Budget line The limits to a household's consumption choices.

Budget surplus A government's budget balance that is positive—revenues exceed outlays.

Business cycle The periodic but irregular up-and-down movement in production.

Canadian interest rate differential The Canadian interest rate minus the foreign interest rate.

Capacity output The output at which average total cost is a minimum—the output at the bottom of the U-shaped *ATC* curve.

Capital The equipment, buildings, tools, and manufactured goods that we use to produce other goods and services.

Capital account A record of foreign investment in a country minus its investment abroad.

Capital accumulation The growth of capital resources.

Capture theory A theory of regulation that states that the regulations are supplied to satisfy the demand of producers to maximize producer surplus—to maximize economic profit.

Cartel A group of firms that has entered into a collusive agreement to restrict output and increase prices and profits.

Central bank A public authority that supervises financial institutions and markets and conducts monetary policy.

Ceteris paribus Other things being equal—all other relevant things remaining the same.

Change in demand A change in buyers' plans that occurs when some influence on those plans changes other than the price of the good. It is illustrated by a shift of the demand curve.

Change in supply A change in sellers' plans that occurs when some influence on those plans changes other than the price of the good. It is illustrated by a shift of the supply curve.

Change in the quantity demanded A change in buyers' plans that occurs when the price of a good changes but all other influences on buyers' plans remain unchanged. It is illustrated by a movement along the demand curve.

Change in the quantity supplied A change in sellers' plans that occurs when the price of a good changes but all other influences on sellers' plans remain unchanged. It is illustrated by a movement along the supply curve.

Chartered bank A private firm chartered under the Bank Act of 1922 to receive deposits and make loans.

Classical growth theory A theory of economic growth based on the view that real GDP growth is temporary and that when real GDP per person rises above the subsistence level, a population explosion eventually brings real GDP per person back to subsistence level.

Coase theorem The proposition that if property rights exist and transactions costs are low, private transactions are efficient—equivalently, with property rights and low transaction costs, there are no externalities.

Collective bargaining A process of negotiation between employers or their representatives and unions.

Collusive agreement An agreement between two (or more) producers to restrict output so as to raise prices and profits.

Command system A system in which some people give orders and other people obey them.

Comparative advantage A person or country has a comparative advantage in an activity if that person or country can perform the activity at a lower opportunity cost than anyone else or any other country.

Complement A good that is used in conjunction with another good.

Constant returns to scale Features of a firm's technology that lead to constant long-run average cost as output increases. When constant returns to scale are present, the *LRAC* curve is horizontal.

Consumer equilibrium A situation in which a consumer has allocated all his or her available income in the way that maximizes his or her total utility.

Consumer Price Index (CPI) An index that measures the average level of prices of the goods and services that a typical urban Canadian family buys.

Consumer surplus The value that the consumer gets from each unit of a good minus the price paid for it.

Consumption expenditure The total amount spent on consumption goods and services.

Consumption function The relationship between consumption expenditure and disposable income, other things remaining the same.

Contestable market A market in which one firm (or a small number of firms) operates but in which entry and exit are free, so the firm (or firms) in the market faces competition from potential entrants.

Contractionary fiscal policy A decrease in government expenditures or an increase in taxes.

Cooperative equilibrium The outcome of a collusive agreement between players when the players make and share the monopoly profit.

Copyright A government-sanctioned exclusive right granted to the inventor of a good, service, or productive process to produce, use, and sell the invention for a given number of years.

Cost-push inflation An inflation that results from an initial increase in costs.

Craft union A group of workers who have a similar range of skills but work for many different firms in many different industries and regions.

Creditor nation A country that during its entire history has invested more in the rest of the world than other countries have invested in it.

Credit union A cooperative organization that operates under the Co-operative Credit Association Act of 1992 and that receives deposits from and makes loans to its members.

Cross elasticity of demand The responsiveness of the demand for a good to a change in the price of a substitute or complement, other things remaining the same. It is calculated as the percentage change in the quantity

demanded of the good divided by the percentage change in the price of the substitute or complement.

Cross-section graph A graph that shows the values of an economic variable for different groups in a population at a point in time.

Crowding in The tendency for expansionary fiscal policy to increase investment.

Crowding out The decrease in investment that results from an expansionary fiscal action.

Crown corporations Publicly owned firms in Canada.

Currency The coins and Bank of Canada notes that we use today.

Currency appreciation The rise in the value of one currency in terms of another currency.

Currency depreciation The fall in the value of one currency in terms of another currency.

Currency drain An increase in currency held by households and firms.

Current account A record of the payments for imports of goods and services from abroad, receipts from exports of goods and services sold abroad, net interest paid abroad, and net transfers (such as foreign aid payments).

Cyclical surplus or deficit The actual surplus or deficit minus the structural surplus or deficit.

Cyclical unemployment The fluctuations in unemployment over the business cycle.

Deadweight loss A measure of inefficiency. It is equal to the loss in total surplus (consumer surplus plus producer surplus) when output is below or above its efficient level.

Debtor nation A country that during its entire history has borrowed more from the rest of the world than it has lent to it.

Deflation A process in which the price level falls—a negative inflation.

Demand The relationship between the quantity of a good that consumers plan to buy and the price of the good, when all other influences on buyers' plans remain the same. It is described by a demand schedule and illustrated by a demand curve.

Demand curve A curve that shows the relationship between the quantity demanded of a good and its price when all other influences on consumers' planned expenditures remain the same.

Demand for labour The relationship between the quantity of labour demanded and the real wage rate when all other influences on firms' hiring plans remain the same.

Demand for money The relationship between the quantity of real money demanded and the interest rate, when all other influences on the amount of money that people wish to hold remain the same.

Demand-pull inflation An inflation that results from an initial increase in aggregate demand.

Deposit multiplier The amount by which an increase in bank reserves is multiplied to calculate the increase in bank deposits.

Depository institution A firm that takes deposits from households and firms and makes loans to other households and firms.

Depreciation The decrease in the capital stock resulting from wear and tear and obsolescence.

Derived demand Demand for a productive resource which is derived from the demand for the goods and services produced by the resource.

Desired reserve ratio The ratio of reserves to deposits that banks wish to hold.

Diminishing marginal rate of substitution The general tendency for the marginal rate of substitution to diminish as the consumer moves along an indifference curve, increasing consumption of the good measured on the x-axis and decreasing consumption of the good measured on the y-axis.

Diminishing marginal returns The tendency for the marginal product of an additional resource eventually to be less than the marginal product of the previous unit of the resource.

Diminishing marginal utility The marginal utility that a consumer gets from a good decreases as more of the good is consumed.

Direct relationship A relationship between two variables that move in the same direction.

Discounting The conversion of a future amount of money to its present value.

Discouraged workers People who do not have jobs, are available and willing to work but who have given up the effort to find work.

Discretionary fiscal policy A policy action that is initiated by an act of Parliament.

Discretionary policy A policy that responds to the state of the economy in a possibly unique way that uses all the information available, including perceived lessons from past "mistakes."

Diseconomies of scale Features of a firm's technology that leads to rising long-run average cost as output increases.

Disposable income Aggregate income minus taxes plus transfer payments.

Dominant strategy equilibrium The outcome of a game in which there is a single best strategy (a dominant strategy) for each player, regardless of the strategy of the other players.

Dumping The sale of a good or service to a foreign country at a price that is less than the cost of producing the good or service.

Duopoly A market structure in which only two producers compete.

Dynamic comparative advantage A comparative advantage that a person or country possesses as a result of having specialized in a particular activity and then, as a result of learning-by-doing, having become the producer with the lowest opportunity cost.

Economic depreciation The change in the market value of capital over a given period.

Economic efficiency A situation that occurs when a firm produces a given output at least cost.

Economic growth The expansion of production possibilities that results from capital accumulation and technological change.

Economic model A description of some aspect of the economic world that includes only those features of the world that are needed for the purpose at hand.

Economic profit A firm's total revenue minus its opportunity cost.

Economic rent The income received by the owner of a resource over and above the amount required to induce that owner to offer the resource for use.

Economics The science that studies the choices that people make when wants exceed the available resources—when resources are scarce.

Economic theory A generalization that summarizes what we think we understand about the economic choices that people make and the performance of industries and entire economies.

Economic welfare A comprehensive measure of the general state of economic well-being.

Economies of scale Features of a firm's technology that lead to falling long-run average cost as output increases.

Economies of scope A situation in which a firm uses specialized (and often expensive) resources to produce a range of goods and services.

Efficiency wage A real wage rate that is set above the full-employment equilibrium wage rate and that balances the costs and benefits of this higher wage rate to maximize the firm's profit.

Efficient Resource use is efficient when we produce the goods and services that we value most highly.

Efficient allocation An allocation of resources that occurs when we produce the goods and services that people value most highly.

Elastic demand Demand with a price elasticity greater than 1; other things remaining the same, the percentage change in the quantity demanded exceeds the percentage change in price.

Elasticity of supply The responsiveness of the quantity supplied of a good to a change in its price when all other influences on selling plans remain the same.

Employment-to-population ratio The percentage of people of working age who have jobs.

Entrants People who enter the labour force.

Entrepreneurship The resource that organizes labour, land, and capital. Entrepreneurs make business decisions, bear the risks that arise from these decisions, and come up with new ideas about what, how, where, and when to produce.

Equation of exchange An equation that states that the quantity of money multiplied by the velocity of circulation equals GDP.

Equilibrium expenditure The level of aggregate expenditure that occurs when aggregate planned expenditure equals real GDP.

Equilibrium price The price at which the quantity demanded equals the quantity supplied.

Equilibrium quantity The quantity bought and sold at the equilibrium price.

Excess reserves A bank's actual reserves minus desired reserves.

Exchange rate The price at which the Canadian dollar exchanges for another currency.

Excise tax A tax on the sale of a particular commodity.

Exhaustible natural resource A natural resource that can be used only once and that cannot be replaced once it has been used.

Expansion A business cycle phase in which real GDP increases.

Expansionary fiscal policy An increase in government expenditures or a decrease in taxes.

Expenditure The price of a good multiplied by the quantity of the good that is bought is the expenditure on a good.

Exports The goods and services that we sell to people in other countries.

External benefits Benefits that accrue to people other than the buyer of the good.

External costs Costs that are not borne by the producer of the good but borne by someone else.

External diseconomies Factors outside the control of a firm that raise the firm's costs as industry output increases.

External economies Factors beyond the control of a firm that lower the firm's costs as the industry output increases.

Externality A cost or a benefit that arises from an economic transaction and that falls on people who do not participate in that transaction.

Factors of production The economy's productive resources—land, labour, capital, and entrepreneurial ability.

Farm marketing board A regulatory agency that intervenes in an agricultural market to stabilize the price of an agricultural product.

Federal budget The annual statement of the expenditures and tax revenues of the government of Canada together with the laws and regulations that approve and support those expenditures and taxes.

Feedback-rule policy A rule that specifies how policy actions respond to changes in the state of the economy.

Firm An institution that hires productive resources and that organizes those resources to produce and sell goods and services.

Fiscal policy The government's attempt to influence the economy by setting and changing taxes, transfer payments, and government expenditures to achieve macroeconomic objectives such as full employment, sustained long-term economic growth, and price level stability.

Fixed-rule policy A rule that specifies an action to be pursued independently of the state of the economy.

Flow A quantity per unit of time.

Foreign exchange market The market in which the currency of one country is exchanged for the currency of another.

Foreign exchange rate The price at which one currency exchanges for another.

Four-firm concentration ratio A measure of market power that is calculated as the percentage of the value of sales accounted for by the four largest firms in an industry.

Free rider A person who consumes a good without paying for it.

Frictional unemployment The unemployment that arises from normal labour turnover—people entering and leaving the labour force and from ongoing creation and destruction of jobs.

Full employment A situation in which the quantity of labour demanded equals the quantity supplied. At full employment, the unemployment rate equals the natural rate of unemployment and all unemployment is frictional, structural, and seasonal.

Game theory The main tool that economists use to analyze strategic behaviour—behaviour that takes into account the expected behavior of others and the mutual recognition of interdependence.

GDP deflator A price index that measures the average level of the prices of all goods and services that are included in GDP.

General Agreement on Tariffs and Trade (GATT) An international agreement designed to reduce tariffs on international trade.

Goods and services All the things that people are willing to pay for.

Government budget deficit The deficit that arises when a government spends more than it collects in taxes.

Government budget surplus The surplus that arises when a government collects more in taxes than it spends.

Government debt The total amount of government borrowing that the government has undertaken. It is the sum of past deficits minus the sum of past surpluses.

Government deposit shifting The transfer of government funds by the Bank of Canada from the government's account at the Bank of Canada to its accounts at the chartered banks or from the government's accounts at chartered banks to its account at the Bank of Canada.

Government expenditures Goods and services bought by the government.

Government expenditures multiplier The magnification effect of a change in government expenditures on goods and services on equilibrium expenditure and real GDP.

Government sector surplus or deficit An amount equal to net taxes minus government expenditures on goods and services.

Great Depression A decade (1929–1939) of high unemployment and stagnant production throughout the world economy.

Gross domestic product (GDP) The value of aggregate production of goods and services in a country during a given time period—usually a year.

Gross investment The total amount spent on adding to the capital stock and on replacing depreciated capital.

Growth accounting A method of calculating how much real GDP growth results from growth of labour and capital and how much is attributable to technological change.

Herfindahl-Hirschman Index A measure of market power that is calculated as the square of the market share of each firm (as a percentage) summed over the largest 50 firms (or over all firms if there are fewer than 50) in a market.

Human capital The skill and knowledge that people obtain from education and on-the-job training.

Implicit rental rate The rent that a firm pays to itself for the use of its own assets.

Imports The goods and services that we buy from people in other countries.

Incentive An inducement to take a particular action.

Incentive system A method of orga-

nizing production that uses a market-like mechanism inside the firm.

Income The amount of money that someone earns by working.

Income effect The change in consumption that results from a change in the consumer's income, other things remaining the same.

Income elasticity of demand The responsiveness of demand to a change in income, other things remaining the same. It is calculated as the percentage change in the quantity demanded divided by the percentage change in income.

Indifference curve A line that shows combinations of goods among which a consumer is indifferent.

Induced expenditure The sum of the components of aggregate expenditure that vary with real GDP.

Induced taxes Taxes that vary with real GDP.

Industrial union A group of workers who have a variety of skills and job types but work for the same firm or industry.

Inelastic demand A demand with a price elasticity between 0 and 1; the percentage change in the quantity demanded is less than the percentage change in price.

Infant-industry argument The argument that protection is necessary to enable an infant industry to grow into a mature industry that can compete in world markets.

Inferior good A good for which demand decreases as income increases.

Inflation A process in which the price level is rising and money is losing value.

Inflationary gap The amount by which real GDP exceeds potential GDP.

Inflation rate The percentage change in the price level from one year to the next.

Injection An expenditure that does not originate with households. The injections are investment, government expenditures, and exports.

Intellectual property rights

Property rights for discoveries owned by the creators of knowledge.

Interest rate The percentage yield on a financial security such as a bond or a stock. It is the amount received by a lender and paid by a borrower expressed as a percentage of the amount of the loan.

Interest rate parity A situation in which the return on assets in different currencies are equal.

Interest-sensitive expenditure curve The relationship between aggregate expenditure plans and the real interest rate when all other influences on expenditure plans remain the same.

Intermediate goods and services Goods and services that firms buy from each other and use as inputs in the goods and services that they eventually sell to final users.

International crowding out The tendency for an expansionary fiscal policy to decrease net exports.

Inverse relationship A relationship between variables that move in opposite directions.

Investment The purchase of new capital including inventories.

Involuntary part-time rate The percentage of the people in the labour force who have part-time jobs and want full-time jobs.

Job leavers People who voluntarily quit their jobs.

Job losers People who are laid off, either permanently or temporarily, from their jobs.

Job rationing The practice of paying a real wage rate above the equilibrium level and then rationing jobs by some method.

Job search The activity of people looking for acceptable vacant jobs.

Keynesian A macroeconomist whose view about the functioning of the economy is based on the theories of John Maynard Keynes.

Keynesian activist An economist who believes that fluctuations in aggregate demand combined with sticky money wage rates (and/or sticky price levels) are the main source of economic fluctuations.

Keynesian theory of the business cycle A theory that regards volatile expectations as the main source of economic fluctuations.

Labour The time and effort that people allocate to producing goods and services.

Labour force The sum of the people who are employed and who are unemployed.

Labour force participation rate The percentage of the working-age population who are members of the labour force.

Labour productivity Real GDP per hour of labour.

Labour union An organized group of workers whose purpose is to increase wages and to influence other job conditions for its members.

Land All the gifts of nature that we use to produce goods and services.

Law of diminishing returns As a firm uses more of a variable input with a given quantity of other inputs (fixed inputs), the marginal product of the variable input eventually diminishes.

Leakage Income that is not spent on domestically produced goods and services. The leakages are saving, net taxes, and imports.

Learning-by-doing People become more productive in an activity (learn) just by repeatedly producing a particular good or service (doing).

Legal monopoly A market in which competition and entry are restricted by the granting of a public franchise, government licence, patent, or copyright.

Limit pricing The practice of charging a price below the monopoly profit-maximizing price and producing a quantity greater than that at which marginal revenue equals marginal cost so as to deter entry.

Linear relationship A relationship between two variables that is illustrated by a straight line.

Liquidity The property of being instantly convertible into a means of payment with little loss in value.

Local public good A public good that is consumed by all the people who live in a particular area.

Long run A time frame in which the quantities of all resources can be varied.

Long-run aggregate supply The relationship between the quantity of real GDP supplied and the price level in the long run when real GDP equals potential GDP.

Long-run aggregate supply curve A curve that shows the relationship between the quantity of real GDP supplied and the price level in the long run when real GDP equals potential GDP.

Long-run average cost curve The relationship between the lowest attainable average total cost and output when both the plant size and labour are varied.

Long-run industry supply curve A curve that shows how the quantity supplied by an industry varies as the market price varies after all the possible adjustments have been made, including changes in plant size and the number of firms in the industry.

Long-run macroeconomic equilibrium A situation that occurs when real GDP equals potential GDP—the economy is on its long-run aggregate supply curve.

Long-run neutrality The proposition that in the long run, a change in the quantity of money changes the price level and leaves all real variables unchanged.

Long-run Phillips curve A curve that shows the relationship between inflation and unemployment when actual inflation rate equals the expected inflation rate.

Lorenz curve A curve that graphs the cumulative percentage of income or wealth against the cumulative percentage of families or population.

Low-income cutoff The income level, determined separately for different types of families (for example, single persons, couples, one parent), that is selected such that families with incomes below that limit normally spend 54.7 percent or more of their income on food, shelter, and clothing.

M1 A measure of money that consists of currency held outside the banks plus demand deposits at chartered banks that are owned by individuals and businesses.

M2+ A measure of money that consists of M1 plus personal savings deposits and nonpersonal notice deposits at chartered banks plus deposits at trust and mortgage companies, credit unions, caisses populaires, and other financial institutions.

Macroeconomic long run A time frame that is sufficiently long for forces operating in the economy to have done their work so that real GDP equals potential GDP and full employment prevails.

Macroeconomics The study of the national economy and the global economy, the way in which economic aggregates grow and fluctuate, and the effects of government actions on them.

Macroeconomic short run A period during which real GDP has fallen below or risen above potential GDP.

Margin When a choice is changed by a small amount or by a little at a time, the choice is made at the margin.

Marginal benefit The benefit that a person receives from consuming one more unit of a good or service. It is measured as the maximum amount that a person is willing to pay for one more unit of the good or service.

Marginal cost The opportunity cost of producing one more unit of a good or service. It is the best alternative forgone. It is calculated as the increase in total cost divided by the increase in output.

Marginal cost pricing rule A rule that sets the price equal to the marginal cost.

Marginal product The change in total product that results from a one-unit increase in the variable input. It is calculated as the increase in total product divided by the increase in the variable input employed, when the quantities of all other resources are constant.

Marginal product of labour The

additional real GDP produced by an additional hour of labour when all other influences on production remain the same.

Marginal propensity to consume The fraction of a change in disposable income that is consumed.

Marginal propensity to import The fraction of an increase in real GDP that is spent on imports.

Marginal propensity to save The fraction of a change in disposable income that is saved.

Marginal rate of substitution The rate at which a person will give up good y (the good measured on the y-axis) to get one additional unit of good x (the good measured on the x-axis) and at the same time remain indifferent (remain on the same indifference curve).

Marginal revenue The change in total revenue that results from a one-unit increase in the quantity sold. It is calculated by dividing the change in total revenue by the change in the quantity sold.

Marginal revenue product The change in total revenue that results from employing one more unit of a resource while the quantity of all other resources remains the same. It is calculated as the increase in total revenue divided by the increase in the quantity of the resource.

Marginal social benefit The marginal benefit received by the buyer of a good (marginal private benefit) plus the marginal benefit received by others (external benefit).

Marginal social cost The marginal cost incurred by the producer of a good (marginal private cost) plus the marginal cost imposed on others (external cost).

Marginal tax rate The percentage of an additional dollar of income that is paid in tax.

Marginal utility The change in total utility resulting from a one-unit increase in the quantity of a good consumed.

Marginal utility per dollar spent The marginal utility obtained from the last unit of a good consumed divided by the price of the good.

Market Any arrangement that enables buyers and sellers to get information and to do business with each other.

Market demand The relationship between the quantity demanded of a good or service by everyone in the population and its price. It is illustrated by the market demand curve.

Market failure A state in which the market does not use resources efficiently.

Market power The ability to influence the market, and in particular the market price, by influencing the total quantity offered for sale.

Means of payment A method of settling a debt.

Microeconomics The study of the decisions of people and businesses, the interactions of those decisions in markets, and the effects of government regulation and taxes on the prices and quantities of goods and services.

Minimum efficient scale The smallest quantity of output at which long-run average cost reaches its lowest level.

Minimum wage The lowest wage rate at which a firm may legally hire labour.

Monetarist An economist who believes that fluctuations in the money stock are the main source of economic fluctuations.

Monetarist theory of the business cycle A theory that regards fluctuations in the money stock as the main source of economic fluctuations.

Monetary base The sum of Bank of Canada notes outside the Bank, chartered banks' deposits at the Bank of Canada, and coins held by households, firms, and banks.

Monetary policy The attempt by the Bank of Canada to control inflation and moderate the business cycle by changing the quantity of money in circulation and adjusting interest rates and the exchange rate.

Monetary policy indicators The current features of the economy that the Bank of Canada looks at to determine whether it needs to apply the

brake or the accelerator to the economy to influence its future real GDP growth, unemployment, and inflation.

Money Any commodity or token that is generally acceptable as a means of payment.

Money multiplier The amount by which a change in the monetary base is multiplied to determine the resulting change in the quantity of money.

Money wage rate The number of dollars that an hour of labour earns.

Monopolistic competition A market structure in which a large number of firms compete by making similar but slightly different products.

Monopoly An industry that produces a good or service for which no close substitute exists and in which there is one supplier that is protected from competition by a barrier preventing the entry of new firms.

Monopsony A market in which there is a single buyer.

Multiplier The amount by which a change in autonomous expenditure is magnified or multiplied to determine the change in equilibrium expenditure and real GDP.

Nash equilibrium The outcome of a game that occurs when player A takes the best possible action given the action of player B and player B takes the best possible action given the action of player A.

National saving Saving by households and businesses—plus government saving.

Natural monopoly A monopoly that occurs when one firm can supply the entire market at a lower price than two or more firms can.

Natural rate of unemployment The unemployment rate when the economy is at full employment. There is no cyclical unemployment; all unemployment is frictional, structural, and seasonal.

Negative income tax A redistribution scheme that gives every family a guaranteed minimum annual income and taxes all income above the guaranteed minimum at a fixed marginal tax rate.

Negative relationship A relationship

between variables that move in opposite directions.

Neoclassical growth theory A theory of economic growth that proposes that real GDP per person grows because technological change induces a level of saving and investment that makes capital per person grow.

Net borrower A country that borrows more from the rest of the world than it lends to it.

Net exports The exports of goods and services minus imports of goods and services.

Net investment Net increase in the capital stock—gross investment minus depreciation.

Net lender A country that lends more to the rest of the world than it borrows from it.

Net present value The present value of the future flow of marginal revenue product generated by the capital minus the cost of the capital.

Net taxes Taxes paid to governments minus transfer payments received from governments.

New classical theory of the business cycle A rational expectations theory of the business cycle that regards unanticipated fluctuations in aggregate demand as the main source of economic fluctuations.

New growth theory A theory of economic growth based on the idea that real GDP per person grows because of the choices people make in the pursuit of profit and that growth can persist indefinitely.

New Keynesian theory of the business cycle A rational expectations theory of the business cycle that regards unanticipated fluctuations in aggregate demand as the main source of economic fluctuations but leaves room for anticipated demand fluctuations to play a role.

Nominal GDP The value of the current period's production in current period prices.

Nominal GDP targeting An attempt to keep the growth rate of nominal GDP steady.

Nominal interest rate The percent-

age return on an asset such as a bond expressed in terms of money.

Nonexhaustible natural resource A natural resource that can be used repeatedly.

Nontariff barrier Any action other than a tariff that restricts international trade.

Normal good A good for which demand increases as income increases.

Normal profit The average return for supplying entrepreneurial ability.

North American Free Trade Agreement An agreement which became effective on January 1, 1994 and under which barriers to international trade between Canada, the United States, and Mexico will be virtually eliminated after a 15-year phasing-in period.

Official Canadian reserves The government's holdings of foreign currency.

Official settlements account A record of the change in a country's official reserves.

Oligopoly A market structure in which a small number of firms compete.

Open market operation The purchase or sale of government of Canada securities—Treasury bills and government bonds—by the Bank of Canada from or to a chartered bank or the public.

Opportunity cost The opportunity cost of an action is the highest-valued alternative forgone.

Overnight loans rate The main monetary policy indicator. It is the interest rate on large-scale loans that chartered banks make to each other and to dealers in financial markets.

Patent A government-sanctioned exclusive right granted to the inventor of a good, service, or productive process to produce, use, and sell the invention for a given number of years.

Pay equity Paying the same wage for different jobs that are judged to be comparable.

Payoff matrix A table that shows the

payoffs for every possible action by each player for every possible action by each other player.

Perfect competition A market in which there are many firms each selling an identical product; there are many buyers; there are no restrictions on entry into the industry; firms in the industry have no advantage over potential new entrants; and firms and buyers are well informed about the price of each firm's product.

Perfectly elastic demand Demand with an infinite price elasticity; the quantity demanded changes by a large percentage in response to a tiny price change.

Perfectly inelastic demand Demand with a price elasticity of zero; the quantity demanded remains constant when the price changes.

Perfect price discrimination Price discrimination that extracts the entire consumer surplus.

Phillips curve A curve that shows a relationship between inflation and unemployment.

Policy conflict A situation that arises when the government and the Bank of Canada pursue different goals and the actions of one make it harder (perhaps impossible) for the other to achieve its goals.

Policy coordination A situation that arises when the government and the Bank of Canada work together to achieve a common set of goals.

Political equilibrium The outcome that results from the choices of voters, politicians, and bureaucrats in which all their choices are compatible and in which no group can improve its position by making a different choice.

Positive relationship A relationship between two variables that move in the same direction.

Potential GDP The value of production (real GDP) when all the economy's labour, land, capital, and entrepreneurial ability are fully employed. Unemployment is at its natural rate, and the economy is at full employment.

Poverty A state in which a family's income is too low to be able to buy the quantities of food, shelter, and clothing that are deemed necessary.

Present value The amount of money that, if invested today, will grow to be as large as a given future amount when the interest that it will earn is taken into account.

Price ceiling A regulation that makes it illegal to charge a price higher than a specified level.

Price discrimination The practice of selling different units of a good or service for different prices.

Price effect The change in consumption that results from a change in the price of a good or service, other things remaining the same.

Price elasticity of demand A measure of the responsiveness of the quantity demanded of a good to a change in its price, when all other influences on buyers' plans remain the same.

Price floor A regulation that makes it illegal to pay a lower price than a specified level.

Price level The average level of prices as measured by a price index.

Price taker A firm that cannot influence the price of the good or service it produces.

Principal-agent problem The problem of devising compensation rules that induce an agent to act in the best interest of a principal.

Principle of minimum differentiation The tendency for competitors to make themselves identical to appeal to the maximum number of clients or voters.

Private sector surplus or deficit An amount equal to saving minus investment.

Privatization The process of selling a publicly owned corporation to private shareholders.

Producer surplus The price a producer gets for a good or service minus the opportunity cost of producing it.

Product differentiation Making a good or service slightly different from that of a competing firm.

Production efficiency A situation in which the economy cannot produce more of one good without producing less of some other good.

Production function The relationship between real GDP and the quantity of labour employed when all other influences on production remain the same.

Production possibility frontier The boundary between those combinations of goods and services that can be produced and those that cannot.

Productivity Production per unit of resource used in the production of goods and services.

Productivity function A relationship that shows how real GDP per hour of labour changes as the amount of capital per hour of labour changes with a given state of technology.

Productivity growth slowdown A slowdown in the growth rate of output per person.

Progressive income tax A tax on income at a marginal rate that increases with the level of income.

Progressive tax A tax on income when the average tax rate increases as income increases.

Property rights Social arrangements that govern the ownership, use, and disposal of resources, goods, and services.

Proportional income tax A tax on income at a constant rate, regardless of the level of income. It is also called a flat-rate income tax.

Proportional tax A tax on income when the average tax rate increases as income increases.

Provincial budget An annual statement of the revenues and outlays of a provincial government together with the laws and regulations that approve or support those revenues and outlays.

Public good A good or service that can be consumed simultaneously by everyone and from which no one can be excluded, even if they don't pay for it.

Public interest theory A theory of regulation that states that regulations are supplied to satisfy the demand of consumers and producers to maximize total surplus—that is, to attain allocative efficiency.

Purchasing power parity The equal value of money.

Quantity demanded The amount of a good or service that consumers plan to buy during a given time period at a particular price.

Quantity of labour demanded The labour hours hired by all the firms in the economy.

Quantity of labour supplied The number of labour hours that all households in the economy plan to work.

Quantity supplied The amount of a good or service that producers plan to sell during a given time period at a particular price.

Quantity theory of money The proposition that in the long run, an increase in the quantity of money brings an equal percentage increase in the price level.

Quota A restriction on the quantity of a good that a farm is permitted to produce or on the quantity of a good that can be imported.

Rand formula A rule (set out by Mr. Justice Ivan Rand in 1945) that makes it compulsory for all workers to contribute funds to the union, whether or not they belong to it.

Rate of return regulation A regulation that determines a regulated price by setting the price at a level that enables the regulated firm to earn a specified target percent return on its capital.

Rational expectation A forecast based on all available relevant information.

Rational ignorance The decision not to acquire information because the cost of doing so exceeds the expected benefit.

Real business cycle theory A theory that regards random fluctuations in productivity as the main source of economic fluctuations.

Real Gross Domestic Product (real GDP) The value of the total production of all the nation's farms, factories, shops, and offices measured in the prices of a single year. Real GDP in Canada is currently measured in the prices of 1992.

Real income   A household's income expressed not as money but as a quantity of goods that the household can afford to buy.

Real interest rate   The percentage return on an asset expressed in terms of what money will buy. It is the nominal interest rate adjusted for inflation and is approximately equal to the nominal interest rate minus the inflation rate.

Real wage rate   The quantity of goods ands services that an hour's work can buy.

Recession   A business cycle phase in which real GDP decreases for at least two successive quarters.

Recessionary gap   The amount by which potential GDP exceeds real GDP.

Re-entrants   People who re-enter the labour force.

Regressive income tax   A tax on income at a marginal rate that decreases with the level of income.

Regressive tax   A tax on income when the average tax rate decreases as income increases.

Relative price   The ratio of the price of one good or service to the price of another good or service. A relative price is an opportunity cost.

Rent ceiling   A regulation that makes it illegal to charge a rent higher than a specified level.

Rent seeking   Any activity that attempts to capture a consumer surplus, a producer surplus, or an economic profit.

Reserve ratio   The fraction of a bank's total deposits that are held in reserves.

Reserves   Cash in a bank's vault plus the bank's deposits at the Bank of Canada.

Saving   The amount of income remaining after meeting consumption expenditures.

Saving function   The relationship between saving and disposable income, other things remaining the same.

Scarcity   The state in which the resources available are insufficient to satisfy people's wants.

Scatter diagram   A diagram that plots the value of one economic variable against the value of another.

Search activity   The time spent looking for someone with whom to do business.

Seasonal unemployment
Unemployment that arises because the number of jobs available has decreased because of the season.

Short run   The short run in microeconomics has two meanings. For the firm, it is the time frame in which the quantities of some resources are fixed. For most firms, the fixed resources are the firm's technology, buildings, and capital. For the industry, the short run is the period of time in which each firm has a given plant size and the number of firms in the industry is fixed.

Short-run aggregate supply   The relationship between the quantity of real GDP supplied and the price level when the money wage rate, the prices of other resources, and potential GDP remain constant.

Short-run aggregate supply curve   A curve that shows the relationship between the quantity of real GDP supplied and the price level in the short run when the money wage rate, other resource prices, and potential GDP remain constant.

Short-run industry supply curve   A curve that shows the quantity supplied by the industry at each price when the plant size of each firm and the number of firms remain constant.

Short-run macroeconomic equilibrium   A situation that occurs when the quantity of real GDP demanded equals the quantity of real GDP supplied—at the point of intersection of the *AD* curve and the *SAS* curve.

Short-run Phillips curve   A curve that shows the tradeoff between inflation and unemployment holding constant the expected inflation rate and the natural unemployment rate.

Shutdown point   The output and price at which the firm just covers its total variable cost. In the short run, the firm is indifferent between producing the profit-maximizing output and shutting down temporarily.

Single-price monopoly   A firm that must sell each unit of its output for the same price to all its customers.

Slope   The change in the value of the variable measured on the *y*-axis divided by the change in the value of the variable measured on the *x*-axis.

Stagflation   The combination of a rise in the price level and a decrease in real GDP.

Stock   A quantity that exists at a point in time.

Strategies   All the possible actions of each player in a game.

Structural surplus or deficit   The budget balance that would occur if the economy were at full employment and real GDP equalled potential GDP.

Structural unemployment   The unemployment that arises when changes in technology or international competition change the skills needed to perform jobs or change the locations of jobs.

Subsidy   A payment made by the government to producers that depends on the level of output.

Subsistence real wage rate   The minimum real wage rate needed to maintain life.

Substitute   A good that can be used in place of another good.

Substitution effect   The effect of a change in price on the quantity bought when the consumer (hypothetically) remains indifferent between the original and the new situation.

Sunk cost   A cost that has been incurred in the past and that cannot be reversed now.

Supply   The relationship between the quantity of a good that producers plan to sell and the price of the good when all other influences on sellers' plans remain the same. It is described by a supply schedule and illustrated by a supply curve.

Supply curve   A curve that shows the relationship between the quantity supplied and the price of a good when all other influences on producers' planned sales remain the same.

Supply of labour   The relationship between the quantity of labour supplied and the real wage rate when all other influences on work plans remain the same.

Symmetry principle   A principle that states that people in similar situations must be treated similarly.

Tariff   A tax that is imposed by the importing country when an imported good crosses its international boundary.

Technological change   The development of new goods and better ways of producing goods and services.

Technological efficiency   A situation that occurs when the firm produces a given output by using the least inputs.

Technology   Any method of producing a good or service.

Terms of trade   The quantity of goods and services that a country exports to pay for its imports of goods and services.

Time-series graph   A graph that measures time (for example, months or years) on the x-axis and the variable or variables in which we are interested on the y-axis.

Total cost   The cost of all the productive resources that a firm uses.

Total fixed cost   The cost of the fixed inputs.

Total product   The total output produced by a firm in a given period of time.

Total revenue   The price of the good multiplied by the quantity sold.

Total revenue test   A method of estimating the price elasticity of demand by observing the change in total revenue that results from a change in the price, with all other influences on the quantity sold remaining unchanged.

Total utility   The total benefit that a person gets from the consumption of goods and services.

Total variable cost   The cost of the firm's variable inputs.

Tradeoff   A constraint that involves giving up one thing to get something else.

Transactions costs   The costs arising from finding someone with whom to do business, in reaching an agreement about the price and other aspects of the exchange, and of ensuring that the terms of the agreement are fulfilled.

Trend   The general direction (rising or falling) in which a variable is moving over the long term.

Trust and mortgage company   A privately owned depository institution that operates under the Trust and Loan Companies Act of 1992. It receives deposits and makes loans and in addition acts as a trustee for pension funds and for estates.

Twin deficits   The tendency for the government budget deficit and the current account deficit to move in the same direction.

Unemployment   Resources that are available but are not being used. Statistics Canada count a person as being unemployed if that person does not have a job but is available for work, willing to work, and has made some effort to find work within the previous four weeks.

Unemployment rate   The percentage of the people in the labour force who are unemployed.

Unit elastic demand   Demand with a price elasticity of 1; the percentage change in the quantity demanded equals the percentage change in price.

Utilitarianism   A principle that states that we should strive to achieve "the greatest happiness for the greatest number."

Utility   The benefit or satisfaction that a person gets from the consumption of a good or service.

Value   The maximum amount that a person is willing to pay for a good. The value of one more unit of the good or service is its marginal benefit.

Value added   The value of a firm's production minus the value of the intermediate goods that the firm buys from other firms.

Value of production   The value of the goods and services produced.

Velocity of circulation   The average number of times a dollar of money is used annually to buy the goods and services that make up GDP.

Voluntary exchange   A transaction between people, businesses, or countries that is undertaken voluntarily.

Voluntary export restraint   An agreement between two governments in which the government of the exporting country agrees to restrain the volume of its own exports.

Wealth   The value of all the things that people own.

Working-age population   The total number of people aged 15 years and over.

World Trade Organization   An international organization that places obligations on its member countries to observe the GATT rules.

Index

Index

Key terms and pages on which they are defined appear in **boldface type**.

Chapter 1
Page 2, Realtor and sign, images copyright 1998 PhotoDisc, Inc.; Page 3, Camping, © Parks Canada, Barrett & Mackay, 06.03.07.04 (10); Page 3, Grape harvester, George Rose/Gamma Liaison; Page 3, Baskets of grapes, Owen Franken/Tony Stone Images; Page 4, Doctors, Prentice Hall Inc.; Page 4, Technician, David Joel, Tony Stone Images; Page 4, Cereal boxes, Charles Gupton/First Light; Page 4, Cars, Paul Conklin/PhotoEdit Inc.; Page 5, Construction, MediaFocus International, LLC ; Page 5, GM closure, Chip Henderson/Tony Stone Images ; Page 6, Students, images copyright 1998 PhotoDisc, Inc.; Page 6, McDonald's, David Young-Wolff/PhotoEdit Inc.; Page 7, Woman and baby, images copyright 1998 PhotoDisc, Inc.; Page 8, Woman buying, Karl Wu; Page 8, Woman selling, Karl Wu; Page 9, Pentium processor, Photo courtesy of Intel Corporation; Page 9, Fishing boat, Michel Thérien, Department of Fisheries & Oceans; Page 10, Coffee beans, Jack Novak/SuperStock; Page 10, Milkshakes, images copyright 1998 PhotoDisc, Inc.; Page 10, Woman and cell phone, David Young-Wolff/Tony Stone Images; Page 10, Auto plant, Bob Sacha/Aurora/PNI; Page 11, Price change, Dick Hemingway; Page 11, Food display, Steven Weinberg/Tony Stone Images; Page 11, Employment office, Dick Hemingway; Page 12, Close-up on board, Scott Foresman/Addison Wesley Longman, Focus on Sports; Page 12, Sports crowd, Scott Foresman/Addison Wesley Longman, Focus on Sports; Page 13, Scientist, images copyright 1998 PhotoDisc, Inc.; Page 13, Parliament, Government of Canada; Page 14, Weather map, Courtesy of The Weather Network; Page 14, Winter road, images copyright 1998 PhotoDisc, Inc.; Page 14, Running race, David Burnett/Contact Press Images/PNI; Page 15, Highway, Dick Hemingway; Page 15, Christmas shopping, Frank Wood/SuperStock; Page 15, Christmas present, images copyright 1998 PhotoDisc, Inc.; Page 16, Gordon Thiessen, The Toronto Sun.

Part 1 Wrap Up
Page 58, Adam Smith, Corbis-Bettmann; Page 59, Pin factory, Culver Pictures; Page 59, Computer chip, Bruce Ando/Tony Stone Images; Page 60, John Whalley, Alan Noon.

Part 2 Wrap Up
Page 154, Alfred Marshall, Stock Montage; Page 155, Train, Courtesy Stoddart Publishing Co. Limited, from *Canada: The Missing Years*; Page 155, Airplanes, Courtesy Air Canada; Page 156, Lawrence A. Boland.

Part 3 Wrap Up
Page 196, Jeremy Bentham, Corbis-Bettmann; Page 197, Women in factory, UCR/California Museum of Photography, University of California, Riverside. All rights reserved; Page 197, Co-workers, PhotoDisc, Inc.; Page 198, Martin Dooley, Dick Hemingway.

Chapter 10
Page 211, Coke and Pepsi machines, Karl Wu; Page 211, Shoe store, Karl Wu; Page 211, Wheat field, PhotoDisc; Page 211, Windows98 boxes, Dick Morton.

Part 4 Wrap Up
Page 316, John von Neumann, Stock Montage; Page 317, King Monopoly cartoon, Culver Pictures; Page 317, Cable repair, Don Wilson, West Stock; Page 318, Nancy Gallini, Dick Hemingway.

Part 5 Wrap Up
Page 386, Thomas Robert Malthus, Corbis-Bettmann; Page 387, Winnipeg in 1913, National Archives of Canada/PA-030176.

Part 6 Wrap Up
Page 450, Ronald Coase, David Joel/David Joel Photography, Inc.; Page 451, Pollution, © Jim Baron/The Image Finders; Page 451, Lake Erie, Patrick Mullen; Page 452, Diane Francis, Dick Hemingway.

Part 7 Wrap Up
Page 538, John Maynard Keynes, Stock Montage; Page 539, Spinning jenny, Corbis-Bettmann; Page 539, Telephone call centre, Mug Shots/First Light; Page 540, Robert E. Lucas, Jr., Loren Santow.

Part 8 Wrap Up
Page 690, Milton Friedman, Marshall Heinrichs/Addison Wesley Longman; Page 691, Woman burning money, Corbis-Bettmann; Page 691, Shopping in Brazil, Carlos Humberto/Contact Stock Images; Page 692, David Laidler, Alan Noon.

Part 9 Wrap Up
Page 796, Joseph Schumpeter, Corbis-Bettmann; Page 797, Mechanical reaper, The Granger Collection, New York; Page 797, Fibre optics, Jon Feingersh/First Light; Page 798, Paul Romer, Christopher Irion.

Part 10 Wrap Up
Page 846, David Ricardo, Corbis-Bettmann; Page 847, Steamship ad, Corbis-Bettmann; Page 847, Container ship, M. Timothy O'Keefe/ West Stock; Page 848, Stanley Fischer, John Skowronski.